New York Marriages

PREVIOUS TO 1784

A reprint of the original edition of 1860

WITH ADDITIONS AND CORRECTIONS

Including:

Supplementary List of Marriage Licenses

New York Marriage Licenses, by Robert H. Kelby

New York Marriage Licenses, 1639-1706,

with Index, by Kenneth Scott

CLEAR~
FIELD

Originally published as
*Names of Persons for Whom Marriage Licenses Were Issued
by the Secretary of the Province of New York, Previous to 1784*
Albany, 1860

With the addition of
Supplementary List of Marriage Licenses
University of the State of New York, *State Library Bulletin,
History*, No. 1, April, 1898.

New York Marriage Licenses
The New York Genealogical and Biographical Record,
Volumes XLVI, Numbers 3-4, and XLVII, Numbers 1-3
July, 1915 through July, 1916

New York Marriage Licenses, 1639-1706, by Kenneth Scott
The New York Genealogical and Biographical Record,
Volume XCVIII, Numbers 1 and 2
January and April, 1967.

With the hitherto unpublished
*Index to New York Marriage Licenses, 1639-1706,
by Kenneth Scott*

First printing in this form, 1968
Second printing in this form, 1984
Genealogical Publishing Co., Inc.

Reprinted for
Clearfield Company, Inc., by
Genealogical Publishing Co., Inc.
1999

Library of Congress Catalogue Card Number 67-30757
International Standard Book Number 0-8063-0259-3
Made in the United States of America

NAMES OF PERSONS

FOR WHOM

MARRIAGE LICENSES

WERE ISSUED BY THE

SECRETARY

OF THE

PROVINCE OF NEW YORK,

PREVIOUS TO 1784.

PRINTED BY ORDER OF

GIDEON J. TUCKER

SECRETARY OF STATE.

ALBANY:

WEED, PARSONS AND COMPANY.

1860.

Table of Contents

Publisher's Preface

This collection constitutes as complete an edition of printed public records of early New York marriage licenses as we could put together. With the various supplements which we have added to the work originally published in 1860 and entitled *Names of Persons for Whom Marriage Licenses Were Issued by the Secretary of the Province of New York, Previous to 1784*, better known as *New York Marriages*, the work as it now stands contains all the published records of the licenses up until the practice of issuing them fell into desuetude on the evacuation of New York by the British in 1783.

The additions and corrections which we have added consist of (1) a 48-page "Supplementary List of Marriage Licenses," which was originally published by the University of the State of New York as a *State Library Bulletin, History*, No. 1, in April, 1898; (2) 44 pages of additions and corrections by Robert H. Kelby entitled "New York Marriage Licenses," which originally appeared in *The New York Genealogical and Biographical Record* from July, 1915, through July, 1916, and which was subsequently issued as an offprint in a limited edition of 100 copies; (3) 19 pages of additional marriage licenses by Kenneth Scott under the title "New York Marriage Licenses, 1639-1706," which was originally published in the January and April, 1967 issues of the *Record;* and (4) with an added index to these licenses published here for the first time from a retyped copy of Mr. Scott's original manuscript.

Fortunately, when we first envisioned such a compilation, we had in our possession a copy of the work generally known as *New York Marriages*, which had been long out-of-print and difficult to obtain at any price. As early as a year ago we began the pre-editorial work for such a definitive edition by searching through the various bibliographies and guides to printed sources, and by consulting the leading genealogists, archivists, and librarians. Our inquiry resulted in our obtaining authoritative bibliographical information on the printed marriage records of the Province of New York. Then, we still had the task of obtaining copies of the various supplements that were suitable for reproduction and of securing permission to reprint them. After some months of correspondence, telephone calls, and personal visits, we finally located copies and received the encouragement of everyone concerned for such a project.

Our work could not have been possible without the help of those who have so generously given of their time and materials. Our special gratitude is extended to Mr. Kenneth Scott who gave us both permission to reprint his lists and supplied us with a manuscript index. We also acknowledge the cooperation of *The New York Genealogical and Biographical Record*, and especially of Miss Marie Berry, for granting us permission to reprint the lists in the *Record*. Finally, we wish to express our appreciation to Miss Juliet F. Wolohan, Librarian of the Manuscripts and History Section of The New York State Library at Albany, who kindly loaned us a copy of the "Supplementary List of Marriage Licenses" for reproduction.

Baltimore, Maryland
1968

INTRODUCTION.

BY E. B. O'CALLAGHAN.

THE origin of Marriage Licenses, in the territory comprised within the State of New York, merits a word or two of explanation.

Under the Roman-Dutch law, which obtained in New-Netherland on its first colonization, the following particulars were requisite to constitute a legal marriage:

All persons desirous of entering the married state were obliged to appear before the Court of Justice, or the Ministers of the Church of their place of abode, where they had their fixed domicil for the last year and day, and to apply there, for three Sundays or Market Days, when publications of the banns were to be made in the Church or the Court House, or other places where the Court of Justice was held; and every one who had any impediment to propose, was obliged to state the same in the meantime, on pain of being otherwise deprived of that right.

These proclamations were designed to preserve the right of a third person; marrying in church being held to be

IV INTRODUCTION.

only an external ceremony of a public confirmation introduced likewise for better security.

As cases, however, might arise where it would be impossible to comply with the general law, provision was made
for dispensing with such proclamations for legal and valid
reasons, by consent of the government, or (some held) of
the judge.*

From these provisions of law, Marriage Licenses—which
are only dispensations from the proclamation of Banns—
took their origin in this country.

When the Colony passed into the hands of the English,
the practice continued to prevail ; Marriage License issued
by them, bearing date as early as 29th December, 1664,†
being found on record. Subsequently, the collating to
Benefices, granting Licenses of Marriage and Probate of
Wills were declared in the Royal Instructions, to be exclu-
sively reserved to the governor.‡

The License was issued from the Provincial Secretary's
office, and in return those obtaining it gave a Penal Bond
in the sum of £500, that there was no "lawful let or impediment of Pre-Contract, Affinity or Consanguinity, to
hinder the parties being joined in the Holy Bonds of Matrimony, and afterwards their living together as Man and
Wife."

There are forty volumes of these Bonds in the office of
the Secretary of State. The names of the parties licensed
to marry, contained in these and in other State Records,
having been indexed in alphabetical order, application was

* Van Leeuwen's Commentaries on the Roman-Dutch Law. London: 1820, p. 72.
† New York General Entries, I. 85.　　‡ New York Colonial Documents, III. 372, 668.

made to the Hon. GIDEON J. TUCKER, late Secretary of State, for authority to print the Index, for public convenience, and it composes the present Volume.

The date prefixed to each name is that of the License or of the Bond. The abbreviation for the title of the volume of Records is affixed to the name.

EXPLANATION OF ABBREVIATIONS

A. R.,   Refers to volumes known as Albany Records, and indorsed—Translations from the Dutch.

C. A.,   "   volumes indorsed—Court of Assize.

C. M.,   "   volumes indorsed—N. Y. Colonial MSS.

C. Min., "   volumes indorsed—Council Minutes.

E.,   "   volume indorsed—Entries.

G. E.,   "   volume indorsed—General Entries.

M. B.,   "   volumes indorsed—Marriage Bonds.

O. W. L., "   volume indorsed—Orders, Warrants and Letters.

O. W.,   "   volume indorsed—Orders, Warrants.

P. B.,   "   volume indorsed—Pass Book.

W. O. P. "   volume indorsed—Warrants, Orders, Passes.

The practice of issuing Marriage Licenses fell into total desuetude in this State, on the Evacuation of New York by the British in 1783. It continued for some years longer in the State of Pennsylvania, as appears by the following letters of Bishop White, to the Governor of that Commonwealth :

Sir,   [1778]

When I had ye Honor, yesterday, of stating to your Excellency my Objections to ye present System of Marriage Licenses, & you condescended to recommend to me ye promoting of a clerical Representation of ye Subject ; I expressed my Doubts as to ye Expediency of such a Measure. My Reason is, that I do not think ye Clergy, as such, materially interested in the correcting of ye Evil. We marry whom we please, under no other Restriction than what should prevail in every Line of Life, if not invading of ye Rights of others. It is true, a Stranger may be imposed on, by his imagining that a License from Government is something more than a blank Paper. But to prevent this, I have made it my Business to advertise every such, of ye Church under my care, of ye State of ye Case & of his own Responsibility.

It was as a citizen that I introduced ye Subject to your Excellency ; And ye Evils which, as such I reprobate in ye present System are as follow :

1. The Practice of issuing Licenses is, as I apprehend, without any Foundation of Law. The only Passage in our Acts of Assembly that can be supposed applicable, & this can be so by Implication only, defines a lawful License to be one which contains ye Consent of the Parent or Guardian expressed in ye Body of it. But such a License I never saw, nor do I know of any Clergyman who has.

2dly. It seems to me (I speak it with submission) disreputable to Government to be in ye Exercise of an Act of Authority, disregarded (as far as I can hear) & that with Impunity, by the most respectable Clergymen in this City ; who instead of thinking themselves under any Obligation, either of Law or of Morals, to ask for ye Licence, consider it rather as a Snare, against which they are to be on their Guard.

3dly. The Licenses, as issued, are a most cruel Invasion of domestic Rights. For, as if it were not enough, that ye Citizen has ye Peace of his Family exposed to ye Acts of ye desperate Adventurer, ye Villain robs him of his Child under a warrant with ye Seal of ye State annexed to it, & signed by ye first Magistrate. I hope your Excellency will not mistake me ; I am as much an Enemy to domestic Tyranny as to ye civil ; And I know that there sho'd be a certain Age when young People may dispose of themselves without the Consent of their Parents. What I contend for is, that there should also be a Period, during which ye Parent should have an uncontroulable Authority over ye Child, in ye Article of preventing Marriage.

As to ye Bond of £100 taken at the office, I think nothing of it. To my certain Knowledge it has been taken, both before & since ye Revolution, from persons not worth 100 pence ; And besides, there are Doubts as to ye Recovery of ye Penalty. I should be sorry to be understood, in this Part of ye Subject, as reflecting either on ye worthy Gentleman who has, nominally, ye Administration of ye Licenses, or on his Deputy, who is supposed to do his Business. On ye contrary, I declare that I believe ye Fault to be, not in them, but in ye System, which while it prevails, must involve ye present Consequences, let who will have ye Administration. And besides, I have not seen above one or two Licenses during Col. Biddle's Secretaryship nor long before.

4thly. It may be of Importance to mention that ye Practice has been stigmatised as illegal by ye Council of Censors. I speak from Report, not having seen their Resolves on ye Subject. But my Authority is such that I cannot doubt ye Truth of it.

And now, Sir, if your Excellency is disposed to listen to my Proposal of a Remedy, it is as follows :

1. In regard to all Persons marrying agreeably to ye Notifications required by their respective religious Societies, ye Clergyman celebrating ye Marriage sh'd be responsible in a pecuniary, or, if you please, on repeated Transgression, in a corporal Penalty. If meer publication be made sufficient, it will amount to Nothing ; because it may be made (& is made in some Congregations) in such a Manner as to be a meer Evasion.

2dly. As to Persons who may not come within ye Rules of any religious Society, some Mode of Publication sh'd be provided for them. There is one indeed, but it is thought insufficient.

3dly. The License sh'd be considered as a Dispensation from ye Notoriety of Publication ; And accordingly, Government sh'd assume ye Responsibility. The dispensing Officer should have a Reward proportioned to his Trouble & Risque. He sh'd be liable to a Penalty, according to ye Damage sustained at ye Discretion of ye Court, within certain Limits. He sh'd therefore, be ye Judge of ye Amount of ye Security to be required ; And if he take insufficient Bondmen, it sh'd be at his Peril. The most material Difficulty that can occur in ye above Plan is ye discretionary Power of ye Court. But I know no other Substitute for ye English Mode, which is ye taking of Oaths that there is no legal Impediment.

Your Excellency's desiring of me to state my Sentiments in writing has occasioned you ye Trouble of reading this long Letter. I am not tenacious of any Advice I have presumed to offer ; But am fixed in my knowledge of ye Fact & I hope ye Freedom of ye Citizen will justify my declaring it, that ye present Practice makes Government contribute to ye sacrificing of ye Peace, Honor & Fortunes of Families.

I have ye Honor to subscribe myself,

Your Excellency's very humble Servant,

WM. WHITE.

His Excell'y, Thos. Mifflin, Esq.

Sir, Dec. 22, 1790.

In Compliance with your Excellency's Intimation, I am emboldened to lay before you briefly, the Substance of what I formerly delivered to you more at large, on the present State of Law and Practice, on ye Subject of Marriage.

The Objections which I had the Honor to state to you against ye Marriage Licenses, were that it is a taking of Money out of ye people's pockets, without even ye Colour of Law, that it had been stigmatized on this Acct. by the Council of Censors; and that to my certain Knowledge, it prostitutes ye Chief Magistrates Name & invades Domestic Rights, by the Sanction it gives to clandestine Marriages.

It is true, the Abuse is considerably lessened, by ye intire Neglect which is shown the License, by ye greater number of the Clergy of all Denominations; who depend on their own Precaution against what they think the Snares of ye govermental License. But I submit to your Excellency whether it be not a great Evil to leave Matters on this Footing.

It is now so well understood that no Man takes out a License, but either thro' Ignorance or for a Cover to an illegal Transaction, that we may presume the Doing without them will more and more prevail. It must be obvious to every Man how much this subjects the Happiness of families to the sudden Determination of very young People. Under such a Dispensation from all preparatory Measures, would it be surprising to hear, that a Girl of the Age at which Matrimony may be contracted, were induced by a Toy or by a Sugar Plumb, to put an artful Man into ye possession of a Fortune; out of which he would only have to pay £50 for ye Irregularity of ye Manner. Impositions may happen far short of this, yet very distressing to Families and ruinous to the Peace of ye Parties.

So far as ye Clergy in particular are concerned, it subjects ye conscientious to great Difficulties; It gives those of ye opposite Description unbounded License; and it subjects to ye Determination of either (and that in situations of great Delicacy) a Question involving Property and Character and Happiness.

In what Manner an evil of so great Magnitude is to be remedied, I presume not to say. But I will hint what I think ye great Outline of ye Business; viz.: That in Favor of these who either cannot, or who, from conscientious Scruples, will not pay for a License, there should be pointed out an unequivocal Mode of Publication; and that a License being a Dispensation from ye Notoriety of Publication, the Officers issuing it should be accountable and should receive a Fee proportioned to ye Trust and to ye Vigilance required in it.

With Sentiments of Respect &
Esteem, I have the honor to write
myself, your Excellency's
very humble Servant,

Directed, His Excellency, the Governor.*   WM. WHITE.

FORM OF BOND

GIVEN on obtaining a Marriage Licence for RICHARD MONT-
GOMERY, Esq., afterwards Major-General in the Ameri-
can Army.

KNOW all Men by these Presents, That *Henry B. Livingston, of
Dutchess County, Esquire, and John Livingston, of New York,
Gentleman,* are held and firmly bound unto our Sovereign Lord
GEORGE the *Third,* by the Grace of GOD, of Great-Britain,
France, and Ireland, King, Defender of the Faith, &c. in the
Sum of *Five Hundred* Pounds, current Money of the Province
of New-York, to be paid to his said Majesty, or his Heirs and
Successors: For the which Payment, well and truly to be made
and done, We do bind Ourselves, and each of Us, our and each
of our Heirs, Executors, and Administrators, and every of them,
firmly by these Presents. Sealed with our Seals, dated the
Fourth Day of *August,* in the *Thirteenth* Year of his said Majesty's Reign. Annoque Domini, One Thousand Seven Hundred
and *Seventy-Three.*

THE CONDITION of this OBLIGATION, is such, That whereas
the above-bounden *Henry B. Livingston and John Livingston* have
obtained a LICENCE OF MARRIAGE for *Richard Montgomery, of the Out-
ward of New-York, Gentleman, & Jennet Livingston, of Dutchess County,*
Spinster, of the other Party. Now if it shall not appear hereafter,
that they, or either of them the said *Richard Montgomery & Jennet
Livingston* have any lawful Let or Impediment of Pre-Contract,
Affinity, or Consanguinity, to hinder their being joined in the Holy
Bands of Matrimony, and afterwards their living together as
Man and Wife: Then this Obligation to be void, and of none
Effect; or else to stand, remain, abide, and be in full Force and
Virtue.

HENRY B. LIVINGSTON, [L. S.]
JOHN LIVINGSTON.   [L. S.]

*Sealed and Delivered in the
    Presence of*
JNO. GRUMLY.

NEW YORK MARRIAGES.

A.

DATE.	NAMES.	RECORD.	VOL.	PAGE.
1765. April 17.	Acker, Catharine, and Peter Van Tassell, ...	M. B.,	IX.	101
1762. June 17.	Acker, Helen, and Walter Hyer,............	"	VI.	194
1758. June 3.	Acker, Jane, and Daniel Scidmore, ...	"	I.	924
1783. Sept. 3.	Acker, Mary, and John Myer,..............	"	XL.	20
1757. Dec. 28.	Ackerly, Robert, and Sarah Smith..........	"	I.	756
1781. April 19.	Ackerman, Ann, and Abram Maybee,........	"	XXXII.	8
1764. Mar. 23.	Ackerman, Catharine, and Nicholas Moore,...	"	VIII.	115
1765. June 27.	Ackerman, Catharine, and Walter De Grauw,.	"	IX.	185
16$\frac{79}{80}$. Mar. 13.	Ackerman, David, Helligond Ver Planck,.....	G. E.,	XXXII.	72
1769. Mar. 22.	Ackerman, Edward, and Susannah Bertine,...	M. B.,	XIV.	58
1778. Sept. 10.	Ackerman, John, and Mary Beekman,.......	"	XXVI.	23
1781. Oct. 5.	Ackerman, John, and Annautia Baldwin, ...	"	XXXIII.	89
1769. Nov. 1.	Ackerman, Leah, and Benjamin Allison,......	"	XV.	73
1765. April 17.	Ackerman, Maritje, and Elbert Onderdonck, ..	"	IX.	100
1760. Mar. 7.	Ackerman, Simon, and Catherine Bowman,...	"	III.	68
1769. April 20.	Ackerman, Susannah, and Peter Tobin, ...	"	XIV.	78
1760. July 14.	Ackerson, Dennes, and Lenea Slingerland, ...	"	III.	213
1779. June 24.	Ackerson, John, and Abigail Olnes,.........	"	XXVIII.	7
1783. Sept. 20.	Ackesen, Thomas, and Hannah Retton, ...	"	XL.	46
1771. Dec. 28.	Acklay, Elizabeth, and Daniel Lawrance,.....	"	XVII.	305
1755. Aug. 16.	Ackle, William, and Mary Newton,..........	"	I.	149
1775. June 28.	Ackley, Ann, and Richard Spencer,.........	"	XXIII.	81
1783. Nov. 2.	Ackley, Daniel, and Mary Harriss,..........	"	XL.	102
1770. Aug. 23.	Ackley, Elizabeth, and Robert Struthan,.....	"	XVI.	169
1782. June 27.	Ackley, Susannah, and Dennis Post,........	"	XXXVI.	64
1757. May 16.	Aclay, Deborah, and William Sands,........	"	I.	534
1781. Jan. 12.	Acres, Thomas, and Mary Hustick (Husten),	"	XXXI.	20
1783. April 28.	Adam, William, and Ally Devoor,..........	"	XXXVIII.	105
1779. July 8.	Adams, Catherine, and John Mitchell,......	"	XXVIII.	18
1759. July 17.	Adams, Elizabeth, and Thomas Liscomb,....	"	II.	358
1763. Oct. 29.	Adams, John, and Charity Smith,..........	"	VII.	412
1771. June 7.	Adams, John, and Hannah Bradburn,.......	"	XVII.	103
1736. May 14.	Adams, Jonas, and Elizabeth Saxton,.......	"	I.	1
1780. Sept. 29.	Adams, James, and Eunice Harned,........	"	XXX.	47
1771. April 25.	Adams, John, and Sarah Wheeler,..........	"	XVII.	68
1775. Aug. 21.	Adams, John, and Mary Con,..............	"	XXIII.	132
1766. Nov. 25.	Adams, Mary, and John Van Vorst,........	"	X.	182
1763. Nov. 21.	Adams, Phebe, and Simon Reeves,.........	"	VII.	460
1762. May 27.	Adams, Sarah, and William Turner,........	"	VI.	170
1762. Jan. 24.	Adams, Susanna, and William Morris,......	"	VII.	33
1759. June 6.	Adams, William, and Susana Van Maple,...	"	II.	304
1762. Jan. 25.	Adams, William, and Jane Jienson,........	"	VII.	34
1760. Sept. 4.	Addy, Jennet, and David Rottery,.........	"	III.	282
1770. April 14.	Adems, John, and Susanah B. Rogers,......	"	XVI.	62
1757. June 10.	Adleton, Abigail, and Alexander Auxburgh,	"	I.	559

Date.	Names.	Record.	Vol.	Page.
1773. May 22.	Adriaanse, Caroline, and Charles Platt,	M. B.,	xx.	121
1773. Oct. 8.	Adriaanse, Cornelius, and Aaltje Swartwout,	"	xxi.	133
1771. Aug. 21.	Adriaense, Elbert, and Sarah Brinckerhoff,..	"	xvii.	161
1768. May 30.	Adriance, Albert, and Hannah Platt,	"	xiii.	119
1766. Sept. 2.	Adriance, Fametie, and Thomas Langdon,..	"	x.	89
1761. Jan. 14.	Adriance, Jacob, and Catherine Hoglandt,..	"	iv.	16
1782. Nov. 23.	Adriance, Jane,' and Cornelius Van Brunt,..	".	xxxvii.	92
1772. Nov. 24.	Adriance, John, and Aneltie Storm,	"	xix.	127
1764. May 11.	Adrianse, Isaac, and Eda Schenck,	"	viii.	188
1755. Nov. 27.	Adrianse, Rem, and Jannetie Van Clief,	"	i.	218
1759. Nov. 21.	Adrianse, Rem, and Elizabeth Ryder,	"	ii.	510
1764. Aug. 13.	Aerhart, Christopher, and Hyler Dey,	"	viii.	279
1760. Nov. 20.	Agen, Timothy, and Elizabeth McGeer,	"	iii.	428
1777. Nov. 8.	Aget, Agness, and Thomas Smith,	"	xxiv.	178
1762. April 8.	Agnew, Abigail, and Caleb Hyatt,	"	vi.	93
1777. Dec. 29.	Ahern, Bridget, and Nathaniel Phillipse,	"	xxiv.	209
1773. Aug. 5.	Aights, Catherine, and Henry Van Woert,..	"	xxi.	57
1783. April 22.	Aikins, John, and Mary Brooks,	"	xxxviii.	108
1773. July 28.	Aim, Martin, and Elinor Harding,	"	xxi.	52
1782. Oct. 17.	Aime, Margaret, and Robert Scott,	"	xxxvii.	44
1779. Jan. 14.	Ainsly, Mary, and Edward Burke,	"	xxvii.	14
1778. Feb. 10.	Airs, Joseph, and Charity Whetten,	"	xxv.	21
1782. Jan. 17.	Airy, Hannah, and Barnard Marling,	"	xxxv.	21
1779. Jan. 20.	Aitkenhead, John, and Ann Hamilton,	"	xxvii.	21
1771. Aug. 19.	Aitkins, Charles, and Cornelia Beekman,	"	xvii.	159
1768. Jan. 28.	Aitun, Robert, and Margaret Ladd,	"	xiii.	19
1759. Dec. 12.	Akely, Elizabeth, and John Stocker,	"	ii.	541
1772. Mar. 7.	Akerly, Jacamiah, and Susannah Dodge,	"	xviii.	51
1781. Sept. 5.	Akerly, Johanah, and Daniel Pine,	"	xxxiii.	59
1770. April 27.	Akerly, Rebecca, and Jacob Sammons,	"	xvi.	71
1775. Dec. 12.	Akin, Abigail, and John Toffey,	"	xxiii.	228
1781. Oct. 16.	Akin, Justice, and Elizabeth Briggs,	"	xxxiii.	103
1780. April 15.	Akinson, John, and Ann McCord,	"	xxix.	25
1764. Nov. 15.	Alberson, Rachel, and Abraham Hill,	"	viii.	411
1760. June 24.	Alberson, Sarah, and Obadiah Green,	"	iii.	195
1761. Mar. 14.	Albertson, Albert, and Phebe Pierce,	"	iv.	102
1772. June 23.	Albertson, Deliverance, and Robert Hinchman,	"	xviii.	148
1778. Dec. 19.	Albertson, Jemima, and John Frazer,	"	xxvi.	126
1780. Oct. 7.	Albertson, William, and Sarah Concklin,	"	xxx.	59
1762. July 31.	Albertus, Antje, and Richard Gosline,	"	vi.	258
1762. Sept. 21.	Albertus, Phebe, and Thomas Sacket,	"	vi.	324
1772. Sept. 29.	Albouy, John, and Catherine Blouw,	"	xix.	63
1779. June 4.	Albouy, Richard, and Mary Lave,	"	xxvii.	158
1768. Sept. 20.	Albouy, Jane, and John De Forrest,	"	xiii.	191
1767. July 17.	Albouy, Martha, and Bernard De Forrest,...	"	xi.	136

4   NEW YORK MARRIAGES.

DATE.	NAMES.	RECORD.	VOL. PAGE.
1762. Dec. 21.	Albouy, Richard, and Sarah Brewerton, ...	M. B.,	VI. 492
1756. Sept. 6.	Albrespy, William, and Hannah Bourdet, . . .	"	I. 290
1769. Mar. 25.	Alburtis, Peter, and Catherine Van Ander, . .	"	XIV. 60
1773. July 22.	Alburtus, Peter, and Martha Denton, ...	"	XXI. 49
1777. April 12.	Aldsworth, John, and Jane Johnson, ...	"	XXIV. 60
1772. Mar. 5.	Alexander, Robert, and Jane Willett, ...	"	XVIII. 49
1760. Feb. 19.	Alford, Margaret, and John Clarke, ...	"	III. 41
1768. Oct. 10.	Alington, Arthur, and Marah Lewis, ...	"	XIII. 206
1780. Nov. 6.	Allaire, Peter A., and Frances Wilmot, ...	"	XXX. 92
1779. Jan. 7.	Allamand, Jonas H., and Mary De Graw, . . .	"	XXVII. 4
1779. July 7.	Allaway, Susanah, and George Person, ...	"	XXVIII. 17
1777. June 18.	Allboy, Sarah, and Isaac Collins, ...	"	XXIV. 105
1756. Aug. 27.	Allee, Peter, and Abigail Borright, ...	"	I. 279
1753. June 6.	Allen, Abraham, and Sarah Outwater, ...	"	I. 50
1775. May 12.	Allen, Agnes, and John Williams, ...	"	XXIII. 31
1782. Mar. 11.	Allen, Agnes, and Jacob Brower, ...	"	XXXV. 86
1780. April 13.	Allen, Ann, and Silas Powel, ...	"	XXIX. 22
1773. Nov. 4.	Allen, David, and Nancy Kissam, ...	"	XXII. 12
1777. Oct. 14.	Allen, Elijah, and Sarah Kissam, ...	"	XXIV. 162
1782. Feb. 2.	Allen, Elizabeth, and John Hurly, ...	"	XXXV. 42
1773. Oct. 28.	Allen, Hannah, and Nathaniel Shaler, ...	"	XXII. 3
1762. Dec. 14.	Allen, Henry, and Elizabeth Smith, ...	"	VI. 479
1761. Aug. 22.	Allen, Jacamiah, and Rachel Hendricks, ...	"	V. 52
1781. Dec. 13.	Allen, James, and Mary Burtis, ...	"	XXXIV. 82
1777. July 30.	Allen, Jane, and John Welsh, ...	"	XXIV. 125
1767. Feb. 14.	Allen, Jerusha, and Amos Powell, ...	"	XI. 26
1757. April 23.	Allen, John, and Elizabeth Annely, ...	"	I. 512
1758. Oct. 26.	Allen, John, and Sovenah Miring, ...	"	II. 69
1770. Dec. 3.	Allen, John, and Ann May Daniel, ...	"	XVI. 280
1779. April 20.	Allen, John, and Ruth Smith, ...	"	XXVII. 110
1782. May 2.	Allen, John, and Susannah Quackenbush, . . .	"	XXXV. 145
1783. June 5.	Allen, John, and Rebecca Wallace, ...	"	XXXIX. 40
1763. Nov. 29.	Allen, Joseph, and Mary Forster, ...	"	VII. 482
1758. Dec. 6.	Allen, Lettetia, and Benjamin Seamans, ...	"	II. 117
1760. Nov. 12.	Allen, Margaret, and Winant Bennett, ...	"	III. 405
1764. June 1.	Allen, Margaret, and Johannes Rosekrans, . .	"	VIII. 203
1759. June 9.	Allen, Mary, and William Luckett, ...	"	II. 316
1759. Sept. 12.	Allen, Mary, and Luke Clarke, ...	"	II. 417
1759. Sept. 28.	Allen, Mary, and Peter De Maree, ...	"	II. 436
1762. Nov. 9.	Allen, Mary, and John Green, ...	"	VI. 420
1765. Aug. 29.	Allen, Mary, and Thomas Robelee, ...	"	IX. 251
1769. Nov. 3.	Allen, Mary, and John Thorne, ...	"	XV. 77
1773. Dec. 20.	Allen, Mary, and Zacharias Flegla, ...	"	XXII. 79
1759. Nov. 3.	Allen, Meriby, and Samuel Townsend, ...	"	II. 487
1770. Dec. 29.	Allen, Nathaniel, and Catherine Lisk, ...	"	XVI. 309

DATE.	NAMES.	RECORD.	VOL.	PAGE.
1779. Oct. 23.	Allen, Nehemiah, and Mary Pearsall,	M. B.,	XXVIII.	118
1761. Aug. 20.	Allen, Patrick, and Mary Young,	"	V.	49
1782. Aug. 24.	Allen, Peter, and Phebe Coole,	"	XXXVI.	123
1769. Jan. 9.	Allen, Phebe, and Joseph Thorne,	"	XIV.	9
1769. Mar. 6.	Allen, Phebe, and Nathaniel Jarvis,	"	XIV.	47
1782. Mar. 6.	Allen, Phebe, and John Kissam,	"	XXXV.	76
1777. June 25.	Allen, Philip, and Sarah Thorne,	"	XXIV.	107
1781. Sept. 17.	Allen, John, and Cloe Yeomans,	"	XXXIII.	68
1762. Nov. 13.	Allen, Richard, and Mary Regan,	"	VI.	465
1770. Feb. 17.	Allen, Samuel, and Pamelia Keese,	"	XVI.	19
1757. April 9.	Allen, Sarah, and Robert Mitchel,	"	I.	494
1769. June 24.	Allen, Sarah, and Jeremiah Hanton,	"	XIV.	130
1761. Nov. 19.	Allen, Stephen, and Mary Vanderhoof,	"	V.	230
1780. May 29.	Allen, Stephen, and Ann Bridgman,	"	XXIX.	71
1778. Jan. 14.	Allery, Stephen, and Bridget Stirling,	"	XXV.	6
1782. May 4.	Allicocke, Abigail, and Thomas Scotland,	"	XXXV.	151
1781. July 21.	Allicocke, Sarah, and James Butcher,	"	XXXIII.	12
1765. April 10.	Alliger, Mary, and John Emans,	"	IX.	85
1759. Nov. 15.	Allin, Penelope, and Simon Noxson,	"	II.	496
1683. May 29.	Allisen, James, and Alse Corbett,	E.,	XXXIII.	59
1769. Nov. 1.	Allison, Benjamin, and Leah Ackerman,	M. B.	XV.	73
1768. May 4.	Allison, Elizabeth, and John Allison,	"	XIII.	92
1768. May 4.	Allison, John, and Elizabeth Allison,	"	XIII.	92
1769. April 10.	Allison, Joseph, and Elcie Parsells,	"	XIV.	68
1773. Nov. 2.	Allison, Sarah, and William Thompson,	"	XXII.	7
1783. April 12.	Alloway, John, and Jane Ris,	"	XXXVIII.	95
1756. Nov. 27.	Ally, Hester, and William Davis,	"	I.	365
1781. June 10.	Almer, Sarah, and Peter Baker,	"	XXXII.	81
1771. Nov. 26.	Alner, Charity, and James Leonard,	"	XVII.	270
1763. Dec. 24.	Alner, James, and Letitia Foster,	"	VII.	524
1758. Sept. 7.	Alsbruken, Catharine E.,and Christopher Rice,	"	II.	6
1766. June 30.	Alsdorph, Gertry, and Samuel Irwin,	"	X.	38
1737. Oct. 28.	Alsop, Amy, and Jonathan Wright,	"	I.	7
1763. July 14.	Alsop, Andrew, and Sarah Brasier,	"	VII.	265
1781. April 26.	Alsop, Elizabeth, and Richard Hawkins,	"	XXXII.	17
1762. Nov. 3.	Alsop, Euphemia, and Thomas Stevenson,	"	VI.	407
1763. July 12.	Alsop, Frances, and Solomon Craft,	"	VII.	261
1766. June 6.	Alsop, John, and Mary Frogat,	"	X.	6
1758. Oct. 24.	Alsop, Mary, and George Willocks Leslie,	"	II.	66
1766. Nov. 20.	Alsop, Richard, and Abigail Whitehead,	"	X.	172
1753. June 5.	Alsop, Sarah, and John Legget,	"	I.	49
1764. June 22.	Alsop, Susannah, and Jacob Hallett,	"	VIII.	232
1761. July 22.	Alsop, Thomas, and Phila Butler,	"	V.	5
1767. April 13.	Alstin, Abraham, and Mary Crab,	"	XI.	61
1763. Mar. 16.	Alstine, Catherine, and James Slover,	"	VII.	100

DATE.	NAMES.	RECORD.	VOL.	PAGE.
1781. Oct. 6.	Alstine, Catharine, and Jeronimus Remsen, M. B.,		XXXIII.	91
1782. April 3.	Alstine, Jane, and James Chadwick, ...	"	XXXV.	111
1737. July 22.	Alstine, Libety, and Abraham Winnegard,	"	I.	6
1760. April 25.	Alstyn, Elizabeth, and Moses Taylor, ...	"	III.	124
1759. June 7.	Alstyn, Jeromus, and Eyda Beekman, ...	"	II.	309
1759. Aug. 3.	Alstyn, Mary, and Robert Tout, ...	"	II.	370
1772. Oct. 26.	Alstyne, Ann, and John Rogers, ...	"	XIX.	91
1761. June 3.	Alstyne, Hermanus, and Rachel Baldwin, . .	"	IV.	224
1763. Mar. 4.	Alstyne, Mary, and Benjamin Barwick, ...	"	VII.	91
1772. May 19.	Alstyne, Meritie Elvyn, and Gose Van Buren,	"	XVIII.	112
1767. July 2.	Altgelt, Jacobus, and Mary Sign, ...	"	XI.	119
1783. July 26.	Althause, John, and Jane Jackson, ...	"	XXXIX.	102
1757. July 15.	Alvey, John, and Geesie Durham, ...	"	I.	592
1782. Jan. 5.	Alward, Joseph, and Frances Childs, ...	"	XXXV.	9
1765. Oct. 24.	Amar, Sharlot, and John Moffit, ...	"	IX.	316
1781. Aug. 28.	Amberman, Sarah, and Barnardus Lamberson,	"	XXXIII.	49
1781. Nov. 17.	Amberman, Sarah, and Simon Lamberson, . .	"	XXXIV.	46
1782. Nov. 8.	Amberman, Elizabeth, and Benjamin Skinner,	"	XXXVII.	74
1781. April 7.	Ambos, Martin T., and Elizabeth Pontine,	"	XXXI.	97
1761. July 9.	Ambrose, Elizabeth, and William Chapman,	"	IV.	292
1766. Aug. 20.	Ame, Mary, and Edward Monton, ...	"	X.	78
1770. May 5.	Amel, John, and Elizabeth Farquhar, ...	"	XVI.	79
1780. April 25.	Amens, Margaret, and John De Mot, ...	"	XXIX.	37
1759. Sept. 5.	Ament, Luke, and Eliza Billins, ...	"	II.	410
1758. Dec. 7.	Amerman, Elbert, and Prudence Montanye,	"	II.	119
1758. Jan. 6.	Amerman, Janetje, and Roeloff Durye, ...	"	I.	772
1769. Mar. 6.	Amerman, Janetje, and Coenrad W. Ham, . .	"	XIV.	48
1755. Nov. 27.	Amerman, John, and Lydia Amerman, ...	"	I.	221
1753. Aug. 3.	Amerman, Lenah, and Samuel Dodge, ...	"	I.	84
1755. Nov. 27.	Amerman, Lydia, and John Amerman, ...	"	I.	221
1768. Feb. 22.	Amerman, Margaret, and John Cowenhoven,	"	XIII.	40
1753. Oct. 17.	Amerman, Petrus, and Willemtie Schenck,	"	I.	142
1773. April 7.	Amerman, Powel, and Mary Voorhis, ...	"	XX.	85
1765. Oct. 21.	Amerman, Richard, and Mary Van Hook, . .	"	IX.	309
1766. July 24.	Amerman, Sarah, and John Remsen, ...	"	X.	61
1737. Sept. 30.	Ames, Mary, and William Green, ...	"	I.	7
1762. June 25.	Amey, Catherine, and Aaron Darling, ...	"	VI.	208
1772. Oct. 29.	Ammerick, Francis, and Catherine Smith, . .	"	XIX.	94
1782. Mar. 9.	Ammerman, Aultye, and Cornelius Mersereau,	"	XXXV.	82
1764. Dec. 22.	Ammerman, Cornelius, and Abigil Okely, . . .	"	VIII.	463
1768. June 15.	Ammerman, Mary, and James Reynolds, . . .	"	XIII.	128
1762. Sept. 3.	Amory, Charles, and Sarah Smith, ...	"	VI.	306
1759. June 21.	Amory, Jane, and John Butler, ...	"	II.	336
1769. Oct. 29.	Amory, John, and Neeltie Staats, ...	"	XV.	66
1777. April 30.	Amory, John, and Mary De Lamontagnie, . .	"	XXIV.	79

DATE.	NAMES.	RECORD.	VOL.	PAGE.
1757. Nov. 22.	Amos, Daniel, and Mary Bell,..............	M. B.,	I.	708
1763. Aug. 12.	Andariesa, Nicholas, Jr., and Hannah Bomer,	"	VII.	298
1762. April 20.	Anderson, Abraham, and Susannah Burger,	"	VI.	117
1768. April 13.	Anderson, Alexander, and Mary Carter,...	"	XIII.	76
1777. Dec. 4.	Anderson, Andrew, and Isabella Brown,...	"	XXIV.	191
1753. Sept. 11.	Anderson, Ann, and John Wendell,.......	"	I.	112
1757. July 5.	Anderson, Ann, and John Smith,.........	"	I.	582
1756. Sept. 10.	Anderson, Catharine, and Jonathan Hughes,	"	I.	293
1761. Mar. 16.	Anderson, George, and Deborah Grant,....	"	IV.	103
1763. May 16.	Anderson, George, and Sarah Brower,.....	"	VII.	188
1780. Aug. 30.	Anderson, John, and Christian Downy,....	"	XXX.	10
1780. April 13.	Anderson, John, and Jane McRobert, ...	"	XXIX.	21
1759. June 7.	Anderson, John, and Martha Evans, ...	"	II.	308
1780. Oct. 25.	Anderson, John, and Mary Wilkinson,.....	"	XXX.	80
1738. Nov. 27.	Anderson, John, and Rachel De Grove,....	"	I.	11
1772. Aug. 6.	Anderson, John, and Sarah Lockwood,....	"	XIX.	14
1757. Feb. 16.	Anderson, Joseph, and Mary Connelly,....	"	I.	439
1760. June 23.	Anderson, Lucretia, and James Dunn,.....	"	III.	195
1764. Jan. 12.	Anderson, Margaret, and Frederick Roorback	"	VIII.	14
1761. Dec. 24.	Anderson, Catharine, and Charles Brewer,..	"	V.	300
1764. Mar. 7.	Anderson, Catharine, and William Grant,..	"	VIII.	96
1770. April 2.	Anderson, Charity, and William Anderson,	"	XVI.	45
1760. May 28.	Anderson, David, and Sarah Lawrence,....	"	III.	165
1762. Oct. 8.	Anderson, Dorothy, and Samuel Treddle,..	"	VI.	354
1767. Oct. 22.	Anderson, Elbert, and Elizabeth Pierce, ...	"	XII.	67
1772. April 27.	Anderson, Elinor, and William Haddon, ...	"	XVIII.	92
1760. Oct. 21.	Anderson, Elijah, and Jemima Bercaw,....	"	III.	375
1780. Nov. 21.	Anderson, Elizabeth, and George Mount,..	"	XXX.	118
1781. June 22.	Anderson, Elizabeth, and William Tilton,..	"	XXXII.	96
1762. July 30.	Anderson, Mary, and John Blanchard,.....	"	VI.	255
1770. Oct. 23.	Anderson, Mary, and Joseph Dorrell,......	"	XVI.	225
1778. April 12.	Anderson, Mary, and John McDonald, ...	"	XXV.	63
1780. Nov. 20.	Anderson, Mary, and William Gibson,.....	"	XXX.	115
1780. Aug. 26.	Anderson, Molly, and Thomas Baker,.....	"	XXX.	2
1759. Sept. 14.	Anderson, Phebe, and Joseph King, ...	"	II.	421
1760. Aug. 15.	Anderson, Phebe, and Garret Wynkoop,...	"	III.	255
1761. Mar. 26.	Anderson, Prudence, and John Hawkins,..	"	IV.	121
1760. Jan. 23.	Anderson, Rebecca, and Hugh Dougherty,	"	III.	4
1760. Sept. 3.	Anderson, Richard, and Margaret Young,..	"	III.	278
1770. April 2.	Anderson, William, and Charity Anderson,	"	XVI.	45
1781. Sept. 6.	Anderson, William, and Elizabeth McBride,	"	XXXIII.	60
1769. Dec. 7.	Andrevet, Ann, and Jacob Cole,...........	"	XV.	117
1760. Sept. 5.	Andrew, Mary, and Richard Sax,.........	"	III.	289
1781. April 30.	Andrews, Ann, and John Adolph Richter,..	"	XXXII.	22
1769. Oct. 28.	Andrews, Phebe, and Absalom Seaman,....	"	XV.	72

DATE.	NAMES.	RECORD.	VOL. PAGE.
1778. Dec. 31.	Andrews, Robert, and Ann Cock, ...	M. B.,	XXVI. 135
1782. April 24.	Andrews, Sarah, and William Denning, ...	"	XXXV. 136
1758. Jan. 3.	Andrewuet, Rachel, and Daniel Wynant, ...	"	I. 766
1763. Mar. 14.	Andries, Nicholas, and Jane Brouwer, ...	"	VII. 96
1773. Sept. 25.	Androvet, John, and Martha Dubois, ...	"	XXI. 122
1780. Dec. 20.	Androvet, Mary, and Joseph Totten, ...	"	XXX. 159
1781. Aug. 29.	Androvett, Catharine, and Daniel Stover, ...	"	XXXIII. 52
1780. Aug. 24.	Androvett, John, and Charity Bogert, ...	"	XXIX. 147
1771. Mar. 25.	Androuet, Elizabeth, and Gilbert Jackson, ..	"	XVII. 40
1783. Feb. 5.	Andrus, Mary, and Elijah Card, ...	"	XXXVIII. 34
1758. Oct. 25.	Anell, Elizabeth, and Thomas Barker, ...	"	II. 68
1686. April 28.	Angell, Mary, and Benjamine Smeedis, ...	C. M.,	XXXIII. 235
1763. Feb. 5.	Angevoine, Ann, and John Martin, ...	M. B.,	VII. 54
1764. Feb. 20.	Anjevoin, Jane, and Ezekiel Legget, ...	"	VIII. 66
1770. Aug. 20.	Annan, Andrew, and Mary Crawford, ...	"	XVI. 163
1757. April 23.	Annely, Elizabeth, and John Allen, ...	"	I. 512
1761. April 4.	Annely, Elizabeth, and William Stewart, ...	"	IV. 132
1773. April 16.	Annet, Mary, and Thomas Boumaer, ...	"	XX. 94
1780. Mar. 20.	Ansley, Amos, and Christiana McMichael, ..	"	XXIX. 23
1782. July 1.	Ansley, Mary, and Richard Bedle, ...	"	XXXVI. 70
1768. Jan. 19.	Ansor, Jonas, and Elizabeth Pugsly, ...	"	XIII. 11
1757. Dec. 14.	Anthony, Abraham, and Ann Careau, ...	"	I. 743
1761. Dec. 18.	Anthony, Abraham, and Charity Suydam, ..	"	V. 286
1767. Sept. 23.	Anthony, Abraham, and Joanna Smith, ...	"	XII. 40
1759. Sept. 25.	Anthony, Angletje, and Theophilus Harden-brook, ...	"	II. 431
1773. May 5.	Anthony, John, and Margaret Pears, ...	"	XX. 104
1758. Sept. 5.	Anthony, Mary, and Henry Brevoort, ...	"	II. 2
1757. Dec. 14.	Anthony, Nicholas, and Catharine Dalley, ..	"	I. 742
1759. June 27.	Anthony, Theophilus, and WellemeyntjeVree-denbergh, ...	"	II. 342
1783. Mar. 25.	Anthony, Wilhelmina, and Robert Gill, ...	"	XXXVIII. 76
1686. Sept. 10.	Antill, Edward, and Elizabeth Bowne, ...	C. M.,	XXXIII. 293
1770. April 21.	Antill, John, and Margaret Colden, ...	M. B.,	XVI. 67
1771. Nov. 30.	Antill, Lewis, and Alice Colden, ...	"	XVII. 274
1773. Aug. 21.	Antoniodis, Catherine, and Joseph Hegeman,	"	XXI. 82
1783. Oct. 14.	Aplee, Jacob, and Sarah Van Winckle, ...	"	XL. 79
1737. Sept. 9.	Appelbee, Jane, and Arthur Heleme, ...	"	I. 7
1759. June 2.	Apple, Anna, and Abraham Birdall, ...	"	II. 301
1768. July 23.	Apple, Anthony, and Mary Marebutton, ...	"	XIII. 163
1758. Nov. 18.	Apple, Jacob, and Rosena Heppie, ...	"	II. 94
1779. Nov. 4.	Applebee, Rebecca, and Jacob Fee, ...	"	XXVIII. 129
1768. June 4.	Appleby, John, and Ann Ennic, ...	"	XIII. 120
1767. Sept. 8.	Appleby, Mary, and Hampton Lillibridge, ..	"	XII. 29
1780. July 22.	Appleby, Mary, and John Cooper, ...	"	XXIX. 118

DATE.	NAMES.	RECORD.	VOL.	PAGE.
1781. July 31.	Appleby, Robert, and Margaret Moore,.....	M. B.,	XXXIII.	22
1672. July 6.	Appleby, Thomas, and Elizabeth Osborne,..	G. E.,	IV.	245
1769. Oct. 27.	Applegate, Esabella, and William Evans,...	M. B.,	XV.	69
1770. Oct. 29.	Applegate, John, and Catharine Willet,....	"	XVI.	233
1764. June 2.	Applestall, Hannah, and John Ryerson,....	"	VIII.	204
1778. Aug. 11.	Appleton, William, and Mary Huggins,....	"	XXVI.	2
1777. Mar. 18.	Appy, Eliza, and William Jephson,.......	"	XXIV.	47
1767. Feb. 4.	Appy, Elizabeth, and Goldsbrow Banyar,..	"	XI.	19
1757. Dec. 7.	Appy, John, and Elizabeth Naden,........	"	I.	727
1779. May 3.	Arbuckle, John, and Mary O'Brien, ...	"	XXVII.	126
1783. Nov. 19.	Archbold, David, and Jemima Reyer, ...	"	XL.	124
1757. Jan. 21.	Archer, Abigail, and Joshua Pell,.........	"	I.	795
1762. May 24.	Archer, Anne, and Frederick Wm. Heeht,..	"	VI.	168
1775. Oct. 26.	Archer, Anthony, and Margaret Mapes,....	"	XXIII.	187
1761. Nov. 10.	Archer, Benjamin, and Rachel Devou,.....	"	V.	205
1762. Dec. 24.	Archer, Bridget, and Samuel Hitchcock, ...	"	VI.	499
1764. Mar. 30.	Archer, Caleb, and Altie Storme,..........	"	VIII.	124
1761. Sept. 1.	Archer, Elihu, and Hannah Hunt, ...	"	V.	66
1763. June 9.	Archer, Ezekiel, and Philena Tippit, ...	"	VII.	219
1772. Mar. 25.	Archer, Gabriel, and Susannah Hunt, ...	"	XVIII.	57
1769. Mar. 9.	Archer, Margaret, and Peter Dorry,,......	"	XIV.	50
1780. Nov. 9.	Archer, Mary, and Abraham Fincher, ...	"	XXX.	100
1780. Jan. 15.	Archer, Rachael, and Charles McDonald,...	"	XXVIII.	196
1758. May 11.	Archer, Rebecca, and Jacob Woolsey,.....	"	I.	900
1764. April 2.	Archer, Rebecca, and John Sneeden,......	"	VIII.	129
1761. Oct. 30.	Archibald, David, and Elizabeth Lawrence,	"	V.	180
1781. Feb. 6.	Archibald, Sarah, and Samuel Clayton, ...	"	XXXI.	38
1763. Feb. 22.	Arden, Abbyjah, and George Wilt,........	"	VII.	75
1768. Jan. 22.	Arden, Elizabeth, and William Ritchce,....	"	XIII.	17
1761. Aug. 22.	Arden, John, and Susanna De St. Croix,...	"	V.	51
1773. Jan. 25.	Arden, Samuel, and Elizabeth Miller,......	"	XX.	20
1773. Feb. 2.	Arden, Thomas, Jr., and Mary Boyle,.....	"	XX.	36
1767. June 30.	Arden, Francis, and Catherine Ryan,.......	"	XI.	117
1738. April 29.	Arding, Charles, and Effie Schuyler,.......	"	I.	9
1766. June 25.	Arding, Charles, and Abigail Van Wyke,...	"	X.	32
1760. Aug. 29.	Arding, Mary, and Thomas Webb,........	"	III.	274
1766. June 23.	Arehart, Froutie, and Peter De Bratt, ...	"	X.	27
1757. June 8.	Arenhoudt, Ann, and Peter Dennels,......	"	I.	557
1770. Oct. 13.	Arentz, James, and Ann Harrison,........	"	XVI.	212
1783. June 7.	Areson, Jacob, and Jane Baley, ...	"	XXXIX.	45
1781. Dec. 13.	Areson, William, and Rebecca Carpenter, ..	"	XXXIV.	83
1758. Dec. 19.	Argan, Thomas, and Elizabeth Morgan,....	"	II.	133
1769. Feb. 7.	Arhart, George, and Margaret Hardon,....	"	XIV.	29
1771. May 24.	Arianse, Arie, and Jane Blauvelt,.........	"	XVII.	91
1771. April 21.	Arison, Mary, and Benjamin Egbert,......	"	XVII.	90

2

DATE.	NAMES.	RECORD.	VOL.	PAGE.
1774. Feb. 22.	Arkles, Jemima, and Joseph Carman, ...	M. B.,	xxii.	132
1772. July 8.	Arksen, John, and Anna Van Antwerp, ...:	"	xviii.	158
1766. July 16.	Arismit, Cornelious, and Adriaantje Coneyn,	"	x.	53
1771. Jan. 5.	Armitage, James, and Abigail Lyle,.......	"	xvii.	2
1770. Dec. 15.	Armitage, James, and Susannah Vandrill,..	"	xvi.	297
1781. Sept. 4.	Armour, Daniel, and Mary Osbourn,......	"	xxxiii.	57
1760. Nov. 17.	Armour, James, and Mary Dunscomb,......	"	iii.	421
1780. May 18.	Armour, William, and Susanah Richardson,	"	xxix.	61
1762. Mar. 30.	Armstrong, Alice, and Thomas Hill, ...	"	vi.	87
1762. April 8.	Armstrong, Ann, and William Robinson,...	"	vi.	95
1775. Nov. 18.	Armstrong, Catharine, and Hugh Welsh,...	"	xxiii.	216
1779. April 27.	Armstrong, Francis, and Sarah Leyster,....	"	xxvii.	121
1761. Aug. 22.	Armstrong, James, and Catherine Cortney,	"	v.	53
1781. Dec. 22.	Armstrong, Jesse, and Hannah Crocker, ...	"	xxxiv.	100
1763. Aug. 31.	Armstrong, Margaret, and John Beek,.....	"	vii.	320
1762. Oct. 18.	Armstrong, Mary, and William Hughes, ...	"	vi.	371
1771. Nov. 13.	Armstrong, Mary, and James Ireland,.....	"	xvii.	253
1763. Feb. 21.	Armstrong, Reginal, and Mary Dobson,....	"	vii.	73
1759. Dec. 29.	Arnes, John, and Bena Scott, ...	"	ii.	559
1781. June 25.	Arno, Charles, and Henrietta Woodword,..	"	xxxii.	97
1761. Nov. 11.	Arnold, Jane, and John McCaffery, ...	"	v.	210
1759. Jan. 22.	Arnold, Valentine, and Tryal Spencer,.....	"	ii.	164
1767. Feb. 19.	Arnold, William, and Mary Sheerwood,....	"	xi.	31
1772. Nov. 27.	Aroe, Elizabeth, and Abraham H. Van Vleck,	"	xix.	134
1782. Sept. 3.	Arrison, Anne, and Frederick De Voue,.....	"	xxxvi.	135
1761. Oct. 6.	Arrison, Arthur, and Marritie Broadhead,...	"	v.	128
173⅞. Feb. 20.	Arrowsmith, Edmund, and Mary Garritson,	"	i.	9
1779. Aug. 22.	Arrowsmith, Letty, and John Heslop,......	"	xxviii.	56
1759. Aug. 21.	Arrowsmith, Martha, and Joseph Morrell,...	"	ii.	385
1764. Oct. 16.	Arrowsmith, Mary, and John Hillyer,......	"	viii.	357
1777. Aug. 6.	Arrowsmith, Miranda, and William Perrine,	"	xxiv.	127
1782. July 15.	Arrowsmith, William, and Elizabeth Mucklevane, ...	"	xxxvi.	83
1757. May 21.	Arthur, Amm, and Joseph Morris,.........	"	i.	539
1758. Mar. 23.	Arthur, Elizabeth, and John Palmer,.......	"	i.	862
1758. April 19.	Arthur, Elizabeth, and Samuel Deal,.......	"	i.	877
1763. Sept. 17.	Arthur, George, and Catharine Puntis,.....	"	vii.	339
1761. June 2.	Arthur, Hugh, and Margaret McDougall,....	"	iv.	223
1771. June 20.	Arthur, John, and Elizabeth Cheesman,....	"	xvii.	118
1757. Feb. 7.	Arthur, Mary, and William Blydenburgh,...	"	i.	436
1760. June 26.	Arthur, Reuben, and Sarah Jerveas,.......	"	iii.	197
1779. Oct. 5.	Arthur, Richard, and Elizabeth Clark,......	"	xxviii.	102
1768. May 5.	Arthur, Samuel, and Elizabeth White,......	"	xiii.	94
1769. April 20.	Arundies, Johannes, and Christena Provost,	"	xiv.	80
1769. Aug. 28.	Ascough, William, and Marian Haines,.....	"	xv.	30

DATE.	NAMES.	RECORD.	VOL.	PAGE.
1757. Dec. 28.	Ash, Catherine, and Gabriel Leget,	M. B.,	I.	754
1757. Oct. 13.	Ash, Miles, and Elenor Way,	"	I.	668
1760. Aug. 12.	Ash, Norman, and Sarah Mason,	"	III.	250
1781. Aug. 16.	Ash, Sarah, and Walter Birk,	"	XXXIII.	38
1763. July 23.	Ash, Thomas, and Elizabeth Stanton,	"	VII.	281
1777. April 18.	Ashfield, Catherine, and Thomas Shreve,	"	XXIV.	66
1781. Nov. 30.	Ashfield, John, and Mary Taylor,	"	XXXIV.	64
1772. Sept. 15.	Ashfield, Vincent P., and Sarah Morris,	"	XIX.	50
1764. April 30.	Ashford, Jane, and John Slidell,	"	VIII.	174
1782. Sept. 15.	Ashford, Nathaniel, and Anne Graham,	"	XXXVII.	2
1753. May 23.	Ashinger, Martha, and Isaac Ball,	"	I.	39
1770. Dec. 29.	Ashworth, Henry, and Elizabeth Tiebout,	"	XVI.	308
1758. Nov. 18.	Askin, Mary, and Isaac Lee,	"	II.	93
1781. Dec. 8.	Askins, William, and Elizabeth Campbell,	"	XXXIV.	77
1766. May 27.	Aspinwall, John, and Rebecca Smith,	"	X.	1
1771. Oct. 29.	Assellstyn, Elizabeth, and Jeremiah Miller,	"	XVII.	230
1767. Sept. 30.	Asselstyn, Jane, and Robert McGinnis, Sen.,	"	XII.	49
1736. May 4.	Asselstyn, John, and Mary Vredenburgh,	"	I.	1
1772. May 25.	Ashton, Elizabeth, and John Neal,	"	XVIII.	124
1685. May 26.	Ashton, Thomas, and Elizabeth Gibbs,	C. M.,	XXXIII.	131
1783. April 11.	Atken, Isaac, and Effee Curtis,	M. B.,	XXXVIII.	91
1761. Nov. 3.	Atkins, Hannah, and John Callahan,	"	V.	190
1782. Feb. 11.	Atkins, James, and Catherine Kelsey,	"	XXXV.	48
1764. May 19.	Atkins, Joseph, and Ann Spear,	"	VIII.	194
1778. July 22.	Atkins, Margaret, and Henry Hodgkinson,	"	XXV.	136
1758. Dec. 5.	Atkins, William, and Ann Claghorn,	"	II.	114
1761. Feb. 3.	Atkison, Mary, and Samuel Gormley,	"	IV.	48
1782. Oct. 11.	Attlay, John, and Elizabeth Covat,	"	XXXVII.	38
1781. April 14.	Attwood, Elizabeth, and Thomas Bruen,	"	XXXII.	5
1778. Dec. 5.	Attwood, Nathan, and Catherine Collard,	"	XXVI.	112
1781. Aug. 10.	Attwood, Thomas B., and Catherine Ten Eyck,	"	XXXIII.	35
1762. May 5.	Aubery, Frederick, and Mary Fannell,	"	VI.	146
1760. April 29.	Audier, Martha, and John Willson,	"	III.	131
1759. Dec. 6.	Austen, Hannah, and Isaac Romine,	"	II.	529
1764. Feb. 20.	Austin, Mathias, and Bridget Van Hoosen,	"	VIII.	64
1764. Aug. 14.	Auterkerck, Anne, and Peter Waldron,	"	VIII.	280
1757. June 10.	Auxburgh, Alexander, and Abigail Adleton,	"	I.	559
1760. Aug. 12.	Avery, Gideon, and Sarah Cille,	"	III.	248
1772. April 9.	Avery, Mary, and Daniel Devoux,	"	XVIII.	72
1781. June 9.	Avery, Mary, and John Hull,	"	XXXII.	79
1762. April 19.	Avery, Mary, and Peter Travellier,	"	VI.	115
1759. June 6.	Avery, Phillip, and Lydia Male,	"	II.	306
1783. April 24.	Avery, Robert, and Mary Bouden,	"	XXXVIII.	113
1779. July 19.	Avery, Thaddeus, and Elizabeth Underhill,	"	XXVIII.	25
1761. Mar. 12.	Ayckley, Abigail, and John Le Gross,	"	IV.	98

DATE.	NAMES.	RECORD.	VOL. PAGE.
1760. Mar. 6.	Aymar, James, and Margaret Brown,......	M. B.,	III. 65
1762. May 13.	Aymar, John, and Jane Bauo,............	"	VI. 159
1760. Jan. 4.	Ayme, Agnes, and George Collet,.........	"	II. 569
1762. Mar. 26.	Ayres, Mary, and James Scott,............	"	VI. 83
1768. May 12.	Ayres, Sarah, and William Everitt,........	"	XIII. 102
1771. April 8.	Ayres, Susannah, and John Inness,........	"	XVII. 79
1761. July 6.	Ayscough, Anne, and Thomas William Moore,	"	IV. 283
1772. Feb. 5.	Ayscough, Sarah, and William Malcom,....	"	XVIII. 29

B.

1779. Mar. 20.	Baar, Elizabeth, and Michael Weaver,......	"	XXVII. 70
1736. May 8.	Babb, John, and Sarah Rowland,..........	"	I. 1
1779. Oct. 2.	Babcock, David, and Barbara Garlick,......	"	XXVIII. 95
1760. Oct. 15.	Bache, Theophilaet, and Ann Barclay,......	"	III. 365
1772. April 15.	Backas, Zacharias, and Rachel Young,......	"	XVIII. 78
1769. June 29.	Backer, Janetje, and Peter Groasbeck,......	"	XIV. 137
1757. July 5.	Backer, Joseph, and Elizabeth Welch,......	"	I. 584
1737. Nov. 19.	Backster, Rebecca, and William Ramsay,...	"	I. 8
1764. July 11.	Backus, Catharine, and Hendrick Fosnar,...	"	VIII. 255
1773. Dec. 22.	Bacon, Salome, and John Sanxay,.........	"	XXII. 83
1779. June 3.	Backhouse, William, and Anne Mahar,.....	"	XXVII. 156
1755. Dec. 20.	Badeau, Hester, and Benjamin Flandreu,...	"	I. 237
1783. June 24.	Baehr, Christian, and Anna Bennet,.......	"	XXXIX. 68
1762. June 30.	Baeley, Esther, and John Stedwell,........	"	VI. 217
1781. Oct. 26.	Bagley, Catharine, and Charles Stewart,....	"	XXXIV. 7
1774. Feb. 25.	Bagley, Elizabeth, and John Burtine,......	"	XXII. 135
1765. Aug. 5.	Bagley, Joseph, and Rachel Jones,.........	"	IX. 255
1758. Jan. 17.	Bagly, Ann, and John Outenbogert,........	"	I. 786
1670. Dec. 6.	Baignoulx, Jean, and Ralph Hall,.........	C. A.,	II. 615
1736. Aug. 2.	Baile, Abigall, and Isaac Platt,............	M. B.,	I. 2
1782. Oct. 9.	Bailey, Elizabeth, and Peter Shute,........	"	XXXVII. 37
1783. May 22.	Bailey, Jane, and Richard Holland,........	"	XXXIX. 24
1782. Oct. 5.	Bailey, Jemima, and Lemuel Carll,........	"	XXXVII. 30
1772. May 6.	Bailey, John, and Ann Brickstock,........	"	XVIII. 102
1762. Oct. 22.	Bailey, John, and Sarah Cornish,..........	"	VI. 379
1758. Oct. 5.	Bailey, Mary, and Increas Carpenter,.......	"	II. 41
1772. April 28.	Bailey, Samuel, and Hanah Butler,........	"	XVIII. 94
1757. Feb. 17.	Bailey, Sarah, and Thomas Wiggins,........	"	I. 440
1761. July 20.	Bailey, William, and Sophia Gravesteen,....	"	V. 1
1779. May 8.	Baily, Lydia, and David Rossett,.........	"	XXVII. 132
1763. Sept. 20.	Baily (Smith), Nathan, and Abigail Pine,..	"	VII. 343
1759. Sept. 11.	Bain, Gilbert, and Mary McCartey,........	"	II. 415
1781. Feb. 6.	Bain, John, and Mary McClean,...........	"	XXXI. 39
1760. Mar. 3.	Baine, ———, and Catharine Beekman,....	"	III. 60

DATE.	NAMES.	RECORD.	VOL.	PAGE.
1759. Nov. 7.	Bakemen, Catharine, and William Elsworth,	M. B.,	II.	489
1781. May 31.	Baker, Andrew, and Catharine Bennet,....	"	XXXII.	66
1718. Sept. 26.	Baker, Ann, and Robert Coles,............	"	XXVI.	34
1777. June 11.	Baker, Barbara, and Joseph Corre,........	"	XXIV.	100
1737. Oct. 21.	Baker, Catherine, and Joseph Drake,.......	"	I.	7
1778. Sept. 28.	Baker, Catherine, and Malachiah Mosely,...	"	XXVI.	37
1782. May 31.	Baker, Charity, and Henry Craft,..........	"	XXXIX.	32
1782. June 5.	Baker, Elizabeth, and Nicholas Pitt,........	"	XXXVI.	38
1763. Jan. 21.	Baker, Elizabeth, and William Morrell,.....	"	VII.	29
1783. July 12.	Baker, Gardner, and Mary Wrighton,......	"	XXXIX.	88
1759. May 12.	Baker, George, and Ann Weekes,.........	"	II.	279
1764. Dec. 11.	Baker, George, and Hannah Lawrence,.....	"	VIII.	451
1736. Dec. 28.	Baker, George, and Phebe Pearce,.........	"	I.	5
1782. Aug. 27.	Baker, Hannah, and Alexander Ogsbury,...	"	XXXVI.	125
1756. Aug. 3.	Baker, Isabella, and Alexander Claxton,....	"	I.	268
1755. Oct. 16.	Baker, James, and Jemima Kirk,..........	"	I.	196
1773. Dec. 23.	Baker, John, and Hannah Lewis,..........	"	XXII.	86
1759. Mar. 27.	Baker, John, and Sarah Page,.............	"	II.	226
1762. July 19.	Baker, John, and Susannah Crisp,.........	"	VI.	245
1763. Nov. 2.	Baker, Jonathan, and Abigail Pears,.......	"	VII.	422
1760. Jan. 18.	Baker, Lyonel, and Phebe Downe,.........	"	II.	585
1761. Dec. 15.	Baker, Margaret, and Thomas Moland,.....	"	V.	279
1761. Dec. 30.	Baker, Mary, and Cornelius Smith,........	"	V.	305
1762. Nov. 20.	Baker, Mary, and Joseph Risley,..........	"	XXXVII.	89
1738. Aug. 24.	Baker, Matthew, and Judah Wood,........	"	I.	10
1760. Mar. 6.	Baker, Nathan, and Eve Poppledurff,......	"	III.	64
1781. June 10.	Baker, Peter, and Sarah Alner,............	"	XXXII.	81
1782. Mar. 27.	Baker, Phebe, and Joshua Carhartt,........	"	XXXV.	99
1771. May 7.	Baker, Rachel, and Jonathan Pine,........	"	XVII.	77
1763. Dec. 1.	Baker, Richard, and Ann Pears,...........	"	VII.	487
1783. May 12.	Baker, Robert, and Jane Oley,............	"	XXXIX.	10
1779. April 20.	Baker, Samuel, and Pamele Craft,.........	"	XXVII.	111
1768. Sept. 29.	Baker, Samuel, and Rachel Ross,..........	"	XIII.	201
1767. Jan. 20.	Baker, Sarah, and John Burger, Jr.,........	"	XI.	9
1771. Dec. 30.	Baker, Sarah, and William Crillin, Jr.,......	"	XVII.	307
1737. May 16.	Baker, Susannah, and John Brazer,........	"	I.	6
1780. Aug. 26.	Baker, Thomas, and Molly Anderson,......	"	XXX.	2
1783. May 20.	Baker, William, and Joanna Keys,.........	"	XXXIX.	22
1764. April 5.	Baker, William, and Sarah Downing,......	"	VIII.	136
1770. Sept. 21.	Balderston, Thomas, and Elsie Deacon,.....	"	XVI.	194
1766. July 23.	Baldin, Susannah, and Garret Stines,......	"	X.	60
1778. April 13.	Balding, Benjamin, and Elizabeth Willis,....	"	XXV.	64
1771. Oct. 18.	Balding, Samuel, and Martha Titus,........	"	XVII.	213
1772. Feb. 26.	Baldwin, Ann, and John Brown,..........	"	XVIII.	43
1781. Oct. 5.	Baldwin, Annautia, and John Ackerman,...	"	XXXIII.	89

14 NEW YORK MARRIAGES.

DATE.	NAMES.	RECORD.	VOL. PAGE.
1762. Mar. 16.	Baldwin, Dorothy, and Jesse Platt,........	M. B.,	VI. 74
1768. June 16.	Baldwin, Elizabeth, and Daniel Raner,.....	"	XIII. 130
1764. Jan. 13.	Baldwin, Hannáh, and Peter Klock,........	"	VIII. 15a
1767. July 10.	Baldwin, Jane, and Thomas Loury,........	"	XI. 128
1778. Nov. 11.	Baldwin, Jesse, and Mary Smith,..........	"	XXVI. 85
1773. Sept. 10.	Baldwin, Joel, and Mary Van Hook,.......	"	XXI. 105
1772. April 13.	Baldwin, John, and Elizabeth Thompson,...	"	XVIII. 74
1761. Sept. 28.	Baldwin, John, and Mary Daldridge,.......	"	V. 101
1782. Feb. 14.	Baldwin, John, and Mary Walker,...........	"	XXXV. 56
1757. July 5.	Baldwin, Mary, and Garret Hyer,.........	"	I. 583
1763. Dec. 1.	Baldwin, Mary, and Isaac Burr,...........	"	VII. 488
1769. July 21.	Baldwin, Mary, and Joseph Colly,.........	"	XV. 2
1773. April 19.	Baldwin, Mary, and Silvanus Smith,......	"	XX. 95
1783. Aug. 11.	Baldwin, Rachael, and Peter McLean,......	"	XXXIX. 122
1761. June 3.	Baldwin, Rachel, and Hermanus Alstyne,...	"	IV. 224
1736. Aug. 30.	Baldwin, Rachel, and John Tenbrooke,.....	"	I. 2
1753. May 30.	Baldwin, Stephen, and Mary Ten Brook,...	"	I. 44
1764. Oct. 31.	Baldwin, William, and Ann Sprainger,.....	"	VIII. 383
1756. Sept. 28.	Baley, Elizabeth, and James Dunne,.......	"	I. 309
1783. June 7.	Baley, Jane, and Jacob Areson,...........	"	XXXIX. 45
1781. Aug. 6.	Ball, Ezabella, and Joseph Palmer,.........	"	XXXIII. 29
1753. May 23.	Ball, Isaac, and Martha Ashinger,..........	"	I. 39
1779. Jan. 1.	Ball, Isaac, Jr., and Mary Breasted,........	"	XXVII. 1
1780. May 30.	Ball, Jamime, and Thomas Swan,..........	"	XXIX. 74
1769. June 29.	Ball, John, and Abigail Peet,.............	"	XIV. 136
1775. May 17.	Ball, John, and Sarah Swanzer,...........	"	XXIII. 36
1777. Dec. 4.	Ball, Matthew, and Mary Forbes,..........	"	XXIV. 190
1782. Dec. 7.	Ball, Peter, and Charity Lott,.............	"	XXXVII. 111
1774. Feb. 16.	Ball, Peter, and Isabella Roberts,..........	"	XXII. 129
1773. May 20.	Ballendine, Isabella, and Edward Ross,.....	"	XX. 119
1759. June 16.	Ballentine, Cicily, and James Sclatter,......	"	II. 329
1763. Nov. 23.	Ballentine, James, and Elizabeth McKay,...	"	VII. 467
1738. Sept. 22.	Baly, Nicholas, and Mary Bargun,.........	"	I. 11
1771. Sept. 16.	Bamper, Margaret, and James McKenney,..	"	XVII. 184
1771. April 20.	Bancker, Abraham, and Abigail King,......	"	XVII. 64
1753. June 7.	Bancker, Ann, and Abraham Heyer,.......	"	I. 52
1764. Sept. 17.	Bancker, Ann, and Robert Lake,..........	"	VIII. 312
1782. Jan. 15.	Bancker, Anne, and John Boyer,.........	"	XXXVIII. 16
1771. Sept. 3.	Bancker, Christopher, and Mary Smith,....	"	XVII. 172
1755. Sept. 10.	Bancker, Elizabeth, and Simon H. Veder,...	"	I. 173
1772. Oct. 20.	Bancker, Evert, Jr., and Ann Taylor,......	"	XIX. 80
1763. April 22.	Bancker, Jane, and Daniel Winne,........	"	VII. 137
1758. Sept. 11.	Bancker, Jane, and James Duthie,.........	"	II. 13
1764. June 6.	Bancker, John, and Aeltje Mesnard,.......	"	VIII. 209

DATE.	NAMES.	RECORD.	VOL.	PAGE.
1771. Mar. 12.	Bancker, Magdalen, and Ulpianus Van Sinderen,	M. B.,	XVII.	32
1769. Mar. 2.	Bancker, Mary, and John Beekman,	"	XIV.	42
1775. Dec. 21.	Bancker, Mary, and Josiah Holmes,	"	XXIII.	234
1753. June 14.	Bancker, Mary, and Josiah Ogden,	"	I.	61
1768. May 4.	Bancker, Nathaniel, and Annetje De Witt,	"	XIII.	93
1768. Mar. 24.	Bancker, Rachel, and Jasper Steymets,	"	XIII.	56
1758. Jan. 23.	Bancker, William, and Anna Rutgers,	"	I.	797
1780. Dec. 1.	Bane, George, and Mary Penney,	"	XXX.	129
1761. Nov. 26.	Bangs, John, and Mahetabel Morris,	"	V.	252
1764. Nov. 12.	Banker, Aaron, and Margaret Stagg,	"	VIII.	401
1757. Oct. 27.	Banker, Catrina, and Jacob Van Aernam,	"	I.	684
1761. Jan. 29.	Banker, Neeltje, and Albert S. Vedder,	"	IV.	38
1764. Jan. 5.	Banks, Jacob, and Anne Burnets,	"	VIII.	7
1761. July 13.	Banks, Jacob, and Sarah Bria,	"	IV.	295
1757. July 6.	Banks, John, and Mary Ingoldsby,	"	I.	585
1772. April 21.	Banks, Justice, and Catharine Graham,	"	XVIII.	86
1776. May 7.	Banks, Rebecca, and David Galatian,	"	XXIII.	307
1773. Mar. 30.	Banks, Richard, and Mary Goff,	"	XX.	78
1781. May 10.	Bannister, Thomas, and Rachel Martin,	"	XXXII.	43
1782. Oct. 29.	Banta, Alida, and John Fairbaien,	"	XXXVII.	67
1773. Jan. 27.	Banta, Jacob, and Jane Stivers,	"	XX.	24
1783. April 26.	Banta, John S., and Rachel Pake,	"	XXXVIII.	114
1760. Nov. 7.	Banter, David, and Hellegont Webber,	"	III.	397
1767. Feb. 4.	Banyar, Goldsbrow, and Elizabeth Appy,	"	XI.	19
1765. June 21.	Barbauck, Peter, and Ariantje Ellis,	"	IX.	178
1771. May 18.	Barber, Margaret, and John Davidson,	"	XVII.	86
1676. Oct. 26.	Barber, Mary, and David Briggs,	W. O. P.,	III.	217
1769. June 19.	Barber, Moses, and Rachel Losee,	M. B.,	XIV.	122
1764. Feb. 16.	Barber, Sarah, and John Gathrey,	"	VIII.	62
1772. May 9.	Barberic, Peter, and Phebe Van Tuyl,	"	XVIII.	105
1780. Sept. 26.	Barberin, Noel, and Ann Pearson,	"	XXX.	42
1761. July 7.	Barcalow, Williamtie, and John Bennet,	"	IV.	286
1781. Dec. 12.	Barckley, Hannah, and Adam Smith,	"	XXXIV.	81
1737. June 14.	Barclay, Andrew, and Helena Rosevelt,	"	I.	6
1778. Jan. 19.	Barclay, Ann Dorothy, and Beverley Robinson, Jr.,	"	XXV.	9
1760. Oct. 15.	Barclay, Anne, and Theophilact Bache,	"	III.	365
1763. Nov. 8.	Barclay, Catharine, and Augustus Van Cortlandt,	"	VII.	434
1778. June 16.	Barclay, Charlotte A., and Richard Bailey,	"	XXV.	104
1773. June 16.	Barclay, Cornelia, and Stephen De Lancey,	"	XXI.	11
1772. Nov. 21.	Barclay, James, and Mary Van Beverhoute,	"	XIX.	122
1771. Aug. 28.	Barclay, John, and Margaret Tenayck,	"	XVII.	165
1760. June 3.	Barclay, Joseph, and Sarah Caduser,	"	III.	175

DATE.	NAMES.	RECORD.	VOL.	PAGE.
1773. Nov. 16.	Barclay, Ann Margaret, and Frederick Jay,	M. B.,	XXII.	31
1764. Dec. 10.	Barclay, Sarah, and Anthony Lispenard,....	"	VIII.	447
1775. Oct. 2.	Barclay, Thomas H., and Susan De Lancey,	"	XXIII.	168
1760. April 5.	Barden, Edward, and Elizabeth Warner,....	"	III.	99
1782. Oct. 18.	Barden, Elizabeth, and Claud Hamilton,....	"	XXXVII.	52
1781. Mar. 12.	Bardine, Darcas, and Richard Webb,.......	"	XXXI.	69
1738. Sept. 22.	Bargan, Mary, and Nicholas Baly,.........	"	I.	11
1770. July 26.	Bargaw, Alletta, and Nicholas Bogart,......	"	XVI.	147
1773. May 26.	Bargaw, Isaac, and Susannah Hallett,......	"	XX.	127
1737. Aug. 3.	Bargeau, Jane, and James Sampell,........	"	I.	7
1781. June 8.	Bargen, Antie, and Aress Ransem,.........	"	XXXII.	75
1760. Feb. 28.	Bargen, John, and Margaret Van Durson,...	"	III.	43
1773. Dec. 8.	Barger, Jacob, and Catherine McLean,.....	"	XXII.	64
1781. Dec. 5.	Barham, Martha, and John Newsted,......	"	XXXIV.	73
1756. Sept. 10.	Barheit, Rachael, and John Yarden,........	"	I.	294
1760. Jan. 14.	Barheyt, Peter, and Jannetye Van Valkenburgh, ...	"	II.	580
1760. Aug. 15.	Barhuyd, John, and Helena Peek,.........	"	III.	254
1760. Feb. 2.	Bark, Mary, and Charles Hanning,.........	"	III.	17
1763. Oct. 29.	Barkeleau, Sarah, and John Durye,........	"	VII.	411
1765. May 31.	Barkelow, Harmanus, and Elizabeth Duryee,	"	IX.	148
1781. May 10.	Barker, Abijah, and Mary Hunt,..........	"	XXXII.	40
1762. Feb. 2.	Barker, Benjamin, and Hannah Wood,.....	"	VII.	49
1771. Aug. 31.	Barker, Christopher, and Abytee Yates,....	"	XVII.	171
1771. Oct. 23.	Barker, Elizabeth, and Francis Denham,....	"	XVII.	220
1760. May 9.	Barker, Elizabeth, and Henry Hartley,.....	"	III.	148
1737. Sept. 23.	Barker, John, and Mary Lawrence,........	"	I.	7
1736. Oct. 16.	Barker, Mary, and Nicholas Deffriest,......	"	I.	3
1765. Feb. 2.	Barker, Mary, and Wright White,.........	"	IX.	60
1772. June 22.	Barker, Peter, and Margaret Brett,........	"	XVIII.	147
1775. Sept. 28.	Barker, Samuel, and Mary Sniffen,........	"	XXIII.	166
1770. Feb. 24.	Barker, Thomas, and Anne Horton,........	"	XVI.	24
1758. Oct. 25.	Barker, Thomas, and Elizabeth Anell,......	"	II.	68
1763. Sept. 10.	Barker, William, and Taman Fowler,......	"	VII.	334
1763. Dec. 8.	Barlow, Thomas, and Hannah Cutler,......	"	VII.	500
1782. Aug. 15.	Barly, Casper, and Rosina Creeman,........	"	XXXVI.	110
1769. Oct. 26.	Barnard, Elizabeth, and Robert Hull,.......	"	XV.	68
1758. May 4.	Barnes, Daniel, and Hannah Wright,.......	"	I.	893
167$\frac{8}{9}$. Jan. 4.	Barnes, Deborah, and Edward Griffen, Jr.,..	G. E.,	XXXII.	21
1772. April 30.	Barnes, Elizabeth, and Paul Mersereau,.....	M. B.,	XVIII.	96
1759. Nov. 23.	Barnes, George, and Catherine McClean,....	"	II.	514
1766. Nov. 12.	Barnes, George, and Dorothy Vanderbeek,..	"	X.	161
1759. Feb. 12.	Barnes, George, and Hannah Van Pelt,....	"	II.	190
1761. Sept. 23.	Barnes, Gilbert, and Mary Bates,..........	"	V.	92
1759. Feb. 2.	Barnes, Isaac, and Lucretia Brested,.......	"	II.	171

DATE.	NAMES.	RECORD	VOL.	PAGE.
1774. Jan 20.	Barnes, James, and Catherine Johnson,.....	M. B.,	XXII.	111
1761. Sept. 15.	Barnes, John, and Statia Ramsey,.........	"	V.	84
1763. Jan. 24.	Barnes, Joshua, and Martha Gidney,.......	"	VII.	32
1757. Dec. 14.	Barnes, Margaret, and Christian Dooper,....	"	I.	741
1778. April 2.	Barnes, Martha, and William Brown,......	"	XXV.	58
1777. May 9.	Barnes, Mary, and Legget Lawrence,.......	"	XXIV.	86
1678. Aug. 14.	Barnes, Mary, and Walter Herbert,........	G. E.,	XXXII.	1
1764. Feb. 21.	Barnes, Merriam, and Minor Hillard,.......	M. B.,	VIII.	69
1761. July 27.	Barnes, Phebe, and Norman Tolmie,.......	"	V.	10
1759. Nov. 8.	Barnes, Rebecca, and Joseph Mullinex,.....	"	II.	490
1782. Dec. 31.	Barnes, Robert, and Hester Lockimin,......	"	XXXVII.	138
1758. Jan. 5.	Barnes, Sarah, and Benjamin Palmer,......	"	I.	767
1763. April 16.	Barnes, Susannah, and Sears Mott,........	"	VII.	130
1668. May 21.	Barnes, Thomas, and Mary Brazier,........	O. W. L.,	II.	223
1759. May 8.	Barnes, William, and Catharine Storm,.....	M. B.,	II.	270
1755. Aug. 16.	Barnet, Jane, and Frederick Lasher,.......	"	I.	147
1768. Aug. 17.	Barnet, Thomas, and Elizabeth Douglass,...	"	XIII.	174
1736. June 12.	Barnet, William, and Elizabeth Baxter,.....	"	I.	1
1777. July 3.	Barnett, Elizabeth, and William Houseman,	"	XXIV.	111
1781. Dec. 12.	Barnett, Joseph, and Jane Bosworth,......	"	XXXIV.	79
1778. Aug. 26.	Barnewall, George, and Elizabeth Willet Lawrence,...............................	"	XXVI.	12
1761. April 1.	Barnhill, David, and Elizabeth Hamilton,...	"	IV.	127
1771. Nov. 1.	Barns, Amelia, and John Currin,...........	"	XVII.	287
1758. May 29.	Barns, Anthony Glen, and Elizabeth Roe,..	"	I.	914
1782. Oct. 7.	Barns, Catharine, and John Reade,........	"	XXXVII.	32
1770. Dec. 12.	Barns, Elizabeth, and William Pugsley,.....	"	XVI.	292
1781. Oct. 20.	Barns, Mary, and Archibald Kerby,........	"	XXXIV.	1
1767. June 18.	Barns, Samuel, and Elizabeth Hatfield,.....	"	XI.	111
1762. Mar. 29.	Barnton, Sarah, and Jacobus Hilton,.......	"	VI.	85
1764. Sept. 20.	Barr, Hendrick, and Mary Tearman,.......	"	VIII.	319
1782. Dec. 30.	Barr, Henry, and Ann Bennet,.............	"	XXXVII.	137
1762. June 2.	Barrack, Adam, and Hellitie Ratcliff,.......	"	VI.	180
1782. Dec. 13.	Barraga, Catharine, and Joseph Lake,......	"	XXXVII.	118
1782. Oct. 16.	Barraga, Catharine, and Samuel Wade,.....	"	XXXVII.	42
1782. June 10.	Barraga, Lametje, and Rutgert Van Brunt,..	"	XXXVI.	47
1780. May 17.	Barraga, Teshey, and Ebenezer Casten,.....	"	XXIX.	58
1782. Oct. 21.	Barratt, John, and Hannah Collin,........	"	XXXVII.	56
1680. June 28.	Barre, James, and Mary Johnson,........	G. E.,	XXXII.	90
1771. April 8.	Barrea, Francis, Jr., and Sarah Kierstead,...	M. B.,	XVII.	50
1773. June 15.	Barrea, Francis, Jr., and Elizabeth Hale,....	"	XXI.	6
1762. June 15.	Barrea, John, and Effe Quick,.............	"	VI.	193
1761. Mar. 3.	Barret, Catharine, and Alexander Leech,....	"	IV.	89
1762. May 11.	Barret, Elenor, and Joseph Rock,..........	"	VI.	514
1778. Aug. 16.	Barret, James, and Margaret Morgan,......	"	XXVI.	5

3

DATE.	NAMES.	RECORD.	VOL.	PAGE.
1760. June 6.	Barret, Mary, and Daniel Hewson, ...	M. B.,	III.	178
1782. June 14.	Barret, Mary, and John Tully, ...	• "	XXXVI.	50
1765. Oct. 26.	Barret, Thomas, and Elizabeth Van Sante,..	"	IX.	323
1667. Dec. 18.	Barrett, Samuel, and Anne Hermitage, ...	O. W. L.,	II.	191
1763. Feb. 1.	Barrett, William, and Mary Ensworth, ...	M. B.,	VII.	46
1760. Feb. 1.	Barrey, Andrew, and Mary Lewis, ...	"	III.	14
1762. Sept. 29.	Barrey, Elisabeth, and Joseph Rigby, ...	"	VI.	335
1757. May 21.	Barrington, Nicholas, and Ariantje Van Pelt,	"	I.	538
1778. Mar. 20.	Barrington, William, and Maria Theresa Clarke, ...	"	XXV.	50
1781. Sept. 17.	Barrit, Catharine, and Archibald Johnson,..	"	XXXIII.	70
1758. Dec. 18.	Barriton, Catherine, and Philder Gryderman,	"	II.	131
1756. Nov. 22.	Barron, Andrew, and Sarah Pierson, ...	"	I.	361
1779. May 22.	Barron, Esther, and Thomas Crowell, ...	"	XXVII.	143
1758. April 19.	Barron, John, and Elizabeth Collon, ...	"	I.	876
1763. Sept. 30.	Barron, Margaret, and John De Clue, ...	"	VII.	363
1781. June 21.	Barron, Mary, and Jeremiah Shotwell, ...	"	XXXII.	93
1778. Feb. 19.	Barrow, James, and Martha Roberts, ...	"	XXV.	27
1769. Aug. 7.	Barrow, James, and Catharine Strachan, ...	"	XV.	20
1763. Dec. 8.	Barroway, Margaret, and Jacobus Pearson,..	"	VII.	499
1755. Aug. 26.	Barry, George, and Carolina Richards, ...	"	I.	157
1778. Oct. 30.	Barry, James, and Elizabeth Cole, ...	"	XXVI.	78
1780. Aug. 19.	Barry, James, and Mary Berry, ...	"	XXIX.	142
1760. Nov. 15.	Barry, Mary, and Patrick Hackit, ...	"	III.	416
1778. Oct. 9.	Barry, Mary Ann, and John Willson, ...	"	XXVI.	52
1755. Aug. 26.	Barry, Thomas, and Maritie Bogardus, ...	"	I.	154
1770. June 16.	Bartell, Andries, and Christina Power, ...	"	XVI.	117
1770. Oct. 2.	Bartell, Philip, and Elebert Michal, ...	"	XVI.	204
1782. Oct. 30.	Barter, Jane, and John Rote, ...	"	XXVI.	79
1782. Dec. 2.	Bartholemew, Violetta, and Dymock Laming,	"	XXXVII.	104
1762. May 17.	Bartine, Martha, and Stephen Rich, ...	"	VII.	191
1760. June 21.	Bartlett, Ann, and William Shooler, ...	"	III.	194
1765. June 14.	Bartley, William, and Mitty Leake, ...	"	IX.	169
1772. Mar. 19.	Barto, Helena, and Ebenezer White, ...	"	XVIII.	55
1738. May 29.	Bartolet, William, and Anne Jones, ...	"	I.	9
1783. Oct. 10.	Barton, Austin, and Rebecca Borbanck, ...	"	XL.	77
1755. Dec. 9.	Barton, Benjamin, and Jane Dusenbury,...	"	I.	229
1779. June 20.	Barton, Elizabeth, and Alexander Morrison,	"	XXVII.	169
1778. Dec. 17.	Barton, Elizabeth, and Ephraim Ludlow,...	"	XXVI.	125
1779. Jan. 19.	Barton, John, and Abby Smith, ...	"	XXVII.	12
1782. Mar. 8.	Barton, John, and Phebe Smith, ...	"	XXXV.	79
1782. Feb. 22.	Barton, Joseph, and Elizabeth Sarly, ...	"	XXXV.	63
1759. Feb. 3.	Barton, Margaret, and James Denton, ...	"	II.	172
1777. Aug. 12.	Barton, Robert, and Ann McGrigor, ...	"	XXIV.	132
1782. Aug. 8.	Barton, Sarah, and John Rundell, ...	"	XXXIX.	120

DATE.	NAMES.	RECORD.	VOL.	PAGE.
1783. July 13.	Bartow, Clarince, and Anthony Lispenard Underhill,	M. B.,	xxxix.	90
1763. Nov. 30.	Bartow, Ephamia, and Daniel White,	"	vii.	485
1768. Mar. 21.	Bartow, Hannah, and Thomas Tucker,	"	xiii.	52
1757. June 29.	Bartow, Basil, and Mary Quimby,	"	i.	576
1761. Nov. 25.	Bartow, John, Jr., and Mary Ryder,	"	v.	247
1771. June 5.	Bartow, John, Jr., and Ann Pell,	"	xvii.	101
1782. Feb. 12.	Bartow, Mary, and John Reid,	"	xxxv.	50
1773. Mar. 15.	Bartow, Servia, and Timothy Mills,	"	xx.	64
1781. Dec. 4.	Bartow, Susannah, and John Gillespie,	"	xxxiv.	71
1772. Oct. 31.	Bartow, Theodosius, and Jemima Abramse,	"	xix.	96
1773. Dec. 14.	Bartow, Thomas, and Mary Vardill,	"	xxii.	74
1759. Dec. 4.	Barnell, Christopher, and Isabella Hayes,	"	ii.	526
1772. July 20.	Barvell, Ann, and James Marshall,	"	xix.	2
1753. June 18.	Barwe, Maria, and Dirick Hempstradt,	"	i.	64
1781. Mar. 25.	Barwell, John, and Ann McDole,	"	xxxi.	86
1763. Mar. 4.	Barwick, Benjamin, and Mary Alstyne,	"	vii.	91
1758. Dec. 9.	Barwick, John, and Sarah Jacobs,	"	ii.	123
1780. Dec. 24.	Barwick, Mary, and David Grim,	"	xxxiv.	104
1778. Jan. 31.	Barwick, William, and Ann Fields,	"	xxv.	14
1761. Oct. 14.	Barwick, William, and Elizabeth Byfield,	"	v.	137
1779. May 16.	Basden, Robert, and Alletta Shearman,	"	xxvii.	139
1779. Sept. 18.	Bashford, Elizabeth, and Thomas Hunt,	"	xxviii.	82
1758. Mar. 9.	Bashford, John, and Lucretia Downen,	"	i.	838
1780. Dec. 7.	Bashford, Lucresha, and William Morrel,	"	xxx.	143
1780. Nov. 16.	Bashford, Mary, and Gilbert Hunt,	'	xxx.	110
1781. May 11.	Basly, Mary, and Gabriel Van Horne,	'	xxxii.	44
1770. Nov. 2.	Bass, Mary, and Robert Thomson,	'	xvi.	237
1773. Jan. 12.	Bass, Robert, and Rebekah Branch,	"	xx.	7
1759. April 21.	Bass, Sarah, and Benjamin Cornish,	"	ii.	249
1757. April 26.	Basset, Francis J., and Mary Hestear,	"	i.	514
1753. June 6.	Basset, Maritie, and Abraham Bogert,	"	i.	51
1764. Mar. 15.	Bassett, Frederick, and Jannetje Vredenburgh,	"	viii.	105
1767. Nov. 27.	Bassett, Michael, and Maritje Van Fronker,	"	xii.	99
1772. Mar. 26.	Bassett, Frederick, and Susannah Bubelot,	"	xviii.	59
1763. Dec. 10.	Bassett, John, and Eleanor Evouts,	"	vii.	501
1759. May 10.	Bassing, Rachal, and James Paulding,	"	ii.	277
1760. Dec. 10.	Bates, Elizabeth, and John Gidney,	"	iii.	470
1764. Mar. 31.	Bates, Elizabeth, and Burger Provoost,	"	viii.	128
1773. April 20.	Bates, Elizabeth, and John Melowny,	"	xx.	98
1771. June 18.	Bates, Gilbert, and Sarah Gibbs,	"	xvii.	113
1757. July 20.	Bates, John, and Rachael Springer,	"	i.	596
1780. Sept. 1.	Bates, Joseph, and Mary Smyth,	"	xxx.	13
1761. Sept. 23.	Bates, Mary, and Gilbert Barnes,	"	v.	92
1779. Dec. 4.	Bates, Mary, and John Hislop,	"	xxviii.	159

Date.	Names.	Record.	Vol.	Page.
1758. Nov. 4.	Bates, Phebe, and Joseph Gidney,.........	M. B.,	II.	82
1782. May 31.	Bates, Rachael, and Leonard Rogers,.......	"	XXXVI.	32
1781. Sept. 17.	Bates, Rachel, and Leonard Rogers,........	"	XXXIII.	69
1761. Sept. 8.	Bates, Samuel, and Mary Blank,.......... .	"	V.	73
1770. June 13.	Bates, Samuel, and Mary Johnston,........	"	XVI.	111
1760. July 19.	Bates, William, and Elizabeth Crum,.......	"	III.	221
1755. Aug. 12.	Batey, Edward, and Mary Lake,...........	"	I.	146
1782. Mar. 9.	Bathram, John, and Mary Gilbertson, ...	"	XXXV.	80
1782. May 22.	Batten, Anne, and John Webb,...........	"	XXXVI.	19
1779. June 7.	Batten, Elizabeth, and Christian Orndoff,....	"	XXVII.	160
1783. Sept. 23.	Baty, Ann, and Barnt Simonson,..........	"	XL.	52
1768. May 9.	Baty, Mary, and John Shay,..............	'	XIII.	99
1769. July 31.	Bauman, John William, and Mary Hiet,....	"	XV.	10
1762. May 13.	Bauo, Jane, and John Aymar,............	"	VI.	159
1760. Sept. 2.	Bavee, Matthias, and Batha Vanderheyden,	"	III.	277
1782. June 19.	Baveridge, Margaret, and Alexander Lister,	"	XXXVI.	58
1783. Feb. 22.	Bavers, Ann, and James Raymond,........	"	XXXVIII.	50
1772. May 12.	Bavier, Elizabeth, and Arthur Morris,......	"	XVIII.	108
1773. July 15.	Bavier, Solomon, and Catherine Eltinge,....	"	XXI.	39
1763. May 9.	Bavington, Alice, and Peter De Riemer,....	"	VII.	170
1770. Nov. 14.	Baxter, Abigail, and John Martin,.........	"	XVI.	251
1736. Nov. 10.	Baxter, Ealse, and Amos Browner,........	"	I.	3
1736. June 12.	Baxter, Elizabeth, and William Barnet,.....	"	I.	1
1783. June 26.	Baxter, James, and Anne Williams,........ : ..	"	XXXIX.	69
1780. Oct. 7.	Baxter, Jonathan, and Mary Gockh,.......	"	XXX.	60
1777. May 26.	Baxter, Keziah, and William Nikols,.......	"	XXIV.	94
1762. Feb. 19.	Baxter, Mitchell, and Hannah Frost,.......	"	VI.	55
1765. Sept. 13.	Baxter, Phebe, and Michael Croos,........	"	IX.	262
1776. Feb. 23.	Baxter, Thomas, and Mary Palmer,........	"	XXIII.	271
1782. May 18.	Bay, Sarah, and Joseph Moore,...........	"	XXXVI.	10
1780. Nov. 4.	Bayan, Edward, and Arabecca Rankin,.....	"	XXX.	91
1780. Nov. 27.	Bayan, Jemime, and John Sels,...........	"	XXX.	126
1777. Dec. 27.	Bayard, Ann, and George Thompson,......	"	XXIV.	208
1778. Dec. 15.	Bayard, Catherine, and Francis Hutcheson,..	"	XXVI.	123
1781. Sept. 20.	Bayard, Elizabeth, and John Ritson,.......	"	XXXIII.	71
1769. Nov. 4.	Bayard, James, and Elizabeth Smith,.......	"	XV.	112
1760. July 3.	Bayard, Judith, and Jeremiah Van Rensselaer,	"	III.	203
1772. May 19.	Bayard, Margaret, and Martin Hoffman,....	"	XVIII.	115
1762. April 20.	Bayard, Nicholas, Jr., and Catharine Livingston, ...	"	VI.	116
1773. Sept. 16.	Bayard Robert, and Elizabeth McEvers,....	"	XXI.	110
1778. April 24.	Bayard, Samuel, and Catherine Van Horne,.	"	XXV.	67
1783. Oct. 4.	Bayard, William, Jr., and Elizabeth Cornell,.	"	XL.	61
1753. Oct. 16.	Bayeaux, Henry, and Charity Fowler,.....	"	I.	141
1753. April 14.	Bayeux, Thomas, and Mary Lispenard,.....	"	I.	22

DATE.	NAMES.	RECORD.	VOL.	PAGE.
1764. May 1.	Beck, Joseph, and Margaret Vincent,	M. B.,	VIII.	176
1781. Feb. 17.	Beck, Margaret, and Robert Laffan,	"	XXXI.	48
1764. Feb. 10.	Beck, Susannah, and John Smith,	"	VIII.	54
1758. May 24.	Beckee, Margaret, and William Hogge,	"	I.	909
1763. May 13.	Becker, Arent, Annatje Van Voort,	"	VII.	187
1761. Feb. 26.	Becker, Frederick, and Elizabeth Skorlock,	"	IV.	84
1758. April 26.	Becker, Fytje, and Jacob De Garmo,	"	I.	886
1767. July 22.	Becker, Hannah, and James Byers,	"	XII.	1
1765. Feb. 4.	Becker, Isaac, and Elizabeth Wendle,	"	IX.	45
1765. Jan. 10.	Becker, Johannes, and Maria Becker,	"	IX.	12
1766. Oct. 14.	Becker, John, and Sarah Van Hoese,	"	X.	122
1765. Jan. 10.	Becker, Maria, and Johannes Becker,	"	IX.	12
1764. Jan. 2.	Becker, Walter, and Annetje De Ridder,	"	VIII.	1
1771. Oct. 28.	Becker, William, and Christiana Jager,	"	XVII.	226
1783. Oct. 20.	Becker, William, and Dorothea Ransier,	"	XL.	95
1761. May 30.	Becket, Hannah, and Richard Smith,	"	IV.	219
1759. Oct. 6.	Becket, John, and Rebecca Collard,	"	II.	450
1757. June 11.	Beckey, Christina, and Henry Buck,	"	I.	560
1758. Nov. 18.	Beckit, Elizabeth, and Andrew Speeding,	"	II.	95
1772. Dec. 21.	Bedel, Benajah, and Phebe Robins,	"	XIX.	160
1781. April 9.	Bedel, Hannah, and Isaac Simonsen,	"	XXXI.	98
1761. Nov. 17.	Bedel, William, and Hannah Bedell,	"	V.	227
1783. Jan. 4.	Bedell, Anne, and John Garrison,	"	XXXVIII.	4
1763. April 13.	Bedell, Charity, and Isaac Bogard,	"	VII.	126
1761. Oct. 16.	Bedell, Elias, and Phebe Parsell,	"	V.	143
1758. Jan. 5.	Bedell, Elisha, and Mary Langdon,	"	I.	768
1761. Nov. 17.	Bedell, Hannah, and William Bedel,	"	V.	227
1770. June 11.	Bedell, John, and Catharine Poilon,	"	XVI.	107
1756. Sept. 3.	Bedell, Mariam, and James Totton,	"	I.	282
1782. July 15.	Bedell, Mary, and Lininton Smith,	"	XXXVI.	82
1781. June 2.	Bedell, Sarah, and Thomas Craddock,	"	XXXII.	68
1781. Nov. 15.	Bedell, Silas, and Martha Burbanks,	"	XXXIV.	36
1769. Nov. 3.	Bedell, Silas, and Mary Pullion,	"	XV.	76
1782. June 19.	Bedell, Silvester, and Mary Hall,	"	XXXVI.	57
1783. Feb. 8.	Bedell, William, and Rachel Van Pelt,	"	XXXVIII.	37
1760. Sept. 11.	Bedford, Dorothy, and John Ferrel,	"	III.	311
1759. May 16.	Bedford, Elizabeth, and John Thorp,	"	II.	285
1780. May 6.	Bedine, Martha, and Peter Laforge,	"	XXIX.	47
1679. Nov. 22.	Bedle, Daniel, and Anne Powle,	G. E.,	XXXII.	63
1757. Aug. 31.	Bedle, Hannah. and Richard Post,	M. B.,	I.	627
1758. Nov. 20.	Bedle, Jemime, and Samuel Brown,	"	II.	98
1782. July 1.	Bedle, Richard, and Mary Ansley,	"	XXXVI.	70
1690. Nov. 3.	Bedloo, Maria, and Joseph Smith,	P. B.,	IV.	71
1759. Dec. 14.	Bedlow, Esther, and Richard Collings,	M. B.,	II.	545
1737. July 26.	Bedlow, Isaac, and Hester Glieves,	"	I.	7

DATE.	NAMES.	RECORD.	VOL.	PAGE.
1763. Dec. 23.	Bedlow, Susanna, and Cornelius Boyce, ...	M. B.,	VII.	523
1766. Oct. 29.	Bedon, Eva, and James McCullough, ...	"	X.	146
1762. Dec. 10.	Be De Vois, George, and Ann Rapalje, ...	"	VI.	476
1760. April 14.	Bergen, Tunis, and Anatje Stothoff, ...	"	III.	105
1758. Oct. 7.	Beebe, Absolum, and Dorothy Plowman, ...	"	II.	42
1783. Dec. 6.	Beeche, Phebe, and Ammi Chase, ...	"	XXXVII.	109
1764. April 6.	Beeckman, Effe, and Philip Verplanck, ...	"	VIII.	139
1764. Aug. 7.	Beeckman, Effy, and John Gaansevort, ...	"	VIII.	276
1762. Sept. 14.	Beeckman, Jemima, and Robert Curtis, ...	"	VI.	316
1782. Mar. 4.	Beedel, Jehiel, and Mary Frost, ...	"	XXXV.	72
1772. Nov. 9.	Beedel, Mordecai, and Charity Carpenter, ...	"	XIX.	104
1780. Oct. 11.	Beedle, Ann, and Thomas Lewis, ...	"	XXX.	62
1736. Nov. 25.	Beedle, Elizabeth, and Samuel Pierson, ...	"	I.	3
1773. Nov. 25.	Beedle, Elizabeth, and Daniel Van Ulser, ...	"	XXII.	45
1736. Nov. 25.	Beedle, Isaac, and Sarah Leosha, ...	"	I.	3
1762. Dec. 17.	Beedle, Mary, and William Williams, ...	"	VI.	486
1780. May 3.	Beedle, Sarah, William Curtis, ...	"	XXIX.	43
1763. Aug. 31.	Beek, John, and Margaret Armstrong, ...	"	VII.	320
1763. Mar. 14.	Beek, Nathaniel, and Sarah Whitney, ...	"	VII.	99
1760. Mar. 3.	Beckman, Catharine, and ——— Bain, ...	"	III.	60
1769. June 28.	Beekman, Catherine, and John Lawrence, ..	"	XIV.	133
1771. Aug. 19.	Beekman, Cornelia, and Charles Aitkins, ...	"	XVII.	159
1755. Sept. 2.	Beeckman, Elizabeth, and Robert Rutgers, ...	"	I.	181
1763. Nov. 12.	Beekman, Eva, and Abraham Schuyler, ...	"	VII.	446
1763. Feb. 21.	Beekman, Eyda, and Erasmus Williams, ...	"	VII.	71
1759. June 7.	Beekman, Eyda, and Jeronemus Alstyne, ...	"	II.	309
1772. Mar. 12.	Beekman, Garret, and Sarah Paines, ...	"	XVIII.	52
1772. Feb. 1.	Beekman, Gerard G., Jr., and Cornelia Court- land, ...	"	XVIII.	25
1761. May 18.	Beekman, Gerardus, and Anne Douw, ...	"	IV.	193
1757. Nov. 2.	Beekman, Henry, and Anna Swits, ...	"	I.	8
1760. Sept. 6.	Beekman, Henry, and Mary Carmer, ...	"	III.	302
1771. Aug. 1.	Beekman, Jane, and Ralph Welsh, ...	"	XVII.	147
1770. July 21.	Beekman, Johannes, and Elizabeth Cuyler, ..	"	XVI.	143
1769. Mar. 2.	Beekman, John, and Mary Bancker, ...	"	XIV.	42
1771. Oct. 14.	Beekman, John, and Mary Rivers, ...	"	XVII.	206
1766. Nov. 15.	Beekman, John H., and Hendrickie Van Bueren, ...	"	X.	165
1759. Oct. 19.	Beekman, John J., and Maria Sanders, ...	"	II.	465
1763. Dec. 28.	Beekman, John M., and Elizabeth Douw, ...	"	VII.	527
1753. July 26.	Beekman, Latitia, and John Taveau, ...	"	I.	78
1757. Feb. 25.	Beekman, Magdaleen, and Abraham Lynsen, Jr., ...	"	I.	451
1771. July 10.	Beekman, Magnus, and Mary Cock, ...	"	XVII.	129
1778. Sept. 10.	Beekman, Mary, and John Ackerman, ...	"	XXVI.	23

DATE.		NAMES.	RECORD.	VOL.	PAGE.
1782. Jan.	9.	Beers, William, and Rachel Butler, ...	M. B.,	xxxv.	13
1775. July	8.	Beesley, Mary, and Joseph Rogers, ...	"	xxiii.	89
1783. Nov.	13.	Beeton, John, and Anne Parker, ...	"	xl.	113
1763. Nov.	9.	Beeton, William, and Mary McFadon, ...	"	vii.	441
1641. April 27.		Beets, Nanne, and Thomas Smith, ...	A. R.,	i.	235
1772. Feb.	13.	Beets, Rachel, and Benjamin Gatfield, ...	M. B.,	xviii.	37
1780. Dec.	1.	Begg, John, and Phebe Willson, ...	"	xxx.	132
1759. Oct.	2.	Begle, Elizabeth, and Jeremiah Green, ...	"	ii.	441
1762. April 10.		Begoom, Rachel, and Isaac Van Duzer, ...	"	vi.	101
1755. Dec.	15.	Belitha, John, and Mary Nobine, ...	"	i.	234
1764. Oct.	29.	Bell, Andrew, and Ann Carter, ...	"	viii.	380
1767. Nov.	14.	Bell, Benjamin, and Jane Marsh, ...	"	xii.	83
1774. Jan.	8.	Bell, Catherine, and Hendrick Bell, ...	"	xxii.	98
1760. Aug.	11.	Bell, Elizabeth, and Henry Dixon, ...	"	iii.	247
1782. Oct.	5.	Bell, George, and Mary Roome, ...	"	xxxvii.	31
1777. Mar.	5.	Bell, George, and Sarah McChain, ...	"	xxiv.	41
1774. Jan.	8.	Bell, Hendrick, and Catherine Bell, ...	"	xxii.	98
1763. June 18.		Bell, Hendrick, and Hannah Lawrence, ...	"	vii.	232
1761. Nov.	10.	Bell, James, and Elizabeth Tate, ...	"	v.	204
173⁶⁄₇. Mar.	16.	Bell, Jane, and Alexander Wiley, ...	"	i.	5
1779. June	3.	Bell, Jared, and Mary Colvill, ...	"	xxvii.	153
1781. Sept. 21.		Bell, John, and Hester Jones, ...	"	xxxiii.	73
1783. Aug.	15.	Bell, John, and Mary Frake, ...	"	xxxix.	127
1770. Oct.	27.	Bell, Mary, and Cornelius Steenbergen, ...	"	xvi.	230
1757. Nov.	22.	Bell, Mary, and Daniel Amos, ...	"	i.	708
1763. May	11.	Bell, Mary, and James Waugh, ...	"	vii.	175
1762. Aug.	18.	Bell, Mary, and Peter Mabee, ...	"	vi.	279
1762. April 22.		Bell, Mary, and Robert Leonard, ...	"	vi.	124
1765. Sept. 30.		Bell, Peter, and Jane Jones, ...	"	ix.	282
1775. June	1.	Bell, Robert, and Magdalen Lownds, ...	"	xxiii.	53
1782. Feb.	13.	Bell, Samuel, and Elizabeth McClain, ...	"	xxxv.	53
1738. Aug.	24.	Bell, Samuel, and Jane Bisset, ...	"	i.	10
1771. June 24.		Bell, Stephen, and Elizabeth Kidney, ...	"	xvii.	121
1757. Aug.	13.	Bell, Thomas, and Elizabeth Nevins, ...	"	i.	612
1772. Jan.	1.	Bell, William, and Elizabeth McCarsey, ...	"	xvii.	308
1781. April 25.		Bellard, William, and Hannah Denton, ...	"	xxxii.	15
1781. Aug.	24.	Belton, Catharine, and Charles White, ...	"	xxxiii.	45
1769. Feb.	6.	Bemper, Ann, and William Pierson, ...	"	xiv.	28
1681. May	19.	Bendall, Bridgett, and James Duncan, ...	O. W.,	xxxii½.	46
1767. Aug.	3.	Bender, Johannes, and Elizabeth Kean, ...	M. B.,	xii.	8
1782. Jan.	15.	Benedict, Jabez, and Mary Weeks, ...	"	xxxv.	18
1759. Oct.	2.	Beneven, Petrus, and Maritje Fort, ...	"	ii.	439
1771. April	3.	Benham, James, and Alathia Pitt, ...	"	xvii.	74
1759. June 14.		Benham, John, and Lena Leake, ...	"	ii.	324
1781. Nov.	14.	Benison, George, and Mary Timothy, ...	"	xxxiv.	32

DATE.	NAMES.	RECORD.	VOL.	PAGE.
1758. May 8.	Benn, Elizabeth, and Cornelius Haight,	M. B.,	I.	897
1768. July 7.	Bennet, Abel, and Phebe Gildersleeve,	"	XIII.	152
1768. Jan. 11.	Bennet, Abraham, and Catherine Hyer,	"	XIII.	5
1763. Nov. 2.	Bennet, Agnes, and James Van Brockle,	"	VII.	424
1776. Mar. 2.	Bennet, Ann, and Benjamin Smith,	"	XXIII.	277
1781. Oct. 12.	Bennet, Ann, and George Hunter,	"	XXXIII.	99
1783. June 24.	Bennet, Anna, and Christian Baehr,	"	XXXIX.	68
1770. Oct. 3.	Bennet, Annatie, and Isaac Brinkerhoff,	"	XVI.	205
1782. Dec. 30.	Bennet, Anne, and Henry Barr,	"	XXXVII.	137
1783. Jan. 18.	Bennet, Anne, and John Enyart,	"	XXXVIII.	20
1781. Aug. 2.	Bennet, Annautie, and James Montfoort,	"	XXXIII.	27
1768. July 22.	Bennet, Anthony, and Mary Hier,	"	XIII.	162
1759. Aug. 4.	Bennet, Antje, and Abraham Snedeker,	"	II.	372
1737. April 22.	Bennet, Augenietie, and Ram Vanderbeck,	"	I.	6
1782. April 3.	Bennet, Barnett, and Charity Striker,	"	XXXV.	110
1765. June 3.	Bennet, Catharine, and Aaron Simonson,	"	IX.	151
1781. May 31.	Bennet, Catharine, and Andrew Baker,	"	XXXII.	66
1762. Nov. 16.	Bennet, Catherine, and George Humphreys,	"	VI.	434
1781. April 4.	Bennet, Charity, and Abraham Vanderveer,	"	XXXI.	93
1770. April 23.	Bennet, Christopher, and Abigail Brundig,	"	XVI.	68
1772. Jan. 19.	Bennet, Cornelius, and Dorothea Voorhis,	"	XX.	14
1757. Oct. 31.	Bennet, Cornelius, and Mary Brewer,	"	I.	691
1781. Nov. 21.	Bennet, Garret, and Sarah Bennet,	"	XXXIV.	54
1769. Aug. 3.	Bennet, George, and Catherine Bogart,	"	XV.	16
1768. Nov. 22.	Bennet, Hannah, and John Van Orst,	"	XIII.	241
1757. Oct. 8.	Bennet, Isaac, and Elizabeth Hitchcock,	"	I.	662
1781. June 19.	Bennet, Isaac, and Sarah Vorhis,	"	XXXII.	90
1763. Oct. 24.	Bennet, Jacob, and Charity Remsen,	"	VII.	401
1769. Dec. 18.	Bennet, Jacob, and Elizabeth Mezerole,	"	XV.	125
1770. Nov. 21.	Bennet, James, and Ann Van Dyck,	"	XVI.	265
1762. Nov. 18.	Bennet, James, and Phebe Pell,	"	VI.	441
1769. May 12.	Bennet, Jeremiah, and Nelly Quinn,	"	XIV.	99
1766. Sept. 24.	Bennet, John, and Ann Wright,	"	X.	103
1761. July 7.	Bennet, John, and Williametie Barcalow,	"	IV.	286
1737. Nov. 1.	Bennet, Joseph, and Rachel Watters,	"	I.	7
1771. Aug. 28.	Bennet, Judith, and Conkling,	"	XVII.	164
1757. April 12.	Bennet (Burnet), Margaret, and Joseph Hunter,	"	I.	498
1761. Feb. 10.	Bennet, Margaret, and Jeremiah Remsen,	"	IV.	55
1773. June 8.	Bennet, Margaret, and Jacob Vandervort,	"	XX.	141
1773. June 19.	Bennet, Margaret, and Peter Bogart,	"	XXI.	16
1757. Dec. 30.	Bennet, Mary, and Peter Walshe,	"	I.	761
1769. Jan. 11.	Bennet, Mary, and Lewis Jones,	"	XIV.	12
1779. May 24.	Bennet, Mary, and Edward Holland,	"	XXVII.	145
1773. Sept. 23.	Bennet, Nicholas, and Mary Duryee,	"	XXI.	123

4

DATE.	NAMES.	RECORD.	VOL.	PAGE.
1781. June 8.	Bennet, Peter, and Margaret Emans,.......	M. B.,	XXXII.	77
1763. June 27.	Bennet, Phebe, and John Voorhis,.........	"	VII.	242
1761. Mar. 19.	Bennet, Rachel, and James Emmens,.......	"	IV.	110
1763. Feb. 28.	Bennet, Robert, and Lydia Mack Neal,.....	"	VII.	80
1761. July 1.	Bennet, Sarah, and Charles De Bevois,.....	"	IV.	271
1736. June 4.	Bennet, Sarah, and Thomas Cockerill,......	"	I.	1
1780. April 11.	Bennet, Sarah, and William Harrison,......	"	XXIX.	17
1781. Nov. 21.	Bennet, Sarah, and Garret Bennet,........	"	XXXIV.	54
1773. May 19.	Bennet, Thomas, and Hannah Hedger,.....	"	XX.	118
1771. June 1.	Bennet, Titus, and Sarah Rogers,..........	"	XVII.	98
1779. June 10.	Bennet, William, and Hannah Van Pelt,....	"	XXVII.	163
1762. Mar. 15.	Bennet, William, and Joanna Wortman,....	"	VI.	71
1755. Oct. 15.	Bennet, William, and Leah Peterson,......	"	I.	192
1758. Nov. 20.	Bennet, William, and Mary Vandevender,..	"	II.	97
1761. Mar. 19.	Bennet, William, and Mary Van Pelt,......	"	IV.	109
1773. Aug. 18.	Bennet, Wynant, and Mintje Van Dyne,....	"	XXI.	73
1670. Feb. 7.	Bennett, Alexander, and Esther Howard,....	C. A.,	II.	639
1783. Jan. 30.	Bennett, Benjamin, and Jane Vanbumlen,...	M. B.,	XXXVIII.	32
1760. Sept. 27.	Bennett, Charles, and Rebecca Pell,........	"	III.	332
1767. Nov. 10.	Bennett, Ellenor, and Andrew Merselus, ...	"	XII.	86
1773. June 11.	Bennett, Freelove, and Ezekiel Brush,......	"	XX.	144
1778. Jan. 5.	Bennett, George, and Ruth Newbury,......	"	XXIV.	9
1758. Nov. 23.	Bennett, Hannah, and George Michael Bush,	"	II.	104
1765. Aug. 14.	Bennett, Jeromus, and Anna Hoghlandt,...	"	IX.	235
1775. June 20.	Bennett, John, and Elizabeth Eagles,.......	"	XXIII.	71
1761. June 15.	Bennett, John, and Mary Finney,.........	"	IV.	240
1761. Jan. 6.	Bennett, Mary, and Philip Concklin,.......	"	IV.	4
1772. Aug. 19.	Bennett, Phebe, and Zebulon Platt,........	"	XIX.	26
1763. May 12.	Bennett, Sarah, and David Devoe,.........	"	VII.	181
1779. Oct. 2.	Bennett, Thomas, and Mary Sexton,.......	"	XXVIII.	97
1782. April 3.	Bennett, William, and Ann Tetetis,........	"	XXXV.	108
1760. Nov. 12.	Bennett, Winant, and Margaret Allen,.....	"	III.	405
1760. Nov. 17.	Benneway, St., and Gertruy Bovye,........	"	III.	420
1772. Aug. 1.	Bennis, Hester, and Anthony Simons,......	"	XIX.	9
1759. April 27.	Bennit, Mary, and Thomas Walker,........	"	II.	258
1764. June 28.	Benon, Mary, and Benjamin Parker,.......	"	VIII.	241
1763. Aug. 30.	Bennoway, Maritie, and Harme Groesbeck,	"	VII.	318
1768. Sept. 28.	Benson, Adolf, and Martha Van Dyck,.....	"	XIII.	200
1737. July 29.	Benson, Catherine, and John Bodin,......,	"	I.	7
1759. May 10.	Benson, Christopher, and Mary Simons,....	"	II.	274
1771. April 10.	Benson, Edward, and Ann Normanton,....	"	XVII.	53
1736. Nov. 5.	Benson, Hanah, and John Man,...........	"	I.	3
1761. Sept. 28.	Benson, John, and Sarah Brower,..........	"	V.	105
1765. Oct. 25.	Benson, Lawrence, and Mary Benson,......	"	IX.	319
1761. May 16.	Benson, Mary, and Vincent Carter,........	"	IV.	192

DATE.	NAMES.	RECORD.	VOL.	PAGE.
1765. Oct. 25.	Benson, Mary, and Lawrence Benson,......	M. B.,	IX.	319
1765. Oct. 9.	Benson, Rebecca, and Mathias Vredenbergh,	"	IX.	293
1738. Aug. 16.	Benson, Robert, and Catherine Van Bosson,	"	I.	10
1736. July 19.	Benson, Sampson, and Catherine Peek,.....	"	I.	2
1737. June 11.	Benson, Sampson, and Elizabeth Williams,..	"	I.	6
1763. Dec. 6.	Benson, Sampson, and Mary Sickels,.......	"	VII.	493
1759. Dec. 22.	Benson, Samuel, and Ann Steel,.......... .	"	II.	554
1763. Mar. 1.	Benson, Samuel, and Rebecca Dyckman,....	"	VII.	86
1763. June 22.	Benson, Sarah, and John Mildeberger,......•	"	VII.	239
1766. Nov. 5.	Benson, William, and Mary Stewart,.......	"	X.	155
1762. Dec. 1.	Bently, Elisabeth, and Peter Noxon,.......	"	VI.	466
1760. Oct. 21.	Bercaw, Jemima, and Elijah Anderson,.....	"	III.	375
1757. Sept. 26.	Berg, Anna Veronica, and Charles Gressmann,	"	I.	648
1773. Aug. 31.	Bergaw, Anna, and Silas Pratt,...........	"	XXI.	91
1764. June 16.	Bergaw, Eleanor, and Jacobus Riker,......	"	VIII.	226
1780. Sept. 5.	Bergaw, Jane, and Tunis Brinkerhoff,.......	"	XXX.	17
1770. April 19.	Bergen, Agnes, and Daniel Rapelje,........	"	XVI.	64
1753. Sept. 11.	Bergen, Jemimah, and William Beatton,....	"	I.	115
1777. July 1.	Bergen, Johannis, and Magdalena Boerum,..	"	XXIV.	109
1780. Nov. 17.	Bergen, John, and Marian Oldfield,........	"	XXX.	96
1759. July 5.	Bergen, Lettitia, and Stephen Terhune,.....	"	II.	348
1759. May 9.	Bergen, Magdelena, and Ebenezar Turell,...	"	II.	273
1780. April 21.	Bergen, Rachel, and Jacob Cowenhoven,....	"	XXIX.	30
1771. Dec. 28.	Bergen, Rachael, and Walter Berry,.......	"	XVII.	306
1778. May 13.	Bergen, Richard, and Mary Boerum,.......	"	XXV.	81
1770. Dec. 7.	Bergen, Sarah, and Hendrick Emmons, Jr.,	"	XXIII.	316
1760. April 14.	Bergen, Tunis, and Anatje Stothoff,........	"	III.	105
1759. Aug. 30.	Berger, Sarah, and John Grant,...........	"	II.	403
1782. Mar. 5.	Bergin, Abraham, and Ann Springsteen,....	"	XXXV.	74
1769. Sept. 2.	Bergin, Jemima, and Joseph Smith,........	"	XV.	34
1760. Sept. 17.	Berrien, Nicholas, and Elizabeth Hallet,....	."	III.	318
1756. Nov. 8.	Berjeau, Sarah, and James Hinderton,.....	"	I.	349
1753. Sept. 13.	Berkaa, Neiltje, and Mathew Moorhead,....	"	I.	117
1762. Aug. 18.	Bernard, Daniel, and Mary Weyley,........	"	VI.	277
1737. June 22.	Bernard, George, and Mary James,........	"	I.	6
1767. Sept. 2.	Bernet, Elizabeth, and Benjamin Underhill,..	"	XII.	25
1760. Feb. 2.	Berret, Margaret, and John Christie,.......	"	III.	18
1771. July 25.	Berrey, John, and Elizabeth Thompson,....	"	XVII.	142
1780. Oct. 18.	Berrian, Abigail, and Alexander Camelon,..	"	XXX.	71
1765. June 15.	Berrian, Cornelius, and Elizabeth Penfold,..	"	IX.	170
1781. Dec. 15.	Berrian, Daniel, and Meriam Wilson,.......	"	XXXIV.	87
1765. Oct. 2.	Berrian, Isaac, and Hannah Vandenbergh,..	"	IX.	286
1763. April 27.	Berrian, John, and Sarah Fish,............	"	VII.	145
1767. Jan. 9.	Berrian, Ruth, and Jacob Hallet,......... ..	"	XI.	6
1783. April 21.	Berrian, Samuel, and Sarah Berrian,.......	"	XXXVIII.	102

DATE.	NAMES.	RECORD.	VOL.	PAGE.
1783. July 17.	Berrian, Sarah, and Daniel James Brooks,..	M. B.,	XXXIX.	94
1780. Oct. 6.	Berrian, Sarah, and Jacob Hagerman,......	"	XXX.	57
1783. April 21.	Berrian, Sarah, and Samuel Berrian,.......	"	XXXVIII.	102
1760. Oct. 14.	Berrien, Amy, and Richard Lawrence,.....	"	III.	363
1763. Jan. 3.	Berrien, Catharine, and Nathan Fish,.......	"	VII.	2
1781. April 14.	Berrien, Cornelius, and Anna Russell,......	"	XXXII.	3
1778. Aug. 22.	Berrien, Elizabeth, and John Bogart,.......	"	XXVI.	9
1758. Mar. 15.	Berrien, Elizabeth, and Richard Betts,......	"	I.	853
173$\frac{7}{8}$. Feb. 15.	Berrien, Jane, and Nathaniel Fish,.........	"	I.	9
1777. Dec. 31.	Berrien, Jane, and John Deakin,...........	"	XXIV.	211
1759. Mar. 3.	Berrien, Nicholas, and Mary Brown,.......	"	II.	206
1779. Sept. 2.	Berrien, Peter, and Deborah Marston,......	"	XXVIII.	64
1763. Dec. 22.	Berrien, Peter, Jr., and Hannah Campbell,..	"	VII.	518
1738. Oct. 10.	Berrien, Trinte, and Rem Remsen,.........	"	I.	11
1773. Oct. 25.	Berringer, Hans Michael, and Leah Bingham,	"	XXI.	147
1781. July 28.	Berrow, Sarah, and Robert Tungate,.......	"	XXXIII.	18
1756. Dec. 22.	Berry, Charles, and Elizabeth Man,........	"	I.	397
1757. Jan. 6.	Berry, David, and Jane Campbell,.........	"	I.	409
1779. Aug. 25.	Berry, Elizabeth, and Samuel Stretch,......	"	XXVIII.	59
1756. Nov. 18.	Berry, John, and Deborah Remeck,........	"	I.	358
1782. May 10.	Berry, Margaret, and Andrew Phair,.......	"	XXXV.	158
1760. Sept. 5.	Berry, Mary, and Gabriel Sprong,.........	"	III.	285
1780. Aug. 19.	Berry, Mary, and James Barry,...........	"	XXIX.	142
1771. Dec. 28.	Berry, Walter, and Rachael Bergen,.......	"	XVII.	306
1756. Aug. 26.	Bertholf, Guilliam, and Osseltie Vesterveldt,	"	I.	277
1765. June 23.	Bertine, John, and Mary Rodman,.........	"	IX.	182
1769. Mar. 22.	Bertine, Susannah, and Edward Ackerman,	"	XIV.	58
1759. Nov. 1.	Bertrand, Anne, and Joseph Lewis,........	"	II.	484
1762. Sept. 14.	Besley, Susanna, and John Guerino,........	"	XI.	315
1773. Sept. 30.	Bessinger, Safereenus, and Mary Young,....	"	XXI.	126
1778. July 23.	Bessonet, John, and Sarah Mitchell,........	"	XXV.	138
1760. Nov. 6.	Bessonett, Charles, and Mary Millington,...	"	III.	395
1762. July 8.	Besswick, Robert, and Margaret Wortman,..	"	VI.	229
1755. Aug. 20.	Best, Edward, and Catharine Ray,.........	"	I.	151
1770. Sept. 5.	Best, Eve, and Jacob J. Miller,............	"	XVI.	180
1773. July 29.	Best, Hannah, and Set Toby,.............	"	XXI.	54
1772. Dec. 14.	Best, Johannes, Jr., and Margaret Musick,..	"	XIX.	155
1773. Jan. 25.	Best, Jury, Jr., and Mary Musick,.........	"	XX.	19
1760. May 7.	Bethell, Nathaniel, and Catharine Ffilkins,..	"	III.	143
1766. Sept. 4.	Bethell, William, and Margaret Willett,.....	"	X.	90
1764. Mar. 9.	Bets, Deborah, and Walters Smith,........	"	VIII.	99
1781. April 4.	Bets, Margaret, and George Corlies,........	"	XXXI.	92
1761. Oct. 30.	Betten, John, and Catharine Watts,........	"	V.	179
1780. May 10.	Bettner, John Henry, and Elizabeth Shonnard,	"	XXIX.	51
1769. June 3.	Betton, David, and Sarah Dring,..........	"	XIV.	114

DATE.	NAMES.	RECORD.	VOL.	PAGE.
1777. Nov. 21.	Betton, George, and Hannah Hindes,	M. B.,	XXIV.	183
1773. April 19.	Betts, Ann, and John Brown,	"	XX.	96
1775. June 23.	Betts, Ann, and John Treadwell Waters,	"	XXIII.	74
1755. Dec. 6.	Betts, Anna, and Samuel Moore,	"	I.	227
1775. May 18.	Betts, Anne, and Joseph Reade De Peyster,	"	XXIII.	37
1772. Aug. 11.	Betts, Anthony, and Jane Hollett,	"	XIX.	20
1758. Oct. 13.	Betts, Daniel, and Deborah Field,	"	II.	55
1764. Aug. 11.	Betts, Dorcas, and Abraham Wheeler,	"	VIII.	278
1762. May 29.	Betts, Hannah, and Jacob Wilkins,	"	VI.	176
1763. Oct. 7.	Betts, Helena, and Tunis Polhemus,	"	VII.	379
1769. Sept. 30.	Betts, James, and Anna Williams,	"	XV.	48
1669. April 20.	Betts, Joanna, and John Scudder, Jr.,	O. W. L.,	II.	417
1764. Aug. 15.	Betts, John, and Ann Percutt,	M. B.,	VIII.	281
176⅞. Mar. 15.	Betts, John, and Sarah Whitehead,	"	I.	9
1763. Sept. 19.	Betts, Mary, and Daniel Kissam, Jr.,	"	VII.	341
1772. Nov. 16.	Betts, Mary, and John Way,	"	XIX.	115
1764. June 27.	Betts, Mary, and Samuel Sacket,	"	VIII.	239
1773. Mar. 29.	Betts, Millisent, and Cornelius Van Nostrand,	"	XX.	75
1758. Mar. 15.	Betts, Richard, and Elizabeth Berrien,	"	I.	853
1781. July 9.	Betts, Richard, Jr., and Ann Frazer,	"	XXXIII.	1
1759. Sept. 27.	Betts, Samuel, and Mary Lawrence,	"	II.	434
1771. Dec. 3.	Betts, Sarah, and Edward Doughty,	"	XVII.	280
1768. Aug. 19.	Betts, Sarah, and John Parsell,	"	XIII.	175
1763. Oct. 4.	Betts, Sarah, and Richard Fish,	"	VII.	370
1775. June 16.	Betts, Susannah, and Thomas Welling,	"	XXIII.	63
1772. July 9.	Betts, Tama, and Isaac Montross,	"	XVIII.	161
1768. Dec. 21.	Betts, Thomas, and Sarah Wey,	"	XIII.	272
1757. Aug. 11.	Betts, William, and Ann Lewis,	"	I.	611
1778. Sept. 10.	Botts, William, and Patience Woodward,	"	XXVI.	24
1771. Nov. 12.	Betty, Bettsey, and Robert Johnson,	"	XVII.	251
1771. Nov. 12.	Betty, Jane, and Henry Watson,	"	XVII.	249
1769. Jan. 7.	Betty, John, and Hannah Post,	"	XIV.	6
1782. Feb. 7.	Betty, Nicholas, and Elenor Higby,	"	XXXV.	45
1766. Oct. 21.	Bevan, John, and Mary Connor,	"	X.	133
1779. Oct. 20.	Beveridge, David, and Margaret McGloan,	"	XXVIII.	116
1764. April 17.	Bevier, Andrew, and Jacamyntje Dubois,	"	VIII.	159
1760. Sept. 27.	Bevier, Benjamin, and Elizabeth Van Keuren,	"	III.	334
1773. Mar. 4.	Bevier, Elizabeth, and Joseph Hasbrouck,	"	XX.	56
1764. Sept. 18.	Bevier, Johannes, and Elizabeth Gonzales,	"	VIII.	313
1762. April 23.	Bevier, Mary, and Johannes Cornelius Vernoi,	"	VI.	129
1773. Dec. 3.	Bevier, Sarah, and Menewal Gonzales, Jr.,	"	XXII.	61
1736. Sept. 6.	Bevois, Jacobus, and Maria Gerrittsen,	"	I.	2
1775. Nov. 16.	Bevois, Sarah, and William Smith,	"	XXIII.	209
1775. Nov. 14.	Bevoise, George, and Elizabeth Van Brunt,	"	XXIII.	208
1772. Oct. 22.	Bezee, Mary, and Francis Veeder,	"	XIX.	87

DATE.	NAMES.	RECORD.	VOL.	PAGE.
1764. Mar. 9.	Bicker, Eve, and Lewis Thibou,...........	M. B.,	VIII.	100
1772. Dec. 2.	Bicker, Walter, and Wilhelmina Mary Welp,	"	XIX.	141
1771. July 25.	Bickers, Ann, and John Kierstead,........	"	XVII.	144
1772. Aug. 28.	Biggcraft, Elizabeth, and Francis Martin,....	"	XIX.	32
1755. Nov. 5.	Biggs, Deborah, and Caleb Hawkins,......	"	I.	206
1759. June 19.	Biggs, Isaac, and Mary Smith,...........	"	II.	330
1782. Jan. 26.	Biggs, John, and Ruth Rudyard,...........	"	XXXV.	34
1773. Mar. 29.	Bill, Ann, and James Minnitt,.............	"	XX.	76
1768. May 21.	Bill, Benjamin, and Ann Smith,...........	"	XIII.	109
1753. Sept. 15.	Bill, Mary, and James Jarvis,.............	"	I.	119
1737. June 22.	Bill, Penelope, and Collin Bussey,.........	"	I.	6
1759. Sept. 5.	Billings, Elizabeth, and Luke Ament,......	"	II.	410
1780. May 3.	Billington, Jane, and Philip Ruckel,........	"	XXIX.	44
1762. Nov. 2.	Billop, Christopher, and Frances Willett,....	"	VI.	405
1773. Feb. 11.	Billopp, Christopher, and Jenny Seaman,...	"	XX.	41
1760. Nov. 22.	Bills, Lydia, and Henry Brookman,........	"	III.	435
1783. May 21.	Binckes, John, and Hannah Klink,.........	"	XXXIX.	23
1763. Aug. 26.	Binckes, John H., and Ann Steenbreaker,..	"	VII.	315
1783. Aug. 16.	Bingham, Anne, and Joseph Hews Burton,..	"	XXXIX.	129
1772. Dec. 7.	Bingham, James, and Catherine Byvanck,..	"	XIX.	145
1773. Oct. 25.	Bingham, Leah, and Hans Michael Berringer,	"	XXI.	147
1758. Dec. 9.	Bird, John, and Mary Lippencut,..........	"	II.	124
1768. Dec. 9.	Bird, Judah, and Peter Waldron,..........	"	XIII.	259
1781. Nov. 16.	Bird, Phebe, and William McConnell,......	"	XXXIV.	41
1759. June 2.	Birdall, Abraham, and Annatje Apple,......	"	II.	301
1772. July 10.	Birdell, Margaret, and David Poyneer,......	"	XVIII.	162
1777. June 11.	Birdsall, Benjamin, and Mariam Mott,......	"	XXIV.	101
1758. Dec. 6.	Birdsall, Deborah, and Ananias Downing,...	"	II.	118
1768. Feb. 13.	Birdsall, Elizabeth, and Permenius Jackson,	"	XIII.	36
1780. July 28.	Birdsall, Elizabeth, and Nehemiah Purdy,...	"	XXIX.	125
1777. April 18.	Birdsall, Martha, and Jacob Smith,.........	"	XXIV.	67
1782. Mar. 25.	Birdsall, Mary, and John Elderd,..........	"	XXXV.	96
1779. Feb. 20.	Birdsall, Phebe, and Gabriel Cock,.........	"	XXVII.	44
1767. Jan. 7.	Birdsall, Sarah, and Amos Hares,..........	"	X.	191
1779. Oct. 18.	Birdsall, Sarah, and John Townsend,.......	"	XXVIII.	115
1762. Dec. 30.	Birdsell, Benjamin, and Freelove Jones,.....	'	VI.	502
1762. May 12.	Birdsell, Mary, and Samuel Simmons,......	"	VI.	157
1780. Jan. 10.	Birdsell, Mary Hannah, and John Titus,....	"	XXVIII.	190
1783. June 21.	Birdsell, Mary Hannah, and William Titus,..	"	XXXIX.	65
1768. Dec. 7.	Birdseye, Ruth, and Leonard Nichol,.......	"	XIII.	256
1781. Aug. 16.	Birk, Walter, and Sarah Ash,.............	"	XXXIII.	38
1777. Aug. 19.	Bininger, Abraham, and Catherine Embury,	"	XXIV.	135
1779. Mar. 23.	Bishop, Elizabeth, and Zachariah Roberts,..	"	XXVII.	74
1780. Sept. 21.	Bishop, Ezekiel, and Marian Fowler,.......	"	XXX.	34
1779. Mar. 27.	Bishop, Joseph, and Elizabeth Groshon,....	"	XXVII.	79

DATE.	NAMES.	RECORD.	VOL.	PAGE.
1762. Sept. 10.	Bishop, Mary, and Elnathan Hunt,	M. B.,	VI.	310
1760. July 5.	Bishop, Mathew, and Catharine Saunders,..	"	III.	205
1761. Sept. 30.	Bishop, Noah, and Sarah Underhill,	"	V.	110
1772. June 10.	Bishop, Tobias, and Christian Livingston,...	"	XVIII.	137
1756. Oct. 6.	Bishop, William, and Ann Varck,	"	I.	320
1737. May 22.	Bisset, Elinor, and Robert Troup,	"	I.	6
1778. Oct. 12.	Bisset, Everet, and Elizabeth Forrester,....	"	XXVI.	56
1738. Aug. 24.	Bisset, Jane, and Samuel Bell,	"	I.	10
1738. Dec. 8.	Bisset, John, and Hester Glover,	"	I.	12
1763. June 2.	Bisset, Thomas, and Hester Downs,	"	VII.	208
1780. Sept. 8.	Bissett, Jane, and Jonathan Hutchins,	"	XXX.	20
1758. Mar. 21.	Blaau, Waldron, and Eleanor Creson,	"	I.	858
1764. Nov. 6.	Black, Ann, and Thomas Handy,	"	VIII.	392
1758. Dec. 16.	Black, Donald, and Jennet McDonald,	"	II.	129
1755. Dec. 20.	Black, Edward, and Mary Morris,	"	I.	236
1769. July 13.	Black, James, and Abigail Bush,	"	XIV.	151
1759. Dec. 6.	Black, Jane, and Henry Millner,...⌡......	"	II.	531
1783. April 22.	Black, William, and Magdalean Gardiner,...	"	XXXVIII.	106
1765. Feb. 12.	Blacklidge, Sarah, and John Peek,	"	IX.	51
1768. May 7.	Blacklock, John, and Elizabeth Staples,.....	"	XIII.	96
1774. Jan. 21.	Blackwell, Joseph, and Mary Hazard,	'	XXII.	113
1676. April 26.	Blackwell, Robert, and Mary Manningham,	W. O. P.,	III.	192
1779. Feb. 16.	Blackwell, Samuel, and Sarah Moore,	M. B.,	XXVII.	41
1770. Feb. 12.	Bladtnar, Frederick, and Resina Musick,....	"	XVI.	16
1773. June 17.	Blagge, John, and Rebecca Drake,	"	XXI.	13
1769. Jan. 12.	Blaggo, Mary, and George Sharp,	"	II.	153
1760. Sept. 10.	Blain, Mary, and Barney Lowree,	"	III.	310
1760. Oct. 13.	Blaine, Alice, and James Parr,	"	III.	360
1763. May 25.	Blaine, Mary, and Charles Stewart,	"	VII.	200
1764. Oct. 12.	Blair, Catharine, and James Sloss,	"	VIII.	355
1687. April 28.	Blair, James, and Sarah Harrison,	C. M.,	LI.	7
1778. May 17.	Blair, John, and Mary Plowman,	M. B.,	XXV.	88
1779. Aug. 18.	Blair, Samuel, and Sarah Ellis,	"	XXVIII.	51
1777. April 24.	Blake, Abigail, and William Mooney,	"	XXIV.	73
1777. May 17.	Blake, Deborah, and John Holtz,	"	XXIV.	88
1764. Mar. 2.	Blake, Edward, and Elizabeth Houseman,..	"	VIII.	90
1769. Sept. 27.	Blake, Elizabeth, and Thomas Mason,	"	XV.	45
1758. Sept. 3.	Blake, John, and Catherine Van Norder,....	"	II.	37
1775. June 14.	Blake, John, and Hannah Van Brunt,	"	XXIII.	60
1778. May 14.	Blake, Margaret, and Isaac Cotgrave,	"	XXV.	83
1762. Oct. 6.	Blake, Martin, and Catherine Fletcher,	"	VI.	347
1759. June 21.	Blake, Martin, and Dorothy Thompson,	"	II.	335
1765. Aug. 27.	Blake, Mary, and Martin Cregier,	"	IX.	245
1756. Nov. 15.	Blake, Richard, and Catharine Spencer,	"	I.	354
1775. Aug. 17.	Blake, Richard, and Elizabeth Bray,	"	XXIII.	130

DATE.	NAMES.	RECORD.	VOL. PAGE.
1759. Aug. 30.	Blake, Richard, and Margaret Turner,......	M. B.,	II. 401
1758. April 15.	Blake, Thomas, and Ann Mary Ducket,.....	"	I. 873
1756. Dec. 20.	Blake, William, and Elizabeth Duglass,.....	"	I. 393
1761. July 4.	Blake, William, and Mary Wooglom,......	"	IV. 277
1761. Nov. 6.	Blaklidge, Mary, and Robert Berne,........	"	V. 193
1758. April 22.	Blanchard, Alatha, and Nicholas Carner,....	"	I. 879
1783. Jan. 22.	Blanchard, Cornelius, and Sarah (Mary) Reynolds,............................	"	XXXVIII. 25
1761. Aug. 1.	Blanchard, Elizabeth, and George Dominick,	"	V. 20
1765. Oct. 3.	Blanchard, James, and Elizabeth Ezlang,....	"	IX. 288
1767. Aug. 14.	Blanchard, James, and Mary Brinkerhoof,...	"	XII. 17
1762. July 30.	Blanchard, John, and Mary Anderson,.....	"	VI. 255
1773. April 5.	Blanchard, Mary, and Walter Grace,.......	"	XX. 83
1736. Aug. 10.	Blancher, John, and Elizabeth Lawdit,.....	"	I. 2
1759. Aug. 4.	Blancher, Margaret, and Francis Dominick,..	"	II. 373
1757. April 23.	Blanck, Agnes, and George Stanton,.......	"	I. 513
1757. Nov. 28.	Blanck, Jeremiah, and Elizabeth Wright,....	"	I. 717
1760. April 14.	Blanck, John, and Ann Titus,.............	"	IV. 149
1778. June 4.	Blanck, Phebe, and Thomas Fling,.........	"	XXV. 97
1763. May 21.	Blanck, Sarah, and William Brown,........	"	VII. 197
1684. Oct. 27.	Blancker, Anitie, and George Brewerton,...	C. M.,	XXXIII. 62
1760. Aug. 7.	Blanford, Elizabeth, and Robert Whary,....	M. B.,	III. 240
173⁶⁄₇. Mar. 4.	Blank, Agnus, and Samuel Tingley,........	"	I. 5
1761. Mar. 11.	Blank, Andrew, and Sarah Myers,.........	"	IV. 96
1766. Sept. 24.	Blank, Cornelius, and Catharine Hyer,.....	"	I. 302
1779. Sept. 18.	Blank, Elisabeth, and John Daniel,........	"	XXVIII. 81
1736. Dec. 23.	Blank, Elizabeth, and Thomas Poole,.......	"	I. 5
1761. Mar. 21.	Blank, Jacob, and Catherine Knecht,.......	"	IV. 112
1772. Aug. 21.	Blank, John, Jr., and Sarah Connet,........	"	XIX. 28
1761. Sept. 8.	Blank, Mary, and Samuel Bates,...........	"	V. 73
1757. Feb. 3.	Blank, Rachael, and Thomas Henderson,....	"	I. 811
1665. April 22.	Blashford, Elizabeth, and Thomas Cox,.....	G. E.,	I. 117
1781. Nov. 8.	Blassly, Rhody, and Zebulon Rogers,.......	M. B.,	XXXIV. 24
1782. Jan. 2.	Blatchly, Ebenezer, and Sarah Jarvis,......	"	XXXV. 5
1764. Feb. 13.	Blatsley, Mary, and Jacobus Hubbs,........	"	VIII. 59
1761. June 13.	Blauvelt, Abraham, and Maria Fleerboome,..	"	IV. 238
1763. Sept. 14.	Blauvelt, Arie, and Altje Smith,..........	"	VII. 335
1757. April 21.	Blauvelt, Catharine, and Peter Herring,....	"	I. 506
1770. Mar. 20.	Blauvelt, Greetye, and Abraham Abramse Haring, Jr.,........................	"	XVI. 34
1764. Sept. 14.	Blauvelt, Hendreck, and Helena Yorkse,...	"	VIII. 306
1771. May 24.	Blauvelt, Jane, and Arie Arianse,..........	"	XVII. 91
1772. Feb. 1.	Blauvelt, Johannes, and Elizabeth Conklin,	"	XVIII. 27
1775. May 3.	Blauvelt, Margaret, and Peter Blauvelt,.....	"	XXIII. 22
1775. May 3.	Blauvelt, Peter, and Margaret Blauvelt,.....	"	XXIII. 22

DATE.	NAMES.	RECORD.	VOL. PAGE.
1764. April 4.	Blauw, Magdalen, and Jacob Boelen,.......	M. B.,	VIII. 132
1758. Mar. 10.	Blawfelt, Johannes, and Elizabeth Smith,...	"	I. 841
1769. Feb. 20.	Blawfield, Elizabeth, and John Thew,......	"	XIV. 38
1758. April 28.	Blawfield, Margaret, and Henry Tourneur,..	"	I. 889
1760. Aug. 13.	Blaw Velt, Abraham, and Elizabeth Ryker,..	"	III. 252
1771. Nov. 13.	Blawvelt, Isaac, and Bridget Lewin,........	"	XVII. 252
1764. Sept. 26.	Blawvelt, Mary, and Jacob Woertendyck,...	"	VIII. 322
1753. Sept. 26.	Blear, John, and Mary Nevin,.............	"	I. 125
1763. May 4.	Bleecker, Anthony L., and Mary Noel,.....	"	VII. 165
1764. Nov. 27.	Bleecker, Catharine, and Goose Van Shaick,	"	VIII. 426
1773. Aug. 18.	Bleecker, David, and Susannah Renoud,....	"	XXI. 74
1769. Oct. 11.	Bleecker, Elizabeth, and William De Hart,..	"	XV. 53
1775. Oct. 4.	Bleecker, Jacob, Jr., and Elizabeth Wendell,	"	XXIII. 173
1772. April 18.	Bleecker, James, and Catherine De Lanoy,..	"	XVIII. 84
1769. Mar. 21.	Bleecker, John, and Ann Elizabeth Schuyler,	"	XIV. 57
1760. Nov. 21.	Bleecker, John J., and Garretie Van Schaick,	"	III. 431
1776. Feb. 8.	Bleecker, Margaret, and Harmanus Ten Eyck,	"	XXIII. 264
1760. Oct. 31.	Bleecker, Rutger, and Catherine Elmendorph,	"	XIII. 220
1736. Oct. 14.	Bleeker, Gertruyd, and Abraham E. Wendall,	"	I. 3
1777. Dec. 20.	Blew, Elinor, and William Van Nuys,......	"	XXIV. 201
1762. Dec. 15.	Blindborough, Almy, and John Philips,.....	"	VI. 481
1783. Jan. 28.	Blindenburrow, Susanah, and Samuel Smith,	"	XXXVIII. 46
1760. Dec. 22.	Bloodgood, Abraham, and Priscilla Ellis,....	"	III. 488
1773. Nov. 8.	Bloodgood, Abraham, and Elizabeth Lynott,	"	XXII. 17
1764. Dec. 7.	Bloodgood, George, and Rachel Thorne,....	"	VIII. 442
1769. Oct. 15.	Bloodgood, James, and Lydia V. Valkenburgh,	"	II. 458
1773. Feb. 25.	Bloodgood, John, and Mary Pudney,.......	"	XX. 53
1758. Jan. 11.	Bloodgood, Joseph, and Ann Stoutenburgh,	"	I. 780
1768. May 25.	Bloodgood, Peperril, and Sarah Tom,.......	"	XIII. 113
1760. June 27.	Bloodgood, Robert, and Sarah Thorn,......	"	III. 198
1763. Sept. 21.	Bloodgood, Sarah, and Thomas Philips,.....	"	VII. 346
1759. Sept. 15.	Bloodgood, William, and Mary Brinkerhoof,	"	II. 422
1761. Mar. 13.	Bloofield, Maria, and John Fleerboome,.....	"	IV. 100
1776. May 2.	Bloom, Barent, and Mary Curshoud,.......	"	XXIII. 305
1771. Dec. 5.	Bloom, Catherine, and Johannes De Wit,...	"	XVII. 285
1763. May 2.	Bloom, Frances, and Cornelius Van Tice,....	"	VII. 162
173⁶⁄₇. Jan. 7.	Bloom, Hester, and Samuel Pell,..........	"	I. 5
1768. July 7.	Bloom, Isaac, and Mary Rowland,.........	"	XIII. 150
1759. July 10.	Bloom, Jacob, and Elizabeth O'Bryan,......	"	II. 353
1761. Jan. 12.	Bloom, Jacob, and Priscilla Meekes,........	"	IV. 12
1761. Oct. 17.	Bloom, Margaret, and Jacob Everson,......	"	V. 146
1764. Nov. 24.	Bloom, Mellisent, and Luke Terbos,........	"	VIII. 423
1758. Mar. 8.	Bloom, Nicholas, and Mietje Vandevoort,...	"	I. 836
1765. Mar. 1.	Bloom, Oke, and Joannah Clowes,.........	"	IX. 59
1765. May 9.	Bloom, Precilla, and John Garrate Schotler,	"	IX. 124

DATE.	NAMES.	RECORD.	VOL. PAGE.
1759. Nov. 21.	Bloom, Rebecca, and Samuel Wright,......	M. B.,	II. 511
1764. Nov. 24.	Bloom, Simon, and Catharine Brinkerhoff,..	"	VIII. 424
1764. Sept. 4.	Bloom, Simon, and Elizabeth Brinkerhoff,..	"	VIII. 297
1760. Oct. 18.	Bloome, Margaret, and Peter Wright,......	"	III. 370
1758. Jan. 18.	Bloomfield, Jonathan, and Elizabeth Wood,	"	I. 788
1758. Jan. 5.	Bloomfield, William, and Elener Patterson,..	"	I. 770
1763. July 18.	Bloomindal, Albertus, and Annatje Harse,..	"	VII. 271
1757. Sept. 7.	Bloomindal, Masil, and Helena Schermerhorne,..............................	"	I. 633
1763. June 27.	Bloon, Mary, and Samuel Harvey,.........	"	VII. 245
1771. Nov. 7.	Bloore, Joshua, and Margaret Brudnel,.....	"	XVII. 243
1772. Sept. 29.	Blouw, Catherine, and John Albony,......	"	XIX. 63
1737. Dec. 29.	Blow, Jeremiah, and Cornelia Waldron,....	"	I. 8
1778. Oct. 30.	Bluck, Stephen, and Margaret Gibbons,.....	"	XXVI. 77
1762. Mar. 18.	Blum, Anne, and Thomas Howell,.........	"	VI. 76
1757. Feb. 7.	Blydenburgh, William, and Mary Arthur,...	"	I. 436
1777. April 15.	Blythe, Jane, and Robert Fox,............	"	XXIV. 63
1737. July 22.	Bochert, Cornelius, and Catherine Kipp,....	"	I. 6
1765. Oct. 31.	Bockee, Abraham, and Martha Van Scise,...	"	IX. 345
1756. Nov. 5.	Bockee, William, and Jane Minthorn,......	"	I. 347
1767. Sept. 16.	Bockey, Martha, and Richard Hitchins,.....	"	XII. 35
1781. Oct. 18.	Bockus, John, and Allctiee Remson,........	"	XXXIII. 107
1768. May 28.	Boderidge, Mary, and George McLaughlan,	"	XIII. 116
1736. Aug. 19.	Bodin, Hester, and Cornelius Brewer,......	"	I. 2
1737. July 29.	Bodin, John, and Catherine Benson,........	"	I. 7
1764. April 14.	Bodine, Hester, and Thomas Graham,......	"	VIII. 154
1778. Aug. 20.	Bodine, John, and Catherine Britain,.......	"	XXVI. 6
1769. Nov. 17.	Bodine, Mary, and Anthony Egberts,......	"	XV. 96
1755. Dec. 15.	Bodine, Mary, and Peter Parke,...........	"	I. 233
1779. Sept. 6.	Bodkin, Mary, and Thomas Stratford,......	"	XXVIII. 69
1738. Oct. 18.	Boeker, Victor, and Anne Turk,...........	"	I. 11
1755. Sept. 24.	Boel, Catharine, and Benjamin Wynkoop,...	"	I. 183
1782. April 29.	Boel, Hannah, and George Brady,.........	"	XXXV. 143
1777. Oct. 1.	Boel, Henry, and Hannah Coombe,........	"	XXIV. 156
1764. April 4.	Boelen, Jacob, and Magdalen Blauw,.......	"	VIII. 132
1773. Aug. 31.	Boelen, Jacob, and Mary Ryckman,........	"	XXI. 92
1780. Jan. 26.	Boerem, John, and Jemime Titus,.........	"	XXVIII. 203
1773. Mar. 13.	Boerhum, Jane, and Isaac Johnson,........	"	XX. 62
1780. Sept. 15.	Boerum, Ann, and Evert Suydam,.........	"	XXX. 29
1763. Nov. 19.	Boerum, Catherine, and Cornelis Voorhies,..	"	VII. 458
1773. Mar. 26.	Boerum, Isaac, and Anne Duryee,.........	"	XX. 73
1778. Feb. 25.	Boerum, Jacob, and Adriantie Remsen,.....	"	XXV. 33
1778. May 13.	Boerum, Mary, and Richard Bergen,.......	"	XXV. 81
1781. May 9.	Boerum, John, and Elizabeth Ward,.......	"	XXXII. 38
1753. May 18.	Boerum, Johannis, and Jane Lose,.........	"	I. 33

DATE.	NAMES.	RECORD.	VOL. PAGE.
1777. July 1.	Boerum, Magdalena, and Johannes Bergen,..	M. B.,	xxiv. 109
1770. May 3.	Boerum, Rebeccah, and Tetus Tetus,.......	"	xvi. 78
1763. May 19.	Boerum, William, and Antje Schenck,......	"	vii. 194
1764. July 7.	Bogard, Catharina, and Garret Van Evre,...	"	viii. 249
1774. Feb. 9.	Bogardus, Catherine, and John Sleght,.....	"	xxii. 124
1642. June 21.	Bogardus, Everardus, and Anna Jansen,....	A. R.,	iii. 37
1770. May 31.	Bogardus, Everardus, and Arreantie Houghtaling,...............................	M. B.,	xvi. 98
1762. June 10.	Bogardus, Francis, and Miriam Losie,......	"	vi. 186
1762. Nov. 11.	Bogardus, Jacob, and Catharine Ten Broeck,	"	vi. 424
1764. Mar. 5.	Bogardus, Jacob, and Patience Hervey,.....	"	viii. 92
1773. May 15.	Bogardus, Hannah, and Johannes Vanderwerg, ...	"	xx. 114
1755. Aug. 26.	Bogardus, Maritie, and Thomas Perry,......	"	i. 154
1775. Sept. 6.	Bogardus, Peter, and Annatie De Witt,.....	"	xxiii. 150
1771. Sept. 25.	Bogardus, Peter, and Rancha Nostrandt,....	"	xvii. 190
1761. June 23.	Bogardus, Peter, and Elizabeth Schoonhover,	"	iv. 257
1772. June 25.	Bogardus, Peter, and Hannah Van Wyck,...	"	xviii. 151
1769. Dec. 21.	Bogardus, Petrus, and Cornelia Teller,......	"	xv. 129
1669. May 13.	Bogardus, William, and Wasburga de Sille,..	O. W. L.,	ii. 407
1772. Nov. 27.	Bogaerdt, Peter I., and Sarah Van Schaick,	M. B.,	xix. 131
1760. Sept. 19.	Bogaert, Anna, and Anthony Quackenbus,..	"	iii. 320
1782. Mar. 22.	Bogart, Abraham, and Anne Garison,......	"	xxxv. 95
1781. Sept. 22.	Bogart, Abraham, and Margaret Lane,......	"	xxxiii. 75
1781. Jan. 4.	Bogart, Ann, and Forbes Newton,.........	"	xxxi. 10
1773. Sept. 1.	Bogart, Annete, and Abraham I.Van Aernum,	"	xxi. 93
1775. Dec. 23.	Bogart, Arres, and Williampy Suydam,....	"	xxiii. 236
1781. June 30.	Bogart, Catharine, and Gerret Nostrand,....	"	xxxii. 100
1783. July 3.	Bogart, Catharine, and Richard Pinfold,....	"	xxxix. 81
1769. Aug. 3.	Bogart, Catherine, and George Bennet,.....	"	xv. 16
1764. May 30.	Bogart, Christiana, and Lawrence Buschalck,	"	viii. 200
1761. June 5.	Bogart, Cornelius, and Margaret Covert,....	"	iv. 227
1783. Oct. 6.	Bogart, Elizabeth, and Abraham Stothoff,...	"	xl. 70
1736. Nov. 29.	Bogart, Elizabeth, and Benjamin Sute,.....	"	i. 3
1781. Jan. 2.	Bogart, Elizabeth, and Eliphalet Jones,.....	"	xxxi. 5
1760. April 5.	Bogart, Elizabeth, and Hugh McEwen, ...	"	iii. 98
1760. Nov. 15.	Bogart, Elizabeth, and James Van Varck,...	"	iii. 417
1760. Dec. 11.	Bogart, Gilbert, and Anne Lott,...........	"	iii. 472
1775. Sept. 5.	Bogart, Helenah, and Peter Winne,........	"	xxiii. 146
1758. Jan. 13.	Bogart, Hendrick, and Barrebar Marcelis,...	"	i. 783
1781. Nov. 27.	Bogart, Henry, and Thamar Huggerford,...	"	xxxiv. 61
1771. Mar. 4.	Bogart, Henry C., and Helena Van Wyck,..	"	xvii. 23
1763. April 13.	Bogart, Isaac, and Charity Bedell,.........	"	vii. 126
1781. Oct. 3.	Bogart, Isaac, Jr., and Hannah Hogeland,...	"	xxxiii. 84
1782. Oct. 18.	Bogart, Jamima, and Thomas Sandon,......	"	xxxvii. 51

DATE.	NAMES.	RECORD.	VOL. PAGE.
1781. Nov. 3.	Bogart, John, and Margaretta Demoray,....	M. B.,	XXXIV. 14
1768. June 28.	Bogart, John N., and Heyltie Gerrebrants,..	"	XIII. 144
1757. Mar. 25.	Bogart, Magdalane, and John Spoore,......	"	I. 482
1763. Dec. 31.	Bogart, Margaret, and David Masterton,....	"	VII. 531
1779. Dec. 24.	Bogart, Margaret, and Oliver Cromwell,....	"	XXVIII. 179
1761. June 8.	Bogart, Mary, and Abraham Verplanck,....	"	IV. 232
1772. Sept. 2.	Bogart, Mary, and Peter Hegeman,........	"	XIX. 39
1760. Dec. 29.	Bogart, Mary, and William Moore,........	"	III. 493
1760. Sept. 1.	Bogart, Mary, and Willet Taylor,..........	"	III. 276
1770. July 26.	Bogart, Nicholas, and Alletta Bargaw,......	"	XVI. 147
1780. Dec. 16.	Bogart, Peter, and Jane Vandine,..........	"	XXX. 155
1783. June 12.	Bogart, Peter, and Mary Lawrence,.......	"	XXXIX. 54
1763. May 26.	Bogart, Rebecca, John Van Ness,.........	"	VII. 203
1767. Nov. 23.	Bogart, Seiche, and Abraham Rapalye,.....	"	XII. 94
1760. Oct. 17.	Bogart, Teunis, Leah Vandervort,..........	"	III. 367
1778. June 17.	Bogart, Teunis, Mary Remsen,............	"	XXV. 110
1772. June 30.	Bogart, Tunis, and Phebe Luister,.........	"	XVIII. 153
1753. June 6.	Bogert, Abraham, and Marrite Basset,......	"	I. 51
1768. May 19.	Bogert, Abraham Outen and Elizabeth Paulding Horton,...........................	"	XIII. 108
1759. Feb. 5.	Bogert, Altje, and Philip Smith,...........	"	II. 175
1777. Feb. 1.	Bogert, Ann, and Nicholas Herring,.......	"	XXIV. 24
1758. Feb. 14.	Bogert, Annatje, and Petrus Byvanck,.....	"	I. 819
1780. Aug. 24.	Bogert, Charity, and John Androvet,.......	"	XXIX. 147
1773. Nov. 16.	Bogert, Isaac, and Catalina Hun,..........	"	XXII. 30
1764. Nov. 27.	Bogert, Isaac, and Rachel Telier,..........	"	VIII. 427
1762. Nov. 3.	Bogert, Jacobus, and Judith Van Sise,.....	"	VI. 408
1773. Dec. 13.	Bogert, Janetye, and Folkert Outhout,......	"	XXII. 72
173⁶⁄₇. Mar. 8.	Bogert, John, and Abigal Quick,...........	"	I. 5
1771. Nov. 21.	Bogert, John N., Philander Forbes,........	"	XVII. 261
1778. Aug. 22.	Bogert, John, and Elizabeth Berrian,.......	"	XXVI. 9
1759. April 2.	Bogert, Léna, and Richard Cullen,.........	"	II. 233
1778. June 1.	Bogert, Margaret, and Alexander McArther,	"	XXV. 96
1764. Dec. 28.	Bogert, Martha, and Francis Coldgrove,.....	"	VIII. 467
1773. Aug. 7.	Bogert, Mary, and Andrew Van Tuyl,......	"	XXI. 59
1762. Jan. 20.	Bogert, Nicholas, and Alida Ritzema,.......	"	VI. 19
1770. Sept. 21.	Bogert, Nicholas P., and Catherine Waldron,	"	XVI. 192
1773. June 19.	Bogert, Peter, and Margaret Bennet,........	"	XXI. 16
1758. Jan. 16.	Bogert, Peter B., and Barbarie Van Vranke,	"	I. 784
1759. Mar. 17	Bogert, Trientje, and Johannes Stoothof,....	"	II. 219
1758. Feb. 27.	Bogg, Richard, and Janet Glaghorn,........	"	I. 831
1764. Oct. 23.	Boggs, Isaac, and Rachel Yardin,..........	"	VIII. 371
1763. July 18.	Boggs, James, and Elizabeth Waiter,.......	"	VII. 270
1765. Oct. 29.	Boggs, James, and Mary Morris,...........	"	IX. 335
1765. April 18.	Boghart, Lambert, and Catharine Van Hoesen,	"	IX. 102

DATE.	NAMES.	RECORD.	VOL.	PAGE.
1770. April 12.	Bogle, William, and Rhoda Weeks,	M. B.,	XVI.	61
1780. Oct. 7.	Bohan, Mary, and George Craig,	"	XXX.	61
1761. June 17.	Bohannan, Jane, and Joseph Groves,	"	IV.	246
1764. April 7.	Bohownen, Robert, and Margaret Ties,	"	VIII.	140
1762. June 19.	Boice, Anne, and Thomas Carmer,	"	VI.	198
1762. Jan. 13.	Boice, Cornelis, and Anne Garretson,	"	VI.	11
1780. July 28.	Boice, George, and Eve Kip,	"	XXIX.	122
1780. Dec. 9.	Boice, Mary, and Reginal Hillery,	"	XXX.	146
1782. Dec. 6.	Boiles, Elizabeth, and George Brown,	"	XXXVII.	107
1736. July 1.	Bois, Cornelis, and Catherine Griggs,	"	I.	2
1738. May 5.	Boiss, Mary, and Cornelius Vanhoven,	"	I.	9
1756. Aug. 19.	Bokey, Hannah, and George Middleton,	"	I.	273
1763. Mar. 7.	Bole, John, and Jane Wiley,	"	VII.	94
1759. May 8.	Bolitho, Mary, and Richard Gilchrist,	"	II.	271
1674. Feb. 15.	Bollen, Elizabeth, and Anthony Watton,	W. O. P.,	III.	53
1761. Dec. 17.	Bollison, Francis, and Mary Hanham,	M. B.,	V.	283
1773. Mar. 30.	Bollmaier, Christian, and Dorothy Nestell,	"	XX.	79
1764. Mar. 31.	Boltenhouse, George, and Jane Breesy,	"	VIII.	125
1763. July 12.	Bolton, Margaret, and John Leveston,	"	VII.	262
1770. Nov. 24.	Bolton, Richard, and Joy Guest,	"	XVI.	269
1779. Sept. 18.	Bolton, Thomas, and Elizabeth Dale,	"	XXVIII.	80
1763. Aug. 12.	Bomer, Hannah, and Nicholas Anderisa,	"	VII.	298
1779. Oct. 6.	Bomon, Mary, and Stephen Feugeas,	"	XXVIII.	103
1769. Feb. 21.	Bond, Abraham, and Ann Mersereau,	"	XIV.	39
1770. Sept. 6.	Bond, Ann, and Peter Levoy,	"	XVI.	182
1761. Nov. 18.	Bond, Barent, and Sarah Fox,	"	V.	220
1760. April 14.	Bond, Catharine, and Renier Nack,	"	III.	103
1760. Mar. 8.	Bond, Jemima, and William Stevens,	"	III.	69
1757. July 4.	Bond, Mary, and Crossfield Rushton,	"	I.	580
1757. April 22.	Bond, Mercy, and William Gilbert,	"	I.	508
1775. Oct. 2.	Bond, Sarah, and Charles Sutton,	"	XXIII.	169
1737. Oct. 24.	Bondmot, Susannah, and Peter Vergersan,	"	I.	7
1772. Sept. 4.	Bonestele, Catherina, and Hendrick D. Steiver,	"	XIX.	42
1772. July 29.	Bonet, Peter, and Patience Hatfield,	"	XIX.	8
1761. Feb. 25.	Bonnel, Mary, and William Clark,	"	IV.	83
1768. Nov. 17.	Bonnet, Jane, and William Schureman,	"	XIII.	237
1762. Oct. 13.	Bonnet, John, and Jane Skureman,	"	VI.	396
1764. July 9.	Bonnet, Mary, and James Buvelot,	"	VIII.	252
1760. June 4.	Bonnet, Peter, and Mary Pine,	"	III.	177
1768. Dec. 16.	Bonnett, Elizabeth, and Benjamin Underhill,	"	XIII.	266
1781. July 12.	Bonney, James, and Elizabeth Fish,	"	XXXIII.	6
1757. Oct. 8.	Bont, Margaret, and Michael Ritter,	"	I.	660
1757. April 16.	Bont, Mercey, and Nathaniel Pettit,	"	I.	501
1783. Mar. 24.	Bonta, Catharine, and Philip Romine,	"	XXXVIII.	75
1766. June 13.	Bonta, Henry, and Joanna Ettsell,	"	X.	16

DATE.	NAMES.	RECORD.	VOL.	PAGE.
1782. June 1.	Bonter, Cathaline, and Lawrence Van Buskirk,	M. B.,	XXXVI.	33
1737. Aug. 9.	Bonter, Frainsante, and Nathaniel Earle,	"	I.	7
1753. Sept. 6.	Bookhout, John, and Deborah Lawrence,	"	I.	108
1761. Feb. 2.	Boom, Mariah, and Mathew Winne,	"	IV.	45
1770. April 2.	Boon, John, and Ruth Whitney,	"	XVI.	46
1767. Jan. 23.	Boon Repo, Elizabeth, and James Shaw,	"	XI.	12
1759. June 2.	Booram, Catharine, and Joseph Mott,	"	II.	303
1761. Oct. 30.	Boos, Wandell, and Catharine Rush,	"	V.	178
1773. June 11.	Boos, Wandel, and Anne Harding,	"	XX.	143
1766. July 26.	Booth, Benjamin, and Elizabeth Willett,	"	X.	62
1770. May 12.	Booth, Mary, and William Jackson,	"	XVI.	83
1767. April 18.	Boots, Christian, and Catherine Strubble,	"	XI.	64
1783. Oct. 10.	Borbanck, Rebecca, and Austin Barton,	"	XL.	77
1759. Jan. 29.	Borden, William, and Rebeccah Haws,	"	II.	169
1765. Mar. 11.	Borgart, Annatje, and Cornelius Vosburgh,	"	IX.	66
1757. Oct. 7.	Borhight, Maritje, and Joseph Praner,	"	I.	659
1769. Aug. 5.	Borkhadds, Santie, and Jacobus Quackenbush,	"	XV.	19
1765. Aug. 17.	Borrow, Samuel, and Catharine Earl,	"	IX.	240
1781. Nov. 1.	Borrowes, Ann, and Samuel Wiseham,	"	XXXIV.	12
1756. Aug. 27.	Borright, Abigail, and Peter Allee,	"	I.	279
1773. Dec. 8.	Borsted, Martytie, and Jacob Eligh,	"	XXII.	63
1762. Oct. 4.	Bortell, Peter, and Eleanor Vredenbergh,	"	VI.	345
1737. Nov. 12.	Boshert, Jonale, and Johannes Volkert,	"	I.	8
1775. May 2.	Boskirk, John, and Catharina Le Beavois,	"	XXIII.	21
1778. July 11.	Boss, Betty, and John Titley,	"	XXV.	124
1736. July 20.	Boss, Elizabeth, and John Parsall,	"	I.	2
1772. Aug. 31.	Boss, Jacobus, and Mary Miller,	"	XIX.	37
1764. April 21.	Boss, Sarah, and Lawrence Harmen,	"	VIII.	166
1758. Sept. 8.	Boss, Susannah, and Simon Losse,	"	II.	11
1758. Oct. 20.	Bossee, Margaret, and Jacob Funda,	"	II.	62
1766. Aug. 23.	Bostwick, Augustus, and Jane Doty,	"	X.	84
1771. May 7.	Bostwick, Ephraim, and Mary Cholwell,	"	XVII.	78
1767. Sept. 26.	Bostwick, Hannah, and Alexander McDougall,	"	XII.	46
1781. Dec. 12.	Bosworth, Jane, and Joseph Barnett,	"	XXXIV.	79
1769. Aug. 5.	Bothwell, Ann, and Alexander Fraser,	"	XV.	18
1783. April 24.	Bouden, Mary, and Robert Avery,	"	XXXVIII.	113
1782. Mar. 19.	Bouler, Elizabeth, and Thomas Pattison,	"	XXXV.	92
1781. Mar. 22.	Boulia, Lavina, and John Stevens,	"	XXXI.	81
1773. April 16.	Boumaer, Thomas, and Mary Annet,	"	XX.	94
1737. Oct. 10.	Bound, Ruth, and John Magran,	"	I.	7
1760. Nov. 21.	Bourch, Neltie, and Courset Wedder,	"	III.	432
1756. Sept. 6.	Bourdet, Hannah, and William Albresty,	"	I.	290
1763. Dec. 12.	Bourdet, Hester, and Philip Horne,	"	VII.	503
1782. Dec. 6.	Bouton, Nathan, and Abigail Burlock,	"	XXXVII.	106

DATE.	NAMES.	RECORD.	VOL.	PAGE.
1764. Nov. 3.	Bovec, Philip, and Gertruyd Vanderbergh,..	M. B.,	VIII.	390
1763. Nov. 29.	Bovier, Sarah, and Johannes Lefever,......	"	VII.	480
1760. Nov. 17.	Bovye, Gertruy, and St. Benneway,........	"	III.	420
1781. Oct. 5.	Bowater, George, and Catherine Brenton,...	"	XXXIII.	88
1768. Sept. 26.	Bowden, Thomas, and Susanna James,.....	"	XIII.	193
1772. Jan. 8.	Bowers, Henry, Jr., and Mary Meyers,.....	"	XVIII.	9
1782. Oct. 12.	Bowie, Daniel, and Hannah Dash,.........	"	XXXVII.	40
1759. July 21.	Bowler, John, and Sarah McKinney,.......	"	II.	360
1767. April 22.	Bowles, John, and Catherine McGuire,.....	"	XI.	67
1782. Dec. 27.	Bowlsby, Rachel, and Jolly Longshore,.....	"	XXXVII.	134
1783. July 2.	Bowman, Andrew, and Mary Lazenbey,....	"	XXXIX.	79
1762. Sept. 26.	Bowman, Catharine, and Isaac Whitney,....	"	VI.	337
1760. Mar. 7.	Bowman, Catharine, and Simon Ackerman,	"	III.	68
1772. June 19.	Bowman, Elizabeth, and Christian Perkile,..	"	XVIII.	144
1738. July 25.	Bowman, Elsha, and John Patterson,.......	"	I.	10
1763. May 12.	Bowman, Esther, and Robert Ely,.........	"	VII.	183
1675. Mar. 21.	Bowman, Henry, and Mary Rawles,.......	W. O. P.,	III.	183
1783. Sept. 10.	Bowman, Henry Richard, and Abigail Parker,	M. B.,	XL.	34
1762. April 10.	Bowman, Mary, and Peter Brown,........	"	VI.	99
1765. July 10.	Bowman, Mary, and William Watters,......	"	IX.	201
1762. April 8.	Bowman, Polly, and William Clift,.........	"	VI.	92
1764. Aug. 18.	Bowman, Sarah, and Joseph Pritchet,......	"	VIII.	287
1766. Sept. 9.	Bowman, Sebastian, and Anna Wetsel,.....	"	X.	93
1778. Dec. 1.	Bowman, William, and Mary Winn,.......	"	XXVI.	104
1765. Aug. 8.	Bown, Amety, and Richard King,.........	"	IX.	234
1758. Sept. 14.	Bown, Catharine, and Samuel French,......	"	II.	23
1686. Sept. 10.	Bowne, Elizabeth, and Edward Antill,......	C. M.,	XXXIII.	293
1757. Aug. 24.	Bowne, Elizabeth, and John Howard,......	M. B.,	I.	622
1773. Dec. 2.	Bowne, Gersham, and Elizabeth Gildersleeves,	"	XXII.	59
1763. Feb. 4.	Bowne, Gershom, and Amity Furman,.....	"	VII.	53
1783. Feb. 24.	Bowne, Hannah, and Townsend Williss,....	"	XXXVIII.	51
1762. Feb. 2.	Bowne, Joseph, and Sarah Mitchell,........	"	VI.	36
1772. Mar. 18.	Bowne, Matilda, and Peter Hunt,..........	"	XVIII.	54
1780. July 18.	Bowne, Obadiah, and Elizabeth Van Dyck,..	"	XXIX.	115
1760. Jan. 18.	Bowne, Phebe, and Lyonel Baker,.........	"	II.	585
1778. Nov. 7.	Bowne, Samuel, and Mary Stocker,........	"	XXVI.	84
1758. Nov. 4.	Bowne, Sarah, and Jacamiah Mitchel,......	"	II.	80
1780. Sept. 30.	Bowne, Sarah, and John Evans,...........	"	XXX.	48
1777. Nov. 25.	Bowne, Thomas, and Elizabeth Carpenter,..	"	XXIV.	185
1757. Jan. 22.	Bowns, Elizabeth, and Francis Van Dike,...	"	I.	425
1764. April 10.	Bowrine, Martin, and Elizabeth Lane,......	"	VIII.	145
1783. Jan. 15.	Bowyer, John, and Anne Bancker,........	"	XXXVIII.	16
1771. June 10.	Boyce, Cornelius, and Hannah Canes,......	"	XVII.	106
1763. Dec. 23.	Boyce, Cornelius, and Sarah Bedlow,.......	"	VII.	523
1764. Oct. 31.	Boyce, Jane, and John Boyce,...........	"	VIII.	384

DATE.	NAMES.	RECORD.	VOL. PAGE.
1764. Oct. 31.	Boyce, John, and Jane Boyce,............	M. B.,	VIII. 384
1764. July 20.	Boyd, Ebenezer, and Sarah Merrit,........	"	VIII. 264
1767. May 5.	Boyd, Elizabeth, and John Siegismund Ferdinand Shutze,.......................	"	XI. 77
1757. April 22.	Boyd, James, and Patty Huestus,..........	"	I. 511
1761. Feb. 3.	Boyd, John, and Anne Morris,............	"	IV. 49
1772. Dec. 8.	Boyd, John, and Helena Hewlet,..........	"	XIX. 147
1762. Oct. 20.	Boyd, Mary, and George Harris,...........	"	VI. 374
1764. Jan. 20.	Boyd, Samuel, and Isabella Dollis,........	"	VIII. 26
1769. Dec. 21.	Boyd, Sarah, and Peter Maybee,..........	"	XV. 127
1765. Sept. 16.	Boyd, William, and Ann Whit,...........	"	IX. 263
1781. Sept. 1.	Boyer, Julia, and John Slone,.............	"	XXXIII. 54
1761. Aug. 14.	Boyer, Samuel, and Judith Tellman,.......	"	V. 43
1782. Sept. 24.	Boyer, Samuel, and Rachel Seamans,.......	"	XXXVII. 10
1757. Jan. 15.	Boyl, Hannah, and Martin Coin,...........	"	I. 418
1758. Mar. 9.	Boyl, Robert, and Affie Waldron,..........	"	I. 839
1763. May 24.	Boylan, Ann, and George Manningham,....	"	VII. 198
1773. June 25.	Boyle, Jane, and Thomas Waters,..........	"	XXI. 22
1773. Feb. 2.	Boyle, Mary, and Thomas Arden, Jr.,......	"	XX. 36
1757. July 28.	Boyle, Robert, and Christian Hill,........	"	I. 605
1764. April 16.	Boyle, Susanna, and Daniel Tear,..........	"	VIII. 156
1759. Dec. 6.	Boyles, Mary, and John Steel,............	"	II. 532
1757. July 15.	Boyd, Catherine, and Garrett Williamson,...	"	I. 591
1758. Nov. 17.	Bozarina, Mary, and William Martin,.......	"	II. 92
1780. May 11.	Braat, Petertie, and Abraham Prior,........	"	XXIX. 53
1773. Aug. 9.	Bracade, Sarah, and Hermanus Ryckman,...	"	XXI. 62
1762. Feb. 10.	Bradbourne, Humphrey, and Hannah Moone,	"	VI. 43
1760. Jan. 10.	Bradbridge, Thomas, and Abigail Reynolds,	"	II. 574
1767. Oct. 7.	Bradburn, Alexander, and Catharine Coleby,	"	XII. 58
1753. Oct. 15.	Bradburn, Elizabeth, and John Cowenhoven,	"	I. 140
1771. June 7.	Bradburn Moon, alias Hannah, and John Adams,...........................	"	XVII. 103
1775. May 26.	Bradburn, Hester, and Wilhelmus Post,.....	"	XXIII. 46
1758. Jan. 30.	Bradburn, John, and Hester Hutton,.......	"	I. 806
1763. Nov. 3.	Braddt, Samuel S., and Highbertie Yates,..	"	VII. 427
1783. Jan. 22.	Bradey, Frances, and Uriah Loshey,.......	"	XXXVIII. 26
1783. Jan. 22.	Bradey, Frances, and Uriah Vanvlaracom,..	"	XXXVIII. 27
1665. Oct. 30.	Bradish, Katharine, and Peter Symons,.....	O. W. L.,	II. 17
1783. April 23.	Bradley, James, and Catharine Farrell,......	M. B.,	XXXVIII. 111
1763. Nov. 2.	Bradley, Jane, and Thomas Doughty, ...	"	VII. 425
1680. July 3.	Bradley, Martha, and John Hendricks,......	G. E.,	XXXII. 90
1761. Mar. 31.	Bradley, William, and Sarah Kipp,.........	M. B.,	IV. 124
1760. Nov. 24.	Bradner, Benoni, and Rebecca Bridges,.....	"	III. 438
1763. June 21.	Bradt, Alida, and Wouter Deforeest,.......	"	VII. 237

DATE.	NAMES.	RECORD.	VOL.	PAGE.
1771. Aug. 29.	Bradt, Anginistje, and Garret Abraham Lansing,	M. B.,	XVII.	168
1736. July 20.	Bradt, Annatie, and Kerjan Muller,	"	I.	2
1764. Jan. 16.	Bradt, Anthony E., and Mary Van Deursen,	"	VIII.	18
1757. June 11.	Bradt, Anthony, and Neeltje Haughwout,	"	I.	561
1757. Feb. 21.	Bradt, Cornelia, and Cornelius Leversie,	"	I.	446
1760. April 14.	Bradt, Engeltje, and Daniel Campbell,	"	III.	106
1736. Aug. 5.	Bradt, Garret, and Maria Ten Eyck,	"	I.	2
1762. Nov. 1.	Bradt, Hendrick, and Agnes Van Wee,	"	VI.	400
1776. Mar. 25.	Bradt, Hendricke, and Mary Eights,	"	XXIII.	290
1761. Oct. 2.	Bradt, Jannetie, and Christopher Yeates,*	"	V.	114
1767. July 22.	Bradt, John, and Gerritje Leansingh,	"	XI.	139
1765. July 8.	Bradt, John, and Sarah Van Antwerpen,	"	IX.	196
173⅞. Feb. 13.	Bradt, Margaret, and Cornelius Vandike,	"	I.	9
1769. June 15.	Bradt, Sister, and John Peeck,	"	XIV.	120
1782. April 29.	Brady, George, and Hannah Boel,	"	XXXV.	143
1770. June 16.	Brady, John, and Mary Diamond,	"	XVI.	113
1760. May 16.	Brady, Mary, and John Wright,	"	III.	158
1782. Aug. 16.	Bragaw, Isaac, and Ann Waldron,	"	XXXVI.	111
1776. April 27.	Bragaw, Richard, and Catherine Gilbert,	"	XXIII.	303
1776. April 27.	Bragraw, Andrew, and Elenor Wiltse,	"	XXIII.	304
1780. April 12.	Braibain, Mary, and Charles Clarke,	"	XXIX.	19
1781. Feb. 15.	Braid, Lois, and Thomas Courtney,	"	XXXI.	45
1773. May 10.	Braiden, Joseph, and Catherine Taylor,	"	XX.	107
1761. July 13.	Brain, Sarah, and Jacob Banks (Barbis),	"	IV.	295
1760. Dec. 10.	Braine, Ann, and Gilbert Comes,	"	X.	107
1778. Oct. 24.	Braine, Daniel, and Elizabeth Lawrence,	"	XXVI.	71
1778. Oct. 15.	Braine, Judah, and Abel Rapelje,	"	XXVI.	62
1764. Jan. 31.	Braine, Mary, and John Hilton,	"	VIII.	45
1772. Jan. 3.	Braine, Merriam, and Henry W. Perry,	"	XVIII.	2
1779. May 17.	Braine, Thomas, and Hannah Harvey,	"	XXVII.	140
1753. July 24.	Braisher, Abigail, and Stephen Leach,	"	I.	77
1781. Oct. 18.	Brambush, William, and Willempy Duryea,	"	XXXIII.	106
1773. Jan. 12.	Branch, Rebekah, and Robert Bass,	"	XX.	7
1760. Mar. 20.	Brand, Catharine, and Jean George Gressand,	"	III.	83
1783. Jan. 11.	Brandon, Ann, and Daniel Gautier,	"	XXXVIII.	13
1782. May 13.	Brandon, Johanna, and John Peters,	"	XXXVI.	1
1763. Mar. 16.	Brandon, John, and Elizabeth Curry,	"	VII.	101
1773. Nov. 24.	Brandow, Sarah, and Peter Overtenbot,	"	XXII.	41
1779. Mar. 11.	Brannon, Ann, and Charles Dunn,	"	XXVII	65
1763. July 22.	Branson, Ann, and William Wood,	"	VII.	280
1767. Nov. 20.	Branson, David, and Rebecca Tylee,	"	XII.	89
1775. July 5.	Branson, Elizabeth, and Daniel Darby,	"	XXIII.	85
1771. Sept. 27.	Branson, Jane, and Daniel Kemper,	"	XVII.	196

* In one part of the Bond the name is "Christophel Lansing." (See *Yeates.*)

6

DATE.	NAMES.	RECORD.	VOL. PAGE.
1767. Sept. 16.	Branson, Mary, and John Bridgwaters,.....	M. B.,	XII. 36
1772. May 23.	Branson, Mary, and Stephen Sands,........	"	XVIII. 122
1776. Mar. 25.	Branson, Ware, and Nancy Palmer,........	"	XXIII. 292
1779. April 19.	Brant, Margaret, and William Elleson,......	"	XXVII. 109
1770. Dec. 13.	Brandt, Philip, and Anne De Beavois,......	"	XVI. 293
1777. April 21.	Brant, Susannah, and James Lowey,.......	"	XXIV 69
1780. Sept. 27.	Branthwaite, William, and Sarah Trotter,..	"	XXX. 44
1771. Aug. 30.	Brantnell, Susanna, and William Hipworth,	"	XVII. 169
1761. Feb. 9.	Bras, Adolph, Jr., and Agnes Tingley,.....	"	IV. 59
1759. Oct. 4.	Bras, Henry, and Mary Oakes,............	"	II. 448
1772. July 10.	Bras, Jane, and William Wischam,.........	"	XVIII. 163
1736. Dec. 23.	Brash, Thomas, and Temperance Denter,...	"	I. 5
1783. April 16.	Brashier, Hannah, and John Balton,.......	"	XXXVIII. 98
1759. June 2.	Brasier, Elenor, and Alexander Dunlap,....	"	II. 302
1766. Nov. 8.	Brasier, Ephraim, and Ann Gilbert,........	'	X. 158
1764. Feb. 6.	Brasier, Henry, and Lucy Clarke,..........	"	VIII. 51
1770. Oct. 23.	Brasier, Meads, and Elizabeth Dash,........	"	XVI. 227
1763. July 14.	Brasier, Sarah, and Andrew Allsop,........	"	VII. 265
1761. Sept. 24.	Brasier, Susanah, and James Gillihen,......	"	V. 96
1764. Jan. 16.	Brasier, Susannah, and John Stiles,........	"	VIII. 19
1761. May 13.	Brasier, William, and Margaret Root,......	"	IV. 188
1782. Sept. 25.	Brass, Catharine, and Thomas Colvill,.	"	XXXVII. 14
1760. June 10.	Brass, Mary, and James Harvey,..........	"	III. 188
1761. April 9.	Brasted, Peter, and Sarah Myngert,........	"	IV. 139
1758. Sept. 12.	Brat, Anthony Danjelse, and Catherine de Forest, ...	"	II. 15
1758. Mar. 13.	Brat, Deborah, and Palmer Coperthwaite,...	"	I. 847
1772. June 24.	Brat, Elizabeth, and John Brat,...........	"	XVIII. 149
1772. June 24.	Brat, John, and Elizabeth Brat,............	"	XVIII. 149
1765. Sept. 10.	Bratt, Aaron, and Gertruy Taalhamer,......	"	IX. 260
1761. Jan. 12.	Bratt, Abraham, and Sarah Van Petten,....	"	IV. 11
1768. June 16.	Bratt, Adam, and Maritje Bratt,...........	"	XIII. 131
1764. Sept. 19.	Bratt, Alida, and Hendrick K. Van Rensselaer,	"	VIII. 314
1738. Sept. 26.	Bratt, Anne, and John Mesnard,...........	"	I. 11
1773. Mar. 26.	Bratt, Anthony E., and Alida Van Schaick,..	"	XX. 74
1765. July 30.	Bratt, Arent Samuel, and Mary Van Slyck,..	"	IX. 221
1738. Aug. 19.	Bratt, Ariantie, and Nicholas Van Petten,...	"	I. 10
1768. April 11.	Bratt, Arreyantie, and Jelles Yates,.......	"	XIII. 73
1760. Dec. 30.	Bratt, Catharine, and Garret Dunbar,.......	"	III. 497
1760. July 28.	Bratt, Deborah, and Jeremiah Wool,.......	"	III. 229
1765. Sept. 18.	Bratt, Dirick, and Eve Christiansoe,.,......	"	IX. 266
1772. Aug. 12.	Bratt, Eaddy, and James Hornbeck,.......	"	XIX. 22
1763. April 20.	Bratt, Elizabeth, and John Vischer,........	"	VII. 131
1761. Nov. 19.	Bratt, Hahnah, and Wilhelmus Smith,..:....	"	V. 231
1750. Nov. 8.	Bratt, Harmanus, and Affia Brower,.......	"	I. 350

DATE.	NAMES.	RECORD.	VOL.	PAGE.
1765. Oct. 18.	Bratt, Helena, and Andrew Winpel,	M. B.,	IX.	308
1770. June 30.	Bratt, Jacobus S., and Susannah Peeck,	"	XVI.	130
1761. July 22.	Bratt, Jannetie, and Abraham Yeates,	"	V.	4
1761. Jan. 29.	Bratt, John, and Folke Wemp,	"	IV.	37
1765. Aug. 14.	Bratt, John A., and Maieka Fonda,	"	IX.	237
1755. Nov. 7.	Bratt, Margarett, and John Kip,	"	I.	207
1770. Oct. 10.	Bratt, Maria, and Jelles Brewer,	"	XVI.	207
1768. June 16.	Bratt, Maritje, and Adam Bratt,	"	XIII.	131
1762. Aug. 26.	Bratt, Mary, and Abraham Quackenbush,	"	VI.	291
1761. July 4.	Bratt, Mary, and Evert Wendell,	"	IV.	276
1753. May 12.	Bratt, Mary, and Jacob Vollenwyder,	"	I.	29
1772. June 11.	Bratt, Mary, and Philip G. Vilia,	"	XVIII.	138
1766. June 17.	Bratt, Mary, and Thomas Lottridge,	"	X.	18
1773. May 12.	Bratt, Pyeterte, and Stewart Dean,	"	XX.	109
1756. July 12.	Bratt, Tunis, and Catalintie Van Ness,	"	I.	251
1760. June 27.	Bratt, Vroutie, and Robert Erhart,	"	III.	199
1780. June 24.	Bratten, Wilson, and Isabella Ewing,	"	XXIX.	94
1737. May 16.	Brazer, John, and Susannah Baker,	"	I.	6
1765. Aug. 6.	Brazier, Jane, and Robert Salmon,	"	IX.	256
1757. Dec. 23.	Brazier, Mary, and Peter Ablin,	"	I.	751
1668. May 21.	Brazier, Mary, and Thomas Barnes,	O. W. L.,	II.	223
1766. Dec. 11.	Brazier, Philip, and Philander Hester Lyng,	M. B.,	X.	198
1665. April 22.	Brazier, Rebecca, and Peter Tilton,	G. E.,	I.	113
1761. July 17.	Brazier, William, and Catharine Norwood,	M. B.,	IV.	301
1775. Aug. 17.	Bray, Elizabeth, and Richard Blake,	"	XXIII.	130
1779. Nov. 12.	Bready, Patrick, and Elisabeth Portor,	"	XXVIII.	138
1753. Sept. 20.	Breasted, Catherin, and Samuel Rue,	"	I.	121
1769. Feb. 1.	Breasted, Margaret, and Henry Vandewater,	"	XIV.	25
1779. Jan. 1.	Breasted, Mary, and Isaac Ball, Jr.,	"	XXVII.	1
1756. Dec. 27.	Breath, John, and Elizabeth Saunders,	"	I.	399
1764. Mar. 29.	Bree, Catharine, and John Groves,	"	VIII.	122
1773. Nov. 25.	Breet, George, and Mary Cooper,	"	XXII.	43
1758. Mar. 18.	Breemer, Martha, and Thomas Hepworth,	"	I.	857
1764. Mar. 12.	Breese, Anne, and Mathew Murphy,	"	VIII.	102
1763. Mar. 12.	Breese, Elizabeth, and Adrian Bross,	"	VII.	98
$173\frac{7}{8}$. Mar. 1.	Breese, John, and Flora Matthews,	"	I.	9
1771. May 23.	Breestead, Elizabeth, and John Cook,	"	XVII.	89
1764. Mar. 31.	Breesy, Jane, and George Bolenhouse,	"	VIII.	125
1764. Mar. 14.	Bregaw, Esther, and Henry Brevoort,	"	VIII.	104
1781. Oct. 5.	Brenton, Catherine, and George Bowater,	"	XXXIII.	88
1755. Sept. 27.	Breuvregny, John, and Frances Heath,	"	I.	184
1780. Dec. 30.	Breseal, Margaret, and William Murchia,	"	XXX.	173
$173\frac{5}{6}$. Mar. 23.	Brested, Anne, and Henry Vanderheule,	"	I.	1
1759. Feb. 2.	Brested, Lucretia, and Isaac Barnes,	"	II.	171
1758. May 25.	Brested, Mary, and John Cook,	"	I.	910

DATE.	NAMES.	RECORD.	VOL. PAGE.
1759. Jan. 13.	Breton, Elizabeth, and Henry Lane,........	M. B.,	II. 156
1765. Oct. 28.	Brett, Cornelius, and Rachel Vantine,......	"	IX. 328
1737. Oct. 5.	Brett, Francis, and Mary Van Wyck,......	"	I. 7
1764. June 7.	Brett, Francis, and Sarah Van Voorhies,....	"	VIII. 215
1763. Feb. 2.	Brett, Hannah, and Henry Schenck,.......	"	VII. 51
1775. June 15.	Brett, Lydia, and Mathew Gault,..........	"	XXIII. 62
1772. June 22.	Brett, Margaret, and Peter Backer,........	"	XVIII. 147
1764.	Brett, Mathew, and Lydia Elliot,..........	"	VIII. 443
1736. May 28.	Brett, Robert, and Catherine De Booyf,....	"	I. 1
1772. May 26.	Brett, Robert, and Elizabeth Fowler,.......	"	XVIII. 126
1768. Nov. 21.	Brett, Rumbout, and Sarah Somerndyck,...	"	XIII. 239
1770. Sept. 26.	Brett, Sarah, and Abraham Brinckerhoff,...	"	XVI. 195
1769. April 26.	Brett, Sarah, and Daniel Van Voorhies,.....	"	XIV. 90
1781. May 29.	Brett, Sarah, and Hassell Pymm,..........	"	XXXII. 60
1779. May 25.	Brevoort, Anna, and John Ousterman,......	"	XXVII. 147
1775. July 5.	Brevoort, Elias, and Mary Stotenburgh,....	"	XXIII. 86
1764. Mar. 14.	Brevoort, Henry, and Esther Bregaw,......	"	VIII. 104
1758. Sept. 5.	Brevoort, Henry, and Mary Anthony,......	"	II. 2
1779. May 25.	Brevoort, Henry, and Sarah Wheaton,.....	"	XXVII. 148
1766. Aug. 22.	Brevoort, Jemima, and Benjamin Stout, Jr.,	"	X. 82
1781. Aug. 10.	Brevoort, Jemime, and Daniel Lawrence,...	"	XXXIII. 33
1782. Nov. 16.	Brevoort, John, and Mary Tweedle,........	"	XXXVII. 82
1775. Oct. 9.	Brevoort, Leah, and John Henry,..........	"	XXIII. 175
1782. April 23.	Brewan, Mary, and Anthony Classon,......	"	XXXV. 133
1758. Oct. 18.	Brewer, Abraham, and Mary Elsworth,.....	"	II. 60
1757. May 13.	Brewer, Abraham, and Mary Locea,.......	"	I. 531
1761. Oct. 29.	Brewer, Catharine, and Thomas Elsworth,..	"	V. 175
1783. Sept. 22.	Brewer, Cene, and Daniel Selover,.........	"	XL. 50
1761. Dec. 24.	Brewer, Charles, and Catharine Anderson,..	"	V. 300
1736. Aug. 19.	Brewer, Cornelius, and Hester Bodin,......	"	I. 2
1761. Nov. 23.	Brewer, David, and Nieltje Snedeker,......	"	V. 241
1761. Aug. 18.	Brewer, Elenor, and John Macow,........	"	V. 45
1758. April 22.	Brewer, Hannah, and John Emmet,........	"	I. 881
1780. July 29.	Brewer, Jane, and William Collins,........	"	XXIX. 128
1670. Oct. 10.	Brewer, Jelles, and Maria Bratt,...........	"	XVI. 207
1757. Sept. 24.	Brewer, Jeremiah, and Elizabeth Vandewater,	"	I. 644
1763. Dec. 28.	Brewer, Jeremiah, and Anne Elsworth,.....	"	VII. 526
1757. Dec. 24.	Brewer, John, and Catherine Vervay,......	"	I. 753
1753. Aug. 9.	Brewer, John, and Hannah Abrams,.......	"	I. 88
1781. Dec. 2.	Brewer, John, Jr., and Jemima Southard,...	"	XXXIV. 66
1760. May 20.	Brewer, Letty, and Isaac Bush,...........	"	III. 160
1775. June 7.	Brewer, Maria, and Roeloff Neefus,........	"	XXIII. 56
1757. Oct. 31.	Brewer, Mary, and Cornelius Bennet,......	"	I. 691
1783. Feb. 15.	Brewer, Moses, and Mary Buflaree,........	"	XXXVIII. 41
1764. Sept. 8.	Brewer, Nazarus, and Bridget Pells,........	"	VIII. 301

DATE.	NAMES.	RECORD.	VOL. PAGE.
1760. Feb. 20.	Brinckerhoff, Altie, and Jacobus Swartout,..	M. B.,	III. 42
1764. Nov. 24.	Brinckerhoff, Catharine, and Simon Bloom,..	"	VIII. 424
1761. May 19.	Brinckerhoff, Derick, Jr., and Rachel Van Rantz, ...	"	IV. 201
1768. Sept. 12.	Brinckerhoff, Dirck, and Mary Schenck,....	"	XIII. 182
1775. Oct. 9.	Brinckerhoff, Elizabeth, and John Jacob Fraesh,............................	"	XXIII. 174
1769. Dec. 21.	Brinckerhoff, George, and Elizabeth Wilcocks,	"	XV. 128
1782. Oct. 22.	Brinckerhoff, Henry, and Elizabeth Hegeman,	"	XXXVII. 60
1767. Jan. 7.	Brinckerhoff, Henry, and Mary Lee,.......	"	XI. 5
1770. Oct. 3.	Brinckerhoff, Isaac, and Annatie Bennet,....	"	XVI. 205
1759. June 2.	Brinckerhoff, John, and Sarah Brinckerhoff,	"	II. 300
1753. Oct. 12.	Brinckerhoff, Joris, and Eyda Monfort,.....	"	I. 137
1772. April 18.	Brinckerhoff, Lucretia, and Jacobus Lefferts,	"	XVIII. 85
1760. May 17.	Brinckerhoff, Margaret, and John Coolbach,	"	III. 159
1760. Nov. 25.	Brinckerhoff, Mary, and Stephen Brincker-hoff, ...	"	III. 445
1760. Mar. 15.	Brinckerhoff, Neltje, and Jacob Vanholer,...	"	III. 78
1761. June 6.	Brinckerhoff, Richard, and Mary Coolback,..	"	IV. 230
1771. Aug. 21.	Brinckerhoff, Sarah, and Elbert Adrianse,...	"	XVII. 161
1759. June 2.	Brinckerhoff, Sarah, and John Brinckerhoff,	"	II. 300
1758. Nov. 21.	Brinckerhoff, Sarah, and Thomas Carman,...	"	II. 99
1760. Nov. 25.	Brinckerhoff, Stephen, and Mary Brincker-hoff, ...	"	III. 445
1782. Feb. 13.	Bringfield, Sarah, and John Mason,........	"	XXXV. 54
1771. Oct. 3.	Brink, Peter, and Sarah Cole,.............	"	XVII. 198
1771. Dec. 14.	Brinkenhoff, Dirck, Jr., and Catrina Van Vlackreh,............................	"	XVII. 294
1782. June 25.	Brinkerhoff, Abraham, and Gertrude Onder-donck, ...	"	XXXVI. 63
1772. April 21.	Brinkerhoff, Albert, and Ann Storn,.......	"	XVIII. 87
1759. Dec. 4.	Brinkerhoff, Antje, and Matthew Debois,...	"	II. 525
1764. Sept. 4.	Brinkerhoff, Elizabeth, and Simon Bloom,...	"	VIII. 297
1771. Sept. 10.	Brinkerhoff, George, and Susanna Fish,.....	"	XVII. 181
1761. Nov. 26.	Brinkerhoff, Jane, and Nicholas Van Osdall,	"	V. 249
1780. Oct. 21.	Brinkerhoff, Jane, and George Vreland,.....	"	XXX. 74
1783. Aug. 20.	Brinkerhoff, Lettitia, and Richard Cooper,...	"	XL. 3
1763. Aug. 9.	Brinkerhoff, Margaret, and Gulian Veearman,	"	VI. 270
1773. April 8.	Brinkerhoff, Tunis, and Catherine Rapalje,..	"	XX. 90
1780. Sept. 5.	Brinkerhoff, Tunis, and Jane Bergaw,......	"	XXX. 17
1781. Sept. 22.	Brinkerhoffs, George, and Sarah Rapalje,....	"	XXXIII. 74
1772. Dec. 17.	Brinkerhoof, Abraham, and Dorothy Remsen,	"	XIX. 157
1767. Mar. 25.	Brinkerhoof, Garrit, and Mary Brinkerhoof,	"	XI. 50
1764. April 3.	Brinkerhoof, Mary, and Cornelius Oostrander,	"	VIII. 130
1767. Mar. 25.	Brinkerhoof, Mary, and Garrit Brinkerhoof,	"	XI. 50

DATE.	NAMES.	RECORD.	VOL.	PAGE.
1767. Aug. 14.	Brinkerhoof, Mary, and James Blanchard,...	M. B.,	XII.	17
1759. Sept. 15.	Brinkerhoof, Mary, and William Bloodgood,	"	II.	422
1736. June 19.	Brinkerhuff, Altie, and William Hooglandt,	"	I.	1
1759. July 29.	Brinley, Pheba, and Zacharias Hawkins,....	"	I.	607
1736. Aug. 7.	Briscow, Edward, and Jane McDermott,....	"	I.	2
1782. Oct. 14.	Brit, Elizabeth, and Abraham Bussing,.....	"	XXXVII.	41
1778. Aug. 20.	Britain, Catherine, and John Bodine,.......	"	XXVI.	6
1779. Oct. 12.	Britain, Nathaniel, and Leah Pue,.........	"	XXVIII.	110
1783. Feb. 25.	Britt, Christian, and Shobel Brush,.........	"	XXXVIII.	53
1738. Mar. 29.	Brittain, Martha, and Samuel Moore,.......	"	I.	9
1773. Dec. 31.	Britten, Abraham, and Phebe Vanderbelt,...	"	XXII.	91
1762. April 15.	Brittine, Mary, and James Rhodes,........	"	VI.	112
1779. May 22.	Britton, Nath, and Ann Buskirk,..........	"	XXVII.	144
1782. April 4.	Broad, William, and Susannah Colder,......	"	XXXV.	114
1778. May 20.	Broadford, Andrew, and Elen Still,........	"	XXV.	94
1760. Dec. 8.	Broadhead, Charles, and Mary Oliver,......	"	III.	467
1755. Dec. 11.	Broadhead, Daniel, and Maritie Constable,..	"	I.	232
1767. May 15.	Broadhead, Elizabeth, and Dirck Romeyn,..	"	XI.	89
1759. Mar. 15.	Broadhead, Garret, and Jane Davis,........	"	II.	217
1773. May 15.	Broadhead, Gertruyde, and Johannis Schoonmaker, ...	"	XX.	113
1761. Oct. 6.	Broadhead, Marritie, and Arthur Arrison,...	"	V.	128
1736. May 5.	Broadhead, Mary, and Robert McGuiness,..	"	I.	1
1773. June 17.	Broadhurst, Benjamin, and Fanny Kenedy,..	"	XXI.	14
1780. June 16.	Broadhurst, Cornelia, and Philip Linn,......	"	XXIX.	89
1760. Aug. 7.	Brockus, Mary, and John Walker,.........	"	III.	241
1772. July 29.	Brockus, Mary, and William Dowdell,......	"	XIX.	7
1766. Oct. 17.	Brodhead, Charles W., and Sarah Hardenbergh,...............................	"	X.	127
1783. Sept. 26.	Brodie, Alexander, and Francis Hamilton,..	"	XL.	55
1779. Dec. 20.	Broeske, William, and Sarah Bunn,........	"	XXVIII.	170
1767. Sept. 29.	Brokaw, Abraham, and Catherine Van Alst,	"	XII.	48
1773. July 23.	Bronck, Antie, and Cornelius P. Hogeboem,	"	XXI.	51
1770. June 30.	Bronck, John, and Mary Goes, ...	"	XVI.	131
1765. Oct. 30.	Bronck, Leonard, and Margaret Bronck,....	"	IX.	337
1765. Oct. 30.	Bronck, Margaret, and Leonard Bronck,....	"	IX.	337
1769. Nov. 24.	Bronck, Maritie, and Johannis Van Deuser,	"	XV.	104
1760. July 23.	Broneek, John Jonas, and Scherlotta Cooyemans, ...	"	III.	222
1756. Nov. 25.	Broock, Walter, and Sarah Dalley,.........	"	I.	364
1778. Jan. 6.	Brooke, Thomas, and Elizabeth Sarly,......	"	XXV.	1
1775. Sept. 21.	Brookman, George, and Jane High,........	"	XXIII.	161
1760. Nov. 22.	Brookman, Henry, and Lydia Bills,........	"	III.	435
1773. Jan. 30.	Brookman, John, and Elinor Garrison,......	"	XX.	33
1755. Oct. 15.	Brooks, Ann, and Petrus Helton,..........	"	I.	195

DATE.	NAMES.	RECORD.	VOL.	PAGE.
1738. July 25.	Brooks, Anne, and John Campbell,........	M. B.,	I.	10
1770. June 16.	Brooks, Catharine, and Abraham Aights,...	"	XVI.	115
1783. July 17.	Brooks, Daniel James, and Sarah Berrian,...	"	XXXIX.	94
1770. Nov. 30.	Brooks, David, and Hannah Sands,........	"	XVI.	275
1753. April 5.	Brooks, Elizabeth, and William Hilton,.....	"	I.	19
1758. Mar. 11.	Brooks, James, and Elizabeth Lowrey,.....	"	I.	844
1773. Feb. 22.	Brooks, James, and Susannah Mills,........	"	XX.	50
1776. Jan. 5.	Brooks, Jane, and Stephen Hendrickson,...	"	XXIII.	241
1758. Dec. 18.	Brooks, Mary, and James Van Sant,.......	"	II.	132
1760. Feb. 2.	Brooks, Mary, and Edmund Mathews,......	"	III.	16
1783. April 22.	Brooks, Mary, and John Aikens,..........	"	XXXVIII.	108
1773. Oct. 18.	Brooks, Michael, and Anne McLean,.......	"	XXI.	144
1771. Oct. 10.	Brooks, Peter, and Fanny Wendell,........	"	XVII.	201
1764. Oct. 8.	Brooks, Phebe, and John Kerns,..........	"	VIII.	337
1779. Feb. 27.	Brooks, Timothy, and Phebe Peters,.......	"	XXVII.	51
1763. Feb. 1.	Broome, Elizabeth, and John Vanderbilt,...	"	VII.	43
1763. June 27.	Broome, Samuel, and Phebe Platt,.........	"	VII.	246
1776. Mar. 23.	Brosh, James, and Sarah Skilman,.........	"	XXIII.	289
1763. Mar. 12.	Bross, Adrian, and Elizabeth Breese,.......	"	VII.	98
1773. June 14.	Bross, Mary, and Theophilus Elsworth,.....	"	XXI.	2
1781. Nov. 20.	Brothers, Catharine, and William Young,...	"	XXXIV.	49
1783. Sept. 17.	Brothers, Dorothea, and Duncan Nicoll,....	"	XL.	42
1763. Sept. 2.	Brothers, Jacob, and Hannah Meredet,.....	"	VII.	325
1755. Nov. 15.	Brouckman, Samuel, and Susannah Hunt,...	"	I.	209
1737. May 12.	Broughton, John, and Alida Gouverneur,....	"	I.	6
1768. June 11.	Broughton, John, and Sarah Sheran,.......	"	XIII.	125
1769. July 5.	Broughton, Mary, and Herman Governeur,..	"	XIV.	142
1760. May 28.	Brouwer, Abram, and Catharine Wilson,....	"	III.	164
1762. Mar. 5.	Brouwer, Daniel, and Hannah Huyck,......	"	VI.	65
1776. Mar. 8.	Brouwer, Garret, and Mary Lefoy, ...	"	XXIII.	281
1763. Nov. 15.	Brouwer, Henry, and Mary Brouwer,......	"	VII.	450
1774. Mar. 16.	Brouwer, Jacob, and Catherina Gander,....	"	XXII.	150
1759. July 26.	Brouwer, Jacob, and Margaret Bralandt,....	"	II.	362
1763. Mar. 14.	Brouwer, Jane, and Nicholas Andries,......	"	VII.	96
1763. Nov. 15.	Brouwer, Mary, and Henry Brouwer,......	"	VII.	450
1783. Sept. 5.	Brouwer, Rachael, and Uzal Ward,.......	"	XL.	25
1761. Nov. 23.	Brower, Abraham, and Gharabrack Brower,.	"	V.	242
1771. Nov. 4.	Brower, Abraham, and Rachel Sebring,.....	"	XVII.	238
1751. Nov. 8.	Brower, Affia, and Harmanus Bratt,.......	"	I.	350
1761. Aug. 27.	Brower, Ann, and Andrew May,..........	"	V.	61
1761. Nov. 6.	Brower, Ann, and Cornelius Hooper,.......	"	V.	195
1764. Feb. 29.	Brower, Ann, and Thomas Colvell,........	"	VIII.	86
1765. Sept. 17.	Brower, Anney, and Theunis Thew,.......	"	IX.	264
1783. Sept. 5.	Brower, Catharine, and John Hyde,........	"	XL.	24
1777. Feb. 22.	Brower, Catherine, and John Lovell,.......	"	XXIV.	33

Date.	Names.	Record.	Vol. Page.
1763. July 18.	Brower, David, and Ariantje Stymets,.....	M. B.,	vii. 269
1768. Jan. 20.	Brower, Effje, and John Burr,............	"	xiii. 13
1768. Feb. 10.	Brower, Elenor, and Garret Kip,..........	"	xiii. 30
1779. Feb. 8.	Brower, Elinor, and Court Johnson,.......	"	xxvii. 38
1764. June 9.	Brower, Elizabeth, and Henry Ustick,......	"	viii. 222
1775. Oct. 28.	Brower, Elizabeth, and Walter Heyer,......	"	xxiii. 191
1761. Nov. 23.	Brower, Gharabrack, and Abraham Brower,	"	v. 242
1774. Jan. 20.	Brower, Hannah, and Samuel Brower,......	"	xxii. 112
1777. Jan. 5.	Brower, Hester, and John Beemsen,.......	"	xxiv. 8
1782. Aug. 31.	Brower, Isaac, and Aggness Gilmoore,.....	"	xxxvi. 133
1767. April 21.	Brower, Isaac, and Mary Knapp,..........	"	xi. 66
1782. Mar. 11.	Brower, Jacob, and Agness Allen,.........	"	xxxv. 86
1774. Mar. 16.	Brower, Jacob, and Catherine Gander,......	"	xxii. 150
1783. June 13.	Brower, Jacob, and Elizabeth Turk,........	"	xl. 108
1783. April 21.	Brower, Jacob, and Jane Brower,..........	"	xxxviii. 103
1760. Nov. 11.	Brower, Jacob, and Mary Spoor, ...	"	iii. 403
1759. May 12.	Brower, Jane, and Henry Van Wenkell,....	"	ii. 281
1783. April 21.	Brower, Jane, and Jacob Brower,..........	"	xxxviii. 103
1764. June 21.	Brower, Jennette, and Peter Sprung,.......	"	viii. 230
1769. Mar. 21.	Brower, John, and Catherine Duryee,......	"	xiv. 56
1760. May 6.	Brower, John, and Elizabeth Speeden,.....	"	iii. 141
1761. April 27.	Brower, Maria, and Abraham Garrison,.....	"	iv. 169
1760. Mar. 24.	Brower, Mary, and John Munro,...........	"	iii. 90
1765. Mar. 18.	Brower, Nicholas, and Sarah Drake,.......	"	ix. 69
1768. Feb. 1.	Brower, Peternellitje, and Anthony Post,...	"	xiii. 25
1760. Mar. 20.	Brower, Rachel, and Nathaniel Marrener,..	"	iii. 84
1778. Dec. 26.	Brower, Rachel, and William Heater,......	"	xxvi. 133
1774. Jan. 20.	Brower, Samuel, and Hannah Brower,.....	"	xxii. 112
1768. June 10.	Brower, Sarah, and Adonija Morehouse,....	"	xiii. 124
1763. May 16.	Brower, Sarah, and George Anderson,......	"	vii. 188
1761. Sept. 28.	Brower, Sarah, and John Benson,..........	"	v. 105
1762. Aug. 25.	Brower, Sarah, and Robert Thomas,.......	"	vi. 286
1755. Aug. 26.	Brower, Susannah, and Jasper Stymetse,....	"	i. 156
1757. Mar. 1.	Brown, Abner, and Joanna Prosher,.......	"	i. 453
1764. Sept. 28.	Brown, Abraham, and Anne Budd,........	"	viii. 324
1767. Nov. 26.	Brown, Abraham, and Nelly Duryee,......	"	xvii. 269
1780. Feb. 17.	Brown, Aitken, and Mary Greggory,.......	"	xxviii. 211
1756. Dec. 9.	Brown, Alexander, and Ann Brown,.......	"	i. 377
1738. Nov. 27.	Brown, Ammy, and Henry Rousby,.......	"	i. 11
1756. Dec. 9.	Brown, Ann, and Alexander Brown,.......	"	i. 377
1761. Feb. 4.	Brown, Ann, and William Mortimer,.......	"	iv. 58
1781. April 30.	Brown, Anna, and Charles Kingsland,......	"	xxxii. 23
1753. July 4.	Brown, Archibald Montague, and Dorothy Roberts,.............................	"	i. 72
1783. Oct. 11.	Brown, Catharine, and Thomas O. Craft,...'.	"	xl. 85

7

DATE.	NAMES.	RECORD.	VOL.	PAGE.
1780. Jan. 12.	Brown, Charles, and Sarah Earl,	M. B.,	XXVIII.	194
1765. June 27.	Brown, Christian, and Peter McClachlan,	"	IX.	186
1762. Sept. 29.	Brown, David, and Esther Wetmore,	"	VI.	340
1757. Nov. 18.	Brown, David, and Hannah Lint,	"	I.	707
1759. Sept. 13.	Brown, Duncan, and Hannah Hewit,	"	II.	418
1764. April 27.	Brown, Elenor, and Jasper Stymetts,	"	VIII.	173
1763. Nov. 19.	Brown, Elisabeth, and George Campbell,	"	VII.	457
1761. Sept. 23.	Brown, Elisabeth, and James Bud,	"	V.	95
1782. July 10.	Brown, Elizabeth, and James Kerr,	"	XXXVI.	77
1760. Oct. 6.	Brown, Elizabeth, and John Sarly,	"	III.	345
1778. July 11.	Brown, Elizabeth, and Mathew Christy,	"	XXV.	126
1778. June 17.	Brown, Elizabeth, and Thomas Randall,	"	XXV.	106
1767. Feb. 17.	Brown, Elizabeth, and Thomas Warner,	"	XI.	28
1755. Nov. 21.	Brown, Francis, and Hannah Cornwell,	"	I.	213
1781. Jan. 13.	Brown, George, and Alice Widowson,	"	XXXI.	22
1782. Dec. 6.	Brown, George, and Elizabeth Boiles,	"	XXXVII.	107
1779. July 21.	Brown, George, and Ellis Marsland,	"	XXVIII.	38
1777. May 2.	Brown, George, and Mary French,	"	XXIV.	81
1781. Nov. 12.	Brown, Hannah, and Abraham Pulliblank,	"	XXXIV.	28
1761. Sept. 28.	Brown, Hannah, and Cornelius Martin,	"	V.	106
1782. Dec. 24.	Brown, Hannah, and Daniel McNiel,	"	XXXVII.	132
1773. Sept. 10.	Brown, Hannah, and Jacobus Dyckman,	"	XXI.	106
1753. Aug. 7.	Brown, Hannah, and Joseph Rayner,	"	I.	86
1782. June 27.	Brown, Hannah, and Levin Turner,	"	XXXVI.	65
1770. Sept. 21.	Brown, Hannah, and Wendel Ham,	"	XVI.	193
1782. Aug. 29.	Brown, Hester, and B. Scuyler Dupton,	"	XXXVI.	130
1765. June 5.	Brown, Isaac, and Ann McGee,	"	IX.	155
1763. Feb. 16.	Brown, Isabel, and James Power,	"	VII.	65
1777. Dec. 4.	Brown, Isabella, and Andrew Anderson,	"	XXIV.	191
1775. July 11.	Brown, Isabella, and Zebulon Pike,	"	XXIII.	94
1737. June 6.	Brown, James, and Sarah Jones,	"	I.	6
1773. Jan. 16.	Brown, Jane, and Benjamin North,	"	XX.	10
1779. Sept. 6.	Brown, Jane, and Henry Elvans,	"	XXVIII.	70
1772. Feb. 26.	Brown, Johh, and Ann Baldwin,	"	XVIII.	43
1773. April 19.	Brown, John, and Ann Betts,	"	XX.	96
1759. Nov. 23.	Brown, John, and Antje Lessier,	"	II.	515
1761. May 8.	Brown, John, and Dinah Stevens,	"	IV.	185
1772. Dec. 4.	Brown, John, and Elizabeth Giffin,	"	XIX.	142
1783. Mar. 28.	Brown, John, and Elizabeth Smith,	"	XXXVIII.	79
1778. Oct. 12.	Brown, John, and Hannah Jenkins,	"	XXVI.	55
1772. June 10.	Brown, John, and Mary Livingston,	"	XVIII.	136
1763. June 27.	Brown, John, and Mary Stagg,	"	VII.	244
1780. Oct. 17.	Brown, Josiah, and Elizabeth Dudley,	"	XXX.	68–70
1759. Dec. 24.	Brown, Juley Ann, and Francis Madick,	"	II.	556
1781. Jan. 23.	Brown, Letty, and Marguelet Willet,	"	XXXI.	27

Simeon S.   Deborah Holmes
Daniel   Sybel Jewett
Benj.   Abigail Blin

DATE.	NAMES.	RECORD.	VOL.	PAGE.
1760. Mar. 6.	Brown, Margaret, and James Aymar,	M. B.,	III.	65
1783. Aug. 21.	Brown, Margaret, and William Dowgen,	"	XL.	6
1759. July 24.	Brown, Margaret, and William Hall,	"	II.	361
1759. April 10.	Brown, Martha, and Dennis Russell,	"	II.	238
1753. May 21.	Brown, Mary, and Benjamin Sniffen,	"	I.	36
1773. Sept. 22.	Brown, Mary, and James Waddick,	"	XXI.	118
1759. Mar. 3.	Brown, Mary, and Nicholas Berrien,	"	II.	206
1781. Dec. 19.	Brown, Mary, and Samuel Doughty,	"	XXXIV.	96
1778. Oct. 27.	Brown, Paul, and Ann Godwin,	"	XXVI.	74
1762. April 10.	Brown, Peter, and Mary Bowman,	"	VI.	99
1737. Sept. 9.	Brown, Peter Nelly, and Jacob Hardenberg,	"	I.	7
1769. May 6.	Brown, Rebecca, and Daniel Willse,	"	XIV.	95
1775. Aug. 7.	Brown, Rebecca, and Richard Shell,	"	XXIII.	121
1760. Oct. 31.	Brown, Robert, and Barbara False,	"	III.	389
1760. Feb. 5.	Brown, Robert, and Catharine Jacklin,	"	III.	23
1780. July 8.	Brown, Ruth, and John Sargent,	"	XXIX.	108
1758. Nov. 20.	Brown, Samuel, and Jemima Bedle,	"	II.	98
1780. Nov. 1.	Brown, Sarah, and Edward Hall,	"	XXX.	87
1777. Jan. 5.	Brown, Sarah, and James Evans,	"	XXIV.	7
1783. May 9.	Brown, Stephen B., and Catharine King,	"	XXXIX.	8
1759. April 9.	Brown, Submit, and James McGown,	"	II.	236
1765. July 24.	Brown, Thomas, and Ann Scott,	"	IX.	216
1770. June 16.	Brown, Thomas, and Elizabeth Haynes,	"	XVI.	114
1781. Nov. 7.	Brown, Thomas, and Mary Ming,	"	XXXIV.	19
1761. Aug. 18.	Brown, Thomas, and Mirtina Hogan,	"	V.	47
1761. Feb. 4.	Brown, William, and Elisaboth Morris,	"	IV.	51
1762. Mar. 15.	Brown, William, and Lydia McDonald,	"	VI.	73
1778. April 2.	Brown, William, and Martha Barnes,	"	XXV.	58
1763. May 21.	Brown, William, and Sarah Blanck,	"	VII.	197
1772. Nov. 11.	Brownbush, Williamanchia, and George Duryee,	"	XIX.	109
1661. Sept. 4.	Browne, Albert, and Ffrowkin Hans,	G. E.,	IV.	25
1763. Nov. 22.	Browne, Isaac, and Ann Van Wyck,	M. B.,	VII.	464
1762. Dec. 30.	Browne, Mercy, and John Jagger,	"	VI.	503
1779. Sept. 29.	Browne, Nicholas, and Hannah Stoutenburgh,	"	XXVIII.	89
1761. Aug. 6.	Browne, Sarah, and Benjamin Soper,	"	V.	27
1763. May 2.	Browne, Thomas, and Elizabeth Townsend,	"	VII.	160
1736. Nov. 10.	Browner, Amos, and Ealsee Baxter,	"	I.	3
1782. Feb. 23.	Brownjohn, Rachel, and John Price,	"	XXXV.	60
1778. Sept. 27.	Brownjohn, Samuel, and Ann Tallman,	"	XXVI.	35
1768. Dec. 22.	Brownjohn, William, Jr., and Deborah Stiles,	"	XIII.	273
1760. Dec. 9.	Brownlee, William, and Gertje Fineout,	"	III.	468
1769. Oct. 28.	Brownly, Geertie, and Reuben Crippen,	"	XV.	71
1666. July 17.	Browning, Margaret, and Daniell Eastall,	O. W. L.,	II.	85
1762. Feb. 2.	Browning, Samuel, and Ann Simmons,	M. B.,	VI.	37

DATE.	NAMES.	RECORD.	VOL. PAGE.
1777. Oct. 8.	Brownrigg, John S., and Lydia Emmes,....	M. B.,	XXIV. 160
1778. Oct. 3.	Browse, Nicholas, and Mary Cowdra,......	"	XXVI. 44
1759. Oct. 22.	Bruce, Anne, and James Powell,..........	"	II. 468
1765. July 20.	Bruce, Anne, and William Murrils,........	"	IX. 213
1770. Jan. 13.	Bruce, Izabella, and Joseph Smith,........	"	XVI. 5
1760. Dec. 2.	Bruce, James, and Jane Stewart,......... .	"	III. 451
1763. Mar. 7.	Bruce, Jane, and Collin McClaron,........	"	VII. 95
1763. Sept. 21.	Bruce, Johanna, and Henry Bryan,........	"	VII. 348
1771. Nov. 7.	Brudnel, Margaret, and Joshua Bloore,.....	"	XVII. 243
1763. Oct. 19.	Bruff, Charles Oliver, and Mary Letelleer,...	"	VII. 393
1738. Oct. 9.	Brughman, Mary, and Samuel Tines,.......	"	I. 11
1771. Sept. 20.	Bruin, Geertruyd, and Cornelius Du Bois, Jr.,	"	XVII. 186
1759. Oct. 31.	Bruister, James, and Sarah Hosler,........	"	II. 482
1761. May 2.	Brummajum, Catharine, and Ambrose Jones,	"	IV. 177
1765. Jan. 31.	Brundidge, Sarah, and Arthur Newman,....	"	IX. 39
1770. April 23.	Brundige, Abigail, and Christopher Bennet,	"	XVI. 68
1778. Dec. 10.	Brundige, James, and Hanah Hunt,........	"	XXVI. 117
1767. July 3.	Brundige, Mary, and Vincent Montange,....	"	XI. 121
1781. Nov. 4.	Brush, Alexander, and Ann Griffix,........	"	XXXIV. 17
1775. Aug. 30.	Brush, Amy, and Isaiah Wetmore,........	"	XXIII. 141
1772. Sept. 3.	Brush, Annanias, and Jemima Stammerson,	"	XIX. 40
1773. Sept. 1.	Brush, Benjamin, and Ann Skilman,.......	"	XXI. 94
1764. April 5.	Brush, Edward, and Hannah Pears,........	"	VIII. 135
1757. Oct. 31.	Brush, Elizabeth, and John Conkling,......	"	I. 692
1782. July 22.	Brush, Elizabeth, and Zebulon Dickinson,..	"	XXXVI. 90
1773. June 11.	Brush, Ezekiel, and Freelove Bennet,......	"	XX. 144
1775. April 12.	Brush, Hannah, and Jesse Whitman.......	"	XXIII. 8
1757. May 4.	Brush, Hannah, and John Walters,........	"	I. 524
1758. Jan. 6.	Brush, Hannah, and Joseph Whitman,.....	"	I. 775
1782. Oct. 4.	Brush, Jacob, and Susannah Veil,..........	"	XXXVII. 27
1763. Feb. 12.	Brush, Jerusha, and March McCoon,.......	"	VII. 60
1774. Jan. 5.	Brush, Jesse, and Arthur Platt,............	"	XXII. 93
1757. Oct. 13.	Brush, Jesse, and Rath Conklin,...........	"	I. 669
1777. Nov. 9.	Brush, John, and Ann Carpenter,..........	"	XXIV. 179
1762. April 27.	Brush, John, and Mary Smith,.............	"	VI. 133
1761. Aug. 24.	Brush, John, and Sarah Smith,.............	"	V. 54
1736. Aug. 24.	Brush, Jonathan, and Elizabeth Smith,.....	"	I. 2
1738. May 5.	Brush, Joseph, and Catherine Peets,.......	"	I. 9
1772. May 2.	Brush, Kesiah, and Jonah Conklin,........	"	XVIII. 97
1757. June 30.	Brush, Keziah, and Thomas Mott,.........	"	I. 578
1780. June 1.	Brush, Margaret, and Patrick Wall,........	"	XXIX. 76
1775. July 4.	Brush, Martha, and John Woods,..........	"	XXIII. 83
1782. Dec. 25.	Brush, Mary, and David Rolph,...........	"	XXXVII. 133
1767. Dec. 30.	Brush, Mary, and Samuel Wood,..........	"	XII. 125
1781. May 16.	Brush, Mary, and Stephen Burtis,.........	"	XXXII. 50

DATE.	NAMES.	RECORD.	VOL. PAGE.
1758. Sept. 20.	Brush, Phebe, and Gilbert Fleet,..........	M. B.,	II. 25
1759. Nov. 16.	Brush, Rebecca, and Gilbert Carll,.........	"	II. 502
1682. Jan. 31.	Brush, Rebecca, and Jeremiah Hubbard,....	G. E.,	XXXIII. 33
1771. Nov. 20.	Brush, Rebecca, and Samuel Young,.......	M. B.,	XVII. 260
1761. Nov. 20.	Brush, Samuel, and Martha Titis,..........	"	V. 235
1782. Jan. 23.	Brush, Sarah, and Benjamin Ralph,........	"	XXXV. 29
1770. Sept. 17.	Brush, Sarah, and Joell Scudder,..........	"	XVI. 189
1762. April 30.	Brush, Sarah, and Thomas Wickes,........	"	VI. 137
1783. Feb. 25.	Brush, Shobel, and Christian Britt,.........	"	XXXVIII. 53
1761. July 31.	Brush, Temperance, and Jesse Ketcham,....	"	V. 18
1773. Dec. 17.	Brush, Zophar, and Margaret Whitman,....	"	XXII. 78
1774. Jan. 19.	Bruyn, Benjamin, and Sarah Depuy,.......	"	XXII. 109
1738. Dec. 1.	Bruyn, Catherine, and Abraham Haasbroock,	"	I. 12
1765. Aug. 4.	Bruyn, Catherine, and Jonathen Elmendorph,	"	IX. 252
1775. Nov. 2.	Bruyn, Mary, and Nicholas Hardenburgh,..	"	XXIII. 196
1770. Sept. 28.	Bruyn, Trientje, and John Graham,........	"	XVI. 200
1767. Oct. 9.	Bryan, Anna, and Micah Hart,............	"	XII. 59
173⁶⁄₇. Mar. 10.	Bryan, Anne, and Thomas Netherway,.....	"	I. 5
1773. April 7.	Bryan, Ebenezer, and Esther Ketcham,.....	"	XX. 86
1779. April 3.	Bryan, Elinor, and John Colvin,...........	"	XXVII. 93
1763. Sept. 9.	Bryan, Hannah, and Thomas Jarvis,.......	"	VII. 333
1763. Sept. 21.	Bryan, Henry, and Johanna Bruce,........	"	VII. 348
1763. Nov. 10.	Bryan, Hugh, and Sarah Convis,..........	"	VII. 442
1765. May 25.	Bryan, Isabella, and Cornelius Ryan,.......	"	IX. 140
1771. Aug. 6.	Bryan, Ruth, and Benjamin Titus,.........	"	XVII. 154
1761. May 19.	Bryan, Sarah, and Jonah Wood,..........	"	IV. 199
1758. Mar. 22.	Bryant, Charity, and Hazael Lewis,........	"	I. 860
1769. April 12.	Bryant, Gilbert, and Mary Chichester,......	"	XIV. 72
1763. Oct. 17.	Bryant, Jacob, and Abigal Rushmur,......	"	VII. 389
1772. Jan. 28.	Bryant, James, and Hannah Scudder,......	"	XVIII. 19
1763. Jan. 10.	Bryant, James, and Ruth Rigby,...........	"	VII. 11
1736. June 3.	Bryant, Jane, and John Coon Oven,.......	"	I. 1
1777. Dec. 12.	Bryant, Thomas, and Elizabeth Hay,.......	"	XXIV. 196
1759. Dec. 1.	Bryant, William, and Jane Howse,........	"	II. 524
1760. June 30.	Bryes, Anthony, and Tryntie Yates,.......	"	III. 200
1778. May 19.	Buchanan, David, and Mary Connell,.......	"	XXV. 87
1771. Dec. 26.	Buchanan, John, and Sarah Harrison,......	"	XVII. 304
1771. Feb. 16.	Buck, Dorothy, and Joseph Smith,..........	"	XVII. 16
1757. June 11.	Buck, Henry, and Christina Beckey,.......	"	I. 560
1782. Jan. 11.	Buckbee, Benjamin, and Ann Morrell,......	"	XXXV. 15
1763. Nov. 10.	Buckbee, Daniel, and Susanna Willse,......	"	VII. 443
1765. Oct. 2.	Buckbee, John, and Mary Hyatt,..........	"	IX. 287
1769. Dec. 29.	Buckbee, Samuel, and Sarah Palmer,......	"	XV. 132a
1761. Oct. 16.	Buckelow, Frederick, and Massey Buckelow,	"	V. 140
1761. Oct. 16.	Buckelow, Massey, and Frederick Buckelow,	"	V. 140

DATE.		NAMES.	RECORD.	VOL.	PAGE.
1759.	Aug. 6.	Buckenhoven, Ann, and Henry Sickles,....	M. B.,	II.	377
1780.	June 2.	Buckett, Catharine, and John Sickles,......	"	XXIX.	78
1761.	Nov. 10.	Buckhout, Elizabeth, and Robert Campbell,	"	V.	206
1755.	Sept. 10.	Buckhout, Hester, and Hendrick Lott,......	"	I.	172
1771.	Nov. 12.	Buckhout, Peter, and Mary Robinson,......	"	XVII.	250
1737.	May 21.	Buckhout, Peter, and Tabitha Chilister,....	"	I.	6
1768.	Nov. 11.	Buckland, Elizabeth, and Philip Painter,....	"	XIII.	231
1761.	Jan. 22.	Buckler, Anne, and Thomas Welch, ...	"	IV.	25
1764.	April 26.	Buckler, James, and Sarah Johnson,.......	"	VIII.	170
1757.	Nov. 25.	Buckley, Hannah, and Thomas Smith,......	"	I.	713
1780.	May 16.	Buckley, James, and Mary Emmas,........	"	XXIX.	57
1783.	Nov. 16.	Buckmaster, Blake, and Deborah Roe, ...	"	XL.	117
1684.	Dec. 2.	Buckmaster, Edward, and Margeret Mathews,	C. M.,	XXXIII.	54
1768.	July 16.	Buckmaster, James, and Sarah Hill,........	M. B.,	XIII.	160
1764.	Sept. 28.	Budd, Anne, and Abraham Brown,........	"	VIII.	324
1755.	Dec. 23.	Budd, Joseph, and Elizabeth Griffin,.......	"	I.	239
1765.	Jan. 18.	Budd, Tamar, and Ebenezer Haviland,.....	"	IX.	23
1769.	Mar. 3.	Budd, Thomas, and Anne Hawxkurst,......	"	XIV.	44
1773.	Nov. 27.	Budd, Thomas, and Anne Hawxhurst,......	"	XXII.	51
1755.	Sept. 4.	Budden, William, and Ann Salter,.........	"	I.	165
1766.	Dec. 4.	Buel, Jerush, and David Gardiner,.........	"	X.	193
1771.	Mar. 18.	Buell, Abel, and Lettice De Voe,..........	"	XVII.	36
1770.	Oct. 17.	Buffet, Jesse, and Sarah Scudder,..........	"	XVI.	217
1770.	June 18.	Buffet, John, and Rebeccah Ketcham,......	"	XVI.	118
1758.	Nov. 21.	Buffet, Joseph, and Sarah Smith,..........	"	II.	100
1783.	Feb. 15.	Buflaree, Mary, and Moses Brewer,........	"	XXXVIII.	41
1782.	Aug. 5.	Bufleree, Jacob, and Anne Stout,..........	"	XXXVI.	101
1755.	Oct. 3.	Bugbie, Sarah, and Thomas Hyatt,.........	"	I.	188
1756.	Oct. 18.	Bugby, William, and Abigail Clemens,......	"	I.	330
1761.	Aug. 8.	Buis, Josyntie, and Baltus Van Kleeck,.....	"	V.	35
1760.	Sept. 8.	Bull, Anne, and James Wilkins,...........	"	III.	304
1760.	Jan. 7.	Bull, Helena, and Michael Rogers,.........	"	II.	571
1761.	Nov. 16.	Bull, Joseph, and Esther Gedney,..........	"	V.	223
1778.	Aug. 10.	Bull, Sarah, and Gideon Lott,.............	"	XXVI.	1
1771.	April 20.	Bull, William, and Sarah Williams,........	"	XVII.	63
1757.	Jan. 25.	Bullock, Susannah, and John Thorne,.... .	"	I.	426
1756.	Dec. 30.	Bun, Catharin, and John Augustus Lauter,..	"	I.	403
1773.	Oct. 15.	Bunce, Anna, and Samuel Lewis,..........	'	XXI.	142
1783.	Oct. 8.	Bunce, Edith, and Thomas Carpenter,......	"	XL.	72
1783.	Aug. 8.	Bunce, Edmund, and Sarah Gildersleve,....	"	XXXIX.	118
1766.	July 14.	Bunce, Isaac, and Sibil Brien,.............	"	X.	47
1762.	Aug. 9.	Bunce, Jacob, and Frances Stringham,.....	"	VI.	271
1670.	Nov. 27.	Bunce, Lemuel, and Eve Sheif,............	"	XVI.	271
1762.	April 16.	Bunn, Mary, and Peter Myer,.............	"	VI.	113
1783.	Jan. 15.	Bunn Mary, and Samuel Tarbett,.........	"	XXXVIII.	18

DATE.	NAMES.	RECORD.	VOL. PAGE.
1779. Dec. 10.	Bunn, Sarah, and William Broeske,	M. B.,	xxviii. 170
1782. Sept. 9.	Bunn, William, and Mary Reid,	"	xxxvi. 140
1769. July 8.	Bunrepo, Sarah, and James Lary,	"	xiv. 145
1760. Feb. 1.	Bunster, John, and Ruth Lewis,	"	iii. 19
1760. Sept. 6.	Bunterbow, Mary, and Roger Magrath,	"	iii. 287
1780. Aug. 24.	Bunts, Hannah, and Benjamin Walker,	"	xxix. 148
1772. May 8.	Bunts, Neamy, and John Jerveis,	"	xviii. 104
1772. May 9.	Bunyan, James, and Juliana Dekay,	"	xviii. 106
1761. July 7.	Burbanck, Altje, and Abraham Lake,	"	iv. 285
1761. Oct. 15.	Burbanck, Charity, and Joachim Stilwell,	"	v. 141
1778. Dec. 16.	Burbank, Ally, and Isaac Decker,	"	xxvi. 124
1763. Sept. 7.	Burbank, Christopher, and Patience Clandenny,	"	vii. 377
1760. Mar. 13.	Burbank, Elizabeth, and Peter White,	"	iii. 75
1763. Oct. 28.	Burbank, Lucas, and Catharine Van De Water,	"	vii. 104
1781. Nov. 15.	Burbanks, Martha, and Silas Bedell,	"	xxxiv. 36
1759. Nov. 12.	Burch, Joseph, and Jane Lamelt,	"	ii. 493
1759. April 28.	Burchall, Mary, and John Charles Sinclair,	"	ii. 259
1764. Sept. 27.	Burchell, Mary, and Isaac Wilkins,	"	viii. 323
1760. Jan. 14.	Burcke, Mary, and Samuel McDonnald,	"	ii. 581
1771. Sept. 25.	Burd, Benjamin, and Sarah McKinstor,	"	xvii. 191
1759. April 12.	Burdet, Samuel, and Sarah Van Voorst,	"	ii. 240
1766. Sept. 15.	Burdett, Sarah, and Robert Towt,	"	x. 96
1757. Feb. 22.	Burdg, Richard, and Hannah Huff,	"	i. 448
1757. Dec. 20.	Burdsall, Daniel, and Hannah Mandevell,	"	i. 747
1738. Oct. 26.	Burgart, Etye, and John Moore,	"	i. 11
1775. Aug. 26.	Burgaw, Hyla, and Jeronimus Rapalje,	"	xxiii. 138
1769. May 3.	Burge, Ann, and John Weaver,	"	xiv. 91
1761. Mar. 11.	Burger, Allida, and John Studdeford,	"	iv. 94
1756. Sept. 4.	Burger, Aneky, and Samuel Mash,	"	i. 283
1781. Nov. 14.	Burger, Ann, and Andrew Snape Douglas,	"	xxxiv. 34
1768. May 11.	Burger, Catherine, and John Whitfield,	"	xiii. 101
1764. Dec. 24.	Burger, David, and Ann Stilwell,	"	viii. 466
1761. July 17.	Burger, Elizabeth, and Henry Constant,	"	iv. 302
1761. Nov. 2.	Burger, Elizabeth, and John Wingodsparding,	"	v. 185
1770. Aug. 20.	Burger, Elizabeth, and John Woodward,	"	xvi. 164
1769. Feb. 9.	Burger, Jane, and Robert Moston,	"	xiv. 30
1778. July 13.	Burger, Jane, and Thomas Hill,	"	xxv. 129
1777. Mar. 11.	Burger, Jane, and William Rose,	"	xxiv. 43
1757. Feb. 3.	Burger, Jannetie, and John Johnson,	"	i. 433
1759. May 31.	Burger, Jannetye, and James Stewart,	"	ii. 295
1767. Jan. 20.	Burger, John, and Sarah Baker,	"	xi. 9
1766. Oct. 21.	Burger, Martin, and Catherine Hooghtyling,	"	x. 132
1781. May 30.	Burger, Nancy, and Thomas Young,	"	xxxii. 65

DATE.	NAMES.	RECORD.	VOL.	PAGE.
1760. Feb. 25.	Burger, Peter, and Elizabeth Eve,.........	M. B.,	III.	50
1762. April 20.	Burger, Susanna, and Abraham Anderson,..	"	VI.	171
1777. April 28.	Burges, Margaret, and William Smythies,...	"	XXIV.	77
1766. Nov. 25.	Burges, Susannah, and Peter Middleton,....	"	X.	183
1775. Nov. 18.	Burgess, Lucy, and John Hillman,.........	"	XXIII.	215
1759. Feb. 19.	Burgess, Olive, and Mary Cole,............	"	II.	160
1782. April 15.	Burgess, Thomas, and Jane Murdock,......	"	XXXV.	124
1736. June 23.	Burgher, Margrett, and Alexander Madole,..	"	I.	1
1761. Sept. 16.	Burhans, Catrina, and Johannis S. Lansingh,	"	V.	85
1763. April 20.	Burhans, Jacob, and Elizabeth Whitaker,...	"	VII.	133
1761. April 13.	Burheyt, Cornelius, and Rachel Vanderbogert,	"	IV.	145
1737. Nov. 11.	Burhite, Margaret, and John Massa,........	"	I.	8
1763. Feb. 28.	Burk, James, and Mary Townsend,........	"	VII.	79
1759. June 20.	Burk, Martha, and Archibald McElroy,.....	"	II.	331
1757. Nov. 22.	Burk, Mary, and James Smith,............	"	I.	709
1759. Nov. 12.	Burk, Mary, and Richard Condon,.........	"	II.	494
1772. Jan. 9.	Burk, Patrick, and Jemima Cursong,.......	"	XX.	6
1763. July 4.	Burk, Sarah, and Archibald McElroy,......	"	VII.	256
1783. Oct. 8.	Burkdaff, Uzley, and John Houseman,.....	"	XL.	71
1779. Jan. 14.	Burke, Edward, and Mary Ainsly,.........	"	XXVII.	14
1758. Mar. 21	Burke, John, and Mary Maygridge,........	"	I.	859
1758. Nov. 8.	Burley, John, and Elizabeth Kenny,.......	"	II.	84
1772. Dec. 10.	Burling, Benjamin, and Sibel Sands,.......	"	XIX.	151
1762. Jan. 28.	Burling, Ebenezer, and Keziah Hunt,......	"	VI.	27
1737. Mar. 21.	Burling, Ebenezer, and Mary Lawrence,....	"	I.	5
1770. June 30.	Burling, George, and Abigail Morrel,.......	"	XVI.	129
1756. Oct. 30.	Burling, James, and Deborah Lawrence,....	"	I.	340
1760. May 2.	Burling, Lancaster, and Elizabeth Latham,..	"	III.	136
1770. May 15.	Burling, Lydia, and John Doughty, ...	"	XVI.	85
1757. April 18.	Burling, Peleg, and Angeneltie Abrahams,...	"	I.	504
1771. Mar. 11.	Burling, Rachel, and Benjamin Helme,.....	"	XVII.	29
1767. Oct. 22.	Burling, Thomas, and Susannah Carter,.....	"	XII.	66
1782. Dec. 6.	Burlock, Abigail, and Nathan Bonton,......	"	XXXVII.	106
1761. Nov. 6.	Burn, Robert, and Mary Blaklidge,........	"	V.	193
1764. Mar. 27.	Burn, Robert, and Rachel Nash,...........	"	VIII.	120
1769. Nov. 29.	Burner, Philip, and Frances Saunders,......	"	XV.	109
1761. July 10.	Burnes, Thomas, and Elizabeth Colegrove...	"	IV.	292b
1757. Dec. 10.	Burnet, Jane, and Henry Kip,............	"	I.	732
1766. July 5.	Burnet, John, and Esther Humphrey,......	"	X.	42
1737. Dec. 10.	Burnet, Justice, and Phebe Rogers,........	"	I.	8
1757. April 12.	Burnet (Bennet), Margaret, and Joseph Hunter, ...	"	I.	498
1766. Dec. 2.	Burnet, Margaret, and William Sorrell,.....	"	X.	192
1762. May 4.	Burnet, Sarah, and Henry McNeely,.......	"	VI.	143
1771. Nov. 22.	Burnet, Thomas, and Mary Johnston,.......	"	XVII.	266

DATE.	NAMES.	RECORD.	VOL.	PAGE.
1753. June 18.	Burnet, William, and Ann Shepperd,.......	M. B.,	I.	63
1764. Jan. 5.	Burnett, Anne, and Jacob Banks,..........	"	VIII.	7
1783. June 2.	Burnett, Henry, and Mary Hallett,.........	"	XXXIX.	37
1764. July 16.	Burnham, Elizabeth, and Divian Devenport,	"	VIII.	260
1778. Sept. 28.	Burnham, John, and Elizabeth Cox,........	"	XXVI.	38
1782. Dec. 7.	Burnham, Robert, and Sarah Dongan,......	"	XXXVII.	110
1762. Oct. 29.	Burns, Anne, and Oliver Wedder,.........	"	VI.	394
1783. June 23.	Burns, Bridget, and James Doty,...........	"	XXXIX.	66
1781. June 13.	Burns, Elizabeth, and James Littlewood,....	"	XXXII.	83
1769. Aug. 16.	Burns, Elizabeth, and Peter Cazellette,.....	"	XV.	24
1767. Sept. 24.	Burns, Elizabeth, and Samuel Shelly,.......	"	XII.	41
1758. Oct. 10.	Burns, Hanah, and William Cobb,.........	"	II.	47
1780. April 5.	Burns, James, and Sarah Norman,.........	"	XXIX.	24
1781. Jan. 9.	Burns, Michael, and Ruth Denton,.........	"	XXXI.	18
1772. Feb. 20.	Burns, Rachel, and Isaac Marvin,..........	"	XVIII.	40
1771. Sept. 25.	Burns, Sarah, and Edward Jones,..........	"	XVII.	192
1773. July 29.	Burns, William, and Alice McMun,........	"	XXI.	53
1781. Feb. 27.	Burnton, Ann, and William Hedges,.......	"	XXXI.	59
1780. Oct. 19.	Burnton, Thomas, and Mary Davis,........	"	XXX.	72
1758. Feb. 8.	Burr, Daniel, and Amey Cheshire,.........	"	I.	814
1782. Nov. 27.	Burr, Daniel, and Sarah Underhill,.........	"	XXXVII.	94
1782. Jan. 24.	Burr, Elizabeth, and Barruck Underhill,....	"	XXXV.	31
1763. Dec. 1.	Burr, Isaac, and Mary Baldwin,...........	"	VII.	488
1768. Jan. 20.	Burr, John, and Effje Brower,............	"	XIII.	13
1756. Oct. 5.	Burrough, Mary, and John Winne,........	"	I.	319
1763. April 20.	Burroughs, Frances, and Adam Smith,......	"	VII.	132
1769. Dec. 12.	Burroughs, James, and Keeshe Corlear,....	"	XV.	120
1761. July 11,	Burroughs, John, and Elizabeth McGlochlin,	"	IV.	294
1764. Mar. 4.	Burroughs, John, and Susannah Wallegrave,	"	VIII.	118
1765. Oct. 29.	Burroughs, Joseph, and Lidya Hallett,......	"	IX.	332
1770. Oct. 27.	Burroughs, Joseph, and Mary Parsel,.......	"	XVI.	229
1756. Dec. 20.	Burroughs, Samuel, and Elizabeth Connel,..	"	I.	392
1755. Aug. 20.	Burroughs, Sarah, and Thomas Woodard,...	"	I.	152
1763. Dec. 22.	Burrowes, Elizabeth, and Patrick Taaffe,....	"	VII.	517
1758. April 15.	Burrows, Rawley, and Elizabeth Laughton,	"	I.	875
1779. Oct. 14.	Burrows, Sarah, and Philip Thompson,.....	"	XXVIII.	111
1762. April 16.	Burrus, Elizabeth, and Richard Sadler,.....	"	VI.	114
1762. Nov. 20.	Burrus, Foster, and Phebe Moore,.........	"	VI.	447
1763. Sept. 27.	Bursen, Mary, and John Sickles, ...	"	VII.	357
1737. June 16.	Bursill, Jacob, and Sarah Weeks,..........	"	I.	6
1766. Nov. 4.	Burt, Hannah, and Arthur Summersby,.....	"	X.	150
1765. May 2.	Burtes, Arthur, and Sarah Clowes,.........	"	IX.	118
1774. Feb. 25.	Burtine, John, and Elizabeth Bagley,.......	"	XXII.	135
1768. Sept. 27.	Burtis, Abigail, and Richard Pearce,........	"	XIII.	197
1782. Dec. 23.	Burtis, Anne, and Lemuel Skidmore,.......	"	XXXVII.	130

8

DATE.	NAMES.	RECORD.	VOL. PAGE.
1762. April 29.	Burtis, Charity, and Peter Thomson,.......	M. B.,	VI. 134
1776. Jan. 6.	Burtis, Elias, and Hannah Dorlan,.........	"	XXIII. 243
1779. Oct. 2.	Burtis, Elizabeth, and George Downing,....	"	XXVIII. 96
1765. July 18.	Burtis, Elizabeth, and Jacob Demaree,......	"	IX. 210
1771. Sept. 12.	Burtis, Elizebeth, and John Duryee,........	"	XVII. 182
1765. Feb. 20.	Burtis, Fordham, and Sarah Cheeseman,....	"	IX. 55
1761. Feb. 23.	Burtis, Henry, and Anna Crooker,.........	"	IV. 78
1767. July 20.	Burtis, Jane, and Anthony Remsen,........	"	XI. 137
1781. Nov. 8.	Burtis, Jane, and Hendrick Munsey,.......	"	XXXIV. 23
1773. Aug. 17.	Burtis, Jane, and Jonathan Mott,..........	"	XXI. 70
1757. Mar. 15.	Burtis, Jane, and Stephen Carman,.........	"	I. 470
1757. Mar. 14.	Burtis, John, and Mary Remsen,...........	"	I. 468
1773. Dec. 23.	Burtis, John, and Sarah Foster,.....	"	XXII. 85
1770. Mar. 22.	Burtis, Margaret, and John Mott, ...	"	XVI. 37
1765. Feb. 14.	Burtis, Martha, and Richard Tatterson,.....	"	IX. 53
1761. Jan. 9.	Burtis, Mary, and Cornelius Vandewater,....	"	IV. 7
1781. Dec. 13.	Burtis, Mary, and James Allen,............	"	XXXIV. 82
1778. Sept. 4.	Burtis, Mary, and John Foster,.............	"	XXVI. 20
1761. Nov. 11.	Burtis, Mary, and Leyy Weekes,...........	"	V. 207
1772. Aug. 29.	Burtis, Paul, and Susannah Morrin,........	"	XIX. 33
1782. Jan. 3.	Burtis, Phebe, and Joseph Fox,...........	"	XXXV. 6
1764. April 25.	Burtis, Phebe, and Rufus Watts,...........	"	VIII. 169
1756. Aug. 2.	Burtis, Simons, and Phebe Carman,........	"	I. 265
1781. May 16.	Burtis, Stephen, and Mary Brush,.........	"	XXXII. 50
1762. Dec. 24.	Burtis, William, and Sarah Carman,........	"	VI. 498
1771. June 19.	Burtle, Philip, and Margaret Miller,........	"	XVII. 115
1759. Sept. 11.	Burthyng, John, and Magdalene Jandine,...	"	II. 416
1736. Aug. 30.	Burton, Elijah, and Margaret Carman,......	"	I. 2
1679. Oct. 14.	Burton, Elizabeth, and John Shottwell,.....	G. E.,	XXXII. 62
1757. Feb. 5.	Burton, Elizabeth, and Thomas Evans,.....	M. B.,	I. 435
1783. Aug. 16.	Burton, Joseph H., and Ann Bingham,.....	"	XXXIX. 129
1774. Feb. 28.	Burton, William, and Isabella Achmuty,...	"	XXII. 136
1781. Oct. 28.	Burtus, Epenetus, and Martha Seamans,....	"	XXXIV. 10
1761. Oct. 21.	Burwell, Mary, and William Weeden,......	"	V. 159
1782. Dec. 11.	Burwick, Catharine, and Morris Earle,......	"	XXXVII. 114
1783. Jan. 22.	Busby, Sarah, and William Miller,...........	"	XXXVIII. 28
1764. May 30.	Buschalck, Lawrence, and Christiana Bogart,	"	VIII. 200
1783. Jan. 16.	Busen, Mary, and Joseph Foard,..........	"	XXXVIII. 19
1769. July 13.	Bush, Abigail, and James Black,...........	"	XIV. 151
1757. Dec. 31.	Bush, Ann, and Richard Wenman,........	"	I. 763
1764. Aug. 14.	Bush, Barnet, and Mary Finley,...........	"	VIII. 282
1772. April 27.	Bush, Catharine, and Hendrick Hagraman,..	"	XVIII. 93
1761. Oct. 30.	Bush, Catharine, and Wandell Boos,.......	"	V. 178
1779. May 20.	Bush, Catherine, and Walter Mitchell,......	"	XXVII. 142
1760. Nov. 14.	Bush, Edward, and Catharine Cannon,.....	"	III. 412

DATE.	NAMES.	RECORD.	VOL.	PAGE.
1766. June 4.	Bush, Elizabeth, and Robert De Groot, ...	M. B.,	x.	29
1766. July 16.	Bush, Elizabeth, and Robert Pikeman, ...	"	x.	50
1782. Nov. 13.	Bush, Garret, and Elizabeth Van Namor, ...	"	xxxvii.	80
1758. Nov. 23.	Bush, George M., and Hannah Bennett, ...	"	ii.	104
1755. Dec. 24.	Bush, Hendrick, and Catharine Rikemond, ..	"	i.	240
1760. May 20.	Bush, Isaac, and Letta Brewer, ...	"	iii.	160
1769. Dec. 7.	Bush, Mary, and Joseph Williams, ...	"	xv.	116
1783. Oct. 5.	Bush, Sarah, and Francis Robins, ...	"	xl.	63
1771. May 31.	Bush, William, and Hannah Hayter, ...	"	xvii.	96
1781. Nov. 7.	Bush, William, and Mary Kendal, ...	"	xxxiv.	20
1766. July 28.	Bushet, Reme, and Mary Jinins, ...	"	x.	65
1757. June 3.	Busing, Peter, and Charity Williams, ...	"	i.	550
1762. Oct. 8.	Buskerk, John, and Trintie Van Lone, ...	"	vi.	353
1770. April 5.	Buskirk, Abraham, and Jane Dey, ...	"	xvi.	49
1779. May 22.	Buskirk, Ann, and Nathaniel Britton, ...	"	xxvii.	144
1781. May 17.	Buskirk, Catharine, and Henry Sharp, ...	"	xxxii.	51
1779. Sept. 26.	Buskirk, Garrit, and Elizabeth Potts, ...	"	xxviii.	84
1778. Feb. 22.	Buskirk, John, and Sarah Ellis, ...	"	xxv.	30
1782. April 20.	Buskirk, Rachel, and John Lewis, ...	"	xxxv.	129
1738. July 5.	Bussen, Eva, and James Man, ...	"	i.	10
1738. Aug. 16.	Bussen, Isaac, and Elizabeth Tillee, ...	"	i.	10
1762. Dec. 18.	Bussey, Catharine, and William Tuckey, ...	"	vi.	487
1758. June 16.	Bussey, Catherine, and John Walker, ...	"	i.	927
1737. June 22.	Bussey, Collin, and Penerope Bill, ...	"	i.	6
1782. Oct. 14.	Bussing, Abraham, and Elizabeth Brit, ...	"	xxxvii.	41
1704. Dec. 22.	Bussing, Abraham, and Margaret Myer, ...	"	viii.	464
1759. Sept. 21.	Bussing, Catharine, and Abraham Storm, ...	"	ii.	428
1782. Oct. 17.	Bussing, Elizabeth, and John Webster, ...	"	xxxvii.	47
1771. Sept. 5.	Bussing, Elizabeth, and Peter Schermerhorn,	"	xvii.	175
1756. Oct. 30.	Bussing, Eva, and Alexander Forbes, ...	"	i.	338
1773. Sept. 3.	Bussing, Jane, and Samuel Schermerhorn, ..	"	xxi.	98
1780. Dec. 29.	Bussing, John, and Mary McCree, ...	"	xxx.	172
1759. Jan. 31.	Bussing, Rebeccah, and John Waldron, ...	"	ii.	170
1760. Sept. 6.	Bussing, Sarah, and Lynear Nack, ...	"	iii.	301
1763. April 29.	Bussing, Timothy, and Jane Crosby, ...	"	vii.	154
1763. Jan. 17.	Bussman, William, and Grace Wishart, ...	"	vii.	18
1755. Sept. 8.	Bussy, Magdalen, and John Stewart, ...	"	i.	170
1782. July 7.	Busteed, John, and Anne Keys, ...	"	xxxvi.	74
1781. July 21.	Butcher, James, and Sarah Allicocke, ...	"	xxxiii.	12
1783. Jan. 13.	Butler, Catharine, and Henry Slaight, ...	"	xxxviii.	14
1783. Nov. 17.	Butler, Catharine, and John Fenton, ...	"	xl.	121
1773. April 16.	Butler, Edmund, and Anne Tillew, ...	"	xx.	84
1778. Nov. 26.	Butler, Elisabeth, and Elias Stilwell, ...	"	xxvi.	100
1762. Dec. 30.	Butler, Elizabeth, and James Debrosses, Jr.,	"	vi.	504
1737. April 21.	Butler, Elizabeth, and William Carlile, ...	"	i.	6

Date.	Names.	Record.	Vol.	Page.
1782. Oct. 24.	Butler, Fanny, and James Butler,..........	M. B.,	xxxvii.	65
1772. April 28.	Butler, Hannah, and Samuel Bailey,.......	"	xviii.	94
1775. July 8.	Butler, Hester, and Mathias Wessels,.......	"	xxiii.	90
1760. Jan. 4.	Butler, Isaac, and Mary Fowler,...........	"	ii.	568
1782. Oct. 24.	Butler, James, and Fanny Butler,..........	"	xxxvii.	65
1757. Dec. 15.	Butler, John, and Catharine Weyser,.......	"	i.	744
1760. Dec. 1.	Butler, John, and Elizabeth Jones,.........	"	iii.	450
1780. June 30.	Butler, John, and Hannah Cooke,.........	"	xxix.	104
1759. June 21.	Butler, John, and Jane Amory,............	"	ii.	336
1783. Oct. 10.	Butler, John, and Margaret Oliver,.........	"	xl.	76
1775. June 23.	Butler, Mary, and Charles McNamee,......	"	xxiii.	75
1762. May 24.	Butler, Mary, and Daniel Murray,.........	"	vi.	167
1779. April 19.	Butler, Mary, and David Laird,............	"	xxvii.	108
1736. Aug. 12.	Butler, Mary, and Matthew Woodford,.....	"	i.	2
1769. Aug. 2.	Butler, Parnell, and William Saunders,.....	"	xv.	15
1761. July 22.	Butler, Phila, and Thomas Alsop,..........	"	v.	5
1780. Mar. 2.	Butler, Rachel, and Jacob Shaw,..........	"	xxviii.	215
1782. Jan. 9.	Butler, Rachell, and William Beers,........	"	xxxv.	13
1781. June 21.	Butler, Susannah, and John Fitzpatrick,....	"	xxxii.	94
1760. Dec. 15.	Butler, Toby, and Ann McFarthing,........	"	iii.	476
1782. Aug. 18.	Butler, William. and Ann Thatford,........	"	xxxvi.	114
1762. Dec. 14.	Butler, William, and Mary Vallintine,......	"	vi.	478
1777. Jan. 10.	Butt, John, and Catherine Thawley,........	"	xxiv.	10.
1761. April 22.	Butt, John, and Martha Sise,..............	"	iv.	162
1764. Feb. 21.	Buttersworth, George, and Margaret Campbell, ...	"	viii.	68
1764. July 9.	Buvelot, James, and Mary Bonnet,.........	"	viii.	252
1772. Mar. 26.	Buvelot, Susannah, and Frederick Bassett, ..	"	xviii.	59
1770. July 20.	Buyce, Hannah, and Benjamin Higgins,....	"	xvi.	142
1780. May 2.	Buyce, John, and Hannah Remine,........	"	xxix.	42
1676. July 21.	Buys, Cornelius, and Mactell Gerritz,.......	W. O. P.,	iii.	202
1757. May 14.	Buys, Volkert, and Hendrickje Praal,......	M. B.,	i.	532
1755. Nov. 3.	Bydder, Dorothy, and John Lewis,........	"	i.	205
1767. July 22.	Byers, James. and Hannah Becker,........	"	xii.	1
1761. Oct. 14.	Byfield, Elizabeth, and William Barwick,...	"	v.	137
173⅞. Jan. 10.	Byfield, Richard, and Elizabeth Rushton,...	"	i.	8
1763. July 18.	Byfield, Sarah, and Warner Richards,......	"	vii.	272
1761. May 2.	Byrd, James, and Deborah Sutton,.........	"	iv.	176
1771. Dec. 3.	Byrns, Mary, and Thomas Nicholson,......	"	xvii.	282
1777. Mar. 4.	Byron, William, and Wilhemina Cannon,...	"	xxiv.	38
1756. Dec. 28.	Byvanck, Anthony, and Frances Duncan,...	"	i.	401
1772. Dec. 7.	Byvanck, Catherine, and James Bingham,...	"	xix.	145
1772. Sept. 18.	Byvanck, Evert, and Mary Van Ranst,.....	"	xix.	52
1761. Oct. 5.	Byvanck, Hannah, and Charles Harrison,...	"	v.	121
1783. Nov. 10.	Byvanck, John, and Elizabeth Decker,.....	"	xl.	110

DATE.	NAMES.	RECORD.	VOL.	PAGE.
1764. Jan. 14.	Byvanck, John, and Elisabets Manfrut,.....	M. B.,	VIII.	16
1769. Nov. 11.	Byvanck, John, and Jane Hougland,.......	"	XVI.	59
1760. Nov. 17.	Byvanck, Mary, and Garret Abeel,........	"	III.	423
1758. Feb. 14.	Byvanck, Petrus, and Annatje Bogart,......	"	I.	819
1765. July 22.	Byvanck, William, and Frances Edsell,.....	"	IX.	215
1736. May 13.	Byvank, Bilikia, and William Cardee, ...	"	I.	1
1666. Oct. 24.	Byvanke, John, and Bellica Dukinke,......	O. W. L.,	II.	105

C.

1775. June 10.	Cabe, Jemima, and James Taylor,.........	M. B.,	XXIII.	59
1762. Oct. 27.	Cabiner, Hannah, and Zachariah Coutten,...	"	VI.	388
1778. May 16.	Cable, Jonathan, and Sarah Ludlow,.......	"	XXV.	84
1782. Aug. 28.	Caddy, Margaret, and John Hembrow,.....	"	XXXVI.	128
1757. April 9.	Cade, Barnabe, and Mary Van Lew,.......	"	I.	496
1762. Jan. 22.	Cadles, Joseph, and Mary Doxey,..........	"	VI.	21
1763. Nov. 22.	Cadman, Sarah, and Asa Lamfear,........	"	VII.	463
1760. June 3.	Caduser, Sarah, and Joseph Barclay,.......	"	III.	175
1779. Aug. 19.	Cady, John, and Jane McKenzie,..........	"	XXVIII.	52
1736. Oct. 11.	Caerten, Albert, and Altie Cartelyoun,......	"	I.	3
1777. July 30.	Cagney, William, and Elinor Lesson,.......	"	XXIV.	123
1758. Jan. 25.	Caho, Thomas, and Ann Fitzgerald,........	"	I.	802
1764. Oct. 8.	Cairnes, John, and Phebe Brooks,.........	"	VIII.	337
1783. April 19.	Cairns, Alexander, and Margaret Pullion,...	"	XXXVIII.	101
1781. Mar. 28.	Cairns, Eleanor, and James Coile,..........	"	XXXI.	80
1783. Oct. 30.	Cairns, Grace, and John McDonagh,.......	"	XL.	96
1762. May 10.	Cairns, James, and Hannah Mezine,........	"	VI.	153
1777. April 28.	Cairns, Thomas, and Elinor Varnet,........	"	XXIV.	76
1771. Feb. 18.	Caithness, Mary, and Robert McWilliams,...	"	XVII.	17
1762. Sept. 16.	Caklen, Martha, and Thomas Nowle,.......	"	VI.	318
1770. Mar. 5.	Calder, Benjamin, and Mary Goddard,......	"	XVI.	30
1763. April 6.	Calder, James, and Mary Coventry,........	"	VII.	116
1764. Feb. 16.	Calder, John, and Hannah Frazier,.........	"	VIII.	60
1761. Oct. 2.	Calder, Mary, and Thomas Denn,..........	"	V.	116
1758. April 12.	Caldwell, Jane, and John Munro,..........	"	I.	872
1769. April 27.	Caldwell, Walter, and Elizabeth Jenkins,....	"	XIV.	87
1758. May 11.	Callahan, Daniel, and Elinor Conner,.......	"	I.	899
1779. Oct. 8.	Callahan, Eleonora, and James McAllister,..	"	XXVIII.	106
1758. Dec. 28.	Callahan, Elizabeth, and John Callahan,.....	"	II.	106
1760. Oct. 2.	Callahan, Elizabeth, and Samuel Walker,....	"	III.	340
1758. Dec. 28.	Callahan, John, and Elizabeth Callahan,.....	"	II.	106
1761. Nov. 3.	Callahan, John, and Hannah Atkins,.......	"	V.	190
1767. July 2.	Callahan, Nicholas, and Sarah Sickels,......	"	XI.	118
1783. Sept. 26.	Callanan, John, and Jane Sawyer,.........	"	XL.	54

DATE.	NAMES.	RECORD.	VOL.	PAGE.
1760. April 15.	Callender,* William, and Mary Johnston, ...	M. B.,	III.	108
1782. Aug. 31.	Calley, Deborah, William Fish, ...	"	XXXVI.	132
1762. Oct. 25.	Callister, Mary, and Abraham Mills, ...	"	VI.	382
1771. Nov. 22.	Callow, Adriana, and Henry Rely, ...	"	XVII.	265
1775. July 5.	Callow, Catharine, and Stacy Stackhouse, . . .	"	XXIII.	84
1781. Dec. 17.	Callow, James, and Anna Myer, ...	"	XXXIV.	91
1760. Mar. 5.	Calvain, John, and Mary Thompson, ...	"	III.	61
1738. July 25.	Cambell, John, and Anne Brooks, ...	"	I.	10
1780. Oct. 18.	Cameron, Alexander, and Abigal Berrian, . . .	"	XXX.	71
1780. Jan. 29.	Cameron, Evan, and Margeret Thomas, ...	"	XXXI.	29
1757. Aug. 24.	Cameron, Francis, and Magdalin Van Kleek,	"	I.	621
1780. Sept. 23.	Cameron, John, and Mary Sibbels, ...	"	XXX.	39
1776. Mar. 12.	Cammel, Jane, and Philip Mulligan, ...	"	XXIII.	283
1779. May 15.	Cammeron, Susanah, and Joshua Mills, ...	"	XXVII.	138
1764. April 30.	Camp, Abraham, and Millisent Jarvis, ...	"	VIII.	175
1780. Sept. 23.	Camp, Margeret, and Lewis Morgan, ...	"	XXX.	37
1765. Oct. 11.	Campbell, Alexander, and Catherine Vedder,	"	IX.	297
1757. Aug. 30.	Campbell, Alexander, and Isabel Read, ...	"	I.	624
1759. Oct. 22.	Campbell, Andrew, and Elizabeth Wheeler, . .	"	II.	467
1769. Nov. 10.	Campbell, Ann, and Joseph Wright, ...	"	XV.	88
1780. July 17.	Campbell, Ann, and Richard Pullet, ...	"	XXIX.	113
1763. Jan. 19.	Campbell, Ann, and William Orr, ...	"	VII.	22
1763. Nov. 18.	Campbell, Anne, and William Crawford, ...	"	VII.	455
1780. April 1.	Campbell, Archibald, and Charlotte Saxton,	"	XXIX.	13
1768. Jan. 8.	Campbell, Archibald, and Christina Starn-bargh, ...	"	XIII.	3
1762. May 5.	Campbell, Catharine, and Benjamin Pearson,	"	VI.	144
1764. Oct. 24.	Campbell, Charles, and Elenor Reed, ...	"	VIII.	374
1773. July 12.	Campbell, Charles, and Sarah Francis, ...	"	XXI.	34
1781. Dec. 26.	Campbell, Colin, and Abigail Mumford Sea-bury, ...	"	XXXIV.	106
1760. April 14.	Campbell, Daniel, and Engeltje Bradt, ...	"	III.	106
1761. Mar. 18.	Campbell, Daniel, and Margaret Power, ...	"	IV.	107
1778. Oct. 26.	Campbell, Donald, and Margaret Mattidale, . .	"	XXVI.	72
1762. July 20.	Campbell, Duncan, and Mary Christie, ...	"	VI.	247
1772. Aug. 15.	Campbell, Eggy, and John Cann, ...	"	XIX.	24
1756. Dec. 13.	Campbell, Elizabeth, and Allan McDugal, . . .	"	I.	381
1766. Nov. 24.	Campbell, Elizabeth, and James Clarke, ...	"	X.	179
1780. July 5.	Campbell, Elizabeth, and Philip Jordan, ...	"	XXIX.	106
1781. Dec. 8.	Campbell, Elizabeth, and William Askins, . . .	"	XXXIV.	77
1760. May 8.	Campbell, Elsie, and Alexander Frazer, ...	"	III.	145
1758. Jan. 9.	Campbell, Ester, and Joseph Letson, ...	"	I.	777
1763. Nov. 19.	Campbell, George, and Elisabeth Brown, ...	"	VII.	457
1763. Dec. 22.	Campbell, Hannah, and Peter Berrien, Jr., . .	"	VII.	518
1762. July 9.	Campbell, Isabella, and William Long, ...	"	VI.	233

DATE.	NAMES.	RECORD.	VOL. PAGE.
1761. Feb. 7.	Campbell, James, and Edrijee Lynerson,....	M. B.,	IV. 54
1757. Jan. 6.	Campbell, Jane, and David Berry,.........	"	I. 409
1760. July 7.	Campbell, Jane, and Isaac Elby,..........	"	III. 206
1756. July 20.	Campbell, John, and Margaret Campbell,....	"	I. 259
1765. April 22.	Campbell, John, and Mary Thompson,......	"	IX. 103
1761. Nov. 3.	Campbell, John, and Sarah Oakley,........	"	V. 189
1782. April 26.	Campbell, Lawrence R., and Mary Henley,..	"	XXXV. 139
1756. July 16.	Campbell, Lilly, and James Murray,........	"	I. 257
1779. April 22.	Campbell, Lydia, and Gilliam Cornell,......	"	XXVII. 115
1764. Feb. 21.	Campbell, Margaret, and George Buttersworth, ...	"	VIII. 68
1762. Nov. 26.	Campbell, Margaret, and James Weekes,...	"	VI. 456
1756. July 20.	Campbell, Margaret, and John Campbell,....	"	I. 259
1772. Oct. 15.	Campbell, Martin, and Mary Rutsen,.......	"	XIX. 72
1761. July 28.	Campbell, Mary, and Francis Panton,......	"	V. 13
1767. July 6.	Campbell, Mary, and Walter Mikljohn,.....	"	XI. 125
1781. Jan. 2.	Campbell, Patrick, and Sarah Pearsall,.....	"	XXXI. 4
1761. Jan. 22.	Campbell, Rachel, and Henry Wyce,.......	"	IV. 26
1764. Nov. 27.	Campbell, Rachel, and Thomas Merrit,......	"	VIII. 429
1773. Mar. 24.	Campbell, Robert, and Abigail Embree,....	"	XX. 70
1761. Nov. 10.	Campbell, Robert, and Elizabeth Buckhout,	"	V. 206
1775. July 26.	Campbell, Robert, and Hannah Kelly,......	"	XXIII. 105
1776. Jan. 25.	Campbell, Robert, and Margaret Lamb,.....	"	XXIII. 250
1765. Mar. 25.	Campbell, Robert, and Margaret Shannon,..	"	IX. 73
1780. Nov. 16.	Campbell, Susanna, and William Hunter,....	"	XXX. 109
1761. Feb. 10.	Campbell, Sylvester, and Lucy Moore,......	"	IV. 56
1765. Oct. 12.	Campbell, Thomas, and Jemimy Oackly,....	"	IX. 299
1769. July 11.	Campble, Christian, and Charles Pitcher Chilcoot, ...	"	XIV. 150
1759. Sept. 15.	Campford, Mary, and Charles Lugg,........	"	II. 423
1760. Aug. 8.	Campion, Charles, and Rebecca Abbot,.....	"	III. 245
1779. Jan. 26.	Camplin, James, and Sarah Willson,........	"	XXVII. 26
1770. Mar. 14.	Candell, William, and Hannah Ellsworth,...	"	XVI. 31
1762. Aug. 30.	Candy, Dennis, and Catharine Rycker,......	"	VI. 298
1776. Mar. 25.	Cane, Robert, and Catherine Graham,......	"	XXIII. 291
1771. June 10.	Canes, Hannah, and Cornelius Boyce,......	"	XVII. 106
1772. Aug. 15.	Cann, John, and Eggy Campbell,..........	"	XIX. 24
1777. Oct. 15.	Cannel, Abraham, and Ann Laturett,.......	"	XXIV. 162a
1760. Feb. 25.	Canner, Francis, and Maria Crounn,........	"	III. 47
1765. Sept. 7.	Cannon, Abraham, and Mary English,......	"	IX. 278
1778. April 28.	Cannon, Abraham, and Susanah Wortman,.	"	XXV. 69
1757. July 26.	Cannon, Arnout, and Phebe Sands,........	"	I. 601
1760. Nov. 14.	Cannon, Catharine, and Edward Bush,......	"	III. 412
1759. Dec. 18.	Cannon, John, and Hendrickea Swan,......	"	II. 549
1756. Oct. 29.	Cannon, John, and Jemimah Mott,........	"	I. 335

DATE.	NAMES.	RECORD.	VOL.	PAGE.
1762. Jan. 20.	Cannon, Margaret, and Amos Ogden, ...	M. B.,	VII.	25
1782. Aug. 17.	Cannon, Mary, and Abner Wood, ...	"	XXXVI.	113
1759. May 9.	Cannon, Mary, and John Denmark, ...	"	II.	272
May	Cannon, Mary, and John Pintard, ...	"	I.	543
1761. Nov. 6.	Cannon, Mary, and William Pile, ...	"	V.	194
1779. Sept. 2.	Cannon, Mott, and Abigail Hitchcock, ...	"	XXVIII.	65
1777. Mar. 4.	Cannon, Wilhelmina, and William Byron, ...	"	XXIV.	38
1763. June 11.	Cannon, William, and Mary Coffren, ..,....	"	VII.	225
1774. Mar. 5.	Cannun, Isabella, and John Smith, ...	"	XXII.	139
1770. Nov. 12.	Cantelun, Richard, and Mary Stoutenburgh,	"	XVI.	247
1758. Feb. 25.	Canterberry, William, and Elizabeth Cramshire, ...	"	I.	828
1769. Oct. 21.	Cantine, Margaret, and Abraham K. Van Vleck, ...	"	XV.	59
1769. July 24.	Cantine, Nathaniel, and Dorothy Newkerk, ..	"	XV.	4
1763. Oct. 20.	Canyne, Alada, and Adam Selen, ...	"	VII.	397
1783. Feb. 5.	Card, Elijah, and Mary Andrus, ...	"	XXXVIII.	34
1776. Jan. 4.	Cardell, Catharine, and Joseph De Groot, ...	"	XXIII.	240
1681. July 28.	Carduall, Ralph, and Elizabeth Read, ...	O.W.,&c.,	XXXII½.	56
1757. Dec. 14.	Careau, Ann, and Abraham Anthony, ...	M. B.,	I.	743
1780. Jan. 15.	Carell, Rebecca, and Edward Dallzall, ...	"	XXVIII.	197
1781. May 30.	Carey, Catharine, and George Ellis, ...	"	XXXII.	64
1782. Dec. 18.	Carey, Edward, and Mary Rian, ...	"	XXXVII.	126
1762. Sept. 23.	Carey, Elias, and Helena De Lancey, ...	"	VI.	327
1783. April 22.	Carey, Stephen, and Anne Gover, ...	"	XXXVIII.	109
1780. Aug. 28.	Cargey, Robert, and Hermione Harrison, ...	"	XXX.	7
1782. July 30.	Carhartt, James, and Elizabeth Vanderbelt, .	"	XXXVI.	95
1782. Mar. 27.	Carhartt, Joshua, and Phebe Baker, ...	"	XXXV.	99
1782. Mar. 11.	Carl, Katurah, and Daniel Udall, ...	"	XXXV.	85
1760. Oct. 28.	Carle, Jacob, and Margaret Pettit, ...	"	III.	383
1767. June 17.	Carle, Jesse, and Hannah Sammons, ...	"	XI.	110
1763. Nov. 30.	Carle, Sarah, and Nathan Valentine, ...	"	VII.	483
1757. July 9.	Carlile, Mary, and John Hendy, ...	"	I.	588
1755. Oct. 11.	Carlile, Mary, and Samuel Francis, ...	"	I.	191
1772. Sept. 25.	Carlile, Thomas, and Margaret Fleming, ...	"	XIX.	56
1737. April 21.	Carlile, William, and Elizabeth Butler, ...	"	I.	6
1759. Nov. 16.	Carll, Gilbert, and Rebeca Brush, ...	"	II.	502
1772. Jan. 5.	Carll, John, and Phebe Hicks, ...	"	XX.	2
1765. Jan. 14.	Carll, Phebe, and Henry Scudder, ...	"	IX.	15
1763. Oct. 13.	Carll, Platt, and Phebe Smith, ...	"	VII.	384
1782. Oct. 5.	Carll, Samuel, and Jemima Bailey, ...	"	XXXVII.	30
1757. Dec. 30.	Carmagh, Daniel, and Hannah Eckels, ...	"	I.	762
1775. June 1.	Carman, Abigail, and Jarvis Coles, ...	"	XXIII.	51
1777. Sept. 10.	Carman, Abigail, and John Day, ...	"	XXIV.	144
1736. July 29.	Carman, Anne, and John De Wint, ...	"	I.	2

DATE.	NAMES.	RECORD.	VOL.	PAGE.
1779. Mar. 31.	Carman, Benjamin, and Elizabeth Powell,...	M. B.,	xxvii.	87
1763. Sept. 22.	Carman, Dinah, and Elkanah Concklin,.....	"	vii.	349
1781. May 3.	Carman, Elizabeth, and Joseph Clowes,.....	"	xxxii.	30
1758. Oct. 25.	Carman, Hannah, and Thomas Southard,...	"	ii.	67
1778. June 15.	Carman, John, and Arabella Pettit,........	"	xxv.	103
1772. Dec. 10.	Carman, John, and Jane Volentine,........	"	xix.	152
1770. Dec. 1.	Carman, John, and Mary Masten,.........	"	xvi.	279
1774. Feb. 22.	Carman, Joseph, and Jemima Arkles,......	"	xxii.	132
1768. Dec. 8.	Carman, Joshua, Jr., and Cabachay Van Kleack,.............................	"	xiii.	257
1736. Aug. 30.	Carman, Margaret, and Elijah Burton,......	"	i.	2
1778. Mar. 20.	Carman, Martha, and Richard Hewlett, ...	"	xxv.	49
1763. May 11.	Carman, Mary, and John Sleght, ...	"	vii.	176
1767. Dec. 15.	Carman, Phebe, and John Rutsen,.........	"	xii.	114
1756. Aug. 2.	Carman, Phebe, and Simmons Burtis,......	"	i.	265
1781. Mar. 6.	Carman, Phebe, and Thomas Fleet,........	"	xxxi.	66
1779. Jan. 22.	Carman, Richard, and Sarah Horsefield,....	"	xxvii.	22
1769. Jan. 25.	Carman, Samuel, and Sarah Carman,.......	"	xiv.	19
1773. June 26.	Carman, Samuel, and Sarah Wright,.......	"	xxi.	24
1777. April 27.	Carman, Samuel, and Theodosia Fish,......	"	xxiv.	74
1764. May 2.	Carman, Sarah, and Cornelius Van Wyck,..	"	viii.	179
1771. May 23.	Carman, Sarah, and Obadiah Simmon, ...	"	xvii.	88
1769. Jan. 25.	Carman, Sarah, and Samuel Carman,.......	"	xiv.	19
1762. Dec. 24.	Carman, Sarah, and William Burtis,........	"	vi.	498
1782. Feb. 11.	Carman, Silas, and Abbe Fleet,............	"	xxxv.	47
1736. May 18.	Carman, Silas, and Hannah Smith,.........	"	i.	1
1763. Nov. 14.	Carman, Stephen, and Elizabeth Roads,....	"	vii.	447
1757. Mar. 15.	Carman, Stephen, and Jane Burtis,........	"	i.	470
1758. Nov. 21.	Carman, Thomas, and Sarah Brinckerhoff,...	"	ii.	99
1762. Dec. 23.	Carman, Thomas, and Susannah Wood,.....	"	vi.	496
1767. June 23.	Carman, William, and Hannah Waters,.....	"	xi.	113
1759. July 12.	Carman, William, and Jane Vanderhoof,....	"	ii.	354
1737. June 18.	Carmar, Anne, and Seth Smith,............	"	i.	6
1682. Jan. 20.	Carmen, John, and Elizabeth Ludlan, ...	E.,	xxxiii.	31
1736. Aug. 5.	Carmen, Phebe, and Benjamin Thorn,......	M. B.,	i.	2
1777. Oct. 18.	Carmer, James, and Jane Thomas,.........	"	xxiv.	165
1760. Sept. 6.	Carmer, Mary, and Henry Beekman,.......	"	iii.	302
1771. April 16.	Carmer, Mary, and John Williamson,......	"	xvii.	61
1758. April 22.	Carmer, Nicholas, and Alatha Blanchard,...	"	i.	879
1773. Dec. 23.	Carmer, Nicholas, and Sarah Wilson,.......	"	xxii.	84
1761. Sept. 2.	Carmer, Ruth, and Joseph Beadell, ...	"	v.	67
1762. June 19.	Carmer, Thomas, and Anne Boice,..........	"	vi.	198
1777. Jan. 30.	Carnes, Thomas, and Jemima Johnson,.....	"	xxiv.	20
1760. May 29.	Carns, John, and Elliner Polhemus,........	"	iii.	167
1753. June 9.	Carolus, John, and Mary Clarkson,.........	"	i.	54

9

DATE.	NAMES.	RECORD.	VOL. PAGE.
1758. Sept. 20.	Carow, Margaret, and Thomas Ladd,........	M. B.,	II. 27
1782. Sept. 24.	Carpenter, Abel, and Elizabeth Stillwell, ...	"	XXXVII. 12
1763. Oct. 15.	Carpenter, Amelia, and Daniel Smith,......	"	VII. 388
1764. June 23.	Carpenter, Ann, and Benjamin Whitehead, Jr.,	"	VIII. 233
1777. Nov. 9.	Carpenter, Ann, and John Brush,..........	"	XXIV. 179
1770. Oct. 17.	Carpenter, Ann, and Lemuel Wicks,.......	"	XVI. 220
1761. Nov. 19.	Carpenter, Anna, and Nathaniel Havens,...	"	V. 232
1772. Mar. 31.	Carpenter, Benjamin, and Jane Edmonds,...	"	XVIII. 66
1760. Nov. 26.	Carpenter, Benjamin, and Jane Leonard,....	"	III. 447
1753. June 23.	Carpenter, Benjamin, and Mary Comes, ...	"	I. 65
1773. Sept. 1.	Carpenter, Benjamin, and Mary Pugsley,...	"	XXI. 95
1772. Nov. 9.	Carpenter, Charity, and Mordecai Bedel,....	"	XIX. 104
1756. Nov. 1.	Carpenter, Coles, and Sarah Lattin,........	"	I. 343
1781. Mar. 20.	Carpenter, Deborah, and Jesse Coles,.......	"	XXXI. 76
1763. June 2.	Carpenter, Elenor, and Benjamin Gale,.....	"	VII. 210
1779. Jan. 5.	Carpenter, Elijah, and Louisa Haddick,.....	"	XXVII. 2
1771. April 25.	Carpenter, Elizabeth, and John Morrell,....	"	XVII. 69
1758. Mar. 14.	Carpenter, Elizabeth, and Joshua Knap,....	"	I. 851
1777. Nov. 25.	Carpenter, Elizabeth, and Thomas Bowne,..	"	XXIV. 185
1783. Nov. 1.	Carpenter, Elizabeth, and Tillit Colvill,.....	"	XL. 100
1781. Nov. 23.	Carpenter, Frances, and Edmund Underhill,.	"	XXXIV. 57
1758. Oct. 5.	Carpenter, Increas, and Mary Bailey,.......｡.	"	II. 41
1778. Dec. 4.	Carpenter, Isaac, and Jane Wortman,......	"	XXVI. 109
1783. Nov. 1.	Carpenter, Jacob, and Hannah Colvill,......	"	XL. 99
1782. Dec. 12.	Carpenter, James, and Pheby Frost,.......	"	XXXVII. 117
1772. March 6.	Carpenter, John, and Sarah Tagart,......	"	XVIII. 50
1782. Mar. 13.	Carpenter, Jonathan, and Easter Cole,......	"	XXXV. 87
1767. May 27.	Carpenter, Joseph, and Darkis Smith,......	"	XI. 99
1772. Dec. 21.	Carpenter, Joseph, and Elizabeth Green,....	"	XIX. 159
1765. Jan. 4.	Carpenter, Judith, and Joshua Mills,.......	"	IX. 7
1775. Aug. 26.	Carpenter, Lewis, and Elizabeth Townsend,.	"	XXIII. 135
1775. July 31.	Carpenter, Martha, and William Mudge,....	"	XXIII. 112
1763. Aug. 29.	Carpenter, Mary, and Henry Van Gelder, ..	"	VII. 319
1780. July 17.	Carpenter, Morris, and Abigail Lawrence,...	"	XXIX. 111
1782. Nov. 18.	Carpenter, Phebe, and John Frost,.........	"	XXXVII. 87
1764. Dec. 13.	Carpenter, Phebe, and John Haviland,.....	"	VIII. 455
1781. Dec. 13.	Carpenter, Rebecca, and William Arason,...	"	XXXIV. 83
1779. Jan. 26.	Carpenter, Rhoda, and Abraham Cock,.....	"	XXVII. 27
1781. Aug. 22.	Carpenter, Samuel, and Easter Hopkins,....	"	XXXIII. 44
1782. April 1.	Carpenter, Samuel, and Rebecca Mott,.....	"	XXXV. 104
1761. April 17.	Carpenter, Sarah, and Abraham Concklin,...	"	IV. 153
1764. Jan. 13.	Carpenter, Sarah, and William Latting,.....	"	VIII. 15
1760. May 3.	Carpenter, Simon, and Catharine Ffiddle,...	"	III. 139
1783. Oct. 8.	Carpenter, Thomas, and Edith Bunce,......	"	XL. 72
1769. Aug. 14.	Carpentor, John, and Mary Carpentor,......	"	XV. 22

DATE.	NAMES.	RECORD.	VOL.	PAGE.
1769. Aug. 14.	Carpentor, Mary, and John Carpentor,	M. B.,	XV.	22
1768. Nov. 28.	Carpentor, Sarah, and Eldert Polhemis, ...	"	XIII.	247
1769. Feb. 14.	Carpentor, Thorne, and Mary Kerby,	"	XIV.	33
1771. Oct. 29.	Carr, Abigail, and Philip Young,	"	XVII.	229
1759. Nov. 30.	Carr, Ann, and James Heuston,	"	II.	522
1769. Nov. 20.	Carr, Elizabeth, and Alexander Wiley,	"	XV.	99
1760. April 15.	Carr, Ffreelove, and Isaac Ketcham,	"	III.	109
1779. July 31.	Carr, George, and Abigail Corington,	"	XXVIII.	39
1767. Aug. 14.	Carr, George, and Fiche Thompson,	"	XII.	16
1772. Nov. 2.	Carr, Hannah, and Timothy Sopea,	"	XIX.	100
1778. Sept. 17.	Carr, Jane, and Thomas Tatham,	"	XXVI.	31
1771. June 21.	Carr, Joseph, and Mary Hazard,	"	XVII.	120
1780. May 6.	Carr, Joshua, and Margeret Templar,	"	XXIX.	49
1757. Nov. 17.	Carr, Margaret, and Matthew Howell,	"	I.	706
1759. Jan. 27.	Carr, Margaret, and Thomas Herbert,	"	II.	168
1780. May 10.	Carr, Mary, and George Grundy,	"	XXIX.	52
1782. Mar. 19.	Carr, Mary, and John Clark,	"	XXXV.	89
1763. Oct. 14.	Carr, Peter, and Mary ———,	"	VII.	387
1781. May 28.	Carr, Rachel, and John Counsely,	"	XXXII.	59
1773. May 14.	Carr, Robert, and Ann Cole,	"	XX.	110
1761. Jan. 12.	Carr, Samuel, and Mary McCoye,	"	IV.	13
1778. July 10.	Carr, Sarah, and Robert Whiting,	"	XXV.	123
1761. Nov. 2.	Carr, Sarah, and Thomas Crawford,	"	V.	186
1783. Feb. 10.	Carr, Thomas, and Catherine De Graw, ...	"	XXXVIII.	39
1672. Mar. 10.	Carr, Walter, and Jannekye Claesen,	G. E.,	IV.	269
1758. Dec. 4.	Carr, William, and Anneke Huise,	M. B,	II.	113
1783. Aug. 21.	Carre, Robert Bulfill, and Catharine Hunt, ..	"	XL.	5
1772. Nov. 21.	Carroll, Elizabeth, and Hosea Lincoln,	"	XIX.	123
1772. Aug. 15.	Carroll, James, and Rebckah Sice,	"	XIX.	25
1775. Sept. 25.	Carroll, Judith, and Martin Van Haugel, ...	"	XXIII.	163
1772. Nov. 2.	Carroll, Mary, and John Kortz,	"	XIX.	98
1779. July 30.	Carrow, John, and Dorothy Kirby,	"	XXVIII.	35
1769. Jan. 4.	Carrow, John, and Mary Conway,	"	XIV.	1
1760. Jan. 3.	Carruthers, Hester, and Thomas Taylor, ...	"	II.	567
1756. July 19.	Carryl, Ann, and William Talman,	"	I.	258
1768. May 24.	Carshauw, Mary, and Oake Voorhuys,	"	XIII.	112
1770. April 10.	Carson, Elizabeth, and Jeremiah Rapalje, ...	"	XVI.	58
1779. May 7.	Carstang, Gideon, and Catherine Fowler, ...	"	XXVII.	129
1783. Sept. 22.	Carte, William, and Allathea Garretson, ...	"	XL.	51
1764. Oct. 29.	Carter, Anne, and Andrew Bell,	"	VIII.	380
1779. Sept. 30.	Carter, Christ., and Priscilla Rogers,	"	XXVIII.	93
1755. Sept. 20.	Carter, Daniel, and Mary Laurence,	"	I.	179
1769. Sept. 27.	Carter, Deborah, and David Potter,	"	XV.	46
1761. Nov. 4.	Carter, Edward, and Mary Linch,	"	V.	191
1769. Feb. 4.	Carter, James, and Jane Cole,	"	XIV.	26

DATE.	NAMES.	RECORD.	VOL. PAGE.
1780. April 25.	Carter, James, and Jemima Collins, ...	M. B.,	XXIX. 34
1759. Sept. 14.	Carter, John, and Frances Hudson, ...	"	II. 420
1765. June 20.	Carter, Mary, and Aenas McKay, ...	"	IX. 175
1768. April 13.	Carter, Mary, and Alexander Anderson, ...	"	XIII. 76
1783. May 7.	Carter, Robert, and Ann Evans, ...	"	XXXIX. 3
1783. Aug. 8.	Carter, Robert, and Anne Gilbert, ...	"	XXXIX. 117
1775. Sept. 7.	Carter, Robert, and Jane Hopper, ...	"	XXIII. 151
1767. Oct. 22.	Carter, Susannah, and Thomas Burling, ...	"	XII. 66
1761. May 16.	Carter, Vincent, and Mary Benson, ...	"	IV. 192
1777. Feb. 10.	Carter, William, and Mary Magdalen Sowers,	"	XXIV. 29
1681. Mar. 26.	Carteret, Phillip, and Elizabeth Lawrence, . . O.W.,&c.		XXXII½. 39
1673. April 15.	Carterett, James, and Frances De Lavall, ...	G. E.,	IV. 277
1760. Feb. 28.	Cartey, Catharine, and Cornelius Ryan, ...	M. B.,	III. 56
1760. June 9.	Cartilo, Ann, and Richard Stillwell, ...	"	III. 181
1759. Oct. 1.	Cartwright, Catharine, and Rensselar Williams, ...	"	II. 438
1767. Oct. 11.	Cartwright, Elizabeth, and Thomas Robison, .	"	XII. 60
1767. May 14.	Carty, Bryan, and Catherine Winslow, ...	"	XI. 88
1757. Mar. 23.	Carty, Bryan, and Elison Edwards, ...	"	I. 480
1781. June 1.	Cary, Rebecca, and William Forster, ...	"	XXXII. 67
1756. July 12.	Case, Henry, and Margery Whiley, ...	"	I. 252
1782. Jan. 2.	Case, Rebecca, and John Gibson, ...	"	XXXV. 3
1769. Aug. 1.	Case, Susannah, and Andrew Gray, ...	"	XV. 12
1756. Dec. 10.	Case, Tabithy, and Thomas Linch, ...	"	I. 379
1665. April 21.	Case, Thomas, and Mary Meacock, ...	G. E.,	I. 111
1763. Sept. 29.	Case, William, and Rachel Sears, ...	M. B.,	VII. 360
1760. April 9.	Casety, James, and Margaret Nixon, ...	"	III. 100
1757. Oct. 15.	Casey, Daniel, and Catharine Smith, ...	"	I. 673
1773. Sept. 2.	Casey, Elizabeth, and Martin Lamb, ...	"	XXI. 97
1779. Dec. 4.	Casey, John, and Mary Kendle, ...	"	XXVIII. 160
1775. May 8.	Casey, Samuel, and Catharine Page, ...	"	XXIII. 24
1783. June 13.	Casey, Sophia, and John Richardson, ...	"	XXXIX. 55
1766. Dec. 11.	Casey, William, and Elizabeth Constant, ...	"	X. 200
1758. May 30.	Casidy, Catherine, and Edward Peters, ...	"	I. 917
1778. Aug. 27.	Caspar, Elizabeth, and Andrew Cropsy, ...	"	XXVI. 14
1770. Dec. 31.	Cassety, Peter, and Mary Davis, ...	"	XVI. 310
1768. July 24.	Casshow, Femmetje, and Johannis Snedecker,	"	XIII. 164
1780. May 17.	Casten, Ebenezer, and Teshey Barraga, ...	"	XXIX. 58
1774. Mar. 14.	Castine, Helena, and Samuel Hobson, ...	"	XXII. 148
1770. June 18.	Casting, Hannah, and William Scott, ...	"	XVI. 119
1757. Feb. 4.	Castle, William, and Mary Shaw, ...	"	I. 434
1773. Oct. 11.	Caston, Abigail, and Daniel Lewis, ...	"	XXI. 136
1771. Oct. 25.	Caston, Hannah, and Gideon Sprague, ...	"	XVII. 223
1783. Feb. 27.	Caston, Martha, and Richard Shephard, ...	"	XXXVIII. 56
1761. Nov. 17.	Castor, William, and Fanny Woodford, ...	"	V. 228

DATE.	NAMES.	RECORD.	VOL.	PAGE.
1760. Oct. 21.	Caswell, Philip, and Sarah Clarke,	M. B.,	III.	378
1763. Sept. 20.	Casy, William, and Susanna Taylor,	"	VII.	342
1762. Mar. 4.	Catack, Jacobus, and Elizabeth Cornell,	"	VI.	63
1779. April 9.	Cathcart, Lord, and Elizabeth Plumsteed Elliot,	"	XXVII.	100
1761. Jan. 29.	Catherine, Anne, and Augustine Drux,	"	IV.	22
1757. Jan. 18.	Caton, Sarah, and John Jones,	"	I.	420
1777. May 21.	Catrine, Mary, and John Reed,	"	XXIV.	91
1769. Dec. 23.	Caulder, Mary, and Lloyd Daubeny,	"	XV.	131
1771. Nov. 11.	Cavalier, Peter, and Sarah Doughty,	"	XVII.	246
1782. Dec. 18.	Cave, James, and Joannah Tyler,	"	XXXVII.	125
1781. Oct. 16.	Cavenagh, Thomas, and Rachael Green,	"	XXXIII.	104
1757. April 21.	Cavenor, James, and Mary Murphy,	"	I.	510
1763. Aug. 12.	Caverly, Abigail, and Thomas Thorne,	"	VII.	297
1756. Nov. 6.	Caverly, Peter, and Ann Cornell,	"	I.	348
1759. Nov. 15.	Caverly, William, and Elizabeth Sebring,	"	II.	497
1671. Feb. 6.	Cavlier, John, and Eleanor La Chare,	G. E.,	IV.	99
1771. July 5.	Caw, Ann, and John Davis,	M. B.,	XVII.	128
1769. Aug. 16.	Cazellett, Peter, and Elizabeth Burns,	"	XV.	24
1761. Nov. 27.	Cebra, Mary, and Joseph Robinson,	"	V.	253
1783. Nov. 19.	Cershow, Jacob, and Rachael Smith,	"	XL.	122
1781. Sept. 3.	Chace, Deadama, and Ebenezer Briggs,	"	XXXIII.	56
1763. Feb. 15.	Chace, Elisha, and Mary White,	"	VII.	64
1771. Dec. 12.	Chace, Mary, and John Clarke,	"	XVII.	292
1757. April 7.	Chadeayne, David, and Catherine Coles,	"	I.	491
1759. Feb. 7.	Chadeayne, Henry, and Ruth Conklin,	"	II.	183
1760. Nov. 8.	Chadeyn, Margaret, and John Wessolls,	"	III.	400
1783. July 15.	Chads, Henry, and Susannah Cornell,	"	XXXIX.	92
1777. April 15.	Chadwell, Benjamin, and Hannah Hammond,	"	XXIV.	64
1759. April 24.	Chadwick, Charles, and Hannah Havens,	"	II.	252
1782. June 15.	Chadwick, Deborah, and William Holmes,	"	XXXVI.	52
1782. April 3.	Chadwick, James, and Jane Alstine,	"	XXXV.	111
1772. Dec. 11.	Chadwick, Sarah, and Joseph Crowell,	"	XIX.	153
1780. Dec. 7.	Chalmers, Charles, and Elizabeth Degrove,	"	XXX.	144
1758. Sept. 12.	Chamberlain, John, and Phebe Stibbins,	"	II.	19
1781. Dec. 24.	Chamberlain, Theophilus, and Lamira Humphervill,	"	XXXIV.	101
1782. June 15.	Chambers, Eleanor, and Robert Roberts,	"	XXXVI.	53
1775. May 20.	Chambers, Jacob, and Hester Davis,	"	XXIII.	41
1737. Mar. 26.	Chambers, John, and Anne Van Cortlandt,	"	I.	6
1761. June 16.	Chambers, John, and Eavis Field,	"	IV.	242
1763. Jan. 3.	Chambers, Mary, and Peter Crolius,	"	VII.	5
1782. July 15.	Chambers, Rachel, and Christopher Durant,	"	XXXVI.	81
1768. Jan. 2.	Chambers, Samuel, and Sarah Walker,	"	XIII.	1
1758. May 8.	Chambers, Thomas, and Mary Lock,	"	I.	896.
1777. April 19.	Chandler, Edward, and Anne Dennis,	"	XXIV.	68

DATE.	NAMES.	RECORD.	VOL.	PAGE.
1765. July 27.	Chantrel, John, and Rebecca Morehouse,...	M. B.,	IX.	219
1782. Dec. 17.	Chapman, Abraham, and Mary Willis,......	"	XXXVII.	122
1777. June 12.	Chapman, George, and Sarah Valentine,....	"	XXIV.	102
1778. Feb. 14.	Chapman, Robert, and Rosana Stevens,.....	"	XXV.	22
1780. Feb. 25.	Chapman, Sarah, and Drummond Simpson,.	"	XXVIII.	213
1761. July 9.	Chapman, William, and Elizabeth Ambrose,.	"	IV.	292
1772. July 7.	Chappell, Annamina, and William Rose,....	"	XVIII.	156
1761. Feb. 23.	Chappel, Christiana, and William Cox,......	"	IV.	77
1764. Oct. 18.	Chappel, Hannah, and Thomas Cox,........	"	VIII.	362
1765. June 21.	Chappel, Peter, and Frances Hutchinson,...	"	IX.	179
1769. April 4.	Chapple, Jemima, and Benjamin Corsa,.....	"	XIV.	64
1772. Mar. 4.	Chardavoyn, Isaac, and Hester Elsworth,...	"	XVIII.	48
1761. April 22.	Chardavoyne, Ann, and Lawrence Wessels,.	"	IV.	161
1758. Feb. 22.	Chardavoyne, Elias, and Johanna Corcilius, ..	"	I.	825
1770. Feb. 23.	Chardavoyne, William, and Magdalen Valleau,	"	XVI.	23
1765. Jan. 17.	Chardevoin, Jane, and William Warner,....	"	IX.	19
1710. April 10.	Charles, Claudius, and Jane Griffith,.......	"	XXXI.	99
1762. Feb. 1.	Charles, William, and Mary Hogen,........	"	VI.	33
1760. Nov. 14.	Charley, Sarah, and Charles Wood,........	"	III.	411
1758. Mar. 27.	Charlick, Henry, and Susanna Rynier,......	"	I.	864
1765. April 24.	Charlick, Mary, and Gilbert Oakley,........	"	IX.	105
1762. Nov. 3.	Charlo, Margaret, and David Frank,........	"	VI.	409
1763. June 8.	Charlotte, Susanna, and Conradt Freitz,....	"	VII.	216
1765. Mar. 29.	Charlton, John, and Mary De Peyster,.....	"	IX.	76
1763. July 29.	Charter, John, and Anne Gerrald,.........	"	VII.	286
1671. Feb. 23.	Chartier, Francois, and Anne Renard,..... .	G. E.,	IV.	100
1782. Dec. 6.	Chase, Ammi, and Phebe Beeche,.........	M. B.,	XXXVII.	109
1764. June 8.	Chatterdon, Shadrach, and Elizabeth Hunt,..	"	VIII.	218
1760. Dec. 19.	Chatterton, Deborah, and John Forster,....	"	III.	485
1777. Sept. 26.	Chatting, Catherine, and Anthony De Mill,..	"	XXVIII.	85
1768. Aug. 27.	Chatwood, Charles, and Margaret Elliot, ...	"	XIII.	178
1759. Mar. 20.	Chavelier, Mary, and Dennis McPeek,......	"	II.	221
1775. Aug. 30.	Chees, Margaret, and Robert McCrubin,....	"	XXIII.	111
1779. Aug. 5.	Cheeseman, Elizabeth, and Philip Thorne,...	"	XXVIII.	47
1769. April 18.	Cheeseman, Hannah, and Peter Duboys,....	"	XIV.	77
1761. Dec. 4.	Cheeseman, Mary, and Isaac Lawrence,....	"	V.	264
1760. Oct. 7.	Cheeseman, Phebe, and William Hutton, ...	"	III.	350
1782. Aug. 10.	Cheeseman, Richard, and Elizabeth Weeks,.	"	XXXVI.	105
1765. Feb. 20.	Cheeseman, Sarah, and Fordham Burtis,....	"	IX.	55
1780. Dec. 7.	Cheesman, Anthony, and Hannah Smith,...	"	XXX.	141
1771. June 20.	Cheesman, Elizabeth, and John Arthur,....	"	XVII.	118
1774. Jan. 26.	Cheesman, Mary, and Benjamin Eyres,.....	"	XXII.	116
1758. Feb. 8.	Cheshire, Amey, and Daniel Burr,.........	"	I.	814
1765. Jan. 18.	Cheshire, Thomas, and Massey Durland,....	"	IX.	22
1761. Oct. 28.	Chesslear, William, and Effey Oman, ...	"	V.	173

DATE.	NAMES.	RECORD.	VOL.	PAGE.
1778. June 13.	Chesley, Robert, and Maria Van Brunt, ...	M. B.,	xxv.	101
1758. Mar. 13.	Chesnut, Archibald, and Judith Funderit, ...	"	I.	848
1675. Mar. 1.	Chew, Richard, and Frances Woodward, ...	W. O. P.,	III.	183
1777. Dec. 19.	Chichester, Edward, and Jane Lamb, ...	M. B.,	xxIV.	200
1758. Sept. 7.	Chichester, Eliphalet, and Mary Pine, ...	"	II.	7
1761. Oct. 23.	Chichester, Martha, and David Van Cot, ...	"	v.	163
1769. April 12.	Chichester, Mary, and Gilbert Bryan, ...	"	xIV.	72
1770. April 11.	Chichester, Merebe, and Joseph Whiteman, .	"	xvI.	60
1781. Feb. 27.	Chichester, Sarah, and Nathaniel Procter, ...	"	xxxI.	58
1769. Mar. 17.	Chichester, Phebe, and Thomas Skidmore, ...	"	xIV.	55
1781. Jan. 26.	Chick, Barbare, and George Happe, ...	"	xxxI.	28
1765. May 21.	Chidister, Eliphalet, and Margaret Oakley, ..	"	Ix.	136
1769. July 11.	Chilcott, Charles Pitcher, and Christian Cample, ...	"	xIV.	150
1760. April 24.	Child, Catharine, and Thomas Stoodly, ...	"	III.	121
1762. Feb. 1.	Child, John, and Frances Filkins, ...	"	vI.	35
1783. Feb. 27.	Child, Jonathan Friend, and Sarah McComb,	"	xxxvIII.	57
1753. Aug. 20.	Child, Joseph, and Catherine Friend, ...	"	I.	94
1782. Oct. 2.	Child, Nathaniel, and Elizabeth Henderson, .	"	xxxvII.	22
1737. Sept. 24.	Children, Thomas, and Elizabeth Muslow, ...	"	I.	7
1764. May 3.	Childs, Catharine, and Pearce Wood, ...	"	vIII.	181
1782. Jan. 5.	Childs, Frances, and Joseph Alward, ...	"	xxxv.	9
1760. Oct. 10.	Childs, John, and Margaret Winner, ...	"	III.	357
1758. Sept. 4.	Childs, Mary, and Eleazer Snell, ...	"	II.	1
1761. Nov. 14.	Childs, Mary, and William Tillou, ...	"	v.	217
1737. May 21.	Chilister, Tabitha, and Peter Buckhourt, ...	"	I.	6
1762. July 22.	Cholwell, Hannah, and Daniel Ten Eyck, ...	"	vI.	253
1771. May 7.	Cholwell, Mary, and Ephraim Bostwick, ...	"	xvII.	78
1760. Feb. 14.	Choulwell, Agnes, and James Dane, ...	"	III.	39
1781. Mar. 20.	Christian, Charles, and Elizabeth Galatian, ..	"	xxxI.	78
1758. Sept. 13.	Christian, Hester, and Francis Dickson, ...	"	II.	20
1765. May 18.	Christian, Margaret, and James Kearns, ...	"	Ix.	131
1761. Nov. 14.	Christian, Margaret, and William Hodge, ...	"	v.	218
1765. Sept. 18.	Christiansse, Eve, and Dirick Bratt, ...	"	Ix.	266
1767. Nov. 21.	Christie, Barbara, and Moses Young, ...	"	xII.	91
1763. April 2.	Christie, Hannah, and Peter Mead, ...	"	vII.	112
1763. Feb. 15.	Christie, John, and Esther Moffet, ...	"	vII.	63
1760. Feb. 2.	Christie, John, and Margaret Berret, ...	"	III.	18
1702. July 20.	Christie, Mary, and Duncan Campbell, ...	"	vI.	247
1758. Feb. 15.	Christie, Mary, and Timothy Macnamara, ...	"	I.	818
1782. Sept. 10.	Christie, Thomas, and Sarah McPherson, ...	"	xxxvI.	141
1763. June 18.	Christina, Anna, and Matthew Hopper, ...	"	vII.	233
1770. Nov. 17.	Christopher, Barent, and Elsie Bass, ...	"	xvI.	263
1762. April 22.	Christopher, Edmund, and Eve Deeker, ...	"	vI.	123
1782. Nov. 30.	Christopher, John, and Altje Zebriskey, ...	"	xxxvII.	102

DATE.		NAMES.	RECORD.	VOL.	PAGE.
1761. Oct. 23.	Christopher, John, and Charity Haughewout,	M. B.,		v.	162
1767. July 28.	Christopher, Richard, and Hester Garrison,.	"		xv.	6
1759. Dec. 17.	Christy, Hannah, and Malcom McPherson,..	"		ii.	547
1760. Mar. 5.	Christy, Mary, and Duncan McGrigore,.....	"		iii.	62
1778. July 11.	Christy, Matth'w, and Elizabeth Brown,....	"		xxv.	126
1666. June 25.	Christy, Sarah, and Humphry Clay,........	O. W. L.,		ii.	77
1660. May 8.	Chronch, Christopher, and Elizabeth Smith,.	"		iii.	146
1672. Mar. 10.	Churcher, William, and Susannah Brasyer,..	G. E.,		iv.	269
1755. Dec. 10.	Churchil, John, and Rebecah Sudred,.......	M. B.,		i.	231
1780. June 5.	Churchill, Sarah, and John Murrow,........	"		xxix.	83
1769. Oct. 24.	Churchward, Thomas, and Sarah Hoff,.....	"		xv.	64
1760. Aug. 12.	Cille, Sarah, and Gideon Avery,...........	"		iii.	248
1684. Oct. 22.	Cinburne, Mary, and William Owing,......	C. M..		xxxiii.	54
1672. Mar. 10.	Claesen, Jannekye, and Walter Carr,.......	G. E.,		iv.	269
1758. Dec. 5.	Claghorn, Ann, and William Atkins,.......	M. B.,		ii.	114
1758. Oct. 12.	Claghorn, Jennet, and Joseph Dennis,......	"		ii.	53
1780. Sept. 6.	Clandenny, Ann, and Abraham Van Winkle,	"		xxx.	19
1763. Sept. 7.	Clandenny,Patience,and Christopher Burbank,	"		vii.	377
1771. Dec. 17.	Clap, Ruth, and John Robinson,...........	"		xvii.	297
1782. May 2.	Clap, Thomas, and Erris Standish,.........	"		xxxv.	148
1757. July 28.	Clapham, George, and Jane Dowers,.......	"		i.	604
1779. May 13.	Clark, Abijah, and Mary Williams,.........	"		xxvii.	135
1763. April 25.	Clark, Alexander, and Catharine Coleman,...	"		vii.	141
1773. July 17.	Clark, Anna, and Joshua Doane,...........	"		xxi.	45
1779. Dec. 10.	Clark, Archebald, and Mary Courtney,.....	"		xxviii.	169
1779. Oct. 5.	Clark, Elizabeth, and Richard Arthur,......	"		xxviii.	102
1779. Sept. 30.	Clark, Eliz. Ann, and Alexander Henderson,	"		xxviii.	92
1767. Oct. 6.	Clark, Ellinor, and James Vanderbergh,....	"		xii.	56
1780. Sept. 9.	Clark, Heman, and Hannah Wortman,.....	"		xxx.	21
1771. July 26.	Clark, James, and Ann Toung,............	"		xvii.	145
1766. Nov. 24.	Clark, James, and Elizabeth Campbell,.....	"		x.	179
1767. June 13.	Clark, Jane, and John Craig,..............	"		xi.	109
1779. June 26.	Clark, Janet, and William Jennings,........	"		xxviii.	10
1770. May 30.	Clark, Jeremiah, and Sarah Hall,..........	"		xvi.	97
1772. Jan. 19.	Clark, John, and Elinor Harper,...........	"		xx.	12
1778. June 17.	Clark, John, and Elizabeth Wilkie,.........	"		xxv.	107
1760. Feb. 19.	Clark, John, and Margaret Alford,.........	"		iii.	41
1771. July 17.	Clark, John, and Margaret Lockerman,.....	"		xvii.	135
1782. Mar. 22.	Clark, John, and Mary Carr,..............	"		xxxv.	89
1777. Dec. 24.	Clark, John, and Mary Sheron,............	"		xxiv.	206
1764. Jan. 25.	Clark, John Wright, and Cornelia Cooper,..	"		viii.	36
1780. Sept. 25.	Clark, Joseph, and Bridget Wright,........	"		xxx.	41
1759. Sept. 12.	Clark, Luke, and Mary Allen,.............	"		ii.	417
1780. June 12.	Clark, Margaret, and Duncan McKnight,....	"		xxix.	86
1761. Oct. 19.	Clark, Margaret, and John Robinson,.......	"		v.	151

DATE.	NAMES.	RECORD.	VOL.	PAGE.
1778. Mar. 20.	Clark, Maria Teresa, and William Barrington,	M. B.,	xxv.	50
1763. Aug. 10.	Clark, Mary, and Joseph Knap,...........	"	vii.	296
1675. Mar. 20.	Clark, Michael, and Johannah Hall,........	W. O. P.,	ii.	183
1770. Oct. 12.	Clark, Phebe, and Obediah Smith,.........	M. B.,	xvi.	210
1771. Oct. 21.	Clark, Reuben, and Mary Peppard,........	"	xvii.	217
1763. April 27.	Clark, Sarah, and Nicholas Smith,.........	"	vii.	147
1777. Feb. 8.	Clark, Sarah, and Robert Timpany, ...	"	xxiv.	26
1767. Dec. 7.	Clarke, Annatje, and Jacob Onderdonck,....	"	xii.	110
1778. April 18.	Clarke, Charity, and Benjamin Moore,......	"	xxv.	65
1764. April 5.	Clarke, Cornelius, and Sarah Bayley,.......	"	viii.	138
1678. Dec. 14.	Clarke, Edward, and Dorothy Reynell, ...	G. E.,	xxxii.	19
1764. July 13.	Clarke, Elenor, and Anning Smith,........	M. B.,	viii.	257
1783. May 29.	Clarke, George, and Ann Graham,.........	G. E.,	xxxix.	27
1780. April 12.	Clarke, George, and Mary Braibain,........	M. B.,	xxix.	19
1736. Sept. 2.	Clarke, Henry, and Elizabeth Welsh,.......	"	i.	2
1765. Aug. 27.	Clarke, James, and Catharine Lynsen,......	"	ix.	247
1783. April 15.	Clarke, John, and Catherine Garrebrants,...	"	xxxviii.	96
1771. Dec. 12.	Clarke, John, and Mary Chace,............	"	xvii.	292
1771. April 9.	Clarke, John, and Mary Duyckman,........	"	xvii.	52
1779. July 28.	Clarke, Joseph, and Mary Lenox,..........	"	xxviii.	34
1764. Feb. 6.	Clarke, Lucy, and Henry Brasier,.........	"	viii.	51
1781. Jan. 4.	Clarke, Lucy, and Lot Strange,............	"	xxxi.	12
1764. Nov. 29.	Clarke, Margaret, and Matthew Lettemore,.	"	viii.	431
1770. Mar. 26.	Clarke, Mary, and Richard Vassall,........	"	xvi.	41
1736. Oct. 26.	Clarke, Nicolas, and Elizabeth Howlent,....	"	i.	3
1760. Oct. 21.	Clarke, Sarah, and Philip Caswell,........	"	iii.	378
1758. May 30.	Clarke, Susannah, and John Leathes,.......	"	i.	918
1759. Dec. 31.	Clarke, Thomas, and Mary Twigg,.........	"	ii.	563
1760. May 31.	Clarke, Thomas, and Rachael Williams,.....	"	iii.	169
1761. Feb. 25.	Clarke, William, and Mary Bonnel, ...	"	iv.	83
1762. Aug. 6.	Clarke, William, and Mary Sing,..........	"	vi.	267
1668. Aug. 17.	Clarke, William, and Susanna Trott,.......	O. W. L.,	ii.	223
1781. Feb. 3.	Clarkson, David M., and Mary Van Horne,.	M. B.,	xxxi.	35
1777. April 12.	Clarkson, Eliza, and Edward Griffiths,......	"	xxiv.	61
1762. Oct. 15.	Clarkson, John, and Elizabeth Conckling,...	"	vi.	366
1763. Feb. 19.	Clarkson, Levinus, and Mary Van Horne,...	"	vii.	69
1753. June 9.	Clarkson, Mary, and John Carolus,........	"	i.	54
1778. Sept. 2.	Clarkson, Mary, and John Murphy,........	"	xxvi.	19
1758. June 1.	Clarkson, Matthew, and Elizabeth De Peyster,	"	i.	920
1773. Aug. 12.	Class, John, and Margaret Many,..........	"	xxi.	66
1781. July 28.	Clatchley, Jamima, and Hubart Ketcham, ..	"	xxxiii.	20
1759. April 23.	Claus, Uliana, and Michael Vooght,...	"	ii.	250
1736. June 3.	Clauseren, Mary, and Andries Frank, ...	"	i.	1
1760. Nov. 25.	Clauw, Henry H., and Deborah Van Volkenburgh,.............................	"	iii.	442

DATE.	NAMES.	RECORD.	VOL.	PAGE.
1768. April 18.	Clauw, Johannis, and Batá Huyck, ...	M. B.,	XIII.	78
1762. Feb. 8.	Claw, Miaca, and James Thomas, ...	"	VI.	41
1772. Feb. 12.	Claw, Rachel, and Caspar Halen Beek, ...	"	XVIII.	35
1775. Aug. 26.	Claw, Rachel, and Thomas Musick, ...	"	XXIII.	137
1756. Aug. 3.	Claxton, Alexander, and Isabella Baker, . . .	"	I.	268
1669. Jan. 16.	Clay, Dorothy, and Richard Wood, ...	C. A.,	II.	450
1666. June 25.	Clay, Humphry, and Sarah Cristy, ...	O. W. L.,	II.	77
1780. April 11.	Clayton, Mary, and Samuel Plumb, ...	M. B.,	XXIX.	16
1780. Feb. 6.	Clayton, Samuel, and Sarah Archibald, ...	"	XXXI.	38
1767. April 25.	Clayton, Stephen, and Martha Sherrard, ...	"	XI.	71
1773. Oct. 27.	Clearwater, Tunis, and Catalina Garrison, . . .	"	XXI.	149
1764. July 4.	Clem, John, and Mary McDowell, ...	"	VIII.	246
1767. Nov. 6.	Clem, Susannah, and Samuel Tingley, ...	"	XII.	78
1756. Oct. 18.	Clemens, Abigail, and William Bugby, ...	"	I.	330
1761. June 24.	Clement, Daniel, and Hannah Thorn, ...	"	IV.	259
1760. July 10.	Clement, Elizabeth, and John Van Sise, ...	"	III.	210
1752. Nov. 28.	Clement, Gilbert, and Hannah Stringham, . .	"	I.	16
1764. April 10.	Clement, James, and Sarah Searing, ...	"	VIII.	148
1777. Aug. 19.	Clement, Jarvis, and Mary Lewis, ...	"	XXIV.	136
1773. July 5.	Clement, John, and Carolina Doughty, ...	"	XXI.	30
1779. Oct. 29.	Clement, Joseph, and Frances Prince, ...	"	XXVIII.	123
1770. Aug. 29.	Clement, Rebeccah, and John Greenoak, ...	"	XVI.	175
1760. Dec. 19.	Clements, Statia, and Thomas Mitchell, ...	"	III.	483
1761. Jan. 30.	Clemison, Edward, and Mary Smith, ...	"	IV.	43
1779. Nov. 25.	Clemmons, Samuel, and Elizabeth Dillingham,	"	XXVIII.	150
1779. July 22.	Clendenny, Elinor, and Thomas Dixon, ...	"	XXVIII.	28
1783. June 29.	Clerdage, Sarah, and John Grant, ...	"	XXXIX.	72
1763. Aug. 9.	Cleve, Elizabeth, and John North, ...	"	VII.	295
1762. April 8.	Clift, William, and Polly Bowman, ...	"	VI.	92
1757. Nov. 25.	Clinton, Alexander, and Mary Keen, ...	"	I.	714
1769. Oct. 28.	Clinton, George, and Cornelia Tappen, ...	"	XV.	70
1765. Feb. 8.	Clinton, James, and Mary De Witt, ...	"	IX.	50
1763. Sept. 29.	Clock, Jacob, and Hannah Forbes, ...	"	VII.	359
1760. Mar. 21.	Cloet, Derick, and Anna Hemstrat, ...	"	III.	85
1753. June 2.	Cloet, Fransyna, and Hendrick Williams, . . .	"	I.	47
1761. May 29.	Cloet, Jacob, and Maica Lansing, ...	"	IV.	211
1772. Mar. 2.	Clopper, Ann, and John Copp, ...	"	XVIII.	44
1778. Jan. 22.	Clopper, Catherine, and George Turnbull, . . .	"	XXIV.	18
1767. Nov. 24.	Clopper, Catherine, and John Van Alen, ...	"	XII.	95
1757. Mar. 7.	Clopper, 3d, Cornelius, and Rachel Lowe, . . .	"	I.	458
1770. June 25.	Clopper, Elizabeth P., and Samuel Schuyler,	"	XVI.	122
1736. Mar. 21.	Clopper, Hyltie, and Jacobus Quick, ...	"	I.	5
1782. April 23.	Closson, Anthony, and Mary Brewau, ...	"	XXXV.	133
1763. April 23.	Clotworthy, Ann, and Arthur Somersby, . . .	"	VII.	138
1779. July 23.	Clotworthy, Ann, and John Faning, ...	"	XVI.	144

DATE.	NAMES.	RECORD.	VOL. PAGE.
1738. Dec. 18.	Cloudy, Mary, and Samuel Bowyer,........	M. B.,	I. 12
1764. Dec. 24.	Clout, Elizabeth, and Jacobus Van Schoon- hoven,...............................	"	VIII. 465
1759. Aug. 11.	Clover, Susannah, and Gilbert Tippit,......	"	II. 382
1764. Oct. 19.	Clow, Judith, and John Legrange,.-........	"	VIII. 365
1768. Jan. 19.	Clowes, Aletta, and Peter Edsall,..........	"	XIII. 12
1761. Nov. 28.	Clowes, Catharine, and Samuel Rowland,...	"	V. 254
1780. Nov. 24.	Clowes, Caty, and William Mott,..........	"	XXX. 123
1765. Mar. 1.	Clowes, Joannah, and Oke Bloom,.........	"	IX. 59
1781. May 3.	Clowes, Joseph, and Elizabeth Carman, ...	"	XXXII. 30
1771. April 19.	Clowes, Lettice, and Morris Simonson,.....	"	XVII. 62
1763. Oct. 8.	Clowes, Mary, and James Southard,........	"	VII. 381
1765. May 2.	Clowes, Sarah, and Arthur Burtis,.........	"	IX. 118
1777. Jan. 11.	Clowes, Thomas, and Catherine Beadell,....	"	XXIV. 11
1769. Sept. 26.	Clowny, Mary Ann, and Robert Cummins,..	"	XV. 44
1761. Aug. 27.	Clows, Hannah, and Jacobus De Kay,......	"	V. 60
1770. Dec. 28.	Clows, Sarah, and Edward Allison, ...	"	XVI. 307
1759. April 24.	Cludie, Catharine, and Robert McCulluck,...	"	II. 251
1760. May 2.	Cluet, Gradus, and Alyda Ffisher,..........	"	III. 135
1781. Jan. 18.	Cluett, John James, and Sarah Mulligan,...	"	XXXI. 26
1763. July 9.	Clute, Barbary, and Walter Quackenbos,....	"	VII. 260
1762. April 20.	Clute, John, and Geesse Vrooman,.........	"	VI. 118
1773. Sept. 21.	Clute, John, and Mary Hugner,...........	"	XXI. 113
1738. Dec. 28.	Cnuttel, Daniel, and Anne Nichols,........	"	I. 12
173$\frac{4}{1}$. Mar. 3.	Coak, Mary, and Isaac Frost,..............	"	I. 9
1768. Oct. 31.	Coal, Charity, and John Field,.............	"	XIII. 219
1781. Sept. 15.	Coals, Zephery, and William Wright,......	"	XXXIII. 66
1762. Aug. 19.	Coates, Benjamin, and Catharine Stilwell,...	"	VI. 281
1758. Oct. 10.	Cobb, William, and Hanah Burns,........	"	II. 47
1760. April 24.	Cobblay, John, and Rachael Knapp,........	"	III. 122
1766. Oct. 13.	Cobham, John, and Jane McDowal, ...	"	X. 121
1761. Aug. 21.	Cobley, Rachel, and Abraham Thew,.......	"	V. 50
1777. Dec. 20.	Cochran, William, and Elizabeth Robinson, .	"	XXIV. 202
1779. Jan. 26.	Cock, Abraham, and Rhoda Carpenter,......	"	XXVII. 27
1778. Dec. 31.	Cock, Ann, and Robert Andrews,..........	"	XXVI. 135
1780. Jan. 17.	Cock, Anna, and Nathaniel Dickinson,......	"	XXXI. 23
1768. Nov. 12.	Cock, Daniel, and Roseannah Townshend, ..	"	XIII. 233
1773. May 29.	Cock, Elijah, and Temperance Townshend,..	"	XX. 131
1780. Dec. 1.	Cock, Elizabeth, and Joshua Cock,.........	"	XXX. 131
1779. Feb. 20.	Cock, Gabriel, and Phebe Birdsall,.........	"	XXVII. 44
1769. Oct. 9.	Cock, Gerhard Daniel, and Christina Ten Broeck,...............................	"	XV. 52
1764. Dec. 10.	Cock, Hannah, and Jeremiah Robins,......	"	VIII. 450
1781. Oct. 6.	Cock, Isaac, and Elizabeth Seaman,........	"	XXXIII. 90
1764. Dec. 18.	Cock, John, and Freelove Latting, ...	"	VIII. 458

DATE.	NAMES.	RECORD.	VOL.	PAGE.
1764. Feb. 22.	Cock, Jordan, and Casia Frost,............	M. B.,	VIII.	72
1780. Dec. 1.	Cock, Joshua, and Elizabeth Cock,.........	"	XXX.	131
1771. July 10.	Cock, Mary, and Magnus Beekman,........	"	XVII.	129
1761. Aug. 29.	Cock, Mary, and Samuel Frost,............	"	V.	63
1772. Jan. 8.	Cock, Penn, and Elizabeth Weekes,........	"	XVIII.	8
1762. Sept. 10.	Cock, Sarah, and Daniel Frost,............	"	VI.	311
1762. Aug. 3.	Cock, Sarah, and Mangel Minthorne,.......	"	VI.	263
1769. May 31.	Cock, Sarah, and Stephen Frost,...........	"	XIV.	110
1763. Oct. 6.	Cock, Thomas, and Mary Smith,...........	"	VII.	374
1782. Mar. 27.	Cock, William, and Dorothy Wallace,......	"	XXXV.	100
1736. June 4.	Cockerill, Thomas, and Sarah Bennet,......	"	I.	1
1767. Jan. 27.	Cockle, John, and Hannah Huskins,.......	"	XI.	15
1763. Oct. 31.	Cockman, Elizabeth, and Jacob Neffzer,....	"	VII.	414
1771. Dec. 2.	Cockram, Elizabeth, and Daniel Marshall,...	"	XVII.	276
1760. Nov. 19.	Cockran, John, and Gertrude Schuyler,.....	"	III.	427
1664. Feb. 13.	Cockrell, John, and Mary Page, ...	G. E.,	I.	85
1766. Nov. 28.	Cockrem, Joseph, and Mary Mathews,.....	M. B.,	X.	186
1781. Oct. 7.	Cocks, Francis, and Mary Robertson,.......	"	XXXIII.	92
1783. Dec. 31.	Cocks, Violetta, and Jacob Weeks,.........	"	XL.	126
1737. Oct. 12.	Codden, Elizabeth, and John Kirten,.......	"	I.	7
1759. Jan. 20.	Codding, Elizabeth, and Thomas Lynott,....	"	II.	163
1757. April 27.	Codebeek, Naomy, and Lodewyck Hoornbeek,	"	I.	518
1781. Oct. 9.	Codmas, Martha, and John Garretson,......	"	XXXIII.	94
1779. June 22.	Codmus, Geo., and Acky Fielding,.........	"	XXVIII.	2
1759. June 15.	Codmus, Peter, and Blendina Kip,.........	"	II.	327
1760. Sept. 13.	Codner, Isaac, and Martha Beadle,.........	"	III.	314
1678. Oct. 2.	Codrington, Thomas, and Margaret Delavall,.	G. E.,	XXXII.	4
1760. Sept. 27.	Codwise,Christopher,and Catharine Remmsen,	M. B.,	III.	335
1760. July 19.	Codwise, George, and Mary Van Rants,....	"	III.	218
1762. June 28.	Codwise, Mary, and Volkert Adouw,.......	"	VI.	212
1759. Dec. 13.	Codwise, Penelope, and Samuel Gilford,....	"	II.	542
1768. Nov. 12.	Codwise, Sarah, and Barent Ten Eyck,.....	"	XIII.	235
1763. Oct. 21.	Cody, Michael, and Lydia Moore,..........	"	VII.	399
1758. Jan. 5.	Coe, Abigail, and Edward Howard,........	"	I.	769
1764. July 23.	Coe, John, and Pomelia Coe,..............	"	VIII.	266
1763. June 25.	Coe, Margaret, and Gabriel Vander Voort,..	"	VII.	241
1767. May 1.	Coe, Mary, and Alathan Leverch, ...	"	XI.	74
1769. Oct. 6.	Coe, Mary, and Samuel Coe,..............	"	XV.	51
1764. July 23.	Coe, Pomelia, and John Coe,..............	"	VIII.	266
1764. June 2.	Coe, Robert, Jr., and Phebe Pettit,........	"	VIII.	206
1769. Oct. 6.	Coe, Samuel, and Mary Coe,..............	"	XV.	51
1782. June 9.	Coeburn, Jane, and Henry Lounsbury,......	"	XXXVI.	45
1779. Oct. 4.	Coen, Daniel, and Deborah Ogilby,.........	"	XXVIII.	99
1773. May 7.	Coevert, Abigail, and Samuel Ryder,.......	"	XX.	105
1761. Mar. 2.	Coffee, Richard, and Catharine Haley,......	"	IV.	87

DATE.	NAMES.	RECORD.	VOL.	PAGE.
1755. Sept. 9.	Coffell, Hester, and John Hall,............	M. B.,	I.	171
1773. Oct. 11.	Coffey, Catherine, and Charles Keeling,.....	"	XXI.	137
1783. Nov. 15.	Coffey, Mary, and Henry Benjamin Schroeder,	"	XL.	115
1772. Mar. 31.	Coffin, Sarah, and Abraham Van Wyck,....	"	XVIII.	65
1763. June 11.	Coffren, Mary, and William Cannon,.......	"	VII.	225
1779. Jan. 17.	Coffy, Catherine, and Joseph Orr,..........	"	XXVII.	15
1760. July 12.	Cofram, Robert, and Mary Livingston,......	"	III.	212
1783. Jan. 7.	Coggrell, Peter, and Phebe Hall,..........	"	XXXVIII.	9
1777. Feb. 24.	Coghlan, John, and Margaret Moncreiffe,...	"	XXIV.	35
1783. April 1.	Cogill, Mary, and Robert Vail,............	"	XXXVIII.	84
1781. Mar. 28.	Coile, James, and Eleanor Cairns,..........	"	XXXI.	89
1757. Jan. 15.	Coin, Martin, and Hannah Boyl,...........	"	I.	418
1763. Nov. 15.	Coin, Mary, and Christopher Rice,.........	"	VII.	451
1766. July 16.	Colden, Alice, and Archibald Hamilton,....	"	X.	51
1771. Nov. 30.	Colden, Alice, and Lewis Antill,...........	"	XVII.	274
1783. Oct. 9.	Colden, Cadwallader, Jr., and Christian Griffith,................................	"	XL.	74
1767. Feb. 24.	Colden, David, and Ann Willett,..........	"	XI.	35
1767. Feb. 12.	Colden, Elcie, and Edward Downes,.......	"	XI.	24
1780. Mar. 20.	Colden, Elizabeth, and Daniel Drake,.......	"	XXIX.	4
173⅞. Jan 7.	Colden, Elizabeth, and Peter De Lansey,....	"	I.	8
1759. Mar. 12.	Colden, Jane, and William Farquhar,.......	"	II.	214
1770. April 21.	Colden, Margaret, and John Antill,........	"	XVI.	67
1782. April 4.	Colder, Susannah, and William Broad,......	"	XXXV.	114
1772. Feb. 13.	Coldwall, James, and Catherine McCargill,..	"	XVIII.	38
1768. Dec. 22.	Cole, Abraham, and Abigail Johnson,......	"	XIII.	271
1761. Feb. 19.	Cole, Abraham, and Catharine Dutree,......	"	IV.	69
1779. April 23.	Cole, Abraham, and Catharine Winants,....	"	XXVII.	116
1761. Aug. 25.	Cole, Abraham, and Hannah Beadle,..... .	"	V.	58
1759. Oct. 8.	Cole, Abraham, and Martha Mersereau,.....	"	II.	452
1770. Oct. 17.	Cole, Abraham, and Susannah Quackenboss,	"	XVI.	219
1759. June 2.	Cole, Actia, and Joseph Craft,............	"	II.	299
1762. Mar. 22.	Cole, Albert, and Anne Dear, ...	"	VI.	81
1779. Jan. 7.	Cole, Ann, and Peter Winants,............	"	XXVII.	5
1773. May 14.	Cole, Ann, and Robert Carr,..............	"	XX.	110
1775. July 26.	Cole, Barnot, and Catharine Eseler,........	"	XXIII.	106
1778. Dec. 3.	Cole, Cornelius, and Patience Rolph,.......	"	XXVI.	108
1756. June 26.	Cole, Deborah, and Robert Warne,.........	"	I.	243
1782. Mar. 13.	Cole, Easter, and Jonathan Carpenter,......	"	XXXV.	87
1778. Oct. 30.	Cole, Elizabeth, and James Barry,.........	"	XXVI.	78
1783. Oct. 7.	Cole, Elizabeth, and Peter Muerenbildt,....	"	XL.	66
1779. Aug. 2.	Cole, Elizabeth, and Stephen Thorn,.......	"	XXVIII.	41
1682. May 12.	Cole, Elizabeth, and William Elston,.......O.W.&c.,	XXXII½.	120
1759. Feb. 5.	Cole, Hester, and Christian Smith,.........	M. B.,	II.	178
1763. Mar. 4.	Cole, Isaac, and Hester Yeates,............	"	VII.	90

DATE.	NAMES.	RECORD.	VOL.	PAGE.
1782. Aug. 24.	Cole, Isaac, and Hannah Taylor,....	M. B.,	XXXVI.	120
1764. Dec. 4.	Cole, Isaac, and Tabita Hannen,..........	"	VIII.	435
1769. Dec. 7.	Cole, Jacob, and Ann Andrevet,..........	"	XV.	117
1769. Feb. 4.	Cole, Jane, and James Carter,............	"	XIV.	26
1759. Dec. 13.	Cole, Jane, and John Hegman,............	"	II.	543
1770. Nov. 23.	Cole, John, and Annatie Daniels,..........	"	XVI.	266
1760. June 21.	Cole, John, and Hannah Thompson,........	"	III.	193
1736. July 3.	Cole, Joseph, and Freelove Weeks,........	"	I.	2
1781. April 30.	Cole, Mary, and Barne Slack,............	"	XXXII.	21
1759. Jan. 19.	Cole, Mary, and Olive Burgess,............	"	II.	160
1771. April 8.	Cole, Mary, and William Lakerman,........	"	XVII.	49
1764. April 7.	Cole, Peter, and Susannah Latourette,......	"	VIII.	143
1757. Dec. 12.	Cole, Rebeccah, and Benjamin Van Steen-bergh,...............................	"	I.	737
1781. May 21.	Cole, Rebecah, and Henry Parlee, ...	"	XXXII.	55
1778. Oct. 29.	Cole, Sarah, and John Sloan,............	"	XXVI.	75
1777. June 20.	Cole, Sarah, and Joshua Willis,............	"	XXIV.	106
1771. Oct. 3.	Cole, Sarah, and Peter Brink,............	"	XVII.	198
1779. Mar. 16.	Cole, Sarah, and Robert Stoddard,........	"	XXVII.	67
1765. April 24.	Cole, Simon Isaac, and Mary Trumpole,....	"	IX.	107
1767. Nov. 20.	Cole, Stephen, and Ann Poilyon,..........	"	XII.	90
1757. June 21.	Cole, Susannah, and Henry Parine,........	"	I.	568
1767. Oct. 7.	Coleby, Catherine, and Alexander Bradburn,	"	XII.	58
1761. July 10.	Colegrove, Elizabeth, and Thomas Burns,...	"	IV.292b
1764. Dec. 28.	Colegrove, Francis, and Martha Bogart,....	"	VIII.	467
1759. Oct. 24.	Colegrove, Susannah, and Jacob Shourt,....	"	II.	472
1760. Sept. 19.	Colegrove, William, and Mary Wheeler,....	"	III.	323
1763. April 25.	Coleman, Catharine, and Alexander Clarke,.	"	VII.	141
1759. Oct. 26.	Coleman, James, and Martha Oates,........	"	I.	680
1768. Feb. 11.	Coles, Abraham, and Hannah Weeks,......	"	XIII.	34
1757. April 7.	Coles, Catharine, and David Chadeayne,....	".	I.	491
1706. Oct. 25.	Coles, Dority, and Coles Mudge,...........	"	I.	3
1760. Jan. 10.	Coles, Ephelanda, and Peter Descoe,........	"	II.	576
1774. Jan. 13.	Coles, Gloriana, and Jackson Mott,........	"	XXII.	102
1775. June 1.	Coles, Jarvis, and Abigail Carman,........	"	XXIII.	51
1781. Mar. 20.	Coles, Jesse, and Deborah Carpenter,.......	"	XXXI.	76
1781. Sept. 21.	Coles, John, and Elizabeth Underhill,......	"	XXXIII.	72
1770. May 23.	Coles, Martha, and Daniel Mudge,.........	"	XVI.	93
1783. Nov. 1.	Coles, Phebe, and Jacob S. Jackson, ...	"	XL.	101
1768. June 18.	Coles, Rebecka, and John Weeks,.........	"	XIII.	132
1769. July 10.	Coles, Rhoda, and Adolph Degrove, Jr., ...	"	XIV.	147
1759. Oct. 31.	Coles, Rhode, and Tunius Wortman,.......	"	II.	483
1778. Sept. 26.	Coles, Robert, and Ann Baker,............	"	XXVI.	34
1736. Nov. 12.	Coles, Zepenah, and William Lawrence,....	"	I.	3
1779. April 27.	Colford, Eleanor, and John Jones,.........	"	XXVII.	123

DATE.		NAMES.	RECORD.	VOL.	PAGE.
1763. Jan.	5.	Colgan, Hannah, and William Newman, ...	M. B.,	VII.	7
1760. Jan.	24.	Colgan, Jane, and Wynant Van Zant,......	"	III.	6
1761. Dec.	18.	Colgan, Sarah, and Thomas Hamersley, ...	"	V.	287
1766. Dec.	1.	Colhoune, Ann, and James Harris,.........	"	X.	190
1779. Sept.	16.	Collard, Affy, and Jacob Scudder,.........	"	XXVIII.	77
1782. Feb.	16.	Collard, Ann, and Johnson Patten,.........	"	XXXV.	57
1778. Dec.	5.	Collard, Catherine, and Nathan Attwood,...	"	XXVI.	112
1756. Aug.	3.	.Collard, Edward, and Elizabeth Moss,......	"	I.	266
1773. Nov.	30.	Collard, Jeremiah, and Mary Cooder,.......	"	XXII.	57
1781. Sept.	13.	Collard, John, and Anne Pengray,.........	"	XXXIII.	63
1757. April	26.	Collard, Margaret, and William Hine,......	"	I.	515
1777. Aug.	3.	Collard, Mary, and Nicholas Perdue Olding,.	"	XXIV.	126
1778. June	27.	Collard, Michael, and Ruth Legget, ...	"	XXV.	113
1759. Oct.	6.	Collard, Rebecca, and John Becket,........	"	II.	450
1764. Jan.	5.	Collard, Susanna, and Thomas Kempe,.....	"	VIII.	6
1669. Aug.	23.	Collard, William, and Elizabeth Jewell,....	O. W. L.,	II.	523
1763. Dec.	28.	Collester, Margaret, and Benjamin Philipse,.	M. B.,	VII.	529
1760. Jan.	4.	Collet, George, and Agnes Ayme,.........	"	II.	569
1757. July	9.	Colley, Joseph, and Sarah Trapaulier,......	"	I.	587
1769. Nov.	14.	Collier, Annetie, and William Miller,.......	"	XV.	94
173⅞. Feb.	9.	Collier, Catherine, and Henry Vandewater,..	"	I.	9
1783. May	20.	Collier, George, and Milley Crosby,........	"	XXXIX.	21
1775. Sept.	1.	Collier, Leentie, and Isaac Huyck,.........	"	XXIII.	144
1773. Nov.	10.	Collier, Mary, and Hope Mills,......... ...	"	XXII.	36
1762. June	12.	Collier, Peter, and Mary Wilson,..........	"	VI.	190
1783. Oct.	21.	Collin, Hannah, and John Barratt,.........	"	XXXVII.	56
1783. Mar.	31.	Collin, John, and Elizabeth Dailley,........	"	XXXVIII.	83
1759. Dec.	14.	Collings, Richard, and Esther Bedlow,......	"	II.	545
1783. June	16.	Collins, Abraham, and Charity Sheffiel,.....	"	XXXIX.	59
1761. Oct.	27.	Collins, Elizabeth, and Robert Symes,......	"	V.	169
1764. April	27.	Collins, George, and Elizabeth Ryker,......	"	VIII.	172
1777. June	18.	Collins, Isaac, and Sarah Allboy,..........	"	XXIV.	105
1780. April	25.	Collins, Jamima, and James Carter,........	"	XXIX.	34
1783. May	8.	Collins, Jane, and John Perry,.............	"	XXXIX.	4
1757. Feb.	19.	Collins, Jane, and Richard Day,...........	"	I.	443
1765. July	17.	Collins, John, and Christiana Truax,........	"	IX.	207
1778. July	11.	Collins, John, and Sarah Watson,..........	"	XXV.	125
1771. April	12.	Collins, Margaret, and Charles Morse,......	"	XVII.	55a
1767. Mar.	24.	Collins, Margaret, and Gilbert Giles,.......	"	XI.	48
1779. Nov.	26.	Collins, Margaret, and Greggs Farish,......	"	XXVIII.	151
1764. Aug.	22.	Collins, Martha, and Isaac Myer,..........	"	VIII.	290
1783. June	16.	Collins. Mary, and Hugh Hays,............	"	XXXIX.	62
1753. Aug.	20.	Collins, Sarah, and Charles Car,...........	"	I.	93
1781. Sept.	12.	Collins, Thomas, and Ann Connell,..... ...	"	XXXIII.	61
1753. April	16.	Collins, Thomas, and Johanna Van Gelden,.	"	I.	23

DATE.	NAMES.	RECORD.	VOL.	PAGE.
1764. Jan. 21.	Collins, Thomas, and Margaret Long,.......	M. B.	VIII.	27
1780. July 29.	Collins, William, and Jane Brewer,.......	"	XXIX.	128
1777. Dec. 13.	Collins, William, and Mary Fulkerson,......	"	XXIV.	197
1759. Feb. 7.	Collis, David, and Margaret Oliver,........	"	II.	182
1774. Feb. 25.	Collison, Mary, and Robert McChesney,....	"	XXII.	134
1772. Jan. 4.	Collister, Margaret, and Thomas Grisdall,....	"	XVIII.	3
1783. Aug. 11.	Collit, Sarah, and James H. Pettit, ...	"	XXXIX.	123
1758. April 19.	Collon, Elizabeth, and John Barrori,.......	"	I.	876
1780. May 13.	Colls, John, and Getty Seloover,..........	"	XXIX.	54
1769. July 21.	Colly, Joseph, and Mary Baldwin,.........	"	XV.	2
1783. July 7.	Colroyd, Catharine, and George Williams,..	"	XXXIX.	83
1762. June 23.	Colton, Anne, and Thomas Howell,........	"	VI.	205
1764. Feb. 29.	Colvell, Thomas, and Ann Brower, ...	"	VIII.	86
1772. June 18.	Colvil, Elizabeth, and David Shedwine,.....	"	XVIII.	142
1766. Oct. 22.	Colvill, Hannah, and David Griffiths,...... .	"	X.	136
1783. Nov. 1.	Colvill, Hannah, and Jacob Carpenter,......	"	XL.	99
1770. Jan. 8.	Colvill, John, and Susannah Sheriff,........	"	XVI.	4
1779. June 3.	Colvill, Mary, and Jared Bell,.............	"	XXVII.	153
1779. Mar. 30.	Colvill, Priscilla, and Isaiah Hait,..........	"	XXVII.	86
1783. Nov. 1.	Colvill, Tillit, and Elizabeth Carpenter,.....	"	XL.	100
1783. Feb. 15.	Colville, Jacob, and Wilmott Craft,........	"	XXXVIII.	40
1778. Oct. 3.	Colville, William, and Elizabeth Murray,...	"	XXVI.	43
1774. Jan. 7.	Colvin, James, and Mary Guion, ...	"	XXII.	94
1779. April 3.	Colvin, John, and Elinor Bryan,...........	"	XXVII.	93
1782. May 3.	Colwell, Amy, and Thomas Larrabee,......	"	XXXV.	149
1760. Oct. 28.	Colwell, Edward, and Amy Wright,........	"	III.	385
1759. Feb. 6.	Colwell, Francis, and Catharine Haley,.....	"	II.	179
1778. July 20.	Colwell, Sarah, and Thomas Sims,.........	"	XXV.	134
1782. Sept. 25.	Colwell, Thomas, and Catherine Brass,......	"	XXXVII.	14
1772. Nov. 18.	Colyer, Jacobus, and Jane Miller,..........	"	XIX.	118
1782. Aug. 5.	Colyer, Sarah, and John Hill,.............	"	XXXVI.	100
1644. July 1.	Combaer (Kombaer), Martha, and Peter Linden,.............................	A. R.,	III.	218
1782. Mar. 21.	Combauld, Richard, and Sarah Van Buskirk,	M. B.,	XXXV.	93
1778. Feb. 19.	Combs, Henry, and Hanah Smith,.........	"	XXV.	28
1756. Sept. 20.	Combs, John, and Charity Vandine,.... ...	"	I.	298
1766. Dec. 10.	Comes, Gilbert, and Ann Braine,..........	"	X.	197
1753. June 23.	Comes, Mary, and Benjamin Carpenter, ...	"	I.	65
1773. June 1.	Comes, Sarah, and William Bayley,........	"	XX.	135
1738. Sept. 18.	Comes, Solomon, and Sarah Lee.	"	I.	11
1737. June 4.	Comfort, Catherine, and Nicholas Rosevelt,..	"	I.	6
1782. July 13.	Comfort, John, and Catharine Harris, ...	"	XXXVI.	79
1783. Sept. 20.	Commindinger, Hannah, and John William Shirmer,.................	"	XL.	47
1769. Oct. 21.	Compton, Catherine, and Samuel Van Vleck,	"	XV.	58

DATE.	NAMES.	RECORD	VOL.	PAGE.
1736. May 12.	Compton, James, and Frances Riggs, ...	M. B.,	I.	1
1765. Oct. 31.	Compton, Mathias, and Catherine Green,....	"	IX.	347
1775. Aug. 21.	Con, Mary, and John Adams,.............	"	XXIII.	132
1761. April 17.	Concklin, Abraham, and Sarah Carpénter, ..	"	IV.	153
1765. May 20.	Concklin, Abraham, and Tjatie Tappan, ...	"	IX.	132
1763. Sept. 22.	Concklin, Elkanah, and Dinah Carman,.....	"	VII.	349
1762. Nov. 29.	Concklin, Ezekiel, and Mary Titus,.........	"	VI.	458
1767. Jan. 28.	Concklin, Jacob, and Elizabeth Jones,......	"	XI.	17
1761. Jan. 6.	Concklin, Philip, and Mary Bennet,........	"	IV.	4
1781. June 18.	Concklin, Rachael, and Joseph Fearly,......	"	XXXII.	89
1780. Oct. 7.	Concklin, Sarah, and William Albertson,....	"	XXX.	59
1764. Oct. 6.	Concklin, Stephen, and Phebe Latting,.....	"	VIII.	336
1776. Feb. 8.	Concklin, Timothy, and Mary Platt,........	"	XXIII.	266
1762. Oct. 15.	Conckling, Elizabeth, and John Clarkson,...	"	VI.	366
1770. Nov. 10.	Conckling, Hannah, and Zebulon Ketcham,..	"	XVI.	246
1761. Aug. 25.	Conckling, Isaac, and Cathalintie Van Bunscoten, ...	"	V.	56
1761. Sept. 12.	Conckling, Margaret, and Francis Watt,.....	"	V.	82
1759. Nov. 12.	Condon, Richard, and Mary Burk,.........	"	II.	494
1762. June 23.	Condy, Jesse, and Parthinia Ogden,........	"	VI.	206
1766. July 16.	Coneyn, Adriantje, and Cornelious Arrowsmith, Jr.,.............................	"	X.	53
1781. Oct. 10.	Conihane, Mary, and Mark Murphy,.......	"	XXXIII.	95
1783. Aug. 30.	Conine, Leonard, and Elizabeth Garabrantse,	"	XI.	16
1775. Oct. 25.	Conine, Peter, and Susannah Mabie,.......	"	XXIII.	186
1771. Aug. 20.	Oonkland, Joseph, and Judith Bennet,.....	"	XVII.	164
1772. Feb. 1.	Conklin, Elizabeth, and Johannes Blauvelt,..	"	XVIII.	27
1782. Oct. 17.	Conklin, Hannah, and John Hendrickson,..	"	XXXVII.	50
1783. Mar. 10.	Conklin, Hanner, and Isaac Rogers, ...	"	XXXVIII.	63
1758. Sept. 12.	Conklin, Isaac, and Jane Titus,............	"	II.	14
1783. June 10.	Conklin, Jacob, and Harmpie Lefferts,.....	"	XXXIX.	47
1767. Nov. 18.	Conklin, Platt, and Phebe Smith,..........	"	XII.	88
1759. Feb. 7.	Conklin, Ruth, and Henry Chadeayne, ...	"	II.	183
1757. Oct. 13.	Conklin, Ruth, and Jesse Brush,..........	"	I.	669
1757. April 7.	Conklin, Tamar, and Dennis Hicks,........	"	I.	489
1756. Sept. 14.	Conkline, David, and Hanah Storm, ...	"	I.	297
1773. April 26.	Conkling, Catherine, and Zophar Hawkins,..	"	XX.	100
1760. July 29.	Conkling, Hannah, and Abraham Jarvis,....	"	III.	230
1753. Aug. 29.	Conkling, Jane, and Daniel McEwen, ...	"	I.	101
1757. Oct. 31.	Conkling, John, and Elizabeth Brush, ...	"	I.	692
1772. May 2.	Conkling, Jonah, and Kisiah Brush,........	"	XVIII.	97
1759. Nov. 1.	Conkling, Naomi, and Joseph Lewis, Jr., ...	"	II.	485
1773. April 30.	Conkling, Nicholas, and Sarah Fowler, ...	"	XX.	102
1782. Sept. 25.	Conkling, Rebecca, and Adam Leffert,......	"	XXXVII.	15
1778. Nov. 16.	Conn, James, and Phebe Stout, ...	"	XXVI.	83

11

DATE.	NAMES.	RECORD.	VOL.	PAGE.
1782. Feb. 4.	Conn, Phebe, and Peter Miller,.............	M. B.,	XXXV.	43
1761. Feb. 19.	Connally, Hannah, and James Surnavey, ...	"	IV.	72
1756. Dec. 20.	Connel, Elizabeth, and Samuel Burroughs,...	"	I.	392
1781. Sept. 12.	Connell, Ann, and Thomas Collins, ...	"	XXXIII.	61
1766. Oct. 11.	Connell, John, and Catherine Titus,........	"	X.	120
1778. May 19.	Connell, Mary, and David Buchanan, ...	"	XXV.	87
1757. Feb. 16.	Connelly, Mary, and Joseph Anderson,.....	"	I.	439
1764. Sept. 28.	Connely, Margaret, and William Mansfield,..	"	VIII.	326
1762. Sept. 27.	Connely, Mary, and Thomas Minn, ...	"	VI.	334
1763. May 12.	Conner, Catharine, and William Wilson,....	"	VII.	182
1759. May 8.	Conner, Charles, and Charlot Williams,.....	"	II.	269
1761. July 9.	Conner, Cicely, and John Davis, ...	"	IV.292a	
1758. May 11.	Conner, Elenor, and Daniel Callahan,.......	"	I.	899
1776. Feb. 16.	Conner, Elenor, and Philip Prosser,........	"	XXIII.	269
1759. April 5.	Conner, Elizabeth, and David Lyons,.......	"	II.	235
1763. Aug. 16.	Conner, Hugh, and Margaret Strong, ...	"	VII.	302
1761. Mar. 4.	Conner, Jeremiah, and Anne Smith, ...	"	IV.	91
1775. April 20.	Conner, Jeremiah, and Catharine Smith,....	"	XXIII.	14
1759. Sept. 7.	Conner, Lenck, and HarrejantieVan Antwerp,	"	II.	412
1780. Mar. 30.	Conner, Sarah, and James Poillon,.........	"	XXIX.	9
1772. Dec. 9.	Connery, Nicholas, and Elizabeth Hurley, ..	"	XIX.	149
1772. Aug. 21.	Connet, Sarah, and John Blank, Jr., ...	"	XIX.	28
1755. Nov. 28.	Connolly, Agnes, and Daniel Sullivan,......	"	I.	222
1773. Mar. 29.	Connor, John, and Elizabeth Wiltse, ...	"	XX.	77
1766. Oct. 21.	Connor, Mary, and John Bevan,...........	"	X.	133
1772. Oct. 28.	Connor, Moses, and Elinor Normoyle,......	"	XIX.	93
1765.	Connoven, John, and Catharine Morris,.....	"	IX.	144
1783. Oct. 6.	Connoway, Catharine, and George Gilladate,	"	XL.	65
1782. May 30.	Conradi, Charles, and Sarah Cortelyou,.....	"	XXXVI.	30
1764. April 19.	Conrey, John, and Margaret McDowell, .. .	"	VIII.	163
1767. Sept. 9.	Conrey, William, and Mary Johnson, ...	"	XII.	32
1775. June 16.	Conry, Patrick, and Elizabeth Swartout,....	"	XXIII.	65
1773. June 19.	Conselly, William, and Mary Skillman,.....	"	XXI.	17
1763. Dec. 22.	Consely, Barent, and Catharine Woortman,..	"	VII.	516
1770. April 21.	Conselyea, Peter, and Antaletta La Quier, ..	"	XVI.	66
1769. June 17.	Conselyee, Deborah, and John Skilman, ...	"	XIV.	121
1765. Oct. 31.	Constable, Dorothy, and John Staple, ...	"	IX.	344
1768. Nov. 3.	Constable, Euretta, and James Phyn, ...	"	XIII.	223
1755. Dec. 11.	Constable, Maritie, and Daniel Broadhead, ..	"	I.	232
1778. Oct. 7.	Constables, Anjet, and Mangle Minthorne,..	"	XXVI.	50
1766. Dec. 11.	Constant, Elizabeth, and William Casey,....	"	X.	200
1761. July 17.	Constant, Henry, and Elizabeth Barger, ...	"	IV.	302
1769. Dec. 5.	Contine, Catherine, and Peter Sleght, ...	"	XII.	108
1756. Dec. 9.	Contine, Nathaniel, and Sarah Rutsen, ...	"	I.	378
1763. Nov. 10.	Convis, Sarah, and Hugh Bryan, ...	"	VII.	442

DATE.	NAMES.	RECORD.	VOL.	PAGE.
1768. Oct. 21.	Conway, John, and Jane Compton, ...	M. B.,	XIII.	215
1769. Jan. 4.	Conway, Mary, and John Carrow, ...	"	XIV.	1
1764. Oct. 23.	Conyn, Casparus, and Tryntie Van Wee, ...	"	VIII.	369
1760. Sept. 17.	Conyn, Maritie, and Peter Van Aelstyn, ...	"	III.	317
1674. Feb. 15.	Coo, Robert, and Jane Rouse, ...	A. R.,	XXIII.	158
1775. Oct. 30.	Coobagh, Stofol, and Catharine Tater, ...	M. B.,	XXIII.	192
1773. Nov. 30.	Cooder, Mary, and Jeremiah Collard, ...	"	XXII.	57
1782. Jan. 19.	Cooe, Elizabeth, and George Shannon, ...	"	XXXV.	24
1759. May 10.	Cook, Alexander, and Elizabeth Sickels, ...	"	II.	275
1765. Jan. 3.	Cook, Ann, and Alexander Riche, ...	"	IX.	2
1769. Nov. 14.	Cook, Ann, and Peter Stewart, ...	"	XV.	93
1779. Aug. 7.	Cook, Cornelius, and Elizabeth Van Vleck, ..	"	XXVIII.	49
1772. May 11.	Cook, George, and Jane Peake, ...	"	XVIII.	107
1737. June 2.	Cook, Hannah, and Francis Dousneck, ...	"	I.	6
1738. June 24.	Cook, Hannah, and William Henry, ...	"	I.	10
1782. June 17.	Cook, Helena, and Jacob Remsen, ...	"	XXXVI.	55
1783. Sept. 29.	Cook, Joanna, and Thomas Mackie, ...	"	XL.	57
1771. May 23.	Cook, John, and Elizabeth Breested, ...	"	XVII.	89
1758. May 25.	Cook, John, and Mary Brested, ...	"	I.	910
1753. Aug. 25.	Cook, John, and Mary Sadlar, ...	"	I.	96
1761. Oct. 31.	Cook, Joseph, and Margaret Lane, ...	"	V.	181
1757. Dec. 13.	Cook, Marytje, and Jacobus Debeavois, ...	"	I.	739
1769. July 14.	Cook, Mathew, and Susannah Glean, ...	"	XIV.	153
1777. April 28.	Cook, Michael, and Hannah Henderson, ...	"	XXIV.	78
1769. July 29.	Cook, Thomas, and Marian Mehon, ...	"	XV.	9
1782. Oct. 17.	Cook, William, and Elenor Devoe, ...	"	XXXVII.	48
1780. Mar. 22.	Cook, William, and Margaret Grayham, ...	"	XXIX.	6
1773. Sept. 22.	Cooke, Effie, and Tunis Kershow, ...	"	XXI.	119
1780. June 30.	Cooke, Hannah, and John Butler, ...	"	XXIX.	104
1762. Aug. 31.	Cool, Jacobus, and Jane Wittbeck, ...	"	VI.	299
1773. Nov. 23.	Cool, Simon, and Mary Steenbergh, ...	"	XXII.	40
1760. May 17.	Coolbach, John, and Margaret Brinckerhoff,.	"	III.	159
1761. June 6.	Coolback, Mary, and Richard Brinckerhoff,..	"	IV.	230
1782. Aug. 5.	Coole, Aaron, and Elizabeth Lutkins, ...	"	XXXVI.	102
1782. Aug. 24.	Coole, Phebe, and Peter Allen, ...	"	XXXVI.	123
1777. Oct. 1.	Coombe, Hanah, and Henry Boel, ...	"	XXIV.	156
1779. June 26.	Coomes, Ann, and John Hilton, ...	"	XXVIII.	9
1780. Mar. 30.	Coon, Elizabeth, and Thomas Charles Man,..	"	XXIX.	10
1767. Nov. 17.	Coony, Catherine, and Abraham Phillips, ...	"	XII.	86
1764. Mar. 31.	Cooper, Annanias, and Elizabeth De Kay,...	"	VIII.	127
1770. Dec. 15.	Cooper, Catherine, and John Deboys, ...	"	XVI.	298
1767. Sept. 11.	Cooper, Catherine, and William Williams,...	"	XII.	33b
1763. Jan. 17.	Cooper, Cornelia, and Abraham Harmans, ..	"	VII.	16
1766. Dec. 1.	Cooper, Cornelia, and Anthoney Hallenbake,	"	X.	189
1764. Jan. 25.	Cooper, Cornelia, and John Wright Clark, ..	"	VIII.	36

DATE.	NAMES.	RECORD.	VOL.	PAGE.
1761. Nov. 6.	Cooper, Cornelius, and Ann Brower,.......	M. B.,	v.	195
1763. Oct. 20.	Cooper, Deborah, and Simon Ter Boss,.....	"	VII.	395
1764. Dec. 31.	Cooper, Ebenezer, and Priscilla Smith, ...	"	VIII.	471
1760. Nov. 25.	Cooper, Eleanor, and William Mannaring, ..	"	III.	444
1780. Sept. 27.	Cooper, Elias, and Sarah Roome, ...	"	XXX.	45
1767. Mar. 12.	Cooper, Elizabeth, and John Foy, ...	"	XI.	43
1762. April 8.	Cooper, Esther, and Simon Cooper, ...	"	VI.	96
1761. Nov. 11.	Cooper, Ezekiel, and Catharine Rote,.......	"	v.	208
1763. Nov. 2.	Cooper, Ezekiel, and Deborah Mott,........	"	VII.	423
1765. Sept. 12.	Cooper, Giles, and Elizabeth Whitfield,.....	"	IX.	261
1776. Mar. 20.	Cooper, Hester, and Amaziah Wheeler,.....	"	XXIII.	286
1764. April 12.	Cooper, James, and Hilah Van Bommell, ...	"	VIII.	152
1764. Nov. 8.	Cooper, Jemima, and Garret Van Clief,.....	" .	VIII.	395
1783. Feb. 15.	Cooper, John, and Jane Van Zant,.........	"	XXXVIII.	42
1780. July 22.	Cooper, John, and Mary Appleby,.........	"	XXIX.	118
1762. April 26.	Cooper, John, and Mary Lowther,.........	"	VI.	132
1780. June 24.	Cooper, John, and Mary Stringham, ...	"	XXIX.	95
1759. Aug. 22.	Cooper, Margaret, and John Smart,........	"	II.	387
1769. Mar. 10.	Cooper, Maria, and Benjamin Thorne,......	"	XIV.	52
1773. Nov. 25.	Cooper, Mary, and George Brett, ...	"	XXII.	43
1779. Nov. 25.	Cooper, Mary, and John Groff,............	"	XXVIII.	148
1768. Nov. 7.	Cooper, Mary, and John Weloer,..........	"	XIII.	230
1768. Oct. 22.	Cooper, Mary, and William Sickels,........	"	XIII.	216
1755. Nov. 28.	Cooper, Mehitabel, and Samuel Smith, ...	"	I.	223
1780. Feb. 7.	Cooper, Nathaniel, and Jane Turner, ...	"	XXVIII.	209
1772. Oct. 20.	Cooper, Obadiah, and Dinah Van Wyck,....	"	XIX.	79
1783. Aug. 20.	Cooper, Richard, and Letticia Brinckerhoff, .	"	XL.	3
1764. Jan. 24.	Cooper, Rosamond, and James Glassford, ...	"	VIII.	33
1772. Nov. 10.	Cooper, Sarah, and Eleazer Du Bois,.......	"	XIX.	107
1762. April 8.	Cooper, Simon, and Esther Cooper,........	"	VI.	96
1766. June 30.	Cooper, Thomas, and Elinor Roberts,.......	"	X.	39
1776. Jan. 27.	Cooper, Thomas, and Frances Moore, ...	"	XXIII.	254
1760. Dec. 24.	Cooper, Thomas, and Jane Miller, ...	"	III.	492
1761. July 27.	Cooper, Thomas, and Mary Lourier,........	"	v.	8
1752. Nov. 27.	Cooper, Zebulon, and Elizabeth Wick,......	"	I.	13
1762. July 22.	Coover, Phebe, and Garret Van Wicken, ...	"	VI.	252
1761. June 5.	Coovert, Margaret, and Cornelius Bogaert,..	"	IV.	227
1760. July 23.	Cooyemans, Scherlotta, and John Jones Bro-			
	neek, ...	"	III.	222
1760. Sept. 6.	Coperthwait, Deborah, and Abraham Labagh,	"	III.	303
1680. Jan. 26.	Copestaffe, John, and Jone Wright, ...	O. W.,	XXXII½.	34
1772. Mar. 2.	Copp, John, and Ann Clopper,............	M. B.,	XVIII.	44
1782. Feb. 12.	Corback, Elizabeth, and Nicholas Lackman,..	"	XXXV.	49
1683. May 29.	Corbet, Alce, and James Allisen, ...	E.,	XXXIII.	59
1759. Sept. 4.	Corbet, Mary, and Francis Dickson,........	M. B.,	II.	409

DATE.	NAMES.	RECORD.	VOL.	PAGE.
1681. Sept. 3.	Corbett, Elizabeth, and Alexander Wardrope,	O. W.,	xxxii½.	67
1783. Jan. 27.	Corby, Ann, and Richard Fletcher,	M. B.,	xxxviii.	29
1758. Feb. 22.	Corcilius, Johanna, and Elias Chardavoyne,.	"	i.	825
1771. Oct. 10.	Corgill, Peter, and Mary Harvey,	"	xvii.	203
1769. Dec. 12.	Corlear, Keeshe, and James Burroughs,	"	xv.	120
1783. Oct. 29.	Corleys, William, and Alada Lindeman,	"	xl.	91
1781. April 4.	Corlies, George, and Margaret Bets,.	"	xxxi.	92
1737. June 2.	Cormichael, Stunford, and Altia Wartnabey,	"	i.	6
1783. Aug. 10.	Corne, Elizabeth, and Charles de Gironwurt,	"	xxxix.	121
1773. June 23.	Corne, Letitia, and Dennis Kennedy,	"	xxi.	21
1762. Mar. 4.	Cornel, Elizabeth, and Jacobus Catack,	"	vi.	63
1764. Dec. 5.	Cornel, Margare, and Peter Smith,	"	viii.	436
1768. Sept. 28.	Cornel, Rem, and Peter Nellie Hegeman,	"	xiii.	199
1685. Aug. 17.	Cornelis, Janite, and Joseph Hopper,	C. M.,	xxxiii.	154
1772. Dec. 7.	Cornelius, Catherine, and Harman Tallman, .	M. B.,	xix.	144
1773. Oct. 6.	Cornelius, Elizabeth, and Tunis Snedeker,	"	xxi.	131
1765. Aug. 5.	Cornelius, John, and Mary Powell,	"	ix.	230
1682. Aug. 7.	Cornelius, John, and Mary Yates,	O. W.,	xxxii½.	144
1782. May 18.	Cornell, Amy, and William Hicks,	M. B.,	xxxvi.	8
1756. Nov. 6.	Cornell, Ann, and Peter Cavarly,	"	i.	348
1767. May 16.	Cornell, Ann, and Samuel Thorn,	"	xi.	90
1780. Dec. 22.	Cornell, Ann, and William Roe,	"	xxx.	163
1763. Nov. 17.	Cornell, Caleb, and Magdalen Headly,	"	vii.	452
1775. Aug. 24.	Cornell, Catharine, and Hendrick Elderd,	"	xxiii.	133
1782. May 24.	Cornell, Cornelia, and Abraham Van Sicklen,.	"	xxxvi.	21
1768. April 27.	Cornell, Deborah, and Isaac Hicks,	"	xiii.	87
1718. Jan. 6.	Cornell, Elizabeth, and Edward Hicks,	"	i.	774
1736. May 10.	Cornell, Elizabeth, and John Sands,	"	i.	1
1779. June 11.	Cornell, Elizabeth, and John White,	"	xxvii.	164
1774. Mar. 9.	Cornell, Elizabeth, and Joseph Marse,	"	xxii.	142
1783. Oct. 4.	Cornell, Elizabeth, and William Bayard, Jr.,	"	xl.	61
1779. Mar. 6.	Cornell, Frances, and Elijah Miles,	"	xxvii.	57
1764. June 19.	Cornell, Geliam, and Jane Suydam,	"	viii.	229
1767. Sept. 21.	Cornell, George, and Amie Hicks,	"	xii.	38
1768. July 13.	Cornell, Gilliam, and Femmetje Wyckof,	"	xiii.	158
1779. April 22.	Cornell, Gulian, and Lydia Campbell,	"	xxvii.	115
1779. Oct. 9.	Cornell, Isaac, and Ann Duyree,	"	xxviii.	107
1775. June 7.	Cornell, Isaac, and Anna Ryder,	"	xxiii.	57
1783. July 12.	Cornell, Isaac, and Hannah Cortelyou,	"	xxxix.	89
1757. Dec. 24.	Cornell, James, and Margaret Hicks,	"	i.	752
1759. April 14.	Cornell, Jamime, and Henry Mardochai,	"	ii.	242
1763. Nov. 23.	Cornell, John, and Altie Williams,	"	vii.	465
1767. April 18.	Cornell, John, and Catherine Smith,	"	xi.	65
1768. Nov. 6.	Cornell, John, and Catherine Suydam,	"	xiii.	228
1761. April 25.	Cornell, John, and Elizabeth Whiting,	"	iv.	167

86   NEW YORK MARRIAGES.

DATE.	NAMES.	RECORD.	VOL. PAGE.
1758. April 24.	Cornell, Joshua, and Hannah Hulet,	M. B.,	I. 884
1775. Oct. 3.	Cornell, Margaret, and Oliver Rowe,	"	XXIII. 172
1773. Feb. 18.	Cornell, Margaret, and Thomas Fowler,	"	XX. 48
1769. June 28.	Cornell, Martha, and Nathaniel Townsend, ..	"	XIV. 134
1772. Nov. 30.	Cornell, Martin, and Elizabeth Vandeburgh,.	"	XIX. 137
1762. Nov. 24.	Cornell, Mary, and John Williams,	"	VI. 452
1761. Oct. 1.	Cornell, Mary, and Joseph McCord,	"	V. 111
1762. Sept. 20.	Cornell, Miriam, and Henry Woolley,	"	VI. 323
1777. Nov. 28.	Cornell, Oliver, and Ann Roe,	"	XXIV. 186
1755. Nov. 27.	Cornell, Peggy, and John Tredwell,	"	I. 217
1780. May 22.	Cornell, Peter, and Mary Matisen,	"	XXIX. 64
1759. Feb. 14.	Cornell, Samuel, and Catharine Smith,	"	II. 191
1777. Oct. 21.	Cornell, Samuel, and Jane Hewlett,	"	XXIV. 168
1761. Nov. 11.	Cornell, Samuel, and Margaret Smith,	"	V. 209
1769. Aug. 4.	Cornell, Sarah, and Abraham Larzelere,	"	XV. 17
1760. May 8.	Cornell, Sarah, and Philip Solomon,	"	III. 144
1774. Mar. 5.	Cornell, Sarah, and Uriah Mitchell,	"	XXII. 140
1775. Dec. 30.	Cornell, Stephen, and Mary Platt,	"	XXIII. 237
1763. Dec. 7.	Cornell, Susanna, and Aaron Van Oostrant,.	"	VII. 496
1783. July 15.	Cornell, Susannah, and Henry Chads,	"	XXXIX. 92
1772. July 1.	Cornell, Thomas, and Anne Gale,	"	XVIII. 154
1765. Jan. 4.	Cornell, Timothy, and Letitia Everett,	"	IX. 6
1770. Sept. 27.	Cornell, William, and Hannah Hicks,	"	XVI. 197
1775. July 10.	Cornish, Abigail, and Abraham W. Hardenbrook,	"	XXIII. 92
1773. Dec. 6.	Cornish, Amy, and Hendrick Googlet,	"	XXII. 62
1759. April 21.	Cornish, Benjamin, and Sarah Bass,	"	II. 249
1762. Oct. 24.	Cornish, Elizabeth, and Gilbert Garrison,	"	VI. 389
1759. Feb. 3.	Cornish, Elizabeth, and Thomas Cumberson,.	"	II. 205
1758. May 2.	Cornish, Rebecca, and Robert Morrell,	"	I. 891
1763. April 6.	Cornish, Richard, and Margaret Kasey,	"	VII. 115
1762. Oct. 22.	Cornish, Sarah, and John Bailey,	"	VI. 379
1765. Feb. 5.	Cornish, Sarah, and John Leveridge,	"	IX. 46
1764. June 8.	Cornish, Timothy, and Mary Weekes,	"	VIII. 216
1761. Sept. 7.	Cornu, Daniel, and Sarah Wessels,	"	V. 69
1767. Mar. 13.	Cornwall, Abigail, and Charles Hicks,	"	XI. 44
1773. Dec. 21.	Cornwall, James, and Rachel Dennis,	"	XXII. 81
1766. June 6.	Cornwall, John, and Patience Oakley,	"	X. 7
1761. Dec. 1.	Cornwall, John, and Phebe Hewlett,	"	V. 259
1766. June 5.	Cornwall, Mary, and Gilbert Hicks,	"	X. 5
1773. Feb. 8.	Cornwall, Thomas, and Deborah Doughty,	"	XX. 38
1780. May 6.	Cornwel, Stephen, and Elizabeth Smyth,	"	XXIX. 46
1767. Sept. 24.	Cornwell, Ann, and Benjamin Floyd,	"	XII. 42
1781. Dec. 2.	Cornwell, Benjamin, and Mary Gibson,	"	XXX. 136
1758. May 6.	Cornwell, Charles, and Abigail Elderd,	"	I. 894

DATE.	NAMES.	RECORD.	VOL.	PAGE.
1770. Oct. 31.	Cornwell, David, and Mary Watson,........	M. B.,	XVI.	236
1778. May 11.	Cornwell, Elizabeth, and Daniel Lefferts, ...	"	XXV.	5
1755. Nov. 21.	Cornwell, Hannah, and Francis Browne,....	"	I.	213
1736. May 11.	Cornwell, Hannah, and Peter Snyder,......	"	I.	1
1779. Jan. 29.	Cornwell, Helena, and Michael Price,......	"	XXVII.	31
1782. July 31.	Cornwell, Hewlett, and Elizabeth Willis,....	"	XXXVI.	96
1766. Aug. 4.	Cornwell, Mary, and William Miller,.......	"	X.	69
1783. Aug. 2.	Cornwell, Rachael, and Joseph Denton,.....	"	XXXIX.	109
1768. Aug. 1.	Cornwell, Samuel, and Susannah Willet,....	"	XIII.	167
1770. Aug. 6.	Cornwell, Thomas, and Elizabeth Thurston,.	"	XVI.	155
1760. Mar. 3.	Correy, Anne, and William Philpot,........	"	III.	59
1779. July 31.	Corrington, Abigail, and George Carr,......	"	XXVIII.	39
1769. April 24.	Corrishon, Catherine, and Matthias Dubois,.	"	XIV.	82
1761. Mar. 23.	Corry, Anne, and Robert Rogers,..........	"	IV.	113
1777. July 7.	Corry, Francis, and Catherine Hopton,.....	"	XXIV.	115
1738. July 13.	Corry, John, and Mary Wytt,.............	"	I.	10
1777. June 11.	Corry, Joseph, and Barbara Baker,........	"	XXIV.	100
1769. April 4.	Corsa, Benjamin, and Jemima Chapple,.....	"	XIV.	64
1761. Jan. 29.	Corsa, Cornelia, and Ernest Ludewig Lende,	"	IV.	36
1765. Jan. 29.	Corsa, Tunis, and Magdalen Everett,.......	"	IX.	33
1765. May 25.	Corselius, Cornelia, and George Lucam,.....	"	IX.	142
1764. April 11.	Corselius, Elizabeth, and Joseph Lock,......	"	VIII.	151
1760. Jan. 3.	Corselius, Mary, and Abraham Smith,.....	"	II.	565
1770. Jan. 4.	Corselus, George, and Barbarie Steel,......	"	XVI.	2
1756. Dec. 14.	Corsen, Catharine, and Cornelius Dasosway,.	"	I.	382
1770. May 10.	Corsen, Daniel, and Charity Spier,.........	"	XXV.	86
1768. June 27.	Corsen, Mary, and John Simonson,........	"	XIII.	140
1773. Feb. 26.	Corsen, Richard, and Closhe Kruser,.......	"	XX.	54
1761. April 9.	Corser, Isaac, and Mary Gibbs,............	"	IV.	140
1761. Mar. 21.	Corson, Peter, and Gertryde Simonson,.....	"	IV.	111
1771. April 23.	Corssin, Jacob, and Lucretia Skillman, ...	"	XVII.	65
1736. Oct. 11.	Cortelyon, Altie, and Albert Coerten,......	"	I.	3
1779. April 20.	Cortelyou, Agnes, and Russell Tomlinson,...	"	XXVII.	112
1772. June 16.	Cortelyou, Elinor, and Edward Beatty,.....	"	XXI.	12
1783. July 12.	Cortelyou, Hannah, and Isaac Cornell,......	"	XXXIX.	89
1766. June 21.	Cortelyou, Isaac, and Altie Lott,...........	"	X.	23
1773. July 5.	Cortelyou, Jacques, and Sarah Townsend, ..	"	XXI.	29
1767. Oct. 26.	Cortelyou, Jaques, and Mary Hewlett,.....	"	XII.	68
1757. June 8.	Cortelyou, Mary, and Rutger Van Brunt,...	"	I.	556
1772. Nov. 14.	Cortelyou, Peter, and Addra Guyon, ...	"	XIX.	113
1782. May 30.	Cortelyou, Sarah, and Charles Conradi,.....	"	XXXVI.	30
1763. May 10.	Cortelyou, Simon, and Sarah Van Wyck,...	"	VII.	173
1781. Nov. 19.	Cortelyow, Mary, and Edward Egberts, ...	"	XXXIV.	48
1761. Aug. 4.	Corter, Mary, and Abel Smith Fisher,......	"	V.	25
1757. Jan. 20.	Cortill, John, and Elenor Peterkin,.........	"	I.	421

DATE	NAMES.	RECORD.	VOL.	PAGE.
1770. Dec. 19.	Cortilyou, Elizabeth, and Richard Seaman,..	M. B.,	XVI.	303
1762. July 30.	Cortlandt, Philip, and Catharine Ogden,....	"	VI.	257
1761. Aug. 22.	Cortney, Catharine, and James Armstrong,..	"	V.	53
1757. Jan. 28.	Cosby, Eliner, and William Ann Skinner,...	"	I.	428
1750. Jan. 15.	Cosby, Thomazin, and David Jenkins,......	"	I.	415
1772. Nov. 17.	Cosine, Walter, and Elizabeth Elsworth,....	"	IX.	116
1775. Oct. 20.	Cosper, Andrew, and Ida Ryerson,........	"	XXIII.	185
1759. Feb. 5.	Cossart, Theophilus, and Catlinetie De Foreest,	"	II.	177
1782. April 6.	Cossean, Jane, and Cornelius Duryea,......	"	XXXV.	116
1775. Oct. 9.	Cosser, Catharine, and Thomas Lawson,....	"	XXIII.	176
1765. Oct. 31.	Costelow, William, and Mary Hages,.......	"	IX.	343
1738. Oct. 23.	Cosyne, Elizabeth, and John Middlemas,...	"	I.	11
1778. May 14.	Cotgrave, Isaac, and Margaret Blake,......	"	XXV.	83
1781. Sept. 14.	Cotheret, John, and Elizabeth Timen,......	"	XXXIII.	65
1758. Nov. 27.	Cothong, John, and Mary Wilson,.........	"	II.	105
1757. April 15.	Cottington, Catharine, and Jacob Feely,....	"	I.	500
1782. May 8.	Cottrell, Mary, and Jonathan Harnad, . ..	"	XXXV.	154
1783. May 19.	Cottrell, Sarah, and Nathaniel Hardned,....	"	XXXIX.	17
1767. Oct. 14.	Cottrell, Sarah, and William Henry,........	"	XII.	61
1778. May 11.	Couenhoven, Ida, and Hendrick Suydam,...	"	XXV.	78
1763. Sept. 21.	Couenhoven, Nicholas, and Jannetje Lott,..	"	VII.	345
1780. April 7.	Coulon, Jonas, and Elizabeth Telier,..:.....	"	XXIX.	14
1772. Oct. 9.	Counhoven, Francis, and Jane Striker,.....	"	XIX.	69
1778. Dec. 1.	Counhoven, William, and Johanna Wyckoff,	"	XXVI.	106
1758. Feb. 14.	Counsalye, Aray, and Hannah Fine,........	"	I.	820
1781. May 28.	Counsely, John, and Rachael Carr,.........	"	XXXII.	59
1759. Mar. 31.	Counselyee, Andries, and Mercy Fine,......	"	II.	231
1767. May 29.	Coupar, Henry, and Jennet Taylor,........	"	XI.	101
1762. June 2.	Courria, John, and Esther Nelson,.........	"	VI.	181
1760. June 10.	Coursey, John, and Jane Forsyth, ...	"	III.	185
1753. June 29.	Courtis, Christian Henry, and Anna Maria Rosina Harnischfegerin,....	"	I.	67
1753. Aug. 24.	Courtis, Ruth, and Warman Duncan,.......	"	I.	95
1772. Feb. 1.	Courtland, Cornelia, and Gerrard Beekman, Jr.,	"	XVIII.	25
1779. Jan. 5.	Courtney, Ann, and Attained A. Lansfield,..	"	XXVII.	3
1779. Dec. 10.	Courtney, Mary, and Archibald Clark,......	"	XXVIII.	169
1780. Dec. 14.	Courtney, Richard, and Sarah Richardson,..	"	XXX.	151
1762. May 10.	Courtney, Richard, and Sarah Stilwell,.....	"	VI.	150
1781. Feb. 15.	Courtney, Thomas, and Lois Braid,........	"	XXXI.	45
1753. May 15.	Courtright, Elizabeth, and Guysbert Gerretson, ...	"	I.	30
1764. June 26.	Coury, James, and Etje Draw,..............	"	VIII.	238
1771. May 9.	Cousins, William, and Elizabeth Howard,...	"	XVII.	81
1781. Dec. 15.	Coutant, John, and Jane Reno,.............	"	XXXIV.	89
1781. Nov. 20.	Coutant, Peter, and Eleaner Secord,........	"	XXXIV.	50

DATE.		NAMES.	RECORD.	VOL.	PAGE.
1765. Jan.	3.	Coutant, Zacharias, and Catharine Haycock,.	M. B.,	IX.	5
1777. Mar.	2.	Couvenhoven, Mary, and William Bayley, ..	"	XXIV.	37
1761. April 24.		Couwenhoven, Niccassie, and NieltjeVan Pelt,	"	IV.	166
1773. June 14.		Couwenhoven, Rem, and Idaa Lefferts,.....	"	XXI.	4
1760. Feb.	1.	Couwenhoven, Rem, and Maggeltye Ffector,	"	III.	20
1783. April	8.	Couwenhoven, Sithje, and Jeremiah Remsen,	"	XXXVIII.	88
1761. June 22.		Couzins, William, and Elizabeth Mullen,....	"	IV.	255
1782. Oct.	11.	Covat, Elizabeth, and John Attlay, ...	"	XXXVII.	38
1783. Aug. 26.		Covenhoven, Abigail, and John Lott,.......	"	XL.	11
1761. May	30.	Covenhoven, Gherje, and John Stockholm,..	"	IV.	220
1759. June 25.		Covenover, Sarah, and Casparus Stuyversant	"	II.	340
1773. June 19.		Covenselly, William, and Mary Skillman,...	"	XXI.	17
1763. April	6.	Coventry, Mary, and James Calder,........	"	VII.	116
1776. Jan.	4.	Covert, Richard, and Catharine Wykoff,....	"	XXIII.	239
1759. Dec.	12.	Covert, Tunis, and Rebecca Rainer, ...	"	II.	538
1758. Mar.	14.	Coward, Catharine, and John Forrest,......	"	I.	850
1779. Oct.	15.	Cowderrey, Sarah, and Thomas Steell,.....	"	XXVIII.	113
1778. Oct.	3.	Cowdra, Mary, and Nicholas Browse, ...	"	XXVI.	44
1783. Oct.	8.	Cowdrey, Benjamin, and Anne Spence,.....	"	XL.	73
1771. Nov.	6.	Cowdrey, Jonathan, and Nelly Venderwater,	"	XVII.	242
1763. July	20.	Cowen, William, and Margaret Duffee,.....	"	VII.	274
1781. July	6.	Cowenhoven, Ann, and Harman Cropsy,...	"	XXXII.	105
1765. May	14.	Cowenhoven, Catharine, and Abraham Luquer,	"	IX.	126
1756. July	29.	Cowenhoven, Dorothy, and Leffert Lefferts,.	"	I.	263
1780. April 21.		Cowenhoven, Jacob, and Rachel Bergen,...	"	XXIX.	30
1781. July	27.	Cowenhoven, Johannes, and Elizabeth Van Pelt, ...	"	XXXIII.	17
1753. Oct.	15.	Cowenhoven, John, and Elizabeth Bradburn,	"	I.	140
1768. Feb.	22.	Cowenhoven, John, and Margaret Amorman,	"	XIII.	40
1765. June	20.	Cowenhoven, Mary, and Abraham Martley,.	"	IX.	176
1760. May	30.	Cowenhoven, Sarah, and Martin Schenck,...	"	III.	168
1757. Aug.	18.	Cowenhover, Famitje, and Hendrick Gulick,	"	I.	616
1736. Aug.	27.	Cowenover, Belatie, and John Eckles, ...	"	I.	2
1737. Nov.	21.	Cowhonoven, Anatie, and John Schenk,....	"	I.	8
1756. Aug.	5.	Cowles, Peter, and Elsie Smith,...........	"	I.	269
1761. Nov.	9.	Cowley, William, and Rebecca Abbot,......	"	V.	196
1737. Sept.	9.	Cownovel, Sarah, and Elias Rice,..........	"	I.	7
1757. Feb.	1.	Cowper, Jeffery, and Dorothy Lewis, ...	"	I.	431
1758. Oct.	11.	Cowper, Matthew, and Elizabeth Tole, ...	"	II.	48
1758. Mar.	13.	Cowperthwaite, Farmer, and Deborah Brat,.	"	I.	847
1781. Aug.	25.	Cox, Ann, and Obadiah Stillwell,..........	"	XXXIII.	47
1761. June	22.	Cox, Charles, and Elizabeth Peffer,........	"	IV.	253
1775. Dec.	11.	Cox, David, and Catherine Fry,...........	"	XXIII.	227
1759. Dec.	5.	Cox, Deborah, and Alexander Ogilvie,......	"	II.	527
1778. Sept. 28.		Cox, Elizabeth, and John Burnham,........	"	XXVI.	38

12

Date.	Names.	Record.	Vol. Page.
1780. Aug. 23.	Cox, Hannah, and John Thomson,.........	M. B.,	xxix. 145
1763. April 30.	Cox, Hannah, and John White,........	"	vii. 156
1737. Nov. 1.	Cox, John, and Ede Stephenson,..........	"	i. 7
1761. July 30.	Cox, Joseph, and Susannah Johnson,.......	"	v. 16
1781. Jan. 18.	Cox, Letitia, and Isaac Robertson,.........	"	xxxi. 24
1757. Feb. 21.	Cox, Martha, and Samuel Bridge,..........	"	i. 444
1781. Mar. 25.	Cox, Mary, and Aeneas Roberts,..........	"	xxxi. 85
1764. June 6.	Cox, Robert, and Catharine Ogden,........	"	viii. 210
1761. May 6.	Cox, Sarah, and Peter Machet,............	"	iv. 181
1665. April 22.	Cox, Thomas, and Elizabeth Blashford,.....	G. E.,	i. 117
1764. Oct. 18.	Cox, Thomas, and Hannah Chappel,........	M. B.,	viii. 362
1761. Feb. 23.	Cox, William, and Christiana Chappel,.....	"	iv. 77
1685. April 17.	Cox, William, and ——— ———, ...	C. M.,	xxxiii. 109
1758. Oct. 12.	Coxell, Mary, and Joseph Hawkins,........	M. B.,	ii. 51
1769. July 17.	Coxeter, Bartholemew, and Lettice Tovow,.	"	xiv. 154
1778. Dec. 7.	Coyd, Janet, and Alexander Houston,......	"	xxvi. 113
1775. Aug. 29.	Coyzer, Jacob, and Jane Rivers,...........	"	xxiii. 140
1781. Oct. 4.	Cozens, Mary, and John McFall,....	"	xxxiii. 86
1760. April 26.	Cozine, Balm Johnson, and Catharine Dyckman,..............	"	iii. 125
1773. Jan. 19.	Cozine, Catherine, and Jacob Horsen,......	"	xx. 13
1767. May 27.	Cozine, Catherine, and William W. Gilbert,.	"	xi. 98
1768. May 10.	Cozine, Cornelius, and Elitje Murphy,......	"	xiii. 100
1771. July 25.	Cozine, Elizabeth, and James Moran,.......	"	xvii. 141
1762. May 22.	Cozine, Jacob, and Freelove Heckbey,......	"	vi. 166
1774. Mar. 10.	Cozine, William, and Elinor Habout,.......	"	xxii. 143
1767. April 13.	Crab, Mary, and Abraham Alstin,..........	"	xi. 61
1760. Oct. 27.	Crabb, John, and Mary Demilt,............	"	iii. 381
1761. Mar. 30.	Crabb, Thomas, and Catharine Lott,........	"	iv. 123
1781. June 2.	Craddock, Thomas, and Sarah Bedell,.......	"	xxxii. 68
1783. Jan. 15.	Craft, Freelove, and Abraham Probasco,....	"	xxxviii. 17
1769. Feb. 14.	Craft, Hannah, and Samuel Harrold,.......	"	xiv. 32
1783. May 31.	Craft, Henry, and Charity Baker,..........	"	xxxix. 32
1762. Dec. 22.	Craft, Isaac, and Jane Secord,............	"	vi. 493
1759. April 25.	Craft, Isaac, and Sarah Rogers, ...	"	ii. 255
1759. June 2.	Craft, Joseph, and Acha Cole,.............	"	ii. 299
1756. Sept. 9.	Craft, Judah, and Silvanus Pine,..........	"	i. 291
1756. June 30.	Craft, Mary, and Michael Rogers,..........	"	i. 244
1779. April 20.	Craft, Pamela, and Samuel Baker,.........	"	xxvii. 111
1762. July 20.	Craft, Rhody, and Nicholass Weeks,.......	"	vi. 246
1764. Jan. 23.	Craft, Robert Thorny, and Jemima Frost,...	"	viii. 30
1775. May 30.	Craft, Ruth, and John Thomas,............	"	xxiii. 49
1763. July 12.	Craft, Solomon, and Frances Alsop,........	"	vii. 261
1783. Feb 15.	Craft, Wilmott, and Jacob Colville,.........	"	xxxviii. 40
1764. Dec. 10.	Crage, Isabel, and George Deniston,.......	"	viii. 448

DATE.	NAMES.	RECORD.	VOL.	PAGE.
1758. Dec. 9.	Crage, Thomas, and Ann Tayler,..........	M. B.,	II.	122
1762. Dec. 4.	Cragg, Archibald, and Elizabeth Frasier,....	"	VI.	467
1762. Jan. 12.	Cragg, Mary, and Edward Grant,..........	"	VI.	9
1780. Oct. 7.	Craig, George, and Mary Bohan,-..........	"	XXX.	61
1767. June 13.	Craig, John, and Jane Clark,..............	"	XI.	109
1763. Jan. 3.	Craig, John, and Lydia King,..............	"	VII.	1
1759. June 6.	Craig, John, and Rebecca McGeer,.........	"	II.	305
1783. Sept. 16.	Craig, Margaret, and James Duncan,.......	"	XL.	41
1736. Nov. 8.	Craig, Samuel, and Gertha Ward,..........	"	I.	3
1763. Dec. 28.	Craige, Rebecca, and James Forbes,........	"	VII.	528
1737. Dec. 12.	Craige, Robert, and Catherine Miller,.......	"	I.	8
1763. Nov. 7.	Cramer, Sophia, and Christopher Long,.....	"	VII.	430
1778. July 7.	Crammell, Margaret, and William Tilton,...	"	XXV.	121
1758. Feb. 25.	Cramsheir, Elizabeth, and William Canterbury,	"	I.	828
1755. Sept. 13.	Cramsheir, Thomas, and Mary Ramsey,....	"	I.	176
1761. Jan. 15.	Crandell, Eleanor, and John Owens,.......	"	IV.	20
1764. Jan. 17.	Crane, Sarah, and John Lockhart,..........	"	VIII.	20
1684. Dec. 10.	Cranesburgh, Oliver, and Helekie Van Korrow,	C. M.,	XXXIII.	70
1770. Nov. 28.	Cranmur, Maria Y., and William Gibbon, ..	M. B.,	XVI.	273
1760. Aug. 20.	Crannel, Geertruydt, and Thomas Fisher,...	"	III.	265
1763. Feb. 19.	Crannell, Catharine, and Gilbert Livingston,.	"	VII.	70
1777. Sept. 4.	Crannell, Effimilah, and Edward Drury,....	"	XXIV.	141
1771. Nov. 6.	Crannell, Elizabeth, and Peter Tappen,.....	"	XVII.	241
1769. Oct. 14.	Crashun, Rachel, and Francis Groome,.....	"	XV.	55
1762. Jan. 30.	Craven, Elizabeth, and James Vance,.......	"	VI.	31
1780. June 2.	Crawford, Alexander, and Jane Button,.....	"	XXIX.	79
1779. Mar. 31.	Crawford, Ann, and John Curtis,..........	"	XXVII.	88
1761. Dec. 22.	Crawford, Ann, and John Pell,............	"	V.	292
1761. Oct. 17.	Crawford, Anne, and Peter Ter Boss,......	"	V.	145
1763. Nov. 1.	Crawford, Catharine, and Stephen Kibble, ..	"	VII.	420
1765. Jan. 19.	Crawford, Elizabeth, and William McGear,..	"	IX.	24
1757. April 1.	Crawford, Euphæma, and Joseph Lowrey,..	"	I.	484
1760. Oct. 14.	Crawford, Jane, and James Denniston,.....	"	III.	361
1761. June 25.	Crawford, Jane, and John Wallace, ...	"	IV.	262
1759. Feb. 9.	Crawford, John, and Sarah Demilt,........	"	II.	186
1777. Oct. 21.	Crawford, Martha, and George Thomas,....	"	XXIV.	167
1772. Nov. 13.	Crawford, Martha, and John Duggen,......	"	XIX.	112
1770. Aug. 20.	Crawford, Mary, and Andrew Annan,......	"	XVI.	163
1763. Sept. 27.	Crawford, Sarah, and Robert Hogg,........	"	VII.	358
1773. June 11.	Crawford, Sidney, and Robert Lewis,......	"	XX.	146
1763. Jan. 21.	Crawford, Susannah and Underhill Horton,.	"	VII.	28
1761. Nov. 2.	Crawford, Thomas, and Sarah Carr,........	"	V.	186
1763. Nov. 18.	Crawford, William, and Anne Campbell,....	"	VII.	455
1782. Mar. 2.	Crawford, William, and Mary Ratoon,......	"	XXXV.	69
1761. April 16.	Crawley, John, and Catharine Sarle,.......	"	IV.	150

DATE.	NAMES.	RECORD.	VOL.	PAGE.
1765. May 30.	Crawley, John, and Catharine Van Zandt, ..	M. B.,	IX.	146
1767. Aug. 1.	Creamer, Belthazar, and Catherine McFall,..	"	XII.	7
1761. Jan. 28.	Creed, Elizabeth, and Peter Taylor,........	"	IV.	57
1783. Nov. 3.	Creed, William, and Anne Duryea,........	"	XL.	103
1759. Jan. 19.	Creed, William, and Elizabeth Pope,......	"	II.	162
1737. Oct. 13.	Creeger, Anne, and Asa King,............	"	I.	7
1771. April 13.	Creegier, Geertruy, and Peter Timoson,....	"	XVII.	56
1759. Oct. 3.	Creeland, Elizabeth, and Thomas Huxland,..	"	II.	446
1737. May 30.	Creeland, William, and Mary Jones,........	"	I.	6
1772. Oct. 21.	Cregeer, Catherine, and James McKenny,...	"	XIX.	83
1769. Nov. 9.	Cregier, Annetie, and Stofel Miller,........	"	XV.	85
1764. Nov. 12.	Cregier, Bastian, and Dericka Fisher,.......	"	VIII.	405
1764. Oct. 18.	Cregier, Hester, and Arent Van Antwerp,..	"	VIII.	361
1763. Mar. 24.	Cregier, John, and Margaret Post,.........	"	VII.	105
1765. Aug. 27.	Cregier, Martin, and Mary Blake,..........	"	IX.	245
1759. July 14.	Cregier, Thomas, and Elizabeth Post,......	"	II.	355
1753. Aug. 9.	Cregill, Elizabeth, and Hugh McColpen, ...	"	I.	87
1736. Nov. 26.	Creighton, Elizabeth, and William Rich,....	"	I.	3
1783. Oct. 2.	Creighton, Peter, and Elizabeth Ferdon,....	"	XL.	59
1782. Aug. 15.	Creman, Rosina, and Casper Barly,.........	"	XXXVI.	110
1760. Mar. 28.	Cremern, Sophia, and Johann Henrick Ernst Teutschbein, ...	"	III.	93
1758. Mar. 21.	Creson, Eleanor, and Waldron Blaau,......	"	I.	858
1759. April 18.	Crib, John, and Mary Smith,....	"	II.	245
1761. Sept. 28.	Cribble, George, and Frances Jones,........	"	V.	102
1737. Dec. 26.	Crieger, Margaret, and Burditt Pilkington Fleetwood,......................	"	L.	8
1758. Nov. 15.	Crigier, Bastean, and Maria Funda,........	"	II.	88
1771. Dec. 30.	Crillin, William, Jr., and Sarah Baker,......	"	XVII.	307
1759. Mar. 5.	Crim, Eve, and Andrew Merrell,..........	"	II.	208
1757. May 25.	Crisp, John, and Elizabeth Evans,.........	"	I.	542
1773. Nov. 3.	Cripeer, Harman, and Elizabeth Lawrence,..	"	XXII.	8
1769. Oct. 28.	Crippen, Reuben, and Geertie Brownly,....	"	XV.	71
1783. Aug. 6.	Crips, Lawrence, and Susannah Fountain,...	"	XXXIX.	114
1783. Sept. 15.	Crips, Mattew, and Anthony Fountain,.....	"	XL.	40
1762. July 19.	Crisp, Susannah, and John Baker,..........	"	VI.	245
1772. Mar. 21.	Crispel, Cornelius, and Geertje Roosa,......	"	XVIII.	56
1763. Nov. 9.	Crispel, Neeltje, and Tobias Van Steenberg,.	"	VII.	440
1775. Nov. 23.	Crispel, Petrus P., and Sarah Du Bois,.....	"	XXIII.	220
1760. Sept. 15.	Crispel, Rebecca, and John Trotter,........	"	III.	316
1762. Nov. 10.	Crispell, Peter, and Gerritje Du Bois,......	"	VI.	423
1775. Aug. 28.	Crist, Mary, and Henry Smith,............	"	XXIII.	139
1767. Sept. 1.	Cro, Mary, and John Corcilius,............	"	XII.	23
1769. May 8.	Crocheron, Abraham, and Margaret Gerritson,	"	XIV.	97
1769. April 25.	Crocheron, Henry, and Ann Decker,.......	"	XIV.	88

DATE.	NAMES.	RECORD.	VOL. PAGE.
1783. Mar. 29.	Crocheron, Jacob, and Ann Morgan, ...	M. B.,	xxxviii. 81
1770. Sept. 17.	Crocheron, John, and Jane Jones, ...	"	xvi. 188
1781. Dec. 22.	Crocker, Hannah, and Jesse Armstrong, ...	"	xxxiv. 100
1778. Mar. 28.	Crocker, Nathan, and Hanah Soper, ...	"	xxv. 54
1760. Nov. 13.	Croff, Jacob, and Mary Heysman, ...	"	iii. 409
1779. Mar. 24.	Crokatt, James, and Mary Kennedy, ...	"	xxvii. 76
1763. Jan. 3.	Crolius, Peter, and Mary Chambers, ...	"	vii. 5
1761. June 5.	Croll, John, and Jane Pendred, ...	"	iv. 197
1737. Sept. 6.	Cromline, Mary, and Guilian Verplank, ...	"	i. 7
1768. April 9.	Crommelin, Charles, and Sarah Fish, ...	"	xiii. 68
1780. Dec. 20.	Crommelin, James, and Julia Smith, ...	"	xxx. 161
1779. Dec. 24.	Cromwell, Oliver, and Margaret Bogart, ...	"	xxviii. 179
1783. June 7.	Cronin, Tady, and Catharine Wilcox, ...	"	xxxix. 46
1762. June 24.	Cronk, Abraham, and Wyntje Huff, ...	"	vi. 207
1768. June 27.	Cronk, Hercules, and Mary Lawrence, ...	"	xiii. 138
1764. May 16.	Crook, Cornelia, and Baltus Van Cleeck, ...	"	viii. 190
1764. Aug. 27.	Crook, Cornelia, and Gabriel W. Ludlow, . .	"	viii. 295
1773. Aug. 10.	Crook, Jane, and Leonard Van Cleeck, ...	"	xxi. 63
1773. May 31.	Crooke, Margaret, and Charles Inglis, ...	"	xx. 134
1761. Feb. 23.	Crooker, Anna, and Henry Burtis, ...	"	iv. 78
1770. June 12.	Crooker, Sampson, and Elizabeth Titus, ...	"	xvi. 109
1761. Dec. 21.	Crooker, Simeon, and Mary Kip, ...	"	v. 290
1762. April 14.	Crooker, William, and Ruth Valentine, ...	"	vi. 109
1758. Mar. 10.	Crooker, William, and Sarah Valentine, ...	"	i. 842
1762. Jan. 11.	Crooks, William, and Elizabeth McGinnis, . . .	"	vi. 7
1703. Oct. 17.	Crookshank, George, and Anne Maschalk, . .	"	xl. 04
1772. Nov. 9.	Crookshanks, Elizabeth, and James Gregg, . .	"	xix. 106
1765. Sept. 13.	Croos, Michael, and Phebe Baxter, ...	"	ix. 262
1779. Feb. 10.	Cropley, William, and Hannah Smith, ...	"	xxvii. 39
1757. Sept. 30.	Cropsey, Barbara, and Duncan Duffie, ...	"	i. 653
1778. Aug. 27.	Cropsy, Andrew, and Elizabeth Caspar, ...	"	xxvi. 14
1781. July 6.	Cropsy, Harman, and Ann Cowenhoven, . . .	"	xxxii. 105
1780. May 26.	Cropsy, William, and Jane Dennis, ...	"	xxix. 69
1799. Oct. 7.	Crosbey, John, and Rebecca Kelly, ...	"	xxviii. 105
1780. Nov. 22.	Crosby, George, and Martha Stevens, ...	"	xxx. 120
1768. Feb. 29.	Crosby, Hannah, and James Davis, ...	"	xiii. 46
1763. April 29.	Crosby, Jane, and Timothy Bussing, ...	"	vii. 154
1783. May 20.	Crosby, Milley, and George Collier, ...	"	xxxix. 21
1761. Aug. 18.	Crosby, Robert, and Elizabeth Tompkins, . . .	"	v. 48
1765. April 3.	Cross, Elizabeth, and Thomas Reynolds, ...	"	ix. 81
1762. Dec. 20.	Cross, Isabella, and James Fisher, ...	"	vi. 491
1772. Jan. 7.	Cross, John, and Jane Demilt, ...	"	xviii. 5
1763. June 21.	Cross, Martha, and Frederick Helmcan, ...	"	vii. 236
1736. Feb. 23.	Cross, Mary, and John Price, ...	"	i. 5
1762. Oct. 25.	Cross, Susanna, and Caleb Hudson, ...	"	vi. 383

DATE.	NAMES	RECORD.	VOL.	PAGE.
1777. July 23.	Cross, William, and Anne Ritchie,.........	M. B.,	XXIV.	120
1668. April 3.	Crosse, Jane, and James Woodward,......:	O. W. L.,	II.	223
1778. May 21.	Crossfield, Stephen, and Hanah Disbury,....	M. B.,	XXV.	90
1771. Dec. 12.	Crossley, Elizabeth, and Nicholas Flinn, ...	"	XVII.	291
1763. May 9.	Crossley, William, and Elizabeth Wooden,..	"	VII.	171
1766. June 12.	Crouscop, Anna B., and Daniel Hess,.......	"	X.	14
1763. Feb. 14.	Crout, Sarah, and John Dubois,...........	"	VII.	62
1760. Feb. 25.	Crouwn, Maria, and Francis Canner,.......	"	III.	47
1762. Mar. 18.	Crow, Mary, and Charles Prosser, Jr.,......	"	VI.	77
1757. Sept. 23.	Crow, Mary, and James Miller,............	"	I.	640
1772. Dec. 11.	Crowell, Joseph, and Sarah Chadwick,......	"	XIX.	153
1779. May 22.	Crowell, Thomas, and Esther Barron,......	"	XXVII.	143
1773. Dec. 9.	Crowl, Jane, and Robert Beaty,.........:...	"	XXII.	68
1757. Feb. 7.	Crown, James P., and Mary Kydney,......	"	I.	437
1781. Oct. 12.	Crowyer, Hannah, and Charles Stackhouse,.	"	XXXIII.	97
1758. May 3.	Cruchley, Magdalin, and Robert Place,.....	"	I.	892
1763. May 9.	Cruck, Charles C., Jr., and Jane Valkenburgh,	"	VII.	172
1780. Oct. 21.	Cruger, George, and Elizabeth Provost,.....	"	XXX.	75
1781. April 17.	Cruger, James, and Mary Smith,..........	"	XXXII.	7
1762. Nov. 25.	Cruger, John H., and Anne De Lancy,.....	"	VI.	454
1763. July 13.	Crukshank, George, and Catharine Muett,...	"	VII.	263
1760. July 19.	Crum, Elizabeth, and William Bates,.......	"	III.	221
1757. April 5.	Crusa, Cornelius, and Beletje De Groot,.....	"	I.	487
1779. July 19.	Cruzer, Mary, and John Simoson,.........	"	XXVIII.	24
1773. Sept. 29.	Crygier, Elizabeth, and Robert Harpur,.....	"	XXI.	125
1770. Nov. 7.	Crygier, Simon, and Elizabeth Rivers,......	"	XVI.	242
1771. Oct. 31.	Cubberley, Joseph, and Andry Jurney,.....	"	XVII.	235
1778. June 16.	Cubberly, Thomas, and Mary Mersereaw,...	"	XXV.	105
1777. Sept. 11.	Culford, Mary, and James McAlpine,.......	"	XXIV.	146
1759. April 2.	Cullin, Richard, and Lenah Bogert,........	"	II.	233
1768. April 5.	Cully, James, and Elizabeth Holmes,.......	"	XIII.	63
1765. July 20.	Culver, John, and Ann Onderdonck,.......	"	IX.	211
1773. Sept. 27.	Culver, John, and Hannah Stilwell,........:	"	XXI.	124
1753. Sept. 5.	Culver, Samuel, and Sarah Renny,.........	"	I.	105
1783. Aug. 23.	Cumberson, Jamima, and Samuel Loughead,	"	XL.	9
1759. Feb. 3.	Cumberson, Thomas, and Elizabeth Cornish,.	"	II.	205
1779. April 5.	Cumming, James, and Mary Williams,......	"	XXVII.	94
1780. Aug. 26.	Cumming, Margaret, and James Watson,...	"	XXX.	4
1757. May 12.	Cumming, William, and Margaret McAllister,	"	I.	529
1761. July 23.	Cumming, William, and Susannah Gregg,...	"	V.	6
1772. June 15.	Cummings, George, and Mary Giffin, ...	"	XVIII.	139
1781. July 7.	Cummings, Thomas, and Lucy Porter,......	"	XXXII.	107
1760. Dec. 5.	Cummins, Eve, and Benjamin Rosse,.......	"	XV.	114
1763. Aug. 18.	Cummins, Luke, and Mary Rowland,.......	"	VII.	305
1763. Jan. 25.	Cummins, Luke, and Rebecca Stivers,......	"	VII.	35

DATE.	NAMES.	RECORD.	VOL.	PAGE.
1775. Dec. 12.	Cummins, Margaret, and James Hanrahan,..	M. B.,	XXIII.	229
1769. Sept. 26.	Cummins, Robert, and Mary Ann Clowny,..	"	XV.	44
1768. Oct. 21.	Cumpton, Jane, and John Conway,........	"	XIII.	215
1781. Mar. 13.	Cunard, Robert, and Elizabeth Travis,......	"	XXXI.	70
1760. Sept. 18.	Cuning, David, and Ann Studdeford,.......	"	III.	319
1766. Dec. 24.	Cunningham, Andrew, and Catherine Shiels,	"	X.	207
1771. Oct. 16.	Cunningham, Francis, and Margaret Stimus- son,.................................	"	XVII.	212
1763. Mar. 25.	Cunningham, Grace, and Richard Mercer,...	"	VII.	106
1763. June 10.	Cunningham, James, and Sarah Hyer,......	"	VII.	222
1781. Mar. 21.	Cunningham, John, and Jane Parsons,......	"	XXXI.	80
1758. June 3.	Cunningham, Mary, and David Kelly,......	"	I.	922
1761. Jan. 2.	Cunningham, Mary, and John Jaison,......	"	IV.	2
1757. Sept. 24.	Cunningham, Sarah, and Gilbert McAdam,..	"	I.	636
1757. June 11.	Cunningham, Thomas, and Elizabeth Evouts,	"	I.	562
1760. Feb. 5.	Cunningham, William, and Elizabeth Noble,.	"	III.	22
1780. June 2.	Cunningham, William, and Nelly Gillespy,..	"	XXIX.	77
1768. April 11.	Cunnington, Rowland, and Jane Ellis,......	"	XIII.	71
1767. Sept. 1.	Curcilius, John, and Mary Cro,............	"	XII.	23
1736. May 13.	Curdee, William, and Bilikia Byvank,......	"	I.	1
1760. June 27.	Cure, John, and Margaret Scott,...........	"	IV.	266
1760. Nov. 13.	Cure, Walter, and Anne Longsword,.......	"	III.	407
1763. Oct. 10.	Cure, Walter, and Catharine Lawson,......	"	VII.	382
1762. Aug. 7.	Cure, Walter, and Elizabeth Lepinget,......	"	VI.	268
1762. July 17.	Cure, William, and Hannah Davis,.........	"	VI.	242
1704. Oct. 22.	Curnew, Ellzabeth, and John Nox,........	"	VIII.	368
1760. Jan. 25.	Curren, James, and Hannah Thornhill,.....	"	III.	7
1777. Jan. 21.	Curren, Mary, and John Hall,.............	"	XXIV.	17
1771. June 11.	Currie, Archibald, and Catherine Sebring,...	"	XVII.	109
1771. Nov. 1.	Currin, John, and Amelia Burns,..........	"	XVII.	237
1777. Aug. 20.	Curry, Elizabeth, and Charles Whitewood,..	"	XXIV.	137
1763. Mar. 16.	Curry, Elizabeth, and John Brandon,.......	"	VII.	101
1768. Jan. 13.	Curry, Jane, and David Gregg, ...	"	XIII.	7
1783. Mar. 8.	Curry, John, and Catharine Joseph,........	"	XXXVIII.	64
1780. Aug. 30.	Curry, John, and Margaret Scadden,.......	"	XXX.	9
1763. Jan. 20.	Curry, Margaret, and David Lion,.........	"	VII.	26
1773. Oct. 28.	Curry, Mary, and James McMullen,........	"	XXII.	4
1758. April 22.	Cursa, Isaac, and Sarah Frankland,........	"	I.	882
1753. Sept. 11.	Curser, Jane, and Abraham Lent,..........	"	I.	114
1776. May 2.	Curshouw, Mary, and Barent Bloom,.......	"	XXIII.	305
1767. Mar. 2.	Curson, Rebecha, and William Seton,......	"	XI.	37
1772. Jan. 9.	Cursong, Jemima, and Patrick Burk,.......	"	XX.	6
1755. Aug. 28.	Curtenius, Peter T., and Catharin Golet,....	"	I.	159
1756. Dec. 15.	Curtine, Francis, and Sarah Secord,........	"	I.	384
1783. April 11.	Curtis, Effee, and Isaac Atkin,............	"	XXXVIII.	91

DATE.	NAMES.	RECORD.	VOL.	PAGE.
1779. Mar. 31.	Curtis, John, and Ann Crawford,..........	M. B.,	XXVII.	88
1761. May 18.	Curtis, John, and Mary Studdeford,........	"	IV.	194
1783. May 31.	Curtis, Margaret, and Ahasuerus Garbrance,.	"	XXXIX.	34, 35
1762. Sept. 14.	Curtis, Robert, and Jemima Beeckman,.....	"	VI.	316
1779. April 10.	Curtis, William, and Margaret Wytt,.......	"	XXVII.	102
1780. May 3.	Curtis, William, and Sarah Beedle,........	"	XXIX.	43
1763. Dec. 8.	Cutler, Hannah, and Thomas Barlow,......	"	VII.	500
1781. Oct. 21.	Cutler, Jane, and Gamaliel Huff,...........	"	XXXIV.	2
1762. Oct. 27.	Cuttant, Zacharias, and Hannah Cabiner,...	"	VI.	388
1762. Mar. 2.	Cuyler, Abraham, and Catharin Wendell,...	"	VI.	72
1764. Mar. 5.	Cuyler, Abraham, and Jane Glen,..........	"	VIII.	93
1768. May 2.	Cuyler, Abraham N., and Margaret Wandell,	"	XIII.	89
1736. Aug. 5.	Cuyler, Catrina, and Jacob Ten Eyck,......	"	I.	2
1763. Jan. 10.	Cuyler, Cornelius, and Anne Wandell,......	"	VII.	13
1770. July 21.	Cuyler, Elizabeth, and Johannes Beekman,..	"	XVI.	143
1760. April 19.	Cuyler, Elsie, and Augustus Van Cortlandt,.	"	III.	115
1755. Oct. 15.	Cuyler, Else, and Barent Ten Eyck,........	"	I.	194
1760. Dec. 6.	Cuyler, Harmanus, and Mary Marcelus,.....	"	III.	463
1771. Nov. 22.	Cuyler, Hermanus, and Elizabeth Van Bergen,	"	XVII.	263
1770. April 10.	Cuyler, Hester, and Leonard Ganswoort, ...	"	XVI.	56
1764. Feb. 27.	Cuyler, Jacob, and Lydia Van Veghten,....	"	VIII.	94
1763. June 15.	Cuyler, John, and Susanna Van Patten,....	"	VII.	228
1757. Sept. 17.	Cuyler, Philip, and Sarah Tweedy,.........	"	I.	635
1766. Oct. 24.	Cuyper, Lambert, and Ann Van Voorhuyse,.	"	X.	139
1762. May 2.	Cypher, Allada, and Jacob Ferdon,........	"	VI.	156
1783. Oct. 30.	Cyrus, Lydia, and Joseph Mott,.......... .	"	XL.	94

D.

1783. Oct. 24.	Daft, Thomas, and Mary Fowler,..........	"	XL.	90
1782. Dec. 19.	Dailey, Owen, and Sarah Lavarrah,........	"	XXXVII.	127
1783. Mar. 31.	Dailley, Elizabeth, and John Collin,........	"	XXXVIII.	83
1761. Sept. 28.	Daldridge, Mary, and John Baldwin,.......	"	V.	101
1779. Sept. 18.	Dale, Elizabeth, and Thomas Bolton,.......	"	XXVIII.	80
1780. May 8.	Dale, Robert, and Alatha Heath,..........	"	XXIX.	50
1777. July 8.	Dalcury, Judith, and Patrick Dooly,........	"	XXIV.	116
1757. Dec. 14.	Dalley, Catharine, and Nicholas Anthony,..	"	I.	742
1757. Nov. 30.	Dalley, Elizabeth, and Samuel Francis,.....	"	I.	719
1767. July 4.	Dalley, Gifford, and Anna Pettit,..........	"	XI.	123
1756. Nov. 25.	Dalley, Sarah, and Walter Broek,..........	"	I.	364
1780. April 21.	Dally, Ann, and William Ross,............	"	XXIX.	31
1756. Sept. 4.	Dally, Catherine, and William Salter,.......	"	I.	284
1773. Mar. 23.	Dally, Christiana, and William Depeyster,...	"	XX.	67
1783. Oct. 17.	Dally, John, and Anne Pearson,...........	"	XL.	83

DATE.	NAMES.	RECORD.	VOL.	PAGE.
1668. Aug. 11.	Dally, John, and Elizabeth Ober, ...	O. W. L.,	II.	223
1779. July 27.	Dally, Philip, and Charity Hunt, ...	M. B.,	XXVIII.	30
1780. Jan. 15.	Dallzal, Edward, and Rebecca Carell, ...	"	XXVIII.	197
1783. April 16.	Dalton, John, and Hannah Brashier, ...	"	XXXVIII.	98
1769. Feb. 16.	Dalton, Walter, and Frances Greenoak, ...	"	XIV.	36
16⅛⁰₈₁. Mar. 12.	Damerill, Elizabeth, and Joseph Ellis, ...	O. W.,	XXXII½.	37
1738. June 13.	Dandy, William, and Margaret McClain, ...	M. B.,	I.	9
1760. Feb. 14.	Dane, James, and Agnes Choulwell, ...	"	III.	39
1770. Dec. 3.	Daniel, Ann May, and John Allen, ...	"	XVI.	280
1779. Sept. 18.	Daniel, John, and Elizabeth Blank, ...	"	XXVIII.	81
1759. Sept. 7.	Daniels, Mary Magdelena, and Charles Wildungen, ...	"	II.	413
1766. Sept. 18.	Daniels, Maria Magdalena, and George Hinnel Burger, ...	"	X.	100
1781. May 15.	Danils, James, and Jane Degroat, ...	"	XXXII.	47
1770. Nov. 23.	Dannels, Annatie, and John Cole, ...	"	XVI.	266
1782. Nov. 9.	Darby, Christopher, and Ruth Wanton, ...	"	XXXVII.	76
1775. July 5.	Darby, Daniel, and Elizabeth Branson, ...	"	XXIII.	85
1783. Sept. 2.	Darby, Theodocia, and James Prior, ...	"	XL.	19
1760. Feb. 14.	Darcey, Elener, and William Hague, ...	"	III.	40
1759. Nov. 16.	Darcey, Mary, and Thomas Humphreys, ...	"	II.	498
1757. April 22.	Darcy, Augustin, and Elinor Nicolls, ...	"	I.	509
1769. June 30.	Darcy, Penelopy, and John Dealing, Jr., ...	"	XIV.	138
1783. Mar. 4.	Darcy, Thomas, and Ann Nellson, ...	"	XXXVIII.	62
1675. July 16.	Darkins, Robert, and Christian Stevenson, ..	W. O. P.,	III.	124
1762. June 25.	Darling, Aaron, and Catherine Amey, ...	M. B.,	VI.	208
1778. Mar. 9.	Dart, John, and Ursula Lee, ...	"	XXV.	37
1781. Aug. 18.	Dartey, Penelopey, and Philip Kissick, ...	"	XXXIII.	41
1753. July 4.	Daryea, Anne, and Cornelius Van Kleef, ...	"	I.	70
1770. Oct. 23.	Dash, Elizabeth, and Meads Brasier, ...	"	XVI.	227
1782. Oct. 12.	Dash, Hannah, and Daniel Bowie, ...	"	XXXVII.	40
1778. Dec. 23.	Dash, John B., and Mary Warner, ...	"	XXVI.	131
1780. May 1.	Dash, Lucretia, and Peter Ritton, ...	"	XXIX.	39
1782. April 15.	Dash, Mary, and John Gassner, ...	"	XXXV.	123
1779. May 29.	Dashwood, Francis, and Ann Ludlow, ...	"	XXVII.	150
1782. Aug. 20.	Date, Samuel, and Sarah Wheat, ...	"	XXXVI.	115
1767. May 11.	Dater, Henry, and Maria Hollenbake, ...	"	XI.	81
1769. Dec. 23.	Daubeny, Lloyd, and Mary Caulder, ...	"	XV.	131
1760. July 23.	Daunt, Francis, and Mary Walker, ...	"	III.	224
1771. Oct. 23.	Davenport, Anna, and John Grosbeeck, ...	"	XVII.	218
1773. Aug. 12.	Davenport, John, and Elizabeth Mekeel, ...	"	XXI.	67
1770. Jan. 4.	Davenport, Martha, and Charles Hewlett, ...	"	XVI.	3
1737. Aug. 16.	Davenport, Mary, and Jacobus Heneon, ...	"	I.	7
1779. Oct. 4.	Davenport, Mary, and Richard Rosamond, ..	"	XXVIII.	100
1774. Feb. 10.	Davenport, Newberry, and Elizabeth Hewlett,	"	XXII.	126

13

DATE.	NAMES.	RECORD.	VOL.	PAGE.
1781. May 19.	Davenport, Samuel, and Hester Oakley,....	M. B.,	XXXII.	54
1763. July 28.	Davenport, Thomas, and Sarah Leanerback,.	"	VII.	284
1771. May 18.	Davidson, John, and Margaret Barber,......	"	XVII.	86
1782. Aug. 10.	Davidson, Peter, and Deborah Purdy,......	"	XXXVI.	104
1780. April 18.	Davie, Adam, and Jane Warren, ...	"	XXIX.	27
1759. May 5.	Davine, William, and Elizabeth Neazer,.....	"	II.	268
1761. July 28.	Davis, Abraham, and Elizabeth Hutchison,..	"	V.	14
1781. July 20.	Davis, Ann, and Peter McLean,...........	"	XXXIII.	11
1753. June 8.	Davis, Benjamin, and Elizabeth Viscount,...	"	I.	53
1736. June 12.	Davis, Benjamin, and Hendrica Gebrink,....	"	I.	1
1781. Oct. 11.	Davis, Catharine, and Ephraim Harvey,....	"	XXXIII.	96
1782. Jan. 21.	Davis, Caturah, and Joseph Tucker,........	"	XXXV.	26
1769. Mar. 15.	Davis, David, and Ruth Gildersleeve,.......	"	XIV.	53
1762. Nov. 26.	Davis, Edward, and Jane Durette,.........	"	VI.	455
1765. Oct. 3.	Davis, Elizabeth, and John Nixon,.........	"	IX.	289
1782. Aug. 26.	Davis, Elizabeth, and Philip Douglas,.......	"	XXXVI.	124
1765. April 2.	Davis, Francis, and Joseph Fairley,........	"	IX.	79
1775. May 20.	Davis, Hester, and Jacob Chambers,........	"	XXIII.	41
1775. May 10.	Davis, Hester, and Robert Noxon,.........	"	XXIII.	28
1762. July 17.	Davis, Hannah, and William Cure,........	"	VI.	242
1778. July 20.	Davis, Henry, and Ann Springall-Jones,....	"	XXV.	135
1763. Nov. 26.	Davis, Isaac, and Mary Marsh,............	"	VII.	475
1770. Nov. 27.	Davis, Jacob, and Hannah Wedge,.........	"	XVI.	272
1768. Feb. 29.	Davis, James, and Hannah Crosby,........	"	XIII.	46
1762. April 22.	Davis, James, and Johanna Roe,...........	"	VI.	127
1759. Mar. 15.	Davis, Jane, and Garret Broadhead,........	"	II.	217
1772. Feb. 1.	Davis, Jane, and William Ferguson,........	"	XVIII	26
1759. Mar. 28.	Davis, Jane, and William Fitz Gerald,......	"	II.	227
1764. Oct. 12.	Davis, Jane, and William Hoare,..........	"	VIII.	354
1771. July 5.	Davis, John, and Ann Caw,...............	"	XVII.	128
1771. Aug. 8.	Davis, John, and Baushe Van Valkenburgh,.	"	XVII.	155
1761. July 9.	Davis, John, and Cicely Conner,...........	"	IV.	292a
1777. April 15.	Davis, John, and Elizabeth Smith,.........	"	XXIV.	62
1761. Oct. 27.	Davis, John, and Elizabeth Walker,........	"	V.	172
1763. Jan. 17.	Davis, John, and Lena Post,..............	"	VII.	17
1782. Aug. 8.	Davy, John, and Martha Kirk,............	"	XXXVI.	103
1759. June 30.	Davis, John, and Mary Williams,..........	"	II.	343
1766. Dec. 12.	Davis, Kessia, and Elijah Wickes, ...	"	X.	202
1757. Nov. 17.	Davis, Mary, and Edmond Kingsland,......	"	I.	705
1770. Dec. 31.	Davis, Mary, and Peter Cassety,...........	"	XVI.	310
1760. July 16.	Davis, Mary, and Peter Sanderson,.... ...	"	III.	214
1779. Nov. 10.	Davis, Mary, and Shadrick Wragden,......	"	XXVIII.	135
1780. Oct. 19.	Davis, Mary, and Thomas Burnton,........	"	XXX.	72
1757. April 27.	Davis, Mary, and Zephaniah Platt,.........	"	I.	516
1781. Feb. 7.	Davis, Rachael, and George Knight,........	"	XXXI.	42

DATE.	NAMES.	RECORD.	VOL.	PAGE.
1771. Aug. 31.	Davis, Rachael, and Moses Patterson,.......	M. B.,	XVII.	170
1757. Sept. 5.	Davis, Richard, and Frances Lewis,........	"	I.	632
1766. Nov. 17.	Davis, Robert, and Catherine Stilwell,......	"	X.	168
1781. July 29.	Davis, Ruth, and Jabez Norton,...........	"	XXXIII.	21
1783. May 29.	Davis, Sarah, and Thomas Hanly,..........	"	XXXIX.	28
1756. Nov. 27.	Davis, William, and Hester Ally,..........	"	I.	365
1781. Dec. 3.	Davison, Ann, and Samuel Taylor,.........	"	XXXIV.	69
1765. Mar. 4.	Davison, Thomas, and Catherine McFargie,.	"	IX.	61
1782. Oct. 8.	Dawkings, Edward, and Sarah Talmage,....	"	XXXVII.	36
1777. Feb. 9.	Dawkins, Edward, and Ann House,........	"	XXIV.	27
1762. Dec. 17.	Dawsey, Eleanor, and John Knowles,......	"	VI.	485
1758. June 3.	Dawson, Boswell, and Phebe Pell,.........	"	I.	923
1760. Nov. 3.	Dawson, Eleanor, and John Surman,.......	"	III.	393
1766. Oct. 14.	Dawson, Elizabeth, and Jacobus Van Norden,	"	X.	123
1778. July 23.	Dawson, Harriet, and Thomas McDonough,.	"	XXV.	139
1763. June 15.	Dawson, Henry, and Catharine Kemper,...	"	VII.	229
1775. April 11.	Dawson, Rachel, and John Reeves,........	"	XXIII.	6
1764. Feb. 28.	Dawson, Richard, and Elizabeth Van Norden,	"	VIII.	58
1778. Mar. 6.	Dawson, Thomas, and Lena Magee,........	"	XXVIII.	216
1760. Dec. 15.	Dawson, Volkert, and Gertrey Denison,....	"	III.	474
1738. June 23.	Dawson, William, and Elizabeth Read,.....	"	I.	10
1783. Aug. 29.	Dawson, William, and Lydia Hallett,.......	"	XL.	14
173⅞. Jan. 5.	Day, Abraham, and Jonaca Ellis,..........	"	I.	5
1758. Sept. 21.	Day, Babary, and John Storm,............	"	II.	30
1783. June 19.	Day, Catharine, and Peter Roome,.........	"	XXXIX.	63
1753. Sept. 8.	Day, Dorothy, and James Jacklin,........	"	I.	111
1780. Dec. 4.	Day, Fanny, and Richard Smyth,..........	"	XXX.	137
1772. May 26.	Day, Jane, and Francis Downman,.........	"	XVIII.	125
1757. Nov. 4.	Day, Jane, and Francis Moore,............	"	I.	696
1777. Sept. 10.	Day, John, and Abigail Carman,...........	"	XXIV.	144
1774. Feb. 19.	Day, Joseph, and Anne Hale,.............	"	XXII.	131
1759. Mar. 26.	Day, Mary, and Jacobus Quick,...........	"	II.	225
1762. Oct. 6.	Day, Mary, and John Waller,.............	"	VI.	349
1759. April 27.	Day, Mary, and Peter Stymets, ...	"	II.	257
1757. Feb. 19.	Day, Richard, and Jane Collins,...........	"	I.	443
1781. Oct. 19.	Day, Sarah, and John Ward,..............	"	XXXIII.	110
1783. July 26.	Day, Sarah, and William Miller,...........	"	XXXIX.	101
1764. Oct. 19.	Day, William, and Adriana Hoghland,......	"	VIII.	364
1781. Mar. 17.	Dayley, Mary, and Jacob Myabrush,.......	"	XXXI.	73
1772. Mar. 25.	Dayly, John, and Mary Miller,............	"	XVIII.	58
1763. Nov. 14.	Dayton, Philathea, and Benjamin Gerrard,..	"	VII.	448
1666. May 14.	Dayton, Samuel, and Mary Dingle,........	O. W. L.,	II.	134
1767. Feb. 24.	Deacon, Elizabeth, and Robert Hargrave,...	M. B.,	XI.	24
1770. Sept. 21.	Deacon, Elsie, and Thomas Balderston,.....	"	XVI.	194
1782. Mar. 27.	Deacon, Jane, and Thomas Murray,........	"	XXXV.	98

DATE.	NAMES.	RECORD.	VOL.	PAGE.
1770. Dec. 15.	Deads, Susannah, and Arthur Hallowell,....	M. B.,	XVI.	296
1777. Dec. 31.	Deakin, John, and Jane Berrien,..........	"	XXIV.	211
1767. Feb. 18.	Deal, Ann, and John Michael..............	"	XI.	29
1759. Jan. 19.	Deal, Catherine, and Jacob Tremper,.......	"	II.	159
1783. May 26.	Deal, Lucretia, and William Frazer,........	"	XXXIX.	25
1757. Oct. 8.	Deal, Robert, and Cretje Mutlow,..........	"	I.	664
1774. Jan. 18.	Deal, Robert, and Elizabeth Lambert,......	"	XXII.	105
1758. April 19.	Deal, Samuel, and Elizabeth Arthur,.......	"	I.	877
1738. Aug. 11.	Dealing, Benjamin, and Elizabeth Freedenbergh,..............................	"	I.	10
1769. June 30.	Dealing, John, Jr., and Penelope Darcy,....	"	XIV.	138
1778. Sept. 12.	Deall, Jane, and John Nicoll,..............	"	XXVI.	28
1782. May 11.	Deall, Samuel, and Sarah Lawrence,.......	"	XXXV.	160
1782. Dec. 6.	Dean, Alexander, and Anne Willis,........	"	XXXVII.	108
1781. Jan. 1.	Dean, Bridget, and James Hallett,.........	"	XXXI.	2
1782. April 8.	Dean, Elizabeth, and Joseph Morris,.......	"	XXXV.	118
1765. July 3.	Dean, George, and Ann Van Deursen,......	"	IX.	192
1766. Aug. 23.	Dean, John, and Bridget Willing,..........	"	X.	83
1775. June 16.	Dean, Rhoda, and William Power,.........	"	XXIII.	66
1773. May 12.	Dean, Stewart, and Pyeterte Bratt,........	"	XX.	109
1767. Aug. 13.	Dean, William, and Adriantie Debevoise,...	"	XII.	15
1771. Oct. 14.	Deane, Ann, and Robert Johnston,........	"	XVII.	205
1780. Aug. 2.	Deane, Ann, and William Wade,..........	"	XXIX.	132
1783. Nov. 11.	Deane, Robert, and Margaret Morgan,......	"	XL.	111
1772. Mar. 28.	Deane, William, and Horiantia Lattin,......	"	XVIII.	63
1762. Mar. 22.	Dear, Anne, and Albert Cole,....	"	VI.	81
1782. Dec. 3.	Deas, James, and Elizabeth Straton, ...	"	XXXVII.	105
1777. Mar. 23.	Deas, John, and Rosanna Taylor,..........	"	XXIV.	50
1777. May 19.	Deas, Mary, and Robert Henderson,.......	"	XXIV.	90
1759. Mar. 29.	De Baan, Joast, and Jennetje Dyckman,....	"	II.	228
1765. May 24.	De Baen, Joseph, and Ghertje Durye,......	"	IX.	138
1770. Dec. 13.	De Beavois, Anne, and Philip Brant,.......	"	XVI.	293
1775. May 2.	De Beavois, Catharina, and John Boskirk,...	"	XXIII.	21
1757. Dec. 13.	Debeavois, Jacobus, and Marytje Cook,.....	"	I.	739
1770. Aug. 4.	De Beavois, Johannes, and Ariantje Remsen,	"	XVI.	159
1765. Aug. 1.	De Beavois, John, and Sarah Rapalje, ...	"	IX.	226
1762. Oct. 13.	De Beavois, Joost, and Elizabeth Vanderbilt,	"	VI.	360
1782. Nov. 29.	De Beveoise, George, and Anne Vanauly, ..	"	XXXVII.	97
1763. Nov. 18.	De Bevoes, Ida, and John Godfrey Miller,..	"	VII.	454
1782. May 24.	De Bevoice, Jacobus, and Lette Rapelyea,..	"	XXXVI.	22
1761. Mar. 9.	De Bevois, Angeltie, and Isaac De Graw,...	"	IV.	93
1776. Jan. 27.	De Bevois, Ann, and Andrew Van Alen,...	"	XXIII.	255
1762. Nov. 4.	De Bevois, Charles, and Nieltie De Bevois,..	"	VI.	410
1761. July 1.	De Bevois, Charles, and Sarah Bennet,.....	"	IV.	271
1760. Aug. 20.	De Bevois, Ida, and Fernandus Suydam,....	"	III.	261

DATE.	NAMES.	RECORD.	VOL.	PAGE.
1736. April 13.	De Bevois, Jacobus, Jr., and Marietia Van Housen,	M. B.,	I.	1
1783. Sept. 13.	De Bevois, Jane, and Isaac Rapalye,	"	XL.	38
1775. Nov. 18.	De Bevois, John, and Jane Beagle,	"	XXIII.	217
1758. Sept. 6.	De Bevois, Margareta, and Peter Calyer,	"	II.	5
1782. Sept. 21.	De Be Vois, Maria, and Basil Jackson,	"	XXXVII.	5
1766. June 23.	Debevois, Mary, and Garret Vandine,	"	X.	24
1768. Nov. 12.	Debevois, Mary, and Thomas Stilwell,	"	XIII.	234
1762. Nov. 4.	De Bevois, Nieltie, and Charles De Bevois,	"	VI.	410
1767. Aug. 13.	Debevoise, Adriantie, and William Dean,	"	XII.	15
1766. July 31.	De Bevoise, George, and Nelly Schenck,	"	X.	67
1777. Aug. 11.	Deblois, George, Jr., and Lydia Scott,	"	XXIV.	130
1763. April 25.	De Bois, Cornelius, and Sarah De Bois,	"	VII.	139
1763. April 25.	De Bois, Deborah, and Tunis De Bois,	"	VII.	140
1773. April 8.	De Bois, Leah, and Christor Kiersted,	"	XX.	88
1760. Oct. 10.	De Bois, Peter, and Mary Van Voorhees,	"	III.	358
1763. April 25.	De Bois, Sarah, and Cornelius De Bois,	"	VII.	139
1763. April 25.	De Bois, Tunis, and Deborah De Bois,	"	VII.	140
1767. May 25.	Debonrepose, John, and Mary Hayse,	"	XI.	96
1736. May 28.	De Booyff, Catherine, and Robert Brett,	"	I.	1
1763. Dec. 7.	Debow, Elizabeth, and John Stevens,	"	VII.	495
1763. Sept. 30.	De Bow, John, Jr., and Mary Elsworth,	"	VII.	364
1770. Dec. 15.	Deboys, John, and Catherine Cooper,	"	XVI.	298
1762. Aug. 26.	De Bratt, Anthony, and Maria Veeder,	"	VI.	289
1766. June 23.	Debratt, Peter, and Froutie Arehart,	"	X.	27
1766. June 27.	Decker, Abraham, and Phebe Wood,	"	X.	34
1764. Jan. 27.	Decker, Alice, and David Tysen,	"	VIII.	40
1769. April 25.	Decker, Ann, and Henry Crokeron,	"	XIV.	88
1783. Sept. 25.	Decker, Benjamin, and Mary Simonson,	"	XL.	53
1768. April 18.	Decker, Catherina, and Daniel Graham,	"	XIII.	81
1779. June 7.	Decker, Charles, and Mary Beagle,	"	XXVII.	159
1766. June 24.	Decker, Cornelious, and Elizabeth Decker,	"	X.	30
1762. May 13.	Decker, Cornelius, and Elizabeth Van Wagenen,	"	VI.	160
1766. June 24.	Decker, Elizabeth, and Cornelious Decker,	"	X.	30
1783. Nov. 10.	Decker Elizabeth, and John Barbank,	"	XL.	110
1759. Aug. 8.	Decker, Esther, and Isaac Decker,	"	II.	379
1778. Dec. 16.	Decker, Isaac, and Elly Burbank,	"	XXVI.	124
1759. Aug. 8.	Decker, Isaac, and Esther Decker,	"	II.	379
1762. Jan. 21.	Decker, Jacob, and Sarah Simonson,	"	VI.	20
1768. Oct. 1.	Decker, Johanis, and Annatje Hasbrouck,	"	XIII.	202
1762. Dec. 7.	Decker, John, and Elizabeth Beagle,	"	VI.	470
1755. Aug. 5.	Decker, John, and Jamima Simmons,	"	I.	143
1773. May 29.	Decker, Mary, and Obadiah Jones,	"	XX.	133
1764. Mar. 16.	Decker, Mathew, and Catharine Jones,	"	VIII.	106

DATE.	NAMES.	RECORD.	VOL. PAGE.
1767. Jan. 7.	Decker, Mathew, and Elizabeth Graham,. .	M. B.,	XI. 3
1764. April 26.	Decker, Mathew, and Elizabeth Pew,......	"	VIII. 171
1757. Feb. 11.	Decker, Mathew, and Else Dupuy,.........	"	I. 438
1773. July 5.	Decker, Richard, aad Wyntie Merrill,.....	"	XXI. 31
1773. Nov. 25.	Decker, Susanna, and John Morgan,.......	"	XXII. 44
1738. Oct. 23.	Deckers, Maria, and Johannis De Latneter,..	"	I. 11
1769. May 5.	De Clark, Jemima, and Daniel Morrell,.....	"	XIV. 94
1763. April 9.	De Clark, Mary, and Peter Lent,..........	"	VII. 120
1766. Dec. 8.	De Clarke, James, and Ellinor Talman,.....	"	X. 195
1764. Nov. 22.	De Clarke, Maritie, and Hendrick Nagle,...	"	VIII. 414
1758. Jan. 28.	Decline, Mary, and Neal Shaw,..........,.	"	I. 805
1763. Sept 30.	De Clous, John, and Margaret Barron,......	"	VII. 363
1639. Sept. 22.	De Conine, Thomas, and Maritje Frans Van Beets, ...	A. R.,	II. 67
1767. Mar. 14.	De Conty, Peter, and Esther Row, ...	M. B.,	XI. 45
1763. Sept. 21.	De Costa, Manuel, and Mary Moore, ...	"	VII. 347
1769. June 2.	Deeds, Soloman, and Susannah Pitts,.......	"	XIV. 113
1762. April 22.	Deeker, Eve, and Edmund Christopher,.....	"	VI. 123
1781. May 15.	Deere, John, and Mary Roach,............	"	XXXII. 48
1736. Oct. 16.	Deffriest, Nicholas, and Mary Barker, .·....	"	I. 3
1765. Oct. 31.	De Fonda, Isaac, and Rebecca Groesbeck,...	"	IX. 342
1758. Nov. 29.	De Foreest, Ann, and James Wells,........	"	II. 108
1767. July 17.	De Foreest, Bernard, and Martha Albouy,..	"	XI. 136
1759. Feb. 5.	De Foreest, Catlinetie, and Theophilus Cossart, ...	"	II. 177
1770. May 3.	Deforeest, David, and Elizabeth Witbeek,...	"	XVI. 77
1764. Feb. 16.	Deforeest, Eleanor, and Thomas Lansing,...	"	VIII. 52
1783. May 3.	Deforeest, John, and Hannah Vanhorne, ...	"	XXXVIII. 124
1775. Aug. 1.	Deforeest, Leah, and Johannis De Graaf,....	"	XXIII. 116
1773. Sept. 25.	De Foreest, Martha, and Nathaniel Harriot,.	"	XXI. 121
1775. May 1.	Deforeest, Peter, and Piertje Van Alstyne,..	"	XXIII. 19
1759. Aug. 1.	Deforeest, Sarah, and William Hun,........	"	II. 369
1761. April 28.	Deforeest, Simon, and Mary McGinnis,.....	"	IV. 170
1779. Jan. 27.	Deforeest, Theodorus, and Susannah Leggett,	"	XXVII. 29
1763. June 21.	Deforeest, Wouter, and Alida Bradt,.......	"	VII. 237
1759. May 11.	Deforest, Caroline, and Richard King,......	"	II. 278
1758. Sept. 12.	De Forest, Catherine, and Anthony Danjelse Brat, ...	"	II. 15
1780. Dec. 20.	Deforest, Jane, and George Scott,.........	"	XXX. 160
1764. June 8.	De Forreest, Catlyna, and Christian Dovebagh,	"	VIII. 219
1768. Sept. 20.	Deforrest, John, and Jane Albony, ...	"	XIII. 191
1766. Sept. 27.	Deforrest, Mary, and Hendrick Mercelis,....	"	X. 113
1776. April 18.	Deforrest, Rebecca, and Ryneer Van Avery,	"	XXIII. 297
1778. Aug. 8.	Deforrest, Theodorus, and Mary Doughty, ..	"	XXV. 144
1761. Jan. 29.	Defoue, Magdalen, and Jeremiah Schurman,.	"	IV. 39

Date.	Names.	Record.	Vol.	Page.
1773. Oct. 20.	De Freeze, Maria, and Joseph Dowers, ...	M. B.,	xxi.	145
1764. Feb. 20.	Defrizee, Maritje, and William Mumbrote, . . .	"	viii.	65
1738. April 29.	De Froseest, Famitic, and Benjamin Stout, . .	"	i.	9
1764. Feb. 6.	De Garemo, Mathew, and Maritje Groesbeek,	"	viii.	49
1758. April 26.	De Garmo, Jacob, and Fytje Becker, ...	"	i.	886
1763. Dec. 31.	De Garmo, John, and Susannah Hogan, ...	"	vii.	530
1765. Aug. 27.	De Garmo, Sarah, and Garret Van Ness, ...	"	ix.	246
1783. Aug. 10.	D'Gironwurt, Charles, and Elizabeth Corne, .	"	xxxix.	121
1756. Oct. 5.	De Graaf, Burwine, and Elizabeth Teller, . . .	"	i.	317
1765. Jan. 29.	De Graaf, Catharine, and William Nixon, . . .	"	ix.	34
1765. Mar. 28.	De Graaf, Johanna, and James Wyness, ...	"	ix.	75
1775. Aug. 1.	De Graaf, Johannes, and Leah Deforest, ...	"	xxiii.	116
1769. Nov. 9.	De Graaff, Jeremiah, and Hannah Quackenboss, ...	"	xv.	84
1763. Oct. 26.	De Graff, John, and Rebecca Van Vrancken,	"	vii.	403
1763. Sept. 2.	De Graff, Sarah, and John Steenbergh, ...	"	vii.	323
1764. Oct. 22.	De Graugh, Catherine, and Martinus Ryerse,	"	viii.	367
1753. April 11.	De Grauw, Garret, Jr., and Hannah Parcel, . .	"	i.	21
1765. June 27.	De Grauw, Walter, and Catharine Ackerman,	"	ix.	185
1783. Feb. 10.	De Graw, Catherine, and Thomas Carr, ...	"	xxxviii.	39
1761. Mar. 9.	Degraw, Isaac, and Angeltie De Bevois, ...	"	iv.	93
1779. Jan. 7.	Degraw, Mary, and Jonas Henry Allamand, .	"	xxvii.	4
1769. May 15.	Degray, Susannah, and Samuel Page, ...	"	xiv.	101
1762. July 15.	De Gree, Doshy, and Richard Edwards, ...	"	vi.	238
1770. July 31.	Degree, Sarah, and William Jacobs, ...	"	xvi.	151
1779. Mar. 17.	De Grey, Hannah, and Littleton Ford, ...	"	xxvii.	00
1781. May 15.	Degroat, Jane, and James Danils, ...	"	xxxii.	47
1773. Oct. 11.	De Groet, Andries, and Ava Swert, ...	"	xxi.	139
1777. Oct. 11.	De Groet, Simon, and Annate Swart, ...	"	xxi.	138
1738. Sept. 4.	De Groets, Staats, and Catherine Van Buskerks,	"	i.	11
1767. June 26.	De Groff, Mary, and Myndert Van Kleeck, . .	"	xi.	114
1764. Oct. 1.	De Groff, Sarah, and Benjamin Rivers, ...	'	viii.	329
1757. April 5.	De Groot, Beletje, and Cornelius Crusa, ...	"	i.	487
1779. Mar. 29.	De Groot, Charity, and Jacob Mersereau, . . . ,	"	xxvii.	82
1763. Dec. 23.	De Groot, Garret, and Elias Slow, ...	"	vii.	522
1763. Feb. 24.	De Groot, Hannah, and Walter Wood, ...	"	vii.	78
1776. Jan. 4.	De Groot, Joseph, and Catharine Cardell, . . .	"	xxiii.	240
1761. Jan. 30.	Degroot, Rachel, and Peter Roome, ...	"	iv.	234
1766. June 24.	Degroot, Robert, and Elizabeth Bush, ...	"	x.	29
1769. July 1.	Degroote, Joseph, and Elizabeth Doran, ...	"	xiv.	140
1763. Mar. 14.	De Grot, John, and Mary Haslet, ...	"	vii.	97
1757. Aug. 20.	Degrote, Mary, and Nicholas Brewer, ...	"	i.	618
1760. Mar. 5.	Degrott, John, and Susannah Rome, ...	"	iii.	63
1769. July 10.	Degrove, Adolph., Jr., and Rhoda Coles, ...	"	xiv.	147
1780. Dec. 7.	Degrove, Elizabeth, and Charles Chalmers, . .	"	xxx.	144

Date.	Names.	Record.	Vol.	Page
1738. Nov. 27.	De Grove, Rachel, and John Anderson, ...	M. B.,	I.	11
1779. July 31.	De Grove, Mary, and John Nichols, ...	"	xxviii.	40
1764. Mar. 3.	De Grushe, Adam, and Jane Stinmets, ...	"	viii.	91
1761. Oct. 17.	Degrushe, Elias, Jr., and Sarah Myer, ...	"	v.	149
1783. Aug. 23.	Degrushe, Sarah, and William Sutton, ...	"	xl.	8
1769. Aug. 26.	Degrushee, Mary, and Edward King, ...	"	xv.	29
1736. Dec. 8.	Dehart, Baltus, and Mary Phillipse, ...	"	I.	3
1779. Nov. 6.	De Hart, Daniel, and Elizabeth Mersereau, . .	"	xxviii.	130
1753. May 30.	De Hart, Elizabeth, and Cornelius Vandenburgh, ...	"	I.	43
1761. Aug. 18.	De Hart, Elizabeth, and John Halsted, Jr., . .	"	v.	46
1764. July 19.	Dehart, Jacobe, and George Brewerton, Jr., .	"	viii.	263
1738. June 26.	De Hart, James, and Elizabeth Morris, ...	"	I.	10
1764. Jan. 7.	De Hart, John, and Mary Van Neme, ...	"	viii.	10
1770. Dec. 7.	De Hart, Mary, and Daniel Hendricksen, . . .	"	xvi.	289
1769. Oct. 11.	D'Hart, William, and Elizabeth Bleecker, . . .	"	xv.	53
1758. Jan. 3.	De Honneur, John, and Rebeccah Sparksman,	"	I.	765
1764. May 2.	De Joncourt, Rachel, and Isaac Noble, ...	"	viii.	180
1764. Mar. 31.	De Kay, Elizabeth, and Annanias Cooper, . . .	"	viii.	127
1772. Sept. 29.	De Kay, Francis, and Nicholas Depeyster, . . .	"	xix.	60
1757. Mar. 11.	De Kay, Jane, and Jacob Morris, ...	"	I.	465
1772. May 9.	De Kay, Juliana, and James Bunyan, ...	"	xviii.	106
1761. Jan. 30.	De Kay, Juliana, and James Howell, ...	"	iv.	42
1770. April 28.	De Kay, Mary, and William Thompson, ...	"	xvi.	72
1782. Jan. 2.	De Keller, Frederick, and Catharine Grim, . .	"	xxxv.	2
1757. June 3.	De Key, Christean, and Samuel Gale, ...	"	I.	551
1761. Aug. 27.	De Key, Jacobus, and Hannah Clows, ...	"	v.	60
1768. April 9.	Deklyn, Barnt, and Mary Van Zandt, ...	"	xiii.	69
1763. Sept. 24.	De Klyn, Leonard, and Margaret Maney, . . .	"	vii.	352
1771. Sept. 9.	De La Marter, Cloudea, and Maria Van Dooser, ...	"	xvii.	179
1769. Nov. 15.	Delamater, Abraham, and Annatie Sleght, . . .	"	xv.	95
1755. Nov. 3.	De Lamater, Abraham I., and Sarah Ten Brook, ...	"	I.	204
1782. April 4.	Delamater, Catharine, and Benjamin Rull, . . .	"	xxxv.	113
1767. Sept. 8.	Delamater, Cornelius, and Rachel Sleght, . . .	"	xii.	30
1770. Oct. 27.	De Lamater, Geertruy, and John Nottingham,	"	xvi.	231
1767. Oct. 16.	Delamater, Hester, and Jacob Elmendorph, . .	"	xii.	63
1775. Oct. 14.	De Lamater, Jacobus, and Hartry Vosburgh,	"	xxiii.	180
1755. Aug. 16.	Delamater, John, and Jane Post, ...	"	I.	148
1756. Sept. 22.	Delamater, Samuel, and Catalintie Waldron, .	"	I.	300
1771. June 11.	Delamater, Sarah, and Andrew Meyer, ...	"	xvii.	108
1770. Dec. 18.	De Lamater, William, and Mary Vandewater,	"	xvi.	300
1762. Nov. 19.	Delamatre, Benjamin, and Anna Hoghtaling,	"	vi.	446
1765. May 20.	De La Matre, Betha, and Garret M. Newkerk,	"	ix.	135

DATE.	NAMES.	RECORD.	VOL.	PAGE.
1772. May 5.	Delamatter, Abraham I., and Maritje Ten Brook,	M. B.,	XVIII.	100
1769. Aug. 1.	Delamatter, Elizabeth, and John Whittbeck,.	"	XV.	14
1770. April 10.	De Lameter, Catalyntje, and Johannes Masten,	"	XVI.	57
1765. Aug. 21.	De Lametter, Allice, and Elbert Rooze,	"	IX.	242
1768. April 14.	Delametter, Catherina, and Jacob Delametter,	"	XIII.	77
1763. Oct. 6.	De Lametter, David D., and Sarah Hoffman,	"	VII.	375
1768. Oct. 13.	De Lametter, Direck, and Catherine Ousterhout,	"	XIII.	208
1768. April 14.	Delametter, Jacob, and Catherina DeLametter,	"	XIII.	77
1763. Dec. 3.	De Lametter, Mary, and Henry Sleght, Jr.,..	"	VII.	490
1766. Oct. 25.	Delamont, Abraham, and Hannah Vedder,..	"	X.	142
1764. Oct. 25.	De Lamont, Eva, and Nicholas Vedder,	"	VIII.	376
1777. April 30.	De Lamontagnie, Mary, and John Amory, ..	"	XXIV.	79
1762. Nov. 25.	De Lancey, Anne, and John Harris Cruger,.	"	VI.	454
1762. Dec. 9.	De Lancey, Anne, and Thomas Jones,	"	VI.	471
1762. Sept. 23.	De Lancey, Helena, and Elias Carey,	"	VI.	327
1775. Oct. 2.	De Lancey, Jane, and John Watts, Jr.,	"	XXIII.	170
1769. May 20.	De Lancey, John, and Dorothy Wickham,..	"	XIV.	104
1757. Oct. 3.	De Lancey, Mary, and William Walton, Jr.,	"	I.	655
1773. June 16.	De Lancey, Stephen, and Cornelia Barclay,.	"	XXI.	11
1775. Oct. 2.	De Lancey, Susan, and Thomas H. Barclay,..	"	XXIII.	168
1767. April 27.	De Lancy, Alice, and Ralph Izard,	"	XI.	72
1759. Oct. 17.	De Laney, Jennet, and John Torry,	"	II.	462
1771. June 27.	De Lano, Jonathan, and Eleanor Yearrow,..	"	XVII.	123
1763. Sept. 27.	De Lanoy, Abraham, and Rachel Marlin,	"	VII.	356
1772. April 18.	De Lanoy, Catherine, and James Bleecker,..	"	XVIII.	84
1757. Feb. 2.	Delanoy, Jane, and Christian Foalk,	"	I.	432
1767. Feb. 5.	Delanoy, Jane, and John Warner,	"	XI.	20
1734. Jan. 7.	De Lansey, Peter, and Elizabeth Colden,	"	I.	8
1761. Sept. 26.	De Le Noy, Magdelin, and Wolvert Van Worden,	"	V.	100
1781. Sept. 4.	Delaplaine, Nicholas, and Mercey Pugsley,..	"	XXXII.	58
1772. May 20.	Delaplaine, Sarah, and Hugh Lindsay,	"	XVIII.	116
1771. Nov. 4.	De La Roche, Gilbert Gibour, and Elizabeth Thompson,	"	XVII.	239
1738. Oct. 23.	De Latneter, Johannes, and Maria Deckers,..	"	I.	11
1673. April 15.	Delavall, Frances, and James Carterett,	G. E.,	IV.	277
1678. Oct. 2.	Delavall, Margaret, and Thomas Codrington,	"	XXXII.	4
1670. Sept. 12.	Delavall, Rebeckah, and William Dervall, ...	C. A.,	II.	589
1780. Nov. 27.	Delavew, Ann, and John Lee,	M. B.,	XXX.	127
1738. July 20.	Delemater, Cornelia, and John Myer,	"	I.	10
1764. May 18.	De Lemetter, Christina, and Abraham Fonda,	"	VIII.	193
1758. Feb. 24.	De Lenoy, Lucy, and John Pattenger,	"	I.	827
1780. Dec. 6.	Dellas, Margaret, and James Sadler,	"	XXX.	140

14

DATE.	NAMES.	RECORD.	VOL.	PAGE.
1783. June 3.	Dellat, Ann, and William Lamarate,........	M. B.,	XXXIX.	38
1763. April 22.	Dellemont, Anne, and Christopher Velthousen,	"	VII.	136
1761. Sept. 8.	Delmont, Johanna, and John Teller,........	"	V.	74
1760. Oct. 20.	Delmont, Margaret, and Abraham Switz, ...	"	III.	373
1758. Jan. 23.	De Long, Jannetje, and Isaiah Essmond,....	"	I.	798
1777. Jan. 27.	Delue, Catherine, and John Knighton, ...	"	XXIV.	19
1778. July 11.	Demare, Rachel, and John Van Houte,......	"	XXV.	127
1765. July 18.	Demaree, Jacob, and Elizabeth Burtis,......	"	IX.	210
1759. Sept. 28.	Demaree, Peter, and Mary Allen,..........	"	II.	436
1779. Oct. 27.	Demarell, Elizabeth, and Francis King,.....	"	XXVIII.	121
1782. April 20.	Demaresk, Frowetje, and Frederick Woerten-dyke, ...	"	XXXV.	130
1782. April 11.	Demarest, Anna, and John Demarest, ...	"	XXXV.	119
1782. April 11.	Demarest, John, and Anna Demarest, ...	"	XXXV.	119
1760. Jan. 23.	Demarest, Peter, and Annetje Smidt,.......	"	III.	3
1770. Mar. 2.	De Marie, Christian, and Hannah Quackenbush,	"	XVI.	28
1762. Nov. 17.	De Marre, Rachel, and Gerardus Ryker, ...	"	VI.	437
1761. Aug. 8.	Demee, Isaac, and Sithia Voorhees, ...	"	V.	33
1777. Mar. 8.	De Ment, William, and Mary Simmons,.....	"	XXIV.	42
1763. May 2.	Demerell, Elizabeth, and Thomas Roberts, ..	"	VII.	161
1779. Sept. 26.	De Mill, Anthony, and Catherine Chatting,..	"	XXVIII.	85
1780. May 16.	Demill, John, and Elizabeth Smyth,........	"	XXIX.	55
1775. Nov. 2.	De Milt, Isaac, and Elizabeth Gordon,......	"	XXIII.	197
1773. Nov. 30.	Demilt, Isaac, and Jane Fine,.............	"	XXII.	56
1760. Oct. 27.	Demilt, Mary, and John Crabb,............	"	III.	381
1772. May 4.	Demilt, Obadiah, and Sarah Frost,.........	"	XVIII.	99
1763. Dec. 20.	De Milt, Peter, and Elizabeth Hicks,.......	"	VII.	515
1772. Jan. 7.	Demilt, Jane, and John Cross,.............	"	XVIII.	5
1759. Feb. 9.	Demilt, Sarah, and John Crawford, ...	"	II.	186
1737. Dec. 10.	De Mire, Agnus, and Edward Nicholls, ...	"	I.	8
1772. Jan. 26.	Demire, Benjamin, and Elizabeth Wynkoop,	"	XI.	14
1760. April 28.	Demont, John, and Caharine Ten Brook,...	"	III.	130
1781. Nov. 3.	Demoray, Margaretta, and John Bogart, ...	"	XXXIV.	14
1774. Jan. 18.	Demorie, Margaret, and Andrew Myer,.....	"	XXII.	104
1780. April 25.	Demot, John, and Margaret Amens,........	"	XXIX.	37
1779. Dec. 8.	Demott, Abraham, and Hannah Foster,.....	"	XXVIII.	166
1770. May 25.	De Mott, Anthony, and Phebe Remsen, ...	"	XVI.	94
1777. April 27.	De Mott, Elizabeth, and John Foster, ...	"	XXIV.	75
1764. June 7.	De Mott, Mary, and John Skidmore,.	"	VIII.	212
1777. July 3.	De Mott, Michael, and Margaret Watts, ...	"	XXIV.	110
1779. Nov. 4.	Demott, Michael, and Mary Heagaman, ...	"	XXVIII.	128
1763. Sept. 22.	Demott, Sarah, and Daniel Durland,........	"	VII.	350
1782. Dec. 22.	Demott, William, and Elizabeth Miller, ...	"	XXXVII.	129
1781. Aug. 9.	Dempsay, William, and Elizabeth Mahany,..	"	XXXIII.	32
1775. Aug. 2.	Demyse, Rymerick, and Peter Wyckoff,....	"	XXIII.	117

DATE.	NAMES.	RECORD.	VOL.	PAGE.
1761. Oct. 2.	Den, Thomas, and Mary Calder,...........	M. B.,	v.	116
1761. Oct. 2.	Denbagh, Mariah, and Simon Van Antwerp,	"	v.	157
1771. Oct. 23.	Denham, Francis, and Elizabeth Barker,....	"	xvii.	220
1760. Nov. 27.	Denicke, Mary, and Michael French,.......	"	iii.	448
1760. June 9.	Denin, Hannah, and Arthur Graham,.......	"	iii.	182
1759. Oct. 4.	Denison, Elizabeth, and Henry Douw,......	"	ii.	449
1760. Dec. 15.	Denison, Gertrey, and Volkert Dawson, ...	"	iii.	474
1757. Sept. 1.	Denison, Hugh, and Rachel Van Volkenburgh,	"	i.	628
1757. Dec. 12.	Denison, Jane, and Samuel Stitt, ...	"	i.	735
1764. Dec. 10.	Deniston, George, and Isabel Crage,........	"	viii.	448
1759. May 9.	Denmark, John, and Mary Cannon,........	"	ii.	272
1762. Mar. 19.	Denn, Mary, and Joseph Noblett,..........	"	vi.	78
1757. June 8.	Dennels, Peter, and Ann Arenhout,........	"	i.	557
1765. June 28.	Denning, William, and Sarah Hawkshurst,..	"	ix.	187
1777. April 19.	Dennis, Anne, and Edward Chandler, ...	"	xxiv.	68
1772. Jan. 28.	Dennis, Benjamin, and Ruth Jervis,........	"	xviii.	18
1773. Feb. 6.	Dennis, Cornelius, and Ruth Hoag,.........	"	xx.	37
1779. Aug. 20.	Dennis, Ezekiel, and Elizabeth Rolph,......	"	xxviii.	54
1780. May 26.	Dennis, Jane, and William Cropsey,........	"	xxix.	69
1758. Oct. 12.	Dennis, Joseph, and Jennet Claghorn,......	"	ii.	53
1773. Dec. 23.	Dennis, Patrick, and Margaret White,......	"	xvii.	303
1782. July 3.	Dennis, Rachel, and Jacob Vanderbilt,......	"	xxxvi.	73
1773. Dec. 21.	Dennis, Rachel, and James Cornwell,...... .	"	xxii.	81
1772. Aug. 12.	Dennison, George, and Mary McClaughry,...	"	xix.	21
1761. June 18.	Dennison, Mary, and Ichabod Higgins,.....	"	iv.	248
1767. Feb. 24.	Dennison, William, and Christiana Carolina Lucum,...............................	"	xi.	36
1760. Oct. 14.	Denniston, James, and Jane Crawford,......	"	iii.	361
1773. Oct. 13.	Denniston, James, and Rachel Falls,........	"	xxi.	140
1765. Aug. 5.	Denniston, Mary, and John Hughes,.......	"	ix.	254
1783. Mar. 28.	Denny, Bridget Anna Maria, and Christopher Pierson, ...	"	xxxviii.	80
1781. Nov. 16.	Denny, David, and Jannet Ross,...........	"	xxxiv.	39
1763. Aug. 30.	De Noyelles, John, and Rachel Stratford,...	"	vii.	317
1763. April 26.	Dent, John, and Elizabeth Welch,.........	"	vii.	144
1736. Dec. 23.	Denter, Temporance, and Thomas Brash,...	"	i.	5
1762. Feb. 1.	Denton, Catharine, and Henry Smith,......	"	vi.	34
1764. Sept. 29.	Denton, Elisabeth, and William Moore,.....	"	viii.	327
1736. May 29.	Denton, Elizabeth, and Jarvis Dusenberre,..	"	i.	1
1759. Dec. 13.	Denton, Elizabeth, and John Dodge,.......	"	ii.	544
1783. Feb. 21.	Denton, Hannah, and Benjamin Seaman,....	"	xxxviii.	49
1781. April 25.	Denton, Hannah, and William Ballard,.....	"	xxxii.	15
1759. Feb. 3.	Denton, James, and Margaret Barton,......	"	ii.	172
1760. Oct. 14.	Denton, James, and Mary Holmes,.........	"	iii.	362
1736. May 14.	Denton, Jane, and Charles Peters,.........	"	i.	1

DATE.	NAMES.	RECORD.	VOL.	PAGE.
1761. Feb. 25.	Denton, John, and Elizabeth Wisner,.........	M. B.,	IV.	82
1758. May 6.	Denton, John, and Mary Lenard,..........	"	I.	895
1765. Nov. 1.	Denton, Jonas, and Eleanor Jackson,.......	"	IX.	340
1783. Aug. 2.	Denton, Joseph, and Rachel Cornwell,......	"	XXXIX.	109
1777. Sept. 20.	Denton, Martha, and James Mills,.........	"	XXIV.	147
1763. Sept. 27.	Denton, Martha, and John Van Lew, ...	"	VII.	355
1773. July 22.	Denton, Martha, and Peter Alburtus,.......	"	XXI.	49
1763. Nov. 26.	Denton Mary, and John Skidmore,........	"	VII.	472
1772. Nov. 23.	Denton, Mary, and Samuel Falls,..........	"	XIX.	125
1770. June 16.	Denton, Mary, and William Puntine,.......	"	XVI.	116
1770. May 7.	Denton, Phebe, and Abel Gale,............	"	XVI.	80
1783. July 20.	Denton, Phebe, and Daniel Lake,..........	"	XXXIX.	97
1782. Oct. 3.	Denton, Robert, and Elizabeth Furman,.....	"	XXXVII.	25
1781. Jan. 9.	Denton, Ruth, and Michael Burns,.........	"	XXXI.	18
1763. Dec. 10.	Denton, Ruth, and William Forster,........	"	VII.	502
1771. Aug. 9.	Denton, Sarah, and Obadiah Mills,.........	"	XVII.	156
1767. Sept. 7.	Denton, Sarah, and Thomas Wickham,.....	"	XII.	26
1767. Oct. 26.	Denton, Thomas, and Phebe Hall, ...	"	XII.	69
1161. Jan. 20.	Denton, William, and Mary Smith, ...	"	IV.	21
1782. Sept. 24.	Denye, Milla, and Samuel Lauddan,........	"	XXXVII.	11
1731. Nov. 1.	Denyke, Jacob, and Ame Wendal,.........	"	I.	8
1771. Aug. 21.	Denyse, Femmitje, and Barnardus Ryder,...	"	XVII.	160
1778. Nov. 25.	Denyse, Helen, and John Taylor,..........	"	XXVI.	94
1783. May 16.	Denyse, Jane, and Hugh Smith,...........	"	XXXIX.	13
1777. Jan. 3.	Denyse, Jane, and William Van Dyck, ...	"	XXIV.	4
1763. June 10.	Denyse, Jaques, and Ann Schenck, ...	"	VII.	220
1767. May 25.	Depeue, Sarah, and Nicholas Larzelere,.....	"	XI.	95
1779. Dec. 7.	De Pertuis, Estienne, and Teresia Piquet,...	"	XXVIII.	165
1736. Mar. 9.	De Peyster, Anne, and Isaac De Peyster,..	"	I.	5
1758. June 1.	De Peyster, Elizabeth, and Matthew Clarkson,	"	I.	920
1763. Feb. 28.	De Peyster, Gerardus, and Elizabeth Rutgers,	"	VII.	81
1736. Mar. 9.	De Peyster, Isaac, and Anne De Peyster,...	"	I.	5
1738. June 13.	De Peyster, Jacobus, and Elizabeth Swartwout, ...	"	I.	10
1753. May 22.	De Peyster, Jannitie, and Johan Sebastian Stephanij,............................	"	I.	37
1769. Sept. 11.	Depeyster, John, Jr., and Elizabeth Harring,	"	XV.	39
1775. May 18.	De Peyster, Joseph Reade, and Ann Betts,..	"	XXIII.	37
1765. Mar. 29.	De Peyster, Mary, and John Charlton, ...	"	IX.	76
1772. Sept. 29.	De Peyster, Nicholas, and Francis De Kay,..	"	XIX.	60
1762. Dec. 18.	De Peyster, Nicholas, and Jane Johnson, ...	"	VI.	488
1773. Mar. 23.	De Peyster, William, and Christiana Dally,..	"	XX.	67
1767. June 3.	Depue, Cornelius, and Helena Wassbrouck,.	"	XI.	104
1756. Dec 6.	Depue, Sarah, and Thomas Marshall, ...	"	I.	375
1757. Feb. 11.	De Puy, Else, and Matthew Decker,.......	"	I.	438

DATE.	NAMES.	RECORD.	VOL.	PAGE.
1773. Sept. 21.	Depuy, Joseph, and Mary Depuy,..........	M. B.,	XXI.	114
1766. Nov. 7.	Depuy, Lena, and Jochem Schoonmaker,...	"	X.	157
1773. Sept. 21.	Depuy, Mary, and Joseph Depuy,......,..	"	XXI.	114
1774. Jan. 19.	Depuy, Sarah, and Benjamin Bruyn, ...	"	XXII.	109
1764. Oct. 4.	Derby, Easter, and Cornelius Lawlor, ...	"	VIII.	333
1763. May 9.	Dercimer, Peter, and Alice Bavington, ...	"	VII.	170
1764. Jan. 2.	De Ridder, Annetje, and Walter Becker,....	"	VIII.	1
1760. April 10.	Deridder, Walter, and Annatje Van Den Bergh	"	III.	102
1760. Oct. 1.	Deriemer, Nicholas,.and Margaret Pool, ...	"	III.	339
1760. Mar. 1.	Dering, William, and Eleanor Pettit, ...	"	III.	58
1760. July 29.	Derkendered, Love, and Henry Roberts,....	"	XXIX.	127
1783. May 19.	Derkinderen, James, and Mary Neavens,....	"	XXXIX.	18
1763. Sept. 22.	Derland, Daniel, and Sarah Demott,........	"	VII.	350
1768. Dec. 16.	Deronda, Mary, and Abraham Lent,........	"	XIII.	264
1761. Feb. 17.	De Ronde, Nicholas, and Anna Sabine Ruehl,	"	IV.	66
1670. Sept. 12.	Dervall, William, and Rebeckah Delavall, ...	C. A.,	II.	589
1738. Sept. 2.	Derye, Anne, and Abraham Hooglandt,.....	M. B.,	I.	11
1762. Dec. 30.	Desbrosses, James, Jr., and Elizabeth Butler,	"	VI.	504
1781. Feb. 6.	Desbrosses, Mary Ann, and Joseph Wadding-ton,................................	"	XXXI.	41
1759. Feb. 7.	De St. Croix, Joshua Temple, and Leah Gal-ladet,..............................	"	II.	184
1762. Aug. 22.	De St. Croix, Susanna, and John Arden,....	"	V.	51
1768. April 8.	Desborough, Margaret, and Thomas Howel Smith,..............................	"	XIII.	67
1760. Jan. 10.	Descoe, Peter, and Ephelanda Coles,.......	"	II.	576
1778. May 21.	Detluff, Sophia, and Christian Eggert, ...	"	XXV.	92
1760. Jan. 30.	Detmars, Abraham, and Elizabeth Johnson, .	"	III.	10
1779. May 8.	Devan, James, and Elinor Ward, ...	"	XXVII.	131
1772. Aug. 24.	Devenny, Mary, and John Russell,.........	"	XIX.	29
1758. Sept. 28.	Devenport, Elenor, and William James,.....	"	II.	36
1783. Aug. 11.	Devenport, Elizabeth, and Cornelius Van Ripey,...............................	"	XXXIX.	124
1783. Aug. 6.	Devenport, Judith, and Caleb Scott,........	"	XXXIX.	115
1764. July 16.	Devenport, Vivian, and Elizabeth Burnham,	"	VIII.	260
1759. Dec. 29.	Devereux, John, and Margaret Morris, ...	"	II.	560
1781. April 6.	Devereux, Margaret, and John Morrel, ...	"	XXXI.	95
1765. April 12.	Devereux, William, and Elizabeth Shearman,	"	IX.	91
1768. June 6.	Deverix, Margaret, and Lawrence Scallon, ..	"	XIII.	122
1758. Mar. 30.	Devine, Abraham, and Else Morse,.........	"	I.	868
1780. Dec. 7.	Devine, John, and Mary Wessells,.........	"	XXX.	145
1782. Dec. 13.	Devine, Mary, and James Smith, ...	"	XXXVII.	119
1765. Dec. 13.	Devine, Robert, and Martha Smith,........	"	VIII.	453
1759. May 23.	Devoe, Abigail, and Henry Odell,..........	"	II.	290
1758. Sept. 23.	Devoe, Abraham, and Elizabeth Persell, ...	"	II.	33

DATE.	NAMES.	RECORD.	VOL.	PAGE.
1763. May 12.	Devoe, David, and Sarah Bennet,..........	M. B.,	VII.	181
1782. Oct. 17.	Devoe, Elenor, and William Cook, ...	"	XXXVII.	48
1757. May 28.	Devoe, Hester, and David Evans,.	"	I.	544
1780. Oct. 2.	Devoe, Hester, and William Rhinelander,...	"	XXX.	50
1779. Mar. 3.	Devoe, Isaac, and Phila Hunt, ...	"	XXVII.	54
1757. July 11.	Devoe, John, and Hester Sea,.............	"	I.	589
1764. Aug. 27.	Devoe, John, and Sarah Frasier,..........	"	VIII.	294
1762. Feb. 27.	Devoe, Joseph, and Lydia High,...........	"	VI.	58
1771. Mar. 18.	De Voe, Lettice, and Abel Buel,...........	"	XVII.	36
1778. Dec. 5.	Devoe, Margaret, and Martin McEvoy, ...	"	XXVI.	111
1783. Mar. 18.	Devoe, Mary, and David Miller, ...	"	XXXVIII.	69
1775. June 27.	Devoe, Mary, and Edward Pell, ...	"	XXIII.	79
1759. July 16.	Devoe, Sarah, and Samuel Lorgange,.......	"	II.	356
1760. April 19.	Devon, Daniel, and Margaret Quackenbos, ..	"	III.	117
1760. April 3.	Devon, Hannah, and Wassal Van Norden,..	"	III.	96
1781. April 26.	Devoo, Sarah, and Nathaniel Golding,......	"	XXXII.	18
1782. Jan. 9.	De Vooe, Catharine, and Gabriel Ward, ...	"	XXXV.	12
1783. April 21.	Devoor, Affey, and Alexander Stephens,....	"	XXXVIII.	104
1783. April 21.	Devoor, Ally, and William Adam, ...	"	XXXVIII.	105
1761. Nov. 10.	Devou, Rachel, and Benjamin Archer,......	"	V.	205
1782. Sept. 3.	De Voue, Frederick, and Anne Arrison, ...	"	XXXVI.	135
1761. Oct. 13.	Devoue, John, and Mary Beavois, ...	"	V.	134
1772. April 9.	Devoux, Daniel, and Mary Avery,.........	"	XVIII.	72
1761. Oct. 29.	Devow, Rachel, and Michael Wyser,.......	"	V.	177
1782. May 8.	De Weber, Francis, and Lucretia Thurston, .	"	XXXV.	153
1782. Sept. 17.	Dewer, David, and Rachel Draisdel,........	"	XXXVII.	3
1761. Dec. 23.	De White, Mary, and Samuel Middleton, ...	"	V.	298
1769. Sept. 19.	De Wint, Ann, and Isaac Kip, ...	"	XV.	41
1767. May 13.	Dewint, Jemima, and John Smith,.........	"	XI.	85
1736. July 29.	De Wint, John, and Anne Carman, ...	"	I.	2
1771. Dec. 5.	De Wit, Johannes, and Catherine Bloom, ...	"	XVII.	285
1757. Nov. 1.	De Witt, Andries T., and Rachel Du Bois,..	"	I.	693
1775. Aug. 3.	De Witt, Ann, and Jacob Smith, ...	"	XXIII.	119
1775. May 31.	De Witt, Annatie, and Peter Bogardus,....	"	XXIII.	150
1768. May 4.	De Witt, Annetje, and Nathaniel Bancker,..	"	XIII.	93
1764. Dec. 21.	De Witt, Catharine, and John Graham,.....	"	VIII.	461
1763. Nov. 9.	De Witt, Catharine, and John Quackenboss,.	"	VII.	437
1769. May 4.	Dewitt, Elizabeth, and Edward Whitaker, ..	"	XIV.	93
1761. July 15.	De Witt, Elizabeth, and William Nottingham,	"	IV.	298
1756. Aug. 11.	De Witt, Garret V. H., and Margaret Van Horne, ...	"	I.	271
1775. Sept. 26.	De Witt, Geddy, and Samuel Harris,.... ..	"	XXIII.	164
1738. Oct. 27.	De Witt, Henry, and Maritie Tenbrooke, ...	"	I.	11
1738. April 20.	De Witt, Johannes, and Catherine Lysler,...	"	I.	9
1765. Feb. 8.	De Witt, Mary, and James Clinton,........	"	IX.	50

DATE.	NAMES.	RECORD.	VOL. PAGE.
1773. Sept. 6.	Dewitt, Tjerck C., and Jannatie Eltinge,....	M. B.,	XXI. 101
1769. Dec. 18.	De Witt, Trentje, and Peter Lent,.........	"	XV. 124
1770. May 17.	De Witt, William, and Hester Duyckman, ..	"	XVI. 90
173⅞. Jan. 26.	De Witt, William, and Mary Parker,.......	"	I. 8
1783. Jan. 21.	Dexter, Abigail, and Mathew Fox,.........	"	XXXVIII. 23
1763. Aug. 26.	Dey, Ann, and Pexall Fowler,............	"	VII. 313
1764. Aug. 13.	Dey, Hyler, and Christopher Aerhart,......	"	VIII. 279
1770. April 5.	Dey, Jane, and Abraham Buskirk,.........	"	XVI. 49
1761. Nov. 23.	Dey, Mary, and David Shaw, ...	"	V. 244
1770. June 16.	Diamond, Mary, and John Bradley,........	"	XVI. 113
1759. Feb. 16.	Dibble, Deborah, and James Varian, ...	"	II. 192
1779. Feb. 12.	Dick, David, Mary Scidmore, ...	"	XXVII. 40
1767. April 23.	Dick, William, and Elizabeth Taylor,.......	"	XI. 69
173⅞. Feb. 13.	Dicke, Anne, and Thomas Dishington,..... .	"	I. 9
1763. Mar. 1.	Dickenson, Beletije, and Robert Ray,.......	"	VII. 85
1764. Feb. 23.	Dickenson, Benjamin, and Katharine Marshall,	"	VIII. 74
1761. Dec. 28.	Dickenson, Cornelia, and Henry Remsen,...	"	V. 304
1781. Jan. 17.	Dickenson, Nathaniel, and Anne Cock,......	"	XXXI. 23
1783. June 24.	Dickenson, Sarah, and Peter Vanderbeek,...	"	XXXIX. 67
1772. Sept. 22.	Dickerson, Jonathan, and Martha Longburn,.	"	XIX. 54
1780. July 28.	Dickey, James, and Mary Rawley,.........	"	XXIX. 126
1770. June 27.	Dickinson, Chloe, and John Wallace,.......	"	XVI. 125
1779. Dec. 20.	Dickinson, Jesse, and Sarah Titus,.........	"	XXVIII. 117
1782. July 22.	Dickinson, Zebulon, and Elizabeth Brush,...	"	XXXVI. 90
1771. Nov. 28.	Dicks, Nancy, and Isaac Vosburgh,........	"	XVII. 271
1760. Nov. 16.	Dickson, Ocasar, and Mary Spikes,.........	"	II. 499
1775. July 14.	Dickson, Elizabeth, and John Evans,.......	"	XXIII. 97
1757. Aug. 15.	Dickson, Elizabeth, and Nicholas Richards,..	"	I. 615
1764. Feb. 25.	Dickson, Flora, and James O'Ham,.........	"	VIII. 77
1758. Sept. 13.	Dickson, Francis, and Hester Christian,.....	"	II. 20
1759. Sept. 4.	Dickson, Francis, and Mary Corbet,........	"	II. 409
1761. Oct. 22.	Dickson, George, and Lenah Kidney,.......	"	V. 161
1757. July 23.	Dickson, James, and Elizabeth Petri,.......	"	I. 599
1779. Feb. 24.	Dickson, John, and Deborah Smith,........	"	XXVII. 48
1782. Nov. 13.	Dickson, John, and Phebe Morgan, ...	"	XXXVII. 81
1757. June 16.	Dickson, Joseph, and Mary Ann McKenny,.	"	I. 564
1780. June 23.	Dickson, Robert, and Jane Gerow,.........	"	XXIX. 93
1764. Oct. 5.	Dickson, Samuel. and Hester Smith, ...	"	VIII. 335
1762. May 28.	Dickson, Thomas, and Ann Johnson,.......	"	VI. 172
1762. Jan. 28.	Dickson, Thomas, and Martha Wright, ...	"	VI. 28
1776. April 20.	Dickson, Thomas, and Sarah White,........	"	XXIII. 298
1778. Nov. 12.	Dicterich, George, and Christian Nestel,....	"	XXVI. 86
1770. Sept. 17.	Diedrick, Christina, and Christian Coeper,...	"	XVI. 190
1780. July 31.	Dikeman, Cathalina, and Peter Grim,.......	"	XXIX. 130
1783. Nov. 6.	Dikeman, Jane, and Charles Hinxman,......	"	XL. 107

DATE.	NAMES.	RECORD.	VOL.	PAGE.
1738. Nov. 3.	Dill, Richard, and Mary Norris,..............	M. B.,	I.	11
1759. Sept. 25.	Dillen, Edward, and Mary Tubbs,..........	"	II.	432
1767. Sept. 25.	Dillin, Judith, and Jacob Rocters Hooper,....	"	XII.	45
1779. Nov. 25.	Dillingham, Elizabeth, and Samuel Clemmons,	"	XXVIII.	150
1764. Jan. 23.	Dillon, John, and Mary McKim,...........	"	VIII.	31
1738. May 1.	Dillon, Patrick, and Sarah William, ...	"	XXIX.	38
1761. Mar. 19.	Dimes, John, and Sarah Welch, ...	"	IV.	108
1759. Feb. 22.	Dingee, Sarah, and Maurice Seaman,...... ..	"	II.	200
1757. Feb. 11.	Dingey, Arthur, and Martha Rogers,.......	"	I.	817
1783. April 23.	Dingey, Elizabeth, and Richard Edwards,...	"	XXXVIII.	110
1769. Nov. 30.	Dingey, Ruth, and Zachariah Rogers,.......	"	XV.	110
1666. Mar. 14.	Dingle, Mary, and Samuel Dayton,.........	O. W. L.,	II.	134
1775. Oct. 18.	Dings, Eve, and Casparus Shultz, Jr., ...	M. B.,	XXIII.	183
1782. July 30.	Dingwall, Arthur, and Elizabeth Evans, ...	"	XXXVI.	94
1767. Sept. 30.	Disborough, Henry, and Emilla Smith, ...	"	XII.	50
1778. May 21.	Disbury, Hannah, and Stephen Crossfield,...	"	XXV.	90
1778. Oct. 23.	Disbury, Henry, and Abigail Fowler,.......	"	XXVI.	69
1763. Dec. 4.	Dischow, Sarah, and Peter Tellott,........	"	VII.	504
173⅞. Feb. 13.	Dishington, Thomas, and Anne Dick,.......	"	I.	9
1770. June 18.	Dissasway, Juthegh, and Gozen Ryersz, ...	"	XVI.	120
1773. Jan. 27.	Dissosway, Ann, and Joseph Guyon, ...	"	XX.	26
1760. Aug. 12.	Ditcher, Catharine, and William Lush,......	"	III.	249
1761. July 9.	Ditmars, Douw, and Sarah Vroom,.........	"	IV.	290
1768. July 11.	Ditmars, Douwe, and Catherine Snedecker,. .	"	XIII.	154
1764. April 10.	Ditmars, Dow, and Mary Johnson,.........	"	VIII.	146
1771. Sept. 26.	Ditmars, Isaac, and Jinne Vroom, ...	"	XVII.	193
1781. July 31.	Ditmars, Jane, and John Vroom, ...	"	XXXIII.	24
1770. Dec. 28.	Ditmars, Jannatje, and Peter Staats, ...	"	XVI.	306
1781. Dec. 12.	Ditmars, Johannis, and Margaret Rapalje,...	"	XXXIV.	80
1762. Sept. 29.	Ditmars, Johannis, and Rebecca Staats,.....	"	VI.	338
1778. Mar. 12.	Ditmars, Maritie, and John Van Der Bilt,...	"	XXV.	40
1761. Dec. 12.	Ditmars, Mary, and Cornelius Voorhis, ...	"	V.	276
1781. Mar. 2.	Ditmas, Abraham, and Mary Scidmore,.....	"	XXXI.	62
1782. June 7.	Ditmass, Cathalina, and Samuel Eldert,.....	"	XXXVI.	40
1780. May 23.	Ditmes, John, Jr, and Jane Nagel,.........	"	XXIX.	65
1737. June 22.	Ditmorse, Janatie, and John Lusasen, ...	"	I.	6
1761. May 5.	Divine, Mary, and Samuel Roberts, ...	"	IV.	180
1762. Feb. 12.	Dixon, Esther, and James O'Neal, ...	"	VI.	48
1760. Aug. 11.	Dixon, Henry, and Elizabeth Bell, ...	"	III.	247
1780. Jan. 8.	Dixon, Thomas, and Elenor Pasman,.......	"	XXVIII.	187
1779. July 22.	Dixon, Thomas, and Elinor Clendenny,.....	"	XXVIII.	28
1779. Sept. 30.	Dixon, William, and Ann Randall,.........	"	XXVIII.	94
1773. July 17.	Doane, Joshua, and Anna Clark,...........	"	XXI.	45
1756. Sept. 28.	Dobbs, Adam, and Affia Snuke,...........	"	I.	308
1762. July 3.	Dobbs, Catherine, and Lovit Thurston, ...	"	VI.	223

DATE.	NAMES.	RECORD.	VOL.	PAGE.
1758. April 15.	Dobbs, Dorothy, and Michael Tannare, ...	M. B.,	I.	874
1770. Sept. 10.	Dobbs, Elinor, and Philip Phenix, ...	"	XVI.	185
1772. Jan. 13.	Dobbs, Elizabeth, and Daniel Dyke,........	"	XVIII.	12
1779. July 22.	Dobbs, George, and Ruth Marks, ...	"	XXVIII.	27
1780. Nov. 14.	Dobbs, Jarvis, and Elizabeth Wortman,.....	"	XXX.	103
1759. Nov. 17.	Dobbs, Mary, and James Deacon,..........	"	II.	503
1764. June 12.	Dobbs, Mary, and Thomas Martin,.........	"	VIII.	223
1766. Dec. 11.	Dobbs, Walter, and Ann Duran,...........	"	X.	199
1757. Jan. 8.	Dobbs, William, and Darcus Harding, ...	"	I.	410
1782. July 2.	Dobs, Mary, and Daniel Odel,.............	"	XXXVI.	71
1763. Feb. 21.	Dobson, Mary, and Reginal Armstrong, ...	"	VII.	73
1759. Oct. 3.	Dodd, Thomas, and Mary Vanderhoof,......	"	II.	445
1771. Feb. 22.	Doddridge, Ann, and William Grant,.......	"	XVII.	19
1782. April 2.	Dodds, Agnes, and John Van Law, ...	"	XXXV.	106
1783. Jan. 7.	Dodg, John, and Mary Smith,.............	"	XXXVIII.	8
1760. May 22.	Dodge, Amos, and Mary Hugeford, ...	"	III.	162
1778. April 30.	Dodge, Charity, and Robert Sutton,........	"	XXV.	70
1762. Jan. 14.	Dodge, Daniel, and Phebe Wooden,........	"	VI.	13
1768. Jan. 11.	Dodge, Deborah, and John Kell,...........	"	XIII.	4
1760. Jan. 28.	Dodge, Elizabeth, and William Hallock, ...	"	III.	9
1761. Dec. 9.	Dodge, Freelove, and Townsend Parish, ...	"	V.	269
1737. Oct. 6.	Dodge, Jeremiah, and Margaret Vandebelt,..	"	I.	7
1770. Feb 26.	Dodge, Joannah, and John Houghton,......	"	XVI.	25
1762. Jan. 31.	Dodge, John, and Anne Smith,............	"	VII.	42
1759. Dec. 13.	Dodge, John, and Elizabeth Denton, ...	"	II.	544
1703. July 20.	Dodge, Joseph, and Sarah Hicks,..........	"	VII.	205
1777. Nov. 7.	Dodge, Margaret, and Jacob Haviland, ...	"	XXIV.	175
1760. Sept. 5.	Dodge, Mary, and Maurice Smith, ...	"	III.	300
1756. Nov. 17.	Dodge, Mary, and Samuel Warner, ...	"	I.	357
1738. Sept. 28.	Dodge, Mary, and Thomas Thorne, ...	"	I.	11
1753. Aug. 3.	Dodge, Samuel, and Lenah Amerman,......	"	I.	84
1769. May 31.	Dodge, Sarah, and Comfort Sands,.........	"	XIV.	111
1772. Mar. 7.	Dodge, Susannah, and Jacamiah Akerly,....	"	XVIII.	51
1779. Nov. 19.	Dodge, Thomas, and Elizabeth Montfoort,...	"	XXVIII.	143
1768. Feb. 11.	Dodge, Thomas, and Susannah Thorn,......	"	XIII.	32
1780. Nov. 7.	Doe, Hannah, and David Wilson,..........	"	XXX.	97
1772. Aug. 3.	Dogherty, Anna, and Daniel McDaniel,. ...	"	XIX.	10
1767. July 10.	Dole, James, and Anna Van Stanvoord, ...	"	XI.	131
1780. June 16.	Doleson, Catharine, and John Willson,......	"	XXIX.	88
1764. Jan. 20.	Dollis, Isabella, and Samuel Boyd, ...	"	VIII.	26
1782. Oct. 21.	Dolowin, Catharine, and Joseph Jones, ...	"	XXXVII.	55
1778. Dec. 15.	Dominick, Francis, and Ann Vandeursen,...	"	XXVI.	121
1759. Aug. 4.	Dominick, Francis, and Margaret Blancher, .	"	II.	373
1761. Aug. 1.	Dominick, George, and Elizabeth Blanchard,	"	V.	20
1782. Nov. 18.	Domminick, Blanch, and Anthony Reece,...	"	XXXVII.	85

15

DATE.	NAMES.	RECORD.	VOL.	PAGE
1764. June 28.	Donaldson, Nemiah, and Sarah Webb,......	M. B.,	VIII.	242
1760. Sept. 1.	Dongan, Richard, and Cornelia Winter,.. ..	"	II.	508
1782. Dec. 7.	Dongan, Sarah, and Robert Burnham,......	"	XXXVII.	110
1782. Nov. 28.	Donnaldson, Jane, and Thomas Ramsey,....	"	XXXVII.	96
1778. Mar. 23.	Donnell, Simon, and Mary Noe,...........	"	XXV.	52
1762. Oct. 18.	Donnely, Sarah, and Robert Garland, ...	"	VI.	370
1763. Aug. 19.	Donnolly, Peter, and Elenor Magragh,......	"	VII.	307
1768. Jan. 26.	Donovan, Pierce, and Ellenor Powel,.......	"	XIII.	18
1777. July 8.	Dooly, Patrick, and Judith Daleury, ...	"	XXIV.	116
1757. Dec. 14.	Dooper, Christian, Jr., and Margaret Barnes,.	"	I.	741
1759. Nov. 27.	Dopking, Henderick, and Catharine Fforrest,	"	II.	519
1769. July 1.	Doran, Elizabeth, and Joseph Degroote, ...	"	XIV.	140
1776. Jan. 6.	Dorlan, Hannah, and Elias Burtis, ...	"	XXIII.	243
1766. Sept. 17.	Dorland, Garrit, and Susanah Van Lue,.....	"	X.	99
1782. June 22.	Dorland, Mary, and Samuel Dorland, Jr., ...	"	XXXVI.	60
1782. June 22.	Dorland, Samuel, Jr., and Mary Dorland, ...	"	XXXVI.	60
1782. Jan. 21.	Dorland, Thomas, Jr., and Mary Hall,......	"	XXXV.	27
1780. Nov. 7.	Dorlon, Joseph, and Elizabeth Smith, ...	"	XXX.	95
1770. Oct. 23.	Dorrell, Joseph, and Mary Anderson,.......	"	XVI.	225
1769. Mar. 9.	Dorry, Peter, and Margaret Acker, ...	"	XIV.	50
173?. Jan. 13.	Dosenbury, Elizabeth, and John Hulet,.....	"	I.	8
1779. Sept. 28.	Doty, Abigail, and William Mitchell,.......	"	XXVIII.	86
1775. Dec. 18.	Doty, Anna, and Joseph Kirby, ...	"	XXIII.	232
1770. Oct. 30.	Doty, Catherine, and John Rudyard, ...	"	XVI.	234
1736. Aug. 4.	Doty, Elizabeth, and Daniel Duning,.......	"	I.	2
1782. Oct. 17.	Doty, Isaac, and Elizabeth Williams,.......	"	XXXVII.	46
1783. June 23.	Doty, James, and Bridget Burns,......... .	"	XXXIX.	66
1766. Aug. 23.	Doty, Jane, and Augustus Bostwick, ...	"	X.	84
1761. Dec. 22.	Doty, John, and Lucy Smith, ...	"	V.	294
1764. Sept. 19.	Doty, Joseph, and Sarah Titus,............	"	VIII.	317
1782. Oct. 17.	Doty, Martha, and Daniel Willets, ...	"	XXXVII.	45
1753. April 10.	Doty, Samuel, and Elizabeth Francklin,.....	"	I.	20
1779. Mar. 7.	Doty, Seaman, and Sarah Gallaudet, ...	"	XXVII.	59
1778. Aug. 26.	Doty, Thomas, and Martha Simmons, ...	"	XXVI.	11
1761. Sept. 25.	Doty, William, and Elizabeth Mott,........	"	V.	99
1762. Jan. 29.	Doty, Zebulon, and Esther Henderson,.....	"	VI.	30
1762. Jan. 18.	Doty, Zebulon, and Hannah McCoon,......	"	VI.	15
1764. June 26.	Doubly, Jane, and Whitehead Skidmore,....	"	VIII.	237
1764. Feb. 25.	Dougan, John, and Mary Gordon, ...	"	VIII.	78
1781. Feb. 19.	Dougherty, Dominick, and Susannah Wilkinson,.....................................	"	XXXI.	51
1760. Jan. 23.	Dougherty, Hugh, and Rebecca Anderson,..	"	III.	4
1762. June 30.	Dougherty, James, and Judith Roome, ...	"	VI.	218
1777. June 16.	Doughty, Benjamin, and Rebecca Doughty, .	"	XXIV.	103
1773. July 5.	Doughty, Carolina, and John Clement, ...	"	XXI.	30

D. TR.	NAMES.	RECORD.	VOL. PAGE.
1780. Mar. 15.	Dow, Aaron, and Margeret Kerby,.........	M. B.,	XXIX. 1
1781. July 5.	Dow, Elizabeth, and John Dow,...........	"	XXXII. 104
1753. Sept. 25.	Dow, Eltje, and Guisbert Fonda, ...	"	I. 124
1757. Oct. 29.	Dow, Folkert, and Annatje Wendell,.......	"	I. 687
1780. Sept. 13.	Dow, Henry, and Mary Marsshalk, ...	"	XXX. 27
1775. April 11.	Dow, James, and Sarah Lewis, ...	"	XXIII. 7
1781. July 5.	Dow, John, and Elizabeth Dow,...........	"	XXXII. 104
1773. Feb. 17.	Dow, Phebe, and Benjamin Oakley,........	"	XX. 46
1765. Sept. 18.	Dow, Rachel, and Henry Van Ranselaer, ...	"	IX. 268
1777. July 15.	Dow, Sarah, and Henry Inness,...........	"	XXIV. 119
1772. July 29.	Dowdall, William, and Mary Brockus,......	"	XIX. 7
1766. July 17.	Dowdell, Richard, and Anna Wisener,......	"	X. 55
1783. Aug. 21.	Dowden, William, and Margaret Brown,....	"	XL. 6
1761. Sept. 24.	Dowe, Abraham, and Catharine Lansingh, ..	"	V. 97
1669. Aug. 23.	Dower, Catharine, and William White, ...	O. W. L.,	II. 523
1757. July 28.	Dowers, Jane, and George Clapham, ...	M. B.,	I. 604
1762. Sept. 22.	Dowers, John, and Elizabeth Seymour, ...	"	VI. 326
1773. Oct. 20.	Dowers, Joseph, and Maria De Freeze, ...	"	XXI. 145
1779. July 21.	Dowlin, Dennis, and Ann McAnalty,.......	"	XXVIII. 26
1776. April 25.	Dowling, Lawrence, and Sarah Marsh, ...	"	XXIII. 302
1758. Mar. 9.	Downen, Lucretia, and John Bashfurd, ...'.	"	I. 838
1767. Feb. 12.	Downes, Edward, and Elcie Colden,.	"	XI. 24
1778. Mar. 23.	Downey, Thomas, and Mary Smith,........	"	XXV. 51
1758. Dec. 6.	Downing, Ananias, and Deborah Birdsall,...	"	II. 118
1766. Nov. 1.	Downing, Anna, and Richard Kirk,........	"	X. 148
1770. Dec. 18.	Downing, Benjamin, and Martha Hopkins,..	"	XVI. 299
1779. May 29.	Downing, Elizabeth, and William Hopkins,..	"	XXVII. 151
1779. Oct. 2.	Downing, George, and Elizabeth Burtis, ...	"	XXVIII. 96
1775. Aug. 16.	Downing, Jacob, and Elizabeth Smith, ...	"	XXIII. 129
1780. Sept. 21.	Downing, Mercey, and Hezekiah Jewell, ...	"	XXX. 35
1763. Feb. 18.	Downing, Sarah, and Abraham Kussow,....	"	VII. 67
1764. April 5.	Downing, Sarah, and William Baker,.......	"	VIII. 136
1772. May 26.	Downman, Francis, and Jane Day,.... ...•	"	XVIII. 125
1763. May 30.	Downs, Hester, and Thomas Bissett, ...	"	VII. 208
1736. Jan. 20.	Downs, Mary, and Thomas Macburn,.......	"	I. 5
1780. Aug. 30.	Downy, Christian, and John Anderson,.....	"	XXX. 10
1773. Dec. 13.	Dox, Peter, and Margreta Ernest,..........	"	XXII. 71
1762. Jan. 22.	Doxey, Mary, and Joseph Cadles,..........	"	VI. 21
1782. Feb. 18.	Doxy, William, and Catharine Abrams,.....	"	XXXV. 58
1757. Mar. 8.	Doyl, Elce, and David Fitzsimmons, ...	"	I. 464
1764. Feb. 25.	Doyle, Derby, and Sophia Sthol,...........	"	VIII. 79
1773. May 18.	Doyle, John, and Sarah Doyle,............	"	XX. 117
1773. May 18.	Doyle, Sarah, and John Doyle,............	"	XX. 117
1782. Sept. 17.	Draisdel, Rachel, and David Dewer,.......	"	XXXVII. 3
1768. Sept. 28.	Drake, Anne, and Elijah Hunter, ...	"	XIII. 198

DATE.	NAMES.	RECORD.	VOL.	PAGE.
1765. Sept. 25.	Drake, Benjamin, and Martha Seaman, ...	M. B.,	IX.	274
1759. Dec. 29.	Drake, Benjamin, and Susanna Pell, ...	"	II.	561
1773. Nov. 27.	Drake, Catherine, and Oliver Smith, ...	"	XXII.	49
1778. Mar. 20.	Drake, Daniel, and Elizabeth Colden, ...	"	XXIX.	4
1767. Oct. 28.	Drake, Elijah, and Sarah Huggeford, ...	"	XII.	72
1764. Jan. 30.	Drake, Elizabeth, and Charles Wood, ...	"	VIII.	42
1757. Dec. 10.	Drake, Gilbert, and Elizabeth Underhill, ...	"	I.	734
1773. Aug. 26.	Drake, Hannah, and William Pinkney, ...	"	XXI.	85
1737. Oct. 21.	Drake, Joseph, and Catharine Baker, ...	"	I.	7
1762. Feb. 10.	Drake, Joseph, and Charity Fowler, ...	"	VI.	44
1757. Jan. 5.	Drake, Mary, and Frederick Steen, ...	"	I.	406
1765. Oct. 28.	Drake, Moses, and Hannah Wright, ...	"	IX.	322
1758. Oct. 18.	Drake, Joseph, and Phebe Hunt, ...	"	II.	61
1773. June 17.	Drake, Rebecca, and John Blagge, ...	"	XXI.	13
1765. Mar. 18.	Drake, Sarah, and Nicolaes Brouwer, ...	"	IX.	69
1758. Nov. 29.	Drake, Sarah, and Timothy Hunt, ...	"	II.	107
1760. Nov. 24.	Drane, William, and Ann Powers, ...	"	III.	437
1764. June 26.	Draw, Etje, and James Courry, ...	"	VIII.	238
1753. July 5.	Drew, Gilbert, and Sarah Hunt, ...	"	I.	73
1780. May 23.	Drew, Lebeus, and Mary Lott, ...	"	XXIX.	66
1763. Feb. 1.	Drinam, Hamilton, and Elizabeth Palmer, ...	"	VII.	45
1769. June 3.	Dring, Sarah, and David Betton, ...	"	XIV.	114
1771. June 15.	Drinker, John, and Minshe Lowereer, ...	"	XVII.	112
1736. July 1.	Drinkwater, Catherine, and David Goodwin,	"	I.	2
1756. Nov. 5.	Drinkwater, Helena, and Alexander Vans, ..	"	I.	346
1763. Sept. 7.	Drinkwater, Jane, and Samuel Thompson, ..	"	VII.	328
1777. May 9.	Driscall, Elizabeth, and George Morrison, ...	"	XXIV.	87
1759. Mar. 6.	Driskill, John, and Christian Tom, ...	"	II.	210
1671. Feb. 26.	Droogstraet, Hendrick, and Mary Jansen, ...	G. F.,	IV.	102
1755. Dec. 8.	Drummond, Donald, and Ann Groesbeck, ...	M. B.,	I.	228
1780. Dec. 23.	Drummond, Mary, and Alexander McGregor,	"	XXX.	166
1777. Oct. 23.	Drummy, Richard, and Mary Whaler, ...	"	XXIV.	170
1777. Sept. 4.	Drury, Edward, and Effimilah Crannell, ...	"	XXIV.	141
1767. Oct. 1.	Drury, Nicholas, and Catherine Smith, ...	"	XII.	53
1761. Jan. 20.	Drux, Augustine, and Anne Catherine, ...	"	IV.	22
1753. Sept. 21.	Duane, James, and Jane Smith, ...	"	I.	123
1782. Sept. 2.	Dubau, Catherine, and William Edey, ...	"	XXXVI.	134
1766. Nov. 20.	Dubois, Anna, and Gilbert Southerd, ...	"	X.	173
1762. Oct. 21.	Dubois, Ariantje, and Solomon Dubois, ...	"	VI.	377
1775. Aug. 7.	Du Bois, Catharine, and John Fonda, ...	"	XXIII.	122
1769. Dec. 8.	Dubois, Catherine, and Benjamin Low, Jr., ..	"	XV.	118
1768. May 14.	Dubois, Catherine, and John McCary, ...	"	XIII.	103
1777. Dec. 23.	Dubois, Charles, and Ann Winants, ...	"	XXIV.	204
1766. Sept. 15.	Dubois. Cornelia, and Cornelius C. Vernoye, .	"	X.	97
1771. Sept. 20.	Du Bois, Cornelius, Jr., and Geertruyd Briun,	"	XVII.	186

DATE.	NAMES.	RECORD.	VOL.	PAGE.
1764. Nov. 12.	Dubois, David, and Annetje Mynderson,....	M. B.,	VIII.	399
1772. Nov. 10.	Du Bois, Eleazer, and Sarah Cooper,.......	"	XIX.	107
1762. June 19.	Du Bois, Elizabeth, and Henry Johnson,....	"	VI.	197
1757. June 1.	Dubois, Elizabeth, and Judah Harlow,......	"	I.	545
1757. Oct. 26.	Du Bois, Esther, and Jesse Odell,..........	"	I.	681
1762. Nov. 10.	Du Bois, Gerritje, and Peter Crispell,.......	"	VI.	423
1760. Sept. 9.	Dubois, Isaac, and Jannitie Rosa,..........	"	III.	305
1764. April 17.	Du Bois, Jacamyntje, and Andrew Bevier,..	"	VIII.	159
1771. May 9.	Du Bois, Jane, and Jonas Kelsey,..........	"	XVII.	80
1767. Oct. 19.	Dubois, Janetje, and Johannes Terbush, ...	"	XII.	64
1770. Oct. 16.	Du Bois, Johannes, and Elizabeth Johnson, .	"	XVI.	215
1772. Sept. 9.	Dubois, John, and Margaret Dubois, ...	"	XIX.	46
1782. April 1.	Dubois, John, and Margrot Randol, ...	"	XXXV.	105
1773. Oct. 28.	Dubois, John, and Mary Gifford, ...	"	XXI.	150
1763. Feb. 14.	Dubois, John, and Sarah Crout,...........	"	VII.	62
1762. April 10.	Dubois, Leah, and Cornelius D. Wynkoop,..	"	VI.	98
1774. Feb. 2.	Du Bois, Lewis, and Abigail Wyer,........	"	XXII.	120
1736. Feb. 9.	Dubois, Lewis, and Catherine Vandike,.....	"	I.	5
1782. May 18.	Du Bois, Lewis, and Lucy Homes,..........	"	XXXV.	157
1756. Dec. 17.	Dubois, Lewis, and Rachel Dubois,..........	"	I.	389
1770. Mar. 19.	Du Bois, Lewis, and Rachel Johnson,......	"	XVI.	32
1772. Sept. 9.	Dubois, Margaret, and John Dubois,.......	"	XIX.	46
1773. Sept. 25.	Dubois, Martha, and John Andreet,.......	"	XXI.	122
1782. April 1.	Dubois, Mathew, and Daniel Winant,......	"	XXXV.	103
1769. April 24.	Dubois, Mathias, and Catherine Corrishon,..	"	XIV.	82
1781. Dec. 4.	Dubois, Mathias, and Margeret Marshall,...	"	XXXIV.	72
1759. Dec. 9.	Dubois, Matthew, and Antje Brinkerhoff,...	"	II.	525
1755. Aug. 28.	Dubois, Peter, and Jacamyntie Kipp,.......	"	I.	158
1757. Nov. 1.	Du Bois, Rachel, and Andries T. De Witt, ..	"	I.	693
1770. June 1.	Du Bois, Rachel, and John A. Hardenbergh,	"	XVI.	100
1756. Dec. 17.	Dubois, Rachel, and Lewis Dubois,........	"	I.	389
1764. Feb. 29.	Dubois, Rennelche, and Samuel Parkhurst,..	"	VIII.	87
1768. Mar. 31.	Dubois, Sarah, and Jacob I. Hasbrouck,....	"	XIII.	59
1773. April 2.	Du Bois, Sarah, and Jacobus Ter Bos, Jr.,..	"	XX.	80
1771. Mar. 11.	Du Bois, Sarah, and Michael Vandercook,..	"	XVII.	31
1763. April 12.	Dubois, Sarah, and Peter Harris,..........	"	VII.	124
1775. Nov. 23.	Du Bois, Sarah, and Petrus P. Crispel,.....	"	XXIII.	220
1762. Oct. 21.	Dubois, Solomon, and Ariantje Dubois,.....	"	VI.	377
1762. Oct. 21.	Dubois, Tyatje, and William Thompson,....	"	VI.	378
1782. May 21.	Du Bon, Elizabeth, and Charles Laforge,...	"	XXXVI.	15
1768. Oct. 19.	Du Boys, Christopher, Jr., and Ellinor Van Vhooris,.............................	"	XIII.	212
1762. Aug. 16.	Du Boys, Joel, and Mary Hooghtelyn,......	"	VI.	274
1764. Dec. 31.	Duboys, Lewis, and Alida Van Kleeck,.....	"	VIII.	470
1769. April 18.	Duboys, Peter, and Hannah Cheeseman,....	"	XIV.	77

DATE.	NAMES.	RECORD.	VOL.	PAGE.
1772. Sept. 23.	Duc, Daniel, and Louisa Stanton,..........	M. B.,	XIX.	55
1767. July 7.	Duchemin, Daniel, and Margaret Mettitel,..	"	XI.	126
1758. April 15.	Ducket, Ann Mary, and Thomas Blake,....	"	I.	873
1773. May 25.	Ducolon, Jane, and Peter Van Volkenburgh,	"	XX.	126
1773. July 16.	Ducolon, Stephen, and Mary Smith,.......	"	XXI.	41
173⅞. Feb. 6.	Ducolong, Claude, and Jane Osborne,......	"	I.	8
1757. April 30.	Ducworth, Sarah, and George Robinson,....	"	I.	521
1670. July 5.	Dudbridge, Angle, and John Marshall,......	C. A.,	II.	564
1762. June 22.	Dudfield, Jonathan, and Catharine Mount,..	M. B.,	VI.	203
1780. Oct. 17.	Dudley, Elizabeth, and Josiah Brown,.....	"	XXX.	68, 70
1780. Sept. 11.	Dudley, Elizabeth, and Peter Laune,..... ..	"	XXX.	24
1758. May 27.	Dudley, John, and Phebe Flinn,...........	"	I.	912
1766. June 17.	Dudley, William, and Mary Ganter,........	"	X.	19
1764. April 7.	Dudly, Stephen, and Cornelia Post,........	"	VIII.	141
1770. Dec. 8.	Duff, Eleanor, and Thomas English,........	"	XVI.	291
1763. July 20.	Duffee, Margaret, and William Cowen,.....	"	VII.	274
1781. Dec. 17.	Duffel, Edward, and Elizabeth Leonard,....	"	XXXIV.	92
1772. Jan. 22.	Duffey, James, and Cornelia Lynda,........	"	XVIII.	14
1756. Sept. 30.	Duffey, Peter, and Elizabeth Reece, ...	"	I.	312
1780. April 18.	Duffie, Cornelie, and Gozen Ryersz,......	"	XXIX.	28
1757. Sept. 30.	Duffie, Duncan, and Barbara Cropsey,......	"	I.	653
1760. Jan. 16.	Duffy, Catharine, and James Kirkwood,....	"	II.	583
1778. Feb. 20.	Duffy, Samuél, and Catharine Scorfield,....	"	XXV.	29
1763. Jan. 12.	Dufouer, Henry, and Mary Ferdon,........	"	VII.	15
1773. June 25.	Duggan, Arthur, and Mary Edwards,......	"	XXI.	23
1772. Nov. 13.	Duggan, John, and Martha Crawford,.....	"	XIX.	112
1758. Sept. 23.	Duglass, Alete, and George Ellis,..........	"	II.	32
1756. Dec. 20.	Duglass, Elizabeth, and William Blake,.....	"	I.	393
1778. Sept. 11.	Duke, John, and Elinor Obrien,...........	"	XXVI.	25
1757. Mar. 8.	Duly, Philip, and Margaret Gilmore,.......	"	I.	460
1776. Mar. 12.	Du Mond, Annatje, and Peter Elmendorph, Jr.,...........................	"	XXIII.	284
1773. May 15.	Dumond, Antonio, and Catharina Dumond,..	"	XX.	112
1773. May 15.	Dumond, Catharina, and Antonio Dumond,..	"	XX.	112
1760. Jan. 10.	Dumond, Egbert, and Margaritje Elmendorph, ...	"	II.	575
1773. Oct. 5.	Dumond, Marjte, and Henry Mours,.......	"	XXI.	130
1770. Nov. 15.	Dumond, Mary, and Henry Staats,........	"	XVI.	257
1772. April 16.	Dumond, Neeltie, and Conradt G. Elmendorph, ...	"	XVIII.	81
1765. Oct. 11.	Dumont, Catrina, and William Wells,......	"	IX.	298
1772. Oct. 2.	Dumont, John Baptist, and Altje Vanderbelt,	"	XIX.	65
1780. Nov. 14.	Dunavon, Hellena, and Neal McKennon,...	"	XXX.	104
1764. June 8.	Dunbar, Catharine, and Rykert Van Vranke,.	"	VIII.	217
1760. Dec. 30.	Dunbar, Garret, and Catherine Bratt,......	"	III.	497

Date.	Names.	Record.	Vol.	Page.
1778. June 12.	Dunbar, John, and Aletta Willet,..........	M. B.,	xxv.	99
1780. Sept. 6.	Dunbar, Joseph, and Phebe Mott,.........	"	xxx.	18
1761. June 13.	Dunbar, Mary, and Jabe Woodruff,........	"	iv.	239
1761. Nov. 16.	Dunbar, Peter, and Mary Oldfield,........	"	v.	220
1770. May 16.	Dunbar, William, and Elizabeth Van Deusen,	"	xvi.	89
1778. Oct. 5.	Duncan, Ann, and Richard Spencer,.......	"	xxvi.	47
1773. Sept. 13.	Duncan, Arabella, and Daniel Ludlow,.....	"	xxi.	107
1782. Sept. 21.	Duncan, Elizabeth, and Abraham Willson, Jr.,	"	xxxvii.	7
1781. Nov. 3.	Duncan, Elizabeth, and William Karr,......	"	xxxiv.	15
1756. Dec. 28.	Duncan, Frances, and Anthony Byvanck,...	"	i.	401
1762. April 29.	Duncan, Frances, and Henry Ludlow, Jr.,...	"	vi.	135
1753. Aug. 24.	Duncan, Warman, and Ruth Courtis,.......	"	i.	95
1681. May 19.	Duncan, James, and Bridgett Bendall,......	O. W.,	xxxii½.	46
1783. Sept. 16.	Duncan, James, and Margaret Craig,.......	M. B.,	xl.	41
1780. Dec. 14.	Duncan, John, and Sarah Hamilton,.......	"	xxx.	153
1760. Dec. 4.	Duncan, Martha, and Nathaniel Lawrence, Jr.,	"	iii.	455
1778. Oct. 13.	Duncan, Ruth, and John Brigs,...	"	xxvi.	58
1768. Feb. 24.	Duncan, Sarah, and William Wickam,......	"	xiii.	42
1763. Aug. 8.	Duncan, Thomas, and Isabell McIntosh,....	"	vii.	294
1773. June 8.	Duncan, Thomas, and Margaret Van Beverhoudt, ...	"	xx.	139
1737. Dec. 14.	Duncan, Thomas, and Mary Ketcham,......	"	i.	8
1779. Dec. 1.	Duncan, William, and Hannah Parsell,.....	"	xxviii.	156
1736. Aug. 4.	Duning, Daniel, and Elizabeth Doty,.......	"	i.	2
1778. Mar. 31.	Dunkell, Ann, and John Kennedy,........	"	xxv.	56
1778. Mar. 28.	Dunkle, Wilhelmina, and John Payne,.....	"	xxv.	55
1765. May 7.	Dunkley, Joseph, and Anne Wood,........	"	ix.	122
1759. June 2.	Dunlap, Alexander, and Elenor Brasier,....	"	ii.	302
1777. Nov. 25.	Dunlap, Janet, and George Keith,.........	"	xxiv.	187
1757. Nov. 3.	Dunlap, Joseph, and Margaret Ware, ...	"	i.	695
1768. Nov. 4.	Dunlap, Mary, and Robert Wells,...	"	xiii.	225
1780. Sept. 12.	Dunlop, Alexander, and Mary Hyat,.......	"	xxx.	25
1781. Nov. 7.	Dunn, Benjamin, and Mary Thorne,.......	"	xxxiv.	21
1779. Mar. 11.	Dunn, Charles, and Ann Brannon,.........	"	xxvii.	65
1763. Oct. 17.	Dunn, Elizabeth, and James Haile,........	"	vii.	390
1760. June 23.	Dunn, James, and Lucretia Anderson,......	"	iii.	195
1782. Mar. 16.	Dunn, John, and Margaret Wealbanch,.....	"	xxxv.	88
1783. Aug. 7.	Dunn, Jonathan, and Rebecca Rikeman,....	"	xxxix.	116
1781. Jan. 29.	Dunnalcha, John, and Hanna Parmer,......	"	xxxi.	30
1756. Sept. 28.	Dunne, James, and Elizabeth Baley,.......	"	i.	309
1779. April 20.	Dunnican, Dorothy, and Obadiah Johnson,..	"	xxvii.	114
1769. Feb. 4.	Dunning, Margaret, and Abijah Yelverton,..	"	xiv.	27
1780. Dec. 28.	Dunscomb, Daniel, and Elizabeth McKenny,	"	xxx.	171
1762. July 8.	Dunscomb, Daniel, and Gertruy Thurman,..	"	vi.	230
1775. May 9.	Dunscomb, Dennis, and Elizabeth Slover,...	"	xxiii.	26

DATE.	NAMES.	RECORD.	VOL. PAGE.
1762. Jan. 18.	Dunscomb, Dennis, and Sarah Schurman,...	M. B.,	VI. 16
1760. Mar. 17.	Dunscomb, Hannah, and Israel Munds,.....	"	III. 79
1760. Jan. 12.	Dunscomb, James, and Dorothy Penny,....	"	II. 578
1762. Dec. 1.	Dunscomb, James, and Mary Sharer,......	"	VI. 461
1760. Nov. 17.	Dunscomb, Mary, and James Armour,......	"	III. 421
1779. Nov. 27.	Dunscomb, Mary, and Samuel Spraggs,.....	"	XXVI. 102
1757. Nov. 29.	Dunstar, Margaret, and Peter Penier,......	"	I. 718
1765. April 4.	Du Pue, Mary, and Richard Wood,........	"	IX. 82
1761. Nov. 4.	Dupuy, Anne Sophia, and Daniel Jaqueri,..	"	V. 192
1769. Aug. 15.	Dupuy, Martha, and Edward Jones,.......	"	XV. 23
1757. Oct. 18.	Dupuy, Moses, and Leah Morgan,..........	"	I. 674
1766. Dec. 11.	Duran, Ann, and Walter Dobbs,...........	"	X. 199
1767. Feb. 21.	Durand, John, and Margret McKinney,.....	"	XI. 33
1782. July 15.	Durant, Christopher, and Rachel Chambers,.	"	XXXVI. 81
1762. Nov. 26.	Durette, Jane, and Edward Davis,.........	"	VI. 455
1757. July 15.	Durham, Geesie, and John Alvey,.........	"	I. 592
1773. July 13.	Durham, Thomas, and Elizabeth Fish,......	"	XXI. 36
1769. July 20.	Durland, Hylitje, and George Van Noorstrandt, ...	"	XV. 1
1762. June 28.	Durland, John, and Catharine Van Loo,....	"	VI. 210
1780. Dec. 14.	Durland, John, and Elizabeth Smith,......	"	XXX. 152
1770. Feb. 3.	Durland, Mary, and Jacob Hicks,.........	"	XVI. 10
1765. Jan. 18.	Durland, Massey, and Thomas Cheshire,....	"	IX. 22
1761. Jan. 4.	Durlandt, Jane, and John Durlandt,.......	"	IV. 50
1761. Jan. 4.	Durlandt, John, and Jane Durlandt,.......	"	IV. 50
1769. Jan. 31.	Durlin, Catherine, and Cornelius Van Noorotrant, ...	"	XIV. 23
1776. Jan. 19.	Durling, Ann, and Thomas Hewlett,.......	"	XXIII. 249
1782. June 22.	Durlon, Mary, and Samuel Durlon,........	"	XXXVI. 60
1782. June 22.	Durlon, Samuel, and Mary Durlon,........	"	XXXVI. 60
1767. April 4.	Durye, Abraham, and Neeltie Nagle,......	"	XI. 55
1765. May 24.	Durye, Ghertje, and Joseph De Baen,......	"	IX. 138
1771. Sept. 24.	Durye, John, and Jane Rappalje,..........	"	XVII. 189
1763. Oct. 29.	Durye, John, and Sarah Barkeleau,........	"	VII. 411
1758. Jan. 6.	Durye, Roeloff, and Jannetie Amerman,....	"	I. 772
1758. Dec. 13.	Durye, Simon, and Jane Vandervoort,.....	"	II. 127
1765. Oct. 1.	Duryea, Abraham, and Sarah Van Bunscouten, ...	"	IX. 283
1783. Nov. 3.	Duryea, Ann, and William Creede,........	"	XL. 103
1782. April 6.	Duryea, Cornelius, and Jane Cosseau,......	"	XXXV. 116
1775. Aug. 31.	Duryea, Elizabeth, and Derick Remsen, Jr.,.	"	XXIII. 143
1770. Nov. 30.	Duryea, Gabriel, and Phebe Hooglandt,....	"	XVI. 276
1780. June 26.	Duryea, Harmty, and John Nostrant,......	"	XXIX. 97
1773. Nov. 12.	Duryea, Phebe, and Rem A. Remsen,.....	"	XXII. 25
1782. Mar. 26.	Duryea, Rulef, and Sarah Roades,........	"	XXXV. 97

DATE.	NAMES.	RECORD.	VOL. PAGE.
1765. April 27.	Duryea, Sarah, and Charles Le Roux,......	M. B.,	IX. 112
1781. Oct. 18.	Duryea, Willimpy, and William Brambush,.	"	XXXIII. 106
1763. Oct. 3.	Duryee, Abraham, and Elizabeth Low,.....	"	VII. 419
1762. July 5.	Duryee, Abraham, and Sarah Van Wyck,...	"	VI. 227
1778. Feb. 24.	Duryee, Affy, and William Ramsen,.......	"	XXV. 31
1773. Mar. 26.	Duryee, Anne, and Isaac Boerum,.........	"	XX. 73
1769. April 25.	Duryee, Catherine, and Cornelius Van Ranst,	"	XIV. 85
1769. Mar. 21.	Duryee, Catherine, and John Brower,......	"	XIV. 56
1776. Feb. 24.	Duryee, Charles, and Catharine Lott,......	"	XXIII. 272
1757. June 2.	Duryee, Cornelia, and Francis Titus, Jr.,....	"	I. 554
1773. Oct. 6.	Duryee, Daniel, and Martha Lane,........	"	XXIX. 131
1765. May 31.	Duryee, Elizabeth, and Harmanus Barkelow,	"	IX. 148
1768. Dec. 16.	Duryee, Elizabeth, and Hendrick Vanderbelt,	"	XIII. 265
1759. Dec. 6.	Duryee, Elizabeth, and Tunis Wortman,....	"	II. 530
1783. Nov. 5.	Duryee, Gabriel, and Hannah Titus,.......	"	XL. 104
1772. Nov. 11.	Duryee, George, and Williamanchia Brownbush, ...	"	XIX. 109
1783. June 29.	Duryee, Jane, and Joseph Howard, ...	"	XXXIX. 71
1779. Mar. 29.	Duryee, Jacob, and Mary Van Wyck,......	"	XXVII. 81
1771. Sept. 12.	Duryee, John, and Elizabeth Burtis,.......	"	XVII. 182
1757. Dec. 15.	Duryee, Maria, and Garret Van Vicklaer,...	"	I. 746
1769. Sept. 25.	Duryee, Mary, and Christopher Roosevelt,..	"	XV. 43
1773. Sept. 27.	Duryee, Mary, and Nicholas Bennet,.......	"	XXI. 123
1771. Nov. 26.	Duryee, Nelly, and Abraham Brown,......	"	XVII. 269
1764. Sept. 15.	Duryee, Stephen, and Antje Lott,.........	"	VIII. 310
1755. Dec. 9.	Dusenberry, Jane, and Benjamin Barton,...	"	I. 229
1762. Nov. 18.	Dusenberry, John, and Hannah Gibbs,.....	"	VI. 442
1769. June 8.	Dusinberry, Elizabeth, and William Hewlett,	"	XIV. 117
1736. May 29.	Dussenberre, Jarvis, and Elizabeth Denton,.	"	I. 1
1756. Dec. 14.	Dussesway, Cornelius, and Catharine Corsel,	"	I. 382
1763. Dec. 23.	Dussoway, Mark, and Judith Poillon,......	"	VII. 520
1761. Dec. 15.	Dutchess, Mary, and Nicholas Brown Seabrook, ...	"	V. 280
1758. Sept. 11.	Duthie, James, and Jane Bancker,.........	"	II. 13
1761. April 18.	Duthie, Jane, and Agins McQuin,.........	"	IV. 155
1761. Feb. 19.	Dutree, Catherine, and Abraham Cole,.....	"	IV. 69
1779. April 7.	Dutton, Richard, and Phebe White,........	"	XXVII. 99
1762. July 21.	Duychinck, Christopher, and Catharine Gautier, ...	"	VI. 249
1773. June 8.	Duyckman, Anna, and Garret Peterson,....	"	XX. 140
1770. May 17.	Duyckman, Hester, and William De Witt,..	"	XVI. 90
1757. Jan. 15.	Duyckman, Janitie, and Charles Spranger,..	"	I. 413
1757. Jan. 15.	Duyckman, Janitie, and Joseph Towers,....	"	I. 414
1767. Feb. 13.	Duyckman, Jemima, and Henry Traphagar,.	"	XI. 25
1771. April 9.	Duyckman, Mary, and John Clarke,.......	"	XVII. 52

Date.	Names.	Record.	Vol. Page.
1775. Nov. 16.	Duykinck, Gerardus, and Susannah Livingston,	M. B.,	xxiii. 212
1779. Oct. 9.	Duyree, Ann, and Isaac Cornell,	"	xxviii. 107
1779. June 23.	Duyree, Cornelia, and Thomas Place,	"	xxviii. 4
1778. Mar. 18.	Duyree, Famitie, and John Van Pelt,	"	xxv. 46
1760. Feb. 9.	Dwight, Joseph, and Margaret Peterson,	"	iii. 29
1757. Sept. 21.	Dwight, Stephen, and Martha Glover,	"	i. 639
1783. Jan. 3.	Dwyer, Edmund, and Catharine Patterson,.	"	xxxviii. 3
1768. Sept. 14.	Dyckman, Angeltje, and Bernardus Rider,	"	xiii. 184
1760. April 26.	Dyckman, Catharine, and Balm Johnson Cozine,	"	iii. 125
1761. Jan. 14.	Dyckman, Charity, and John Middlemass,	"	iv. 18
1763. Sept. 10.	Dyckman, Jacobus, and Hannah Brown,	"	xxi. 106
1777. Dec. 9.	Dyckman, Jane, and John Vredenbergh,	"	xxiv. 192
1759. Mar. 29.	Dyckman, Jannetje, and Joast Debaam,	"	ii. 228
1773. June 15.	Dyckman, Mary, and Jacob Vermilya,	"	xxi. 10
1760. Jan. 24.	Dyckman, Oliker, and Wessell Hopper,	"	iii. 5
1763. Mar. 1.	Dyckman, Rebecca, and Samuel Benson,	"	vii. 86
1770. Aug. 27.	Dyckman, Samuel, and Rebecca Odell,	"	xvi. 174
1759. April 19.	Dyckman, Wyntje, and John Hopper,	"	ii. 246
1682. Aug. 28.	Dyer, Elizabeth, and John White,.	O. W.,	xxxii½. 159
1780. Dec. 16.	Dyer, Sarah, and Thomas Bealy,	M. B.,	xxx. 156
1772. Jan. 13.	Dyke, Daniel, and Elizabeth Dobbs,	"	xviii. 12
1760. Mar. 19.	Dyke, Margaret, and James Thomas,	"	iii. 82

E.

1770. Aug. 23.	Eackker, Maria, and Hendrick Wartt,	M. B.,	xvi. 168
1760. June 27.	Eaerhart, Robert, and Vroutie Bratt,	"	iii. 199
1763. Dec. 17.	Eagan, Elizabeth, and Alexander White,	"	vii. 507
1775. June 20.	Eagles, Elizabeth, and John Bennett,	"	xxiii. 71
1762. Feb. 11.	Eagles, John, and Mary Tallman,	"	vi. 46
1764. Nov. 22.	Eagleson, Elizabeth, and Alexander Manson,	"	viii. 421
1770. April 4.	Eaglin, John, and Ann Howell,	"	xvi. 48
1781. May 2.	Earl, Abigail, and James Rose,	"	xxxii. 29
1760. Aug. 30.	Earl, Alice, and Edward Smith,	"	iii. 275
1765. Aug. 17.	Earl, Catharine, and Samuel Borrowe,	"	ix. 240
1781. Sept. 1.	Earl, Charity, and John Watt,	"	xxxiii. 53
1773. Nov. 12.	Earl, Hannah, and George Fisher,	"	xxii. 22
1782. July 9.	Earl, Latey, and Stephen Ryder,	"	xxxvi. 76
1763. Dec. 1.	Earl, Marmaduke, and Martha Van Gelder,	"	vii. 489
1759. June 12.	Earl, Rebecca, and James Elliot,	"	ii. 320
1780. July 20.	Earl, Samuel, and Mary Langsbury,	"	xxix. 116
1780. Jan. 12.	Earl, Sarah, and Charles Brown,	"	xxviii. 194

DATE.	NAMES.	RECORD.	VOL.	PAGE.
1779. Sept. 14.	Earle, Elinor, and Thomas Lawrence,	M. B.,	XXVIII.	76
1737. Aug. 6.	Earle, Enock, and Chatie Vanderhoof,	"	I.	7
1778. Sept. 5.	Earle, Justus, and Ann Lawrence,	"	XXVI.	22
1779. Sept. 14.	Earle, Mary, and William Parker,	"	XXVIII.	74
1761. May 23.	Earle, Morris, and Abigail Leach,	"	IV.	203
1782. Dec. 11.	Earle, Morris, and Catharine Burwick,	"	XXXVII.	114
1778. Mar. 10.	Earle, Morris, and Elizabeth Terhune,	"	XXV.	38
1737. Aug. 9.	Earle, Nathaniel, and Fransainte Bonter,	"	I.	7
1778. Sept. 29.	Earle, Rebecca, and William I. Roome,	"	XXVI.	39
1774. Feb. 15.	Early, Emilia, and Andrew Van Duzer,	"	XXII.	128
1760. Sept. 9.	Earnest, John, and Sarah Ten Eyk,	"	III.	306
1671. June 3.	Earwin, William, and Jannekey Stevens,	C. A.,	II.	709
1666. July 17.	Eastall, Daniel, and Margaret Browning,	O. W. L.,	II.	85
1763. April 30.	Eastham, Emanuel, and Elizabeth Walker,	M. B.,	VII.	157
1759. July 5.	Eastley, Isaac, and Dorothy Lovet,	"	II.	349
1767. Aug. 6.	Easton, Elizabeth, and Joshua Marriner,	"	XII.	10
1758. Oct. 4.	Easton, Margaret, and William Grimes,	"	II.	39
1779. July 10.	Ebart, John, and Mary Elizabeth Pelletreau,	"	XXVIII.	20
1736. April 15.	Ebbets, Ellenor, and John Nevill,	"	I.	1
1753. Sept. 12.	Ebbets, Richard, and Jane Waldron,	"	I.	116
1758. Oct. 4.	Ebbitt, John, and Margaret Smith,	"	II.	40
1667. Sept. 28.	Ebell, Alice, and William Trotter,	O. W. L.,	II.	185
1781. May 16.	Ebert, Catherine, and William Powers,	M. B.,	XXXII.	49
1770. Dec. 14.	Ebert, Margaret, and Charles Meal,	"	XVI.	294
1762. Sept. 15.	Ebet, John J., and Mary Loman,	"	VI.	317
1738. June 3.	Ebon, John, and Vrontie Heyer,	"	I.	9
1772. Sept. 29.	Echts, Elizabeth, and Peter Hilton,	"	XIX.	62
1763. Nov. 29.	Ecker, Elizabeth, and John Sealie,	"	VII.	478
1753. May 17.	Ecker, Rachel, and Isaac Post,	"	I.	32
1770. Feb. 19.	Eckerson, Cornelius, and Rebecca Van Sant-ford,	"	XVI.	21
1770. May 1.	Eckert, Frederick, and Mary Zuricher,	"	XVI.	75
1757. Dec. 30.	Eckles, Hannah, and Daniel Carmagh,	"	I.	762
1736. Aug. 27.	Eckles, John, and Belatie Cowenover,	"	I.	2
1768. Dec. 10.	Eddey, William, and Mary Stevens,	"	XIII.	260
1775. Sept. 6.	Eden, Medcaf, and Martha Peltreau,	"	XXIII.	147
1782. Sept. 2.	Edey, William, and Catharine Duban,	"	XXXVI.	134
1767. May 6.	Edgar, Jane, and Thomas Wallace,	"	XI.	82
1783. Feb. 25.	Edgar, William, and Elizabeth Rice,	"	XXXVIII.	54
1772. Mar. 31.	Edmonds, Jane, and Benjamin Carpenter,	"	XVIII.	66
1738. July 25.	Edmondson, Jane, and John Triby,	"	I.	10
1780. Dec. 23.	Edo, Lellis, and John Gould,	"	XXX.	167
167⅝. Mar. 9.	Edsal, Anne, and William Laurence,	W. O. P.,	III.	183
1762. May 29.	Edsall, Catharine, and John Farrel,	M. B.,	VI.	174
1759. Mar. 2.	Edsall, Mary, and James Wendell,	"	II.	204

DATE.	NAMES.	RECORD.	VOL. PAGE.
1768. Jan. 19.	Edsall, Peter, and Alleta Clowes,..........	M. B.,	XIII. 12
1765. July 22.	Edsell, Francis, and William Byvanck,......	"	IX. 215
1757. Nov. 22.	Edwards, Anne, and Philip Welch, ...	"	I. 711
1771. Dec. 19.	Edwards, Benjamin, and Phebe Moore,....	"	XVII. 301
1767. Aug. 6.	Edwards, Daniel, and Margaret Hedger,....	"	XII. 11
1765. Jan. 7.	Edwards, Eleanor, and Jacob Morris,......	"	IX. 10
1757. Mar. 23.	Edwards, Elinor, and Bryan Carter,.......	"	I. 480
1778. Sept. 14.	Edwards, John, and Mary Hays,..........	"	XXVI. 29
1756. Sept. 13.	Edwards, John, and Mary Shampow,......	"	I. 295
1762. Nov. 1.	Edwards, Margaret, and Christopher Francis,	"	VI. 404
1737. Aug. 6.	Edwards, Marjetie, and John March, ...	"	I. 7
1773. June 25.	Edwards, Mary, and Arthur Duggan,......	"	XXI. 23
1771. Mar. 18.	Edwards, Mary, and Jonathan Worth,.....	"	XVII. 37
1759. Mar. 31.	Edwards, Mary, and Robert Gilmore,......	"	II. 230
1762. July 10.	Edwards, Mary, and Thomas Smith,.......	"	VI. 234
1737. Dec. 23.	Edwards, Phebe, and John Little,..... ...	"	I. 8
1769. Sept. 4.	Edwards, Pierpont, and Frances Ogden,....	"	XV. 35
1766. Nov. 17.	Edwards, Rebecka, and John Vandervoort,.	"	X. 167
1762. July 15.	Edwards, Richard, and Doshy D'Gree,.....	"	VI. 238
1783. April 23.	Edwards, Richard, and Elizabeth Dingey,...	"	XXXVIII. 110
1758. Dec. 12.	Edwards, Samuel, and Mary Rose,.........	"	II. 125
1757. Oct. 20.	Edwards, William, and Margaret Miller, ...	"	I. 676
1757. Oct. 25.	Egbersen, Mary, and Henry Knoll,........	"	I. 679
1771. Oct. 28.	Egberson, Martin, and Sinea Scharmehorn,..	"	XVII. 227
1781. Nov. 19.	Egbert, Edward, and Mary Cortelyow,.....	"	XXXIV. 48
1783. May 31.	Egbert, Jane, and William Williams,.......	"	XXXIX. 30
1782. Feb. 22.	Egbert, John, and Molly Holmes,.........	"	XXXV. 59
1781. Dec. 6.	Egbert, Walling, and Sarah Stager,........	"	XXXIV. 75
1779. Mar. 10.	Egberts, Abraham, and Ann Ridgeway,....	"	XXVII. 63
1767. May 12.	Egberts, Abraham, and Elizabeth Van Cleaf,	"	XI. 83
1769. Dec. 22.	Egberts, Anne, and William Waddle,.......	"	XV. 130
1769. Nov. 17.	Egberts, Anthony, and Mary Bodine,......	"	XV. 96
1771. April 23.	Egberts, Benjamin, and Mary Arison,......	"	XVII. 90
1767. May 12.	Egberts, Catherine, and John Egberts,.....	"	XI. 84
1736. Nov. 3.	Egberts, Christian, and John Wenshaer,....	"	I. 3
1763. Feb. 23.	Egberts, Elizabeth, and Joseph Van Pelts,..	"	VII. 76
1781. July 21.	Egberts, Frances, and Joseph Lake,........	"	XXXIII. 13
1767. May 12.	Egberts, John, and Catherine Egberts,.....	"	XI. 84
1760. Aug. 18.	Egberts, Mary, and Abraham Hopper,.....	"	III. 258
1775. Nov. 10.	Egberts, Mary, and Anthony Ten Eyck,....	"	XXIII. 205
1768. Feb. 10.	Egberts, Sarah, and Jyon Merrell,.........	"	XIII. 31
1766. July 31.	Egburson, Barbary, and Joseph Rose,......	"	X. 68
1778. May 9.	Egerton, Louisa, and John Lewey,.........	"	XXV. 77
1778. May 21.	Eggert, Christian, and Sophia Detluff,.......	"	XXV. 92
1761. Sept. 30.	Ehl, Elizabeth, and John Tice,.............	"	V. 107

DATE.	NAMES.	RECORD.	VOL.	PAGE.
1762. Nov. 17.	Ehl, Mary, and Peter Ehl,	M. B.,	VI.	439
1762. Nov. 17.	Ehl, Peter, and Mary Ehl,	"	VI.	439
1770. June 16.	Eights, Abraham, and Catharine Brooks,...	"	XVI.	115
1776. Mar. 25.	Eights, Mary, and Hendrickse Bradt,	"	XXIII.	290
1759. June 25.	Eim, George, and Catharine Punt,	"	II.	339
1765. May 18.	Elder, Margaret, and John Vanderveer, Jr.,.	"	IX.	130
1758. May 6.	Elderd, Abigail, and Charles Cornwell,	"	I.	894
1775. Aug. 24.	Elderd, Hendrich, and Catharine Cornell,...	"	XXIII.	133
1782. Mar. 25.	Elderd, John, and Mary Birdsall,	"	XXXV.	96
1775. April 20.	Eldert, Isaac, and Mary Wykoff,	"	XXIII.	13
1769. April 3.	Eldert, Jannatje, and Pieter Lott,	"	XIV.	63
1757. Jan. 11.	Eldert, Lucas, and Martha Mott,	"	I.	411
1782. June 7.	Eldert, Samuel, and Cathalina Ditmass,	"	XXXVI.	40
1685. April 9.	Elderts, Neltie, and Cornels Nicholls,	C. M.,	XXXIII.	110
1772. Feb. 12.	Eldred, Luke, and Jane Sidam,	M. B.,	XVIII.	36
1737. Sept. 7.	Eldridge, Elizabeth, and Henry Beackman,.	"	I.	7
1761. Feb. 12.	Eldridge, Mary, and Joseph Fitch,	"	IV.	60
1765. Sept. 21.	Eley, Robert, and Catherine McCloud,	"	IX.	269
1763. May 12.	Eley, Robert, and Esther Bowman,	"	VII.	183
1773. Dec. 8.	Eligh, Jacob, and Marytie Borsted,	"	XXII.	63
1771. Nov. 29.	Eligh, Margaret, and Phillip Moore,	"	XVII.	273
1772. Sept. 14.	Eligh, Margaret, and William Fiero,	"	XIX.	49
1762. July 3.	Eliot, John, and Mary Renolds,	"	VI.	224
1768. Feb. 29.	Elkins, Margaret, and William Harrald,....	"	XIII.	45
1756. Aug. 18.	Elkins, William, and Margaret Higby,	"	I.	272
1779. April 9.	Elliot, Elizabeth Plumstead, and Lord Cathcart,	"	XXVII.	100
1759. June 12.	Elliot, James, and Rebecca Earl,	"	II.	320
	Elliot, Lydia, and Mathew Brett,	"	VIII.	443
1768. Aug. 27.	Elliot, Margaret, and Charles Chatwood,....	"	XIII.	178
1773. Nov. 20.	Elliot, Eleanor, and James Jauncey, Jr.,....	"	XXII.	35
1759. Jan. 13.	Elliott, Andrew, and Letty Turk,	"	II.	155
1774. Feb. 5.	Elliott, Letitia, and Robert Stein,	"	XXII.	123
1764. Nov. 22.	Elliott, Samuel, and Margaret McCaller,....	"	VIII.	419
1761. July 22.	Ellis, Apphia, and Nicholas Stillwell,	"	V.	2
1765. June 21.	Ellis, Ariantje, and Peter Barbank,	"	IX.	178
1772. Sept. 4.	Ellis, Catherine, and Gabriel Ellison,	"	XIX.	41
1760. Nov. 7.	Ellis, Charles, and Susannah Webb,	"	III.	398
1783. Aug. 16.	Ellis, Elizabeth, and George Ryerson,	"	XXXIX.	128
1763. Feb. 8.	Ellis, Franuntje, and Benjamin Quackenboss, Jr.,	"	VII.	56
1758. Sept. 23.	Ellis, George, and Aleta Duglass,	"	II.	32
1781. May 30.	Ellis, George, and Catharine Carey,	"	XXXII.	64
1763. May 13.	Ellis, Henry, and Elizabeth Van Bommell,..	"	VII.	184
1768. April 11.	Ellis, Jane, and Rowland Cunnington,	"	XIII.	71

DATE.	NAMES.	RECORD.	VOL.	PAGE.
1761. Nov. 1.	Elmendorph, Cornelius, and Margaret Witteker, ...	M. B.,	v.	238
1770. Oct. 2.	Elmendorph, Jacobus, Jr., and Elizabeth Sammons, ...	"	XVI.	203
1765. Aug. 4.	Elmendorph, Jonathan, and Catherine Bruyn,	"	IX.	252
1760. Jan. 10.	Elmendorph, Margaritje, and Egbert Dumond,	"	II.	575
1775. April 22.	Elmendorph, Mary, and Philip Hardenbergh,	"	XXIII.	16
1776. Mar. 12.	Elmendorph, Peter, Jr., and Annetje Du Mond, ...	"	XXIII.	284
1779. Nov. 30.	Elpingston, Rebecca, and Alexander Hackett,	"	XXVIII.	154
1777. Mar. 15.	Elsden, Benjamin, and Elizabeth Gray, ...,	"	XXIV.	45
1757. Dec. 29.	Elsom, Allin, and Hester Van Als, ...	"	I.	758
1682. May 12.	Elston, William, and Elizabeth Cole, ...	O. W.,	XXXII½.	120
1763. Dec. 28.	Elsworth, Anne, and Jeremiah Brower, ...	M. B.,	VII.	526
1737. May 11.	Elsworth, Anne, and Thomas Seamour, ...	"	I.	6
1759. Feb. 16.	Elsworth, Christopher, and Sarah Brewer, ...	"	II.	194
1737. May 9.	Elsworth, Elizabeth, and Richard Leasraft, ..	"	I.	6
1765. April 30.	Elsworth, Elizabeth, and Walter Cosine, ...	"	IX.	116
1770. Mar. 14.	Elsworth, Hannah, and William Candell, ...	"	XVI.	31
1775. July 31.	Elsworth, Henrietta, and William Lary, ...	"	XXIII.	115
1772. Mar. 4.	Elsworth, Hester, and Isaac Chadravoyne, ..	"	XVIII.	48
1771. Dec. 21.	Elsworth, Hilletye, and Abraham Russell, ..	"	XVII.	302
1778. Oct. 15.	Elsworth, John, and Margaret King, ...	"	XXVI.	61
1758. Sept. 12.	Elsworth, Margaret, and John Fine, ...	"	II.	16
1758. Oct. 18.	Elsworth, Mary, and Abraham Brower, ...	"	II.	60
1753. Aug. 13.	Elsworth, Mary, and Christopher Stymes, ..	"	I.	90
1766. Sept. 25.	Elsworth, Mary, and George Shaw, ...	"	X.	106
1763. Sept. 30.	Elsworth, Mary, and John Debow, Jr., ...	"	VII.	364
1773. June 14.	Elsworth, Theophilus, and Mary Bross, ...	"	XXI.	2
1778. June 23.	Elsworth, Theophilus, and Mary Stymets, ..	"	XXV.	111
1761. Oct. 29.	Elsworth, Thomas, and Catharine Brewer, ..	"	v.	175
1772. May 19.	Elsworth, Thomas, and Maria Vannise, ...	"	XVIII.	113
1759. May 16.	Elsworth, Verdine, and Dorothy Gale, ...	"	II.	286
1756. Oct. 5.	Elsworth, William, Jr., and Hendrika Stoutenburgh, ...	"	I.	318
1759. Nov. 7.	Elsworth, William, and Catharine Bakeman,	"	II.	489
1767. July 17.	Elsworth, William, and Elizabeth Van Schaick,	"	XI.	135
1769. Mar. 25.	Elsworth, William I., and Ann Van Dalsam,	"	XIV.	59
1770. Sept. 20.	Elting, Elizabeth, and James Rowe, ...	"	XVI.	191
1776. April 25.	Eltinge, Annatje, and Dirck D. Wynekoop, .	"	XXIII.	301
1773. July 15.	Eltinge, Catherine, and Solomon Bavier, ...	"	XXI.	39
1776. Mar. 21.	Eltinge, Cornelius, and Blandion Elmendorph,	"	XXIII.	288
1766. Oct. 22.	Eltinge, Elsie, and Silvester Salisbury, ...	"	X.	138
1763. Nov. 24.	Eltinge, Janetje, and Peter Hoghteling, ...	"	VII.	470
1773. Sept. 6.	Eltinge, Jannatie, and Tjerck C. Dewitt, ...	"	XXI.	101

DATE.	NAMES.	RECORD.	VOL.	PAGE.
1770. Aug. 17.	Eltinge, Peter, and Richard Van Gaesbeek,.	M. B.,	XVI.	161
1765. Oct. 29.	Eltinge, Sarah, and Derick D. Wynkoop,...	"	IX.	331
1772. Dec. 7.	Eltinge, Tryntje, and Jacobus G. Hardenbergh,	"	XIX.	143
1779. Sept. 6.	Elvans, Henry, and Jane Brown,	"	XXVIII.	70
1773. Sept. 21.	Elvendorp, Margaret, and John Hardenbergh,	"	XXI.	117
1760. July 7.	Elvy, Isaac, and Jane Campbell,.'.	"	III.	206
1759. Feb. 7.	Eman, Lawrens, and Catharine Van Vleek,.	"	II.	181
1760. Aug. 5.	Eman, Margaret, and David Frederick Geller,	"	III.	234
1778. May 25.	Emans, Cornelius, and Margaret Schenck,...	"	XXV.	93
1776. Dec. 7.	Emans, Hendrick, Jr., and Sarah Bergen,...	"	XXIII.	316
1767. Jan. 13.	Emans, Jacobus, and Catherine Snederger,..	"	XI.	7
1768. May 19.	Emans, Johannes, and Maria Wyckoff,....	"	XIII.	106
1773. Nov. 3.	Emans, John, and Lucretia Williamson,....	"	XXII.	10
1778. Aug. 21.	Emans, John, and Margaret Schenck,	"	XXVI.	8
1765. April 10.	Emans, John, and Mary Alleger,	"	IX.	85
1779. May 8.	Emans, Margaret, and John Noorstrant,...:	"	XXVII.	130
1781. June 8.	Emans, Margeret, and Peter Bennet,.	"	XXXII.	77
1764. Oct. 24.	Emans, Sarah, and Hendrick Wyckoff,	"	VIII.	373
1779. April 3.	Embre, Ann, and William Nelson,	"	XXVII.	92
1773. Mar. 24.	Embree, Abigail, and Robert Campbell,....	"	XX.	70
1780. Dec. 26.	Embree, Effingham, and Mary Lawrence,...	"	XXX.	169
1779. July 28.	Embree, John, and Elizabeth Webb,	"	XXVIII.	31
1757. Oct. 11.	Embree, Mary, and Thomas Willet,	"	I.	665
1771. Jan. 11.	Embree, Samuel, and Sarah Hyat,	"	XVII.	4
1776. Feb. 5.	Embree, Stephen, and Hannah Emmery,...	"	XXIII.	258
1761. April 17.	Embree, Thomas, and Catherine Stevens,...	"	IV.	152
1777. Aug. 19.	Embury, Catherine, and Abraham Bininger,	"	XXIV.	135
1774. Mar. 12.	Emens, Antje, and Samuel Hubbard,	"	XXII.	145
1757. Feb. 11.	Emerson, Ann, and Sylvanus Ludlam,	"	I.	816
1783. Oct. 29.	Emery, Elenor, and James Molloy,	"	XL.	93
1781. July 12.	Emery, Jane, and William Nelson,	"	XXXIII.	5
1761. Mar. 19.	Emmans, James, and Rachel Bennet,	"	IV.	110
1780. May 16.	Emmas, Mary, and James Buckley,	"	XXIX.	57
1771. April 30.	Emmens, Jacob, and Elizabeth Glean,	"	XVII.	73
1776. Feb. 5.	Emmery, Hannah, and Stephen Embree,...	"	XXIII.	258
1777. Oct. 8.	Emmes, Lydia, and John S. Brownrig,	"	XXIV.	160
1783. Mar. 4.	Emmons, Mary, and Nicholas Van Brunt,...	"	XXXVIII.	61
1753. June 1.	Emmons, Rebeccah, and Hendrick Suydam, Jr.,	"	I.	54
1758. April 22.	Emmot, John, and Hannah Brewer,	"	I.	881
1779. May 15.	Emmot, Rachel, and George Wighton,	"	XXVII.	137
1780. Aug. 9.	Emory, Deborah, and Paul Trumpour,	"	XXIX.	137
1761. July 13.	Emott, Esther, and Thomas Nevill,	"	IV.	296
1756. Nov. 11.	Emptye, Johannes, and Catlyna Wempel,...	"	I.	351

17

DATE.		NAMES.	RECORD.	VOL.	PAGE.
1762. Jan.	22.	Emry, William, and Hannah Outerkerk, ...	M. B.,	VI.	22
1782. Jan.	3.	Ende, Francis Hartman, and Penelope Forsy,	"	XXXV.	7
1759. Oct.	1.	Endover, Prudence, and Thoman Isemonger, .	"	II.	437
1756. Sept.	28.	Engelsfred, Maria Catrina, and Samuel Martin Rebstook, ...:.	"	I.	310ᶜ
1761. April	4.	England, Ann, and Thomas Meek, ...	"	IV.	134
1763. May	25.	English, John, and Barbary Oliver, ...	"	VII.	202
1770. Aug.	21.	English, John, and Hester Neil, ...	"	XVI.	165
1761. Oct.	6.	English, John, and Jane Harper, ...	"	V.	123
1765. Sept.	27.	English, Mary, and Abraham Cannon, ...	"	IX.	278
1770. Dec.	8.	English, Thomas, and Eleanor Duff, ...	"	XVI.	291
1760. Oct.	2.	English, Thomas, and Mary Reyan, ...	"	III.	341
1780. Sept.	2.	Engslete, Rebecca, and Christien de Molitor,	"	XXX.	15
1756. Sept.	30.	Enlew, Sarah, and Hugh Maginnis, ...	"	I.	311
1768. June	4.	Ennic, Ann, and Jane Appleby, ...	"	XIII.	120
1783. July	31.	Ennis, Hannah, and Daniel Beck, ...	"	XXXIX.	106
1764. April	19.	Ennis, Henry, and Rebecca Simmonds, ...	"	VIII.	162
1767. Mar.	24.	Ennis, James, and Ann Oakley, ...	"	XI.	49
1761. Aug.	15.	Ennis, Peter, and Nieltje Stagg, ...	"	V.	44
1763. Feb.	1.	Ensworth, Mary, and William Barrett, ...	"	VII.	46
1756. Dec.	7	Ent, John, and Ann Wessels, ...	"	I.	376
1770. June	27.	Enters, John, and Mary See, ...	"	XVI.	123
1783. Jan.	18.	Enyard, John, and Anne Bennet, ...	"	XXXVIII.	20
1772. Dec.	2.	Erle, Hannah, and James Parsell, ...	"	XIX.	140
1763. June	21.	Ernest, Catharine, and John Lasher, ...	"	VII.	235
1773. Dec.	13.	Ernest, Margreta, and Peter Dox, ...	"	XXII.	71
1755. Oct.	24.	Erskin, John, and Ann Flanagan, ...	"	I.	199
1761. Feb.	4.	Erskine, Thomas, and Mary Gano, ...	"	IV.	52
1778. Oct.	7.	Erving, John, and Frances Ramsay, ...	"	XXVI.	48
1762. Aug.	27.	Erwin, Alexander, and Elizabeth Johnson, ..	"	VI.	295
1764. Sept.	6.	Erwin, Anne, and Peter Quackenbuss, ...	"	VIII.	299
1758. Oct.	9.	Erwin, Edward, and Elizabeth Johnson, ...	"	II.	43
1675. July	16.	Erwin, Jannitie, and Clement Sebra, ...	W., O., P.,	III.	124
1775. July	26.	Eseler, Catharine, and Barent Cole, ...	M. B.,	XXIII.	106
1764. Nov.	15.	Esiel, Maria, and Jacob Van Hoesen, ...	"	VIII.	409
1758. Jan.	23.	Esmond, Isaiah, and Jannetje De Long, ...	"	I.	798
1763. May	11.	Esmond, Jacob, and Mary Smith, ...	"	VII.	178
1770. Jan.	17.	Eson, Jane, and Andrew Spence, ...	"	XVI.	7
1769. July	4.	Esselstyn, Elizabeth, and Michael Horton, ..	"	XIV.	141
1769. Oct.	23.	Esselstyne, Gabriel, and Catlyne Van Valkenburgh, ...	"	XV.	62
1760. Dec.	29.	Estilltine, Weamthy, and John Upham, Jr., .	"	III.	495
1761. Feb.	19.	Ethrington, John, and Elizabeth Powell, ...	"	IV.	70
1766. June	13.	Ettsell, Joanna, and Henry Bonta, ...	"	X.	16
1768. Oct.	14.	Etwards, Sarah, and Henry Heder, ...	"	XIII.	210

DATE.	NAMES.	RECORD.	VOL.	PAGE.
1763. June 21.	Euen, Elizabeth, and William Whitnell, ...	M. B.,	VII.	238
1783. April 12.	Eurine, Elinor, and Abraham Sarvant, ...	"	XXXVIII.	92
1675. June 15.	Eustace, Honor, and Thomas Williams, ...	W., O., P.,	III.	97
1783. May 7.	Evans, Ann, and Robert Carter, ...	M. B.,	XXXIX.	3
1783. Sept. 7.	Evans, Catharine, and Richard Way, ...	"	XL.	30
1780. Oct. 16.	Evans, Catharine, and Thomas Kelly, ...	"	XXX.	66
1757. May 28.	Evans, David, and Hester Devoe, ...	"	I.	544
1760. July 19.	Evans, David, and Mary Nixon, ...	"	III.	219
1782. July 30.	Evans, Elizabeth, and Arthur Dingwall, ...	"	XXXVI.	94
1757. May 25.	Evans, Elizabeth, and John Crisp, ...	"	I.	542
1758. Oct. 12.	Evans, George, and Elizabeth Brewerton, ...	"	II.	54
1777. April 4.	Evans, Hannah, and William Letteney, ...	"	XXIV.	57
1777. Jan. 5.	Evans, James, and Sarah Brown, ...	"	XXIV.	7
1780. July 4.	Evans, Jane, and John Wells, ...	"	XXIX.	105
1775. July 14.	Evans, John, and Elizabeth Dickson, ...	"	XXIII.	97
1759. April 26.	Evans, John, and Mary Hinchman, ...	"	II.	256
1780. Sept. 30.	Evans, John, and Sarah Bowne, ...	"	XXX.	48
1762. Dec. 29.	Evans, Margaret, and Hector McKenzie, ...	"	VI.	462
1759. June 7.	Evans, Martha, and John Anderson, ...	"	II.	308
1778. Sept. 12.	Evans, Rachel, and John Tench, ...	"	XXVI.	27
1761. April 6.	Evans, Robert, and Mary Kendall, ...	"	IV.	135
1783. Aug. 30.	Evans, Sarah, and Alexander Pringel, ...	"	XL.	17
1757. Feb. 5.	Evans, Thomas, and Elizabeth Burton, ...	"	P.	435
1769. Oct. 27.	Evans, William, and Isabella Applegate, ...	"	XV.	69
1760. Feb. 25.	Eve, Elizabeth, and Peter Burger, ...	"	III.	50
1781. March 3.	Eve, Joseph, and Martha Moore, ...	"	XXXI.	64
1764. Nov. 21.	Everett, John, and Deborah Moore, ...	"	VIII.	417
1765. Jan. 4.	Everett, Latitia, and Timothy Cornell, ...	"	IX.	6
1782. Jan. 26.	Everit, Benjamin, and Sarah Higby, ...	"	XXXV.	33
1760. Aug. 16.	Everit, Elizabeth, and John Faulkner, ...	"	III.	256
1773. Dec. 14.	Everit, Emilia, and Richard Wilkinson, ...	"	XXII.	75
1772. May 13.	Everit, Esther, and Daniel McGuin, ...	"	XVIII.	110
1765. Jan. 29.	Everit, Magdalen, and Teunis Corsa, ...	"	IX.	33
1771. Sept. 30.	Everit, Phebe, and John Jackson, ...	"	XVII.	197
1761. Feb. 18.	Everit, Phebe, and William Martin, ...	"	IV.	68
1757. Mar. 12.	Everit, Richard, and Susannah Hendrickson,	"	I.	466
1779. Mar. 30.	Everitt, Hannah, and Stephen Post, ...	"	XXVII.	84
1782. Oct. 22.	Everitt, Jane, and David Purdy, ...	"	XXXVII.	59
1780. April 17.	Everitt, John, and Mary Polhamus, ...	"	XXIX.	26
1763. Oct. 5.	Everitt, Mary, and Hugh Van Kleeck, ...	"	VII.	372
1768. May 12.	Everitt, William, and Sarah Ayres, ...	"	XIII.	102
1759. Mar. 20.	Everson, Catherine, and Robert Patterson, .	"	II.	222
1773. Oct. 2.	Everson, Elizabeth, and Henry Van Houser,	"	XXI.	129
1761. Oct. 17.	Everson, Jacob, and Margaret Bloom, ...	"	V.	146
1780. Oct. 26.	Evert, Jacob, and Catherine Smith, ...	"	XXX.	81

DATE.	NAMES.	RECORD.	VOL. PAGE.
1756. Aug. 27.	Evertse, Maria, and Jacob Jacobs,.........	M. B.,	I. 278
1771. April 15.	Evertsen, Bernardus, and Martina Hogen,..	"	XVII. 59
1764. Sept. 19.	Evonet, John, and Lydia Marsh, ...	"	VIII. 315
1763. Dec. 10.	Evouts, Elinor, and John Bassett,.........	"	VII. 501
1757. June 11.	Evouts, Elizabeth, and Thomas Cunningham,	"	I. 562
1764. Oct. 20.	Ewetse, Mary, and Jacob Van Wagener,....	"	VIII. 381
1778. July 29.	Ewing, Daniel, and Isabella Macbeth,......	"	XXV. 142
1780. June 24.	Ewing, Isabella, and Wilson Bratten,......	"	XXIX. 94
1769. April 13.	Exceen, Alexander, and Catharine Waldron,	"	XIV. 73
1765. Oct. 3.	Eylang, Elizabeth, and James Blanchard,...	"	IX. 288
1763. May 30.	Eyles, John, and Margaret Holliday,.......	"	VII. 207
1764. Aug. 16.	Eyles, John, and Sarah Fraser,............	"	VIII. 285
1765. Sept. 25.	Eyles, Sarah, and Thomas King,..........	"	IX. 275
1761. June 24.	Eyraud, Judith, and Lawrence Killbrunn,...	"	IV. 258
1774. Jan. 26.	Eyre, Benjamin, and Mary Cheesman,......	"	XXII. 116
1759. June 8.	Ezeler, Henry, and Cornelia Vanderwater,..	"	II. 313

F.

1772. Aug. 28.	Fach, Henry, and Gedey Weaver,.........	"	XIX. 31
1772. June 4.	Factory, Nicholas, and Abebgeltie Seydam,.	"	XVIII. 132
1775. Oct. 9.	Faesh, John Jacob, and Elizabeth Brincker-		
	hoff, ...	"	XXIII. 174
1760. Dec. 5.	Fagg, Roger, and Johanna Loring,.........	"	III. 457
1767. Dec. 21.	Fagg, Roger, and Martha McGillicuddy,....	"	XII. 118
1777. Oct. 7.	Fagh, Mary Margaret, and Frederick Joseph		
	Heysen, ...	"	XXIV. 159
1782. Oct. 29.	Fairbaien, John, and Alida Banta,.........	"	XXXVII. 67
1781. Aug. 1.	Fairchild, Anne, and Jacob Simmons,......	"	XXXIII. 26
1760. Mar. 24.	Fairchild, Reuben, and Mary Wells,.......	"	III. 91
1778. Dec. 22.	Fairchild, Thomas, and Elizabeth Vanderwa-		
	ter, ...	"	XXVI. 129
1771. Mar. 18.	Faircloy, George, and Elizabeth Garrick,....	"	XVII. 35
1765. April 2.	Fairley, Joseph, and Frances Davis,........	"	IX. 79
1773. Nov. 12.	Fairley, Martha, and Seth Young,.........	"	XXII. 23
1757 June 2.	Fairlie, James, and Phebe Mitchell, ...	"	I. 549
1765. July 4,	Fallansby, Mary, and Daniel McClure,. ...	"	IX. 194
1760. May 16.	Falls, George, and Rachael Mulliner, ...	"	III. 154
1773. Oct. 13.	Falls, Rachel, and James Denniston, ...	"	XXI. 140
1772. Nov. 23.	Falls, Samuel, and Mary Denton,..........	"	XIX. 125
1760. Oct. 31.	False, Barbary, and Robert Brown,........	"	III. 389
1762. May 5.	Fannell, Mary, and Frederick Aubery,.....	"	VI. 146
1770. July 3.	Fanning, John, and Ann Clotworthy,......	"	XVI. 144
1764. Feb. 23.	Fardon, Isaac, and Elisabeth King,........	"	VIII. 75

DATE.		NAMES.	RECORD.	VOL.	PAGE.
1753. July	2.	Fardon, Jacob, and Catalina Fells,.........	M. B.,	I.	69
1782. June	1.	Fargie, Anne, and Samuel Nicoll,..........	"	XXXVI.	34
1757. May	24.	Fargie, Winter, and Eve Holland,.........	"	I.	540
1779. Nov.	26.	Farish, Greggs, and Margaret Collins,......	"	XXVIII.	151
1679. Oct.	14.	Farley, Anne, and William Dove,.........	G. E.,	XXXII.	62
1770. Oct.	11.	Farley, James, and Zerviah Latting,.......	M. B.,	XVI.	208
1772. June	5.	Farley, Mary, and Benjamin Yongs,.......	"	XVIII.	134
1759. Mar.	8.	Farman, Sarah, and Michael B. Goldthwait,..	"	II.	213
1764. July	25.	Farmer, Christian, and John Marschalk,....	"	VIII.	268
1772. Dec.	10.	Farmer, Elizabeth, and Thomas Farmer,....	"	XIX.	150
1758. Sept.	11.	Farmer, Jasper, and Mary Grant,..........	"	II.	12
1759. Jan.	19.	Farmer, Mary, and Richard Nickleson,.....	"	II.	161
1760. Sept.	24.	Farmer, Peter, and Mary Leacraft,........	"	III.	326
1772. Dec.	10.	Farmer, Thomas, and Elizabeth Farmer,....	"	XIX.	150
1770. May	5.	Farquhar, Elizabeth, and John Amiel,.....	"	XVI.	79
1759. Mar.	12.	Farquhar, William, and Jane Colden,......	"	II.	214
1769. July	11.	Farr, Hester, and John O'Brien,...........	"	XIV.	148
1761. Oct.	24.	Farr, Martha, and Thomas Needham,......	"	V.	167
1760. May	29.	Farrel, John, and Catharine Edsall,........	"	VI.	174
1761. May	25.	Farrel, Margaret, and Anthony Rose,......	"	IV.	206
173⅞. Feb.	9.	Farrel, Mary, and Lew Nodine,...........	"	I.	8
1783. April	23.	Farrell, Catharine, and James Bradley,.....	"	XXXVIII.	111
1762. Dec.	23.	Farrell, Catharine, and William Kirby,.....	"	VI.	497
1783. Aug.	2.	Farrell, John, and Jane Ellison,...........	"	XXXIX.	108
1758. Sept.	12.	Farrell, John, and Mary Galloway, ...	"	II.	18
1757. Dec.	12.	Farroll, Margaret, and Martin Farrell,	'	I.	738
1757. Dec.	12.	Farrell, Martin, and Margaret Farrell,......	"	I.	738
1762. Sept.	10.	Farrell, Mary, and Joshua Thomason,......	"	VI.	313
1761. Jan.	23.	Farrington, Benjamin, and Susanna Tonkins,	"	IV.	27
1780. Dec.	9.	Farrington, Catharine, and Thomas Tom,...	'	XXX.	147
1783. Oct.	7.	Farrington, Charles, and Mary Way,.......	"	XL.	69
1766. July	19.	Farrington, Dorothy, and Edward Hopper,..	"	X.	57
1780. Oct.	5.	Farrington, George, and Elizabeth Pinfold, .	"	XXX.	55
1760. Feb.	27.	Ffarrington, Hannah, and William Haywood,	"	III.	53
1780. Dec.	11.	Farrington, Isabella, and John Heitman,....	"	XXX.	149
1758. Dec.	21.	Farrington, James, and Sarah Lawrence,...	"	II.	135
1781. April	28.	Farrington, Jonas, and Euphaney Lawrence,	"	XXXII.	20
1780. Aug.	30.	Farrington, Matthew, and Phebe McCollin,.	"	XXX.	8
1775. June	24.	Farrington, Matthew, and Sarah Woodward,	"	XXIII.	76
1757. Feb.	19.	Farris, Robert, and Esther Merrit,.........	"	I.	442
1761. April	21.	Fashee, Mary, and Joseph Waldron,.......	"	IV.	156
1766. June	27.	Faulk, Chrishe, and William Garret,.......	"	X.	37
1758. Oct.	2.	Faulkner, John, and Ann Phillips,.........	"	II.	63
1760. Aug.	16.	Faulkner, John, and Elizabeth Everit,......	"	III.	256
1769. July	11.	Faulkner, William, and Garritje Ten Eyck,..	"	XIV.	149

DATE.	NAMES.	RECORD.	VOL.	PAGE.
1781. Dec. 13.	Faunote, Phebe, and John Murry,.........	M. B.,	XXXIV.	85
1783. Aug. 6.	Fea, Catharine, and John Gaber,..........	"	XXXIX.	113
1777. Feb. 21.	Fea, Charles, and Mary Johnson,..........	"	XXIV.	32
1781. June 18.	Fearly, Joseph, and Rachel Concklin, ...	"	XXXII.	89
1760. Feb. 1.	Ffector, Maggeltye, and Rem Couwenhoven,	"	III.	20
1779. Nov. 14.	Fee, Jacob, and Rebecca Applebee,........	"	XXVIII.	129
1757. April 15.	Feely, Jacob, and Catharine Cottington,....	"	I.	500
1781. April 24.	Fegan, John, and Jane Grigg,.............	"	XXXII.	12
1782. April 24.	Feilding, Catharine, and Jacob Vanhourn,..	"	XXXV.	134
1764. Mar. 24.	Feks, Mary, and William Roe,............	"	VIII.	117
1762. Nov. 12.	Felinch, William, and Jannetje Van Vranken,.	"	VI.	429
1782. Nov. 11.	Feley, Ezekiel, and Anne Vandine,........	"	XXXVII.	78
1763. April 15.	Felmer, George, and Esther Green,........	"	VII.	128
1761. Aug. 14.	Fellman, Judith, and Samuel Boyer,.......	"	V.	43
1778. Aug. 10.	Fenton, Elenor, and David O'Bryan,.......	"	XXV.	147
1783. Nov. 17.	Fenton, John. and Catharine Butler,.......	"	XL.	121
1682. Mar. 16.	Fenton, Joseph, and Mary Nixon,.........	E.,	XXXIII.	44
1783. Oct. 2.	Ferdon, Elizabeth, and Peter Creighton,....	M. B.,	XL.	59
1762. May 2.	Ferdon, Jacob, and Allada Cypher,........	"	VI.	156
1763. Jan. 12.	Ferdon, Mary, and Henry Dufouer,........	"	VII.	15
1757. Sept. 23.	Fayerweather, Samuel, and Mary Sutton, ..	"	I.	642
1761. Jan. 29.	Ferguson, Daniel, and Anne Strong,.......	"	IV.	40
1760. June 2.	Fferguson, John, and Christian Yoole,.	"	III.	172
1783. Feb. 23.	Ferguson, Mary, and James Leslie,........	"	XXXVIII.	55
1780. Oct. 3.	Ferguson, Mary, and Samuel Milligan,.....	"	XXX.	25
1779. Dec. 23.	Ferguson, Robert, and Catharine Milford,..,	"	XXVIII.	176
1757. Oct. 5.	Ferguson, Robert, and Elizabeth Wylley,...	"	I.	658
1772. Feb. 1.	Ferguson, William, and Jane Davis,.......	"	XVIII.	26
1680. Jan. 18.	Ferior, Sarah, and Gustavus Kingsland,....	O. W.,	XXXII½.	33
1778. Nov. 25.	Feris, Mary, and Benjamin Pell,...........	M. B.,	XXVI.	96
1756. Oct. 12.	Ferrari, Hannah, and Thomas Robinson,....	"	I.	328
1778. May 13.	Ferrers, John, and Marcy Stilwell,........	"	XXV.	82
1760. Sept. 11.	Ferrel, John, and Dorothy Bedford,........	"	III.	311
1737. April 7.	Ferrington, Benjamin, and Deborah Wright,	"	I.	5
1778. Oct. 16.	Ferris, Elizabeth, and John White,........	"	XXVI.	64
1761. Oct. 3.	Ferris, Elizabeth, and Samuel Webb,......	"	V.	120
1753. Sept. 19.	Ferris, James, and Charity Thomas,........	"	I.	120
1756. Dec. 15.	Ferris, John, and Mianah Hunt,...........	"	I.	385
1763. June 16.	Ferris, Josiah, and Letitia Van Alst,.......	"	VII.	231
1773. Nov. 17.	Ferris, Samuel, and Mary Riche, ...	"	XXII.	32
1766. June 6.	Ferris, Sarah, and Gilead Hunt,...........	"	X.	8
1772. June 2.	Fettie, Amy, and Vincent Fountain,.......	"	XVIII.	129
1779. Oct. 6.	Feugeas, Stephen, and Mary Bomon,......	"	XXVIII.	103
1761. May 4.	Fey, Anne, and Robert Kinnear, ...	"	IV.	178
1760. May 3.	Ffiddle, Catharine, and Simon Carpenter,...	"	III.	139

DATE.		NAMES.	RECORD.	VOL.	PAGE.
1757. April	9.	Field, Benjamin, and Elizabeth Pettit,.....	M. B.,	I.	493
1764. Jan.	4.	Field, Benjamin, and Violetta Lawrence,...	"	VIII.	5
1772. Aug.	25.	Field, Charles, and Anne Sands,...........	"	XIX.	30
1758. Oct.	13.	Field, Deborah, and Daniel Betts, Jr.,......	"	II.	55
1761. June	16.	Field, Eavis, and John Chambers,.........	"	IV.	242
1756. Dec.	2.	Field, Elnathan, and Mary Willet, ...	"	I.	370
1769. July	8.	Field, Gilbert, and Hannah Thorne,........	"	XIV.	144
1761. June	24.	Field, Hannah, and Ebenezer Beamun,.....	"	IV.	260
1765. June	28.	Field, Jacob, and Charity Whitehead,......	"	IX.	190
1757. May	4.	Field, Jeremiah, and Mary Stafford,........	"	I.	523
1768. Oct.	31.	Field, John, and Charity Cole,............	"	XIII.	219
1758. Mar.	8.	Field, John, and Mariam Hunt,...........	"	I.	837
1753. Oct.	10.	Field, Joseph, and Elizabeth Willet, ...	"	I.	136
1764. Mar.	17.	Field, Nicholas, and Ann Murphy,.........	"	VIII.	110
1761. Oct.	31.	Field, Robert, and Anna Renne,...........	"	V.	183
1762. Sept.	4.	Field, Stephen, and Elleanor Whitehead,....	"	VI.	307
1779. June	22.	Fielding, Acky, and George Codmus, ...	"	XXVIII.	2
1759. July	26.	Fielding, Deborah, and Bynear Van Yeveren,	"	II.	363
1772. Aug.	7.	Fielding, Jane, and John Metsger,.........	"	XIX.	15
1778. Jan.	31.	Fields, Ann, and William Barwick,.... ...	"	XXV.	14
1758. Nov.	16.	Fiele, Jannetie, and John Sybrant Quackenbus, ...	"	II.	90
1756. Oct.	23.	Fiele, Rebecca, and Abram Slingerland,....	"	I.	332
1772. Sept.	14.	Fiero, Catherina, and Ludwigh Roessell,....	"	XIX.	48
1772. Sept.	14.	Fiero, William, and Margaret Eligh,.......	"	XIX.	49
1759. Sept.	7.	Filkin, Catharine, and Christian Tobias,.....	"	II.	411
1762. Feb.	1.	Filkin, Frances, and John Child,...........	"	VI.	35
1761. April	3.	Filkin, Geesie, and William Waddel,.......	"	IV.	128
1763. Aug.	13.	Filkin, Henry, and Catharine Van Tine, ...	"	VII.	301
1760. May	7.	Ffilkins, Catharine, and Nathaniel Bethel, ..	"	III.	143
1780. Nov.	9.	Fincher, Abraham, and Mary Archer, ...	"	XXX.	100
1763. Dec.	16.	Fine, Elizabeth, and John Ritter,..........	"	VII.	506
1779. Oct.	28.	Fine, Frederick, and Catharine Heylian,....	"	XXVIII.	122
1758. Feb.	14.	Fine, Hannah, and Aray Counsalyee,......	"	I.	820
1756. July	12.	Fine, Hendrick, and Catharine Pain,.......	"	I.	253
1773. Nov.	30.	Fine, Jane, and Isaac Demilt,.............	"	XXII.	56
1758. Sept.	12.	Fine, John, and Margaret Elsworth,.......	"	II.	16
1759. Mar.	31.	Fine, Mercy, and Andries Counselyee, ...	"	II.	231
1760. Dec.	9.	Fineout, Gertje, and William Brownly,.....	"	III.	468
1757. June	28.	Fines, Johan Philip, and Maria Stiene,.....	"	I.	575
1775. July	31.	Finglass, James, and Catherine Van Dyck,..	"	XXIII.	114
1761. Aug.	14.	Finigin, Catharine, and James Meldrum,...	"	V.	41
1781. Nov.	13.	Fink, Elizabeth, and Lawrence Hyer,.	"	XXXIV.	30
1758. Jan.	21.	Finley, Ann, and Robert Midwinter,.......	"	I.	796
1768. July	12.	Finley, Catherine, and James Holland,.....	"	XIII.	156

　　　　NEW YORK MARRIAGES.

DATE.	NAMES.	RECORD.	VOL.	PAGE.
1760. Oct. 7.	Finley, James, and Christian Youll,........	M. B.,	III.	349
1766. Nov. 21.	Finley, John, and Elizabeth McCloughry,...	"	X.	177
1773. Mar. 9.	Finley, John, and Martha Pantine,.........	"	XX.	57
1764. Aug. 14.	Finley, Mary, and Barnet Bush,...........	"	VIII.	282
1765. July 8.	Finley, Sarah, and Thomas Lawson,.......	"	IX.	198
1767. May 23.	Finn, Elizabeth, and Augustus Stine,......	"	XI.	94
1761. July 6.	Finney, Jane, and Philip Hower,....	"	IV.	281
1761. June 15.	Finney, Mary, and John Bennet,..........	"	IV.	240
1767. Dec. 17.	Fish, Abigail, and Johannis Lott,......*...	"	XII.	116
1780. Dec. 2.	Fish, Ambrush, and Hannah Wortman,....	"	XXX.	134
1770. July 24.	Fish, Ann, and Jacob Palmer,............	"	XVI.	145
1765. July 29.	Fish, Benjamin, and Phebe Vandervort,....	"	IX.	220
1772. Jan. 22.	Fish, Daniel, and Rachel Ellis,...........	"	XX.	16
1781. July 12.	Fish, Elizabeth, and James Benney,.......	"	XXXIII.	6
1773. July 13.	Fish, Elizabeth, and Thomas Durham,......	"	XXI.	36
1760. Aug. 27.	Fish, Elizabeth, and Thomas Lawrence,....	"	III.	269
1782. Jan. 30.	Fish, Jane, and William Moore,...........	"	XXXV.	39
1780. Dec. 11.	Fish, Jesse, and Jemime Moore,...........	"	XXX.	150
1761. Dec. 24.	Fish, Mary, and Samuel Renne,...........	"	V.	301
1763. Jan. 3.	Fish, Nathan, and Catharine Berrien,......	"	VII.	2
173⅞. Feb. 15.	Fish, Nathaniel, and Jane Berrien,........	"	I.	9
1763. Oct. 4.	Fish, Richard, and Sarah Betts,...........	"	VII.	370
1737. Nov. 4.	Fish, Ruth, and Daniel Rapalie,...........	"	I.	8
1765. June 28.	Fish, Ruth, and Jesse Warner,............	"	IX.	189
1768. April 9.	Fish, Sarah, and Charles Cromelian,........	"	XIII.	68
1759. Oct. 30.	Ffish, Sarah, and Daniel Searean,.........	"	II.	480
1763. April 27.	Fish, Sarah, and John Berrian,............	"	VII.	145
1781. Dec. 14.	Fish, Sarah, and William Palmer,.........	"	XXXIV.	86
1759. Aug. 31.	Fish, Sarah, and William Sackett,.........	"	II.	405
1771. Sept. 10.	Fish, Susanna, and George Brinkerhoff,....	"	XVII.	181
1771. Nov. 14.	Fish, Susannah, and John Riker,..........	"	XVII.	257
1760. April 15.	Ffish, Temperance, and John Simonson,....	"	III.	107
1736. Oct. 16.	Ffish, Temperance, and Joseph Woodward,.	"	I.	3
1777. April 27.	Fish, Theodosia, and Samuel Carman,......	"	XXIV.	74
1737. Sept. 20.	Fishee, Peter, and Elizabeth Post, ...	"	I.	7
1772. Nov. 17.	Fisheir, John, and Elizabeth Sitcher,.......	"	XIX.	117
1761. Aug. 4.	Fisher, Abel Smith, and Mary Corter,......	"	V.	25
1759. Feb. 16.	Fisher, Agnes, and James Pudney,........	"	II.	193
1753. Aug. 29.	Fisher, Alida, and Gerret Roorbeck,.......	"	I.	100
1760. May 2.	Ffisher, Alyda, and Gradus Cluet,.........	"	III.	135
1758. Sept. 7.	Fisher, Ann, and Abraham Van Gelder,....	"	II.	8
1781. Mar. 26.	Fisher, Bethia, and Gibbert Purdy,.........	"	XXXI.	87
1758. Sept. 7.	Fisher, Catharine, and Andrew Marseles,...	"	II.	9
1770. Nov. 29.	Fisher, Catherine, and Dirck Woortman,...	"	XVI.	274
1763. Feb. 2.	Fisher, Cornelius, and Catherine Lawrence,.	"	VII.	50

DATE.	NAMES.	RECORD.	VOL. PAGE.
1764. Nov. 12.	Fisher, Dericka, and Bastian Cregier,......	M. B.,	VIII. 405
1768. Nov. 23.	Fisher, Dirckje, and Jacob Fonda, Jr.,......	"	XIII. 243
1775. Nov. 24.	Fishor, Donald, and Elizabeth Monroe,.....	"	XXIII. 221
1773. Nov. 12.	Fisher, George, and Hannah Earl,.........	"	XXII. 22
1769. Jan. 30.	Fisher, Gerret, and Hannah Smatt,........	"	XIV. 22
1762. Sept. 30.	Fisher, Gerrit, and Alida Fonda,..........	"	VI. 336
1770. Nov. 17.	Fisher, Gertruy, and Gerret G. Van Vranken,	"	XVI. 260
1765. May 31.	Fisher, Hester, and Ahasuerus Mercellus,...	"	IX. 150
1762. Dec. 20.	Fisher, James, and Isabella Cross,.........	"	VI. 491
1768. Sept. 19.	Fisher, John, and Annatje Pearse,.........	"	XIII. 188
1772. Sept. 15.	Fisher, Matthew, and Lydia Fryer,........	"	XIX. 51
1763. Nov. 24.	Fisher, Minne, and Elizabeth Loun,........	"	VII. 469
1760. July 29.	Fisher, Nanning, and Catherina Wendell,...	"	III. 231
1764. Oct. 11.	Fisher, Nanning, Jr., and Helena Lansingh,.	"	VIII. 353
1767. Jan. 15.	Fisher, Rachael, and John Weatherhead,...	"	XI. 8
1737. Oct. 6.	Fisher, Sarah, and Harmon Slyk,..........	"	J. 7
1760. Aug. 20.	Fisher, Thomas, and Geertruydt Crannel,...	"	III. 265
1774. Jan. 26.	Fisheron, Joanna, and John Wynant,......	"	XXII. 115
1782. Aug. 31.	Fisk, William, and Deborah Calley,.... ...	"	XXXVI. 132
1761. Feb. 12.	Fitch, Joseph, and Mary Eldridge,....	"	IV. 60
1738. April 14.	Fitch, Mary, and George McNeese,........	"	I. 9
1736. Sept. 22.	Fitch, Mary, and Timothy Titus,.........:..	"	I. 2
1734. Feb. 28.	Fitch, Phebe, and Philip Pell,..............	"	I. 5
1760. Sept. 25.	Fitch, William, and Altje Wheeler,........	"	III. 329
1758. Jan. 25.	Fitzgerald, Ann, and Thomas Caho,........	"	I. 802
1760. Mar. 24.	Fitzgerald, Mary, and Colin Minnics,.......	"	XXXVIII. 74
1779. Mar. 11.	Fitzgerald, Mary, and John Smith,........	"	XXVII. 66
1759. Mar. 28.	Fitz Gerald, William, and Jane Davis,......	"	II. 227
1781. June 21.	Fitzpatrick, John, and Susannah Butler,....	"	XXXII. 94
1757. Mar. 8.	Fitzsimmons, David, and Elce Doyl,.......	"	I. 464
1781. June 9.	Fitzsimons, Peter, and Eunes Woodruff,....	"	XXXII. 80
1779. Nov. 25.	Flack, Henry, and Catherine Weger,.......	"	XXVIII. 147
1755. Oct. 24.	Flanagan, Ann, and John Erskin,..........	"	I. 199
1758. April 22.	Flanagan, Mary, and Thomas Snowden,....	"	I. 880
1755. Dec. 20.	Flandreau, Benjamin, and Hester Badeau, ..	"	I. 237
1778. Dec. 14.	Flandereau, Esther, and Nathan Stilwill,...	"	XXVI. 119
1763. July 1.	Flandreau, Peter, and Anne Le Comte,.....	"	VII. 253
1783. May 17.	Flandro, Magdalen, and Daniel Secord,.....	"	XXXIX. 15
1779. Dec. 28.	Flannagen, Jane, and Alexander Achyndaey,	"	XXVIII. 183
1783. Jan. 9.	Fleat, Mary, and Richard Long,...........	"	XXXVIII. 12
1761. Mar. 13.	Fleerboome, John, and Maria Bloofield,.....	"	IV. 100
1761. June 13.	Fleerboome, Maria, and Abraham Blauvelt,.	"	IV. 238
1782. Feb. 11.	Fleet, Abbe, and Silas Carman,...........	"	XXXV. 47
1767. Dec. 1.	Fleet, Anna, and Jesse Oakes,............,...	"	XII. 102
1780. Jan. 29.	Fleet, Arnold, and Judith Woodward,......	"	XXVIII. 204

18

DATE.	NAMES.	RECORD.	VOL.	PAGE.
1768. Nov. 2.	Fleet, Deborah, and Zebulon Smyth, Jr.,...	M. B.,	XIII.	222
1758. Sept. 20.	Fleet, Gilbert, and Phebe Brush,..........	"	II.	25
1764. May 22.	Fleet, Jeremiah, and Deborah Samis,.......	"	VIII.	197
1781. June 14.	Fleet, John, and Margery Tobias,..........	"	XXXII.	86
1675. June 22.	Fleet, Mary, and Shedrake Manton,.......	W. O. P.,	III.	101
1764. Nov. 26.	Fleet, Thankful, and Justus Sammis,.......	M. B.,	VIII.	425
1768. Jan. 5.	Fleet, Thomas, and Hannah McCoon,......	"	XIII.	2
1781. Mar. 6.	Fleet, Thomas, and Phebe Carman,.... ...	"	XXXI.	66
1737. Dec. 26.	Fleetwood, Burditt Pilkington, and Margaret Creger,..................	"	I.	8
1761. Dec. 12.	Fleetwood, Mary, and Henry Stryken,.....	"	V.	277
1773. Dec. 20.	Fleglea, Zacharias, and Mary Allen,........	"	XXII.	79
1764. Sept. 10.	Flegler, Simon, and Esther Lott,..........	"	VIII.	302
1778. April 4.	Fleming, John, and Sarah May,...........	"	XXV.	59
1778. Oct. 5.	Flemming, Anstice, and Thomas Robinson,..	"	XXVI.	46
1763. Nov. 9.	Flemming, Elisabeth, and James Sandes,...	"	VII.	435
1772. Sept. 25.	Flemming, Margaret, and Thomas Carlile,...	"	XIX.	56
1762. Oct. 6.	Fletcher, Catherine, and Martin Blake,.....	"	VI.	347
1758. Mar. 25.	Fletcher, Esther, and Hugh Heany,........	"	I.	863
1781. May 2.	Fletcher, Lette, and Peter Hegeman,.......	"	XXXII.	27
1781. Jan. 3.	Fletcher, Margaret, and Alexander Watson,.	"	XXXI.	8
1761. Sept. 1.	Fletcher, Mary, and John Robertson,......	"	V.	65
1759. April 24.	Fletcher, Mary, and William Newton,......	"	II.	254
1767. July 8.	Fletcher, Nicholas, and Aletta Murphy,....	"	XI.	127
1770. May 1.	Fletcher, Nicholas, and Margaret Weber,...	"	XVI.	74
1780. Mar. 25.	Fletcher, Nicholas, and Mary Martin,......	"	XXIX.	7
1783. Jan. 27.	Fletcher, Richard, and Ann Colby,........	"	XXXVIII.	29
1762. Sept. 25.	Fletcher, Richard, and Margaret Hogelandt,.	"	VI.	332
1681. May 16.	Fletcher, Seth, and Mary Byson,..........	O. W.,	XXXII½.	46
1782. Dec. 11.	Flewelling, Maplit, and Samuel McCoon,...	M. B.,	XXXVII.	116
1781. Aug. 10.	Fling, Phebe, and William Beach,.........	"	XXXIII.	34
1778. June 4.	Fling, Thomas, and Phebe Blanck,.........	"	XXV.	97
1771. Dec. 12.	Flinn, Nicholas, and Elizabeth Crossley,....	"	XVII.	291
1758. May 27.	Flinn, Phebe, and John Dudley,..........	"	I.	912
1769. May 26.	Flock, Hendrick, and Elizabeth Reker,.....	"	XIV.	108
1782. Feb. 6.	Flockady, Elizabeth, and George Paddison,.	"	XXXV.	44
1779. July 3.	Flood, Catherine, and John Jaffray,........	"	XXVIII.	15
1763. April 20.	Flood, Christiana, and Stephen Wilkinson,..	"	VII.	134
1759. Jan. 18.	Flood, James, and Anapel Legget,.........	"	II.	158
1757. May 11.	Flood, James, and Rebecah Pilot,..........	"	I.	527
1769. June 12.	Flood, Loronah, and Robert James,........	"	XIV.	118
1778. Jan. 12.	Flood, Mary, and Charles Thompson,......	"	XXV.	4
1762. Nov. 17.	Flood, Mary, and Thomas Wisely,..........	"	VI.	438
1765. Aug. 5.	Florentine, Catherine, and Monson Ward,..	"	IX.	253
1781. Aug. 28.	Florintine, Ann, and John Pafford,.......	"	XXXIII.	51

Date.	Names.	Record.	Vol.	Page.
1781. Aug. 11.	Flower, John, and Mary Flower, ...	M. B.,	xxxiii.	36
1781. Aug. 11.	Flower, Mary, and John Flower, ...	"	xxxiii.	36
1773. June 29.	Flowers, George, and Rebekah Taylor, ...	"	xxi.	25
1778. May 21.	Floyd, Ann, and Thomas Longley, ...	"	xxv.	91
1767. Sept. 24.	Floyd, Benjamin, and Ann Cornwell, ...	"	xii.	42
1769. July 29.	Floyd, Catherine, and Thomas Thomas, ...	"	xv.	8
1761. April 28.	Floyd, Charles, and Margaret Thomas, ...	"	iv.	171
1759. Nov. 9.	Floyd, John, and Leanah Vandue, ...	"	ii.	491
1783. Jan. 4.	Floyd, Margaret, and John Wright, ...	"	xxxviii.	5
1763. May 3.	Floyd, Mary, and Edmund Smith, ...	"	vii.	164
1769. May 22.	Floyd, Mary, and William Ellison, ...	"	xiv.	106
1755. Aug. 8.	Floyd, Mary, and William Montz Summers, .	"	i.	144
1769. Oct. 5.	Floyd, Nancy, and Hugh Smith, ...	"	xv.	50
1757. Sept. 26.	Floyd, Richard, and Arrabella Jones, ...	"	i.	649
1760. Aug. 20.	Floyd, William, and Hannah Jones, ...	"	iii.	262
1778. April 24.	Flugger, Metta, and Diederick Heyer, ...	"	xxv.	68
1782. Jan. 28.	Fly, Hannah, and Ephraim Golding, ...	"	xxxv.	35
1769. May 16.	Flynn, James, and Ann Walker, ...	"	xiv.	102
1783. Jan. 16.	Foard, Joseph, and Mary Busen, ...	"	xxxviii.	19
1780. May 2.	Fogarty, Sarah, and John Pearse, ...	"	xxix.	41
1771. Jan. 12.	Foght, John Morris, and Sarah Rynders, ...	"	xvii.	5
1762. Oct. 16.	Folkens, Johannes, and Mary Smith, ...	"	vi.	369
1771. Aug. 5.	Folker, John Casper, and Ann King, ...	"	xvii.	153
1773. Dec. 1.	Follan, Tyney, and William Douglass, ...	"	xxii.	58
1766. Dec. 1.	Follensby, Margaret, and John Schermer-horne,	"	x	188
1758. Nov. 16.	Folliot, George, and Jane Harison, ...	"	ii.	89
1764. May 18.	Fonda, Abraham, and Christina D. Lematter,	'	viii.	193
1771. Aug. 5.	Fonda, Abraham, and Hendricke Lansingh, .	"	xvii.	151
1763. Mar. 17.	Fonda, Abraham, and Maria Outerkirk, ...	"	vii.	102
1769. Nov. 13.	Fonda, Abraham A., and Rachel Van Valkenburgh, ...	"	xv.	90
1762. Sept. 30.	Fonda, Alida, and Gerrit Fisher, ...	"	vi.	336
1773. May 12.	Fonda, Alleda, and Gerret I. Lansing, ...	"	xx.	108
1768. Aug. 30.	Fonda, Elizabeth, and Peter H. Veelie, ...	"	xiii.	180
1755. Aug. 26.	Fonda, Elizabeth, and Peter Williams, ...	"	i.	155
1753. Sept. 25.	Fonda, Guisbert, and Eltje Douw, ...	"	i.	124
1766. July 14.	Fonda, Isaac, and Francyntie Perry, ...	"	x.	48
1770. Nov. 17.	Fonda, Isaac, and Sanakie Clausie Vanden Bergh, ...	"	xvi.	262
1768. Nov. 23.	Fonda, Jacob, Jr., and Dirckje Fisher, ...	"	xiii.	243
1775. Aug. 7.	Fonda, John, and Catharine Du Bois, ...	"	xxiii.	122
1758. Nov. 22.	Fonda, John, and Egje Vander See, ...	"	ii.	101
1763. Oct. 31.	Fonda, Lawrence, and Catlyntie Van Volkenburgh, ...	"	vii.	416

DATE.	NAMES.	RECORD.	VOL.	PAGE.
1765. Aug. 4.	Fonda, Maieka, and John A. Bratt,........	M. B.,	IX.	237
1770. April 20.	Fonda, Mary, and Anthony Van Veghten,..	"	XVI.	65
1763. June 1.	Fonda, Peter A., and Christina Van Loon,..	"	VII.	209
1770. July 13.	Fonda, Rachel, and Philip Veele,..........	"	XVI.	139
1775. July 10.	Fonda, Rebecca, and Arent Vander Kar,...	"	XXIII.	93
1769. Nov. 9.	Fonda, Rebecca, and Garret Vanderbarrack,.	"	XV.	83
1767. May 22.	Fonsens, Catherine, and John Gassra,......	"	XI.	93
1761. Oct. 31.	Foot, Robert, and Mary Sulivan,..........	"	V.	184
1767. Aug. 11.	Forbes, Agnes, and John McIntosh,.......	"	XII.	13
1756. Oct. 30.	Forbes, Alexander, and Eva Bussing,......	"	I.	338
1769. Aug. 29.	Forbes, Gilbert, and Elizabeth Totten,......	"	XV.	32
1763. Sept. 29.	Forbes, Hannah, and Jacob Clock,.........	"	VII.	359
1764. July 28.	Forbes, James, and Dorothy Koster,.......	"	VIII.	270
1763. Dec. 28.	Forbes, James, and Rebecca Craige,.......	"	VII.	528
1777. Dec. 4.	Forbes, Mary, and Mathew Ball,..........	"	XXIV.	190
1778. Dec. 8.	Forbes, Mary, and Samuel Harrisson,......	"	XXVI.	114
1771. Nov. 21.	Forbes, Philander, and John N. Bogert,....	"	XVII.	261
1767. Feb. 7.	Forbes, Robert, and Mary Smith,..........	"	XI.	21
1779. Nov. 9.	Forbes, Sarah, and Nicholas White,........	"	XXVIII.	133
1771. Nov. 5.	Forbes, William, and Catherine Van Gelder,.	"	XVII.	240
1762. Sept. 24.	Forbes, William, and Elizabeth Herring,....	"	VI.	329
1783. Jan. 22.	Forbes, William, and Mary Thorne,........	"	XXXVIII.	24
1771. July 16.	Forbes, William A., and Catherine Van Zandt,	"	XVII.	133
1782. April 24.	Forbess, Dorothy, and John Plantain,......	"	XXXV.	135
1753. June 30.	Forbos, Alexander, and Lucretia Hagerman (Hagerdorn),.........................	"	I.	68
1762. June 21.	Forbus, Daniel, and Agnes Pool,..........	"	VI.	201
1760. Sept. 22.	Forbus, Elizabeth, and Duncan McPherson,.	"	III.	325
1781. Dec. 29.	Forbush, Elizabeth, and Nathaniel Rhoads,..	"	XXXIV.	110
1667. April —.	Fforce, Matthew, and Elizabeth Palmer,....	O. W. L.,	II.	134
1764. Feb. 16.	Ford, Anthony, and Jemimie Michaelson,...	M. B.,	VIII.	61
1778. Aug. 8.	Ford, Elizabeth, and Thomas Smith,.......	"	XXV.	145
1773. Dec. 8.	Ford, James, and Martha Oakes,..........	"	XXII.	65
1780. Aug. 25.	Ford, John, and Elizabeth Gaskin,.........	"	XXX.	1
1760. Oct. 7.	Ford, John, and Elizabeth Ward,..........	"	III.	348
1783. Sept. 8.	Ford, John, and Hannah Lasher,..........	"	XL.	32
1779. Mar. 17.	Ford, Littleton, and Hannah De Grey,.....	"	XXVII.	68
1759. Mar. 7.	Fordham, Martha, and Benjamin Wright,...	"	II.	212
1777. Mar. 15.	Foreman, James, and Elizabeth Lawson,...	"	XXIV.	44
1782. Nov. 30.	Foreman, John, and Anne Acker,..........	"	XXXVII.	100
1759. Oct. 16.	Foreman, John, and Hanah Griffiths,......	"	II.	459
1771. Nov. 19.	Foresayth, Mary, and Nathaniel Wheeler,..	"	XVII.	259
1781 Feb. 16.	Foreseyth, Sarah, and Alexander Penny,...	"	XXXI.	46
1778. Oct. 12.	Forester, Elizabeth, and Everet Bisset,.....	"	XXVI.	56
1762. June 30.	Forester, Susannah, and William Preston,..	"	VI.	219

DATE.	NAMES.	RECORD.	VOL.	PAGE.
1676. April 1.	Forgison, Mary, and Robert Manning,......	W. O. P.,	III.	183
1766. Nov. 27.	Forgorson, John, and Hannah Gardiner,....	M. B.,	X.	184, 185
1783. Mar. 20.	Fork, John, and Gertrude Rikeman,.......	"	XXXVIII.	70
1781. June 21.	Fork, John, and Susannah Rider,..........	"	XXXII.	92
1779. July 23.	Forman, Abigail, and Abraham Springsteen,	"	XXVIII.	29
1778. Aug. 31.	Forman, Gabriel, and Sally Wall,..........	"	XXVI.	17
1778. May 12.	Forman, Hannah, and Robert Prince,......		XXV.	80
1763. Feb. 22.	Forman, Rhode, and Matthew Whitemen,..	··	VII.	74
1777. Sept. 25.	Forman, Sarah, and John Seely,..........	"	XXIV.	151
1759. Nov. 27.	Fforrest, Catharine, and Henderick Dopking,	"	II.	519
1758. Mar. 14.	Forrest, John, and Catharine Coward,......	"	I.	850
1758. Oct. 17.	Forrest, John, and Hannah Hayter,........	"	II.	59
1772. Aug. 11.	Forrest, Thomas Mitchell, and Sarah Howard,	"	XIX.	19
1779. June 10.	Forrester, Deborah, and James Rowland,...	"	XXVII.	161
1779. Feb. 22.	Forrester, Joseph, and Else Majesty,.......	"	XXVII.	46
1767. Sept. 21.	Forrgster, Lillis, and Jacob Van Benthuysen,	"	XII.	39
1758. April 28.	Forsburgh, Margaret, and Myndert Goes,...	"	I.	519
1762. Oct. 5.	Forsey, Benjamin, and Mary Van Voort,...	"	VI.	346
1757. Nov. 17.	Forst, Thomas, and Phebe Thornycraft,.....	"	I.	704
1759. Oct. 16.	Forster, Catharine, and Lewis Smith,......	"	II.	460
1760. Dec. 19.	Forster, John, and Deborah Chatterton,.....	"	III.	485
1737. June 2.	Forster, John, and Juneah Jygels,.........	"	I.	6
1771. June 7.	Forster, John, and Phebe Rowe,..........	"	XVII.	104
1763. Nov. 29.	Forster, Mary, and Joseph Allen,..........	"	VII.	482
1761. Aug. 10.	Forster, Thomas, and Catherine Wall,......	"	V.	36
1781. June 1.	Forster, William, and Rebecca Cary,.......	"	XXXII.	67
1763. Dec. 10.	Forster, William, and Ruth Denton,........	"	VII.	502
1782. Jan. 3.	Forsy, Penelope, and Frances Hartman Ende,	"	XXXV.	7
1760. June 10.	Fforsyth, Jane, and John Coursey,.........	"	III.	185
1764. July 18.	Forsyth, John, and Catharine Gadey,......	"	VIII.	262
1753. June 29.	Fort, Hannah, and Johannes Van Vranck,...	"	I.	66
1760. Aug. 19.	Fort, Harme, and Rebecca Van Woort,.....	"	III.	260
1762. May 10.	Fort, John Isaac, and Elizabeth Quokenboss,	"	VI.	152
1759. Oct. 2.	Fort, Maritje, and Petrus Beneven,........	"	II.	439
1762. Sept. 7.	Fort, Simon, and Ann Van Vranke,........	"	VI.	309
1764. July 11.	Fosmar, Hendrick, and Catharine Backus,..	"	VIII.	255
1767. Aug. 11.	Foster, Abigail, and Hope Mills,..........	"	XII.	12
1776. April 24.	Foster, Anna, and James Brewster,........	"	XXIII.	300
1773. Aug. 27.	Foster. Catherine, and Abraham Skinner,...	"	XXI.	87
1781. Oct. 15.	Foster, Elizabeth, and John Todd,...	"	XXXIII.	102
1779. Dec. 8.	Foster, Hannah, and Abraham Demott,.....	"	XXVIII.	166
1782. Oct. 19.	Foster, Hannah, and Nathan Foster,.......	"	XXXVII.	53
1781. Sept. 13.	Foster, Henry, and Sarah Brush,..........	"	XXXIII.	64
1780. Dec. 18.	Foster, Hester, and Henry Vinnell,........	"	XXX.	157
1781. Feb. 24.	Foster, Jacob, and Ann Stuart,............	"	XXXI.	56

DATE.	NAMES.	RECORD.	VOL.	PAGE.
1779. July 1.	Foster, Jane, and John Hendrickson, ...	M. B.,	XXVIII.	13
1777. April 27.	Foster, John, and Elizabeth De Mott, ...	"	XXIV.	75
1778. Sept. 4.	Foster, John, and Mary Burtis, ...	"	XXVI.	20
1768. June 27.	Foster, John, and Sarah Hansen, ...	"	XIII.	142
1764. Jan. 16.	Foster, John, and Sarah Langdon, ...	"	VIII.	17
1763. Dec. 24.	Foster, Letitia, and James Alner, ...	"	VII.	524
1781. Oct. 15.	Foster, Letitia, and John Rothery, ...	"	XXXIII.	101
1759. Nov. 23.	Foster, Marmaduke, and Elliner Vander Belt,	"	II.	513
1761. July 28.	Foster, Marmaduke, and Jemima Mertons, . .	"	V.	12
1773. June 9.	Foster, Mary, and Hugh Gelston, ...	"	XX.	142
1781. Dec. 24.	Foster, Mary, and Joseph Northrup, ...	"	XXXIV.	103
1781. July 3.	Foster, Mary, and Swete Luscom, ...	"	XXXII.	102
1782. Oct. 19.	Foster, Nathan, and Hannah Foster, ...	"	XXXVII.	53
1780. Sept. 13.	Foster, Nathaniel, and Sarah Van Wick, ...	"	XXX.	26
1779. Mar. 22.	Foster, Rachel, and Hugh Shannon, ...	"	XXVII.	73
1781. Dec. 18.	Foster, Rachel, and Johnson Kierstead, ...	"	XXXIV.	94
1756. Sept. 30.	Foster, Samuel, and Magdalin Gotier, ...	"	I.	314
1764. June 28.	Foster, Sarah, and Garret Springar, ...	"	VIII.	240
1773. Dec. 23.	Foster, Sarah, and John Burtis, ...	"	XXII.	85
1772. Aug. 5.	Foster, Solomon, and Phebe Hendrickson, . .	"	XIX.	12
1757. Mar. 12.	Foster, Thomas, and Martha Morril, ...	"	I.	467
1779. Jan. 26.	Foster, Thomas, and Mary Stymers, ...	"	XXVII.	28
1674. Mar. 10.	Foster, William, and Deborah Valentine, . . .	W. O. P.,	III.	60
1757. Sept. 26.	Fotherby, Mary, and William Hatley, ...	M. B.,	I.	650
1782. Oct. 7.	Fouler, Mariam, and William Williams, ...	"	XXXVII.	35
1780. May 20.	Fountain, Anthony, and Catharine Journeay,	"	XXIX.	63
1783. Sept. 15.	Fountain, Anthony, and Matthew Crips, ...	"	XL.	40
1771. Oct. 29.	Fountain, Peter, and Eleanor Wickham, ...	"	XVII.	232
1783. Aug. 6.	Fountain, Susannah, and Lawrence Crips, . . .	"	XXXIX.	114
1772. June 2.	Fountain, Vincent, and Amy Fettie, ...	"	XVIII.	129
1778. Oct. 23.	Fowler, Abigail, and Henry Disbury, ...	"	XXVI.	69
1760. Dec. 24.	Fowler, Abigail, and John Johnson, ...	"	III.	490
1759. Jan. 11.	Fowler, Abigail, and Lewis Vincent, ...	"	II.	151
1777. May 17.	Fowler, Abigail, and Moses Ward, ...	"	XXIV.	89
1782. July 30.	Fowler, Anne, and William Seaman, ...	"	XXXVI.	93
1776. Feb. 15.	Fowler, Bersheba, and Daniel Thorn, ...	"	XXIII.	267
1779. May 7.	Fowler, Catherine, and Gideon Carstang, . . .	"	XXVII.	129
1753. Oct. 16.	Fowler, Charity, and Henry Bayeux, ...	"	I.	141
1762. Feb. 10.	Fowler, Charity, and Joseph Drake, ...	"	VI.	44
1781. May 12.	Fowler, Dorothy, and Elijah Fowler, ...	"	XXXII.	45
1780. Oct. 26.	Fowler, Edmund, and Elenor Harbourd, ...	"	XXX.	82
1761. Nov. 14.	Fowler, Edward, and Susannah Shute, ...	"	V.	216
1781. May 12.	Fowler, Elijah, and Dorothy Fowler, ...	"	XXXII.	45
1760. Dec. 29.	Fowler, Elizabeth, and John Warner, ...	"	III.	494
1772. May 26.	Fowler, Elizabeth, and Robert Brett, ...	"	XVIII.	126

DATE.		NAMES.	RECORD.	VOL.	PAGE.
1775. June	28.	Fowler, George, and Jane Townsend,	M. B.,	XXIII.	80
1764. Dec.	5.	Fowler, Hanna, and Henry Fowler,	"	VIII.	440
1764. Dec.	5.	Fowler, Henry, and Hanna Fowler,	"	VIII.	440
1783. Sept.	13.	Fowler, Jane, and Samuel Jones,	"	XL.	39
1761. Feb.	23.	Fowler, Jeremiah, and Maritje Pels,	"	IV.	76
1783. April	29.	Fowler, Juliana, and David Roe,	"	XXXVIII.	120
1782. May	28.	Fowler, Mariam, and Robert Sneden,	"	XXXVI.	27
1780. Sept.	21.	Fowler, Marian, and Ezekiel Bishop,	"	XXX.	34
1764. Sept.	14.	Fowler, Mary, and Henry Lowerer,	"	VIII.	307
1760. Jan.	4.	Fowler, Mary, and Isaac Butler,	"	II.	568
1782. Oct.	7.	Fowler, Mary, and Jacob Vanwart,	"	XXXVII.	34
1783. Feb.	17.	Fowler, Mary, and John Peters,	"	XXXVIII.	43
1763. Feb.	28.	Fowler, Mary, and Richard Wood,	"	VII.	84
1783. Oct.	24.	Fowler, Mary, and Thomas Daft,	"	XL.	90
1780. Mar.	11.	Fowler, Moses, and Ann Smith,	"	XXVIII.	219
1763. Nov.	1.	Fowler, Moses, and Elisabeth Jones,	"	VII.	421
1779. Nov.	19.	Fowler, Oliver, and Elizabeth Rowe,	"	XXVIII.	144a
1763. Aug.	26.	Fowler, Pexall, and Ann Dey,	"	VII.	313
1783. July	15.	Fowler, Purdy, Sr., and Abigael Roe,	"	XXXIX.	93
1782. Oct.	16.	Fowler, Sarah, and David Lawrence,	"	XXXVII.	43
1773. April	30.	Fowler, Sarah, and Nicholas Conkling,	"	XX.	102
1761. May	30.	Fowler, Solomon, and Sarah Hunt,	"	IV.	217
1761. May	29.	Fowler, Susannah, and William Hunt,	"	IV.	216
1763. Sept.	10.	Fowler, Tamar, and William Barker,	"	VII.	334
1769. Dec.	2.	Fowler, Thomas, and Abigail Hedger,	"	XV.	111
1773. Feb.	18.	Fowler, Thomas, and Margaret Cornell,	"	XX.	48
1775. July	24.	Fowler, Thomas, and Mary Guion,	"	XXIII.	103
1768. Jan.	30.	Fowler, Vincent, and Dorothy Valentine,	"	XIII.	20
1736. Sept.	13.	Fowler, William, and Elizabeth Griffin,	"	I.	2
1777. Aug.	21.	Fowler, William, and Jane Watson,	"	XXIV.	138
1770. Nov.	3.	Fowlkes, Mary, and Peter Vianey,	"	XVI.	239
1758. Dec.	21.	Fox, Anne, and George Vogel,	"	II.	137
1761. Jan.	27.	Fox, Catherine, and Francis Runwa,	"	IV.	33
1761. Jan.	10.	Fox, John, and Mary Saunders,	"	IV.	10
1782. Jan.	3.	Fox, Joseph, and Phebe Burtis,	"	XXXV.	6
1783. Jan.	21.	Fox, Matthew, and Abigail Dexter,	"	XXXVIII.	23
1777. Mar.	18.	Fox, Matthew, and Sarah Potts,	"	XXIV.	46
1777. April	15.	Fox, Robert, and Jane Blythe,	"	XXIV.	63
1761. Nov.	18.	Fox, Sarah, and Barent Bond,	"	V.	229
1782. April	13.	Fox, Susannah, and Robert Knight,	"	XXXV.	120
1767. Mar.	12.	Foy, John, and Elizabeth Cooper,	"	XI.	43
1767. Feb.	18.	Foy, Mary, and James Robbins,	"	XI.	30
1780. Sept.	20.	Foy, Thomas, and Sarah Ann Munday,	"	XXX.	32
1759. Feb.	17.	Fraizer, William, and Catharine Morrison,	"	II.	196
1783. Aug.	15.	Frake, Mary, and John Bell,	"	XXXIX.	127

DATE.	NAMES.	RECORD.	VOL.	PAGE.
1762. Aug. 3.	Fraly, Jacob, and Christina Metsger, ...	M. B.,	VI.	262
1783. Aug. 18.	Frances, Mary, and John Smith, ...	"	XL.	1
1757. Nov. 30.	Frances, Samuel, and Elizabeth Dalley, ...	"	I.	719
1762. Nov. 14.	Francis, Christopher, and Margaret Edwards,	"	VI.	404
1761. May 8.	Francis, Helen, and George Hawkins, ...	"	IV.	184
1755. Oct. 11.	Francis, Samuel, and Mary Carlile, ...	"	I.	191
1773. July 12.	Francis, Sarah, and Charles Campbell, ...	"	XXI.	34
1681. Sept. 4.	Francisco, ———, and Honour Griffin, ...	O. W.,	XXXII½.	67
1753. April 13.	Francklin, Elizabeth, and Samuel Doty	M. B.,	I.	20
1779. June 3.	Francois, John, and Mary Kendrick, ...	"	XXVII.	155
1779. Nov. 2.	Franehommy, John, and Hannah Harcourt,.	"	XXVIII.	126
1736. June 3.	Frank, Andries, and Mary Clauseren, ...	"	I.	1
1762. Nov. 3.	Frank, David, and Margaret Charlo, ...	"	VI.	409
1779. Aug. 20.	Frankfort, Catherine, and Matthew Young,.	"	XXVIII.	53
1758. April 22.	Frankland, Sarah, and Isaac Cursen (Cursa),.	"	I.	882
1770. Oct. 18.	Franklin, James, and Gloriana Thomas, ...	"	XVI.	223
1782. Jan. 17.	Franks, Rebecca, and Henry Johnson, ...	"	XXXV.	22
1768. Feb. 23.	Frasee, Jemima, and George Smart, ...	"	XIII.	41
1769. Aug. 5.	Fraser, Alexander, and Ann Bothwell, ...	"	XV.	18
1779. Sept. 29.	Fraser, Alexander, and Ann Kennion, ...	"	XXVIII.	90
1781. Feb. 21.	Fraser, Hugh, and Elizabeth Nicolls, ...	"	XXXI.	53
1780. Dec. 1.	Fraser, John Daniel, and Jemima Pinckney,.	"	XXX.	130
1764. Aug. 16.	Fraser, Sarah, and John Eyles, ...	"	VIII.	285
1778. Nov. 21.	Fraser, William, and Catharine McDonald,..	"	XXVI.	91
1783. May 26.	Fraser, William, and Lucretia Deal, ...	"	XXXIX.	25
1767. Aug. 5.	Frasher, Sarah, and John McNeil, ...	"	XII.	9
1762. Dec. 4.	Frasier, Elisabeth, and Archibald Cragg, ...	"	VI.	467
1764. Aug. 27.	Frasier, Sarah, and John Devoe, ...	"	VIII.	294
1753. May 24.	Frayer, Elizabeth, and Jacob Kip, ...	"	I.	40
1781. July 9.	Frazer, Ann, and Richard Betts, Jr., ...	"	XXXIII.	1
1779. Aug. 28.	Frazer, Catherine, and Thomas Mason, ...	"	XXVIII.	61
1778. Dec. 19.	Frazer, John, and Jemima Albertson, ...	"	XXVI.	126
1670. March 9.	Frazer, Richard, and Louis Howard, ...	C. A.,	II.	655
1780. July 11.	Frazer, Walter, and Martha Harris, ...	M. B.,	XXIX.	110
1764. Jan. 7.	Frazier, Alexander, and Elizabeth Frazier,..	"	VIII.	11
1760. May 8.	Ffrazier, Alexander, and Elsie Campbell, ...	"	III.	145
1764. Jan. 7.	Frazier, Elizabeth, and Alexander Frazier,..	"	VIII.	11
1760. Mar. 22.	Frazier, Elizabeth, and William Vielliock, ...	"	III.	87
1764. Feb. 16.	Frazier, Hannah, and John Calder, ...	"	VIII.	60
1738. Sept. 23.	Frazier, Thomas, and Hester Walker, ...	"	I.	11
1781. Dec. 24.	Frazur, Lewis, and Catharine Thorn, ...	"	XXXIV.	102
1775. Sept. 2.	Frear, Simeon, and Sarah Van Cleeck, ...	"	XXIII.	145
1760. Jan. 5.	Frederick, Andrew, and Mary Friedz, ...	"	II.	570
1769. Nov. 21.	Frederick, John, and Elizabeth White, ...	"	XV.	101
1772. Dec. 30.	Frederick, Michael, and Margaret Sneyder,..	"	XIX.	167

DATE.	NAMES.	RECORD.	VOL.	PAGE.
1767. April 24.	Fredherring, John, and Lucretia Van Duersen,	M. B.,	XI.	70
1779. Sept..10.	Freeborn, John, and Elizabeth Ramadge, ...	"	XXVIII.	72
1760. April 9.	Freeborn, John, and Mary Smith,.........	"	III.	101
1781. April 27.	Freeborn, Sarah Pricilla, and Samuel Harrison,	"	XXXII.	19
1738. Aug. 11.	Freedenbergh, Elizabeth, and Benjamin Dealing, ...	"	I.	10
1770. Feb. 12.	Freek, James, and Mary Suydam,.........	"	XVI.	15
1773. July 6.	Freeland, Amy, and John Silvester,........	"	XXI.	33
1767. April 29.	Freeland, John, and Cornelia Hoogeland,...	"	XI.	73
1774. Jan. 18.	Freeland, Mary, and Isaac Palmore,........	"	XXII.	107
1756. July 6.	Freelinhousen, Margaret, and Thomas Romein, ...	"	I.	246
1778. Feb. 4.	Freeman, Augustus John, and Mary Lathwhite, ...	"	XXV.	15
1762. Sept. 29.	Freeman, Edward, and Anne Porry,.......	"	VI.	339
1738. Nov. 9.	Freeman, Grace, and Joseph Murray,......	"	I.	11
1738. Aug. 9.	Freeman, Isaac, and Ellinor Ridden,.......	"	I.	10
1777. Nov. 15.	Freeman, John, and Elizabeth Valentine,...	"	XXIV.	182
1761. July 6.	Freeman, Phebe, and Benjamin Wheten,...	"	IV.	280
1782. Oct. 5.	Freeman, Seth, and Hannah Hitchcock,....	"	XXXVII.	28
1766. Nov. 29.	Freeman, Thomas, and Hannah Manville,...	"	X.	187
1775. Nov. 23.	Freer, Maritie, and John Kater,...........	"	XXIII.	219
1774. Jan. 19.	Freer, Samuel, and Sarah Roosa,..........	"	XXII.	108
1771. Mar. 30.	Freese, Hannah, and Abraham Polhemus,...	"	XVII.	46
1773. Jan. 27.	Freidenburgh, Catherine, and John I. Person,	"	XX.	21
1763. June 8.	Freitz, Conradt, and Susanna Charlotte,....	"	VII.	216
1771. Nov. 12.	Freley, Solomon, and Rachel Vanderbeck,..	"	XVII.	247
1775. June 14.	Freligh, Abraham, and Charity Van Fleet,..	"	XXIII.	61
1761. June 6.	French, Catharine, and Thomas Guest,.....	"	IV.	228
1761. Oct. 21.	French, Catherine, and Samuel Hunt,......	"	V.	158
1755. Dec. 10.	French, Joseph, and Mary Jarvis,.........	"	I.	230
1763. Aug. 27.	French, Judith, and Henry Kip,...........	"	VII.	316
1771. Sept. 10.	French, Margaret, and Henry McCloskey,...	"	XVII.	180
1777. May 2.	French, Mary, and George Brown,........	"	XXIV.	81
1760. Nov. 27.	French, Michael, and Mary Denicke:.......	"	III.	448
1758. Sept. 14.	French, Samuel, and Catharine Bown,.....	"	II.	23
1772. Feb. 24.	French, Sarah, and William Robertson,.....	"	XVIII.	41
1755. Dec. 12.	Frer, Arryantie, and Evert Pils,...........	"	I.	238
1760. June 17.	Fresneau, Helena, and Jacob Brewerton,...	"	III.	189
1759. Feb. 24.	Freyer, John, and Elizabeth Van Voorte, ...	"	II.	201
1760. Jan. 5.	Friedz, Mary, and Andrew Frederick,......	"	II.	570
1757. Aug. 2.	Frielinghouse, Anne, and William Jackson,.	"	I.	629
1753. Aug. 20.	Friend, Catherine, and Joseph Child,......	"	I.	94
1755. Dec. 1.	Frilinghuysen, Theodorus, and Elizabeth Syms, ...	"	I.	224

19

DATE.		NAMES.	RECORD.	VOL.	PAGE.
1761. Oct.	6.	Frizer, Elizabeth, and John Teal, ...	M. B.,	v.	126
1766. June	6.	Frogat, Mary, and John Alsop, ...	"	x.	6
1772. Jan.	28.	Frost, Amy, and Benjamin Lewis, ...	"	xviii.	20
1763. Dec.	23.	Frost, Anne, and Micajah Townsend, ...	"	vii.	519
1764. Feb.	22.	Frost, Casia, and Jordan Cock, ...	"	viii.	72
1782. Oct.	24.	Frost, Charles, and Phebe Harriss, ...	"	xxxvii.	64
1762. Sept.	10.	Frost, Daniel, and Sarah Cock, ...	"	vi.	311
1773. Nov.	26.	Frost, Elizabeth, and Stephen Horton, ...	"	xxii.	48
1781. May	30.	Frost, Elizabeth, and Thomas Merritt, ...	"	xxxii.	62
1758. Jan.	5.	Frost, Freelove, and Harmanus Ramsen, ...	"	i.	771
1759. Jan.	15.	Frost, Hannah, and John Salt, ...	"	ii.	157
1762. Feb.	19.	Frost, Hannah, and Richard Baxter, ...	"	vi.	55
173⁷⁄. Mar.	3.	Frost, Isaac, and Mary Coak, ...	"	i.	9
1764. Jan.	23.	Frost, Jemima, and Robert Thorny Craft, ..	"	viii.	30
1782. Nov.	18.	Frost, John, and Phebe Carpenter, ...	"	xxxvii.	87
173⁴⁄. Jan.	12.	Frost, John, and Rache Wright, ...	"	i.	5
1762. Jan.	22.	Frost, Mary, and Charles Valentine, ...	"	vi.	24
1782. March 4.		Frost, Mary, and Jehiel Beedel, ...	"	xxxv.	72
1761. Oct.	14.	Frost, Pen, and Sarah Underhill, ...	"	v.	135
1782. Dec.	12.	Frost, Pheby, and James Carpenter, ...	"	xxxvii.	117
1761. Aug.	29.	Frost, Samuel, and Mary Cock, ...	"	v.	63
1756. Jan.	6.	Frost, Sarah, and Daniel Underhill, ...	"	i.	407
1772. May	4.	Frost, Sarah, and Obadiah De Milt, ...	"	xviii.	99
1769. May	31.	Frost, Stephen, and Sarah Cock, ...	"	xiv.	110
1778. Nov.	14.	Frost, Susanah, and Francis Towse, ...	"	xxvi.	87
1764. Dec.	5.	Frost, Theodotia, and Sylvanus Townsend, .	"	viii.	438
1757. Nov.	17.	Frost, Thomas, and Phebe Thornycraft, ...	"	i.	704
1756. Nov.	1.	Frost, William, and Ethelinda Lattin, ...	"	i.	344
1775. Dec.	11.	Fry, Catherine, and David Cox, ...	"	xxiii.	227
1761. Oct.	19.	Fry, Elizabeth, and Thomas North, ...	"	v.	150
1774. Jan.	31.	Fry, Maria, and Christopher P. Yates, ...	"	xxii.	118
1772. Sept.	15.	Fryar, Lydia, and Matthew Fisher, ...	"	xix.	51
1771. April 30.		Fryenmoet, Ann, and John E. Van Alen, ..	"	xvii.	72
1771. Sept.	12.	Fryenmoet, Dorothy, and Peter B. Van Bu-			
		ren, ...	"	xvii.	183
1771. Feb.	18.	Fryenmoet, Mary, and Abraham E. Van Alen,	"	xvii.	18
1776. Jan.	25.	Fryer, Elizabeth, and John A. Lansingh, ...	'	xxiii.	252
1758. Sept.	5.	Fryer, Hannah, and Edward Simmonds, ...	"	ii.	3
1760. Nov.	15.	Fryer, Isaac, and Elizabeth Hinton, ...	"	iii.	418
1774. Jan.	31.	Fryer, Sarah, and Edward S. Willet, ...	"	xxii.	119
1780. May	30.	Fueter, Daniel Christian, and Martha Leonard,	"	xxix.	75
1777. Dec.	30.	Fulkerson, Mary, and William Collins, ...	"	xxiv.	197
1783. April	8.	Fuller, Barsheba, and Edward Trigleth, ...	"	xxxviii.	87
1763. Sept.	6.	Fuller, Samuel, and Anne Hall, ...	"	vii.	376
1781. May	12.	Fullham, Michael, and Catharine Goff, ...	"	xxxii.	46

DATE.	NAMES.	RECORD.	VOL.	PAGE.
1772. Sept. 29.	Fulver, Susannah, and Lemuel Winchel, ...	M. B.,	XIX.	64
1760. Feb. 10.	Funbubble, Marquis, and Sarah Lauson, ...	"	III.	30
1779. June 23.	Funck, John, and Priscilla Potter, ...	"	XXVIII.	3
1763. Aug. 25.	Funck, Hannah, and Thomas Leech, ...	"	VII.	312
1757. July 20.	Funda, Dow, and Deborah Wemp, ...	"	I.	595
1758. Oct. 20.	Funda, Jacob, and Margaret Bossee, ...	"	II.	62
1758. Nov. 15.	Funda, Maria, and Bastean Crigier, ...	"	II.	88
1757. Oct. 12.	Funda, Mary, and Peter Lieuse, ...	"	I.	666
1758. Mar. 13.	Funderit, Judith, and Archibald Chesnut, ...	"	I.	848
1682. Dec. 17.	Furbush, Margaret, and Matthias Harvie, ...	E.,	XXXIII.	24
1763. Feb. 4.	Furman, Amity, and Gershom Bowne, ...	M. B.,	VII.	53
1775. June 16.	Furman, Elizabeth, and John Tyler, ...	"	XXIII.	64
1782. Oct. 3.	Furman, Elizabeth, and Robert Denton, ...	"	XXXVII.	25
173⅞. Feb. 10.	Furman, Gabriel, and Elizabeth Roberts, ...	"	I.	9
1772. Mar. 2.	Furman, Gabriel, and Temperance Woodward, ...	"	XVIII.	45
1781. May 2.	Furman, Hannah, and Demenicas Van Dine,	"	XXXII.	26
1783. May 20.	Furman, John, and Rachael Furman, ...	"	XXXIX.	20
1762. Feb. 13.	Furman, Jonathan, and Susannah Titus, ...	"	VI.	50
1738. Mar. 27.	Furman, Newel, and Susanah Titus, ...	"	I.	9
1783. May 20.	Furman, Rachel, and John Furman, ...	"	XXXIX.	20
1782. June 8.	Furman, William, and Syntje Vandine, ...	"	XXXVI.	43
1779. April 24.	Furnivall, William, and Hester Scandrett, ..	"	XXVII.	117
1781. Jan. 3.	Fyers, William, and Ann Walton, ...	"	XXXI.	9

G.

1764. Aug. 7.	Gaanswort, John, and Effy Beeckman, ...	"	VIII.	276
1783. Aug. 6.	Gabel, John, and Catharine Fea, ...	"	XXXIX.	113
1762. April 10.	Gaddus, Joseph, and Ann Glenn, ...	"	VI.	102
1764. July 18.	Gadey, Catharine, and John Forsyth, ...	"	VIII.	262
1778. Dec. 15.	Gage, Arthur, and Mary Jebereau, ...	"	XXVI.	122
1769. Sept. 5.	Gaine, Hugh, and Cornelia Wallace, ...	"	XV.	37
1759. Oct. 23.	Gaine, Hugh, and Sarah Robbins, ...	"	II.	471
1781. Mar. 20.	Galatian, Elizabeth, and Charles Christian, ..	"	XXXI.	78
1770. Dec. 22.	Galatian, Peter, and Elizabeth Warner, ...	"	XVI.	305
1777. Dec. 16.	Galbreath, James, and Rachel Hunter, ...	"	XXIV.	198
1779. May 7.	Galbreath, Robert, and Elizabeth Tucker, ...	"	XXVII.	127
1781. Feb. 17.	Galbreath, Sarah, and Thomas Ellis, ...	"	XXXI.	47
1770. May 7.	Gale, Abel, and Phebe Denton, ...	"	XVI.	80
1772. July 1.	Gale, Anne, and Thomas Cornell, ...	"	XVIII.	154
1763. June 2.	Gale, Benjamin, and Elenor Carpenter, ...	"	VII.	210
1759. May 16.	Gale, Dorothy, and Verdine Elsworth, ...	"	II.	286
1765. July 30.	Gale, Keziah, and Roger Townsend, ...	"	IX.	223

DATE.		NAMES.	RECORD.	VOL.	PAGE.
1757. May	9.	Gale, Joseph, and Catharine Haviland,.....	"	I.	526
1762. Aug.	27.	Gale, Mary, and Edward Willett,..........	"	VI.	294
1757. June	3.	Gale, Samuel, and Christina De Key,.......	"	I.	551
1773. June	15.	Gale, Samuel, and Rebecca Wells,.........	"	XXI.	5
1780. Aug.	22.	Galilee, Roger, and Ann Simons,.........	"	XXIX.	144
1759. Feb.	7.	Galladet, Leah, and Joshua Temple De St. Croix, ...	"	II.	184
1768. July	13.	Gallant, Susannah, and Willliam Ross,......	"	XIII.	159
1760. Sept.	26.	Gallasha, Mary, and Matthias Warner,.....	"	III.	330
1776. May	7.	Gallatian, David, and Rebecca Banks,......	"	XXIII.	307
1770. Nov.	24.	Gallaudet, Elisha, and Næmoe Reade,......	"	XVI.	268
1760. Aug.	7.	Gallaudet, John, and Charity Richards,.....	"	III.	242
1783. July	14.	Gallaudet, John, and Mary Williams,.......	"	XXXIX.	91
1765. Jan.	21.	Gallaudet, Paul, and Anna Hazard,........	"	IX.	27
1779. Mar.	7.	Gallaudet, Sarah, and Seaman Doty,.......	"	XXVII.	59
1758. Jan.	17.	Gallot, Joseph, and Jane Van Valkenbergh,.	"	I.	785
1775. Sept.	19.	Galloway, James, and Catharine Thurston,..	"	XXIII.	158
1756. Sept.	6.	Galloway, James, and Isabel St. Clear,.....	"	I.	286
1779. Aug.	25.	Galloway, Joseph, and Isabella Williams,...	"	XXVIII.	58
1758. Sept.	12.	Galloway, Mary, and John Farrell,........	"	II.	18
1757. Sept.	3.	Gambauld, Catherine, and Christopher Holt,	"	I.	631
1758. Jan.	3.	Gamble, Jane, and Aaron Van Gelder,.....	"	I.	764
1783. April	11.	Gamble, John, and Catharine Lefferd,......	"	XXXVIII.	90
1760. Feb.	7.	Gamble, Samuel, and Mary Tobin, ...	"	III.	25
1759. June.	25.	Gandell, William, and Mary Ann Marchant,.	"	II.	338
1774. Mar.	16.	Gander, Catharina, and Jacob Brouwer,....	"	XXII.	150
1761. Feb.	4.	Gano, Mary, and Thomas Erskine,.........	"	IV.	52
1752. Nov.	27.	Gansevoort, Elsie, and Barent Ten Eyck,...	"	I.	15
1770. April	10.	Gansevoort, Leonard, and Hester Cuyler,...	"	XVI.	56
1762. May	4.	Gansevoort, Sarah, and John Ten Broeck,..	"	VI.	142
1766. June	17.	Ganter, Mary, and William Dudley,.......	"	X.	19
1776. May	2.	Ganter, Michael, and Mary Hemelsburgh,...	"	XXIII.	306
1773. Aug.	20.	Ganter, Peter, and Elizabeth Trenchard,....	"	XXI.	78
1760. Feb.	2.	Ganthy, Michael, and Apoloney Greenwalden,	"	III.	21
1783. Aug.	30.	Garabrance, Elizabeth, and Leonard Conine,	"	XL.	16
1781. Jan.	6.	Garabrants, Mary, and Daniel Hugunie,....	"	XXXI.	14
1783. May	31.	Garbrance, Ahasuerus, and Margaret Curtis,.	"	XXXIX.	34, 35
1757. Aug.	10.	Garbrants, Cornelius, and Jannetje Van Horne,.......	"	I.	610
1766. July	9.	Garbrants, Elizabeth, and Jacobus Van Sice,.	"	X.	45
1758. Sept.	21.	Garbrantz, Christian, and Mary Post,......	"	II.	28
1782. May	21.	Garden, William, and Jane Rapelye,.......	"	XXXVI.	14
1758. Feb.	16.	Gardenear, Susannah, and Peter Miltonberry,	"	I.	823
1759. Aug.	9.	Gardener, Andries, and Sarah Hanson,.....	"	II.	381
1775. May	31.	Gardenier, Derick, and Elizabeth Van Alen,.	"	XXIII.	50

DATE.	NAMES.	RECORD.	VOL.	PAGE.
1765. Sept. 18.	Gardenier, Johannis, and Cornelia Vosburgh,	M. B.,	IX.	267
1760. Sept. 19.	Gardenier, Neltie, and Johannis Vosburgh,.	"	III.	321
1773. Sept. 23.	Gardenier, Nicholas, and Mary Missick,....	"	XXI.	120
1771. Sept. 26.	Gardenier, Rachel, and Samuel Moral,......	"	XVII.	195
1761. June 27.	Gardinear, Susannah, and Richard Varian,..	"	IV.	265
1772. May 14.	Gardineer, Castintye, and Nicholas Miller,:.	"	XVIII.	111
1770. Sept. 15.	Gardiner, Charles, and Susannah Lynon,...	"	XVI.	187
1766. Dec. 4.	Gardiner, David, and Jerusha Buel,........	"	X.	193
1764. May 11.	Gardiner, David, and Mary Stiren,........	"	VIII.	187
1761. Dec. 23.	Gardiner, Elizabeth, and William Thorn,....	"	V.	297
1766. Nov. 27.	Gardiner, Hannah, and John Forgorsen,....	"	X. 184,	185
1763. June 30.	Gardiner, Helena, and Johannis Van Slik,..	"	VII.	252
1737. April 21.	Gardiner, Isaac, and Mary Woodward,.....	"	I.	6
1766. June 24.	Gardiner, Janetie, and Mathew Vosburgh,..	"	X.	28
1783. April 22.	Gardiner, Magdalean, and William Black,...	"	XXXVIII.	106
1772. May 19.	Gardiner, Mary, and Isaac Thompson,......	"	XVIII.	114
1763. Sept. 8.	Gardiner, Samuel, and Christiana Groadt,...	"	VII.	330
1765. May 15.	Gardiner, Sarah, and John Abraham Vosburgh, ...	"	IX.	127
1768. June 16.	Gardinier, Abraham, and Arriantje Verplank,	"	XIII.	129
1778. July 24.	Gardinier, Jacob, and Catherine Garlick,....	"	XXV.	140
1773. Nov. 30.	Gardinier, Joanna, and Evert Vosburgh,....	"	XXII.	54
1760. Nov. 25.	Gardinier, Seyntie, and Peter Van Slyck,...	"	III.	443
1780. June 10.	Gardner, Elizabeth, and Robert Morris,....	"	XXIX.	85
1770. Dec. 31.	Gardner, Fytie, and Philip Harder,........	"	XVI.	311
1782. Sept. 21.	Gardner, Isabella, and Walter McDonald,..	"	XXXVII.	8
1765. May 31.	Gardner, James, and Margaret Way,......	"	IX.	149
1781. Jan. 6.	Gardner, Mary, and James Selkrig,........	"	XXXI.	15
1771. Nov. 9.	Gardner, Sarah, and Henry Humphrys,....	"	XVII.	244
1779. Jan. 22.	Gardner, Susanah, and George Smith,......	"	XXVII.	23
1773. Sept. 16.	Gardner, Thomas, and Jane Hart,.........	"	XXI.	111
1780. Nov. 9.	Gardner, William, and Magdalean McWhirten,	"	XXX.	99
1777. Mar. 24.	Garing, Catherine, and Robert Hill,........	"	XXIV.	51
1781. May 28.	Garish, Elizabeth, and William Willson,....	"	XXXII.	58
1758. Oct. 4.	Garison, Amey, and William Steves,.......	"	II.	38
1782. Mar. 22.	Garison, Ann, and Abraham Bogart,.......	"	XXXV.	95
1669. April 20.	Garland, John, and Susannah Verplanck,...	O. W. L.,	II.	417
1762. Oct. 18.	Garland, Robert, and Sarah Donnely,......	M. B.,	VI.	370
1779. Oct. 2.	Garlick, Barbara, and David Babcock,......	"	XXVIII.	95
1778. July 24.	Garlick, Catherine, and Jacob Gardinier,...	"	XXV.	140
1762. April 22.	Garman, Rueben, and Esther Vail,........	"	VI.	126
1762. Feb. 25.	Garrabrants, Eleanor, and Egbert Haughwout, ...	"	VI.	57
1761. Aug. 14.	Garrabrants, Peter, and Eleanor Lang,.....	"	V.	42
1783. April 15.	Garrebrants, Catharine, and John Clarke,...	"	XXXVIII.	96

DATE.	NAMES.	RECORD.	VOL.	PAGE.
1766. June 27.	Garret, William, and Chrishe Faulke,......	M. B.,	x.	37
1762. Nov. 27.	Garretse, Esther, and John Vanness,.......	"	vi.	464
1769. Oct. 5.	Garretsen, Samuel, and Margaret Remsen,..	"	xv.	49
1783. Sept. 22.	Garretson, Allathea, and William Carty,....	"	xl.	51
1781. April 2.	Garretson, Ann, and Nicholas Journeay,....	"	xxxi.	90
1762. Jan. 13.	Garretson, Anne, and Cornelius Boyce,.....	"	vi.	11
1769. Nov. 2.	Garretson, Annetje, and Peter Van Der Belt,	"	xv.	74
1783. Aug. 28.	Garretson, Gertrude, and Xenophon Jouett,	"	xl.	13
1781. Oct. 9.	Garretson, John, and Martha Codmas,.....	"	xxxiii.	94
1762. April 14.	Garretson, Margaret, and Richard Osborne,.	"	vi.	103
1771. Mar. 18.	Garrick, Elizabeth, and George Faircloy,...	"	xvii.	35
1764. April 25.	Garrick, Margaret, and James Gordon,.....	"	viii.	167
1779. July 9.	Garrish, Thomas, and Elizabeth Jordan,....	"	xxviii.	19
1761. April 27.	Garrison, Abraham, and Maria Brower,....	"	iv.	169
1762. Mar. 15.	Garrison, Anne, and Daniel Lake,.........	"	vi.	70
1773. Oct. 27.	Garrison, Catalina, and Tunis Clearwater,...	"	xxi.	149
1780. June 12.	Garrison, Catharine, and Charles Johnston,..	"	xxix.	87
1773. Jan. 30.	Garrison, Elinor, and John Brookman,.....	"	xx.	33
1775. July · 24.	Garrison, Elizabeth, and Cornelius Van Cleft,	"	xxiii.	104
1781. Aug. 20.	Garrison, Elizabeth, and Henry Miller,.....	"	xxxiii.	42
1737. Dec. 27.	Garrison, Elizabeth, and Simon Vaname,...	"	i.	8
1762. Oct. 28.	Garrison, Gilbert, and Elizabeth Cornish,..	"	vi.	389
1764. Oct. 11.	Garrison, Hannah, and Simon Swain,......	"	viii.	352
1779. Mar. 25.	Garrison, Hannah, and William Jacocks,...	"	xxvii.	146
1769. July 28.	Garrison, Hester, and Richard Christopher,..	"	xv.	6
1783. Jan. 4.	Garrison, John, and Anne Bedell,.........	"	xxxviii.	4
1777. Oct. 11.	Garrison, Lenah, and Samuel Stillwell,.....	"	xxiv.	161
1779. April 10.	Garrisen, Mary, and John Kingston,.......	"	xxvii.	103
1772. April 28.	Garrison, Nathaniel, and Tamer Rickaw,...	"	xviii.	95
1770. Sept. 6.	Garrison, Samuel, and Ealtie Ryder,.......	"	xvi.	181
173⁷⁄₈. Feb. 20.	Garritson, Mary, and Edmund Arrowsmith,.	"	i.	9
1767. Oct. 14.	Gasherie, Joseph, and Catharine Wynkoop,.	"	xii.	62
1780. Aug. 25.	Gaskin, Elizabeth, and John Ford,.........	"	xxx.	1
1778. Mar. 7.	Gasling, Jacob, and Mary Lawrence,......	"	xxv.	34
1771. Sept. 18.	Gasner, John, and Entye Underdunk,......	"	xvii.	185
1767. May 22.	Gassra, John, and Catherine Fonseus,......	"	xi.	93
1766. Oct. 24.	Gatfield, Archibald, and Mary Van Evera,..	"	x.	140
1772. Feb. 13.	Gatfield, Benjamin, and Rachel Beets,.....	"	xviii.	37
1764. Feb. 16.	Gathry, John, and Sarah Barber,..........	"	viii.	62
1779. July 5.	Gault, Robert, and Elizabeth Hallett,......	"	xxviii.	16
1775. June 15.	Gault, Mathew, and Lydia Brett,..........	"	xxiii.	62
1779. Dec. 14.	Gautier, Apoline, and Francois Girom,.....	"	xxviii.	171
1762. July 21.	Gautier, Catharine, and Christopher Duyckinck, ...	"	vi.	249
1783. Jan. 11.	Gautier, Daniel, and Ann Brandon,........	"	xxxviii.	13

DATE.	NAMES.	RECORD.	VOL.	PAGE.
1760. Feb. 11.	Gautier, Hunty, and Jenkin Williams, ...	M. B.,	III.	31
1783. Oct. 6.	Gautier, Margaret, and Andrew Hamersly, . .	"	XL.	64
1783. Oct. 16.	Gay, Alexander, and Elizabeth Long, ...	"	XL.	81
1771. July 25.	Gay, Charles, and Rebeccah Smith, ...	"	XVII.	143
1774. Jan. 7.	Geamester, William, and Catherine Walsh, . .	"	XXII.	96
1782. Aug. 23.	Geary, Martha, and Stephen Shakespear, . . .	"	XXXVI.	118
1736. June 12.	Gebrink, Hendrica, and Benjamin Davis, . . .	"	I.	1
1761. Nov. 16.	Gedney, Ester, and Joseph Bull, ...	"	V.	223
1783. April 10.	Geldersleve, Ruth, and John Smith, ...	"	XXXVIII.	89
1769. July 18.	Gell, John, and Ann Tate, ...	"	XIV.	155
1760. Aug. 5.	Geller, David Frederick, and Margaret Eman,	"	III.	234
1769. Aug. 24.	Gelston, David, and Phebe Mitchel, ...	"	XV.	28
1764. Nov. 20.	Gelston, Elizabeth, and David Pearson, ...	"	VIII.	413
1773. June 9.	Gelston, Hugh, and Mary Foster, ...	"	XX.	142
1765. June 5.	Gelston, John, and Margaret Thompson, ...	"	IX.	157
1737. Oct. 15.	George, Hannah, and John Richards, ...	"	I.	7
1764. Mar. 29.	George, Hannah, and Thomas Whitefield, . . .	"	VIII.	123
1769. Jan. 10.	George, Joseph, and Ellinor Vanderbelt, ...	"	XIV.	10
1780. May 17.	Gerard, William, and Christiana Glass, ...	"	XXIX.	60
1760. Nov. 14.	Gerbrantz, Elizabeth, and Peter Post, ...	"	III.	415
1768. Sept. 19.	Gerdenier, Elizabeth, and Hans Muller, ...	"	XIII.	189
1757. June 30.	Gereau, Mary, and John Shields, ...	"	I.	577
1780. May 30.	Geree, William, and Rebecca Van Denham, . .	"	XXIX.	72
1760. Oct. 7.	German, Elizabeth, and Richard Hussey, . . .	"	III.	347
1762. Oct. 20.	German, Elizabeth, and William Sands, ...	"	VI.	375
1736. Nov. 22.	German, Isaac, and Catherine Huff, ...	"	I.	3
1736. July 26.	German, Susannah, and Lawrence Huff, ...	"	I.	2
1780. Sept. 21.	German, William, and Jane Ludet, ...	"	XXX.	33
1773. Jan. 14.	Germond, Susanna, and Turpin Holroyd, . . .	"	XVIII.	13
1780. June 23.	Gerow, Jane, and Robert Dickson, ...	"	XXIX.	93
1782. Aug. 2.	Gerow, Phebe, and Jonathan Sherwood, . . .	"	XXXVI.	97
1763. July 29.	Gerrald, Ann, and John Charter, ...	"	VII.	286
1763. Nov. 14.	Gerrard, Benjamin, and Philethea Dayton, . .	"	VII.	448
1768. June 28.	Gerrebrants, Heyltye, and John N. Bogert, .	"	XIII.	144
1760. Dec. 6.	Gerretie, Annatje, and Barent Vosburgh, . . .	"	III.	462
1764. Mar. 17.	Gerretsen, Johannes, and Jannetje William- son, ...	"	VIII.	107
1753. May 15.	Gerretson, Guysbert, and Elizabeth Court- right, ...	"	I.	30
1675. May 26.	Gerritse, Peter, and Christien Pieterse, ...	W. O. P.,	III.	96
1757. Dec. 8.	Gerritsen, Samuel, and Matje Hagerman, . . .	M. B.,	I.	730
1759. April 19.	Gerritson, Harmanus, and Altje Simerson, . .	"	II.	247
1764. Jan. 6.	Gerritson, John, and Cornelia Middigh, ...	"	VIII.	8
1769. May 8.	Gerritson, Margaret, and Abraham Crocheron,	"	XIV.	97
1736. Sept. 6.	Gerrittsen, Maria, and Jacobus Bevois, ...	"	I.	2

DATE.	NAMES.	RECORD.	VOL.	PAGE.
1676. July 21.	Gerritz, Mactell, and Cornelys Buys,.......	W. O. P.,	III.	202
1767. Oct. 26.	Gertson, Mary, and Isaac Hogen,.........	M. B.,	XII.	67a
1757. April 27.	Gest, Elizabeth, and John Griffith,.........	"	I.	517
1782. April 15.	Gestner, John, and Mary Dash,...........	"	XXXV.	123
1763. Aug. 18.	Gettens, Phillip, and Catharine McIntosh,.,.	"	VII.	306
1771. Oct. 15.	Geuero, Jacob, and Catherine Powers,.....	"	XVII.	209
1737. Aug. 17.	Gibb, Richard, and Catherine Vannenburgh,	"	I.	7
1757. May 17.	Gibb, Robert, and Jane Taylor,...........	"	I.	535
1778. Oct. 30.	Gibbons, Margaret, and Stephen Bluck,....	"	XXVI.	77
1770. Nov. 28.	Gibbons, William, and Maria Yandel Cranmur, ...	"	XVI.	273
1685. May 26.	Gibbs, Elizabeth, and Thomas Ashton,.....	C. M.,	XXXIII.	131
1762. Nov. 18.	Gibbs, Hannah, and John Dusenberry,.....	M. B.,	VI.	442
1760. June 3.	Gibbs, John, and Sarah Leycraft,..........	"	III.	174
1761. April 9.	Gibbs, Mary, and Isaac Corsa,............	"	IV.	140
1764. Jan. 27.	Gibbs, Patience, and John Storm,.........	"	VIII.	39
1771. June 18.	Gibbs, Sarah, and Gilbert Bates,..........	"	XVII.	113
1771. Mar. 9.	Gibbs, Sarah, and John Sebring,...... ...	"	XVII.	28
1769. Dec. 13.	Gibson, Ann, and John Jonsline,..	"	XV.	122
1768. Dec. 21.	Gibson, Elizabeth, and Abraham Vandervoort,...............................	"	XIII.	270
1782. Jan. 2.	Gibson, John, and Rebecca Case,..........	"	XXXV.	3
1763. April 30.	Gibson, James, and Mary McCaller,.......	"	VII.	159
1780. Dec. 2.	Gibson, Mary, and Benjamin Cornwell,.....	"	XXX.	136
1773. Aug. 20.	Gibson, Mary, and Charles Sprainger,......	"	XXI.	80
1760. May 28.	Gibson, Mary, and James Brewster,.......	"	III.	166
1759. Feb. 12.	Gibson, Mathew, and Ann Haney,.........	"	II.	189
1782. May 28.	Gibson, Thomas, and Hannah Vandebargh,..	"	XXXVI.	28
1780. Nov. 20.	Gibson, William, and Mary Anderson,.....	"	XXX.	115
1783. June 13.	Gidney, Deborah, and Bernard Rapelye,....	"	XXXIX.	57
1778. Dec. 31.	Gidney, Elizabeth, and Benjamin Hunt,....	"	XXVI.	136
1783. June 6.	Gidney, Elizabeth, and David Hallett,......	"	XXXIX.	43
1780. Dec. 9.	Gidney, Frances, and Alexander Morrison,..	"	XXX.	148
1779. Dec. 23.	Gidney, Hester, and Williams Hunt,........	"	XXVIII.	177
1736. July 31.	Gidney, Isaac, and Sibe Nelson,...........	"	I.	2
1763. Feb. 1.	Gidney, Jacob, and Mary Seacord,........	"	VII.	48
1760. Dec. 10.	Gidney, John, and Elizabeth Bates,........	"	III.	470
1758. Nov. 4.	Gidney, Joseph, and Phebe Bates,.........	"	II.	82
1763. Jan. 24.	Gidney, Martha, and Joshua Barnes,.......	"	VII.	32
1783. June 10.	Gidney, Patty, and Nathaniel Moore,......	":	XXXIX.	48
1758. Nov. 4.	Gidney, Phebe, and Robert Sutton,.......	"	II.	81
1773. Nov. 2.	Gidney, Solomon, and Hannah Horton,....	"	XXII.	60
1757. April 9.	Gidney, Tamar, and William Sutton,.......	"	I.	495
1782. Aug. 3.	Gidney, Teamor, and Thomas O'Brien,.....	"	XXXVI.	99
1780. Sept. 11.	Gierson, James, and Ann Hardman,.......	"	XXX.	23

DATE.	NAMES.	RECORD.	VOL.	PAGE.
1769. Oct. 23.	Giew, Jane, and John Townsend,.........	M. B.,	xv.	60
1772. Dec. 4.	Giffin, Elizabeth, and John Brown,.......	"	xix.	142
1772. June 15.	Giffin, Mary, and George Cummings,......	"	xviii.	139
1772. April 13.	Giffin, Rachel, and John Mandevel,.......	"	xviii.	75
1773. Oct. 28.	Gifford, Mary, and John Dubois,..........	"	xxi.	150
1762. Oct. 13.	Gifford, William, and Mary Ryder,........	"	vi.	363
1780. April 1.	Gifford, William Bernard, and Ann Voorhies,	"	xxix.	11
1756. July 9.	Gilbert, Aaron, and Hannah Mandavel,.....	"	i.	248
1776. Feb. 7.	Gilbert, Alitha, and John Sickles,.	"	xxiii.	263
1766. Nov. 8.	Gilbert, Ann, and Ephraim Brasher,.......	"	x.	158
1783. Aug. 8.	Gilbert, Anne, and Robert Carter,.........	"	xxxix.	117
1776. April 27.	Gilbert, Catherine, and Richard Bragaw,...	"	xxiii.	303
1766. Nov. 19.	Gilbert, Cornelia, and Martin Vosburgh,....	"	x.	171
1781. Feb. 23.	Gilbert, Ebeneazer, and Margaret Sprung,..	"	xxxi.	55
1756. Dec. 24.	Gilbert, Elizabeth, and Beekman Van Bueren,	"	i.	398
1769. Dec. 28.	Gilbert, Henry, and Ann Shaw,...........	"	xv.	132
1762. Aug. 17.	Gilbert, Mary, and William Gilbert,.......	"	vi.	276
1762. Aug. 17.	Gilbert, William, and Mary Gilbert,........	"	vi.	276
1757. April 22.	Gilbert, William, and Mercy Bond,........	"	i.	508
1767. May 27.	Gilbert, William W., and Catherine Cozine,.	"	xi.	98
1782. Mar. 9.	Gilbertson, Mary, and John Barthram,.....	"	xxxv.	80
1780. May 16.	Gilbertson, William, and Mary Regen,.....	"	xxix.	56
1770. April 26.	Gilchrist, Margaret, and William Stephens,..	"	xvi.	70
1768. Jan. 18.	Gilchrist, Rebecka, and James Taylor,......	"	xiii.	10
1759. May 8.	Gilchrist, Richard, and Mary Bolitho,......	"	ii.	271
1781. Jan. 1.	Gildersleeve, John, and Kezia Ketcham,....	"	xxxi.	1
1763. May 3.	Gildersleeve, Joseph, and Jane Wiley,.....	"	vii.	163
1768. July 7.	Gildersleeve, Phebe, and Abel Bennett,....	"	xiii.	152
1737. Dec. 23.	Gildersleeve, Richard, and Phebe Oldfield,..	"	i.	8
1769. Mar. 15.	Gildersleeve, Ruth, and David Davis,......	"	xiv.	53
1782. June 5.	Gildersleeve, Sarah, and Zopher Roggers,...	"	xxxvi.	39
1773. Dec. 2.	Gildersleeves, Elizabeth, and Gershom Bowne,	"	xxii.	59
1783. Aug. 8.	Gildersleve, Sarah, and Edmund Bunce,....	"	xxxix.	118
1738. June 17.	Gildersleves, Mary, and Joseph Griffen,.....	"	i.	10
1759. Oct. 27.	Gildo, Mary, and James Hill,.............	"	ii.	475
1755. Aug. 20.	Giles, Gilbert, and Elizabeth Nelson,.......	"	i.	153
1767. Mar. 24.	Giles, Gilbert, and Margaret Collins,.......	"	xi.	48
1763. Mar. 5.	Giles, James, and Sarah Young,...........	"	vii.	93
1781. Nov. 13.	Giles, John, and Hester Marschalk,........	"	xxxiv.	29
1759. May 12.	Giles, Samuel, and Frances Helme,........	"	ii.	280
1759. Dec. 13.	Gilford, Samuel, and Penelope Codwise,....	"	ii.	542
1783. Mar. 25.	Gill, Robert, and Wilhelmina Anthony,....	"	xxxviii.	76
1783. Oct. 6.	Gilladate, George, and Catharine Connoway,	"	xl.	65
1773. Nov. 10.	Gilleas, Robert, and Hester Steel,.........	"	xxii.	19
1782. April 23.	Gilledet, Charity, and Ludwick Herman,...	"	xxxv.	132

20

DATE.	NAMES.	RECORD.	VOL.	PAGE.
1780. Dec. 5.	Gilles, Archibald, and Sarah Whitehand,...	M. B.,	XXX.	138
1771. Aug. 5.	Gilles, William, and Mary Maer,..........	"	XVII.	152
1768. Feb. 25.	Gillesby, John, and Mary Elsworth,.......	"	XIII.	43
1781. Dec. 4.	Gillespie, John, and Susannah Bartow,.....	"	XXXIV.	71
1780. June 2.	Gillespy, Nelly, and William Cuningham,...	"	XXIX.	77
1761. Sept. 24.	Gillihen, James, and Susanah Brasier, ...	"	V.	96
1762. July 9.	Gilliland, James, and Judith Rose,.	"	VI.	232
1769. Dec. 30.	Gilliland, John, and Catherine Zeegaart,....	"	XV.	135
1759. Feb. 8.	Gilliland, William, and Elizabeth Phagen,...	"	II.	185
1782. Aug. 31.	Gilmore, Aggness, and Isaac Brower,......	"	XXXVI.	133
1757. July 25.	Gilmore, Hugh, and Catharine Pinkeman,...	"	I.	600
1757. Mar. 8.	Gilmore, Margaret, and Philip Duly,.......	"	I.	460
1777. Feb. 1.	Gilmore, Margaret, and William Haggs,....	"	XXIV.	22
1759. Mar. 31.	Gilmore, Robert, and Mary Edwards,......	"	II.	230
1763. July 14.	Giraud, Andrew, and Elizabeth Henderson,.	"	VII.	266
1758. April 24.	Giraud, Ann, and John Tomlinson,........	"	I.	883
1779. Dec. 14.	Girom, Francois, and Apoline Gautier,.....	"	XXVIII.	171
1763. Aug. 4.	Gisling, Elias, and Elizabeth Quackenboss,..	"	VII.	290
1763. Jan. 18.	Gislingh, Breghtie, and Gerret Van Vranke,	"	VII.	21
1758. Jan. 28.	Gittins, John, and Mary Kemp,...........	"	I.	804
1758. Feb. 27.	Glaghorn, Janet, and Richard Bogg,.......	"	I.	831
1780. May 17.	Glass, Christiana, and William Gerard,.....	"	XXIX.	60
1764. Jan. 24.	Glassford, James, and Rosamond Cooper,...	"	VIII.	33
1779. Mar. 30.	Glean, Anthony, and Martha Tippet,.......	"	XXVII.	85
1771. April 30.	Glean, Elizabeth, and Jacob Emmens,.....	"	XVII.	73
1779. Mar. 24.	Glean, Mary, and Peter Prindle,..........	"	XXVII.	75
1775. June 6.	Glean, Samuel, aud Jane Parsons,.........	"	XXIII.	54
1769. July 14.	Glean, Susannah, and Matthew Cook,......	"	XIV.	153
1775. April 15.	Glean, Susannah, and Matthew Smith,.....	"	XXIII.	10
1779. April 11.	Gleaves, Brachey, and James Tillery,......	"	XXVII.	105
1764. May 3.	Gleen, Abigail, and Thomas Ogilvie,...'..	"	VIII.	183
1761. April 27.	Gleen, James, and Mary Williams,.........	"	IV.	168
1760. Mar. 1.	Gleghorne, Violet, and William Hall,.......	"	III.	57
1762. April 10.	Glen, Ann, and Joseph Gaddus,...........	"	VI.	102
1765. June 5.	Glen, Annatje Sanderse, and Hermans Van Slyck, ...	"	IX.	159
1762. May 21.	Glen, Catharine, and Harmanus Wendell,...	"	VI.	163
1764. Aug. 16.	Glen, Cornelius, and Elizabeth Nicholls,....	"	VIII.	283
1762. Nov. 9.	Glen, Henry, and Elisabeth Visher,........	"	VI.	422
1764. Mar. 5.	Glen, Jane, and Abraham Cuyler,.........	"	VIII.	93
1759. May 4.	Glen, John, Jr., and Catharine Veeder,.....	"	II.	266
1762. Sept. 3.	Glenn, John S., and Sarah Saunders,......	"	VI.	304
1765. April 9.	Glenn, Thomas, and Margaret Mahony,.....	"	IX.	84
1755. Sept. 16.	Gleson, Catharine, and John Stevens,......	"	I.	178
1760. Nov. 22.	Gleves, Matthew, and Margaret Rote,......	"	III.	434

DATE.	NAMES.	RECORD.	VOL.	PAGE.
1737. July 26.	Glieves, Hester, and Isaac Bedlow,........	M. B.,	I.	7
1783. April 22.	Glover, Anne, and Stephen Carey,........	"	XXXVIII.	109
1738. Dec. 8.	Glover, Hester, and John Bisset,..........	"	I.	12
1771. June 15.	Glover, John, and Esther Grondine,.......	"	XVII.	111
1757. Sept. 21.	Glover, Martha, and Stephen Dwight,......	"	I.	639
1755. Sept. 8.	Goar, John, and Effie Van Veghte,.........	"	I.	169
1780. Oct. 7.	Gockh, Mary, and Jonathan Baxter,.......	"	XXX.	60
1737. Dec. 3.	Goddard, Christopher, and Mary Kennedy,.	"	I.	8
1770. Mar. 5.	Goddard, Mary, and Benjamin Calder,.....	"	XVI.	30
1778. Oct. 27.	Godwin, Ann, and Paul Brown,..........	"	XXVI.	74
1763. Jan. 3.	Godwin, Samuel, and Magdalen Wallagrave,	"	VII.	4
1757. Jan. 20.	Godwood, Mary, and Robert Moore,.......	"	I.	422
1780. Dec. 21.	Goeddecy, Charles, and Mary Moutchell,...	"	XXX.	162
1776. Jan. 30.	Goelet, Alice, and Andrew Lott,..........	"	XXIII.	256
1755. Aug. 28.	Goelet, Catharin, and Peter T. Curtenius,..	"	I.	159
1764. Nov. 20.	Goelet, Jane, and John Zabriski,..........	"	VIII.	412
1770. Dec. 4.	Goelet, Peter, and Mary Ludlow,..........	"	XVI.	283
1770. Oct. 12.	Goes, Elizabeth, and Burger Huick,.......	"	XVI.	209
1775. May 10.	Goes, Jane, and Cornelius Sebring,........	"	XXIII.	27
1766. Nov. 21.	Goes, Johannis, Jr., and Elizabeth Vosburgh,	"	X.	174
1776. Jan. 25.	Goes, John D., and Mary Quackenboss,.....	"	XXIII.	251
1764. Nov. 22.	Goes, Louris, and Catharine Hoffman,......	"	VIII.	418
1767. Nov. 24.	Goes, Mary, and Johannes I. Van Alen,....	"	XII.	97
1770. June 30.	Goes, Mary, and John Bronck,............	"	XVI.	131
1760. June 2.	Goes, Mathew, and Helena Van Duesen,...	"	III.	171
1757. April 28.	Goes, Myndert, and Margaret Forsburgh,..	"	I.	519
1776. Feb. 24.	Goetchius, Catherine, and Rynier Van Nest,.	"	XXIII.	273
1758. Oct. 14.	Goetschius, Johannes Mauritius, and Catrina Huger,................................	"	II.	56
1759. May 2.	Goetz, John Michael, and Catharine Webern,	"	II.	264
1760. Jan. 21.	Goewy, Catlyna, and John Gerse Yates,....	"	II.	586
1781. May 12.	Goff, Catherine, and Michael Fullhan,......	"	XXXII.	46
1775. May 20.	Goff, Elizabeth, and Jacob Roose,.........	"	XXIII.	40
1760. Nov. 8.	Goff, Jane, and John Smith,..............	"	III.	399
1765. Aug. 14.	Goff, Jenny, and Coenradt Wolfe,.........	"	IX.	236
1773. Mar. 30.	Goff, Mary, and Richard Banks,...........	"	XX.	78
1760. May 16.	Goforth, William, and Catharine Weeks,...	"	III.	155
1760. Sept. 3.	Gold, Anne, and John McColme,..........	"	III.	280
1781. July 24.	Golden, John, and Pheby Volintine,.......	"	XXXIII.	14
1760. Nov. 14.	Golder, Dorothy, and Thomas Southerd,....	"	III.	413
1774. Feb. 9.	Golder, Joseph, and Elizabeth Gripman,...	"	XXII.	125
1782. Dec. 17.	Golder, Letitia, and John Staats,..........	"	XXXVII.	123
1761. Dec. 18.	Golder, Michael, and Altje Van Noorstrandt,	"	V.	285
1737. April 14.	Golder, Wanechy, and Abraham Hendrickson, ...	"	I.	5

DATE.	NAMES.	RECORD.	VOL.	PAGE
1763. Feb. 10.	Golding, Ann, and Daniel Polhemus,.......	M. B.,	VII.	58
1782. Jan. 28.	Golding, Ephraim, and Hannah Fly,.......	"	XXXV.	35
1781. April 26.	Golding, Nathaniel, and Sarah Devoo,.....	"	XXXII.	18
1765. April 10.	Golding, Rebecca, and Daniel Libbey,.....	"	IX.	87
1773. Nov. 15.	Goldsmith, Richard, and Lydia Rider,......	"	XXII.	28
1759. Mar. 8.	Goldthwait, Michael Burrell, and Sarah Farman,................................	"	II.	213
1761. Jan. 26.	Goldtrap, Thomas, and Margaret Martin,...	"	IV.	29
1759. Oct. 29.	Goldwin, Sarah, and Dennis MacGwier,....	"	II.	477
1768. Aug. 5.	Gons, Francis, and Ann Kingston,.........	"	XIII.	169
1764. Sept. 18.	Gonzales, Elizabeth, and Johannes Bevier,..	"	VIII.	313
1773. Dec. 3.	Gonzales, Manewal, Jr., and Sarah Bevier,..	"	XXII.	61
1773. Mar. 23.	Goodbylet, Catherine, and John Parker,....	"	XX.	68
1737. May 16.	Goodland, Mary, and Dennis Hicks,.......	"	I.	6
1781. Oct. 15.	Goodman, John, and Hannah Pennell,.....	"	XXXIII.	100
1778. Oct. 5.	Goodrich, Bartlett, and Mary Wilson,......	"	XXVI.	110
1736. July 1.	Goodwin, David, and Catharine Drinkwater,	"	I.	2
1764. April 14.	Goodwin, Elizabeth, and Thomas Wiggins,..	"	VIII.	155
1771. Jan. 18.	Goodwin, Richard, and Elizabeth Lewis,...	"	XVII.	7
1773. Dec. 6.	Googlet, Hendrick, and Amy Cornish,......	"	XXII.	62
1782. Jan. 16.	Goold, Amy, and Alexander Sammis,......	"	XXXV.	19
1782. Oct. 3.	Goold, Benjamin, and Elizabeth Platt,......	"	XXXVII.	26
1774. Mar. 2.	Goold, Edward, and Sarah Child Huggins,..	"	XXII.	138
1773. Nov. 17.	Goot, Dirck G., and Harantie Wimp,.......	"	XXII.	33
1762. Feb. 22.	Gorbacker, John, and Elizabeth Stanton,...	"	VI.	56
1761. Aug. 5.	Gordan, John, and Catharine Bayley,......	"	V.	26
1771. June 26.	Gordon, Alice, and William White,.......	"	XVII.	122
1772. Feb. 12.	Gordon, Catherine, and Valentine Nutter,...	"	XVIII.	34
1775. Nov. 2.	Gordon, Elizabeth, and Isaac Demilt,......	"	XXIII.	197
1770. Oct. 13.	Gordon, Elizabeth, and Joshua H. Smith,...	"	XVI.	211
1764. April 25.	Gordon, James, and Margaret Garrick,.....	"	VIII.	167
1770. Nov. 10.	Gordon, Margaret, and Alexander Richie,..	"	XVI.	245
1764. Feb. 25.	Gordon, Mary, and John Dougan,.........	"	VIII.	78
1763. Jan. 29.	Gordon, Thomas, and Martha Needham,...	"	VII.	39
1761. Feb. 3.	Gormley, Samuel, and Mary Atkison,......	"	IV.	48
1761. Dec. 7.	Gorsline, Jost, and Martha Smith,.........	"	V.	266
1770. June 1.	Gortser, Christiana, and Hendrick Andrew Smith, ...	"	XVI.	101
1772. July 15.	Gose, Elizabeth, and Leonard Van Alstyne,.	"	XVIII.	167
1773. Aug. 20.	Gose, Matthew, and Jane Van Valkenbergh,	"	XXI.	79
1773. April 21.	Gose, Stantia, and Thomas L. Witbeek,....	"	XX.	99
1669. Feb. 12.	Gosen, Maria, and James Matthews,.......	C. A.,	II.	467
1756. Sept. 14.	Gosline, John, and Judith Realer,.........	M. B.,	I.	296
1759. Oct. 2.	Gosline, Joseph, and Sarah Leverich,......	"	II.	442
1773. June 14.	Gosline, Patience, and William Loweree,...	"	XXI.	3

DATE.		NAMES.	RECORD.	VOL.	PAGE.
1762. July	31.	Gosline, Richard, and Antje Albertus,......	M. B.,	VI.	258
1738. Oct.	11.	Gosline, Samuel, and Judah Wood,........	"	I.	11
1780. Nov.	14.	Gosling, Elizabeth, and Normand McLeod,..	"	XXX.	105
1764. Feb.	6.	Gosling, Jacob, and Sarah Hallett,........	"	VIII.	53
1782. May	28.	Goswelling, Mary, and John Hatch,.......	"	XXXVI.	29
1756. Sept.	30.	Gotier, Magdalin, and Samuel Foster,......	"	I.	314
1758. Feb.	23.	Gould, John, and Catherine Menee,........	"	I.	826
1780. Dec.	23.	Gould, John, and Lellis Edo,.............	"	XXX.	167
1757. July	19.	Gould, Rebeccah, and John Kerly,.........	"	I.	594
1737. May	12.	Gouverneur, Alida, and John Broughton,...	"	I.	6
1769. July	5.	Gouverneur, Herman, and Mary Broughton,.	"	XIV.	142
1779. July	12.	Govier, Joseph, and Phebe Lewis,.........	"	XXVIII.	21
1779. Nov.	11.	Gowey, William, and Ann Watkins,.......	"	XXVIII.	136
1758. Oct.	10.	Grace, John, and Sarah Stone,............	"	II.	46
1761. July	7.	Grace, Rebecca, and Abraham Post,.......	"	IV.	288
1771. Dec.	2.	Grace, Robert, and Ann Wilkins,..........	"	XVII.	278
1773. April	5.	Grace, Walter, and Mary Blanchard,.......	"	XX.	83
1757. Aug.	5.	Grage, Elizabeth, and Peter Rose,.	"	I.	608
1761. Dec.	3.	Graghburgher, Hannah, and Johan Bastian Kuysrock,...................	"	V.	263
1771. Aug.	16.	Graham, Annanias, and Jane Kempton,....	"	XVII.	158
1737. Nov.	4.	Granger, Anne, and David Mersereau,.....	"	I.	8
1782. Sept.	15.	Graham, Anne, and Nathaniel Ashfoard,...	"	XXXVII.	2
1783. Aug.	13.	Graham, Anne, and William Reynolds,.....	"	XXXIX.	125
1760. June	9.	Graham, Arthur. and Hannah Denin,......	"	III.	182
1770. Feb.	17.	Graham, Austin, and Mary Van Ranst,.....	"	XVI.	18
1772. April	21.	Graham, Catharine, and Justice Banks,.....	"	XVIII.	86
1776. Mar.	25.	Graham, Catherine, and Robert Cane,......	"	XXIII.	291
1768. April	18.	Graham, Daniel, and Catherina Decker,....	"	XIII.	81
1768. Oct.	29.	Graham, Duncan, and Mary McCavey,.....	"	XIII.	218
1767. Jan.	7.	Graham, Elizabeth, and Mathew Decker,...	"	XI.	3
1771. Mar.	23.	Graham, Elizabeth, and Thomas Storm,....	"	XVII.	39
1763. July	21.	Graham, Ennis, and Elizabeth Wilcox,.....	"	VII.	279
1771. Dec.	11.	Graham, Isabella, and Jonathan Landon,...	"	XVII.	288
1738. Nov.	30.	Graham, James, and Arabella Morris,......	"	I.	12
1764. Dec.	21.	Graham, John, and Catharine De Witt,.....	"	VIII.	461
1768. Dec.	20.	Graham, John, and Elizabeth Irvin,........	"	XIII.	268
1770. Sept.	28.	Graham, John, and Trientje Bruyn,.......	"	XVI.	200
1781. Sept.	25.	Graham, Robert, and Anne Hunter,.......	"	XXXIII.	78
1773. June	22.	Graham, John, and Mary Winter,.........	"	XXI.	19
1781. Dec.	4.	Graham, Joseph, and Hannah Hallet,......	"	XXXIV.	70
1765. Aug.	23.	Graham, Malcolm, and Elinor Groves,......	"	IX.	244
1773. Aug.	20.	Graham, Mary, and Edward Patten,......;.	"	XXI.	77
1763. June	30.	Graham, Mary, and James Johnson,.......	"	VII.	248
1736. Dec.	14.	Graham, Mary, and John Lattimer,........	"	I.	5

DATE.	NAMES.	RECORD.	VOL.	PAGE.
1764. July 16.	Graham, Peter, and Mary Revoe,	M. B.,	VIII.	261
1760. April 16.	Graham, Robert, and Mary McIntosh,	"	III.	110
1772. Sept. 28.	Graham, Sarah, and James Monnell,	"	XIX.	59
1779. Aug. 5.	Graham, Susannah, and Robert Pattullo,	"	XXVIII.	46
1764. April 14.	Graham, Thomas, and Hester Bodine,	"	VIII.	154
1766. Nov. 25.	Graham, William, and Elizabeth Wermoct,	"	X.	181
1758. Oct. 4.	Graham, William, and Margaret Easton,	"	II.	39
1763. Nov. 29.	Grahms, George, and Phebe Irwin,	"	VII.	481
1764. July 14.	Grainger, Henry, and Elenor Parsols,	"	VIII.	259
1780. July 26.	Grandine, John, and Elizabeth Shepherd,	"	XXIX.	120
1768. Oct. 7.	Grandine, Mary, and Matthias Swame,	"	XIII.	205
1765. May 23.	Grant, Daniel, and Anne McPherson,	"	IX.	137
1759. Feb. 10.	Grant, Daniel, and Ruth Moore,	"	II.	187
1761. Mar. 16.	Grant, Deborah, and George Anderson,	"	IV.	103
1762. Jan. 12.	Grant, Edward, and Mary Cragg,	"	VI.	9
1781. Feb. 10.	Grant, Elinor, and George Ross,	"	XXXI.	44
1770. Oct. 25.	Grant, John, and Rachel Wessells,	"	XVI.	228
1759. Aug. 30.	Grant, John, and Sarah Berger,	"	II.	403
1783. June 29.	Grant, John, and Sarah Clerdage,	"	XXXIX.	72
1758. Sept. 11.	Grant, Mary, and Jasper Farmer,	"	II.	12
1763. June 11.	Grant, Robert, and Esther Robinson,	"	VII.	226
1755. Oct. 30.	Grant, Thomas, and Catharine Stephens,	"	I.	201
1771. Feb. 21.	Grant, William, and Ann Doddridge,	"	XVII.	19
1764. Mar. 7.	Grant, William, and Catharine Anderson,	"	VIII.	96
1761. Aug. 8.	Grass, Othilia, and Martine Lange,	"	V.	34
1677. July 3.	Graves, Deliverance, and Josiah Hallett,	W. O. P.,	III.	252
1761. July 20.	Gravesteen, Sophia, and William Bailey,	M. B.,	V.	1
1672. May 7.	Gray, Affyance, and William Pyles,	G. E.,	IV.	134
1783. Sept. 10.	Gray, Andrew, and Elizabeth Moorehead,	M. B.,	XL.	35
1769. Aug. 1.	Gray, Andrew, and Susannah Case,	"	XV.	12
1760. Aug. 18.	Gray, Catharine, and Edmund Savage,	"	III.	257
1777. Mar. 15.	Gray, Elizabeth, and Benjamin Elsden,	"	XXIV.	45
1761. Nov. 14.	Gray, Elizabeth, and Joseph Whitehouse,	"	V.	219
1769. Nov. 6.	Gray, Jane, and Daniel Miller,	"	XV.	80
1759. Jan. 10.	Gray, James, and Elizabeth Kernaghen,	"	II.	148
1783. April 26.	Gray, James, and Eunice Thorp,	"	XXXVIII.	117
1671. Feb. 26.	Gray, Mary, and John Watson,	G. E.,	IV.	102
1760. Feb. 9.	Gray, Sarah, and Francis Turner,	M. B.,	III.	27
1779. Sept. 28.	Gray, Thomas, and Elizabeth Massane,	"	XXVIII.	87
1781. July 7.	Gray, William, and Lusina Spry,	"	XXXII.	106
1783. May 29.	Grayham, Ann, and George Clark,	"	XXXIX.	27
1780. Mar. 22.	Grayham, Margaret, and William Cook,	"	XXIX.	6
1783. June 13.	Gready, Aria, and Jacob Langrange,	"	XXXIX.	56
1765. Oct. 31.	Green, Catherine, and Matthias Compton,	"	IX.	347
1761. Nov. 16.	Green, Elisabeth, and Benajah Wiggins,	"	V.	221

DATE.	NAMES.	RECORD.	VOL. PAGE.
1772. Dec. 21.	Green, Elizabeth, and Joseph Carpenter,...	M. B.,	XIX. 159
1763. April 15.	Green, Esther, and George Felmer,........	"	VII. 128
1759. Nov. 19.	Green, Jamime, and John Tur Bose,.......	"	II. 504
1759. Oct. 2.	Green, Jeremiah, and Elizabeth Begle,.....	"	II. 441
1762. Nov. 9.	Green, John, and Mary Allen,............	"	VI. 420
1775. June 1.	Green, Lucy, and Thomas Wood,..........	"	XXIII. 52
1760. June 24.	Green, Obadiah, and Sarah Alberson,......	"	III. 195a
1770. Feb. 7.	Green, Phebe, and Andrew Lyon,.........	"	XVI. 13
1781. Oct. 16.	Green, Rachel, and Thomas Cavenagh,....	"	XXXIII. 104
1765. April 27.	Green, Rebecca, and John Jabwain,.......	"	IX. 111
1763. Jan. 2.	Green, Sarah, and Plat Smith,............	"	VII. 534
1782. June 3.	Green, Thomas, and Debby Tucker,.......	"	XXXVI. 35
1737. Sept. 30.	Green, William, and Mary Amos,..........	"	I. 7
1777. Jan. 3.	Greene, Joseph, and Hanah Townsend,.....	"	XXIV. 2
1764. June 22.	Greenill, Mary, and John Sloss Hobart,....	"	VIII. 231
1769. Feb. 16.	Greenoak, Frances, and Walter Dalton,....	"	XIV. 36
1775. June 7.	Greenoak, John, and Lydia Hallet,........	"	XXIII. 55
1770. Aug. 29.	Greenoak, John, and Rebecca Clement,.....	"	XVI. 175
1764. Sept. 14.	Greenock, Mary, and Ludly Hare,.........	"	VIII. 309
1775. June 24.	Greenock, Sarah, and Melancton Lawrence,.	"	XXIII. 77
1760. Feb. 2.	Greenwalden, Apoleney, and Michael Ganthy,	"	III. 21
1762. Oct. 11.	Greenwood, Joseph, and Catharine McCarty,	"	VI. 358
1781. June 26.	Greer, Samuel, and Jane McMurdy,.......	"	XXXII. 99
1768. Jan. 13.	Gregg, David, and Jane Curry,...........	"	XIII. 7
1763. Sept. 9.	Gregg, Higginbottom, and Elizabeth Sutton,	"	VII. 332
1772. Nov. 0.	Gregg, James, and Elizabeth Crookshanks,..	"	XIX. 100
1760. Feb. 11.	Gregg, Jane, and Stewart Wilson,.........	"	III. 32
1780. Feb. 17.	Greggory, Mary, and Aitken Brown,......	"	XXVIII. 211
1781. Dec. 15.	Gregory, Elenor, and Benjaman Shepherd,..	"	XXXIV. 90
1782. Mar. 18.	Gregory, Mary, and Andrew Rogers,......	"	XXXVI. 9
1783. Aug. 6.	Gregory, Mary, and John Patterson,.......	"	XXXIX. 119
173⅞. Jan. 11.	Gregory, Robert, and Mary Robinson,.....	"	I. 8
1758. Dec. 18.	Greiderman, Philder, and Catherine Barriton,	"	II. 181
1767. June 12.	Grenell, John, and Catherine Smith,.......	"	XI. 107
1766. Aug. 9.	Grenell, Thomas, and Elizabeth Stanton,...	"	X. 72
1760. Mar. 20.	Gressand, Jean George, and Catharine Brand,	"	III. 83
1757. Sept. 26.	Gressman, Charles, and Anna Veronica Berg,	"	I. 648
1779. Nov. 10.	Greswould, Susannah, and Benjamin Hilton,	"	XXVIII. 134
1773. Feb. 24.	Grevorate, Henry, and Mary Van Driesen,..	"	XX. 52
1736. Feb. 16.	Griffen, Elizabeth, and Job Hadden,.......	"	I. 5
1764. Oct. 20.	Griffin, Ame, and James Haight,..........	"	VIII. 366
1759. Oct. 3.	Griffin, Bridget, and Moses Griffin,........	"	II. 447
1678. Jan. 4.	Griffin, Edward, Jr., and Deborah Barns,...	G. E.,	XXXII. 21
1761. Oct. 14.	Griffin, Elizabeth, and James Peck,........	M. B.,	V. 138
1755. Dec. 23.	Griffin, Elizabeth, and Joseph Budd,.......	"	I. 239

DATE.	NAMES.	RECORD.	VOL.	PAGE.
1777. April 15.	Griffin, Elizabeth, and Matthias Shacker,...	M. B.,	XXIV.	65
1736. Sept. 13.	Griffin, Elizabeth, and William Fowler,.....	"	I.	2
1779. July 15.	Griffin, Ephraim, and Hester Vanderburgh,.	"	XXVIII.	23
1681. Sept. 4.	Griffin, Honour, and Francisco,...........	O. W.,	XXXII½.	67
1738. June 17.	Griffin, Joseph, and Mary Gildersleves,.....	M. B.,	I.	10
1759. Oct. 3.	Griffin, Moses, and Bridget Griffin,........	"	II.	447
1684. Jan. 7.	Griffin, Samuel, and Elizabeth Platt,.......	C. M.,	XXXIII.	75
1760. Oct. 15.	Griffin, Susannah, and Peleg Ransom,......	M. B.,	III.	366
1768. April 6.	Griffin, William, and Mary Lowrea,........	"	XIII.	64
1781. Nov. 4.	Griffis, Ann, and Alexander Brush,.......	"	XXXIV.	17
1759. Dec. 5.	Griffis, Margaret, and Richard Tatterson,...	"	II.	528
1783. Oct. 9.	Griffith, Christian, and Cadwallader Colden, Jr.,..................................	"	XL.	74
173⁶⁄₇. Mar. 21.	Griffith, David, and Sarah Humble,........	"	I.	5
1781. April 10.	Griffith, Jane, and Claudius Charles,......	"	XXXI.	99
1757. April 29.	Griffith, John, and Elizabeth Gest,.........	"	I.	517
1762. Nov. 8.	Griffiths, Agnes, and Andrew Murray,.....	"	VI.	418
1766. Oct. 26.	Griffiths, David, and Hannah Colvill,.......	"	X.	136
1777. April 12.	Griffiths, Edward, and Eliza Clarkson,.....	"	XXIV.	61
1759. Oct. 16.	Griffiths, Hanah, and John Foreman,......	"	II.	459
1782. Jan. 29.	Griffiths, Jane, and William Lewis,........	"	XXXV.	37
1775. July 21.	Griffiths, Johanna, and James Light, Jr.,...	"	XXIII.	113
1781. April 11.	Griffiths, Joseph, and Agness Van Wagenen,	"	XXXI.	101
1775. July 19.	Griffiths, Joseph, and Sarah Leonard,......	"	XXIII.	99
1781. Mar. 19.	Grigg, Catharine, and James Peevey,......	"	XXXI.	75
	Grigg, Hannah, and Joseph Hildreth,......	"	VII.	391
1756. July 31.	Grigg, Henry, and Catherine Ward,.......	"	I.	264
1781. April 24.	Grigg, Jane, and John Fegan,.............	"	XXXII.	12
1782. April 25.	Grigg, John, and Hannah Roome,.........	"	XXXV.	138
1762. Sept. 22.	Grigg, Joseph, and Helena Mills,..........	"	VI.	325
1761. July 23.	Grigg, Susannah, and William Cummings,..	"	V.	6
1766. Sept. 29.	Grigg, William, and Helena Stout,.........	"	X.	115
1755. Aug. 12.	Griggs, Ann, and Bernardus Van Vorhes,...	"	I.	145
1736. July 1.	Griggs, Catherine, and Cornelius Bois,.....	"	I.	2
1758. Feb. 2.	Griggs, John, and Martha Schenk,.........	"	I.	810
1757. June 8.	Griggs, Lydia, and Joost Van Brunt,......	"	I.	555
1782. Jan. 2.	Grim, Catharine, and Frederick De Keller,..	"	XXXV.	2
1781. Dec. 24.	Grim, David, and Mary Barwick,....... ..	"	XXXIV.	104
1781. May 2.	Grim, Elizabeth, and Joham Carl Von Altenstein, ...	"	XXXII.	28
1780. July 31.	Grim, Peter, and Cathalina Dikeman,......	"	XXIX.	130
1770. Sept. 27.	Grimes, Mary, and James Lemusny,.......	"	XVI.	196
1770. Dec. 7.	Grimesly, Charles, and Mary Ryan,........	"	XVI.	288
1770. Aug. 6.	Grimesly, Sarah, and Richard Northover,...	"	XVI.	153
1770. Aug. 22.	Grinjard, Nicholas, and Margaret Heborn,..	"	XVI.	167

Date.		Names.	Record.	Vol.	Page.
1775. Feb.	9.	Gripman, Elizabeth, and Joseph Golder,...	M. B.,	xxii.	125
1772. Jan.	4.	Grisdall, Thomas, and Margaret Collister,...	"	xviii.	3
1760. Mar.	14.	Grisner, John, and Altje Lamberson,..	"	iii.	77
1772. Feb.	10.	Griswold, Elizabeth, and Benjamin Hildreth, Jr., ...	"	xviii.	32
1753. Aug.	30.	Griswold, Joseph, and Sarah Karley, ...	"	i.	104
1763. Sept.	8.	Groadt, Christiana, and Samuel Gardiner,...	"	vii.	330
1769. June	29.	Groasbeck, Peter, and Janetje Backer,.....	"	xiv.	137
1759. Dec.	20.	Groasbeek, Catharine, and Thomas Lynch,..	"	ii.	553
1765. Oct.	24.	Groat, Anne, and Peter Philip,...........	"	ix.	315
1765. April	24.	Groenendyck, Mayaka, and Gerrit Probasco,	"	ix.	106
1755. Dec.	8.	Groesbeck, Ann, and Donald Drummond,...	"	i.	228
1762. Nov.	4.	Groesbeck, Catharine, and Casparus Pruyn,.	"	vi.	411
1765. July	17.	Groesbeck, Catlina, and Philip Wendell,....	"	ix.	208
1765. Sept.	9.	Groesbeck, David, and Sarah Winne,......	"	ix.	257
1766. Dec.	11.	Groesbeck, Gertrude, and Jonathan Lewis,.	"	x.	201
1763. Aug.	30.	Groesbeck, Harme, and Maritie Bennoway,.	"	vii.	318
1765. June	17.	Groesbeck, John, and Altje Van Aernam,..	"	ix.	173
1766. June	25.	Groesbeck, Margaret, and Nicholas Marsellis,	"	x.	31
1764. Feb.	6.	Groesbeck, Maritje, and Mathew De Garemo,	"	viii.	49
1766. June	27.	Groesbeck, Nicholas, and Gertrude Waldron,	"	x.	35
1765. Oct.	31.	Groesbeck, Rebecca, and Isaac De Fonda,..	"	ix.	342
1761. May	27.	Groesbeck, Walter N., and Alida Quackenbosch, ...·...................	"	iv.	209
1764. Jan.	30.	Groesbeek, Maria, and Garret Van Groesbook, ...	"	viii.	13
1779. Nov.	25.	Groff, John, and Mary Cooper,........ ...	"	xxviii.	148
1756. Dec.	3.	Gromell, James, and Elizabeth McDonach,..	"	i.	371
1757. Dec.	20.	Grondarn, Mary, and Peter Noe, ...	"	i.	748
1771. June	15.	Grondine, Esther, and John Glover,.......	"	xvii.	111
1765. April	11.	Grondine, Margaret, and John Wood,......	"	ix.	90
1756. Oct.	14.	Gronendick, Nicholas, and Catharine Peterson, ...	"	i.	329
1769. Oct.	17.	Groome, Francis, and Rachel Crashum,.....	"	xv.	55
1764. April	13.	Groosbeeck, Alida, and Jacob Harsin, Jr.,..	"	viii.	153
1773. Sept.	30.	Groosbeek, John, and Cathalina Van Schaick,	"	xxi.	128
1773. June	3.	Groostine, Conrad, and Lucy Knap,.......	"	xx.	137
1762. Aug.	26.	Groot, Abraham, and Catherine Kittel,.....	"	vi.	293
1770. Aug.	10.	Groot, Catrena, and John Hall,............	"	xvi.	157
1767. Nov.	6.	Groot, Hester, and Cornelius Maebie,......	"	xii.	76
1762. Oct.	14.	Groot, Jacomentje, and Jesse Van Slyck,...	"	vi.	365
1762. Feb.	10.	Groot, John, and Engeltje Van Patten,.....	"	vi.	45
1770. April	25.	Groot, Maria, and Phineas Leach,.........	"	xvi.	69
1773. Mar.	20.	Groote, Neltie, and Petrus Groote,........	"	xx.	66
1773. Mar.	20.	Groote, Petrus, and Neltie Groote,........	"	xx.	66

21

DATE.	NAMES.	RECORD.	VOL.	PAGE.
1771. Oct. 23.	Grosbeeck, John, and Anna Davenport,....	M. B.,	XVII.	218
1764. Feb. 27.	Grosehanck, Catharine, and John Christian Wiesener, ...	"	VIII.	82
1779. Mar. 27.	Groshon, Elizabeth, and Joseph Bishop,....	"	XXVII.	79
1768. Nov. 2.	Grote, Rebecca, and Aaron Peeke,.........	"	XIII.	221
1779. June 19.	Grover, Barzillai, and Catherine Simonson,..	"	XXVII.	168
1765. Aug. 23.	Groves, Elinor, and Malcolm Graham,......	"	IX.	244
1760. Oct. 30.	Groves, Catharine, and Anthony O'Niel,...	"	III.	388
1778. Dec. 1.	Groves, Jane, and Joseph Pile,............	"	XXVI.	105
1764. Mar. 29.	Groves, John, and Catharine Bree,........	"	VIII.	122
1761. June 17.	Groves, Joseph, and Jane Bohannan,......	"	IV.	246
1761. July 20.	Grovesteen, Sophia, and William Bailey,...	"	V.	1
1760. April 19.	Growsekop, Elizabeth, and Henry Reese,...	"	III.	116
1780. May 10.	Grundy, George, and Mary Carr,..........	"	XXIX.	52
1772. April 21.	Gruver, Catharine, and George Masserve,...	"	XVIII.	89
1764. Aug. 2.	Gue, Jane, and Michael Onray,...........	"	VIII.	273
1762. Sept. 14.	Guerino, John, and Susanna Besley,.......	"	VI.	315
1765. June 21.	Guest, Anne, and George Power,.........	"	IX.	180
1772. May 13.	Guest, Elizabeth, and James Rote,........	"	XVIII.	109
1778. Oct. 22.	Guest, Henry, and Elizabeth Hodgson,.....	"	XXVI.	65
1770. Nov. 24.	Guest, Joy, and Richard Bolton,..........	"	XVI.	269
1777. Nov. 1.	Guest, Letty, and James Rollin,...........	"	XXIV.	173
1772. July 18.	Guest, Lewis, and Jane Van Sickler,.......	"	XIX.	1
1764. April 11.	Guest, Mary, and Barent Jansen,..........	"	VIII.	149
1778. July 16.	Guest, Mary, and George Oates,...........	"	XXV.	131
1761. June 6.	Guest, Thomas, and Catharine French,.....	"	IV.	228
1772. Nov. 23.	Guildersleive, Jennetye, and Roger McNeill,	"	XIX.	126a
1779. Feb. 27.	Guinnell, Thomas, and Milleson Haight,....	"	XXVII.	52
1767. Mar. 19.	Guion, Aletta, and Joseph Purdy,...........	"	XI.	46
1769. Jan. 27.	Guion, Alida, and Joseph Rodman, Jr.,.....	"	XIV.	21
1773. Sept. 6.	Guion, Benjamin, and Sarah Pell,.........	"	XXI.	99
1770. Dec. 5.	Guion, Elias, and Magdalen Soulis,........	"	XVI.	285
1778. July 18.	Guion, Frederick, and Jemima Hackett, ..	"	XXV.	133
1771. Jan. 3.	Guion, Lewis, and Elizabeth Hooglar,... ..	"	XVII.	309
1774. Jan. 7.	Guion, Mary, and James Colvin,..........	"	XXII.	94
1775. July 24.	Guion, Mary, and Thomas Fowler,.........	"	XXIII.	103
1782. Dec. 1.	Guire, Anne, and Samuel Whitney,........	"	XXXVII.	103
1757. Aug. 18.	Gulick, Hendrick, and Famitje Cowenhover,	"	I.	616
1757. Sept. 24.	Gunther, Johan Heinrich, and Elenor Hendrick, ...	"	I.	647
1778. May 9.	Guyion, Agnes, and John Stevens,........	"	XXV.	74
1765. Oct. 31.	Guyon, Abraham, and Mary Rodman,......	"	IX.	341
1772. Nov. 14.	Guyon, Addra, and Peter Cortelyou,.......	"	XIX.	113
1765. Aug. 28.	Guyon, Addra, and Samuel Ward,.........	"	IX.	250
1782. May 7.	Guyon, James, and Margaret Lake,.......	"	XXXV.	152

DATE.	NAMES.	RECORD.	VOL.	PAGE.
1782. Sept. 2.	Hageman, Jacobus, and Sarah Van Der Bilt,	M. B.,	xxxvii.	16
1758. Nov. 17.	Hageman, Joost, and Gertruyd Hageman,..	"	ii.	91
1755. Oct. 31.	Hageman, Maria, and Adriaen Onderdonck,.	"	i.	203
1775. Nov. 1.	Hageman, Nelly, and Hendrick Suydam,...	"	xxiii.	194
1765. July 4.	Hageman, Peter, and Christina Pearsall,....	"	ix.	193
1779. July 28.	Hageman, Sarah, and Daniel Rappelje,.....	"	xxviii.	32
1760. Mar. 10.	Hagendorn, Catharine, and Harmonus Hagendorn, ...	"	iii.	73
1760. Mar. 10.	Hagendorn, Harmonus, and Catharine Hagendorn, ...	"	iii.	73
1763. Oct. 27.	Hagens, Alice, and Christopher Pears,.....	"	vii.	408
1753. June 30.	Hagerdorn (Hagerman), Lucretia, and Alexander Forbus, ...	"	i.	68
1772. April 24.	Hagerman, Anna, and William Huskins,....	"	xviii.	91
1758. May 29.	Hagerman, Hendrick, and Eliza Vanderbergh,	"	i.	913
1753. June 30.	Hagerman (Hagerdorn), Lucretia, and Alexander Forbus, ...	"	i.	68
1757. Dec. 8.	Hagerman, Matje, and Samuel Garison,....	"	i.	730
1757. Oct. 31.	Hagerman, Rem, and Idey Vande Belt,....	"	i.	690
1773. Jan. 30.	Hagner, Hendrick, and Phebe Rowland,...	"	xx.	29
1772. April 27.	Hagraman, Hendrick, and Catharine Bush,.	"	xviii.	93
1760. Feb. 14.	Hague, William, and Elener Darcey,.	"	iii.	40
1763. May 11.	Haight, Anne, and Joseph Strang,.........	"	vii.	180
1780. Feb. 9.	Haight, Benjamin, and Mary Kip,.........	"	xxviii.	210
1758. May 8.	Haight, Cornelius, and Elizabeth Benn,.....	"	i.	897
1779. Mar. 30.	Haight, Isaiah, and Priscilla Colvill,........	"	xxvii.	86
1764. Oct. 20.	Haight, James, and Amy Griffin,..........	"	viii.	366
1777. Sept. 4.	Haight, Joseph, and Lydia Post,..........	"	xxiv.	142
1779. Feb. 27.	Haight, Milleson, and Thomas Guinell,.....	"	xxvii.	52
1771. April 12.	Haight, Samuel, and Abigail Simmons,.....	"	xvii.	55
1763. Sept. 6.	Haight, Sarah, and John Ogden,..........	"	vii.	327
1773. Mar. 9.	Haight, Susanah, and John Siemont,.......	"	xx.	58
1762. Aug. 21.	Haigs, John, and Mary Outenbogart,......	"	vi.	284
1763. Oct. 17.	Haile, James, and Elizabeth Dunn,........	"	vii.	390
1678. Nov. 21.	Hailstone, Mary, and William Pinhorne,....	G. E.,	xxxii.	17
1767. Sept. 11.	Haines, Joseph, and Elizabeth Saunders,....	M. B.,	xii.	33a
1769. Aug. 28.	Haines, Marian, and William Ascough,.....	"	xv.	30
1684. June 15.	Haines, William, and Elizabeth Hussy,.....	C. M.,	xxxi.	151
1771. Sept. 9.	Hains, Sarah, and Philip Rollens,.........	M. B.,	xvii.	178
1753. July 14.	Haiter, Susanah, and Jacob Lasshar,..	"	i.	76
1769. Jan. 4.	Hake, Samuel, and Helen Livingston,......	"	xiv.	2
1771. June 5.	Haldane, Elizabeth, and John Leaycraft,....	"	xvii.	102
1763. Aug. 5.	Halden, William, and Hannah Randle,.....	"	vii.	291
1772. Sept. 9.	Halding, Hannah, and Duncan McDugall,..	"	xix.	45
1774. Feb. 19.	Hale, Anne, and Joseph Day,.............	"	xxii.	131

DATE.	NAMES.	RECORD.	VOL.	PAGE.
1773. June 15.	Hale, Elizabeth, and Francis Barrea, Jr.,....	M. B.,	XXI.	6
1768. Feb. 1.	Halenbake, Margaret, and Peter Van Buren,	"	XIII.	26
1763. July 21.	Halenbeck, Catharine, and Isaac Van Loon,.	"	VII.	277
1759. Feb. 19.	Halenbeck, Gertruy, and Barent Van Ben-thuysen, ...	"	II.	197
1766. July 5.	Halenbeck, Michael, and Mary Thornton,..	"	IX.	199
1771. Oct. 5.	Halenbeeck, Nicholas, and Jane Willes,.....	"	XVII.	199
1772. Feb. 12.	Halen Beek, Casper, and Rachel Claw,......	"	XVIII.	35
1759. Feb. 6.	Haley, Catharine, and Francis Colwell,.....	"	II.	179
1761. Mar. 2.	Haley, Catharine, and Richard Coffey,......	"	IV.	87
1764. Feb. 10.	Haley, Elizabeth, and James Patterson,.....	"	VIII.	56
1781. May 1.	Hall, Adam, and Martha Weeks,..........	"	XXXII.	25
1763. Sept. 6.	Hall, Anne, and Samuel Fuller,...........	"	VII.	376
1777. Jan. 21.	Hall, Catharine, and George Povey,........	"	XXIV.	16
1775. July 27.	Hall, Charlotte, and John Ablin,..........	"	XXIII.	107
1780. Nov. 1.	Hall, Edward, and Sarah Brown,..,.......	"	XXX.	87
1670. Dec. 6.	Hall, Elizabeth, and Jean Baignouke,......	C. A.,	II.	615
1758. Dec. 2.	Hall, Elizabeth, and John Parr,..........	M. B.,	II.	109
1764. Feb. 27.	Hall, Eve, and Benjamin Roberts,.........	"	VIII.	84
1771. April 15.	Hall, Hannah, and Nathaniel Moore,.......	"	XVII.	58
1777. Aug. 16.	Hall, Henry, and Mary Thomas,..........	"	XXIV.	133
1771. May 27.	Hall, James, and Keziah Wilcox,..........	"	XVII.	93
167⅝. Mar. 20.	Hall, Johannah, and Michael Clarke,.......	W. O. P.,	III.	183
1737. Dec. 17.	Hall, John, and Elizabeth Sherrard,........	M. B.,	I.	8
1763. April 7.	Hall, John, and Anne Ripel,..............	"	V.	117
1770. Aug. 10.	Hall, John, and Catrina Groot,...........	"	XVI.	157
1755. Sept. 9.	Hall, John, and Hester Coffell,...........	"	I.	171
1756. Oct. 6.	Hall, John, and Margaret Mutlow,........	"	I.	321
1777. Jan. 21.	Hall, John, and Mary Curren,.............	"	XXIV.	17
1671. Dec. 27.	Hall, Joseph, and Joanna Smellidge,.......	G. E.,	IV.	80
1762. Oct. 6.	Hall, Margaret, and John Tackker,........	M. B.,	VI.	348
1782. June 19.	Hall, Mary, and Silvester Bedell,..........	"	XXXVI.	57
1782. Jan. 21.	Hall, Mary, and Thomas Dorland, Jr.,......	"	XXXV.	27
1766. Oct. 7.	Hall, Peter, and Margaret Brickell,........	"	X.	119
1783. Jan. 7.	Hall, Phebe, and Peter Coggrell,..........	"	XXXVIII.	9
1767. Oct. 26.	Hall, Phebe, and Thomas Denton,.........	"	XII.	69
1758. Feb. 14.	Hall, Sarah, and George Weeks,...........	"	I.	821
1770. May 30.	Hall, Sarah, and Jeremiah Clark,..........	"	XVI.	97
1779. Sept. 17.	Hall, Thomas, and Elizabeth Seymour,.....	"	XXVIII.	78
1759. July 24.	Hall, William, and Margaret Brown,.......	"	II.	361
1763. Feb. 3.	Hall, William, and Margaret Harper,.......	"	VII.	52
1761. Dec. 2.	Hall, William, and Maritie Veder,.........	"	V.	260
1760. Mar. 1.	Hall, William, and Violet Gleghorne,......	"	III.	57
1759. Oct. 31.	Hallam, Ann, and Henry Robinson,.......	"	II.	481
1759. Oct. 11.	Hallam, Lewis, and Sarah Perry,..........	"	II.	455

DATE.	NAMES.	RECORD.	VOL.	PAGE.
1780. Mar. 15.	Halleck, Noah, and Sarah Thorn,..........	M. B.,	XXIX.	2
1766. Dec. 1.	Hallenbake, Anthony, and Cornelia Cooper,.	"	X.	189
1776. Feb. 29.	Hallenbeck, Abraham, and Mary Pruyne,...	"	XXIII.	275
1738. Oct. 18.	Hallenbeck, Allida, and Johannes Staats,...	"	I.	11
1769. Oct. 23.	Hallenbeck, Jacob, and Elizabeth Van Lone,.	"	XV.	61
1772. Aug. 10.	Hallenbeeck, Rachel, and Conrat E. Ten Eyck,	"	XIX.	16
1778. April 4.	Hallet, Eliza, and Richard Stephens,.......	"	XXV.	60
1760. Sept. 17.	Hallet, Elizabeth, and Nicholas Berrian,....	"	III.	318
1781. Dec. 4.	Hallet, Hannah, and Joseph Graham,......	"	XXXIV.	70
1779. Mar. 2.	Hallet, Hannah, and William Walters,.....	"	XXVII.	53
1760. Nov. 13.	Hallet, James, and Elizabeth Welling,......	"	III.	410
1760. Dec. 10.	Hallet, Joseph, and Elizabeth Hazard,......	"	III.	471
1775. June 7.	Hallet, Lydia, and John Greenoak,........	"	XXIII.	55
1765. Oct. 29.	Hallet, Lydia, and Joseph Burroughs,......	"	IX.	332
173⁷⁄₈. Feb. 25.	Hallet, Phebe, and Robert Hallet,.........	"	I.	9
173⁷⁄₈. Feb. 25.	Hallet, Robert, and Phebe Hallet,.........	"	I.	9
1764. Feb. 6.	Hallet, Sarah, and Jacob Gosling,.........	"	VIII.	53
1781. Mar. 19.	Hallett, Daniel, and Charity Moore,.......	"	XXXI.	74
1783. June 6.	Hallett, David, and Elizabeth Gidney,......	"	XXXIX.	43
1780. Nov. 21.	Hallett, Elizabeth, and Charles Kendle,....	"	XXX.	117
1779. July 5.	Hallett, Elizabeth, and Robert Gault,.......	"	XXVIII.	16
1757. June 24.	Hallett, Elizabeth, and William Hallett,.....	"	I.	573
1767. Jan. 9.	Hallett, Jacob, and Ruth Berrian,.........	"	XI.	6
1764. June 22.	Hallett, Jacob, and Susannah Alsop,.......	"	VIII.	232
1781. Jan. 1.	Hallett, James, and Bridget Dean,.........	"	XXXI.	2
1770. July 30.	Hallett, James, and Mary Hallett,.........	"	XVI.	150
1780. May 25.	Hallett, Jemima, and David Moore,........	"	XXIX.	68
1762. Aug. 18.	Hallett, Jemimah, and William Hallett,.....	"	VI.	280
1780. April 1.	Hallett, John, and Charity Wright,........	"	XXIX.	12
1768. May 29.	Hallett, Jonathan, and Joanna Woodard,...	"	XIII.	117
1677. July 3.	Hallett, Josiah, and Deliverance Graves,....	O. W. P.,	II.	252
1783. Aug. 29.	Hallett, Lidia, and William Dawson,.......	M. B.,	XL.	14
1783. June 2.	Hallett, Mary, and Henry Burnett,........	"	XXXIX.	37
1770. July 30.	Hallett, Mary, and James Hallett,..........	"	XVI.	150
1781. Mar. 17.	Hallett, Mary, and John Waters,..........	"	XXXI.	72
1783. Aug. 30.	Hallett, Moses, and Elizabeth McConney,...	"	XL.	15
1782. Sept. 30.	Hallett, Pheby, and Samuel Hallett,.......	"	XXXVII.	20
1759. Dec. 18.	Hallett, Richard, and Elizabeth Titus, ...	"	II.	548
1767. Dec. 11.	Hallett, Richard, and Hannah Washbun,....	"	XII.	112
1762. May 29.	Hallett, Robert, and Ruth Leverage,.......	"	VI.	169
1761. Dec. 18.	Hallett, Samuel, and Elizabeth Wilson,. ...	"	V.	284
1765. Oct. 29.	Hallett, Samuel, and Mary Jackson,.......	"	IX.	334
1782. Sept. 30.	Hallett, Samuel, and Pheby Hallett,.......	"	XXXVII.	20
1764. Sept. 6.	Hallett, Samuel, and Sarah Wright,........	"	VIII.	298
1773. May 26.	Hallett, Susannah, and Isaac Bargaw,......	"	XX.	127

Date.		Names.	Record.	Vol.	Page.
1772. May	6.	Hallett, Thomas, and Elizabeth Willett,.....	M. B.,	xviii.	101
1757. June	24.	Hallett, William, and Elizabeth Hallett,.....	"	i.	573
1762. Aug.	18.	Hallett, William, and Jemimah Hallett,.....	"	vi.	280
1759. Mar.	17.	Halley, Jane, and Thomas Pears,..........	"	ii.	218
1779. July	30.	Hallibert, Mary, and Jonathan Strickland,..	"	xxviii.	36
1764. Nov.	15.	Hallinbeck, Maria, and Coenradt Johnson,..	"	viii.	408
1780. Oct.	30.	Hallock, Henry, and Mary Jane,..........	"	xxx.	85
1760. Jan.	28.	Hallock, William, and Elizabeth Dodge,....	"	iii.	9
1770. Dec.	15.	Hallowell, Arthur, and Susannah Deads,...	"	xvi.	296
1766. June	26.	Hallowell, Samuel, and Margaret Seader,...	"	x.	33
1683. April	11.	Halsie, Jamima, and John Laurison,.......	E.,	xxxiii.	49
1780. July	7.	Halsey, Melescent, and Allison Wright,.....	M. B.,	xxix.	107
1759. Feb.	10.	Hallstead, John, and Mary Haasbrough,....	"	ii.	188
1767. Mar.	27.	Hallstead, Jonas, and Phebe Mitchel,......	"	xi.	51
1773. May	29.	Halstead, Daniel, and Elizabeth Schuyler,...	"	xx.	132
1775. Oct.	11.	Halstead, Elizabeth, and Joseph Hunt,.....	"	xxiii.	178
1763. Mar.	26.	Halstead, Jemima, and Rossil Wilcocks,....	"	vii.	107
1753. June	12.	Halstead, Mary, and William Haviland,.....	"	i.	59
1759. Oct.	2.	Halstead, Pearson, and Phebe Lyon,.......	"	ii.	444
1770. Aug.	22.	Halstead, Phebe, and Joseph Lawrence,....	"	xvi.	166
1769. April	1.	Halstead, Philemon, and Jane King,.......	"	xiv.	62
1780. Oct.	21.	Halstead, Sarah, and John Sears,..........	"	xxx.	76
1765. Oct.	22.	Halsted, Benjamin, and Sarah Tredwell,....	"	ix.	311
1761. Aug.	18.	Halsted, John, Jr., and Elizabeth De Hart,..	"	v.	46
1736. April	27.	Halsted, Joseph, and Elizabeth Smith,.....	"	i.	1
1773. April	8.	Halsted, Robert, and Mary Wiley,.........	"	xx.	89
1769. Mar.	6.	Ham, Coenrad W., and Jannetje Amerman,.	"	xiv.	48
1765. June	10.	Ham, Coenrad W., and Maria Schenck,.....	"	ix.	163
1759. Nov.	19.	Ham, Margaret, and John Oull,...........	"	ii.	505
1766. July	21.	Ham, Rachel, and Elisha Powell,..........	"	x.	58
1770. Sept.	21.	Ham, Wendel, and Hannah Brown,........	"	xvi.	193
1767. Nov.	14.	Ham, William, and Elizabeth McCallar;.....	"	xii.	84
1775. July	24.	Hamands, Seaity, and Nicholas Schenck,...	"	xxiii.	102
1782. Nov.	30.	Hamble, Charles, and Susannah Jackson,...	"	xxxvii.	101
1764. Nov.	6.	Hambly, Thomas, and Ann Black,..........	"	viii.	392
1782. Aug.	28.	Hambrow, John, and Margaret Caddy,.....	"	xxxvi.	128
1783. Oct.	6.	Hamersley, Andrew, and Margaret Gautier,.	"	xl.	64
1761. July	16.	Hamersley, Andrew, and Margaret Still,...	"	iv.	300
1779. Jan.	20.	Hamilton, Ann, and John Aitkenhead,.....	"	xxvii.	21
1766. July	16.	Hamilton, Archibald, and Alice Colden,.....	"	x.	51
1757. April	6.	Hamilton, Archibald, and Mary McDugal,..	"	i.	488
1782. Oct.	18.	Hamilton, Cloud, and Elizabeth Barden,....	"	xxxvii.	52
1757. May	11.	Hamilton, Elizabeth, and Hugh McCabe,...	"	i.	528
1760. Feb.	13.	Hamilton, Elizabeth, and Daniel Ramson,..	"	iii.	34
1761. April	1.	Hamilton, Elizabeth, and David Barnhill,...	"	iv.	127

Date.		Names.	Record.	Vol.	Page.
1772. June	5.	Hamilton, Ellen, and John Kirkby, ...	M. B.,	xviii.	133
1783. Sept.	26.	Hamilton, Frances, and Alexander Brodie, . .	"	xl.	55
1761. Oct.	24.	Hamilton, James, and Maria Schoonmaker, .	"	v.	166
1765. Jan.	15.	Hamilton, John, and Ann Taylor, ...	"	ix.	16
1779. Nov.	15.	Hamilton, John, and Mary Harvey, ...	"	xxviii.	140
1781. May	8.	Hamilton, Joshua, and Frances Irwin, ...	"	xxxii.	37
1760. Oct.	9.	Hamilton, Mary, and John Thompson, ...	"	iii.	355
1760. June	9.	Hamilton, Rebecca, and Andrew Morley, . . .	"	iii.	180
1780. Dec.	14.	Hamilton, Sarah, and John Duncan, ...	"	xxx.	153
1778. June	15.	Hamilton, Thomas, and Mary Sears, ...	"	xxv.	102
1779. Nov.	27.	Hammell, John, and Hannah Roome, ...	"	xxviii.	152
1761. Dec.	18.	Hammersley, Thomas, and Sarah Colgan, . . .	"	v.	287
1777. April	15.	Hammond, Hannah, and Benjamin Chadwell,	"	xxiv.	64
1772. Feb.	10.	Hammond, Susan, and Nichols James, ...	"	xviii.	33
1781. Nov.	16.	Hampton, Ann, and William Thomas, ...	"	xxxiv.	42
1781. Feb.	2.	Hampton, Elizabeth, and Joseph Marsh, ...	"	xxxi.	34
1780. Aug.	24.	Hampton, Hester, and John McKoun, ...	"	xxix.	146
1777. Feb.	19.	Hampton, Jonathan, and Ann Harding, ...	"	xxiv.	31
1775. April	15.	Hampton, Margaret, and Joseph Sheppard, .	"	xxiii.	9
1779. Jan.	7.	Hampton, Mary, and James Stuart, ...	"	xxvii.	7
1761. Nov.	30.	Hampton, Mary Ann, and Isaac Lawrence, . .	"	v.	258
1777. Sept.	29.	Hanah, Elizabeth, and William Witnell, ...	"	xxiv.	153
1782. Nov.	16.	Hancock, Mary, and James Meade, ...	"	xxxvii.	83
1758. Sept.	23.	Hancock, Mary, and Jeremiah Sullivan, ...	"	ii.	34
1764. June	18.	Handcock, John, and Mary Sharpe, ...	"	viii.	227
1764. June	9.	Handcock, Thomas, and Elenora Johnson, . .	"	viii.	221
1781. May	5.	Handford, Nehemiah, and Sarah Smith, ...	"	xxxii.	33
1778. Feb.	18.	Handford, Thomas, and Ann Townsend, ...	"	xxv.	24
1761. June	22.	Handlin, Mary, and Thomas Jones, ...	"	iv.	252
1759. Feb.	12.	Haney, Ann, and Mathew Gibson, ...	"	ii.	189
1761. Dec.	17.	Hanham, Mary, and Francis Bollison, ...	"	v.	283
1757. Nov.	7.	Hanion, Catharine, and John Quintin, ...	"	i.	697
1736. April	5.	Hanks, William, and Anne Prat, ...	"	i.	1
1763. Nov.	9.	Hanly, Edward, and Mary Ross, ...	"	vii.	436
1783. May	29.	Hanly, Thomas, and Sarah Davis, ...	"	xxxix.	28
1780. Oct.	20.	Hanna, John, and Jemima Tarren, ...	"	xxx.	73
1780. May	17.	Hannah, Nathaniel, and Agness Merrily, ...	"	xxix.	59
1761. Oct.	6.	Hannah, William, and Hannah Lawrence, . .	"	v.	124
1767. Nov.	2.	Hannan, John, and Hannah Levy, ...	"	xii.	74
1764. Dec.	4.	Hannen, Tabita, and Isaac Cole, ...	"	viii.	435
1766. July	7.	Hanneon, Christopher, and Lenah Regar, . . .	"	x.	43
1760. June	10.	Hannigan, Ida, and Nishie Waldron, ...	"	iii.	183
1760. Feb.	2.	Hanning, Charles, and Mary Bark, ...	"	iii.	17
1764. Feb.	21.	Hannon, Mary, and Abraham Rice, ...	"	viii.	70
1765. May	30.	Hannon, Patrick, and Jane Gylard, ...	"	ix.	145

DATE.	NAMES.	RECORD.	VOL. PAGE.
1775. Dec. 12.	Hanrahan, James, and Margaret Cummins,.	M. B.,	xxiii. 229
1671. Sept. 4.	Hans, Ffiowkin, and Albert Browne, ...	G. E.,	iv. 25
1764. Aug. 22.	Hanse, John Isaac, and Gertruy Slingerland,	M. B.,	viii. 289
1766. Sept. 24.	Hansen, Alida, and Martin Hoffman, ...	"	x. 105
1753. Aug. 18.	Hansen, David, and Sarah Onderdanck, ...	"	i. 92
1762. May 29.	Hansen, David, and Sarah Seloover, ...	"	vi. 173
1764. Dec. 10.	Hansen, John, and Rachel Lane, ...	"	viii. 445
1738. May 24.	Hansen, Rykert, and Catherine Ten Brook,.	"	i. 9
1773. Nov. 20.	Hansen, Sarah, and Abraham Veeder, ...	"	xxii. 37
1759. Aug. 9.	Hansen, Sarah, and Andries Gardener, ...	"	ii. 381
1768. June 27.	Hansen, Sarah, and John Foster, ...	"	xiii. 142
1771. Nov. 22.	Hanson, John P., and Elizabeth Vanderhey-		
	den, ...	"	xvii. 264
1762. Jan. 29.	Hanson, John Wilkinson, and Mary Kortright,	'	vii. 41
1765. May 17.	Hanson, Margaret, and Frederick Hawes, . . .	"	ix. 129
1783. Oct. 16.	Hanstein, John, and Christianna Wilkinson,.	"	xl. 82
1769. June 24.	Hanton, Jeremiah, and Sarah Allen, ...	"	xiv. 130
1760. April 30.	Hapey, Hannah, and James Welch, ...	"	iii. 132
1781. Jan. 26.	Happe, George, and Barabare Chick, ...	"	xxxi. 28
1768. June 20.	Harbeck, John, and Catherine Tiers, ...	"	xiii. 135
1765. Oct. 31.	Harbour, Richard, and Mary Wool, ...	"	ix. 338
1781. Oct. 26.	Harbourd, Elinor, and Edmond Fowler, ...	"	xxx. 82
1779. Nov. 2.	Harcourt, Hannah, and John Franhomme,. .	"	xxviii. 126
1759. July 2.	Harden, Isabella, and Moses Roach, ...	"	ii. 344
1762. June 8.	Hardenberg, Charles, and Jane Van Alst, . . .	"	vi. 183
1737. Sept. 9.	Hardenberg, Jacob, and Peter Nelly Brown,	"	i. 7
1757. Dec. 21.	Hardenbergh, Ann, and Andrew Maerschalk,	"	i. 749
1759. Oct. 25.	Hardenbergh, Catharina, and Conraat J. El-		
	mendorph, ...	"	ii. 473
1773. Oct. 28.	Hardenbergh, Cornelia, and Elias Harden-		
	bergh, ...	"	xxii. 1
1773. Oct. 28.	Hardenbergh, Elias, and Cornelia Harden-		
	bergh, ...	"	xxii. 1
1771. Jan. 4.	Hardenbergh, Garret, and Jane Remsen, . . .	"	xvii. 1
1775. Nov. 16.	Hardenbergh, Graas, and Elizabeth Oliver, . .	"	xxiii. 211
1772. Dec. 7.	Hardenbergh, Jacobus G., and Tryntje El-		
	tinge, ...	"	xix. 143
1778. Mar. 9.	Hardenbergh, Jane, and Benjamin Seaman,.	"	xxv. 35
1773. Sept. 21.	Hardenbergh, John, and Margaret Elven-		
	dorp, ...	"	xxi. 117
1770. June 1.	Hardenbergh, John A., and Rachel Du Bois,	"	xvi. 100
1738. Oct. 11.	Hardenbergh, Leonard, and Rachel Hoog-		
	teeling, ...	"	i. 11
1765. Jan. 22.	Hardenbergh, Margaret, and Christopher		
	Remsen, ...	"	ix. 29

22

DATE.	NAMES.	RECORD.	VOL.	PAGE.
1775. Aug. 3.	Hardenbergh, Margaret L., and Garton Nottingham,	M. B.,	XXIII.	120
1762. July 6.	Hardenbergh, Mary, and Abraham Polhemis,	"	VI.	228
1775. Nov. 2.	Hardenbergh, Nicholas, and Mary Bruyn,..	"	XXIII.	196
1775. April 22.	Hardenbergh, Philip, and Mary Elmendorph,	"	XXIII.	16
1764. April 17.	Hardenbergh, Rachel, and Harmanus Myer,	"	VIII.	158
1766. Oct. 17.	Hardenbergh, Sarah, and Charles W. Brodhead,	"	X.	127
1775. July 10.	Hardenbrook, Abraham W., and Abigail Cornish,	"	XXIII.	92
1761. May 7.	Hardenbrook, Catharine, and James Linkletar,	"	IV.	183
1770. April 6.	Hardenbrook, Gerardus, and Damarius Tucker,	"	XVI.	50
1758. Mar. 14.	Hardenbrook, Gerardus, and Rebecca Parson,	"	I.	849
1753. Sept. 21.	Hardenbrook, Lewis, and Catherine Waldron,	"	I.	122
1759. Sept. 25.	Hardenbrook, Theophilus, and Angeltje Anthony,	"	II.	431
1770. Dec. 31.	Harder, Philip, and Fytie Gardner,	"	XVI.	311
1762. Aug. 9.	Hardick, Garret, and Mary Vanderkarr, ...	"	VI.	269
1777. Feb. 19.	Harding, Ann, and John Hampton,	"	XXIV.	31
1759. April 2.	Harding, Ann, and John Pitt,	"	II.	234
1756. Nov. 1.	Harding, Ann, and Thomas Taylor,	"	I.	342
1773. June 11.	Harding, Anne, and Wandal Boos,	"	XX.	143
1757. Jan. 8.	Harding, Darcus, and William Dobbs,	"	I.	410
1773. July 28.	Harding, Elinor, and Martin Aim,	"	XXI.	52
1672. Feb. 7.	Harding, Joan, and Willliam Leyton,	G. E.,	IV.	257
1778. Oct. 8.	Harding, John, and Kasiah Lewis,	M. B.,	XXVI.	51
1736. April 26.	Harding, Mary, and John Stephens,	"	I.	1
1783. April 16.	Harding, Sarah, and Augustus Nicoll,	"	XXXVIII.	99
1780. Sept. 11.	Hardman, Ann, and James Grierson,	"	XXX.	23
1764. April 21.	Hardman, Lawrence, and Sarah Boss,	"	VIII.	166
1769. Feb. 7.	Hardon, Margaret, and George Arhart,	"	XIV.	29
1781. Oct. 27.	Hardy, Elias, and Martha Huggeford,	"	XXXIV.	9
1782. Sept. 6.	Hare, Elizabeth, and Simon Weeks,	"	XXXVI.	138
1764. Sept. 14.	Hare, Ludly, and Mary Greenock,	"	VIII.	309
1767. Jan. 7.	Hares, Amos, and Sarah Birdsall,	"	X.	191
1779. April 12.	Hargill, William, and Sarah Triglith,	"	XXVII.	106
1767. Feb. 24.	Hargrave, Robert, and Elizabeth Deacon,...	"	XI.	34
1760. June 25.	Haring, Abraham, and Jannetie Vertruyck,.	"	III.	195b
1770. Mar. 20.	Haring, Abraham A., Jr., and Greetye Blauvelt,	"	XVI.	34
1764. June 7.	Haring, Ann, and Samuel Kip,	"	VIII.	211
1763. Oct. 21.	Haring, John, and Gertruy Sickels,	"	X.	134

DATE.	NAMES.	RECORD.	VOL.	PAGE.
1773. Oct. 30.	Haring, John, and Mary Haring,..........	M. B.,	XXII.	5
1773. Oct. 30.	Haring, Mary, and John Haring,..........	"	XXII.	5
1774. Mar. 14.	Haring, Sarah, and Gardiner Jones,........	"	XXII.	147
1758. Nov. 16.	Harison, Jane, and George Folliott,........	"	II.	89
1758. Feb. 28.	Harison, Morley, and Elizabeth Rue,.......	"	I.	833
1782. May 17.	Harlin, Ann, and John Harris,............	"	XXXVI.	7
1757. June 1.	Harlow, Judah, and Elizabeth Dubois,......	"	I.	545
1771. Dec. 3.	Harman, Mary, and Joseph Abbot,........	"	XVII.	281
1781. Sept. 13.	Harman, Thomas L., and Mary Howel,.....	"	XXXIII.	62
1772. May 30.	Harmance, Philip, and Sarah Vangwaggenen, ...	"	XVIII.	127
1763. Jan. 17.	Harmans, Abraham, and Cornelia Cooper,..	"	VII.	16
1780. Sept. 29.	Harned, Eunice, and James Adams,.......	"	XXX.	47
1782. May 27.	Harned, Jacob, and Mary Nicoll,..........	"	XXXVI.	26
1782. May 8.	Harned, Jonathan, and Mary Cottrell,.....	"	XXXV.	154
1781. Nov. 15.	Harned, Mary, and George Younghusband,.	"	XXXIV.	38
1783. May 19.	Harned, Nathaniel, and Sarah Cottrell,.....	"	XXXIX.	17
1782. June 14.	Harned, Phineas, and Mary Winance,.....	"	XXXVI.	49
1671. Dec. 11.	Harnett, Edward, and Mary Marsh,.......	G. E.,	IV.	73
1753. June 29.	Harnischfegerin, Anna Maria Rosina, and Christian Henry Courtis,..............	M. B.,	I.	67
1772. Jan. 19.	Harper, Elinor, and John Clark,...........	"	XX.	12
1761. Oct. 6.	Harper, Jane, and John English,....	"	V.	123
1763. Mar. 3.	Harper, John, and Ann Vandewater,.......	"	VII.	87
1763. Feb. 3.	Harper, Margaret, and William Hall,.......	"	VII.	52
1759. July 20.	Harper, Robert, and Catharine Ten Brook,..	"	II.	364
1760. Mar. 10.	Harper, William, and Margaret Williams,...	"	III.	72
1773. Sept. 29.	Harpur, Robert, and Elizabeth Crygier,.....	"	XXI.	125
1768. Feb. 29.	Harrald, William, and Margaret Elkins,.....	"	XIII.	45
1762. Nov. 1.	Harrington, Elizabeth. and John Miller,....	"	VI.	399
1780. July 22.	Harrington, Silvester, and Mary Jones,.....	"	XXIX.	117
1769. Dec. 6.	Harrington, Valentine, and Alida Pemberton,	"	XV.	115
1773. Sept. 25.	Harriott, Nathaniel, and Martha De Foreest,.	"	XXI.	121
1759. June 12.	Harriott, Thomas, and Claetje Wynants,...	"	II.	321
1766. June 21.	Harris, Abraham, and Rachel Mersereau,...	"	X.	22
1759. Aug. 15.	Harris, Catharine, and Daniel Roberts,.....	"	II.	384
1782. July 30.	Harris, Catharine, and John Comfort,......	"	XXXVI.	79
1765. Oct. 17.	Harris, Catharine, and Joseph Loosie,......	"	IX.	306
1738. Sept. 22.	Harris, Elizabeth, and Josiah Leonard,.....	"	I.	11
1765. Aug. 5.	Harris, Elizabeth, and Peter Truman,......	"	IX.	231
1762. Oct. 20.	Harris, George, and Mary Boyd,..........	"	VI.	374
1738. Dec. 1.	Harris, Gertrie, and Tunis Somerendick,....	"	I.	12
1764. April 17.	Harris, Isaac, and Margaret Person,.......	"	VIII.	161
1766. Dec. 1.	Harris, James, and Ann Colhoune, ...	"	X.	190
1782. May 17.	Harris, John, and Ann Harlin,............	"	XXXVI.	7

DATE.	NAMES.	RECORD.	VOL.	PAGE.
1760. Oct. 6.	Harris, John, and Elizabeth Seawood,......	M. B.,	III.	346
1778. Oct. 7.	Harris, John, and Mary Vance,..........	"	XXVI.	49
1773. Nov. 5.	Harris, John, and Nancy Leonard,........	"	XXII.	15
1780. July 11.	Harris, Martha, and Walter Frazer,........	"	XXIX.	110
1674. Feb. 5.	Harris, Mary, and Ralph Doxy,..........	A. R.,	XXIII.	168
1761. Nov. 12.	Harris, Mary, and Thomas Power,........	M. B.,	V.	213
1763. May 25.	Harris, Mary, and Walter McLintock,......	"	VII.	199
1756. Aug. 21.	Harris, Nathaniel, and Phebae Steel,.......	"	I.	276
1763. April 12.	Harris, Peter, and Sarah Dubois,..........	"	VII.	124
1761. Mar. 11.	Harris, Robert, and Sarah Peet,..........	"	IV.	95
1775. Sept. 26.	Harris, Samuel, and Geddy De Witt,.......	"	XXIII.	164
1782. May 17.	Harris, Samuel, and Hendricke Remson,....	"	XXXVI.	4
1781. July 26.	Harris, Sarah, and Samuel Herbert,........	"	XXXIII.	16
1761. Dec. 22.	Harris, Tryntje, and Aaron Moggeridge,....	"	V.	293
1782. Mar. 30.	Harris, William, and Mary Thompson,.....	"	XXXV.	102
1770. Oct. 13.	Harrison, Ann, and James Arentz,........	"	XVI.	212
1762. May 15.	Harrison, Arabella, and John Rutter,......	"	VI.	161
1761. Oct. 5.	Harrison, Charles, and Hannah Byvanck,...	"	V.	121
1782. April 17.	Harrison, Elizabeth, and John Jordan,.....	"	XXXV.	126
1761. Nov. 25.	Harrison, Elizabeth, and Thomas Truxtun,..	"	V.	248
1780. Aug. 28.	Harrison, Hermione, and Robert Cargey,...	"	XXX.	7
1781. Mar. 20.	Harrison, Lydia, and George McCall,.......	"	XXXI.	77
1761. April 21.	Harrison, Margaret, and Matthew Rogers,..	"	IV.	158
1782. July 19.	Harrison, Rebecca, and Thomas Potts,.....	"	XXXVI.	88
1783. Sept. 4.	Harrison, Richard, and Frances Ludlow,....	"	XL.	23
1771. Dec. 26.	Harrison, Sarah, and John Buchanan,......	"	XVII.	304
1778. Dec. 8.	Harrison, Samuel, and Margaret Forbes,....	"	XXVI.	114
1781. April 27.	Harrison, Samuel, and Sarah Pricilla Freeborn, ...	"	XXXII.	19
1765. May 13.	Harrison, Thomas, and Elizabeth North,....	"	IX.	125
1768. April 23.	Harrison, William, and Abigail Sutton,.....	"	XIII.	84
1783. Nov. 17.	Harrison, William, and Margaret Mansfield,.	"	XL.	119
1780. April 20.	Harrison, William, and Sarah Bennet,......	"	XXIX.	17
1783. Nov. 2.	Harriss, Mary, and Daniel Ackley,.... ...	"	XL.	102
1782. Oct. 24.	Harriss, Pheby, and Charles Frost,........	"	XXXVII.	64
1769. Feb. 14.	Harrold, Samuel, and Hannah Craft,.......	"	XIV.	32
1763. July 18.	Harse, Annatje, and Albertus Bloomindal,..	"	VII.	271
1758. Feb. 1.	Harsen, Sarah, and Cornelius Heyer,.......	"	I.	809
173⁶₇. Jan. 17.	Harsin, Barnardus, and Catherine Bryne,...	"	I.	5
1774. Jan. 12.	Harsin, Garrit, and Catherine Van Fleet,...	"	XXII.	100
1772. Nov. 16.	Harsin, George, and Elizabeth Van Gelder,..	"	XIX.	114
1764. April 13.	Harsin, Jacob, Jr., and Alida Groosbeck,...	"	VIII.	153
1760. Oct. 20.	Hart, Cornelia, and Richard Harbert,......	"	III.	374
1778. Dec. 21.	Hart, Elizabeth, and Christian Smily,......	"	XXVI.	128
1772. Oct. 22.	Hart, Elizabeth, and Peter Hatfield, Jr.,....	"	XIX.	85

DATE.	NAMES.	RECORD.	VOL.	PAGE.
1773. Aug. 9.	Hart, Esther, and William Williams,	M. B.,	XXI.	61
1777. Feb. 10.	Hart, George, and Ann Barbara Sowers,	"	XXIV.	28
1783. Jan. 14.	Hart, James, and Catharine Latorette,	"	XXXVIII.	15
1773. Sept. 16.	Hart, Jane, and Thomas Gardner,	"	XXI.	111
1782. Dec. 30.	Hart, Keturah, and Peter Losey,	"	XXXVII.	136
1781. Nov. 27.	Hart, Mary, and Patrick McDermott,	"	XXXIV.	60
1761. May 29.	Hart, Thomas, and Esther Wiley,	"	IV.	213
1738. Aug. 28.	Hartily, James, and Elenor Kingsley,	"	I.	10
1775. Nov. 8.	Hartley, Elizabeth, and Daniel McOnulty,	"	XXIII.	202
1773. Aug. 20.	Hartley, Hannah, and William Pyls,	"	XXI.	81
1760. May 9.	Hartley, Henry, and Elizabeth Barker,	"	III.	148
1761. Dec. 24.	Hartley, Richard, and Mary Magdalen Leddel,	"	V.	303
1773. Nov. 2.	Harton, Hannah, and Solomon Gidney,	"	XXII.	60
1757. April 16.	Harts, Christeena, and William Ruger,	"	I.	502
1782. Sept. 7.	Hartshorn, Beriah, and Lidey Hunt,	"	XXXVI.	139
1780. Jan. 20.	Hartshorn, Elizabeth, and Elizabeth Ustick,	"	XXVIII.	199
1773. Jan. 28.	Hartt, Joshua, and Abigail Howell,	"	XX.	27
1767. Oct. 9.	Hartt, Micah, and Anna Bryan,	"	XII.	59
1781. Oct. 11.	Harvey, Ephraim, and Catharine Davis,	"	XXXIII.	96
1759. Dec. 8.	Harvey, George, and Mary Wright,	"	II.	535
1779. May 17.	Harvey, Hannah, and Thomas Braine,	"	XXVII.	140
1760. June 16.	Harvey, James, and Mary Brass,	"	III.	188
1779. Nov. 15.	Harvey, Mary, and John Hamilton,	"	XXVIII.	140
1771. Oct. 10.	Harvey, Mary, and Peter Corgill,	"	XVII.	203
1779. June 26.	Harvey, Mary, and Robert Robinson,	"	XXVII.	119
1763. June 27.	Harvey, Samuel, and Mary Bloon,	"	VII.	245
1767. Jan. 21.	Harvey, Samuel, and Sarah Haselep,	"	XI.	10
1763. Dec. 24.	Harvey, William, and Rachel Lester,	"	VII.	525
1682. Dec. 17.	Harvie, Matthias, and Margarett Furbush,	E.,	XXXIII.	24
1772. May 25.	Hasbrock, Esther, and George Wirtz,	M. B.,	XVIII.	123
1766. July 2.	Hasbrook, Isaac, and Ann Van Gosbeck,	"	X.	40
1768. Oct. 1.	Hasbrouck, Annatje, and Johanis Decker,	"	XIII.	202
1770. Oct. 2.	Hasbrouck, Catherine, and Abraham Hoghteling,	"	XVI.	202
1767. July 4.	Hasbrouck, Daniel, and Deentie Van Vlecker,	"	XI.	124
1762. Oct. 26.	Hasbrouck, Elias, and Elizabeth Sleght,	"	VI.	387
1770. Oct. 2.	Hasbrouck, Elsie, and Abraham Salisbury,	"	XVI.	201
1764. Nov. 7.	Hasbrouck, Jane, and Theodorus Van Wyck,	"	VIII.	394
1776. Feb. 5.	Hasbrouck, John, and Mary Hasbrouck,	"	XXIII.	261
1773. Mar. 4.	Hasbrouck, Joseph, and Elizabeth Bevier,	"	XX.	56
1776. Feb. 5.	Hasbrouck, Mary, and John Hasbrouck,	"	XXIII.	261
1767. Jan. 21.	Haselep, Sarah, and Samuel Harvey,	"	XI.	10
1763. Mar. 14.	Haslet, Mary, and John De Grot,	"	VII.	97
1758. Oct. 9.	Hassie, George, and Mary Magdalin Siderlin,	"	II.	44
1761. Mar. 12.	Hastier, Elizabeth, and William Lucy,	"	IV.	97

DATE.	NAMES.	RECORD.	VOL.	PAGE.
1771. Nov. 23.	Haston, Joseph, and Sarah Tonnery,.......	M. B.,	XVII.	267
1782. May 28.	Hatch, John, and Mary Goswelling,........	"	XXXVI.	29
1767. June 18.	Hatfield, Elizabeth, and Samuel Barns,.....	"	XI.	111
1780. Nov. 11.	Hatfield, Job, and Jane Smith,........	"	XXX.	102
1778. June 27.	Hatfield, John; and Mary Lockerman,......	"	XXV.	116
1762. Dec. 9.	Hatfield, Martha, and Arthur Williams,.....	"	VI.	472
1772. July 29.	Hatfield, Patience, and Peter Bonet,.......	"	XIX.	8
1772. Oct. 22.	Hatfield, Peter, Jr., and Elizabeth Hart,....	"	XIX.	85
1771. Dec. 18.	Hathorn, John, and Elizabeth Wellin,......	"	XVII.	300
1757. Sept. 26.	Hatley, William, and Mary Fotherly,.......	"	I.	650
1783. Aug. 28.	Hatten, Anne, and Daniel Williams,.......	"	XL.	12
1761. Oct. 23.	Haughewout, Charity, and John Christopher,	"	V.	162
1764. Aug. 10.	Haughewout, Dorcas, and Mathias Smith,..	"	VIII.	277
1783. June 16.	Haughwout, Anne, and Richard Webb,....	"	XXXIX.	60
1762. Feb. 25.	Haughwout, Egbert, and Eleanor Garrabrants, ...	"	VI.	57
1757. June 11.	Haughwout, Neeltje, and Antony Brat,....	"	I.	561
1778. Mar. 17.	Haughwout, Peter, and Mary Martino,.....	"	XXV.	43
1758. April 4.	Haun, Coenradt, and Mary Ann Pendrey,..	"	I.	870
1783. Jan. 8.	Hausser, Nauchey, and Thomas Hayes,.....	"	XXXVIII.	10
1759. April 24.	Havens, Hannah, and Charles Chadwick,...	"	II.	252
1761. Nov. 19.	Havens, Nathaniel, and Anna Carpenter,...	"	V.	232
1759. July 31.	Havens, Peter, and Rebecca Smith,........	"	II.	368
1781. Jan. 29.	Havens, Selah, and Sarah Strong,.........	"	XXXI.	31
1761. July 8.	Haviland, Benjamin, and Rohamay Steed,..	"	IV.	289
1757. May 9.	Haviland, Catharine, and Joseph Gale,.....	"	I.	526
1762. Mar. 7.	Haviland, Catharine, and William Lawson,..	"	VI.	84
1779. June 22.	Haviland, David, and Mary Tom,..........	"	XXVIII.	1
1763. Jan. 21.	Haviland, Ebenezer, and Mary Tredwell,...	"	VII.	27
1765. Jan. 18.	Haviland, Ebenezer, and Tamar Budd,.....	"	IX.	23
1777. Nov. 7.	Haviland, Jacob, and Margaret Dodge,.....	"	XXIV.	175
1762. Aug. 26.	Haviland, James, and Ann Honeywell,.....	"	VI.	290
1759. Jan. 3.	Haviland, James, and Mary Pell,..........	"	II.	143
1782. Nov. 25.	Haviland, Jane, and Robert Hubbs, ...	"	XXXVII.	93
1764. Dec. 13.	Haviland, John, and Phebe Carpenter,.....	"	VIII.	455
1738. Dec. 16.	Haviland, Luke, and Sarah Oakley,........	"	I.	12
1769. May 26.	Haviland, Margaret, and James Nairne,.....	"	XIV.	109
1778. Jan. 21.	Haviland, Sarah, and Henderson Moore,....	"	XXV.	10
1762. Sept. 23.	Haviland, Sarah, and Isaac Oakley,........	"	VI.	328
1772. June 18.	Haviland, William, and Deborah Smith,....	"	XVIII.	143
1753. June 12.	Haviland, William, and Mary Halstead,.....	"	I.	59
1765. May 17.	Hawes, Frederick, and Margaret Hanson,...	"	IX.	129
1783. June 11.	Hawking, Deborah, and Adom Watson,....	"	XXXIX.	49
1755. Nov. 5.	Hawkins, Caleb, and Deborah Biggs,......	"	I.	206
1764. May 14.	Hawkins, Deliverance, and James Mapes,...	"	VIII.	189

DATE.	NAMES.	RECORD.	VOL.	PAGE.
1761. May 8.	Hawkins, George, and Hellen Francis,.....	M. B.,	IV.	184
1769. June 28.	Hawkins, Israel, and Susannah Skidmore,..	"	XIV.	135
1769. June 19.	Hawkins, John, and Martha Hildreth,.....	"	XIV.	123
1737. Oct. 28.	Hawkins, John, and Phebe Williams,......	"	I.	7
1761. Mar. 26.	Hawkins, John, and Prudence Anderson,...	"	IV.	121
1758. Oct. 12.	Hawkins, Joseph, and Mary Coxell,.......	"	II.	51
1763. Sept. 30.	Hawkins, Martha, and Joseph Smith,......	"	VII.	361
1781. April 26.	Hawkins, Richard, and Elizabeth Alsop,....	"	XXXII.	17
1757. Oct. 19.	Hawkins, Stephen, and Elizabeth Samon,...	"	I.	675
1781. June 3.	Hawkins, William, and Elizabeth Nuton,...	"	XXXII.	69
1757. July 29.	Hawkins, Zacharias, and Phebe Brinley,...	"	I.	607
1773. April 26.	Hawkins, Zophar, and Catherine Conkling,.	"	XX.	100
1773. Nov. 27.	Hawkshurst, Anne, and Thomas Budd,.....	"	XXII.	51
1761. Feb. 14.	Hawkshurst, Hannah, and Peter Townsend,.	"	IV.	64
1764. Jan. 19.	Hawkshurst, Jotham, and Phebe Oakley,...	"	VIII.	24
1765. June 28.	Hawkshurst, Sarah, and William Denning,..	"	IX.	187
1763. Mar. 21.	Hawley, Eunice, and William McIntosh,...	"	VII.	104
1783. April 28.	Haws, Jemime, and Moses West,..........	"	XXXVIII.	119
1759. Jan. 29.	Haws, Rebeccah, and William Borden,.....	"	II.	169
1768. Aug. 10.	Hawse, Hannah, and James Warner,......	"	XIII.	172
1769. Mar. 3.	Hawxhurst, Anne, and Thomas Budd,.....	"	XIV.	44
1755. Dec. 5.	Hawxhurst, Hosea, and Sarah Saults,......	"	I.	225
1773. Nov. 12.	Hawxhurst, Jesse, and Jane Reynolds,.....	"	XXII.	26
1768. Aug. 20.	Hawxhurst, Mary, and Solomon Wright,...	"	XIII.	177
1768. June 21.	Hawxhurst, Mary, and White Matlack,.....	"	XIII.	136
1763. Sept. 30.	Hay, Ann Hawkes, and Martha Smith,.....	"	VII.	362
1777. Dec. 12.	Hay, Elizabeth, and Thomas Bryant,.......	"	XXIV.	196
1778. Jan. 17.	Hay, Helen, and Robert Keith,...........	"	XXV.	8
1781. Feb. 5.	Hay, Hugh, and Magdelen Henry,........	"	XXXI.	37
1765. Jan. 3.	Haycock, Catharine, and Zacharias Cutant,..	"	IX.	5
1759. Nov. 30.	Haycock, John, and Catharine Manbret,....	"	II.	523
1779. May 19.	Hayden, Stephen, and Susanah Scidmore,..	"	XXVII.	141
1759. Dec. 4.	Hayes, Isabella, and Christopher Barwell,...	"	II.	526
168⅞. Feb. 2.	Hayes, Jane, and William Morris,.........	C. Min.,	V.	217
1768. Dec. 30.	Hayes, Mary, and Stephen Morland,.......	M. B.,	XIII.	275
1758. Sept. 22.	Hayes, Tamer, and Samuel Roe,..........	"	II.	31
1783. Jan. 8.	Hayes, Thomas, and Nauchey Hausser,.....	"	XXXVIII.	10
1777. Feb. 1.	Hayes, William, and Margaret Gilmore,....	"	XXIV.	22
1770. June 16.	Haynes, Elizabeth, and Thomas Brown,....	"	XVI.	114
1763. May 17.	Haynes, John, and Sarah Levige,..........	"	VII.	190
1759. June 13.	Haynes, Mary, and George Read,.........	"	II.	323
1783. June 16.	Hays, Hugh, and Mary Collins,...........	"	XXXIX.	62
1771. Sept. 24.	Hays, John, and Sarah Moore,............	"	XVII.	187
1778. Sept. 14.	Hays, Mary, and John Edwards,..........	"	XXVI.	29
1767. May 25.	Hayse, Mary, and John Debonerepose,.....	"	XI.	96

DATE.	NAMES.	RECORD.	VOL.	PAGE.
1780. Oct. 12.	Hayt, Elna, and Sarah Sacket, ...	M. B.,	xxx.	63
1758. Oct. 17.	Hayter, Hannah, and John Forrest,.......	"	II.	59
1771. May 31.	Hayter, Hannah, and William Bush,.......	"	XVII.	96
1753. Aug. 28.	Haywood, John, and Mary Schuyler,......	"	I.	99
1757. Oct. 27.	Haywood, Susannah, and John Letson,.....	"	I.	686
1760. Feb. 27.	Haywood, William, and Hannah Ffarrington,	"	III.	53
1765. Oct. 23.	Hazard, Ann, and Thomas Tredwell,.......	"	IX.	314
1765. Jan. 21.	Hazard, Anna, and Paul Gallaudet,........	"	IX.	27
1760. Dec. 10.	Hazard, Elizabeth, and Joseph Hallett,.....	"	III.	471
1768. Feb. 12.	Hazard, Elizabeth, and Samuel Lawrence,...	"	XIII.	35
1770. July 28.	Hazard, Mary, and Cornelius Turk,........	"	XVI.	148
1774. Jan. 21.	Hazard, Mary, and Joseph Blackwell,......	"	XXII.	113
1771. June 21.	Hazard, Mary, and Joseph Carr,...........	"	XVII.	120
1766. Nov. 3.	Hazard, Morriss, and Catherine Skenck,....	"	X.	149
1783. July 18.	Hazard, Pamela, and Henry Knipschild,...	"	XXXIX.	95
1769. Dec. 14.	Hazard, Thomas, and Martha Smith,.......	"	XV.	123
1761. Oct. 10.	Hazel, Sarah, and James Jackson,.........	"	V.	131
1763. Nov. 17.	Headly, Magdalen, and Caleb Cornwall,....	"	VII.	452
1779. Nov. 4.	Heagamen, Mary, and Michael Demott,.....	"	XXVIII.	128
1755. Sept. 4.	Healand, John, and Ann Willkenson,......	"	I.	166
1737. Sept. 13.	Healy, Anne, and Hardman Long,........	"	I.	7
1669. Sept. 8.	Heamore, Richard, and Joane Richardson,..	O. W. L.,	II.	524
1753. Oct. 3.	Heamstraat, Johannes, and Elizabeth Vandervolver, ...	M. B.,	I.	130
1758. Mar. 25.	Heaney, Hugh, and Esther Fletcher,......	"	I.	863
1772. Jan. 29.	Hearmans, Nelly, and John Mynderse,.....	"	XVIII.	22
1778. Mar. 17.	Hearn, James, and Mary Ellison,..........	"	XXV.	42
1778. Dec. 26.	Heater, William, and Rachel Brower,......	"	XXVI.	133
1780. May 8.	Heath, Elatha, and Robert Dale,..........	"	XXIX.	50
1755. Sept. 27.	Heath, Frances, and John Breuvregny,.....	"	I.	184
1760. Oct. 18.	Heath, John, and Eletha Pell,.............	"	III.	369
1777. July 8.	Heath, William, and Sarah Reily,.........	"	XXIV.	117
1782. Feb. 14.	Heaton, Peter, and Mary Vanburen,.......	"	XXXV.	55
1770. Aug. 22.	Heborn, Margaret, and Nicholas Grinjard,..	"	XVI.	167
1760. Feb. 23.	Hedden, Arrabella, and Ffloyd Stevenson,..	"	III.	46
1768. Oct. 14.	Heder, Henry, and Sarah Etwards,........	"	XIII.	210
1769. Dec. 2.	Hedger, Abigail, and Thomas Fowler,......	"	XV.	111
1773. May 19.	Hedger, Hannah, and Thomas Bennet,.....	"	XX.	118
1770. Jan. 27.	Hedger, Helena, and George Smart,.......	"	XVI.	8
1767. Aug. 6.	Hedger, Margaret, and Daniel Edwards,....	"	XII.	11
1781. Feb. 27.	Hedges, William, and Ann Burnton,.......	"	XXXI.	59
1779. Mar. 25.	Hedges, William, and Mary Richardson,....	"	XXVII.	77
1762. May 24.	Heeht, Frederick William, and Anne Archer,	"	VI.	168
1762. May 22.	Heekby, Freelove, and Jacob Cosyn,......	"	VI.	166
1770. Aug. 14.	Heermans, Catherine, and David Van Ness,.	"	XVI.	160

DATE.	NAMES.	RECORD.	VOL. PAGE.
1763. Sept. 2.	Helme, Jane, and Francis Panton,.........	M. B.,	VII. 322
1767. July 10.	Helmes, Ann Mary, and Peter W. Yates,....	"	XI. 129
1762. Nov. 13.	Helmes, Phineas, and Mary Wisner,.......	"	VI. 433
1782. Nov. 4.	Helms, Deborah, and Jeremiah Wood,.....	"	XXXVII. 71
1755. Oct. 15.	Helton, Petrus, and Ann Brooks,..........	"	I. 195
1776. May 2.	Hemelsburgh, Mary, and Michael Ganter,...	"	XXIII. 306
1768. Aug. 20.	Hempsted, Robert, and Mehitabel Reeve,...	"	XIII. 176
1753. June 18.	Hempstradt, Dirick, and Maria Barwe,.....	"	I. 64
1760. Mar. 21.	Hemstrat, Anna, and Derick Cloet,........	"	III. 85
1737. Aug. 16.	Hencen, Jacobus, and Mary Davanport,....	"	I. 7
1779. Sept. 30.	Henderson, Alexander, and Elizabeth Ann Clark,...............................	"	XXVIII. 92
1762. April —.	Henderson, Catharine, and John Imlay,....	"	VI. 104
1771. May 13.	Henderson, David, and Mary Tody,.......	"	XVII. 83
1760. Dec. 18.	Henderson, Eapheme, and William Proctor,.	"	III. 482
1763. July 14.	Henderson, Elizabeth, and Andrew Giraud,.	"	VII. 266
1782. Oct. 2.	Henderson, Elizabeth, and Nathaniel Child,.	"	XXXVII. 22
1762. Jan. 29.	Henderson, Esther, and Zebulon Doty,.....	"	VI. 30
1777. April 28.	Henderson, Hannah, and Michael Cook,....	"	XXIV. 78
1773. Dec. 13.	Henderson, Hendrick, and Jane Rierson,...	"	XXII. 73
1774. Mar. 14.	Henderson, James, and Mary Hobson,.....	"	XXII. 146
1765. April 10.	Henderson, John, and Elizabeth McClean,..	"	IX. 86
1759. Oct. 23.	Henderson, Mary, and Paul Miller, Jr.,.....	"	II. 407
1782. May 20.	Henderson, Masey, and Thomas Manuel,...	"	XXXVI. 12
1738. June 22.	Henderson, Michael, and Sarah Van Horne,.	"	I. 10
1777. May 19.	Henderson, Robert, and May Deas,........	"	XXIV. 90
1757. Feb. 3.	Henderson, Thomas, and Rachael Blank,...	"	I. 811
1738. June 13.	Henderson, Titia, and Alexander Moore,...	"	I. 10
1756. Nov. 8.	Henderton, James, and Sarah Berjeau,.....	"	I. 349
1782. Mar. 4.	Hendren, Downing, and Hannah Scudder,..	"	XXXV. 71
1757. Sept. 24.	Hendrick, Elenor, and Johan Heinrich Gunther, ...	"	I. 647
1670. Sept. 19.	Hendricks, Abigail, and Francis Leigh,.....	C. A.,	II. 594
1768. Oct. 27.	Hendricks, Cornelius, and Rachel Van Waghenan, ...	M. B.,	XIII. 217
1678. Oct. 4.	Hendricks, Gretye, and John Robinson,....	G. E.,	XXXII. 4
1773. Feb. 18.	Hendricks, John, and Catherine Sadler,....	M. B.,	XX. 47
1680. July 3.	Hendricks, John, and Martha Bradly,......	G. E.,	XXXII. 90
1761. Aug. 22.	Hendricks, Rachel, and Jacamiah Allen, ...	M. B.,	V. 52
1737. April 14.	Hendrickson, Abraham, and Wanechy Golder,	"	I. 5
1757. May 25.	Hendrickson, Aeltje, and Peter Van Gelder,	"	I. 541
1756. June 21.	Hendrickson, Daniel, and Catherine Van Brunt,	"	I. 242
1770. Dec. 7.	Hendrickson, Daniel, and Mary De Hart,...	"	XVI. 289
1758. May 27.	Hendrickson, Hannah, and Andries Stockholm, ...	"	I. 911

DATE.	NAMES.	RECORD.	VOL.	PAGE.
1770. May 16.	Hendrickson, Hendrick, and Hannah Hubbard,	M. B.,	XVI.	87
1782. Nov. 23.	Hendrickson, Isaac, and Sarah Monfort,	"	XXXVII.	90
1765. May 4.	Hendrickson, Jane, and Abraham Lott,	"	IX.	119
1782. June 23.	Hendrickson, John, and Abigail Seaman,	"	XXXVI.	61
1782. Oct. 17.	Hendrickson, John, and Hannah Conklin,	"	XXXVII.	50
1779. July 1.	Hendrickson, John, and Jane Foster,	"	XXVIII.	13
1782. Feb. 23.	Hendrickson, John, and Rhodey Wood,	"	XXXV.	62
1771. Feb. 5.	Hendrickson, Marcey, and Anthony Van Noorstrant,	"	XVII.	14
1780. Mar. 20.	Hendrickson, Martha, and Richard Robbins,	"	XXIX.	3
1756. Nov. 13.	Hendrickson, Peter, and Ann Stillwell,	"	I.	353
1783. May 31.	Hendrickson, Peter, and Mary Skidmore,	"	XXXIX.	33
1772. Aug. 5.	Hendrickson, Phebe, and Solomon Foster,	"	XIX.	12
1776. Jan. 5.	Hendrickson, Stephen, and Jane Brooks,	"	XXIII.	241
1757. Mar. 12.	Hendrickson, Susannah, and Richard Everit,	"	I.	466
1764. Jan. 24.	Hendrickson, William, and Ann Snedaker,	"	VIII.	34
1760. Dec. 19.	Hendrie, James, and Jane Traphager,	"	III.	484
1763. April 7.	Hendrie, Margaret, and Harman Ledru,	"	VII.	117
1757. July 9.	Hendy, John, and Mary Carlile,	"	I.	588
1782. April 26.	Henley, Mary, and Lawrence R. Campbell,	"	XXXV.	139
1781. Mar. 10.	Hennesy, Hester, and Jonathan Smith,	"	XXXI.	68
1782. April 27.	Henning, Thomas, and Elizabeth Vangelder,	"	XXXV.	141
1761. Jan. 31.	Henry, Alexander, and Mary Jones,	"	IV.	44
1685. May 26.	Henry, John, and Ann Price,	C. M.,	XXXIII.	130
1763. April 21.	Henry, John, and Elizabeth Van Vorst,	M. B.,	VII.	135
1775. Oct. 9.	Henry, John, and Leah Brevoort,	"	XXIII.	175
1781. Feb. 5.	Henry, Magdalen, and Hugh Hay,	"	XXXI.	37
1774. Jan. 8.	Henry, Margery, and Joseph Bridemore,	"	XXII.	97
1782. May 25.	Henry, Margret, and William Wright,	"	XXXVI.	24
1767. Feb. 21.	Henry, Mary, and Andrew McMyer,	"	XI.	32
1766. June 12.	Henry, Robert, and Elizabeth Vernor,	"	X.	15
1738. June 24.	Henry, William, and Hannah Cook,	"	I.	10
1767. Oct. 14.	Henry, William, and Sarah Cottrell,	"	XII.	61
1772. Dec. 22.	Henrys, Silas, and Ann Turner,	"	XIX.	161
1770. May 17.	Henshaw, Mehitable, and Samuel Nesbitt,	"	XVI.	91
1764. Aug. 20.	Henshaw, Samuel, and Elizabeth Tingley,	"	VIII.	288
1770. Oct. 31.	Henshaw, Samuel, and Mary King,	"	XVI.	235
1758. Nov. 18.	Heppie, Rosena, and Jacob Appel,	"	II.	94
1758. Mar. 18.	Hepworth, Thomas, and Martha Reemer,	"	I.	857
1781. July 26.	Herbert, Samuel, and Sarah Harris,	"	XXXIII.	16
1759. Jan. 27.	Herbert, Thomas, and Margaret Carr,	"	II.	168
1678. Aug. 14.	Herbert, Walter, and Mary Barnes,	G. E.,	XXXII.	1
1758. Mar. 18.	Herkemer, Annetje, and John Van Alen,	M. B.,	I.	856

DATE.		NAMES.	RECORD.	VOL.	PAGE.
1758. April	28.	Herkemer, Mary, and Abraham Rosencranz,	M. B.,	I.	888
1782. April	27.	Herman, Frederick Ludwick, and Charity Gelledet,	"	XXXV.	132
1667. Dec.	18.	Hermitage, Anne, and Samuel Barrett, ...	O. W. L.,	II.	191
1762. Nov.	22.	Heroy, Jane, and Louis Riviere, ...	M. B.,	VI.	449
1783. July	11.	Herriman, Stephen, and Elizabeth Smith, ..	"	XXXIX.	86
1771. May	31.	Herring, Aeltie, and John Hogen Kamp,...	"	XVII.	97
1759. Dec.	12.	Herring, Catharine, and Philip Kull,.......	"	II.	540
1768. July	7.	Herring, Cornelia, and Samuel Jones,......	"	XIII.	151
1769. Sept.	11.	Herring, Elizabeth, and John De Peyster, Jr.,	"	XV.	39
1762. Sept.	24.	Herring, Elizabeth, and William Forbes,...	"	VI.	329
1777. Feb.	1.	Herring, Nicholas, and Ann Bogert,.......	"	XXIV.	24
1757. April	21.	Herring, Peter, and Catharine Blauvelt,....	"	I.	506
1762. Nov.	5.	Herrington, Christopher, and Rosanna Haddock, ...	"	VI.	413
1734/5. Mar.	9.	Hertie, Ghertse, and Isaac King,..........	"	I.	9
1764. Mar.	5.	Hervey, Patience, and Jacob Bogardus, ...	"	VIII.	92
1767. Jan.	21.	Hervey, Samuel, and Sarah Haselep, ...	"	XI.	10
1779. Aug.	22.	Heslop, John, and Letty Arrowsmith, ...	"	XXVIII.	56
1766. June	12.	Hess, Daniel, and Anna Barbara Crouscop, .	"	X.	14
1763. July	6.	Hess, John, and Mary Reigler,.............	. "	VII.	259
1760. April	14.	Hesson, Catharine, and Jacob Loch, ...	"	III.	104
1757. April	26.	Hestear, Mary, and Francis J. Bassett,.....	"	I.	514
1780. April	12.	Hetfield, James, and Mary Ten Eyck, ...	"	XXIX.	20
1779. Nov.	1.	Hetly, Mary, and James Todd, ...	"	XXVIII.	125
1773. July	17.	Heughan, John, and Anna Beck,..........	"	XXI.	44
1759. Nov.	30.	Heuston, James, and Ann Carr,...........	"	II.	522
1759. Sept.	13.	Hewit, Hannah, and Duncan Brown,......	"	II.	418
1766. Oct.	7.	Hewlet, Benjamin, and Jemima Hewlet,...	"	X.	118
1779. Mar.	7.	Hewlet, Hannah, and John Jones, ...	"	XXVII.	60
1760. Oct.	29.	Hewlet, Hannah, and Joseph Smith, ...	"	III.	386
1766. Aug.	30.	Hewlet, Hannah, and Samuel Van Wyck, ..	"	X.	86
1772. Dec.	8.	Hewlet, Helena, and John Boyd, ...	"	XIX.	147
1779. Jan.	12.	Hewlet, Isaac, and Rhoda Van Wyck, ...	"	XXVII.	11
1760. Dec.	16.	Hewlet, Jane, and Benjamin Creed, ...	"	III.	478
1766. Oct.	7.	Hewlet, Jemima, and Benjamin Hewlet,...	"	X.	118
1772. Jan.	7.	Hewlet, Mary, and Isaac Youngs,.........	"	XX.	5
1761. Mar.	31.	Hewlet, Mary, and William Horsfield,.....	"	IV.	126
1761. Dec.	1.	Hewlet, Phebe, and John Cornwall, ...	"	V.	259
1770. Jan.	4.	Hewlett, Charles, and Martha Davenport, ..	"	XVI.	3
1766. Nov.	22.	Hewlett, Elizabeth, and Adam Mott, ...	"	X.	178
1774. Feb.	10.	Hewlett, Elizabeth, and Newberry Davenport,................................	"	XXII.	126
1766. June	5.	Hewlett, George, and Susannah Peters, ...	"	X.	4
1778. Feb.	18.	Hewlett, Hannah, and Richard Hewlett, ...	"	XXV.	25

DATE.	NAMES.	RECORD.	VOL.	PAGE.
1761. Sept. 8.	Hewlett, Hannah, and Stephen Hewlett, ...	M. B.,	v.	72
1772. Oct. 2.	Hewlett, James, and Jemima Jackson, ...	"	xix.	67
1777. Oct. 21.	Hewlett, Jane, and Samuel Cornell, ...	"	xxiv.	168
1766. Aug. 22.	Hewlett, John, and Ann Jackson, ...	"	x.	81
1777. June 18.	Hewlett, Lawrence, and Charity Peters, ...	"	xxiv.	104
1773. Dec. 17.	Hewlett, Martha, and Benjamin Kissam, Jr.,	"	xxii.	77
1767. Oct. 26.	Hewlett, Mary, and Jaques Cortelyou, ...	"	xii.	68
1781. April 20.	Hewlett, Mary, and Richard Townsend, ...	"	xxxii.	9
1777. Oct. 21.	Hewlett, Mary, and Stephen Hicks, ...	"	xxiv.	169
1778. Feb. 18.	Hewlett, Richard, and Hannah Hewlett, ...	"	xxv.	25
1778. Mar. 20.	Hewlett, Richard, and Martha Carman, ...	"	xxv.	49
1761. Sept. 8.	Hewlett, Stephen, and Hannah Hewlett, ...	"	v.	72
1764. Nov. 21.	Hewlett, Susannah, and Samuel Tredwell, ..	"	viii.	416
1776. Jan. 19.	Hewlett, Thomas, and Ann Durling, ...	"	xxiii.	249
1779. Jan. 12.	Hewlett, Townsend, and Margaret Jones, ...	"	xxvii.	10
1769. June 8.	Hewlett, William, and Elizabeth Dusinberry,	"	xiv.	117
1762. Aug. 26.	Hewlett, William, and Phebe Kirby, ...	"	vi.	288
1781. Nov. 21.	Hewlick, Jacob, and Levina Tiginer, ...	"	xxxiv.	53
1764. May 4.	Hewson, Anne, and David Smith, ...	"	viii.	184
1760. June 6.	Hewson, Daniel, and Mary Barret, ...	"	iii.	178
1760. Oct. 2.	Heyan, Mary, and Thomas English, ...	"	iii.	341
1764. Aug. 23.	Heyder, Margaret, and John Jauncey, ...	"	viii.	291
1768. Jan. 11.	Heyer, Catherine, and Abraham Bennet, ...	"	xiii.	5
1778. April 24.	Heyer, Diederick, and Metta Flugger, ...	"	xxv.	68
1779. Jan. 30.	Heyer, Mary, and William Scott, ...	"	xxvii.	33
1738. June 3.	Heyer, Viontie, and John Elbow, ...	"	i.	9
1775. Oct. 28.	Heyer, Walter, and Elizabeth Brower, ...	"	xxiii.	191
1779. Oct. 28.	Heylian, Catharine, and Frederick Fine, ...	"	xxviii.	122
1780. Jan. 20.	Heymell, Bartholomew Ernest, and Margaret Tarrant, ...	"	xxviii.	201
1777. Oct. 7.	Heysen, Frederick Joseph, and Mary Margaret Fagh, ...	"	xxiv.	159
1757. Dec. 8.	Hibben, William, and Margery West, ...	"	i.	729
1765. June 5.	Hickby, Sarah, and John Pringle, ... ·	"	ix.	156
1780. Jan. 4.	Hickman, Julie, and George Lilly, ...	"	xxviii.	185
1781. Mar. 24.	Hickock, Rachel, and Robert Ray, ...	"	xxxi.	84
1761. April 21.	Hicks, Abigail, and Caleb Smith, ...	"	iv.	160
1767. Sept. 21.	Hicks, Amie, and George Cornell, ...	"	xii.	38
1778. May 11.	Hicks, Ann, and Andrew Walker, ...	"	xxv.	79
1758. Jan. 18.	Hicks, Ann, and James Smith, ...	"	i.	789
1782. Mar. 2.	Hicks, Ann, and Ralph Smith, ...	"	xxxv.	70
1765. April 26.	Hicks, Benjamin, and Elizabeth Mott, ...	"	ix.	110
1767. Mar. 13.	Hicks, Charles, and Abigail Cornwall, ...	"	xi.	44
1768. Feb. 22.	Hicks, Charles, and Hannah Hyman, ...	"	xiii.	39
1767. Feb. 3.	Hicks, Charles, and Mary Hicks, ...	"	xi.	18

DATE.		NAMES.	RECORD.	VOL.	PAGE.
1737. May	16.	Hicks, Dennis, and Mary Goodland,.......	M. B.,	I.	6
1757. April	7.	Hicks, Dennis, and Tamar Conklin,........	"	I.	489
1758. Jan.	6.	Hicks, Edward, and Elizabeth Cornell,.....	"	I.	774
1761. Aug.	1.	Hicks, Elizabeth, and John Jauncey, Jr.,...	"	V.	21
1763. Dec.	20.	Hicks, Elizabeth, and Peter De Milt, ...	"	VII.	515
1762. May	4.	Hicks, Elizabeth, and Stephen Thorne,.....	"	VI.	141
1781. April	6.	Hicks, Elizabeth, and Timothy Hicks,......	"	XXXI.	96
1773. Aug.	18.	Hicks, Elizabeth R., and Nathaniel Tom,...	"	XXI.	71
1782. Sept.	28.	Hicks, Evan, and Rachel North, ...	"	XXXVII.	19
1757. Sept.	30.	Hicks, George, and Elizabeth Ryder, ...	"	I.	652
1760. Aug.	26.	Hicks, George, and Teetie King,..........	"	III.	268
1762. June	1.	Hicks, Hannah, and David Seaman, ...	"	VI.	177
1770. Sept.	27.	Hicks, Hannah, and William Cornell,......	"	XVI.	197
1768. April	27.	Hicks, Isaac, and Deborah Cornell,........	"	XIII.	87
1770. Feb.	3.	Hicks, Jacob, and Mary Durland,..........	"	XVI.	10
1775. Sept.	8.	Hicks, James, and Jane Randell,..........,.	"	XXIII.	153
1761. June	11.	Hicks, James, and Lydia Youry,....	"	IV.	235
1766. June	5.	Hicks, Jeffery, and Mary Cornwall,........	'.	X.	5
1738. July	5.	Hicks, John, and Martha Mott, ...	"	I.	10
1780. Aug.	14.	Hicks, John, and Ruth Serin,.............	"	XXIX.	141
173⁶⁄₇. Mar.	24.	Hicks, Joseph, and Margret Lester,........	"	I.	5
1761. Feb.	17.	Hicks, Joseph, and Sarah Valentine,.......	"	IV.	67
1758. Dec.	7.	Hicks, Margaret, and Thomas Poyer, ...	"	II.	120
1757. Dec.	24.	Hicks, Margret, and James Cornell, ...	"	I.	752
1767. Feb.	3.	Hicks, Mary, and Charles Hicks,..........	"	XI.	18
1781. June	8.	Hicks, Mary, and Jacob Suydam, ...	"	XXXII.	76
1757. Mar.	15.	Hicks, Mary, and James Townsend,.......	"	I.	469
1756. Oct.	12.	Hicks, Mary, and Samuel Seabury,........	"	I.	326
1780. Aug.	28.	Hicks, Mary, and Stephen Hicks, ...	"	XXX.	6
1781. Dec.	20.	Hicks, Norris, and Sarah Lawrence,.......	"	XXXIV.	97
1772. Jan.	5.	Hicks, Phebe, and John Carll, ...	"	XX.	2
1676. May	24.	Hicks, Rachel, and John Spencer, ...	W. O. P.,	III.	198
1781. July	9.	Hicks, Richard, and Hannah Mullenerex,...	M. B.,	XXXIII.	3
1780. Oct.	5.	Hicks, Samuel, and Elizabeth Kilman, ...	"	XXX.	54
1762. Aug.	23.	Hicks, Samuel, and Jane Smith,..........	"	VI.	285
1769. June	3.	Hicks, Sarah, and Cornelius Van Wyck,....	"	XIV.	115
1763. July	28.	Hicks, Sarah, and Joseph Dodge, ...	"	VII.	285
1770. Feb.	3.	Hicks, Silas, and Mary Pearson, ...	"	XVI.	11
1777. Oct.	21.	Hicks, Stephen, and Mary Hewlett, ...	"	XXIV.	169
1780. Aug.	28.	Hicks, Stephen, and Mary Hicks, ...	"	XXX.	6
1677. July	6.	Hicks, Thomas, and Mary Doughty, ...	W. O. P.,	III.	252
1781. April	6.	Hicks, Timothy, and Elizabeth Hicks,......	M. B.,	XXXI.	96
1758. Dec.	14.	Hicks, Timothy, and Rachel Schurri, ...	"	II.	128
1782. May	18.	Hicks, William, and Amy Cornell, ...	"	XXXVI.	8
1780. Nov.	8.	Hicks, William, and Sarah Serrin,.........	"	XXX.	98

DATE.	NAMES.	RECORD.	VOL. PAGE.
1768. July 22.	Hier, Mary, and Anthony Bennet, ...	M. B.,	XIII. 162
1769. July 31.	Hiet, Mary, and John William Bauman,....	"	XV. 10
1782. May 17.	Hieth, Catharine, and William Weaver,....	"	XXXVI. 5
1753. June 4.	Higbee, Elizabeth, and Samuel Rayner, ...	"	I. 48
1755. Sept. 5.	Higbee, Sarah, and Richard Sallisbury,.....	"	I. 167
1782. Feb. 7.	Higbey, Elenor, and Nicholas Betty, ...	"	XXXV. 45
1761. June 18.	Higby, Henry, and Herodia Mott,.........	"	IV. 247
1756. Aug. 18.	Highy, Margaret, and William Elkins,.....	"	I. 272
1779. April 7.	Higby, Phebe, and Elijah Pettet, ...	"	XXVII. 97
1782. Jan. 26.	Higby, Sarah, and Benjamin Everit,.......	"	XXXV. 33
1682. July 4.	Higby, Thomas, and Mary Taylor,........	O. W.,	XXXII½. 132
1767. May 4.	Higday, Mary, and John Payne, ...	M. B.,	XI. 76
1779. July 2.	Higgin, Ann, and Andrew Jantzen,.......	"	XXVIII. 14
1770. July 20.	Higgins, Benjamin, and Hannah Rayce,....	"	XVI. 142
1760. May 2.	Higgins, Benjamin, and Phebe Teller,......	"	III. 137
1753. Aug. 1.	Higgins, Daniel, and Catherine Viele,......	"	I. 82
1768. Mar. 15.	Higgins, Ichabod, and Hannah Turk,......	"	XIII. 49
1761. June 18.	Higgins, Ichabod, and Mary Dennison,.....	"	IV. 248
1762. July 12.	Higgins, Sarah, and Francis Perry,........	"	VI. 235
1759. Sept. 3.	High, David, and Jennet Williams,........	"	II. 407
1775. Sept. 21.	High, Jane, and George Brookman,........	"	XXIII. 161
1762. Feb. 27.	High, Lydia, and Joseph Devoe, ...	"	VI. 58
1773. Dec. 21.	Hike, Gertruyd, and Alexander Wiley,.....	"	XXII. 80
1756. Sept. 25.	Hiklarie, Ester, and Hendrick Pruyn,.....	"	I. 305
1772. Feb. 10.	Hildreth, Benjamin, and Elizabeth Greswold,............................	"	XVIII. 32
	Hildreth, Joseph, and Hannah Grigg,......	"	VII. 391
1769. June 19.	Hildreth, Martha, and John Hawkins,.....	"	XIV. 123
1764. Nov. 15.	Hill, Abraham, and Rachel Elberson,......	"	VIII. 411
1682. June 1.	Hill, Ann, and Elyas Leyston,............	O. W.,	XXXII½. 125
1760. Oct. 9.	Hill, Catherine, and David Jones,.........	M. B.,	III. 356
1761. July 18.	Hill, Christian, and Gregory Springall,.....	"	IV. 303
1757. July 28.	Hill, Christian, and Robert Boyle,.........	"	I. 605
1777. June 11.	Hill, Elizabeth, and Gregory Springall,.....	"	XXIV. 99
1763. Aug. 1.	Hill, Henry, and Martha Riddle,..........	"	VII. 289
1759. Oct. 27.	Hill, James, and Mary Gildo,.............	"	II. 475
1765. June 8.	Hill, John, and Jane Monnell,............	"	IX. 162
1782. Aug. 5.	Hill, John, and Sarah Colyer,............	"	XXXVI. 100
1781. Mar. 8.	Hill, Joshua, and Mary Rose,............	"	XXXI. 67
1756. Oct. 11.	Hill, Mary, and Benjamin Loring, ...	"	I. 325
1777. Mar. 24.	Hill, Robert, and Catherine Garing,.......	"	XXIV. 51
1776. Jan. 13.	Hill, Robert, and Catherine Van Wickelen,..	"	XXIII. 246
1768. July 16.	Hill, Sarah, and James Buckmaster,.......	"	XIII. 160
1685. Nov. 15.	Hill, Thomas, and Abigail Wakeman,......	C. M.,	XXXIII. 198
1762. Mar. 13.	Hill, Thomas, and Alice Armstrong,.......	M. B.,	VI. 87

DATE.	NAMES.	RECORD.	VOL.	PAGE.
1778. Feb. 24.	Hill, Thomas, and Catherine Wigmore,	M B.,	xxv.	129
1778. July 13.	Hill, Thomas, and Jane Burger,	"	xxv.	32
1760. Aug. 20.	Hill, William, and Mary Thorn,	"	III.	264
1761. Nov. 24.	Hilliar, Elizabeth, and George Pitts,	"	v.	245
1764. Feb. 21.	Hillard, Minor, and Merriam Barnes,	"	VIII.	69
1777. July 30.	Hillier, Isaac, and Jane Reynolds,	"	xxiv.	124
1775. Nov. 18.	Hillman, John, and Lucy Burgess,	"	xxiii.	215
1783. Sept. 12.	Hillyer, Edward and Sarah Perine,	"	xl.	37
1760. May 23.	Hillyer, Elizabeth, and Abraham Lakerman,	"	III.	163
1769. Nov. 4.	Hillyer, Hester, and James Way,	"	xv.	78
1764. Oct. 16.	Hillyer, John, and Mary Arrowsmith,	"	VIII.	357
1759. Feb. 5.	Hillyer, Lawrence, and Ann Lakerman,	"	II.	176
1770. Dec. 7.	Hillyer, Mary, and William Smith,	"	xvi.	287
1783. Sept. 12.	Hillyer, Sarah, and Edward Perine,	"	xl.	37
1770. June 1.	Hillyer, Sarah, and Oliver Taylor,	"	xvi.	102
1767. Oct. 6.	Hilton, Anne, and Abraham Hoghkerk,	"	xii.	57
1779. Nov. 10.	Hilton, Benjamin, and Susannah Greswold,	"	xxviii.	134
1762. Mar. 29.	Hilton, Jacobus, and Sarah Barnton,	"	vi.	85
1758. Oct. 17.	Hilton, Jerusha, and Solomon Powell,	"	II.	58
1773. Aug. 28.	Hilton, John, and Catherine Van Bueren,	"	xxi.	89
1762. Aug. 2.	Hilton, Marcey, and Walter Michaeljohn,	"	vi.	261
1772. Sept. 29.	Hilton, Peter, and Elizabeth Echts,	"	xix.	62
1753. April 5.	Hilton, William, and Elizabeth Brooks,	"	I.	19
1736. July 16.	Hilton, William, and Margrett Jones,	"	I.	2
1766. Sept. 18.	Himmelsburger, George, and Maria Magde-			
	lana Daniels,	"	x.	100
1760. Aug. 18.	Himmons, Lydia, and John Yeamons,	"	III.	259
1765. Oct. 16.	Hinchman, Elizabeth, and Daniel Robert,	"	ix.	302
1780. Dec. 2.	Hinchman, Letitia, and David Lamberson,	"	xxx.	133
1759. April 26.	Hinchman, Mary, and John Evans,	"	II.	256
1772. June 23.	Hinchman, Robert, and Deliverance Albertson,	"	xviii.	148
1757. Sept. 24.	Hinchman, Robert, and Joanna Ludlam,	"	I.	643
1768. Mar. 23.	Hinckman, John, and Mary Tanner,	"	xiii.	55
1761. Dec. 10.	Hincksman, Thomas, and Patience Reed,	"	v.	272
1762. July 31.	Hind, Margaret, and Thomas White,	"	vi.	259
1777. Nov. 21.	Hindes, Hannah, and George Belton,	"	xxiv.	183
1760. Dec. 15.	Hindmore, Ann, and Paul Postle,	"	III.	477
1757. April 26.	Hine, William, and Margaret Collard,	"	I.	515
1779. Aug. 2.	Hines, James, and Mary Widner,	"	xxviii.	43
1760. May 7.	Hinson, Anne, and Thomas White,	"	I.	822
1736. Sept. 4.	Hinson, Nathaniel, and Elizabeth Marschalk,	"	I.	2
1765. Jan. 22.	Hinton, Abigail, and John Richar,	"	ix.	30
1760. Nov. 15.	Hinton, Elizabeth, and Isaac Fryer,	"	III.	418
1772. April 16.	Hinton, William, and Phebe Smith,	"	xviii.	82
1783. Nov. 6.	Hinxman, Charles, and Jane Dikeman,	"	xl.	107

DATE.	NAMES.	RECORD.	VOL.	PAGE.
1779. Sept. 29.	Hipp, Sarah, and Thomas Hodson,........	M. B.,	XXVIII.	91
1771. Aug. 30.	Hipworth, William, and Susanna Brantnell,	"	XVII.	169
1737. Oct. 5.	Hire, Frederick, and Margaret Vandewater,.	"	I.	7
1779. Dec. 4.	Hislop, John, and Mary Bates,............	"	XXVIII.	159
1736. Dec. 10.	Hitcham, Joshua, and Jerusha Whitmon,...	"	I.	3
1779. Sept. 2.	Hitchcock, Abigail, and Mott Cannon,.....	"	XXVIII.	65
1757. Oct. 8.	Hitchcock, Elizabeth, and Isaac Bennet,....	"	I.	662
1782. Oct. 5.	Hitchcock, Hannah, and Seth Freeman,....	"	XXXVII.	28
1753. Oct. 8.	Hitchcock, Mary, and Richard Howard,....	"	I.	133
1763. July 28.	Hitchcock, Miles, and Margaret Secord,....	"	VII.	283
1762. Dec. 24.	Hitchcock, Samuel, and Bridget Archer,....	"	VI.	499
1767. Sept. 16.	Hitchings, Richard, and Martha Bockey,...	"	XII.	35
1757. Dec. 12.	Hitt, Samuel, and Jane Denison, ...	"	I.	735
1736. Dec. 13.	Hix, Thomas, and Elizabeth Lefoy,........	"	I.	3
1773. Feb. 6.	Hoag, Ruth, and Cornelius Dennis,........	"	XX.	37
1760. Jan. 3.	Hoanch, Anthony, and Deborah Wood,.....	"	II.	564
1778. July 24.	Hoar, Jane, and Mathew Taylor,..........	"	XXV.	141
1764. Oct. 12.	Hoare, William, and Jane Davis,..........	"	VIII.	354
1764. June 22.	Hobart, John Sloss, and Mary Greenill,....	"	VIII.	231
1768. Mar. 29.	Hobbs, Oliver, and Mary Lent,...........	"	XIII.	57
1778. June 27.	Hobbs, William, and Jane Main,..........	"	XXV.	114
1781. Dec. 13.	Hobby, Jabez, and Abigail Theal,.........	"	XXXIV.	84
1774. Mar. 14.	Hobson, Mary, and James Henderson,.....	"	XXII.	146
1774. Mar. 14.	Hobson, Samuel, and Helena Castine,......	"	XXII.	148
1762. Feb. 1.	Hodge, Ralph, and Elizabeth Walker,......	"	VI.	32
1782. Nov. 9.	Hodge, Thomas, and Jane McCloud,.......	"	XXXVII.	77
1761. Jan. 10.	Hodge, William, and Gerthry Wilson,......	"	IV.	8
1761. Nov. 14.	Hodge, William, and Margaret Christian,...	"	V.	218
1761. Aug. 11.	Hodges, Isabella, and Ephorim Shaw,......	"	V.	39
1778. July 22.	Hodgkinson, Henry, and Margaret Atkins,.	"	XXV.	136
1778. Oct. 28.	Hodgson, Elizabeth, and Henry Guest,.....	"	XXVI.	65
1772. July 7.	Hodgson, Thomas, and Catherine Hutchinson,	"	XVIII.	157
1772. Jan. 29.	Hodkisson, Mary, and Ralph Mellor,.......	"	XVIII.	23
1779. Sept. 29.	Hodson, Thomas, and Sarah Hipp,........	"	XXVIII.	91
1766. Sept. 24.	Hoel, Phebe, and William Smith, ...	"	X.	104
1768. June 1.	Hoff, Hannah, and Simeon Losee,.........	"	XIII.	121
1775. June 20.	Hoff, Joseph, and Sarah Weygand,........	"	XXIII.	69
1769. Oct. 24.	Hoff, Sarah, and Thomas Churchward,.....	"	XV.	64
1769. Aug. 17.	Hoff, William, and Rebecca Talman,.......	"	XV.	25
1773. Sept. 6.	Hoffman, Annatie, and Philip Van Beuren,.	"	XXI.	100
1737. Nov. 24.	Hoffman, Anthony, and Catherina Van Groosbeck, ...	"	I.	8
1764. Nov. 22.	Hoffman, Catharine, and Louris Goes, ...	"	VII.	418
1763. Nov. 9.	Hoffman, Esther, and Jacobus Vanderlign,.	"	VII.	439
1770. Nov. 14.	Hoffman, Herman, and Catherine Douw,...	"	XVI.	254

24

DATE.	NAMES.	RECORD.	VOL.	PAGE.
1766. Oct. 16.	Hoffman, Janatie, and John Kierstada, ...	M. B.,	x.	126
1772. April 18.	Hoffman, Jane, and Zachariah Hoffman, ...	"	xviii.	83
1760. Dec. 17.	Hoffman, John Nicholas, and Rebecca Myers,	"	iii.	480
1766. Sept. 24.	Hoffman, Martin, and Alida Hansen, ...	"	x.	105
1772. May 19.	Hoffman, Martin, Jr., and Margaret Bayard,	"	xviii.	115
1768. July 18.	Hoffman, Mary, and Archibald Laidlie, ...	"	xiii.	161
1770. Nov. 14.	Hoffman, Nicholas, Jr., and Ede Sylvester, .	"	xvi.	253
1761. April 10.	Hoffman, Robert, and Sarah Van Alstyn, . . .	"	iv.	143
1763. Oct. 6.	Hoffman, Sarah, and David D. De Lametter,	"	vii.	375
1772. April 18.	Hoffman, Zachariah, and Jane Hoffman, . . .	"	xviii.	83
1775. June 17.	Hoffman, Zacharias, and Aeltje Van Wyck, .	"	xxiii.	68
1766. June 9.	Hoffnaul, Barbara, and Nicholas Michael, . . .	"	x.	11
1770. Nov. 12.	Hofth, John, and Mary McDaniel, ...	"	xvi.	248
1781. Oct. 3.	Hogaland, Hannah, and Isaac Bogart, Jr., . .	"	xxxiii.	84
1772. Jan. 29.	Hogan, Hannah, and Rynear Van Yeveron, .	"	xviii.	21
1760. Oct. 2.	Hogan (Reyan), Mary, and Thomas English,	"	iii.	341
1761. Aug. 18.	Hogan, Mirtina, and Thomas Brown, ...	"	v.	47
1757. May 12.	Hogan, Rachel, and Jacob Luke, ...	"	i.	530
1763. Dec. 31.	Hogan, Susanna, and John De Garmo, ...	"	vii.	530
1773. July 23.	Hogeboem, Cornelius P., and Antie Bronck,	"	xxi.	51
1769. Nov. 9.	Hogeboom, Abraham, and Mary Vosburgh, .	"	xv.	86
1771. Oct. 29.	Hogeboom, Bartholomew, and Polly Van Valkenburgh, ...	"	xvii.	231
1769. Sept. 5.	Hogeboom, Catherine, and Thomas Storm, .	"	xv.	36
1761. June 29.	Hogeboom, Cornelius, and Sarah Vosburgh, .	"	iv.	269
1766. Sept. 27.	Hogeboom, Elbertie, and Peter Van Ness, . .	"	x.	112
1773. Nov. 30.	Hogeboom, Jacobus, and Elberty Van Alen, .	"	xxii.	55
1760. Oct. 28.	Hogeboom, Jeremiah, and Anati Van Hoosen, ...	"	iii.	384
1761. May 28.	Hogeboom, Johannis, and Gertrey Muller, . .	"	iv.	210
1764. Feb. 27.	Hogeboom, Lawrence, and Hester Legget, . .	"	viii.	81
1764. Nov. 27.	Hogeboom, Sarah, and Jeremiah Miller, ...	"	viii.	428
1763. Nov. 24.	Hogeboom, Stephen, and Helletje Muller, . . .	"	vii.	468
1762. Oct. 22.	Hogeland, George, and Mary Schenck, ...	"	iii.	342
1761. Oct. 20.	Hogelandt, Altje, and John Low, ...	"	v.	154
1763. Nov. 26.	Hogelandt, Frances, and Anthony Stonbacke,	"	vii.	471
1762. Sept. 25.	Hogelandt, Margaret, and Richard Fletcher,	"	vi.	332
1762. Sept. 2.	Hogelandt, William, and Sarah Moore, ...	"	vi.	303
1759. May 31.	Hogelent, Benjamin, and Elizabeth Van Wyck, ...	"	ii.	296
1757. June 24.	Hogen, Alida, and Andries Van Schaick, . . .	"	i.	574
1767. Oct. 26.	Hogen, Isaac, and Mary Gertson, ...	"	xii.	67a
1771. April 15.	Hogen, Martina, and Bernardus Evertsen, . .	"	xvii.	59
1770. Feb. 26.	Hogen, Mary, and James McCrea, ...	"	xvi.	26
1762. Feb. 1.	Hogen, Mary, and William Charles, ...	"	vi.	33

Date.		Names.	Record.	Vol.	Page.
1771.	May 31.	Hogenkamp, John, and Aeltie Herring,....	M. B.,	XVII.	97
1781.	July 3.	Hogg, Elizabeth, and Charles Ortzen,.......	"	XXXII	103
1777.	April 27.	Hogg, George, and Magdalen Van Beuren,.	"	XXIV.	75a
1763.	Sept. 27.	Hogg, Robert, and Sarah Crawford,.......	"	VII.	358
1758.	May 24.	Hogge, William, and Margaret Beckee,....	"	I.	909
1763.	Oct. 3.	Hoghkarck, Isaac, and Rachel Van Sante,..	"	VII.	369
1767.	Oct. 6.	Hoghkerk, Abraham, and Anne Hilton,....	"	XII.	57
1772.	Dec. 9.	Hoghkirk, Alla, and John I. Wendell,......	"	XIX.	148
1783.	July 22.	Hoghland, Elizabeth, and Daniel Ritter,....	"	XXXIX.	99
1758.	April 21.	Hoghland, Sarah, and Jeremiah Williamson,.	"	I.	878
1764.	Oct. 19.	Hoghlandt, Adriana, and William Day,.....	"	VIII.	364
1765.	Aug. 14.	Hoghlandt, Anna, and Jeromus Bennet,....	"	IX.	235
1738	June 26.	Hoghlandt, Sarah, and Jacob Janeway, ...	"	I.	10
1761.	July 22.	Hoghtelengh, Catherine, and Daniel Winne,.	"	V.	3
1760.	Nov. 17.	Hoghtelin, David, and Helligont Vandensee,	"	III.	419
1770.	Oct. 2.	Hoghteling, Abraham, and Catherine Hasbrouck, ...	"	XVI.	202
1762.	Nov. 19.	Hoghteling, Anna, and Benjamin Delamatre,	"	VI.	446
1763.	Nov. 24.	Hoghteling, Philip, and Jannetje Eltinge,...	"	VII.	470
1761.	Jan. 14.	Hoglandt, Catherine, and Jacob Adriance,..	"	IV.	16
1782.	April 17.	Holcomb, Jechamiah, and Ruth Sealy,.....	"	XXXV.	125
1783.	June 11.	Holden, James, and Ann Watt, ...	"	XXXIX.	51
1669.	July 28.	Holdren, Denis, and Sara Wilkins, ...	O. W. L.,	II.	492
1760.	Oct. 27.	Holdridge, Mary, and John Williams,......	M. B.,	III.	382
1782.	Oct. 23.	Holdstock, Joseph, and Elizabeth Wier,....	"	XXXVII.	63
1738.	April 4.	Hollanbeck, Jane, and Benjamin Ilslee,.....	"	I.	9
1779.	May 24.	Holland, Edward, and Mary Bennet, ...	"	XXVII.	145
1762.	Mar. 19.	Holland, Elizabeth, and James Waldron,...	"	VI.	79
1758.	Jan. 6.	Holland, Elizabeth, and Tunis Vandolphson,.	"	I.	773
1757.	May 24.	Holland, Eve, and Winter Fargie,.........	"	I.	540
1768.	July 12.	Holland, James, and Catherine Finley,.....	"	XIII.	156
1760.	Mar. 17.	Holland, Jane, and Hannah Van Schaack,..	"	III.	80
1757.	Jan. 31.	Holland, Jane, and Lambert Moore,.......	"	I.	430
1781.	April 12.	Holland, John, and Elizabeth Weldridge,...	"	XXXII.	1
1770.	Aug. 9.	Holland, Margaret, and Ephraim Van Bury,	"	XVI.	156
1765.	Jan. 26.	Holland, Mary, and Jonathan Roberts,.....	"	IX.	31
1783.	May 22.	Holland, Richard, and Jane Bailey,........	"	XXXIX.	24
1737.	July 11.	Hollenback, Rachel, and James Marshall,...	"	I.	6
1767.	May 11.	Hollenbake, Maria, and Henry Dater,......	"	XI.	81
1772.	Aug. 11.	Hollet, Jane, and Anthony Betts, ...	"	XIX.	20
1763.	July 20.	Hollet, Rebecca, and Nathaniel Provoost,...	"	VII.	273
1757.	Nov. 22.	Hollet, Robert, and Lydia Pidgeon,........	"	I.	710
1761.	Jan. 13.	Hollet, Samuel, and Agness Rapelje,.......	"	IV.	14
1761.	Sept. 15.	Hollet, Sarah, and Richard Moore, ...	"	V.	83
1768.	Mar. 21.	Holley, Sarah, and Josiah Sealy,..........	"	XIII.	53

DATE.	NAMES.	RECORD.	VOL.	PAGE
1767. Sept. 2.	Holliday, John, and 'Catherine Wheeler, ...	M. B.,	XII	24
1763. May 30.	Holliday, Margaret, and John Eyles, ...	"	VII.	207
1665. Aug.' 15.	Hollis, Robert, and Mary Page,...........	O. W. L.,	II.	18
1684. Oct. 12.	Hollitt, Deliverance, and Edward Taylor,...	C. M.,	XXXIII.	54
1767. Sept. 24.	Hollock, Joshua, and Mary Peters,........	M. B.,	XII.	43
1761. Aug. 25.	Hollock, Margaret, and Henry Tiebout, ...	"	V.	55
1782. Sept. 15.	Hollondshead, Elizabeth, and Peter McMullen,	"	XXXVII.	1
1759. Nov. 21.	Hollyday, Samuel, and Hellatie Scott, ...	"	II.	512
1738. Aug. 17.	Hollyer, Margaret, and Aaron Hyatt, ...	"	I.	10
1760. May 31.	Hollyway, Isabel, and William Spotten,....	"	III.	170
1755. Sept. 16.	Hollywood, Nicholas, and Sarah Jury,.....	"	I.	177
16⅞⅝. Feb. 7.	Holmes, Alice, and William Osburne, ...	G. E.,	XXXII.	67
1761. Oct. 3.	Holmes, Anne, and John Scott,...........	M. B.,	V.	118
1762. Dec. 16.	Holmes, Deliverance, and Samuel Cotterel, .	"	VI.	484
1762. Sept. 17.	Holmes, Elizabeth, and Benjamin Lever,....	"	VI.	319
1768. April 5.	Holmes, Elizabeth, and James Cully,.......	"	XIII.	63
1773. Dec. 15.	Holmes, Elizabeth, and Thomas Lattin, ...	"	XXII.	76
1775. Dec. 21.	Holmes, Josiah, and Mary Bancker, ...	"	XXIII.	234
1760. Oct. 14.	Holmes, Mary, and James Denton,........	"	III.	362
1779. Sept. 1.	Holmes, Ninian, and Ann Mann,..........	"	XXVIII.	63
1737. Nov. 18.	Holmes, Sarah, and Edward Smith,........	"	I.	8
1738. June 17.	Holmes, Sarah, and William Lane, ...	"	I.	10
1771. April 24.	Holmes, Sarah, and William Lee, ...	"	XVII.	66
1764. June 5.	Holmes, Stephen, and Elenor Miller, ...	"	VIII.	207
1768. Dec. 21.	Holmes, Unice, and Leonard Robinson, ...	"	XIII.	271
1782. June 15.	Holmes, William, and Deborah Chadwick,..	"	XXXVI.	52
1757. July 28.	Holms, Jonathan, and Sarah Potter, ...	"	I.	606
1772. Jan. 14.	Holroyd, Turpin, and Susanna Jermond,...	"	XVIII.	13
1778. Nov. 2.	Holsman, John, and Catherina Loriat, ...	"	XXVI.	81
1757. Sept. 3.	Holt, Christopher, and Catherine Gambauld,	"	I.	631
1771. Dec. 31.	Holt, Elizabeth, and Eleazer Oswald, ...	"	XVII.	310
1761. Feb. 19.	Holt, Elizabeth, and Francis James, ...	"	IV.	71
1777. May 17.	Holtz, John, and Deborah Blake,..........	"	XXIV.	88
1770. Oct. 18.	Homan, Massey, and Thomas Hagerman,...	"	XVI.	221
1780. Nov. 23.	Homan, Morris, and Temme Platt,.........	"	XXX.	122
1772. Oct. 28.	Homen, Benjamin, Jr., and Elizabeth Noble,	"	XIX.	92
1781. Dec. 8.	Homes, Joseph, and Catharine Wintworth, .	"	XXXIV.	78
1781. Oct. 2.	Homes, Lucy, and Daniel Perine, ...	"	XXXIII.	81
1782. May 10.	Homes, Lucy, and Lewis Du Bois, ...	"	XXXV.	157
1782. Feb. 22.	Homes, Molly, and John Egberts,.........	"	XXXV.	59
1770. April 30.	Hommel, George, and Margaret Merkel,....	"	XVI.	73
1763. Dec. 12.	Hone, Philip, and Hester Bourdet, ...	"	VII.	503
1759. Nov. 15.	Honeyman, Mary, and Richard Smith,.....	"	II.	495
1762. Aug. 26.	Honeywell, Ann, and James Haviland,.....	↲	VI.	290
1768. June 27.	Honeywell, Israel, and Pheby Stevenson, ..	"	XIII.	141

DATE.	NAMES.	RECORD.	VOL.	PAGE.
1780. Jan. 24.	Honeywell, Mary, and Gilbert Pell, ...	M. B.,	XXVIII.	202
1766. Nov. 21.	Honeywill, Effeme, and Elvin Hunt,.......	"	X.	175
1783. Sept. 28.	Honseal, Michael, and Mary Shand (Strand),	"	XXXVII.	18
1761. Jan. 19.	Hoobbard, Margaret, and Ebenezer Wood,..	"	XIV.	15
1761. July 2.	Hooff, Jemmima, and Arent Van Dyck,....	"	IV.	273
1738. April 1.	Hooffa, Orionta, and Mathias Van Dyck, ...	"	I.	9
1771. Aug. 28.	Hoofman, Eve, and James McDavit, ...	"	XVII.	166
1753. Sept. 14.	Hoofman, Maritje, and John Ten Brook, ...	"	I.	118
1771. June 3.	Hoog, Thomas Andrew, and Maria Wilhelmina Ritzema,......................	"	XVII.	100
1736. Aug. 2.	Hoogeboom, Maria, and Jochem Van Valkenburgh, ...	"	I.	2
1760. Oct. 7.	Hoogeland, Abraham, and Mary Hegeman,.	"	III.	353
1767. April 29.	Hoogeland, Cornelia, and John Freeland,...	"	XI.	73
1773. Nov. 4.	Hoogen, Maria, and Albert Meebie, ...	"	XXII.	11
1764. Nov. 12.	Hooghtclin, Hester, and Albert Vander Zee, Jr., ...	"	VIII.	402
1765. Oct. 21.	Hooghtelingh, Coenradt, and Sarah Van Sleght,.............................	"	IX.	333
1768. May 25.	Hooghtelle, Arriantje, and David Seyver, ..	"	XIII.	114
1762. Aug. 16.	Hooghtclyn, Mary, and Joel Du Bois, ...	"	VI.	274
1766. Oct. 21.	Houghtyling, Catherine, and Martin Burger,	"	X.	132
1780. June 28.	Hoogland, Cornelius, and Elizabeth Lester, .	"	XXIX.	101
1772. Mar. 30.	Hoogland, Helen, and Peter Ven Der Bilt,..	"	XVIII.	64
1770. Sept. 5.	Hoogland, Oliver, and Susannah Ludlow,...	"	XVI.	179
1768. Oct. 12.	Hoogland, William, and Margaret Wood,...	"	XIII.	207
1738. Sept. 2.	Hooglandt, Abraham, and Anne Derye,....	"	I.	11
1769. Dec. 18.	Hooglandt, Catharina, and Abraham Schenck,	"	XV.	126
1737. April 30.	Hooglandt, Cornelius, and Sarah Woertman,	"	I.	6
1770. Nov. 30.	Hooglandt, Phebe, and Gabriel Duryea,....	"	XVI.	276
1736. June 19.	Hooglandt, William, and Altie Brinkerhuff,.	"	I.	1
1771. Jan. 3.	Hooglar, Elizabeth, and Lewis Guion,......	"	XVII.	309
1738. Oct. 11.	Hoogteeling, Rachel, and Leonard Hardenberg, ...	"	I.	11
1760. Oct. 14.	Hoome, David, and Mary Wiley,..........	"	III.	364
1761. Oct. 1.	Hooper, Elizabeth, and John Marshall,.....	"	V.	112
1767. Sept. 25.	Hooper, Jacob Roeters, and Judith Dillin, ..	"	XII.	45
1757. April 27.	Hoornbeek, Lodewyck, and Naomy Codebeek, ...	"	I.	518
1753. July 12.	Hoes, Barent, and Jannetie Van Valkenbergh, ...	"	I.	75
1782. April 7.	Hooton, John, and Rachael Mott,.........	"	XXXV.	117
1759. Dec. 10.	Hope, Catherine, and James Richards,.....	"	II.	536
1776. Mar. 1.	Hope, Elizabeth, and James Long, ...	"	XXIII.	276
1755. Sept. 20.	Hope, Elizabeth, and Peter Wessels, ...	"	I.	180

DATE.	NAMES.	RECORD.	VOL.	PAGE.
1759. Dec. 8.	Hope, Elizabeth, and William Richardson,..	M. B.,	II.	533
1781. Aug. 22.	Hopkins, Easter, and Samuel Carpenter, ...	"	XXXIII.	44
1759. May 14.	Hopkins, George, and Mary Van Sice,.....	"	II.	282
1762. April 8.	Hopkins, Hannah, and John Trip,.........	"	VI.	97
1765. Jan. 10.	Hopkins, John, and Elizabeth Phisong, ...	"	IX.	14
1770. Dec. 18.	Hopkins, Martha, and Benjamin Downing,..	"	XVI.	299
1755. Oct. 3.	Hopkins, Mary, and David Tilley,.........	"	I.	187
1759. Sept. 3.	Hopkins, Mary, and William Taylor, ...	"	II.	408
1772. Dec. 28.	Hopkins, Samuel, and Elizabeth Robinson, .	"	XIX.	164
1780. Nov. 6.	Hopkins, Samuel, and Elizabeth Wood- hull,............	"	XXX.	94
1736. Dec. 22.	Hopkins, Sarah, and Joseph Merritt,.......	"	I.	5
1764. Jan. 3.	Hopkins, Sarah, and Joseph Robinson,.....	"	VIII.	3
1736. Oct. 25.	Hopkins, Sarah, and Michael Mudge,......	"	I.	3
1738. May 5.	Hopkins, Thomas, and Margaret Pine,.....	"	I.	9
1779. May 29.	Hopkins, William, and Elizabeth Down- ing, ...	"	XXVII.	151
1777. July 10.	Hopkins, William, and Mary Sands, ...	"	XXIV.	118
1760. Aug. 18.	Hopper, Abraham, and Mary Egberts, ...	"	III.	258
1760. June 30.	Hopper, Alltie, and Cornelius Vorhis,......	"	III.	201
1758. Jan. 23.	Hopper, Andrew, and Catharine Steymets,..	"	I.	799
1782. Jan. 25.	Hopper, Ann, and Cornelious Horsen, ...	"	XXXV.	32
1766. July 19.	Hopper, Edward, and Dorothy Farrington,.	"	X.	57
1736. Oct. 22.	Hopper, Edward, and Elizabeth Salya,.....	"	I.	3
1759. Sept. 26.	Hopper, Elenor, and Samuel Hopson, ...	"	II.	433
1757. Oct. 8.	Hopper, Elizabeth, and James Mullen, ...	"	I.	663
1775. Sept. 7.	Hopper, Jane, and Robert Carter,.........	"	XXIII.	151
1770. June 22.	Hopper, Jemima, and John Horn,.........	"	XVI.	121
1759. Dec. 8.	Hopper, Jemime, and John McDonnald,....	"	II.	534
1759. April 19.	Hopper, John, and Wyntje Dyckman, ...	"	II.	246
1685. Aug. 17.	Hopper, Joseph, and Jannitie Cornelis,.....	C. M.,	XXXIII.	154
1780. Sept. 23.	Hopper, Mary, and James Striker,........	M. B.,	XXX.	40
1764. Nov. 12.	Hopper, Mary, and John Pickton,.........	"	VIII.	403
1778. Nov. 20.	Hopper, Mary, and Lawrance Ohlwine,....	"	XXVI.	90
1760. Mar. 7.	Hopper, Mary, and Thomas Canpi, ...	"	III.	67
1763. June 18.	Hopper, Mathew, and Anna Christina,.....	"	VII.	233
1760. Feb. 27.	Hopper, Matthew, and Mary Hugens,......	"	III.	55
1760. Jan. 24.	Hopper, Wessell, and Oliker Dyckman,.....	"	III.	5
1759. July 10.	Hopper, Yalloss, and Elizabeth Waldron,...	"	II.	352
1765. Aug. 10.	Hopson, Alice, and John Lawell,..........	"	IX.	258
1757. Mar. 8.	Hopson, George, and Seviah Speedy,......	"	I.	461
1763. Jan. 28.	Hopson, Mary, and John Van Zandt,.......	"	VII.	38
1759. Sept. 28.	Hopson, Samuel, and Elenor Hopper,......	"	II.	433
1761. Feb. 28.	Hopson, Samuel, and Margaret Savage,....	"	IV.	86
1777. July 7.	Hopton, Catherine, and Francis Corry,.....	"	XXIV.	115

DATE.	NAMES.	RECORD.	VOL.	PAGE.
1773. April 16.	Horenbeek, Maria, and Jacob de Witt Schonmaker, ...	M. B.,	xx.	93
1770. June 22.	Horn, John, and Jemima Hopper, ...	"	xvi.	121
1775. May 30.	Hornbeeck, Catherine, and Andrew Witbeeck, ...	"	xxiii.	48
1772. Aug. 12.	Hornbeek, James, and Eaddy Bratt, ...	"	xix.	22
1772. July 21.	Hornbeek, Matthias, and Mary Miller, ...	"	xix.	4
1780. April 8.	Hornby, Ellen, and Thomas Williams, ...	"	xxix.	15
1778. Dec. 27.	Horne, Rachel, and William Johnston, ...	"	xxvi.	134
1783. Nov. 5.	Horner, Charlotte, and John Munds, ...	"	xl.	105
1772. Aug. 14.	Horner, James, and Mary McGraw, ...	"	xix.	23
1760. Mar. 13.	Hornsen, Ann, and Phillip Norris, ...	"	iii.	76
1773. Nov. 26.	Horse, Catharine, and John Sinclair, ...	"	xxii.	47
1765. Feb. 22.	Horsefield, Joseph, and Sarah Whitehead,...	"	ix.	57
1779. Jan. 22.	Horsefield, Sarah, and Richard Carman, ...	"	xxvii.	22
1764. July 27.	Horsefield, Thomas, and Ann Peters, ...	"	viii.	269
1761. Sept. 9.	Horseman, Catharine, and Robert McDowall,	"	v.	76
1782. Jan. 25.	Horsen, Cornelious, and Anne Hopper, ...	"	xxxv.	32
1773. Jan. 19.	Horsen, Jacob, and Catherine Cozine, ...	"	xx.	13
1775. May 24.	Horser, Catharine, and Tunis Somarindyke,.	"	xxiii.	42
1772. Feb. 25.	Horser, Cornelia, and Michael Varian, ...	"	xviii.	42
1761. Mar. 31.	Horsfield, William, and Mary Hewlet, ...	"	iv.	126
1775. May 16.	Horsford, Eleanor, and Samuel Pruyn, ...	"	xxiii.	35
1770. Feb. 24.	Horton, Anne, and Thomas Barker, ...	"	xvi.	24
1782. Sept. 21.	Horton, Bethiah, and John Hubbard,... ..	"	xxxvii.	9
1768. May 19.	Horton, Elizabeth Paulding, and Abraham Outen Bogert, ...	"	xiii.	108
1782. Dec. 28.	Horton, James, and Anne Styne, ...	"	xxxvii.	135
1760. Aug. 29.	Horton, Jonathan, and Guertry Purdy, ...	"	iii.	273
1769. July 4.	Horton, Michael, and Elizabeth Esselstyn,..	"	xiv.	141
1761. Aug. 4.	Horton, Nathan, and Freelove Wright, ...	"	v.	23
1773. Sept. 10.	Horton, Sarah, and Samuel Townsend, ...	"	xxi.	104
1773. Nov. 26.	Horton, Stephen, and Elizabeth Frost, ...	"	xxii.	48
1758. Nov. 22.	Horton, Tamer, and Morris Salts, ...	"	ii.	103
1763. Jan. 21.	Horton, Underhill, and Susannah Crawford,.	"	vii.	28
1772. June 29.	Hortwick, Lawrence, and Anne Rivers, ...	"	xviii.	152
1763. May 7.	Horwser, Mary, and Philip Miller, ...	"	vii.	169
1737. Oct. 12.	Hosbrook, Sarah, and William Osterheet,...	"	i.	7
1759. Oct. 31.	Hosler, Sarah, and James Brewster, ...	"	ii.	482
1782. Sept. 30.	Hosser, Mary, and James Rikeman, ...	"	xxxvii.	21
1770. May 31.	Houghtaling, Arreantie, and Everardus Bogardus, ...	"	xvi.	98
1765. Oct. 17.	Houghteling, Maritie, and John C. Kingland,	"	ix.	307
1770. Feb. 20.	Houghton, John, and Susannah Dodge, ...	"	xvi.	25
1769. April 10.	Houghton, Mary, and John McDowl, ...	"	xiv.	67

Date.	Names.	Record.	Vol.	Page.
1770. Nov. 11.	Hougland, Jane, and John Byvanck, ...	M. B.,	xvi.	59
1760. Jan. 11.	Hounam, James, and Margaret Steward, . . .	"	ii.	577
1767. Sept. 7.	Hous, Henry, and Jane Vosburgh, ...	"	xii.	28
1777. Feb. 9.	House, Ann, and Edward Dawkins, ...	"	xxiv.	27
1760. May 14.	Houseman, Aart, and Elizabeth Morschalk, .	"	iii.	151
1764. Mar. 2.	Houseman, Elizabeth, and Edward Blake, . .	"	viii.	90
1783. Oct. 8.	Houseman, John, and Uzeley Burkdaff, . . .	"	xl.	71
1780. Dec. 30.	Houseman, Mary, and John Tysen, ...	"	xxx.	174
1777. July 3.	Houseman, William, and Elizabeth Barnett, .	"	xxiv.	111
1772. May 13.	Housman, Peter, and Lena Kruse, ...	"	xviii.	117
1778. Dec. 7.	Houston, Alexander, and Janet Coyd, ...	"	xxvi.	113
1761. May 29.	Houston, Ann, and William Stewart, ...	"	iv.	215
1765. Sept. 30.	Houtvat, Margarita, and John Smith, ...	"	ix.	281
1768. Sept. 13.	Houtvat, Susannah Catherine, and Thomas Simpson, ...	"	xiii.	183
1757. Oct. 5.	Houtvatt, Elizabeth, and Joshua Paine, ...	"	i.	657
1769. June 17.	Houwy, Alida, and Cornelius Waldron, ...	"	xiv.	116
1778. Aug. 5.	Howard, Abraham, and Sarah Ross, ...	"	xxv.	143
1758. Jan. 5.	Howard, Edward, and Abigail Coe, ...	"	i.	769
1771. May 9.	Howard, Elizabeth, and William Cousin, ...	"	xvii.	81
1670. Feb. 7.	Howard, Esther, and Alexander Bennett Cooper, ...	C. A.,	ii.	639
1757. Aug. 24.	Howard, John, and Elizabeth Bowne, ...	M. B.,	i.	622
1783. June 29.	Howard, Joseph, and Jane Duryee, ...	"	xxxix.	71
1757. Oct. 15.	Howard, Judith, and Isaac Lawrence, ...	"	i.	672
1670. Mar. 9.	Howard, Louis, and Richard Frazer, ...	C. A.,	ii.	655
1764. Mar. 12.	Howard, Margaret, and Robert Munrow, . . .	M. B.,	viii.	101
1765. Aug. 15.	Howard, Phebe, and Philip Pine, ...	"	ix.	239
1753. Oct. 8.	Howard, Richard, and Mary Hitchcock, ...	"	i.	133
1764. July 10.	Howard, Ruth, and James Smith, ...	"	viii.	254
1783. June 16.	Howard, Samuel, and Ann Teple, ...	"	xxxix.	61
1772. Dec. 23.	Howard, Sarah, and Jacob Pozer, ...	"	xix.	163
1772. Aug. 11.	Howard, Sarah, and Thomas Mitchell Forrest, ...	"	xix.	19
1763. Mar. 4.	Howard, Thomas, and Catharine Jabwaine, '	"	vii.	88
1760. Feb. 13.	Howbran, Mary, and John Moor, ...	"	iii.	35
1773. Jan. 28.	Howell, Abigail, and Joshua Hartt, ...	"	xx.	27
1770. April 4.	Howell, Ann, and John Eaglin, ...	"	xvi.	48
1761. April 28.	Howell, Hannah, and Stephen Rogers, ...	"	iv.	172
1767. Oct. 1.	Howell, Hezekiah, and Julianna Woodhull, .	"	xii.	52
1761. Jan. 30.	Howell, James, and Juliana De Kay, ...	"	iv.	42
1758. Oct. 30.	Howell, Mary, and Josiah Smith, ...	"	ii.	73
1781. Sept. 13.	Howell, Mary, and Thomas Lear Harman, . .	"	xxxiii.	62
1757. Nov. 17.	Howell, Mathew, and Margaret Carr, ...	"	i.	706
1769. Aug. 12.	Howell, Phebe, and Arthur Parks, ...	"	xv.	21

Date.		Names.	Record.	Vol. Page.
1760. Dec.	15.	Howell, Phebe, and Edward Hoy,.........	M. B.,	iii. 475
1775. Nov.	15.	Howell, Phebe, and Thomas Sandford,.....	"	xxiii. 210
1769. April	25.	Howell, Stephen, and Susannah Smith,.....	"	xiv. 86
1773. Sept.	20.	Howell, Susannah, and Thomas Moffet, ...	"	xxi. 112
1762. Mar.	18.	Howell, Thomas, and Anne Blum,........	"	vi. 76
1762. June	23.	Howell, Thomas, and Anne Colton,.......	"	vi. 205
1761. July	6.	Hower, Philip, and Jane Finney,..........	"	iv. 281
1776. Feb.	6.	Howes, Margaret, and Peter Switzer, ...	"	xxiii. 262
1772. Oct.	21.	Howetson, James, and Engeltje Wendel, ...	"	xix. 82
1757. June	8.	Howghteling, Thomas, and Elizabeth Whitbeck, ...	"	i. 558
1736. Oct.	26.	Howlent, Elizabeth, and Nicolas Clarke,....	"	i. 3
1759. Dec.	1.	Howse, Jane, and William Bryant,........	"	ii. 524
1760. Dec.	15.	Hoy, Edward, and Phebe Howell,.........	"	iii. 475
1753. May	17.	Hoyer, Peter, and Elizabeth Telyou,.......	"	i. 31
1778. Oct.	30.	Hoyer, Rebecca, and Thomas Snowdon,....	"	xxvi. 76
1763. Jan.	22.	Hoyct, Jonathan, and Elizabeth Rogers,....	"	vii. 31
1756. Dec.	16.	Hubbard, Adriantie, and Adriaen Voorhees,.	"	i. 387
1765. Oct.	28.	Hubbard, Ariantje, and Jacobus Lake,......	"	ix. 327
1756. Nov.	16.	Hubbard, Bernardus, and Neeltje Lake,....	"	i. 356
1769. April	7.	Hubbard, Catherine, and Peter Sierget,....	"	xiv. 66
1670. Mar.	2.	Hubbard, Edward, and Martha Turner,....	C. A.,	ii. 655
1770. May	16.	Hubbard, Hannah, and Hendrick Hendrickson, ...	M. B.,	xvi. 87
1682. Jan.	31.	Hubbard, Jeremiah, and Rebecca Brush,....	G. E.,	xxxiii. 33
1782. Sept.	21.	Hubbard, John, and Bethiah Horton, ...	M. D.,	xxxvii. 9
1762. July	1.	Hubbard, John, and Mary Tyrrel,.........	"	vi. 221
1762. Oct.	13.	Hubbard, John, and Sarah Skilman,.......	"	vi. 362
1774. Mar.	12.	Hubbard, Samuel, and Antje Emens,......	"	xxii. 145
1664. Dec.	29.	Hubbart, James, and Elizabeth Bayly, ...	G. E.,	i. 85
1775. Sept.	19.	Hubbedd, Mercy, and Isaac Latham,.......	M. B.,	xxiii. 159
1764. Feb.	13.	Hubbs, Jacobus, and Mary Blatsley,.......	"	viii. 59
1764. Oct.	10.	Hubbs, Job, and Phebe Smith,...........	"	viii. 363
1782. Nov.	25.	Hubbs, Robert, and Jane Haviland,........	"	xxxvii. 93
1775. June	22.	Hubbs, Sarah, and Joseph Wilson,........	"	xxiii. 73
1772. Oct.	19.	Hubner, George, and Mary Size,..........	"	xix. 78
1782. Aug.	28.	Huchinson, Catharine, and Robert Roberts,.	"	xxxvi. 127
1772. Sept.	29.	Huck, Catherine, and John Ver Planck,....	"	xix. 61
1765. Jan.	7.	Huck, Cornelia, and John Whitbeeck,......	"	ix. 11
1782. May	9.	Huck, Elizabeth, and John Swift,.........	"	xxxv. 156
1782. June	7.	Huck, Michael, and Mary Van Horne,.....	"	xxxvi. 41
1771. Oct.	23.	Huck, Nicholas, and Jenny Williams,......	"	xvii. 219
1760. Oct.	7.	Hudden, William, and Phebe Cheeseman, ..	"	iii. 350
1762. Oct.	25.	Hudson, Caleb, and Susanna Cross,........	"	vi. 383
1759. Sept.	14.	Hudson, Frances, and John Carter,........	"	ii. 420

25

DATE.	NAMES.	RECORD.	VOL.	PAGE.
1768. Aug. 10.	Hudson, Frederick, and Sarah Youngs, ...	M. B.,	XIII.	173
1761. Mar. 31.	Hudson, William, and Elenor Murphy, ...	"	IV.	125
1772. Jan. 13.	Hueick, Elbertie, and Tobias Van Bueren, ..	' "	XX.	8
1778. Dec. 10.	Huestis, Edward, and Hanah McConnell,...	"	XXVI.	118
1757. April 22.	Huestus, Patty, and James Boyd, ...	"	I.	511
1736. Nov. 22.	Huff, Catherine, and Isaac German, ...	"	I.	3
1781. Oct. 21.	Huff, Gamaliel, and Jane Cutler,..........	"	XXXIV.	2
1757. Feb. 22.	Huff, Hannah, and Richard Burdg, ...	"	I.	448
1762. Sept. 1.	Huff, Henry, and Susannah Hyatt,........	"	VI.	301
1736. July 26.	Huff, Lawrence, and Susannah German,....	"	I.	2
1782. April 29.	Huff, Uriah, and Deborah Townsend,......	"	XXXV.	144
1760. May 22.	Hugeford, Mary, and Amos Dodge, ...	"	III.	162
1760. Feb. 27.	Hugens, Mary, and Mathew Hopper, ...	"	III.	55
1768. Nov. 7.	Hugeny, Margrietta, and Abraham C. Vosburgh, ...	"	XIII.	229
1758. Oct. 14.	Huger, Catrina, and Johannes Mauritius Goetschius, ...	"	II.	56
1781. Oct. 27.	Huggeford, Martha, and Elias Hardy,......	"	XXXIV.	9
1767. Oct. 28.	Huggeford, Sarah, and Elijah Drake,.......	"	XII.	72
1781. Nov. 27.	Huggerford, Thamar, and Henry Bogert,...	"	XXXIV.	61
1778. Aug. 11.	Huggins, Mary, and William Appleton, ...	"	XXVI.	2
1774. Mar. 2.	Huggins, Sarah Child, and Edwin Goold,...	"	XXII.	138
1763. Aug. 5.	Hughes, Catharine, and James Simpson,....	"	VII.	292
1770. Aug. 25.	Hughes, Hannah, and Samuel Tate, ...	"	XVI.	171
1761. July 6.	Hughes, James, and Phebe Lowther, ...	"	IV.	284
1765. Aug. 5.	Hughes, John, and Mary Denniston,.......	"	IX.	254
1756. Sept. 30.	Hughes, Jonathan, and Catharine Anderson,	"	I.	293
1764. Dec. 6.	Hughes, Margaret, and Robert Johnson,....	"	VIII.	441
1763. June 6.	Hughes, Meredith, and Margaret Humphries,	"	VII.	214
1762. Jan. 2.	Hughes, Nathaniel, and Eleanor Stuart,....	"	VI.	1
1761. June 5.	Hughes, Nathaniel, and Sarah Langford, ...	"	IV.	196
1762. Oct. 18.	Hughes, William, and Mary Armstrong,....	"	VI.	371
1773. Sept. 21.	Hugner, Mary, and John Clute, ...	"	XXI.	113
1781. Jan. 6.	Hugunie, Daniel, and Mary Garabrants,....	"	XXXI.	14
1759. May 23.	Huick, Andries, and Lenah Shaver,........	"	II.	289
1770. Oct. 12.	Huick, Burger, and Elizabeth Goes,........	"	XVI.	209
1755. Sept. 12.	Huick, Direck, and Sarah Vanduersen,.....	"	I.	174
1758. Dec. 4.	Huise, Anneke, and William Carr, ...	"	II.	113
1764. Sept. 12.	Huleat, Rebecca, and John Mitchell,.......	"	VIII.	304
1738. April 21.	Hulet, Benjamin, and Susannah Whitehead,	"	I.	9
1769. Jan. 9.	Hewlett, Daniel, and Mary Mott, ...	"	XIV.	7
1758. April 24.	Hulet, Hannah, and Joshua Cornwall, ...	"	I.	884
173⅞. Jan. 13.	Hulet, John, and Elizabeth Dosenbury, ...	"	I.	8
1761. Oct. 17.	Hulet, William, and Abigail Still,..........	"	V.	144
1780. Nov. 21.	Hulett, Elizabeth, and William Maffett, ...	"	XXX.	119

DATE.		NAMES.	RECORD.	VOL.	PAGE.
1775. Nov.	8.	Hulett, Samuel, and Ruth Willis, ...	M. B.,	XXIII.	201
173⅞. Feb.	7.	Hulit, Sarah, and Timothy Townsend, ...	"	I.	8
1781. Juno	9.	Hull, John, and Mary Avery,.............	"	XXXII.	79
1769. Oct.	26.	Hull, Robert, and Elizabeth Barnard,......	"	XV.	68
1758. Sept.	14.	Hull, Stelle, and Hanah Winter,..........	"	II.	21
1781. June	9.	Hulse, Ruth, and Ephraim Smith,.........	"	XXXII.	78
1771. Sept.	7.	Hulse, Thomas, and Margaret Sweesy,.....	"	XVII.	177
1768. May	9.	Hum, Peter, and Mary Michel, ...	"	XIII.	97
1736. Mar.	21.	Humble, Sarah, and David Griffith, ...	"	I.	5
1781. May	8.	Hume, James, and Patty Remsen, ...	"	XXXII.	35
1781. Dec.	24.	Humpherville, Lamira, and Theophilus Chamberlain, ...	"	XXXIV.	101
1767. May	26.	Humphrevil, Timothy, and Elizabeth Reed, .	"	XI.	97
1763. Nov.	28.	Humphrey, Agnes, and James McClaughry,	"	VII.	476
1766. July	5.	Humphrey, Ester, and John Burnet,.......	"	X.	42
1762. Nov.	16.	Humphreys, George, and Catherine Bennet,	"	VI.	434
1759. Nov.	16.	Humphreys, Thomas, and Mary Darcey, ...	"	II.	498
1763. June	6.	Humphries, Margaret, and Meredith Hughes,	"	VII.	214
1763. April	28.	Humphries, Morris, and Judith Woodby,...	"	VII.	153
1771. Nov.	9.	Humphrys, Henry, and Sarah Gardner,....	"	XVII.	244
1761. Mar.	25.	Humphrys, Mary, and Moses Knap,.......	"	IV.	118
1773. Nov.	16.	Hun, Catlina, and Isaac Bogert,...........	"	XXII.	30
1757. April	19.	Hun, Elsie, and Philip Lansing,...........	"	I.	505
1765. Mar.	18.	Hun, John, and Catharine Tigley, ...	"	IX.	70
1758. Nov.	22.	Hun, Majeka, and Cornelius Van Buren,....	"	II.	102
1761. July	16.	Hun, Thomas I., and Elisabeth Wendell,...	"	IV.	299
1759. Aug.	1.	Hun, William, and Sarah Deforeest, ...	"	II.	369
1762. Nov.	17.	Hunn, Jane, and Volkert Van Veghten,....	"	VI.	440
1761. Oct.	21.	Hunn, Thomas, and Baatja Van Deusen,....	"	V.	160
1768. Nov.	4.	Hunt, Ann, and Robert Hunt, Jr.,.........	"	XIII.	224
1764. Nov.	21.	Hunt, Arnold, and Phebe Hunt,..........	"	VIII.	415
1778. Dec.	31.	Hunt, Benjamin, and Elizabeth Gidney,....	"	XXVI.	136
1783. Aug.	21.	Hunt, Catharine, and Robert Bulfill Carre,.	"	XL.	5
1779. July	27.	Hunt, Charity, and Philip Dally,..........	"	XXVIII.	30
1762. Oct.	22.	Hunt, Elisabeth, and William Rodgers,....	"	VI.	357
1760. Mar.	17.	Hunt, Elizabeth, and John Steuart,........	"	III.	81
1764. June	8.	Hunt, Elizabeth, and Shadrach Chatterdon,.	"	VIII.	218
1762. Sept.	10.	Hunt, Elnathan, and Mary Bishop,........	"	VI.	310
1758. Jan.	20.	Hunt, Elnathan, and Mary Nelson,........	"	I.	792
1766. Nov.	21.	Hunt, Elven, and Effeme Honeywill,......	"	X.	175
1772. April	16.	Hunt, Eudocia, and Lancaster Underhill,...	"	XVIII.	80
1773. Jan.	15.	Hunt, Euphemia, and Gilbert Williams,....	"	XX.	9
1780. Nov.	16.	Hunt, Gilbert, and Mary Bashford,........	"	XXX.	110
1766 June	6.	Hunt, Gilead, and Sarah Ferris,...........	"	X.	8
1761. Jan.	15.	Hunt, Grizell, and John Moore,...........	"	IV.	19

DATE.		NAMES.	RECORD.	VOL.	PAGE.
1778. Dec.	10.	Hunt, Hanah, and James Brundige,.......	M. B.,	XXVI.	117
1761. Sept.	1.	Hunt, Hannah, and Elihu Archer,.........	"	V.	66
1753. Sept.	7.	Hunt, John, and Phebe Williams,.........	"	I.	110
1764. Feb.	3.	Hunt, John, Jr., and Jane Ryan,..........	"	VIII.	47
1775. Oct.	11.	Hunt, Joseph, and Elizabeth Halstead,.....	"	XXIII.	178
1768. Feb.	11.	Hunt, Joshua, and Mary Simmons,........	"	XIII.	33
1762. Jan.	28.	Hunt, Keziah, and Ebenezer Burling,......	"	VI.	27
1761. Feb.	20.	Hunt, Keziah, and Jacob Wilkins,.........	"	IV.	73
1763. July	14.	Hunt, Levy, and Sarah Valentine,.........	"	VII.	264
1782. Sept.	7.	Hunt, Lidey, and Beriah Hartshorn,.......	"	XXXVI.	139
1772. Sept.	21.	Hunt, Margaret, and John Stout, Jr.,......	"	XIX.	53
1758. Mar.	8.	Hunt, Mariam, and John Field,...........	"	I.	837
1773. July	1.	Hunt, Martha, and Samuel Thorn,.........	"	XXI.	28
1781. May	10.	Hunt, Mary, and Abijah Barker,..........	"	XXXII.	40
1768. July	2.	Hunt, Mary, and James Smith,...........	"	XIII.	147
1772. July	8.	Hunt, Mary, and Jeremiah Regan,.........	"	XVIII.	160
1759. Mar.	26.	Hunt, Mary, and John Pugsley,...........	"	II.	224
1756. Dec.	15.	Hunt, Mianah, and John Ferris,..........	"	I.	385
1756. Dec.	11.	Hunt, Nathaniel, and Sarah Peets,........	"	I.	380
1772. Mar.	18.	Hunt, Peter, and Matilda Bowne,.........	"	XVIII.	54
1764. Nov.	21.	Hunt, Phebe, and Arnold Hunt,..........	"	VIII.	415
1758. Oct.	18.	Hunt, Phebe, and Joseph Drake,..........	"	II.	61
1759. Sept.	19.	Hunt, Phebe, and Samuel Warner,........	"	II.	427
1779. Mar.	3.	Hunt, Phila, and Isaac Devoe,...........	"	XXVII.	54
1775. Oct.	9.	Hunt, Philena, and Benjamin Palmer,.....	"	XXIII.	177
1763. June	9.	Hunt, Phineas, and Sarah Rich,...........	"	VII.	218
1779. Feb.	25.	Hunt, Rachel, and Michael Sloot,.........	"	XXVII.	50
1768. Nov.	4.	Hunt, Robert, Jr., and Ann Hunt,.........	"	XIII.	224
1761. Oct.	21.	Hunt, Samuel, and Catharine French,......	"	V.	158
1753. July	5.	Hunt, Sarah, and Gilbert Drew,..........	"	I.	73
1761. May	30.	Hunt, Sarah, and Solomon Fowler,........	"	IV.	217
1766. July	16.	Hunt, Solomon, and Mary Sutton,........	"	X.	52
1761. Nov.	2.	Hunt, Susannah, and Daniel Knap,........	"	V.	188
1772. Mar.	25.	Hunt, Susannah, and Gabriel Archer,......	"	XVIII.	57
1771. Aug.	28.	Hunt, Susannah, and Joseph Peirson,......	"	XVII.	167
1755. Nov.	15.	Hunt, Susannah, and Samuel Brouckman,..	"	I.	209
1738. July	21.	Hunt, Susannah, and Thomas Palmer,.....	"	I.	10
1768. Jan.	16.	Hunt, Thamar, and Gilbert Pell,..........	"	XIII.	9
1783. Sept.	22.	Hunt, Theodosius, and Elizabeth Moore,...	"	XL.	49
1779. Sept.	18.	Hunt, Thomas, and Elizabeth Bashford,....	"	XXVIII.	82
1737. Dec.	2.	Hunt, Thomas, and Mary Pattrick,........	"	I.	8
1758. Jan.	20.	Hunt, Thomas, and Mileson Wright,......	"	I.	794
1756. Nov.	18.	Hunt, Thomas, and Rachel Pears,.........	"	I.	360
1758. Nov.	29.	Hunt, Timothy, and Sarah Drake,.........	"	II.	107
1765. Oct.	31.	Hunt, William, and Mary Storm,..........	"	IX.	348

DATE.	NAMES.	RECORD.	VOL.	PAGE.
1761. May 29.	Hunt, William, and Susannah Fowler,.....	M. B.,	IV.	216
1779. Dec. 23.	Hunt, Williams, and Hester Gidney,.......	"	XXVIII.	177
1780. Nov. 16.	Hunten, William, and Susannah Campbell,..	"	XXX.	109
1765. May 20.	Hunter, Agnes, and William Wallace,......	"	IX.	134
1781. Sept. 25.	Hunter, Anne, and Robert Graham,.......	"	XXXIII.	78
1763. Nov. 2.	Hunter, Elenor, and Christopher Sweedland,	"	VII.	426
1768. Sept. 28.	Hunter, Elijah, and Anne Drake,.........	"	XIII.	198
1737. June 4.	Hunter, Elizabeth, and John Ward, ...	"	I.	6
1760. Nov. 13.	Hunter, Elizabeth, and William Taylor,....	"	III.	408
1781. Oct. 12.	Hunter, George, and Ann Bennet,.........	"	XXXIII.	99
1757. April 12.	Hunter, Joseph, and Margaret Burnet,.....	"	I.	498
1769. Feb. 16.	Hunter, Mary, and John Schuyler,........	"	XIV.	35
1737. Nov. 19.	Hunter, Rachael, and Edward Smith,......	"	I.	8
1777. Dec. 16.	Hunter, Rachel, and James Galbreath,.....	"	XXIV.	198
1764. Oct. 9.	Hunter, William, and Eleanor McNeil,.....	"	VIII.	343
1780. Nov. 6.	Hunting, Zeruihia, and Zebulon Jessup,....	"	XXX.	93
1757. Aug. 5.	Hunton, Mary, and David Osborne,........	"	I.	609
1771. July 1.	Hurd, Ralph, and Susannah Rofft,.........	"	XVII.	127
1773. Dec. 9.	Hurley, Elizabeth, and Nicholas Connery,..	"	XIX.	149
1758. April 7.	Hurley, William, and Elizabeth Mills,......	"	I.	871
1783. Jan. 29.	Hurry, Frances, and Amos Lefurge,.......	"	XXXVIII.	81
1780. Dec. 6.	Hurst, Henry, and Margaret Waley,.......	"	XXX.	139
1761. Dec. 3.	Hurtman, Mary, and Frederick Shannort,..	"	V.	262
1783. Jan. 18.	Husbands, William, and Jane Ryals, ...	"	XXXVIII.	22
1772. Oct. 15.	Husk, Lydia, and David Post,.............	"	XIX.	71
1767. Jan. 27.	Huskins, Hannah, and John Cockle, Jr.,....	"	XI.	15
1772. April 24.	Huskins, William, and Anna Hagerman,...	"	XVIII.	91
1765. June 23.	Huson, Mary, and Michael Kortright,......	"	IX.	181
1684. June 15.	Hussy, Elizabeth, and William Haines,.....	C. M.,	XXXI.	151
1760. Oct. 7.	Hussy, Richard, and Elizabeth German,....	M. B.,	III.	347
1765. Jan. 30.	Hustice, David, and Abigal Morgan,.......	"	IX.	35
1781. Jan. 12.	Hustick (Husten), Mary, and Thomas Acres,	"	XXXI.	20
1771. Dec. 5.	Huston, George, and Elizabeth Quick,.....	"	XVII.	284
1760. April 24.	Hutchens, Ann, and Adam Trout,.........	"	III.	123
1764. Nov. 14.	Hutchings, Amos, and Mary Ellison,......	"	VIII.	407
1778. July 11.	Hutchings, John, and Mary Stogdell,......	"	XXV.	128
1779. Dec. 27.	Hutchings, William, and Margaret Ross,....	"	XXVIII.	182
1783. May 27.	Hutchins, Abigail, and James Stinet,......	"	XXXIX.	26
1763. June 15.	Hutchins, Abigal, and William Judkins, ...	"	VII.	230
1775. Aug. 11.	Hutchins, Charity, and William Tillman,...	"	XXIII.	123
1758. Sept. 12.	Hutchins, Deborah, and John Sullivan,.....	"	II.	17
1782. May 4.	Hutchins, John, and Catharine Remsen,....	"	XXXV.	150
1780. Sept. 8.	Hutchins, Jonathan, and Jane Bissett,.....	"	XXX.	20
1762. Nov. 13.	Hutchins, Jonathan, and Letitia Langdon,..	"	VI.	432
1766. Nov. 14.	Hutchins, Sarah, and Lewis Seely,........	"	X.	164

DATE.	NAMES.	RECORD.	VOL.	PAGE.
1671. Sept. 13.	Hutchinson, Agnes, and Daniel Sutton,....	G. E.,	IV.	31
1782. Nov. 5.	Hutchinson, Benjamin, and Theodosia Smith,	M. B.,	XXXVII.	72
1772. July 7.	Hutchinson, Catherine, and Thomas Hodgson, ...	"	XVIII.	157
1765. June 21.	Hutchinson, Frances, and Peter Chappell,..	"	IX.	179
1778. Dec. 15.	Hutchinson, Francis, and Catherine Bayard,	"	XXVI.	123
1761. July 28.	Hutchison, Elizabets, and Abraham Davids,	"	V.	14
1758. Jan. 30.	Hutton, Hester, and John Bradbrin,.......	"	I.	806
1761. Sept. 28.	Hutton, Mary, and John Peirse,..........	"	V.	103
1779. Nov. 30.	Hutton, Mary, and William Giffing,........	"	XXVIII.	153
1756. July 10.	Hutton, Peter, and Mary Innes,...........	"	I.	250
1759. Oct. 3.	Huxland, Thomas, and Elizabeth Creeland,..	"	II.	446
1768. April 18.	Huyck, Bata, and Johannes Clauw,........	"	XIII.	78
1763. Sept. 8.	Huyck, Catharine, and Isaac Van Slyck,...	"	VII.	329
1771. Mar. 11.	Huyck, Cornelius A., and Eitie Vosburgh,..	"	XVII.	30
1762. Mar. 5.	Huyck, Hannah, and Daniel Brower,......	"	VI.	65
1759. Nov. 26.	Huyck, Isaac, and Catalintje Schermerhorn,	"	II.	517
1775. Sept. 1.	Huyck, Isaac, and Leentie Collier,.........	"	XXIII.	144
1753. Sept. 5.	Huyck, Johannes, and Gerritje Jansen,....	"	I.	106
1771. May 30.	Huyck, Johannis I., and Jane Staats,......	"	XVII.	95
1783. Aug. 14.	Huyck, John, and Sarah Mantaney,.......	"	XXXIX.	126
1765. Sept. 30.	Huyck, John Johannes, and Mary Vanderpool,................................	"	IX.	280
1772. Nov. 10.	Huyck, Marretie, and Cornelius Rhyne, ...	"	XIX.	108
1764. Oct. 23.	Huyck, Rachael, and Stephen Van Allen,...	"	VIII.	370
1762. Mar. 8.	Huycke, Johannes A., and Fitie Vanderkarre,	"	VI.	67
1771. Jan. 11.	Hyat, Sarah, and Samuel Embree,.........	"	XVII.	4
1764. Jan. 11.	Hyatt, Abijah, and Massey Soper,.........	"	VIII.	13
1738. Aug. 17.	Hyatt, Aron, and Margaret Hollyer,......	"	I.	10
1762. April 8.	Hyatt, Caleb, and Abigail Agnew,........	"	VI.	93
1777. Nov. 24.	Hyatt, Hanah, and Jonathan Underhill,....	"	XXIV.	184
1773. Dec. 22.	Hyatt, Jane, and William Kennedy,.......	"	XXII.	82
1758. May 19.	Hyatt, Mary, and Benjamin Lyan,.........	"	I.	902
1765. Oct. 2.	Hyatt, Mary, and John Buckbee, ...	"	IX.	287
1738. June 8.	Hyatt, Mary, and Richard Thorne,........	"	I.	9
1758. Oct. 27.	Hyatt, Sarah, and Jonathan Griffin Tompkins,..	"	II.	70
1762. Sept. 1.	Hyatt, Susannah, and Henry Huff,........	"	VI.	301
1755. Oct. 3.	Hyatt, Thomas, and Sarah Bugbie,........	"	I.	188
1783. Sept. 5.	Hyde, John, and Catharine Brower,.......	"	XL.	24
1777. June 25.	Hyde, William, and Mary Pollard, ...	"	XXIV.	108
1753. June 7.	Hyer, Abraham, and Ann Bancker,........	"	I.	52
1780. June 22.	Hyer, Andrew, Jr., and Mary McFall,.....	"	XXIX.	92
1765. Feb. 22.	Hyer, Ann, and Isaac Van Gelder, ...	"	IX.	56
1756. Sept. 24.	Hyer, Catharine, and Cornelius Blanck,....	"	I.	302

DATE.	NAMES.	RECORD.	VOL.	PAGE.
1758. Feb. 1.	Hyer, Cornelius, and Sarah Harsen, ...	M. B.,	I.	809
1772. Nov. 12.	Hyer, Garret, and Jane Van Slyck, ...	"	XIX.	111
1757. July 5.	Hyer, Garret, and Mary Baldwin, ...	"	I.	583
1774. Jan. 27.	Hyer, Hannah, and Abraham Sanders, ...	"	XXII.	117
1781. Nov. 13.	Hyer, Lawrence, and Elizabeth Fink, ...	"	XXXIV.	30
1763. June 30.	Hyer, Mary, and Winant Van Pelt, ...	"	VII.	247
1779. June 23.	Hyer, Michael, and Sarah Tucker, ...	"	XXVIII.	5
1763. June 10.	Hyer, Sarah, and James Cunningham, ...	"	VII.	222
1765. Jan. 31.	Hyer, Walter, and Elizabeth Rusco, ...	"	IX.	41
1762. June 17.	Hyer, Walter, and Helen Acker, ...	"	VI.	194
1738. July 7.	Hyer, William, and Tabitha Simpson, ...	"	I.	10
1780. Sept. 12.	Hyet, Mary, and Alexander Dunlop, ...	"	XXX.	25
1779. June 26.	Hylton, John, and Ann Coomes, ...	"	XXVIII.	9
1764. Jan. 21.	Hylton, John, and Mary Braine, ...	"	VIII.	45
1768. Feb. 22.	Hyman, Hannah, and Charles Hicks, ...	"	XIII.	39
1780. Sept. 2.	Hyman, Hester, and Emmanuel Rinedollar,	"	XXX.	16
1757. July 2.	Hyne, Patrick, and Hannah Van Sice, ...	"	I.	570
1760. Jan. 17.	Hynes, Patrick, and Elizabeth Winthrop, ...	"	II.	584
1765. July 27.	Hyre, Jane, and Garret Peterson, ...	"	IX.	218

I.

1781. Oct. 18.	I'Ans, Francis, and Mary Thorne, ...	"	XXXIII.	108
1738. April 4.	Ilslee, Benjamin, and Jane Hollanbeck, ...	"	I.	9
1762. April —.	Imlay, John, and Catharine Henderson, ...	"	VI.	104
1760. Nov. 1.	Ingilsby, Frances, and James Kip, ...	"	III.	391
1773. May 31.	Inglis, Charles, and Margaret Crooke, ...	"	XX.	134
1762. May 10.	Ingoldaby, Ann, and William Needham, ...	"	VI.	151
1766. Aug. 21.	Ingoldsby, Catharine, and Francis Moon, ...	"	X.	80
1763. Oct. 3.	Ingoldsby, Grace, and Emanuel Roberts, ...	"	VII.	368
1757. July 6.	Ingoldsby, Mary, and John Banks, ...	"	I.	585
1761. June 26.	Ingraham, John, and Mary L'Hommedieu, .	"	IV.	264
1783. Sept. 18.	Ingram, Ann, and William Peneyead, ...	"	XL.	45
1756. July 10.	Innes, Mary, and Peter Hutton, ...	"	I.	250
1777. July 15.	Inness, Henry, and Sarah Dow, ...	"	XXIV.	119
1771. April 8.	Inness, John, and Susannah Ayres, ...	"	XVII.	79
1769. Mar. 9.	Innis, Catherine, and Nicholas Jones, ...	"	XIV.	51
1763. Oct. 27.	Inslar, Lodwick, and Ann Van Deursen, ...	"	VII.	407
1782. July 1.	Iredell, Abraham, and Hester Marsh, ...	"	XXXVI.	68
1771. Mar. 30.	Ireland, Elizabeth, and John Morgan, ...	"	XVII.	43
1775. Sept. 12.	Ireland, Jacob, and Elizabeth Kelsey, ...	"	XXIII.	155
1771. Nov. 13.	Ireland, James, and Mary Armstrong, ...	"	XVII.	253
1670. Aug. 24.	Ireland, Joane, and Richard Lattin, ...	C. A.,	II.	580
1758. Feb. 21.	Ireland, Loose, and Elizabeth Jervas, ...	M. B.,	I.	824

DATE.	NAMES.	RECORD.	VOL.	PAGE.
1768. May 2.	Ireland, Thomas, and Jerusha Kirk, ...	M. B.,	XIII.	90
1781. Jan. 6.	Ireland, Thomas, and Patience Oakley,.....	"	XXXI.	16
1769. Nov. 23.	Ireland, Thomas, and Phebe Valentine, ...	"	XV.	102
1758. Jan. 10.	Irons, William, and Susannah Nicoll, ...	"	I.	778
1767. Jan. 26.	Irons, Susannah, and William Sheriff,......	"	XI.	13
1765. July 5.	Irvin, Christiana, and James Marshall, ...	"	IX.	195
1768. Dec. 20.	Irvin, Elizabeth, and John Graham, ...	"	XIII.	268
1781. May 8.	Irvin, Francis, and Joshua Hamilton,......	"	XXXII.	37
1763. Nov. 29.	Irwin, Phebe, and George Grahms,........	"	VII.	481
1766. June 30.	Irwin, Samuel, and Gerty Alsdorph,.......	"	X.	38
1757. Nov. 9.	Isbuster, Thomas, and Hannah Van Arnem,	"	I.	700
1759. Oct. 1.	Isemonger, Thomas, and Prudence Endover,	"	II.	437
1761. Mar. 3.	Isleton, Mary, and Patrick Welch, ...	"	IV.	88
1763. Dec. 17.	Isman, Jacob, and Mercy Thorne, ...	"	VII.	509
1775. Sept. 16.	Ivers, Mary, and Moses Smith,...........	"	XXIII.	157
1759. Nov. 10.	Ives, Susannah, and John Barney, ...	"	II.	492
1767. April 27.	Izard, Ralph, and Alice Delancey,.........	"	XI.	72

J.

1765. April 27.	Jabwain, John, and Rebecca Green, ...	"	IX.	111
1763. Mar. 4.	Jabwaine, Catharine, and Thomas Howard,.	"	VII.	88
1753. Sept. 8.	Jackleen, James, and Dorothy Day, ...	"	I.	111
1760. Feb. 5.	Jacklin, Catharine, and Robert Brown,.....	"	III.	23
1782. Nov. 1.	Jackson, Abigael, and Jacob Robbins,......	"	XXXVII.	68
1766. Aug. 21.	Jackson, Ann, and John Hewlett,.........	"	X.	81
1782. Sept. 21.	Jackson, Basil, and Maria De Be Vois,.....	"	XXXVII.	5
1781. Mar. 28.	Jackson, Charles, and Sarah Whitson, ...	"	XXXI.	88
1765. Nov. 1.	Jackson, Elenor, and Jonas Denton,.......	"	IX.	340
1780. Nov. 23.	Jackson, Elizabeth, and John Jackson, Jr., .	"	XXX.	121
1757. Mar. 16.	Jackson, Elizabeth, and John Sands, ...	"	I.	472
1782. Feb. 12.	Jackson, Elizabeth, and Thomas Jackson,...	"	XXXV.	51
1771. Mar. 25.	Jackson, Gilbert, and Elizabeth Androvet,..	"	XVII.	40
1766. Nov. 10.	Jackson, Hannah, and Samuel Jones,......	"	X.	159
1776. Jan. 11.	Jackson, Henry, and Ann Sidman, ...	"	XXIII.	245
1770. July 4.	Jackson, Jacob, and Catherine Peters, ...	"	XVI.	135
1773. Jan. 30.	Jackson, Jacob, and Mariam Sering,.......	"	XX.	31
1783. Nov. 1.	Jackson, Jacob S., and Phebe Coles,.......	"	XL.	101
1761. Oct. 10.	Jackson, James, and Sarah Hazel,.........	"	V.	131
1783. July 26.	Jackson, Jane, and John Althause, ...	"	XXXIX.	102
1771. June 1.	Jackson, Jane, and Zebulon Seaman, ...	"	XVII.	99
1772. Oct. 2.	Jackson, Jemima, and James Hewlett,.....	"	XIX.	67
1766. Oct. 29.	Jackson, Jerusha, and Maurice Pleas,......	"	X.	145
1781. April 14.	Jackson, John, and Ann Shannon, ...	"	XXXII.	6

DATE.	NAMES.	RECORD.	VOL.	PAGE.
1738. June 20.	Jackson, John, and Mary Townsend,......	M. B.,	I.	10
1771. Sept. 30.	Jackson, John, and Phebe Everit,.........	"	XVII.	197
1780. Nov. 23.	Jackson, John, Jr., and Elizabeth Jackson,..	"	XXX.	121
1766. Sept. 8.	Jackson, Lettitia, and Soloman Poole,.....	"	X.	92
1778. Mar. 12.	Jackson, Margaret, and Stephen Lawrence,.	"	XXV.	39
1765. Jan. 16.	Jackson, Martha, and Joseph Ryder,.......	"	IX.	18
1758. Oct. 20.	Jackson, Mary, and Benjamin Sands,......	"	II.	64
1779. May 11.	Jackson, Mary, and John Pratt,...........	"	XXVII.	133
1771. July 13.	Jackson, Mary, and John Roberts,........	"	XVII.	131
1769. Jan. 5.	Jackson, Mary, and John Tredwell,........	"	XIV.	4
1765. Oct. 29.	Jackson, Mary, and Samuel Hallett,.......	"	IX.	334
1756. July 26.	Jackson, Obadiah, and Ame Simmons,.....	"	I.	261
1768. Feb. 13.	Jackson, Permenius, and Elizabeth Birdsall,.	"	XIII.	36
1769. Nov. 7.	Jackson, Phebe, and Gilbert Wright,......	"	XV.	82
1763. July 5.	Jackson, Phebe, and Isaac Seaman,.......	"	VII.	257
1770. June 30.	Jackson, Rebecca, and John McDonnough, .	"	XVI.	128
1767. Mar. 11.	Jackson, Richard, and Phebe Kissam,.....	"	XI.	42
1777. April 24.	Jackson, Richard, and Rachel Suthard,.....	"	XXIV.	72
1768. Feb. 1.	Jackson, Richard, and Rosetta Jackson, ...	"	XIII.	24
1768. Feb. 1.	Jackson, Rosetta, and Richard Jackson,....	"	XIII.	24
1773. June 20.	Jackson, Samuel, and Deborah Seaman,....	"	XXI.	20
1782. Nov. 30.	Jackson, Susannah, and Charles Hamble,...	"	XXXVII.	101
1760. Sept. 24.	Jackson, Thomas, and Catherine Truman, ..	"	III.	328
1782. Feb. 12.	Jackson, Thomas, and Elizabeth Jackson, ..	"	XXXV.	51
1782. Nov. 29.	Jackson, Thomas, and Rebecca Smith,.....	"	XXXVII.	99
1783. April 16.	Jackson, Thomas, and Elizabeth Winters, ..	"	XXXVIII.	97
1778. Feb. 7.	Jackson, Townsend, and Poley Seaman, ...	"	XXV.	19
1757. Aug. 2.	Jackson, William, and Ann Frielinghouse,..	"	I.	629
1770. May 12.	Jackson, William, and Mary Booth,.......	"	XVI.	83
1767. Aug. 21.	Jackson, William, Jr., and Mary Veghte,...	"	XII.	1
1684. Oct. 9.	Jacobs, Hendrick, and Antie Symons,......	C. M.,	XXXIII.	54
1762. Dec. 29.	Jacobs, Henry, and Catharine Van Alst,....	M. B.,	VI.	500
1773. Dec. 9.	Jacobs, Henry, and Hester Vanorse,.......	"	XXII.	67
1757. Dec. 3.	Jacobs, Mary, and William Rescarla,.......	"	I.	724
1765. June 17.	Jacobs, Matthew, and Elenor Pipkin,......	"	IX.	174
1760. Dec. 22.	Jacobs, Phebe, and Evert Sharman,........	"	III.	489
1771. June 19.	Jacobs, Philip, and Sophia Whiteman,......	"	XVII.	117
1758. Dec. 9.	Jacobs, Sarah, and John Barwick,.........	"	II.	123
1764. Aug. 3.	Jacobs, Susannah, and Thomas Timpson,...	"	VIII.	274
1770. July 31.	Jacobs, William, and Sarah Degree,..	"	XVI.	151
1756. Aug. 27.	Jacobse, Jacob, and Maria Evertse,........	"	I.	278
1775. July 10.	Jacobson, John Jacob, and Catharine Hagadorn, ...	"	XXIII.	91
1779. Mar. 25.	Jacocks, William, and Hannah Garrison,...	"	XXVII.	146
1738. Sept. 14.	Jadwin, Joseph, and Elinor Martin,.......	"	I.	11

Date.		Names.	Record.	Vol.	Page.
1763. Mar.	26.	Jadwin, Joseph, and Phebe Warner,	M. B.,	vii.	108
1761. July	24.	Jadwin, Joseph, and Sarah Warner,	"	v.	7
1779. July	3.	Jaffray, John, and Catherine Flood,	"	xxviii.	15
1771. Oct.	28.	Jager, Christiana, and William Becker,	"	xvii.	226
1762. Dec.	30.	Jager, John, and Mercy Browne,	"	vi.	503
1766. July	17.	Jagger, Steven, and Meriam Wicks,	"	x.	56
1782. July	17.	Jakways, John, and Mary Turner,	"	xxxvi.	86
1765. Mar.	25.	James, Benjamin, and Elizabeth Wright,	"	ix.	72
1762. Oct.	28.	James, Eleanor, and Thomas Wills,	"	vi.	392
1761. Oct.	5.	James, Elenor, and John Lawrence,	"	v.	122
1781. Feb.	3.	James, Francis, and Ann Messavey,	"	xxxi.	36
1761. Feb.	19.	James, Francis, and Elizabeth Holt,	"	iv.	71
1782. Dec.	14.	James, George, and Mary Taylor,	"	xxxvii.	120
1779. Aug.	14.	James, George, and Sarah Rosell,	"	xxviii.	50
1758. May	24.	James, James, and Abigail Lawrence,	"	i.	908
1780. May	6.	James, Juliane, and David Melville,	"	xxix.	48
1781. Sept.	26.	James, Lewis, and Margaret Maradith,	"	xxxiii.	79
1737. June	22.	James, Mary, and George Bernard,	"	i.	6
1772. Feb.	10.	James, Nicholas, and Susan Hammond,	"	xviii.	33
1769. June	12.	James, Robert, and Loronah Flood,	"	xiv.	118
1768. Sept.	26.	James, Susanna, and Thomas Bowder,	"	xiii.	193
1758. Sept.	28.	James, William, and Elenor Davenport,	"	'i.	36
1763. July	21.	Jameson, William, and Isabella Obrine,	"	vii.	278
1759. Jan.	13.	Jamine, Lucy, and Peter Many,	"	ii.	154
1763. Nov.	6.	Jamison, David, and Elizabeth Johnston,	"	vi.	414
1761. Jan.	2.	Jamison, John, and Mary Cunningham,	"	iv.	2
1755. Nov.	13.	Jandine, Catherine, and John Lamb,	"	i.	208
1759. Sept.	11.	Jandine, Magdalene, and John Burt Lyng,	"	ii.	416
1766. July	22.	Jandine, Mary, and James Lamb,	"	x.	59
1778. Oct.	13.	Janet, Margareta, and Jacob Nicolaus Lackman,	"	xxvi.	57
1767. Dec.	12.	Janeway, George, and Effie Poppeldorph,	"	xii.	113
1738. June	26.	Janeway, Jacob, and Sarah Hoghlandt,	"	i.	10
1763. July	25.	Janse, Jannetje, and Andries Ten Eyck,	"	vii.	282
1753. Sept.	5.	Jansen, Gerritje, and Johannes Huyck,	"	i.	106
1770. Oct.	11.	Jansen, Hanny, and Henry Van Dresin,	"	xvii.	204
1671. Feb.	26.	Jansen, Mary, and Hendrick Droogstraet,	G. E.,	iv.	102
1737. Sept.	7.	Jansey, John, and Sarah Tinover,	M. B.,	i.	7
1779. July	2.	Jantzen, Andreas, and Ann Higgin,	"	xxviii.	14
1780. Feb.	4.	Jappi, Paul, and Ann White,	"	xxviii.	208
1761. Nov.	4.	Jaqueri, Daniel, and Anne Sophia Dupuy,	"	v.	192
1777. Sept.	29.	Jarvis, Abigail, and John Sayre,	"	xxiv.	154
1760. July	29.	Jarvis, Abraham, and Hannah Conkling,	"	iii.	230
1782. Jan.	2.	Jarvis, Drusela, and Zophar Nichols,	"	xxxv.	4
1783. Feb.	20.	Jarvis, Grace, and Joseph Smith,	"	xxxviii.	45

DATE.	NAMES.	RECORD.	VOL.	PAGE.
1782. Nov. 29.	Jarvis, Isaiah, and Phebe Whitman,	M. B.,	XXXVII.	98
1753. Sept. 15.	Jarvis, James, and Mary Bell,	"	I.	119
1755. Dec. 10.	Jarvis, Mary, and Joseph French,	"	I.	230
1764. April 30.	Jarvis, Millisent, and Abraham Camp,	"	VIII.	175
1769. Mar. 6.	Jarvis, Nathaniel, and Phebe Allen,	"	XIV.	47
1782. Jan. 2.	Jarvis, Sarah, and Ebenezer Blatchly,	"	XXXV.	5
1763. Sept. 9.	Jarvis, Thomas, and Hannah Bryan,	"	VII.	333
1773. Nov. 20.	Jauncey, James, Jr., and Eleanor Elliot,	"	XXII.	35
1764. Aug. 23.	Jauncey, John, and Margaret Heyder,	"	VIII.	291
1761. Aug. 1.	Jauncey, John, Jr., and Elizabeth Hicks,	"	V.	21
1766. Sept. 13.	Jauncey, Joseph, and Susannah Nichols,	"	X.	94
1781. May 9.	Jauncey, Susannah, and Thomas Vardill,	"	XXXII.	39
1773. Nov. 16.	Jay, Frederick, and Ann Margaret Barclay,	"	XXII.	31
1757. June 24.	Jayne, Elizabeth, and Nathaniel Owen,	"	I.	572
1781. April 10.	Jayne, Robert, Jr., and Sarah Robinson,	"	XXXI.	100
1783. Aug. 22.	Jayne, Tabitha, and Benjamin Jones,	"	XI.	7
1767. June 22.	Jean, John, and Mary Smith,	"	XI.	112
1778. Dec. 15.	Jebereau, Mary, and Arthur Gage,	"	XXVI.	122
1665. Oct. 31.	Jefford, John, and Olive Low,	O. W. L.,	II.	18
1760. April 18.	Jeffrey, Charles, and Sarah White,	M. B.,	III.	114
1759. Dec. 24.	Jemison, Elizabeth, and Philip Pettinger,	"	II.	557
1780. Nov. 18.	Jenings, Thomas, and Sarah White,	"	XXX.	114
1757. Jan. 15.	Jenkins, David, and Thomazin Cosby,	"	I.	415
1780. Sept. 16.	Jenkins, Elizabeth, and Archibald Paterson,	"	XXX.	31
1769. April 25.	Jenkins, Elizabeth, and Walter Caldwell,	"	XIV.	87
1778. Oct. 12.	Jenkins, Hannah, and John Brown,	"	XXVI.	55
1768. June 29.	Jenkins, John, and Elizabeth Mollenar,	"	XIII.	145
1775. May 27.	Jenkins, Joseph, and Elizabeth Wallgrove,	"	XXIII.	47
1774. Jan. 14.	Jenkins, Richard, and Elizabeth Poppledorff,	"	XXII.	103
1760. Dec. 20.	Jenner, Mary, and John Kien,	"	III.	487
1781. Aug. 6.	Jennins, Catharine, and John Segoin,	"	XXXIII.	28
1736. April 7.	Jennins, Richard, and Aeltie Kettletas,	"	I.	1
1772. Sept. 14.	Jennye, Patty, and David Randolph,	"	XIX.	47
1777. Mar. 18.	Jephsen, William. and Eliza Appy,	"	XXIV.	47
1772. May 8.	Jervais, John, and Neamy Bunts,	"	XVIII.	104
1772. Jan. 28.	Jervais, Ruth, and Benjamin Dennis,	"	XVIII.	18
1778. Feb. 21.	Jervas, Elizabeth, and Loose Ireland,	"	I.	824
1760. June 26.	Jerveas, Sarah, and Reuben Arthur,	"	III.	197
1738. Nov. 22.	Jervers, Hannah, and Jonathan Piersee,	"	I.	11
1762. July 14.	Jervis, Eliphalet, and Ruth Whitman,	"	VI.	237
1763. Oct. 20.	Jervis, John, Jr., and Susanna Thomas,	"	VII.	398
1668. Nov. 4.	Jessop, Elizabeth, and Robert Beacham,	O. W. L.,	II.	240
1758. Oct. 15.	Jessop, Mary, and John Young,	M. B.,	II.	49
1780. Nov. 6.	Jessup, Zebulon, and Zeruihia Hunting,	"	XXX.	93
1765. Jan. 22.	Jewel, Cornilwell, and Elenor Lyons,	"	IX.	28

DATE.	NAMES.	RECORD.	VOL.	PAGE.
1782. July 1.	Johnson, Elizabeth, and William Sharp, ...	M B.,	XXXVI.	67
1773. Feb. 19.	Johnson, George, and Rachel Kain, ...	"	XX.	49
1778. July 18.	Johnson, Hanah, and Matthew West, ...	"	XXV.	132
1777. May 23.	Johnson, Hannah, and Benjamin Pollard, ...	"	XXIV.	92
1773. July 6.	Johnson, Helena, and John Lane, ...	"	XXI.	32
1761. April 24.	Johnson, Hendrick, and Tientje Lott, ...	"	IV.	164
1762. June 19.	Johnson, Henry, and Elisabeth Du Bois, ...	"	VI.	197
1759. Dec. 11.	Johnson, Henry, and Elizabeth Vanbrunt, ..	"	II.	537
1760. Nov. 14.	Johnson, Henry, and Lena Slaight, ...	"	III.	414
1758. June 1.	Johnson, Henry, and Rachel Minee, ...	"	I.	921
1782. Jan. 17.	Johnson, Henry, and Rebecca Franks, ...	"	XXXV.	22
1773. Aug. 11.	Johnson, Isaac, and Ann Romney, ...	"	XXI.	65
1773. Mar. 13.	Johnson, Isaac, and Jane Boerhum, ...	"	XX.	62
1783. May 19.	Johnson, Issabel, and Caleb Morgan, ...	"	XXXIX.	19
1768. Aug. 27.	Johnson, Jabes, and Joanna Waters, ...	"	XIII.	179
1757. Dec. 14.	Johnson, James, and Elizabeth Tate, ...	"	I.	740
1763. June 30.	Johnson, James, and Mary Graham, ...	"	VII.	248
1779. May 1.	Johnson, James, and Mary Wood, ...	"	XXVII.	125
1756. Sept. 24.	Johnson, Jane, and Aron King, ...	"	I.	303
1777. April 12.	Johnson, Jane, and John Aldworth, ...	"	XXIV.	60
1762. Dec. 18.	Johnson, Jane, and Nicholas De Peyster, ...	"	VI.	488
1777. Jan. 30.	Johnson, Jemima, and Thomas Carnes, ...	"	XXIV.	20
1763. Dec. 24.	Johnson, John, and Abigail Fowler, ...	"	III.	490
1760. Aug. 5.	Johnson, John, and Ann Querreau, ...	"	III.	235
1764. April 16.	Johnson, John, and Christiana Van Wyck, ..	"	VIII.	157
1761. Oct. 19.	Johnson, John, and Flora McKeller, ...	"	V.	153
1773. June 21.	Johnson, John, and Jane Winterton, ...	'	XXI.	18
1757. Feb. 3.	Johnson, John, and Jannetie Burger, ...	"	I.	433
1778. May 18.	Johnson, John, and Mary Murphy, ...	"	XXV.	85
1771. Oct. 31.	Johnson, John, and Mary Tiebout, ...	"	XVII.	234
1780. June 20.	Johnson, John, and Sealeah Vanwaglum, ...	"	XXIX.	90
1782. Mar. 4.	Johnson, John, and Susannah Toddy, ...	"	XXXV.	73
1775. May 25.	Johnson, Maria, and Jaques Van Brunt, ...	"	XXIII.	45
1769. Mar. 29.	Johnson, Martha, and John Van Dyck, ...	"	XIV.	61
1763. Aug. 13.	Johnson, Martha, and Samuel Johnson, ...	"	VII.	299
1772. May 7.	Johnson, Martin, and Phebe Rapelje, ...	"	XVIII.	103
1777. Feb. 21.	Johnson, Mary, and Charles Fea, ...	"	XXIV.	32
1764. April 10.	Johnson, Mary, and Dow Ditmes, ...	"	VIII.	146
1680. June 28.	Johnson, Mary, and James Barre, ...	G. E.,	XXXII.	90
1766. Aug. 16.	Johnson, Mary, and Peter Praa Van Zandt, .	M. B.,	X.	76
1760. May 15.	Johnson, Mary, and Richard Steves, ...	"	III.	153
1768. June 10.	Johnson, Mary, and Richard Stilwill, ...	"	XIII.	123
1767. Sept. 9.	Johnson, Mary, and William Conrey, ...	"	XII.	32
1764. July 9.	Johnson, Michael, and Elizabeth Kein, ...	"	VIII.	251
1765. Sept. 26.	Johnson, Nathaniel, and Eleanor Vanderbelt,	"	IX.	277

DATE.	NAMES.	RECORD.	VOL.	PAGE.
1768. April 11.	Johnson, Nathaniel, and Sarah Mersereau,..	M. B.,	XIII.	70
1770. Mar. 1.	Johnson, Nicholas, and Mary O'Brien,.....	"	XVI.	27
1764. Sept. 29.	Johnson, Nieltie, and Joseph Morrell,......	"	VIII.	328
1779. April 20.	Johnson, Obadiah, and Dorothy Dunnican,..	"	XXVII.	114
1783. Mar. 11.	Johnson, Rachel, and Barent Parley,......	"	XXXVIII.	65
1770. Mar. 19.	Johnson, Rachel, and Lewis Du Bois,......	"	XVI.	32
1783. Feb. 7.	Johnson, Reuben, and Vianah Rogers,.....	"	XXXVIII.	36
1756. Nov. 23.	Johnson, Richard, and Catharine Rilents,...	"	I.	362
1762. Sept. 24.	Johnson, Richard, and Wyntje Rezeau,....	"	VI.	330
1778. Jan. 23.	Johnson, Robert, and Ann Page,....	"	XXV.	11
1771. Nov. 12.	Johnson, Robert, and Bettsey Betty,......	"	XVII.	251
1764. Dec. 6.	Johnson, Robert, and Margaret Hughes,....	"	VIII.	441
1763. Aug. 13.	Johnson, Samuel, and Martha Johnson,....	"	VII.	299
1775. April 5.	Johnson, Samuel, and Mary Seebring,......	"	XXIII.	1
1753. June 9.	Johnson, Sarah, and Edward Paddon,......	"	I.	57
1764. April 26.	Johnson, Sarah, and James Buckler,.......	"	VIII.	170
1762. Feb. 17.	Johnson, Sarah, and Samuel Southern,.....	"	VI.	52
1737. Nov. 7.	Johnson, Simon, and Margett Vanhorne, ...	"	I.	8
1757. Aug. 23.	Johnson, Stephen, and Sarah Whaley,.....	"	I.	620
1761. July 30.	Johnson, Susannah, and Joseph Cox, ...	"	V.	16
1759. July 28.	Johnson, Susannah, and Matthew Tankard,.	"	II.	366
1760. Oct. 20.	Johnson, Thomas, and Else Ousterhout,....	"	III.	372
1783. Jan. 3.	Johnson, Uzal, and Jane Wilmott,.........	"	XXXVIII.	2
1762. Oct. 26.	Johnson, William, and Mary Van Clief, ...	"	VI.	385
1779. Nov. 17.	Johnson, William, and Sarah Stanger, ...	"	XXVIII.	142
1769. April 12.	Johnson, Wynant, and Mary Laforge,......	"	XIV.	71
1779. May 7.	Johnston, Ann, and Abraham Manee,......	"	XXVII.	128
1766. Sept. 22.	Johnston, Ann, and James Perine, ...	"	X.	102
1780. June 12.	Johnston, Charles, and Catharine Garrison,.	"	XXIX.	87
1766. Oct. 22.	Johnston, Cornelius, Jr., and Hannah Ellsworth, ...	"	X.	137
1760. July 16.	Johnston, David, and Elizabeth Salmon, ...	"	III.	215
1762. Nov. 6.	Johnston, Elisabeth, and David Jamison,...	"	VI.	414
1783. April 30.	Johnston, Elizabeth, and Elliot Salter, ...	"	XXXVIII.	122
1773. Dec. 9.	Johnston, Esther, and Joshua Mersereau,..	"	XXII.	66
1781. Nov. 17.	Johnston, Jane, and William Moody, ...	"	XXXIV.	44
1777. April 24.	Johnston, Jane, and William Mountford, ...	"	XXIV.	71
1763. Nov. 27.	Johnston, Keziah, and Thomas Morrel,.....	"	VI.	457
1762. April 14.	Johnston, Mary, and John Mason, ...	"	VI.	107
1771. June 13.	Johnston, Mary, and Samuel Bates, ...	"	XVI.	111
1771. Nov. 22.	Johnston, Mary, and Thomas Burnet,......	"	XVII.	266
1760. April 15.	Johnston, Mary, and William Callander,....	"	III.	108
1770. Oct. 14.	Johnston, Robert, and Ann Deane,........	"	XVII.	205
1761. May 29.	Johnston, Thomas, and Mary Utt,.........	"	IV.	195
1778. Dec. 27.	Johnston, William, and Rachel Horne, ...	"	XXVI.	134

DATE.		NAMES.	RECORD.	VOL.	PAGE.
1761. May	2.	Jones, Ambrose, and Catharine Brummajum,	M. B.,	IV.	177
1736. May	13.	Jones, Anne, and Thomas Sickle, ...	"	I.	1
1738. May	29.	Jones, Anne, and William Bartolet, ...	"	I.	9
1757. Sept.	26.	Jones, Arrabella, and Richard Floyd, ...	"	I.	649
1783. Aug.	22.	Jones, Benjamin, and Tabitha Jayne, ...	"	XL.	7
1772. Nov.	20.	Jones, Catharine, and Austin Roe, ...	"	XIX.	119
1764. Mar.	16.	Jones, Catharine, and Matthew Decker,....	"	VIII.	106
1771. Oct.	16.	Jones, Catherine, and Baltis Van Kleeck,...	"	XVII.	211
1766. Sept.	16.	Jones, Cave, and Lydia Marriss, ...	"	X.	98
1783. April	26.	Jones, Charlotte, and John McMullen, ...	"	XXXVIII.	115
1781. June	14.	Jones, Daniel, and Jane Van Dyck,........	"	XXXII.	85
1760. Oct.	9.	Jones, David, and Catherine Hill,.........	"	III.	356
1770. July	6.	Jones, David, and Deborah Wing,.........	"	XVI.	137
1777. April	7.	Jones, David, and Mary McCoy, ...	"	XXIV.	59
1768. Jan.	4.	Jones, David, Jr., and Elizabeth Seaman,...	"	XIV.	3
1761. May	30.	Jones, Dorothy, and Benajah Smith,.......	"	IV.	221
1769. Aug.	15.	Jones, Edward, and Martha Dupuy, ...	"	XV.	23
1771. Sept.	25.	Jones, Edward, and Sarah Burns,.........	"	XVII.	192
1781. Jan.	2.	Jones, Eliphalet, and Elizabeth Bogart, ...	"	XXXI.	5
1763. Nov.	1.	Jones, Elisabeth, and Moses Fowler, ...	"	VII.	421
1761. June	12.	Jones, Elizabeth, and Barent Sleght, ...	"	IV.	237
1767. Jan.	28.	Jones, Elizabeth, and Jacob Concklin,......	"	XI.	17
1772. Nov.	23.	Jones, Elizabeth, and James Smith,........	"	XIX.	126
1760. Dec.	1.	Jones, Elizabeth, and John Butler, ...	"	III.	450
1760. July	9.	Jones, Elizabeth, and Michael Thodey,.....	"	III.	209
1772. May	22.	Jones, Elizabeth, and Thomas Ridgway,....	"	XVIII.	120
1762. Dec.	16.	Jones, Erasmus Guilford, and Jane Mansfield,	"	VI.	483
1761. Sept.	8.	Jones, Francis, and George Cribble,........	"	V.	102
1762. Dec.	30.	Jones, Freelove, and Benjamin Birdsall,....	"	VI.	502
1774. Mar.	14.	Jones, Gardiner, and Sarah Haring,.......	"	XXII.	147
1771. Aug.	27.	Jones, Hanna, and Edward McCollom,.....	"	XVII.	163
1760. Aug.	20.	Jones, Hannah, and William Floyd,.......	"	III.	262
1781. Sept.	21.	Jones, Hester, and John Bell,.............	"	XXXIII.	73
1737. May	18.	Jones, Hester, and William Walker,.......	"	I.	6
1770. May	16.	Jones, Humphry, and Margaret Rutgers, ...	"	XVI.	88
1783. Sept.	26.	Jones, Isaac, and Mary Lasher,...........	"	XL.	56
1762. Aug.	28.	Jones, Jane, and Charles Read, Jr.,........	"	VI.	297
1770. Sept.	17.	Jones, Jane, and John Crocheron,.........	"	XVI.	188
1765. Sept.	30.	Jones, Jane, and Peter Bell,..............	"	IX.	282
1758. Nov.	2.	Jones, Jeremiah, and Elizabeth Schurri,....	"	II.	77
1777. Sept.	25.	Jones, John, and Adriana Zegers,.........	"	XXIV.	149
1763. June	3.	Jones, John, and Catherine Pelts,.........	"	VII.	211
1772. Aug.	31.	Jones, John, and Catherine Trotter, ...	"	XIX.	38
1779. April	27.	Jones, John, and Eleanor Colford,.........	"	XXVII.	123
1753. May	9.	Jones, John, and Frances Quereau,........	"	I.	26

DATE.		NAMES.	RECORD.	VOL.	PAGE.
1779. Mar.	7.	Jones, John, and Hannah Hewlet, ...	M. B.,	XXVII.	60
1765. May	8.	Jones, John, and Mary Reemer, ...	"	IX.	123
1760. Nov.	6.	Jones, John, and Mary Rich, ...	"	III.	396
1757. Jan.	18.	Jones, John, and Sarah Caton, ...	"	I.	420
1778. July	7.	Jones, John, and Susanah Nailer, ...	"	XXV.	122
1782. Dec.	9.	Jones, Jonathan, and Rebecca Stillwell, ...	"	XXXVII.	112
1768. May	30.	Jones, Jonathan, and Sarah Sampson, ...	"	XIII.	118
1782. Oct.	21.	Jones, Joseph, and Catharine Dulowin, ...	"	XXXVII.	55
1782. Jan.	24.	Jones, Joshua, and Margaret Ranshaw, ...	"	XXXV.	30
1769. Jan.	11.	Jones, Lewis, and Mary Bennet, ...	"	XIV.	12
17.7. Nov.	12.	Jones, Lydia, and John Sarell, ...	"	XXIV.	181
1779. Jan.	12.	Jones, Margaret, and Townsend Hewlett, ..	"	XXVII.	10
1736. July	16.	Jones, Margrett, and William Hilton, ...	"	I.	2
1761. Jan.	31.	Jones, Mary, and Alexander Henry, ...	"	IV.	44
1779. Dec.	24.	Jones, Mary, and Daniel Ravo, ...	"	XXVIII.	181
1780. July	22.	Jones, Mary, and Silvester Harrington, ...	"	XXIX.	117
1777. Jan.	1.	Jones, Mary, and Smith Ramadge, ...	"	XXIV.	1
1764. May	24.	Jones, Mary, and Thomas Jones, ...	"	VIII.	198
1737. May	30.	Jones, Mary, and William Creeland, ...	"	I.	6
1761. Oct.	27.	Jones, Mary, and William Wright, ...	"	V.	170
1769. Mar.	9.	Jones, Nicholas, and Catherine Innis, ...	"	XIV.	51
1773. May	29.	Jones, Obadiah, and Mary Decker, ...	"	XX.	133
1773. June	1.	Jones, Obadiah, and Mary Smith, ...	"	XX.	136
1763. Feb.	18.	Jones, Rachel, and John Seaman, ...	"	VII.	68
1765. Aug.	5.	Jones, Rachel, and Joseph Bagley, ...	"	IX.	255
1768. July	7.	Jones, Samuel, and Cornelia Herring, ...	"	XIII.	151
1765. Oct.	31.	Jones, Samuel, and Eleanor Turk, ...	"	IX.	339
1766. Nov.	10.	Jones, Samuel, and Hannah Jackson, ...	"	X.	159
1783. Sept.	13.	Jones, Samuel, and Jane Fowler, ...	"	XL.	39
1738. May	24.	Jones, Sarah, and Abraham Lakerman, ...	"	I.	9
1779. Feb.	4.	Jones, Sarah, and Daniel Peabody, ...	"	XXVII.	36
1737. June	6.	Jones, Sarah, and James Brown, ...	"	I.	6
1762. Dec.	9.	Jones, Thomas, and Anne Delancey, ...	"	VI.	471
1783. May	3.	Jones, Thomas, and Elizabeth Morrison, ...	"	XXXIX.	1
1761. June	22.	Jones, Thomas, and Mary Handlin, ...	"	IV.	252
1764. May	24.	Jones, Thomas, and Mary Jones, ...	"	VIII.	198
1777. May	7.	Jones, Thomas, and Rachel Russell, ...	"	XXIV.	84
1758. Feb.	3.	Jones, William, and Caroline Lake, ...	"	I.	813
1781. July	31.	Jones, William, and Catharine Voorhies, ...	"	XXXIII.	23
1758. Mar.	31.	Jones, William, and Elizabeth Wall, ...	"	I.	869
1771. Oct.	19.	Jones, William, and Rachel Murphy, ...	"	XVII.	216
1777. April	1.	Jones, William, and Rebecca Mollineux, ...	"	XXIV.	55
1762. June	11.	Jones, William, Jr., and Mary Townsend, ..	"	VI.	187
1783. May	16.	Jonson, Benjamin, and Elizabeth Simmons, .	"	XXXIX.	12
1760. July	29.	Joralemon, Henry, and Mary Pool, ...	"	III.	232

DATE.	NAMES.	RECORD.	VOL.	PAGE.
1779. July 9.	Jordan, Elizabeth, and Thomas Garrish,....	M. B.,	XXVIII.	19
1782. April 17.	Jordan, John, and Elizabeth Harrison,.....	"	XXXV.	126
1766. June 16.	Jordan, Mary, and John Morgan,..........	"	X.	17
1780. July 5.	Jordan, Philip, and Elizabeth Campbell,....	"	XXIX.	106
1783. Mar. 8.	Joseph, Catharine, and John Curry,.......	"	XXXVIII.	64
1783. Aug. 28.	Jouett, Xenophon, and Gertrude Garretson,	"	XL.	13
1762. Feb. 12.	Journal, Sarah, and John Joy,............	"	VI.	47
1778. May 18.	Journeay, Albert, and Mary Perine,.......	"	XXV.	95
1780. May 20.	Journeay, Catharine, and Anthony Fountain,	"	XXIX.	63
1781. April 2.	Journey, Nicholas, and Ann Garretson,....	"	XXXI.	90
1762. Feb. 12.	Joy, John, and Sarah Journal,............	"	VI.	47
1783. June 2.	Judd, Richard, and Catharine Miller,.......	"	XXXIX.	36
1763. June 15.	Judkens, William, and Abigail Hutchins,...	"	VII.	230
1780. Jan. 5.	Julang, Margaret, and Charles Swan,......	"	XXVIII.	186
1771. Oct. 31.	Jurney, Andry, and Joseph Cubberley,.....	"	XVII.	235
1755. Sept. 16.	Jury, Sarah, and Nicholas Hollywood,.....	"	I.	177
1737. June 2.	Jygels, Juneah, and John Forster,.........	"	I.	6
1672. Oct. 22.	Jylett, Jeremy, and Rachel Kelly,.........	G. E.,	IV.	223

K.

DATE.	NAMES.	RECORD.	VOL.	PAGE.
1773. Feb. 19.	Kain, Rachel, and George Johnson,........	M. B.,	XX.	49
1760. June 18.	Kairsted, Sarah, and John Machet, ...	"	III.	191
1763. Sept. 27.	Kaiser, Barbara, and Michael Weaver,......	"	VII.	353
1763. Oct. 1.	Kaljer, Magiel, and Wyntle Koonyn,.......	"	VII.	367
1774. Feb. 3.	Kane, Isaac, and Rose Weeks,......	"	XXII.	121
1770. July 25.	Kane, Jane, and Thomas Welsh,..........	"	XVI.	146
1765. Oct. 30.	Kennaday, Christopher, and Sarah Pelton,..	"	IX.	336
1767. June 30.	Karr, William, and Mary Rumsey,........	"	XI.	116
1763. April 6.	Kasey, Margaret, and Richard Cornish,.....	"	VII.	115
1775. May 19.	Kashow, Jacob, and Sarah Probasco,......	"	XXIII.	39
1775. Nov. 23.	Kater, John, and Maritie Freer,...........	"	XXIII.	219
1762. Oct. 20.	Kattenhorne, Peter, and Sarah Lyen,......	"	VI.	373
1765. Sept. 24.	Kavanagh, James, and Frances Mar,.......	"	IX.	272
1773. Jan. 29.	Kautzman, Thomas, and Catherine Poole,...	"	XX.	28
1762. May 3.	Kay, Joshua, and Mary Ward, ...	"	VI.	140
1762. Mar. 16.	Kean, Anne, and Peter McCarty,.........	"	VI.	75
1767. Aug. 3.	Kean, Elizabeth, and Johannes Bender,....	"	XII.	8
1783. Sept. 22.	Kearney, Edward, and Hannah Rowland,..	"	XL.	48
1779. Nov. 16.	Kearney, Isabella, and Henry Rogers,.....	"	XXVIII.	141
1766. Sept. 18.	Kearney, Mary, and Edward Shields,......	"	X.	101
1770. July 4.	Kearney, Philip, and Susannah Watts,.....	"	XVI.	134
1765. May 16.	Kearns, James, and Margaret Christian, ...	"	IX.	131
1780. Oct. 30.	Keaquick, John, and Darkus Lightfoot,.....	"	XXX.	86

27

DATE.		NAMES.	RECORD.	VOL.	PAGE.
1783. June	4.	Keech, Jane, and John McGie, ...	M. B.,	XXXIX.	39
1761. Jan.	13.	Keech, Robert, and Elizabeth Liver, ...	"	IV.	15
1760. Dec.	16.	Keeler, Ebenezer, and Anne McNeal, ...	"	III.	479
1773. Oct.	11.	Keeling, Charles, and Catherine Coffey, ...	"	XXI.	137
1769. Mar.	4.	Keen, Martha, and Jacob Titus, ...	"	XIV.	45
1757. Nov.	25.	Keen, Mary, and Alexander Clinton, ...	"	I.	714
1762. Dec.	10.	Keen, Mary, and Henry Powell, ...	"	VI.	474
1779. June	30.	Keese, Elizabeth, and James Rice, ...	"	XXVIII.	11
1770. Feb.	17.	Keese, Pamela, and Samuel Allen, ...	"	XVI.	19
1764. July	9.	Kein, Elizabeth, and Michael Johnson, ...	"	VIII.	251
1778. April	6.	Keirstead, Catherine, and John Neeslet, ...	"	XXV.	61
1764. Nov.	2.	Keirstead, Christopher, and Aurontie Tappan,	"	VIII.	389
1781. Dec.	18.	Keirstead, Johnson, and Rachel Foster, ...	"	XXXIV.	94
1777. Nov.	28.	Keith, George, and Janet Dunlap, ...	"	XXIV.	187
1778. Jan.	17.	Keith, Robert, and Helen Hay, ...	"	XXV.	8
1768. Jan.	11.	Kell, John, and Deborah Dodge, ...	"	XIII.	4
1761. Aug.	1.	Kelley, James, and Letitia Pitt, ...	"	V.	22
1778. June	25.	Kelley, Samuel, and Joana Provoost, ...	"	XXV.	112
1779. April	27.	Kellie, Michael, and Sarah Wallace, ...	"	XXVII.	120
1763. Aug.	1.	Kelly, Ann, and Thomas Woodward, ...	"	VII.	287
1759. Jan.	11.	Kelly, Catherine, and James Wall, ...	"	II.	150
1758. June	3.	Kelly, David, and Mary Cunningham, ...	"	I.	922
1756. Dec.	6.	Kelly, Elenor, and William Davenport, ...	"	I.	374
1764. Mar.	7.	Kelly, Elizabeth, and Frederick Malco, ...	"	VIII.	97
1772. July	11.	Kelly, Elizabeth, and John Simson, ...	"	XVIII.	165
1780. May	23.	Kelly, Elizabeth, and William Lewis, ...	"	XXIX.	67
1775. July	26.	Kelly, Hannah, and Robert Campbell, ...	"	XXIII.	105
1757. April	29.	Kelly, Mary, and Samuel Lyons, ...	"	I.	520
1672. Oct.	22.	Kelly, Rachel, and Jeremy Jyllett, ...	G. E.,	IV.	223
1779. Oct.	7.	Kelly, Rebecca, and John Crosby, ...	M. B.,	XXVIII.	105
1780. Oct.	16.	Kelly, Thomas, and Catharine Evans, ...	"	XXX.	66
1782. Feb.	11.	Kelsey, Catharine, and James Atkins, ...	"	XXXV.	48
1775. Sept.	12.	Kelsey, Elizabeth, and Jacob Ireland, ...	"	XXIII.	155
1775. May	24.	Kelsey, Elizabeth, and Patrick McHugh, ...	"	XXIII.	44
1771. May	9.	Kelsy, Jonas, and Jane Du Bois, ...	"	XVII.	80
1768. Mar.	19.	Kemble, Lawrence, and Frances Peacock, ..	"	XIII.	51
1778. Jan.	11.	Kemble, Robert T., and Mary Marsten, ...	"	XXVIII.	191
1761. Mar.	25.	Kemp, Leah, and Richard Webb, ...	"	IV.	117
1778. Nov.	26.	Kemp, Mary, and Paul Mersereau, ...	"	XXVI.	98
1760. Mar.	7.	Kemp, Thomas, and Mary Hopper, ...	"	III.	67
1758. Jan.	28.	Kempe, Mary, and John Gittins, ...	"	I.	804
1764. Jan.	5.	Kempe, Thomas, and Susanna Collard, ...	"	VIII.	6
1763. June	15.	Kemper, Catharine, and Henry Dawson, ...	"	VII.	229
1771. Sept.	27.	Kemper, Daniel, and Jane Branson, ...	"	XVII.	196
1760. July	17.	Kemper, Gertrude, and Christian Miller, ...	"	III.	216

DATE.		NAMES.	RECORD.	VOL.	PAGE.
1760. Aug.	28.	Kemper, Sophia, and John Morton,.......	M. B.,	III.	272
1771. Aug.	16.	Kempton, Jane, and Ananias Graham,.....	"	XVII.	158
1772. Sept.	26.	Kempton, Samuel, and Martha Wilson,....	"	XIX.	58
1757. Dec.	29.	Kendall, Joseph, and Abigail Wheeler,.....	"	I.	759
1761. April	6.	Kendall, Mary, and Robert Evans,........	"	IV.	135
1781. Nov.	7.	Kendel, Mary, and William Bush,.........	"	XXXIV.	20
1780. Nov.	21.	Kendle, Charles, and Elizabeth Hallett,.....	"	XXX.	117
1779. Dec.	4.	Kendle, Mary, and John Casey,...........	"	XXVIII.	160
1779. June	3.	Kendrick, Mary, and John Francois,.......	"	XXVII.	155
1773. June	17.	Kenedy, Fanny, and Benjamin Broadhurst,.	"	XXI.	14
1772. April	4.	Kenedy, Mary, and John Van Winckel,....	"	XVIII.	67
1783. April	12.	Kenneday, Rachael, and James Willett,....	"	XXXVIII.	93
1757. Mar.	25.	Kennedy, Anna, and Patrick McConegall,..	"	I.	481
1769. April	26.	Kennedy, Archibald, and Ann Watts,.	"	XIV.	89
1736. Dec.	1.	Kennedy, Archibald, and Mary Schuyler,...	"	I.	3
1765. June	13.	Kennedy, Catharine, and Jonathan Mallet,..	"	IX.	165
1773. June	23.	Kennedy, Dennis, and Letitia Corne,.......	"	XXI.	21
1765. Oct.	4.	Kennedy, Elizabeth, and Robert McMennomy, ...	"	IX.	290
1778. Mar.	31.	Kennedy, John, and Ann Dunkell,........	"	XXV.	56
1737. Dec.	3.	Kennedy, Mary, and Christopher Goddard,.	"	I.	8
1779. Mar.	24.	Kennedy, Mary, and James Crokatt,.......	"	XXVII.	76
1764. Nov.	15.	Kennedy, Thomas, and Mary Murphy,.....	"	VIII.	410
1761. Oct.	6.	Kennedy, William, and Annistes Lattemore,.....	"	V.	125
1773. Dec.	22.	Kennedy, William, and Jane Hyatt,.......	"	XXII.	82
1779. Sept.	29.	Kennion, Ann, and Alexander Fraser,.....	"	XXVIII.	90
1758. Nov.	8.	Kenny, Elizabeth, and John Burley,.......	"	II.	84
1770. Nov.	2.	Kenny, Margaret, and Down Johnson,.....	"	XVI.	238
1783. July	1.	Kenrich, Mary, and Thomas Renshaw,.....	"	XXXIX.	77
1781. Nov.	23.	Kerby, Anne, and William Randall, ...	"	XXXIV.	56
1781. Oct.	20.	Kerby, Archibald, and Mary Barns,.......	"	XXXIV.	1
1781. Mar.	15.	Kerby, Margaret, and Aaron Dow,........	"	XXIX.	1
1769. Feb.	14.	Kerby, Mary, and Thorne Carpentor,......	"	XIV.	33
1757. June	21.	Kerby, Thomas, and Mary Walker,........	"	I.	569
1757. July	19.	Kerly, John, and Rebecca Gould,..........	"	I.	594
1753. Aug.	30.	Kerly, Sarah, and Joseph Greswold, ...	"	I.	104
1759. Jan.	10.	Kernaghen, Elizabeth, and James Gray,....	"	II.	148
1758. Oct.	12.	Kernickerbacker, Aleda, and Derick Van Veghten, ...	"	II.	50
1782. July	10.	Kerr, James, and Elizabeth Brown,........	"	XXXVI.	77
1738. Nov.	6.	Kerr, Timothy, and Jernsea Scudder,......	"	I.	11
1781. Nov.	3.	Kerr, William, and Elizabeth Duncan,.....	"	XXXIV.	15
1779. May	31.	Kershow, Jacob, and Elizabeth Rapelje,....	"	XXVII.	152
1773. Sept.	22.	Kershow (Cershow), Tunis, and Effee Cooke,	"	XXI.	119

DATE.	NAMES.	RECORD.	VOL. PAGE.
1761. May 15.	Kerster, Sarah, and Tobias Ryckman,......	M. B.,	IV. 190
1779. Jan. 22.	Keshow, Margaret, and Samuel Mott,......	"	XXVII. 24
1782. July 20.	Ketcham, Caleb, and Abigal Rogers,.......	"	XXXVI. 89
1781. Sept. 22.	Ketcham, Charity, and Foster Vanostrandt,.	"	XXXIII. 76
1781. Oct. 28.	Ketcham, Deborah, and David Sammis,....	"	XXXIV. 11
1773. April 7.	Ketcham, Esther, and Ebenezer Bryan,.....	"	XX. 86
1673. April 25.	Ketcham, Hester, and John Wicks,........	G. E.,	IV. 280
1781. July 28.	Ketcham, Hubart, and Jamima Clatchley, ..	M. B.,	XXXIII. 20
1760. April 15.	Ketcham, Isaac, and Ffreelove Carr,.......	"	III. 109
1761. July 31.	Ketcham, Jesse, and Temperance Brush,...	"	V. 18
167⁴⁄₅. Feb. 26.	Ketcham, John, and Bethia Richardson,....	W. O. P.,	III. 241
1781. Jan. 1.	Ketcham, Kezia, and John Gildersleeve,....	M. B.,	XXXI. 1
1763. Oct. 26.	Ketcham, Mary, and Jesse Bryant,........	"	VII. 406
1737. Dec. 17.	Ketcham, Mary, and Thomas Duncan,.....	"	I. 8
1770. June 18.	Ketcham, Rebeccah, and John Buffet, ...	"	XVI. 118
1756. July 3.	Ketcham, Sarah, and James Oman,........	"	I. 245
1770. Nov. 10.	Ketcham, Zebulon, and Hannah Conckling,.	"	XVI. 246
1774. Feb. 18.	Ketcham, Zophar, and Jemima Luskew,....	"	XXII. 130
1779. Mar. 17.	Ketchison, William, and Mary Rull, ...	"	XXVII. 69
1781. Mar. 6.	Ketchum, Phebe, and Seth Purdy,........	"	XXXI. 65
1771. June 20.	Ketchum, Reuben, and Temperance Smith,.	"	XVII. 119
1755. Oct. 22.	Keteltas, Abraham, and Sarah Smith, ...	"	I. 198
1777. Jan. 19.	Ketletass, Catharine, and Peter Guion,.....	"	XXIV. 15
1764. Feb. 27.	Keton, Elinor, and James Shaw,.....	"	VIII. 83
1759. Nov. 26.	Kettel, Hendryck, and Dorote Van Valken-		
	burgh, ...	"	II. 516
1765. Jan. 30.	Kettenhorn, Sarah, and William McDermot,	"	IX. 38
1781. July 9.	Ketter, John, and Frances Vansyth,.......	"	XXXIII. 2
1753. May 24.	Kettle, Mary, and William Lawrence, ...	"	I. 41
1736. April 7.	Kettletas, Aeltie, and Richard Jennins,....	"	I. 1
1778. Sept. 30.	Key, Christiana, and Thomas Sellars,......	"	XXVI. 41
1782. July 7.	Keys, Ann, and John Busteed, ...	"	XXXVI. 74
1783. May 20.	Keys, Joanna, and William Baker, ...	"	XXXIX. 22
1758. Mar. 13.	Keys, Joseph, and Sarah Vandewater,.....	"	I. 846
1783. Feb. 28.	Keys, Sophia, and Ruth Van Norden, ...	"	XXXVIII. 59
1779. July 12.	Keyser, Barbara, and Philip Righter,......	"	XXVIII. 22
1760. Nov. 13.	Keysman, Mary, and Jacob Croff,.........	"	III. 409
1761. Dec. 3.	Keysrok, Johan Bastian, and Hannah Gragh-		
	burgher, ...	"	V. 263
1763. Nov. 1.	Kibble, Joseph, and Catharine Crawford,...	"	VII. 420
1764. Dec. 8.	Kickwood, Catharine, and Duncan McDugal,	"	VIII. 444
1783. Oct. 31.	Kidd, John, and Sarah Roberts, ...	"	XL. 98
1773. Mar. 24.	Kidney, Angeltie, and John McMichael, ...	"	XX. 72
1771. June 24.	Kidney, Elizabeth, and Stephen Bell,......	"	XVII. 121
1761. Oct. 22.	Kidney, Lena, and George Dickson,.......	"	V. 161

Date.		Names.	Record.	Vol. Page.
1769. April	1.	King, Jane, and Philemon Halstead,.......	M. B.,	xiv. 62
1764. Oct.	11.	King, John, and Annatje Acker,..........	"	viii. 351
1777. Mar.	25.	King, John, and Elenor London,..........	"	xxiv. 52
1783. April	17.	King, John, and Margaret Lindsay,........	"	xxxviii. 100
1782. May	22.	King, John, and Tiddy Lewis,............	"	xxxvi. 16
1783. Sept.	10.	King, Joseph, and Isabella Catharine Winslow, ...	"	xl. 33
1759. Sept.	14.	King, Joseph, and Phebe Anderson,.......	"	ii. 421
1763. Jan.	1.	King, Lydia, and John Craig,.............	"	vii. 1
1778. Oct.	15.	King, Margaret, and John Elsworth,.......	"	xxvi. 61
1774. Jan.	5.	King, Mary, and Ethan Sickels,....	"	xxii. 92
1782. Aug.	16.	King, Mary, and Mathew Taylor, ...	"	xxxvi. 112
1770. Oct.	31.	King, Mary, and Samuel Henshaw, ...	"	xvi. 235
1777. April	5.	King, Patrick, and Elizabeth Williams,.....	"	xxiv. 58
1762. Feb.	8.	King, Rachel, and Daniel Lawrence,.......	"	vi. 40
1762. June	21.	King, Rachel, and George Snowdon, ...	"	vi. 200
1765. Aug.	8.	King, Richard, and Amity Bown,.........	"	ix. 234
1759. May	11.	King, Richard, and Caroline Deforest, ...	"	ii. 278
1766. Sept.	1.	King, Richard, and Rachel Sutton, ...,...	"	x. 87
1778. Oct.	15.	King, Sarah, and Oliver Vanderbilt, ...	"	xxvi. 60
1760. Aug.	26.	King, Teetie, and George Hicks,..........	"	iii. 268
1765. Sept.	25.	King, Thomas, and Sarah Eyles,..........	"	ix. 275
1781. April	30.	Kingsland, Charles, and Anna Brown, ...	"	xxxii. 23
1778. July	6.	Kingland, Claradia, and David Moncreif, ...	"	xxv. 120
1757. Nov.	17.	Kingsland, Edmund, and Mary Davis,......	"	i. 705
1781. Dec.	27.	Kingsland, Elizabeth, and John Lely, ...	"	xxxiv. 108
1680. Jan.	24.	Kingsland, Gustavus, and Sarah Ferior, ...	O. W.,	xxxii½. 33
1782. Jan.	14.	Kingsland, Hetty, and Abraham Van Buskirk,...............................	M. B.,	xxxv. 17
1783. June	30.	Kingsland, Jane, and John Kingsland, ...	"	xxxix. 74
1778. Dec.	25.	Kingsland, John, and Frances Martin, ...	"	xxvi. 132
1783. June	30.	Kingsland, John, and Jane Kingsland, ...	"	xxxix. 74
1779. Aug.	4.	Kingsland, Sarah, and John Pugsley, ...	"	xxviii. 45
1738. Aug.	28.	Kingsley, Elenor, and James Hartily,......	"	i. 10
1768. Aug.	5.	Kingston, Ann, and Francis Gons, ...	"	xiii. 169
1779. April	10.	Kingston, John, and Mary Garrison,.......	"	xxvii. 103
1779. Oct.	2.	Kingston, Sarah, and Charles Roubalet, ...	"	xxviii. 98
1757. Oct.	13.	Kinman, Sarah, and Nehemiah Smith, ...	"	i. 667
1771. April	29.	Kinnan, Ann, and William Boggs, ...,...	"	xvii. 71
1761. May	4.	Kinnear, Robert, and Anne Fey,..........	"	iv. 178
1767. June	2.	Kinsey, Edmund, and Hannah Shino,......	"	xi. 103
1760. Nov.	3.	Kip, Abraham, and Helena Tremper, ...	"	iii. 392
1759. June	15.	Kip, Blendina, and Peter Codmus, ...	"	ii. 327
1757. Dec.	6.	Kip, Catherine, and Peter Teller,..........	"	i. 725
1758. Oct.	10.	Kip, Elizabeth, and Isaac Kip,............	"	ii. 45

DATE.	NAMES.	RECORD.	VOL.	PAGE.
1781. Nov. 17.	Kirk, Elizabeth, and David Wilson, ...	M. B.,	XXXIV.	43
1755. Oct. 16.	Kirk, Jamimah, and James Baker, ...	"	I.	196
1768. May 2.	Kirk, Jerusha, and Thomas Ireland, ...	"	XIII.	90
1782. Aug. 8.	Kirk, Martha, and John Davy,............	"	XXXVI.	103
1766. Nov. 1.	Kirk, Richard, and Anna Downing,........	"	X.	148
173⅘. Mar. 8.	Kirk, Temperance, and Joseph Wright, ...	"	I.	9
1772. June 5.	Kirkby, John, and Ellen Hamilton,........	"	XVIII.	133
1763. Feb. 1.	Kirkes, Thomas, and Ann Abel,..........	"	VII.	44
1760. Jan. 16.	Kirkwood, James, and Catharine Duffy,....	"	II.	583
1736. Nov. 30.	Kirton, Anne, and John Waddel, ...	"	I.	3
1737. Oct. 12.	Kirton, John, and Elizabeth Codden, ...	"	I.	7
1755. Oct. 1.	Kissam, Benjamin, and Catharin Rutgers,...	"	I.	186
1773. Dec. 17.	Kissam, Benjamin, Jr., and Martha Hewlett,	"	XXII.	77
1763. Sept. 19.	Kissam, Daniel, Jr., and Mary Betts, ...	"	VII.	341
1763. Sept. 2.	Kissam, Deborah, and Edmund Smith,.....	"	VII.	324
1761. Oct. 20.	Kissam, Elizabeth, and Jacob Mott, ...	"	V.	152
1782. Mar. 6.	Kissam, John, and Phebe Allen, ...	"	XXXV.	76
1773. Nov. 4.	Kissam, Nancy, and David Allen,........	"	XXII.	12
1779. July 3.	Kissam, Peter R., and Deborah Townsend, .	"	XXVIII.	37
1767. Mar. 11.	Kissam, Phebe, and Richard Jackson,......	"	XI.	42
1777. Oct. 14.	Kissam, Sarah, and Elijah Allen,..........	"	XXIV.	162
1761. Jan. 14.	Kissawny, Elizabeth, and Samuel Thistle,...	"	IV.	17
1781. Aug. 18.	Kissick, Philip, and Penelopey Dartey,.....	"	XXXIII.	41
1762. Aug. 26.	Kittel, Catherine, and Abraham Groot,.....	"	VI.	293
1760. Nov. 25.	Kittell, Johannis, and Geesie Moor, ...	"	III.	441
1762. Nov. 12.	Kittle, William, and Ann Toll,............	"	VI.	428
1773. Nov. 10.	Klien, Margaret, and Peter Romp, ...	"	XXII.	20
1783. May 21.	Klink, Hannah, and John Binckes,........	"	XXXIX.	23
1759. April 30.	Klissnam, Anna Maria, and John Merkler,..	"	II.	263
1766. June 12.	Klock, George, and Cathrina Pellinger, ...	"	X.	13
1763. Jan. 18.	Klock, Jacob G., and Hannah Nellis, ...	"	VII.	20
1771. July 23.	Klock, Margaret, and Stephen March, ...	"	XVII.	139
1764. Jan. 13.	Klock, Peter, and Hannah Baldwin,.......	"	VIII.	15a
1773. July 30.	Klum, Geertry, and William Pulver,.......	"	XXI.	55
1757. Dec. 28.	Klump, Peter, and Maria Wearerlen, ...	"	I.	755
1761. Nov. 2.	Knap, Daniel, and Susannah Hunt,........	"	V.	188
1765. May 25.	Knap, Amos, and Jane Ogilvie, ...	"	IX.	141
1758. Dec. 21.	Knap, Elizabeth, and Benjamin Wise, ...	"	II.	136
1772. Oct. 3.	Knap, Epinetus, and Mary Abbot, ...	"	XIX.	68
1763. Aug. 10.	Knap, Joseph, and Mary Clark,...........	"	VII.	296
1758. Mar. 14.	Knap, Joshua, and Elizabeth Carpenter,....	"	I.	851
1773. June 3.	Knap, Lucy, and Conrad Groostine, ...	"	XX.	137
1761. Mar. 25.	Knap, Moses, and Mary Humphrys,.......	"	IV.	118
1763. May 16.	Knap, Susannah, and Abraham Sneden,....	"	VII.	189
1770. May 7.	Knap, Tamar, and Saul Robinson,........	"	XVI.	81

DATE.	NAMES.	RECORD.	VOL. PAGE.
1768. Aug. 8.	Knapp, Deborah, and James Palmer,	M. B.,	XIII. 170
1768. Sept. 22.	Knapp, Hannah, and Henry Palmer,	"	XIII. 192
1767. April 21.	Knapp, Mary, and Isaac Brower,	"	XI. 66
1760. April 24.	Knapp, Rachael, and John Cobblay,	"	III. 122
1761. Mar. 21.	Knecht, Catharine, and Jacob Blanck,	"	IV. 112
1770. Sept. 10.	Knickerbacker, Ann, and Abraham Vielen,.	"	XVI. 184
1757. Nov. 8.	Knickerbacker, Annetje, and Cornelius Van Veghte,	"	I. 699
1762. Sept. 17.	Knickerbacker, Catharine, and William Van Alstyn,	"	VI. 320
1757. Nov. 2.	Knickerbacker, Elizabeth, and William Pasman,	"	I. 694
1775. May 24.	Knickerbacker, Margery, and Hugh Rea,	"	XXIII. 43
1775. Oct. 30.	Kniffen, Elizabeth, and Dennis McKaven,	"	XXIII. 193
1783. April 30.	Knight, Charles, and Margaret L. Loyd,	"	XXXVIII. 123
1737. Mar. 25.	Knight, Charles, and Rebecca Winter,	"	I. 5
1781. Feb. 7.	Knight, George, and Rachel Davis,	"	XXXI. 42
1783. Jan. 30.	Knight, John, and Sarah Shepherd,	"	XXXVIII. 33
1782. April 13.	Knight, Robert, and Susanah Fox,	"	XXXV. 120
1777. Jan 27.	Knighton, John, and Catherine Delue,	"	XXIV. 19
1783. July 18.	Knipschild, Henry, and Pamela Hazard,	"	XXXIX. 95
1757. Oct. 25.	Knoll, Henry, and Mary Egbersen,	"	I. 679
1766. Sept. 13.	Knolton, Christian David, and Jeanneta Arabella Pilkington,	"	X. 95
1753. Aug. 29.	Knout, Johannes, and Jannetje Ouderkirk, .	"	I. 102
1759. Sept. 22.	Knouts, Mary, and John Abeel,	"	II. 429
1760. Dec. 17.	Knowles, John, and Eleanor Dawsey,	"	VI. 485
1755. Oct. 6.	Knowlin, Thomas, and Margaret Webber,	"	I. 189
1763. Feb. 1.	Knox, Catharine, and Joshua Lose,	"	VII. 47
1780. July 18.	Knox, James, and Margaret Maud,	"	XXIX. 114
1773. Nov. 12.	Knut, Gertruy, and Tark Van Ness,	"	XXII. 24
1770. Sept. 17.	Koeper, Christian, and Christina Diedrick,	"	XVI. 190
1760. May 15.	Koffman, John, and Barbara Rape,	"	III. 152
1764. Jan. 21.	Koning, Elizabeth, and Coenradt Rende,	"	VIII. 29
1763. Oct. 1.	Koonyn, Wyntie, and Magiel Kaljer,	"	VII. 367
1772. Dec. 8.	Kool, Cornelius, and Catherina Pick,	"	XIX. 146
1762 Dec. 29.	Koolaback, Margaret, and John Van Alla,	"	VI. 501
1773. Oct. 17.	Kooper, Mary, and Dennis McKibby,	"	XXI. 132
1765. Jan. 3.	Kortright, Elizabeth, and William Ricketts Van Cortland,	"	IX. 3
1761. Sept. 30.	Kortright, Frances, and John Norris,	"	V. 109
1763. Jan. 29.	Kortright, Mary, and John Wilkinson Hanson,	"	VII. 41
1765. June 23.	Kortright, Michael, and Mary Huson,	"	IX. 181
1775. Nov. 4.	Kortz, Elizabeth, and Peter Wiesmer,	"	XXIII. 199

28

DATE.	NAMES.	RECORD.	VOL.	PAGE.
1772. Nov. 2.	Kortz, John, and Mary Carroll, ...	M. B.,	XIX.	98
1762. Dec. 16.	Kottorel, Samuel, and Deliverance Holmes,.	"	VI.	484
1771. Sept. 3.	Kouwenhoven, Anna, and Peter Vander Voort, ...	"	XVII.	173
1782. Oct. 5.	Kowood, Joseph, and Margaret Pingra, ...	"	XXXVII.	29
1763. July 15.	Kramer, Samuel, and Catharine Oglesby,. . .	"	VII.	267
1771. Mar. 8.	Krindlemeyer, Margaret, and John Jogh, . .	"	XVII.	26
1762. Mar. 3.	Krous, Mary, and Lodowick Krouscup, ...	"	VI.	62
1762. Mar. 3.	Krouscup, Lodowick, and Mary Krous, ...	"	VI.	62
1781. Oct. 23.	Kruse, John, and Jamima Simonson, ...	"	XXXIV.	3
1772. May 13.	Kruse, Lena, and Peter Housman, ...	"	XVIII.	117
1773. Feb. 26.	Kruser, Closhe, and Richard Corsen, ...	"	XX.	54
1760. May 12.	Kuaggs, George, and Gartruy Schuyler, ...	"	III.	149
1777. May 6.	Kouwenhoven, Peter, and Lamitie Lott, . . .	"	XXIV.	82
1764. Sept. 8.	Kowenhouen, William, and Deborah Voorhees, ...	"	VIII.	300
1759. Dec. 12.	Kull, Philip, and Catharine Herring, ...	"	II.	540
1763. Feb. 18.	Kussow, Abraham, and Sarah Downing, . . .	"	VII.	67
1757. June 1.	Kwackenbus, Adderyaen, and Folkie Vandenbergh, ...	"	I.	546
1757. Feb. 7.	Kydney, Mary, and James Philip Crown, . .	"	I.	437

L.

1760. Sept. 6.	Labagh, Abraham, and Deborah Coperthwait,	"	III.	303
1762. July 21.	Labagh, Isaac, and Judith Uzza, ...	"	VI.	248
1778. Oct. 24.	Labon, Ann, and Compte Thompson, ...	"	XXVI.	70
1762. Oct. 22.	Laboyteu, John, and Hannah Smith, ...	"	VI.	380
1671. Feb. 6.	La Chare, Eleanor, and John Cavlier, ...	G. E.,	IV.	99
1782. Mar. 9.	Lackerman, Sarah, and John Wilson, ...	M. B.,	XXXV.	83
1762. Dec. 10.	Lackey, Jane, and William Webber, ...	"	VI.	473
1779. Mar. 17.	Lackman, Amy, and Williem Merrell, ...	"	XX.	59
1778. Oct. 13.	Lackman, Jacob Nicholas, and Margareta Janch, ...	"	XXVI.	57
1782. Feb. 12.	Lackman, Nicholas, and Elizabeth Corback,.	"	XXXV.	49
1782. Jan. 19.	Lacy, Lawrence, and Jane Warner, ...	"	XXXV.	25
1768. Jan. 28.	Ladd, Margaret, and Robert Aitun, ...	"	XIII.	19
1758. Sept. 20.	Ladd, Thomas, and Margaret Carow, ...	"	II.	27
1782. Feb. 26.	Laferty, Daniel, and Isabella Woods, ...	"	XXXV.	66
1783. May 16.	Laffan, Margaret, and Flourence Sullivan, . . .	"	XXXIX.	14
1781. Feb. 17.	Laffan, Robert, and Margeret Beck, ...	"	XXXI.	48
1762. Mar. 15.	Laffraa, William, and Margaret Webber, ...	"	VI.	69
1766. Dec. 23.	Lafong, Margaret, and Robert Michner, ...	"	X.	205
1781. April 14.	Laforge, David, and Catharine Sequine, ...	"	XXXII.	2

DATE.	NAMES.	RECORD.	VOL.	PAGE.
1782. Mar. 6.	Laforge, John, and Sarah Moore,..........	M. B.,	XXXV.	75
1783. Sept. 5.	Laforge, Mary, and Teunis Van Pelt,......	"	XL.	27
1769. April 12.	Laforge, Mary, and Wynant Johnson,......	"	XIV.	71
1768. Dec. 31.	Laforge, Peter, and Elizabeth Reed,.......	"	XIII.	277
1780. May 6.	Laforge, Peter, and Martha Bedine,........	"	XXIX.	47
1769. Nov. 21.	Lafoy, Rebecca, and James Wendell,.......	"	XV.	100
1761. April 9.	Lafurgee, Tunis, and Jane Lent,...........	"	IV.	141
1763. April 2.	Laghlieu, John, and Mary Abberfield,......	"	VII.	111
1768. Dec. 6.	Lagier, Cornelia, and Fardeandes Van Sickelen, ...	"	XIII.	254
1768. Sept. 6.	Lagrange, Annatje, and Conradt Lagrange,..	"	XIII.	181
1763. April 28.	Lagrange, Arie, and Elenor Legrange,.....	"	VII.	150
1768. Sept. 6.	Lagrange, Conradt, and Annatje Lagrange,..	"	XIII.	181
1761. Sept. 18.	Lagrange, John, and Elisabeth Mersereau,..	"	V.	89
1768. July 18.	Laidlie, Archibald, and Mary Hoffman,.....	"	XIII.	161
1772. Nov. 2.	Laight, William, and Frances Sackett,......	"	XIX.	99
1770. April 19.	Laird, David, and Mary Butler,....	"	XXVII.	108
1771. Aug. 3.	Lajire, Ann, and William Terrett,.........	"	XVII.	149
1761. July 7.	Lake, Abraham, and Altje Burbanck,......	"	IV.	285
1783. Aug. 1.	Lake, Abraham, and Patience Perbanck,...	"	XXXIX.	107
1758. Feb. 3.	Lake, Caroline, and William Jones........	"	I.	813
1782. April 3.	Lake, Court, and Idea Rider,.............	"	XXXV.	107
1762. Mar. 15.	Lake, Daniel, and Anne Garrison,........	"	VI.	70
1783. July 20.	Lake, Daniel. and Phebe Denton,.........	"	XXXIX.	97
1765. Oct. 28.	Lake, Jacob, and Ariantje Hubbard,.......	"	IX.	327
1770. Dec. 1.	Lake, James, and Rachael Mullineux,......	"	LXVIII.	157
1782. Dec. 13.	Lake, Joseph, and Catharine Barraga,......	"	XXXVII.	118
1781. July 21.	Lake, Joseph, and Frances Egberts,........	"	XXXIII.	13
1753. Oct. 6.	Lake, Latiche, and Charles Sickels,........	"	I.	132
1782. May 7.	Lake, Margaret, and James Guyon,........	"	XXXV.	152
1755. Aug. 12.	Lake, Mary, and Edward Batey,..........	"	I.	146
1767. July 16.	Lake, Mary, and Joshua Mersereau,........	"	XI.	134
1783. May 19.	Lake, Mary, and Richard Stillwell,........	"	XXXIX.	16
1753. Oct. 9.	Lake, Mary, and Stephen Voorhees,.......	"	I.	134
1756. Nov. 16.	Lake, Neeltje, and Bernardus Hubbard, ...	"	I.	356
1764. April 4.	Lake, Patience, and Lawrance Rolph,......	"	VIII.	133
1765. Oct. 22.	Lake, Rebecca, and Peter Mersereau, ...	"	IX.	310
1764. Sept. 17.	Lake, Robert, and Ann Bancker,..........	"	VIII.	312
1773. June 14.	Lake, Sarah, and Nicholas Snyder,........	"	XXI.	1
1760. Dec. 17.	Lake, Sarah, and Obadiah Wilkins,........	"	III.	481
1763. Dec. 23.	Lake, Sarah, and Richard Williams,........	"	VII.	521
1775. June 21.	Lake, William, and Elizabeth Poilon,......	"	XXIII.	72
1769. Feb. 18.	Lake, William, and Mary Tisen,...........	"	XIV.	37
1770. Nov. 27.	Lakeman, Mary, and Anthony Neill,.......	"	XVI.	270
1760. May 23.	Lakerman, Abraham, and Elizabeth Hillyer,.	"	III.	163

DATE.		NAMES.	RECORD.	VOL.	PAGE.
1738. May	24.	Lakerman, Abraham, and Sarah Jones,....	M. B.,	I.	9
1759. Feb.	5.	Lakerman, Ann, and Lawrence Hillyer,....	"	II.	176
1765. May	30.	Lakerman, Isaac, and Martha Mercereau,...	"	IX.	147
1765. June	13.	Lakerman, James, and Catherine Valleau,..	"	IX.	167
1759. Jan.	12.	Lakerman, Richard, and Mary Smith,......	"	II.	152
1783. June	3.	Lamacrate, William, and Ann Dellat,......	"	XXXIX.	38
1763. May	4.	Laman, James, and Elinor McDougall,.....	"	VII.	167
1763. May	7.	Laman, Malkar, and Rosanna Styler,......	"	VII.	168
1770. Sept.	27.	Lamasny, James, and Mary Grimes,.......	"	XVI.	196
1738. Nov.	14.	Lamb, Alexander, Anne Matticks,.........	"	I.	11
1769. Nov.	6.	Lamb, Alexander, and Rachel Savage,.....	"	XV.	79
1770. Sept.	27.	Lamb, Cornelia, and James William Payne,	"	XVI.	198
1753. April	16.	Lamb, Elizabeth, and Tunis Tyebout,......	"	I.	24
1778. Sept.	2.	Lamb, James, and Catalina Matthews,.....	"	XXVI.	18
1766. July	22.	Lamb, James, and Mary Jandine,.........	"	X.	59
1777. Dec.	19.	Lamb, Jane, and Edward Chichester,......	"	XXIV.	200
1755. Nov.	13.	Lamb, John, and Catherine Jandine,.......	"	I.	208
1763. Oct.	26.	Lamb, John, and Mary Van Winkle,.......	"	VII.	402
1762. Feb.	5.	Lamb, Leah, and Thomas Parratt,.........	"	VI.	39
1776. Jan.	25.	Lamb, Margaret, and Robert Campbell,....	"	XXIII.	250
1773. Sept.	2.	Lamb, Martin, and Elizabeth Casey,.......	"	XXI.	97
1763. Nov.	30.	Lamb, Rachel, and Mindert Van Evra,.....	"	VII.	484
1771. July	31.	Lambersen, Elizabeth, and William McDermott, ...	"	XVII.	146
1760. Mar.	14.	Lamberson, Altje, and John Grisner,......	"	III.	77
1781. Aug.	28.	Lamberson, Barnardus, and Sarah Amberman, ...	"	XXXIII.	49
1780. Dec.	2.	Lamberson, David, and Letitia Hinchman,..	"	XXX.	133
1767. Nov.	23.	Lamberson, David, and Sarah Van Nostrant,	"	XII.	92
1783. Jan.	2.	Lamberson, Letitia, and John Mills,.......	"	XXXVIII.	1
1781. Nov.	17.	Lamberson, Simon, and Sarah Amberman,..	"	XXXIV.	46
1777. Aug.	12.	Lambert, Edward, and Lucy Provoost,.....	"	XXIV.	131
1774. Jan.	18.	Lambert, Elizabeth, and Robert Deal,......	"	XXII.	105
1782. April	3.	Lambert, Robert, and Mary Lucas,........	"	XXXV.	109
1758. Mar.	3.	Lambertson, Nicholas, and Famatje Mauntaunge, ...	"	I.	834
1759. Nov.	12.	Lamelt, Jane, and Joseph Burch,.........	"	II.	493
1763. Nov.	22.	Lamfear, Asa, and Sarah Cadman,.........	"	VII.	463
1782. Dec.	2.	Laming, Dymock, and Violetta Bartholomew,	"	XXXVII.	104
1783. Oct.	4.	Lamont, Elizabeth, and Samuel Street,.....	"	XL.	62
1782. Aug.	15.	Lamoureuex, Jesse, and Jane Wetmore,....	"	XXXVI.	107
1760. Feb.	23.	Lampkin, Michael George, and Freelove Lewis, ...	"	III.	45
1783. June	6.	Lance, Sarah, and Hassel Pym,...........	"	XXXIX.	42
1782. Sept.	24.	Landdon, Samuel, and Milla Denye,.......	"	XXXVII.	11

DATE.	NAMES.	RECORD.	VOL.	PAGE.
1780. April 12.	Lander, John, and Mary McCoy,	M. B.,	XXIX.	18
1771. Dec. 11.	Landon, Jonathan, and Isabella Graham, ...	"	XVII.	288
1762. June 26.	Landrine, Susannah, and Joshua Soulies,	"	VI.	209
1764. April 10.	Lane, Elizabeth, and Martin Bowrin,	"	VIII.	145
1762. Feb. 18.	Lane, Frederick, and Elizabeth Van Deurer,	"	VI.	54
1765. April 13.	Lane, George, and Mary Shaw,	"	IX.	113
1759. Jan. 13.	Lane, Henry, and Elizabeth Breton,	"	II.	156
1757. Dec. 9.	Lane, Henry, and Elizabeth Van Law,	"	I.	731
1773. July 6.	Lane, John, and Helena Johnson,	"	XXI.	32
1781. Sept. 22.	Lane, Margaret, and Abraham Bogart,	"	XXXIII.	75
1761. Oct. 31.	Lane, Margaret, and Joseph Cook,	"	V.	181
1780. Aug. 2.	Lane, Martha, and Daniel Duryee,	"	XXIX.	131
1763. Dec. 7.	Lane, Mathias, and Martha Losee,	"	VII.	497
1764. Dec. 10.	Lane, Rachel, and John Hansen,	"	VIII.	445
1753. Aug. 30.	Lane, Sarah,' and Jochim Rieck,	"	I.	103
1760. Jan. 14.	Lane, Stephen, and Elsie Legg,	"	II.	579
1762. Jan. 8.	Lane, Thomas, and Jane Abel,	"	VI.	5
1738. June 17.	Lane, William, and Sarah Holmes,	"	I.'	10
1761. Aug. 14.	Lang, Eleanor, and Peter Garrebrants,	"	V.	42
1775. Aug. 26.	Langdon, Hannah, and William Pearsall, ...	"	XXIII.	134
1736. Oct. 14.	Langdon, Joseph, and Abigail Lee,	"	I.	3
1762. Nov. 13.	Langdon, Lititia, and Jonathan Hutchins, ...	"	VI.	432
1758. Jan. 5.	Langdon, Mary, and Elisha Bedel,	"	I.	768
1764. Jan. 16.	Langdon, Sarah, and John Foster,	"	VIII.	17
1766. Sept. 2.	Langdon, Thomas, and Fametie Adriance, ..	"	X.	89
1701. Aug. 8.	Lange, Martin, and Othelia Grass,	"	V.	34
1761. June 5.	Langford, Sarah, and Nathaniel Hughes, ...	"	IV.	196
1781. June 22.	Langrall, Charles, and Margeret Kip,	"	XXXII.	95
1783. June 13.	Langrange, Jacob, and Aria Gready,	"	XXXIX.	56
1780. July 20.	Langsbury, Mary, and Samuel Earl,	"	XXIX.	116
1779. Jan. 5.	Lansfield, Attained A., and Ann Courtney,.	"	XXVII.	3
1768. July 13.	Lansing, Anna, and Cornelius Wendell, Jr.,.	"	XIII.	157
1761. June 17.	Lansing, Catharine, and Christopher Yeates,	"	IV.	245
1771. Aug. 29.	Lansing, Garrit Abraham, and Angenietje Bradt,	"	XVII.	168
1768. May 25.	Lansing, Garrit A., and Ruth Man,	"	XIII.	115
1768. Feb. 15.	Lansing, Gerret A., and Cathalina Van Alstyn,	"	XIII.	37
1738. Nov. 8.	Lansing, Gerrit, and Machtel Beakman, ...	"	I.	11
1769. April 24.	Lansing, Hendrick James, and Helena Winne,	"	XIV.	83
1761. May 29.	Lansing, Isaac, and Anne Van Arnem,	"	IV.	212
1762. June 14.	Lansing, Jacob, and Jannetie Visher,	"	VI.	192
1764. Oct. 25.	Lansing, Jacob, and Williamtie Winne, ...	"	VIII.	375
1760. Nov. 21.	Lansing, Jannetie, and John Baptist Van Eps,	"	III.	430

DATE.	NAMES.	RECORD.	VOL. PAGE.
1761. Sept. 16.	Lansing, Johannis S., and Catrina Burhans,.	M. B.,	v. 85
1761. May 29.	Lansing, Maica, and Jacob Cloet,..........	"	IV. 211
1767. Oct. 1.	Lansing, Margaret, and Abraham Oothout,..	"	XII. 54
1757. April 12.	Lansing, Maria, and Hendrick Wendell,....	"	I. 497
1757. April 19.	Lansing, Philip, and Elsie Hun,...........	"	I. 505
1773. Mar. 13.	Lansingh, Abraham H., and Anna Van Denbergh, ...	"	XX. 60
1775. Sept. 21.	Lansingh, Annatie, and Jacob Van Alstyne,.	"	XXIII. 162
1761. Sept. 24.	Lansingh, Catharine, and Abraham Douw,..	"	v. 97
1760. Aug. 6.	Lansingh, Catharine, and Abraham Myndertse, ...	"	III. 237
1762. Aug. 21.	Lansingh, Catharine, and Gerrit Van Wie,..	"	VI. 282
1770. June 8.	Lansingh, Catharine, and John Van Woert,.	"	XVI. 106
1766. Oct. 20.	Lansingh, Catherine, and Cornelius C. Vanderbergh,.............................	"	X. 129
1761. Oct. 2.	Lansingh, Christopher, and Jannetie Bradt,..	"	v. 114
1773. Nov. 23.	Lansingh, Cornelia, and Abraham Staats,...	"	XXII. 30
1762. Nov. 1.	Lansingh, Cornelia, and Henry Schermerhorne, ...	"	VI. 403
1773. Mar. 13.	Lansingh, Cornelius, and Esther Vander Heyden, ...;	"	XX. 61
1771. Mar. 30.	Lansingh, Elsie, and Jacob Van Dusen,.....	"	XVII. 45
1736. Nov. 2.	Lansingh, Franciscus, and Marritie Liervorse,	"	I. 3
1773. May 12.	Lansingh, Gerret I., and Alleda Fonda,.....	"	XX. 108
1767. July 22.	Lansingh, Gerritie, and John Bradt,.......	"	XI. 139
1766. Nov. 15.	Lansingh, Gertruy, and Peter Schuyler, Jr.,.	"	X. 166
1772. June 20.	Lansingh, Helena, and Abraham Verplanck,	"	XVIII. 145
1764. Feb. 11.	Lansingh, Helena, and Jeremiah Van Rensselaer, ...	"	VIII. 57
1764. Oct. 11.	Lansingh, Helena, and Nanning Fisher, Jr.,.	"	VIII. 353
1771. Aug. 5.	Lansingh, Hendricke, and Abraham Fonda,.	"	XVII. 151
1762. Sept. 11.	Lansingh, Henry, and Mary Merselis,......	"	VI. 312
1763. Jan. 10.	Lansingh, Hester, and Jacob Roseboom,....	"	VII. 12
1761. Dec. 7.	Lansingh, Jacob H., and Maria Ouderkerk,.	"	v. 267
1767. May 11.	Lansingh, Jannatie, and William Van Wie,..	"	XI. 80
1776. Jan. 25.	Lansingh, John A., and Elizabeth Fryer,...	"	XXIII. 252
1766. Sept. 5.	Lansingh, John E., and Mary Staats,......	"	X. 91
1775. Dec. 7.	Lansingh, Leentje, and John J. Zabriski, ...	"	XXIII. 225
1770. Mar. 5.	Lansingh, Levinus, and Catherine Vanderheyden, ...	"	XVI. 29
1772. June 3.	Lansingh, Obadiah, and Cornelia Van Banthousen,...................	"	XVIII. 130
1764. Sept. 20.	Lansingh, Rutger, and Susannah Van Schoonhoven, ...	"	VIII. 318
1753. Sept. 26.	Lansingh, Sander J., and Abigail Ver Planck,	"	I. 126

DATE.	NAMES.	RECORD.	VOL.	PAGE.
1763. Aug. 17.	Lansingh, Saunders, and Elinor Van Eps,...	M. B.,	VII.	303
1764. Feb. 6.	Lansingh, Thomas, and Eleanor Deforeest,...	"	VIII.	52
1770. April 1.	Lapevick, Thomas, and Dorcas White, ...	"	XXVII.	89
1770. April 21.	La Quier, Antaletta, and Peter Corneye,...	"	XVI.	66
1769. July 8.	Larcy, James, and Sarah Bunrepo,.........	"	XIV.	145
1764. June 14.	Lariman, Henry, and Catharine Runaway,..	"	VIII.	225
1779. Sept. 14.	Laroy, Peter P., and Jane Lott,...........	"	XXVIII.	75
1782. May 3.	Larrabee, Thomas, and Amy Colwell,......	"	XXXV.	149
1769. Aug. 4.	Larzelere, Abraham, and Sarah Cornell,....	"	XV.	17
1762. Oct. 28.	Larzelere, Benjamin, and Sarah Wood,.....	"	VI.	391
1770. April 6.	Larzelere, Elizabeth, and Peter Prull, ...	"	XVI.	52
1757. Jan. 22.	Larzelere, Jacob, and Elce Leake,..........	"	I.	424
1767. May 25.	Larzelere, Nicholas, and Sarah Depue,.....	"	XI.	95
1755. Aug. 16.	Lashar, Frederick, and Jane Barnet,.......	"	I.	147
1783. Sept. 8.	Lasher, Hannah, and John Ford,..........	"	XL.	32
1763. June 21.	Lasher, John, and Catharine Ernest,.......	"	VII.	235
1783. Sept. 26.	Lasher, Mary, and Isaac Jones,...........	"	XL.	56
1764. July 6.	Lasher, Sarah, and Henry Riker,..........	"	VIII.	247
1782. Nov. 6.	Lashire, Elizabeth, and William Sebeston,..	"	XXXVII.	73
1771. Aug. 10.	Lashly, Mary, and Joseph Right,..........	"	XVII.	157
1780. April 25.	Lashore, Catharine, and James Tobine,.....	"	XXIX.	35
1779. Dec. 7.	Lasier, Margaret, and Stephen Sprung,.....	"	XXVIII.	164
1753. July 14.	Lasshar, Jacob, and Susannah Haiter,......	"	I.	76
1753. May 19.	Lassher, John, Jr., and Helena Pearse,.....	"	I.	35
1762. June 29.	Laten, Fametee, and Barnardus Voorhees,..	"	VI.	215
1775. Sept. 19.	Latham, Isaac, and Mercy Hubbedd,......	"	XXIII.	159
1763. Dec. 20.	Latham, Mary, and Abraham Simonson,....	"	VII.	514
1760. May 2.	Latham, Elizabeth, and Lancaster Burling,..	"	III.	136
1782. July 23.	Latham, John, and Jane Van Evere,.......	"	XXXVI.	91
1773. Aug. 28.	Latham, John, and Mary Waters,.........	"	XXI.	88
1759. June 12.	Latham, Mary, and Robert Mitchill,.......	"	II.	319
1759. June 7.	Latham, Rachel, and Charles Peters,.......	"	II.	310
1761. July 1.	Latham, Rebecca, and John McDonald,.....	"	IV.	272
1778. Feb. 4.	Lathwhite, Mary, and Augustus John Free- man, ...	"	XXV.	15
1761. May 4.	Latin, Richard, and Ann Weeks,..........	"	IV.	179
1761. June 17.	Laton, John, and Elenor Simerson,........	"	IV.	244
1780. Aug. 6.	Latouch, Jane, and Patrick Rice,..........	"	XXIX.	134
1783. Jan. 14.	Latorette, Catharine, and James Hart, ...	"	XXXVIII.	15
1781. Oct. 4.	La Tourette, David, and Margaret Perine,..	"	XXXIII.	85
1764. April 7.	Latourette, Susannah, and Peter Cole,.....	"	VIII.	143
1783. Mar. 22.	Latourrette, David, and Mary Evendor, ...	"	XXXVIII.	73
1764. Sept. 28.	Latourrette, Henry, and Sarah Wood,.....	"	VIII.	325
1780. Sept. 15.	Latourrette, James, and Mary Stoutenbourgh,	"	XXX.	30
1761. Oct. 6.	Lattemore, Annestes, and Walter Kennedy,	"	V.	125

DATE.	NAMES.	RECORD.	VOL.	PAGE.
1764. Nov. 29.	Lattemore, Mathew, and Margaret Clark,...	M. B.,	VIII.	431
1780. Dec. 2.	Latten, Jane, and John Vandervoort,.......	"	XXX.	135
1763. May 19.	Latten, Phebe, and William Laurence,......	"	VII.	193
1736. Dec. 14.	Lattimer, John, and Mary Graham,........	"	I.	5
1757. Nov. 12.	Lattin, Elizabeth, and Augustine Weekes,..	"	I.	703
1756. Nov. 1.	Lattin, Ethelinda, and William Frost,......	"	I.	344
1772. Mar. 28.	Lattin, Horiontia, and William Deane,.....	"	XVIII.	63
1670. Aug. 24.	Lattin, Richard, and Joane Ireland,........	C. A.,	II.	580
1756. Nov. 1.	Lattin, Sarah, and Coles Carpenter,........	M. B.,	I.	343
1773. Dec. 15.	Lattin, Thomas, and Elizabeth Holmes,....	"	XXII.	76
1764. Dec. 18.	Latting, Freelove, and John Cock,.........	"	VIII.	458
1765. Jan. 4.	Latting, Joseph, and Martha Wright,.......	"	IX.	8
1764. Oct. 6.	Latting, Phebe, and Stephen Concklin,.....	"	VIII.	336
1764. Jan. 13.	Latting, William, and Sarah Carpenter,.....	"	VIII.	15
1770. Oct. 11.	Latting, Zerviah, and James Farley,.......	"	XVI.	208
1783. Feb. 25.	Lattoretee, Susanna, and John Wandel,....	"	XXXVIII.	52
1777. Oct. 15.	Laturett, Ann, and Abraham Cannon, ...	"	XXIV.	162a
1773. July 22.	Laugharne, Arthur, and Ann Phillips,......	"	XXI.	48
1758. April 15.	Laughton, Elizabeth, and Crawley Borrows,	"	I.	875
1782. Dec. 14.	Laughton, John, and Elizabeth Whitehead,.	"	XXXVII.	121
1765. Jan. 28.	Laughton, John, and Mary Beaton, ...	"	IX.	32
1780. Sept. 11.	Laune, Peter, and Elizabeth Dudley,.......	"	XXX.	24
1778. Sept. 5.	Laurence, Ann, and Justus Earle, ...	"	XXVI.	22
1736. Jan. 24.	Laurence, Debor, and John Van Wyck,.....	"	I.	5
1753. Sept. 6.	Laurence, Deborah, and John Bookhout,...	"	I.	108
1778. Aug. 26.	Laurence, Elizabeth Willet, and George Barnewall, ...	"	XXVI.	12
1672. Feb. 1.	Laurence, Elizabeth, and Thomas Stevens,..	G. E.,	IV.	251
1780. Aug. 12.	Laurence, Hannah, and Jacob Schieffelin,...	M. B.,	XXIX.	140
1755. Sept. 20.	Laurence, Mary, and Daniel Carter, ...	"	I.	179
167⁶⁄₇. Jan. 25.	Laurence, Susannah, and Gabriell Minviele,	W. O. P.,	III.	237
167⁵⁄₆. Mar. 9.	Laurence, William, and Ann Edsall, ...	"	III.	183
1664. Mar. 4.	Laurence, William, and Elizabeth Smith,...	G. E.,	I.	98
1753. May 24.	Laurence, William, and Mary Kettle,......	M. B.,	I.	41
1763. May 19.	Laurence, William, and Phebe Latten,.....	"	VII.	193
1683. April 11.	Laurison, John, and Jamima Halsie,........	E.,	XXXIII.	49
1760. Feb. 10.	Lauson, Sarah, and Marquis Ffunbubble,...	M. B.,	III.	30
1756. Dec. 30.	Lauter, John Augustus, and Catharine Bun,	"	I.	403
1782. Dec. 19.	Lavarrah, Sarah, and Owen Dealy,........	"	XXXVII.	127
1768. Mar. 17.	Lave, Ann, and Hugh McDowll,......... ...	"	XIII.	50
1779. June 4.	Lave, Mary, and Richard Albouy,.........	"	XXVII.	158
1777. Jan. 13.	Lavender, Margaret, and Robert Rouse,....	"	XXIV.	12
1768. Oct. 15.	Lavine, Abraham, and Hannah Parcell,.....	"	XIII.	211
1770. Sept. 6.	Lavoy, Peter, and Ann Bond,.............	"	XVI.	182
1736. Aug. 10.	Lawdit, Elizabeth, and John Blancker,.....	"	I.	2

DATE.	NAMES.	RECORD.	VOL.	PAGE.
1765. Aug. 10.	Lawell, John, and Alice Hopson,.........	M. B.,	IX.	258
1764. Oct. 4.	Lawler, Cornelius, and Easter Derby,......	"	VIII.	333
1762. Jan. 19.	Lawn, George, and Hannah Stokes,.......	"	VI.	17
1781. Aug. 10.	Lawrance, Daniel, and Jemime Brevoort,...	"	XXXIII.	33
1773. Nov. 3.	Lawrance, Elizabeth, and Harman Cripcer,..	"	XXII.	8
1767. July 10.	Lawrance, Gilbert, and Elizabeth Rushmore,	"	XI.	132
1758. May 24.	Lawrence, Abigail, and James James,......	"	I.	908
1780. July 17.	Lawrence, Abigail, and Morris Carpenter,..	"	XXIX.	111
1706. Dec. 6.	Lawrence, Abraham, and Mary Smith,.....	"	I.	373
1771. July 23.	Lawrence, Ann, and Baltus Van Kleeck, ...	"	XVII.	140
1764. April 9.	Lawrence, Ann, and George Yeomans,.....	"	VIII.	144
1775. June 9.	Lawrence, Ann, and Joseph Roe,..........	"	XXIII.	58
1781. June 16.	Lawrence, Ann, and Samuel Moore, 3d,....	"	XXXII.	87
1768. Jan. 16.	Lawrence, Anna, and Samuel Riker,.......	"	XIV.	13
1772. Jan. 21.	Lawrence, Anna, and Zachariah Vanvorhis,.	"	XVIII.	15
1780. Nov. 10.	Lawrence, Benjamin, and Ann Seabury,....	"	XXX.	101
1758. Oct. 30.	Lawrence, Benjamin, and Elizabeth Roberts,	"	II.	72
1780. Oct. 6.	Lawrence, Catharine, and Jacob Winants,..	"	XXX.	58
1781. Nov. 15.	Lawrence, Catharine, and Philip Lawrence,.	"	XXXIV.	37
1762. Sept. 25.	Lawrence, Catharine, and William Sutherland,...............................	"	VI.	333
1763. Feb. 2.	Lawrence, Catherine, and Cornelius Fisher,..	"	VII.	50
1753. June 12.	Lawrence, Catherine, and Epenetus Platt, ..	"	I.	58
1771. Dec. 16.	Lawrence, Catherine, and John Rider,.....	"	XVII.	295
1757. July 2.	Lawrence, Clarke, and Mary Mudge,.......	"	I.	579
1766. Nov. 4.	Lawrence, Daniel, and Ann Talman,.......	"	X.	152
1771. Dec. 28.	Lawrence, Daniel, and Elizabeth Acklay,...	"	XVII.	305
1765. Jan. 10.	Lawrence, Daniel, and Eva Van Horne,....	"	IX.	13
1773. Nov. 30.	Lawrence, Daniel, and Phebe Simons,.....	"	XXII.	53
1762. Feb. 8.	Lawrence, Daniel, and Rachel King,.......	"	VI.	40
1782. Oct. 16.	Lawrence, David, and Sarah Fowler,......	"	XXXVII.	43
1756. Oct. 30.	Lawrence, Deborah, and James Burling,....	"	I.	340
1762. Oct. 25.	Lawrence, Elison, and John Sneden,.......	"	VI.	381
1778. Oct. 24.	Lawrence, Elizabeth, and Daniel Braine,....	"	XXVI.	71
1761. Oct. 30.	Lawrence, Elizabeth, and David Archibald,.	"	V.	180
1683. July 26.	Lawrence, Elizabeth, and John Sanders,...	E.,	XXXIII.	74
1772. Aug. 29.	Lawrence, Elizabeth, and Peearcy Poole,...	M. B.,	XIX.	34
1681. Mar. 26.	Lawrence, Elizabeth, and Phillip Carterett,.	O. W.,	XXXII½.	39
1771. Mar. 15.	Lawrence, Elizabeth, and Richard Seaman,.	M. B.,	XVII.	34
1737. Oct. 15.	Lawrence, Elizabeth, and Thomas Willet,...	"	I.	7
1765. Aug. 2.	Lawrence, Elizabeth, and William Titchbourn, ...	"	IX.	229
1781. April 28.	Lawrence, Euphaney, and Jonas Farrington,	"	XXXII.	20
1776. Dec. 23.	Lawrence, Fanny, and John Vanderbelt,....	"	XXIV.	205
1763. Feb. 9.	Lawrence, Frances, and Sebastian Ellis,.....	"	VII.	57

29

DATE.	NAMES.	RECORD.	VOL.	PAGE.
1764. Dec. 11.	Lawrence, Hanna, and George Baker,.....	M. B.,	VIII.	451
1763. June 18.	Lawrence, Hannah, and Hendrick Bell,....	"	VII.	232
1761. Oct. 6.	Lawrence, Hannah, and William Hannah,..	"	V.	124
1757. Oct. 15.	Lawrence, Isaac, and Judith Howard,......	"	I.	672
1761. Nov. 30.	Lawrence, Isaac, and Mary Ann Hampton,.	"	V.	258
1761. Dec. 4.	Lawrence, Isaac, and Mary Cheeseman,....	"	V.	264
1770. Mar. 24.	Lawrence, Jacob, and Massey Rhoads,.....	" -	XVI.	38
1759. April 18.	Lawrence, John, and Catharine Livingston,.	"	II.	244
1769. June 28.	Lawrence, John, and Catherine Beekman,..	"	XIV.	133
1761. Oct. 5.	Lawrence, John, and Elenor James,.......	"	V.	122
1753. Oct. 1.	Lawrence, John, and Elizabeth Youngs,....	"	I.	129
1776. Feb. 27.	Lawrence, John and Mary Pinfold, ...	"	XXIII.	274
1783. May 3.	Lawrence, John, and Mary Reazau,.......	"	XXXVIII.	125
1778. July 4.	Lawrence, John, and Vally Heldredge,.....	"	XXV.	119
1682. Nov. 20.	Lawrence, John, Jr., and Sarah Bridges,....	E.,	XXXIII.	20
1768. Aug. 5.	Lawrence, Jonathan, and Ruth Riker,.....	M. B.,	XIII.	168
1763. Nov. 7.	Lawrence, Jordan, and Ruth Mott,........	"	VII.	432
1775. May 11.	Lawrence, Joseph, and Margaret Van Valkenburgh, ...	"	XXIII.	30
1770. Aug. 22.	Lawrence, Joseph, and Phebe Halstead,....	"	XVI.	166
1764. Mar. 17.	Lawrence, Joseph, and Phebe Townsend,..	"	VIII.	108
1777. May 9.	Lawrence, Leggett, and Mary Barnes,......	"	XXIV.	86
1771. Nov. 13.	Lawrence, Leonard, and Margaret Doughty,	"	XVII.	255
1675. Aug. 22.	Lawrence, Martha, and Thomas Snawsell,..	W. O. P.,	III.	126
1772. July 15.	Lawrence, Mary, and David Johnson, ...	M. B.,	XVIII.	166
173⁶⁄₇. Mar. 21.	Lawrence, Mary, and Ebenezor Burling, ...	"	I.	5
1780. Dec. 26.	Lawrence, Mary, and Effingham Embree, ..	"	XXX.	169
1768. June 27.	Lawrence, Mary, and Hercules Cronk,.....	"	XIII.	138
1766. Oct. 20.	Lawrence, Mary, and Isaac Post, ...	"	X.	131
1757. Jan. 15.	Lawrence, Mary, and Isaac Woodward,....	"	I.	417
1778. Mar. 7.	Lawrence, Mary, and Jacob Gasling, ...	"	XXV.	34
1737. Sept. 23.	Lawrence, Mary, and John Barker, ...	"	I.	7
1770. July 28.	Lawrence, Mary, and John Lefferts,.......	"	XVI.	149
1783. June 12.	Lawrence, Mary, and Peter Bogert,.......	"	XXXIX.	54
1780. Oct. 5.	Lawrence, Mary, and Richard Lawrence,...	"	XXX.	56
1782. Oct. 2.	Lawrence, Mary, and Robert Lawrence,...	"	XXXVII.	23
1759. Sept. 27.	Lawrence, Mary, and Samuel Betts,.......	"	II.	434
1769. Dec. 12.	Lawrence, Mary, and Thomas Skidmore,...	"	XV.	121
1782. June 3.	Lawrence, Mary, and William Kippin,.....	"	XXXVI.	36
1757. Sept. 24.	Lawrence, Mary, and William Milburne,...	"	I.	645
1775. June 24.	Lawrence, Melancton, and Sarah Greenock,.	"	XXIII.	77
1671. Dec. 16.	Lawrence, Miss, and Thomas Walton,......	G. E.,	IV.	73
1760. Dec. 4.	Lawrence, Nathaniel,Jr., and Martha Duncan,	M. B.,	III.	455
1781. Nov. 15.	Lawrence, Philip, and Catharine Lawrence,.	"	XXXIV.	37
1762. Nov. 14.	Lawrence, Rachel, and John Wright,..,..	"	VII.	449

DATE.	NAMES.	RECORD.	VOL.	PAGE.
1760. Oct. 14.	Lawrence, Richard, and Amy Berrien,.....	M. B.,	III.	363
1778. Dec. 22.	Lawrence, Richard, and Elizabeth Oakley,...	"	XXVI.	130
1780. Oct. 5.	Lawrence, Richard, and Mary Lawrence,...	"	XXX.	56
1782. Oct. 2.	Lawrence, Robert, and Mary Lawrence,....	"	XXXVII.	23
1768. Feb. 12.	Lawrence, Samuel, and Elizabeth Hazard,..	"	XIII.	35
1765. June 11.	Lawrence, Samuel, and Mary Sneden,.....	"	IX.	160
1760. May 28.	Lawrence, Sarah, and David Anderson,....	"	III.	165
1758. Dec. 21.	Lawrence, Sarah, and James Farrington,....	"	II.	135
1781. Dec. 20.	Lawrence, Sarah, and Norris Hicks,.......	"	XXXIV.	97
1771. June 19.	Lawrence, Sarah, and Peter Van Pelt,......	"	XVII.	116
1782. May 11.	Lawrence, Sarah, and Samuel Deall,.......	"	XXXV.	160
1760. Dec. 5.	Lawrence, Silas, and Deborah Roe,........	"	III.	459
1778. Mar. 12.	Lawrence, Stephen, and Margaret Jackson,.	"	XXV.	39
1779. Sept. 14.	Lawrence, Thomas, and Elinor Earle,......	"	XXVIII.	76
1760. Aug. 27.	Lawrence, Thomas, and Elizabeth Fish,....	"	III.	269
1757. Dec. 29.	Lawrence, Thomas, and Elizabeth Hadley,..	"	I.	760
1775. June 26.	Lawrence, Thomas, and Mary Morris,......	"	XXIII.	78
1764. Jan. 4.	Lawrence, Violetta, and Benjamin Field,...	"	VIII.	5
1680. June 1.	Lawrence, William, and Deborah Smith, ...	G. E.,	XXXII.	86
1771. April 6.	Lawrence, William, and Mary Palmer,.....	M. B.,	XVII.	48
1756. Dec. 16.	Lawrence, William, and Rachel Brewer, ...	"	I.	386
1736. Nov. 12.	Lawrence, William, and Zeperah Coles, ...	"	I.	3
1672. Feb. 1.	Lawrenson, Hannah, and Joseph Thorne,...	G. E.,	IV.	251
1761. July 7.	Lawsing, John, and Catharine Shearer,.....	M. B.,	IV.	287
1763. Oct. 10.	Lawson, Catharine, and Walter Cure,......	"	VII.	382
1777. Mar. 15.	Lawson, Elizabeth, and James Foreman,...	"	XXIV.	44
1782. April 15.	Lawson, Janett, and Thomas Stovey, ...	"	XXXV.	122
1775. Oct. 9.	Lawson, Thomas, and Catharine Cosser,. ..	"	XXIII.	176
1765. July 8.	Lawson, Thomas, and Sarah Finley, ...	"	IX.	198
1762. Mar. 27.	Lawson, William, and Catharine Haviland,.	"	VI.	84
1761. July 6.	Lawyer, Johannes, and Anna Maria Michael,	"	IV.	278
1763. Aug. 6.	Layton, Elizabeth, and John Schenck,.....	"	VII.	293
1783. July 2.	Lazenby, Mary, and Andrew Bouman,.....	"	XXXIX.	79
1761. May 23.	Leach, Abigail, and Morris Earle, ...	"	IV.	203
1780. Dec. 23.	Leach, Elizabeth, and John Love,.........	"	XXX.	168
1770. April 25.	Leach, Phineas, and Maria Groot,.........	"	XVI.	69
1753. July 24.	Leach, Stephen, and Abigail Braisher,.....	"	I.	77
1764. April 5.	Leacraft, Elizabeth, and Jacob Suydam,....	"	VIII.	134
1736. May 8.	Leacraft, George, and Sarah Norbury,.....	"	I.	1
1760. Sept. 24.	Leacraft, Mary, and Peter Farmer,........	"	III.	326
1737. May 9.	Leacraft, Richard, and Elizabeth Elsworth,..	"	I.	6
1771. Oct. 24.	Leadbetter, James, and Esther Vanduersen,.	"	XVII.	221
1771. Mar. 5.	Leadbetter, Letitia, and William Mott,.....	"	XVII.	24
1765. Feb. 15.	Leadbetter, William, and Lettice Wright,...	"	IX.	54
1766. June 26.	Leader, Margaret, and Samuel Hallowell,...	"	X.	33

DATE.	NAMES.	RECORD.	VOL.	PAGE.
1783. Mar. 27.	Leadson, Easter, and Samuel Murgatroyd,..	M. B.,	XXXVIII.	78
1757. Jan. 22.	Leake, Elce, and Jacob Larzelere,.........	"	I.	424
1759. June 14.	Leake, Lena, and John Benham,..........	"	II.	324
1765. June 14.	Leake, Mitty, and William Bartley,.......	"	IX.	169
1757. July 27.	Leake, Sarah, and John Micheau,.........	'	I.	602
1755. Oct. 30.	Leaming, Jeremiah, Jr., and Elizabeth Peck,	'	I.	202
1759. Dec. 24.	Lean, Margaret, and John Wigmore, ...	"	II.	558
1763. July 28.	Leanerback, Sarah, and Thomas Davenport,.	"	VII.	284
1779. June 3.	Lear, Jesse, and Elinor Mitchell, ...	"	XXVII.	154
1778. June 6.	Lear, Rachel, and Francis Redmond,.......	"	XXV.	98
1775. July 31.	Leary, William, and Henrietta Elsworth,...	"	XXIII.	115
1758. May 30.	Leathes, John, and Susannah Clarke,......	"	I.	918
1771. June 5.	Leaycraft, John, and Elizabeth Haldane,...	"	XVII.	102
1763. May 28.	Leaycraft, Mary, and James Riker,........	"	VII.	206
1765. May 28.	Leaycraft, Richard,and Mary Van Steenbergh,	"	IX.	143
1764. July 10.	Leaycraft, Viner, Jr., and Rachel Willet,....	"	VIII.	253
1782. Nov. 6.	Lebeston, William, and Elizabeth Lashire,..	"	XXXVII.	73
1764. Nov. 1.	Le Brown, Elizabeth, and Richard Ten Eyck,.............................	"	VIII.	387
1762. Oct. 29.	Le Cont, Josiah, and Susannah Soulice,....	"	VI.	393
1763. Oct. 20.	Le Cont, Sarah, and John Steenbergh,.....	"	VII.	396
1763. July 1.	Leconte, Anne, and Peter Flandreau,......	"	VII.	253
1752. Jan. 8.	Leddel, Joseph, and Mary Patterson,......	"	I.	925
1761. Dec. 24.	Leddel, Mary Magdalen, and Richard Hartley,..............................	"	V.	303
1778. Jan. 28.	Ledner, Catharine, and Pierre Nery,.......	"	XXV.	13
1763. April 7.	Ledru, Harman, and Margaret Hendrie,....	"	VII.	117
1736. Oct. 14.	Lee, Abigail, and Joseph Langdon,........	"	I.	3
1760. July 23.	Lee, Isaac, and Elizabeth Wouters,........	"	III.	223
1758. Nov. 18.	Lee, Isaac, and Mary Askin,..............	"	II.	93
1780. Nov. 27.	Lee, John, and Ann Dela Vew,...........	"	XXX.	127
1767. Jan. 7.	Lee, Mary, and Henry Brinckerhoff,.......	"	XI.	5
1768. April 28.	Lee, Misper, and Catherine Killman, ...	"	XIII.	88
1773. Jan. 30.	Lee, Peter, and Hannah Sandsbury, ...	"	XX.	32
1736. June 22.	Lee, Ruth, and Isaac Wright,.............	"	I.	1
1738. Sept. 18.	Lee, Sarah, and Solomon Comes,..........	"	I.	11
1778. Mar. 9.	Lee, Ursula, and John Dart,..............	"	XXV.	37
1771. April 24.	Lee, William, and Sarah Holmes,.........	"	XVII.	66
1761. Mar. 3.	Leech, Alexander, and Catherine Barret,...	"	IV.	89
1763. Aug. 25.	Leech, Thomas, and Hannah Funck,.......	"	VII.	312
1767. Feb. 7.	Lees, Janet, and Samuel Willis,...........	"	XI.	22
1772. Oct. 23.	Leevie, John, and Mary Romer, ...	"	XIX.	88
1763. Nov. 29.	Lefever, Johannes, and Sarah Bovier,......	"	VII.	480
1758. Nov. 8.	Lefever, Stephen, and Ann Wheeler,.......	"	II.	85
1760. Dec. 5.	Lefferd, Hannah, and John Smith,.........	"	III.	456

DATE.	NAMES.	RECORD.	VOL.	PAGE.
1782. Sept. 25.	Lefferts, Adam, and Rebecca Conckling, ...	M. B.,	XXXVII.	15
1780. Jan. 18.	Lefferts, Abigail, and Bateman Loyd, ...	"	XXVIII.	198
1778. Jan. 14.	Lefferts, Daniel, and Elizabeth Cornwell, ...	"	XXV.	5
1782. July 13.	Lefferts, Daniel, and Susanah Skidmore, ...	"	XXXVI.	80
1761. April 29.	Lefferts, Dirck, and Annatie Provoost, ...	"	IV.	173
1777. Mar. 29.	Lefferts, Elenor, and John Vannostrand, ...	"	XXIV.	54
1772. Mar. 4.	Lefferts, Garret, and Elizabeth Van Kleck, ..	'	XVIII.	47
1766. Oct. 15.	Lefferts, Harempy, and Hendrick Suydam, .	"	X.	124
1783. June 10.	Lefferts, Harmpie, and Jacob Conklin, ...	"	XXXIX.	47
1767. Nov. 27.	Lefferts. Ida, and Ram Van Pelt, ...	"	XII.	100
1773. June 14.	Lefferts, Idaa, and Rem Couwenhoven, ...	"	XXI.	4
1777. Jan. 20.	Lefferts, Jacob, and Ida Vanderveer, ...	"	XXIV.	14
1772. April 18.	Lefferts, Jacobus, and Lucretia Brinckerhoff,	"	XVIII.	85
1756. July 12.	Lefferts, Jacobus, Jr., and Mary Vanderhuyl,	"	I.	254
1766. Nov. 13.	Lefferts, Jane, and Jacob Sebring, ...	"	X.	162
1775. April 29.	Lefferts, Jane, and Peter Lefferts, ...	"	XXIII.	17
1765. April 17.	Lefferts, John, and Lammatje Van Der Bilt, .	"	IX.	98
1770. July 28.	Lefferts, John, and Mary Lawrence, ...	"	XVI.	149
1756. July 29.	Lefferts, Leffert, and Dorothy Cowenhoven, .	"	I.	263
1775. April 29.	Lefferts, Peter, and Jane Lefferts, ...	"	XXIII.	17
1757. Dec. 6.	Leffertse, Barent, and Famitje Remsen, ...	"	I.	726
1783. April 11.	Lefford, Catharine, and John Gamble, ...	"	XXXVIII.	90
1780. Sept. 11.	Lefford, James, and Mary Waters, ...	"	XXX.	22
1783. April 26.	Lefford, Titus, and Sarah Doughty, ...	"	XXXVIII.	118
1782. May 21.	Leforge, Charles, and Elizabeth Du Bou, ...	"	XXXVI.	15
1790. Dec. 19.	Lefoy, Elizabeth, and Thomas Hix, ...	"	I.	3
1776. Mar. 8.	Lefoy, Mary, and Garret Brouwer, ...	"	XXIII.	281
1783. Jan. 29.	Lefurge, Amos, and Frances Hurry, ...	"	XXXVIII.	31
1782. Jan. 1.	Legang, Ann, and James Linvill, ...	"	XXXV.	1
1760. Jan. 14.	Legg, Elsie, and Stephen Lane, ...	"	II.	579
1775. Sept. 6.	Legg, Neeltje, and Hendrick I. Mesick, ...	"	XXIII.	149
1759. Jan. 18.	Legget, Anapel, and James Flood, ...	"	II.	158
1772. May 15.	Legget, Anna, and John Russel, ...	"	XVIII.	119
1764. Jan. 30.	Legget, Catharine, and James Tomlinsson, ..	"	VIII.	44
1764. Feb. 27.	Legget, Esther, and Lawrence Hogeboom, ..	"	VIII.	81
1757. Dec. 28.	Legget, Gabriel, and Catherine Ash, ...	"	I.	754
1763. June 30.	Legget, Gertrude, and Jacob Vosburgh, ...	"	VII.	250
1764. April 19.	Legget, John, and Rachel Lemetter, ...	"	VIII.	164
1778. June 27.	Legget, Ruth, and Michael Collord, ...	"	XXV.	113
1764. Feb. 20.	Leggett, Ezekiel, and Jane Anjevoin, ...	"	VIII.	66
1765. July 9.	Leggett, Gabriel, and Mary Wiggins, ...	"	IX.	200
1761. Feb. 2.	Leggett, Isaac, and Hannah Wiggins, ...	"	IV.	47
1771. Oct. 15.	Leggett, Isaac, and Mary Oakley, ...	"	XVII.	208
1753. June 5.	Leggett, John, and Sarah Alsop, ...	"	I.	49
1779. Jan. 27.	Leggett, Susanah, and Theodorus Deforeest,	"	XXVII.	29

DATE.	NAMES.	RECORD.	VOL.	PAGE.
1760. Nov. 21.	Leghorn, Jane, and William Satchell,	M. B.,	III.	433
1763. April 28.	Legrange, Elenor, and Arie Lagrange,	"	VII.	150
1764. Oct. 19.	Le Grange, John, and Judith Clow,	"	VIII.	365
1782. June 8.	Legrange, Mary, and Moses Van Namer,	"	XXXVI.	42
1761. Nov. 20.	Le Grange, Orre, and Mary Van Antwerp, .	"	V.	237
1764. Mar. 12.	Le Gross, John, and Abigail Ayckley,	"	IV.	98
1670. Sept. 19.	Leigh, Francis, and Abigale Hendricks,	C. A.,	II.	594
1690. Feb. 3.	Leisler, Mary, and Jacob Milborne,	P. B.,	IV.	71
1756. Nov. 24.	Leister, Antje, and John Neefus,	M. B.,	I.	363
1767. Aug. 1.	Leister, Sarah, and Alexander Menzies,	"	XII.	6
1753. Oct. 9.	Leiyter, Garret, and Willemtje Wyckoff,	"	I.	135
1781. Dec. 27.	Lely, John, and Elizabeth Kingsland,	"	XXXIV.	108
1764. April 19.	Lemetter, Rachel, and John Legget,	"	VIII.	164
1777. Sept. 29.	Lemote, Susanah, and James Nash,	"	XXIV.	152
1686. Sept. 17.	Lemouletz, Jean, and Helena Fell,	C. M.,	XXXIII.	296
1758. May 6.	Lenard, Mary, and John Denton,	M. B.,	I.	895
1761. Jan. 29.	Lende, Ernest Ludewig, and Cornelia Corsa,	"	IV.	36
1759. Jan. 24.	Lenerton, Elizabeth, and John Wood,	"	II.	165
1782. Jan. 31.	Lennox, David, and Susannah Webster,	"	XXXV.	40
1759. July 19.	Lennox, Samuel, and Agnus Rose,	"	II.	359
1758. May 24.	Lenonton, Mary, and Daniel Pearce,	"	I.	900
1779. July 28.	Lenox, Mary, and Joseph Clarke,	"	XXVIII.	34
1768. Dec. 16.	Lent, Abraham, and Mary Deronda,	"	XIII.	264
1753. Sept. 11.	Lent, Abram, and Jane Curser,	"	I.	114
1764. Nov. 9.	Lent, Aletic, and George Rapalie,	"	VIII.	398
1761. April 9.	Lent, Jane, and Tunis Lafurgee,	"	IV.	141
1768. Jan. 20.	Lent, Margaret, and Garret Snedeker,	"	XIII.	14
1768. Mar. 29.	Lent, Mary, and Oliver Hobbs,	"	XIII.	57
1769. Dec. 18.	Lent, Peter, and Trentje De Witt,	"	XV.	124
1775. Oct. 16.	Lent, Sarah, and William McKellop,	"	XXIII.	181
1762. Nov. 6.	Leonard, Catharine, and Henry Smith,	"	VI.	416
1782. Feb. 24.	Leonard, Daniel, and Amy Morrell,	"	XXXV.	64
1761. Jan. 16.	Leonard, Elizabeth, and Benjamin Smith,	"	IV.	241
1781. Dec. 17.	Leonard, Elizabeth, and Edward Duffel,	"	XXXIV.	92
1782. June 12.	Leonard, Elizabeth, and Jonathan Pell,	"	XXXVI.	48
1738. July 11.	Leonard, Jacob, and Mary Moore,	"	I.	10
1771. Nov. 26.	Leonard, James, and Charity Alner,	"	XVII.	270
1760. Nov. 26.	Leonard, Jane, and Benjamin Carpenter,	"	III.	447
1759. Aug. 21.	Leonard, Jeffery, and Mary Steddiford,	"	II.	386
1738. Sept. 22.	Leonard, Josiah, and Elizabeth Harris,	"	I.	11
1780. May 30.	Leonard, Martha, and Daniel Cristian Fueter,	"	XXIX.	75
1761. Sept. 23.	Leonard, Martha, and Dennis McGillycuddy,	"	V.	93
1772. Oct. 14.	Leonard, Mary, and Andrew Thompson,	"	XIX.	70
1773. Nov. 5.	Leonard, Nancy, and John Harris,	"	XXII.	15
1762. April 22.	Leonard, Robert, and Mary Bell,	"	VI.	124

DATE.			NAMES.	RECORD.	VOL.	PAGE.
1761.	Nov.	26.	Leonard, Samuel, and Deborah West, ...	M. B.,	v.	250
1775.	July	19.	Leonard, Sarah, and Joseph Griffith, ...	"	xxiii.	99
1767.	Dec.	7.	Leonard, Temperance, and Thomas Smith, . .	"	xii.	109
1736.	Nov.	25.	Leosha, Sarah, and Isaac Beedle, ...	"	i.	3
1762.	Aug.	7.	Lepinget, Elizabeth, and Walter Cure, ...	"	vi.	268
1761.	May	27.	Leppard, Sarah, and Henry Shutze, ...	"	iv.	208
1765.	May	14.	Lequer, Abraham, and Catharine Cowenhoven, ...	"	ix.	126
1736.	Mar.	21.	Lequie, Ame, and Jacob Sowdam, ...	"	i.	5
1738.	Oct.	7.	Lequier, Jonathan, and Elizabeth Schank, . .	"	i.	11
1763.	Oct.	28.	Lequiere, Catharine, and Abraham Marlatt, .	"	vii.	409
1763.	Jan.	7.	Lequire, Elisabeth, and Martin Rappelje, . . .	"	vii.	9
1765.	April	27.	Le Roux, Charles, and Sarah Duryea, ...	"	ix.	112
1763.	Jan.	26.	Lerow, Selata, and Samuel Niscombe, ...	"	vii.	36
1763.	April	12.	Le Roy, Francis, and Sarah Ellis, ...	"	vii.	125
1766.	May	30.	Le Roy, Jacob, and Catherine Rutgers, . . .	"	x.	2
1775.	May	11.	Le Roy, Mary, and John Livingston, Jr., . . .	"	xxiii.	29
1780.	Dec.	22.	Leslie, Alexander, and Mary Ellis, ...	"	xxx.	165
1758.	Oct.	24.	Leslie, George Willocks, and Mary Alsop, . .	"	ii.	66
1783.	Feb.	26.	Leslie, James, and Mary Ferguson, ...	"	xxxviii.	55
1759.	Nov.	23.	Lessier, Antje, and John Brower, Jr., ...	"	ii.	515
1767.	Oct.	27.	Lester, Christian, and Tobias Norwood, ...	"	xii.	71
1780.	June	28.	Lester, Elizabeth, and Cornelis Hoogland, . .	'	xxix.	101
1767.	June	12.	Lester, Margaret, and James Peters, ...	"	xi.	106
1736.	Mar.	24.	Lester, Margret, and Joseph Hicks, ...	"	i.	5
1763.	Dec.	24.	Lester, Rachel, and William Harvey, ...	"	vii.	525
1758.	Mar.	11.	Lester, Samuel, and Christiana Riffle, ...	"	i.	845
1763.	Oct.	19.	Letelleer, Mary, and Charles Oliver Bruff, . .	"	vii.	393
1757.	Oct.	27.	Letson, John, and Susannah Haywood, ...	"	i.	686
1758.	Jan.	9.	Letson, Joseph, and Ester Campbell, ...	"	i.	777
1779.	Sept.	3.	Letson, Robert, and Elizabeth Norris, ...	"	xxviii.	66
1777.	April	4.	Letteny, William, and Hanah Evans, ...	"	xxiv.	57
1770.	April	4.	Leuon, David, and Mary Russell, ...	"	xvi.	47
1762.	Sept.	17.	Lever, Benjamin, and Benjamin Holmes, . . .	"	vi.	319
1779.	Feb.	19.	Lever, Elizabeth, and Humphrey Massenburg, ...	"	xxvii.	43
1761.	Jan.	13.	Lever, Elizabeth, and Robert Keech, ...	"	iv.	15
1762.	May	25.	Leverage, Ruth, and Robert Hallett, ...	"	vi.	169
1767.	May	1.	Leverch, Elathan, and Mary Coe, ...	"	xi.	74
1768.	Dec.	31.	Leverich, Ann, and Samuel Moore, ...	"	xiii.	276
1782.	May	15.	Leverich, Patience, and Henry Stanton, ...	"	xxxvi.	3
1781.	Nov.	14.	Leverich, Richard, and Ame Titus, ...	"	xxxiv.	33
1759.	Oct.	2.	Leverich, Sarah, and Joseph Gosline, ...	"	ii.	442
1765.	Feb.	5.	Leveridge, John, and Sarah Cornish, ...	"	ix.	46
1757.	Feb.	21.	Leversie, Cornelius, and Cornelia Bradt, ...	"	i.	446

DATE.	NAMES.	RECORD.	VOL.	PAGE.
1759. June 20.	Leverson, Lydia, and William Verplanck,...	M. B.,	III.	333
1763. July 12.	Leveston, John, and Margaret Bolton, ...	"	VII.	262
1763. May 17.	Levige, Sarah, and John Hains,..........	"	VII.	190
1760. Sept. 9.	Levinus, Charity, and John Melwood, ...	"	III.	307
1760. Sept. 26.	Levison, Harman, and Catherine Winne,...	"	III.	331
1782. May 22.	Levy, Asher, and Mary Thompson, ...	"	XXXVI.	18
1684. Dec. 23.	Levy, Asser, and Maria Levy,.............	C. M.,	XXXIII.	76
1767. Nov. 2.	Levy, Hannah, and John Hannan, ...	M. B.,	XII.	74
1684. Dec. 23.	Levy, Maria, and Asser Levy, ...	C. M.,	XXXIII.	76
1778. May 9.	Lewey, John, and Louisa Egerton,........	M. B.,	XXV.	77
1780. Nov. 16.	Lewis, Abigail, and Thomas Seaman,......	"	XXX.	108
1770. April 6.	Lewis, Abraham, and Leah Van Wagener,..	"	XVI.	51
1764. June 6.	Lewis, Ann, and John Thompson,.........	"	VIII.	208
1761. April 7.	Lewis, Ann, and Peter Van Kleeck,.......	"	IV.	137
1757. Aug. 11.	Lewis, Ann, and William Betts,..........	"	I.	611
1763. Dec. 19.	Lewis, Archelaus, and Susannah Roome,...	"	VII.	513
1756. Oct. 9.	Lewis, Barent, and Christiena Van Benthuysen, ...	"	I.	323
1761. Oct. 29.	Lewis, Barent, and Leah Van Etta, ...	"	V.	176
1772. Jan. 28.	Lewis, Benjamin, and Amy Frost,.........	"	XVIII.	20
1759. Oct. 29.	Lewis, Charles, and Elizabeth Kindal,.....	"	II.	476
1773. Oct. 11.	Lewis, Daniel, and Abigail Caston,.......	"	XXI.	136
1762. April 2.	Lewis, Deliverance, and Abraham Snedaker,	"	VI.	89
1773. Oct. 28.	Lewis, Dorothy, and Hubert Van Wagenen,.	"	XXII.	2
1759. Feb. 1.	Lewis, Dorothy, and Jeffery Cowper,......	"	I.	431
1758. Mar. 17.	Lewis, Elizabeth, and John Mitchell,.......	"	I.	854
1782. Oct. 17.	Lewis, Elizabeth, and John Robinson,......	"	XXXVII.	49
1771. Jan. 18.	Lewis, Elizabeth, and Richard Goodwin, ...	"	XVII.	7
1760. June 27.	Lewis, Elizabeth, and Thomas Richardson,..	"	XVI.	124
1770. Mar. 21.	Lewis, Foster, and Sarah Smith,..........	"	XVI.	36
1738. Nov. 11.	Lewis, Frances, and Garat Van Banthonsen,	"	I.	11
1757. Sept. 5.	Lewis, Frances, and Richard Davis,........	"	I.	632
1758. Oct. 24.	Lewis, Francis, and Mary Power,.........	"	II.	65
1760. Feb. 23.	Lewis, Freelove, and Michael George Lampkin, ...	"	III.	45
1773. Dec. 23.	Lewis, Hannah, and John Baker,..........	"	XXII.	86
1758. Mar. 22.	Lewis, Hazael, and Charity Bryant, ...	"	I.	860
1763. Mar. 30.	Lewis, Israel, and Hannah Norton,........	"	VII.	109
1782. May 25.	Lewis, James, and Elinor Stewart, ...	"	XXXVI.	23
1779. April 16.	Lewis, James, and Mary Vandewater, ...	"	XXVII.	107
1765. Jan. 31.	Lewis, Jemima, and Joseph Van Emburgh,.	"	IX.	40
1755. Nov. 3.	Lewis, John, and Dorothy Bydder,....... .	"	I.	205
1760. June 18.	Lewis, John, and Margaret Macguire,......	"	III.	192
1782. April 20.	Lewis, John, and Rachel Buskirk,.........	"	XXXV.	129
1766. Dec. 11.	Lewis, Jonathan, and Gertrude Goesbeck,..	"	X.	201

DATE.	NAMES.	RECORD.	VOL.	PAGE.
1759. Nov. 1.	Lewis, Joseph, and Anne Bertrand, ...	M. B.,	II.	484
1759. Oct. 29.	Lewis, Joseph, and Anne Montange, ...	"	II.	479
1759. Nov. 1.	Lewis, Joseph, Jr., and Naomi Conkling,...	"	II.	485
1778. Oct. 8.	Lewis, Kasiah, and John Harding, ...	"	XXVI.	51
1768. Oct. 10.	Lewis, Marah, and Arthur Alington,.......	"	XIII.	206
1758. Mar. 7.	Lewis, Margaret, and John Van Pelt,......	"	I.	835
1760. Feb. 1.	Lewis, Mary, and Andrew Barrey,........	"	III.	14
1777. Aug. 19.	Lewis, Mary, and Jarvis Clement,........	"	XXIV.	136
1770. May 15.	Lewis, Mary, and John Rhoades,..........	"	XVI.	86
1780. Nov. 20.	Lewis, Mary, and Robert Patterson,.......	"	XXX.	116
1777. July 12.	Lewis, Phebe, and Joseph Govier,.........	"	XXVIII.	21
1773. June 11.	Lewis, Robert, and Sidney Crawford,......	"	XX.	146
1760. Feb. 1.	Lewis, Ruth, and John Bunster,..........	"	III.	19
1773. Oct. 15.	Lewis, Samuel, and Anna Bunce, ...	"	XXI.	142
1767. Mar. 28.	Lewis, Samuel, and Mary Smith, ...	"	XI.	52
1775. April 11.	Lewis, Sarah, and James Dow, ...	"	XXIII.	7
1764. July 28.	Lewis, Susannah, and John Stout,.........	"	VIII.	271
1780. Oct. 11.	Lewis, Thomas, and Ann Beedle, ...	"	XXX.	62
1782. May 22.	Lewis, Tiddy, and John King,............	"	XXXVI.	16
1780. May 23.	Lewis, William, and Elizabeth Kelly, ...	"	XXIX.	67
1782. Jan. 29.	Lewis, William, and Jane Griffiths,........	"	XXXV.	37
1760. June 3.	Leycraft, Sarah, and John Gibbs,..........	"	III.	174
1777. Mar. 21.	Leydebach, Godfry, and Elizabeth Prills,...	"	XXIV.	40
1762. July 21.	Leydig, Frederick, and Mary Shearen, ...	"	VI.	251
1779. April 27.	Leyster, Sarah, and Francis Armstrong,....	"	XXVII.	121
1761. Dec. 19.	Leyster, Sarah, and Stephen Ryder, ...	"	V.	288
1682. June 1.	Leyston, Elyas, and Ann Hill, ...	O. W.,	XXXII½.	125
1672. Feb. 7.	Leyton, William, and Joan Harding,.......	G. E.,	IV.	257
1769. Dec. 29.	Lezier, Catharine, and James Reynolds,....	M. D.,	XV.	133
1768. June 27.	Lezier, Elizabeth, and Jacob Terhuen,......	"	XIII.	139
1761. June 26.	L'Hommedieu, Mary, and John Ingraham,..	"	IV.	264
1765. April 10.	Libbey, Daniel, and Rebecca Golding, ...	"	IX.	87
1736. Nov. 2.	Lierverse, Maritie, and Franciscus Lansingh,	"	I.	3
1760. Sept. 5.	Liester, Margaret, and Johannes Williamson,	"	III.	288
1757. Oct. 12.	Lieuse, Peter, and Maria Funda, ...	"	I.	666
1773. Mar. 3.	Light, James, and Jane Salisbury,.........	"	XX.	55
1775. July 31.	Light, James, Jr., and Johanna Griffiths,....	"	XXIII.	113
1780. Oct. 30.	Lightfoot, Darkus, and John Keaquick, ...	"	XXX.	86
1780. Sept. 30.	Lightfoot, Elizabeth, and Joseph Montgomery,................................	"	XXX.	49
1759. June 20.	Lightfoot, Sarah, and Thomas Steel,.......	"	II.	332
1767. Sept. 8.	Lillibridg, Hampton, and Mary Appleby, ...	"	XII.	29
1786. Jan. 4.	Lilly, George, and Julie Hickman,.........	"	XXVIII.	185
1754. Dec. 21.	Lilly, James, and Sarah Wytt,............	"	I.	210
1761. Nov. 4.	Linch, Mary, and Edward Carter,.........	"	V.	191

DATE.	NAMES.	RECORD.	VOL.	PAGE.
1756. Dec. 10.	Linch, Thomas, and Tabithy Case, ...	M. B.,	I.	379
1772. Nov. 21.	Lincoln, Hosea, and Elizabeth Carroll, ...	"	XIX.	123
1783. Oct. 29.	Lindeman, Allada, and William Corleys, . . .	"	XL.	91
1644. July 1.	Linden, Peter, and Martha Kombaer, ...	A. R.,	III.	218
1779. May 26.	Lindesay, Grace, and John Megger, ...	M. B.,	XXVII.	149
1763. Oct. 4.	Lindsay, Elizabeth, and Hugh Philips, ...	"	VII.	371
1772. May 20.	Lindsay, Hugh, and Sarah Delaplaine, ...	"	XVIII.	116
1783. April 17.	Lindsay, Margaret, and John King, ...	"	XXXVIII.	100
1763. Oct. 1.	Lindsay, William, and Elizabeth Pell, ...	"	VII.	366
1778. Jan. 26.	Lines, Stephen, and Martha Underhill, ...	"	XXV.	12
1769. Oct. 25.	Lines, Thomas, and Sarah Nickerson, ...	"	XV.	67
1761. July 27.	Linford, James, and Christian Van Ryper, . .	"	V.	9
1760. Nov. 18.	Lininton, John, and Lucretia Williamson, . . .	"	III.	426
1769. Aug. 1.	Lininton, Samuel, and Mary Van Siclen, . . .	"	XV.	13
1761. May 7.	Linkletar, James, and Catharine Hardenbrook,	"	IV.	183
1775. Oct. 28.	Linn, Philip, and Abigail Sickells, ...	"	XXIII.	189
1780. June 16.	Linn, Philip, and Cornelia Broadhurst, ...	"	XXIX.	89
1757. Nov. 18.	Lint, Hannah, and David Brown, ...	"	I.	707
1763. April 9.	Lint, Peter, and Mary De Clark, ...	"	VII.	120
1760. Sept. 10.	Lintot, Bernard, and Catharine Trotter, . . .	"	III.	308
1782. Jan. 1.	Linvill, James, and Ann Legang, ...	"	XXXV.	1
1758. Dec. 4.	Linzen, Mary, and Jacob Lyckfar, ...	"	II.	112
1770. July 12.	Lion, Henry, and Mary Van Bury, ...	"	XVI.	138
1764. Sept. 21.	Lipe, Marcelus, and John Savage, ...	"	VIII.	321
1758. Dec. 9.	Lippencut, Mary, and John Bird, ...	"	II.	124
1760. Dec. 19.	Lippingcutt, Dinah, and Thomas White, . . .	"	III.	486
1759. July 17.	Liscomb, Thomas, and Elizabeth Adams, . . .	"	II.	358
1760. Feb. 12.	Liscum, Catharine, and Everston Smith, ...	"	III.	33
1770. Dec. 29.	Lisk, Catherine, and Nathaniel Allen, ...	"	XVI.	309
1770. May 1.	Lisk, William, and Catharine Nesbit, ...	"	XVI.	76
1783. Dec. 31.	Lisle, Warren Pitt, and Sarah Morgan, ...	"	XL.	125
1761. Mar. 4.	Lispenard, Abigail, and Israel Underhill, . . .	"	IV.	90
1764. Dec. 10.	Lispenard, Anthony, and Sarah Barclay, . . .	"	VIII.	447
1759. Feb. 7.	Lispenard, Cornelia, and Thomas Marston, . .	"	II.	180
1775. Sept. 14.	Lispenard, Elizabeth, and Abraham T. Schenck, ...	"	XXIII.	156
1759. May 3.	Lispenard, Elizabeth, and Samuel Tredwell, .	"	II.	265
1753. April 14.	Lispenard, Mary, and Thomas Bayeux, ...	"	I.	22
1782. Mar. 19.	List, Mary, and John Manson, ...	"	XXXV.	90
1782. June 19.	Lister, Alexander, and Margaret Baveridge, .	"	XXXVI.	58
1772. Mar. 27.	Lister, Mary, and Richard Nassau Stephens,	"	XVIII.	62
1666. Sept. 18.	Litscho, Hannah, and Thomas Tiddeman, . . .	O. W. L.,	II.	134
1760. June 12.	Litsjer, Geertruy, and Martin Vosburgh, . . .	M. B.,	III.	187
1762. June 10.	Little, Elizabeth, and John McLean, ...	"	VI.	185
1769. Jan. 21.	Little, Fardinand, and Leddia Oliver, ...	"	XIV.	18

DATE.	NAMES.	RECORD.	VOL.	PAGE.
1758. May 8.	Lock, Mary, and Thomas Chambers,.......	M. B.,	I.	896
1783. June 28.	Lockerman, John, and Mary Turett,.......	"	XXXIX.	70
1771. July 17.	Lockerman, Margaret, and John Clark,.....	"	XVII.	135
1778. June 27.	Lockerman, Mary, and John Hatfield,.....	"	XXV.	116
1771. April 8.	Lockerman, William, and Mary Cole,......	"	XVII.	49
1760. Jan. 17.	Lockhart, John, and Sarah Crane,.........	"	VIII.	20
1686. Sept. 17.	Lockhartt, Jane, and John Merritt,........	C. M.,	XXXIII.	296
1782. Dec. 31.	Lockimin, Hester, and Robert Barnes,.....	M. B.,	XXXVII.	118
1778. April 1.	Lockman, Elizabeth, and Albert Rightman,.	"	XXV.	57
1679. Nov. 11.	Lockwood, Judith, and Daniel Maulsten,...	G. E.,	XXXII.	63
1763. May 11.	Lockwood, Phineas, and Ann Pettinger, ...	M. B.,	VII.	179
1762. June 14.	Lockwood, Ruth, and Seymour Sherwood,.	"	VI.	191
1772. Aug. 6.	Lockwood, Sarah, and John Anderson, ...	"	XIX.	14
1770. Oct. 15.	Lodewick, John, and Elizabeth Miller,.....	"	XVI.	213
1770. Sept. 2.	Lodewick, Rebecca, and Andrew Rous,....	"	XVI.	177
1761. June 17.	Logan, Elizabeth, and James Beard,.......	"	IV.	243
1738. Sept. 30.	Logan, Elizabeth, and James Wiley, ...	"	I.	11
1781. July 31.	Logan, John, and Catharine Nesbit, ...	"	XXXIII.	25
1782. Aug. 15.	Loise, Mary, and Epenetus Wood,........	"	XXXVI.	108
1782. Nov. 28.	Lokerman, Elizabeth, and Peter Wrightmen,	"	XXXVII.	95
1779. Feb. 6.	Lomax, John, and Ann Proffit, ...	"	XXVII.	37
1777. Mar. 25.	London, Elenor, and John King,..........	"	XXIV.	52
1763. Nov. 7.	Long, Christopher, and Sophia Cramer, ...	"	VII.	430
1783. Oct. 16.	Long, Elizabeth, and Alexander Gay,......	"	XL.	81
1765. Jan. 16.	Long, Elizabeth, and William Snow Steel,..	"	IX.	17
1762. July 30.	Long, Gertruy, and John Wiley,..........	"	VI.	256
1737. Sept. 13.	Long, Hardman, and Anne Healy, ...	"	I.	7
1776. Mar. 1.	Long, James, and Elizabeth Hope, ...	"	XXIII.	276
1764. Jan. 21.	Long, Margaret, and Thomas Collins, ...	"	VIII.	27
1777. Feb. 1.	Long, Richard, and Margaret Smith,.......	"	XXIV.	23
1783. Jan. 9.	Long, Richard, and Mary Fleat,...........	"	XXXVIII.	12
1762. July 9.	Long, William, and Isabella Campbell,.....	"	VI.	233
1779. Dec. 23.	Longbottom, Mary, and George Muirson,...	"	XXVIII.	178
1772. Sept. 22.	Longburn, Martha, and Jonathan Dickerson,	"	XIX.	54
1763. July 4.	Longendijck, Eva, and Albert Van Nors-trandt, ...	"	VII.	255
1778. May 21.	Longley, Thomas, and Ann Floyd, ...	"	XXV.	91
1782. Dec. 27.	Longshore, Jolly, and Rachael Bowlsby,....	"	XXXVII.	134
1760. Nov. 13.	Longsword, Anna, and Walter Cure, ...'	"	III.	407
1772. June 17.	Look, Phillip, and Madalena Van Wie,.....	"	XVIII.	141
1773. May 24.	Loose, Jane, and Pelig Randall,...........	"	XX.	124
1782. Mar. 9.	Loosely, Robert, and Catharine Roosehill, ..	"	XXXV.	81
1758. Mar. 22.	Loosie, Anne, and Bartholomew Noxon, Jr.,	"	I.	861
1765. Oct. 17.	Loosie, Joseph, and Catherine Harris,......	"	IX.	306
1759. July 16.	Lorgange, Samuel, and Sarah Devoe, ...	"	II.	356

DATE.	NAMES.	RECORD.	VOL.	PAGE
1778. Nov. 2.	Loriat, Catherina, and John Holsman, ...	M. B.,	XXVI.	81
1763. Aug. 19.	Lorilliard, John, and Hannah Moore, ...	"	VII.	309
1763. Aug. 19.	Lorilliard, Peter, and Catharine Moore, ...	"	VII.	308
1756. Oct. 11.	Loring, Benjamin, and Mary Hill, ...	"	I.	325
1760. Dec. 5.	Loring, Johanna, and Roger Fagg, ...	"	III.	457
1670. Oct. 7.	Lorrison, Hans, and Mary Sartell, ...	C. A.,	II.	594
1757. Aug. 26.	Lorway, Maretje, and Frans Winne, ...	M. B.,	I.	623
1768. Oct. 19.	Lose, Elizabeth, and David Masterton, ...	"	XIII.	213
1753. May 18.	Lose, Jane, and Johannes Boerum, ...	"	I.	33
1763. Feb. 1.	Lose, Joshua, and Catharine Knox, ...	"	VII.	47
1763. Dec. 1.	Losee, Ann, and James Pettet, ...	"	VII.	486
1765. May 1.	Losee, Catharine, and Baltus Vielee, ...	"	IX.	117
1773. May 17.	Losee, George, and Zena Vanderhuffen, ...	"	XX.	116
1764. Mar. 31.	Losee, James, and Anne Pettit, ...	"	VIII.	126
1759. Jan. 3.	Losee, Janetje, and Levinus Vandewater, ..	"	II.	144
1763. Dec. 7.	Losee, Martha, and Mathias Lane, ...	"	VII.	497
1764. Mar. 22.	Losee, Phebe, and Henry Sharpensteen, ...	"	VIII.	113
1769. June 19.	Losee, Rachel, and Moses Barber, ...	"	XIV.	122
1764. July 31.	Losee, Sarah, and John Nostran, ...	"	VIII.	272
1767. Nov. 5.	Losey, Abraham, and Sarah Hegeman, ...	"	XII.	121
1782. Dec. 30.	Losey, Peter, and Ketureh Hart, ...	"	XXXVII.	136
1783. Jan. 22.	Loshey, Uriah, and Frances Bradey, ...	"	XXXVIII.	26
1760. June 10.	Losie, Elizabeth, and Reuben Beagle, ...	"	III.	186
1762. June 10.	Losie, Miriam, and Francis Bogardus, ...	"	VI.	186
1768. June 1.	Losie, Simeon, and Hannah Hoff, ...	"	XIII.	121
1758. Sept. 8.	Losecc, Simon, and Susannah Boss, ...	"	II.	11
1772. Nov. 28.	Lot, George, and Jane Miserole, ...	"	XIX.	135
1765. May 4.	Lott, Abraham, and Jane Hendrickson, ...	"	IX.	119
1763. April 28.	Lott, Abraham, and Mary Van Wyck, ...	"	VII.	151
1766. June 21.	Lott, Altie, and Isaac Cortelyou, ...	"	X.	23
1776. Jan. 30.	Lott, Andrew, and Alice Goelet, ...	"	XXIII.	256
1760. Dec. 11.	Lott, Anne, and Gilbert Bogart, ...	"	III.	472
1782. June 19.	Lott, Anne, and Henry Statts, ...	"	XXXVI.	56
1781. April 26.	Lott, Anne, and William Williamson, ...	"	XXXII.	16
1764. Sept. 15.	Lott, Antje, and Stephen Duryee, ...	"	VIII.	310
1759. Jan. 8.	Lott, Antje, and Stephen Lott, ...	"	II.	147
1776. Feb. 24.	Lott, Catharine, and Charles Duryee, ...	"	XXIII.	272
1761. Mar. 30.	Lott, Catharine, and Thomas Crabb, ...	"	IV.	123
1782. Dec. 7.	Lott, Charity, and Peter Ball, ...	"	XXXVII.	111
1772. Oct. 21.	Lott, Dennis H., and Maria Schenck, ...	"	XIX.	81
1759. May 14.	Lott, Dorothy, and John Van Louwe, ...	"	II.	283
1782. Oct. 22.	Lott, Elizabeth, and Nicholas Williamson, ..	"	XXXVII.	61
1764. Sept. 10.	Lott, Esther, and Simon Flegler, ...	"	VIII.	302
1779. Jan. 19.	Lott, Else, and James Van Beuren, ...	"	XXVII.	18
1778. Aug. 10.	Lott, Gideon, and Sarah Bull, ...	"	XXVI.	1

DATE.		NAMES.	RECORD.	VOL.	PAGE.
1761. Sept.	31.	Lupton, William, and Johanna Schuyler,...	M. B.,	v.	64
1738. May	4.	Lurtraet, Maria, and Urin Tupper,.........	"	I.	9
1737. June	22.	Lusasen, John, and Janatie Ditmorse,......	"	I.	6
1781. Oct.	8.	Luse, Bethiah, and Daniel Joanes,.........	"	XXXIII.	93
1783. May	9.	Lush, Mary, and David Maitland, ...	"	XXXIX.	5
1771. Sept.	26.	Lush, Mary, and Wright Southgate,.......	"	XVII.	194
1760. Aug.	12.	Lush, William, and Catharine Ditcher, ...	"	III.	249
1774. Feb.	18.	Luskew, Jemima, and Zophar Ketcham, ...	"	XXII.	130
1779. Sept.	11.	Luther, Henry, and Sarah Shadden,.......	"	XXVIII.	73
1782. Aug.	5.	Lutkins, Elizabeth, and Aaron Cole,.......	"	XXXVI.	102
1777. Mar.	5.	Lutwyche, Edward Goldston, and Jane Rapelje,.............................	"	XXIV.	40
1781. Oct.	12.	Luyster, Cornelious, and Sarah Luyster,....	"	XXXIII.	98
1783. Oct.	7.	Luyster, Matthias, and Ann Van Bomlen,..	"	XL.	67
1760. Oct.	22.	Luyster, Peter, and Neltye Wickof,........	"	III.	379
1769. April	21.	Luyster, Peter, and Willemtje Luyster, ...	"	XIV.	81
1781. Oct.	12.	Luyster, Sarah, and Cornelious Luyster,....	"	XXXIII.	98
1768. Dec.	1.	Luyster, Sarah, and Joost Wyckoff,.......	"	XIII.	250
1769. April	21.	Luyster, Willemtje, and Peter Luyster, ...	"	XIV.	81
1757. Jan.	31.	Lyal, Alexander, and Sarah Osborn,.......	"	I.	429
1758. May	19.	Lyan, Benjamin, and Mary Hyatt, ...	"	I.	902
1781. Aug.	7.	Lyans, Eli, and Leah Smith,..............	"	XXXIII.	30
1758. Dec.	4.	Lyckfar, Jacob, and Mary Linzen,.........	"	II.	112
1768. Dec.	20.	Lydecker, Albert, and Sarah Sickels,.......	"	XIII.	269
1778. Mar.	18.	Lydekker, Elizabeth, and Jacob Roome, ...	"	XXV.	47
1762. Oct.	20.	Lyen, Sarah, and Peter Kattenhorn,.......	"	VI.	373
1771. Jan.	5.	Lyle, Abigail, and James Armitage, ...	"	XVII.	2
1761. Jan.	6.	Lyle, Abraham, and Jane Van Allen,......	"	IV.	5
1761. Aug.	11.	Lyn, Benjamin, and Mary Odell,..........	"	v.	37
1766. Dec.	11.	Lyn, Philander Hester, and Philip Brosher,.	"	x.	198
1769. June	26.	Lynal, Barbara, and John Richardson, ...	"	XIV.	131
1779. Jan.	20.	Lynch, Ann, and Michael McDonnell,......	"	XXVII.	19
1764. Feb.	25.	Lynch, John, and Pamela Simmonds,......	"	VIII.	80
1759. Dec.	20.	Lynch, Thomas, and Catharine Groasbeek,..	"	II.	553
1757. Sept.	19.	Lynd, Archelaus, and Sarah Abrahams,....	"	I.	638
1762. Dec.	4.	Lynd, John, and Hannah McJervis, ...	"	VI.	468
1772. Jan.	21.	Lynda, Cornelia, and James Duffey,.......	"	XVIII.	14
1761. July	14.	Lynde, Archelaus, and Mary Dovebagh,....	"	IV.	297
1770. Sept.	5.	Lyne, Anne, and David Seabury, ...	"	XVI.	178
1760. Sept.	4.	Lyneal, Dorothy, and William Tongue, ...	"	III.	283
1761. Feb.	7.	Lynerson, Adrijee, and James Campbell, ...	"	IV.	54
1782. Oct.	22.	Lynes, Holley, and Martha Pass,..........	"	XXXVII.	58
1755. Dec.	5.	Lynes, Mary, and Jonathan Smith,........	"	I.	226
1779. Jan.	10.	Lyng, John Burt, and Hester Moore, ...	"	XXVII.	9
1759. Sept.	11.	Lyng, John Burt, and Magdalane Jandine, .	"	II.	416

31

DATE.	NAMES.	RECORD.	VOL.	PAGE.
1760. May 5.	Lynn, Mary, and Thomas Lovegrove,......	M. B.,	III.	140
1770. Sept. 15.	Lynon, Susannah, and Charles Gardner, ...	"	XVI.	187
1773. Nov. 8.	Lynott, Elizabeth, and Abraham Bloodgood,	"	XXII.	17
1759. Jan. 20.	Lynott, Thomas, and Elizabeth Codding, ...	"	II.	163
1764. April 10.	Lynott, Thomas, and Elizabeth Van Valkin- burgh, ...	"	VIII.	147
1757. Feb. 25.	Lynsen, Abraham, Jr., and Magdalen Beek- man,................................	"	I.	451
1765. Aug. 27.	Lynsen, Catharine, and James Clarke, ...	"	IX.	247
1756. Oct. 22.	Lynsen, Joseph, and Hannah Vorse,.......	"	I.	331
1758. Feb. 1.	Lynser, Elizabeth, and Gilbert Outenbogert,	"	I.	808
1737. May 31.	Lynson, Elizabeth, and Ephraim Sayre, ...	"	I.	6
1782. Mar. 21.	Lynson, Jane, and James Moody,.........	"	XXXV.	94
1770. Feb. 7.	Lyon, Andrew, and Phebe Green,........	"	XVI.	13
1776. Jan. 11.	Lyon, Ann, and Richard Kip, Jr., ...	"	XXIII.	244
1763. Jan. 20.	Lyon, David, and Margaret Curry, ...	"	VII.	26
1764. Dec. 13.	Lyon, Gloriana, and Andrew Sniffen,......	"	VIII.	454
1759. Oct. 2.	Lyon, Phebe, and Pearson Halstead, ...	"	II.	444
1781. Feb. 19.	Lyon, Walker, and Sener Van Northwick,..	"	XXXI.	50
1759. April 5.	Lyons, David, and Elizabeth Conner, ...	"	II.	235
1765. Jan. 22.	Lyons, Elenor, and Cornelwell Jewell,.....	"	IX.	28
1761. May 2.	Lyons, Isaac, and Eleanor Skobey,.......	"	IV.	174
1757. April 29.	Lyons, Samuel, and Mary Kelly,..........	"	I.	520
1761. Aug. 4.	Lyset, William, and Jemima Weekes,......	"	V.	24
1764. Nov. 22.	Lyster, Altje, and Cornelius Smock,.......	"	VIII.	420
1738. April 20.	Lyster, Catherine, and Johannis De Witt,...	"	I.	9
1761. Oct. 7.	Lyster, Jane, and Abrahan Rapelye,.......	"	V.	130
1757. Aug. 13.	Lyster, John, and Hillitie Snedeker, ...	"	I.	614

M.

1762. Oct. 13.	Mabee, Ann, and Henry Sickles,..........	"	VI.	359
1760. Dec. 8.	Mabee, Harmanus, and Susannah Wimpell,..	"	III.	464
1757. Oct. 25.	Mabee, Margaret, and John R. Wempell, ..	"	I.	678
1773. May 26.	Mabey, Abraham, and Winchea Quackenboss,	"	XX.	128
1762. June 11.	Mabey, Mary, and John Westerveldt,......	"	VI.	188
1775. Oct. 25.	Mabie, Susannah, and Peter Conine,.......	"	XXIII.	186
1762. Aug. 18.	Maby, Peter, and Mary Bell, ...	"	VI.	279
1757. Sept. 24.	McAdam, Gilbert, and Sarah Cunningham,.	"	I.	636
1778. Mar. 14.	McAdam, John London, and Gloriana Nicoll,	"	XXV.	41
1779. Oct. 8.	McAllister, James, and Eleonora Callahan,..	"	XXVIII.	106
1757. May 12.	McAllister, Margaret, and William Cumming,	"	I.	529
1777. Sept. 11.	McAlpine, James, and Mary Culford, ...	"	XXIV.	146
1782. Aug. 13.	McAlpine, James, and Mary Turner,.......	"	XXXVI.	106

Date.	Names.	Record.	Vol.	Page.
1779. Dec. 21.	McAlpine, Margaret, and Daniel McDonold,	M. B.,	xxviii.	175
1779. July 21.	McAnalty, Ann, and Denis Dowlin, ...	"	xxviii.	26
1778. June 1.	McArthur, Alexander, and Margaret Bogert,	"	xxv.	96
1757. Oct. 8.	McArthur, Mary, and John Robson, ...	"	i.	661
1768. June 28.	McArthur, Mary, and Thomas McFarran,...	"	xiii.	143
1782. Jan. 10.	McAtee, James, and Grace Thetcher, ...	"	xxxv.	14
1782. June 8.	McBean, Sarah, and William Mulock, ...	"	xxxvi.	44
1778. July 29.	Macbeth, Isabella, and Daniel Ewing, ...	"	xxv.	142
1777. Feb. 18.	McBride, Elenor, and Patrick Murphey,....	"	xxiv.	30
1779. Aug. 2.	McBride, Elizabeth, and John Young, ...	"	xxviii.	42
1781. Sept. 6.	McBride, Elizabeth, and William Anderson,	"	xxxiii.	60
1736. Jan. 20.	Macburn, Thomas, and Mary Downs, ...	"	i.	5
1757. May 11.	McCabe, Hugh, and Elizabeth Hamilton,...	"	i.	528
1778. Nov. 26.	McCachan, Catherine, and John Stewart,...	"	xxvi.	101
1761. Nov. 11.	McCaffery, John, and Jane Arnold,........	"	v.	210
1781. Mar. 20.	McCall, George, and Lydia Harrison, ...	"	xxxi.	77
1759. Dec. 18.	McCallar, Catharine, and Hugh Montgomery,	"	ii.	550
1767. Nov. 14.	McCallar, Elizabeth, and William Ham,....	"	xii.	84
1764. Nov. 22.	McCallar, Margaret, and Samuel Elliot, ...	"	viii.	419
1766. Sept. 30.	McCaller, Elinor, and Peter Smilley, ...	"	x.	116
1780. Jan. 10.	McCaller, Elizabeth, and Joseph Menus,....	"	xxviii.	189
1763. April 30.	McCaller, Mary, and James Gibson, ...	"	vii.	159
1781. Aug. 27.	McCallor, Mary, and Niel McKinnon, ...	"	xxxiii.	48
1762. Dec. 15.	McCallow, Catharine, and John Stevenson,.	"	vi.	480
1760. Dec. 6.	McCandliss, David, and Isabella Nelson,....	"	iii.	460
1768. Dec. 15.	McCandliss, James, and Mary Orey, ...	"	xiii.	262
1762. Jan. 14.	McCann, Mary, and Stephen Pullen,.......	"	vi.	14
1772. Feb. 13.	McCargill, Catherine, and James Coldwell,..	"	xviii.	38
1767. Aug. 12.	McCarrick, Patrick, and Sarah Neal, ...	"	xii.	14
1772. Jan. 1.	McCarsey, Elizabeth, and William Bell,....	"	xvii.	308
1762. Dec. 22.	McCarter, John, and Abigail Van Bursen, ..	"	vi.	494
1759. Sept. 11.	McCartey, Mary, and Gilbert Bain,........	"	ii.	415
1780. Nov. 27.	McCarthy, Elizabeth, and Hiel Pemley,....	"	xxx.	125
1762. Oct. 11.	McCarty, Catharine, and Joseph Greenwood, Jr., ...	"	vi.	358
1771. May 6.	McCarty, David, and Charlotta Witbeck, ...	"	xvii.	75
1767. Sept. 30.	McCarty, Elizabeth, and Thomas Smart, ...	"	xii.	51
1762. Mar. 16.	McCarty, Peter, and Anne Kean,.........	"	vi.	75
1757. May 2.	McCaul, Nathaniel, and Elizabeth McGowen,	"	i.	522
1768. Oct. 29.	McCavey, Mary, and Duncan Graham,.....	"	xiii.	218
1768. May 14.	McCavy, John, and Catherine Dubois, ...	"	xiii.	103
1778. April 6.	McCay, Kennith, and Sarah Magrath, ...	"	xxv.	62
1777. Mar. 5.	McChain, Sarah, and George Bell, ...	"	xxiv.	41
1774. Feb. 25.	McChesney, Robert, and Mary Collison,....	"	xxii.	134
1765. June 27.	McClachlan, Peter, and Christian Brown,...	"	ix.	186

DATE.	NAMES.	RECORD.	VOL.	PAGE
1758. Dec. 6.	McClaghery, Jane, and James McCobb, ...	M. B.,	II.	115
1782. Feb. 13.	McClain, Elizabeth, and Samuel Bell,......	"	XXXV.	53
1761. Mar. 25.	McClain, Margaret, and John Murray, ...	"	IV.	116
1738. June 13.	McClain, Margaret, and William Dandy,....	"	I.	9
1771. April 29.	McClallen, Robert, and Jane Williams,.....	"	XVII.	70
1779. April 29.	McClan, Charles, and Elizabeth Swaim, ...	"	XXVII.	124
1767. Jan. 2.	McClanah, John, and Margaret Tulle,......	"	XI.	1
1780. Dec. 22.	McClaren, Mary, and Collen Reid, ...	"	XXX.	164
1763. Mar. 7.	McClaron, Collin, and Jane Bruce, ...	"	VII.	95
1763. Nov. 28.	McClaughry, James, and Agnes Humphry,.	"	VII.	476
1772. Aug. 12.	McClaughry, Mary, and George Dennison,..	"	XIX.	21
1772. Jan. 6.	McClean, Ann, and John Willson,.........	"	XVIII.	4
1759. Nov. 23.	McClean, Catherine, and George Barnes,...	"	II.	514
1765. April 10.	McClean, Elizabeth, and John Henderson,..	"	IX.	86
1762. June 10.	McClean, John, and Elizabeth Little, ...	"	VI.	185
1738. April 25.	McClean, Mary, and Arent Van Name, ...	"	I.	9
1772. Jan. 16.	McClean, Mary, and Jeremiah Simonson,...	"	XX.	11
1781. Feb. 6.	McClean, Mary, and John Bain, ...	"	XXXI.	39
1778. Oct. 31.	McClean, Mary, and Patrick McCollem,....	"	XXVI.	80
1760. Aug. 6.	McCleland, Andrew, and Rachel Low,... .	"	III.	236
1767. Dec. 11.	McClister, John, and Elizabeth McMasters, .	"	XII.	111
1771. Sept. 10.	McCloskey, Henry, and Margaret French,..	"	XVII.	180
1764. July 3.	McCloud, Ann, and George Wylle,........	"	VIII.	244
1778. Oct. 26.	McCloud, Barbara, and Robert McKay,....	"	XXVI.	73
1778. Sept. 21.	McCloud, Catherine, and Charles McPherson, ...	"	XXVI.	33
1765. Sept. 21.	McCloud, Catherine, and Robert Eley,.....	"	IX.	269
1756. Sept. 30.	McCloud, Daniel, and Elizabeth McDugal,..	"	I.	313
1782. Nov. 9.	McCloud, Jane, and Thomas Hodge,.......	"	XXXVII.	77
1763. Aug. 31.	McCloud, Mary Ann, and John McKinnon,.	"	VII.	321
1766. Nov. 21.	McCloughry, Elizabeth, and John Finley, ..	"	X.	177
1765. July 4.	McClure, Daniel, and Mary Fallansby, ...	"	IX.	194
1758. Dec. 6.	McCobb, James, and Jane McClaghery,....	"	II.	115
1778. Oct. 31.	McCollem, Patrick, and Mary McClean,....	"	XXVI.	80
1780. Aug. 30.	McCollin, Phebe, and Matthew Farrington,.	"	XXX.	8
1771. Aug. 27.	McCollom, Edward, and Hanna Jones,.....	"	XVII.	163
1766. Oct. 30.	McCollough, James, and Eva Bedon, ...	"	X.	146
1777. Jan. 3.	McCollough, Robert, and Dorothy Parsley, .	"	XXIV.	3
1760. Sept. 3.	McColme, John, and Anne Gold, ...	"	III.	280
1753. Aug. 9.	McColpen, Hugh, and Elizabeth Cregill,....	"	I.	87
1783. Feb. 27.	McComb, Sarah, and Jonathan Friend Child,	"	XXXVIII.	57
1763. Jan. 5.	McCombs, James, and Bridget Mott,......	"	VII.	8
1757. Mar. 25.	McConegall, Patrick, and Anna Kennedy,..	"	I.	481
1764. Feb. 24.	McConnel, Hugh, and Ann Waylin, ...	"	VIII.	76
1760. Feb. 25.	McConnell, Ann, and John McKnaight,....	"	III.	49

DATE.	NAMES.	RECORD.	VOL.	PAGE.
1778. Dec. 10.	McConnell, Hanah, and Edward Huestis,...	M. B.,	XXVI.	118
1781. Nov. 16.	McConnell, William, and Phebe Bird,......	"	XXXIV.	41
1783. Aug. 30.	McConney, Elizabeth, and Moses Hallett, ..	"	XL.	15
1760. Oct. 24.	Maccoon, Hannah, and Daniel Young, ...	"	III.	380
1768. Jan. 5.	McCoon, Hannah, and Thomas Fleet,......	"	XIII.	2
1762. Jan. 18.	McCoon, Hannah, and Zebulon Doty,......	"	VI.	15
1763. Feb. 12.	McCoon, March, and Jerusha Brush,.......	"	VII.	60
1782. Dec. 11.	McCoon, Samuel, and Maplet Flewelling, ..	"	XXXVII.	116
1780. April 15.	McCord, Ann, and John Atkinson,........	"	XXIX.	25
1761. Oct. 1.	McCord, Joseph, and Mary Cornell, ...	"	V.	111
1782. April 25.	McCorneck. Janett, and Gilbert McKenna,..	"	XXXV.	137
1780. May 30.	McCorrick, Agness, and James Moore,.....	"	XXIX.	73
1778. Feb. 7.	McCouen, William, and Sarah Townsend, ..	"	XXV.	18
1761. June 3.	Maccoun, John, and Elizabeth Townsend,..	"	IV.	225
1759. Nov. 3.	McCoun, Martha, and Stephen Seaman,....	"	II.	486
1759. Sept. 15.	McCown, Procolus, and Sarah Totton,.....	"	II.	424
1760. May 2.	McCoy, Edward, and Catharine McKenzie,.	"	III.	138
1777. April 7.	McCoy, Mary, and David Jones, ...	"	XXIV.	59
1760. Nov. 17.	McCoy, Mary, and Duncan McDougall, ...	"	III.	424
1761. Nov. 9.	MacCoy, Mary, and William McKenzie,....	"	V.	202
1761. Jan. 12.	McCoye, Mary, and Samuel Carr,.........	"	IV.	13
1760. Aug. 20.	McCray, Elizabeth, and Charles Mulford,...	"	III.	263
1770. Feb. 26.	McCrea, James, and Mary Hogen,.........	"	XVI.	26
1768. Jan. 30.	McCready, James, and Elizabeth Young,...	"	XIII.	21
1780. Dec. 29.	McCree, Mary, and John Bussing, ...	"	XXX.	172
1775. July 30.	McCrubins, Robert, and Margaret Chees,...	"	XXIII.	111
1759. April 24.	McCulluck, Robert, and Catharine Cludie, ..	"	II.	251'
1773. Oct. 28.	McCullen, James, and Mary Curry,........	"	XXII.	4
1781. Oct. 24.	McCullen, Phebe, and Stephen Reeves, ...	"	XXXIV.	4
1781. Aug. 16.	McCutchen, Elizabeth, and James Watson, .	"	XXXIII.	39
1771. April 15.	McDaniel, Ann, and William Schermerhorn,	"	XVII.	57
1772. Aug. 3.	McDaniel, Daniel, and Anna Dogherty, ...	"	XIX.	10
1760. Sept. 4.	McDaniel, John, and Catharine Rardon,....	"	III.	281
1764. Jan. 19.	McDaniel, John, and Margaret Morrison,...	"	VIII.	23
1770. Nov. 12.	McDaniel, Mary, and John Hofth,.........	"	XVI.	248
1757. Sept. 12.	McDaniel, Thomas, and Latitia Woll, ...	"	I.	634
1770. Aug. 28.	McDavit, James, and Eve Hoofman,.......	"	XVII.	166
1777. Nov. 1.	McDavitt, Catherine, and Patrick McNiff, ..	"	XXIII.	195
1764. July 9.	McDermot, Alexander, and Catharine Nevens, ...	"	VIII.	250
1736. Aug. 7.	McDermot, Jane, and Edward Briscow,....	"	I.	2
1765. Jan. 30.	McDermot, William, and Sarah Kettenhorn,	"	IX.	38
1781. Nov. 27.	McDermott, Patrick, and Mary Hart,......	"	XXXIV.	60
1771. July 31.	McDermott, William, and Elizabeth Lambersen, ...	"	XVII.	146

DATE.		NAMES.	RECORD.	VOL.	PAGE.
1781. Mar.	25.	McDole, Ann, and John Barwell, ...	M. B.,	xxxi.	86
1756. Dec.	3.	McDonach, Elizabeth, and James Gromell,..	"	i.	371
1764. Oct.	1.	McDonald, Alexander, and Susannah Myer,.	"	viii.	331
1759. Feb.	5.	McDonald, Allen, and Catharine McMullen,.	"	ii.	173
1736. Sept.	28.	McDonald, Catherine, and John Shurmur,..	"	i.	2
1772. Mar.	4.	McDonald, Catherine, and John Thomas,...	"	xviii.	46
1778. Nov.	21.	McDonald, Catherine, and William Fraser,..	"	xxvi.	91
1780. Jan.	15.	McDonald, Charles, and Rachel Archer,....	"	xxviii.	196
1769. Nov.	23.	McDonald, Collin, and Kaert Plass,........	"	xv.	103
1763. July	2.	McDonald, Elisabeth, and Robert Beattie,..	"	vii.	254
1771. Jan.	18.	McDonald, Elizabeth, and Barnaby McFadden, ...	"	xvii.	8
1758. Dec.	16.	McDonald, Jennet, and Donald Black, ...	"	ii.	129
1778. April	12.	McDonald, John, and Mary Anderson,.....	"	xxv.	63
1761. July	1.	MacDonald, John, and Rebecca Latham, ...	"	iv.	272
1772. Mar.	15.	McDonald, Lydia, and William Brown, ...	"	vi.	73
1770. Mar.	24.	McDonald, Mary, and William Scores,.....	"	xvi.	40
1777. Oct.	30.	McDonald, Rebecca, and Jacob Wright,....	"	xxiv.	172
1775. June	20.	McDonald, Richard, and Hannah Weygand,	"	xxiii.	70
1782. Sept.	21.	McDonald, Walter, and Isabella Gardner, ..	"	xxxvii.	8
1767. Nov.	3.	McDonel, Mathew, and Jane Whyley,.....	"	xii.	75
1761. Nov.	17.	McDonell, Hannah, and Samuel Shakeshaft, ...	"	v.	226
1780. June	20.	McDonell, Henrietta, and Donald McLean, .	"	xxix.	99
1760. Jan.	14.	McDonnald, Samuel, and Mary Burcke,....	"	ii.	581
1779. Jan.	20.	McDonnell, Michael, and Ann Lynch,......	"	xxvii.	19
1757. June	6.	McDonnell, Patrick, and Mary Tusener,....	"	i.	553
1759. Dec.	8.	McDonnold, John, and Jemime Hopper,....	"	ii.	534
1770. June	30.	McDonnough, John, and Rebecca Jackson, .	"	xvi.	128
1779. Dec.	21.	McDonold, Daniel, and Margaret McAlpine,.	"	xxviii.	175
1763. Oct.	19.	McDonold, Ronold, and Catharine Walker, .	"	vii.	392
1768. Feb.	6.	McDonough, Bridgett, and John Snow,....	"	xiii.	28
1783. Oct.	30.	McDonough, John, and Grace Cairns,......	"	xl.	96
1778. July	23.	McDonough, Thomas, and Harriot Dawson,.	"	xxv.	139
1760. Nov.	24.	McDougal, Alexander, and Margaret Shaw,.	"	iii.	439
1758. May	20.	McDougal, Catharine, and John Lowrear, ..	"	i.	904
1759. May	10.	McDougal, Catherine, and Hugh McLaughlin, ...	"	ii.	276
1764. Dec.	8.	McDougal, Duncan, and Catharine Kickwood,.............................	"	viii.	444
1760. Nov.	17.	McDougal, Duncan, and Mary McCoy,.....	"	iii.	424
1783. April	22.	McDougal, Mary, and John Charles Struve,.	"	xxxviii.	107
1767. Sept.	26.	McDougal,Alexander, and Hannah Bostwick,	"	xii.	46
1781. Nov.	2.	McDougall, Alexander, and Mary Stymets,.	"	xxxiv.	13
1765. Oct.	17.	McDougall, Allan, and Mary Price,........	"	ix.	305

DATE.	NAMES.	RECORD.	VOL. PAGE.
1775. Dec. 11.	McDougall, Donald, and Eve Sommer,.....	M. B.,	XXIII. 226
1763. May 4.	McDougall, Elinor, and James Laman,.....	"	VII. 167
1762. Feb. 4.	McDougall, Margaret, and Charles Ross,....	"	VI. 38
1761. June 2.	McDougall, Margaret, and Hugh Arthur,...	"	IV. 223
1761. Jan. 24.	McDougall, Mary, and John Habbot,.......	"	IV. 28
1759. Dec. 19.	McDounick, Jane, and Peter Terrell,.......	"	II. 551
1766. Oct. 13.	McDowal, Jane, and John Cobham, ...	"	X. 121
1763. Aug. 13.	McDowall, Hannah, and Nathaniel Tylee....	"	VII. 300
1761. Sept. 9.	McDowall, Robert, and Catharine Horseman,	"	V. 76
1764. April 19.	McDowell, Margaret, and John Conrey,....	"	VIII. 163
1764. July 4.	McDowell, Mary, and John Clom,.........	"	VIII. 246
1770. Aug. 6.	McDowell, Sarah, and Stephen Weeks, ...	"	XVI. 154
1769. April 10.	McDowl, John, and Mary Houghton,......	"	XIV. 67
1768. Mar. 17.	McDowll, Hugh, and Ann Lave, ...	"	XIII. 50
1756. Dec. 13.	McDugal, Allen, and Elizabeth Campbell, ..	"	I. 381
1759. Jan. 25.	McDugal, Dugall, and Mary Shaw,.........	"	II. 166
1756. Sept. 30.	McDugal, Elizabeth, and Daniel McCloud,..	"	I. 313
1758. April 6.	McDugal, Mary, and Archibald Hamilton,..	"	I. 488
1772. Sept. 9.	McDugall, Duncan, and Hannah Halding,..	"	XIX. 45
1759. June 20.	McElroy, Archibald, and Martha Burk, ...	"	II. 331
1763. July 4.	McElroy, Archibald, and Sarah Burk,......	"	VII. 256
1769. Nov. 25.	McEuen, Elizabeth, and Thomas Warburton Powell, ...	"	XV. 106
1760. April 5.	McEuen, Hugh, and Elizabeth Bogart,.....	"	III. 98
1762. July 16.	McEuen, Malcom, and Mary McKenzie, ...	"	VI. 241
1770. Sept. 8.	McEuen, Mary, and John Patrick, ...	"	XXVIII. 71
1783. Oct. 31.	McEvers, Catharine, and Thomas Martin Palmer, ...	"	XL. 97
1773. Sept. 16.	McEvers, Elizabeth, and Robert Bayard, ...	"	XXI. 110
1779. Aug. 23.	McEvers, Elizabeth, and William Myers,...	"	XXVIII. 57
1778. Dec. 5.	McEvoy, Martin, and Margaret Devoe,.....	"	XXVI. 111
1782. Jan. 29.	McEwen, Ann, and James Sparkman, ...	"	XXXV. 38
1753. Aug. 29.	McEwen, Daniel, and Jane Conkling,......	"	I. 101
1763. Nov. 9.	McFadon, Mary, and William Beeton, ...	"	VII. 441
1771. Jan. 18.	McFadden, Barnaby, and Elizabeth McDonald,................................	"	XVII. 8
1767. Aug. 1.	McFall, Catherine, and Belthazar Creamer,.	"	XII. 7
1781. Oct. 4.	McFall, John, and Mary Cozens,..........	"	XXXIII. 86
1780. June 22.	McFall, Mary, and Andrew Hyer, Jr., ...	"	XXIX. 92
1771. July 12.	McFall, Nail, and Margaret Mason,........	"	XVII. 130
1773. Nov. 3.	McFardin, Jane, and Nicholas Morall,......	"	XXII. 9
1765. Mar. 4.	McFargie, Catharine, and Thomas Davison,.	"	IX. 61
1764. Jan. 17.	McFarlan, Andrew, and Anne Peters,.....	"	VIII. 21
1767. Jan. 7.	McFarlan, Catherine, and Ignatius Peter White,................................	"	XI. 4

DATE.	NAMES.	RECORD.	VOL.	PAGE.
1779. June 14.	McFarland, Mary, and Thomas Pearce,.....	M. B.,	xxvii.	164a
1764. Feb. 22.	McFarlane, John, and Jane Steele,........	"	viii.	73
1783. Mar. 12.	McFarlane, William, and Penelopa Newall,.	"	xxxviii.	66
1768. June 28.	McFarran, Thomas, and Mary McArthur,...	"	xiii.	143
1760. Dec. 15.	McFarthing, Ann, and Toby Butler,........	"	iii.	476
1782. Oct. 7.	McFee, John, and Ellinor Van Pelt, ...	"	xxxvii.	33
1773. Aug. 16.	McGarr, Elizabeth, and James Mitchell,....	"	xxi.	69
1753. June 29.	McGear, John, and Martha Stratton, ...	"	i.	55
1762. May 5.	McGear, Sarah, and John Williss,.........	"	vi.	147
1765. Jan. 19.	McGear, William, and Elizabeth Crawford,.	"	ix.	24
1765. June 5.	McGee, Anne, and Isaac Brown,..........	"	ix.	155
1768. June 30.	McGee, Catherine, and Joseph Peck,.......	"	xiii.	146
1781. Nov. 5.	McGee, Margaret, and Robert Westwick,...	"	xxxiv.	18
1763. April 29.	McGee, Samuel, and Mary Ritter,.........	"	vii.	155
1760. Nov. 20.	McGeer, Elizabeth, and Timothy Egan,....	"	iii.	428
1759. June 6.	McGeer, Rebecca, and John Craig, ...	"	ii.	305
1783. June 4.	McGie, John, and Jane Keech, ...	"	xxxix.	39
1761. Sept. 23.	McGillicuddy, Dennis, and Martha Leonard,	"	v.	93
1767. Dec. 21.	McGillicuddy, Martha, and Roger Fagg,....	"	xii.	118
1765. Aug. 15.	McGillivrey, John, and Mary Willis,.......	"	ix.	238
1761. Mar. 21.	McGinnis, Elizabeth, and Robert McGinnis,	"	iv.	120
1762. Jan. 11.	McGinnis, Elizabeth, and William Crooks,..	"	vi.	7
1758. Feb. 1.	McGinnis, Hugh, and Elizabeth Morris, ...	"	i.	807
1761. April 28.	McGinnis, Mary, and Simon Deforeest, ...	"	iv.	170
1761. Mar. 21.	McGinnis, Robert, and Elizabeth McGinnis,	"	iv.	120
1767. Sept. 30.	McGinnis, Robert, Sr., and Jane Asselstyn,.	"	xii.	49
1759. Sept. 6.	McGinnis, Sarah, and Edward Muckelroy,..	"	ii.	411
1779. Oct. 20.	McGloan, Margaret, and David Beveridge,..	"	xxviii.	116
1761. July 11.	McGlochlin, Elizabeth, and John Burroughs,	"	iv.	294
1759. Sept. 17.	McGlocline, Mary, and Michael Power, ...	"	ii.	426
1757. May 2.	McGowen, Elizabeth, and Nathaniel McCaul,	"	i.	522
1781. July 16.	McGowen, Janet, and Archibald Nesbit, ...	"	xxxiii.	8
1782. April 18.	McGowen, Jannet, and Ronald McIntyre,..	"	xxxv.	127
1759. April 9.	McGown, James, and Submit Brown,......	"	ii.	236
1777. Aug. 12.	McGrigor, Ann, and Robert Barton,.......	"	xxiv.	132
1760. Mar. 5.	McGrigore, Duncan, and Mary Christy,....	"	iii.	62
1760. Dec. 4.	McGrah, Alexander, and Ann Elliot, ...	"	iii.	453
1772. Aug. 14.	McGraw, Mary, and James Horner, ...	"	xix.	23
1780. Dec. 23.	Macgregor, Alexander, and Mary Drummond,	"	xxx.	166
1759. Mar. 23.	McGugen, Richard, and Lydia Thomas, ...	"	ii.	223
1772. May 13.	McGuin, Daniel, and Esther Everit, ...	"	xviii.	110
1761. Feb. 16.	McGuineas, Dorothy, and John Thompson,.	"	iv.	65
1736. May 5.	McGuinness, Robert, and Mary Broadhead,	"	i.	1
1767. April 22.	McGuire, Catherine, and John Bowles,.....	"	xi.	67
1760. June 18.	Macguire, Margaret, and John Lewis,......	"	iii.	192

DATE.	NAMES.	RECORD.	VOL.	PAGE.
1758. Sept. 15.	McGuire, Sarah,and Richard Matthias Sweetman, ...	M. B.,	II.	24
1759. Oct. 29.	McGwier, Dennis, and Sarah Goldwin,.....	"	II.	477
1761. Mar. 17.	Machain, John, and Christeen Van Emburg.,	"	IV.	105
1760. June 18.	Machet, John, and Sarah Kairsted, ...	"	III.	191
1761. May 6.	Machet, Peter, and Sarah Cox, ...	"	IV.	181
1775. May 24.	McHugh, Patrick, and Elizabeth Kelsey,...	"	XXIII.	44
1760. Oct. 3.	McIlworth, Thomas, and Anna Statia Willet,	"	III.	343
1756. Dec. 20.	McIntire, Margaret, and Hezekias Travis,...	"	I.	395
1764. Dec. 10.	McIntosh, Aneas, and Ebetye Vandenbergh,	"	VIII.	446
1763. Aug. 18.	MacIntosh, Catharine, and Phillip Gettens, .	"	VII.	306
1763. Aug. 8.	McIntosh, Isabell, and Thomas Duncan,....	"	VII.	294
1767. Aug. 11.	McIntosh, John, and Agnes Forbes,.......	"	XII.	13
1760. April 16.	McIntosh, Mary, and Robert Graham, ...	"	III.	110
1763. Mar. 21.	McIntosh, William, and Eunice Hawley,...	"	VII.	104
1782. Jan. 28.	McIntyer, Malcom, and Elizabeth Ramadge,	"	XXXV.	36
1782. April 18.	McIntyre, Ronald, and Jannet McGowen,..	"	XXXV.	127
1762. Dec. 4.	McJervis, Hannah, and John Lynd,.......	"	VI.	468
1783. Jan. 29.	McJoy, Patty, and Samuel Mason,........	"	XXXVIII.	30
1773. Aug. 25.	McKave, Catherine, and Henry Kilburn,...	"	XXI.	84
1775. Oct. 30.	McKaven, Dennis, and Elizabeth Kniffen, ..	"	XXIII.	193
1765. June 20.	McKay, Æneas, and Mary Carter,.........	"	IX.	175
1775. Aug. 30.	McKay, Ann, and Alastor McLean, ...	"	XXIII.	142
1761. Jan. 21.	McKay, Charles, and Moyckie Ouderkirk, ..	"	IV.	23
1781. June 11.	Mackay, Donald, and Hellena Robinson, ...	"	XXXII.	82
1763. Nov. 29.	McKay, Elizabeth, and James Dallentine,...	"	VII.	467
1760. Feb. 26.	McKay, Robert, and Ann Waters,.........	"	III.	51
1778. Oct. 26.	McKay, Robert, and Barbara McCloud, ...	"	XXVI.	73
1779. Dec. 9.	McKay, William, and Ann Williams, ...	"	XXVIII.	168
1766. June 27.	McKeavy, William, and Jane Sutton,......	"	X.	36
1772. April 9.	McKell, Catherine, and David Stanley, ...	"	XVIII.	71
1761. Oct. 19.	McKeller, Flora, and John Johnson,.......	"	V.	153
1775. Oct. 16.	McKellop, William, and Sarah Lent,.......	"	XXIII.	181
1782. April 25.	McKenna, Gilbert, and Janett McCorneck,..	"	XXXV.	137
1780. Dec. 28.	McKenney, Elizabeth, and Daniel Dunscomb,	"	XXX.	171
1780. Nov. 14.	McKennon, Neal, and Hellena Dunavon,...	"	XXX.	104
1764. Feb. 17.	McKenny, Eleanor, and James Powell,.....	"	VIII.	63
1772. Oct. 21.	McKenny, James, and Catherine Cregeer, ..	"	XIX.	83
1757. June 16.	McKenny, Mary Ann, and Joseph Dickson,.	"	I.	564
1759. Nov. 19.	McKenny, Sarah, and John McNealy, ...	"	II.	507
1760. May 2.	McKenzie, Catharine, and Edward McCoy,.	"	III.	138
1758. Feb. 27.	Mackenzie, Hector, and Elizabeth Pool,....	"	I.	830
1762. Dec. 29.	McKenzie, Hector, and Margaret Evans, ...	"	VII.	462
1769. Oct. 12.	McKenzie, James, and Margery Margueson,	"	XV.	54
1779. Aug. 19.	McKenzie, Jane, and John Keady, ...	"	XXVIII.	52

32

DATE.		NAMES.	RECORD.	VOL. PAGE.
1762. July	16.	McKenzie, Mary, and Malcom McEuen, ...	M. B.,	VI. 241
1761. Dec.	8.	Mackey, John, and Ann Rolf, ...	"	V. 268
1758. Feb.	3.	Mackey, Mary, and Patrick Smith, ...	"	I. 812
1773. Oct.	7.	McKibby, Dennis, and Mary Kooper, ...	"	XXI. 132
1757. Sept.	28.	McKichin, Elizabeth, and Alexander Wylley,	"	I. 651
1783. Sept.	29.	Mackie, Thomas, and Joanna Cook, ...	"	XL. 57
1779. Nov.	12.	McKildo, Richard, and Elizabeth York, ...	"	XXVIII. 137
1760. July	2.	McKilop, Neil, and Catharine Morrison, ...	"	III. 202
1764. Jan.	23.	McKim, Mary, and John Dillon, ...	"	VIII. 31
1780. June	5.	McKindlas, Isabel, and Samuel Tanner, ...	"	XXIX. 82
1753. Aug.	14.	McKinney, Daniel, and Margaret Stienhouse,	"	I. 91
1771. Sept.	16.	McKinney, James, and Margaret Bamper, ..	"	XVII. 184
1767. Feb.	21.	McKinney, Margret, and John Durand, ...	"	XI. 33
1759. July	21.	McKinney, Sarah, and John Bowler, ...	"	II. 360
1763. Aug.	31.	McKinnon, John, and Mary Ann McCloud, .	"	VII. 321
1781. Aug.	27.	McKinnon, Neal, and Mary McCallon, ...	"	XXXIII. 48
1778. Mar.	27.	McKinny, Catherine, and John Minzies, ...	"	XXV. 53
1771. Sept.	25.	McKinstor, Sarah, and Benjamin Burd, ...	"	XVII. 191
1762. Jan.	20.	McKlen, Mary, and Peter Waller, ...	"	VI. 18
1761. Sept.	10.	McKlenney, John, and Mary Shans, ...	"	V. 79
1760. Feb.	25.	McKnaight, John, and Ann McConnell, ...	"	III. 49
1763. Feb.	28.	Mackneal, Lydia, and Robert Bennet, ...	"	VII. 80
1738. April	14.	Mack Neese, George, and Mary Fitch, ...	"	I. 9
1780. Aug.	24.	McKoun, John, and Hester Hampton, ...	"	XXIX. 146
1780. April	12.	McKoy, Mary, and John Lander, ...	"	XXIX. 18
1780. Aug.	28.	McKoy, Sophia, and Robert Narren, ...	"	XXX. 5
1761. Feb.	2.	Macknamar, James, and Martha Kierstead, .	"	IV. 46
1760. July	25.	Macknamar, James, and Mary Nicolls, ...	"	III. 226
1768. May	28.	McLaughlin, George, and Mary Boderidge, .	"	XIII. 116
1759. May	10.	McLaughlin, Hugh, and Catharine McDougal,	"	II. 276
1775. Aug.	30.	McLean, Alastor, and Ann McKay, ...	"	XXIII. 142
1776. Jan.	31.	McLean, Alexander, and Eleanor Watson, ..	"	XXIII. 257
1773. Oct.	18.	McLean, Anne, and Michael Brooks, ...	"	XXI. 144
1773. Dec.	8.	McLean, Catherine, and Jacob Barger, ...	"	XXII. 64
1780. June	27.	McLean, Donald, and Henrietta McDonell, .	"	XXIX. 99
1783. Mar.	26.	McLean, Donald, and Henrietta McLean, ...	"	XXXVIII. 77
1756. Sept.	27.	McLean, Elizabeth, and John Willsher, ...	"	I. 306
1783. Mar.	26.	McLean, Henrietta, and Donald McLean, ...	"	XXXVIII. 77
1773. Nov.	10.	McLean, John, and Chloe Phelps, ...	"	XXII. 18
1770. Aug.	13.	McLean, Mary, and Benjamin Swan, ...	"	XVI. 158
1780. April	25.	McLean, Mary, and William Smith, ...	"	XXIX. 33
1781. July	20.	McLean, Peter, and Ann Davis, ...	"	XXXIII. 11
1783. Aug.	11.	McLean, Peter, and Rachel Baldwin, ...	"	XXXIX. 122
1770. Feb.	23.	McLean, William, and Anne Simonson, ...	"	XVI. 22
1783. June	30.	McLeod, Donald, and Ann Masterton, ...	"	XXXIX. 73

Date.	Names.	Record.	Vol. Page.
1780. Nov. 14.	McLeod, Norman, and Elizabeth Gosling, ..	M. B.,	xxx. 105
1763. May 25.	McLintock, Walter, and Mary Harris, ...	"	vii. 199
1762. July 3.	McLutwidge, John, and Hannah Taylor, ...	"	vi. 225
1768. Feb. 2.	McMahon, James, and Jane Hagaman,.....	"	xiii. 27
1770. Aug. 25.	McMahon, Peter, and Jane Ryan,.........	"	xvi. 172
1772. Sept. 8.	McMaster, David, and Isabell Moore,......	"	xix. 44
1760. May 12.	McMasters, Ann, and Thomas Peck,.......	"	iii. 150
1767. Dec. 11.	McMasters, Elizabeth, and John McClister,.	"	xii. 111
1765. Oct. 4.	McMennomy, Robert, and Elizabeth Kennedy,............................	"	ix. 290
1780. Mar. 20.	McMichael, Christiana, and Amos Ansley,..	"	xxix. 23
1782. Aug. 28.	McMichael, Dugal, and Jane Muckleherring,	"	xxxvi. 129
1773. Mar. 24.	McMichael, John, and Angeltie Kidney,....	"	xx. 72
1772. Nov. 25.	McMullan, Elizabeth, and Joseph Mintrige,.	"	xix. 128
1759. Feb. 5.	McMullen, Catharine, and Allen McDonald,.	"	ii. 173
1764. Mar. 8.	McMullen, Isabella, and Edward Painter,...	"	viii. 98
1783. April 16.	McMullen, John, and Charlotte Jones, ...	"	xxxviii. 115
1779. Sept. 25.	McMullen, Neal, and Mary Rankin, ...	"	xxviii. 83
1782. Sept. 15.	McMullen, Peter,and Elizabeth Hollondshead,	"	xxxvii. 1
1773. July 29.	McMun, Alice, and William Burns,........	"	xxi. 53
1781. June 26.	McMurdy, Jane, and Samuel Gaur,........	"	xxxii. 99
1767. Feb. 21.	McMyer, Andrew, and Mary Henry, ...	"	xi. 32
1762. Aug. 28.	McNab, John, and Elizabeth Martin, ...	"	vi. 296
1757. Nov. 30.	McNamar, Timothy, and Mary Weeks, ...	"	i. 720
1758. Feb. 15.	MacNamara, Timothy, and Mary Christie,..	"	i. 818
1775. June 23.	McNamee, Charles, and Mary Butler,......	"	xxiii. 76
1760. Dec. 16.	McNeal, Anne, and Ebenezer Keeter,......	"	iii. 479
1783. June 12.	McNeal, Charles, and Mary Van Orden,....	"	xxxix. 52
1782. Dec. 24.	McNeal, Daniel, and Hannah Brown,......	"	xxxvii. 132
1765. May 16.	McNeal, John, and Sarah Parsells,.........	"	ix. 128
1759. Nov. 19.	McNealy, John, and Sarah McKenny, ...	"	ii. 507
1759. Dec. 12.	McNeel, John, and Margaret Ellison, ...	"	ii. 539
1762. May 4.	McNeely, Henry, and Sarah Burnet,.......	"	vi. 143
1765. April 29.	McNeil, Archibald, and Rachel Starkes,....	"	ix. 115
1764. Oct. 9.	McNeil, Eleanor, and William Hunter,.....	"	viii. 343
1766. Dec. 23.	McNeil, Ellenor, and Alexander Quarry,...	"	x. 206
1767. Aug. 6.	McNeil, John, and Sarah Frasher,.........	"	xii. 9
1783. Sept. 3.	McNeil, Mary, and James McPherson,.....	"	xl. 21
1773. Feb. 22.	McNeil, William, and Elizabeth Wiltse, ...	"	xx. 51
1777. Aug. 8.	McNeill, Charles, and Sarah Prince,.......	"	xxiv. 129
1772. Nov. 23.	McNeill, Roger, and Jennetye Guildersleive,	"	xix. 126a
1775. Nov. 1.	McNiff, Patrick, and Catharine McDavitt, ..	"	xxiii. 195
1780. June 12.	McNight, Duncan, and Margaret Clark, ...	"	xxix. 86
1782. Feb. 26.	McNight, Nancy, and Timothy Mahone, ...	"	xxxv. 67
1775. Nov. 8.	McOnulty, Daniel, and Elizabeth Hartley, ..	"	xxiii. 202

31

DATE.		NAMES.	RECORD.	VOL.	PAGE.
1780. Mar.	6.	McOnulty, Jenken, and Catharine Stedford,	M. B.,	xxviii.	217
1761. Aug.	18.	Macow, John, and Elenor Brewer, ...	"	v.	45
1759. Mar.	20.	McPeek, Dennis, and Mary Chavelier, ...	"	ii.	221
1765. May	23.	McPherson, Ann, and Donald Grant,.......	"	ix.	137
1779. Sept.	21.	McPherson, Charles, and Catharine McCloud,	"	xxvi.	33
1760. Sept.	22.	McPherson, Duncan, and Elizabeth Forbus,.	"	iii.	325
1783. Sept.	3.	McPherson, James, and Mary McNeil,.....	"	xl.	21
1779. Nov.	6.	McPherson, John, and Elizabeth Schenck,..	"	xxviii.	131
1759. Dec.	17.	McPherson, Malcon, and Hannah Christy,..	"	ii.	547
1782. Sept.	10.	McPherson, Sarah, and Thomas Christie,...	"	xxxvi.	141
1781. April	4.	McQueen, John, and Jane Hegerman,......	"	xxxi.	91
1761. April	18.	McQuin, Agins, and Jane Duthie, ...	"	iv.	155
1761. Nov.	9.	McQuirrey, Mary, and Thomas Wright,....	"	v.	200
1782. Feb.	25.	McReady, Mary, and Thomas O'Sullivan,...	"	xxxv.	65
1780. April	13.	McRobert, Jane, and John Anderson,......	"	xxix.	21
1757. July	14.	McTer, William, and Ann Sprung, ...	"	i.	590
1768. April	4.	McTier, William, and Charity Miller,........	"	xiii.	60
1781. May	19.	McVickar, John, and Anna Moore,........	"	xxxii.	53
1762. Nov.	9.	McVicker, Isabel, and Christopher Murdy,..	"	vi.	421
1762. April	21.	McWherter, Margaret, and Daniel Baien, ...	"	vi.	120
1780. Nov.	9.	McWhirten, Magdalean, and William Gardner, ...	"	xxx.	99
1771. Feb.	18.	McWilliams, Robert, and Mary Caithness,..	"	xvii.	17
1758. Sept.	5.	Maddox, Else, and Daniel Veal,...........	'	ii.	4
1761. July	31.	Maddux, Benjamin, and Mary Lowe, ...	"	v.	19
1759. Dec.	24.	Madick, Francis, and Julianna Brown, ...	"	ii.	556
1736. June	23.	Madole, Alexander, and Margrett Burgher,.	"	i.	1
1771. Aug.	5.	Maer, Mary, and William Gilles,..........	"	xvii.	152
1757. Dec.	21.	Maerschalk, Andrew, and Ann Hardenbergh,	"	i.	749
1758. Jan.	9.	Maerschalk, Sarah, and Peter Van Zandt, ..	"	i.	776
1780. Nov.	21.	Maffett, William, and Elizabeth Hulett, ...	"	xxx.	119
1779. April	6.	Magaw, Robert, and Marrite Van Brunt, ...	"	xxvii.	95
1766. June	5.	Magdalen, Mary, and Cornelius Tiebout,....	"	x.	3
1779. Nov.	3.	Magee, Cicile, and John Wile,.............	"	xxviii.	127
1780. Mar.	6.	Magee, Lena, and Thomas Dawson,........	"	xxviii.	216
1756. Aug.	28.	Maghee, Samuel, and Mary Vors,.........	"	i.	280
1767. Dec.	7.	Maghee, Samuel, and Sarah Somarindike, ..	"	xii.	117
1756. Sept.	30.	Maginnes, Hugh, and Sarah Enlew, ...	"	i.	311
1761. May	23.	Magknight, Margaret, and John Faverat,...	"	iv.	205
1756. Sept.	24.	Maglaghlin, William, and Elizabeth Pepinger, ...	"	i.	301
1783. Oct.	7.	Magra, Sarah, and Mark Wright,..........	"	xl.	68
1763. Aug.	19.	Magragh, Elenor, and Peter Donnally,.....	"	vii.	307
1737. Oct.	10.	Magran, John, and Ruth Bound,..........	"	i.	7
1760. Sept.	6.	Magrath, Roger, and Mary Bunterbow, ...	"	iii.	287

DATE.	NAMES.	RECORD.	VOL.	PAGE.
1778. April 6.	Magrath, Sarah, and Kennith McCay, ...	M. B.,	XXV.	62
1781. Aug. 9.	Mahany, Elizabeth, and William Dempsay (Dempos), ...	"	XXXIII.	32
1764. Nov. 12.	Mahany, John, and Teuntje Turck, ...	"	VIII.	404
1779. June 3.	Mahar, Ann, and William Backhouse, ...	"	XXVII.	156
1765. Oct. 15.	Maharry, William, and Rebecca Vermylie, ..	"	IX.	300
1782. Feb. 26.	Mahone, Timothy, and Nancy McKnight, ..	"	XXXV.	67
1765. April 9.	Mahony, Margaret, and Thomas Glenn, ...	"	IX.	84
1765. Feb. 6.	Maid, Hannah, and Charles Sabaton, ...	"	IX.	47
1762. Nov. 16.	Mail, Martha, and Francis Webster, ...	"	VI.	435
1759. May 24.	Main, Henry, and Ann Pearl, ...	"	II.	291
1778. June 27.	Main, Jane, and William Hobbs, ...	"	XXV.	114
1783. July 20.	Maine, Magdaleen, and John Van Norden, ..	"	XXXIX.	98
1780. Mar. 29.	Maine, Margaret, and Gabriel Van Norden, ...	"	XXIX.	8
1783. May 9.	Maitland, David, and Mary Lush, ...	"	XXXIX.	5
1779. Feb. 22.	Majesty, Else, and Joseph Forster, ...	"	XXVII.	46
1773. Aug. 12.	Makeel, Elizabeth, and John Davenport, ...	"	XXI.	67
1764. Mar. 7.	Malco, Frederick, and Elizabeth Kelly, ...	"	VIII.	97
1765. Oct. 5.	Malcolm, William, and Abigall Tingley, ...	"	IX.	291
1772. Feb. 5.	Malcom, William, and Sarah Aysoough, ...	"	XVIII.	29
1761. Sept. 10.	Maldrom, David, and Elizabeth Nixon, ...	"	V.	77
1759. June 6.	Male, Lydia, and Philip Avery, ...	"	II.	306
1769. Jan. 10.	Mallam, Elizabeth, and Daniel Neil, ...	"	XIV.	11
1761. June 3.	Mallery, Thomas, and Susannah Peterson, ..	"	IV.	226
1765. June 13.	Mallet, Jonathan, and Catharine Kennedy, ..	"	IX.	105
1764. Jan. 14.	Mambrut, Elizabeth, and John Byvanck, ...	"	VIII.	16
1761. Aug. 11.	Man, Ann, and Samuel Short, ...	"	V.	38
1771. Dec. 18.	Man, David, and Sarah Douse, ...	"	XVII.	299
1756. Dec. 22.	Man, Elizabeth, and Charles Berrow, ...	"	I.	397
1764. June 7.	Man, Elizabeth, and John Ruger, ...	"	VIII.	213
1738. July 5.	Man, James, and Eva Bussen, ...	"	I.	10
1771. Feb. 7.	Man, Johanna, and John Young, ...	"	XVII.	15
1764. May 7.	Man, John, and Anne Marschalk, ...	"	VIII.	185
1760. Feb. 2.	Man, Latitia, and John Prest, ...	"	III.	15
1768. May 25.	Man, Ruth, and Garrit A. Lansing, ...	"	XIII.	115
1773. April 8.	Man, Thomas Charles, and Catherine Smith,	"	XX.	87
1780. Mar. 30.	Man, Thomas Charles, and Elizabeth Coon, .	"	XXIX.	10
1759. Nov. 30.	Manbret, Catharine, and John Haycock, ...	"	II.	523
1758. Feb. 28.	Manbret, John, and Catherine Parrow, ...	"	I.	832
1771. Oct. 25.	Mancius, Cesparius, and Mary Rosekrants, ..	"	XVII.	225
1738. April 18.	Mancius, Georgius Wilhelmus, and Cornelia Kierstead, ...	"	I.	9
1766. Oct. 27.	Mancius, Wilhelmus, and Annatie Ten Eyck,	"	X.	143
1756. July 9.	Mandavel, Hannah, and Aaron Gilbert, ...	"	I.	248

DATE.	NAMES.	RECORD.	VOL.	PAGE.
1756. Oct. 7.	Mandevel, Hannah, and Gerret Van Den Bergh,	M. B.,	I.	322
1772. April 13.	Mandevel, John, and Rachel Giffin,	"	XVIII.	75
1757. Dec. 20.	Mandevell, Hannah, and Daniel Burdsall,	"	I.	747
173⅞. Mar. 17.	Mandevill, John, and Hannah Somerdyke,	"	I.	9
1775. Nov. 29.	Mandevill, Yellis, and Mary Smith,	"	XXIII.	222
1779. May 7.	Manee, Abraham, and Ann Johnston,	"	XXVII.	128
1778. Feb. 16.	Manee, James, and Elizabeth Stocker,	"	XXV.	23
1776. Feb. 5.	Manee, Richard, and Abigal Valentine,	"	XXIII.	260
1763. Sept. 24.	Maney, Margaret, and Leonard De Klyn,	"	VII.	352
1765. Jan. 18.	Manford, Ann, and Philip Pines,	"	IX.	21
1762. Nov. 22.	Manger, Nicholas, and Margaret Seelig,	"	VI.	448
1757. Jan. 17.	Manley, Margaret, and Edward Welch,	"	I.	419
1761. Sept. 25.	Manley, Robert, and Catharine Poppels-dorffche,	"	V.	98
1738. Oct. 27.	Manltsby, Anthony, and Sarah White,	"	I.	11
1779. Sept. 1.	Mann, Ann, and Ninian Holmes,	"	XXVIII.	63
1779. April 20.	Mann (Moell), Jacob, and Elizabeth Young,	"	XXVII.	113
1780. Nov. 3.	Mann, Sarah, and Isaac Stanbery,	"	XXX.	89
1760. Nov. 25.	Mannaring, William, and Eleanor Cooper,	"	III.	444
1738. Oct. 26.	Manner, Anne, and John Whibben,	"	I.	11
1762. Jan. 25.	Mannerley, Mary, and Benjamin Hageman,	"	VI.	25
1763. May 24.	Mannighan, George, and Ann Boylan,	"	VII.	198
1665. Feb. 13.	Manning, Hannah, and John Smith,	O. W. L.,	II.	27
1676. April 1.	Manning, Robert, and Mary Fforgison,	W. O. P.,	III.	183
1676. April 26.	Manningham, Mary, and Robert Blackwell,	"	III.	192
1762. Dec. 16.	Mansfield, Jane, and Erasmus Guilford Jones,	M. B.,	VI.	483
1783. Nov. 17.	Mansfield, Margaret, and William Harrison,	"	XL.	119
1764. Sept. 28.	Mansfield, William, and Margaret Connely,	"	VIII.	326
1766. Aug. 20.	Mansius, Cornelia, and Cornelius E. Wyn-koop,	"	X.	79
1764. Nov. 22.	Manson, Alexander, and Elizabeth Eagleson,	"	VIII.	421
1782. Mar. 19.	Manson, John, and Mary List,	"	XXXV.	90
1783. Aug. 14.	Mantaney, Sarah, and John Huyck,	"	XXXIX.	126
1675. June 22.	Manton, Shedrake, and Mary Ffleet,	W. O. P.,	III.	101
1757. Feb. 21.	Manual, Elizabeth, and William Wood,	M. B.,	I.	445
1782. May 20.	Manuel, Thomas, and Masey Henderson,	"	XXXVI.	12
1766. Nov. 29.	Manville, Hannah, and Thomas Freeman,	"	X.	187
1770. Oct. 27.	Many, Frances, and Samuel Wentworth,	"	XVI.	232
1773. Aug. 12.	Many, Margaret, and John Class,	"	XXI.	66
1759. Jan. 13.	Many, Peter, and Lucy Jamine,	"	II.	154
1758. May 1.	Mapes, Benjamin, and Elizabeth White,	"	I.	890
1764. May 14.	Mapes, James, and Deliverance Hawkins,	"	VIII.	189
1775. Oct. 26.	Mapes, Margaret, and Anthony Archer,	"	XXIII.	187

DATE.	NAMES.	RECORD.	VOL. PAGE.
1765. Sept. 24.	Mar, Frances, and James Kavanagh,.......	M. B.,	IX. 272
1778. Aug. 16.	Mara, Robert, and Elizabeth Terrot,......	"	XXVI. 4
1781. Sept. 26.	Maradith, Margaret, and Lewis James,.....	"	XXXIII. 79
1736. Oct. 19.	Marce, Hiley, and George Row, ...	"	I. 3
1758. Jan. 13.	Marcelis, Barreber, and Hendrick Bogart,..	"	I. 783
1769. Nov. 27.	Marcellis, John, and Margretje Vandenbergh,	"	XV. 107
1767. Nov. 10.	Marcelus, Andrew, and Ellenor Bennett,...	"	XII. 80
1781. June 6.	Marcereu, Martha, and Amos Rooke,......	"	XXXII. 74
1737. Aug. 6.	March, John, and Marjetie Edwards,......	"	I. 7
1771. July 23.	March, Stephen, and Margaret Klock, ...	"	XVII. 139
1759. Nov. 29.	Marchant, Shadrack, and Susannah Van-duresen, ...	"	II. 521
1759. April 14.	Mardochai, Henry, and Jamime Cornell,...	"	II. 242
1775. Sept. 28.	Marea, Mary, and Lewis Ryan,...	"	XXIII. 165
1768. July 23.	Marebutton, Mary, and Antson Appel,.....	"	XIII. 163
1758. Mar. 29.	Marener, William, and Elizabeth Van Nor-der,.................................	"	I. 866
1778. Aug. 20.	Margeson, Catherine, and Robert Wiely,...	"	XXVI. 7
1756. Aug. 7.	Margeson, John, and Elizabeth Woortman,.	"	I. 270
1758. Mar. 21.	Margridge, Mary, and John Burk,........	"	I. 859
1769. Oct. 12.	Margueson, Margery, and James McKenzie,.	"	XV. 54
1770. Nov. 17.	Marinus, Ratie, and Jacob Van Evera,.....	"	XVI. 261
1779. July 22.	Marks, Ruth, and George Dobbs, ...	"	XXVIII. 27
1779. Oct. 25.	Marks, Ruth, and John O'Brien,..........	"	XXVIII. 120
1763. Oct. 28.	Marlett, Abraham, and Catharine Lequiere,.	"	VII. 409
1768. Oct. 4.	Marley, Catherine, and Abraham Speer,. ..	"	XIII. 204
1763. Sept. 27.	Marlin, Rachel, and Abraham De Lanois,...	"	VII. 356
1782. Jan. 17.	Marling, Barnard, and Hannah Airy, ...	"	XXXV. 21
1782. Mar. 6.	Marr, John, and Abigail Patchan,.........	"	XXXV. 77
1760. Mar. 20.	Marrener, Nathaniel, and Rachel Brower,..	"	III. 84
1767. Aug. 6.	Marriner, Joshua, and Elizabeth Easton,....	"	XII. 10
1781. Feb. 6.	Marris, Lydia, and Wright Southgate, ...	"	XXXI. 40
1766. Sept. 16.	Marriss, Lydia, and Cave Jones, ...	"	X. 98
1763. April 11.	Marschalck, Elizabeth, and Leonard Kipp,..	"	VII. 122
1763. May 4.	Marschalk, Andrew, and Sarah Newel, ...	"	VII. 166
1783. Oct. 17.	Marschalk, Anne, and George Crookshank,.	"	XL. 84
1764. May 7.	Marschalk, Anne, and John Man, ...	"	VIII. 185
1760. May 14.	Marschalk, Elizabeth, and Aart Houseman,.	"	III. 151
1736. Sept. 4.	Marschalk, Elizabeth, and Nathaniel Hin-son, ...	"	I. 2
1781. Nov. 13.	Marschalk, Hester, and John Giles,........	"	XXXIV. 29
1764. July 25.	Marschalk, John, and Christian Farmer,....	"	VIII. 268
1762. Jan. 12.	Marschalk, Joseph, and Mary Schermer-horne, ...	"	VI. 8
1761. Jan. 20.	Marschalk, Mary, and Abraham Morris,....	"	IV. 30

DATE.	NAMES.	RECORD.	VOL.	PAGE.
1760. April 3.	Marseles, Marie, and Ryckert R. Van Vranken,	M. B.,	III.	95
1758. Sept. 7.	Marselis, Andrew, and Catharine Fisher, ...	"	II.	9
1779. July 1.	Marselis, Elizabeth, and John Pierce,	"	XXVIII.	12
1766. June 25.	Marsellis, Nicholas, and Margaret Groesbeck,	"	X.	31
1760. Dec. 8.	Marselus, Guysbert, and Anne Staats,	"	III.	465
1760. Dec. 6.	Marselus, Mary, and Harmanus Cuyler, ...	"	III.	463
1668. Aug. 12.	Marsh, Deborah, and Thomas Lovell,	O. W. L.,	II.	223
1669. July 22.	Marsh, Dorothy, and Francis Yates,	"	II.	474
1766. Sept. 2.	Marsh, Elizabeth, and Samuel Smith,	M. B.,	X.	88
1782. July 1.	Marsh, Hester, and Abraham Iredell,	"	XXXVI.	68
1767. Nov. 14.	Marsh, Jane, and Benjamin Bell,	"	XII.	83
1774. Mar. 9.	Marsh, Joseph, and Elizabeth Cornell,	"	XXII.	142
1781. Feb. 2.	Marsh, Joseph, and Elizabeth Hampton, ...	"	XXXI.	34
1764. Sept. 19.	Marsh, Lydia, and John Evonet,	"	VIII.	315
1767. Mar. 21.	Marsh, Mary, and Andreas Lucam,	"	XI.	47
1671. Dec. 11.	Marsh, Mary, and Edward Harnett,	G. E.,	IV.	73
1763. Nov. 26.	Marsh, Mary, and Isaac Davis,	M. B.,	VII.	475
1768. May 21.	Marsh, Richard, and Sarah Thorn,	"	XIII.	110
1756. Sept. 4.	Marsh, Samuel, and Anaky Burger,	"	I.	283
1782. May 2.	Marsh, Sarah, and John Brien,	"	XXXV.	146
1776. April 25.	Marsh, Sarah, and Lawrence Dowling,	"	XXIII.	302
1756. Dec. 6.	Marshal, Thomas, and Sarah Depue,	"	I.	375
1767. July 20.	Marshall, Abraham, and Rachel Moore, ...	"	XI.	138
1771. Dec. 2.	Marshall, Daniel, and Elizabeth Cockran,...	"	XVII.	276
1772. July 20.	Marshall, James, and Ann Barvell,	"	XIX.	2
1765. July 6.	Marshall, James, and Christiana Irvin,	"	IX.	195
1737. July 11.	Marshall, James, and Rachel Hollenback,...	"	I.	6
1670. July 5.	Marshall, John, and Angle Dudbridge,	C. A.,	II.	564
1762. April 26.	Marshall, John, and Ann Ten Eyck,	M. B.,	VI.	131
1761. Oct. 1.	Marshall, John, and Elizabeth Hooper,	"	V.	112
1764. Feb. 23.	Marshall, Katharine, and Benjamin Dickinson,	"	VIII.	74
1759. Oct. 2.	Marshall, Margaret, and John Mabee,	"	II.	443
1781. Dec. 4.	Marshall, Margeret, and Mathias Dubois, ...	"	XXXIV.	72
1761. Sept. 8.	Marshall, Martha, and Daniel Van Clefe, ...	"	V.	75
1771. July 20.	Marshel, Johannah, and Andrew Abel,	"	XVII.	137
1774. Mar. 8.	Marsine, Margaret, and Henry Reden,	"	XXII.	141
1779. July 31.	Marsland, Ellis, and George Brown,	"	XXVIII.	38
1780. Sept. 13.	Marsshalk, Mary, and Henry Dow,	"	XXX.	27
1765. Feb. 13.	Marston, Ann, and Augustus Van Horne, ..	"	IX.	52
1767. Feb. 14.	Marston, Bailey, and Catherine Ridgeway, .	"	XI.	27
1779. Sept. 2.	Marston, Deborah, and Peter Berrian,	"	XXVIII.	64
1781. Jan. 30.	Marston, Elizabeth, and Daniel Smith,.....	"	XXXI.	32

DATE.	NAMES.	RECORD.	VOL.	PAGE.
1779. Feb. 18.	Marston, Frances, and Charles Mongan, ...	M. B.,	XXVII.	42
1777. Mar. 19.	Marston, Mary, and Frederick Philipse, ...	"	XXIV.	48
1780. Jan. 11.	Marston, Mary, and Robert T. Kemble, . ..	"	XXVIII.	191
1764. Jan. 4.	Marston, Tabitha, and Palatiah Thurston, ..	"	VIII.	4
1759. Feb. 7.	Marston, Thomas, and Cornelia Lispenard, ..	"	II.	180
1761. Sept. 1.	Marten, Cornelius, and Hannah Brown, ...	"	V.	106
1762. Aug. 28.	Marten, Elisabeth, and John McNab, ...	"	VI.	296
1762. Aug. 18.	Marten, George, and Leah Vanderhyden, ...	"	VI.	278
1763. July 20.	Marten, John, and Mary Luddin, ...	"	VII.	275
1756. Dec. 31.	Marteneau, Charity, and William Ward, ...	"	I.	405
1775. Oct. 28.	Martense, Isaac, and Mary Misserol, ...	"	XXIII.	190
1738. Sept. 14.	Martin, Elinor, and Joseph Jadwin, ...:	"	I.	11
1764. Nov. 12.	Martin, Elizabeth, and John Shaw, ...	"	VIII.	400
1760. Nov. 17.	Martin, Elizabeth, and Riner Low, ...	"	III.	425
1780. Oct. 28.	Martin, Frances, and Edward Wilkie, ...	"	XXX.	83
1778. Dec. 25.	Martin, Frances, and John Kingsland, ...	"	XXVI.	132
1772. Aug. 28.	Martin, Francis, and Elizabeth Biggcraft, ...	"	XIX.	32
1765. April 17.	Martin, George, and Jannetje Vander Bilt, ..	"	IX.	99
1736. July 14.	Martin, Jane, and Jacob Swan, ...	"	I.	2
1770. Nov. 14.	Martin, John, and Abigail Baxter, ...	"	XVI.	251
1763. Feb. 5.	Martin, John, and Ann Angevoine, ...	"	VII.	54
1778. Aug. 29.	Martin, John, and Susanah Molineux, ...	"	XXVI.	16
1779. Sept. 18.	Martin, Josiah, and Martha Vanwinckel, ...	"	XXVIII.	79
1761. Jan. 26.	Martin, Margaret, and Thomas Goldtrap, ...	"	IV.	29
1777. July 26.	Martin, Mary, and Abraham Peterson, ...	"	XXIV.	122
1762. April 30.	Martin, Mary, and Jeremiah Spencer, ...	"	VI.	136
1780. Mar. 25.	Martin, Mary, and Nicholas Fletcher, ...	"	XXIX.	7
1762. Dec. 20.	Martin, Mary, and Peter Rougont, ...	"	VI.	490
1756. July 22.	Martin, Peter, and Elizabeth Troy, ...	"	I.	260
1765. July 15.	Martin, Peter, and Mary Staates, ...	"	IX.	205
1781. May 10.	Martin, Rachel, and Thomas Banister, ...	"	XXXII.	43
1758. Sept. 21.	Martin, Rebeccah, and Richard Richards, ...	"	II.	29
1756. Nov. 15.	Martin, Richard, and Rebecca Montanic, ...	"	I.	355
1780. Nov. 16.	Martin, Robert, and Catharine Summerdeck,	"	XXX.	112
1766. July 3.	Martin, Sarah, and Solomon Whitehouse, ..	"	X.	41
1764. June 12.	Martin, Thomas, and Mary Dobbs, ...	"	VIII.	223
1782. July 19.	Martin, Thomas, and Precilla Smith, ...	"	XXXVI.	87
1758. Nov. 17.	Martin, William, and Mary Bozarina, ...	"	II.	92
1761. Feb. 18.	Martin, William, and Phebe Everit, ...	"	IV.	68
1769. Nov. 10.	Martine, Effie, and Aurt Polhemus, ...	"	XV.	87
1725. Oct. 6.	Martine, Mary, and Daniel Parine, ...	C. M.,	LXVII.	72
1761. Sept. 19.	Martineau, Cornelius, and Rebecca Walton, .	M. B.,	V.	90
1772. Sept. 26.	Martineaux, Susannah, and James Guyon, ..	"	XIX.	57
1769. May 19.	Martino, Abraham, and Charity Simonson, .	"	XIV.	103
1778. Mar. 17.	Martino, Mary, and Peter Haughwout, ...	"	XXV.	43

DATE.		NAMES.	RECORD.	VOL.	PAGE.
1781. Oct.	5.	Martino, Sarah, and Peter Guyon, ...	M. B.,	XXXIII.	87
1765. Oct.	28.	Martinson, Adrian, and Adrianse Ryder,...	"	IX.	324
1753. May	9.	Martisen, Susannah, and Peter Monfoort,...	"	I.	27
1765. June	20.	Martley, Abraham, and Mary Cowenhoven,.	"	IX.	176
1765. Jan.	18.	Marvel, Francis, and Margaret Sower, ...	"	IX.	20
1772. Feb.	20.	Marvin, Isaac, and Rachel Burns, ...	"	XVIII.	40
1780. June	22.	Marvin, Jacob, and Mary Peters,..........	"	XXIX.	91
1783. May	31.	Marvin, Phebe, and Daniel Willis, ...	"	XXXIX.	31
1779. June	17.	Marvin, Sarah, and Oliver Willis, ...	"	XXVII.	167
1779. Jan.	28.	Marvin, Susanah, and Ichabod Smith, ...	"	XXVII.	30
1763. Oct.	14.	———, Mary, and Peter Carr, ...	"	VII.	387
1781. April	14.	Masemore, James, and Ann Johnson,......	"	XXXII.	4
1764. Mar.	27.	Mash, Rachel, and Robert Burn, ...	"	VIII.	120
1777. May	6.	Mason, George, and Rebecca Lawther, ...	"	XXIV.	83
1762. April	14.	Mason, John, and Mary Johnston,.........	"	VI.	107
1782. Feb.	13.	Mason, John, and Sarah Bringfield, ...	"	XXXV.	54
1760. May	16.	Mason, John, and Sarah Vanhorne, ...	"	III.	157
1771. July	12.	Mason, Margaret, and Nail McFall,........	"	XVII.	130
1783. Jan.	29.	Mason, Samuel, and Patty McJoy, ...	"	XXXVIII.	30
1763. Nov.	9.	Mason, Sarah, and George Suthrenland,....	"	VII.	438
1760. Aug.	12.	Mason, Sarah, and Norman Ash,..........	"	III.	250
1779. Aug.	28.	Mason, Thomas, and Catherine Frazer,.....	"	XXVIII.	61
1777. Mar.	2.	Mason, Thomas, and Catherine Rogers,....	"	XXIV.	36
1769. Sept.	27.	Mason, Thomas, and Elizabeth Blake, ...	"	XV.	45
1737. Nov.	11.	Massa, John, and Margaret Burhite,.......	"	I.	8
1779. Sept.	28.	Massane, Elizabeth, and Thomas Gray, ...	"	XXVIII.	87
1779. Feb.	19.	Massenburg, Humphrey, and Elizabeth Lever, ...	"	XXVII.	43
1776. Jan.	18.	Masten, Annatie, and Peter Roggen, ...	"	XXIII.	248
1773. Sept.	6.	Masten, Catherine, and John Van Steenbergh, ...	"	XXI.	102
1770. Aug.	1.	Masten, Elizabeth, and Cornelius Persen,...	"	XVI.	152
1770. April	10.	Masten, Johannes, and Catalyntje De Lameter,................................	"	XVI.	57
1770. Dec.	1.	Masten, Mary, and John Carman,.........	"	XVI.	279
1759. Aug.	4.	Masters, John, and Phebe Rogers, ...	"	II.	371
1783. June	30.	Masterton, Ann, and Donald McLeod, ...	"	XXXIX.	73
1768. Oct.	19.	Masterton, David, and Elizabeth Lose,.....	"	XIII.	213
1763. Dec.	31.	Masterton, David, and Margaret Bogart, ...	"	VII.	531
1764. April	25.	Matcalf, Susannah, and John Johns,.......	"	VIII.	168
1783. May	6.	Mathers, Jane, and John Scot Bride, ...	"	XXXIX.	2
1773. Aug.	6.	Mathewman, Elizabeth, and Stephen Van Voorhis,............................	"	XXI.	58
1758. Nov.	6.	Mathews, David, and Sarah Seymour, ...	"	II.	83
1760. Feb.	2.	Mathews, Edmund, and Mary Brooks, ...	"	III.	16

DATE.	NAMES.	RECORD.	VOL.	PAGE.
1762. Feb. 18.	Mathews, James, and Hannah Strong, ...	M. B.,	VI.	53
1684. Dec. 2.	Mathews, Margaret, and Edward Buckmaster, ...	C. M.,	XXXIII.	54
1766. Nov. 28.	Mathews, Mary, and Joseph Cockrem, ...	M. B.,	X.	186
1780. May 22.	Matisen, Mary, and Peter Cornell, ...	"	XXIX.	64
1768. June 21.	Matlack, White, and Mary Hawxhurst, ...	"	XIII.	136
1773. Aug. 24.	Matthewman, Luke, and Elizabeth Sise, ...	"	XXI.	83
1778. Sept. 2.	Matthews, Catalina, and James Lamb, ...	"	XXVI.	18
1758. Jan. 24.	Matthews, Fletcher, and Sarah Woodhull, ..	'	I.	800
173⅞. Mar. 1.	Matthews, Flora, and John Breese, ...	"	I.	9
1669. Feb. 12.	Matthews, James, and Mary Gosen, ...	C. A.,	II.	467
1736. Aug. 30.	Matthews, James, and Phebe Wood, ...	M. B.,	I.	2
1779. Mar. 22.	Matthews, Sarah, and William Littlewood, .	"	XXVII.	72
1738. Nov. 14.	Matticks, Anne, and Alexander Lamb, ...	"	I.	11
1778. Oct. 26.	Mattidale, Margaret, and Donald Campbell, .	"	XXVI.	72
1765. Oct. 29.	Maturin, Gabriel, and Mary Livingston, ...	"	IX.	329
1780. July 18.	Maud, Margaret, and James Knox, ...	"	XXIX.	114
1679. Nov. 11.	Maulster, Daniel, and Judith Lockwood, ...	G. E.,	XXXII.	63
1771. July 22.	Mauncius, Elizabeth, and Eldert Smeads, ...	M. B.,	XVII.	138
1763. June 10.	Maunsell, John, and Elizabeth Wraxall, ...	"	VII.	223
1758. Mar. 3.	Mauntanye, Famatje, and Nicholas Lamberse, ...	"	I.	834
1769. April 17.	Maurkwat, Agnes, and Francis Vandyke, ..	"	XIV.	76
1772. July 4.	Maverick, Peter Rushton, and Anne Reynolds, ...	"	XVIII.	155
1779. June 25.	Maxfield, Ann, and Joseph Morrison, ...	"	XXVIII.	8
1783. Jan. 6.	Maxly, William, and Margaret Wallenburgh,	"	XXXVIII.	7
1781. Dec. 6.	Maxwell, Eleonora, and Andrew Snodgrass,	"	XXXIV.	76
1761. Aug. 27.	May, Andrew, and Ann Brower, ...	"	V.	61
1778. April 4.	May, Sarah, and John Fleming, ...	"	XXV.	59
1770. Mar. 21.	May, William, and Sarah Santford, ...	"	XVI.	35
1761. Mar. 30.	Maybe, Margaret, and Nicholas Stevens, ...	"	IV.	122
1781. April 19.	Maybee, Abraham, and Ann Ackerman, ...	"	XXXII.	8
1753. May 28.	Maybee, Angeltjee, and Hendrick Vandyck,	"	I.	42
1764. Oct. 10.	Maybee, Arent, and Sarah Swart, ...	"	VIII.	350
1759. Oct. 2.	Maybee, John, and Margaret Marshall, ...	"	II.	443
1769. Dec. 21.	Maybey, Peter, and Sarah Boyd, ...	"	XV.	127
1665. April 21.	Meacock, Mary, and Thomas Case, ...	G. E.,	I.	111
1763. April 2.	Mead, Peter, and Hannah Christie, ...	M. B.,	VII.	112
1763. April 15.	Mead, Sylvanus, and Sybil Wood, ...	"	VII.	129
1773. Feb. 16.	Meade, Andrew, and Margaret Outerbergh, .	"	XX.	45
1782. Nov. 16.	Meade, James, and Mary Hancock, ...	"	XXXVII.	83
1770. Dec. 14.	Meal, Charles, and Margaret Ebert, ...	"	XVI.	294
1779. May 15.	Meals, Joshua, and Susanah Cameron, ...	"	XXVII.	138
1771. Aug. 2.	Measick, Catherine, and Stephen Muller, ...	"	XVII.	148

DATE.	NAMES.	RECORD.	VOL.	PAGE.
1781. May 26.	Mebie, Isaac, and Sarah Post,............	M. B.,	XXXII.	56
1779. Oct. 25.	Mecien, Andrew, and Elizabeth Rice,......	"	XXVIII.	119
1760. Oct. 30.	Meebie, Albert, and Engettie Vroman,.....	"	III.	387
1773. Nov. 4.	Meebie, Albert, and Maria Hoogen,.......	"	XXII.	11
1767. Nov. 6.	Meebie, Cornelius, and Hester Groot,......	"	XII.	76
1767. June 2.	Meebie, Petrus, and Alida Peeck,.........	"	XI.	102
1783. Oct. 3.	Meed, Nicholas, and Jane Van Garden,....	"	XL.	60
1761. April 4.	Meek, Thomas, and Ann England,........	"	IV.	134
1761. Jan. 12.	Meekes, Priscilla, and Jacob Bloom,.......	"	IV.	12
1759. Aug. 6.	Meeks, Catharine, and Duncan Robertson,..	"	II.	374
1767. May 1.	Meeks, John, and Susannah Mary Moulinaus,	"	XI.	75
1779. May 26.	Megger, John, and Grace Lindsay,........	"	XXVII.	149
1781. April 24.	Megraw, Catherine, and Nicholas Soman-dyke,........	"	XXXII.	14
1769. July 29.	Mehon, Marian, and Thomas Cook,........	"	XV.	9
1772. Dec. 29.	Mekee, William, and Sarah Whitney,......	"	XIX.	166
1764. Jan. 20.	Mel, Charles, and Mary Venice,..........	"	VIII.	25
1761. Aug. 14.	Meldrum, James, and Catharine Finigan,...	"	V.	41
1772. Jan. 29.	Mellor, Ralph, and Mary Hodkisson,......	"	XVIII.	23
1778. Dec. 21.	Mellows, David, Jr., and Catherine Parsell,.	"	XXVI.	127
1773. April 20.	Melowny, John, and Elizabeth Bates,......	"	XX.	98
1782. Jan. 17.	Melvill, Alexander, and Elizabeth Spencer,.	"	XXXV.	20
1780. May 6.	Melville, David, and Juliana James;.......	"	XXIX.	48
1782. May 18.	Melvin, William, and Sarah Wilcocks,.....	"	XXXVI.	11
1760. Sept. 9.	Melwood, John, and Charity Levinus, ...	"	III.	307
1758. Feb. 28.	Menee, Catherine, and John Gould,........	"	I.	826
1765. June 23.	Menfore, Yanatie, and John Jewel,........	"	IX.	183
1780. Jan. 10.	Menus, Joseph, and Elizabeth McKeller, ...	"	XXVIII.	189
1767. Aug. 1.	Menzies, Alexander, and Sarah Leister,....	"	XII.	6
1765. May 31.	Mercellus, Ahasuerus, and Hester Fisher,..	"	IX.	150
1755. Aug. 20.	Mercelus, John, and Bailtie Van Waganen,.	"	I.	150
1773. Feb. 1.	Mercer, Alexander, and Leonora Patterson,.	"	XX.	34
1763. Mar. 25.	Mercer, Richard, and Grace Cunningham,..	"	VII.	106
1778. Sept. 27.	Mercereau, Bartholomew, and Ann Sparling,	"	XXVI.	36
1761. Sept. 18.	Mercereau, Elisabeth, and John Lagrange,..	"	V.	89
1779. Mar. 29.	Mercereau, Jacob, and Charity De Groot,..	"	XXVII.	82
1771. Oct. 15.	Mercereau, John, and Barbara Van Pelt,...	"	XVII.	207
1765. May 30.	Mercereau, Martha, and Isaac Lakerman,..	"	IX.	147
1776. Jan. 2.	Merchant, Harriot, and John Robertson,...	"	XXIII.	238
1759. June 25.	Merchant, Mary Ann, and William Gandal,.	"	II.	338
1769. June 14.	Mercier, Christena, and David Morris,.....	"	XIV.	119
1763. Sept. 2.	Meredet, Hannah, and Jacob Brothers, ...	"	VII.	325
1780. June 6.	Meredith, John, and Gertrude Skinner,....	"	XXIX.	84
1770. July 14.	Meredith, Jonathan, and Elizabeth Tuckey,.	"	XVI.	140
1762. April 18.	Meril, Elizabeth, and Jacob Vanpelt,......	"	VI.	322

DATE.	NAMES.	RECORD.	VOL.	PAGE.
1771. Jan. 28.	Mesick, Hendrick J., and Angeltie Witbeck,	M. B.,	XVII.	9
1775. Sept. 6.	Mesick, Hendrick J., and Neltje Legg, ...	"	XXIII.	149
1764. Feb. 1.	Mesier, Peter, Jr., and Catharine Sleght,...	"	VIII.	46
1764. June 6.	Mesnard, Aeltje, and John Bancker,.......	"	VIII.	209
1738. Sept. 26.	Mesnard, John, and Anne Bratt,..........	'	I.	11
1781. Feb. 3.	Messavey, Ann, and Frances James,.......	"	XXXI.	36
1772. June 1.	Messenger, Rachel, and William Puntine,..	"	XVIII.	128
1669. April 20.	Messenger, Samuel, and —— ——,......	O. W. L.,	II.	417
1773. Oct. 9.	Messerol, Anne, and George Vanness,.....	M. B.,	XXI.	134
1772. April 21.	Messerve, George, and Catharine Gruver,..	"	XVIII.	89
1760. Sept. 22.	Metcalf, Thomas, and Susannah Wood,....	"	III.	324
1762. Aug. 3.	Metsger, Christina, and Jacob Fraly, ...	"	VI.	262
1772. Aug. 7.	Metsger, John, and Jane Fielding, ...	"	XIX.	15
1736. Mar. 1.	Mett, Richbell, and Mary Semans,.........	"	I.	5
1767. July 7.	Mettital, Margaret, and Daniel Duchemin,..	"	XI.	126
1762. Nov. 1.	Meurenus, Clara, and Jacob Van Voorst,...	"	VI.	402
1772. Jan. 8.	Meyers, Mary, and Henry Bowers, Jr., ...	"	XVIII.	9
1769. Dec. 18.	Mezerole, Elizabeth, and Jacob Bennett, ...	"	XV.	125
1762. May 10.	Mezine, Hannah, and James Cairns,.......	"	VI.	153
1781. Mar. 17.	Miabrush, Jacob, and Mary Dayley,.......	"	XXXI.	73
1761. July 6.	Michael, Anna Maria, and Johannes Lawyer, ...	"	IV.	278
1767. Feb. 18.	Michael, John, and Ann Deal, ...	"	XI.	29
1766. June 9.	Michael, Nicholas, and Barbara Hoffnaul,...	"	X.	11
1762. Aug. 2.	Michaeljohn, Walter, and Marcy Hilton,....	"	VI.	261
1764. Feb. 16.	Michaelson, Jemimie, and Anthony Ford,..	"	VIII.	61
1770. Oct. 2.	Michal, Elebert, and Philip Bartell,........	"	XVI.	204
1757. July 27.	Micheau, John, and Sarah Leake,..........	"	I.	602
1759. Aug. 6.	Micheau, Paul, and Mary Seaman, ...	"	II.	376
1768. May 9.	Michel, Mary, and Peter Hum, ...	"	XIII.	97
1685. April 9.	Michells, Cornelis, and Neltie Elderts, ...	C. M.,	XXXIII.	110
1763. Nov. 22.	Middagh, John, and Sarah Ryerson,.......	M. B.,	VII.	461
1767. Dec. 5.	Middagh, Magdalena, and Folkert Sprong,..	"	XII.	106
1760. Dec. 29.	Middagh, Margaret, and George Moore,....	"	III.	496
1764. Jan. 6.	Middigh, Cornelia, and John Gerritson, ...	"	VIII.	8
1738. Oct. 23.	Middlemas, John, and Elizabeth Cosyne, ...	"	I.	11
1761. Jan. 14.	Middlemass, John, and Charity Dyckman, ..	"	IV.	18
1762. June 29.	Middlemus, Jennet, and John Smith, ...	"	VI.	214
1756. Aug. 19.	Middleton, George, and Hannah Bokey, ...	"	I.	273
1781. Oct. 27.	Middleton, Hannah, and George Remsen,...	"	XXXIV.	8
1766. Nov. 25.	Middleton, Peter, and Susannah Burges, ...	"	X.	183
1761. Dec. 23.	Middleton, Samuel, and Mary De White,...	"	V.	298
1758. Jan. 21.	Midwinter, Robert, and Ann Finley,.......	"	I.	796
1767. July 6.	Mikljohn, Walter, and Mary Campbell,.....	"	XI.	125
1690. Feb. 3.	Milborne, Jacob, and Mary Leisler,........	P. B.,	IV.	71

Date.	Names.	Record.	Vol.	Page.
1757. Sept. 24.	Milburne, William, and Mary Lawrence, ...	M. B.,	i.	645
1763. June 22.	Mildeberger, John, and Sarah Benson,.....	"	vii.	239
1779. Mar. 6.	Miles, Elijah, and Frances Cornell, ...	"	xxvii.	57
1783. Jan. 18.	Miles, John, and Jane Parcells, ...	"	xxxviii.	21
1779. Dec. 23.	Milford, Catharine, and Rober Ferguson, ...	"	xxviii.	176
1772. Feb. 3.	Miller, Ann, and Edward Reynolds, ...	"	xviii.	28
1764. May 30.	Miller, Catharine, and Elias Smith,........	"	viii.	182
1783. June 2.	Miller, Catharine, and Richard Judd,.......	"	xxxix.	36
1772. April 14.	Miller, Catherine, and Joseph Withten,.....	"	xviii.	76
1737. Dec. 12.	Miller, Catherine, and Robert Craige,......	"	i.	8
1768. April 4.	Miller, Charity, and William McTier, ...	"	xiii.	60
1760. July 17.	Miller, Christian, and Gertrude Kemper, ...	"	iii.	216
1772. July 21.	Miller, Christopher, and Linechea Miller, ...	"	xix.	5
1769. Nov. 6.	Miller, Daniel, and Jane Gray,............	"	xv.	80
1783. Mar. 18.	Miller, David, and Mary Devoe, ...	"	xxxviii.	69
1776. Jan. 25.	Miller, Dorothy, and Philip Schermerhorn,..	"	xxiii.	253
1771. Sept. 24.	Miller, Eleazer, and Ann Waddell, ...	"	xvii.	188
1764. June 5.	Miller, Elenor, and Stephen Holmes, ...	"	viii.	207
1770. Oct. 15.	Miller, Elizabeth, and John Lodewick, ...	"	xvi.	213
1773. Jan. 25.	Miller, Elizabeth, and Samuel Arden, ...	"	xx.	20
1782. Dec. 22.	Miller, Elizabeth, and William Demott, ...	"	xxxvii.	129
1763. July 16.	Miller, Elizabeth, and William Thompson,..	"	vii.	268
1783. June 6.	Miller, Frederick, and Elizabeth Shearwood,	"	xxxix.	41
1781. Aug. 20.	Miller, Henry, and Elizabeth Garrison,.....	"	xxxiii.	42
1770. Sept. 5.	Miller, Jacob J., and Eve Best, ...	"	xvi.	180
1757. Sept. 23.	Miller, James, and Mary Crow,...........	"	i.	640
1772. Nov. 18.	Miller, Jane, and Jacobus Colyer, ...	"	xix.	118
1775. Nov. 22.	Miller, Jane, and John Walmsley,.........	"	xxiii.	218
1760. Dec. 24.	Miller, Jane, and Thomas Cooper,....	"	iii.	492
1771. Oct. 29.	Miller, Jeremiah, and Elizabeth Assellstyn, .	"	xvii.	230
1764. Nov. 27.	Miller, Jeremiah, and Sarah Hogeboom,....	"	viii.	428
1760. Mar. 27.	Miller, John, and Ann Mitchell, ...	"	iii.	66
1762. Nov. 1.	Miller, John, and Elizabeth Harrington,....	"	vi.	399
1782. May 14.	Miller, John, and Elizabeth Spangler,......	"	xxxvi.	2
1769. Aug. 22.	Miller, John, and Hannah Rowley,........	"	xv.	27
1765. Mar. 16.	Miller, John, and Lena Stockholm,........	"	ix.	68
1763. Nov. 18.	Miller, John Godfrey, and Ida De Bevoos,..	"	vii.	454
1763. Dec. 15.	Miller, John, Jr., and Hannah Welder,.....	"	vii.	505
1772. July 21.	Miller, Linechea, and Christopher Miller, ...	"	xix.	5
1771. June 19.	Miller, Margaret, and Philip Burtle, ...	"	xvii.	115
1757. Oct. 20.	Miller, Margaret, and William Edwards,....	"	i.	676
1782. Nov. 1.	Miller, Martha, and Nathaniel Miller, ...	"	xxxvii.	69
1772. Aug. 31.	Miller, Mary, and Jacobus Boss, ...	"	xix.	37
1757. Nov. 28.	Miller, Mary, and James Scott, ...	"	ii.	520
1772. Mar. 25.	Miller, Mary, and John Dayly, ...	"	xviii.	58

DATE.		NAMES.	RECORD.	VOL.	PAGE.
1772. July	21.	Miller, Mary, and Matthias Hornbeck, ...	M. B.,	XIX.	4
1782. Nov.	1.	Miller, Nathaniel, and Martha Miller, ...	"	XXXVII.	69
1772. May	14.	Miller, Nicholas, and Castintye Gardineer, . .	"	XVIII.	111
1759. Oct.	23.	Miller, Paul, Jr., and Mary Henderson, ...	"	II.	470
1778. Dec.	14.	Miller, Peter, and Elizabeth Titus, ...	"	XXVI.	120
1782. Feb.	4.	Miller, Peter, and' Phebe Conn, ...	"	XXXV.	43
1763. May	7.	Miller, Philip, and Mary Horwser, ...	"	VII.	169
1755. Oct.	10.	Miller, Samuel, and Elizabeth Oats, ...	"	I.	190
1757. June	17.	Miller, Sarah, and Daniel Shaw, ...	"	I.	566
1780. Oct.	23.	Miller, Sarah, and John Ousterman, ...	"	XXX.	78
1768. July	6.	Miller, Sarah, and Richard Woodhull, ...	"	XIII.	148
1769. Mar.	9.	Miller, Stofel, and Annetie Cregier, ...	"	XV.	85
1780. Sept.	26.	Miller, Susanna, and John Wedders, ...	"	XXX.	43
1756. Oct.	12.	Miller, Thomas, and Martha Willett, ...	"	I.	327
1769. Nov.	14.	Miller, William, and Annetie Collier, ...	"	XV.	94
1766. Aug.	4.	Miller, William, and Mary Cornwell, ...	"	X.	69
1783. Jan.	22.	Miller, William, and Sarah Busby, ...	"	XXXVIII.	28
1783. July	26.	Miller, William, and Sarah Day, ...	"	XXXIX.	101
1780. Oct.	3.	Milligan, Samuel, and Mary Ferguson, ...	"	XXX.	52
1764. Mar.	21.	Milliner, Phebe, and John Rhenor, ...	"	VIII.	112
1760. Nov.	6.	Millington, Mary, and Charles Bessonett, . . .	"	III.	395
1759. Dec.	6.	Millner, Henry, and Jane Black, ...	"	II.	531
1762. Oct.	25.	Mills, Abraham, and Mary Callester, ...	"	VI.	382
1760. Sept.	30.	Mills, Catherine, and John Vanosdall, ...	"	III.	337
1758. April	7.	Mills, Elizabeth, and William Hurley, ...	"	I.	871
1762. Sept.	22.	Mills, Helena, and Joseph Grigg, ...	"	VI.	325
1767. Sept.	10.	Mills, Hezekiah, and Mary Peterson, ...	"	XII.	33
1767. Aug.	11.	Mills, Hope, and Abigail Foster, ...	"	XII.	12
1773. Nov.	20.	Mills, Hope, and Mary Collier, ...	"	XXII.	36
1766. Dec.	8.	Mills, Jacob, and Catherine Murphae, ...	"	X.	196
1777. Sept.	20.	Mills, James, and Martha Denton, ...	"	XXIV.	147
1780. Nov.	24.	Mills, Jerusha, and Reuben Pine, ...	"	XXX.	124
1783. Jan.	2.	Mills, John, and Letitia Lamberson, ...	"	XXXVIII.	1
1765. Jan.	4.	Mills, Joshua, and Judith Carpenter, ...	"	IX.	7
1783. Sept.	1.	Mills, Mary, and Isaac Roop, ...	"	XL.	18
1757. Oct.	22.	Mills, Mary, and John Sexon, ...	"	I.	677
1771. Aug.	9.	Mills, Obadiah, and Sarah Denton, ...	"	XVII.	156
1762. July	17.	Mills, Phebe, and George Christopher Pack,	"	VI.	243
1762. July	1.	Mills, Phebe, and Peter Tilton.	"	VI.	220
1781. July	10.	Mills, Robert, and Hannah Willis, ...	"	XXXIII.	4
1773. Feb.	22.	Mills, Susannah, and James Brooks, ...	"	XX.	50
1773. Mar.	15.	Mills, Timothy, and Servia Bartow, ...	"	XX.	64
1777. Dec.	10.	Milne, Alexander, and Elizabeth Pearsall, . .	"	XXIV.	194
1768. Nov.	26.	Milton, Benjamin, and Elizabeth Nicholson,	"	XIII.	245
1758. Feb.	16.	Miltonberry, Peter, and Susanah Gardenear,	"	. I.	823

DATE.	NAMES.	RECORD.	VOL.	PAGE.
1766. Oct. 28.	Minderse, Susannah, and Volkert Veeder,..	M. B.,	x.	144
1764. Jan. 23.	Minderson, Elisabeth, and John Van Volken- burgh, ...	"	VIII.	32
1758. June 1.	Minee, Rachel, and Henry Johnson,.......	"	I.	921
1781. Nov. 7.	Ming, Mary, and Thomas Brown,.........	"	XXXIV.	19
1762. Sept. 27.	Ming, Thomas, and Mary Connely,........	"	VI.	314
1783. Mar. 24.	Minzies, Colin, and Mary Fitzgerald, ...	"	XXXVIII.	74
1772. July 29.	Minifie, Richard, and Elizabeth Stilwell, ...	"	XIX.	6
1773. Mar. 29.	Minnitt, James, and Ann Bill,............	"	XX.	76
1772. Oct. 17.	Minshall, John, and Mary Stanton,........	"	XIX.	76
1756. Nov. 5.	Minthorn, Jane, and William Bockee,......	"	I.	347
1783. July 9.	Minthorn, Sarah, and Joshua Pell, Jr.,.....	"	XXXIX.	85
1770. Aug. 30.	Minthorne, Henry, and Mary Van Vleck, ..	"	XVI.	176
1762. Aug. 3.	Minthorne, Mangel, and Sarah Cock,.......	"	VI.	263
1778. Oct. 7.	Minthorne, Mangle, and Anjet Constables,..	"	XXVI.	50
1753. June 9.	Minthorne, Margaret, and Netkles Romein. .	"	I.	56
1773. Mar. 15.	Minthorne, Philip, and Catherine Montanye,	"	XX.	63
1772. Nov. 25.	Mintrige, Joseph, and Elizabeth McMullan,.	"	XIX.	128
1783. May 10.	Minues, Hannah, and William Pearson,....	"	XXXIX.	9
167?. Jan. 25.	Minviele, Gabriel, and Susannah Laurence, .	W. O. P.,	III.	237
1778. Mar. 27.	Minzies, John, and Catherine McKinny,....	M. B.,	XXV.	53
1767. Feb. 9.	Mioitt, Francois, and Catherine Pelagie,....	"	XI.	23
1758. Oct. 26.	Miring, Sovenah, and John Allen,.........	"	II.	69
1780. Aug. 26.	Miserol, Elizabeth, and John Morrell,......	"	XXX.	3
1772. Nov. 28.	Miserole, Jane, and George Lot, ...	"	XIX.	135
1778. Jan. 16.	Misplee, Thomas, and Elizabeth Thomas, ...	"	AAV.	7
1775. Oct. 28.	Misserol, Mary, and Isaac Martense,.......	"	XXIII.	190
1773. Sept. 23.	Missick, Mary, and Nicholas Gardeneir,....	"	XXI.	120
1781. Mar. 18.	Mitchel, Andrew, and Margaret Stiles,.....	"	XXXIII.	9
1768. Nov. 14.	Mitchel, Hugh, and Sophia Peters,........	"	XIII.	236
1758. Mar. 17.	Mitchel. John, and Elizabeth Lewis,.......	"	I.	854
1764. Sept. 12.	Mitchel, John, and Rebecca Huleat, ...	"	VIII.	304
1772. Jan. 4.	Mitchel, Margaret, and Stephen Ryder, ...	"	XX.	1
1769. Aug. 24.	Mitchel, Phebe, and David Gelston, ...	"	XV.	28
1757. April 9.	Mitchel, Robert, and Sarah Allen,.........	"	I.	494
1780. Oct. 23.	Mitchell, Andrew, and Ann Steele,........	"	XXX.	77
1760. Sept. 12.	Mitchell, Andrew, and Mary Van Eppe,....	"	III.	312
1760. Mar. 7.	Mitchell, Ann, and John Miller, ...	"	III.	66
1779. June 3.	Mitchell, Elinor, and Jesse Lear,..........	"	XXVII.	154
1758. Nov. 4.	Mitchell, Jacamiah, and Sarah Bown,......	"	II.	80
1773. Aug. 16.	Mitchell, James, and Elizabeth McGarr,....	"	XXI.	69
1779. July 8.	Mitchell, John, and Catharine Adams, ...	"	XXVIII.	18
1760. May 22.	Mitchell, John, and Deborah Prince,.......	"	III.	161
1760. Feb. 25.	Mitchell, Mary, and Jacob Smith,.........	"	III.	48
1757. June 2.	Mitchell, Phebe, and James Fairlie,.......	"	I.	549

34

DATE.		NAMES.	RECORD.	VOL.	PAGE.
1737. Dec.	2.	Mitchell, Phebe, and John Nuttman,	M. B.,	I.	8
1767. Mar.	27.	Mitchell, Phebe, and Jonas Halstead,	"	XI.	51
1778. July	23.	Mitchell, Sarah, and John Bessonet,	"	XXV.	138
1762. Feb.	2.	Mitchell, Sarah, and Joseph Bowne,	"	VI.	36
1781. Dec.	22.	Mitchell, Susannah, and John Morrell,	"	XXXIV.	98
1783. July	1.	Mitchell, Thomas, and Loretta Hegaman,	"	XXXIX.	78
1760. Dec.	19.	Mitchell, Thomas, and Statia Clements,	"	III.	483
1770. May	14.	Mitchell, Uriah, and Freelove Smith,	"	XVI.	84
1774. Mar.	5.	Mitchell, Uriah, and Sarah Cornell,	"	XXII.	140
1779. May	20.	Mitchell, Walter, and Catherine Bush,	"	XXVII.	142
1779. Sept.	28.	Mitchell, William, and Abigail Doty,	"	XXVIII.	86
1759. June	12.	Mitchill, Robert, and Mary Latham,	"	II.	319
1766. Dec.	23.	Mitchner, Robert, and Margaret Lafong,	"	X.	205
1737. Feb.	4.	Moby, Charity, and Nathaniel Smith,	"	I.	8
1779. April	20.	Moell (Mann), Jacob, and Elizabeth Young,	"	XXVII.	113
1781. Jan.	4.	Moffatt, James, and Mary Ross,	"	XXXI.	11
1763. Feb.	15.	Moffet, Esther, and John Christie,	"	VII.	63
1773. Sept.	20.	Moffet, Thomas, and Susannah Howell,	"	XXI.	112
1765. Oct.	24.	Moffit, John, and Charlotte Amar,	"	IX.	316
1761. Dec.	22.	Moggeridge, Aaron, and Tryntje Harris,	"	V.	293
1757. July	27.	Moit, Elizabeth, and George Slater,	"	I.	603
1760. Nov.	24.	Moke, Elizabeth, and Albert Slingerlant,	"	III.	436
1759. Oct.	15.	Moke, Francis, and Anglitje Slingerlandt,	"	II.	457
1761. Dec.	15.	Moland, Thomas, and Margaret Baker,	"	V.	279
1760. Oct.	4.	Molaran, Abraham, and Rachael Van Cot,	"	III.	344
1778. Aug.	21.	Molineux, Susanah, and John Martin,	"	XXVI.	16
1780. Sept.	2.	Molitor, Chretiende, and Rebecca Engslete,	"	XXX.	15
1768. June	29.	Mollenar, Elizabeth, and John Jenkins,	"	XIII.	145
1777. April	1.	Mollineux, Rebecca, and William Jones,	"	XXIV.	55
1783. Oct.	29.	Molloy, James, and Elenor Emery,	"	XL.	93
1780. Aug.	21.	Monck, Andrew, and Abigail Noe,	"	XXIX.	143
1779. Feb.	20.	Moncrieff, Christian, and John Turner,	"	XXVII.	45
1777. Feb.	24.	Moncreiffe, Margaret, and John Coghlan,	"	XXIV.	35
1764. Oct.	9.	Moncrieffe, Thomas, and Mary Livingston,	"	VIII.	341
1778. July	6.	Moncrif, David, and Claradia Kingland,	"	XXV.	120
1738. Aug.	3.	Monell, George, and Jane Wherry,	"	I.	10
1765. June	8.	Monell, Jane, and John Hill,	"	IX.	162
1772. Dec.	12.	Monfoont, Anna, and Abraham Shear,	"	XIX.	154
1778. Oct.	10.	Monfoort, Abraham, and Rancey Monfort,	"	XXVI.	53
1779. Nov.	19.	Monfoort, Elizabeth, and Thomas Dodge, Jr.,	"	XXVIII.	143
1771. May	14.	Monfoort, Elsie, and Thomas Oakes,	"	XVII.	84
1781. Aug.	2.	Monfoort, James, and Anautia Bennet,	"	XXXIII.	27
1767. Sept.	28.	Monfort, John, and Sarah Van Wickler,	"	XII.	47
1762. April	13.	Monfoort, Peter, and Margaret Schenck,	"	VI.	105
1753. May	9.	Monfoort, Peter, and Susannah Martisen,	"	I.	27

DATE.	NAMES.	RECORD.	VOL.	PAGE.
1762. June 28.	Monfoort, Peter H., and Ann Thorne,	M. B.,	VI.	213
1770. Aug. 25.	Monfoort, Rem, and Susannah Vantassel,	"	XVI.	170
1760. Mar. 12.	Monfor, Maria, and Abraham Polhemus,	"	III.	74
1766. Aug. 13.	Monford, Ann, and Isaac Terbush,	"	X.	74
1772. Oct. 21.	Monfore, Garret, and Edah Ryder,	"	XIX.	84
1753. Oct. 12.	Monfort, Eyda, and Joris Brinkerhoff,	"	I.	137
1778. Oct. 10.	Monfort, Rancey, and Abraham Monfoort,	"	XXVI.	53
1782. Nov. 23.	Monfort, Sarah, and Isaac Hendrickson,	"	XXXVII.	90
1779. Feb. 18.	Mongan, Charles, and Frances Marston,	"	XXVII.	42
1763. Sept. 17.	Monier, John, and Mary Sharp,	"	VII.	340
1781. July 26.	Monkhouse, Ralph, and Ann Stevens,	"	XXXIII.	15
1755. Aug. 8.	Monksommers, William, and Mary Floyd,	"	I.	144
1772. Sept. 28.	Monnell, James, and Sarah Graham,	"	XIX.	59
1767. July 3.	Montang, Vincent, and Mary Brundige,	"	XI.	121
1761. April 10.	Montange, Vincent, and Gertrey Vonck,	"	IV.	142
1775. Nov. 10.	Montanje, Ann, and Thomas Parsells,	"	XXIII.	204
1759. Oct. 29.	Montanje, Anne, and Joseph Lewies,	"	II.	479
1759. June 8.	Montanje, Hester, and Lazarus Pepperall,	"	II.	311
1771. Jan. 14.	Montanje, Teunis, and Sarah Nicoll,	"	XVII.	6
1768. June 24.	Montanye, Ann, and John Tomkins,	"	XIII.	137
1768. April 13.	Montanye, Benjamin, and Elizabeth Norris,	"	XIII.	74
1773. Mar. 15.	Montanye, Catherine, and Philip Minthorne,	"	XX.	63
1757. Nov. 9.	Montanye, Jane, and John Wright,	"	I.	701
1767. April 1.	Montanye, John, and Abigail Wilsey,	"	XI.	54
1767. Mar. 4.	Montanye, Nelly, and Isaac Vredenburgh,	"	XI.	39
1758. Dec. 7.	Montanyo, Prudence, and Albert Amerman,	"	II.	119
1773. May 24.	Montanye, Rebekah, and Peter Truman,	"	XX.	122
1779. June 4.	Montfoort, Peter, and Sarah Luister,	"	XXVII.	157
1759. Dec. 18.	Montgomery, Hugh, and Catharine McCallar,	"	II.	550
1763. Jan. 8.	Montgomery, Jane, and William Palmer,	"	VII.	10
1780. Sept. 30.	Montgomery, Joseph, and Elizabeth Lightfoot,	"	XXX.	49
1773. Aug. 4.	Montgomery, Richard, and Jennet Livingston,	"	XXI.	56
1766. Aug. 20.	Monton, Edward, and Mary Ame,	"	X.	78
1760. Aug. 8.	Montonje, John, and Catharine White,	"	III.	243
1772. July 9.	Montross, Isaac, and Tama Betts,	"	XVIII.	161
1775. April 6.	Montross, Wyntie, and John Pell Sutton,	"	XXIII.	4
1769. July 26.	Monvoort, Dorothy, and Anderies Hegeman,	"	XV.	5
1756. Sept. 24.	Money, Anne, and Daniel Lamar,	"	I.	304
1782. Mar. 21.	Moody, James, and Jane Lynson,	"	XXXV.	94
1778. May 9.	Moody, Thomas, and Janet Haburn,	"	XXV.	75
1781. Nov. 17.	Moody, William, and James Johnston,	"	XXXIV.	44
1766. Aug. 21.	Moon, Francis, and Catharine Ingoldsby,	"	X.	80

DATE.	NAMES.	RECORD.	VOL.	PAGE.
1762. Feb. 10.	Moone, Hannah, and Humphry Jones Bradbourne,	M. B.,	VI.	43
1761. Sept. 15.	Moone, Richard, and Sarah Hollet,	"	V.	83
1778. Oct. 10.	Mooney, Amby, and Ann O'Brien,	"	XXVI.	54
1777. April 24.	Mooney, William, and Abigail Blake,	"	XXIV.	73
1781. Nov. 14.	Moony, Mary, and Henry O'Brien,	"	XXXIV.	35
1738. Aug. 8.	Moor, Charity, and John Pepper,	"	I.	10
1760. Nov. 25.	Moor, Geesie, and Johannis Kittel,	"	III.	441
1775. Sept. 21.	Moor, James, and Elizabeth Peters,	"	XXIII.	160
1760. Feb. 13.	Moor, John, and Mary Howbran,	"	III.	35
1738. June 13.	Moore, Alexander, and Titia Henderson, ...	"	I.	10
1781. May 19.	Moore, Anna, and John McVickar,	"	XXXII.	53
1778. April 18.	Moore, Benjamin, and Charity Clarke,	"	XXV.	65
1757. May 21.	Moore, Benjamin, and Elizabeth Moore,	"	I.	537
1762. June 2.	Moore, Benjamin, and Margaret Morrell, ...	"	VI.	179
1776. April 3.	Moore, Benjamin, Jr., and Margaret Wessells,	"	XXIII.	295
1762. Nov. 12.	Moore, Catharine, and Jeremiah Muller, Jr.,	"	VI.	427
1763. Aug. 19.	Moore, Catharine, and Peter Lorilliard,	"	VII.	308
1767. July 6.	Moore, Catherine, and Isaac Stonehouse, ...	"	XI.	125
1781. Mar. 19.	Moore, Charity, and Daniel Hallett,	"	XXXI.	74
1763. Nov. 22.	Moore, Content, and John Wilkinson,	"	VII.	462
1780. May 25.	Moore, David, and Jemima Hallett,	"	XXIX.	68
1764. Nov. 21.	Moore, Deborah, and John Everitt,	"	VIII.	417
1757. May 21.	Moore, Elizabeth, and Benjamin Moore, ...	"	I.	537
1780. Jan. 12.	Moore, Elizabeth, and John Robinson,	"	XXVIII.	193
1783. Sept. 22.	Moore, Elizabeth, and Theodosius Hunt, ...	"	XL.	49
1670. Jan. 1.	Moore, Elizabeth, and William Osborne, ...	C. A.,	II.	639
1776. Mar. 29.	Moore, Elizabeth, and William Smith,	M. B.,	XXIII.	293
1779. Oct. 15.	Moore, Frances, and Joseph Pentland,	"	XXVIII.	112
1776. Jan. 27.	Moore, Frances, and Thomas Cooper,	"	XXIII.	254
1757. Nov. 4.	Moore, Francis, and Jane Day,	"	I.	696
1772. June 7.	Moore, Garrott, and Susannah O'Bryan, ...	"	XVIII.	135
1760. Dec. 29.	Moore, George, and Margaret Middagh,	"	III.	496
1767. Sept. 15.	Moore, Hannah, and Jacob Roeckser,	"	XII.	33d
1763. Aug. 19.	Moore, Hannah, and John Lorilliard,	"	VII.	309
1778. Jan. 21.	Moore, Henderson, and Sarah Haviland, ...	"	XXV.	10
1779. Jan. 10.	Moore, Hester, and John Burt Lyng,	"	XXVII.	9
1769. June 26.	Moore, Hugh, and Catherine Murphy,	"	XIV.	132
1772. Sept. 8.	Moore, Isabell, and David McMaster,	"	XIX.	44
1781. May 28.	Moore, Jacob, and Elizabeth Waters,	"	XXXII.	57
1779. April 11.	Moore, Jacob, and Hannah Waters,	"	XXVII.	104
1759. May 15.	Moore, Jacob, and Maria Whetbeck,	"	II.	284
1783. Sept. 5.	Moore, James, and Catharine Rikeman,	"	XL.	26
1780. Dec. 11.	Moore, Jemime, and Jesse Fish,	'	XXX.	150
1759. June 6.	Moore, John, and Elizabeth Taylor,	"	II.	307

DATE.	NAMES.	RECORD.	VOL.	PAGE.
1738. Oct. 26.	Moore, John, and Etye Burgart,..........	M. B.,	I.	11
1761. Jan. 15.	Moore, John, and Grizell Hunt,...	"	IV.	19
1783. July 11.	Moore, John, and Helen Parkinson,.......	"	XXXIX.	87
1773. Oct. 16.	Moore, John, and Judith Livingston, ...	"	XXI.	143
1781. Feb. 24.	Moore, John, and Margaret Smith,........	"	XXXI.	57
1772. Mar. 26.	Moore, John, and Mary Van Dyck,.......	"	XVIII.	60
1769. May 20.	Moore, John B., and Aryetta Kiersted,....	"	XIV.	105
1778. Nov. 25.	Moore, John B., and Elizabeth Wessells,...	"	XXVI.	93
1782. May 18.	Moore, Joseph M., and Sarah Bay,........	"	XXXVI.	10
1757. Jan. 31.	Moore, Lambert, and Jane Holland,.......	"	I.	430
1780. Mar. 22.	Moore, Leah, and Joel Stone,............	"	XXIX.	5
1761. Feb. 10.	Moore, Lucy, and Sylvester Cavanaugh,....	"	IV.	56
1763. Oct. 21.	Moore, Lydia, and Michael Cody,.........	"	VII.	399
1781. July 31.	Moore, Margaret, and Rober Appleby,.....	"	XXXIII.	22
1781. Mar. 3.	Moore, Martha, and Joseph Eve, ...	"	XXXI.	64
1775. April 5.	Moore, Martha, and Joseph Titus,.........	"	XXIII.	2
1761. April 7.	Moore, Mary, and Isaiah Valleau,.........	"	IV.	136
1738. July 11.	Moore, Mary, and Jacob Leonard,.........	"	I.	10
1781. June 25.	Moore, Mary, and James Powers,.........	"	XXXII.	98
1763. Sept. 21.	Moore, Mary, and Manuel De Costa, ...	"	VII.	347
1771. April 15.	Moore, Nathaniel, and Hannah Hall, ...	"	XVII.	58
1783. June 10.	Moore, Nathaniel, and Patty Gidney,......	"	XXXIX.	48
1764. Mar. 23.	Moore, Nicholas, and Catharine Acherman,.	"	VIII.	115
1771. Dec. 19.	Moore, Phebe, and Benjamin Edwards,....	"	XVII.	301
1762. Nov. 20.	Moore, Phebe, and Foster Burrus, ...	"	VI.	447
1771. Nov. 29.	Moore, Philip, and Margaret Eligh, ...	"	XVII.	273
1767. July 20.	Moore, Rachel, and Abraham Marshall, ...	"	XI.	138
1780. Feb. 22.	Moore. Robert, and Catharine Steymets, ...	"	XXVIII.	212
1757. Jan. 20.	Moore, Robert, and Mary Godwood, ...	"	I.	422
1781. April 24.	Moore, Roseny, and Barnyby Bauer,......	"	XXXII.	13
1759. Feb. 10.	Moore, Ruth, and Daniel Grant, ...	"	II.	187
1767. April 23.	Moore, Ruth, and Thomas Perry, ...	"	XI.	68
1768. Dec. 31.	Moore, Samuel, and Amy Levrich,........	"	XIII.	276
1781. June 16.	Moore, Samuel, and Ann Lawrence,.......	"	XXXII.	87
1738. Mar. 29.	Moore, Samuel, and Martha Brittain,......	"	I.	9
1755. Dec. 6.	Moore, Samuel, Jr., and Anna Betts, ...	"	I.	227
1781. May 29.	Moore, Sarah, and Hugh Webster,........	"	XXXII.	61
1771. Sept. 24.	Moore, Sarah, and John Hays, ...	"	XVII.	187
1782. Mar. 6.	Moore, Sarah, and John Laforge, ...	"	XXXV.	75
1779. Feb. 16.	Moore, Sarah, and Samuel Blackwell,......	"	XXVII.	41
1762. Sept. 2.	Moore, Sarah, and William Hogeland,.....	"	VI.	303
1672. Feb. 7.	Moore, Thomas, and Susanna ———, ...	G. E.,	IV.	257
1761. July 6.	Moore, Thomas William, and Anne Ays- cough, ...	M. B.,	IV.	283
1764. Sept. 29.	Moore, William, and Elisabeth Denton,....	"	VIII.	327

Date.	Names.	Record.	Vol.	Page.
1782. Jan. 30.	Moore, William, and Jane Fish,............	M. B.,	xxxv.	39
1760. Dec. 29.	Moore, William, and Mary Bogart,........	"	iii.	493
1783. Sept. 10.	Moorehead, Elizabeth, and Andrew Gray,..	"	xl.	35
1753. Sept. 13.	Moorehead, Matthew, and Neiltje Berkaa,.	"	i.	117
1783. Mar. 17.	Moorewise, Catharine, and Nicholas Wethershien, ...	"	xxxviii.	67
1771. Sept. 26.	Moral, Samuel, and Rachel Gardenier, ...	"	xvii.	195
1773. Nov. 3.	Morall, Nicholas, and Jane McFardin, ...	"	xxii.	9
1771. July 25.	Moran, James, and Elizabeth Cozine,......	"	xvii.	141
1763. July 20.	Moran, James, and Margaret Price, ...	"	vii.	276
1764. June 23.	Moran, Mary, and John Wilson, ...	"	viii.	234
1773. Aug. 30.	Morcomb, Mary, and Philip Sykes,........	"	xxi.	90
1768. June 10.	Morehouse, Adonijah, and Sarah Brower, ..	"	xiii.	124
1780. Oct. 29.	Morehouse, John, and Mary Joanes,.......	"	xxx.	84
1765. July 27.	Morehouse, Rebecca, and John Chantrel,...	"	ix.	219
1773. Feb. 12.	Morel, Sarah, and Thomas Roe,...........	"	xx.	42
1765. Jan. 30.	Morgan, Abigal, and David Hustice,.......	"	ix.	35
1773. June 3.	Morgan, Ann, and Edward Treadwell,.....	"	xx.	138
1783. Mar. 29.	Morgan, Ann, and Jacob Crocheron, ...	"	xxxviii.	81
1779. Nov. 22.	Morgan, Ann, and Thomas Musgrove Snow,	"	xxviii.	145
1738. May 16.	Morgan, Benjamin, and Maria Tiebout, ...	"	i.	9
1777. July 5.	Morgan, Bridget, and John Nash,..........	"	xxiv.	113
1783. May 19.	Morgan, Caleb, and Issabel Johnson, ...	"	xxxix.	19
1767. Dec. 26.	Morgan, Caleb, and Phebe Ward,........	"	xii.	123
1762. June 21.	Morgan, Daniel, and Hannah Saunders,....	"	vi.	199
1761. Dec. 31.	Morgan, Elizabeth, and David Latourrette, .	"	v.	306
1758. Dec. 19.	Morgan, Elizabeth, and Thomas Argan,....	"	ii.	133
1769. Nov. 13.	Morgan, Elleonor, and John Simonson,....	"	xv.	92
1671. Aug. 29.	Morgan, Katherine, and Nicholas Stillwell,.	G. E.,	iv.	22
1781. June 4.	Morgan, James, and Anna Townsend, ...	M. B.,	xxxii.	71
1759. Mar. 14.	Morgan, James, and Helena Underhill, ...	"	ii.	215
1771. Dec. 11.	Morgan, James, and Phebe Treaddle,......	"	xvii.	290
1783. Feb. 21.	Morgan, Jessee, and Catharine Stilwell,. ..	"	xxxviii.	47
1761. May 30.	Morgan, John, and Deborah Winant, ...	"	iv.	218
1771. Mar. 30.	Morgan, John, and Elizabeth Ireland,.....	"	xvii.	43
1766. June 16.	Morgan, John, and Mary Jordan, ...	"	x.	17
1779. Aug. 6.	Morgan, John, and Phebe Roberts,........	"	xxviii.	48
1773. Nov. 25.	Morgan, John, and Susannah Decker, ...	"	xxii.	44
1757. Oct. 18.	Morgan, Lea, and Moses Dupue,..........	"	i.	674
1780. Sept. 23.	Morgan, Lewis, and Margeret Camp,......	"	xxx.	37
1778. Aug. 16.	Morgan, Margaret, and John Barrett,......	"	xxvi.	5
1783. Nov. 11.	Morgan, Margaret, and Robert Deane,.....	"	xl.	111
1772. Jan. 9.	Morgan, Mary, and Gilbert Vollentine,.....	"	xviii.	10
1773. April 3.	Morgan, Phebe, and Elisha Shute, ...	"	xx.	81
1782. Nov. 13.	Morgan, Phebe, and John Dickson,........	"	xxxvii.	81

DATE.	NAMES.	RECORD.	VOL. PAGE.
1763. May 22.	Morgan, Rachel, and Abraham Johnson, ...	M. B.,	VII. 195
1781. Dec. 24.	Morgan, Rebecca, and John Beauvx, ...	"	XXXIV. 105
1783. Dec. 31.	Morgan, Sarah, and Warren Pitt Lisle,.....	"	XL. 125
1766. Oct. 20.	Morgan, Susannah, and John Townsend,...	"	X. 128
1758. Mar. 9.	Morgan, Thomas, and Martha Spragg, ...	"	I. 840
1774. Jan. 7.	Morgan, William, and Hannah Somarandike,	"	XXII. 95
1768. Feb. 29.	Morgat, John, and Mary Rodman, ...	"	XIII. 47
1780. Dec. 9.	Morison, Alexander, and Frances Gidney,..	"	XXX. 148
1763. Nov. 7.	Morison, George, and Margaret Thompson,.	"	VII. 431
1768. Dec. 30.	Morland, Stephen, and Mary Hayes, ...	"	XIII. 275
1760. June 9.	Morley, Andrew, and Rebella Hamilton, ...	"	III. 180
1769. May 5.	Morrel, Daniel, and Jemima D. Clark,......	"	XIV. 94
1781. April 6.	Morrel, John, and Margaret Devereux,.....	"	XXXI. 95
1759. Aug. 21.	Morrel, Joseph, and Martha Arrowsmith,...	"	II. 385
1764. Sept. 29.	Morrel, Joseph, and Nieltie Johnson, ...	"	VIII. 328
1762. Nov. 27.	Morrel, Thomas, and Kesiah Johnston,.....	"	VI. 457
1780. Dec. 7.	Morrel, William, and Lucresha Bashford,...	"	XXX. 143
1770. June 30.	Morrell, Abigail, and George Burling,......	"	XVI. 129
1782. Feb. 24.	Morrell, Amy, and Daniel Leonard,........	"	XXXV. 64
1782. Jan. 11.	Morrell, Ann, and Benjamin Buckbie, ...	"	XXXV. 15
1778. Mar. 17.	Morrell, Elizabeth, and John Philips, ...	"	XXV. 44
1767. Nov. 12.	Morrell, James, and Sarah Willett, ...	"	XII. 81
1762. April 21.	Morrell, Jane, and John Whipple,.........	"	VI. 121
1781. Dec. 22.	Morrell, John, and Ann Stillwell, ...	"	XXXIV. 99
1771. April 25.	Morrell, John, and Elizabeth Carpenter,....	"	XVII. 69
1760. Aug. 20.	Morrell, John, and Elizabeth Miserol,......	"	XXX. 3
1781. Dec. 22.	Morrell, John, and Susannah Mitchell,.....	"	XXXIV. 98
1762. June 2.	Morrell, Margaret, and Benjamin Moore,...	"	VI. 179
1775. Sept. 17.	Morrell, Margaret, and Samuel Woolley, ...	"	XXIII. 213
1782. July 16.	Morrell, Phebe, and Nathaniel Woodruff,...	"	XXXVI. 84
1783. Mar. 29.	Morrell, Phebe, and William Smith,.......	"	XXXVIII. 82
1758. May 2.	Morrell, Robert, and Rebecca Cornish,.. ...	"	I. 891
1773. Mar. 12.	Morrell, William, and Amy Lackman, ...	"	XX. 59
1763. Jan. 21.	Morrell, William, and Elizabeth Baker,.....	"	VII. 29
1753. Sept. 29.	Morriceu, John, and Catherin Vandebogert,.	"	I. 128
1756. Oct. 30.	Morril, John, and Elizabeth Skilman,......	"	I. 339
1757. Mar. 12.	Morril, Martha, and Thomas Foster,.......	"	I. 467
1772. Aug. 29.	Morrin, Susannah, and Paul Burtus,.......	"	XIX. 33
1761. Jan. 20.	Morris, Abraham, and Mary Marschalk,....	"	IV. 30
1763. April 26.	Morris, Ann, and Jacob Shafer,...........	"	VII. 143
1761. Feb. 3.	Morris, Ann, and John Boyd,.............	"	IV. 49
1738. Nov. 30.	Morris, Arabella, and James Graham,......	"	I. 12
1772. May 12.	Morris, Arthur, and Elizabeth Bavier,......	"	XVIII. 108
1765. May —.	Morris, Catharine, and John Connoven,....	"	IX. 144
1769. June 14.	Morris, David, and Christena Mercier,......	"	XIV. 119

DATE.	NAMES.	RECORD.	VOL.	PAGE.
1758. Feb. 1.	Morris, Elizabeth, and Hugh McGinnis, ...	M. B.,	I.	807
1738. June 26.	Morris, Elizabeth, and James De Hart,.....	"	I.	10
1779. Sept. 3.	Morris, Elizabeth, and Robert Letson, ...	"	XXVIII.	66
1761. Feb. 4.	Morris, Elizabeth, and William Brown, ...	"	IV.	51
1762. Nov. 6.	Morris, Isabella, and Isaac Wilkins, ...	"	VI.	415
1765. Jan. 7.	Morris, Jacob, and Eleanor Edwards, ...	"	IX.	10
1757. Mar. 11.	Morris, Jacob, and Jane De Kay, ...	"	I.	465
1757. May 21.	Morris, Joseph, and Amm Arthur, ...	"	I.	539
1782. April 8.	Morris, Joseph, and Elizabeth Dean,.......	"	XXXV.	118
1761. Nov. 26.	Morris, Mahetabel, and John Baggs,.......	"	V.	252
1759. Dec. 29.	Morris, Margaret, and John Devareux,.....	"	II.	560
1777. Dec. 27.	Morris, Margaret, and Christopher Doughty,	"	XXIV.	207
1768. May 24.	Morris, Mary, and Amos Smith, ...	"	XIII.	111
1755. Dec. 20.	Morris, Mary, and Edward Black,.........	"	I.	236
1765. Oct. 29.	Morris, Mary, and James Boggs, ...	"	IX.	335
1775. June 26.	Morris, Mary, and Thomas Lawrence, ...	"	XXIII.	78
1759. June 13.	Morris, Richard, and Sarah Ludlow,.......	"	II.	322
1780. June 10.	Morris, Robert, and Elizabeth Gardner, ...	"	XXIX.	85
1758. Jan. 19.	Morris, Roger, and Mary Philipse, ...	"	I.	790
1761. June 22.	Morris, Sarah, and John Willson, ...	"	IV.	254
1762. Mar. 1.	Morris, Sarah, and Robert Smith, ...	"	VI.	60
1772. Sept. 15.	Morris, Sarah, and Vincent Pearse Ashfield,	"	XIX.	50
1757. Sept. 23.	Morris, William, and Ann Ramsey, ...	"	I.	641
1760. Sept. 15.	Morris, William, and Rachel Perry, ...	"	III.	315
1763. Jan. 24.	Morris, William, and Susanna Adams, ...	"	VII.	33
1760. July 2.	Morrison, Catharine, and Neil McKilop,....	"	III.	202
1759. Feb. 17.	Morrison, Catharine, and William Fraizer,..	"	II.	196
1781. May 4.	Morrison, Dorathy, and John Tollckimett,..	"	XXXII.	31
1783. May 3.	Morrison, Elizabeth, and Thomas Jones, ...	"	XXXIX.	1
1777. May 9.	Morrison, George, and Elizabeth Driscall,..	"	XXIV.	87
1779. June 25.	Morrison, Joseph, and Ann Maxfield,......	"	XXVIII.	8
1764. Jan. 19.	Morrison, Margaret, and John McDaniel,...	"	VIII.	23
1780. June 30.	Morrison, Mary, and Alexander Morton,...	"	XXXIX.	75
1779. June 20.	Morrisson, Alexander, and Elizabeth Barton,	"	XXVII.	169
1764. May 22.	Morrus, James, and Jemimie Terry, ...	"	VIII.	196
1771. April 12.	Morse, Charles, and Margaret Collins,......	"	XVII.	55a
1782. May 17.	Morse, Ebenezer, and Hannah Siverly, ...	"	XXXVI.	6
1758. Mar. 30.	Morse, Else, and Abraham Devine,........	"	I.	868
1775. May 2.	Morss, William, and Lydia Pew,..........	"	XXIII.	20
1757. Mar. 21.	Morsereau, Mary, and Abraham Winant,...	"	I.	477
1758. Oct. 1.	Morson, Daniel, and Ann Watson, ...	"	II.	75
1760. Jan. 28.	Morss, Ephram, and Susannah Titus, ...	"	III.	8
1761. Feb. 4.	Mortimer, William, and Ann Brown,......	"	IV.	58
1771. Oct. 10.	Mortisoe, Nelly, and John Vendine,.......	"	XVII.	200
1769. Jan. 7.	Mortison, Garret, and Sytie Suydam,......	"	XIV.	5

DATE.	NAMES.	RECORD.	VOL.	PAGE.
1780. June 30.	Morton, Alexander, and Mary Morrison, ...	M. B.,	XXXIX.	75
1776. Dec. 7.	Morton, Jane, and John Waters, ...	"	XXIII.	315
1760. Aug. 28.	Morton, John, and Sophiah Kemper, ...	"	III.	272
1782. Aug. 24.	Morton, William, and Mary Love, ...	"	XXXVI.	121
1773. Jan. 20.	Moscholick, Catherine, and Joseph Robinson,	"	XX.	15
1773. April 29.	Moscholick, Mary, and Cornelius Turk, Jr., .	"	XX.	101
1778. Sept. 28.	Mosely, Malachi, and Catherine Baker, ...	"	XXVI.	37
1772. Dec. 31.	Moses, Jacob, and Elizabeth Roberts, ...	"	XIX.	168
1771. Dec. 18.	Mosher, Margaret, and Samuel Russell, ...	"	XVII.	298
1756. Aug. 3.	Moss, Elizabeth, and Edward Collard, ...	"	I.	266
1769. Feb. 9.	Mosteon, Robert, and Jane Burger, ...	"	XIV.	30
1766. Nov. 22.	Mott, Adam, and Elizabeth Hewlett, ...	"	X.	178
1737. Nov. 4.	Mott, Adam, and Elizabeth Smith, ...	"	I.	8
1781. Nov. 22.	Mott, Amelia, and John Ryan, ...	"	XXXIV.	55
1775. Oct. 18.	Mott, Benjamin, and Rachel Whitson, ...	"	XXIII.	184
1763. Jan. 5.	Mott, Bridget, and James McCombs, ...	"	VII.	8
1763. April 16.	Mott, Ceeors, and Susannah Barnes, ...	"	VII.	130
1763. Nov. 2.	Mott, Deborah, and Ezekiel Cooper, ...	"	VII.	423
1753. Oct. 13.	Mott, Edmund, and Deborah Sands, ...	"	I.	139
1761. Sept. 25.	Mott, Elisabeth, and William Doty, ...	"	V.	99
1765. April 26.	Mott, Elizabeth, and Benjamin Hicks, ...	"	IX.	110
1782. Sept. 10.	Mott, Elizabeth, and John Whitehand, ...	"	XXXVI.	143
1766. June 10.	Mott, Elizabeth, and Philip Smith Platt, ...	"	X.	12
1761. June 18.	Mott, Herodia, and Henry Higbie, ...	"	IV.	247
1763. Jan. 26.	Mott, Kesiah, and James Whippo, ...	"	VII.	37
1774. Jan. 13.	Mott, Jackson, and Gloriana Coles, ...	"	XXII.	102
1761. Oct. 20.	Mott, Jacob, and Elizabeth Kissam, ...	"	V.	152
1763. Mar. 5.	Mott, James, and Catharine Sibly, ...	"	VII.	92
1670. Sept. 5.	Mott, James, and Mary Redman, ...	C. A.,	II.	589
1756. Oct. 29.	Mott, Jamimah, and John Cannon, ...	M. B.,	I.	335
1758. Sept. 7.	Mott, John, and Ann Somerendike, ...	"	II.	10
1770. Mar. 22.	Mott, John, and Margaret Burtis, ...	"	XVI.	37
1771. Aug. 3.	Mott, John, and Martha Sammons, ...	"	XVII.	150
1773. Aug. 17.	Mott, Jonathan, and Jan Burtis, ...	"	XXI.	70
1759. June 2.	Mott, Joseph, and Catharine Boorem, ...	"	II.	303
1783. Oct. 30.	Mott, Joseph, and Lidia Cyrus, ...	"	XL.	94
1772. Mar. 17.	Mott, Margaret, and Melancton Smith, ...	"	XVIII.	53
1777. June 11.	Mott, Mariam, and Benjamin Birdsall, ...	"	XXIV.	101
1738. July 5.	Mott, Martha, and John Hicks, ...	"	I.	10
1757. Jan. 11.	Mott, Martha, and Lucas Eldert, ...	"	I.	411
1769. Jan. 9.	Mott, Mary, and Daniel Hewlett, ...	"	XIV.	7
1773. Nov. 11.	Mott, Mary, and Jacob Pratt, ...	"	XXII.	21
1780. Sept. 6.	Mott, Phebe, and Joseph Dunbar, ...	"	XXX.	18
1782. April 7.	Mott, Rachael, and John Hooton, ...	"	XXXV.	117
1782. April 1.	Mott, Rebecca, and Samuel Carpenter, ...	"	XXXV.	104

35

DATE.	NAMES.	RECORD.	VOL. PAGE.
1779. Dec. 24.	Mott, Rebecca, and William Simpson,......	M. B.,	XXVIII. 180
1760. Sept. 30.	Mott, Richard, and Jane Perrit,...........	"	III. 338
1780. Oct. 3.	Mott, Richard, and Martha Sutton,..	"	XXX. 53
1763. Nov. 7.	Mott, Ruth, and Jordan Lawrence,........	"	VII. 432
1779. Jan. 22.	Mott, Samuel, and Margaret Keshow,......	"	XXVII. 24
1762. Oct. 7.	Mott, Sarah, and James Raynor,..........	"	VI. 351
1757. June 30.	Mott, Thomas, and Keziah Brush,.........	"	I. 578
1771. Mar. 5.	Mott, William, and Letitia Leadbetter,.....	"	XVII. 24
1780. Nov. 24.	Mott, William, and Caty Clowes, ...	"	XXX. 123
1761. May 6.	Moudd, Hugh, and Catharine Norris, ...	"	IV. 182
1763. April 14.	Moule, Frederick, and Gertrude Sharp, ...	"	VII. 127
1767. May 1.	Moulinaus, Susannah Mary, and John Meeks,	"	XI. 75
1762. June 22.	Mount, Catharine, and Jonathan Dudfield,..	"	VI. 203
1781. Aug. 21.	Mount, Cloe, and James Theam, ...	"	XXXIII. 43
1781. Oct. 17.	Mount, Frances, and Christopher Platt, ...	"	XXXIII. 105
1780. Nov. 21.	Mount, George, and Elizabeth Anderson,...	"	XXX. 118
1780. July 8.	Mount, Margaret, and John Shepherd, Jr.,..	"	XXIX. 109
1756. Nov. 15.	Mountanie, Rebecca, and Richard Martin,..	"	I. 355
1738. May 4.	Mountany, Maritie, and Patrick Smith, ...	"	I. 9
1777. April 24.	Mountfordt, William, and Jane Johnston, ..	"	XXIV. 71
1773. Oct. 5.	Mours, Henry, and Marjte Dumond,.......	"	XXI. 130
1758. Mar. 11.	Moutton, Peter, and Hann Van Arder,.....	"	I. 843
1765. July 8.	Mowatt, John, and Jane Quereau, ...	"	IX. 197
1775. Aug. 26.	Mowl, Christina, and Petrus Musick,......	"	XXIII. 136
1763. July 13.	Muat, Catharine, and George Cruksank, ...	"	VII. 263
1781. Nov. 8.	Muay, Hendrick, and Jane Burtis, ...	"	XXXIV. 23
1759. Sept. 6.	Muckelroy, Edward, and Sarah McGinnis,..	"	II. 411
1757. Aug. 30.	Muckelvain, Mary, and Hendrick Sullivan, .	"	I. 625
1782. Aug. 28.	Muckleherring, Jane, and Dugal McMichael,	"	XXXVI. 129
1759. April 14.	Mucklevain, William, and Susannah Titus,..	"	II. 241
1782. July 15.	Mucklevane, Elizabeth, and William Arrow-		
	smith,.............	"	XXXVI. 83
1736. Oct. 25.	Mudge, Coles, and Dority Coles, ...	"	I. 3
1770. May 23.	Mudge, Daniel, and Martha Coles,.........	"	XVI. 93
1779. Nov. 19.	Mudge, Dorathy, and Willet Weeks, ...	"	XXVIII. 144
1765. Oct. 7.	Mudge, Elizabeth, and John Oakley, ...,...	"	IX. 292
1765. Jan. 3.	Mudge, Elizabeth, and Peter Titus,........	"	IX. 4
1757. July 2.	Mudge, Mary, and Clark Lawrence, ...	"	I. 579
1736. Oct. 25.	Mudge, Michael, and Sarah Hopkins, ...	"	I. 3
1765. Oct. 1.	Mudge, Sarah, and Daniel Merritt, ...	"	IX. 285
1775. July 31.	Mudge, William, and Martha Carpenter, ...	"	XXIII. 112
1783. Oct. 7.	Muerenbeldt, Peter, and Elizabeth Cole,....	"	XL. 66
1780. May 30.	Muir, James, and Agness McCorrick,......	"	XXIX. 73
1765. July 20.	Muirils, William, and Ann Bruce,.........	"	IX. 213
1779. Dec. 23.	Muirson, George, and Mary Longbottom,...	"	XXVIII. 178

DATE.	NAMES.	RECORD.	VOL.	PAGE.
1767. Sept. 7.	Muirson, Gloriana, and Thomas Rice, ...	M. B.,	XII.	27
1760. Aug. 20.	Mulford, Charles, and Elizabeth McCray, ...	"	III.	263
1761. Mar. 3.	Mulford, Phebe, and Joseph Tillinghast, ...	"	IV.	114
1760. Mar. 8.	Mulligan, Hugh, and Catherine Pool, ...	"	III.	70
1769. Sept. 23.	Mullen, Elizabeth, and Oliver Sweeney, ...	"	XV.	42
1761. June 22.	Mullen, Elizabeth, and William Couzins, ...	"	IV.	255
1757. Oct. 8.	Mullen, James, and Elizabeth Hopper, ...	"	I.	663
1778. Aug. 22.	Mullen, Mark, and Susanah Tufton, ...	"	XXVI.	10
1781. July 9.	Mullenuex, Hannah, and Richard Hicks, ...	"	XXXIII.	3
1761. May 28.	Muller, Gertrey, and Johannis Hogeboom, ..	"	IV.	210
1768. Sept. 19.	Muller, Hans, and Elizabeth Gerdenier, ...	"	XIII.	189
1763. Nov. 24.	Muller, Helletje, and Stephen Hogeboom, ..	"	VII.	468
1771. April 8.	Muller, Hilitie, and Dirck Van D. Carr, ...	"	XVII.	51
1762. Nov. 12.	Muller, Jeremiah, Jr., and Catharine Moore,	"	VI.	427
1768. Nov. 24.	Muller, John Isaac, and Elizabeth Skinkle, ..	"	XII.	96
1736. July 20.	Muller, Kerjan, and Annatie Bradt, ...	"	I.	2
1761. Sept. 16.	Muller, Maria, and Peter Muller, ...	"	V.	86
1771. Sept. 16.	Muller, Peter, and Maria Muller, ...	"	V.	86
1771. Aug. 2.	Muller, Stephen, and Catherine Measick, ...	"	XVII.	148
1773. Oct. 27.	Mulligan, Hercules, and Elizabeth Sanders, .	"	XXI.	148
1776. Mar. 12.	Mulligen, Philip, and Jane Cammel, ...	"	XXIII.	283
1781. Jan. 18.	Mulligan, Sarah, and John James Cluett, ...	"	XXXI.	26
1779. Dec. 1.	Mullineaux, Rachael, and James Lake, ...	"	XXVIII.	157
1760. May 16.	Mulliner, Rachael, and George Falls, ...	"	III.	154
1759. Nov. 8.	Mullinix, Joseph, and Rebecca Barnes, ...	"	II.	490
1782. June 8.	Mullock, William, and Sarah McBean, ...	"	XXXVI.	44
1764. Feb. 20.	Mumbrole, William, and Maritje Defrizee, ..	"	VIII.	65
1780. May 26.	Mumford, Elizabeth, and Abraham Ellison, .	"	XXIX.	70
1736. Nov. 5.	Mun, John, and Hanah Benson, ...	"	I.	3
1675. June 11.	Muncy, Hannah, and John Ramsden, ...	W. O. P.,	III.	97
1780. Sept. 20.	Munday, Sarah Ann, and Thomas Fay, ...	M. B.,	XXX.	32
1760. Mar. 17.	Munds, Israel, and Hannah Dunscomb, ...	"	III.	79
1783. Nov. 5.	Munds, John, and Charlotte Horner, ...	"	XL.	105
1758. April 12.	Munro, John, and Jane Caldwell, ...	"	I.	872
1760. Mar. 24.	Munro, John, and Mary Brower, ...	"	III.	90
1773. Feb. 9.	Munro, Margaret, and Adam Schaumburg, .	"	XX.	39
1764. Mar. 12.	Munro, Robert, and Margaret Howard, ...	"	VIII.	101
1781. Feb. 19.	Munro, Sarah, and John Stuart, ...	"	XXXI.	49
1783. April 26.	Munro, Susannah, and James Littlewood, ..	"	XXXVIII.	116
1775. Nov. 24.	Munroe, Elizabeth, and Donald Fisher, ...	"	XXIII.	221
1780. Dec. 30.	Murchia, William, and Margret Breseal, ...	"	XXX.	173
1759. July 27.	Murdigh, Elenor, and Leothes Smith, ...	"	II.	365
1782. April 15.	Murdock, Jane, and Thomas Burgess, ...	"	XXXV.	124
1762. Nov. 9.	Murdy, Christopher, and Isabel McVicker, ..	"	VI.	421
1783. Mar. 27.	Murgatroyd, Samuel, and Easter Ledson, ..	"	XXXVIII.	78

DATE.		NAMES.	RECORD.	VOL.	PAGE.
1762. Aug.	9.	Muriahn, Anna Maria, and John Biniling, ..	M. B.,	VI.	272
1777. Feb.	18.	Murphey, Patrick, and Elenor McBride,....	"	XXIV.	30
1777. Oct.	4.	Murphey, Peter, and Lucretia Smith,......	"	XXIV.	157
1766. Dec.	8.	Murphore, Catherine, and Jacob Mills,.....	"	X.	196
1767. July	8.	Murphy, Aletta, and Nicholas Fletcher,....	"	XI.	127
1764. Mar.	17.	Murphy, Ann, and Nicholas Feild, ...	"	VIII.	110
1769. June	26.	Murphy, Catherine, and Hugh Moore,.....	"	XIV.	132
1761. Mar.	1.	Murphy, Elenor, and William Hudson, ...	"	IV.	125
1761. Dec.	5.	Murphy, Ellen, and John Ryan, ...	"	VIII.	437
1768. May	10.	Murphy, Ellitje, and Cornelius Cozine,.....	"	XIII.	100
1765. Oct.	16.	Murphy, John, and Maria Van Nice, ...	"	IX.	301
1778. Sept.	2.	Murphy, John, and Mary Clarkson, ...	"	XXVI.	19
1781. Oct.	10.	Murphy, Mark, and Mary Conihane, ...	"	XXXIII.	95
1757. April	21.	Murphy, Mary, and James Cavenor,.......	"	I.	510
1778. May	18.	Murphy, Mary, and John Johnson,........	"	XXV.	85
1761. June	6.	Murphy, Mary, and John Omand,.........	"	IV.	231
1764. Nov.	15.	Murphy, Mary, and Thomas Kennedy,.....	"	VIII.	410
1783. Jan.	14.	Murphy, Mary, and Thomas Welch,.......	"	XXXIX.	58
1764. Mar.	12.	Murphy, Mathew, and Anne Breese,......	"	VIII.	102
1781. May	1.	Murphy, Rachael, and John Smith,........	"	XXXII.	24
1771. Oct.	11.	Murphy, Rachel, and William Jones, ...	"	XVII.	216
1759. Feb.	20.	Murphy, Thomas, and Letitia Patroue,.....	"	II.	199
1778. July	13.	Murray, Alexander, and Ann Scudder,.....	"	XXV.	130
1762. May	24.	Murray, Daniel, and Mary Butler,.........	"	VI.	167
1766. Oct.	25.	Murray, Elenor, and George Rogers, ...	"	X.	141
1762. Dec.	18.	Murray, Elisabeth, and Edward Williams,..	"	VI.	489
1763. Oct.	1.	Murray, Elizabeth, and Michael Wyser,....	"	VII.	365
1778. Oct.	3.	Murray, Elizabeth, and William Colville,...	"	XXVI.	43
1762. Oct.	7.	Murray, George, and Elizabeth Talkington,.	"	VI.	352
1783. Oct.	23.	Murray, George, and Mary Sinnet,........	"	XL.	89
1758. Dec.	27.	Murray, Hannah, and John Smith,........	"	II.	140
1756. July	16.	Murray, James, and Lilly Campbell, ...	"	I.	257
1764. May	30.	Murray, John, and Alithea Power,........	"	VIII.	201
1761. Mar.	25.	Murray, John, and Margaret McClain, ...	"	IV.	116
1738. Nov.	9.	Murray, Joseph, and Grace Freeman,......	"	I.	11
1777. May	9.	Murray, Mary, and Robert Richardson, ...	"	XXIV.	85
1782. Mar.	27.	Murray, Thomas, and Jane Deacon,.......	"	XXXV.	98
1762. Nov.	8.	Murrey, Andrew, and Agnes Griffiths,.....	"	VI.	418
1780. June	5.	Murrow, John, and Sarah Churchill,.......	"	XXIX.	83
1763. Aug.	18.	Murrills, William, and Elizabeth Pedley, ...	"	VII.	304
1781. Dec.	13.	Murry, John, and Phebe Faunote, ...	"	XXXIV.	85
1765. Oct.	22.	Murseroe, Peter, and Rebecca Lake,.......	"	IX.	310
1772. Dec.	14.	Musick, Margaret, and Johannis Best, Jr.,.	"	XIX.	155
1773. Jan.	25.	Musick, Mary, and Jury Best, Jr.,........	"	XX.	19
1775. Aug.	26.	Musick, Petrus, and Christina Mowl, ...	"	XXIII.	136

DATE.	NAMES.	RECORD.	VOL.	PAGE.
1770. Feb. 12.	Musick, Resina, and Frederick Bladtner, ...	M. B.,	XVI.	16
1775. Aug. 26.	Musick, Thomas, and Rachael Claw,.......	"	XXIII.	137
1737. Sept. 24.	Muslow, Elizabeth, and Thomas Children,..	"	I.	7
1757. Oct. 8.	Mutlow, Cretje, and Robert Dale,.........	"	I.	664
1756. Oct. 6.	Mutlow, Margaret, and John Hall, ...	"	I.	321
1771. June 29.	Myer, Abraham, Jr., and Agnus Roome,...	"	XVII.	126
1762. Sept. 24.	Myer, Andrew, and Elleanor Southerd,....	"	VI.	331
1774. Jan. 18.	Myer, Andrew, and Margaret Demorie,....	"	XXII.	104
1771. June 11.	Myer, Andrew, and Sarah De Lamater,....	"	XVII.	108
1762. Jan. 21.	Myer, Angeltje, and Peter Waldron, Jr., ...	"	IX.	25
1769. June 23.	Myer, Ann, and Thomas Sowers, ...	"	XIV.	127
1781. Dec. 17.	Myer, Anna, and James Callow,..........	"	XXXIV.	91
1765. June 17.	Myer, Bridget, and John Low,............	"	IX.	171
1772. Dec. 19.	Myer, Catherina, and Frederick Westfalt, ..	"	XIX.	158
1770. July 5.	Myer, Catherine, and Jonathan Randel,....	"	XVI.	136
1775. April 20.	Myer, Catherine, and William Vredenburgh, Jr.,..............................	"	XXIII.	12
1759. May 28.	Myer, Garret Hendrick, and Alida Roberts,.	"	II.	292
1764. Mar. 24.	Myer, George, and Christene Wall, ...	"	III.	89
1764. Aug. 22.	Myer, Isaac, and Martha Collins,..........	"	VIII.	290
1761. July 11.	Myer, John, and Ann Waldron, ...	"	IV.	293
1738. July 20.	Myer, John, and Cornelia Delemater,......	"	I.	10
1783. Sept. 3.	Myer, John, and Mary Acker,............	"	XL.	20
1757. Jan. 15.	Myer, John, Jr., and Mercy Roe, ...	"	I.	416
1764. Dec. 22.	Myer, Margaret, and Abraham Bussing,....	"	VIII.	464
1767. July 4.	Myer, Mary, and William Shipman, ...	"	XI.	125
1762. April 6.	Myer, Peter, and Mary Bunn, ...,	"	VI.	113
1761. Oct. 17.	Myer, Sarah, and Elias Degrushe, Jr., ...	"	V.	149
1764. Oct. 1.	Myer, Susannah, and Alexander McDonald,..............................	"	VIII.	331
1779. Oct. 16.	Myere, Frowey, and Thomas Ridley, ,.....	"	XXVIII.	114
1780. Aug. 30.	Myers, Eleanor, and William Rodman,.....	"	XXX.	12
1763. Jan. 20.	Myers, Gertrude, and James Sinclair,......	"	VII.	23
1765. Sept. 24.	Myers, John, and Sarah Rusco,...........	"	IX.	273
1765. Oct. 28.	Myers, Lawrence, and Angeltje Waldrone,.	"	IX.	325
1773. Jan. 25.	Myers, Peter, and Sarah Kilpatrick, ...	"	XX.	18
1760. Dec. 17.	Myers, Rebecca, and John Nicholas Hoffman, ...	"	III.	480
1761. Mar. 11.	Myers, Sarah, and Andrew Blanck, ...	"	IV.	96
1779. Aug. 23.	Myers, William, and Elizabeth McEvers,...	"	XXVIII.	57
1779. Jan. 14.	Myford, Elizabeth, and Thomas Weston, ...	"	XXVII.	13
1738. Aug. 22.	Mynders, Burger, and Madelane Van Vyve,	"	I.	10
1770. Nov. 14.	Mynderse, Barent, and Jane Van Vrankin, .	"	XVI.	250
1765. April 15.	Mynderse, Frederick, and Catharine Van Valkenburgh, ...	"	IX.	93

DATE.		NAMES.	RECORD.	VOL.	PAGE.
1761. Oct.	10.	Mynderse, Gertrude, and Petrus Van De Volgen, ...	M. B.,	v.	132
1772. Jan.	29.	Mynderse, John, and Nelly Hearmans, ...	"	xviii.	22
1767. July	13.	Mynderse, Margaret, and Teunis Swart, Jr.,	"	xii.	3
1764. Nov.	12.	Mynderson, Annatje, and David Dubois, ...	"	viii.	399
1768. April	8.	Mynderson, John, and Catherine Yates,....	"	xiii.	66
1761. April	9.	Myndert (Mynderson), Sarah, and Peter Breested,...........................	"	iv.	139
1755. Sept.	6.	Myndertse, Abraham, and Catherina Ostranden, ...	"	i.	168
1760. Aug.	6.	Myndertse, Abraham, and Catharine Lansingh,............................	"	iii.	237
1779. Mar.	20.	Myres, Samuel, and Patience Willet,......	"	xxvii.	71
1757. June	17.	Myring, Barbara, and Jacob Sumard,......	"	i.	567

N.

1760. April	14.	Nack, Rinier, and Catharine Bond, ...	"	iii.	103
1760. Sept.	6.	Nack, Rinier, and Sarah Bussing, ...	"	iii.	301
1757. Dec.	7.	Naden, Elizabeth, and John Appy,........	"	i.	727
1768. Dec.	19.	Nafins, Catherine, and Nicholas Van Brunt,	"	xiii.	267
1762. July	14.	Nagel, Deborah, and Benjamin Waldron,...	"	vi.	236
1764. Nov.	22.	Nagel, Hendrik, and Maritie De Clarke,....	"	viii.	414
1764. Dec.	5.	Nagle, Annetie, and Art Vanderbilt,.......	"	viii.	439
1780. May	23.	Nagle, Jane, and John Ditmes, Jr.,........	"	xxix.	65
1767. April	4.	Nagle, Neeltie, and Abraham Duryee, ...	"	xi.	55
1759. Aug.	30.	Nagle, Thomas, and Elizabeth Stevens, ...	"	ii.	404
1778. July	7.	Nailer, Susanah, and John Jones, ...	"	xxv.	122
1763. Oct.	12.	Nairn, James, and Deborah Snethen,......	"	vii.	383
1769. May	26.	Nairne, James, and Margaret Haviland,....	"	xiv.	109
1780. Aug.	28.	Narren, Robert, and Sophia McKoy, ...	"	xxx.	5
1777. Sept.	29.	Nash, James, and Susanah Lemote, ...	"	xxiv.	152
1777. July	5.	Nash, John, and Bridget Morgan,.........	"	xxiv.	113
1783. April	30.	Naylor, Charles, and Hester Swanser,......	"	xxxviii.	121
1668. April	3.	Naylor (Woodward), James, and Jane Crosse,	O. W. L.,	ii.	223
1668. May	14.	Naylor, Mary, and Richard Stiles,.........	"	ii.	223
1762. Aug.	13.	Neal, James, and Elisabeth Tilly, ...	M. B.,	vi.	273
1778. May	7.	Neal, James, and Margaret Smith, ...	"	xxv.	73
1772. May	25.	Neal, John, and Elizabeth Ashton,........	"	xviii.	124
1767. Aug.	12.	Neal, Sarah, and Patrick McCarrick,.......	"	xii.	14
1755. Aug.	20.	Nealson, Elizabeth, and Gilber Giles, ...	"	i.	153
1783. May	19.	Neavens, Mary, and Jelm Der Kinderen, ...	"	xxxix.	18
1759. May	5.	Neazer, Elizabeth, and William Divine, ...	"	ii.	268
1782. May	22.	Neck, Elizabeth, and Lewis Taylor, ...	"	xxxvi.	20

DATE.	NAMES.	RECORD.	VOL.	PAGE.
1783. Mar. 12.	Newall, Penelopa, and William McFarlane,.	M. B.,	xxxviii.	66
1771. Nov. 30.	Newberry, Elizabeth, and Benjamin Lowe,.	"	xvii.	275
1758. May 20.	Newbold, Richard, and Margaret Shourt,...	"	i.	903
1777. Jan. 5.	Newbury, Ruth, and George Bennet,......	"	xxiv.	9
1763. May 4.	Newel, Sarah, and Andrew Marschalck,....	"	vii.	166
1781. Nov. 10.	Newkam, John, and Ann Smith,..........	"	xxxiv.	25
1759. Sept. 3.	Newkerk, Annatje, and Wessell Van Dyck,.	"	ii.	406
1767. May 19.	Newkerk, Benjamin, and Catherine Rutsen,	"	xi.	92
1769. July 24.	Newkerk, Dorothy, and Nathaniel Cantine,.	"	xv.	4
1765. May 20.	Newkerk, Garret M., and Betha De Lematre,	"	ix.	135
1768. Dec. 2.	Newkerk, Jacob, and Mary Patterson,.....	"	xiii.	251
1773. Oct. 30.	Newkerk, Philip, and Jannetje Rosa, ...	"	xxii.	6
1765. Oct. 17.	Newkirck, Mary, and Evert Wynkoop, ...	"	ix.	304
1765. April 2.	Newkirk, Barney, and Ann Teurs, ...	"	ix.	78
1738. Oct. 31.	Newkirk, Elizabeth, and Isaac Wimple,....	"	i.	11
1765. Jan. 31.	Newman, Arthur, and Sarah Brundidge,...	"	ix.	39
1781. Dec. 5.	Newsted, John, and Martha Barham,......	"	xxxiv.	73
1781. Jan. 4.	Newton, Forbes, and Ann Bogart, ...	"	xxxi.	10
1755. Aug. 16.	Newton, Mary, and William Ackle, ...	"	i.	149
1782. July 1.	Newton, Richard, and Jane Ogden,........	"	xxxvi.	69
1780. June 24.	Newton, Richard, and Mary Otis,.........	"	xxix.	96
1759. April 24.	Newton, William, and Mary Fletcher, ...	"	ii.	254
1779. June 24.	Newton, William, Jr., and Elizabeth Ogsbury, ...	"	xxviii.	6
1770. May 18.	Nexsen, Elias, and Mary Pels,............	"	xvi.	92
1775. Oct. 3.	Nexsen, Elias, and Mary Waldron,........	"	xxiii.	171
1765. Jan. 29.	Nexsen, William, and Catharine De Graff,..	"	ix.	34
1738. Dec. 28.	Nicholls, Anne, and Daniel Cnuttel, ...	"	i.	12
1737. Dec. 10.	Nicholls, Edward, and Agnus De Mire,.....	"	i.	8
1764. Aug. 16.	Nicholls, Elizabeth, and Cornelius Glen,....	"	viii.	283
1765. Mar. 7.	Nicholls, George, and Catherine Tillenborough, ...	"	ix.	65
1736. Sept. 7.	Nicholls, John, Jr., and Frances Little, ...	"	i.	2
1770. May 25.	Nichols, Jane, and William Nutting,.......	"	xvi.	95
1779. July 31.	Nichols, John, and Mary De Grove,.......	"	xxviii.	40
1767. Dec. 24.	Nichols, Lewis, and Mary Thompson,......	"	xii.	122
1759. Oct. 26.	Nichols, Rebecca, and Thomas Smith,......	"	ii.	474
1769. May 10.	Nichols, Ruth, and Joseph Woodward,.....	"	xiv.	98
1768. July 26.	Nichols, Samuel, and Freelove Wood, ...	"	xiii.	166
1766. Sept. 13.	Nichols, Susannah, and Joseph Jauncey, ...	"	x.	94
1782. Jan. 2.	Nichols, Zophar, and Drusela Jarvis........	"	xxxv.	4
1768. Nov. 26.	Nicholson, Elizabeth, and Benjamin Milton,	"	xiii.	245
1763. April 30.	Nicholson, James, and Frances Witter,.....	"	vii.	158
1779. Dec. 9.	Nicholson, Richard, and Mary Webb,......	"	xxviii.	167
1771. Dec. 3.	Nicholson, Thomas, and Mary Byrns,......	"	xvii.	282

DATE.	NAMES.	RECORD.	VOL.	PAGE.
1769. Oct. 25.	Nickerson, Sarah, and Thomas Lines,......	M. B.,	XV.	67
1759. Jan. 19.	Nickleson, Richard, and Mary Farmer,.....	"	II.	161
1779. Aug. 3.	Nicklin, Samuel, and Catherine Roebuck,...	"	XXVIII.	44
1777. May 26.	Nickols, William, and Keziah Baxter, ...	"	XXIV.	94
1768. Dec. 7.	Nicol, Leonard, and Ruth Birdseye, ...	"	XIII.	256
1765. April 12.	Nicoll, Agnes, and Benjamin Helme, ...	"	IX.	94
1783. April 16.	Nicoll, Augustus, and Sarah Harding,......	"	XXXVIII.	99
1771. Oct. 30.	Nicoll, Charity, and George Keteltas,......	"	XVII.	233
1759. Oct. 11.	Nicoll, Charles, and Elenor Pinyard,.......	"	II.	456
1783. Sept. 17.	Nicoll, Duncan, and Dorathea Brothers,....	"	XL.	42
1763. June 30.	Nicoll, Edward, and Sarah Ross,..........	"	VII.	249
1752. Sept. 3.	Nicoll, Francis, and Margaret Van Rense-laer, ...	"	VI.	305
1778. Mar. 14.	Nicoll, Gloriana, and John London McAdam,	"	XXV.	41
1779. June 16.	Nicoll, Henry, and Alice Willett,..........	"	XXVII.	166
1781. Nov. 17.	Nicoll, Henry, and Elizabeth Woodhull,....	"	XXXIV.	45
1763. May 11.	Nicoll, Isaac, and Deborah Woodhull,......	"	VII.	177
1778. Sept. 12.	Nicoll, John, and Jane Deall,.............	"	XXVI.	28
1782. May 27.	Nicoll, Mary, and Jacob Harned,..........	"	XXXVI.	26
1777. June 4.	Nicoll, Matthias, and Sarah Taylor, ...	"	XXIV.	96
1782. June 1.	Nicoll, Samuel, and Anne Fargie, ...	"	XXXVI.	34
1771. Jan. 14.	Nicoll, Sarah, and Tunis Mountanye, ...	"	XVII.	6
1758. Jan. 10.	Nicoll, Susannah, and William Irons, ...	"	I.	778
1757. April 22.	Nicolls, Elinor, and Augustine Darcy,......	"	I.	509
1781. Feb. 21.	Nicolls, Elizabeth, and Hugh Fraser,.......	"	XXXI.	53
1782. Nov. 18.	Nicolls, Hannah, and John Prim, ...	"	XXXVII.	88
1760. July 25.	Nicolls, Mary, and James McNamarr,......	"	III.	226
1761. Oct. 2.	Nicolls, Sarah, and James Searing, ...	"	V.	115
1673. Mar. 29.	Nicolls, Thomasin, and Thomas Griffin, ...	G. E.,	IV.	274
1783. Oct. 22.	Niper, John, and Batey Tire,..............	M. B.,	XL.	87
1759. June 2.	Nisbit, Benjamin, and Maritje Van Kats,...	"	II.	297
1763. Jan. 26.	Niscombe, Samuel, and Selata Lerow, ...	"	VII.	36
1736. Mar. 18.	Niven, Amy, and Jacob Sominindike, ...	"	I.	5
1761. Sept. 10.	Nixon, Elizabeth, and David Maldrom, ...	"	V.	77
1761. Dec. 22.	Nixon, Jane, and John Wright,...........	"	V.	291
1765. Oct. 3.	Nixon, John, and Elizabeth Davis, ...	"	IX.	289
1760. April 9.	Nixon, Margaret, and James Casety, ...	"	III.	100
1760. July 19.	Nixon, Mary, and David Evans, ...	"	III.	219
1682. Mar. 16.	Nixon, Mary, and Joseph Ffenton,........	E.,	XXXIII.	44
1772. Jan. 7.	Nixon, Sarah, and Thomas Price, ...	M. B.,	XX.	4
1761. Nov. 9.	Nixon, Sophia, and Thomas Porter, ...	"	V.	198
1762. Jan. 25.	Noble, Abel, and Phebe Townsend,........	"	VI.	26
1738. Aug. 23.	Noble, Catherine, and William Tennant,....	"	I.	10
1772. Oct. 28.	Noble, Elizabeth, and Benjamin Homen, Jr.,	"	XIX.	92
1759. Aug. 13.	Noble, Elizabeth, and James Wilkie,.......	"	II.	383

DATE.	NAMES.	RECORD.	VOL.	PAGE.
1760. Feb. 5.	Noble, Elizabeth, and William Cunningham,	M. B.,	III.	22
1764. May 2.	Noble, Isaac, and Rache Dejoncourt,......	"	VIII.	180
1783. Feb. 8.	Nóble, Mungo, and Sarah Phillips, ...	"	XXXVIII.	38
1768. April 11.	Nobles, Joanna, and Nathan Sherwood,....	"	XIII.	72
1762. Mar. 19.	Noblett, Joseph, and Mary Denn,.........	"	VI.	78
1763. May 27.	Nodine, Catharine, and Frederick Vermilye,	"	VII.	204
173⅞. Feb. 9.	Nodine, Lewis, and Mary Farrel,..........	"	I.	8
1755. Dec. 15.	Nodine, Mary, and John Belitha,..........	"	I.	234
1780. Aug. 21.	Noe, Abigail, and Andrew Monck, ...	"	XXIX.	143
1782. Oct. 11.	Noe, Loris, and Mary Wright, ...	"	XXXVII.	39
1778. Mar. 23.	Noe, Mary, and Simon Donnel, ...	"	XXV.	52
1757. Dec. 20.	Noe, Peter, and Mary Grondarn,..........	"	I.	748
1756. Sept. 21.	Noel, Garrat, and Experience Young,......	"	I.	299
1763. May 4.	Noel, Mary, and Anthony D. Bleecker, ...	"	VII.	165
1737. May 25.	Noghill, Rebecca, and Jahendrick Poust,...	"	I.	6
1762. Dec. 30.	Noorstradt, Garret, and Wyntje Van Noors-			
	trandt,...............................	"	VI.	341
1779. May 8.	Noorstrant, John, and Margaret Emans,...	"	XXVII.	130
1778. Sept. 30.	Noostrandt, Greetie, and John Rider,......	"	XXVI.	40
1780. Sept. 18.	Noostrant, Peter, and Peggy White, ...	"	XXX.	14
1736. May 8.	Norbury, Sarah, and George Leacraft, ...	"	I.	1
1780. April 5.	Norman, Sarah, and James Burnes,........	"	XXIX.	24
1771. April 10.	Normanton, Ann, and Edward Benson,....	"	XVII.	53
1772. Oct. 28.	Normoyle, Elinor, and Moses Connor, ...	"	XIX.	93
1761. May 6.	Norris, Catharine, and Hugh Moudd,......	"	IV.	182
1768. April 13.	Norris, Elizabeth, and Benjamin Montanye,.	"	XIII.	74
1764. Aug. 16.	Norris, Hannah, and Michel Taylor,.......	"	VIII.	286
1761. Sept. 30.	Norris, John, and Frances Kortright,..,...	"	V.	109
1738. Nov. 3.	Norris, Mary, and Richard Dill,...........	"	I.	11
1760. Mar. 13.	Norris, Phillip, and Ann Hornsen, ...	"	III.	76
1764. Jan. 26.	Norstrandt, James, and Phebe Whitman,...	"	VIII.	38
1767. Mar. 7.	North, Abigail, and Lucas Ramsen,........	"	XI.	40
1778. Feb. 6.	North, Ann, and Caleb Valentine,.........	"	XXV.	17
1773. Jan. 16.	North, Benjamin, and Jane Brown, ...	"	XX.	10
1757. Dec. 29.	North, Daniel, and Rachel Smith,.........	"	I.	757
1773. June 29.	North, Elizabeth, and James Stoker,.......	"	XXI.	26
1765. May 13.	North, Elizabeth, and Thomas Harrisson,...	"	IX.	125
1763. Aug. 9.	North, John, and Elizabeth Cleve, ...	"	VII.	295
1774. Jan. 18.	North, Mary, and Gabriel Smith,..........	"	XXII.	106
1782. Sept. 28.	North, Rachel, and Evan Hicks,..........	"	XXXVII.	19
1762. Nov. 13.	North, Robert, and Elizabeth Peneer,......	"	VI.	430
1761. Oct. 19.	North, Thomas, and Elizabeth Fry,........	"	V.	150
1765. Oct. 10.	North, Thomas, and Hannah Play,........	"	IX.	294
1766. July 28.	Northen, Elizabeth, and John Titts,........	"	X.	64
1770. Aug. 6.	Northover, Richard, and Sarah Grimesly,...	"	XVI.	153

DATE.	NAMES.	RECORD.	VOL. PAGE.
1781. Dec. 24.	Northrup, Joseph, and Mary Foster,.......	M. B.,	xxxiv. 103
1767. Aug. 22.	Norton, George, Jr., and Sarah Titus,......	"	xii. 21
1763. Mar. 30.	Norton, Hannah, and Israel Lewis,........	"	vii. 109
1781. July 29.	Norton, Jabez, and Ruth Davis,...........	"	xxxiii. 21
1775. Sept. 12.	Norton, Sarah, and John Titus,...........	"	xxiii. 154
1761. July 17.	Norwood, Catharine, and William Brasier,...............................	"	iv. 301
1781. Jan. 18.	Norwood, Charlotte, and Thomas Stewart McClellen,..........................	"	xxxi. 25
1782. Nov. 23.	Norwood, Jane, and Alida Sandford,......	"	xxxvii. 91
1767. Oct. 27.	Norwood, Tobias, and Christian Lester,....	"	xii. 71
1764. July 31.	Nostran, John, and Sarah Losee,.........	"	viii. 272
1783. Oct. 14.	Nostrand, Anna, and Henry Suydam,......	"	xl. 78
1781. June 30.	Nostrand, Garret, and Catharine Bogart, ...	"	xxxii. 100
1761. Aug. 7.	Nostrand, John, and Elizabeth Oakley, ...	"	v. 30
1780. July 26.	Nostrand, Maria, and Jacob Sharpe,.......	"	xxix. 119
1782. May 8.	Nostrand, Mary, and John Willett,........	"	xxxv. 155
1783. April 24.	Nostrandt, Hannah, and Noah Seaman,....	"	xxxviii. 112
1771. Sept. 25.	Nostrandt, Rancha, and Peter Bogardus,...	"	xvii. 190
1773. May 10.	Nostrandt, Sarah, and John Schenck,......	"	xx. 106
1767. Nov. 5.	Nostrant, James, and Rebecka Killsey,.....	"	xii. 120
1780. June 26.	Nostrant, John, and Harmty Duryea,......	"	xxix. 97
1767. Nov. 10.	Nostrant, Mary, and John Wyckoff,.......	"	xii. 79
1769. Mar. 1.	Nostrant, Peter, and Mary Seaman,.......	"	xiv. 40
1775. Aug. 3.	Nottingham, Garton, and Margaret L. Hardenbergh, ...	"	xxiii. 120
1770. Oct. 27.	Nottingham, John, and Geertruy De Lamater,................................	"	xvi. 231
1761. July 15.	Nottingham, William, and Elizabeth De Witt, ...	"	iv. 298
1780. Dec. 21.	Noutchell, Mary, and Charles Goedduy,....	"	xxx. 162
1762. Sept. 16.	Nowlan, Thomas, and Martha Caklen, ...	"	vi. 318
1764. Oct. 22.	Nox, John, and Elisaboth Curnow,........	"	viii. 368
1758. Mar. 22.	Noxon, Bartholomew, Jr., and Ann Loosie,................................	"	i. 861
1753. Sept. 5.	Noxon, Margaret, and James Vander Burgh,	"	i. 107
1762. Dec. 1.	Noxon, Peter, and Elisabeth Bentley, ...	"	vi. 466
1775. May 10.	Noxon, Robert, and Hester Davis, ...	"	xxiii. 28
1759. Nov. 15.	Noxson, Simon, and Penelope Allin, ...	"	ii. 496
1759. Oct. 9.	Nugent, Robert, and Phebe Pearson,......	"	ii. 454
1758. Dec. 28.	Numan, William, and Abigail Suckfield,....	"	ii. 142
1763. Jan. 5.	Numan, William, and Hannah Colgan,.....	"	vii. 7
1781. June 4.	Nuton, Charity, and Isaiah Smith, Jr.,.....	"	xxxii. 70
1781. June 3.	Nuton, Elisebeth, and William Hawkins,...	"	xxxii. 69
1648. April 16.	Nuton, Tomas, and Joons Smith,..........	A. R.,	vii. 145

DATE.	NAMES.	RECORD.	VOL.	PAGE.
1657. Aug. 22.	Nutt, John, and Catharine Wright,.... ...	M. B.,	I.	619
1772. Feb. 12.	Nutter, Valentine, and Catherine Gordon, ..	"	XVIII.	34
1770. May 25.	Nutting, William, and Jane Nichols,.......	"	XVI.	95
1737. Dec. 2.	Nuttman, John, and Phebe Mitchell,.......	"	I.	8

O.

1765. Oct. 12.	Oackly, Jemimy, and Thomas Campbell, ...	"	IX.	299
1762. April 1.	Oakeley, Samuel, and Abigail Wood,......	"	VI.	88
1772. Nov. 9.	Oakes, Elizabeth, and John Waldron,......	"	XIX.	103
1767. Dec. 1.	Oakes, Jesse, and Anna Fleet,............	"	XII.	102
1773. Dec. 8.	Oakes, Martha, and James Ford,..........	"	XXII.	65
1759. Oct. 4.	Oakes, Mary, and Henry Bras, ...	"	II.	448
1771. May 14.	Oakes, Thomas, and Elsie Monfoort,.......	"	XVII.	84
1767. Mar. 24.	Oakley, Anne, and James Ennis,..........	"	XI.	49
1773. Feb. 17.	Oakley, Benjamin, and Phebe Dow, ...	"	XX.	46
1761. Dec. 9.	Oakley, Elizabeth, and Jacob Stringham,...	"	V.	270
1761. Aug. 7.	Oakley, Elizabeth, and John Norstrand, ...	"	V.	30
1781. Oct. 19.	Oakley, Elizabeth, and Peter Thompson, ...	"	XXXIII.	109
1778. Dec. 22.	Oakley, Elizabeth, and Richard Lawrence,..	"	XXVI.	130
1765. April 24.	Oakley, Gilbert, and Mary Charlick,.......	"	IX.	105
1781. May 19.	Oakley, Hester, and Samuel Davenport,....	"	XXXII.	54
1762. Sept. 23.	Oakley, Isaac, and Sarah Haviland,........	"	VI.	328
1765. Oct. 7.	Oakley, John, and Elizabeth Mudge,.......	"	IX.	292
1761. Dec. 4.	Oakley, Martha, and Gilbert Willett, ...	"	V.	265
1771. Oct. 15.	Oakley, Mary, and Isaac Leggett, ...	"	XVII.	208
1773. July 15.	Oakley, Mary, and Richard Vollentine, ...	"	XXI.	38
1766. June 6.	Oakley, Patience, and John Cornwall, ...	"	X.	7
1781. Jan. 6.	Oakley, Patience, and Thomas Ireland,.....	"	XXXI.	16
1764. Jan. 19.	Oakley, Phebe, and Jotham Hawkshurst,...	"	VIII.	24
1781. Dec. 19.	Oakley, Samuel, and Rebecca Roff,........	"	XXXIV.	95
1761. Nov. 3.	Oakley, Sarah, and John Campbell,........	"	V.	189
1738. Dec. 16.	Oakley, Sarah, and Luke Haviland, ...	"	I.	12
1775. Jan. 15.	Oakley, Sarah, and Tolman Pugsley, ...	"	XXIII.	247
1761. June 20.	Oakley, William, and Elizabeth Johnson,...	"	IV.	250
1767. April 4.	Oakly, Andrew, and Patience Smith,......	"	XI.	56
1765. Sept. 26.	Oakly, John, and Ruth Rogers,...........	"	IX.	276
1765. May 21.	Oakly, Margaret, and Eliphelet Chidister, ..	"	IX.	136
1778. July 16.	Oates, George, and Mary Guest, ...	"	XXV.	131
1757. Oct. 26.	Oates, Martha, and James Coleman, ...	"	I.	680
1755. Oct. 10.	Oats, Elizabeth, and Samuel Miller,........	"	I.	190
1668. Aug. 11.	Ober, Elizabeth, and John Dally,...........	O. W. L.,	II.	223
1764. May 2.	Oblenus, Dennis, and Catharine Parsell,....	M. B.,	VIII.	177
1762. Mar. 5.	O'Brian, Margaret, and Thomas Smith, ...	"	VI.	66

DATE.	NAMES.	RECORD.	VOL.	PAGE.
1772. June 7.	Obrian, Susannah, and Garrott Moore,	M. B.,	XVIII.	135
1778. Oct. 10.	Obrien, Ann, and Amby Mooney,	"	XXVI.	54
1778. Sept. 11.	Obrien, Elinor, and John Duke,	"	XXVI.	25
1781. Nov. 14.	O'Brien, Henry, and Mary Moony,	"	XXXIV.	35
1761. Aug. 28.	O'Brien, James, and Mary Plume,	"	V.	62
1769. July 11.	Obrien, John, and Hester Farr,	"	XIV.	148
1779. Oct. 25.	O'Brien, John, and Ruth Marks,	"	XXVIII.	120
1779. May 3.	O'Brien, Mary, and John Arbuckle,	"	XXVII.	126
1770. Mar. 1.	Obrien, Mary, and Nicholas Johnson,	"	XVI.	27
1782. Aug. 3.	O'Brien, Thomas, and Teamor Gidney,	"	XXXVI.	99
1763. July 21.	Obrine, Isabella, and William Jameson,	"	VII.	278
1778 .Aug. 10.	O'Bryan, David, and Elenor Fenton,	"	XXV.	147
1759. July 10.	O'Bryan, Elisabeth, and Jacob Bloom,	"	II.	353
1762. Aug. 9.	Ocearman, Gulian, and Margaret Brinkerhoff,	"	VI.	270
1667. July 10.	Ockeson, John, and Susannah Thorne,	O. W. L.,	II.	134
1759. June 15.	O'Conner, Timothy, and Elizabeth Rotteridge,	M. B.,	II.	326
1766. Nov. 24.	O'Connor, Mary, and James Williams,	"	X.	180
1783. Oct. 18.	O'Craft, Thomas, and Catharine Brown,	"	XL.	85
1782. July 2.	Odel, Daniel, and Mary Dobs,	"	XXXVI.	71
1759. May 23.	Odell, Henry, and Abigail Devoe,	"	II.	290
1757. Oct. 26.	Odell, Jesse, and Esther Du Bois,	"	I.	681
1782. May 11.	Odell, John, and May Vandenburgh,	"	XXXV.	159
1761. Aug. 11.	Odell, Mary, and Benjamin Lent,	"	V.	37
1770. Aug. 27.	Odell, Rebecca, and Samuel Dyckman,	"	XVI.	174
1773. Nov. 24.	Oder, Jenny, and Abraham Valentine,	"	XXII.	42
1730. Oct. 22.	Oethout, Margurita, and John Van Driesen,.	"	I.	3
1776. Dec. 18.	O'Farrell, Richard, and Anna Stephens,	"	XXIV.	199
1753. May 7.	Offenmout, Mary, and John Young,	"	I.	25
1767. Dec. 22.	Ogden, Abraham, and Sarah Ludlow,	"	XII.	119
1763. Jan. 20.	Ogden, Amos, and Margaret Cannon,	"	VII.	25
1762. July 30.	Ogden, Catharine, and Philip V. Cortland, .	"	VI.	257
1764. June 6.	Ogden, Catharine, and Robert Cox,	"	VIII.	210
1762. July 24.	Ogden, Catharine, and William Paulding,...	"	VI.	254
1777. Dec. 30.	Ogden, Euphame, and Thomas Roach,	"	XXIV.	210
1769. Sept. 4.	Ogden, Frances, and Pierpont Edwards,	"	XV.	35
1778. Mar. 3.	Ogden, Jacob, and Rachel Sandford,	"	XXXI.	63
1782. July 1.	Ogden, Jane, and Richard Newton,	"	XXXVI.	69
1764. April 5.	Ogden, John, and Jane Schermerhorn,	"	VIII.	137
1763. Sept. 6.	Ogden, John, and Sarah Haight,	"	VII.	327
1753. June 14.	Ogden, Josiah, and Mary Bancker,	"	I.	61
1765. Jan. 2.	Ogden, Margaret, and John White,	"	IX.	1
1762. June 23.	Ogden, Parthinia, and Jesse Condy,	"	VI.	206
1777. Sept. 11.	Ogden, Rachell, and George Wetmore,	"	XXIV.	145
1772. May 2.	Ogden, Robert, Jr., and Sarah Platt,	"	XVIII.	98
1782. Nov. 9.	Ogden, Sarah, and Robert Randall,	"	XXXVII.	75

DATE.		NAMES.	RECORD.	VOL.	PAGE.
1779. Oct.	4.	Ogilby, Deborah, and Daniel Coen,........	M. B.,	XXVIII.	99
1783. May	14.	Ogilvey, Rebecca, and Edward Sainthill, ...	"	XXXIX.	11
1759. Dec.	5.	Ogilvie, Alexander, and Deborah Cox,.....	"	II.	527
1777. Aug.	6.	Ogilvie, George, and Amelia Willett, ...	"	XXIV.	128
1769. April	15.	Ogilvie, John, and Margaret Philips,.......	"	XIV.	75
1777. Oct.	17.	Ogilvie, Mary, and B. Roorbach,..........	"	XXIV.	164
1764. May	3.	Ogilvie, Thomas, and Abigail Gleen,.......	"	VIII.	183
1775. Nov.	3.	Ogilvie, Thomas, and Catharine Whitfield,..	"	XXIII.	198
1763. July	15.	Oglesby, Catharine, and Samuel Kramer,....	"	VII.	267
1764. May	25.	Oglevie, Jane, and Amos Knap,...........	"	IX.	141
1782. Aug.	27.	Ogsbury, Alexander, and Hannah Baker,...	"	XXXVI.	125
1779. June	24.	Ogsbury, Elizabeth, and William Newton, Jr.,	"	XXVIII.	6
1764. Feb.	25.	O'Ham, James, and Flora Dickson,........	"	VIII.	77
1778. Nov.	20.	Ohlwine, Lawrance, and Mary Hopper,....	"	XXVI.	90
1764. Dec.	22.	Okeley, Abigil, and Cornelius Ammerman, .	"	VIII.	463
1764. Nov.	7.	Okely, Miles, and Deborah Wood,.........	"	VIII.	393
1782. Mar.	7.	Okye, Harre, and Mary Waderef,.........	"	XXXV.	78
1780. Nov.	7.	Oldfield, Mariam, and John Barin, ...	"	XXX.	96
1761. Nov.	16.	Oldfield, Mary, and Peter Dunbar, ...	"	V.	220
1737. Dec.	23.	Oldfield, Phebe, and Richard Gildersleeve,..	"	I.	8
1777. Aug.	3.	Olding, Nicholas Perdue, and Mary Collard,	"	XXIV.	126
1783. May	12.	Oley, Jane, and Robert Baker,............	"	XXXIX.	10
1763. May	25.	Oliver, Barbary, and John English,........	"	VII.	202
1775. Nov.	16.	Oliver, Elizabeth, and Gross Hardenbergh,.	"	XXIII.	211
1777. July	6.	Oliver, George, and Eunice Otheroff, ...	"	XXIV.	114
1769. Jan.	21.	Oliver, Leddia, and Ferdinand Little, ...	"	XIV.	18
1759. Feb.	7.	Oliver, Margaret, and David Collis,........	"	II.	182
1736. July	3.	Oliver, Margaret, and George Lubeken, ...	"	I.	2
1783. Oct.	10.	Oliver, Margaret, and John Butler,........	"	XL.	76
1760. Dec.	8.	Oliver, Mary, and Charles Broadhead,......	"	III.	467
1782. Sept.	27.	Oliver, Mary, and Jasper Stanton, ...	"	XXXVII.	17
1765. July	22.	Oliver, Mary, and Richard Smith,.........	"	IX.	214
1779. June	24.	Olnes, Abigail, and John Ackerson,........	"	XXVIII.	7
1777. Jan.	30.	Olphord, Ann, and Samuel Small,.........	"	XXIV.	21
1761. Oct.	28.	Oman, Effey, and William Chesslear, ...	"	V.	173
1756. July	3.	Oman, James, and Sarah Ketcham,........	"	I.	245
1761. June	8.	Omand, John, and Mary Murphy,.........	"	IV.	231
1782. Aug.	15.	Omond, Robert, and Sybbel Heetman,.....	"	XXXVI.	109
1753. Aug.	18.	Onderdanck, Sarah, and David Hansen,....	"	I.	92
1755. Oct.	31.	Onderdonck, Adriæn, and Maria Hageman,.	"	I.	203
1767. Nov.	12.	Onderdonck, Andrew, and Elizabeth Rider,	"	XII.	82
1765. July	20.	Onderdonck, Ann, and John Culver,.......	"	IX.	211
1758. Feb.	27.	Onderdonck, Charity, and Aury Smith, ...	"	I.	829
1765. April	17.	Onderdonck, Elbert, and Maritje Ackerman,	"	IX.	100
1736. Nov.	6.	Onderdonck, Garrit, and Sarah Hegreman,.	"	I.	3

DATE.	NAMES.	RECORD.	VOL. PAGE.
1782. June 25.	Onderdonck (Underdunk), Gertrude, and Abraham Brinckerhoff,	M. B.,	xxxvi. 63
1767. Dec. 7.	Onderdonck, Jacob, and Annatje Clarke, ...	"	xii. 110
1764. Mar. 22.	Onderdonck, Sarah, and Abraham Brincker-hoff,	"	viii. 114
1781. Oct. 2.	Onderdunck, Geertruy, and Peter Luister, ..	"	xxxiii. 82
1765. June 5.	Onderkerck, Mayeke, and Cornelius Vander-berg,	"	ix. 158
1761. May 29.	O'Neal, Catharine, and Norris Palmer, ...	"	iv. 214
1762. Feb. 12.	O'Neal, James, and Esther Dixon, ...	"	vi. 48
1769. Aug. 28.	O'Neal, Margaret, and James Robins, ...	"	xv. 31
1760. Oct. 30.	O'Neil, Anthony, and Catharine Groves, ...	"	iii. 388
1761. May 21.	O'Niel, Elenor, and John Thorp, ...	"	iv. 202
1764. Aug. 2.	Onray, Michael, and Jane Gue, ...	"	viii. 273
1771. Feb. 4.	Oosterhout, Hendrickus P., and Margaret Schoonmaker, ...	"	xvii. 11
1765. Oct. 31.	Oosterhout, John, and Eve Van Valken-burgh,	"	ix. 346
1770. June 6.	Oosterhout, Joseph, and Sarah Van Gaasbeek,	"	xvi. 104
1761. Feb. 23.	Oosterhout, Marytie, and Garret Van Alen, .	"	iv. 75
1772. Nov. 27.	Oostrander, Catherine, and Jacob Phillips, ..	"	xix. 132
1764. April 3.	Oostrander, Cornelius, and Mary Brinkerhoff,	"	viii. 130
1761. Sept. 11.	Oostrander, Garret, and Christina Vanden-berg,	"	v. 81
1760. Oct. 31.	Oostrander, Jane, and Henry Rosekrans, ...	"	iii. 390
1767. Oct. 1.	Oothout, Abraham, and Margaret Lansing, .	"	xii. 54
1765. July 12.	Oothout, Henry, Jr., and Lydia Down, ...	"	ix. 203
1763. Dec. 5.	Orchard, Jane, and Peter White, ...	"	vii. 492
1768. Dec. 15.	Orey, Mary, and James McCandless, ...	"	xiii. 262
1783. Sept. 7.	Ormond, George, and Elizabeth Smith, ...	"	xl. 31
1779. June 7.	Orndorff, Christian, and Elizabeth Batten, ..	"	xxvii. 160
1779. Jan. 17.	Orr, Joseph, and Catherine Coffy, ...	"	xxvii. 15
1765. April 25.	Orr, Robert, and Sarah Taylor, ...	"	ix. 109
1763. Jan. 19.	Orr, William, and Ann Campbell, ...	"	vii. 22
1759. Nov. 20.	Orstin, Hannah, and Owen Sullivan, ...	"	ii. 509
1781. July 3.	Ortzen, Charles, and Elizabeth Hogg, ...	"	xxxii. 103
1770. Mar. 20.	Osborn, Elizabeth, and James Rumsay, ...	"	xvi. 33
1777. Aug. 27.	Osborn, Else, and William Smith, ...	"	xxiv. 140
1758. May 22.	Osborn, Jane, and John Rider, ...	"	i. 905
1757. Jan. 31.	Osborn, Sarah, and Alexander Lyal, ...	"	i. 429
1764. Sept. 17.	Osborne, Alida, and Robert Robson, ...	M. B.,	viii. 311
1757. Aug. 5.	Osborne, David, and Mary Hunton, ...	"	i. 609
1672. Jan. 7.	Osborne, Elizabeth, and Thomas Appleby, ..	G. E.,	iv. 245
173⅞. Feb. 6.	Osborne, Jane, and Claude Ducelong, ...	M. B.,	i. 8
1762. April 14.	Osborne, Richard, and Margaret Garretson, .	"	vi. 103

DATE.		NAMES.	RECORD.	VOL. PAGE.
1759. June	27.	Osborne, Robert, and Agnes Van Husen,...	M. B.,	II. 341
1670. Jan.	1.	Osborne, William, and Elizabeth Moore,....'	C. A.,	II. 639
1781. Sept.	4.	Osbourn, Mary, and Daniel Armour,.......	M. B.,	XXXIII. 57
1769. May	26.	Osburn, Elizabeth, and John Robinson, Jr...	"	XIV. 107
16⁷⁹⁄₈₀. Feb.	7.	Osburn, William, and Alice Holm,.........	G. E.,	XXXII. 67
1737. Oct.	12.	Osterheet, William, and Sarah Hosbrook,...	M. B.,	I. 7
1775. Aug.	15.	Osterhout, John, and Aga Winne,.........	"	XXIII. 128
1775. May	6.	Osterhout, Mary, and Peter Winne,.......	"	XXIII. 23
1768. July	11.	Ostrande, Annatje, and Isaac Van Valkenburgh,............................	"	XIII. 155
1755. Sept.	6.	Ostranden, Catherina, and Abraham Myndertse,............................	"	I. 168
1771. Feb.	4.	Ostrander, Hendrick, and Mary Van Den Bergh,............................	"	XVII. 12
1771. Dec.	31.	Oswald, Eleazer, and Elisabeth Holt,......	"	XVII. 310
1767. May	6.	Oswald, Mary, and Alexander Bridges, ...	"	XI. 78
1767. Dec.	2.	Oswald, Philip, and Catharine Haan, ...	"	XII. 103
1761. May	23.	Ostrum, Roeluf, and Elisabeth Yelvington,..	"	IV. 204
1782. Feb.	25.	O'Sullivan, Thomas, and Mary McReady,...	"	XXXV. 65
1777. July	6.	Otheroff, Eunice, and George Oliver, ...	"	XXIV. 114
1780. June	24.	Otis, Mary, and Richard Newton,.........	"	XXIX. 96
1760. May	2.	Ott, Catharine, and George Smith, ...	"	III. 134
1762. Oct.	19.	Ott, Jacob, and Appolonia Vindlern,.......	"	VI. 372
1771. Dec.	2.	Oudderceak, Aladey, and John Quackingbush, ...	"	XVII. 277
1756. July	27.	Oudenaarde, Hendrick, and Sarah Van Dyck,	"	I. 262
1761. Nov.	21.	Ouderkerk, John, and Annatie Van Ness, ..	"	V. 239
1761. Dec.	7.	Ouderkerk, Maria, and Jacob H. Lansingh,.	"	V. 267
1769. Nov.	24.	Ouderkerk, Mayekie, and Johannes I. Vandenbergh, ...	"	XV. 105
1753. Aug.	29.	Ouderkirk, Jannetje, and Johannes Knout,.	"	I. 102
1761. Jan.	21.	Ouderkirk, Moyckie, and Charles McKay, ..	"	IV. 23
1759. Nov.	19.	Oull, John, and Margaret Ham, ...	"	II. 505
1768. Oct.	13.	Ousterhout, Catharine, and Dirck De Lametter, ...	"	XIII. 208
1760. Oct.	20.	Ousterhout, Else, and Thomas Johnson,....	"	III. 372
1755. Sept.	23.	Ousterhout, Kalleticot, and Lambert Van Alstyne,....	"	I. 182
1779. May	25.	Ousterman, John, and Anna Brevoort,.....	"	XXVII. 147
1780. Oct.	23.	Ousterman, John, and Sarah Miller, ...	"	XXX. 78
1773. Dec.	13.	Outhout, Folkert, and Jannetye Bogert,....	"	XXII. 72
1760. Nov.	11.	Outhout, Henry, and Neltie Van Bergen,...	"	III. 401
1772. Nov.	28.	Outenbogart, Catherine, and James Russel,.	"	XIX. 136
1758. Jan.	17.	Outenbogart, John, and Ann Bagly, ...	"	I. 786
1764. Nov.	2.	Outen Bogart, Joseph, and Elizabeth Skinner,	"	VIII. 388

DATE.	NAMES.	RECORD.	VOL.	PAGE.
1762. Mar. 4.	Outenbogart, Joseph, and Martha Hadden,.	M. B.,	VI.	64
1762. Aug. 21.	Outenbogart, Mary, and John Haigs,	"	VI.	284
1772. Jan. 6.	Outen Bogert, Catherine, and Peter Van Kleck,	"	XX.	3
1758. Feb. 1.	Outenbogert, Gilbert, and Elizabeth Lynser,	"	I.	808
1772. April 7.	Outen Bogert, Jane, and Francis Sawyer,..	"	XVIII.	70
1757. Mar. 3.	Outenbogert, John, and Mary Vredenburgh,	"	I.	454
1773. Feb. 16.	Outer Bergh, Margaret, and Andrew Meade,	"	XX.	45
1762. Jan. 22.	Outerkerk, Hannah, and William Emry, ...	"	VI.	22
1763. Mar. 17.	Outerkirk, Maria, and Abraham Fonda,....	"	VII.	102
1771. Mar. 19.	Outwater, Catharine, and Barends R. Van Kleeck,	"	XVII.	38
1753. June 6.	Outwater, Sarah, and Abraham Allen,	"	I.	50
1770. Dec. 19.	Outwater, Thomas, and Catherine Vander Ruff,	"	XVI.	302
1781. July 20.	Outwater, Thomas, and Francintje Quackenbus,	"	XXXIII.	10
1737. Aug. 20.	Overhall, Captain, and Mary Stilwell,	"	I.	7
1773. Nov. 24.	Overtenbot, Peter, and Sarah Brandew,....	"	XXII.	41
1759. Aug. 6.	Owen, Elizabeth, and Joseph Woodruff,....	"	II.	375
1757. June 24.	Owen, Nathaniel, and Elizabeth Jayne, ...	"	I.	572
1761. Jan. 15.	Owens, John, and Eleanor Crandell,	"	IV.	20
1684. Oct. 22.	Owing, William, and Mary Cinburne,... ..	C. M.,	XXXIII.	54

P.

1762. July 17.	Pack, George Christopher, and Phebe Mills,	M. B.,	VI.	243
1782. Feb. 6.	Paddison, George, and Elizabeth Flockady,.	"	XXXV.	44
1753. June 9.	Paddon, Edward, and Sarah Johnson,	"	I.	57
1770. Dec. 3.	Paddy, Samuel, and Helena Van Evra, ...	"	XVI.	282
1781. Aug. 28.	Pafford, John, and Ann Florintine,	"	XXXIII.	51
1778. Jan. 23.	Page, Ann, and Robert Johnson,	"	XXV.	11
1775. May 8.	Page, Catharine, and Samuel Casey,	"	XXIII.	24
1664. Feb. 13.	Page, Mary, and John Cockrell,	G. E.,	I.	85
1665. Aug. 15.	Page, Mary, and Robert Hollis,	O. W. L.,	II.	18
1769. May 15.	Page, Samuel, and Susannah Degray,	M. B.,	XIV.	101
1759. Mar. 27.	Page, Sarah, and John Baker,	"	II.	226
1781. Jan. 2.	Pain, Benjamin, and Mary Heges,	"	XXXI.	3
1756. July 12.	Pain, Catharine, and Hendrick Fine,	"	I.	253
1761. Oct. 14.	Pain, George, and Sarah Parsalls,	"	V.	139
1783. Aug. 2.	Pain, John, and Susannah Stilwell,	"	XXXIX.	110
1757. Oct. 5.	Paine, Joshua, and Elizabeth Houtvat,	"	I.	657
1772. Mar. 12.	Paines, Sarah, and Garret Beakman,	"	XVIII.	52
1764. Mar. 8.	Painter, Edward, and Isabella McMillen,...	"	VIII.	98

DATE.	NAMES.	RECORD.	VOL.	PAGE.
1768. Nov. 11.	Painter, Philip, and Elizabeth Buckland,...	M. B.,	XIII.	231
1761. Aug. 7.	Pake, Margaret, and Harmanus Peters, ...	"	V.	32
1783. April 26.	Pake, Rachel, and John S. Banta,.........	"	XXXVIII.	114
1783. July 3.	Pakeman, Elias, and Sophia Pemberton,...	"	XXXIX.	82
1763. Feb. 17.	Palding, Cornelius, and Catharine Stillwell,.	"	VII.	66
1773. Dec. 28.	Palmateer, Ariantje, and Cornelius Wilie,..	"	XXII.	88
1782. April 27.	Palmer, Ann, and Peter Perine, ...	"	XXXV.	140
173⅞. Mar. 15.	Palmer, Benjamin, and Mary Palmer,......	"	I.	9
1775. Oct. 9.	Palmer, Benjamin, and Philena Hunt,......	"	XXIII.	177
1758. Jan. 5.	Palmer, Benjamin, and Sarah Barnes,......	"	I.	767
173⅔. Mar. 12.	Palmer, Drake, and Mary Pell, ...	"	I.	1
1763. Feb. 1.	Palmer, Elisabeth, and Hamilton Drinam,..	"	VII.	45
1667. April —.	Palmer, Elizabeth, and Matthew Fforce, ...	O. W. L.,	II.	134
1779. Mar. 5.	Palmer, Euphemia, and Jonathan Williams,	M. B.,	XXVII.	56
1768. Sept. 22.	Palmer, Henry, and Hannah Knapp, ...	"	XIII.	192
1774. Jan. 18.	Palmore, Isaac, and Mary Freeland,.......	"	XXII.	107
1770. July 24.	Palmer, Jacob, and Ann Fish, ...	"	XVI.	145
1768. Aug. 8.	Palmer, James, and Deborah Knapp, ...	"	XIII.	170
1758. Mar. 23.	Palmer, John, and Elizabeth Arthur, ...	"	I.	862
1677. April 13.	Palmer, John, and Sarah Ffinder, ...	W. O. P.,	II.	245
1778. Mar. 9.	Palmer, John, and Mary Wood, ...	M. B.,	XXV.	36
1781. Aug. 6.	Palmer, Joseph, and Ezabella Ball,........	"	XXXIII.	29
1761. Jan. 28.	Palmer, Marmeduke, and Jemima Plumb, ..	"	IV.	34
173⅞. Mar. 15.	Palmer, Mary, and Benjamin Palmer,......	"	I.	9
1783. April 5.	Palmer, Mary, and John Sullivan,.........	"	XXXVIII.	86
1776. Feb. 23.	Palmer, Mary, and Thomas Baxter,........	"	XXIII.	271
1771. April 6.	Palmer, Mary, and William Lawrence,.....	"	XVII.	48
1776. Mar. 25.	Palmer, Nancey, and Ware Branson,......	"	XXIII.	292
1761. May 29.	Palmer, Norris, and Catharine O'Neal,.....	"	IV.	214
1769. Dec. 29.	Palmer, Sarah, and Samuel Buckbee,......	"	XV.	132a
1764. Nov. 6.	Palmer, Susanna, and Charles Wright,.....	"	VIII.	391
1782. Aug. 21.	Palmer, Thomas, and Hester Wolsey, ...	"	XXXVI.	117
1738. July 21.	Palmer, Thomas, and Susannah Hunt, ...	"	I.	10
1783. Oct. 31.	Palmer, Thomas Martin, and Catharine McEvers,............................	"	XL.	97
1762. Jan. 9.	Palmer, William, and Ann White,.........	"	VI.	6
1763. Jan. 18.	Palmer, William, and Jane Montgomery,...	"	VII.	10
1781. Dec. 14.	Palmer, William, and Sarah Fish, ...	"	XXXIV.	86
1764. Dec. 10.	Palmetier, Helena, and Parent Van Kleeck,.	"	VIII.	449
1755. Oct. 15.	Palmetier, Peter, and Catharine Van Kleeck,	"	I.	193
1757. Dec. 15.	Panter, Catherine, and Henry Wood,......	"	I.	745
1773. Mar. 9.	Pantine, Martha, and John Finley,........	"	XX.	57
1773. Aug. 26.	Pantine, Mary, and Peter Gant, ...	"	XXI.	86
1763. Sept. 2.	Panton, Francis, and Jane Helme, ...	"	VII.	322
1761. July 28.	Panton, Francis, and Mary Campbell,......	"	V.	13

DATE.	NAMES.	RECORD.	VOL.	PAGE.
1737. Oct. 10.	Parangue, Daniel, and Elizabeth Poullon,...	M. B.,	I.	7
1780. June 28.	Parbirt, George, and Elizabeth Taylor,.....	"	XXIX.	102
1768. Oct. 15.	Parcell, Hannah, and Abraham Lavine, ...	"	XIII.	211
1770. Oct. 27.	Parcell, Mary, and Joseph Burroughs,......	"	XVI.	229
1783. Jan. 18.	Parcells, Jane, and John Miles,...........	"	XXXVIII.	21
1764. Oct. 29.	Parent, Judith, and Leonard Whitmey, ...	"	VIII.	378
1760. May 1.	Parent, Magdalen, and Jacob Schurman,...	"	III.	133
1725. Oct. 6.	Parine, Daniel, and Mary Martin,.........	C. M.,	LXVII.	72
1757. June 21.	Parine, Henry, and Susannah Cole,........	M. B.,	I.	568
1761. Feb. 21.	Paris, James, and Christiana Parsons,......	"	IV.	74
1759. April 19.	Paris, Lewis, and Catharine Ryley,........	"	II.	248
1761. Dec. 9.	Parish, Townsend, and Freelove Dodge,....	"	V.	269
1769. July 14.	Park, Sarah, and Thomas Paul,...........	"	XIV.	152
1755. Dec. 15.	Parke, Peter, and Mary Bodine,..........	"	I.	233
1783. June 6.	Parks, Peter, and Elizabeth Roberts, ...	"	XXXIX.	44
1783. Sept. 10.	Parker, Abigail, and Henry Richard Bowman,	"	XL.	34
1781. Sept. 1.	Parker, Alice, and William Ward,.........	"	XXXIII.	55
1783. Nov. 13.	Parker, Anne, and John Beeton,..........	"	XL.	113
1780. Jan. 31.	Parker, Benjamin, and Elizabeth Turk,.....	"	XXVIII.	205
1764. June 28.	Parker, Benjamin, and Mary Benon,.......	"	VIII.	241
1783. May 30.	Parker, Elizabeth, and Moses Trembles,....	"	XXXIX.	29
1779. April 2.	Parker, John, and Ann Popplesdorff, ...	"	XXVII.	91
1773. Mar. 23.	Parker, John, and Catherine Goodbylet,....	"	XX.	68
1778. Nov. 5.	Parker, Joseph, and Elizabeth Swan, ...	"	XXVI.	82
1756. Oct. 29.	Parker, Mary, and John Simson,..........	"	I.	337
1780. Feb. 1.	Parker, Mary, and John Watson,..........	"	XXVIII.	206
173⅞. Jan. 26.	Parker, Mary, and William De Witt,.......	"	I.	8
1779. Sept. 14.	Parker, William, and Mary Earle,.........	"	XXVIII.	74
1778. July 1.	Parkes, Phœbe, and Henry Weatherby,....	"	XXV.	118
1764. Feb. 24.	Parkhurst, Samuel, and Rennelche Dubois,..	"	VIII.	87
1782. May 21.	Parkinson, Catharine, and William Doughty,	"	XXXVI.	13
1783. July 11.	Parkinson, Helen, and John Moore, ...	"	XXXIX.	87
1769. Aug. 12.	Parks, Arthur, and Phebe Howell, ...	"	XV.	21
1768. July 7.	Parlee, Abraham, and Ann Simonson,......	"	XIII.	149
1783. Mar. 11.	Parlee, Bornt, and Rachel Johnson, ...	"	XXXVIII.	65
1781. May 21.	Parlee, Henry, and Rebecah Cole,.........	"	XXXII.	55
1781. Jan. 29.	Parmer, Hanna, and John Dunnalcha, ...	"	XXXI.	30
1760. Oct. 13.	Parr, James, and Alice Blaine,............	"	III.	360
1758. Dec. 2.	Parr, John, and Elizabeth Hall,...........	"	II.	109
1762. Oct. 16.	Parrager, Catharine, and Peter Sharpe,.....	"	VI.	368
1762. Feb. 5.	Parratt, Thomas, and Leah Lamb,.........	"	VI.	39
1758. Feb. 28.	Parrow, Catherine, and John Manbrut,.....	"	I.	832
1736. July 20.	Parsall, John, and Elizabeth Boss,.........	"	I.	2
1761. Dec. 24.	Parsall, John, and Margaret Van Alst, ...	"	V.	299
1762. Oct. 15.	Parsall, Nicholas, and Elizabeth Parsalls, ...	"	VI.	367

DATE.		NAMES.	RECORD.	VOL.	PAGE.
1764. May	2.	Parsalls, Catharine, and Dennis Oblenus, ...	M. B.,	VIII.	177
1762. Oct.	15.	Parsalls, Elizabeth, and Nicholas Parsall, ...	"	VI.	367
1761. Oct.	14.	Parsalls, Sarah, and George Pain, ...	"	V.	139
1753. April	11.	Parsel, Hannah, and Garret De Grauw, ...	"	I.	21
1778. Dec.	21.	Parsell, Catherine, and David Mellows, Jr., ..	"	XXVI.	127
1779. Dec.	1.	Parsell, Hannah, and William Duncan, ...	"	XXVIII.	156
1772. Dec.	2.	Parsell, James, and Hannah Erle, ...	"	XIX.	140
1768. Aug.	19.	Parsell, John, and Sarah Betts, ...	"	XIII.	175
1761. Oct.	16.	Parsell, Phebe, and Elias Bedell, ...	"	V.	143
1781. Nov.	10.	Parsell, Richard, and Mary Powers, ...	"	XXXIV.	26
1781. Dec.	18.	Parsell, Robert, and Polly Furman, ...	"	XXXIV.	93
1780. Dec.	16.	Parsell, William, and Carie Van Alts, ...	"	XXX.	154
1769. April	10.	Parsells, Elcie, and Joseph Allison, ...	"	XIV.	68
1765. May	16.	Parsells, Sarah, and John McNeil, ...	"	IX.	128
1775. Nov.	10.	Parsells, Thomas, and Ann Montanje, ...	"	XXIII.	204
1777. Jan.	3.	Parsley, Dorothy, and Robert McCollough, .	"	XXIV.	3
1761. Feb.	14.	Parsley, Sarah, and George Weekes, ...	"	IV.	62
1764. July	14.	Parsols, Elenor, and Henry Grainger, ...	"	VIII.	259
1753. Aug.	3.	Parson, Lydia, and Edward Thorn, ...	"	I.	85
1761. Feb.	21.	Parsons, Christiana, and James Paris, ...	"	IV.	74
1761. Sept.	7.	Parsons, Eletta, and Daniel Pearce, ...	"	V.	70
1781. Mar.	21.	Parsons, Jane, and John Cunningham, ...	"	XXXI.	80
1775. June	6.	Parsons, Jane, and Samuel Glean, ...	"	XXIII.	54
1764. July	7.	Parsons, Janitie, and Wessels Ten Brook, ..	"	VIII.	248
1758. Mar.	14.	Parsons, Rebeccah, and Gerardus Harden- brook, ...	"	I.	849
1775. Aug.	17.	Parsons, William, and Catharine Sanders, ...	"	XXIII.	131
1762. July	16.	Paschall, George, and Mary Roberts, ...	"	VI.	240
1770. Oct.	18.	Pasen, John, and Martha Townsend, ...	"	XVI.	224
1780. Jan.	8.	Pasman, Elener, and Thomas Dixon, ...	"	XXVIII.	187
1757. Nov.	2.	Pasman, William, and Elizabeth Knicker- backer, ...	"	I.	694
1782. Oct.	22.	Pass, Martha, and Holley Lynes, ...	"	XXXVII.	58
1664. Mar.	9.	Passill, Mary, and John Thorne, ...	G. E.,	I.	98
1779. Aug.	26.	Patch, Caspar, and Mary Patch, ...	M. B.,	XXVIII.	60
1779. Aug.	26.	Patch, Mary, and Caspar Patch, ...	"	XXVIII.	60
1782. Mar.	6.	Patcham, Abigail, and John Marr, ...	"	XXXV.	77
1782. Mar.	11.	Patchen, Andrew, and Elizabeth Read, ...	"	XXXV.	84
1780. Sept.	16.	Paterson, Archibald, and Elizabeth Jenkins, .	"	XXX.	31
1764. Feb.	10.	Paterson, James, and Elizabeth Haley, ...	"	VIII.	56
1772. Oct.	23.	Paterson, John, and Mary Van Alstyne, ...	"	XIX.	90
1761. Dec.	23.	Paterson, Mathew, and Sarah Thorp, ...	"	V.	295
1759. Mar.	20.	Paterson, Robert, and Catherine Everson, ..	"	II.	222
1780. Nov.	30.	Patmer, Richard, and Sophia Stover, ...	"	XXX.	128
1779. Sept.	8.	Patrick, John, and Margaret McEuen, ...	"	XXVIII.	71

DATE.		NAMES.	RECORD.	VOL. PAGE.
1759. Feb.	20.	Patroue, Letitia, and Thomas Murphy,.....	M. B.,	II. 199
1779. Feb.	3.	Patten, Edward, and Gitty Van Horne,....	"	XXVII. 35
1773. Aug.	20.	Patten, Edward, and Mary Graham,.......	"	XXI. 77
1782. Feb.	16.	Patten, Johnson, and Ann Collard,........	"	XXXV. 57
1761. Dec.	23.	Patten, Mary, and David Caithness,........	"	V. 296
1783. Jan.	3.	Patterson, Catharine, and Edmund Dwyer,.	"	XXXVIII. 3
1758. Jan.	5.	Patterson, Elener, and William Bloomfield,.	"	I. 770
1778. Nov.	30.	Patterson, Isabella, and Joseph Veasey, ...	"	XXVI. 103
1738. July	25.	Patterson, John, and Elsha Bowman, ...	"	I. 10
1783. Aug.	8.	Patterson, John, and Mary Gregory, ...	"	XXXIX. 119
1773. Feb.	1.	Patterson, Leonora, and Alexander Mercer,.	"	XX. 34
1783. Oct.	29.	Patterson, Margaret, and William Louttit,..	"	XL. 92
1782. Sept.	18.	Patterson, Mary, and Daniel Stilwell,......	"	XXXVII. 6
1768. Dec.	2.	Patterson, Mary, and Jacob Newkerk,.....	"	XIII. 251
1752. Jan.	8.	Patterson, Mary, and Joseph Leddel, ...	"	I. 925
1771. Aug.	31.	Patterson, Moses, and Rachael Davis,......	"	XVII. 170
1780. Nov.	20.	Patterson, Robert, and Mary Lewis,.......	"	XXX. 116
1760. Nov.	12.	Patterson, Thomas, and Mary Walker,.....	"	III. 404
1730. April	20.	Patterson, Yufins, and Robert Wirling, ...	"	XXIX. 29
1782. Mar.	19.	Pattison, Thomas, and Elizabeth Bouler, ...	"	XXXV. 92
1763. June	27.	Patton, Francis Landey, and Elizabeth Richard, ...	"	VII. 243
1737. Dec.	2.	Pattrick, Mary, and Thomas Hunt,........	"	I. 8
1779. Aug.	5.	Pattullo, Robert, and Susanah Graham, ...	"	XXVIII. 46
1762. Oct.	4.	Paul, Elisabeth, and Joseph Willis,........	"	VI. 344
1730. April	21.	Paul, Rebecca, and Francis Young,........	"	XXIX. 32
1769. July	14.	Paul, Thomas, and Sarah Park, ...	"	XIV. 152
1763. Nov.	21.	Paulding, Elenor, and Robert Wilson,.....	"	VII. 459
1762. July	24.	Paulding, William, and Catharine Ogden,...	"	VI. 254
1761. April	23.	Paulin, Joseph, and Judith Shields, ...	"	IV. 163
1770. Sept.	27.	Payne, James William, and Cornelia Lamb,	"	XVI. 198
1767. May	4.	Payne, John, and Mary Higday, ...	"	XI. 76
1779. Dec.	31.	Payne, Joseph, and Ann Van Cleaf,.......	"	XXVIII. 184
1772. Nov.	5.	Payne, Mary, and Benjamin Williams,.....	"	XIX. 102
1780. June	3.	Payne, Wilhelmina, and William Ranken,..	"	XXIX. 81
1764. Mar.	12.	Payntar, William, and Hester Skillman,....	"	VIII. 103
1779. Feb.	4.	Peabody, Daniel, and Sarah Jones, ...	"	XXVII. 36
1768. Mar.	19.	Peacock, Frances, and Lawrence Kemble,..	"	XIII. 51
1783. Nov.	19.	Peacock, John, and Caroline Doughty,.....	"	XL. 123
1772. May	11.	Peake, Jane, and George Cook,...........	"	XVIII. 107
1761. Sept.	7.	Pearce, Daniel, and Eletta Parsons,........	"	V. 70
1758. May	24.	Pearce, Daniel, and Mary Lenonton,.......	"	I. 906
1736. Nov.	17.	Pearce, Elizabeth, and Jeremiah Wood,....	"	I. 3
1736. Dec.	28.	Pearce, Phebe, and George Baker,........	"	I. 5
1768. Sept.	27.	Pearce, Richard, and Abigal Burtis,.......	"	XIII. 197

DATE.		NAMES.	RECORD.	VOL.	PAGE.
1738. May	20.	Pearce, Samuel, and Abigael Powel,.......	M. B.,	I.	9
1775. Nov.	8.	Pearce, Samuel, and Ann Taggart,........	"	XXIII.	203
1779. June	14.	Pearce, Thomas, and Mary McFarland,....	"	XXVII.	164a
1772. Aug.	29.	Pearcy, Poole, and Elizabeth Lawrence, ...	"	XIX.	34
1759. May	24.	Pearl, Ann, and Henry Main,............	"	II.	291
1763. Nov.	2.	Pears, Abigail, and Jonathan Baker,.......	"	VII.	422
1763. Dec.	1.	Pears, Ann, and Richard Baker,..........	"	VII.	487
1763. Oct.	27.	Pears, Christopher, and Alice Hagens,......	"	VII.	408
1764. April	5.	Pears, Hannah, and Edward Brush, ...	"	VIII.	135
1756. Nov.	18.	Pears, Rachel, and Thomas Hunt,.........	"	I.	360
1759. Mar.	17.	Pears, Thomas, and Jane Haley,...........	"	II.	218
1765. July	4.	Pearsall, Christina, and Peter Hageman,....	"	IX.	193
1777. Dec.	10.	Pearsall, Elizabeth, and Alexander Milne,..	"	XXIV.	194
1778. Nov.	5.	Pearsall, Hester, and Isaac Smith,.........	"	XXVI.	83
1779. Oct.	23.	Pearsall, Mary, and Nehemiah Allen,......	"	XXVIII.	118
1781. Jan.	2.	Pearsall, Sarah, and Patrick Campbell,.....	"	XXXI.	4
1765. Mar.	5.	Pearsall, Sarah, and Samuel Searing,......	"	IX.	64
1777. June	10.	Pearsall, Thomas, and Mary Vanderhoeven,.	"	XXIV.	98
1781. Aug.	8.	Pearsall, Uriah, and Catherine Roebuck,....	"	XXXIII.	31
1775. Aug.	26.	Pearsall, William, and Hannah Langdon,...	"	XXIII.	134
1768. Sept.	19.	Pearse, Annatje, and John Fisher,........	"	XIII.	188
1759. Jan.	27.	Pearse, Elizabeth, and Joseph Tillet,.......	"	II.	167
1753. May	19.	Pearse, Helena, and John Lassher, Jr.,... .	"	I.	35
1780. May	2.	Pearse, John, and Sarah Fogarty,.........	"	XXIX.	41
1773. May	5.	Pearse, Margaret, and John Anthony, ...	"	XX.	104
1760. April	2.	Pearsee, Mary, and Marinus Willett,......	"	III.	94
1780. Sept.	26.	Pearson, Ann, and Noel Barberin,........	"	XXX.	42
1783. Oct.	17.	Pearson, Anne, and John Dally,..........	"	XL.	83
1783. Mar.	28.	Pearson, Christopher, and Bridget Anna Maria Denny,......................	"	XXXVIII.	80
1782. June	24.	Pearson, David, and Catharin Pennil,......	"	XXXVI.	62
1764. Nov.	20.	Pearson, David, and Elizabeth Gelston,....	"	VIII.	413
1779. July	7.	Pearson, George, and Susanah Allaway,...	"	XXVIII.	17
1763. Dec.	8.	Pearson, Jacobus, and Margaret Barroway,.	"	VII.	499
1762. Dec.	13.	Pearson, John, and Margaret Heleges,.....	"	VI.	477
1764. April	17.	Pearson, Margaret, and Isaac Harris, ...	"	VIII.	161
1770. Feb.	3.	Pearson, Mary, and Silas Hicks,..........	"	XVI.	11
1778. Nov.	26.	Pearson, Mary, and William Watts,.......	"	XXVI.	99
1759. Oct.	9.	Pearson, Phebe, and Robert Nugent,......	"	II.	454
1783. May	10.	Pearson, William, and Hannah Mineus, ...	"	XXXIX.	9
1763. Aug.	1.	Pearson, William, and Mary Smith,........	"	VII.	288
167⅚. Mar.	14.	Peartree, William, and Anne Tiddeman,...	W. O. P.,	III.	183
1761. Oct.	6.	Peasley, Francis, and Mary Villanaaux,....	M. B.,	V.	129
1772. July	20.	Peck, Jacobus C., and Hannah Van Vorst,..	"	XIX.	3
1761. Oct.	14.	Peck, James, and Elizabeth Griffen, ...	"	V.	138

DATE.	NAMES.	RECORD.	VOL.	PAGE.
1778. Nov. 23.	Peck, James, and Elizabeth Woodward,....	M. B.,	XXVI.	92
1768. June 30.	Peck, Joseph, and Catherine McGee,......	"	XIII.	146
1761. Nov. 10.	Peck, Mary, and Thomas Ellison, Jr.,......	"	V.	203
1760. May 12.	Peck, Thomas, and Ann McMasters,.......	"	III.	150
1763. Aug. 18.	Pedley, Elizabeth, and William Murrills,....	"	VII.	304
1767. June 2.	Peeck, Alida, and Petrus Meebie, ...	"	XI.	102
1764. July 24.	Peeck, Daniel, and Eva Peeck,............	"	VIII.	267
1764. July 24.	Peeck, Eva, and Daniel Peeck,............	"	VIII.	267
1769. June 15.	Peeck, John, and Sister Bradt,............	"	XIV.	120
1773. June 30.	Peeck, Margaret, and John Jacob Van Eps,	"	XXI.	27
1770. June 30.	Peeck, Susannah, and Jacobus S. Bradt,....	"	XVI.	130
1757. Mar. 5.	Peck, Catherine, and John Wylley,........	"	I.	457
1736. July 19.	Peck, Catherine, and Sampson Benson, ...	"	I.	2
1772. Oct. 15.	Peck, George, and Susannah Saunders, ...	"	XIX.	73
1760. Aug. 15.	Peek, Helena, and John Barhuyd,.........	"	III.	254
1761. Dec. 2.	Peck, Johannes, and Eva Yates, ...	"	V.	261
1765. Feb. 12.	Peek, John, and Sarah Blacklidge,........	"	IX.	51
1763. April 22.	Peek, Joseph, and Lucretia Bayley,........	"	VI.	125
1758. Sept. 14.	Peek, Mary, and Daniel Johnson,.........	"	II.	22
1768. Nov. 2.	Peeke, Aaron, and Rebecca,..............	"	XIII.	221
1770. May 31.	Peet, Mary, and Richard Sibley,..........	"	XVI.	99
761. Mar. 11.	Peet, Sarah, and Robert Harris, ...	"	IV.	95
765. June 25.	Peet, Simon, and Ruth Salmons,....	"	IX.	184
761. Aug. 26.	Peet, Thomas, and Mary Spock,..........	"	V.	59
738. May 5.	Peets, Catherine, and Joseph Brush,.......	"	I.	9
756. Dec. 11.	Peets, Sarah, and Nathaniel Hunt, ...	"	I.	380
1758. Dec. 16.	Peffer, Anne Marea, and Robert Williams,..	"	II.	130
1761. June 22.	Peffer, Elizabeth, and Charles Cox,........	"	IV.	253
1765. July 11.	Peffer, Michael, and Sarah Ryan,..........	"	IX.	202
1762. June 28.	Pegrem, Hannah, and Henry Harps, ...	"	VI.	211
1761. Mar. 14.	Peirce, Phebe, and Albert Albertson,......	"	IV.	102
1761. Sept. 28.	Peirse, John, and Mary Hutton, ...	"	V.	103
1765. July 27.	Peirson, Garret, and Jane Hyre,..........	"	IX.	218
1764. Oct. 31.	Peirson, Joseph, and Ann Villee,..........	"	VIII.	385
1771. Aug. 28.	Peirson, Joseph, and Susanna Hunt,.......	"	XVII.	167
1781. Mar. 19.	Peivey, James, and Catherine Grigg,......	"	XXXI.	75
1767. Feb. 9.	Pelagie, Catherine, and Francois Mioitt,....	"	XI.	23
1771. June 5.	Pell, Ann, and John Bartow, Jr., ...	"	XVII.	101
1778. Nov. 25.	Pell, Benjamin, and Mary Ferris, ...	"	XXVI.	96
1736. Dec. 10.	Pell, Catherine, and Jacob Write, ...	"	I.	3
1775. June 27.	Pell, Edward, and Mary Devoe, ...	"	XXIII.	79
1760. Oct. 18.	Pell, Eletha, and John Heath, ...	"	III.	369
1763. Oct. 1.	Pell, Elizabeth, and William Lindsay,......	"	VII.	366
1780. Jan. 24.	Pell, Gilbert, and Mary Honeywell, ...	"	XXVIII.	202
1768. Jan. 16.	Pell, Gilbert, and Thamar Hunt, ...	"	XIII.	9

DATE.	NAMES.	RECORD.	VOL.	PAGE.
1775. July 14.	Pell, James, and Martha Rigsley, ...	M. B.,	XXIII.	98
1761. Dec. 22.	Pell, John, and Ann Crawford, ...	"	V.	292
1782. June 12.	Pell, Jonathan, and Elizabeth Leonard, ...	"	XXXVI.	48
1778. Nov. 25.	Pell, Joseph, and Phila Pell, ...	"	XXVI.	97
1757. Jan. 21.	Pell, Joshua, and Abigail Archer, ...	"	I.	795
1783. July 9.	Pell, Joshua, Jr., and Sarah Minthorn,.....	"	XXXIX.	85
173⅝. Mar. 12.	Pell, Mary, and Drake Palmer, ...	"	I.	1
1759. Jan. 3.	Pell, Mary, and James Haviland,..........	"	II.	143
1758. June 3.	Pell, Phebe, and Boswell Dawson, ...	"	I.	923
1762. Nov. 18.	Pell, Phebe, and James Bennett,..........	"	VI.	441
1736. Sept. 11.	Pell, Pheby, and John Tredwell,..........	"	XL.	36
1778. Nov. 25.	Pell, Phila, and Joseph Pell,.............	"	XXVI.	97
1774. Jan. 11.	Pell, Philip, and Mary Stevegier,..........	"	XXII.	99
173⁴⁄₇. Feb. 28.	Pell, Phillip, and Phebe Fitch,...........	"	I.	5
1760. Sept. 27.	Pell, Rebecca, and Charles Bennet,........	"	III.	332
173⁴⁄₇. Jan. 7.	Pell, Samuel, and Hester Bloom,..........	"	I.	5
1773. Sept. 6.	Pell, Sarah, and Benjamin Guyon, ...	"	XXI.	99
1780. Sept. 28.	Pell, Sarah, and Joshua Watson,..........	"	XXX.	46
1771. June 10.	Pell, Sarah, and William Bayley, ...	"	XVII.	107
1759. Dec. 29.	Pell, Susanna, and Benjamin Drake,.......	"	II.	561
1779. July 10.	Pelletreau, Mary Elizabeth, and John Ebart,	"	XXVIII.	20
1757. June 15.	Pelletreau, Susannah, and William Ustick,..	"	I.	56.
1766. June 12.	Pellinger, Cathrina, and George Klock, ...	"	X.	13
1764. Sept. 8.	Pells, Bridget, and Nazarus Brewer,.......	"	VIII.	301
1753. July 2.	Pells, Catalina, and Jacob Fardon,.........	"	I.	69
1770. Nov. 15.	Pells, Francis, and Catherine Van Kleeck,..	"	XVI.	258
1760. July 9.	Pels, Evert, and Sarah Smith, ...	"	III.	208
1762. April 6.	Pels, Henry, and Sarah Vandenbergh, ...	"	VI.	90
1761. Feb. 23.	Pels, Maritje, and Jeremiah Ffowler,.......	"	IV.	76
1770. May 18.	Pels, Mary, and Elias Nexsen,............	"	XVI.	92
1765. Oct. 30.	Pelton, Sarah, and Christopher Kannady,...	"	IX.	336
1775. Sept. 6.	Peltreau, Martha, and Medcaf Eden,......	"	XXIII.	147
1763. June 3.	Pelts, Catharine, and John Jones,.........	"	VII.	211
1769. Dec. 6.	Pemberton, Alida, and Valentine Farrington,	"	XV.	115
1783. July 3.	Pemberton, Sophiah, and Elias Pakeman,...	"	XXXIX.	82
1780. Nov. 14.	Pemberton, Sophiah, and Samuel John,....		XXX.	106
1780. Nov. 27.	Pemley, Hiel, and Elizabeth McCarthy,....		XXX.	125
1773. Aug. 16.	Pemper, Anna Savenah, and Henrech Wessel,	"	XXI.	68
1761. June 5.	Pendred, Jane, and John Croll,...........	"	IV.	197
1758. April 4.	Pendry, Mary Ann, and Coenradt Haun,...	"	I.	870
1762. Nov. 13.	Peneer, Elizabeth, and Robert North,......	"	VI.	430
1760. Mar. 22.	Peneer, Elizabeth, and William Scott, ...	"	III.	88
1759. June 9.	Peneur, Penelope, and Cornelius Turner,...	"	II.	317
1783. Sept. 18.	Peneyead, William, and Ann Ingram,.....	"	XL.	45
1765. June 15.	Penfold, Elisabeth, and Cornelius Berrien,..	"	IX.	170

DATE.	NAMES.	RECORD.	VOL. PAGE.
1783. July 3.	Penfold, Richard, and Catharine Bogart,....	M. B.,	xxxix. 81
1781. Sept. 13.	Pengray, Anne, and John Collard,........	"	xxxiii. 63
1757. Nov. 29.	Penier, Peter, and Margaret Dunstar,......	"	i. 718
1781. Oct. 15.	Pennell, Hannah, and John Goodman,.....	"	xxxiii. 100
1757. June 2.	Pennell, Hayes, and Mary White,.........	"	i. 548
1782. June 24.	Pennil, Catharin, and David Pearson,......	"	xxxvi. 62
1781. Feb. 15.	Penny, Alexander, and Sarah Foreseyth,...	"	xxxi. 46
1760. Jan. 12.	Penny, Dorothy, and James Dunscomb,....	"	ii. 578
1780. Dec. 1.	Penny, Mary, and George Bane,..........	"	xxx. 129
1670. Aug. 1.	Pennyer, Elizabeth, and Richard Lownesberry, ...	C. A.,	ii. 572
1761. Feb. 12.	Pens, Louis, and Jane Tyrrel, ...	M. B.,	iv. 61
1757. Nov. 11.	Pensinger, Ann, and Cornelius Van Vaghten,	"	i. 702
1779. Oct. 15.	Pentland, Joseph, and Frances Moore,.....	"	xxviii. 112
1756. Sept. 24.	Pepinger, Elizabeth, and William Maghlaghlin, ...	"	i. 301
1771. Oct. 21.	Peppard, Mary, and Rueben Clark,........	"	xvii. 217
1738. Aug. 8.	Pepper, John, and Charity Moor, ...	"	i. 10
1759. June 8.	Pepperal, Lazeras, and Hester Montanje,...	"	ii. 311
1770. Nov. 13.	Pepson, Thomas, and Catherine Treyner,...	"	xvi. 249
1783. Aug. 1.	Perbanck, Patience, and Abraham Lake, ...	"	xxxix. 107
1764. Aug. 15.	Percutt, Anne, and John Betts,...........	"	viii. 281
1778. Dec. 2.	Percy, Elenor, and William Rider,........	"	xxvi. 107
1760. Mar. 22.	Percut, Jane, and Benjamin Seacord,......	"	iii. 86
1773. Aug. 19.	Periam, Thomas P., and Dinah Van Varck,.	"	xxi. 76
1781. Oct. 2.	Perine, Daniel, and Lucy Homes,..........	"	xxxiii. 81
1783. Sept. 12.	Perine, Edward, and Sarah Hillyard,......	"	xl. 37
1768. Sept. 26.	Perine, Elizabeth, and David Mersereau,....	"	xiii. 194
1766. Sept. 22.	Perine, James, and Ann Johnston, ...	"	x. 102
1782. Sept. 25.	Perine, Joseph, and Catharine Swame, ...	"	xxxvii. 13
1781. Oct. 4.	Perine, Margaret, and David La Tourette,..	"	xxxiii. 85
1778. May 30.	Perine, Mary, and Albert Journeay,.......	'	xxv. 95
1782. April 27.	Perine, Peter, and Ann Palmer,...........	"	xxxv. 140
1772. June 19.	Perkile, Christian, and Elizabeth Bowman,.	"	xviii. 144
1759. Aug. 8.	Pero, John, and Anne Van Norder, ...	"	ii. 380
1782. Feb. 9.	Perrey, Stephen, and Margaret Scudder, ...	"	xxxv. 46
1777. Aug. 6.	Perrine, William, and Miranda Arow Smith,	"	xxiv. 127
1760. Sept. 30.	Perrit, Jane, and Richard Mott,...........	"	iii. 338
1762. July 12.	Perry, Francis, and Sarah Higgins,........	"	vi. 235
1766. July 14.	Perry, Francyntie, and Isaac Fonda,.......	"	x. 48
1772. Jan. 3.	Perry, Henry W., and Miriam Braine,.....	"	xviii. 2
1783. May 8.	Perry, John, and Jane Collins,...........	"	xxxix. 4
1770. Jan. 8.	Perry, Mary, and John Vance,............	"	xvii. 3
1777. Dec. 22.	Perry, Mary, and William Van Assendelft,..	"	xxiv. 203
1769. Jan. 9.	Perry, Mervine, and Alletta Wessells,......	"	xiv. 8

DATE.	NAMES.	RECORD.	VOL. PAGE.
1760. Sept. 15.	Perry, Rachel, and William Morris,.......	M. B.,	III. 315
1759. Oct. 11.	Perry, Sarah, and Lewis Hallam,..........	"	II. 455
1736. April 9.	Perry, Susannah, and Hugh Shaw,........	"	I. 1
1780. Mar. 7.	Perry, Susannah, and James Turnbull,.....	"	XXVIII. 218
1767. April 23.	Perry, Thomas, and Ruth Moore, ...	"	XI. 68
1758. Sept. 23.	Persell, Elizabeth, and Abraham Devoe,....	"	II. 33
1770. Aug. 1.	Persen, Cornelius, and Elizabeth Masten,...	"	XVI. 152
1767. Aug. 21.	Persen, Jannetie, and Peter Swart,........	"	XII. 20
1762. May 5.	Person, Benjamin, and Catharine Campbell,.	"	VI. 144
1773. Jan. 27.	Person, John I., and Catherine Freidenburgh,	"	XX. 21
1681. May 16.	Person, Mary, and Setch Fletcher, ...	O. W.,	XXXII½. 46
1779. Dec. 7.	Pertuis, Estienne de, and Teresia Piquet,...	M. B.,	XXVIII. 165
1770. Oct. 23.	Pest, Eve, and Hendrick Platner,..........	"	XVI. 226
1757. Jan. 27.	Peterkin, Elenor, and John Cortill,........	"	I. 421
1764. Jan. 17.	Peters, Ann, and Andrew McFarlan, ...	"	VIII. 21
1764. July 24.	Peters, Ann, and Thomas Horsefield,......	"	VIII. 269
1772. Nov. 26.	Peters, Benjamin, and Maria Van Wagoner,	"	XIX. 130
1770. July 4.	Peters, Catherine, and Jacob Jackson,.....	"	XVI. 135
1777. June 18.	Peters, Charity, and Lawrence Hewlett,....	"	XXIV. 104
1736. May 14.	Peters, Charles, and Jane Denton, ...	"	I. 1
1759. June 7.	Peters, Charles, and Rachel Latham,.......	"	II. 310
1758. May 30.	Peters, Edward, and Catherine Cassidy,....	"	I. 917
1762. Nov. 5.	Peters, Elisabeth, and Daniel Searing, ...	"	VI. 412
1775. Sept. 21.	Peters, Elizabeth, and James Moor, ...	"	XXIII. 160
1761. Aug. 7.	Peters, Harmanus, and Margaret Pake, ...	"	V. 32
1767. June 12.	Peters, James, and Margaret Lester,.......	"	XI. 106
1759. Aug. 7.	Peters, Jane, and Samuel Skidmore,.......	"	II. 378
1782. May 13.	Peters, John, and Johanna Brandon,......	"	XXXVI. 1
1783. Feb. 17.	Peters, John, and Mary Fowler, ...	"	XXXVIII. 43
1780. June 22.	Peters, Mary, and Jacob Marvin,..........	"	XXIX. 91
1761. Sept. 21.	Peters, Mary, and James Willis,..........	"	V. 91
1767. Sept. 24.	Peters, Mary, and Joshua Hallock,........	"	XII. 43
1736. April 8.	Peters, Mary, and Richard Titus,..........	"	I. 1
1762. April 14.	Peters, Miriam, and Adam Seabury,.......	"	VI. 108
1779. Feb. 27.	Peters, Phebe, and Timothy Brooks,.......	"	XXVII. 51
1768. Nov. 12.	Peters, Rachel, and John Simonson,.......	"	XIII. 232
1767. July 10.	Peters, Rebeka, and Jacob Smith, ...	"	XI. 130
1782. Jan. 3.	Peters, Richard, and Elizabeth Smith,......	"	XXXV. 8
1768. Nov. 14.	Peters, Sophia, and Hugh Mitchel, ...	"	XIII. 236
1766. June 5.	Peters, Susannah, and Georg Hewlett,.....	"	X. 4
1777. July 26.	Peterson, Abraham, and Mary Martin,.....	"	XXIV. 122
1769. July 5.	Peterson, Agnes, and Alexander Smith,....	"	XIV. 143
1763. Dec. 8.	Peterson, Annatje, and Peter Wilson,......	"	VII. 498
1756. Oct. 14.	Peterson, Catharine, and Nicolaes Goenendyck, ...	"	I. 329

DATE.	NAMES.	RECORD	VOL.	PAGE.
1736. Dec. 20.	Peterson, Christina, and Peter Vandike, ...	M. B.,	I.	5
1772. June 8.	Peterson, Garret, and Anna Duyckman, ...	"	XX.	140
1783. Nov. 5.	Peterson, Garret, and Catharine Somering-dike, ...	"	XL.	106
1738. May 27.	Peterson, John, and Anne Turner, ...	"	I.	9
1773. May 17.	Peterson, John, and Mary Reshong, ...	"	XX.	115
1755. Oct. 15.	Peterson, Leah, and William Bennet, ...	"	I.	192
1761. Oct. 13.	Peterson, Margaret, and James Shuter, ...	"	V.	133
1760. Feb. 9.	Peterson, Margaret, and Joseph Dwight, ...	"	III.	29
1767. Sept. 10.	Peterson, Mary, and Hezekiah Mills, ...,.	"	XII.	33
1783. Sept. 3.	Peterson, Susannah, and Prince Royal, ...	"	XL.	22
1761. June 3.	Peterson, Susannah, and Thomas Mallery, ..	"	IV.	226
1757. July 23.	Petri, Elisabeth, and James Dickson, ...	"	I.	599
1763. Oct. 20.	Pettenger, Hannah, and Jacob Tabeley, ...	"	VII.	394
1779. April 7.	Pettet, Elijah, and Phebe Higby, ...	"	XXVII.	97
1757. April 9.	Pettet, Elizabeth, and Benjamin Field, ...	"	I.	493
1763. Dec. 1.	Pettet, James, and Anne Losee, ...	"	VII.	486
1764. June 2.	Pettet, Phebe, and Robert Coe, Jr., ...	"	VIII.	206
1778. Feb. 5.	Pettet, Robert, and Ruth Powell, ...	"	XXV.	16
1763. May 11.	Pettinger, Ann, and Phineas Lockwood, ...	"	VII.	179
1758. Feb. 24.	Pettinger, John, and Lucy De Lenoy, ...	"	I.	827
1764. June 23.	Pettinger, Mary, and Jacob Smith, ...	"	VIII.	236
1759. Dec. 24.	Pettinger, Philip, and Elizabeth Jemison, ..	"	II.	557
1767. July 4.	Pettit, Anna, and Gifford Dalley, ...	"	XI.	123
1764. Mar. 31.	Pettit, Anne, and James Losee, ...	"	VIII.	126
1778. June 15.	Pettit, Arabella, and John Oarman, ...	"	XXV.	103
1760. Mar. 1.	Pettit, Eleanor, and William Dering, ...	"	III.	58
1766. June 19.	Pettit, Elizabeth, and Abraham Warner, ...	"	X.	21
1766. Aug. 28.	Pettit, Elizabeth, and John Vandervort, ...	"	X.	85
1779. Jan. 8.	Pettit, Esther, and Simon Vooris, ...	"	XXVII.	8
1783. Aug. 11.	Pettit, James H., and Sarah Collit, ...	"	XXXIX.	123
1777. Sept. 20.	Pettit, Jane, and Gilbert Willson, ...	"	XXIV.	148
1760. Oct. 28.	Pettit, Margaret, and Jacob Carle, ...	"	III.	383
1757. April 16.	Pettit, Nathaniel, and Mercy Bont, ...	"	I.	501
1782. April 13.	Pettit, Nelly, and John Spencer, ...	"	XXXV.	121
1778. Oct. 16.	Pettit, Patty, and Peter Sniffen, ...	"	XXVI.	63
1779. April 7.	Pettit, Sarah, and John Vannostran, ...	"	XXVII.	98
1778. June 13.	Pettit, Wyntie, and Daniel Caen, ...	"	XXV.	100
1765. Oct. 23.	Petton, Mary, and John Walcot, ...	"	IX.	312
1764. April 26.	Pew, Elizabeth, and Matthew Decker, ...	"	VIII.	171
1775. May 2.	Pew, Lydia, and William Morss, ...	"	XXIII.	20
1759. Feb. 8.	Phagen, Elizabeth, and William Gilliland, ..	"	II.	185
1782. May 10.	Phair, Andrew, and Margeret Berry, ...	"	XXXV.	158
1773. Nov. 10.	Phelps, Chloe, and John McLean, ...	"	XXII.	18
1772. Nov. 2.	Phenix, Daniel, and Elizabeth Platt, ...	"	XIX.	97

DATE.	NAMES.	RECORD.	VOL.	PAGE.
1738. Oct. 28.	Phenix, Jacob, and Mary Rome, ...	M. B.,	I.	11
1770. Sept. 10.	Phenix, Philip, and Elinor Dobbs, ...	"	XVI.	185
1765. Oct. 24.	Philip, Peter, and Anne Groat, ...	"	IX.	315
1758. Oct. 20.	Philips, Ann, and John Faulkner, ...	"	II.	63
1763. Oct. 4.	Philips, Hugh, and Elizabeth Lindsay, ...	"	VII.	371
1772. Nov. 27.	Philips, Jacob, Jr., and Catherine Oostrander,	"	XIX.	132
1762. Dec. 15.	Philips, John, and Almy Blindborough, ...	"	VI.	481
1769. April 15.	Philips, Margaret, and John Ogilvie, ...	"	XIV.	75
1758. April 26.	Philips, Margaret, and William Sole, ...	"	I.	887
1773. Dec. 30.	Philips, Sarah, and David Roe, ...	"	XXII.	89
1763. Sept. 21.	Philips, Thomas, and Sarah Bloodgood, ...	"	VII.	346
1763. Dec. 28.	Philipse, Benjamin, and Margaret Collister,.	"	VII.	529
1756. Aug. 31.	Philipse, Frederick, and Elizabeth Rutgers, .	"	I.	281
1777. Mar. 19.	Philipse, Frederick, and Mary Marsten, ...	"	XXIV.	48
1779. Sept. 4.	Philipse, Maria Eliza, and Lionel Smythe,..	"	XXVIII.	68
1738. July 17.	Philipse, Mary, and George Little, ...	"	I.	10
1758. Jan. 19.	Philipse, Mary, and Roger Morris, ...	"	I.	790
1779. Nov. 17.	Phillips, Abraham, and Catherine Coony,...	"	XII.	86
1773. July 22.	Phillips, Ann, and Arthur Lougharne, ...	"	XXI.	48
1782. Dec. 9.	Phillips, Else, and Moses Smith, ...	"	XXXVII.	113
1778. Mar. 17.	Phillips, John, and Elizabeth Morrell, ...	"	XXV.	44
1768. Jan. 22.	Phillips, Moses, and Sarah Wisner, ...	"	XIII.	16
1783. Feb. 8.	Phillips, Sarah, and Mungo Noble, ...	"	XXXVIII.	38
1736. Dec. 8.	Phillipse, Mary, and Baltus Dehart, ...	"	I.	3
1777. Dec. 29.	Phillipse, Nathaniel, and Bridget Ahern, ...	"	XXIV.	209
1736. Oct. 21.	Phillipse, Samuel, and Mary Sanders, ...	"	I.	3
1760. Mar. 3.	Philpot, William, and Ann Correy, ...	"	III.	59
1765. Jan. 10.	Phisong, Elizabeth, and John Hopkins, ...	"	IX.	14
1758. Mar. 15.	Phœnix, Catherine, and Adolph Waldron,..	"	I.	852
1770. Feb. 8.	Phœnix, Daniel, and Hannah Tredwell, ...	"	XVI.	14
1768. Nov. 3.	Phyn, James, and Euretta Constable, ...	"	XIII.	223
1772. Dec. 8.	Pick, Catherina, and Cornelius Kool, ...	"	XIX.	146
1756. Nov. 18.	Pick, Sarah, and Niclaas Vender Lyn, ...	"	I.	359
1766. July 16.	Pickeman, Robert, and Elizabeth Bush, ...	"	X.	50
1760. Jan. 30.	Pickeman, Robert, and Rebecca Sample, ...	"	III.	11
1779. Dec. 1.	Pickering, Hallser, and Ann Lloyd, ...	"	XXVIII.	158
1782. Sept. 6.	Pickles, Anne, and James Pryor, ...	"	XXXVI.	137
1764. Nov. 12.	Pickton, John, and Mary Hopper, ...	"	VIII.	403
1757. Nov. 22.	Pidgeon, Lydia, and Robert Hollet, ...	"	I.	710
1767. Oct. 22.	Pierce, Elizabeth, and Elbert Anderson, ...	"	XII.	67
1779. July 1.	Pierce, John, and Elizabeth Marselis, ...	"	XXVIII.	12
1736. Nov. 30.	Pierce, John, and Marytie Tibout, ...	"	I.	3
1783. Feb. 21.	Pierce, Samuel, and Leah Stout, ...	"	XXXVIII.	48
1761. Nov. 19.	Pierce, William, and Abigail Young, ...	"	V.	234
1738. Nov. 22.	Piersee, Jonathan, and Hannah Jervers, ...	"	I.	11

DATE.	NAMES.	RECORD.	VOL. PAGE.
1759. Oct. 11.	Pinyard, Elenor, and Charles Nicoll, ...	M. B.,	II. 456
1757. Mar. 4.	Piper, Mary, and John Taylor, ...	"	I. 456
1765. June 17.	Pipkin, Elenor, and Matthew Jacobs, ...	"	IX. 174
1770. Nov. 24.	Pitcher, William, and Marritie Righter, ...	"	XVI. 267
1755. Dec. 12.	Pits, Evert, and Arryantie Frer, ...	"	I. 238
1771. April 3.	Pitt, Alathia, and James Benham, ...	"	XVII. 74
1775. Dec. 22.	Pitt, Hannah, and Andrew Van Every, ...	"	XXIII. 235
1761. Aug. 1.	Pitt, Letitia, and James Kelley, ...	"	V. 22
1782. June 5.	Pitt, Nichols, and Elizabeth Baker, ...	"	XXXVI. 38
1768. Sept. 14.	Pitt, Jacob, and Mary Shepherd, ...	"	XIII. 186
1759. April 2.	Pitt, John, and Ann Harding, ...	"	II. 234
1761. Nov. 24.	Pitts, George, and Elisabeth Hilliar, ...	"	V. 245
1769. June 2.	Pitts, Susannah, and Solomon Deeds, ...	"	XIV. 113
1762. July 21.	Place, Clement, and Susannah Tomkins, ...	"	VI. 250
1759. Mar. 5.	Place, Joseph, and Martha Smith, ...	"	II. 209
1779. Jan. 18.	Place, Sarah, and Nathaniel Weeks, ...	"	XXVII. 16
1779. Jan. 18.	Place, Thomas, and Amelia Smith, ...	"	XXVII. 17
1779. June 23.	Place, Thomas, and Cornelia Duyree, ...	"	XXVIII. 4
1756. Nov. 30.	Place, Thomas, and Sarah Tillot, ...	"	I. 367
1780. May 19.	Place, Thomas, and Ziprey Weeks, ...	"	XXIX. 62
1760. Nov. 12.	Place, William, and Anna Totten, ...	"	III. 406
1780. Feb. 3.	Place, Zophia, and Peter Walters, ...	"	XXVIII. 207
1780. Nov. 16.	Plant, William, and Sarah Lowey, ...	"	XXX. 111
1782. April 24.	Plantain, John, and Dorothy Forbess, ...	"	XXXV. 135
1781. April 5.	Plas, Hendrick, and Sarah Wickoff, ...	"	XXXI. 94
1769. Sept. 23.	Plass, Kaert, and Collin McDonald, ...	"	XV. 103
1770. Oct. 23.	Platner, Hendrick, and Eve Pest, ...	"	XVI. 226
1783. Aug. 6.	Platt, Benjamin, and Hannah Whooley, ...	"	XXXIX. 112
1773. May 22.	Platt, Charles, and Caroline Adriaanse, ...	"	XX. 121
1781. Oct. 17.	Platt, Christopher, and Frances Mount, ...	"	XXXIII. 105
1774. Jan. 5.	Platt, Dorothy, and Jesse Brush, ...	"	XXII. 93
1757. Nov. 23.	Platt, Eliphilet, and Elizabeth Scudder, ...	"	I. 712
1782. Oct. 3.	Platt, Elizabeth, and Benjamin Goold, ...	"	XXXVII. 26
1772. Nov. 2.	Platt, Elizabeth, and Daniel Phenix, ...	"	XIX. 97
1763. June 3.	Platt, Elizabeth, and James Rogers, ...	"	VII. 212
1684. Jan. 7.	Platt, Elizabeth, and Samuel Griffin, ...	C. M.,	XXXIII. 75
1753. June 12.	Platt, Epenetus, and Catherine Lawrence, ..	M. B.,	I. 58
1780. Oct. 14.	Platt, Hanah, and Charles Whitehead, ...	"	XXX. 65
1768. May 30.	Platt, Hannah, and Albert Adriance, ...	"	XIII. 119
1736. Aug. 2.	Platt, Isaac, and Abigall Baile, ...	"	I. 2
1762. April 27.	Platt, Isaac, Jr., and Mary Smith, ...	"	VI. 133
1761. April 7.	Platt, Israel, and Abigail Scudder, ...	"	IV. 138
1769. Aug. 29.	Platt, Jeremiah, and Mary Ann Vanderspiegle, ...	"	XV. 33
1762. Mar. 16.	Platt, Jesse, and Dorothy Baldwin, ...	"	VI. 74

Date.		Names.	Record.	Vol.	Page.
1775. June	29.	Platt, Mary, and John Roney,............	M. B.,	XXIII.	82
1769. June	24.	Platt, Mary, and John Tallman,...........	"	XIV.	129
1736. Aug.	31.	Platt, Mary, and Josiah Wheeler, ...	"	I.	2
1775. Dec.	30.	Platt, Mary, and Stephen Cornwall,.......	"	XXIII.	237
1776. Feb.	8.	Platt, Mary, and Timothy Concklin,.......	"	XXIII.	266
1738. Dec.	14.	Platt, Mary, and Timothy Tredwell,.......	"	I.	12
1766. Nov.	10.	Platt, Nathaniel, and Phebe Smith,........	"	X.	160
1766. Nov.	5.	Platt, Phebe, and Daniel Wiggins, ...	"	X.	153
1763. June	27.	Platt, Phebe, and Samuel Broome, ...	"	VII.	246
1766. June	10.	Platt, Philip Smith, and Elizabeth Mott,....	"	X.	12
1772. May	2.	Platt, Sarah, and Robert Ogden, ...	"	XVIII.	98
1773. Oct.	14.	Platt, Sarah, and Stephen Thorne, Jr.,.....	"	XXI.	141
1780. Nov.	23.	Platt, Temme, and Morris Homan, ...	"	XXX.	122
1761. Jan.	21.	Platt, Uriah, and Sarah Tredwell, ...	"	IV.	24
1762. April	8.	Platt, Vashty, and Israel Wood, ...	"	VI.	94
1772. Aug.	19.	Platt, Zebulon, and Phebe Bennett, ...	"	XIX.	26
1762. Oct.	14.	Platt, Zephaniah, and Mellisent Roe, ...	"	VI.	364
1757. April	27.	Platt, Zephaniah, Jr., and Mary Davis,.....	"	I.	516
1761. Nov.	23.	Platt, Zephaniah, Jr., and Mary Van Wyck,	"	V.	243
1765. Oct.	10.	Play, Hannah, and Thomas North, ...	"	IX.	294
1758. May	3.	Pleace, Robert, and Magdelin Crutchley,...	"	I.	892
1766. Oct.	29.	Pleas, Maurice, and Jerusha Jackson,......	"	X.	145
1771. Oct.	19.	Plenderbath, John, and Jennet Smith, ...	"	XVII.	215
1758. Oct.	7.	Plowman, Dorothy, and Absalom Beebe,...	"	II.	42
1778. May	19.	Plowman, Mary, and John Blair, ...	"	XXV.	88
1759. May	16.	Plum, Justus, and Margaret Summons,.....	"	II.	287
1761. Jan.	28.	Plumb, Jemima, and Marmeduke Palmer, ..	"	IV.	34
1780. April	11.	Plumb, Samuel, and Mary Clayton,........	"	XXIX.	16
1760. Jan.	8.	Plumbe, Samuel, and Jane Wilson,........	"	II.	572
1761. Aug.	28.	Plume, Mary, and James O'Briern,........	"	V.	62
1757. Jan.	6.	Plumstead, Dorothy, and Charles Wheeler, .	"	I.	408
1765. Feb.	8.	Plumsted, Margaret, and Abraham Wheeler,	"	IX.	49
1758. Nov.	4.	Plunket, Mary, and William Richardson, ...	"	II.	79
1761. Dec.	10.	Poilion, Mary, and Peter Rezeau,..........	"	V.	271
1775. June	21.	Poillon, Elizabeth, and William Lake,......	"	XXIII.	72
1763. Oct.	31.	Poillon, Hellitje, and Jeremiah Stillwell,....	"	VII.	417
1780. Mar.	30.	Poillon, James, and Sarah Conner,.........	'	XXIX.	9
1781. Feb.	23.	Poillon, Judith, and John Mersereau, ...	"	XXXI.	54
1763. Dec.	23.	Poillon, Judith, and Mark Dusosway,......	"	VII.	520
1770. June	11.	Poilon, Catharine, and John Bedell, Jr.,....	"	XVI.	107
1778. Nov.	17.	Poilon, Catherine, and Joseph Precket, ...	"	XXVI.	89
1767. Nov.	20.	Poilyon, Ann, and Stephen Cole,..........	"	XII.	90
1780. April	17.	Polhamos, Mary, and John Everitt,........	"	XXIX.	26
1768. Nov.	28.	Polhanus, Ealor, and Sarah Carpenter,.....	"	XIII.	247
1772. Nov.	20.	Polhelmus, Elizabeth, and Daniel Rapelye, .	"	XIX.	121

DATE.		NAMES.	RECORD.	VOL.	PAGE.
1770. July	2.	Polhemus, Abraham, and Cretia Titus, ...	M. B.,	XVI.	132
1771. Mar.	30.	Polhemus, Abraham, and Hannah Freese, ..	"	XVII.	46
1773. Nov.	27.	Polhemus, Abraham, and Letitia Rapelye, ..	"	XXII.	50
1760. Mar.	12.	Polhemus, Abraham, and Maria Monfor, ...	"	III.	74
1762. July	6.	Polhemus, Abraham, and Mary Hardenbergh,	"	VI.	228
1769. Nov.	10.	Polhemus, Aurt, and Effie Martine, ...	"	XV.	87
1783. Mar.	3.	Polhemus, Charity, and Jacob Polhemus, ...	"	XXXVIII.	60
1763. Feb.	10.	Polhemus, Daniel, and Ann Golding, ...	"	VII.	58
1759. Jan.	10.	Polhemus, Elizabeth (Catherine), and William Barre, ...	"	II.	149
1760. May	29.	Polhemus, Elliner, and John Carns, ...	"	III.	167
1760. Dec.	3.	Polhemus, George, and Elizabeth Titus, ...	"	III.	452
1766. Dec.	6.	Polhemus, Gitty, and Paul Vandervoort, ...	"	X.	194
1783. Mar.	3.	Polhemus, Jacob, and Charity Polhemus, ..	"	XXXVIII.	60
1769. Feb.	11.	Polhemus, Johannis, and Mary Vanlew, ...	"	XIV.	31
1770. Dec.	7.	Polhemus, John, and Catherine Vanderhover, ...	"	XVI.	290
1762. Mar.	22.	Polhemus, John, and Mary Van Wyck, ...	"	VI.	82
1783. June	20.	Polhemus, Letitia, and Thomas Stagg, ...	"	XXXIX.	64
1771. Oct.	25.	Polhemus, Sarah, and Peter Sneyder, ...	"	XVII.	222
1762. April	14.	Polhemus, Sarah, and Rodolves Swartwout, ...	"	VI.	106
1763. Oct.	7.	Polhemus, Tunis, and Helena Betts, ...	"	VII.	379
1738. Oct.	3.	Polimius, Jacob, and Rebecca Snedega, ...	"	I.	11
1777. May	23.	Pollard, Benjamin, and Hannah Johnson, ...	"	XXIV.	92
1777. June	25.	Pollard, Mary, and William Hyde, ...	"	XXIV.	108
1759. Mar.	15.	Polluke, Catharine, and Adrian Hagaman, ..	"	II.	216
1783. April	7.	Pontine, Elizabeth, and Martin Taylor Ambos, ...	"	XXXI.	97
1773. Jan.	29.	Pooke, Catherine, and Thomas Kautzman, ..	"	XX.	28
1762. June	21.	Pool, Agnes, and Daniel Forbus, ...	'	VI.	201
1760. Mar.	8.	Pool, Catherine, and Hugh Mulligen, ...	"	III.	70
1778. Feb.	27.	Pool, Elizabeth, and Hector McKenzie, ...	"	I.	830
1760. Oct.	1.	Pool, Margaret, and Nicholas De Riemer, ...	"	III.	339
1760. July	29.	Pool, Mary, and Henry Joralemon, ...	"	III.	232
1766. Sept.	8.	Poole, Solomon, and Lettitia Jackson, ...	"	X.	92
1736. Dec.	23.	Poole, Thomas, and Elizabeth Blank, ...	"	I.	5
1762. June	8.	Pooley, Thomas, and Magdalen Vanderbergh,	"	VI.	184
1759. Jan.	19.	Pope, Elizabeth, and William Creed, ...	"	II.	162
1779. April	2.	Poppelsdorff, Ann, and John Parker, ...	"	XXVII.	91
1761. Sept.	25.	Poppelsdorff, Catharine, and Robert Manley,	"	V.	98
1758. Jan.	20.	Poppelsdorff, Wilhelmus, and Elizabeth Walter, ...	"	I.	793
1763. Jan.	20.	Poppelsdorff, William, Jr., and Apphia Ten Eyck, ...	"	VII.	24

Date.	Names.	Record.	Vol.	Page.
1767. Dec. 12.	Poppelsdorph, Effie, and George Janeway,..	M. B.,	xii.	113
1774. Jan. 14.	Poppledorff, Elizabeth, and Richard Jenkins,	"	xxii.	103
1760. Mar. 6.	Poppledurff, Eve, and Nathan Baker,......	"	iii.	64
1762. Sept. 29.	Porry, Ann, and Edward Freeman, ...	"	vi.	339
1779. Nov. 12.	Porter, Elizabeth, and Patrick Bready,.....	"	xxviii.	138
1781. July 17.	Porter, Lucy, and Thomas Commings,.....	"	xxxii.	107
1761. Nov. 9.	Porter, Thomas, and Sophia Nixom,.......	"	v.	198
1765. Oct. 28.	Porter, Thomas, and Mary Winfield,.......	"	ix.	326
1761. July 7.	Post, Abraham, and Rebecca Grace,.......	"	iv.	288
1768. Feb. 1.	Post, Anthony, and Peternellitje Brower, ..	"	xiii.	25
1783. Oct. 22.	Post, Catharine, and Peter Ritter,........	"	xl.	88
1764. April 7.	Post, Cornelia, and Stephen Dudly,........	"	viii.	141
1772. Oct. 15.	Post, David, and Lydia Husk, ...	"	xix.	71
1782. June 27.	Post, Dennis, and Susannah Ackley,.......	"	xxxvi.	64
1737. Sept. 20.	Post, Elizabeth, and Peter Fishee,........	"	i.	7
1759. July 14.	Post, Elizabeth, and Thomas Cregier,......	"	ii.	355
1779. April 24.	Post, Garritye, and Garrit Wauters,.......	"	xxvii.	118
1768. Jan. 7.	Post, Hannah, and John Betty,...........	"	xiv.	6
1766. July 26.	Post, Hendrick, and Phebe Reed,.........	"	x.	63
1766. Oct. 20.	Post, Isaac, and Mary Lawrence,..........	"	x.	131
1753. May 17.	Post, Isaac, and Rachel Ecker,...........	"	i.	32
1755. Aug. 16.	Post, Jane, and John De Lameter, ...	"	i.	148
1765. Aug. 8.	Post, John, and Deborah Smith, ...	"	ix.	233
173⅚. Mar. 10.	Post, Joseph, and Mary Smith, ...	"	i.	1
1763. April 6.	Post, Jotham, and Winifred Wright,.......	"	vii.	114
1763. Jan. 17.	Post, Lenah, and John Davis, ...	"	vii.	17
1777. Sept. 4.	Post, Lydia, and Joseph Haight,..........	"	xxiv.	142
1763. Mar. 24.	Post, Margaret, and John Cregier, ...	"	vii.	105
1775. April 15.	Post, Martha, and William Salt, ...	"	xxiii.	11
1758. Sept. 21.	Post, Mary, and Christian Garbrantz,......	"	ii.	28
1762. June 1.	Post, Mary, and Gilbert Seaman,..........	"	vi.	178
1761. June 6.	Post, Mary, and Richard Read,...........	"	iv.	229
1773. Dec. 9.	Post, Peter, and Dorothy Warner, ...	"	xxii.	69
1760. Nov. 14.	Post, Peter, and Elizabeth Gerbrantz,......	"	iii.	415
1782. June 21.	Post, Peter, and Mary Vannamer,.........	"	xxxvi.	59
1757. Aug. 31.	Post, Richard, and Hannah Bedle, ...	"	i.	627
1781. Feb. 20.	Post, Sarah, and Henry Rutherford,.......	"	xxxi.	52
1781. May 26.	Post, Sarah, and Isaac Mebie, ...	"	xxxii.	56
1779. Mar. 30.	Post, Stephen, and Hannah Everitt,.......	"	xxvii.	84
1775. May 26.	Post, Wilhelmus, and Hester Bradburn,....	"	xxiii.	46
1767. April 18.	Post, William, and Jerusha Smith, ...	"	xi.	63
1756. Aug. 3.	Poste, Jacob, and Rachael Pinkney,.......	"	i.	267
1760. Dec. 15.	Postle, Paul, and Ann Hindmore,.........	"	iii.	477
1781. Sept. 22.	Postlethwaite, James, and Jane Shepherd,..	"	xxxiii.	77
1737. Aug. 11.	Postley, Mary, and John Wiley, ...	"	i.	7

DATE.	NAMES.	RECORD.	VOL.	PAGE.
1769. Sept. 27.	Potter, David, and Doborah Carter, ...	M. B.,	XV.	46
1756. Nov. 12.	Potter, Mary, and John Smith, ...	"	I.	352
1779. June 23.	Potter, Priscilla, and John Funck, ...	"	XXVIII.	3
1757. July 28.	Potter, Sarah, and Jonathan Holmes, ...	"	I.	606
1775. Nov. 17.	Potter, Sarah, and William Rodgers, ...	"	XXIII.	214
1762. Sept. 17.	Pottman, Margaret, and Jacob Snook, ...	"	VI.	321
1779. Sept. 26.	Potts, Elisabeth, and Garrit Boskark, ...	"	XXVIII.	84
1777. Mar. 18.	Potts, Sarah, and Matthew Fox, ...	"	XXIV.	46
1782. July 19.	Potts, Thomas, and Rebecca Harrison, ...	"	XXXVI.	88
1737: Oct. 10.	Poullon, Elizabeth, and Daniel Parangue, ..	"	I.	7
1737. May 25.	Poust, Jahendrick, and Rebecca Noghill,...	"	I.	6
1777. Jan. 21.	Povey, George, and Catherine Hall, ...	"	XXIV.	16
1738. May 20.	Powel, Abigael, and Samuel Pearce, ...	"	I.	9
1767. July 30.	Powel, Nathaniel, and Ann Sutton, ...	"	XII.	3a
1780. April 13.	Powel, Silas, and Ann Allen, ...	"	XXIX.	22
1773. Nov. 5.	Powell, Amos, and Jemima Willets, ...	"	XXII.	14
1767. Feb. 14.	Powell, Amos, and Jerusha Allen, ...	"	XI.	26
1761. June 20.	Powell, Edmund, and Mery Rowland, ...	"	IV.	251
1766. July 21.	Powell, Elisha, and Rachel Ham, ...	"	X.	58
1779. Mar. 31.	Powell, Elizabeth, and Benjamin Carman,..	"	XXVII.	87
1761. Feb. 19.	Powell, Elizabeth, and John Etherington, ..	"	IV.	70
1768. Jan. 26.	Powell, Ellenor, and Pierce Donovan, ...	"	XIII.	18
1762. Dec. 10.	Powell, Henry, and Mary Keen, ...	"	VI.	474
1759. Oct. 22.	Powell, James, and Anne Bruce, ...	"	II.	468
1764. Feb. 17.	Powell, James, and Eleanor McKenny, ...	"	VIII.	63
1760. April 26.	Powell, Joseph, and Amey Stagg, ...	"	III.	128
1757. Dec. 2.	Powell, Joseph, and Deborah Scott, ...	"	I.	723
1779. July 28.	Powell, Jonah, and Jane Ryder, ...	"	XXVIII.	33
1765. Aug. 3.	Powell, Mary, and John Cornelus, ...	"	IX.	230
1781. May 30.	Powell, Richard, and Jemime Pratt, ...	"	XXXII.	63
1778. Feb. 5.	Powell, Ruth, and Robert Pettet, ...	"	XXV.	16
1772. Aug. 10.	Powell, Sarah, and Silas Whitson, ...	"	XIX.	18
1758. Oct. 17.	Powell, Solmon, and Jerusha Hilton, ...	"	II.	58
1781. Dec. 2.	Powell, Thomas, and Martha Smith, ...	"	XXXIV.	68
1755. Oct. 28.	Powell, Thomas, and Sarah Sands, ...	"	I.	200
1769. Nov. 25.	Powell, Thomas Warburton, and Elizabeth McEuen, ...	"	XV.	106
1779. June 16.	Powell, Willets, and Catherine Simmons,...	"	XXVII.	165
1781. Nov. 14.	Powell, Willets, and Ruth Whiston, ...	"	XXXIV.	31
1773. Nov. 19.	Powell, Zebulun, and Anna Willets, ...	"	XXII.	34
1764. May 30.	Power, Alithea, and John Murray, ...	"	VIII.	201
1770. June 16.	Power, Christina, and Andries Bartell, ...	•	XVI.	117
1765. June 21.	Power, George, and Anne Guest, ...	"	IX.	180
1763. Feb. 16.	Power, James, and Isabel Brown,.	"	VII.	65
1761. Mar. 18.	Power, Margaret, and Daniel Campbell, ...	"	IV.	107

DATE.	NAMES.	RECORD.	VOL.	PAGE.
1758. Oct. 24.	Power, Mary, and Francis Lewis,.........	M. B.,	II.	65
1759. Sept. 17.	Power, Michael, and Mary McGlocline,....	"	II.	426
1761. Nov. 12.	Power, Thomas, and Mary Harris, ...	"	V.	213
1775. June 16.	Power, William, and Rhoda Dean, ...	"	XXIII.	66
1760. Nov. 24.	Powers, Ann, and William Drian,.........	"	III.	437
1771. Oct. 15.	Powers, Catharine, and Jacob Guero,......	"	XVII.	209
1781. June 25.	Powers, James, and Mary Moore,.........	"	XXXII.	98
1781. Nov. 10.	Powers, Mary, and Richard Parsell,.......	"	XXXIV.	26
1781. May 16.	Powers, William, and Catharine Ebert, ...	"	XXXII.	49
1679. Nov. 22.	Powle, Anne, and Daniel Bidle,...........	G. E.,	XXXII.	63
1760. June 4.	Poyer, Sarah, and Aaron Van Norstrandt,..	M. B.,	III.	176
1758. Dec. 7.	Poyer, Thomas, and Margaret Hicks, ...	"	II.	120
1768. April 25.	Poyllon, Margaret, and Peter Poyllon,.....	"	XIII.	86
1768. April 25.	Poyllon, Peter, and Margaret Poyllon,.....	"	XIII.	86
1772. July 10.	Poyneer, David, and Margaret Birdell,.....	"	XVIII.	162
1772. Dec. 23.	Pozer, Jacob, and Sarah Howard,.........	"	XIX.	163
1757. May 14.	Praal, Hendrickje, and Volkert Buys,......	"	I.	532
1768. May 11.	Prall, Abraham, and Mary Stillwell,.......	"	XIII.	98
1779. June 10.	Prall, Benjamin, and Margaret Simonson,..	"	XXVII.	162
1782. April 29.	Prall, Peter, and Elizabeth Ridgway, ...	"	XXXV.	142
1767. Nov. 17.	Prall, Peter, and Mary Van Pelt, ...	"	XII.	87
1757. Oct. 7.	Praner, Joseph, and Maritje Borhight, ...	"	I.	659
1736. April 5.	Prat, Ann, and William Hawks, ...	"	I.	1
1773. Aug. 31.	Prat, Silas, and Anna Bergaw, ...	"	XXI.	91
1773. Nov. 11.	Pratt, Jacob, and Mary Mott, ...	"	XXII.	21
1781. May 30.	Pratt, Jemime, and Richard Powell,.......	"	XXXII.	63
1779. May 11.	Pratt, John, and Mary Jackson, ...	"	XXVII.	133
1756. Oct. 29.	Prawn, Mary, and John Mercereau, ...	"	I.	336
1779. Jan. 22.	Pray, Isaac, and Elizabeth Woglam, ...	"	XXVII.	25
1778. Nov. 17.	Precket, Joseph, and Catherine Poilon, ...	"	XXVI.	89
1778. Sept. 11.	Prendergast, John, and Mary Simpson,....	"	XXVI.	26
1763. Dec. 19.	Preslow, Daniel, and Millesant Smith, ...	"	VII.	512
1738. Dec. 14.	Pressing, Judah, and Nicholas Valet, ...	"	I.	12
1760. Aug. 7.	Prest, Aletta, and Uzail Shearman,........	"	III.	238
1760. Feb. 2.	Prest, John, and Latitia Man, ...	"	III.	15
1757. July 19.	Prest, Richard, and Lena Van Brunt,......	"	I.	593
1762. Oct. 29.	Preston, Achelles, and Abigail Webb,......	"	VI.	395
1738. July 11.	Preston, John, and Elizabeth Smith,.......	"	I.	10
1762. June 30.	Preston, William, and Susannah Forrester,.	"	VI.	219
1736. Jan. 14.	Prevoost, Elizabeth, and Cornelius Vonck,..	"	I.	5
1685. May 26.	Price, Ann, and John Henry, ...	C. M.,	XXXIII.	130
1736. Feb. 23.	Price, John, and Mary Cross,.............	M. B.,	I.	5
1782. Feb. 23.	Price, John, and Rachel Brownjohn, ...	"	XXXV.	60
1763. July 20.	Price, Margaret, and James Moran,........	"	VII.	276
1765. Oct. 17.	Price, Mary, and Allan McDougall,........	"	IX.	305

DATE.	NAMES.	RECORD.	VOL.	PAGE.
1761. Dec. 11.	Price, Mary, and Luke Thomas,............	M. B.,	v.	274
1779. Jan. 29.	Price, Michael, and Helena Cornwell,......	"	XXVII.	31
1761. Sept. 23.	Price, Thomas, and Grace Tempie,........	"	v.	94
1772. Jan. 7.	Price, Thomas, and Sarah Nixon, ...	"	XX.	4
1777. Mar. 21.	Prills, Elizabeth, and Gottfried Leydebak,..	"	XXIV.	49
1782. Nov. 18.	Prim, John, and Hannah Nicolls,..........	"	XXXVII.	88
1753. Aug. 3.	Prime, Mary, and Israel Wood,...........	"	I.	83
1760. May 22.	Prince, Deborah, and John Mitchill, ...	"	III.	161
1779. Oct. 29.	Prince, Frances, and Joseph Clement, ...	"	XXVIII.	123
1762. June 19.	Prince, James, and Mary Saunders, ...	"	VI.	196
1778. May 12.	Prince, Robert, and Hanah Forman,.......	"	XXV.	80
1777. Aug. 8.	Prince, Sarah, and Charles McNeile,.......	"	XXIV.	129
1779. Mar. 24.	Prindle, Peter, and Mary Glean,..........	"	XXVII.	75
1783. Aug. 30.	Pringel, Alexander, and Sarah Evans, ...	"	XL.	17
1765. June 5.	Pringle, John, and Sarah Hickby,.........	"	IX.	156
1782. Nov. 11.	Prior, Casparus, and Ann Van Wagenen,...	"	XXXVII.	79
1783. Sept. 2.	Prior, James, and Theodocia Darby,.......	"	XL.	19
1764. Aug. 18.	Pritchet, Joseph, and Sarah Bowman, ...	"	VIII.	287
1783. Jan. 15.	Probasco, Abraham, and Freelove Craft,....	"	XXXVIII.	17
1783. Nov. 17.	Probasco, Ann, and John Van Cott,.......	"	XL.	120
1765. April 24.	Probasco, Gerrit, and Mayaka Groenendyck,	"	IX.	106
1775. May 19.	Probasco, Sarah, and Jacob Kashow, ...	"	XXIII.	39
1781. Feb. 27.	Proctor, Nathaniel, and Sarah Chichester, ..	"	XXXI.	58
1760. Dec. 18.	Proctor, William, and Eapheme Henderson,	"	III.	482
1779. Feb. 6.	Proffit, Ann, and John Lomax, ...	"	XXVII.	37
1757. Mar. 1.	Prosher, Johana, and Abner Browne,......	"	I.	453
1762. Mar. 18.	Prosser, Charles, Jr., and Mary Crow, ...	"	VI.	77
1776. Feb. 16.	Prossor, Philip, and Elener Conner,........	"	XXIII.	269
1775. July 28.	Provoost, Abraham, and Annatie Staats,...	"	XXIII.	108
1761. April 29.	Provoost, Annake, and Dirck Lefferts,.....	"	IV.	173
1764. Mar. 31.	Provoost, Burger, and Elizabeth Bates, ...	"	VIII.	128
1737. Aug. 23.	Provoost, Catherine, and Garret Brested,...	"	I.	7
1761. July 28.	Provoost, Christiana, and Stephen Teppet,..	"	v.	11
1736. July 23.	Provoost, Cornelia, and Peregrine Vanenburgh, ...…	"	I.	2
1778. June 25.	Provoost, Joana, and Samuel Kelley,......	"	XXV.	112
1777. Aug. 12.	Provoost, Lucy, and Edward Lambert, ...	"	XXIV.	131
1763. July 20.	Provoost, Nathaniel, and Rebecca Hollet, ..	"	VII.	273
1758. May 30.	Provoost, William, and Elizabeth Van Wyck,	"	I.	919
1769. April 20.	Provost, Christena, and Johannes Arundies,	"	XIV.	80
1780. Oct. 21.	Provost, Elizabeth, and George Cruger,....	"	XXX.	75
1778. Aug. 27.	Prout, Timothy, and Ann Wright, ...	"	XXVI.	15
1770. April 6.	Prull, Peter, and Elizabeth Larzelere,......	"	XVI.	52
1762. Nov. 4.	Pruyn, Casparus, and Catharine Groesbeck,.	"	VI.	411
1756. Sept. 25.	Pruyn, Hendrick, and Ester Hiklarie, ...	"	I.	305

DATE.	NAMES.	RECORD.	VOL.	PAGE.
1773. Dec. 24.	Pruyn, Jacob, and Hendrickje Van Buren,..	M. B.,	XXII.	87
1769. May 4.	Pruyn, Johannes, and Geertje Ten Eyck, ..	"	XIV.	92
1775. May 16.	Pruyn, Samuel, and Eleanor Horsford, ...	"	XXIII.	35
1755. Nov. 27.	Pruyn, Samuel, and Nieltie Ten Eyck,.....	"	I.	219
1767. Oct. 27.	Pruyne, John, and Catherine Vanderpool,..	"	XII.	70
1776. Feb. 29.	Pruyne, Mary, and Abraham Hallenbeck, ..	"	XXIII.	275
1783. Mar. 21.	Pruyor, Matthew, and Martha Thatford, ...	"	XXXVIII.	71
1761. Mar. 18.	Pryer, Hannah, and Abraham Rickhow, ...	"	IV.	106
1736. Jan. 17.	Pryne, Catherine, and Barnardus Harsin,...	"	I.	5
1780. May 11.	Pryor, Abraham, and Petertie Braat,......	"	XXIX.	53
1766. Aug. 15.	Pryor, Ann, and Jacob Reary,.............	"	X.	75
1767. April 13.	Pryor, Edward, and Jane Vermillyea, ...	"	XI.	60
1782. Sept. 6.	Pryor, James, and Anne Pickles, ...	"	XXXVI.	137
1667. Jan. 31.	Puddington, Sarah, and Nehemiah Smith,..	O. W. L.,	II.	192
1759. Feb. 16.	Pudney, James, and Agnes Fisher, ...	M. B.,	II.	193
1773. Feb. 25.	Pudney, Mary, and John Bloodgood,......	"	XX.	53
1779. Oct. 12.	Pue, Leah, and Nathaniel Britain, ...	"	XXVIII.	110
1778. Aug. 27.	Pugh, Frances, and John Robinson, ...	"	XXVI.	13
1759. Mar. 26.	Pugsley, John, and Mary Hunt, ...	"	II.	224
1779. Aug. 4.	Pugsley, John, and Sarah Kingsland,......	"	XXVIII.	45
1773. Sept. 1.	Pugsley, Mary, and Benjamin Carpenter,..	"	XXI.	95
1781. Sept. 4.	Pugsley, Mercey, and Nicholas Delaplaine,.	"	XXXIII.	58
1776. Jan. 15.	Pugsley, Tolmon, and Sarah Oakley, ...	"	XXIII.	247
1759. Feb. 26.	Pugsly, David, and Hanah Vail,...........	"	II.	203
1768. Jan. 19.	Pugsly, Elizabeth, and Jonas Ansor, ...	"	XIII.	11
1770. Dec. 12.	Pugsly, William, and Elizabeth Barnes, ...	"	XVI.	292
1762. Jan. 14.	Pullen, Stephen, and Mary McCann,.......	"	VI.	14
1780. July 17.	Puller, Richard, and Ann Campbell, ...	"	XXIX.	113
1781. Nov. 12.	Pulliblank, Abraham, and Hannah Brown,..	"	XXXIV.	28
1783. April 19.	Pullion, Margaret, and Alexander Cairns,...	"	XXXVIII.	101
1769. Nov. 3.	Pullion, Mary, and Silas Bedell,...........	"	XV.	76
1773. July 30.	Pulver, William, and Geertry Klum,.......	"	XXI.	55
1759. June 25.	Punt, Catharine, and George Eim, ...	"	II.	339
1765. Sept. 30.	Puntine, William, and Ann Robinson, ...	"	IX.	279
1770. June 16.	Puntine, William, and Mary Denton, ...	"	XVI.	116
1772. June 1.	Puntine, William, and Rachel Messenger, ..	"	XVIII.	128
1763. Sept. 17.	Puntis, Catharine, and George Arthar,.....	"	VII.	339
1669. Jan. 14.	Purchase, Roger, and Katherine Evans,....	C. A.,	II.	450
1764. July 21.	Purcutt, Frances, and Thomas Steele,......	M. B.,	VIII.	265
1783. Sept. 17.	Purdy, Anthony, and Frances Russell,.....	"	XL.	44
1781. April 11.	Purdy, Bathia, and Benjamin Stearns, ...	"	XXXI.	103
1782. Oct. 22.	Purdy, David, and Jane Everitt,..........	"	XXXVII.	59
1780. Aug. 30.	Purdy, David, and Mary Rapelye,.........	"	XXX.	11
1782. Aug. 10.	Purdy, Deborah, and Peter Davidson,......	"	XXXVI.	104
1781. Mar. 26.	Purdy, Gilbert, and Bethia Fisher, ...	"	XXXI.	87

DATE.		NAMES.	RECORD.	VOL.	PAGE.
1760. Aug.	29.	Purdy, Guertry, and Jonathan Horton, ...	M. B.,	III.	273
1779. Jan.	20.	Purdy, Hachaliah, and Temperance Weeks,.	"	XXVII.	20
1773. Feb.	16.	Purdy, Henry, and Tamer Sniffen, ...	"	XX.	44
1781. Dec.	28.	Purdy, John, and Sarah Vanblarkam,......	"	XXXIV.	109
1767. Mar.	19.	Purdy, Joseph, and Aletta Guion, ...	"	XI.	46
1780. July	28.	Purdy, Nehemiah, and Elizabeth Birdsall,..	"	XXIX.	125
1781. Mar.	6.	Purdy, Seth, and Phebe Ketchum, ...	"	XXXI.	65
1757. May	16.	Purdy, Stephen, and Hester Bayley, ...	"	I.	533
1672. May	7.	Pyles, William, and Affyance Gray, ...	G. E.,	IV.	134
1773. Aug.	20.	Pyls, William, and Hannah Hartley,.......	M. B.,	XXI.	81
1761. Nov.	6.	Pyls, William, and Mary Cannon,.........	"	V.	194
1783. June	6.	Pym, Hassel, and Sarah Lance,...........	"	XXXIX.	42
1781. May	29.	Pymm, Hassel, and Sarah Britt,..........	"	XXXII.	60
1756. Sept.	9.	Pyne, Silvanes, and Juda Craft, ...	"	I.	291

Q.

1761. May 27.	Quackenbosch, Alida, and Walter N. Groesbeck, ...	"	IV.	209
1759. April 30.	Quackenbosh, Catharine, and Daniel Hellenbeck, ...	"	II.	262
1767. July 13.	Quackenboss, Catherine, and Peter Van Bueren, ...	"	XI.	133
1768. April 7.	Quackenboss, Cornelia, and John Peter Quackenboss, ...	"	XIII.	65
1763. Aug. 4.	Quackenboss, Elisabeth, and Elias Gisleng, .	"	VII.	290
1769. Sept. 9.	Quackenboss, Hannah, and Jeremiah De Graaff, ...	"	XV.	84
1763. Nov. 9.	Quackenboss, John, and Catharine D'Witt, .	"	VII.	437
1768. April 7.	Quackenboss, John Peter, and Cornelia Quackenboss, ...	"	XIII.	65
1776. Jan. 25.	Quackenboss, Mary, and John D. Goes, ...	"	XXIII.	251
1770. Oct. 17.	Quackenboss, Susannah, and Abram Kool,..	"	XVI.	219
1763. July 9.	Quackenboss, Walter, and Barbary Clute, ..	"	VII.	260
1757. Oct. 27.	Quackenboss, Walter, and Sophia Roorback, ...	"	I.	685
1773. May 26.	Quackenboss, Winchea, and Abraham Mabey, ...	"	XX.	128
1760. Sept. 19.	Quackenbus, Anthony, and Anna Bogaert, .	"	III.	320
1781. July 20.	Quackenbus, Francintje, and Thomas Outwater, ...	"	XXXIII.	10
1758. Nov. 16.	Quackenbus, John Sybrant, and Jannetie Fiele, ...	"	II.	90
1762. Aug. 26.	Quackenbush, Abraham, and Mary Bratt, ..	"	VI.	291

DATE.		NAMES.	RECORD.	VOL.	PAGE.
1763. Feb.	8.	Quackenbush, Benjamin, Jr., and Francintje Ellis, ...	M. B.,	VII.	56
1770. Mar.	2.	Quackenbush, Hannah, and Christian De Marie, ...	"	XVI.	28
1769. Aug.	5.	Quackenbush, Jacobus, and Santie Berkhadds, ...	"	XV.	19
1760. April	19.	Quackenbush, Margaret, and Daniel Devou,.	"	III.	117
1764. Sept.	6.	Quackenbush, Peter, and Anne Erwin,.....	"	VIII.	299
1782. May	2.	Quackenbush, Susannah, and John Allen, ..	"	XXXV.	145
1769. June	23.	Quackinbush, Ann, and Joseph Bauldwin,..	"	XIV.	126
1737. July	22.	Quackinbush, Lia, and William Weynat, ...	"	I.	7
1771. Dec.	2.	Quackingbush, John, and Aladey Oudderceak,	"	XVII.	277
1737. Sept.	24.	Quacumbush, Benjamin, and Margaret Ellis,	"	I.	7
1776. Mar.	21.	Quakenboss, Henry, and Elizabeth Roeseboom, ...	"	XXIII.	287
1766. Dec.	23.	Quary, Alexander, and Ellenor McNeil,....	"	X.	206
1760. Aug.	5.	Quearreau, Ann, and John Johnson,.......	"	III.	235
1738. Oct.	26.	Queman, Elizabeth, and Abraham Vanderpool, ...	"	I.	11
1753. May	9.	Quereau, Frances, and John Jones, ...	"	I.	26
1765. July	8.	Quereau, Jane, and John Mowatt,.........	"	IX.	197
173⁷⁄. Mar.	8.	Quick, Abigal, and John Bogert,..........	"	I.	5
1762. June	15.	Quick, Effie, and John Barrea,.............	"	VI.	193
1771. Dec.	5.	Quick, Elizabeth, and George Huston,......:	"	XVII.	284
173⁴⁄. Mar.	21.	Quick, Jacobus, and Hyltie Clopper,.......	"	I.	5
1759. Mar.	26.	Quick, Jacobus, and Mary Day,...........	"	II.	235
1762. May	17.	Quick, Luke C., and Sarah Van De Water,.	"	VI.	162
1737. May	20.	Quick, Nealta, and John Thurman, ...	"	I.	6
1769. Jan.	21.	Quick, Robert, and Elizabeth Sparks,......	"	XIV.	17
1757. July	4.	Quick, William, and Ann Van Gelder, ...	"	I.	581
1763. Feb.	11.	Quigley, Thomas, and Anne Simerson,.....	"	VII.	59
1759. Oct.	18.	Quill, Thomas, and Mary Sourin,..........	"	II.	464
1757. June	29.	Quimby, Mary, and Basil Barton, ...	"	I.	576
1769. Nov.	3.	Quinby, Phebe, and Reuben Wright, ...	"	XV.	76a
1769. May	12.	Quinn, Nelly, and Jeremiah Bennet,.......	"	XIV.	99
1757. Nov.	7.	Quintin, John, and Catharine Hanion, ...	"	I.	697
1762. May	10.	Quokenboss, Elizabeth, and John Isaac Fort,	"	VI.	152

R.

1759. Dec.	15.	Radliff, John, and Elizabeth Wilkinson,....	"	II.	546
1777. April	4.	Raft, Anne, and James Rich,............,..	"	XXIV.	56
1772. Dec.	23.	Rafter, Thomas, and Rachel Young,.......	"	XIX.	162
1779. Mar.	6.	Rainer, Ann, and Stephen Wilson,........	"	XXVII.	58

DATE.	NAMES.	RECORD.	VOL.	PAGE.
1759. Dec. 12.	Rainer, Rebecca, and Tunus Covert, ...	M. B.,	II.	538
1764. Jan. 11.	Rainor, Elijah, ánd Rebecca Smith, ...	"	VIII.	12
1777. Nov. 5.	Rainsley, Catherine, and Thomas Winepress,	"	XXIV.	174
1764. Jan. 14.	Ralston, William, and Mary Robinson, ...	"	VIII.	15b
1779. Sept. 10.	Ramadge, Elizabeth, and John Freeborn, . . .	"	XXVIII.	72
1782. Jan. 28.	Ramadge, Elizabeth, and Malcom McIntyre,	"	XXXV.	36
1777. Jan. 1.	Ramadge, Smith, and Mary Jones, ...	"	XXIV.	1
1783. Oct. 30.	Ramier, Dorathea, and William Becker, ...	"	XL.	95
1778. Oct. 7.	Ramsay, Frances, and John Irvine, ...	"	XXVI.	48
1737. Nov. 19.	Ramsay, William, and Rebecca Backster, . . .	"	I.	8
1675. June 11.	Ramsden, John, and Hannah Muncy, ...	W. O. P.,	III.	97
1771. Nov. 13.	Ramsen, Elizabeth, and John Williamson, . .	M. B.,	XVII.	254
1758. Jan. 5.	Ramsen, Harmanus, and Freelove Frost, . . .	"	I.	771
1767. Mar. 7.	Ramsen, Lucas, and Abigail North, ...	"	XI.	40
1772. Oct. 17.	Ramsen, Luke, and Judah Titus, ...	"	XIX.	74
1778. June 17.	Ramsen, Mary, and Theunis Bogart, ...	"	XXV.	110
1781. May 8.	Ramsen, Patty, and James Hume, ...	"	XXXII.	35
1778. Feb. 24.	Ramsen, William, and Affy Duryee, ...	"	XXV.	31
1757. Sept. 23.	Ramsey, Ann, and William Morris, ...	"	I.	641
1761. Feb. 14.	Ramsey, David, and Wilet Cleghorne, ...	"	IV.	63
1755. Sept. 13.	Ramsey, Mary, and Thomas Cramsheir, ...	"	I.	176
1761. Sept. 15.	Ramsey, Statia, and John Barnes, ...	"	V.	84
1782. Nov. 28.	Ramsey, Thomas, and Jane Donnaldson, . . .	"	XXXVII.	96
1767. July 20.	Ramson, Anthony, and Jane Burtis, ...	"	XI.	137
1781. June 8.	Ramson, Aress, and Antie Bargen, ...	"	XXXII.	75
1760. Feb. 13.	Ramson, Daniel, and Elizabeth Hamilton, . .	"	III.	34
1778. Jan. 10.	Ramson, Isaac, and Mary Snedeker, ...	"	XXV.	2
1781. May 8.	Ramson, Jacob, and Rebecca Wortman, ...	"	XXXII.	36
1766. July 24.	Ramson, John, and Sarah Amerman, ...	"	X.	61
1779. Sept. 30.	Randall, Ann, and William Dixon, ...	"	XXVIII.	94
1763. June 20.	Randall, John, and Catharine Stump, ...	"	VII.	234
1761. Mar. 25.	Randall, Martin, and Catharine Van De Bogart, ... :	"	IV.	119
1773. May 24.	Randall, Pelig, and Jane Loose, ...	"	XX.	124
1782. Nov. 9.	Randall, Robert, and Sarah Ogden, ...	"	XXXVII.	75
1778. June 17.	Randall, Thomas, and Elizabeth Brown, ...	"	XXV.	106
1781. Nov. 23.	Randall, William, and Ann Kerby, ...	"	XXXIV.	56
1763. Jan. 3.	Randeker, Samuel, and Dorothy Windish, . .	"	VII.	3
1770. July 5.	Randel, Jonathan, and Catherine Myer, ...	"	XVI.	136
1763. Feb. 24.	Randel, William, and Mary Wiley, ...	"	VII.	77
1775. Sept. 8.	Randell, Jane, and James Hicks, ...	"	XXIII.	153
1763. Aug. 5.	Randle, Hannah, and William Haldan, ...	"	VII.	291
1782. April 1.	Randol, Margrot, and John Du Bois, ...	"	XXXV.	105
1772. Sept. 14.	Randolph, David, and Patty Jennye, ...	"	XIX.	47
1768. June 16.	Raner, Daniel, and Elizabeth Baldwin, ...	"	XIII.	130

DATE.		NAMES.	RECORD.	VOL.	PAGE.
1767. July	6.	Raner, William, and Margaret Searring,....	M. B.,	XI.	125
1780. June	3.	Ranken, William, and Wilhelmina Payne,..	"	XXIX.	81
1780. Nov.	4.	Rankin, Arabccca, and Edward Bayan, ...	"	XXX.	91
1779. Sept.	25.	Rankin, Mary, and Neal McMullian,.......	"	XXVIII.	83
1779. Sept.	4.	Rankin, Sarah, and Daniel Wheaton,......	"	XXVIII.	67
1780. Aug.	13.	Rannels, William, and Ann Graham, ...	"	XXXIX.	125
1765. Oct.	11.	Ranoud, John, and Mary Siccore,.........	"	IX.	295
1782. Jan.	24.	Ranshaw, Margeret, and Joshua Jones, ...	"	XXXV.	30
1760. Oct.	15.	Ransom, Peleg, and Susannah Griffin,......	"	III.	366
1737. Nov.	4.	Rapalie, Daniel, and Ruth Fish,...........	"	I.	8
1762. Dec.	16.	Rapalje, Agnes, and Cornelius Turck,......	"	VI.	482
1770. April	18.	Rapalje, Alletta, and Simon Remsen, ...	"	XVI.	63
1761. Jan.	6.	Rapalje, Altie, and Johannis Lott,.........	"	VI.	3
1670. Mar.	30.	Rap ", Catharine, and Johannis Remsen,..	"	XVI.	44
1767. Dec.	3.	Rapalje, Daniel, and Jane Schenck,........	"	XII.	105
1779. July	28.	Rapalje, Daniel, and Sarah Hageman,......	"	XXVIII.	32
1773. April	15.	Rapalje, Jane, and Edward Thorne, ...	"	XX.	92
1770. April	10.	Rapalje, Jeremiah, and Elizabeth Carson,...	"	XVI.	58
1753. Oct.	12.	Rapalje, Joris, and Elizabeth Schenck,.....	"	I.	138
1772. May	7.	Rapalje, Phebe, and Martin Johnson, ...	"	XVIII.	103
1765. Aug.	1.	Rapalje, Sarah, and Charles Debevoeise,....	"	IX.	226
1782. April	22.	Rapalje, Syntje, and Richard Vandcrburgh,.	"	XXXV.	131
1761. Oct.	7.	Rapalye, Abraham, and Jane Lyster, ...	"	V.	130
1783. Aug.	21.	Rapalye, Agness, and Martin Schenck,.....	"	XL.	4
1773. April	8.	Rapalye, Catherine, and Tunis Brinkerhoff,.	"	XX.	90
1760. May	15.	Rape, Barbara, and John Koffman,........	"	III.	152
1778. Oct.	15.	Rapelje, Abel, and Judah Braine, ...	"	XXVI.	62
1761. Jan.	13.	Rapelje, Agness, and Samuel Hollett,......	"	IV.	14
1761. Jan.	29.	Rapelje, Ann Catherine, and Jacobus Riiken,	"	IV.	35
1770. April	19.	Rapelje, Daniel, and Agnes Bergen, ...	"	XVI.	64
1779. May	31.	Rapelje, Elizabeth, and Jacob Kershow,....	"	XXVII.	152
1770. Mar.	5.	Rapelje, Jane, and Edward Goldston Lutwycke, ...	"	XXIV.	40
1781. Dec.	12.	Rapelje, Margaret, and Johannis Ditmars, ..	"	XXXIV.	80
1767. May	7.	Rapelje, Maritie, and Albert Snedeker,......	"	XI.	79
1781. Sept.	22.	Rapelje, Sarah, and George Brinkerhoff,....	"	XXXIII.	74
1757. Mar.	10.	Rapelje, Teunis, and Catharine Stockholm, .	"	I.	462
1757. Jan.	12.	Rapeljea, Idea, and Rick Suydam,.........	"	I.	412
1763. May	27.	Rapeljie, Lambertie, and Jeromus Lott, ...	"	VII.	205
1737. Sept.	22.	Rapellie, Johannes, and Maria Van Dike,...	"	I.	7
1767. Nov.	23.	Rapelye, Abraham, and Seiche Bogart, ...	"	XII.	94
1768. Jan.	13.	Rapelye, Agnes, and Martin Schenck, Jr.,..	"	XIII.	6
1762. Dec.	10.	Rapelye, Anne, and George Be De Vois,...	"	VI.	476
1783. June	13.	Rapelye, Bernard, and Deborah Gidney, ...	"	XXXIX.	57
1772. Nov.	20.	Rapelye, Daniel, and Elizabeth Polhemus, ..	"	XIX.	121

40

DATE.		NAMES.	RECORD.	VOL.	PAGE.
1760. Jan.	3:	Rapelye, Eanquelty, and Andrew Van Brunt,	M. B.,	II.	566
1764. Nov.	9.	Rapelye, George, and Aletie Lent, ...	"	VIII.	398
1783. Sept.	13.	Rapelye, Isaac, and Jane De Be Vois, ...	"	XL.	38
1782. May	21.	Rapelye, Jane, and William Garden, ...	"	XXXVI.	14
1773. Nov.	27.	Rapelye, Letitia, and Abraham Polhemus,..	"	XXII.	50
1780. Aug.	30.	Rapelye, Mary, and David Purdy, ...	"	XXX.	11
1768. April	25.	Rapelyea, Ann, and Jeromus Remsen, ...	"	XIII.	85
1767. May	14.	Rapelyea, Ann, and Nickles Wickoff, ...	"	XI.	87
1782. May	24.	Rapelyea, Lette, and Jacobus Debevoice,...	"	XXXVI.	22
1766. Dec.	21.	Rapelyea, Nelly, and Jeremiah Remsen, ...	"	X.	210
1780. Nov.	15.	Rapleye, Cornelius, and Moriah Riker, ...	"	XXX.	107
1771. Sept.	24.	Rappalje, Jane, and John Durye, Jr., ...	"	XVII.	189
1763. Jan.	7.	Rappalje, Martin, and Elisabeth Lequire, ...	"	VII.	9
1775. Aug.	26.	Rappelje, Jeronimus, and Hyla Burgaw,....	"	XXIII.	138
1760. April	22.	Rappleye, Jane, and Henry Ryker, ...	"	III.	118
1760. Sept.	4.	Rardon, Catharine, and John McDaniel,....	"	III.	281
1770. Nov.	17.	Rass, Elsie, and Barent Christopher, ...	"	XVI.	263
1762. June	2.	Ratcliff, Hillitie, and Adam Barrack, ...	"	VI.	180
1772. July	10.	Ratclift, Peter, and Catazene Trophauga, ...	"	XVIII.	164
1760. Dec.	31.	Rathbun, Thomas, and Mary Waldrom, ...	"	III.	498
1782. Mar.	2.	Ratoon, Mary, and William Crawford,.....	"	XXXV.	69
1762. May	13.	Rauo, Jane, and John Aymar,............	"	VI.	159
1779. Dec.	24.	Ravo, Daniel, and Mary Jones, ...	"	XXVIII.	181
1675. Mar.	21.	Rawles, Mary, and Henry Bowman,.......	W. O. P.,	III.	183
1780. July	28.	Rawley, Mary, and James Dickey, ...	M. B.,	XXIX.	126
1755. Aug.	20.	Ray, Catharine, and Edward Best, ...	"	I.	151
1769. Nov.	27.	Ray, John, and Hannah Williams, ...	"	XV.	108
1763. Mar.	1.	Ray, Robert, and Beletije Dickenson, ...	• "	VII.	85
1781. Mar.	24.	Ray, Robert, and Rachael Hickock, ...	"	XXXI.	84
1783. Feb.	22.	Raymond, James, and Ann Bowers,.......	"	XXXVIII.	50
1759. May	31.	Rayner, Amy, and Sylvanus Rayner,......	"	II.	294
1753. Aug.	28.	Rayner, James, and Mary Serien,.........	"	I.	98
1753. Aug.	7.	Rayner, Joseph, and Hannah Brown,......	"	I.	86
1753. June	4.	Rayner, Samuel, and Elizabeth Higbee,....	"	I.	48
1759. May	31.	Rayner, Sylvanus, and Amy Rayner,......	"	II.	294
1764. Feb.	3.	Raynor, Anne, and Samuel Smith, ...	"	VIII.	48
1760. Sept.	5.	Raynor, Hannah, and Carman Rushmore, ..	"	III.	286
1762. Oct.	7.	Raynor, James, and Sarah Mott,........	"	VI.	351
1775. May	24.	Rea, Hugh, and Margery Knickerbacker,...	"	XXIII.	43
1762. Aug.	28.	Read, Charles, Jr., and Jane Jones,........	"	VI.	297
1760. July	11.	Read, David, and Jane Lovell,............	"	III.	211
1681. July	28.	Read, Elizabeth, and Ralph Cardnall,......	O. W.,	XXXII½.	56
1738. June	23.	Read, Elizabeth, and William Dawson,.....	M. B.,	I.	10
1759. June	13.	Read, George, and Mary Haynes,.........	"	II.	323
1757. Aug.	30.	Read, Isabel, and Alexander Campbell, ...	"	I.	624

DATE.	NAMES.	RECORD.	VOL. PAGE.
1761. June 6.	Read, Richard, and Mary Post, ...	M. B.,	IV. 229
1782. Oct. 7.	Reade, John, and Catharine Barns, ...	"	XXXVII. 32
1770. Nov. 24.	Reade, Næmoe, and Elisha Gallaudet,......	"	XVI. 268
1756. Sept. 14.	Realer, Judith, and John Gosline,.........	"	I. 296
1766. Aug. 15.	Reary, Jacob, and Ann Pryor,............	"	X. 75
1783. May 3.	Reazau, Mary, and John Lawrence, ...	"	XXXVIII. 125
1756. Sept. 28.	Rebstock, Samuel Martin, and Maria Catrina Engelsped,........................	"	I. 310
1762. Oct. 25.	Recoy, Rachel, and Joseph Stevens,.......	"	VI. 384
1769. Oct. 18.	Reddens, Mary, and John Wilson, ...	"	XV. 56
1760. Oct. 7.	Redder, Rachel, and Petrus Jacob Van Woort,	"	III. 352
1774. Mar. 8.	Reden, Henry, and Margaret Marsine,.....	"	XXII. 141
1676. July 27.	Reder, Jeremiah, and Elizabeth Wattells Simpson, ...	W. O. P.,	III. 203
1764. Dec. 31.	Redgrove, Elenor, and James Wilson, ...	M. B.,	VIII. 468
1760. July 9.	Redliffs, Catherine, and Johannes Redliffs,..	"	IH. 207
1760. July 9.	Redliffs, Johannes, and Catherine Redliffs,..	"	III. 207
1670. Sept. 5.	Redman, Mary, and Adam Mott, ...	C. A.,	II. 589
1778. June 6.	Redmond, Francis, and Rachel Lear,.......	M. B.,	XXV. 98
1782. Nov. 18.	Reece, Anthony, and Blanch Domminick, ..	"	XXXVII. 85
1756. Sept. 30.	Reece, Elizabeth, and Peter Duffy,........	"	I. 312
1764. Oct. 24.	Reed, Elenor, and Charles Campbell, ...	"	VIII. 374
1782. Mar. 11.	Reed, Elizabeth, and Andrew Patchen, ...	"	XXXV. 84
1768. Dec. 31.	Reed, Elizabeth, and Peter Lefurge, ...	"	XIII. 277
1767. May 26.	Reed, Elizabeth, and Timothy Humphrevil,.	"	XI. 97
1757. Mar. 22.	Reed, James, and Claetle Ryckman, ...	"	I. 478
1761. Sept. 23.	Reed, James, and Elisabeth Brown,,......	"	V. 95
1783. Aug. 4.	Reed, James, and Wright Springsteen,.....	"	XXXIX. 111
1768. May 18.	Reed, Jane, and Henry Spingler, ...	"	XIII. 105
1761. Dec. 10.	Reed, Patience, and Thomas Hinksman, ...	"	V. 272
1766. July 26.	Reed, Phebe, and Hendrick Post,.........	"	X. 63
1737. Oct. 20.	Reed, Samuel, and Susannah Sullier, ...	"	I. 7
1765. May 8.	Reemer, Mary, and Jan Jonas,............	"	IX. 123
1760. April 19.	Reese, Henry, and Elizabeth Growsekop, ..	"	III. 116
1763. Nov. 4.	Reeve, Abigail, and Peter Reeve, ...	"	VII. 428
1768. Aug. 20.	Reeve, Mehetable, and Robert Hempsted,..	"	XIII. 176
1763. Nov. 4.	Reeve, Peter, and Abigail Reeve, ...	"	VII. 428
1775. April 11.	Reeves, John, and Rachel Dawson,........	"	XXIII. 6
1763. Nov. 21.	Reeves, Simon, and Phebe Adams,........	"	VII. 460
1781. Oct. 24.	Reeves, Stephen, and Phebe McCullem,....	"	XXXIV. 4
1767. April 6.	Regan, Ellenor, and William Tribe,........	"	XI. 57
1772. July 8.	Regan, Jeremiah, and Mary Hunt, ...	"	XVIII. 160
1762. Nov. 30.	Regan, Mary, and Richard Allen, ...	"	VI. 465
1766. July 7.	Regar, Lenah, and Christopher Hanneon,...	"	X. 43
1780. May 16.	Regen, Mary, and William Gilbertson,.....	"	XXIX. 56

DATE.	NAMES.	RECORD.	VOL.	PAGE.
1780. Dec. 22.	Reid, Collen, and Mary McClaren, ...	M. B.,	xxx.	164
1778. Mar. 17.	Reid, James, and Ann Stevenson, ...	"	xxv.	45
1782. Feb. 12.	Reid, John, and Mary Bartow, ...	"	xxxv.	50
1777. May 21.	Reid, John, and Mary Catrine, ...	"	xxiv.	91
1780. Dec. 7.	Reid, Margret, and Peter Trotter, ...	"	xxx.	142
1782. Sept. 9.	Reid, Mary, and William Bunn, ...	"	xxxvi.	140
1763. July 6.	Reigler, Mary, and John Hess, ...	"	vii.	259
1782. Dec. 18.	Reilly, Terence, and Sarah Wright, ...	"	xxxvii.	124
1773. Mar. 23.	Reilly, Terence, and Susannah Watts, ...	"	xx.	69
1777. July 8.	Reily, Sarah, and William Heath, ...	"	xxiv.	117
1738. Aug. 30.	Reinsen, Jane, and John Hegeman, ...	"	i.	10
1769. May 26.	Reker, Elizabeth, and Hendrick Flock, ...	"	xiv.	108
1771. Nov. 22.	Relay, Henry, and Adriana Callow, ...	"	xvii.	265
1779. Dec. 6.	Reley, Ellena, and Richard Whiston Yorke,.	"	xxviii.	162
1756. Nov. 18.	Remeck, Deborah, and John Berry, ...	"	i.	358
1780. May 2.	Remine, Hannah, and John Buyce, ...	"	xxix.	42
1763. Nov. 28.	Remmis, Ann Mary, and Gottfried Schwahn,.	"	vii.	477
1760. Sept. 27.	Remsem, Catherine, and Christopher Cod-wise, ...	"	iii.	335
1761. Sept. 8.	Remsem, Haltje, and John Remsem, ...	"	v.	71
1761. Sept. 8.	Remsem, John, and Haltje Remsem, ...	"	v.	71
1778. Feb. 25.	Remsen, Adriantie, and Jacob Boerum, ...	"	xxv.	33
1764. Aug. 27.	Remsen, Ann, and Barnt Johnson, ...	"	viii.	296
1756. Nov. 30.	Remsen, Anne, and Thomas Robeson, ...	"	i.	368
1770. Aug. 14.	Remsen, Ariantje, and Johannes De Beavois,	"	xvi.	159
1763. May 13.	Remsen, Aultje, and Christopher Stymest,..	"	vii.	185
1782. May 4.	Remsen, Catharine, and John Hutchins, ...	"	xxxv.	150
1755. Nov. 17.	Remsen, Charity, and Christofel Remsen,...	"	i.	211
1763. Oct. 24.	Remsen, Charity, and Jacob Bennet, ...	"	vii.	401
1767. Jan. 3.	Remsen, Charity, and Joseph Hegeman, ...	"	xi.	2
1755. Nov. 17.	Remsen, Christofel, and Charity Remsen,...	"	i.	211
1765. Jan. 22.	Remsen, Christopher, and Margaret Harden-bergh, ...	"	ix.	29
1775. Aug. 31.	Remsen, Derick, Jr., and Elizabeth Duryea,.	"	xxiii.	143
1772. Dec. 17.	Remsen, Dorothy, and Abraham Brincker-hoff, ...	"	xix.	157
1781. June 16.	Remsen, Dorothy, and John Remsen, ...	"	xxxii.	88
1764. Oct. 3.	Remsen, Elizabeth, and John Smith, ...	"	viii.	332
1757. Dec. 6.	Remsen, Famitje, and Barent Lefferts, ...	"	i.	726
1781. Oct. 27.	Remsen, George, and Hannah Middleton, ..	"	xxxiv.	8
1753. Aug. 28.	Remsen, Hendricka, and Johannes Lott, ...	"	i.	97
1761. Dec. 28.	Remsen, Henry, Jr., and Cornelia Dickenson,	"	v.	304
1768. Dec. 7.	Remsen, Hilitje, and Peter Wyckoff, ...	"	xiii.	255
1782. June 17.	Remsen, Jacob, and Helena Cook, ...	"	xxxvi.	55
1777. Jan. 15.	Remsen, Jane, and Abraham Snedeker, ...	"	xxiv.	13

DATE.		NAMES.	RECORD.	VOL. PAGE.
1771. Jan.	4.	Remsen, Jane, and Garret Hardenbergh, ...	M. B.,	XVII. 1
1781. June	19.	Remsen, Jane, and William Sailer, ...	"	XXXII. 91
1760. Dec.	31.	Remsen, Jeremiah, and Nelly Rapelyea,....	"	X. 210
1783. April	18.	Remsen, Jeremiah, and Sithje Couwenhoven,	"	XXXVIII. 88
1768. April	25.	Remsen, Jeromus, and Ann Rapelyea,.....	"	XIII. 85
1781. Oct.	6.	Remsen, Jeronimus, and Câtherine Alstine,.	"	XXXIII. 91
1773. May	24.	Remsen, Jeronimus A., and Phebe Remsen,	"	XX. 123
1737. Dec.	17.	Remsen, Johannes, and Elizabeth Waldron,.	"	I. 8
1770. Mar.	30.	Remsen, Johannis, and Catharine Rapalje,..	"	XVI. 44
1779. Nov.	13.	Remsen, John, and Ann Stoothoff, ...	"	XXVIII. 139
1781. June	16.	Remsen, John, and Dorothy Remsen,......	"	XXXII. 88
1777. Jan.	5.	Remsen, John, and Hester Brower, ...	"	XXIV. 8
1769. Oct.	5.	Remsen, Margaret, and Samuel Gerrtsen, ..	"	XV. 49
1757. Mar.	14.	Remsen, Mary, and John Burtis,..........	"	I. 468
1770. May	25.	Remsen, Phebe, and Anthony De Mott, ...	"	XVI. 94
1773. May	24.	Remsen, Phebe, and Jeronimus A. Remsen,	"	XX. 123
1761. July	29.	Remsen, Rebecca, and Isaac Teller,........	"	V. 15
1762. June	22.	Remsen, Rem, and Maria Schenck,........	"	VI. 204
1738. Oct.	10.	Remsen, Rem, and Trinte Berrien, ...	"	I. 11
1773. Nov.	12.	Remsen, Rem A., and Phebe Duryea,......	"	XXII. 25
1770. April	18.	Remsen, Simon, and Alletta Rapalje, ...	"	XVI. 63
1781. Oct.	18.	Remson, Alletie, and John Bockus,........	"	XXXIII. 107
1782. May	17.	Remson, Hendricke, and Samuel Harris,....	"	XXXVI. 4
1761. Feb.	10.	Remson, Jeremiah, and Margaret Bennet, ..	"	IV. 55
1671. Feb.	23.	Renard, Anne, and Ffrancois Chartier,.....	G. E.,	IV. 100
1778. May	27.	Renaud, Magdalen, and William Rhineland-er, Jr.,...............................	M. B.,	XX. 130
1764. Jan.	4.	Rende, Coonradt, and Elisabeth Koning, ...	"	VIII. 29
1762. Oct.	31.	Renne, Anna, and Robert Field, ...	"	V. 183
1761. Dec.	24.	Renne, Samuel, and Mary Fish, ...	"	V. 301
1782. Dec.	15.	Reno, Jane, and John Coutant, ...	"	XXXIV. 89
1762. July	3.	Renolds, Mary, and John Elliott,..........	"	VI. 224
1773. Aug.	18.	Renoud, Susannah, and David Bleecker,....	"	XXI. 74
1783. July	1.	Renshow, Thomas, and Mary Kenrich,.....	"	XXXIX. 77
1762. Nov.	30.	Rescau, Susanna, and Peter Winat, ...	"	VI. 459
1757. Dec.	3.	Resconla, William, and Mary Jacobs,......	"	I. 724
1773. May	17.	Reshong, Mary, and John Petersen,.......	"	XX. 115
1782. Mar.	30.	Resler, Jacob, Jr., and Mary Stanton,......	"	XXXV. 101
1771. April	11.	Resslur, Mary, and John Stephens,........	"	XVII. 54
1783. Sept.	20.	Retton, Hannah, and Thomas Ackesen, ...	"	XL. 46
1764. July	16.	Revoe, Mary, and Peter Graham, ...	"	VIII. 261
1781. May	5.	Rexorla, James, and Mary Smith,.........	"	XXXII. 32
1765. June	21.	Rey, William, and Maritje Wells, ...	"	IX. 177
1760. Oct.	2.	Reyan, Mary, and Thomas English, ...	"	III. 341
1764. Aug.	24.	Reyder, Hannah, and Johann Weigand,....	"	VIII. 293

DATE.	NAMES.	RECORD.	VOL. PAGE.
1783. Nov. 19.	Reyer, Jemima, and David Archbold,......	M. B.,	xl. 124
1678. Dec. 14.	Reynells, Dorothy, and Edward Clarke,....	G. E.,	xxxii. 19
1760. Jan. 10.	Reynolds, Abigail, and Thomas Bradbridge,.	M. B.,	ii. 574
1772. July 4.	Reynolds, Anne, and Peter Rushton Maverick,	"	xviii. 155
1762. July 8.	Reynolds, Austin, and Hila Wright, ...	"	vi. 231
1772. Feb. 3.	Reynolds, Edward, and Ann Miller, ...	"	xviii. 28
1769. Dec. 29.	Reynolds, James, and Catharine Lezier,....	"	xv. 133
1768. June 15.	Reynolds, James, and Mary Ammerman,...	"	xiii. 128
1777. July 30.	Reynolds, Jane, and Isaac Hillier,.........	"	xxiv. 124
1773. Nov. 12.	Reynolds, Jane, and Jesse Hawxhurst, ...	"	xxii. 26
1759. Nov. 20.	Reynolds, John, and Elizabeth Smith, ...	"	ii. 508
1760. Oct. 17.	Reynolds, Joshua, and Elizabeth Richardson,	"	iii. 368
1783. Jan. 22.	Reynolds, Mary, and Cornelius Blanchard,..	"	xxxviii. 25
1757. April 4.	Reynolds, Robert, and Isabel Weeks,......	"	i. 485
1765. April 3.	Reynolds, Thomas, and Elizabeth Cross, ...	"	ix. 81
1761. Dec. 10.	Rezeau, Peter, and Mary Poilion,.........	"	v. 271
1762. Sept. 24.	Rezeau, Wyntje, and Richard Johnson, ...	"	vi. 330
1772. April 14.	Rhemp, Michael, and Phebe Wood,........	"	xviii. 77
1762. Jan. 12.	Rhenehart, Valentine, and Sybil Heidlar,...	"	vi. 10
1764. Mar. 21.	Rhener, John, and Phebe Milliner,........	"	viii. 112
1765. May 4.	Rhinelander, Fredrick, and Mary Speeder,..	"	ix. 153
1780. Oct. 2.	Rhinelander, William, and Hester Devoe, ..	"	xxx. 50
1774. May 29.	Rhinelander, William, Jr., and Magdalen Renaud, ...·............	"	xx. 130
1782. Nov. 10.	Rhoades, George, and Sarah Smith,........	"	xxxiv. 27
1770. May 15.	Rhoades, Jonah, and Mary Lewis,.........	"	xvi. 86
1770. Mar. 24.	Rhoads, Massey, and Jacob Lawrence,.....	"	xvi. 38
1782. Dec. 29.	Rhoads, Nathaniel, and Elizabeth Forbush,.	"	xxxiv. 110
1761. Sept. 18.	Rhodes, Elenor, and Nathaniel Smith,.....	"	v. 88
1761. Aug. 11.	Rhodes, Elethe, and Nicholas Van Dam,....	"	v. 40
1760. Feb. 22.	Rhodes, Elizabeth, and Stephen Wood, ...	"	iii. 44
1762. April 15.	Rhodes, James, and Mary Brittine,........	"	vi. 112
1772. Nov. 10.	Rhyne, Cornelis, and Marretie Huyck,.....	"	xix. 108
1753. July 17.	Rhypell, Annatje, and John Staklen, ...	"	i. 247
1782. Dec. 18.	Rian, Mary, and Edward Carey, ...	"	xxxvii. 126
1764. Feb. 21.	Rice, Abraham, and Mary Hannon, ...	"	viii. 70
1758. Sept. 7.	Rice, Christopher, and Catharine Elizabeth Alsbruken, ...	"	ii. 6
1763. Nov. 15.	Rice, Christopher, and Mary Cain, ...	"	vii. 451
1737. Sept. 9.	Rice, Elias, and Sarah Connovel, ...	"	i. 7
1779. Oct. 25.	Rice, Elizabeth, and Andrew Mecien,......	"	xxviii. 119
1783. Feb. 25.	Rice, Elizabeth, and William Edgar,.......	"	xxxviii. 54
1779. June 30.	Rice, James, and Elizabeth Keese,.........	"	xxviii. 11
1789. Aug. 6.	Rice, Patrick, and Jane Latouch,..........	"	xxix. 134
1767. Sept. 7.	Rice, Thomas, and Gloriana Muirson,......	"	xii. 27

DATE.		NAMES.	RECORD.	VOL.	PAGE.
1761. Dec.	16.	Riegler, Catharine, and George Ludwig Wachtel,	M. B.,	v.	282
1777. April	4.	Rich, James, and Anne Raft,	"	xxiv.	56
1760. Nov.	6.	Rich, Mary, and John Jones,	"	iii.	396
1763. June	9.	Rich, Sarah, and Phinehas Hunt,	"	vii.	218
1783. July	20.	Rich, Sarah, and Searing Williams,	"	xxxix.	96
1762. May	17.	Rich, Stephen, and Martha Bartine,	"	vii.	191
1736. Nov.	26.	Rich, William, and Elizabeth Creighton, ...	"	i.	3
1765. Jan.	22.	Richar, John, and Abigail Hinton,	"	ix.	30
1763. June	27.	Richard, Elisabeth, and Francis Landey Patton,	"	vii.	243
1755. Aug.	26.	Richards, Carolina, and George Barry,	"	i.	157
1760. Aug.	7.	Richards, Charity, and John Galladett,	"	iii.	242
1759. Dec.	10.	Richards, James, and Catherine Hope,	"	ii.	536
1737. Oct.	15.	Richards, John, and Hannah George,	"	i.	7
1757. Aug.	15.	Richards, Nicholas, and Elizabeth Dickson,.	"	i.	615
1758. Sept.	21.	Richards, Richard, and Rebecca Martin,	"	ii.	29
1763. Oct.	5.	Richards, Roger, and Susannah Salmon,	"	vii.	373
1738. Nov.	15.	Richards, Samuel, and Elizabeth Staats,	"	i.	11
1772. Feb.	8.	Richards, Smith, and Rachel Low,	"	xviii.	31
1763. July	18.	Richards, Warner, and Sarah Byfield,	"	vii.	272
1753. May	22.	Richards, William, and Mary Elizabeth Row,	"	i.	38
1676. Feb.	26.	Richardson, Bethia, and John Ketcham,	W. O. P.,	iii.	241
1760. Oct.	7.	Richardson, Elizabeth, and Joshua Reynolds,	M. B.,	iii.	368
1669. Sept.	8.	Richardson, Joan, and Richard Heamore,...	O. W. L.,	ii.	524
1769. June	26.	Richardson, John, and Barbara Lynal,	M. B.,	xiv.	131
1783. June	13.	Richardson, John, and Sophia Casey,	"	xxxix.	55
1683. July	24.	Richardson, Margarett, and Thomas Williams,	E.,	xxxiii.	73
1758. Jan.	25.	Richardson, Mary, and Christian Sheperla,..	M. B.,	i.	801
1775. Oct.	11.	Richardson, Mary, and Henry Rihl,	"	xxiii.	179
1779. Mar.	25.	Richardson, Mary, and William Hedges,	"	xxvii.	77
1777. May	9.	Richardson, Robert, and Mary Murry,	"	xxiv.	85
1780. Dec.	14.	Richardson, Sarah, and Richard Courtney,..	"	xxx.	151
1780. July	28.	Richardson, Sarah, and Thomas Wellham,..	"	xxix.	121
1780. May	18.	Richardson, Susanah, and William Armour,.	"	xxix.	61
1770. June	27.	Richardson, Thomas, and Elizabeth Lewis,..	"	xvi.	124
1759. Dec.	8.	Richardson, William, and Elizabeth Hope,..	"	ii.	533
1758. Nov.	4.	Richardson, William, and Mary Plunket,...	"	ii.	79
1764. Dec.	17.	Richardson, William, and Mary Wortman,..	"	viii.	456
1765. Jan.	6.	Riche, Alexander, and Anne Cook,	"	ix.	2
1773. Nov.	17.	Riche, Mary, and Samuel Ferris,	"	xxii.	32
1760. April	26.	Richey, George, and Catharine Tillou,	"	iii.	127
1769. June	2.	Richey, James, and Catherine Johnson,	"	xiv.	112
1764. Feb.	21.	Richey, James, and Jane Wells,	"	viii.	67
1770. Nov.	10.	Richie, Alexander, and Margaret Gordon, ..	"	xvi.	245

DATE.		NAMES.	RECORD.	VOL.	PAGE.
1781. April 30.	Richter, John Adolph, and Ann Andrews,..	M. B.,	xxxii.	22
1766. July 16.	Richy, John, and Machtel Veldtman, ...	"	x.	54
1772. April 28.	Rickaw, Tamer, and Richard Garrison,. ...	"	xviii.	95
1738. May 6.	Rickets, Mary Walton, and Stephen Van Cortlandt, ...	"	i.	9
1773. Mar. 24.	Ricketts, Jacob, and Mary Thompson, ...	"	xx.	71
1738. Nov. 9.	Rickew, Jacob, and Elizabeth Wright,.....	"	i.	11
1761. Mar. 18.	Rickhow, Abraham, and Hannah Pryer, ...	"	iv.	106
1759. Mar. 19.	Rickman, Cornelia, and Daniel Terbos,.....	"	ii.	220
1774. Mar. 10.	Rickman, Cornelia, and James Kip, ...	"	xxii.	144
1760. Jan. 16.	Riddell, James, and Elizabeth Ryder, ...	"	ii.	582
1738. Aug. 9.	Ridden, Ellinor, and Isaac Freeman,........	"	i.	10
1759. Dec. 31.	Ridder, Maria, and Wynant W. Vandenbergh,	"	ii.	562
1763. Aug. 1.	Riddle, Martha, and Henry Hill,..........	"	vii.	289
1764. May 19.	Rideout, Magdalen, and Joseph Russell,....	"	viii.	195
1783. Nov. 17.	Rider, Catharine, and Isaac Styles,........	"	xl.	118
1767. Nov. 12.	Rider, Elizabeth, and Andrew Onderdonck,.	"	xii.	82
1782. April 3.	Rider, Idea, and Court Lake,.............	"	xxxv.	107
1771. Dec. 16.	Rider, John, and Catherine Lawrence,.....	"	xvii.	295
1778. Sept. 30.	Rider, John, and Greetie Noostrandt,......	"	xxvi.	40
1758. May 22.	Rider, John, and Jane Osborn, ...	"	i.	905
1773. Nov. 15.	Rider, Lydia, and Richard Goldsmith,......	"	xxii.	28
1781. June 21.	Rider, Susannah, and John Fork, ...	"	xxxii.	92
1778. Dec. 2.	Rider, William, and Elenor Person, ...	"	xxvi.	107
1778. Nov. 25.	Ridge, Sampson, and Phebe Webster,......	"	xxvi.	95
1779. Mar. 10.	Ridgeway, Ann, and Abraham Egburts,....	"	xxvii.	63
1767. Feb. 14.	Ridgeway, Catherine, and Bailey Marston,..	"	xi.	27
1781. April 11.	Ridgway, Caturey, and John Wood,.......	"	xxxi.	102
1782. April 29.	Ridgway, Elizabeth, and Peter Prall, ...	'	xxxv.	142
1772. May 22.	Ridgway, Thomas, and Elizabeth Jones,....	"	xviii.	120
1779. Mar. 3.	Ridley, James, and Ann Barbara Sowers, ..	"	xxvii.	55
1779. Oct. 16.	Ridley, Thomas, and Frowey Myere,......	"	xxviii.	114
1781. Nov. 29.	Ridly, Frowy, and Joseph Zaney,.........	"	xxxiv.	63
1782. Jan. 22.	Ridly, Ralph, and Margeret Kip,..........	"	xxxv.	28
1753. Aug. 30.	Rieck, Jochim, and Sarah Lane, ...	"	i.	103
1780. Sept. 5.	Riersen, Jacob, and Heliet Schanck,.......	"	iii.	284
1775. Sept. 30.	Rierson, Elizabeth, and John Schenk, ...	"	xxiii.	167
1773. Dec. 30.	Rierson, Jane, and Hendrick Henderson, ..	"	xxii.	73
1777. Sept. 30.	Rierson, Sarah, and Gilbert Van Wyck,....	"	xxiv.	155
1758. Mar. 11.	Riffle, Christiana, and Samuel Lester,......	"	i.	845
1783. July 29.	Rigbey, William, and Margaret Stout, ...	"	xxxix.	104
1758. Dec. 6.	Rigby, James, and Ruth Wandewater,.....	"	ii.	116
1763. Jan. 10.	Rigby, Ruth, and James Bryant,..........	"	vii.	11
1736. May 12.	Riggs, Frances, and James Compton,......	"	i.	1
1762. Sept. 29.	Righby, Joseph, and Elizabeth Barrea,.....	"	vi.	335

DATE.	NAMES.	RECORD.	VOL.	PAGE.
1781. Jan. 5.	Right, Nathaniel, and Mary Skidmore, ...	M. B.,	XXXI.	13
1770. Nov. 24.	Righter, Maritie, and William Pitcher,.....	"	XVI.	267
1778. April 1.	Rightman, Albert, and Elizabeth Lockman,.	"	XXV.	57
1762. Sept. 4.	Rigler, Leonard, and Angletie Vander Voort,	"	VI.	308
1775. July 14.	Rigsley, Martha, and James Pell, ...	"	XXIII.	98
1775. Oct. 11.	Rihl, Henry, and Mary Richardson, ...	"	XXIII.	179
1761. Jan. 29.	Riiken, Jacobus, and Ann Catherine Rapelje,	"	IV.	35
1783. Sept. 15.	Rikeman, Catharine, and James Moore, ...	"	XL.	26
1783. Mar. 20.	Rikeman, Gertrude, and John Fork,.......	"	XXXVIII.	70
1782. Sept. 30.	Rikeman, James, and Mary Hosser, ...	"	XXXVII.	21
1783. Aug. 7.	Rikeman, Rebecca, and Jonathan Dunn,....	"	XXXIX.	116
1755. Dec. 24.	Rikemond, Catharine, and Hendrick Bush,..	"	I.	240
1766. Aug. 9.	Riker, Abraham, and Margaret Riker.......	"	X.	73
1764. July 6.	Riker, Henry, and Sarah Lasher,..........	"	VIII.	247
1764. June 16.	Riker, Jacobus, and Eleanor Bergaw,..... .	"	VIII.	226
1763. May 28.	Riker, James, and Mary Leaycraft, ...	"	VII.	206
1771. Dec. 1.	Riker, John, and Mary Underdonk,........	"	XVII.	289
1771. Nov. 14.	Riker, John, and Susanna Fish,...........	"	XVII.	257
1766. Aug. 9.	Riker, Margaret, and Abraham Riker, ...	"	X.	73
1780. Nov. 15.	Riker, Moriah, and Cornelius Rapelye,.....	"	XXX.	107
1768. Aug. 5.	Riker, Ruth, and Jonathan Lawrence, ...	"	XIII.	168
1769. Jan. 16.	Riker, Samuel, and Anna Lawrence,.......	"	XIV.	13
1759. Oct. 29.	Rikey, John, and Catherina Vanantwarp, ..	"	II.	478
1756. Nov. 23.	Rilents, Catharine, and Richard Johnson,...	"	I.	362
1764. May 17.	Riley, Gertruy, and William Rogers, Jr.,...	"	VIII.	192
1760. Sept. 2.	Rinedollar, Emmanuel, and Hester Hyman,.	"	XXX.	16
1762. Aug. 9.	Rineling, Johann, and Anna Maria Muriahn,	"	VI.	272
1765. Oct. 17.	Ringland, John C., and Maritie Howghteling,	"	IX.	307
1758. Nov. 3.	Ringo, Cornelius, and Margaret Twitcher, ..	"	II.	78
1762. Nov. 22.	Riniere, Louis, and Jane Heroy, ...	"	VI.	449
1761. Oct. 3.	Ripel, Ann, and John Hall, ...	"	V.	117
1767. Sept. 24.	Risedurpe, Margaret, and Wynant Van Alstyne, ...	"	XII.	44
1782. Nov. 20.	Risley, Joseph, and Mary Baker,..........	"	XXXVII.	89
1777. July 23.	Ritchie, Anne, and William Cross,........	"	XXIV.	120
1782. Jan. 12.	Ritchie, John, and Cornelia Wilson, ...	"	XXXV.	16
1768. Jan. 22.	Ritchie, William, and Elizabeth Arden, ...	"	XIII.	17
1768. May 16.	Ritchie, William, and Elizabeth Silvester, ..	"	XIII.	104
1781. Sept. 20.	Ritson, John, and Elizebeth Bayard, ...	"	XXXIII.	71
1783. July 22.	Ritter, Daniel, and Elizabeth Hoghland,....	"	XXXIX.	99
1763. Dec. 16.	Ritter, John, and Elisabeth Fine, ...	"	VII.	506
1763. April 29.	Ritter, Mary, and Samuel Maghee,........	"	VII.	155
1757. Oct. 8.	Ritter, Michael, and Margret Bont,........	"	I.	660
1783. Oct. 22.	Ritter, Peter, and Catharine Post,........	"	XL.	88
1780. May 1.	Ritton, Peter, and Lucretia Dash, ...	"	XXIX.	39

41

Date.	Names.	Record.	Vol.	Page.
1761. Dec. 14.	Ritts, Edward, and Elizabeth Smith,... ...	M. B.,	v.	278
1762. Jan. 20.	Ritzema, Alida, and Nicholas Bogert,......	"	vi.	19
1771. June 3.	Ritzema, Maria Wilhelmina, and Thomas Andrew Hoog,.........................	"	xvii.	100
1772. June 29.	Rivers, Anne, and Lawrance Hortwick,....	"	xviii.	152
1764. Oct. 1.	Rivers, Benjamin, and Sarah De Groff, ...	"	viii.	329
1770. Nov. 7.	Rivers, Elizabeth, and Simon Crygier, ...	"	xvi.	242
1775. Aug. 29.	Rivers, Jane, and Jacob Coyzer, ...	"	xxiii.	140
1771. Oct. 14.	Rivers, Mary, and John Beekman, ...	"	xvii.	206
1769. Mar. 9.	Rivington, James, and Elizabeth Vanhorne,	"	xiv.	49
1783. April 12.	Rix, Jane, and John Alloway,.............	"	xxxviii.	95
1767. June 30.	Roach, James, and Susannah Thorn,.......	"	xi.	115
1781. May 15.	Roach, Mary, and John Dare,.............	"	xxxii.	48
1759. July 2.	Roach, Moses, and Isabella Harden, ...	"	ii.	344
1777. Dec. 30.	Roach, Thomas, and Euphame Ogden, ...	"	xxiv.	210
1782. Mar. 26.	Roades, Sarah, and Rulef Duryea, ...	"	xxxv.	97
1767. July 3.	Roads, Anthony, and Susannah Hegeman,..	"	xi.	120
1763. Nov. 14.	Roads, Elizabeth, and Stephen Carman, ...	"	vii.	447
1781. Mar. 21.	Roads, Hannah, and Stephen Voris, ...	"	xxxi.	79
1767. Aug. 25.	Roan, Mary, and William Smith,..........	"	xii.	22
1773. Nov. 4.	Robbins, Abigal, and Samuel Titus, ...	"	xxii.	13
1770. Mar. 24.	Robbins, Isaac, and Margaret Titus,.......	"	xvi.	39
1782. Nov. 1.	Robbins, Jacob, and Abigail Jackson,......	"	xxxvii.	68
1767. Feb. 18.	Robbins, James, and Mary Foy, ...	"	xi.	30
1779. Mar. 10.	Robbins, Jane, and Henry Titus,..........	"	xxvii.	64
1760. Mar. 10.	Robbins, Martha, and Theodorus Vanwyck,.	'	iii.	71
1780. Mar. 20.	Robbins, Richard, and Martha Hendrickson,	"	xxix.	3
1759. Oct. 23.	Robbins, Sarah, and Hugh Gaine,.........	"	ii.	471
1765. Aug. 29.	Robblee, Thomas, and Mary Allen,........	"	ix.	251
1783. Oct. 5.	Robeno, Francis, and Sarah Bush,.........	"	xl.	63
1765. Oct. 16.	Robert, Daniel, and Elizabeth Hincksman,..	"	ix.	302
1781. Mar. 25.	Roberts, Æneas, and Mary Cox,..........	"	xxxi.	85
1759. May 28.	Roberts, Alida, and Garret Hendrick Myer,.	"	ii.	292
1777. Aug. 16.	Roberts, Arabella, and Edward Peirce Willington, ...	"	xxiv.	134
1764. Feb. 27.	Roberts, Benjamin, and Eve Hall,.........	"	viii.	84
1759. Aug. 15.	Roberts, Daniel, and Catharine Harris,.....	"	ii.	384
1778. Feb. 19.	Roberts, David, and Mary Pinkney, ...	"	xxv.	26
1750. July 4.	Roberts, Dorithy, and Archibald Mountegue Brown, ...	"	i.	72
1766. June 30.	Roberts, Elinor, and Thomas Cooper, ...	"	x.	39
1758. Oct. 30.	Roberts, Elizabeth, and Benjamin Lawrence,	"	ii.	72
173⅟. Feb. 10.	Roberts, Elizabeth, and Gabriel Furman,...	"	i.	9
1762. Dec. 31.	Roberts, Elizabeth, and Jacob Moses,......	"	xix.	168
1783. June 6.	Roberts, Elizabeth, and Peter Parks, ...	"	xxxix.	44

DATE.	NAMES.	RECORD.	VOL.	PAGE.
1763. Oct. 3.	Roberts, Emanuel, and Grace Ingoldsby,...	M. B.,	VII.	368
1777. Nov. 8.	Roberts, Frederick, and Hanah Roberts, ...	"	XXIV.	177
1777. Nov. 8.	Roberts, Hanah, and Frederick Roberts, ...	"	XXIV.	177
1780. July 29.	Roberts, Henry, and Love Derkendered, ...	"	XXIX.	127
1774. Feb. 16.	Roberts, Isabella, and Peter Ball, ...	"	XXII.	129
1782. June 5.	Roberts, John, and Abigail Stevens,.......	"	XXXVI.	37
1771. July 13.	Roberts, John, and Mary Jackson, ...	"	XVII.	131
1762. June 17.	Roberts, John, and Rebecca Sadler,........	"	VI.	195
1766. Jan. 26.	Roberts, Jonathan, and Mary Holland,.....	"	IX.	31
1778. Feb. 19.	Roberts, Martha, and James Barrow, ...	"	XXV.	27
1762. July 16.	Roberts, Mary, and George Paschall, ...	"	VI.	240
1779. Aug. 6.	Roberts, Phebe, and John Morgan, ...	"	XXVIII.	48
1782. Aug. 22.	Roberts, Robert, and Catharine Huchinson,.	"	XXXVI.	127
1782. June 15.	Roberts, Robert, and Eleanor Chambers,...	"	XXXVI.	53
1765. April 15.	Roberts, Samuel, and Alice Webb, ...	"	IX.	92
1761. May 5.	Roberts, Samuel, and Mary Divine,........	"	IV.	180
1783. Oct. 31.	Roberts, Sarah, and John Kidd,...........	"	XL.	98
1762. June 5.	Roberts, Thomas, and Cornelia Van Evera,.	"	VI.	182
1763. May 2.	Roberts, Thomas, and Elizabeth Demerell,..	"	VII.	161
1779. Mar. 23.	Roberts, Zachariah, and Elizabeth Bishop,..	"	XXVII.	74
1759. Aug. 6.	Robertson, Duncan, and Catharine Meeks,..	"	II.	374
1781. Jan. 18.	Robertson, Isaac, and Letitia Cox, ...	"	XXXI.	24
1761. Sept. 1.	Robertson, John, and Mary Fletcher,......	"	V.	65
1776. Jan. 2.	Robertson, John, and Harriot Merchant, ...	"	XXIII.	238
1781. Oct. 7.	Robertson, Mary, and Francis Cocks, ...	"	XXXIII.	92
1777. June 5.	Robertson, Richard, and Catherine Thorne,.	"	XXIV.	07
1781. April 10.	Robertson (Robinson), Sarah, and Robert Jayne, Jr.,............................	"	XXXI.	100
1772. Feb. 24.	Robertson, William, and Sarah French, ...	"	XVIII.	41
1756. Nov. 30.	Robeson, Thomas, and Ann Remsen, ...	"	I.	368
1783. Jan. 4.	Robins, Elizabeth, and Augustus Sidell, ...	"	XXXVIII.	6
1777. Mar. 17.	Robins, Elizabeth, and Valentine Williams,.	"	XXIV.	53
1769. Aug. 28.	Robins, James, and Margaret O'Neal,......	"	XV.	31
1764. Dec. 10.	Robins, Jeremiah, and Hannah Cock,......	"	VIII.	450
1778. April 23.	Robins, Job, and Mary Searing,...........	"	XXV.	66
1760. Feb. 9.	Robins, Mary, and John Strange,..........	"	III.	28
1772. Dec. 21.	Robins, Phebe, and Benajah Bedlel, ...	"	XIX.	160
1765. Sept. 30.	Robinson, Ann, and William Puntine, ...	"	IX.	279
1778. Jan. 19.	Robinson, Beverly, Jr., and Ann Dorothy Barclay,............................	"	XXV.	9
1773. Sept. 1.	Robinson, Edward, and Janetie Van Slyck,.	"	XXI.	96
1736. Nov. 9.	Robinson, Elizabeth, and George Witts,....	"	I.	3
1759. Aug. 25.	Robinson, Elizabeth, and Godfrey Streyd,..	"	II.	400
1772. Dec. 28.	Robinson, Elizabeth, and Samuel Hopkins,.	"	XIX.	164
1777. Dec. 20.	Robinson, Elizabeth, and William Cochran,.	"	XXIV.	202

DATE.		NAMES.	RECORD.	VOL.	PAGE.
1763.	June 11.	Robinson, Esther, and Robert Grant, ...	M. B.,	VII.	226
1757.	April 30.	Robinson, George, and Sarah Ducworth, ...	"	I.	521
1781.	June 11.	Robinson, Hellena, and Donald Mackay, ...	"	XXXII.	82
1759.	Oct. 31.	Robinson, Henry, and Ann Hallam, ...	"	II.	481
1782.	Oct. 17.	Robinson, John, and Elizabeth Lewis, ...	"	XXXVII.	49
1780.	Jan. 12.	Robinson, John, and Elizabeth Moore, ...	"	XXVIII.	193
1778.	Aug. 27.	Robinson, John, and Frances Pugh, ...	"	XXVI.	13
1678.	Oct. 4.	Robinson, John, and Greetye Hendryckes,..	G. E.,	XXXII.	4
1783.	Nov. 15.	Robinson, John, and Lidie Wilson, ...	M. B.,	XL.	114
1761.	Oct. 19.	Robinson, John, and Margaret Clark,......	"	V.	151
1783.	May 24.	Robinson, John, and Mary Syms, ...	"	I.	9
1771.	Dec. 17.	Robinson, John, and Ruth Clap, ...	"	XVII.	297
1769.	May 26.	Robinson, John, Jr., and Elizabeth Osburn,.	"	XIV.	107
1761.	Nov. 27.	Robinson, Joseph, and Mary Cebra, ...	"	V.	253
1764.	Jan. 3.	Robinson, Joseph, and Sarah Hopkins,.. ..	"	VIII.	3
1773.	Jan. 20.	Robinson, Joseph, and Catherine Moscholick,	"	XX.	15
1774.	Mar. 15.	Robinson, Joseph, and Mary Smith,.......	"	XXII.	149
1768.	Dec. 21.	Robinson, Leonard, and Unice Holmes,....	"	XIII.	271
1771.	Nov. 12.	Robinson, Mary, and Peter Buckhout, ...	"	XVII.	250
173⅞.	Jan. 11.	Robinson, Mary, and Robert Gregory,.....	"	I.	8
1764.	Jan. 14.	Robinson, Mary, and William Ralston,.....	"	VIII.	15b
1779.	April 27.	Robinson, Rachel, and James Storey,......	"	XXVII.	122
1761.	Jan. 10.	Robinson, Richard, and Elizabeth Whitfield,	"	IV.	9
1779.	April 26.	Robinson, Robert, and Mary Harvey,......	"	XXVII.	119
1757.	July 22.	Robinson, Samuel, and Elizabeth Ward,....	"	I.	598
1757.	Mar. 22.	Robinson, Sarah, and Alexander Simpson,..	"	I.	479
1760.	Feb. 14.	Robinson, Sarah, and Jacob Taylor,........	"	III.	36
1781.	April 10.	Robinson (Robertson), Sarah, and Robert Jayne, Jr., ...	"	XXXI.	100
1770.	May 7.	Robinson, Saul, and Tamar Knap,.........	"	XVI.	81
1761.	April 24.	Robinson, Sciah, and Margaret Winfield,...	"	IV.	165
1778.	Oct. 5.	Robinson, Thomas, and Anstice Flemming,.	"	XXVI.	46
1756.	Oct. 12.	Robinson, Thomas, and Hannah Ferrari, ...	"	I.	328
1762.	April 8.	Robinson, William, and Ann Armstrong,...	"	VI.	95
1767.	Oct. 11.	Robison, Thomas, and Elizabeth Cartwright,	"	XII.	60
1757.	Oct. 8.	Robson, John, and Mary McArthur,.......	"	I.	661
1764.	Sept. 17.	Robson, Robert, and Alida Osborne,.......	"	VIII.	311
1781.	Aug. 8.	Robuck, Catherine, and Vriah Pearsall, ...	"	XXXIII.	31
1755.	Nov. 22.	Rochell, Elizabeth, and Thomas Wright,....	"	I.	214
1762.	May 11.	Rock, Joseph, and Elenor Barret,.........	"	VI.	154
1777.	Mar. 5.	Rock, Nathaniel Smith, and Phebe Beagle,.	"	XXIV.	39
173⅞.	Jan. 11.	Rock, Peter, and Catherine Van Horne,....	"	I.	8
1768.	Sept. 19.	Rockefeller, Philip, and Catherine Sharp,...	"	XIII.	187
1765.	Oct. 25.	Rodbin, Mary, and John Vredenburgh, ...	"	IX.	320
1779.	Mar. 27.	Rode, Andrew, and Lanah Ullick,.........	"	XXVII.	78

DATE.	NAMES.	RECORD.	VOL.	PAGE.
1781. Dec. 15.	Rodgers, Edward, and Rebecca Taylor, ...	M. B.,	XXXIV.	88
1776. Mar. 6.	Rodgers, Lydia, and John Taylor,.........	"	XXIII.	278
1762. Oct. 22.	Rodgers, William, and Elisabeth Hunt, ...	"	VI.	357
1775. Nov. 17.	Rodgers, William, and Sarah Potter, ...	"	XXIII.	214
1769. Jan. 27.	Rodman, Joseph, Jr., and Allida Guion,....	"	XIV.	21
1765. Oct. 31.	Rodman, Mary, and Abram Guion,........	"	IX.	341
1765. June 23.	Rodman, Mary, and John Bertine, ...	"	IX.	182
1768. Feb. 29.	Rodman, Mary, and John Morgat, ...	"	XIII.	47
1780. Aug. 30.	Rodman, William, and Eleanor Myers,.....	"	XXX.	12
1783. July 15.	Roe, Abigail, and Purday Fowler,.........	"	XXXIX.	93
1777. Nov. 28.	Roe, Ann, and Oliver Cornell, ...	"	XXIV.	186
1772. Nov. 20.	Roe, Austin, and Catharine Jones, ...	"	XIX.	119
1769. May 6.	Roe, Betsey, and Solomon Smith,.........	"	XIV.	96
1762. April 22.	Roe, Daniel, and Deborah Brewster,.......	"	VI.	128
1783. April 29.	Roe, David, and Juliana Fowler,..........	"	XXXVIII.	120
1773. Dec. 30.	Roe, David, and Sarah Philips, ...	"	XXII.	89
1783. Nov. 16.	Roe, Deborah, and Blake Buckmaster,.....	"	XL.	117
1760. Dec. 5.	Roe, Deborah, and Silas Lawrence,........	"	III.	459
1758. May 29.	Roe, Elizabeth, and Anthony Glen Barns,..	"	I.	914
1762. April 22.	Roe, Johanna, and James Davis,..........	"	VI.	127
1783. Oct. 16.	Roe, John, and Caroline Lowree,..........	"	XL.	80
1775. June 9.	Roe, Joseph, and Ann Lawrence, ...	"	XXIII.	58
1783. Mar. 18.	Roe, Mary, and George Thorn, ...	"	XXXVIII.	68
1763. Oct. 7.	Roe, Mary, and Lanckford Thorne,........	"	VII.	380
1762. Oct. 14.	Roe, Mellisent, and Zephaniah Platt, ...	"	VI.	364
1757. Jan. 15.	Roe, Mercy, and John Myer,.............	"	I.	416
1775. Oct. 3.	Roe, Oliver, and Margaret Cornell,........	"	XXIII.	172
1758. Sept. 22.	Roe, Samuel, and Tamer Haynes,.........	"	II.	31
1761. Nov. 13.	Roe, Sophia, and Andries Zeegaerd,.......	"	V.	214
1773. Feb. 12.	Roe, Thomas, and Sarah Morel,...........	"	XX.	42
1780. Dec. 22.	Roe, William, and Ann Cornell,...........	"	XXX.	163
1764. Mar. 24.	Roe, William, and Mary Feks,............	"	VIII.	117
1770. Aug. 3.	Roebuck, Catherine, and Samuel Nicklir,...	"	XXVIII.	44
1767. Sept. 15.	Roeckser, Jacob, and Hannah Moore,......	"	XII.	33d
1776. Mar. 21.	Roeseboom, Elizabeth, and Henry Quaken-boss, ...	"	XXIII.	287
1772. Sept. 14.	Roessell, Ludwigh, and Catherine Fiero, ...	"	XIX.	48
1781. Dec. 19.	Roff, Rebecca, and Samuel Oakley,........	"	XXXIV.	95
1771. July 1.	Rofft, Susannah, and Ralph Hurd, ...	"	XVII.	127
1764. July 28.	Rofter, Dorothy, and James Forbes,.......	"	VIII.	270
1783. Feb. 28.	Roger, Ruth, and Jacob Titus, ...	"	XXXVIII.	58
1779. Aug. 22.	Rogero, Francois Mant, and Mary Locan,...	"	XXVIII.	55
1782. July 20.	Rogers, Abigail, and Caleb Ketcham, ...	"	XXXVI.	89
1782. Mar. 18.	Rogers, Andrew, and Mary Gregory,......	"	XXXVI.	9
1761. July 3.	Rogers, Annanias, and Mary Smith, ...	"	IV.	274

DATE.	NAMES.	RECORD.	VOL.	PAGE.
1777. Mar. 2.	Rogers, Catherine, and Thomas Mason, ...	M. B.,	XXIV.	36
1762. Jan. 22.	Rogers, Elisabeth, and Jonathan Hoyet, ...	"	VII.	31
1766. Oct. 25.	Rogers, George, and Ellenor Murray,......	"	X.	141
1779. April 2.	Rogers, Henry, and Catherine Van Ranst,..	"	XXVII.	90
1779. Nov. 16.	Rogers, Henry, and Isabella Kearny, ...	"	XXVIII.	141
1783. Mar. 10.	Rogers, Isaac, and Hannah Conklin,.......	"	XXXVIII.	63
1763. June 6.	Rogers, James, and Elizabeth Platt, ...	"	VII.	212
1772. Oct. 26.	Rogers, John, and Ann Alstyne,..........	"	XIX.	91
1761. Nov. 26.	Rogers, John, and Ruth Woods,..........	"	V.	251
1775. July 8.	Rogers, Joseph, and Mary Beesly,.........	"	XXIII.	89
1761. May 19.	Rogers, Joshua, and Hannah Smith,.......	"	IV.	200
1782. May 31.	Rogers, Leonard, and Rachael Bates, ...	"	XXXVI.	32
1781. Sept. 17.	Rogers, Leonard, and Rachel Bates, ...	"	XXXIII.	69
1757. Feb. 11.	Rogers, Martha, and Arthur Dingey, ...	"	I.	817
1760. July 26.	Rogers, Martha, and Nicolas Viel,.........	"	III.	227
1758. Nov. 20.	Rogers, Mary, and John Simons,..........	"	II.	96
1759. Jan. 3.	Rogers, Mary, and Nathaniel Sackett, ...	"	II.	145
1760. Sept. 24.	Rogers, Mary, and William Ryan,.........	"	III.	327
1761. April 21.	Rogers, Matthew, and Margaret Harrison,..	"	IV.	158
1760. Jan. 7.	Rogers, Michael, and Helena Bull,.........	"	II.	571
1756. June 30.	Rogers, Michael, and Mary Craft, ...	"	I.	244
1779. Nov. 6.	Rogers, Obediah, and Hannah Sayre,......	"	XXVIII.	132
1764. April 2.	Rogers, Patrick, and Ida Wiltse,..........	"	VIII.	178
1759. Aug. 4.	Rogers, Phebe, and John Masters, ...	"	II.	371
1737. Dec. 10.	Rogers, Phebe, and Justice Burnett,.......	"	I.	8
1779. Sept. 30.	Rogers, Priscilla, and Christopher Carter, ..	"	XXVIII.	93
1761. Mar. 23.	Rogers, Robert, and Anne Corry,.........	"	IV.	113
1765. Sept. 26.	Rogers, Ruth, and John Oakly,...........	"	IX.	276
1759. April 25.	Rogers, Sarah, and Isaac Craft, ...	"	II.	255
1765. Oct. 24.	Rogers, Sarah, and Nicholas Williams,.....	"	IX.	317
1771. June 1.	Rogers, Sarah, and Titus Bennett,.........	"	XVII.	98
1761. April 28.	Rogers, Stephen, and Hannah Howell,.....	"	IV.	172
1773. Sept. 21.	Rogers, Susannah, and William Mackey Tennent, ...	"	XXI.	115
1770. April 14.	Rogers, Susannah B., and John Adems,....	"	XVI.	62
1759. Sept. 28.	Rogers, Timothy, and Mary Thomas,......	"	II.	435
1783. Feb. 7.	Rogers, Vianah, and Rueben Johnson,......	"	XXXVIII.	36
1764. May 17.	Rogers, William, Jr., and Gertruy Riley,...	"	VIII.	192
1769. Nov. 30.	Rogers, Zachariah, and Ruth Dingey,......	"	XV.	110
1781. Nov. 8.	Rogers, Zebulon, and Rhoda Blassly, ...	"	XXXIV.	24
1776. Jan. 18.	Roggen, Peter, and Annatie Masten, ...	"	XXIII.	248
1782. June 5.	Roggen, Zopher, and Sarah Gilden Sleeve, .	"	XXXVI.	39
1771. April 29.	Roggs, William, and Ann Kinnan, ...	"	XVII.	71
1771. Sept. 9.	Rolens, Philip, and Sarah Hains,..........	"	XVII.	178
1761. Dec. 8.	Rolf, Ann, and John Mackey, ...	"	V.	268

DATE.	NAMES.	RECORD.	VOL. PAGE.
1738. Oct. 14.	Roll, John, and Hilie Van Boskerk,........	M. B.,	I. 11
1755. Oct. 17.	Roll, Sophia, and Jacob Mersereau,........	"	I. 197
1782. Jan. 23.	Rolph, Benjamin, and Sarah Brush,........	"	xxxv. 29
1782. Dec. 25.	Rolph, Daniel, and Mary Brush, ...	"	xxxvii. 133
1779. Aug. 20.	Rolph, Elizabeth, and Ezekiel Dennis, ...	"	xxviii. 54
1764. April 4.	Rolph, Lawrence, and Patience Lake,......	"	viii. 133
1761. Oct. 19.	Rolph, Mary, and Abraham Swaim, ...	"	v. 148
1778. Dec. 3.	Rolph, Patience, and Cornelius Cole, ...	"	xxvi. 108
1761. Feb. 24.	Romans, Barent, and Mary Wendell, ...	"	iv. 80
1738. Oct. 28.	Rome, Mary, and Jacob Phenix,..........	"	I. 11
1760. Mar. 5.	Rome, Susannah, and John Degoot,.......	"	iii. 63
1753. June 9.	Romein, Netkles, and Margaret Minthorne,.	"	I. 56
1772. Oct. 23.	Romer, Mary, and John Leevie, ...	"	xix. 88
1737. May 16.	Romer, Mary, and Richard Fenyck,........	"	I. 6
1767. May 15.	Romeyn, Dirck, and Elizabeth Brodhead, ..	"	xi. 89
1759. Dec. 6.	Romine, Isaac, and Hannah Austen,.......	"	ii. 529
1762. Nov. 8.	Romine, Lamatje, and Teunis Van Vliet,...	"	vi. 419
1761. Nov. 9.	Romine, Mary, and Peter Low, ...	"	v. 201
1783. Mar. 24.	Romine, Philip, and Catharine Bonta, ...	"	xxxviii. 75
1757. Dec. 22.	Romme, Cornelius, and Susannah Waldron,.	"	I. 750
1737. Oct. 27.	Romme, Sarah, and John Stirrup,..... ...	"	I. 7
1773. Aug. 11.	Romney, Ann, and Isaac Johnson, ...	"	xxi. 65
1773. Nov. 3.	Romp, Peter, and Margaret Klien, ...	"	xxii. 20
1756. July 6.	Romyne, Thomas, and Margaret Freelinhousen, ...	"	I. 246
1776. June 20.	Roncy, John, and Mary Platt,............	"	xxiii. 82
1760. Aug. 28.	Ronson, William, and Elisabeth Rose, ...	"	iii. 271
1781. June 6.	Rooke, Amos, and Martha Marcereu, ...	"	xxxii. 74
1771. June 29.	Roome, Agnus, and Abraham Myey, Jr.,...	"	xvii. 126
1782. April 25.	Roome, Hannah, and John Grigg,....	"	xxxv. 138
1779. Nov. 27.	Roome, Hannah, and John Hammell,......	"	xxviii. 152
1778. Mar. 18.	Roome, Jacob, and Elizabeth Lydekker, ...	"	xxv. 47
1762. June 30.	Roome, Judith, and James Dougherty,.....	"	vi. 218
1738. Aug. 28.	Roome, Lawrence, and Nieltie Turck, ...	"	I. 10
1782. Oct. 5.	Roome, Mary, and George Bell, ...	"	xxxvii. 31
1783. June 19.	Roome, Peter, and Catherine Day, ...	"	xxxix. 63
1761. June 10.	Roome, Peter, and Rachel Degroot, ...	"	iv. 234
1770. Dec. 19.	Roome, Rachel, and Christopher Steymets,..	"	xvi. 301
1780. Sept. 27.	Roome, Sarah, and Elias Cooper, ...	"	xxx. 45
1763. Dec. 19.	Roome, Susannah, and Archelaus Lewis, ...	"	vii. 513
1778. Sept. 29.	Roome, William I., and Rebecca Earle, ...	"	xxvi. 39
1783. Sept. 1.	Roop, Isaac, and Mary Mills,............	"	xl. 18
1764. Jan. 12.	Roorbach, Frederick, and Margaret Anderson, ...	"	viii. 14
1755. Nov. 27.	Roorbach, Frederick, and Neilte Ten Eyck,.	"	I. 220

DATE.	NAMES.	RECORD.	VOL. PAGE.
1758. June 15.	Roorbach, Johannes, and Mary Van Dueren,	M. B.,	I. 926
1777. Oct. 17.	Roorback, B., and Mary Ogilvie,.....	"	XXIV. 164
1753. Aug. 29.	Roorback, Gerret, and Alleda Fisher,......	"	I. 100
1757. Oct. 27.	Roorback, Sophia, and Walter Quackenboss,	"	I. 685
1765. April 11.	Roos, Evert, and Gertrude Van Steenbergh,	"	IX. 89
1772. Mar. 21.	Roosa, Geertje, and Cornelius Crispel,......	"	XVIII. 56
1774. Jan. 19.	Roosa, Sarah, and Samuel Freer,..........	"	XXII. 108
1765. Sept. 23.	Roosbach, Garret, and Jantie Van Sleck,...	"	IX. 270
1775. May 20.	Roose, Jacob, and Elizabeth Goff,.........	"	XXIII. 40
1781. April 20.	Roose, Sarah, and John Wilkee, ...	"	XXXII. 10
1782. Mar. 9.	Roosehill, Catharine, and Robert Loosely,..	"	XXXV. 81
1766. Sept. 26.	Roosevelt, Catherine, and Abraham Van Ranst, ...	"	X. 107
1769. Sept. 25.	Roosevelt, Christopher, and Mary Duryee,..	"	XV. 43
1770. Oct. 18.	Roosevelt, Elizabeth, and William Lupton,..	"	XVI. 222
1771. June 28.	Roosevelt, Hannah, and Andries Heermanse,	"	XVII. 125
1772. Nov. 27.	Roosevelt, Margaret, and Isaac Van Vleck, .	"	XIX. 133
1780. Nov. 2.	Roosevelt, Mary, and Thomas Stagg, ...	"	XXX, 88
1761. Dec. 15.	Roosevelt, Nicholas, Jr., and Sarah Van Ranst, ...	"	V. 281
1780. May 6.	Roosevelt, Oliver, and Rebecca Taylor,.....	"	XXIX. 45
1762. May 11.	Roosevelt, Peter, and Eelizabeth Vreelenhue-sen, ...	"	VI. 155
1761. May 13.	Root, Margaret, and William Brasier,......	"	IV. 188
1765. Aug. 21.	Rooze, Ebbert, and Alice De Lametter, ...	"	IX. 242
1773. Oct. 30.	Rosa, Jannetje, and Philip Newkerk, ...	"	XXII. 6
1760. Sept. 9.	Rosa, Jannitie, and Isaac Duboies,........	"	III. 305
1779. Oct. 4.	Rosamond, Richard, and Mary Davenport,..	"	XXVIII. 100
1759. July 19.	Rose, Agnus, and Samuel Lennox, ...	"	II. 359
1761. May 25.	Rose, Anthony, and Margaret Farrel,......	"	IV. 206
1762. Oct. 26.	Rose, Eghtje, and Samuel Swart, ...	"	VI. 386
1736. April 30.	Rose, Elizabeth, and Gerardus Waldron, ...	"	I. 1
1760. Aug. 28.	Rose, Elizabeth, and William Ronson, ...	"	III. 271
1763. Nov. 17.	Rose, Isaac, and Mary Van Vranka,.......	"	VII. 453
1781. May 2.	Rose, James, and Abigail Earl, ...	"	XXXII. 29
1766. July 31.	Rose, Joseph, and Barbary Egburson,......	"	X. 68
1762. July 9.	Rose, Judith, and James Gilliland, ...	"	VI. 232
1781. Mar. 8.	Rose, Mary, and Joshua Hill,.............	"	XXXI. 67
1758. Dec. 12.	Rose, Mary, and Samuel Edwards, ...	"	II. 125
1764. July 12.	Rose, Mary, and Theophilus Nelson,.......	"	VIII. 256
1757. Aug. 5.	Rose, Peter, and Elizabeth Grage, ...	"	I. 608
1772. July 7.	Rose, William, and Annamina Chappell,....	"	XVIII. 156
1777. Mar. 11.	Rose, William, and Jane Burger,..........	"	XXIV. 43
1767. Oct. 21.	Roseboom, Elcie, and Garrit A. Roseboom,.	"	XII. 65
1767. Sept. 9.	Roseboom, Elcie, and Gosen Van Schaick,..	"	XII. 31

DATE.	NAMES.	RECORD.	VOL.	PAGE.
1767. Oct. 31.	Roseboom, Elizabeth, and Cornelius Van Schurliunse,	M. B.,	XII.	73
1767. Oct. 21.	Roseboom, Garrit A., and Elcie Roseboom,.	"	XII.	65
1769. Sept. 11.	Roseboom, Gerretie, and John Ten Broeck,.	"	XV.	38
1763. Jan. 10.	Roseboom, Jacob, and Hester Lansingh,....	"	VII.	12
1763. Jan. 29.	Roseboom, John, and Susannah Veeder, ...	"	VII.	40
1765. April 29.	Roseboom, Myndert, and Gertrude Switts,..	"	IX.	114
1760. Oct. 29.	Rosekrans, Henry, and Jane Oostrander,...	"	III.	390
1764. June 1.	Rosekrans, Johannes, and Margaret Allen,..	"	VIII.	203
1771. Oct. 25.	Rosekrants, Mary, and Casparus Mancius,..	"	XVII.	225
1773. Jan. 28.	Rosekranz, Benjamin, and Phebe Vincent,..	"	XX.	27a
1779. Aug. 14.	Rosell, Sarah, and George James,.........	"	XXVIII.	50
1758. April 27.	Rosencranz, Abraham, and Mary Herhemer,	"	I.	888
1779. May 8.	Rosett, David, and Lydia Baily,...........	"	XXVII.	132
1760. Feb. 6.	Rosevelt, Catharine, and William Kirby, ...	"	III.	24
1737. June 14.	Rosevelt, Helena, and Andrew Barclay,....	"	I.	6
1737. June 4.	Rosevelt, Nicholas, and Catherine Comfort,.	"	I.	6
1769. Dec. 5.	Ross, Benjamin, and Eve Cummins, ...	"	XV.	114
1762. Feb. 4.	Ross, Charles, and Margaret McDougall,....	"	VI.	38
1761. April 3.	Ross, David, and Rachel Stymets,.........	"	IV.	131
1773. May 20.	Ross, Edward, and Isabella Ballendine, ...	"	XX.	119
1781. Feb. 10.	Ross, George, and Elenor Grant,..........	"	XXXI.	44
1770. Oct. 16.	Ross, Hester, and Samuel Neilson, ...	"	XVI.	216
1759. Dec. 20.	Ross, Jane, and Robert Welsh, ...	"	II.	552
1781. Nov. 16.	Ross, Jennet, and David Denny,..........	"	XXXIV.	39
1780. Dec. 27.	Ross, John, and Frances Van Evera,.......	"	XXX.	170
1781. Aug. 25.	Ross, John, and Hannah Ellison,..........	"	XXXIII.	46
1778. Aug. 8.	Ross, Juliet, and John White, ...	"	XXV.	146
1779. Dec. 27.	Ross, Margaret, and William Hutchings, ...	"	XXVIII.	182
1763. Nov. 9.	Ross, Mary, and Edward Hanly,..........	"	VII.	436
1781. Jan. 4.	Ross, Mary, and James Moffatt,...........	"	XXXI.	11
1768. Sept. 29.	Ross, Rachel, and Samuel Baker, ...	"	XIII.	201
1769. June 22.	Ross, Robert, and Deborah White, ...	"	XIV.	125
1778. Aug. 5.	Ross, Sarah, and Abraham Howard, ...	"	XXV.	143
1763. June 30.	Ross, Sarah, and Edward Nicoll,..........	"	VII.	249
1780. April 21.	Ross, William, and Ann Dally,............	"	XXIX.	31
1768. July 13.	Ross, William, and Susannah Gallant,......	"	XIII.	159
1762. July 16.	Rosseter, Robert, and Abigail Wright, ...	"	VI.	239
1761. Nov. 11.	Rote, Catharine, and Ezekiel Cooper,......	"	V.	208
1772. May 13.	Rote, James, and Elizabeth Guest, ...	"	XVIII.	109
1778. Oct. 30.	Rote, John, and Jane Barker, ...	"	XXVI.	79
1760. Nov. 22.	Rote, Margaret, and Matthew Gleves, ...	"	III.	434
1781. Oct. 15.	Rothery, John, and Letitia Foster, ...	"	XXXIII.	101
1760. Sept. 4.	Rottery, David, and Jennet Addy, ...	"	III.	282
1767. Mar. 14.	Rou, Esther, and Peter de Conty,.	"	XI.	45

42

DATE.	NAMES.	RECORD.	VOL.	PAGE.
1753. May 22.	Rou, Mary Elizabeth, and William Richards,	M. B.,	I.	38
1779. Oct. 2.	Roubalet, Charles, and Sarah Kingston,....	"	XXVIII.	98
1762. Dec. 20.	Rougont, Peitre, and Mary Martin,........	"	VI.	490
1770. Sept. 2.	Rous, Andrew, and Rebecca Lodewick,....	"	XVI.	177
1738. Nov. 27.	Rousby, Henry, and Ammy Brown,.......	"	I.	11
1757. Oct. 29.	Rousby, Sarah, and Abraham Ryker,......	"	I.	688
1777. Jan. 13.	Rouse, Robert, and Margaret Lavender,....	"	XXIV.	12
1736. Oct. 8.	Rousen, Hester, and Thomas Timson,......	"	I.	2
1771. Dec. 3.	Row, Catherine, and William Stewart,.....	"	XVII.	279
1736. Oct. 19.	Row, George, and Hiley Marce, ...	"	I.	3
1780. Oct. 14.	Row, John, and Etebert Hagarman,.,......	"	XXX.	64
1763. Sept. 15.	Rowan, Abraham, and Mary Van Orland,..	"	VII.	337
1779. Nov. 19.	Rowe, Elizabeth, and Oliver Fowler, ...	"	XXVIII.	144a
1770. Sept. 20.	Rowe, James, and Elizabeth Elting,.......	"	XVI.	191
1762. April 15.	Rowe, Johanna, and John Van Voorhis, ...	"	VI.	110
1771. June 7.	Rowe, Phebe, and John Forster,..........	"	XVII.	104
1764. Dec. 3.	Rowland, Abigal, and Philip Thorne, ...	"	VIII.	433
1783. Sept. 22.	Rowland, Hannah, and Edward Kearney,..	"	XL.	48
1779. June 10.	Rowland, James, and Deborah Forrester,...	"	XXVII.	161
1761. June 20.	Rowland, Mary, and Edmund Powell, ...	"	IV.	251
1768. July 7.	Rowland, Mary, and Isaac Bloom,.........	"	XIII.	150
1763. Aug. 18.	Rowland, Mary, and Luke Cummins,......	"	VII.	305
1773. Jan. 30.	Rowland, Phebe, and Hendrick Hagner, ...	"	XX.	29
1761. Nov. 28.	Rowland, Samuel, and Catharine Clowes, ..	"	V.	254
1779. Mar. 30.	Rowland, Sarah, and Israel Seaman,.......	"	XXVII.	83
1736. May 8.	Rowland, Sarah, and John Babb, ...	"	I.	1
1779. Jan. 7.	Rowland, Zorada, and William Williams,...	"	XXVII.	6
1769. Aug. 22.	Rowly, Hannah, and John Miller,.........	"	XV.	27
1761. June 25.	Rowlin, Martha, and Thomas Simmonds,...	"	IV.	261
1768. Feb. 10.	Roy, John, and Mary Young, ...	"	XIII.	29
1777. Jan. 3.	Royal, Elizabeth, and Matthew Ryan,......	'	XXIV.	5
1783. Sept. 3.	Royal, Prince, and Susannah Peterson, ...	"	XL.	22
1767. July 10.	Ruchmore, Elizabeth, and Gilbert Lawrance,	"	XI.	132
1780. May 3.	Ruckel, Philip, and Jane Billington, ...	"	XXIX.	44
1781. Nov. 20.	Ruckhow, Anne, and William Thorn,......	"	XXXIV.	51
1760. Aug. 26.	Rudgard, Thomas, and Charity Smith, ...	"	III.	266
1684. Oct. 25.	Rudgars, Ann, and John West,...........	C. M.,	XXXIII.	54
1684. Oct. 25.	Rudgars, Margaret, and Samuel Winder,...	"	XXXIII.	54
1758. Sept. 27.	Rudolph, George, and Christian Wagnren, .	M. B.,	II.	35
1770. Oct. 30.	Rudyard, John, and Catherine Doty, ...	"	XVI.	234
1782. Jan. 26.	Rudyard, Ruth, and John Biggs,..........	"	XXXV.	34
1758. Feb. 28.	Rue, Elizabeth, and Morley Harison, ...	"	I.	833
1753. Sept. 20.	Rue, Samuel, and Catherin Breasted,......	"	I.	121
1760. April 17.	Ruehle, Maria Catharine, and Cornelius Wynkoop,...............................	"	III.	112

DATE.	NAMES.	RECORD.	VOL.	PAGE.
1761. Feb. 17.	Ruehl, Anna Sabina, and Nicolaes de Ronde,.	M. B.,	IV.	66
1759. Feb. 16.	Ruger, Catharine, and Robert Nesbit,......	"	II.	195
1764. June 7.	Ruger, John, and Elizabeth Man, ...	"	VIII.	213
1757. April 16.	Ruger, William, and Christeena Harts,.....	"	I.	502
1779. Feb. 24.	Ruggles, John, and Hannah Sacket, ...	"	XXVII.	49
1779. July 12.	Rukler, Philipp, and Barbara Keyser,......	"	XXVIII.	22
1781. Aug. 28.	Ruland, Henry, and Joanna Smith,........	"	XXXIII.	50
1782. April 4.	Rull, Benjamin, and Catharine Delamater, ..	"	XXXV.	113
1779. Mar. 17.	Rull, Mary, and William Ketchison, ...	"	XXVII.	69.
1770. Mar. 20.	Rumsay, James, and Elizabeth Osborne, ...	"	XVI.	33
1765. June 30.	Rumsey, Mary, and William Karr, ...	"	XI.	116
1764. June 14.	Runaway, Catharine, and Henry McLorman,	"	VIII.	225
1783. Aug. 8.	Rundell, John, and Sarah Barton, ...	"	XXXIX.	120
1761. Jan. 27.	Runeva, Francis, and Catherine Fox, ...	"	IV.	33
1761. May 15.	Runshaw, Edward, and Rachel Wheeler,...	"	IV.	189
1765. Jan. 31.	Rusco, Elizabeth, and Walter Hyer, ...	"	IX.	41
1765. Sept. 24.	Rusco, Sarah, and John Myers,...........	"	IX.	273
1781. July 3.	Ruscom, Sweet, and Mary Foster,........	"	XXXII.	102
1760. Sept. 5.	Rushmore, Carman, and Hannah Raynor, ..	"	III.	286
1769. Jan. 31.	Rushmore, Elizabeth, and Jacob Vallentine,.	"	XIV.	24
1757. April 18.	Rushmore, Isaac, and Sarah Titus, ...	"	I.	503
1761. June 20.	Rushmore, Phelena, and Elias Darling,.....	"	IV.	249
1763. Oct. 17.	Rushmur, Abigal, and Jacob Briant, ...	"	VII.	389
1757. July 4.	Rushton, Crossfield, and Mary Bond, ...	"	I.	580
173⅞. Jan. 10.	Rushton, Elizabeth, and Richard Byfield,...	"	I.	8
1737. Nov. 16.	Ruskey, Mary, and Theodorus Vanwyk, ...	"	I.	8
1778. Aug. 12.	Rusler, Zachariah, and Elizabeth Vredenbergh, ...	"	XXVI.	3
1772. Nov. 28.	Russel, James, and Catherine Outenbogart,.	"	XIX.	136
1772. May 15.	Russel, John, and Anna Legget, ...	"	XVIII.	119
1771. Dec. 21.	Russell, Abraham, and Hilletye Elsworth,..	"	XVII.	302
1781. April 14.	Russell, Anna, and Cornelius Berrien,......	"	XXXII.	3
1764. Feb. 22.	Russell, David, and Elizabeth Williams,....	"	VIII.	71
1759. April 10.	Russell, Dennis, and Martha Brown,.......	"	II.	238
1783. Sept. 17.	Russell, Frances, and Anthony Purdy,.....	"	XL.	44
1781. June 5.	Russell, James, and Christiana Shepperd,...	"	XXXII.	73
1772. Aug. 24.	Russell, John, and Mary Devenny,........	"	XIX.	29
1764. May 19.	Russell, Joseph, and Magdalen Rideout,....	"	VIII.	195
1770. April 4.	Russell, Mary, and David Leuon,..........	"	XVI.	47
1777. May 7.	Russell, Rachel, and Thomas Jones,........	"	XXIV.	84
1771. Dec. 18.	Russell, Samuel, and Margaret Mosher, ...	"	XVII.	298
1782. June 10.	Rutan, William, and Margaret Steel,.......	"	XXXVI.	46
1758. Jan. 23.	Rutgers, Anna, and William Bancker,......	"	I.	797
1755. Oct. 1.	Rutgers, Catharin, and Benjamin Kissam, ..	"	I.	186
1766. May 30.	Rutgers, Catherine, and Jacob Le Roy, ...	"	X.	2

DATE.		NAMES.	RECORD.	VOL.	PAGE.
1763. Feb.	28.	Rutgers, Elisabeth, and Gerard De Peyster,.	M. B.,	VII.	81
1756. Aug.	31.	Rutgers, Elizabeth, and Frederick Philipse,.	"	I.	281
1773. July	19.	Rutgers, Harman, and Darkes Tippet,	"	XXI.	46
1770. May	16.	Rutgers, Margaret, and Humphry Jones, ...	"	XVI.	88
1755. Sept.	22.	Rutgers, Robert, and Elizabeth Beekman, ..	"	I.	181
1781. Feb.	20.	Rutherford, Henry, and Sarah Post,	"	XXXI.	52
1762. Oct.	8.	Rutsen, Alida, and Henry Van Renselaer,..	"	VI.	355
1767. May	19.	Rutsen, Catherine, and Benjamin Newkirk,.	"	XI.	92
1737. Oct.	25.	Rutsen, Jacob, Jr., and Allaida Livingston, .	"	I.	7
1767. Dec.	15.	Rutsen, John, and Phebe Carman,	"	XII.	114
1772. Oct.	15.	Rutsen, Mary, and Martin Campbell,	"	XIX.	72
1756. Dec.	9.	Rutsen, Sarah, and Nathaniel Contine,	"	I.	378
1765. April	23.	Rutser, Cornelia, and Robert Van Rensse- laer,	"	IX.	104
1762. May	5.	Rutter, John, and Arabella Harrison,	"	VI.	161
1783. Jan.	18.	Ryals, Jane, and William Husbands,	"	XXXVIII.	22
1767. June	30.	Ryan, Catherine, and Francis Arden,	"	XI.	117
1765. May	25.	Ryan, Cornelius, and Isabella Bryan,	"	IX.	140
1760. Feb.	28.	Ryan, Cornelous, and Catharine Cartey,....	"	III.	56
1768. Oct.	13.	Ryan, Elliner, and Bartholomew Vosburgh,.	"	XIII.	209
1764. Feb.	3.	Ryan, Jane, and John Hunt, Jr.,	"	VIII.	47
1770. Aug.	25.	Ryan, Jane, and Peter McMahon,	"	XVI.	172
1781. Nov.	22.	Ryan, John, and Amelia Mott,	"	XXXIV.	55
1763. Mar.	31.	Ryan, John, and Elizabeth Shea,	"	VII.	110
1764. Dec.	5.	Ryan, John, and Ellen Murphy,	"	VIII.	437
1775. Sept.	28.	Ryan, Lewis, and Mary Marea,	"	XXIII.	165
1770. Dec.	7.	Ryan, Mary, and Charles Grimesly,	"	XVI.	288
1777. Jan.	3.	Ryan, Mathew, and Elizabeth Royal,	"	XXIV.	5
1760. Mar.	24.	Ryan, Peter, and Jane Lowie,	"	III.	92
1765. July	11.	Ryan, Sarah, and Michael Peffer,	"	IX.	202
1760. Sept.	24.	Ryan, William, and Mary Rogers,	"	III.	327
1757. Feb.	18.	Ryason, John, and Maria Leffertse,	"	I.	441
1762. Aug.	30.	Rycker, Catharine, and Dennis Candy,	"	VI.	298
1757. Mar.	22.	Ryckman, Clactie, and James Reid,	"	I.	478
1769. Nov.	13.	Ryckman, Garret, and Elizabeth Vanbury, .	"	XV.	89
1773. Aug.	9.	Ryckman, Harmanus, and Sarah Bracade,..	"	XXI.	62
1773. Aug.	31.	Ryckman, Mary, and Jacob Boeler,	"	XXI.	92
1758. Nov.	1.	Ryckman, Peter, and Lydia Vandenbergh, .	"	II.	76
1761. May	15.	Ryckman, Tobias, and Sarah Kerser,	"	IV.	190
1765. Oct.	28.	Ryder, Adrianse, and Adreiaen Martensen,.	"	IX.	324
1770. Sept.	6.	Ryder, Aeltie, and Samuel Garrison,	"	XVI.	181
1778. Oct.	23.	Ryder, Amos, and Margaret Wyckoff,	"	XXVI.	68
1775. June	7.	Ryder, Anna, and Isaac Cornell,	"	XXIII.	57
1772. June	22.	Ryder, Anne, and John Hegeman,	"	XVIII.	146
1768. Sept.	14.	Ryder, Barnardus, and Angeltje Dyckman, .	"	XIII.	184

NEW YORK MARRIAGES. 333

DATE.	NAMES.	RECORD.	VOL.	PAGE.
1771. Aug. 21.	Ryder, Barnardus, and Femmitje Denyse, ..	M. B.,	XVII.	160
1772. Oct. 21.	Ryder, Edah, and Garret Monfore,........	"	XIX.	84
1757. Sept. 30.	Ryder, Elizabeth, and George Hicks, ...	"	I.	652
1760. Jan. 16.	Ryder, Elizabeth, and James Riddell,......	"	II.	582
1759. Nov. 21.	Ryder, Elizabeth, and Rem Adrianse,......	"	II.	510
1770. Feb. 17.	Ryder, Jane, and John Vorheis,...........	"	XVI.	20
1779. July 28.	Ryder, Jane, and Jonah Powell,..........	"	XXVIII.	33
1765. Jan. 16.	Ryder, Joseph, and Martha Jackson,.......	"	IX.	18
1783. Aug. 19.	Ryder, Joseph, and Sarah Stilwell,........	"	XL.	2
1778. Sept. 4.	Ryder, Laurence, and Catherine Williamson,	"	XXVI.	21
1779. Oct. 30.	Ryder, Letty, and Wilhelmus Stoothoff,....	"	XXVIII.	124
1761. Nov. 25.	Ryder, Mary, and John Bartow, Jr.,.......	"	V.	247
1762. Oct. 13.	Ryder, Mary, and William Gifford,........	"	VI.	363
1767. May 19.	Ryder, Phebe, and Stephen Voorhees, ...	"	XI.	91
1773. May 7.	Ryder, Samuel, and Abigail Coevert, ...	"	XX.	105
1768. Nov. 22.	Ryder, Stephen, and Jenny Simonson,.....	"	XIII.	240
1782. July 9.	Ryder, Stephen, and Latey Earl,..........	"	XXXVI.	76
1773. Jan. 4.	Ryder, Stephen, and Margaret Mitchel, ...	"	XX.	1
1761. Dec. 19.	Ryder, Stephen, and Sarah Leyster,.......	"	V.	288
1771. Dec. 15.	Ryder, William, and Mary Sands,.........	"	XVII.	296
1759. Feb. 19.	Rye, Catharine, and John Scobble, ...	"	II.	198
1736. June 30.	Ryers, James, and Apolonia Vredenbergh,..	"	I.	1
1764. Oct. 22.	Ryerse, Martinus, and Catherine De Graugh,	"	VIII.	367
1762. Aug. 2.	Ryerson, Antee, and Jeremyas Vanderbilt, .	"	VI.	260
1777. April 22.	Ryerson, Peter, and Sarah Welling, ...	"	XXIV.	70
1763. Nov. 22.	Ryerson, Sarah, and John Middagh,.......	"	VII.	461
1783. Aug. 16.	Ryerson, George, and Elizabeth Ellis, ...	"	XXXIX.	128
1775. Oct. 20.	Ryerson, Ida, and Andrew Cosper,........	"	XXIII.	185
1764. June 2.	Ryerson, Johannes, and Hannah Applestall,	"	VIII.	204
1779. Sept. 29.	Ryersz, Aris, and Sarah Stout,...........	"	XXVIII.	88
1780. April 18.	Ryersz, Gozen, and Cornelia Duffie, ...	"	XXIX.	28
1770. June 18.	Ryersz, Gozen, and Juthegh Dissasway, ...	"	XVI.	120
1781. Oct. 25.	Ryersz, Phebe, and John Thompson, ...	"	XXXIV.	5
1764. Mar. 8.	Rykeman, Albert, and Frances Stillwell, ...	"	VIII.	121
1757. Oct. 29.	Ryker, Abraham, and Sarah Rousby, ...	"	I.	688
1764. April 27.	Ryker, Elizabeth, and George Collins, ...	"	VIII.	172
1760. Aug. 13.	Ryker, Elizabets, and Abraham Blau Velt, .	"	III.	252
1762. Nov. 17.	Ryker, Gerardus, and Rachel De Marree,...	"	VI.	437
1760. April 22.	Ryker, Henry, and Jane Rappleye,........	"	III.	118
1759. June 16.	Ryker, Margaret, and John Bragra, ...	"	II.	328
1759. April 19.	Ryley, Catharine, and Lewis Harris,.......	"	II.	248
1755. Sept. 12.	Ryley, Philip, and Jannetie Jacobus Van Slyck, ...	"	I.	175
1765. Jan. 21.	Ryly, Alida, and Garret Van Francke,.....	"	IX.	26
1766. Aug. 20.	Rynders, Jacob, and Sarah Vandle,........	"	X.	77

DATE.	NAMES.	RECORD.	VOL. PAGE.
1771. Jan. 12.	Rynders, Sarah, and John Morris Foght, ...	M. B.,	XVII. 5
1770. June 29.	Ryndollar, Emanuel, and Elizabeth Smith, .	"	XVI. 126
1758. Mar. 27.	Rynier, Susannah, and Henry Charlick,....	"	I. 864
1762. Oct. 2.	Rynus, Elisabeth, and Christopher Torn, ...	"	VI. 343

S.

1771. Nov. 25.	Saats, Else, and Francis Salisbury, ...	"	XVII. 268
1765. Feb. 6.	Sabaton, Charles, and Hannah Maid, ...	"	IX. 47
1737. Oct. 28.	Sacket, Deborah, and James Stringham,....	"	I: 7
1779. Feb. 24.	Sacket, Hannah, and John Ruggles, ...	"	XXVII. 49
1780. Oct. 12.	Sacket, Sarah, and Elna Hayt,............	"	XXX. 63
1782. Sept. 11.	Sacket, Sarah, and John Woods,..........	"	XXXVI. 144
1762. Sept. 21.	Sacket, Thomas, and Phebe Albertus, ...	"	VI. 324
1772. Nov. 2.	Sackett, Frances, and William Laight, ...	"	XIX. 99
1759. Jan. 3.	Sackett, Nathaniel, and Mary Rogers, ...	"	II. 145
1764. June 27.	Sackett, Samuel, and Mary Betts,.........	"	VIII. 239
1759. Aug. 31.	Sackett, William, and Sarah Fish,.........	"	II. 405
1772. April 15.	Sackrider, Moses, and Hannah Wright, ...	"	XVIII. 79
1753. Aug. 25.	Sadlar, Mary, and John Cook,............	"	I. 96
1773. Feb. 18.	Sadler, Catherine, and John Hendricks,....	"	XX. 47
1762. June 17.	Sadler, Rebecca, and John Roberts, ...	"	VI. 195
1762. April 16.	Sadler, Richard, and Elizabeth Burrus,.....	"	VI. 114
1780. Dec. 6.	Saidlar, James, and Margaret Dellas, ...	"	XXX. 140
1756. Sept. 6.	St. Clear, Isabel, and James Galloway,.....	"	I. 286
1759. Feb. 7.	St. Croix, Joshua Temple De, and Leah Galladet, ...	"	II. 184
1783. May 14.	Sainthill, Edward, and Rebecca Ogilvey, ...	"	XXXIX. 11
1775. Aug. 11.	St. John, John, and Martha Wilkinson, ...	"	XXIII. 124
1773. July 12.	St. Morris, Susannah, and John Taylor, ...	"	XXI. 35
1761. July 9.	Salders, Daniel, and Jemima Towers, ...	"	IV. 291
1781. June 19.	Sailer, William, and Jane Remsen, ...	"	XXXII. 91
1770. Oct. 2.	Salisbury, Abraham, and Elsie Hasbrouck,..	"	XVI. 201
1759. Oct. 22.	Salisbury, Jane, and Edward York, ...	"	II. 469
1761. Nov. 20.	Salisbury, Mary, and Anthony Van Bergen,	"	V. 236
1771. Nov. 25.	Salisbury, Francis, and Elsie Saats,........	"	XVII. 268
1765. May 4.	Salisbury, Francis, and Lydia Van Veghte,.	"	IX. 120
1773. Mar. 3.	Salisbury, Jane, and James Light,.........	"	XX. 55
1768. June 11.	Salisbury, Lucas, and Mary Vanbueren,....	"	XIII. 126
1766. Oct. 22.	Salisbury, Silvester, and Elsie Eltinge,.....	"	X. 138
1764. Sept. 13.	Salisbury, Sylvester, and Nellie Staats, ...	"	VIII. 305
1770. Dec. 3.	Salisbury, Wessell, and Annatje Witbeck, ..	"	XVI. 281
1737. Oct. 20.	Sallier, Susannah, and Samuel Reed,.......	"	I. 7
1765. Sept. 5.	Sallisbury, Richard, and Sarah Higbee,.....	"	I. 167

DATE.	NAMES.	RECORD.	VOL.	PAGE.
1765. July 16.	Salmon, Elizâbeth, and David Johnston, ...	M. B.,	III.	215
1765. Aug. 6.	Salmon, Robert, and Jane Brazier, ...	"	IX.	256
1763. Oct. 5.	Salmon, Susannah, and Roger Richards, ...	"	VII.	373
1765. June 25.	Salmons, Ruth, and Simon Peet,....	"	IX.	184
1763. Nov. 11.	Salsbury, Elinor, and Henry Van Bergen,..	"	VII.	444
1769. Oct. 24.	Salsbury, Mary, and Nicholas Staats, ...	"	XV.	65
1759. Jan. 15.	Salt, John, and Hannah Frost,............	"	II.	157
1775. April 15.	Salt, William, and Martha Post, ...	"	XXIII.	11
1755. Sept. 4.	Salter, Ann, and William Budden, ...	"	I.	165
1758. Dec. 21.	Salter, Catharine, and John Simmons, ...	"	II.	138
1783. April 30.	Salter, Elliot, and Elizabeth Johnston, ...	"	XXXVIII.	122
1764. Jan. 6.	Salter, Manasseh, and Catherine Wright, ...	"	VIII.	9
1756. Sept. 4.	Salter, William, and Catherine Dally, ...	"	I.	284
1763. July 5.	Salts, Catharine, and Ezekiel Smith,.......	"	VII.	258
1758. Nov. 22.	Salts, Morris, and Tamer Horton, ...	"	II.	103
1772. April 25.	Saltus, Solomon, and Soncha Van Dyck, ...	"	XVIII.	88
1736. Oct. 22.	Salya, Elizabeth, and Edward Hopper,.....	"	I.	3
1762. Sept. 15.	Samen, Mary, and John James Ebet,......	"	VI.	317
1764. May 22.	Samis, Deborah, and Jeremiah Fleet, ...	"	VIII.	197
1782. Jan. 16.	Sammis, Alexander, and Amy Goold,......	"	XXXV.	19
1781. Oct. 28.	Sammis, David, and Deborah Ketchem,....	"	XXXIV.	11
1764. Nov. 26.	Sammis, Justus, and Thankful Fleet, ...	"	VIII.	425
1781. Nov. 18.	Sammis, Philip, and Martha White, ...	"	XXXIV.	47
1762. April 21.	Sammis, Timothy, and Elizabeth Scudder,..	"	VI.	122
1756. Dec. 21.	Sammon, Azuby, and William Saterly, ...	"	I.	396
1770. Oct. 2.	Sammons, Elizabeth, and Jacobus Elmendorph, Jr.,.....................	"	XVI.	203
1765. June 17.	Sammons, Hannah, and Jesse Carle,.......	"	XI.	110
1770. April 27.	Sammons, Jacob, and Rebecca Akerly,.....	"	XVI.	71
1771. Aug. 3.	Sammons, Martha, and John Mott,.... ...	"	XVII.	150
1770. Dec. 7.	Sammons, Rhode, and Jonas Titus,........	"	XVI.	286
1771. April 3.	Samons, Ruth, and Samuel Skidmore, ...	"	XVII.	47
1737. Aug. 3.	Sampell, James, and Jane Bargeau,........	"	I.	7
1760. Jan. 30.	Sample, Rebecca, and Robert Pickeman, ...	"	III.	11
1775. July 12.	Sample, Thomas, and Elizabeth Young,....	"	XXIII.	96
1768. May 30.	Sampson, Sarah, and Jonathan Jones, ...	"	XIII.	118
1772. April 10.	Samson, Frederick, and Mary Lott,........	"	XVIII.	73
1764. April 20.	Sandallan, William, and Elizabeth Waldron,	"	VIII.	165
1774. Jan. 27.	Sanders, Abraham, and Hannah Hyer,.....	"	XXII.	117
1775. Aug. 17.	Sanders, Catharine, and William Parsons, ..	"	XXIII.	131
1773. Oct. 27.	Sanders, Elizabeth, and Hercules Mulligan, .	"	XXI.	148
1683. July 26.	Sanders, John, and Ellzabeth Lawrence, ...	E.,	XXXIII.	74
1736. Oct. 21.	Sanders, Maria, and Samuel Phillipse,......	M. B.,	I.	3
1759. Oct. 19.	Sanders, Mary, and John J. Beekman,.....	"	II.	465
1782. Oct. 2.	Sanders, Sarah, and William Van Pelt, ...	"	XXXVII.	24

336 NEW YORK MARRIAGES.

Date.		Names.	Record.	Vol.	Page.
1769. Aug.	2.	Sanders, William, and Parnell Butler,	M. B.,	xv.	15
1760. July	16.	Sanderson, Peter, and Mary Davis,	"	iii.	214
1763. Nov.	9.	Sandes, James, and Elisabeth Flemming,	"	vii.	435
1782. Nov.	23.	Sandford, Elijah, and Jane Norwood,	"	xxxvii.	91
1777. Oct.	4.	Sandford, Mary, and John Thomson,	"	xxiv.	158
1781. Mar.	3.	Sandford, Rachel, and Jacob Ogden,	"	xxxi.	63
1775. Nov.	15.	Sandford, Thomas, and Phebe Howell,	"	xxiii.	210
1758. Dec.	12.	Sando, Margaret, and Jacob Pinno,	"	ii.	126
1782. Oct.	18.	Sandon, Thomas, and Jemima Bogart,	"	xxxvii.	51
1777. May	1.	Sands, Abigail, and Thomas Thorne,	"	xxiv.	80
1772. Aug.	25.	Sands, Anne, and Charles Field,	"	xix.	30
1758. Oct.	20.	Sands, Benjamin, and Mary Jackson,	"	ii.	64
1769. May	31.	Sands, Comfort, and Sarah Dodge,	"	xiv.	111
1753. Oct.	13.	Sands, Deborah, and Edmond Mott,	"	i.	139
1757. Mar.	16.	Sands, George, and Jamima Smith,	"	i.	471
1770. Nov.	30.	Sands, Hannah, and David Brooks,	"	xvi.	275
1736. May	10.	Sands, John, and Elizabeth Cornell,	"	i.	1
1757. Mar.	16.	Sands, John, and Elizabeth Jackson,	"	i.	472
1777. July	10.	Sands, Mary, and William Hopkins,	"	xxiv.	118
1771. Dec.	16.	Sands, Mary, and William Ryder,	"	xvii.	296
1757. July	26.	Sands, Phebe, and Arnout Cannon,	"	i.	601
1777. July	21.	Sands, Samuel, and Hester Simmons,	"	xxiv.	121
1779. May	14.	Sands, Sarah, and Richard Seaman,	"	xxvii.	136
1765. Oct.	11.	Sands, Sarah, and Symon Sands,	"	ix.	296
1755. Oct.	28.	Sands, Sarah, and Thomas Powell,	'	i.	200
1772. Dec.	10.	Sands, Sibel, and Benjamin Burling,	"	xix.	151
1772. May	23.	Sands, Stephen, and Mary Branson,	"	xviii.	122
1765. Oct.	11.	Sands, Symon, and Sarah Sands,	"	ix.	296
1757. May	16.	Sands, William, and Deborah Aclay,	"	i.	534
1762. Oct.	20.	Sands, William, and Elisabeth German,	"	vi.	375
1773. Jan.	30.	Sandsbury, Hannah, and Peter Lee,	"	xx.	32
1770. Mar.	1.	Santford, Sarah, and William May,	"	xvi.	35
1773. Dec.	22.	Sanxay, John, and Salome Bacon,	"	xxii.	83
1777. Nov.	12.	Sarell, John, and Lydia Jones,	"	xxiv.	181
1769. Mar.	6.	Sargent, Ann, and John Sigell,	"	xiv.	46
1780. July	8.	Sargent, John, and Ruth Brown,	"	xxix.	108
1757. Sept.	17.	Sarjeant, William, and Catherine Douglass,	"	i.	637
1761. April	16.	Sarle, Catharine, and John Crawley,	"	iv.	150
1782. Feb.	23.	Sarly, Elizabeth, and Joseph Barton,,	"	xxxv.	63
1778. Jan.	6.	Sarly, Elizabeth, and Thomas Brooke,	"	xxv.	1
1760. Oct.	6.	Sarly, John, and Elizabeth Brown John,	"	iii.	345
1670. Oct.	7.	Sartell, Mary, and Hans Lorrison,	C. A.,	ii.	594
1783. April	12.	Sarvant, Abraham, and Elinor Urine,	M. B.,	xxxviii.	92
1782. Jan.	8.	Sarvant, John, and Margaret Yeany,	"	xxxv.	11
1760. Nov.	21.	Satchell, William, and Jane Leghorn,	"	iii.	433

DATE.		NAMES.	RECORD.	VOL.	PAGE.
1781. Jan.	6.	Saterly, Phebe, and Samuel Thompson, ...	M. B.,	XXXI.	17
1756. Dec.	21.	Saterly, William, and Azuby Sammon,.....	"	I.	396
1781. Dec.	26.	Satterly, Samuel, and Hannah Woodhull, ..	"	XXXIV.	107
1761. Sept.	11.	Satturley, Mary, and William Tooker, ...	"	V.	80
1772. Jan.	3.	Saul, Eve, and John Shoemakar,.....	"	XVIII.	1
1755. Dec.	5.	Saults, Sarah, and Hozeah Hawxhurst, ...	"	I.	225
1777. June	2.	Saunders, Ann, and John Wm. Livingston,.	"	XXIV.	95
1770. June	1.	Saunders, Catherine, and Henry B. Ten Eyck,.............................	"	XVI.	103
1760. July	5.	Saunders, Catharine, and Mathew Bishop,..	"	III.	205
1756. Dec.	27.	Saunders, Elizabeth, and John Breath,.....	"	I.	399
1767. Sept.	11.	Saunders, Elizabeth, and Joseph Haines,...	"	XII.	33a
1769. Nov.	29.	Saunders, Frances, and Philip Burner, ...	"	XV.	109
1762. June	21.	Saunders, Hannah, and Daniel Morgan,....	"	VI.	199
1737. July	20.	Saunders, John, and Elizabeth Singeon,....	"	I.	6
1762. Nov.	13.	Saunders, Margaret, and Henry Whyte,....	"	VI.	431
1768. Feb.	13.	Saunders, Maria, and Stephen Van Renselaer, ...	"	XIII.	38
1762. June	19.	Saunders, Mary, and James Prince, ...	"	VI.	196
1761. Jan.	10.	Saunders, Mary, and John Fox,...........	"	IV.	10
1781. Nov.	16.	Saunders, Peter, and Lette Skinner,.......	"	XXXIV.	40
1762. Sept.	3.	Saunders, Sarah, and John S. Glenn,......	"	VI.	304
1772. Oct.	15.	Saunders, Susannah, and George Peek, ...	"	XIX.	73
1760. Aug.	18.	Savage, Edmund, and Catharine Gray,.....	"	III.	257
1764. Sept.	21.	Savage, John, and Marcelus Lipe,.........	"	VIII.	321
1761. Feb.	8.	Savage, Margaret, and Samuel Hopson,....	"	IV.	86
1767. April	7.	Savage, Mary, and Peter Thompson, ...	"	XI.	58
1769. Nov.	6.	Savage, Rachel, and Alexander Lamb,. ...	"	XV.	79
1772. April	7.	Sawyer, Francis, and Jane Outen Bogert, ..	"	XVIII.	70
1783. Sept.	26.	Sawyer, Jane, and John Callanan, ...	"	XL.	54
1771. Nov.	18.	Sax, John, and Catherine Weaver, ...	"	XVII.	258
1760. Sept.	5.	Sax, Richard, and Mary Andrews, ...	"	III.	289
1780. April	1.	Saxton, Charlotte, and Archibald Campbell,.	"	XXIX.	13
1736. May	14.	Saxton, Elizabeth, and Jonas Adams,......	"	I.	1
1737. Nov.	26.	Saybrant, Elizabeth, and Jacobus Kiersted,.	"	I.	8
1761. Dec.	18.	Saydam, Charity, and Abraham Anthony,..	"	V.	286
1760. Dec.	6.	Sayer, Samuel, and Rachel Sprung,........	"	III.	461
1737. May	31.	Sayre, Ephram, and Elizabeth Lynson, ...	"	I.	6
1779. Nov.	6.	Sayre, Hannah, and Obediah Rogers,......	"	XXVIII.	132
1777. May	24.	Sayre, Jane, and Obadiah Wright, ...	"	XXIV.	93
1777. Sept.	29.	Sayre, John, and Abigail Jarvis,..........	"	XXIV.	154
1780. Aug.	30.	Scadden, Margeret, and John Curry, ...	"	XXX.	9
1781. June	4.	Scales, William, and Jane Spence,.........	"	XXXII.	72
1768. June	6.	Scallon, Laurance, and Margeret Deverix,..	"	XIII.	122
1768. Aug.	8.	Scandlin, John, and Mary Hacket, ...	"	XIII.	171

43

DATE.	NAMES.	RECORD.	VOL. PAGE.
1738. June 5.	Scandling, Patrick, and Jane Stricker,.....	M. B.,	I. 9
1779. April 24.	Scandrett, Hester, and William Furnivall,..	"	XXVII. 117
1770. Oct. 15.	Scankel, Hendrick, and Mary Tocloan,.....	"	XVI. 214
1764. Oct. 29.	Scarp, Jane, and Johannis Schermerhorn, ..	"	VIII. 377
1775. May 18.	Schams, Anna, and Gerrit A. Van Den Bergh,	"	XXIII. 38
1760. Sept. 5.	Schanck, Heliet, and Jacob Riersen,.......	"	III. 284
1760. Jan. 8.	Schank, Anna, and John Voorhies,........	"	II. 573
1738. Oct. 7.	Schank, Elizabeth, and Jonathan Lequier,..	"	I. 11
1771. Oct. 28.	Scharmehorn, Sinea, and Martin Egberson,.	"	XVII. 227
1767. Nov. 6.	Scharp, Augustinus, and Mary Van Alstyne,	"	XII. 77
1773. Feb. 9.	Schaumburg, Adam, and Margaret Munro,..	"	XX. 39
1775. Aug. 17.	Schell, Richard, and Rebecca Brown,......	"	XXIII. 121
1766. Nov. 5.	Schelp, Solomon A., and Sarah Thomas, ...	"	X. 154
1768. Dec. 18.	Schenck, Abraham, and Catharine Hooglandt,......	"	XV. 126
1763. Jan. 10.	Schenck, Ann, and Jaques Denyse,........	"	VII. 220
1773. Mar. 17.	Schenck, Ann, and John Tanner, ...	"	XX. 65
1763. May 19.	Schenck, Antje, and William Boerum,.....	"	VII. 194
1764. May 11.	Schenck, Eda, and Isaac Adriance,........	"	VIII. 188
1779. May 13.	Schenck, Elinor, and James Waters,.......	"	XXVII. 134
1753. Oct. 12.	Schenck, Elizabeth, and Joris Rapalje, ...	"	I. 138
1767. Dec. 3.	Schenck, Jane, and Daniel Rapalje,........	"	XII. 105
1783. Jan. 9.	Schenck, John, and Anne Williamsen......	"	XXXVIII. 11
1763. Aug. 6.	Schenck, John, and Elizabeth Layton, ...	"	VII. 293
1773. May 10.	Schenck, John, Jr., and Sarah Nostrandt, ..	"	XX. 106
1778. May 25.	Schenck, Margaret, and Cornelius Emans,..	"	XXV. 93
1762. April 13.	Schenck, Margaret, and Peter F. Monfoort,.	"	VI. 105
1755. June 10.	Schenck, Maria, and Coenrad W. Ham,....	"	IX. 163
1772. Oct. 21.	Schenck, Maria, and Dennis H. Lott, ...	"	XIX. 81
1762. June 22.	Schenck, Maria, and Rem Remsen,........	"	VI. 204
1768. Nov. 23.	Schenck, Maritje, and Samuel Stryker,.....	"	XIII. 242
1783. Aug. 21.	Schenck, Martin, and Agnes Rapalye, ...	"	XL. 4
1760. May 30.	Schenck, Martin, and Sarah Cowenhoven,..	"	III. 168
1768. Jan. 13.	Schenck, Martin, Jr., and Agnes Rapelye, ..	"	XIII. 6
1768. Sept. 12.	Schenck, Mary, and Dirck Brinckerhoff, ...	"	XIII. 182
1760. Oct. 2.	Schenck, Mary, and George Hogeland, ...	"	III. 342
1778. Aug. 21.	Schenck, Mary, and John Emens,.........	"	XXVI. 8
1777. Nov. 8.	Schenck, Mary, and John Williamson, ...	"	XXIV. 176
1766. July 31.	Schenck, Nelly, and George De Bevoise,...	"	X. 67
1775. July 24.	Schenck, Nicholas, and Seaity Hamands,...	"	XXIII. 102
1757. Aug. 13.	Schenck, Nicholas, and Willentie Wickoff,..	"	I. 613
1776. Jan. 16.	Schenck, Paul, and Joana Livingston, ...	"	XXIII. 242
1764. June 1.	Schenck, Phebe, and Peter Stryker,.......	"	VIII. 202
1779. Dec. 1.	Schenck, Sarah, and Jacob Vaullintine, ...	"	XXVIII. 155
1753. Oct. 17.	Schenck, Willemtie, and Petrus Amerman,.	"	I. 142

DATE.		NAMES.	RECORD.	VOL.	PAGE.
1769. Oct.	19.	Schermerhorne, Gerrity, and Wilhelmus Van Steenbergh, ...	M. B.,	XV.	57
1762. Mar.	29.	Schermerhorne, Gertie, and Jacob Schermerhorne, ...	"	VI.	86
1757. Sept.	7.	Schermerhorne, Helena, and Masil Bloomindale, ...	"	I.	633
1762. Nov.	1.	Schermerhorne, Henry, and Cornelia Lansingh, ...	"	VI.	403
1762. Mar.	29.	Schermerhorne, Jacob, and Gertie Schermerhorne, ...	"	VI.	86
1762. Oct.	13.	Schermerhorne, Jacob, and Mary Vedder, ..	"	VI.	397
1762. Aug.	21.	Schermerhorne, Jacobus, and Ann P. Vrooman, ...	"	VI.	283
1757. Sept.	2.	Schermerhorne, Jannetje, and Barent Veeder,	"	I.	630
1766. Dec.	1.	Schermerhorne, John, and Margaret Follensby, ...	"	X.	188
1757. April	16.	Schermerhorne, Lientie, and James Willson,	"	I.	499
1768. Sept.	19.	Schermerhorne, Maritje, and Peter Vanvalkenburgh, ...	"	XIII.	190
1762. Jan.	12.	Schermerhorne, Mary, and Joseph Marschalk,	"	VI.	8
1770. Nov.	5.	Schermerhorne, Mary, and Peter Van Geyseling, ...	"	XVI.	240
1776. Jan.	25.	Schermerhorne, Philip, and Dorothy Miller, .	"	XXIII.	253
1761. Oct.	6.	Schermerhorne, William, and Magdelain Van Bueren, ...	"	V.	127
1738. Oct.	18.	Scherp, Neltia, and Johannes Schermehoon,	"	I.	11
1780. Aug.	12.	Schieffelin, Jacob, and Hannah Laurence, ..	"	XXIX.	140
1776. Feb.	8.	Schinckel, Johannis, and Jan Van Valkenburgh, ...	"	XXIII.	265
1782. June	28.	Schlaesman, Johan Michael, and Susannah Stuvenge, ...	"	XXXVI.	66
1760. Dec.	8.	Schoenmaker, Peter, and Jane Wesbrook, ..	"	III.	466
1761. Dec.	11.	Schoenmaker, Susannah, and Felte Smith, ..	"	V.	275
1759. June	21.	Schonmaker, Cornelius, and Ariantje Turwilegen, ...	"	II.	334
1761. Aug.	25.	Schonmaker, Edward, and Lydia Schepmus, .	"	V.	57
1773. April	16.	Schonmaker, Jacob De Witt, and Maria Hozenbeek, ...	"	XX.	93
1761. June	23.	Schoonhover, Elisabeth, and Peter Bogardus,	"	IV.	257
1776. April	22.	Schoonmaker, Benjamin, and Catrina Vroome,	"	XXIII.	299
1765. June	14.	Schoonmaker, Catharine, and Johannes Schoonmaker, ...	"	IX.	168
1768. April	5.	Schoonmaker, Catherine, and Jacobus Schoonmaker, ...	"	XIII.	62
1771. Aug.	26.	Schoonmaker, Daniel, and Moyaca Slack, ...	"	XVII.	162

DATE.	NAMES.	RECORD.	VOL. PAGE.
1766. Oct. 31.	Schoonmaker, Deborah, and Hezekiah Schoonmaker, Jr., ...	M. B.,	x. 147
1760. Aug. 27.	Schoonmaker, Elizabeth, and Frederick Schoonmaker, ...	"	III. 270
1760. Aug. 27.	Schoonmaker, Frederick, and Elizabeth Schoonmaker, ...	"	III. 270
1760. May 9.	Schoonmaker, Helena, and John Wanshaer, Jr., ...	"	III. 147
1766. Oct. 31.	Schoonmaker, Hezekiah, Jr., and Deborah Schoonmaker, ...	"	x. 147
1772. Oct. 17.	Schoonmaker, Jacobus, and Annetje Sleght,	"	XIX. 77
1768. April 5.	Schoonmaker, Jacobus, and Catherine Schoonmaker, ...	"	XIII. 62
1766. Nov. 7.	Schoonmaker, Jochem, and Lena Depuy,...	"	x. 157
1765. June 14.	Schoonmaker, Johannes, and Catharine Schoonmaker, ...	"	IX. 168
1773. May 15.	Schoonmaker, Johannes, and Gertruyde Broadhead, ...	"	xx. 113
1771. Feb. 4.	Schoonmaker, Margaret, and Hendrickus P. Oosterhout, ...	"	XVII. 11
1761. Oct. 24.	Schoonmaker, Maria, and James Hamilton,.	"	v. 166
1765. May 9.	Schotler, John Garrat, and Precilla Bloom, .	'	IX. 124
1758. May 10.	Schram, John, and Eva Van Volkenburgh, .	"	I. 898
1783. Nov. 15.	Schroeder, Henry Benjamin, and Mary Coffey, ...	"	XL. 115
1773. May 27.	Schryver, Jacob, and Rachel Tenbroock, ...	"	xx. 129
1759. April 12.	Schureman, Catharine, and Stephen Steel,..	"	II. 239
1768. Nov. 17.	Schureman, William, and Jane Bonnet,....	"	XIII. 237
1760. May 1.	Schurman, Jacob, and Magdalen Parent, ...	"	III. 133
1761. Jan. 29.	Schurman, Jeremiah, and Magdalen De Foue,	"	IV. 39
1762. Jan. 18.	Schurman, Sarah, and Dennis Dunscomb, ..	"	VI. 16
1758. Nov. 2.	Schurri, Elizabeth, and Jeremiah Jones,....	"	II. 77
1758. Dec. 14.	Schurri, Rachel, and Timothy Hicks,.......	"	II. 128
1765. Aug. 7.	Schut, Johannes, and Phebe Van Voorhees,	"	IX. 232
1767. May 5.	Schutze, John Sigismund Ferdinand, and Elizabeth Boyd, ...	"	XI. 77
1763. Nov. 12.	Schuyler, Abraham, and Eva Beeckman,...	"	VII. 446
1769. Mar. 21.	Schuyler, Ann Elizabeth, and John Bleecker,	"	XIV. 57
1757. Aug. 10.	Schuyler, Anthon, and Rachel Vanburen, ..	"	I. 10
1772. Nov. 2.	Schuyler, Arent I., and Swen Schuyler,....	"	XIX. 101
1762. Jan. 14.	Schuyler, Catharine, and Cornelius Swits, ..	"	VI. 12
1764. Nov. 14.	Schuyler, David Hermanus, and Elizabeth Simmonds, ...	"	VIII. 406
1764. April 17.	Schuyler, Dirck, Jr., and Mary Van Duersen, ...	"	VIII. 160

DATE.	NAMES.	RECORD.	VOL.	PAGE.
1738. April 29.	Schuyler, Effie, and Charles Arding,.......	M. B.,	I.	9
1773. May 29.	Schuyler, Elizabeth, and Daniel Halstead, ..	"	XX.	132
1760. May 12.	Schuyler, Gurtruy, and George Kuaggs,....	"	III.	149
1760. Nov. 19.	Schuyler, Gertrude, and John Charlton,....	"	III.	427
1766. Sept. 27.	Schuyler, Gertruydt, and Robert Livingston,	"	X.	109
1761. Sept. 1.	Schuyler, Johanna, and William Lupton,...	"	V.	64
1769. Feb. 16.	Schuyler, John, and Mary Hunter, ...	"	XIV.	35
1760. Aug. 7.	Schuyler, Margaret, and Anthony Ten Eyck,	"	III.	239
1761. Nov. 9.	Schuyler, Margaret, and Goshen Van Schaick,	"	V.	199
1736. Dec. 1.	Schuyler, Mary, and Archibald Kennedy, ..	"	I.	3
1753. Aug. 28.	Schuyler, Mary, and John Haywood,......	"	I.	99
1776. Nov. 15.	Schuyler, Peter, Jr., and Gertruy Lansingh,	"	X.	166
1755. Sept. 4.	Schuyler, Philip John, and Catherin Van Renselaer, ...	"	I.	160
1765. Mar. 26.	Schuyler, Philip P., and Annatje Wendell,..	"	IX.	74
1770. June 25.	Schuyler, Samuel, and Elizabeth P. Clopper,	"	XVI.	122
1757. Mar. 19.	Schuyler, Stephen, and Angeltie Van Veghten, ...	"	I.	475
1763. April 11.	Schuyler, Stephen, and Helena Ten Eyck,..	"	VII.	121
1772. Nov. 2.	Schuyler, Swen, and Arent I. Schuyler,....	"	XIX.	101
1763. Nov. 28.	Schwahnn, Gottfried, and Ann Mary Remmis, ...	"	VII.	477
1758. June 3.	Scidmore, Daniel, and Jane Acker,........	"	I.	924
1764. Feb. 10.	Scidmore, Jane, and Ephraim Bayly,.......	"	VIII.	55
1781. Mar. 2.	Scidmore, Mary, and Abraham Ditmas, ...	"	XXXI.	62
1779. Feb. 12.	Scidmore, Mary, and David Dick,.........	"	XXVII.	40
1779. May 19.	Scidmore, Susanah, and Stephen Hayden,..	"	XXVII.	141
1759. June 16.	Sclatter, James, and Cicily Ballantine,......	"	II.	329
1759. Feb. 19.	Scobble, John, and Catharine Rye, ...	"	II.	198
1768. Jan. 30.	Scobey, William, and Ann White,.........	"	XIII.	23
1770. Mar. 24.	Scores, William, and Mary McDonald,.....	"	XVI.	40
1778. Feb. 20.	Scorfield, Catherine, and Samuel Duffy,....	"	XXV.	29
1765. Jan. 5.	Scorfield, Thomas, and Catharine Smith, ...	"	IX.	9
1782. May 4.	Scotland, Thomas, and Abigail Allicoke,....	"	XXXV.	151
1765. July 24.	Scott, Ann, and Thomas Brown,..........	"	IX.	216
1759. Dec. 29.	Scott, Bena, and John Arnes, ...	"	II.	559
1783. Aug. 6.	Scott, Caleb, and Judith Devenport,.......	"	XXXIX.	115
1759. July 10.	Scott, David, and Mary Wendell,..........	"	II.	351
1757. Dec. 2.	Scott, Deborah, and Joseph Powell, ...	"	I.	723
1778. May 9.	Scott, Elizabeth, and Leonard Tarrant,.....	'	XXV.	76
1780. Dec. 20.	Scott, George, and Jane Deforrest, ...	'	XXX.	160
1759. Nov. 21.	Scott, Hellatie, and Samuel Holliday,......	"	II.	512
1759. Nov. 28.	Scott, James, and Jane (Mary) Miller, ...	"	II.	520
1762. Mar. 26.	Scott, James, and Mary Ayres,...........	"	VI.	83
1761. Oct. 3.	Scott, John, and Anne Holmes,...........	"	V.	118

DATE.	NAMES.	RECORD	VOL.	PAGE.
1738. Aug. 7.	Scott, Joseph, and Sarah Vanderspiegel,....	M. B.,	I.	10
1777. Aug. 11.	Scott, Lydia, and George Deblois, Jr., ...	"	XXIV.	130
1760. June 27.	Scott, Margaret, and John Cure, ...	"	IV.	266
1736. April 16.	Scott, Robert, and Annanekie Williams,....	"	I.	1
1782. Oct. 17.	Scott, Robert, and Margaret Aime,........	"	XXXVII.	44
1678. Feb. 7.	Scott, William, and Abigail Warner,......	G. E.,	XXXII.	21
1760. Mar. 22.	Scott, William, and Elizabeth Peneer, ...	M. B.,	III.	88
1760. July 28.	Scott, William, and Elizabeth Wright, ...	"	III.	228
1770. June 18.	Scott, William, and Hannah Casting, ...	"	XVI.	119
1779. Jan. 30.	Scott, William, and Mary Heyer,..........	"	XXVII.	33
1782. Mar. 19.	Scudden, Timothy, and Rebeckah Wiseen,..	"	XXXV.	91
1761. April 7.	Scudder, Abigail, and Israel Platt,.........	"	IV.	138
1778. July 13.	Scudder, Ann, and Alexander Murray,.....	"	XXV.	130
1757. Nov. 23.	Scudder, Elizabeth, and Elphilet Platt,.....	"	I.	712
1762. April 21.	Scudder, Elizabeth, and Timothy Sammis,..	"	VI.	122
1782. Mar. 4.	Scudder, Hannah, and Downing Hendren,..	"	XXXV.	71
1772. Jan. 28.	Scudder, Hannah, and James Bryan, ...	"	XVIII.	19
1668. Jan. 4.	Scudder, Hannah, and William Smith,.....	O. W. L.,	II.	321
1765. Jan. 14.	Scudder, Henry, and Phebe Carll,.........	M. B.,	IX.	15
1779. Sept. 16.	Scudder, Jacob, and Affy Collard,.........	"	XXVIII.	77
1738. Nov. 6.	Scudder, Jernsea, and Timothy Kerr,......	"	I.	11
1770. Sept. 17.	Scudder, Joel, and Sarah Brush,..........	"	XVI.	189
1669. April 20.	Scudder, John, Jr., and Joannah Betts, ...	O. W. L.,	II.	417
1773. Jan. 20.	Scudder, Jonas, and Sarah Taylor, ...	M. B.,	XX.	23
1782. Feb. 9.	Scudder, Margreet, and Stephen Penney,...	"	XXXV.	46
1770. Oct. 17.	Scudder, Sarah, and Jooso Russot,........	"	XVI.	217
1768. May 25.	Scyver, David, and Arreantje Hooghtelle,..	"	XIII.	114
1757. July 11.	Sea, Hester, and John Devoe, ...	"	I.	589
1779. June 11.	Seabring, Catherine, and Archibald Currie, .	"	XVII.	109
1761. Dec. 15.	Seabrook, Nicholas Brown, and Mary Duch-			
	ess,................................	"	V.	280
1768. Jan. 14.	Seabury, Abigail, and Gilbert Van Wyck,..	"	XIII.	8
1781. Dec. 26.	Seabury, Abigail Mumford, and Colin Camp-			
	bell, ...	"	XXXIV.	106
1762. April 14.	Seabury, Adam, and Mirian Peters, ...	"	VI.	108
1780. Nov. 10.	Seabury, Ann, and Benjamin Lawrence, ...	"	XXX.	101
1770. Sept. 5.	Seabury, David, and Anne Lyne, ...	"	XVI.	178
1762. Nov. 24.	Seabury, Elisabeth, and Benjamin Tredwell,	"	VI.	450
1756. Oct. 12.	Seabury, Samuel, and Mary Hicks,........	"	I.	326
1783. July 8.	Seabury, Violette Ricketts, and Charles Ni-			
	coll Taylor, ...	"	XXXIX.	84
1760. Mar. 22.	Seacord, Benjamin, and Jane Perent,......	"	III.	86
1765. May 20.	Seacord, Christian, and Tunis Willsey,.....	"	IX.	133
1762. Dec. 22.	Seacord, Jane, and Isaac Craft, ...	"	VI.	493
1763. Feb. 1.	Seacord, Mary, and Jacob Gidney, ...	"	VII.	48

DATE.	NAMES.	RECORD.	VOL.	PAGE.
1773. Jan. 23.	Sealy, Benjamin, and Elizabeth Solds, ...	M. B.,	xx.	17
1768. Mar. 21.	Sealy, Josiah, and Sarah Holley,..........	"	xiii.	53
1782. April 17.	Sealy, Ruth, and Jechaniah Holcomb, ...	"	xxxv.	125
1782. June 23.	Seaman, Abigail, and John Hendrickson,...	"	xxxvi.	61
1769. Oct. 28.	Seaman, Absalom, and Phebe Andrews,....	"	xv.	72
1783. Feb. 21.	Seaman, Benjamin, and Hannah Denton,...	"	xxxviii.	49
1762. June 1.	Seaman, David, and Hannah Hicks,.......	"	vi.	177
1769. Nov. 18.	Seaman, David, and Martha Wilson, ...	"	xv.	97
1773. June 22.	Seaman, Deborah, and Samuel Jackson,....	"	xxi.	20
1768. Jan. 4.	Seaman, Elizabeth, and David Jones, Jr.,...	"	xiv.	3
1781. Oct. 6.	Seaman, Elizabeth, and Isaac Cock, ...	"	xxxiii.	90
1781. Oct. 26.	Seaman, Elizabeth, and Robert Stewart, ...	"	xxxiv.	6
1773. April 19.	Seaman, Elizabeth, and Solomon Seman,...	"	xx.	97
1780. Aug. 9.	Seaman, Enoc, and Mary Smith,..........	"	xxix.	136
1762. June 1.	Seaman, Gilbert. and Mary Post,..........	"	vi.	178
1763. July 5.	Seaman, Isaac, and Phebe Jackson,........	"	vii.	257
1779. Mar. 30.	Seaman, Israel, and Sarah Rowland, ...	"	xxvii.	83
1773. Feb. 11.	Seaman, Jenny, and Christopher Billopp,...	"	xx.	41
1763. Feb. 18.	Seaman, John, and Rachel Jones, ...	"	vii.	68
1764. Jan. 24.	Seaman, Jordan, and Mary Seaman,.......	"	viii.	35
1765. Sept. 25.	Seaman, Martha, and Benjamin Drake, ...	"	ix.	274
1764. Jan. 24.	Seaman, Mary, and Jordan Seaman,.......	"	viii.	35
1759. Aug. 6.	Seaman, Mary, and Paul Micheau, ...	"	ii.	376
1769. Mar. 1.	Seaman, Mary, and Peter Nostrant,.......	"	xiv.	40
1759. Feb. 22.	Seaman, Maurice, and Sarah Dingee, ...	"	ii.	200
1759. July 28.	Seaman, Millia, and Jonathan Smith, ...	"	ii.	367
1783. April 24.	Seaman, Noah, and Hannah Nostrandt,....	"	xxxviii.	112
1767. June 5.	Seaman, Obadiah, and Phebe Vallentine,...	"	xi.	105
1755. Dec. 19.	Seaman, Obediah, and Deborah Smith,.....	"	i.	235
1778. Feb. 7.	Seaman, Poley, and Townsend Jackson, ...	"	xxv.	19
1770. Dec. 19.	Seaman, Richard, and Elizabeth Cortelyou,.	"	xvi.	303
1771. Mar. 15.	Seaman, Richard, and Elizabeth Lawrence,.	"	xvii.	34
1780. July 31.	Seaman, Robert, and Mary Straton, ...	"	xxix.	129
1779. May 14.	Seaman, Richard, and Sarah Sands, ...	"	xxvii.	136
1763. Nov. 7.	Seaman, Sarah, and Thomas Shadbolt,.....	"	vii.	429
1759. Nov. 3.	Seaman, Stephen, and Martha McCoun,....	"	ii.	486
1780. Nov. 16.	Seaman, Thomas, and Abigail Lewis,......	"	xxx.	108
1762. Feb. 9.	Seaman, Willett, and Mary Serring, ...	"	vi.	42
1782. July 30.	Seaman, William, and Anne Fowler, ...	"	xxxvi.	93
1764. Oct. 29.	Seaman, William, and Philena Smith,......	"	viii.	382
1771. June 1.	Seaman, Zebulon, and Jane Jackson, ...	"	xvii.	99
1758. Dec. 6.	Seamans, Benjamin, and Lettetia Allen,....	"	ii.	117
1756. July 10.	Seamans, James, and Sarah Weekes, ...	"	i.	249
1781. Oct. 28.	Seamans, Martha, and Epinetus Burtis, ...	"	xxxiv.	10
1756. Dec. 1.	Seamans, Peleg, and Urselah Akerly,......	"	i.	369

DATE.	NAMES.	RECORD.	VOL.	PAGE.
1778. Mar. 9.	Seamen, Benjamin, and Jane Hardenbergh,.	M. B.,	xxv.	35
1770. Oct. 17.	Seamen, Rosetta, and Richard Townsend,..	"	xvi.	218
1715. May 31.	Seamon, Almy, and Robert Warne, ...	"	ii.	293
1782. Sept. 24.	Seamons, Rachel, and Samuel Boyer,......	"	xxxvii.	10
1737. May 11.	Seamour, Thomas, and Anne Elsworth,....	"	i.	6
1759. Oct. 30.	Searean, Daniel, and Sarah Ffish, ...	"	ii.	480
1778. Oct. 22.	Searing, Abigail, and Albert Vannorstrand,.	"	xxvi.	66
1753. May 10.	Searing, Ame, and James Smith,..........	"	i.	28
1762. Nov. 5.	Searing, Daniel, and Elisabeth Peters, ...	"	vi.	412
1761. Oct. 2.	Searing, James, and Sarah Nicolls, ...	"	v.	115
1777. April 23.	Searing, Mary, and Job Robbins, ...	"	xxv.	66
1762. Mar. 15.	Searing, Samuel, and Phebe Tredwell,.....	"	vi.	68
1765. Mar. 5.	Searing, Samuel, and Sarah Pearsall, ...	"	ix.	64
1764. April 10.	Searing, Sarah, and James Clement,.......	"	viii.	148
1767. July 6.	Searring, Margaret, and William Raner,....	"	xi.	125
1774. Feb. 14.	Sears, Hesther, and Paschal N. Smith,.....	"	xxii.	127
1780. Oct. 21.	Sears, John, and Sarah Halstead, ...	"	xxx.	76
1780. April 20.	Sears, Joseph, and Hester Wheaton,.......	"	xxix.	36
1778. June 15.	Sears, Mary, and Thomas Hamilton,.......	"	xxv.	102
1763. Sept. 29.	Sears, Rachel, and William Case, ...	"	vii.	360
1772. Dec. 16.	Scarvent, Phillip, and Sarah Underdunk,...	"	xix.	156
1760. Oct. 6.	Seawood, Elizabeth, and John Harriss,.....	"	iii.	346
1782. Nov. 6.	Sebeston, William, and Elizabeth Lashire,..	"	xxxvii.	73
1675. July 16.	Sebra, Clement, and Janitie Erwin,........	W. O. P.,	iii.	124
1737. Dec. 17.	Sebring, Catherine, and Jerrard Smith, ...	M. B.,	i.	8
1775. May 10.	Sebring, Cornelius, and Jane Goes,........	"	xxiii.	27
1759. Nov. 15.	Sebring, Elizabeth, and William Caverly,...	"	ii.	497
1764. Oct. 10.	Sebring, Femitje, and Reyneer Suydam, ...	"	viii.	345
1766. Nov. 13.	Sebring, Jacob, and Jane Lefferts,.........	"	x.	162
1771. Mar. 9.	Sebring, John, and Sarah Gibbs,..........	"	xvii.	28
1762. Oct. 28.	Sebring, Lettice, and Hendrick Suydam, ...	"	vi.	390
1771. Nov. 4.	Sebring, Rachel, and Abraham Brouwer,...	"	xvii.	238
1764. Oct. 13.	Secord, Abraham, and Hannah Simmonds, .	"	viii.	356
1783. May 17.	Secord, Daniel, and Magdalean Flandro,....	"	xxxix.	15
1781. Nov. 20.	Secord, Eleaner, and Peter Coutant,.......	"	xxxiv.	50
1763. July 18.	Secord, Martha, and Mills Hitchcock, ...	"	vii.	283
1756. Dec. 15.	Secord, Sarah, and Francis Curtine,........	"	i.	384
1770. June 27.	See, Mary, and John Enters, ...	"	xvi.	123
1775. April 5.	Seebring, Mary, and Samuel Johnson, ...	"	xxiii.	1
1763. Nov. 29.	Seelie, John, and Elizabeth Ecker, ...	"	vii.	478
1762. Nov. 22.	Seelig, Margaret, and Nicholas Manger,....	"	vi.	448
1777. Sept. 25.	Seely, John, and Sarah Forman,..........	"	xxiv.	151
1766. Nov. 14.	Seely, Lewis, and Sarah Hutchins, ...	"	x.	164
1666. Dec. 22.	Seely, Robert, and Mary Walker, ...	O. W. L.,	ii.	{105 {134

44

DATE.	NAMES.	RECORD.	VOL.	PAGE.
1781. April 14.	Shannon, Ann, and John Jackson, ...	M. B.,	XXXII.	6
1782. Jan. 19.	Shannon, George, and Elizabeth Cooe,.....	"	XXXV.	24
1779. Mar. 22.	Shannon, Hugh, and Rachel Foster,.......	"	XXVII.	73
1766. Dec. 24.	Shannon, Judith, and James Tattersall, ...	"	X.	208
1765. Mar. 25.	Shannon, Margaret, and Robert Campbell,..	"	IX.	73
1761. Sept. 10.	Shans, Mary, and John McKlenney,.......	"	V.	79
1764. Mar. 6.	Shappel, Margret, and Matthias Tear,......	"	VIII.	95
1756. Nov. 3.	Sharer, James, and Hannah Shaw,........	"	I.	345
1765. July 26.	Sharer, Margaret, and Roilf Vanhouten, ...	"	IX.	217
1762. Dec. 1.	Sharer, Mary, and James Dunscomb, ...	"	VI.	461
1760. Dec. 22.	Sharman, Evert, and Phebe Jacobs, ...	"	III.	489
1768. Sept. 19.	Sharp, Catherine, and Philip Rockefeller,...	"	XIII.	187
1771. Oct. 10.	Sharp, Coenraed, and Elizabeth Steets,.....	"	XVII.	202
1759. Jan. 12.	Sharp, George, and Mary Blagge,.........	"	II.	153
1772. April 23.	Sharp, George, and Rebecca Teator,.......	"	XVIII.	90
1769. Nov. 13.	Sharp, Gysbert, and Alabart Van Alner, ...	"	XV.	91
1781. May 17.	Sharp, Henry, and Catharine Buskirk, ...	"	XXXII.	51
1781. May 10.	Sharp, John, and Sarah Shippy,...........	"	XXXII.	42
1763. Sept. 20.	Sharp, Lena, and James Van Alstyne, ...	"	VII.	344
1763. Sept. 17.	Sharp, Mary, and John Monier,...........	"	VII.	340
1775. Dec. 16.	Sharp, Mary, and Pieter Wiesmer, ...	"	XXIII.	231
1782. July 1.	Sharp, William, and Elizabeth Johnson,....	"	XXXVI.	67
1763. April 14.	Sharpe, Gertrude, and Frederick Moule,....	"	VII.	127
1760. Feb. 14.	Sharpe, Jacob, and Ffrances Skates,.......	"	III.	38
1780. July 26.	Sharpe, Jacob, and Maria Nostrandt, ...	"	XXIX.	119
1763. Feb. 28.	Sharpe, James, and Hannah Wendell,......	"	VII.	88
1764. June 18.	Sharpe, Mary, and John Handcock, ...	"	VIII.	227
1779. Jan. 10.	Sharpe, Mary, and John Sutphen,.........	"	XXVIII.	188
1762. Oct. 16.	Sharpe, Peter, Jr., and Catharine Parrager,.	"	VI.	368
1764. Mar. 22.	Sharpensteen, Henry, and Phebe Lose,.....	"	VIII.	113
1765. Aug. 2.	Shauknassy, Catharine, and Thomas Pynn Williams, ...	"	IX.	227
1769. Dec. 29.	Shaver, Anna, and Johannes Snell, ...	"	XV.	134
1782. Nov. 1.	Shaver, Hannah, and John Lovell, ...	"	XXXVII.	70
1759. May 23.	Shaver, Lenah, and Andries Huick,........	"	II.	289
1769. Dec. 28.	Shaw, Ann, and Henry Gilbert, ...	"	XV.	132
1771. May 21.	Shaw, Charles, and Elizabeth Ludlow,.....	"	XVII.	87
1757. June 17.	Shaw, Daniel, and Sarah Miller, ...	"	I.	566
1761. Nov. 23.	Shaw, David, and Mary Dey,.............	"	V.	244
1760. Sept. 29.	Shaw, Deborah, and Joseph Webb,........	"	III.	336
1761. Aug. 11.	Shaw, Ephorim, and Isabella Hodges,......	"	V.	39
1766. Sept. 25.	Shaw, George, and Mary Elsworth, ...	"	X.	106
1756. Nov. 3.	Shaw, Hannah, and James Sharer,........	"	I.	345
1736. April 9.	Shaw, Hugh, and Susannah Perry,........	"	I.	1
1780. Mar. 2.	Shaw, Jacob, and Rachel Butler,..........	"	XXVIII.	215

DATE.	NAMES.	RECORD.	VOL.	PAGE.
1764. Feb. 24.	Shaw, James, and Elinor Keton,....	M. B.,	VIII.	83
1767. Jan. 23.	Shaw, James, and Elizabeth Boon Repo,...	"	XI.	12
1764. Nov. 12.	Shaw, John, and Elizabeth Martin,........	"	VIII.	400
1779. Mar. 10.	Shaw, Jonathan, and Mary Lott,..........	"	XXVII.	61
1760. Nov. 24.	Shaw, Margaret, and Alexander McDougall,	"	III.	439
1759. Jan. 25.	Shaw, Mary, and Dugall McDugal,........	"	II.	166
1765. April 29.	Shaw, Mary, and George Lane,...........	"	IX.	113
1782. Dec. 11.	Shaw, Mary, and Jacob Wheate,..........	"	XXXVII.	115
1757. Feb. 4.	Shaw, Mary, and William Castle, ...	"	I.	434
1758. Jan. 28.	Shaw, Neal, and Mary Decline,...........	"	I.	805
1768. May 9.	Shay, John, and Mary Baty, ...	"	XIII.	99
1765. Feb. 4.	Shea, John, and Ann Vedder, ...	"	IX.	42
1763. Mar. 31.	Shead, Elizabeth, and John Ryan,........	"	VII.	110
1782. April 4.	Sheaff, Henry, and Phebe Vanvyck,.......	"	XXXV.	115
1781. Dec. 13.	Sheal, Abigail, and Jabez Hobby, ...	"	XXXIV.	84
1772. Dec. 12.	Shear, Abraham, and Anna Monfoont,.....	"	XIX.	154
1773. Feb. 10.	Shear, Catherine, and Sovereign Sybrandt, .	"	XX.	40
1762. July 21.	Shearen, Mary, and Frederick Leydig,.....	"	VI.	251
1761. July 7.	Shearer, Catherine, and John Lawsing, ...	"	IV.	287
1760. Feb. 8.	Shearer, Gilbert, and Susannah Wrightman,	"	III.	26
1779. May 16.	Shearman, Aletta, and Robert Basden,.....	"	XXVII.	139
1765. April 12.	Shearman, Elizabeth, and William Devereux,	"	IX.	91
1760. Aug. 7.	Shearman, Uzail, and Aletta Prest,........	"	III.	238
1783. June 6.	Shearwood, Elizabeth, and Fredrick Miller,.	"	XXXIX.	41
1772. June 18.	Shedwine, David, and Elizabeth Colvil, ...	"	XVIII.	142
1767. Feb. 19.	Sheerwood, Mary, and William Arnold,....	"	XI.	31
1760. Jan. 22.	Shefer, Maria, and Mathias Heyer, ...	"	III.	2
1783. June 16.	Shefliel, Charity, and Abraham Collins, ...,	"	XXXIX.	59
1770. Nov. 27.	Sheif, Eve, and Lemuel Bunce, ...	"	XVI.	271
1766. Sept. 18.	Shelds, Edward, and Mary Kearney, ...	"	X.	101
1779. Oct. 4.	Shelly, Mary, and Joseph Wayne,.........	"	XXVIII.	101
1767. Sept. 24.	Shelly, Samuel, and Elizabeth Burns,......	"	XII.	41
1757. Aug. 18.	Shelton, Cyntje, and Benjamin Douglass,...	"	I.	617
1764. Sept. 10.	Shelton, William, and Susannah Strong,....	"	VIII.	303
1772. Sept. 7.	Shepard, Jane, and James Kiersted,.......	"	XIX.	43
1772. May 15.	Shepard, Sebina, and George Walgrove, ...	"	XVIII.	118
1753. June 18.	Sheperd, Anne, and William Burnett,......	"	I.	63
1758. Jan. 25.	Sheperla, Christian, and Mary Richardson,..	"	I.	801
1781. Dec. 15.	Shepherd, Benjamin, and Elenor Gregory,..	"	XXXIV.	90
1760. Feb. 14.	Shepherd, Edward, and Ruth Shepherd,....	"	III.	37
1780. July 26.	Shepherd, Elizabeth, and John Grandine,...	'	XXIX.	120
1780. July 8.	Shepherd, John, and Margaret Mount,.....	'	XXIX.	109
1768. Sept. 14.	Shepherd, Mary, and Jacob Pitt,..........	"	XIII.	186
1768. Sept. 14.	Shepherd, Mary, and Matthew Douglass,...	"	XIII.	185
1783. Feb. 27.	Shepherd, Richard, and Martha Caston,....	"	XXXVIII.	56

Date.	Names.	Record.	Vol.	Page.
1760. Feb. 14.	Shepherd, Ruth, and Edward Shepherd, ...	M. B.,	III.	37
1783. Jan. 30.	Shepherd, Sarah, and John Knight, ..., ...	"	XXXVIII.	33
1781. Sept. 22.	Shepherd, Jane, and James Postlethwaite, ..	"	XXXIII.	77
1775. April 15.	Sheppard, Joseph, and Margaret Hampton,.	"	XXIII.	9
1781. June 5.	Shepperd, Christiana, and James Russell, ...	"	XXXII.	73
1768. June 11.	Sherar, Sarah, and John Broughton, ...	'	XIII.	125
1778. Oct. 3.	Sheriff, James, and Elizabeth King, ...	"	XXVI.	45
1770. Jan. 8.	Sheriff, Susannah, and John Colvill, ...	"	XVI.	4
1767. Jan. 26.	Sheriff, William, and Susannah Irons, ...	"	XI.	13
1777. Dec. 24.	Sheron, Mary, and John Clark, ...	"	XXIV.	206
1737. Dec. 17.	Sherrard, Elizabeth, and John Hall, ...	"	I.	8
1767. April 25.	Sherrard, Martha, and Stephen Clayton, ...	"	XI.	71
1738. Dec. 11.	Sherwood, Anne, and Robert Young, ...	"	I.	12
1757. June 16.	Sherwood, Isaac, and Mary Wheeler, ...	"	I.	565
1773. Aug. 7.	Sherwood, John, and Mary Stanton, ...	"	XXI.	60
1782. Mar. 26.	Sherwood, Jonathan, and Phebe Gerow, ...	"	XXXVI.	97
1768. April 11.	Sherwood, Nathan, and Joanna Nobles, ...	"	XIII.	72
1762. June 14.	Sherwood, Seymour, and Ruth Lockwood, .	"	VI.	191
1761. April 23.	Shields, Judith, and Joseph Paulin, ...	"	IV.	163
1760. Nov. 24.	Shields, Timothy, and Letty Vanderrife, ...	"	III.	440
1766. Dec. 24.	Shiels, Catherine, and Andrew Cunningham,	"	X.	207
1757. June 30.	Shilds, John, and Mary Gereau, ...	"	I.	577
1762. Oct. 13.	Shilman, Sarah, and John Hubbard, ...	"	VI.	362
1780. Aug. 5.	Shimell. Valentine, and Elizabeth Nestle, ...	"	XXIX.	133
1767. June 2.	Shino, Hannah, and Edmund Kinsey, ...	"	XI.	103
1765. April 25.	Shipboy, Thomas, and Ann Van Veghte, ...	"	IX.	108
1767. July 4.	Shipman, William, and Mary Myer, ...	"	XI.	125
1781. May 10.	Shippey, Sarah, and John Sharp, ...	"	XXXII.	42
1761. April 13.	Shippy, Luke, and Mary Webber, ...	"	IV.	148
1769. Jan. 18.	Shire, Henry, and Elizabeth Beaty, ...	"	XIV.	14
1783. Sept. 20.	Shirmer, John William, and Hannah Commindinger, ...	"	XL.	47
1761. Dec. 3.	Shoanertt, Freidrich, and Mary Hurtman, ..	"	V.	262
1772. Jan. 3.	Shoemaker, John, and Eve Saul, ...	"	XVIII.	1
1780. May 10.	Shonnard, Elizabeth, and John Henry Bettner, ...	"	XXIX.	51
1760. June 21.	Shooler, William, and Ann Bartlet, ...	"	III.	194
1756. July 12.	Short, Adam, and Jannetie Winne, ...	"	I.	255
1761. Aug. 11.	Short, Samuel, and Ann Man, ...	"	V.	38
1762. Nov. 2.	Shortell, William, and Elizabeth Trepeger, ..	"	VI.	406
1679. Oct. 14.	Shottwell, John, and Elizabeth Burton, ...	G. E.,	XXXII.	62
1781. June 21.	Shotwell, Jeremiah, and Mary Barron, ...	M. B.,	XXXII.	93
1781. Aug. 15.	Shotwell, Joseph, and Sarah Wilson, ...	"	XXXIII.	37
1758. May 20.	Shourt, Margaret, and Richard Newbold, ..	"	I.	903
1757. Nov. 20.	Shourt, Rebeccah, and Thomas Moore, ...	"	I.	716

DATE.	NAMES.	RECORD.	VOL.	PAGE
1759. Oct. 24.	Shourt, Jacob, and Susannah Colegrove, ...	M. B.,	II.	472
1777. April 18.	Shrieve, Thomas, and Catherine Ashfield, ..	"	XXIV.	66
1766. Oct. 1.	Shuckburgh, Elizabeth, and James Stewart,	"	X.	117
1775. Oct. 18.	Shultz, Casparus, Jr., and Eve Dings,......	"	XXIII.	183
1736. Sept. 28.	Shurmur, John, and Catherine McDonald,..	"	I.	2
1756. Dec. 16.	Shurmur, Mary, and Fridricg von Weissenfels, ...	"	I.	388
1773. April 3.	Shute, Elisha, and Phebe Morgan, ...	"	XX.	81
1782. Oct. 9.	Shute, Peter, and Elizabeth Bailey,........	"	XXXVII.	37
1761. Nov. 14.	Shute, Susannah, and Edward Fowler,.....	"	V.	216
1761. Oct. 13.	Shuter, James, and Margaret Peterson, ...	"	V.	133
1761. May 27.	Shutze, Henry, and Sarah Leppard,........	"	IV.	208
1780. Sept. 29.	Sibbles, Mary, and John Cameron,........	"	XXX.	39
1770. May 31.	Sibby, Richard, and Mary Peet, ...	"	XVI.	99
1763. Mar. 5.	Sibly, Catharine, and James Mott, ...	"	VII.	92
1765. Oct. 11.	Siccore, Mary, and John Ranoud, ...	"	IX.	295
1772. Aug. 15.	Sice, Rebekah, and James Carroll, ...	"	XIX.	25
1775. Oct. 28.	Sickels, Abigail, and Philip Linn, ...	"	XXIII.	189
1753. Oct. 6.	Sickels, Charles, and Latiche Lake,........	"	I.	132
1774. Jan. 5.	Sickels, Ethan, and Mary Kings,..........	"	XXII.	92
1766. Oct. 21.	Sickels, Gertruy, and John Haring,........	"	X.	134
1760. Nov. 11.	Sickels, Hannah, and Philip Young,.......	"	III.	402
1759. Aug. 6.	Sickels, Henry, and Ann Buckenhoven,....	"	II.	377
1762. Oct. 13.	Sickels, Henry, and Ann Mabee,..........	"	VI.	359
1766. Nov. 21.	Sickels, Henry, and Peternele Brouwer,....	"	X.	176
1763. Dec. 6.	Sickels, Mary, and Samson Benson, Jr.,....	"	VII.	493
1768. Dec. 20.	Sickels, Sarah, and Albert Lydecker, ...	"	XIII.	269
1758. Jan. 12.	Sickels, Sarah, and John Stanger,.........	"	I.	782
1767. July 2.	Sickels, Sarah, and Nicholas Callahan, ...	"	XI.	118
1768. Oct. 22.	Sickels, William, and Mary Cooper, ...	"	XIII.	216
1781. May 7.	Sickes, Anstance, and Daniel Killing,......	"	XXXII.	34
1764. Oct. 29.	Sickle, Albertus, and Mary Sopes,........	"	VIII.	379
1736. May 13.	Sickle, Thomas, and Anne Jones, ...	"	I.	1
1759. May 10.	Sickles, Elizabeth, and Alexander Cook,....	"	II.	275
1776. Feb. 7.	Sickles, John, and Alitha Gilbert, ...	"	XXIII.	263
1780. June 2.	Sickles, John, and Catharine Buckett, ...	"	XXIX.	78
1763. Sept. 27.	Sickles, John, and Mary Bursen,..........	"	VII.	357
1760. Sept. 10.	Sickles, Letty, and William Kirby, ...	"	III.	309
1772. Feb. 12.	Sidam, Jane, and Luke Elderd, ...	"	XVIII.	36
1783. Jan. 4.	Sidell, Augustus, and Elizabeth Robins, ...	"	XXXVIII.	6
1758. Oct. 9.	Siderlin, Mary Magdelin, and George Hassie,	"	II.	44
1776. Jan. 11.	Sidman, Ann, and Heny Jackson,.........	"	XXIII.	245
1773. Mar. 9.	Siemont, John, and Susanah Haight, ...	"	XX.	58
1769. Mar. 6.	Sigell, John, and Ann Sargent,...........	"	XIV.	46
1767. July 2.	Sign, Mary, and Jacobus Altgelt,...........	"	XI.	119

DATE.		NAMES.	RECORD.	VOL.	PAGE.
1669. May	13.	Sille, Washburga, de, and William Bogardus,	O. W. L.,	II.	407
1736. Sept.	7.	Sills, Jane, and William Smith,...........	M. B.,	I.	2
1768. May	16.	Silvester, Elizabeth, and William Ritchie,...	"	XIII.	104
1676. July	13.	Silvester, Grizell, and James Lloyd, ...	W. O. P.,	III.	203
1773. July	6.	Silvester, John, and Amy Freeland, ...	M. B.,	XXI.	33
1763. Feb.	11.	Simerson, Anne, and Thomas Quigley,.....	"	VII.	59
1761. June	17.	Simerson, Elenor, and John Laton,........	"	IV.	244
1762. Dec.	10.	Simerson, Maria, and Andries Hegeman,...	"	VI.	475
1678. Sept.	26.	Simkins, Mary, and Samuel Tilley,........	G. E.,	XXXII.	3
1762. Feb.	2.	Simmonds, Ann, and Samuel Browning,....	M. B.,	VI.	37
1758. Sept.	5.	Simmonds, Edward, Jr., and Hannah Fryer,.	"	II.	3
1764. Nov.	14.	Simmonds, Elizabeth, and David Hermanus Schuyler,...............	"	VIII.	406
1764. Oct.	13.	Simmonds, Hannah, and Abraham Secord,.	"	VIII.	356
1764. Feb.	25.	Simmonds, Pamela, and John Lynch,......	"	VIII.	80
1764. April	19.	Simmonds, Rebecca, and Henry Ennis, ...	"	VIII.	162
1761. July	30.	Simmonds, Thomas, and Phebe Hinton,....	"	V.	17
1771. April	12.	Simmons, Abigail, and Samuel Haight, ...	"	XVII.	55
1756. July	26.	Simmons, Ame, and Obadiah Jackson,... .	"	I.	261
1779. June	16.	Simmons, Catherine, and Willets Powell, ..	"	XXVII.	165
1737. April	7.	Simmons, David, and Mary Willett, ...	"	I.	5
1783. May	16.	Simmons, Elizabeth, and Benjamin Jonson,.	"	XXXIX.	12
1736. Mar.	11.	Simmons, Henry, and Jane Williams, ...	"	I.	5
1777. July	26.	Simmons, Hester, and Samuel Sands,......	"	XXIV.	121
1781. Aug.	1.	Simmons, Jacob, and Anne Fairchild,......	"	XXXIII.	26
1755. Aug.	5.	Simmons, Jamima, and John Decker,......	"	I.	143
1758. Dec.	21.	Simmons, John, and Catharine Salter, ...	"	II.	138
1768. Nov.	5.	Simmons, Martha, and Henry Titus,.......	"	XIII.	226
1778. Aug.	26.	Simmons, Martha, and Thomas Doty,.....	"	XXXVI.	11
1768. Feb.	11.	Simmons, Mary, and Joshua Hunt,........	"	XIII.	33
1755. Nov.	25.	Simmons, Mary, and Silas Smith, ...	"	I.	215
1777. Mar.	8.	Simmons, Mary, and William Dement, ...	"	XXIV.	42
1771. May	23.	Simmons, Obadiah, and Sarah Carman, ...	"	XVII.	88
1762. May	12.	Simmons, Samuel, and Mary Birdsell, ...	"	VI.	157
1761. June	25.	Simmons, Thomas, and Martha Rowlin,....	"	IV.	261
1780. Aug.	22.	Simons, Ann, and Roger Galilee,..........	"	XXIX.	144
1772. Aug.	1.	Simons, Anthony, and Hester Bemus, ...	"	XIX.	9
1758. Nov.	20.	Simons, John, and Mary Rogers,..........	"	II.	96
1759. May	10.	Simons, Mary, and Christopher Benson,....	"	II.	274
1773. April	9.	Simons, Phebe, and Barnardus V. d'Water,.	"	XX.	91
1773. Nov.	30.	Simons, Phebe, and Daniel Laurence,......	"	XXII.	53
1781. April	9.	Simonsen, Isaac, and Hannah Bedel, ...	"	XXXI.	98
1763. Dec.	20.	Simonson, Abraham, and Mary Latham,....	"	VII.	514
1768. July	7.	Simonson, Ann, and Abraham Parlee, ...	"	XIII.	149
1770. Feb.	23.	Simonson, Anne, and William Macklane,...	"	XVI.	22

DATE.	NAMES.	RECORD.	VOL.	PAGE.
1783. Sept. 23.	Simonson, Barnt, and Anne Baty, ...	M. B.,	XL.	52
1779. June 19.	Simonson, Catherine, and Barzilla Grover, . .	"	XXVII.	168
1766. Aug. 8.	Simonson, Fredrick, and Hiltie Pilyon, ...	"	X.	71
1761. Mar. 21.	Simonson, Gertryde, and Peter Carson, ...	"	IV.	111
1768. Sept. 26.	Simonson, Helena, and Mortines Swaim, . . .	"	XIII.	195
1772. Oct. 23.	Simonson, Henry, and Joanna Spragge, ...	"	XIX.	89
1781. Oct. 23.	Simonson, Jamima, and John Kruse, ...	"	XXXIV.	3
1768. Nov. 22.	Simonson, Jenny, and Stephen Ryder, ...	"	XIII.	240
1773. Jan. 16.	Simonson, Jeremiah, and Mary McLean, . . .	"	XX.	11
1766. Dec. 12.	Simonson, John, and Anna Beagle, ...	"	X.	203
1769. Nov. 13.	Simonson, John, and Ellenor Morgan, ...	"	XV.	92
1780. Oct. 2.	Simonson, John, and Gitty Swame, ...	"	XXX.	51
1768. June 27.	Simonson, John, and Mary Corsen, ...	"	XIII.	140
1768. Nov. 12.	Simonson, John, and Rachel Peters, ...	"	XIII.	232
1760. April 15.	Simonson, John, and Temperance Ffish, ...	"	FII.	107
1763. Sept. 3.	Simonson, Lena, and John Suydam, ...	"	VII.	326
1779. June 10.	Simonson, Margaret, and Beruamin Prall, . .	"	XXVII.	162
1763. Jan. 18.	Simonson, Mary, and Abraham Vandeventer,	"	VII.	19
1779. Nov. 25.	Simonson, Mary, and Adriaen Hegeman, Jr.,	"	XXVIII.	149
1783. Sept. 25.	Simonson, Mary, and Benjamin Decker, ...	"	XL.	53
1771. April 19.	Simonson, Morris, and Lettice Clowes, ...	"	XVII.	62
1780. Mar. 12.	Simonson, Patty, and Isaac Van Noorstrand,	"	XXVIII.	214
1762. Jan. 21.	Simonson, Sarah, and Jacob Decker, ...	"	VI.	20
1770. Jan. 30.	Simonson, William, and Jane Suydam, ...	"	XVI.	9
1779. July 19.	Simoson, John, and Mary Cruzer, ...	"	XXVIII.	24
1757. Mar. 22.	Simpson, Alexander, and Sarah Robinson, . .	"	I.	479
1780. Feb. 25.	Simpson, Drummond, and Sarah Chapman, .	"	XXVIII.	213
1777. Sept. 25.	Simpson, Isabella, and John Swan, ...	"	XXIV.	150
1763. Aug. 5.	Simpson, James, and Catharine Hughes, ...	"	VII.	292
1762. July 5.	Simpson, Margaret, and Hendrick Sleght, . .	"	VI.	226
1778. Sept. 11.	Simpson, Mary, and John Pendergast, ...	"	XXVI.	26
1738. July 7.	Simpson, Tabitha, and William Hyer, ...	"	I.	10
1768. Sept. 13.	Simpson, Thomas, and Johannah Catherine Houtvat, ...	"	XIII.	183
1779. Dec. 24.	Simpson, William, and Rebeccah Mott, ...	"	XXVIII.	180
1778. July 20.	Sims, Thomas, and Sarah Colwell, ...	"	XXV.	134
1772. July 11.	Simson, John, and Elizabeth Kelly, ...	"	XVIII.	165
1756. Oct. 29.	Simson, John, and Mary Parker, ...	"	I.	337
1759. April 28.	Sinclair, John Charles, and Mary Bunhall, . .	"	II.	259
1763. Jan. 20.	Sinclair, James, and Gertrude Myers, ...	"	VII.	23
1773. Nov. 26.	Sinclair, John, and Catharine Horse, ...	"	XXII.	47
1762. Aug. 6.	Sing, Mary, and William Clarke, ...	"	VI.	267
1737. July 20.	Singeon, Elizabeth, and John Saunders, . . .	"	I.	6
1783. Oct. 23.	Sinnet, Mary, and George Murray, ...	"	XL.	89
1773. Aug. 24.	Sise, Elizabeth, and Luke Matthewman, . . .	"	XXI.	83

DATE.		NAMES.	RECORD.	VOL.	PAGE.
1761. April	22.	Sise, Martha, and John Butt,.............	M. B.,	IV.	162
1767. Nov.	27.	Sise, Michael, and Catharine Ellison,.......	"	XII.	98
1772. Nov.	17.	Sitcher, Elizabeth, and John Fisheir,.......	"	XIX.	117
1782. May	17.	Siverly, Hannah, and Ebenezer Morse, ...	"	XXXVI.	6
1772. Oct.	19.	Size, Mary, and George Hubner,..........	"	XIX.	78
1760. Feb.	14.	Skates, Ffrances, and Jacob Sharpe, ...	"	III.	38
1766. Nov.	3.	Skenck, Catherine, and Morriss Hazard,....	"	X.	149
1764. June	7.	Skidmore, John, and Mary De Mott, ...	"	VIII.	212
1763. Nov.	26.	Skidmore, John, and Mary Denton, ...	"	VII.	472
1782. Dec.	23.	Skidmore, Lemuel, and Anne Burtis, ...	"	XXXVII.	130
1781. Jan.	5.	Skidmore, Mary, and Nathaniel Right,.....	"	XXXI.	13
1783. May	31.	Skidmore, Mary, and Peter Hendrickson, ..	"	XXXIX.	33
1765. Oct.	28.	Skidmore, Nathan, and Sarah Smith,......	"	IX.	321
1769. Aug.	1.	Skidmore, Phebe, and Hendrick Suydam, ..	"	XV.	11
1772. May	23.	Skidmore, Phillip, and Margaret Weekes, ..	"	XVIII.	121
1764. Dec.	20.	Skidmore, Samuel, and Abigal Whitehead, .	"	VIII.	460
1759. Aug.	7.	Skidmore, Samuel, and Jane Peters,.......	"	II.	378
1771. April	3.	Skidmore, Samuel, and Ruth Samons, ...	"	XVII.	47
1782. July	13.	Skidmore, Susannah, and Daniel Lefferts, ..	"	XXXVI.	80
1769. June	28.	Skidmore, Susannah, and Israel Hawkins,..	"	XIV.	135
1765. Mar.	12.	Skidmore, Thomas, and Jane Wright, ...	"	IX.	67
1769. Dec.	12.	Skidmore, Thomas, and Mary Lawrence,...	"	XV.	121
1769. Mar.	17.	Skidmore, Thomas, and Phebe Chichester, .	"	XIV.	55
1770. Feb.	3.	Skidmore, Walter, and Catherine Wood,...	"	XVI.	12
1764. June	26.	Skidmore, Whitehead, and Jane Doubley,..	"	VIII.	237
1762. May	20.	Skillman, Elisabeth, and Albertus Vande Water,...........	"	VI.	171
1764. Mar.	12.	Skillman, Hester, and William Payntar,....	"	VIII.	103
1769. June	17.	Skillman, John, and Deborah Conselyee, ...	"	XIV.	121
1771. April	23.	Skillman, Lucretia, and Jacob Corssin,.....	"	XVII.	65
1773. June	19.	Skillman, Mary, and William Conselly, ...	"	XXI.	17
1773. Mar.	26.	Skillman, Sarah, and Richard Smith, ...	"	XX.	72a
1761. April	11.	Skillman, Thomas, and Jannetie Titus, ...	"	IV.	144
1773. Sept.	1.	Skilman, Ann, and Benjamin Brush, ...	"	XXI.	94
1756. Oct.	30.	Skilman, Elisabeth, and John Morrel, Jr., ..	"	I.	339
1776. Mar.	23.	Skilman, Sarah, and James Brosh, ...	"	XXIII.	289
1769. July	10.	Skinkel, Hannah, and Mathew Van Valkenburgh, ...	"	XIV.	146
1767. Nov.	24.	Skinkle, Elizabeth, and John Isaac Muller,..	"	XII.	96
1773. Aug.	27.	Skinner, Abraham, and Catherine Foster,...	"	XXI.	87
1782. Nov.	8.	Skinner, Benjamin, and Elizabeth Amberman, ...	"	XXXVII.	74
1764. Nov.	2.	Skinner, Elizabeth, and Joseph Outen Bogart, ...	"	VIII.	388
1780. June	6.	Skinner, Gertrude, and John Meredith, ...	"	XXIX.	84

45

DATE.	NAMES.	RECORD.	VOL.	PAGE.
1775. April 6.	Skinner, Jonathan, and Ann Mary Van Varck,	M. B.,	XXIII.	3
1777. Nov. 16.	Skinner, Lette, and Peter Saunders,	"	XXXIV.	40
1757. Jan. 28.	Skinner, William Ann, and Eliner Cosby, ..	"	I.	428
1761. May 2.	Skobey, Eleanor, and Isaac Lyons,	"	IV.	174
1761. Feb. 26.	Skorlock, Elizabeth, and Frederick Becker, .	"	IV.	84
1762. Oct. 30.	Skureman, Jane, and John Bonnet,	"	VI.	396
1781. April 30.	Slack, Barne, and Mary Cole,	"	XXXII.	21
1771. Aug. 26.	Slack, Moyaca, and Daniel Schoonmaker, ..	"	XVII.	162
1761. June 12.	Slaght, Barnt, and Elizabeth Jones,	"	IV.	237
1783. Jan. 13.	Slaght, Henry, and Catharine Butler,	"	XXXVIII.	14
1760. Nov. 14.	Slaight, Lena, and Henry Johnson,	"	III.	414
1757. July 27.	Slater, George, and Elizabeth Moit,	"	I.	603
1762. Feb. 15.	Slegell, Eve, and John Slegell,	"	VI.	51
1762. Feb. 15.	Slegell, John, and Eve Slegell,	"	VI.	51
1772. Oct. 17.	Sleght, Annatje, and Jacobus Schoonmaker,	"	XIX.	77
1769. Nov. 15.	Sleght, Annetie, and Abraham De Lameter,	"	XV.	95
1756. Dec. 15.	Sleght, Catharine, and James Segene,	"	I.	383
1764. Feb. 1.	Sleght, Catharine, and Peter Mesier, Jr., ...	"	VIII.	46
1762. Oct. 26.	Sleght, Elizabeth, and Elias Hasbrouck, ...	"	VI.	387
1768. April 11.	Sleght, Elizabeth, and Oack Suydam,	"	XIII.	75
1762. July 5.	Sleght, Hendrick, and Margaret Simpson, ..	"	VI.	226
1763. Dec. 3.	Sleght, Henry, Jr., and Mary De Lametter, .	"	VII.	490
1774. Feb. 9.	Sleght, John, and Catherine Bogardus,	"	XXII.	124
1763. May 11.	Sleght, John H., and Mary Carman,	"	VII.	176
1767. Dec. 5.	Sleght, Peter, and Catherine Contine,	"	XII.	108
1767. Sept. 8.	Sleght, Rachel, and Cornelius Delamater, ...	"	XII.	30
1763. June 8.	Sleght, Rachel, and Peter Van Auke,	"	VII.	217
1756. July 14.	Sleeth, Abraham, and Elizabeth Wright, ...	"	I.	256
1736. Nov. 29.	Sleigh, Tuntye, and Henry Wessells,	"	I.	3
1764. April 30.	Slidell, John, and Jane Ashford,	"	VIII.	174
1756. Oct. 23.	Slingerland, Abram, and Rebecca Fiele, . .	"	I.	332
1763. Sept. 27.	Slingerland, Albert, and Christeena Van Vroncka,	"	VII.	354
1757. Oct. 14.	Slingerland, Albert, and Mary Wingont, ...	"	I.	671
1763. April 28.	Slingerland, Engeltie, and Abraham Van Alstyn,	"	VII.	148
1764. Aug. 22.	Slingerland, Gertruy, and John Isaac Hanse,	"	VIII.	289
1760. July 14.	Slingerland, Lenea, and Dinnes Ackerson, ..	"	III.	213
1759. Oct. 15.	Slingerlandt, Anglitje, and Francis Moke, ..	"	II.	457
1760. Nov. 27.	Slingerlandt, Isaac, and Eva Van Woort, ...	"	III.	449
1760. Nov. 24.	Slingerlant, Albert, and Elizabeth Moke, ...	"	III.	436
1757. Oct. 21.	Slingerlant, Garrett T., and Eghtje Van Dersea,	"	I.	689
1759. Aug. 30.	Slingerlant, Geesye, and John Vielen,	"	II.	402

DATE.	NAMES.	RECORD.	VOL.	PAGE.
1756. Oct. 4.	Slingsby, Rebeccah, and John Spartman, ..	M. B.,	I.	316
1778. Oct. 29.	Sloan, John, and Sarah Cole,.............	"	XXVI.	75
1781. Sept. 1.	Slone, John, and Julia Boyer, ...	"	XXXIII.	54
1763. Dec. 23.	Sloo, Alida, and Garret De Groot,.........	"	VII.	522
1779. Feb. 25.	Slood, Michael, and Rachel Hunt,.........	"	XXVII.	50
1764. Oct. 12.	Sloss, James, and Catharine Blair,.........	"	VIII.	355
1775. May 9.	Slover, Elizabeth, and Dennis Dunscomb,...	"	XXIII.	26
1737. Oct. 6.	Slyk, Harmen, and Sarah Fisher, ...	"	I.	7
1761. Aug. 4.	Slyke, Catharine, and Nicholas White,.....	"	V.	31
1769. Jan. 30.	Small, Hannah, and Garret Fisher, ...	"	XIV.	22
1782. July 27.	Small, Mary, and Coneraut Wort,.........	"	XXXVI.	92
1777. Jan. 30.	Small, Samuel, and Ann Olphord,.........	"	XXIV.	21
1770. Jan. 27.	Smart, George, and Helena Hedger,.......	"	XVI.	8
1768. Feb. 23.	Smart, George, and Jemime Frasee,.......	"	XIII.	41
1759. Aug. 22.	Smart, John, and Margaret Cooper, ...	"	II.	387
1767. Sept. 30.	Smart, Thomas, and Elizabeth McCarthy, ..	"	XII.	51
1771. July 22.	Smeades, Eldert, and Elizabeth Mauncius,..	"	XVII.	138
1767. May 20.	Smedes, Elizabeth, and Luke Kiersted,.....	"	XI.	92a
1760. Nov. 17.	Smedus, Sarah, and Derrick Wynkoop, Jr.,	"	III.	422
1686. April 29.	Smeedis, Benjamine, and Mary Angell, ...	C. M.,	XXXIII.	235
1671. Dec. 27.	Smellidge, Joanna, and Joseph Hall,.......	G. E.,	IV.	80
1778. June 17.	Smelzel, Mary, and Nicodemus Ungerer,...	M. B.,	XXV.	109
1766. Sept. 30.	Smilley, Peter, and Elinor McCaller,.......	"	X.	116
1778. Dec. 21.	Smily, Christian, and Elizabeth Hart,......	"	XXVI.	128
1779. Jan. 13.	Smith, Abby, and John Barton,...........	"	XXVII.	12
1761. Feb. 5.	Smith, Abner, and Ann Smith, ...	"	IV.	53
1760. Jan. 3.	Smith, Abraham, and Mary Corselius, ...	"	II.	565
1763. April 20.	Smith, Adam, and Frances Burroughs,.....	"	VII.	132
1781. Dec. 12.	Smith, Adam, and Hannah Barckley,......	"	XXXIV.	81
1752. Nov. 27.	Smith, Affie, and Thomas Smith,..........	"	I.	14
1769. July 5.	Smith, Alexander, and Agnes Peterson,....	"	XIV.	143
1772. Nov. 9.	Smith, Alliday, and John Ten Broock,.....	"	XIX.	105
1763. Sept. 14.	Smith, Altje, and Arie Blauvelt, ...	"	VII.	335
1763. Jan. 3.	Smith, Amelia, and Jeremiah Smith, ...	"	VII.	6
1779. Jan. 18.	Smith, Amelia, and Thomas Place, ...	"	XXVII.	17
1764. Oct. 10.	Smith, Amos, and Amy Smith,...........	"	VIII.	344
1768. May 24.	Smith, Amos, and Mary Morris, ...	"	XIII.	111
1764. Oct. 10.	Smith, Amy, and Amos Smith,...........	"	VIII.	344
1778. Sept. 18.	Smith, Amy, and Isaac Seloover, ...	"	XXVI.	32
1760. Jan. 23.	Smith, Anatje, and Pieter Demarest, ...	"	III.	3
1761. Feb. 5.	Smith, Ann, and Abner Smith, ...	"	IV.	53
1768. May 21.	Smith, Ann, and Benjamin Bill, ...	"	XIII.	109
1772. Nov. 11.	Smith, Ann, and Benjamin Smith, ...	"	XIX.	110
1781. Nov. 10.	Smith, Ann, and John Newkam, ...	"	XXXIV.	25
1780. Mar. 11.	Smith, Ann, and Moses Fowler, ...	"	XXVIII.	219

Date.	Names.	Record.	Vol.	Page.
1757. Nov. 3.	Smith, Ann, and Timothy Doughty, ...	M. B.,	i.	698
1760. Dec. 10.	Smith, Anne, and Isaac Smith, ...	"	iii.	469
1761. Mar. 4.	Smith, Anne, and Jeremiah Connor, ...	"	iv.	91
1763. Jan. 31.	Smith, Anne, and John Dodge, ...	"	vii.	42
1764. July 13.	Smith, Anning, and Elenor Clarke, ...	"	viii.	257
1762. Aug. 26.	Smith, Aron, and Catharine Valing, ...	"	vi.	292
1758. Feb. 27.	Smith, Aury, and Charity Onderdonck, ...	"	i.	829
1782. Oct. 23.	Smith, Barnadus, and Esther Smith, ...	"	xxxvii.	62
1761. May 30.	Smith, Benajah, and Dorothy Jones, ...	"	iv.	221
1762. May 6.	Smith, Benjamin, and Amy Spragge, ...	"	vi.	148
1776. Mar. 2.	Smith, Benjamin, and Ann Bennet, ...	"	xxiii.	277
1772. Nov. 11.	Smith, Benjamin, and Ann Smith, ...	"	xix.	110
1761. June 16.	Smith, Benjamin, and Elizabeth Leonard, . .	"	iv.	241
1757. April 7.	Smith, Benjamin, and Martha Underhill, . . .	"	i.	490
1780. May 2.	Smith, Benjamin, and Mary Smyth, ...	"	xxix.	40
1777. Feb. 24.	Smith, Blackwell, and Catherine Udall, ...	"	xxiv.	34
1761. April 21.	Smith, Caleb, and Abigail Hicks, ...	"	iv.	160
1765. Mar. 5.	Smith, Caroline,-and Daniel Terry, ...	"	ix.	63
1757. Oct. 15.	Smith, Catharine, and Daniel Casey, ...	"	i.	673
1775. April 20.	Smith, Catharine, and Jeremiah Connor, . . .	"	xxiii.	14
1764. Feb. 11.	Smith, Catharine, and Richard Smith, ...	"	viii.	58
1759. Feb. 14.	Smith, Catharine, and Samuel Cornell, ...	"	ii.	191
1765. Jan. 5.	Smith, Catharine, and Thomas Scorfield, . . .	"	ix.	9
1772. Oct. 29.	Smith, Catherine, and Francis Ammerick, . .	"	xix.	94
1781. Oct. 26.	Smith, Catherine, and Jacob Evert, ...	"	xxx.	81
1767. April 18.	Smith, Catherine, and John Cornell, ...	"	xi.	65
1767. June 12.	Smith, Catherine, and John Grenell, ...	"	xi.	107
1767. Oct. 1.	Smith, Catherine, and Nicholas Drury, ...	"	xii.	53
1773. April 8.	Smith, Catherine, and Thomas Charles Man,	"	xx.	87
1763. Oct. 29.	Smith, Charity, and John Adams, ...	"	vii.	412
1760. Aug. 21.	Smith, Charity, and Thomas Rudgard, ...	"	iii.	266
1738. June 19.	Smith, Charles, and Cornelia Willocks, ...	"	i.	10
1759. Feb. 5.	Smith, Christian, and Hester Cole, ...	"	ii.	178
1771. Oct. 29.	Smith, Christina, and Cloudea Van Volkin-burgh, ...	"	xvii.	228
1761. Nov. 30.	Smith, Cornelius, and Mary Baker, ...	"	v.	305
1764. Mar. 17.	Smith, Cornelius, and Altje Van Nostrandt, .	"	viii.	109
1767. May 27.	Smith, Darkis, and Joseph Carpenter, ...	"	xi.	99
1763. Oct. 15.	Smith, Daniel, and Amelia Carpenter, ...	"	vii.	388
1781. Jan. 30.	Smith, Daniel, and Elizabeth Marston, . . , . .	"	xxxi.	32
1764. May 4.	Smith, David, and Anne Hewson, ...	"	viii.	184
1778. Dec. 9.	Smith, Deborah, and Jacob Williams, ...	"	xxvi.	115
1779. Feb. 24.	Smith, Deborah, and John Dickson, ...	"	xxvii.	48
1765. Aug. 8.	Smith, Deborah, and John Post, ...	"	ix.	233
1755. Dec. 19.	Smith, Deborah, and Obadiah Seaman, ...	"	i.	235

DATE.		NAMES.	RECORD.	VOL.	PAGE.
1772. June	18.	Smith, Deborah, and William Haviland,....	M. B.,	XVIII.	143
1680. June	1.	Smith, Deborah, and William Lawrence,....	G. E.,	XXXII.	86
1763. Sept.	2.	Smith, Edmund, and Deborah Kissam, ...	M. B.,	VII.	324
1763. May	3.	Smith, Edmund, and Mary Floyd,.........	"	VII.	164
1760. Aug.	13.	Smith, Edward, and Alice Earl,...........	"	III.	275
1737. Nov.	19.	Smith, Edward, and Rachael Hunter,......	"	I.	8
1737. Nov.	18.	Smith, Edward, and Sarah Holmes, ...	"	I.	8
1756. Aug.	5.	Smith, Elsie, and Peter Cowles, ...	"	I.	269
1764. May	30.	Smith, Elias, and Catharine Miller,........	"	VIII.	182
1762. Dec.	14.	Smith, Elisabeth, and Henry Allen, ...	"	VI.	479
1762. Nov.	30.	Smith, Elisabeth, and Jacob Wood, ...	"	VI.	460
1782. Jan.	3.	Smith, Elisabeth, and Richard Peters,......	"	XXXV.	8
1783. Mar.	28.	Smith, Elisebeth, and John Brown, ...	"	XXXVIII.	79
1737. Nov.	4.	Smith, Elizabeth, and Adam Mott, ...	"	I.	8
1768. April	20.	Smith, Elizabeth, and Benjamin Douglass,..	"	XIII.	83
1760. May	8.	Smith, Elizabeth, and Christopher Chrouch,.	"	III.	146
1761. Dec.	14.	Smith, Elizabeth, and Edward Bitts,.......	"	V.	278
1757. May	4.	Smith, Elizabeth, and Edward Lowerare,...	"	I.	525
1770. June	29.	Smith, Elizabeth, and Emanuel Ryndollar,..	"	XVI.	126
1783. Sept.	7.	Smith, Elizabeth, and George Ormond, ...	"	XL.	31
1775. Aug.	16.	Smith, Elizabeth, and Jacob Downing,.....	"	XXIII.	129
1764. Nov.	4.	Smith, Elizabeth, and James Bayard,......	"	XV.	112
1758. Mar.	10.	Smith, Elizabeth, and Johannes Blauvelt, ..	"	I.	841
1777. April	15.	Smith, Elizabeth, and John Davis, ...	"	XXIV.	62
1780. Dec.	14.	Smith, Elizabeth, and John Durland,.......	"	XXX.	152
1738. July	11.	Smith, Elizabeth, and John Preston........	"	I.	10
1759. Nov.	20.	Smith, Elizabeth, and John Reynolds, ...	"	II.	508
1736. Aug.	24.	Smith, Elizabeth, and Jonathan Brush, ...	"	I.	2
1780. Nov.	7.	Smith, Elizabeth, and Joseph Dorlon,......	"	XXX.	95
1736. April	27.	Smith, Elizabeth, and Joseph Halsted,.....	"	I.	1
1770. Jan.	2.	Smith, Elizabeth, and Samuel Townsend, ..	"	XVI.	1
1783. July	11.	Smith, Elizabeth, and Stephen Herriman,...	"	XXXIX.	86
1664. Mar.	4.	Smith, Elizabeth, and William Laurence,...	G. E.,	I.	198
1767. Sept.	30.	Smith, Emilla, and Henry Disborough,.....	M. B.,	XII.	50
1781. June	9.	Smith, Ephraim, and Ruth Hulse,.........	"	XXXII.	78
1782. Oct.	23.	Smith, Esther, and Barnardus Smith,......	"	XXXVII.	62
1760. Feb.	12.	Smith, Everston, and Catharine Liscum,....	"	III.	33
1763. July	5.	Smith, Ezekiel, and Catharine Salts,.......	"	VII.	258
1761. Dec.	11.	Smith, Felte, and Susannah Schoenmaker,..	"	V.	275
1770. May	14.	Smith, Freelove, and Uriah Mitchell, ...	"	XVI.	84
1774. Jan.	18.	Smith, Gabriel, and Mary North,..........	"	XXII.	106
1760. May	2.	Smith, George, and Catharine Ott, ...	"	III.	134
1779. Jan.	22.	Smith, George, and Susanah Gardner, ...	"	XXVII.	23
1778. Feb.	19.	Smith, Hanah, and Henry Combs, ...	"	XXV.	28
1780. Dec.	7.	Smith, Hannah, and Anthony Cheesman,...	"	XXX.	141

DATE.		NAMES.	RECORD.	VOL.	PAGE.
1762. Oct.	22.	Smith, Hannah, and John Laboyten,.......	M. B.,	VI.	380
1761. May	19.	Smith, Hannah, and Joshua Rogers,.......	"	IV.	200
1761. June	1.	Smith, Hannah, and Nicolas Wortman,.....	"	IV.	222
1736. May	18.	Smith, Hannah, and Silas Carman,........	"	I.	1
1760. Jan.	31.	Smith, Hannah, and Thomas Williams,.....	"	III.	13
1779. Feb.	10.	Smith, Hannah, and William Cropley, ...	"	XXVII.	39
1757. Oct.	5.	Smith, Hebseba, and Eliphalet Wheeler,....	"	I.	654
1770. June	1.	Smith, Hendrick Andrew, and Christiana Gortser,............................	"	XVI.	101
1762. Feb.	1.	Smith, Henry, and Catharine Denton, ...	"	VI.	34
1762. Nov.	16.	Smith, Henry, and Catharine Leonard,.....	"	VI.	416
1775. Aug.	28.	Smith, Henry, and Mary Crist,...........	"	XXIII.	139
1738. Nov.	28.	Smith, Henry, and Ruth Smith, ...	"	I.	11
1758. Dec.	8.	Smith, Hepseby, and William Smith, ...	"	II.	121
1764. Oct.	5.	Smith, Hester, and Samuel Dickson,.......	"	VIII.	335
1788. May	16.	Smith, Hugh, and Jane Denyse, ...	"	XXXIX.	13
1769. Oct.	5.	Smith, Hugh, and Nancy Floyd,..........	"	XV.	50
1779. Jan.	28.	Smith, Ichabod, and Susanah Marvin, ...	"	XXVII.	30
1760. Dec.	10.	Smith, Isaac, and Anne Smith, ...	"	III.	469
1778. Nov.	5.	Smith, Isaac, and Hester Pearsall,.........	"	XXVI.	83
1770. Dec.	19.	Smith, Isaac, and Margaret Theal,.........	"	XVI.	304
1757. July	9.	Smith, Isaac, and Phebe Mervin,..........	"	I.	586
1781. June	4.	Smith, Isaiah, Jr., and Charity Nuton,.....	"	XXXII.	70
1782. Aug.	2.	Smith, Jacob, and Hannah Whaley,..	"	XXXVI.	98
1777. April	18.	Smith, Jacob, and Martha Birdsall,........	"	XXIV.	67
1764. June	23.	Smith, Jacob, and Mary Pettinger,........	"	VIII.	236
1767. July	10.	Smith, Jacob, and Rebecka Peters, ...	"	XI.	130
1753. May	10.	Smith, James, and Ame Searing,..........	"	I.	28
1758. Jan.	18.	Smith, James, and Ann Hicks,............	"	I.	789
1772. Nov.	21.	Smith, James, and Anna Volentine, ...	"	XIX.	124
1772. Nov.	23.	Smith, James, and Elizabeth Jones, ...	"	XIX.	126
1737. April	2.	Smith, James, and Elizabeth Thompson,....	"	I.	5
1757. Nov.	22.	Smith, James, and Mary Burk, ...	"	I.	709
1768. July	2.	Smith, James, and Mary Hunt, ...	"	XIII.	147
1771. July	18.	Smith, James, and Rebecca Neely, ...	"	XVII.	136
1764. July	10.	Smith, James, and Ruth Howard,.........	"	VIII.	254
1757. Mar.	16.	Smith, Jamima, and George Sands,........	"	I.	471
1760. Sept.	13.	Smith, Jamima, and Thomas Smith,.......	"	III.	313
1753. Sept.	21.	Smith, Jane, and James Duane,...........	"	I.	123
1780. Nov.	11.	Smith, Jane, and Job Hatfield, ...	"	XXX.	102
1783. April	12.	Smith, Jane, and Joseph Stout,...........	"	XXXVIII.	94
1762. Aug.	23.	Smith, Jane, and Samuel Hicks, ...	"	VI.	285
1771. Oct.	19.	Smith, Jennit, and John Plenderleath,.....	"	XVII.	215
1763. Jan.	3.	Smith, Jeremiah, and Amelia Smith, ...	"	VII.	6
1737. Dec.	17.	Smith, Jerrard, and Catherine Sebring, ...	"	I.	8

DATE.	NAMES.	RECORD.	VOL.	PAGE.
1767. April 18.	Smith, Jerusha, and William Post, ...	M. B.,	XI.	63
1767. Oct. 5.	Smith, Jesse, and Charity Willett, ...	"	XII.	55
1767. Sept. 23.	Smith, Joanna, and Abraham Anthony, ...	"	XII.	40
1781. Aug. .28.	Smith, Joanna, and Henry Ruland, ...	"	XXXIII.	50
1768. Jan. 30.	Smith, Joel, and Elizabeth Wright, ...	"	XIII.	22
1757. July 5.	Smith, John, and Ann Anderson, ...	"	I.	582
1778. July 23.	Smith, John, and Dorothy Willson, ...	"	XXV.	137
1764. Oct. 3.	Smith, John, and Elizabeth Remsen, ...	"	VIII.	332
1760. Dec. 5.	Smith, John, and Hannah Lefferd, ...	"	III.	456
1665. Feb. 13.	Smith, John, and Hannah Manning, ...	O. W. L.,	II.	27
1758. Dec. 27.	Smith, John, and Hannah Murray, ...	M. B.,	II.	140
1774. Mar. 5.	Smith, John, and Isabella Cannun, ...	"	XXII.	139
1760. Nov. 8.	Smith, John, and Jane Goff, ...	"	III.	399
1767. May 13.	Smith, John, and Jemima Dewint, ...	"	XI.	85
1762. June 29.	Smith, John, and Jennet Middlemas, ...	"	VI.	214
1765. Sept. 30.	Smith, John, and Margarita Houtvat, ...	"	IX.	281
1781. Sept. 29.	Smith, John, and Martha Woods, ...	"	XXXIII.	80
1779. Mar. 11.	Smith, John, and Mary Fitzgerald, ...	"	XXVII.	66
1783. Aug. 18.	Smith, John, and Mary Frances, ...	"	XL.	1
1775. Oct. 15.	Smith, John, and Mary Pine, ...	"	XXIII.	182
1756. Nov. 12.	Smith, John, and Mary Potter, ...	"	I.	352
1771. June 27.	Smith, John, and Priscilla Bayley, ...	"	XVII.	124
1781. May 1.	Smith, John, and Rachel Murphy, ...	"	XXXII.	24
1783. April 10.	Smith, John, and Ruth Geldersleve, ...	"	XXXVIII.	89
1764. Feb. 10.	Smith, John, and Susannah Beck, ...	"	VIII.	54
1737. Jan. 3.	Smith, Jonathan, and Filana Weeks, ...	"	I.	5
1781. Mar. 10.	Smith, Jonathan, and Hester Hennesy, ...	"	XXXI.	68
1755. Dec. 5.	Smith, Jonathan, and Mary Lynes, ...	"	I.	226
1738. Oct. 4.	Smith, Jonathan, and Mary Smith, ...	"	I.	11
1759. July 28.	Smith, Jonathan, and Millia Seaman, ...	"	II.	367
1648. April 16.	Smith, Joons, and Tomas Nuton, ...	A. R.,	VII.	145
1771. Feb. 16.	Smith, Joseph, and Dorothy Ruck, ...	M. B.,	XVII.	16
1783. Feb. 20.	Smith, Joseph, and Grace Jarvis, ...	"	XXXVIII.	45
1760. Oct. 29.	Smith, Joseph, and Hannah Hewlet, ...	"	III.	386
1770. Jan. 13.	Smith, Joseph, and Izabella Bruce, ...	"	XVI.	5
1769. Sept. 2.	Smith, Joseph, and Jemima Bergin, ...	"	XV.	34
1690. Nov. 3.	Smith, Joseph, and Maria Bedloo, ...	P. B.,	IV.	71
1763. Sept. 30.	Smith, Joseph, and Martha Hawkins, ...	M. B.,	VII.	361
1780. Oct. 17.	Smith, Joseph, and Mary Smith, ...	"	XXX.	67
1770. Oct. 13.	Smith, Joshua H., and Elizabeth Gordon, ..	"	XVI.	211
1758. Oct. 30.	Smith, Josiah, and Mary Howell, ...	"	II.	73
1780. Dec. 20.	Smith, Julia, and James Crommelin, ...	"	XXX.	161
1781. Aug. 7.	Smith, Leah, and Eli Lyons, ...	"	XXXIII.	30
1759. July 27.	Smith, Leathes, and Eleanor Murdigh, ...	"	II.	365
1756. Dec. 18.	Smith, Lette, and Anthony Swan, ...	"	I.	391

DATE.	NAMES.	RECORD.	VOL.	PAGE.
1759. Oct. 16.	Smith, Lewis, and Catharine Forster,	M. B.,	II.	460
1782. July 15.	Smith, Linninton, and Mary Bedell,	'	XXXVI.	82
1771. Feb. 4.	Smith, Littish, and John Van Buren,	"	XVII.	13
1777. Oct. 4.	Smith, Lucretia, and Peter Murphy,	"	XXIV.	157
1761. Dec. 22.	Smith, Lucy, and John Doty,	"	V.	294
1763. Sept. 15.	Smith, Margaret, and Benjamin Strong,	"	VII.	338
1778. May 7.	Smith, Margaret, and James Neal,	"	XXV.	73
1758. Oct. 4.	Smith, Margaret, and John Ebbit,	"	II.	40
1777. Feb. 1.	Smith, Margaret, and Richard Long,	"	XXIV.	23
1768. May 2.	Smith, Margaret, and Robert Watts,	"	XIII.	91
1761. Nov. 11.	Smith, Margaret, and Samuel Cornell,	"	V.	209
1768. Nov. 25.	Smith, Margaret, and Tunes Tallman,	"	XIII.	244
1781. Feb. 24.	Smith, Margret, and John Moore,	"	XXXI.	57
1763. Sept. 30.	Smith, Martha, and Ann Hawkes Hay,	"	VII.	362
1765. May 28.	Smith, Martha, and Eliphelet Whitman,	"	XI.	100
1759. Mar. 5.	Smith, Martha, and Joseph Place,	"	II.	209
1761. Dec. 7.	Smith, Martha, and Jost Gorsline,	"	V.	266
1763. April 27.	Smith, Martha, and Nathaniel Whitmen,	"	VII.	146
1765. Dec. 13.	Smith, Martha, and Robert Divine,	"	VIII.	453
1770. Dec. 14.	Smith, Martha, and Thomas Hazard,	"	XV.	123
1781. Dec. 2.	Smith, Martha, and Thomas Powell,	"	XXXIV.	68
1762. Aug. 25.	Smith, Mary, and Abijah Abbot,	"	VI.	287
1756. Dec. 6.	Smith, Mary, and Abraham Lawrence,	"	I.	373
1781. Nov. 24.	Smith, Mary, and Abraham Woodhull,	"	XXXIV.	58
1761. July 3.	Smith, Mary, and Annanias Rogers,	"	IV.	274
1738. May 1.	Smith, Mary, and Benjamin Wright,	"	I.	9
1771. Sept. 3.	Smith, Mary, and Christopher Bancker,	"	XVII.	172
1761. Jan. 30.	Smith, Mary, and Edward Clemison,	"	IV.	43
1772. Feb. 19.	Smith, Mary, and Elbert Aegeman,	"	XVIII.	39
1780. Aug. 9.	Smith, Mary, and Enoc Seaman,	"	XXIX.	136
1759. June 19.	Smith, Mary, and Isaac Biggs,	"	II.	330
1762. April 27.	Smith, Mary, and Isaac Platt,	"	VI.	133
1763. May 11.	Smith, Mary, and Jacob Essmond,	"	VII.	178
1781. April 17.	Smith, Mary, and James Cruger,	"	XXXII.	7
1781. May 5.	Smith, Mary, and James Rexorla,	"	XXXII.	32
1778. Nov. 11.	Smith, Mary, and Jesse Baldwin,	"	XXVI.	85
1762. Oct. 16.	Smith, Mary, and Johannes Folkens,	"	VI.	369
1759. April 18.	Smith, Mary, and John Crib,	"	II.	245
1783. Jan. 7.	Smith, Mary, and John Dodg,	"	XXXVIII.	8
1760. April 9.	Smith, Mary, and John Freeborn,	"	III.	101
1767. June 22.	Smith, Mary, and John Jean,	"	XI.	112
1760. May 16.	Smith, Mary, and John Wall,	"	III.	156
1738. Oct. 4.	Smith, Mary, and Jonathan Smith,	"	I.	11
173$\frac{8}{9}$. Mar. 10.	Smith, Mary, and Joseph Post,	"	I.	1
1774. Mar. 15.	Smith, Mary, and Joseph Robinson,	"	XXII.	149

DATE.	NAMES.	RECORD.	VOL.	PAGE.
1778. Oct. 17.	Smith, Mary, and Joseph Smith, ...	M. B.,	xxx.	67
1762. May 29.	Smith, Mary, and Morris Smith, ...	"	vi.	175
1782. Juno 15.	Smith, Mary, and Nicholas Ludlum, ...	"	xxxvi.	51
1773. June 1.	Smith, Mary, and Obadiah Jones, ...	"	xx.	136
1759. Jan. 12.	Smith, Mary, and Richard Lakerman, ...	"	ii.	152
1767. Feb. 7.	Smith, Mary, and Robert Forbes, ...	"	xi.	21
1767. Mar. 28.	Smith, Mary, and Samuel Lewis, ...	"	xi.	52
1773. July 16.	Smith, Mary, and Stephen Ducolon, ...	"	xxi.	41
1763. Oct. 6.	Smith, Mary, and Thomas Cock, ...	"	vii.	374
1778. Mar. 23.	Smith, Mary, and Thomas Downey, ...	"	xxv.	51
1777. Nov. 12.	Smith, Mary, and Thomas Williams, ...	"	xxiv.	180
1763. Aug. 1.	Smith, Mary, and William Pearson, ...	"	vii.	288
1775. Nov. 29.	Smith, Mary, and Yellis Mandevill, ...	"	xxiii.	222
1764. Aug. 10.	Smith, Mathias, and Dorcas Haughewout, ..	"	viii.	277
1775. April 15.	Smith, Matthew, and Susannah Glean, ...	"	xxiii.	10
1760. Sept. 5.	Smith, Maurice, and Mary Dodge, ...	"	iii.	300
1758. Mar. 30.	Smith, Maurice, and Mary Sering, ...	"	i.	867
1772. Mar. 17.	Smith, Melancton, and Margaret Mott, ...	"	xviii.	53
1766. June 18.	Smith, Melancton, and Sarah Smith, ...	"	x.	20
1781. Feb. 12.	Smith, Mercey, and Charles Wheeler, ...	"	xxxi.	21
1779. Oct. 6.	Smith, Michel, and Mary Steel, ...	"	xxviii.	104
1763. Dec. 19.	Smith, Millesant, and Daniel Preslow, ...	'	vii.	512
1762. May 29.	Smith, Morris, and Mary Smith, ...	"	vi.	175
1782. Dec. 9.	Smith, Moses, and Else Philips, ...	"	xxxvii.	113
1775. Sept. 16.	Smith, Moses, and Mary Ivers, ...	"	xxiii.	157
1763. Sept. 20.	Smith, Nathan, and Abigail Pine, ...	"	vii.	343
1737. Feb. 4.	Smith, Nathaniel, and Charity Meby, ...	"	i.	8
1761. Sept. 18.	Smith, Nathaniel, and Eleonor Rhodes, ...	"	v.	88
1771. Nov. 11.	Smith, Nathanicl, and Susannah Ludlow, ..	"	xvii.	245
1757. Oct. 13.	Smith, Nehemiah, and Sarah Kinman, ...	"	i.	667
1667. Jan. 31.	Smith, Nehemiah, and Sarah Luddington, ..	O. W. L.,	ii.	192
1763. April 27.	Smith, Nicholas, and Sarah Clark, ...	M. B.,	vii.	147
1770. Oct. 12.	Smith, Obediah, and Phebe Clark, ...	"	xvi.	210
1773. Nov. 27.	Smith, Oliver, and Catherine Drake, ...	"	xxii.	49
1774. Feb. 14.	Smith, Paschal N., and Hesther Sears, ...	"	xxii.	127
1765. April 4.	Smith, Patience, and Andrew Oakly, ...	"	xi.	56
1738. May 4.	Smith, Patrick, and Maritie Mountany, ...	"	i.	9
1758. Feb. 3.	Smith, Patrick, and Mary Mackey, ...	"	i.	812
1764. Dec. 5.	Smith, Peter, and Margaret Cornell, ...	"	viii.	436
1764. Oct. 19.	Smith, Phebe, and Job Hubbs, ...	"	viii.	363
1766. Nov. 10.	Smith, Phebe, and Nathaniel Platt, ...	"	x.	160
1763. Oct. 13.	Smith, Phebe, and Platt Carll, ...	"	vii.	384
1767. Nov. 18.	Smith, Phebe, and Platt Conklin, ...	"	xii.	88
1772. April 16.	Smith, Phebe, and William Hinton, ...	"	xviii.	82
1782. Mar. 8.	Smith, Pheby, and John Barton, ...	"	xxxv.	79

46

DATE.		NAMES.	RECORD.	VOL.	PAGE.
1764. Oct.	29.	Smith, Philena, and William Seaman,......	M. B.,	VIII.	382
1759. Feb.	5.	Smith, Phillip, and Altje Bogert,..........	"	II.	175
1761. June	9.	Smith, Philip, and Mary Shadbolt, ...	"	IV.	233
1763. Jan.	2.	Smith, Platt, and Sarah Green, ...	"	VII.	534
1782. July	19.	Smith, Precilla, and Thomas Martin,.......	"	XXXVI.	87
1764. Dec.	31.	Smith, Priscilla, and Ebenezer Cooper,.....	"	VIII.	471
1783. Nov.	19.	Smith, Rachael, and Jacob Cershow,.......	"	XL.	122
1761. Dec.	24.	Smith, Rachel, and Benjamin Kiersted, ...	"	V.	302
1757. Dec.	29.	Smith, Rachel, and Daniel North,.........	"	I.	757
1782. Mar.	2.	Smith, Ralph, and Ann Hicks, ...	"	XXXV.	70
1764. Jan.	11.	Smith, Rebecca, and Elijah Rainor,........	"	VIII.	12
1766. May	27.	Smith, Rebecca, and John Aspinwall,......	"	X.	1
1759. July	31.	Smith, Rebecca, and Peter Havens,........	"	II.	368
1782. Nov.	29.	Smith, Rebecca, and Thomas Jackson, ...	"	XXXVII.	99
1763. Oct.	26.	Smith, Rebecca, and Volkert Vedder,......	"	VII.	405
1771. July	25.	Smith, Rebeccah, and Charles Gay,........	"	XVII.	143
1764. Feb.	11.	Smith, Richard, and Catherine Smith,......	"	VIII.	58
173⁷⁄₈. Mar.	4.	Smith, Richard, and Hanna Totten,........	"	I.	5
1761. May	30.	Smith, Richard, and Hannah Becket, ...	"	IV.	219
1765. July	22.	Smith, Richard, and Mary Oliver,....	"	IX.	214
1773. Mar.	26.	Smith, Richard, and Sarah Skillman, ...	"	XX.	72a
1768. June	20.	Smith, Richard, and Sarah Smith, ...	"	XIII.	134
1670. June	20.	Smith, Richard, Jr., [and Hannah Tooker,*].	C. A.,	II.	550
1762. Mar.	1.	Smith, Robert, and Sarah Morris, ...	M. B.,	VI.	60
1738. Nov.	28.	Smith, Ruth, and Henry Smith, ...	"	I.	11
1779. April	20.	Smith, Ruth, and John Allen, ...	"	XXVII.	110
1770. Jan.	17.	Smith, Ruth, and John Watts,............	"	XVI.	6
1764. Mar.	23.	Smith, Ruth, and William Valentine,......	"	VIII.	116
1764. Feb.	3.	Smith, Samuel, and Anne Raynor, ...	"	VIII.	48
1766. Sept.	2.	Smith, Samuel, and Elizabeth Marsh,......	"	X.	88
1755. Nov.	28.	Smith, Samuel, and Mehitabel Cooper,.....	"	I.	223
1783. Jan.	28.	Smith, Samuel, and Susanah Blindenburrow,	"	XXXVIII.	46
1767. Jan.	22.	Smith, Samuel, Jr., and Hannah Stringham,	"	XI.	11
1755. Oct.	22.	Smith, Sarah, and Abraham Keteltas,......	"	I.	198
1764. Dec.	31.	Smith, Sarah, and Abraham Ten Eyck, ...	"	VIII.	469
1762. Sept.	3.	Smith, Sarah, and Charles Amory, ...	"	VI.	306
1761. Jan.	6.	Smith, Sarah, and David Tyler,...........	"	IV.	3
1760. July	9.	Smith, Sarah, and Evert Pels, ...	"	III.	208
1770. Mar.	21.	Smith, Sarah, and Foster Lewis,....	"	XVI.	36
1779. Mar.	10.	Smith, Sarah, and Garret Dorland,........	"	XXVII.	62
1781. Nov.	10.	Smith, Sarah, and George Rhoades, ...	"	XXXIV.	27
1769. April	28.	Smith, Sarah, and James Sutton,..........	"	XIV.	84
1761. Aug.	24.	Smith, Sarah, and John Brush, ...	"	V.	54

* The name of the woman is not mentioned in the Record. It is taken from Thompson's History of Long Island, vol. II, p. 452.

DATE.		NAMES.	RECORD.	VOL.	PAGE.
1758. Nov.	21.	Smith, Sarah, and Joseph Buffet, ...	M. B.,	II.	100
1781. Mar.	23.	Smith, Sarah, and Joseph Willabe, ...	"	XXXI.	82
1766. June	18.	Smith, Sarah, and Melancton Smith, ...	"	X.	20
1781. July	28.	Smith, Sarah, and Michael Williams, ...	"	XXXIII.	19
1765. Oct.	28.	Smith, Sarah, and Nathan Skidmore, ...	"	IX.	321
1781. May	5.	Smith, Sarah, and Nehemiah Hanford, ...	"	XXXII.	33
1768. June	20.	Smith, Sarah, and Richard Smith, ...	"	XIII.	134
1757. Dec.	28.	Smith, Sarah, and Robert Akerly, ...	"	I.	756
1782. May	30.	Smith, Sarah, and Robert Bridgeford, ...	"	XXXVI.	31
1765. May	7.	Smith, Sarah, and Robert Watts, ...	"	IX.	121
1762. Aug.	31.	Smith, Sarah, and Stephen Willis, ...	"	VI.	300
1736. Jan.	25.	Smith, Sarah, and Thomas Williams, ...	"	I.	5
1737. June	18.	Smith, Seth, and Anne Carman, ...	"	I.	6
1755. Nov.	25.	Smith, Silas, and Mary Simmons, ...	"	I.	215
1760. June	6.	Smith, Silvanus, and Elizabeth Wesner, ...	"	III.	179
1773. April	19.	Smith, Silvanus, and Mary Baldwin, ...	"	XX.	95
1769. May	6.	Smith, Solomon, and Betsey Roe, ...	"	XIV.	96
1769. April	25.	Smith, Susannah, and Stephen Howell, ...	"	XIV.	86
1771. June	20.	Smith, Temperance, and Rueben Ketchum,.	"	XVII.	119
1782. Nov.	5.	Smith, Theodotia, and Benjamin Hutchinson,	"	XXXVII.	72
1752. Nov.	27.	Smith, Thomas, and Affie Smith, ...	"	I.	14
1777. Nov.	8.	Smith, Thomas, and Agness Aget, ...	"	XXIV.	178
1782. July	9.	Smith, Thomas, and Amy Southard, ...	"	XXXVI.	75
1778. Aug.	8.	Smith, Thomas, and Elizabeth Ford, ...	"	XXV.	145
1757. Nov.	25.	Smith, Thomas, and Hannah Buckley, ...	"	I.	713
1760. Sept.	13.	Smith, Thomas, and Jamima Smith, ...	"	III.	313
1764. Nov.	9.	Smith, Thomas, and Letitia Van Loo, ...	"	VIII.	397
1762. Mar.	25.	Smith, Thomas, and Margaret O'Brian, ...	"	VI.	66
1762. July	10.	Smith, Thomas, and Mary Edwards, ...	"	VI.	234
1763. Mar.	17.	Smith, Thomas, and Mary Thompson, ...	"	VII.	103
1760. May	7.	Smith, Thomas, and Mary Waters, ...	"	III.	142
1641. April	27.	Smith, Thomas, and Naune Beets, ...	A. R.,	I.	235
1759. Oct.	26.	Smith, Thomas, and Rebecca Nicholls, ...	M. B.,	II.	474
1780. July	28.	Smith, Thomas, and Sarah Toffey, ...	"	XXIX.	123
1767. Dec.	7.	Smith, Thomas, and Temperance Leonard,..	"	XII.	109
1768. April	8.	Smith, Thomas Howel, and Margaret Desborough, ...	"	XIII.	67
1764. Mar.	9.	Smith, Waters, and Deborah Betts, ...	"	VIII.	99
1761. Nov.	19.	Smith, Wilhelmus, and Hannah Bratt, ...	"	V.	231
1776. Mar.	27.	Smith, William, and Elizabeth Moore, ...	"	XXIII.	293
1777. Aug.	27.	Smith, William, and Else Osborn, ...	"	XXIV.	140
1668. Jan.	4.	Smith, William, and Hannah Scudder, ...	O. W. L.,	II.	321
1758. Dec.	8.	Smith, William, and Hepsebie Smith, ...	M. B.,	II.	121
1736. Sept.	7.	Smith, William, and Jane Sills, ...	"	I.	2
1780. Aug.	8.	Smith, William, and Martha Ludlam, ...	"	XXIX.	135

DATE.	NAMES.	RECORD.	VOL. PAGE.
1770. Dec. 7.	Smith, William, and Mary Hillyer,........	M. B.,	XVI. 287
1780. April 25.	Smith, William, and Mary McLean, ...	"	XXIX. 33
1767. Aug. 25.	Smith, William, and Mary Roan,..........	"	XII. 22
1766. Sept. 24.	Smith, William, and Phebe Hoel,.........	"	X. 104
1783. Mar. 29.	Smith, William, and Phebe Morrell,.......	"	XXXVIII. 82
1762. Mar. 2.	Smith, William, and Ruth Woodhull,......	"	VI. 61
1775. Nov. 14.	Smith, William, and Sarah Bevoise,.......	"	XXIII. 209
1759. May 4.	Smith, William, and Sarah Wilks,........	"	II. 267
1768. Nov. 2.	Smith, Zebulun, Jr., and Debroa Fleet,.....	"	XIII. 222
1764. Nov. 22.	Smock, Cornelius, and Altje Lyster, ...	"	VIII. 420
1780. May 16.	Smyth, Elizabeth, and John Demill,.......	"	XXIX. 55
1780. May 6.	Smyth, Elizabeth, and Stephen Cornwell,...	"	XXIX. 46
1780. Sept. 22.	Smyth, Hannah, and William Summers, ...	"	XXX. 36
1775. Aug. 3.	Smyth, Jacob, and Ann De Witt,..........	"	XXIII. 119
1782. Dec. 13.	Smyth, James, and Mary Devine, ...	"	XXXVII. 119
1780. May 2.	Smyth, Mary, and Benjamin Smith,.......	"	XXIX. 40
1780. Sept. 1.	Smyth, Mary (Margaret), and Joseph Bates,.	'	XXX. 13
1780. Dec. 4.	Smyth, Richard, and Fanny Day, ...	"	XXX. 137
1779. Sept. 4.	Smythe, Lionel, and Maria Eliza Philipse,..	"	XXVIII. 68
1777. April 28.	Smythies, William, and Margaret Burges,..	"	XXIV. 77
1675. Aug. 22.	Snawsell, Thomas, and Martha Lawrence,..	W. O. P.,	III. 126
1762. April 2.	Snedaker, Abraham, and Deliverance Lewis,	M. B.,	VI. 89
1764. May 24.	Snedaker, Ann, and William Hendrickson, .	"	VIII. 34
1768. July 24.	Snedaker, Johannes, and Femmetje Cas-show,.............................	"	XIII. 164
1761. Nov. 23.	Snedaker, Nieltje, and David Browder,.....	"	V. 241
1737. June 23.	Snedecar, Williampia, and Johannes Wil-liamson,............................	"	I. 6
1768. July 11.	Snedecker, Catherine, and Douwe Ditmars,.	"	XIII. 154
1768. Nov. 28.	Snedecker, Effje, and Theodorus Snedecker,	"	XIII. 246
1768. Nov. 28.	Snedecker, Theodorus, and Effje Snedecker,	"	XIII. 246
1738. Oct. 3.	Snedega, Rebecca, and Jacob Polimius, ...	"	I. 11
1759. Aug. 4.	Snedeker, Abraham, and Antje Bennet,....	"	II. 372
1767. May 7.	Snedeker, Albert, and Maritie Rapelje,.....	"	XI. 79
1768. Jan. 20.	Snedeker, Garret, and Margaret Lent, ...	"	XIII. 14
1760. Nov. 5.	Snedeker, Harriantie, and Solomon Waring,	"	III. 394
1757. Aug. 13.	Snedeker, Hillittié, and John Lyster, ...	"	I. 614
1778. Jan. 10.	Snedeker, Mary, and Isaac Ramson,.......	"	XXV. 2
1771. Nov. 20.	Snedeker, Nelly, and Adreyoan Onderdonck,	"	XVII. 262
1765. Oct. 16.	Snedeker, Sarah, and Luke Teller,.........	"	IX. 303
1773. Oct. 6.	Snedeker, Tunis, and Elizabeth Cornelius,..	"	XXI. 131
1763. May 16.	Sneden, Abraham, and Susannah Knap, ...	"	VII. 189
1765. June 7.	Sneden, Mary, and Samuel Lawrence, ...	"	IX. 160
1782. May 28.	Sneden, Robert, and Mariam Fowler,......	"	XXXVI. 27
1763. Oct. 13.	Sneden, Stephen, and Margaret Townsend,.	"	VII. 413

DATE.		NAMES.	RECORD.	VOL.	PAGE.
1737. Jan.	13.	Suederger, Catherine, and Jacobus Emans,..	M. B.,	XI.	7
1765. April	16.	Snedicker, James, and Jane Welling, ...	"	IX.	97
1777. Jan.	15.	Snediker, Abraham, and Jane Remsen, ...	"	XXIV.	13
1757. Mar.	21.	Sneed, Ezekiel, and Mary Willson, ...	"	I.	476
1762. Oct.	25.	Sneeden, John, and Elison Lawrence,......	"	VI.	381
1764. April	2.	Sneeden, John, and Rebecca Archer, ...	"	VIII.	129
1765. May	24.	Sneeden, Mary, and George Calhoun,......	"	IX.	139
1768. Jan.	20.	Sneelen, Hannah, and Samuel Bayley,.....	"	XIII.	15
1758. Sept.	4.	Snell, Eliezer, and Mary Childs, ...	"	II.	1
1783. Nov.	7.	Snell, Elizabeth, and Daniel Stanbury,.....	"	XL.	108
1769. Dec.	29.	Snell, John, and Anna Shaver, ...	"	XV.	134
1767. Jan.	28.	Snell, John, and Elizabeth Wiley,..........	"	XI.	16
1763. Oct.	12.	Snethen, Deborah, and James Nairn, ...	"	VII.	383
1772. Dec.	30.	Sneyder, Margaret, and Michael Frederick,.	"	XIX.	167
1771. Oct.	25.	Sneyder, Peter, and Sarah Polhemus,......	"	XVII.	222
1773. Feb.	16.	Snifen, Tamar, and Henry Purdy,.........	"	XX.	44
1764. Dec.	13.	Sniffen, Andrew, and Gloriana Lyon,......	"	VIII.	454
1753. May	21.	Sniffen, Benjamin, and Mary Brown,......	"	I.	36
1778. Sept.	28.	Sniffen, Mary, and Samuel Barker,........	"	XXIII.	166
1779. Oct.	16.	Sniffen, Peter, and Patty Pettit, ...	"	XXVI.	63
1781. Dec.	6.	Snodgrass, Andrew, and Eleonora Maxwell,	"	XXXIV.	76
1762. Sept.	17.	Snook, Jacob, and Margaret Pottman, ...	"	VI.	321
1768. Feb.	6.	Snow, John, and Bridgett McDonough, ...	"	XIII.	28
1779. Nov.	29.	Snow, Thomas Musgrove, and Ann Morgan,	"	XXVIII.	145
1758. April	22.	Snowden, Thomas, and Mary Flanagan,....	"	I.	880
1762. June	21.	Snowdon, George, and Rachel King, ...	"	VI.	200
1778. Oct.	30.	Snowdon, Thomas, and Rebecca Hoyer,....	"	XXVI.	76
1756. Sept.	28.	Snuke, Effia, and Adam Dobbs, ...	"	I.	308
1758. Jan.	28.	Snyder, Amey, and Jacob Wiltse,.........	"	I.	803
1769. Nov.	7.	Snyder, Benjamin, and Annetie Brinck,....	"	XV.	81
1756. Dec.	29.	Snyder, John, and Ann Johnson, ...	"	I.	402
1773. June	14.	Snyder, Nicholas, and Sarah Lake,........	"	XXI.	1
1736. May	11.	Snyder, Peter, and Hannah Cornwell, ...	"	I.	1
1773. Jan.	23.	Solds, Elizabeth, and Benjamin Sealy, ...	"	XX.	17
1758. April	26.	Sole, William, and Margaret Philips,.......	"	I.	887
1758. May	15.	Solis, John, and Anne Williams, ...	"	I.	901
1760. May	8.	Solomon, Philip, and Sarah Cornell,.......	"	III.	144
1767. Dec.	17.	Somandike, Sarah, and Samuel Maghee,....	"	XII.	117
1781. April	24.	Somandyke, Nicholas, and Catharine Magraw,	"	XXXII.	14
1774. Jan.	7.	Somarandike, Hannah, and William Morgan,	"	XXII.	95
1768. Nov.	18.	Somarindike, Richard, and Elizabeth Stout,.	"	XIII.	238
1769. April	20.	Somarindyck, John, and Sarah Willis, ...	"	XIV.	79
1775. May	24.	Somarindyke, Tunis, and Catharine Horser,.	"	XXIII.	42
1780. Jan.	12.	Somendyck, Catharine, and John Wright, ..	"	XXVIII.	195
1760. April	22.	Somendyck, Isaac, and Elizabeth States, ...	"	III.	119

DATE.	NAMES.	RECORD.	VOL.	PAGE.
1757. June 17.	Somer, Jacob, and Barbara Myring, ...	M. B.,	I.	567
173⅝. Mar. 17.	Somerdyke, Hannah, and John Mandeville, .	"	I.	9
1738. Dec. 1.	Somerendick, Tunis, and Gertrie Harris, ...	"	I.	12
1758. Sept. 7.	Somerendike, Ann, and John Mott, ...	"	II.	10
1783. Oct. 20.	Someringdike, Coenrod, and Anne Southerd, ...	"	XL.	86
1783. Nov. 5.	Someringdyke, Catharine, and Garret Peterson, ...	"	XL.	106
1768. Nov. 21.	Somerndyck, Sarah, and Rumbout Brett, . . .	"	XIII.	239
173⁶₉. Mar. 18.	Sominindike, Jacob, and Amy Niven, ...	"	I.	5
1775. Dec. 11.	Sommer, Eve, and Donald McDougall, ...	"	XXIII.	226
1763. April 23.	Sommersby, Arthur, and Ann Clotworthy, .	"	VII.	138
1772. Nov. 2.	Sopea, Timothy, and Hannah Carr, ...	"	XIX.	100
1761. Aug. 6.	Soper, Benjamin, and Sarah Brown, ...	"	V.	27
1761. Nov. 30.	Soper, Charity, and Moses Hayt, ...	"	V.	257
1778. Mar. 28.	Soper, Hanah, and Nathan Crocker, ...	"	XXV.	54
1764. Jan. 11.	Soper, Massey, and Abijah Hyat, ...	"	VIII.	13
1764. Oct. 29.	Sopes, Mary, and Albertus Sickle, ...	"	VIII.	379
1766. Dec. 2.	Sorrell, William, and Margaret Burnet, ...	"	X.	192
1762. Oct. 29.	Soulice, Susanna, and Josiah Le Conte, ...	"	VI.	393
1770. Dec. 5.	Soulis, Magdalen, and Elias Guion, ...	"	XVI.	285
1762. June 26.	Souliss, Joshua, and Susannah Landrine, . . .	"	VI.	209
1759. Oct. 18.	Sourin, Mary, and Thomas Quill, ∙.	"	II.	464
1764. April 7.	South, Ann, and James Steel, ...	"	VIII.	142
1782. July 9.	Southard, Amy, and Thomas Smith, ...	"	XXXVI.	75
1782. Nov. 17.	Southard, Elizabeth, and John Vallance, . . .	"	XXXVII.	84
1763. Oct. 8.	Southard, James, and Mary Clowes, ...	"	VII.	381
1781. Dec. 2.	Southard, Jemimah, and John Brewer, Jr., .	"	XXXIV.	66
1758. Oct. 25.	Southard, Thomas, and Hannah Carman, . . .	"	II.	67
1783. Oct. 20.	Southerd, Anne, and Coenrad Someringdyke,	"	XL.	86
1761. Nov. 13.	Southerd, Daniel, and Sarah Van Voorhees,	"	V.	215
1762. Sept. 24.	Southerd, Eleanor, and Andrew Myer, ...	"	VI.	331
1766. Nov. 20.	Southerd, Gilbert, and Anna Dubois, ...	"	X.	173
1760. Nov. 14.	Southerd, Thomas, and Dorothy Golder, . . .	"	III.	413
1763. Dec. 19.	Southerd, Zebulon, and Jannetje Van Voorhees, ...	"	VII.	510
1762. Feb. 17.	Southern, Samuel, and Sarah Johnson, ...	"	VI.	52
1781. Feb. 6.	Southgate, Wright, and Lydia McCarris, . . .	"	XXXI.	40
1771. Sept. 26.	Southgate, Wright, and Mary Lush, ...	"	XVII.	194
173₄¹. Mar. 21.	Sowdam, Jacob, and Ame Lequie, ...	"	I.	5
1765. Jan. 18.	Sower, Margaret, and Francis Marvel, ...	"	IX.	20
1777. Feb. 10.	Sowers, Ann Barbara, and George Hart, . . .	"	XXIV.	28
1779. Mar. 3.	Sowers, Ann Barbara, and James Ridley, . .	"	XXVII.	55
1777. Feb. 10.	Sowers, Mary Magadalen, and William Carter, ...	"	XXIV.	29

DATE.	NAMES.	RECORD.	VOL.	PAGE.
1769. June 23.	Sowers, Thomas, and Ann Myer,..........	M. B.,	XIV.	127
1782. May 14.	Spangler, Elizabeth, and John Miller,......	"	XXXVI.	2
1761. Nov. 2.	Sparding, John Wingod, and Elizabeth Burger, ...	"	V.	185
1782. Jan. 29.	Sparkman, James, and Ann McEwen, ...	"	XXXV.	38
1769. Jan. 21.	Sparks, Elizabeth, and Robert Quick, ...	"	XIV.	17
1758. Jan. 3.	Sparksman, Rebeccah, and John De Houneur,	"	I.	765
1778. Sept. 27.	Sparling, Ann, and Bartholomew Mercereau,	"	XXVI.	36
1778. June 27.	Sparracks, Katharine, and Richard Wood, ..	"	XXV.	115
1756. Oct. 4.	Spartman, John, and Rebeccah Slingsby,...	"	I.	316
1776. Mar. 27.	Spawn, Eitie, and Philip Luke,...........	"	XXIII.	294
1770. Nov. 8.	Speaight, Richard, and Mary Thomas,......	"	XVI.	244
1764. May 19.	Spear, Ann, and Joseph Atkins, ...	"	VIII.	194
1763. Sept. 22.	Spear, Barrent, and Juditt Utt,...........	"	VII.	351
1770. Dec. 5.	Speece, Catherine, and Bissett Weeks, ...	"	XVI.	284
1760. May 6.	Speeden, Elizabeth, and John Brower,.....	"	III.	141
1765. May 4.	Speeder, Mary, and Frederick Rhinelander,.	"	IX.	153
1758. Nov. 18.	Speeding, Andrew, and Elizabeth Bekit, ...	"	II.	95
1757. Mar. 18.	Speedy, Seviah, and George Hopson,......	"	I.	461
1768. Oct. 4.	Speer, Abraham, and Catharine Marley,....	"	XIII.	204
1770. Jan. 17.	Spence, Andrew, and Jane Eson, ...	"	XVI.	7
1783. Oct. 8.	Spence, Anne, and Benjamin Cowdrey, ...	"	XL.	73
1781. June 4.	Spence, Jane, and William Scales, ...	"	XXXII.	72
1753. June 2.	Spencer, Agnus, and Churchil James Abel, .	"	I.	46
1756. Nov. 15.	Spencer, Catharine, and Richard Blacke,....	"	I.	354
1782. Jan. 17.	Spencer, Elizabeth, and Alexander Melvill,..	"	XXXV.	20
1738. June 13.	Spencer, George, and Florida Pinlard, ...	"	I.	10
1762. April 30.	Spencer, Jeremiah, and Mary Martin,......	"	VI.	136
1782. April 30.	Spencer, John, and Nelly Pettit,..........	"	XXXV.	121
1676. May 24.	Spencer, John, and Rachell Hicks, ...	W. O. P.,	III.,	198
1775. June 28.	Spencer, Richard, and Ann Ackley, ...	M. B.,	XXIII.	81
1778. Oct. 5.	Spencer, Richard, and Ann Duncan,.......	"	XXVI.	47
1759. Jan. 22.	Spencer, Tryal, and Valintine Arnold, ...	"	II.	164
1773. Feb. 15.	Spicer, Moses, and Abigail Wall,..........	"	XX.	43
1779. Nov. 15.	Spier, Abraham, and Ann Vanderbelt,.....	"	XXVIII.	140a
1778. May 19.	Spier, Charity, and Daniel Corser,.........	"	XXV.	86
1768. May 19.	Spier, Cornelius, and Hannah Stimets,.....	"	XIII.	107
1759. Nov. 16.	Spikes, Mary, and Cæser Dickson, ...	"	II.	499
1761. Aug. 26.	Spock, Mary, and Thomas Peet, ...	"	V.	59
1760. Nov. 11.	Spoor, Mary, and Jacob Brouwer,.........	"	III.	403
1757. Mar. 25.	Spoore, John, and Magdelane Bogart, ...	"	I.	482
1760. May 31.	Spotten, William, and Isabel Hollyway,....	"	III.	170
1758. Mar. 9.	Spragg, Martha, and Thomas Morgan, ...	"	I.	840
1773. Dec. 13.	Spragg, Samuel, and Sarah Way, ...	"	XXII.	70
1762. May 6.	Spragge, Amy, and Benjamin Smith,......	"	VI.	148

DATE.	NAMES.	RECORD.	VOL. PAGE.
1772. Oct. 23.	Spragge, Joanna, and Henry Simonson,....	M. B.,	XIX. 89
1778. Nov. 27.	Spraggs, Samuel, and Mary Dunscomb, ...	"	XXVI. 102
1771. Oct. 25.	Sprague, Gideon, and Hannah Caston,.....	"	XVII. 223
1764. Oct. 31.	Sprainger, Ann, and William Baldwin,.....	"	VIII. 383
1773. Aug. 20.	Sprainger, Charles, and Mary Gibson,......	"	XXI. 80
1757. Jan. 15.	Spranger, Charles, and Janitie Duyckman,..	"	I. 413
1758. Feb. 9.	Spranger, Susanah, and Joseph Tower,.....	"	I. 815
1781. Jan. 2.	Spring, Mary, and George Taunton,.... ...	"	XXXI. 6
1761. July 18.	Springall, Gregory, and Christian Hill,.....	"	IV. 303
1777. June 11.	Springall, Gregory, and Elizabeth Hill,.....	"	XXIV. 99
1764. June 28.	Springar, Garret, and Sarah Foster,........	"	VIII. 240
1757. July 20.	Springer, Rachel, and John Bates,.........	"	I. 596
1768. May 18.	Springler, Henry, and Jane Reed,.........	"	XIII. 105
1779. July 23.	Springsteen, Abraham, and Abigail Forman,	"	XXVIII. 29
1782. Mar. 5.	Springsteen, Ann, and Abraham Bergin,...	"	XXXV. 74
1771. Dec. 5.	Springsteen, Cobus, and Cornelia Vorhis,...	"	XVII. 286
1777. Dec. 2.	Springsteen, Hannah, and Douw Van Dine,.	"	XXIV. 188
1760. Oct. 18.	Springsteen, Maria, and Abraham Cannon,..	"	III. 371
1783. Aug. 21.	Springsteen, Right, and James Reed,......	"	XXXIX. 111
1767. Dec. 5.	Sprong, Folkert, and Magdalena Middagh, .	"	XII. 106
1760. Sept. 5.	Sprong, Gabriel, and Mary Berry,.........	"	III. 285
1767. Sept. 15.	Sprong, Phebe, and John Suydam,....... .	"	XII. 34
1764. Aug. 6.	Sproung, Antje, and Leonard Van Bomel, ..	"	VIII. 275
1757. July 14.	Sprung, Ann, and William Macktear,......	"	I. 590
1781. Feb. 23.	Sprung, Margret, and Ebenezer Gilbert,....	"	XXXI. 55
1764. June 21.	Sprung, Peter, and Jennette Brower,......	"	VIII. 230
1760. Dec. 6.	Sprung, Rachel, and Samuel Sayer,........	"	III. 461
1779. Dec. 7.	Sprung, Stephen, and Margaret Leasier,....	"	XXVIII. 164
1781. July 7.	Spry, Lucine, and William Gray,..........	"	XXXII. 106
1765. July 15.	Staates, Mary, and Peter Martin,..........	"	IX. 205
1773. Nov. 23.	Staats, Abraham, and Cornelia Lansingh,...	"	XXII. 39
1766. July 11.	Staats, Abraham, and Elizabeth Staats,.....	"	X. 46
1775. July 25.	Staats, Annatie, and Abraham Provoost, ...	"	XXIII. 108
1760. Dec. 8.	Staats, Anne, and Guysbert Marselus,......	'	III. 465
1767. July 31.	Staats, Barent, and Antie Winne, ...	"	XII. 5
1759. Dec. 22.	Staats, Barent, and Elizabeth Wendell,.....	"	II. 555
1766. July 11.	Staats, Elizabeth, and Abraham Staats, ...	"	X. 46
1738. Nov. 15.	Staats, Elizabeth, and Samuel Richards,....	"	I. 11
1770. Nov. 15.	Staats, Henry, and Mary Dumond,........	"	XVI. 257
1769. July 21.	Staats, Henry, and Rachel Villee, ...	"	XV. 3
1771. May 30.	Staats, Jane, and Johannis I. Huyck,......	"	XVII. 95
1775. Nov. 6.	Staats, Jane, and Rem Hegeman, ...	"	XXIII. 200
1761. Feb. 24.	Staats, Jochem Isaac, and Geesie Veeder,..	"	IV. 79
1738. Oct. 18.	Staats, Johannes, and Allida Hallenbeck,...	"	I. 11
1782. Dec. 17.	Staats, John, and Letetia Golder,..........	"	XXXVII. 123

DATE.		NAMES.	RECORD.	VOL.	PAGE.
1768. Oct.	31.	Staats, Maria, and Nicholas Van Voort, ...	M. B.,	VII.	418
1766. Sept.	5.	Staats, Mary, and John E. Lansingh, ...	"	X.	91
1769. Oct.	25.	Staats, Neeltie, and John Amory, ...	'	XV.	66
1764. Sept.	13.	Staats, Nellie, and Sylvester Salisbury, ...	"	VIII.	305
1769. Oct.	24.	Staats, Nicholas, and Mary Salsbury, ...	"	XV.	65
1770. Dec.	28.	Staats, Peter, and Jannatje Ditmars, ...	"	XVI.	306
1762. Sept.	29.	Staats, Rebecca, and Johannis Ditmars, ...	"	VI.	338
1736. Nov.	8.	Staats, Sarah, and Johannes Vanderpoole, ..	"	I.	3
1771. Mar.	28.	Staats, William, and Hannah Yates, ...	"	XVII.	42
1781. Oct.	12.	Stackhouse, Charles, and Hannah Crowyer, .	"	XXXIII.	97
1775. July	15.	Stackhouse, Stacy, and Catharine Callow, ..	"	XXIII.	84
1780. Dec.	18.	Stacy, Mathew, and Jane Thomson, ...	"	XXX.	158
1757. May	4.	Stafford, Mary, and Jeremiah Field, ...	"	I.	523
1765. June	3.	Stag, Jemima, and Johannes Symonson, ...	"	IX.	152
1781. Dec.	6.	Stager, Sarah, and Walleng Egbert, ...	"	XXXIV.	75
1760. April	26.	Stagg, Amey, and Joseph Powell, ...	"	III.	128
1765. April	13.	Stagg, Jane, and Thomas Stagg, ...	"	IX.	95
1769. May	13.	Stagg, John, and Annaka Stoutenburgh, ...	"	XIV.	100
1761. Oct.	1.	Stagg, John, and Catharine Van Duzer, ...	"	V.	113
1764. Nov.	12.	Stagg, Margaret, and Aron Banker, ...	"	VIII.	401
1763. June	27.	Stagg, Mary, and John Brown, ...	"	VII.	244
1761. Aug.	15.	Stagg, Nieltje, and Peter Ennis, ...	"	V.	44
1765. April	13.	Stagg, Thomas, and Jane Stagg, ...	"	IX.	95
1783. June	20.	Stagg, Thomas, and Letecise Polhemus, ...	"	XXXIX.	64
1780. Nov.	2.	Stagg, Thomas, and Mary Roosevelt, ...	"	XXX.	88
1756. July	7.	Staklen, John, and Annatje Rhypell, ...	"	I.	247
1781. Dec.	1.	Stallinwarf, Jacob, and Gearthry Suydam, ..	"	XXXIV.	65
1772. Sept.	3.	Stammerson, Jemima, and Annanias Brush,	"	XIX.	40
1783. Nov.	7.	Stanbury, Daniel, and Elizabeth Snell, ...	"	XI.	108
1780. Nov.	3.	Stanbury, Isaac, and Sarah Mann, ...	"	XXX.	89
1782. May	2.	Standish, Erris, and Thomas Clapp, ...	"	XXXV.	148
1758. Jan.	12.	Stanger, John, and Sarah Sickels, ...	"	I.	782
1779. Nov.	17.	Stanger, Sarah, and William Johnson, ...	"	XXVIII.	142
1772. April	9.	Stanley, David, and Catherine McKell, ...	"	XVIII.	71
1779. Aug.	30.	Stanton, Abigail, and John Stanton, ...	"	XXVIII.	62
1762. Feb.	22.	Stanton, Elizabeth, and Johan Chorbacher, .	"	VI.	56
1763. July	23.	Stanton, Elizabeth, and Thomas Ash, ...	"	VII.	281
1766. Aug.	9.	Stanton, Elizabeth, and Thomas Grenell, ...	"	X.	72
1757. April	23.	Stanton, George, and Agnes Blanck, ...	"	I.	513
1782. May	15.	Stanton, Henry, and Patience Leverich, ...	"	XXXVI.	3
1757. Dec.	10.	Stanton, Henry, and Rebeccah Van Blaercum,	"	I.	733
1782. Sept.	27.	Stanton, Jasper, and Mary Oliver, ...	"	XXXVII.	17
1779. Aug.	30.	Stanton, John, and Abigail Stanton, ...	"	XXVIII.	62
1772. Sept.	23.	Stanton, Louisa, and Daniel Duc, ...	"	XIX.	55
1782. Mar.	30.	Stanton, Mary, and Jacob Resler, Jr., ...	"	XXXV.	101

47

Date.		Names.	Record.	Vol. Page.
1772. Oct.	17.	Stanton, Mary, and John Minshall, ...	M. B.,	xix. 76
1773. Aug.	7.	Stanton, Mary, and John Sherwood, ...	"	xxi. 60
1763. Jan.	22.	Staple, Francis, and Mary Vannaple, ...	"	vii. 30
1765. Oct.	31.	Staple, John, and Dorothy Constable, ...	"	ix. 344
1768. May	7.	Staples, Elizabeth, and John Blacklock, ...	"	xiii. 96
1759. Jan.	6.	Starkes, Ann, and Nicholas White, ...	"	ii. 146
1765. April	29.	Starkes, Rachel, and Archibald McNeil, ...	"	ix. 115
1768. Jan.	9.	Starnbargh, Christina, and Archibald Camp-bell, ...	"	xiii. 3
1666. Mar.	6.	Starre, Elizabeth, and John Treadwell, ...	O. W. L.,	ii. 134
1760. April	22.	States, Elizabeth, and Isaac Somendyck, ...	M. B.,	iii. 119
1782. June	19.	Statts, Henry, and Anne Lott, ...	"	xxxvi. 56
1764. June	2.	Stead, William, and Hannah Utten, ...	"	viii. 205
1781. April	11.	Stearns, Benjamin, and Bathia Purdy, ...	"	xxxi. 103
1759. Aug.	21.	Steddiford, Mary, and Jeffery Leonard, ...	"	ii. 386
1738. Nov.	16.	Steddiford, William, and Hannah Van Golder,	"	i. 11
1780. Mar.	6.	Stedford, Catharine, and Jenkin McOnulty,.	"	xxviii. 217
1762. June	30.	Stedwell, John, and Esther Bailey, ...	"	vi. 217
1768. Dec.	3.	Steed, Elizabeth, and Peter Vandewater,...	"	xiii. 253
1761. July	8.	Steed, Rohamay, and Benjamin Haviland,..	"	iv. 289
1759. Dec.	22.	Steel, Ann, and Samuel Benson, ...	"	ii. 554
1770. Jan.	4.	Steel, Barbarie, and George Corselus, ...	"	xvi. 2
1773. Nov.	10.	Steel, Hester, and Robert Gillees, ...	"	xxii. 19
1764. April	7.	Steel, James, and Ann South, ...	"	viii. 142
1759. Dec.	6.	Steel, John, and Mary Boyles, ...	"	ii. 532
1782. June	10.	Steel, Margaret, and William Rutan, ...	"	xxxvi. 46
1779. Oct.	6.	Steel, Mary, and Michel Smith, ...	"	xxviii. 104
1756. Aug.	21.	Steel, Pheba, and Nathaniel Harris, ...	"	i. 276
1759. April	12.	Steel, Stephen, and Catharine Schureman,..	"	ii. 239
1759. June	20.	Steel, Thomas, and Sarah Lightfoot, ...	"	ii. 332
1765. Jan.	16.	Steel, William Snow, and Elizabeth Long,..	"	ix. 17
1780. Oct.	23.	Steele, Ann, and Andrew Mitchell, ...	"	xxx. 77
1764. Feb.	22.	Steele, Jane, and John McFarlane, ...	"	viii. 73
1764. July	21.	Steele, Thomas, and Frances Purcutt, ...	"	viii. 265
1779. Oct.	15.	Steell, Thomas, and Sarah Cowderey, ...	"	xxviii. 113
1770. Nov.	30.	Steellinwarf, Phebe, and Arent Van Pelt, ..	"	xvi. 278
1757. Jan.	5.	Steen, Frederick, and Mary Drake, ...	"	i. 406
1770. Oct.	27.	Steenbergen, Cornelius, and Mary Bell, ...	"	xvi. 230
1763. Sept.	2.	Steenbergh, John, and Sarah De Graeff, ...	"	vii. 323
1763. Oct.	20.	Steenbergh, John, and Sarah Le Cont, ...	"	vii. 396
1773. Nov.	23.	Steenbergh, Mary, and Simon Cool, ...	"	xxii. 40
1756. Dec.	28.	Steenbergh, Rachel, and William Wood, ...	"	i. 400
1763. Aug.	26.	Steenbreaker, Ann, and John Henry Binckes,	"	vii. 315
1764. Oct.	10.	Steers, Peter, and Geetje Vrooman, ...	"	viii. 348
1771. Oct.	10.	Steets, Elizabeth, and Coenraed Sharp, ...	"	xvii. 202

DATE.	NAMES.	RECORD.	VOL. PAGE.
1763. Dec. 5.	Steggens, Mary Ann, and John Thomas,....	M. B.,	VII. 491
1774. Feb. 5.	Stein, Robert, and Letitia Elliot,..........	"	XXII. 123
1772. Sept. 4.	Steiver, Hendrick D., and Catherina Bone-ste'e, ...	"	XIX. 42
1764. Oct. 10.	Stellenwerf, Jacob, and Magdalen Van Nyss,	"	VIII. 346
1753. May 22.	Stephany, John Sebastian, and Jannitie De Peyster,............	"	I. 37
1783. April 21.	Stephens, Alexander, and Affey Devore, ...	"	XXXVIII. 104
1776. Dec. 18.	Stephens, Anna, and Richard O'Farrell,....	"	XXIV. 199
1755. Oct. 30.	Stephens, Catharine, and Thomas Grant, ...	"	I. 201
1736. April 26.	Stephens, John, and Mary Harding,.......	"	I. 1
1763. Dec. 7.	Stephens, John, Jr., and Elizabeth Debow,..	"	VII. 495
1771. April 11.	Stephens, John, and Mary Resslur,.........	"	XVII. 54
1772. Mar. 27.	Stephens, Richard Nassau, and Mary Lister,	"	XVIII. 62
1770. April 26.	Stephens, William, and Margaret Gilchrist,.	"	XVI. 70
1734. Feb. 17.	Stephenson, Abigail, and Thomas Willett, ..	"	I. 5
1778. Mar. 17.	Stephensòn, Ann, and James Reid,........	"	XXV. 45
1737. Nov. 1.	Stephenson, Ede, and John Cox,..........	"	I. 7
1770. June 16.	Stephenson, Mary, and Abraham Storm,...	"	XVI. 112
1760. Mar. 17.	Steuart, John, and Elizabeth Hunt, ...	"	III. 81
1783. July 1.	Steuart, John, and Unice Briggs,..........	"	XXXIX. 76
1782. April 3.	Stevans, Phenas, and Mary Woodward,....	"	XXXV. 112
1771. Mar. 30.	Stevens, Abigail, and Arondt Van Hook, ..	"	XVII. 44
1782. June 5.	Stevens, Abigail, and John Roberts,..	"	XXXVII. 37
1781. July 26.	Stevens, Ann, and Ralph Monkhouse,......	"	XXXIII. 15
1763. Oct. 14.	Stevens, Benjamin, and Mary Treddell, ...	"	VII. 380
1761. April 17.	Stevens, Catherine, and Thomas Embree, ..	"	IV. 152
1761. Mar. 8.	Stevens, Dinah, and John Brown,....	"	IV. 185
1759. Aug. 30.	Stevens, Elizabeth, and Thomas Nagle, ...	"	III. 404
1773. June 15.	Stevens, George, and Hannah Waldron,....	"	XXI. 7
1676. Jan. 4.	Stevens, Gozen, and Annetye Jans Loursens,	W. O. P.,	III. 231
1671. June 3.	Stevens, Jannekey, and William Earwin,...	C. A.,	III. 709
1778. May 9.	Stevens, John, and Agnes Guyion,........	M. B.,	XXV. 74
1772. Jan. 24.	Stevens, John, and Cathalyna Van Schayck,	"	XVIII. 17
1756. Sept. 16.	Stevens, John, and Catharine Gleson,......	"	I. 178
1781. Mar. 22.	Stevens, John, and Lavinia Boulia,........	"	XXXI. 81
1762. Oct. 25.	Stevens, Joseph, and Rachel Recoy,.......	"	VI. 384
1780. Nov. 22.	Stevens, Martha, and George Crosby, ...	"	XXX. 120
1769. Sept. 28.	Stevens, Mary, and Edward Townsend,....	"	XV. 47
1772. Jan. 8.	Stevens, Mary, and John Stewart, ...	"	XVIII. 7
1770. Sept. 7.	Stevens, Mary, and Robert R. Livingston, Jr.,	"	XVI. 183
1768. Dec. 10.	Stevens, Mary, and William Eddey,.......	"	XIII. 260
1761. Mar. 30.	Stevens, Nicholas, and Margaret Maybe,...	"	IV. 122
1778. April 4.	Stevens, Richard, and Eliza Hallet,.........	"	XXV. 60
1780. Nov. 17.	Stevens, Robert, and Nelly Taylor,.	"	XXX. 113

Date.		Names.	Record.	Vol.	Page.
1778. Feb.	14.	Stevens, Rosana, and Robert Chapman,....	M. B.,	xxv.	22
1672. Feb.	1.	Stevens, Thomas, and Elizabeth Laurence,..	G. E.,	iv.	251
1770. Sept.	30.	Stevens, William, and Geertruy Van Eps,..	M. B.,	xvi.	186
1760. Mar.	8.	Stevens, William, and Jemima Bond,... ..	"	iii.	69
1768. Nov.	29.	Stevenson, Abigail, and Alexander Watson,	"	xiii.	248
1675. July	16.	Stevenson, Christian, and Robert Darkins,..	W. O. P.,	iii.	124
1760. Feb.	23.	Stevenson, Ffloyd, and Arrabella Hedden,..	M. B.,	iii.	46
1780. Aug.	10.	Stevenson, Francis, and Nelly Townsend,..	"	xxix.	138
1682. May	12.	Stevenson, Issack, and Margaret Vanderveen,	O. W.,	xxxii½.	119
1770. Aug.	18.	Stevenson, John, and Magdalen Dow, ...	M. B.,	xvi.	162
1767. Sept.	17.	Stevenson, Martha, and Robert Woffendale,	"	xii.	37
1768. June	27.	Stevenson, Pheby, and Israel Honywell,....	"	xiii.	141
1762. Nov.	3.	Stevenson, Thomas, and Euphemia Alsop,..	"	vi.	407
1760. May	15.	Steves, Richard, and Mary Johnson,.......	"	iii.	153
1758. Oct.	4.	Steves, William, and Amey Garison, ...	"	ii.	38
1781. Oct.	26.	Steward, Charles, and Catharine Bagley,...	"	xxxiv.	7
1758. Nov.	9.	Steward, Jane, and William Vesey, .'.....	"	ii.	87
1760. Jan.	11.	Steward, Margaret, and James Hounam, ...	"	ii.	577
1763. Dec.	19.	Stewart, Alexander, and Mary Thompson,..	"	vii.	511
1781. Feb.	28.	Stewart, Charles, and Jannet Thorn,.......	"	xxxi.	61
1763. May	25.	Stewart, Charles, and Mary Blaine,........	"	vii.	200
1782. May	25.	Stewart, Elinor, and James Lewis,........	"	xxxvi.	23
1759. Oct.	16.	Stewart, George, and Sarah Vankleek,.....	"	ii.	461
1780. July	28.	Stewart, James, and Ann Guzlin, ...	"	xxix.	124
1766. Oct.	1.	Stewart, James, and Elizabeth Shuckburgh,	"	x.	117
1759. May	31.	Stewart, James, and Jannetje Burger, ...	"	ii.	295
1771. May	6.	Stewart, James A., and Sarah Schermerhorn,	"	xvii.	76
1777. Nov.	26.	Stewart, John, and Catharine McCachan, ..	"	xxvi.	101
1772. Jan.	8.	Stewart, John, and Mary Stevens, ...	"	xviii.	7
1766. Nov.	5.	Stewart, Mary, and William Benson, ...	"	x.	155
1769. Nov.	14.	Stewart, Peter, and Ann Cook,...........	"	xv.	93
1764. Jan.	25.	Stewart, Peter, and Mary Stuart, ...	"	viii.	37
1781. Oct.	26.	Stewart, Robert, and Elizabeth Seaman,....	"	xxxiv.	6
1761. May	29.	Stewart, William, and Ann Houston,......	"	iv.	215
1771. Dec.	3.	Stewart, William, and Catherine Row,.....	"	xvii.	279
1761. April	4.	Stewart, William, and Elizabeth Annely,...	"	iv.	132
1758. Jan.	23.	Steymets, Catherine, and Andrew Hopper,..	"	i.	799
1780. Feb.	22.	Steymets, Catharine, and Robert Maer,....	"	xxviii.	212
1768. Mar.	24.	Steymets, Jasper, and Rachel Bancker, ...	"	xiii.	56
1768. Mar.	31.	Steymets, Mary, and Philip Thompson,....	"	xiii.	58
1764. Feb.	25.	Sthol, Sophia, and Derby Doyle,..........	"	viii.	79
1758. Sept.	12.	Stibbins, Phebe, and John Chamberlain,....	"	ii.	19
1757. June	28.	Stiene, Maria, and Johan Philip Fines,.....	"	i.	575
1753. Aug.	14.	Stienhouse, Margaret, and Daniel McKinney,	"	i.	91
1768. Dec.	22.	Stiles, Deborah, and William Brownejohn, Jr.,	"	xiii.	273

DATE.	NAMES.	RECORD.	VOL.	PAGE.
1764. Jan. 16.	Stiles, John, and Susannah Brasier, ...	M. B.,	VIII.	19
1668. May 14.	Stiles, Richard, and Mary Naylor,.........	O. W. L.,	II.	223
1761. Oct. 17.	Still, Abigail, and William Hulet,.........	M. B.,	V.	229
1759. Mar. 31.	Still, Effie, and William Williams,.........	"	II.	144
1778. May 28.	Still, Elen, and Andrew Broadford,........	"	XXV.	94
1759. April 28.	Still, Johonn Albertus, and Jane Wood,....	"	II.	261
1761. July 16.	Still, Margaret, and Andrew Hamersley, ...	"	IV.	300
1753. May 18.	Still, Margaret, and John Wilt,...........	"	I.	34
1761. Mar. 24.	Stiller, Jane, and Dennis Sulevan,.........	"	IV.	115
1762. Jan. 8.	Stillwell, Ann, and Hendrick Van Wagenen,	"	VI.	4
1756. Nov. 13.	Stillwell, Ann, and Peter Hendrickson, ...	"	I.	353
1763. Feb. 17.	Stillwell, Catharine, and Cornelius Palding,.	"	VII.	66
1782. Sept. 24.	Stillwell, Elizabeth, and Abel Carpenter,...	"	XXXVII.	12
1764. Mar. 28.	Stillwell, Francis, and Albert Rykeman, ...	"	VIII.	121
1763. Oct. 31.	Stillwell, Jeremiah, and Hellitje Poillon,....	"	VII.	417
1765. Sept. 18.	Stillwell, Joseph, and Ann Williamson, ...	"	IX.	265
1768. May 11.	Stillwell, Mary, and Abraham Prall,.......	"	XIII.	98
1761. July 22.	Stillwell, Nicholas, and Apphia Ellis, ...	"	V.	2
1671. Aug. 29.	Stillwell, Nicholas, and Katherine Morgan,..	G. E.,	IV.	22
1781. Dec. 9.	Stillwell, Rebecca, and Jonathan Jones, ...	M. B.,	XXXVII.	112
1760. June 9.	Stillwell, Richard, and Ann Cartilo, ...	"	III.	181
1768. June 10.	Stillwell, Richard, and Mary Johnson, ...	"	XIII.	123
1783. May 19.	Stillwell, Richard, and Mary Lake, ...	"	XXXIX.	16
1777. Oct. 11.	Stillwell, Samuel, and Lenah Garrison, ...	"	XXIV.	161
1768. Nov. 12.	Stillwell, Thomas, and Mary Debevois,.....	"	XIII.	234
1764. Dec. 24.	Stilwell, Ann, and David Burger, ...	"	VIII.	400
1762. Aug. 19.	Stilwell, Catharine, and Benjamin Coates, ..	"	VI.	281
1783. Feb. 21.	Stilwell, Catharine, and Jesse Morgan,.....	"	XXXVIII.	47
1767. Nov. 16.	Stilwell, Catherine, and Thomas Hadden, .	"	XII.	85
1736. Oct. 11.	Stilwell, Daniel, and Catherine Johnson, ...	"	I.	2
1782. Sept. 18.	Stilwell, Daniel, and Mary Patterson,......	"	XXXVII.	6
1772. July 29.	Stilwell, Elizabeth, and Richard Minifie,....	"	XIX.	6
1773. Sept. 28.	Stilwell, Hannah, and John Culver, ...	"	XXI.	124
1768. Sept. 26.	Stilwell, Jane, and Barant Johnson, ...	"	XIII.	196
1738. Aug. 25.	Stilwell, Martha, and George Waker,......	"	I.	10
1737. Aug. 20.	Stilwell, Mary, and Captain Overhall,......	"	I.	7
1778. May 13.	Stilwell, Mary, and John Ferrers,..........	"	XXV.	82
1778. Dec. 14.	Stilwell, Nathan, and Esther Flandereau,...	"	XXVI.	119
1783. Aug. 19.	Stilwell, Sarah, and Joseph Ryder,........	"	XL.	2
1783. Aug. 2.	Stilwell, Susannah, and John Pain,........	"	XXXIX.	110
1781. Aug. 25.	Stillwill, Obadiah, and Ann Cox,..........	"	XXXIII.	47
1781. Dec. 22.	Stilwill, Anna, and John Morrall, ...	"	XXXIV.	99
1777. Oct. 15.	Stilwill, Abraham, and Susanah Van Pelt,.	"	XXIV.	163
1766. Nov. 17.	Stilwill, Catherine, and Robert Davis, ...	"	X.	168
1778. Nov. 26.	Stilwill, Elias, and Elizabeth Butler, ...	"	XXVI.	100

DATE.	NAMES.	RECORD.	VOL.	PAGE.
1761. Oct. 15.	Stilwill, Joachim, and Charity Burbanck,...	M. B.,	v.	141
1762. May 10.	Stilwill, Sarah, and Richard Courtney,.....	"	vi.	150
1764. April 27.	Stimes, Jasper, and Elenor Brown,........	"	viii.	173
1768. May 19.	Stimets, Hannah, and Cornelius Spier, ...	"	xiii.	107
1771. Oct. 16.	Stimusson, Margaret, and Francis Cunning-ham, ...	"	xvii.	212
1767. May 23.	Stine, Augustus, and Elizabeth Finn, ...	"	xi.	94
1783. May 27.	Stinet, James, and Abigail Hutchins, ...	"	xxxix.	26
1764. Mar. 3.	Stinmetts, Jane, and Adam De Grushe,....	"	viii.	91
1764. May 11.	Stiren, Mary, and David Gardiner, ...	"	viii.	187
1778. Jan. 14.	Stirling, Bridget, and Stephen Allery,......	"	xxv.	6
1737. Oct. 27.	Stirrup, John, and Sarah Romme,..........	"	i.	7
1781. Mar. 18.	Stites, Margaret, and Andrew Mitchell, ...	"	xxxiii.	9
1762. Dec. 15.	Stivenson, John, and Catharine McCallow, .	"	vi.	480
1773. Jan. 27.	Stivers, Jane, and Jacob Banta,...........	"	xx.	24
1763. Jan. 25.	Stivers, Rebecca, and Luke Cummings, ...	"	vii.	35
1782. May 2.	Stives, Ann, and Peter Vallentine, ...	"	xxxv.	147
1757. Feb. 24.	Stock, James, and Anne Williams, ...	"	i.	449
1778. Feb. 16.	Stocker, Elizabeth, and James Manee,......	"	xxv.	23
1759. Dec. 12.	Stocker, John, and Elizabeth Akely,.......	"	ii.	541
1778. Nov. 7.	Stocker, Mary, and Samuel Bowne, ...	"	xxvi.	84
1768. Nov. 30.	Stocker, Susannah, and Benjamin Woolley,.	"	xiii.	249
1758. May 27.	Stockholm, Anderies, Jr., and Hannah Hen-drickson, ...	"	i.	911
1757. Mar. 10.	Stockholm, Catharina, and Teunis Rapelje,..	"	i.	462
1761. May 30.	Stockholm, John, and Gherje Covenhoven,.	"	iv.	220
1765. Mar. 16.	Stockholm, Lena, and John Miller,........	"	ix.	68
1779. Mar. 16.	Stoddard, Robert, and Sarah Coles,........	"	xxvii.	67
1781. Feb. 28.	Stoddart, John, and Mary Thomson,.......	"	xxxi.	60
1759. Nov. 19.	Stoffs, Alexander, and Mary Wilson, ...	"	ii.	506
1778. July 11.	Stogdell, Mary, and John Hutchins, ...	"	xxv.	128
1762. Jan. 19.	Stoker, Hannah, and George Lawn, ...	"	vi.	17
1773. June 29.	Stoker, James, and Elizabeth North, ...	"	xxi.	26
1763. Nov. 26.	Stonbacke, Anthony, and Frances Hogelandt,	"	vii.	471
1780. Mar. 22.	Stone, Joel, and Leah Moore, ...	"	xxix.	5
1758. Oct. 10.	Stone, Sarah, and John Grace,............	"	ii.	46
1773. July 19.	Stone, William, and Mary Douglass,.......	"	xxi.	47
1767. July 6.	Stonehouse, Isaac, and Catherine Moore,...	"	xi.	125
1760. April 24.	Stoodly, Thomas, and Catharine Child,.....	"	iii.	121
1773. Nov. 15.	Stoothof, Peter, and Laco Vanderbilt,......	"	xxii.	29
1783. Oct. 8.	Stoothoff, Abraham, and Elizabeth Bogart, .	"	xl.	70
1779. Nov. 13.	Stoothoff, Ann, and John Remsen,........	"	xxviii.	139
1762. May 13.	Stoothoff, Gerret, and Mary Voorhees,.....	"	vi.	158
1779. Oct. 30.	Stoothoff, Wilhelmus, and Letty Ryder,....	"	xxviii.	124
1762. Nov. 24.	Stoothoff, William, and Hellitje Voorhies,..	"	vi.	451

DATE.	NAMES.	RECORD.	VOL. PAGE.
1779. April 27.	Storey, James, and Rachel Robinson,......	M B.,	XXVII. 122
1759. Sept. 21.	Storm, Abraham, and Catharine Bussing,...	"	II. 428
1770. June 16.	Storm, Abraham, and Mary Stephenson, ...	"	XVI. 112
1772. Nov. 24.	Storm, Aneltie, and John Adriance, ...	"	XIX. 127
1759. May 8.	Storm, Catharine, and William Barnes......	"	II. 270
1756. Sept. 14.	Storm, Hanah, and David Conkline,.......	"	I. 297
1758. Sept. 21.	Storm, John, and Barbary Day, ...	"	II. 30
1761. April 11.	Storm, John, and Esther Van Anden,......	"	IV. 147
1764. Jan. 27.	Storm, John, and Patience Gibbs,.........	"	VIII. 39
1771. May 18.	Storm, Maria, and John Benneway, ...	"	XVII. 85
1765. Oct. 31.	Storm, Mary, and William Hunt,..........	"	IX. 348
1781. Jan. 30.	Storm, Peter, and Catharine Vandervoort,..	"	XXXI. 33
1769. Sept. 5.	Storm, Thomas, and Catherine Hoogeboom,	"	XV. 36
1771. Mar. 23.	Storm, Thomas, and Elizabeth Graham,....	"	XVII. 39
1764. Mar. 13.	Storme, Altie, and Caleb Archer, ...	"	VIII. 124
1772. April 21.	Storn, Ann, and Elbert Brinkerhoff, ...	"	XVIII. 87
1775. July 5.	Stotenburgh, Mary, and Elias Brevoort,....	"	XXIII. 86
1700. April 14.	Stothoff, Anatje, and Tunis Bergen,........	"	III. 105
1770. Feb. 15.	Stout, Abigail, and Jonathan Tremian, ...	"	XVI. 17
1780. Sept. 14.	Stout, Abraham, and Sarah Terrat,........	"	XXX. 28
1782. Aug. 5.	Stout, Anne, and Jacob Busleree,.........	"	XXXVI. 101
1738. April 29.	Stout, Benjamin, and Ffamitie De Froseest,.	"	I. 9
1766. Aug. 22.	Stout, Benjamin, Jr., and Jemima Brevoort,..................................	"	X. 82
1760. April 23.	Stout, Catharine, and John Shaghnussy, ...	"	III. 120
1768. Nov. 18.	Stout, Elizabeth, and Richard Somarindike,.	"	XIII. 288
1764. May 26.	Stout, Hannah, and Henry Wells,.........	"	VIII. 199
1766. Sept. 29.	Stout, Helena, and William Grigg, ...	"	X. 115
1772. Jan. 23.	Stout, John, and Effee Van Varck,........	"	XVIII. 16
1764. July 28.	Stout, John, and Susannah Lewis,.........	"	VIII. 271
1772. Sept. 21.	Stout, John, Jr., and Margaret Hunt, ...	"	XIX. 53
1783. April 12.	Stout, Joseph, and Jane Smith,...........	"	XXXVIII. 94
1783. Feb. 21.	Stout, Leah, and Samuel Pierce, ...	"	XXXVIII. 48
1783. July 29.	Stout, Margaret, and William Rigby, ...	"	XXXIX. 104
1778. Nov. 16.	Stout, Phebe, and James Conn,.....	"	XXVI. 88
1779. Sept. 29.	Stout, Sarah, and Aris Ryersz, ...	"	XXVIII. 88
1756. Nov. 1.	Stout, Sarah, and James Taggart, ...	"	I. 341
1761. May 26.	Stoutenbergh, Ann, and Henry Hermans,..	"	IV. 207
1758. Jan. 11.	Stoutenbergh, Ann, and Joseph Bloodgood,.	"	I. 780
1764. Oct. 8.	Stoutenbergh, Margaret, and John Teller, ..	"	VIII. 338
1780. Sept. 15.	Stoutenbourgh, Mary, and James La Tourrette, ...	"	XXX. 30
1769. May 13.	Stoutenburgh, Annaka, and John Stagg, ...	"	XIV. 100
1776. Mar. 9.	Stoutenburgh, Catherine, and Isaac Vannass,......	"	XXIII. 282

DATE.		NAMES.	RECORD.	VOL.	PAGE.
1779. Sept.	29.	Stoutenburgh, Hannah,and Nicholas Browne,	M. B.,	XXVIII.	89
1756. Oct.	5.	Stoutenburgh, Hendrika, and William Elsworth, Jr.,	"	I.	318
1761. Jan.	27.	Stoutenburgh, Isaac, and Elizabeth Wall,...	"	IV.	32
1766. July	29.	Stoutenburgh, Isaac, and Hannah Brewerton,	"	X.	66
1764. June	23.	Stoutenburgh, Jacobus, and Jesyntje Teller,	"	VIII.	235
1773. Nov.	25.	Stoutenburgh, John, and Catharine Taller,..	"	XXII.	46
1762. Aug.	2.	Stoutenburgh, Luke, and Rachel Teller,....	"	VI.	264
1770. Nov.	12.	Stoutenburgh, Mary, and Richard Cantelun,	"	XVI.	247
1767. July	27.	Stoutenburgh, Peter, and Johannah Treadwell,	"	XII.	2
1753. July	11.	Stoutenburgh, William, and Mary Van Vleck,	"	I.	71
1781. Aug.	29.	Stover, Daniel, and Catharine Androvett,...	"	XXXIII.	52
1780. Nov.	30.	Stover, Sophia, and Richard Patmer,	" .	XXX.	128
1782. April	15.	Stovey, Thomas, and Janett, Lawson,	"	XXXV.	122
1769. Aug.	7.	Strachan, Catherine, and James Barrow,...	"	XV.	20
1763. May	11.	Strang, Joseph, and Anne Haight,	"	VII.	180
1761. Mar.	17.	Strang, Levinah, and John Woods,	"	IV.	104
1781. Jan.	29.	Strang, Sarah; and Selah Havens,	"	XXXI.	31
1758. Sept.	20.	Strange, Henry, and Hanah Susberry,	"	II.	26
1760. Feb.	9.	Strange, John, and Mary Robins,	"	III.	28
1781. Jan.	4.	Strange, Lot, and Lucy Clarke,	"	XXXI.	12
1763. Aug.	30.	Stratford, Rachel, and John De Noyelles,...	"	VII.	317
1779. Sept.	6.	Stratford, Thomas, and Mary Bodkin,	"	XXVIII.	69
1782. Dec.	3.	Straton, Elizabeth, and James Deas,	"	XXXVII.	105
1780. July	31.	Straton, Mary, and Robert Seaman,	"	XXIX.	129
1761. Sept.	10.	Stratton, Cornelius, and Mary Weeks,	"	V.	78
1767. Sept.	15.	Stratton, Eliphilet, and Mary Valentine, ...	"	XII.	33c
1765. June	11.	Stratton, Elizabeth, and Samuel Cook Sullivan,	"	IX.	164
1753. June	9.	Stratton, Martha, and John McGear,	"	I.	55
1783. Oct.	4.	Street, Samuel, and Elizabeth Lamont,	"	XL.	62
1779. Aug.	25.	Stretch, Samuel, and Elizabeth Berry,	"	XXVIII.	59
1759. Aug.	25.	Streyd, Godfrey, and Elizabeth Robinson,..	"	II.	400
1738. June	5.	Stricker, Jane, and Patrick Scandling,	"	I.	9
1779. July	30.	Strickland, Jonathan, and Mary Hallibert,..	"	XXVIII.	36
1782. April	3.	Striker, Charity, and Barnett Bennet,	"	XXXV.	110
1771. Dec.	13.	Striker, Elizabeth, and Roelof Lott,	"	XVII.	293
1780. Sept.	23.	Striker, James, and Mary Hopper,	"	XXX.	40
1772. Oct.	9.	Striker, Jane, and Francis Couenhoven,....	"	XIX.	69
1778. May	5.	Striker, Sarah, and Peter Neefus,	"	XXV.	72

DATE.		NAMES.	RECORD.	VOL.	PAGE.
1758. Nov.	8.	Stringer, Samuel, and Rachel Vander Heyden, ...	M. B.,	II.	86
1762. Aug.	9.	Stringham, Frances, and Jacob Bunce, ...	"	VI.	271
1752. Nov.	28.	Stringham, Hannah, and Gilbert Clement, ..	"	I.	16
1767. Jan.	22.	Stringham, Hannah, and Samuel Smith, Jr.,	"	XI.	11
1761. Dec.	9.	Stringham, Jacob, and Elizabeth Oakley, ...	"	V.	270
1737. Oct.	28.	Stringham, James, and Deborah Sacket, ...	"	I.	7
1782. Jan.	5.	Stringham, James, and Mary Van Horne, ..	"	XXXV.	10
1780. June	24.	Stringham, Mary, and John Cooper, ...	"	XXIX.	95
1761. Jan.	29.	Strong, Anne, and Daniel Ferguson, ...	"	IV.	40
1763. Sept.	15.	Strong, Benjamin, and Margaret Smith, ...	"	VII.	338
1762. Feb.	18.	Strong, Hannah, and James Mathews, ...	"	VI.	53
1736. Aug.	25.	Strong, Hannah, and Richard Willets, ...	"	I.	2
1782. Aug.	23.	Strong, Keturah, and James Woodhull, ...	"	XXXVI.	119
1763. Aug.	16.	Strong, Margaret, and Hugh Connor, ...	"	VII.	302
1762. April	21.	Strong, Rachel, and Birdseye Young, ...	"	VI.	119
1764. Sept.	10.	Strong, Susannah, and William Shelton, ...	"	VIII.	303
1760. July	18.	Strope, Elizabeth, and Derrick Van Dyck, ..	"	III.	217
1767. April	18.	Strubble, Catherine, and Christian Boots, ...	"	XI.	64
1770. Aug.	23.	Struthens, Robert, and Elizabeth Ackley, ...	"	XVI.	169
1783. April	22.	Struve, John Charles, and Mary McDougal, .	"	XXXVIII.	107
1764. Nov.	8.	Strycker, John, and Catherine Vander Veer,	"	VIII.	396
1760. Aug.	5.	Stryker, Elizabeth, and Archibald Thompson, ...	"	III.	233
1756. June	15.	Stryker, Garrit, and Ida Vanderventer, ...	"	I.	241
1761. Dec.	12.	Stryker, Henry, and Mary Fleetwood, ...	"	V.	277
1777. July	4.	Stryker, John, and Jane Lot, ...	"	XXIV.	112
1764. June	1.	Stryker, Peter, Jr., and Phebe Schenck, ...	"	VIII.	202
1768. Nov.	23.	Stryker, Samuel, and Maritje Schenck, ...	"	XIII.	242
1755. Sept.	8.	Stuard, John, and Magdalen Bussy, ...	"	I.	170
1781. Feb.	24.	Stuart, Ann, and Jacob Foster, ...	"	XXXI.	56
1762. Jan.	2.	Stuart, Eleanor, and Nathaniel Hughes, ...	"	VI.	1
1779. Jan.	7.	Stuart, James, and Mary Hampton, ...	"	XXVII.	7
1760. Dec.	2.	Stuart, Jane, and James Bruce, ...	"	III.	451
1781. Feb.	19.	Stuart, John, and Sarah Munro, ...	"	XXXI.	49
1764. Jan.	25.	Stuart, Mary, and Peter Stewart, ········	"	VIII.	37
1760. Sept.	18.	Studdeford, Ann, and David Canning, ...	"	III.	319
1761. Mar.	11.	Studdeford, John, and Allida Burger, ...	"	IV.	94
1761. May	11.	Studdeford, Mary, and John Curtis, ...	"	IV.	194
1763. June	20.	Stump, Catharine, and John Randall, ...	"	VII.	234
1774. Dec.	10.	Stunill, Lucy, and John Lownds, ...	"	XXIV.	193
1774. Jan.	11.	Sturgier, Mary, and Philip Pell, ...	"	XXII.	99
1759. Mar.	17.	Stoothof, Johannis, and Trientje Bogart, ...	"	II.	219
1782. June	28.	Stuvenge, Susannah, and Johan Michael Schlaesman, ...	"	XXXVI.	66

48

DATE.	NAMES.	RECORD.	VOL. PAGE.
1759. June 25.	Stuyversant, Casparays, and Sarah Coven-over,	M. B.,	II. 340
1764. Oct. 17.	Stuyvesant, Petrus, and Margaret Livingston,	"	VIII. 359
1783. Nov. 17.	Style, Isaac, and Catharlne Rider,	"	XL. 118
1763. May 7.	Styler, Rosanna, and Malker Leman,	"	VII. 168
1779. Jan. 26.	Stymers, Mary, and Thomas Foster,	"	XXVII. 28
1753. Aug. 13.	Stymes, Christopher, and Mary Elsworth,	"	I. 90
1763. May 13.	Stymest, Christopher, and Altje Remsen,	"	VII. 185
1766. July 23.	Stymest, Garret, and Susannah Baldin,	"	X. 60
1762. June 30.	Stymest, Thomas, and Margaret Williams,	"	VI. 216
1763. July 18.	Stymets, Ariantje, and David Brower,	"	VII. 269
1781. July 14.	Stymets, John, and Elizabeth Taylor,	"	XXXIII. 7
1781. Nov. 2.	Stymets, Mary, and Alexander McDougall,	"	XXXIV. 13
1778. June 23.	Stymets, Mary, and Theophilus Elsworth,	"	XXV. 111
1759. April 27.	Stymets, Peter, and Mary Day,	"	II. 257
1761. April 3.	Stymets, Rachel, and David Ross,	"	IV. 131
1782. Dec. 28.	Styne, Anne, and James Horton,	"	XXXVII. 135
1758. Dec. 28.	Suckfield, Abigail, and William Numan,	"	II. 142
1755. Dec. 10.	Sudred, Rebecah, and John Churchil,	"	I. 231
1761. Mar. 24.	Sulevan, Dennis, and Jane Stiller,	"	IV. 115
1757. Aug. 30.	Sulivan, Hendrick, and Mary Muckelvain,	"	I. 625
1761. Oct. 31.	Sulivan, Mary, and Robert Foott,	"	V. 184
1772. June 28.	Sullivan, Cornelius W., and Ann Vaughan,	"	XVIII. 150
1755. Nov. 28.	Sullivan, Daniel, and Agnes Connolly,	"	I. 222
1783. May 16.	Sullivan, Florence, and Margaret Laffan,	"	XXXIX. 14
1758. Sept. 23.	Sullivan, Jeremiah, and Mary Hancock,	"	II. 34
1758. Sept. 12.	Sullivan, John, and Deborah Hutchins,	"	II. 17
1783. April 5.	Sullivan, John, and Mary Palmer,	"	XXXVIII. 86
1759. Nov. 20.	Sullivan, Owen, and Hannah Orstin,	"	II. 509
1765. June 11.	Sullivan, Samuel Cook, and Elizabeth Stratton,	"	IX. 164
1761. May 15.	Summer, Barbery, and John Wendall,	"	IV. 191
1780. Nov. 16.	Summerdeck, Catharine, and Robert Martin,	"	XXX. 112
1762. April 7.	Summerman, John, and Elizabeth Abraham,	"	VI. 91
1780. Sept. 22.	Summers, William, and Hannah Smyth,	"	XXX. 36
1766. Nov. 4.	Summersbey, Arthur, and Hannah Burt,	"	X. 150
1759. May 16.	Summons, Margaret, and Justus Plum,	"	II. 287
1769. April 7.	Surget, Peter, and Catherine Hubbard,	"	XIV. 66
1760. Nov. 3.	Surman, John, and Eleanor Dawson,	"	III. 393
1769. April 10.	Surmon, Elizabeth, and Thomas Yarrow,	"	XIV. 69
1761. Feb. 19.	Surnavey, James, and Hannah Connally,	"	IV. 72
1672. Feb. 7.	Susanna, ———, and Thomas Moore,	G. E.,	IV. 257
1758. Sept. 20.	Susberry, Hanah, and Henry Strange,	M. B.,	II. 26

DATE.	NAMES.	RECORD.	VOL.	PAGE.
1736. Nov. 29.	Sute, Benjamin, and Elizabeth Bogart,.....	M. B.,	I.	3
1777. April 24.	Suthard, Rachel, and Richard Jackson,.....	"	XXIV.	72
1762. Sept. 25.	Sutherland, William, and Catharine Lawrence, ...	"	VI.	333
1763. Nov. 9.	Sutherenland, George, and Sarah Mason,...	"	VII.	438
1780. Jan. 10.	Sutphen, John, and Mary Sharpe,....	"	XXVIII.	188
1768. April 23.	Sutton, Abigail, and William Harrison, ...	"	XIII.	84
1767. July 30.	Sutton, Ann, and Nathaniel Powel, ...	"	XII.	3a
1775. Oct. 2.	Sutton, Charles, and Sarah Bond, ...	"	XXIII.	169
1671. Sept. 13.	Sutton, Daniel, and Agnes Hutchinson,....	G. E.,	IV.	31
1761. May 22.	Sutton, Deborah, and James Byrd,........	M. B.,	IV.	176
1763. Sept. 9.	Sutton, Elizabeth, and Gregg Higginbotham,....	"	VII.	332
1769. April 25.	Sutton, James, and Sarah Smith,..........	"	XIV.	84
1780. June 2.	Sutton, Jane, and Alexander Crawford,....	"	XXIX.	79
1766. June 27.	Sutton, Jane, and William McKeavy,......	"	X.	36
1775. April 6.	Sutton, John Pell, and Wyntie Montross, ..	"	XXIII.	4
1763. May 25.	Sutton, Joseph, and Martha Young,.......	"	VII.	201
1753. July 27.	Sutton, Martha, and Luke Kiersted, ...	"	I.	79
1780. Oct. 2.	Sutton, Martha, and Richard Mott,........	"	XXX.	53
1757. Sept. 23.	Sutton, Mary, and Samuel Fayerweather,..	"	I.	642
1766. July 16.	Sutton, Mary, and Solomon Hunt, ...	"	X.	52
1766. Sept. 1.	Sutton, Rachel, and Richard King,........	"	X.	87
1758. Nov. 4.	Sutton, Robert, and Pheby Gidney, ...	"	II.	81
1778. April 30.	Sutton, Robert, and Charity Dodge,.......	"	XXV.	70
1783. Aug. 23.	Sutton, William, and Sarah Degrushe,......	"	XL.	8
1757. April 9.	Sutton, William, and Tamar Gidney, ...	"	I.	495
1768. Nov. 6.	Suydam, Catherine, and John Cornell, ...	"	XIII.	228
1780. Sept. 15.	Suydam, Evert, and Ann Bocrum, ...	"	XXX.	29
1764. June 9.	Suydam, Eyda, and Martin Schenk,.......	"	VIII.	220
1760. Aug. 20.	Suydam, Farnandus, and Ida De Bevois,...	"	III.	261
1781. Dec. 1.	Suydam, Gearthry, and Jacob Stallinwarf,..	"	XXXIV.	65
1766. Oct. 15.	Suydam, Henderick, and Harempy Lefferts, ...	"	X.	124
1778. May 11.	Suydam, Hendrick, and Ida Couenhoven,...	"	XXV.	78
1762. Oct. 28.	Suydam, Hendrick, and Lettice Sebring, ...	"	VI.	390
1775. Nov. 1.	Suydam, Hendrick, and Nelly Hageman,...	"	XXIII.	194
1769. Aug. 1.	Suydam, Hendrick, and Phebe Skidmore,..	"	XV.	11
1753. June 1.	Suydam, Hendrick, Jr., and Rebeccah Emmons,.......	"	I.	45
1783. Oct. 14.	Suydam, Henry, and Anna Nostrand,......	"	XL.	78
1770. Nov. 20.	Suydam, Ida, and Jacob Thorne,..........	"	XVI.	264
1764. April 5.	Suydam, Jacob, and Elisabeth Leacraft,....	"	VIII.	134
1781. June 8.	Suydam, Jacob, and Mary Hicks, ...	"	XXXII.	76
1772. Jan. 31.	Suydam, Jacob, and Mary Totton,, ...	"	XVIII.	24

DATE.	NAMES.	RECORD.	VOL.	PAGE.
1769. April 10.	Suydam, Jacobus, and Arreantje Van Sicklen,	M. B.,	XIV.	70
1764. June 19.	Suydam, Jane, and Geliam Cornell,	"	VIII.	229
1770. Jan. 30.	Suydam, Jane, and William Simonson,	"	XVI.	9
1763. Sept. 3.	Suydam, John, and Lena Simonson,	"	VII.	326
1767. Sept. 15.	Suydam, John, and Phebe Sprong,	"	XII.	34
1770. Feb. 12.	Suydam, Mary, and James Freek,	"	XVI.	15
1768. April 11.	Suydam, Oack, and Elizabeth Sleght,	"	XIII.	75
1764. Oct. 10.	Suydam, Reyneer, and Famitje Sebring,	"	VIII.	345
1757. Jan. 12.	Suydam, Rick, and Idea Rapeljea,	"	I.	412
1769. Jan. 7.	Suydam, Sytie, and Garret Martense,	"	XIV.	5
1778. Mar. 19.	Suydam, Teunis, and Ida Voorhees,	"	XXV.	48
1775. Dec. 23.	Suydam, Williampy, and Arres Bogart,	"	XXIII.	236
1761. Oct. 19.	Swaim, Abraham, and Mary Rolph,	"	V.	148
1768. Sept. 26.	Swaim, Mortines, and Helena Simonson,	"	XIII.	195
1764. Oct. 11.	Swaim, Simon, and Hannah Garrison,	"	VIII.	352
1779. April 29.	Swain, Elizabeth, and Charles McClan,	"	XXVII.	124
1782. Sept. 25.	Swame, Catharine, and Joseph Perine,	"	XXXVII.	13
1780. Oct. 2.	Swame, Getty, and John Simonson,	"	XXX.	51
1768. Oct. 7.	Swame, Matthias, and Mary Grandine,	"	XIII.	205
1756. Dec. 18.	Swan, Anthony, and Lette Smith,	"	I.	391
1770. Aug. 13.	Swan, Benjamin, and Mary McLean,	"	XVI.	158
1780. Jan. 5.	Swan, Charles, and Margaret Julang,	"	XXVIII.	186
1778. Nov. 5.	Swan, Elizabeth, and Joseph Parker,	"	XXVI.	82
1759. Dec. 18.	Swan, Hendrickea, and John Cannon,	"	II.	549
1736. July 14.	Swan, Jacob, and Jane Martin,	"	I.	2
1777. Sept. 25.	Swan, John, and Isabella Simpson,	"	XXIV.	150
1761. July 4.	Swan, Lititia, and John Wandel,	"	IV.	275
1780. May 30.	Swan, Thomas, and Jamime Ball,	"	XXIX.	74
1783. April 30.	Swanser, Hester, and Charles Naylor,	"	XXXVIII.	121
1762. July 17.	Swanser, Mary, and John Woodard,	"	VI.	244
1775. May 17.	Swanzer, Sarah, and John Ball,	"	XXIII.	36
1769. April 15.	Swart, Abraham, and Cornelia Waldron,	"	XIV.	74
1773. Oct. 11.	Swart, Ava, and Andries De Groat,	"	XXI.	139
1762. Nov. 19.	Swart, Evert Wynkoop, and Margaret Van Steenbergh,	"	VI.	445
1763. May 13.	Swart, Gertruy, and Albert Vedder,	"	VII.	186
1772. Nov. 20.	Swart, Mary, and Ryer Heermans,	"	XIX.	120
1773. Oct. 11.	Swart, Nicholas, and Angenitie Vedder,	"	XXI.	135
1767. Aug. 21.	Swart, Peter, and Jannetie Persen,	"	XII.	20
1762. Oct. 26.	Swart, Samuel, and Eghje Rose,	"	VI.	386
1764. Oct. 10.	Swart, Sarah, and Arent Maybe,	"	VIII	350
1761. April 3.	Swart, Sartje, and Peter B. Vroman,	"	IV.	129
1763. Oct. 26.	Swart, Teunis, and Sarah Van Vorst,	"	VII.	404
1767. July 30.	Swart, Teunis, Jr., and Margaret Mynderse,	"	XII.	3

DATE.	NAMES.	RECORD.	VOL. PAGE.
1770. Sept. 28.	Swart, Tobias, and Rachel Wydecker, ...	M. B.,	XVI. 199
1775. June 16.	Swartout, Elizabeth, and Patrick Conry, ...	"	XXIII. 65
1760. Feb. 20.	Swartout, Jacobus, and Altie Brincker hoff, ...	"	III. 42
1759. Nov. 3.	Swartout, Rachael, and Abraham Sneden,..	"	II. 488
1773. Oct. 8.	Swartwout, Aaltje, and Cornelius Adriaanse,	"	XXI. 133
1773. Feb. 2.	Swartwout, Annatje, and Samuel Van Steenbergh, ...	"	XX. 35
1738. June 13.	Swartwout, Elizabeth, and Jacobus De Peyster, ...	"	I. 10
1762. April 14.	Swartwout, Rodolves, and Sarah Polhemus, ...	"	VI. 106
1763. Nov. 2.	Sweedland, Christopher, and Elinor Hunter,.	"	VII. 426
1769. Sept. 23.	Sweeney, Oliver, and Elizabeth Mullen,....	"	XV. 42
1767. Mar. 9.	Sweeny, Edmond, and Ann Wellean,......	"	XI. 41
1756. Oct. 9.	Sweeny, Mathew, and Mary Thorn,.......	"	I. 324
1771. Sept. 7.	Sweesy, Margaret, and Thomas Hulse,.....	"	XVII. 177
1772. Aug. 5.	Sweet, John, and Hannah Tuthill, ...	"	XIX. 13
1758. Sept. 15.	Sweetman, Richard Matthias, and Sarah McGuire,.........................	"	II. 24
1773. Oct. 11.	Swert, Annate, and Simon De Groet,......	"	XXI. 138
1782. May 9.	Swift, John, and Elizabeth Huck,.........	"	XXXV. 156
1762. Oct. 1.	Swinney, Elizabeth, and John Young,.....	"	VI. 342
1758. Nov. 3.	Switcher, Margaret, and Cornelius Ringo,..	"	II. 78
1737. Nov. 2.	Swits, Anna, and Henry Beekman,........	"	I. 8
1702. Jan. 14.	Swits, Cornelius, and Catharine Schuyler, ..	"	VI. 12
1757. Oct. 26.	Swits, Jannetje, and John Hendrickse Vrooman, ...	"	I. 682
1771. Feb. 23.	Swits, Mary, and John Isaac Wemp, ...	"	XVII. 20
1765. April 29.	Switts, Gertrude, and Myndert Roseboom, .	"	IX. 114
1738. Oct. 28.	Switts, Susannah, and Cornelius Van Nesse, ...	"	I. 11
1775. June 16.	Switts, Susannah, and Daniel Foll, ...	"	XXIII. 67
1760. Oct. 20.	Switz, Abraham, and Margaret Delmont,...	"	III. 373
1776. Feb. 6.	Switzer, Peter, and Margaret Howes,......	"	XXIII. 262
1773. Feb. 10.	Sybrandt, Sovereign, and Catherina Shear,..	"	XX. 40
1665. Nov. 4.	Sybrants, Alice, and Peter Van Cowenhoven,..............................	O. W. L.,	II. 18
1773. Aug. 30.	Sykes, Philip, and Mary Morcomb,........	M. B.,	XXI. 90
1770. Nov. 8.	Sylvester, Ann, and John Woodward,.....	"	XVI. 243
1770. Nov. 14.	Sylvester, Ede, and Nicholas Hoffman, Jr.,.	"	XVI. 253
1764. Aug. 16.	Sylvester, Peter, and Jane Van Schaick, ...	"	VIII. 284
1761. Oct. 27.	Symes, Robert, and Elisabeth Collins, ...	"	V. 169
1665. Oct. 30.	Symonds, Peter, and Katharine Bradish, ...	O. W. L.,	II. 17
1684. Oct. 9.	Symons, Antie, and Hendricks Jacobs,.....	C. M.,	XXXIII. 54

DATE.		NAMES.	RECORD.	VOL. PAGE.
1765. June	3.	Symonson, Johannes, and Jemima Stag, ...	M. B.,	IX. 125
1755. Dec.	1.	Syms, Elizabeth, and Theodorus Frilinghuysen, ...	"	I. 224
1738. May	24.	Syms, Mary, and John Robinson, ...	"	I. 9
1765. June	3.	Symmson, Aron, and Catharine Bennet, ...	"	IX. 151

T.

1763. Dec.	22.	Taaffe, Patrick, and Elisabeth Burrowes, ...	"	VII. 517
1765. Sept.	10.	Taalhamer, Gertruy, and Aaron Bratt, ...	"	IX. 260
1763. Oct.	20.	Tabeley, Jacob, and Hannah Pettenger, ...	"	VII. 394
1762. Oct.	6.	Tackker, John, and Margaret Hall, ...	"	VI. 348
1772. Mar.	6.	Tagart, Sarah, and John Carpenter, ...	"	XVIII. 50
1775. Nov.	8.	Taggart, Ann, and Samuel Pearce, ...	"	XXIII. 203
1756. Nov.	1.	Taggart, James, and Sarah Stout, ...	"	I. 341
1762. Oct.	7.	Talkington, Elisabeth, and George Murray, .	"	VI. 352
1777. Sept.	27.	Tallman, Ann, and Samuel Brownejohn, ...	"	XXVI. 35
1766. Dec.	8.	Tallman, Ellenor, and James De Clarke, ...	"	X. 195
1772. Dec.	7.	Tallman, Harman, and Catherine Cornelius, .	"	XIX. 144
1778. Sept.	20.	Tallman, Jane, and Oliver Waters, ...	"	XXVI. 30
1769. June	24.	Tallman, John, and Mary Platt, ...	"	XIV. 129
1762. Feb.	11.	Tallman, Mary, and John Eagles, ...	"	VI. 46
1768. Nov.	25.	Tallman, Tunes, and Margaret Smith, ...	"	XIII. 244
1778. Jan.	11.	Tallman, William, and Sarah Willett, ...	"	XXV. 3
1756. Sept.	9.	Tallor, Sarah, and Solomon Taylor, ...	"	I. 292
1782. Oct.	8.	Talmage, Sarah, and Edward Dawkins, ...	"	XXXVII. 36
1766. Nov.	4.	Talman, Ann, and Daniel Lawrence, ...	"	X. 152
1760. Dec.	4.	Talman, Catherine, and Edmond Pinfold, ...	"	III. 454
1769. Aug.	17.	Talman, Rebecca, and William Hoff, ...	"	XV. 25
1781. Mar.	15.	Talman, Samuel, and Phebe Townsend, ...	"	XXXI. 71
1756. July	19.	Talman, William, and Ann Carryl, ...	"	I. 258
1759. June	15.	Tanare, Peter, and Sarah Warne, ...	"	II. 325
1759. July	28.	Tankard, Matthew, and Susannah Johnson, .	"	II. 366
1685. Aug.	17.	Tankirs, John, and Jannitie Haddock, ...	C. M.,	XXXIII. 154
1758. April	15.	Tannare, Mickel, and Dorothy Dobbs, ...	M. B.,	I. 874
1764. Nov.	23.	Tannely, Dorothy, and William Webb, ...	"	VIII. 422
1771. April	24.	Tanner, Ann, and Thomas Welling, ...	"	XVII. 67
1763. Jan.	12.	Tanner, Elizabeth, and Edward Wilkinson, ..	"	VII. 14
1778. Feb.	10.	Tanner, Elizabeth, and Samuel Welling, ...	"	XXV. 20
1773. Mar.	17.	Tanner, John, and Ann Schenck, ...	"	XX. 65
1768. Mar.	23.	Tanner, Mary, and John Hinchman, ...	"	XIII. 55
1780. June	5.	Tanner, Samuel, and Isabel McKindlas, ...	"	XXIX. 82
1764. Nov.	2.	Tappan, Aurontie, and Christopher Kierstead, Jr., ...	"	VIII. 389

DATE.	NAMES.	RECORD.	VOL.	PAGE.
1769. Oct. 28.	Tappan, Cornelia, and George Clinton,.....	M. B.,	xv.	70
1765. May 20.	Tappan, Tjatie, and Abraham Concklin,....	"	ix.	132
1761. April 16.	Tappen, Christopher, and Annatje Wynkoop,	"	iv.	151
1782. Dec. 24.	Tappen, Mary, and Garret Elliss,..........	"	xxxvii.	131
1771. Nov. 6.	Tappen, Peter, and Elizabeth Crannell, ...	"	xvii.	241
1768. Dec. 9.	Tappen, Saretje, and Nicholas Vanderlyn, ..	"	xiii.	258
1738. May 4.	Tapper, Urin, and Maria Lurtraet, ...	"	i.	9
1783. Jan. 15.	Tarbell, Samuel, and Mary Bunn,.........	"	xxxviii.	18
1769. Mar. 2.	Targe, John, and Sarah Kip, ...	"	xiv.	43
1778. May 9.	Tarrant, Leonard, and Elizabeth Scott,.....	"	xxv.	76
1780. Jan. 20.	Tarrant, Margaret, and Bartholomew Ernest Heymell,......................	"	xxviii.	201
1780. Oct. 20.	Tarren, Jemima, and John Hanna, ...:.	"	xxx.	73
1769. July 18.	Tate, Ann, and John Gell,...............	"	xiv.	155
1761. Nov. 10.	Tate, Elizabeth, and James Bell, ...	"	v.	204
1757. Dec. 14.	Tate, Elizabeth, and James Johnson,.......	"	i.	740
1770. Aug. 25.	Tate, Samuel, and Hannah Hughes, ...	"	xvi.	171
1775. Oct. 30.	Tater, Catharine, and Stofol Coobagh,......	"	xxiii.	192
1778. Sept. 17.	Tatham, Thomas, and Jane Carr,..........	"	xxvi.	31
1766. Dec. 24.	Tattersall, James, and Judith Shannon,.....	"	x.	208
1765. April 3.	Tatterson, Margaret, and John Luddra,.....	"	ix.	80
1759. Dec. 5.	Tatterson, Richard, and Margaret Griffis,...	"	ii.	528
1765. Feb. 14.	Tatterson, Richard, and Martha Burtis,.....	"	ix.	53
1781. Jan. 2.	Taunton, George, and Mary Spring,.......	"	xxxi.	6
1753. July 26.	Taveau, John, and Latitia Beekman,...... .	"	i.	78
1761. May 23.	Taverat, Jean, and Margaret Magknight, ...	"	iv.	205
1758. Dec. 9.	Tayler, Ann, and Thomas Crag, ...	"	ii.	122
1757. April 1.	Tayler, Elizabeth, and Robert Tayler,......	"	i.	483
1768. Jan. 18.	Tayler, James, and Rebecca Gilchrist, ...	"	xiii.	10
1757. April 1.	Tayler, Robert, and Elizabeth Tayler,......	"	i.	483
1768. Dec. 16.	Taylor, Abijah, and Isabella Wyley, ...	"	xiii.	263
1737. June 24.	Taylor, Alexander, and Anne Wright, ...	"	i.	6
1772. Oct. 20.	Taylor, Ann, and Evert Bancker, Jr.,.:....	"	xix.	80
1765. Jan. 15.	Taylor, Ann, and John Hamilton,.........	"	ix.	16
1773. May 10.	Taylor, Catherine, and Joseph Braiden, ...	"	xx.	107
1783. July 8.	Taylor, Charles Nicoll, and Violette Ricketts Seabury,...................	"	xxxix.	84
1684. Oct. 12.	Taylor, Edward, and Deliverance Hewitt, ..	C. M.,	xxxiii.	54
1780. June 28.	Taylor, Elizabeth, and George Parbirt,.....	M. B.,	xxix.	102
1759. June 6.	Taylor, Elizabeth, and John Moore, ...	"	ii.	307
1781. July 14.	Taylor, Elizabeth, and John Stymets,......	"	xxxiii.	7
1767. April 23.	Taylor, Elizabeth, and William Dick, ...	"	xi.	69
1763. Nov. 11.	Taylor, George, and Mary Williams,.......	"	vii.	445
1782. Aug. 24.	Taylor, Hannah, and Isaac Cole,..........	"	xxxvi.	120
1762. July 3.	Taylor, Hannah, and John McLutwidge, ...	"	vi.	225

DATE.		NAMES.	RECORD.	VOL.	PAGE.
1760.	Feb. 14.	Taylor, Jacob, and Sarah Robinson, ...	M. B.,	III.	36
1775.	June 10.	Taylor, James, and Jemima Cabe,.........	"	XXIII.	59
1757.	May 17.	Taylor, Jane, and Robert Gibb,...........	"	I.	535
1767.	May 29.	Taylor, Jennet, and Henry Coupar, ...	"	XI.	101
1778.	Nov. 25.	Taylor, John, and Helen Denyse, ...	"	XXVI.	94
1776.	Mar. 6.	Taylor, John, and Lydia Rodgers,.........	"	XXIII.	278
1764.	Mar. 19.	Taylor, John, and Margaret Van Valkenburgh, ...	"	VIII.	111
1757.	Mar. 4.	Taylor, John, and Mary Piper, ...	"	I.	456
1761.	Oct. 17.	Taylor, John, and Mary Waddell, ...	"	V.	147
1773.	July 12.	Taylor, John, and Susannah St. Morris, ...	"	XX.	35
1782.	Feb. 23.	Taylor, Joseph, and Catharine Vandyck,...	"	XXXV.	61
1770.	July 2.	Taylor, Leah, and Isaac Walmsley, ...	"	XVI.	133
1782.	May 22.	Taylor, Lewis, and Elizabeth Neck, ...	"	XXXVI.	20
1782.	Dec. 14.	Taylor, Mary, and George James,.........	"	XXXVII.	120
1781.	Nov. 30.	Taylor, Mary, and John Ashfield, ...	"	XXXIV.	64
1781.	June 30.	Taylor, Mary, and John Mersereau, ...	"	XXXII.	84
1682.	July 4.	Taylor, Mary, and Thomas Higby, ...	O. W.,	XXXII$\frac{1}{2}$.	132
1783.	July 30.	Taylor, Mathew, and Eleanora Van Ever,..	M. B.,	XXXIX.	105
1778.	July 24.	Taylor, Mathew, and Jane Hoar, ...	"	XXV.	141
1782.	Aug. 16.	Taylor, Mathew, and Mary King,.........	"	XXXVI.	112
1764.	Aug. 16.	Taylor, Michael, and Hannah Norris, ...	"	VIII.	286
1760.	April 25.	Taylor, Moses, Jr., and Elizabeth Alstyn,...	"	III.	124
1758.	Dec. 2.	Taylor, Nathaniel, and Ann Welch, ...	"	II.	110
1780.	Nov. 17.	Taylor, Nelly, and Robert Stevens,........	"	XXX.	113
1770.	June 1.	Taylor, Oliver, and Sarah Hillyer,.........	"	XVI.	102
1761.	Jan. 28.	Taylor, Peter, and Elizabeth Creed,........	"	IV.	57
1781.	Dec. 15.	Taylor, Rebecca, and Edward Rodgers, ...	"	XXXIV.	88
1780.	May 6.	Taylor, Rebecca, and Oliver Roosevelt,.....	"	XXIX.	45
1773.	June 29.	Taylor, Rebekah, and George Flowers,.....	"	XXI.	25
1777.	Mar. 23.	Taylor, Rosana, and John Deas, ...	"	XXIV.	50
1781.	Dec. 3.	Taylor, Samuel, and Ann Davison, ...	"	XXXIV.	69
1765.	July 31.	Taylor, Sarah, and John Schermerhorne,...	"	IX.	224
1773.	Jan. 27.	Taylor, Sarah, and Jonas Scudder,.........	"	XX.	23
1780.	June 2.	Taylor, Sarah, and Joseph Webb, ...	"	XXIX.	80
1777.	June 4.	Taylor, Sarah, and Matthias Nicoll,........	"	XXIV.	96
1765.	April 25.	Taylor, Sarah, and Robert Orr, ...	"	IX.	109
1756.	Sept. 9.	Taylor, Solomon, and Sarah Tallor,........	"	I.	292
1763.	Sept. 17.	Taylor, Susanna, and William Cassy, ...	"	VII.	342
1756.	Nov. 1.	Taylor, Thomas', and Ann Harding,........	"	I.	342
1760.	Jan. 3.	Taylor, Thomas, and Hester Carruthers,....	"	II.	567
1760.	Sept. 1.	Taylor, Willet, and Mary Bogart, ...	"	III.	276
1760.	Nov. 13.	Taylor, William, and Elizabeth Hunter, ...	"	III.	408
1759.	Sept. 3.	Taylor, William, and Mary Hopkins, ...	"	II.	408
1761.	Oct. 6.	Teal, John, and Elisabeth Frizer,..........	"	V.	126

DATE.	NAMES.	RECORD.	VOL.	PAGE.
1764. April 16.	Tear, Daniel, and Susannah Boyle, ...	M. B.,	VIII.	156
1764. Mar. 6.	Tear, Mathias, and Margrat Shappel,.......	"	VIII.	95
1782. Oct. 21.	Teare, John, and Mary Tittle, ...	"	XXXVII.	57
1764. Sept. 20.	Tearman, Mary, and Hendrick Barr,.......	"	VIII.	319
1772. April 23.	Teator, Rebecca, and George Sharp,.......	"	XVIII.	90
1736. Nov. 13.	Tebout, Francis, and Constantia King, ...	"	I.	3
1764. Nov. 23.	Telier, Rachel, and Isaac Bogart,..........	"	VIII.	427
1766. Nov. 17.	Tell, Affie, and Lowickes Veeler, ...	"	X.	169
1773. Nov. 25.	Teller, Catherine, and John Stoutenburgh,..	"	XXII.	46
1769. Dec. 21.	Teller, Cornelia, and Petrus Bogardus,.....	"	XV.	129
1756. Oct. 5.	Teller, Elizabeth, and Burrivine De Graaf,..	"	I.	317
1780. April 17.	Teller, Elizabeth, and Joseph Coulon,......	"	XXIX.	14
1762. Nov. 8.	Teller, Isaac, and Catharine Brewerton,....	"	VI.	417
1761. July 29.	Teller, Isaac, and Rebecca Remsen,........	"	V.	15
1762. Oct. 7.	Teller, Jacobus, and Mary Yeates,.........	"	VI.	350
1764. June 23.	Teller, Jesyntje, and Jacobus Stoutenburgh,	"	VIII.	235
1760. Sept. 8.	Teller, John, and Johanna Delmont,.......	"	V.	74
1764. Oct. 8.	Teller, John, and Margaret Stoutenbergh, ..	"	VIII.	338
1757. Dec. 12.	Teller, John, and Margaret Van Steenbergh,	"	I.	736
1765. Oct. 16.	Teller, Luke, and Sarah Snedeker, ...	"	IX.	303
1757. Dec. 6.	Teller, Peter, and Catherine Kip,..........	"	I.	725
1760. May 2.	Teller, Phebe, and Benjamin Higgins,......	"	III.	137
1762. Aug. 4.	Teller, Rachel, and Luke Stoutenburgh,....	"	VI.	264
1763. June 13.	Teller, Sineche, and Jacob Valentine,... ..	"	VII.	227
1766. Nov. 6.	Teller, William, and Helena Van Eps, ...	"	X.	156
1761. Mar. 23.	Tellinghast, Joseph, and Phebe Mulford, ...	"	IV.	114
1753. May 17.	Telyou, Elizabeth, and Peter Hoyer,.......	"	I.	31
1761. Sept. 23.	Tempie, Grace, and Thomas Price, ...	"	V.	94
1780. May 6.	Templar, Margeret, and Joshua Carr, ...	"	XXIX.	49
1771. Aug. 28.	Tenayck, Margaret, and John Barclay,.....	"	XVII.	165
1766. Nov. 14.	Ten Broeck, Abraham, and Catharine Whitaker, ...	"	X.	163
1765. June 8.	Ten Broeck, Catharine, and George Wray, .	"	IX.	161
1762. Nov. 11.	Ten Broeck, Catharine, and Jacob Bogardus,	"	VI.	424
1769. Oct. 9.	Ten Broeck, Christina, and Gerhard Daniel Cock,.............................	"	XV.	52
1769. Sept. 11.	Ten Broeck, John, and Gerretie Roseboom,.	"	XV.	38
1762. May 4.	Ten Broeck, John, and Sarah Gansevoort,..	"	VI.	142
1776. Mar. 7.	Ten Broeck, Leonard, and Geartje Schermerhorn, ...	"	XXIII.	279
1770. Nov. 15.	Ten Broeck, Mary, and Goose Van Schaick,	"	XVI.	256
1768. Feb. 23.	Tenbroeck, Samuel, and Emmetje Van Alstyn, ...	"	XIII.	44
1772. Nov. 9.	Ten Broock, John, and Alliday Smith,.....	"	XIX.	105
1759. July 17.	Tenbroock, Lenah, and Philip Van Ness,...	"	II.	357

386   NEW YORK MARRIAGES.

DATE.	NAMES.	RECORD.	VOL.	PAGE.
1760. April 28.	Ten Brook, Catharine, and John Demont,..	M. B.,	III.	130
1759. July 26.	Ten Brook, Catharine, and Robert Harper,.	"	II.	364
1738. May 24.	Ten Brook, Catherine, and Rykert Hanson,.	"	I.	9
1736. May 5.	Tenbrook, Cathrina Johana, and Dirick Van Hall, ...	"	I.	1
1780. Aug. 12.	Tenbrook, Hannah, and William Welch,....	"	XXIX.	139
1753. Sept. 14.	Ten Brook, John, and Maritje Hoofman,...	"	I.	118
1772. May 5.	Tenbrook, Maritje, and Abraham I. Delametter,..............................	"	XVIII.	100
1753. May 30.	Ten Brook, Mary, and Stephen Baldwin,...	"	I.	44
1773. May 27.	Tenbrook, Rachel, and Jacob Schryver, ...	"	XX.	129
1755. Nov. 3.	Ten Brook, Sarah, and Abraham J. De Lametter, ...	"	I.	204
1764. July 7.	Ten Brook, Wessels, and Janitie Parsons, ..	"	VIII.	248
1737. Sept. 3.	Tenbrooke, Christina, and Dirick Van Slyck,	"	I.	7
1736. Aug. 30.	Tenbrooke, John, and Rachel Baldwin, ...	"	I.	2
1738. Oct. 27.	Tenbrooke, Maritie, and Henry De Witt, ..	"	I.	11
1778. Sept. 12.	Tench, John, and Rachel Evans,..........	"	XXVI.	27
1737. July 2.	Tenet, Mary, and Henry Witfield, ...	"	I.	6
1764. Dec. 31.	Ten Eyck, Abraham, and Sarah Smith, ...	"	VIII.	469
1738. April 21.	Ten Eyck, Affia, and Andrew Varck,......	"	I.	9
1764. Dec. 18.	Ten Eyck, Andrew, and Jane Welp, ...	"	VIII.	457
1763. July 25.	Ten Eyck, Andries, and Jannetje Janse,....	"	VII.	282
1762. April 26.	Ten Eyck, Ann, and John Marshall,.......	"	VI.	131
1766. Oct. 27.	Ten Eyck, Annatie, and Wilhelmus Mancius,	"	X.	143
1760. Aug. 7.	Ten Eyck, Anthony, and Margaret Schuyler,	"	III.	239
1775. Nov. 10.	Ten Eyck, Anthony, and Mary Egberts,....	"	XXIII.	205
1763. Jan. 20.	Ten Eyck, Appia, and William Popplesdorff, Jr.,....	"	VII.	24
1755. Oct. 15.	Ten Eyck, Barent, and Elsie Cuyler, ...	"	I.	194
1752. Nov. 27.	Ten Eyck, Barent, and Elsie Gansevoort, ..	"	I.	15
1768. Nov. 12.	Ten Eyck, Barent J., and Sarah Codwise, ..	"	XIII.	235
1781. Aug. 10.	Ten Eyck, Catherine, and Thomas Bridgen Attwood, ...	"	XXXIII.	35
1768. Nov. 5.	Ten Eyck, Charlotta, and Coenradt Ten Eyck,	"	XIII.	227
1768. Nov. 5.	Ten Eyck, Coenradt, and Charlotta Ten Eyck,	"	XIII.	227
1770. April 9.	Ten Eyck, Coenradt A., and Elizabeth Johnson, ...	"	XVI.	53
1772. Aug. 10.	Ten Eyck, Conrat E., and Rachel Hallenbeeck, ...	"	XIX.	16
1762. July 22.	Ten Eyck, Daniel, and Hannah Cholwell, ..	"	VI.	253
1769. May 4.	Ten Eyck, Geertje, and Johannes Pruyn, ..	"	XIV.	92
1769. July 11.	Ten Eyck, Gerritje, and William Faulkner, .	"	XIV.	149
1776. Feb. 8.	Ten Eyck, Harmanus, and Margaret Bleecker,	"	XXIII.	264
1763. April 11.	Ten Eyck, Helena, and Stephen Schuyler,..	"	VII.	121

DATE.	NAMES.	RECORD.	VOL.	PAGE.
1767. May 13.	Ten Eyck, Henry, Jr., and Margaret Douw,	M. B.,	XI.	86
1770. June 1.	Ten Eyck, Henry B., and Catherine Saunders,	"	XVI.	103
1736. Aug. 5.	Ten Eyck, Jacob, and Catrina Cuyler,	"	I.	2
1760. April 16.	Ten Eyck, Jacob, and Rachael Thornton,	"	III.	111
1783. Sept. 7.	Ten Eyck, John, and Sarah Lowere,	"	XL.	29
1736. Aug. 5.	Ten Eyck, Maria, and Gerret Bradt,	"	I.	2
1780. April 12.	Ten Eyck, Mary, and James Hetfield,	"	XXIX.	20
1763. April 26.	Ten Eyck, Mary, and John Walter,	"	VII.	142
1755. Nov. 27.	Ten Eyck, Neiltie, and Frederick Roorbach,	"	I.	220
1755. Nov. 27.	Ten Eyck, Neiltie, and Samuel Pruyn,	"	I.	219
1764. Nov. 1.	Ten Eyck, Richard, and Elizabeth L. Brown,	"	VIII.	387
1760. Sept. 9.	Ten Eyck, Sarah, and John Ernest,	"	III.	306
1755. Nov. 25.	Ten Eyck, Tobias, and Judith Van Buren,	"	I.	216
1781. May 10.	Tenier, Barshaba, and Thomas Lufborrow,	"	XXXII.	41
1738. Aug. 23.	Tennant, William, and Catherine Noble,	"	I.	10
1773. Sept. 21.	Tennent, William Mackey, and Susannah Rogers,	"	XXI.	115
1783. June 16.	Teple, Ann, and Samuel Howard,	"	XXXIX.	61
1761. July 28.	Teppet, Stephen, and Christiana Provoost,	"	V.	11
1759. Mar. 19.	Terbos, Daniel, and Cornelia Rickman,	"	II.	220
1773. April 2.	Ter Bos, Jacob, Jr., and Sarah Du Bois,	"	XX.	80
1764. Nov. 24.	Terbos, Luke, and Mellisent Bloom,	"	VIII.	423
1761. Oct. 17.	Ter Boss, Peter, and Anne Crawford,	"	V.	145
1763. Oct. 20.	Ter Boss, Simon, and Deborah Cooper,	"	VII.	395
1763. Oct. 23.	Terbush, Abraham, and Mitty Pine,	"	IX.	313
1766. Aug. 13.	Terbush, Isaac, and Ann Munford,	"	X.	74
1767. Oct. 19.	Terbush, Johannes, and Janitje Dubois,	"	XII.	64
1753. June 15.	Terbush, Johannis, and Catherine Van Wyck,	"	I	62
1768. June 27.	Terhuen, Jacob, and Elizabeth Lezier,	"	XIII.	139
1778. Mar. 10.	Terhune, Elizabeth, and Morris Earle,	"	XXV.	38
1781. Feb. 9.	Terhune, Margaret, and John Wyckoff,	"	XXXI.	43
1759. July 5.	Terhune, Stephen, and Lettitia Bergen,	"	II.	348
1771. Aug. 3.	Terrett, William, and Ann Lajire,	"	XVII.	149
1778. Aug. 16.	Terrot, Elizabeth, and Robert Mara,	"	XXVI.	4
1780. Sept. 14.	Terrot, Salah, and Abraham Stout,	"	XXX.	28
1765. Mar. 5.	Terry, Daniel, and Carolina Smith,	"	IX.	63
1764. May 22.	Terry, Jemimie, and James Marcus,	"	VIII.	196
1782. April 3.	Tetetis, Ann, and William Bennett,	"	XXXV.	108
1782. Mar. 22.	Tetis, Hester, and David Van Cotts,	"	XXXI.	83
1775. May 13.	Tetus, Tetus, and Jemima Townsend,	"	XXIII.	34
1770. May 3.	Tetus, Tetus, and Rebeccah Boerum,	"	XVI.	78
1765. April 2.	Teurs, Ann, and Barney Newkirk,	"	IX.	78
1760. Mar. 28.	Teutschbern, Johann Henrich Ernst, and Sophia Creman,	"	III.	93

DATE.	NAMES.	RECORD.	VOL.	PAGE.
1780. Sept. 23.	Tharp, Mary, and Joshua Tull, ...	M. B.,	xxx.	38
1782. Aug. 18.	Thatford, Ann, and William Butler, ...	"	xxxvi.	114
1783. Mar. 21.	Thatford, Martha, and Matthew Pruyor, ...	"	xxxviii.	71
1777. Jan. 10.	Thawley, Catherine, and John Butt, ...	"	xxiv.	10
1770. Dec. 19.	Theal, Margaret, and Isaac Smith, ...	"	xvi.	304
1781. Aug. 21.	Thean, James, and Cloe Mount, ...	"	xxxiii.	43
1782. Jan. 19.	Thetcher, Grace, and James McAtee, ...	"	xxxv.	14
1761. Aug. 21.	Thew, Abraham, and Rachel Cobby, ...	"	v.	50
1769. Feb. 20.	Thew, John, and Elizabeth Blawfield, ...	"	xiv.	38
1765. Sept. 17.	Thew, Theunis, and Anney Brower, ...	"	ix.	264
1764. Mar. 9.	Thibou, Lewis, and Eve Bicker, ...	"	viii.	100
1756. Dec. 4.	Thibou, Mary, and William Young, ...	"	i.	372
1761. Jan. 14.	Thistle, Samuel, and Elizabeth Kissawny, ..	"	iv.	17
1760. July 9.	Thodey, Michael, and Elizabeth Jones, ...	"	iii.	209
1753. Sept. 19.	Thomas, Charity, and James Fferris, ...	"	i.	120
1778. Jan. 16.	Thomas, Elizabeth, and Thomas Misplee, ...	"	xxv.	7
1777. Oct. 21.	Thomas, George, and Martha Crawford, ...	"	xxiv.	167
1770. Oct. 18.	Thomas, Gloriana, and James Franklin, ...	"	xvi.	223
1760. Mar. 19.	Thomas, James, and Margaret Dyke, ...	"	iii.	82
1762. Feb. 8.	Thomas, James, and Miaca Claw, ...	"	vi.	41
1777. Oct. 18.	Thomas, Jane, and James Carmer, ...	"	xxiv.	165
1772. Mar. 4.	Thomas, John, and Catherine McDonald, ...	"	xviii.	46
1777. Sept. 4.	Thomas, John, and Margaret Watson, ...	"	xxiv.	143
1778. May 5.	Thomas, John, and Martha Wilson, ...	"	xxv.	71
1763. Dec. 5.	Thomas, John, and Maryann Stiggens, ...	"	vii.	491
1775. May 30.	Thomas, John, and Ruth Craft, ...	"	xxiii.	49
1761. Dec. 11.	Thomas, Luke, and Mary Price, ...	"	v.	274
1759. Mar. 23.	Thomas, Lydia, and Richard McGugen, ...	"	ii.	223
1761. April 28.	Thomas, Margaret, and Charles Floyd, ...	"	iv.	171
1781. Jan. 29.	Thomas, Margaret, and Even Cameron, ...	"	xxxi.	29
1777. Aug. 16.	Thomas, Mary, and Henry Hall, ...	"	xxiv.	133
1770. Nov. 8.	Thomas, Mary, and Richard Speaight, ...	"	xvi.	244
1759. Sept. 28.	Thomas, Mary, and Timothy Rogers, ...	"	ii.	435
1762. Aug. 25.	Thomas, Robert, and Sarah Brower, ...	"	vi.	286
1783. June 11.	Thomas, Samuel, and Sarah Vanderhoof, ...	"	xxxix.	50
1766. Nov. 5.	Thomas, Sarah, and Solomon A. Schelp, ...	"	x.	154
1763. Oct. 20.	Thomas, Susanna, and John Jervis, Jr., ...	"	vii.	398
1769. July 29.	Thomas, Thomas, and Catherine Floyd, ...	"	xv.	8
1781. Nov. 16.	Thomas, William, and Ann Hampton, ...	"	xxxiv.	42
1762. Sept. 10.	Thomason, Joshua, and Mary Farrell, ...	"	vi.	313
1760. Jan. 21.	Thompson, Andrew, and Margaret Little, ..	"	iii.	1
1772. Oct. 14.	Thompson, Andrew, and Mary Leonard, ...	"	xix.	70
1760. Aug. 5.	Thompson, Archibald, and Elizabeth Stryker,	"	iii.	233
1761. Oct. 14.	Thompson, Archibald, and Margaret Kidney,	"	v.	136
1778. Jan. 12.	Thompson, Charles, and Mary Flood, ...	"	xxv.	4

DATE.	NAMES.	RECORD.	VOL.	PAGE.
1759. June 21.	Thompson, Dorothy, and Martin Blake,....	M. B.,	II.	335
1737. April 2.	Thompson, Elizabeth, and James Smith,....	"	I.	5
1772. April 13.	Thompson, Elizabeth, and John Baldwin, ..	"	XVIII.	74
1771. July 23.	Thompson, Elizabeth, and John Berrey,....	"	XVII.	142
1767. Aug. 14.	Thompson, Fiche, and George Carr,.......	"	XII.	16
1777. Dec. 27.	Thompson, George, and Ann Bayard,......	"	XXIV.	208
1771. Nov. 4.	Thompson, Elizabeth, and Gilbert Gibour De La Roche,.......................	"	XVII.	239
1760. June 2.	Thompson, Hannah, and John Cole,.......	"	III.	193
1778. Oct. 24.	Thompson, Hupty, and Ann Labon, ...	"	XXVI.	70
1772. May 19.	Thompson, Isaac, and Mary Gardiner,.....	"	XVIII.	114
1764. June 6.	Thompson, John, and Ann Lewis, ...	"	VIII.	208
1761. Feb. 16.	Thompson, John, and Dorothy McGuineas,.	"	IV.	65
1760. Oct. 9.	Thompson, John, and Mary Hamilton,.....	"	III.	355
1781. Oct. 25.	Thompson, John, and Phebe Ryersz,......	"	XXXIV.	5
1763. Nov. 7.	Thompson, Margaret, and George Morison,.	"	VII.	431
1765. June 5.	Thompson, Margaret, and John Gelston, ...	"	IX.	157
1763. Dec. 19.	Thompson, Mary, and Alexander Steuart, ..	"	VII.	511
1782. May 22.	Thompson, Mary, and Asher Levy,........	"	XXXVI.	18
1773. Mar. 24.	Thompson, Mary, and Jacob Ricketts,.....	"	XX.	71
1760. Mar. 5.	Thompson, Mary, and John Calvein, ...	"	III.	61
1765. April 22.	Thompson, Mary, and John Campbell,.....	"	IX.	103
1767. Dec. 24.	Thompson, Mary, and Lewis Nichols,......	"	XII.	122
1763. Mar. 17.	Thompson, Mary, and Thomas Smith, ...	"	VII.	103
1782. Mar. 30.	Thompson, Mary, and William Harris,.....	"	XXXV.	102
1737. July 19.	Thompson, Mathew Edward, and Cornelia Van Ulitt,.......................	"	I.	6
1781. Oct. 19.	Thompson, Peter, and Elizabeth Oakley,...	"	XXXIII.	109
1767. April 7.	Thompson, Peter, and Mary Savage,.......	"	XI.	58
1779. Oct. 14.	Thompson, Philip, and Sarah Burrows, ...	"	XXVIII.	111
1770. Nov. 2.	Thompson, Robert, and Mary Bass,........	"	XVI.	237
1763. Sept. 7.	Thompson, Samuel, and Jane Drinkwater,..	"	VII.	328
1781. Jan. 6.	Thompson, Samuel, and Phebe Saterly, ...	"	XXXI.	17
1778. Dec. 10.	Thompson, Thomas, and Sarah Walker,....	"	XXVI.	116
1763. July 16.	Thompson, William, and Elizabeth Miller,..	"	VII.	268
1770. April 28.	Thompson, William, and Mary De Kay,....	"	XVI.	72
1773. Nov. 2.	Thompson, William, and Sarah Allison,....	"	XXII.	7
1762. Oct. 21.	Thompson, William, and Tyatje Dubois,....	"	VI.	378
1768. Mar. 31.	Thompsons, Philip, and Mary Steymets, ...	"	XIII.	58
1780. Dec. 18.	Thomson, Jane, and Mathew Stacey,......	"	XXX.	158
1777. Oct. 4.	Thomson, Johen, and Mary Sandford, ...	"	XXIV.	158
1780. Aug. 23.	Thomson, John, and Hannah Cox, ...	"	XXIX.	145
1781. Feb. 28.	Thomson, Mary, and John Stoddart,.......	"	XXXI.	60
1762. April 29.	Thomson, Peter, and Charity Burtis, ...	"	VI.	134
1736. Aug. 5.	Thorn, Benjamin, and Phebe Carmen, ...	"	I.	2

DATE.	NAMES.	RECORD.	VOL.	PAGE.
1781. Dec. 24.	Thorn, Catharine, and Lewis Frazur,	M. B.,	xxxiv.	102
1774. Jan. 13.	Thorn, Charles, and Ann Kirby,	"	xxii.	101
1776. Feb. 15.	Thorn, Daniel, and Bersheba Fowler,	"	xxiii.	267
1765. Mar. 20.	Thorn, Daniel, and Margaret Townsend,	"	ix.	71
1751. Aug. 3.	Thorn, Edward, and Lydia Parsons,	"	i.	85
1783. Mar. 18.	Thorn, George, and Mary Roe,	"	xxxviii.	68
1761. June 24.	Thorn, Hannah, and Daniel Clement,	"	iv.	259
1781. Feb. 28.	Thorn, Jannet, and Charles Stewart,	"	xxxi.	61
1737. May 7.	Thorn, John, and Mercy Willson,	"	i.	6
1759. Jan. 2.	Thorn, Joseph, and Lydia Thorne,	"	ii.	298
1781. Nov. 7.	Thorn, Mary, and Benjamin Dunn,	"	xxxiv.	21
1756. Oct. 9.	Thorn, Mary, and Mathew Sweeny,	"	i.	324
1760. Aug. 20.	Thorn, Mary, and William Hill,	"	iii.	264
1763. Dec. 17.	Thorn, Mercy, and Jacob Isman,	"	vii.	509
1767. May 16.	Thorn, Samuel, and Ann Cornell,	"	xi.	90
1773. July 1.	Thorn, Samuel, and Martha Hunt,	"	xxi.	28
1780. Mar. 15.	Thorn, Sarah, and Noah Hallock,	"	xxix.	2
1768. May 21.	Thorn, Sarah, and Richard Marsh,	"	xiii.	110
1760. June 27.	Thorn, Sarah, and Robert Bloodgood,	"	iii.	198
1779. Aug. 2.	Thorn, Stephen, and Elizabeth Cole,	"	xxviii.	41
1779. Feb. 23.	Thorn, Stephen, Jr., and Sarah Kippen,	"	xxvii.	47
1767. June 30.	Thorn, Susannah, and James Roach,	"	xi.	115
1768. Feb. 11.	Thorn, Susannah, and Thomas Dodge,	"	xiii.	32
1781. Nov. 20.	Thorn, William, and Anne Ruckhow,	"	xxxiv.	51
1776. Feb. 16.	Thorn, William, and Hester Townsend,	"	xxiii.	270
1762. June 28.	Thorne, Ann, and Peter H. Monfoort,	"	vi.	213
1769. Mar. 10.	Thorne, Benjamin, and Maria Cooper,	"	xiv.	52
1777. June 5.	Thorne, Catherine, and Richard Robertson,.	"	xxiv.	97
1779. Oct. 9.	Thorne, Daniel, and Hester Nevaro,	"	xxviii.	108
1763. Dec. 6.	Thorne, Deborah, and Samuel Woodard,	"	vii.	494
1773. April 15.	Thorne, Edward, and Jane Rapalje,	"	xx.	92
1779. Nov. 25.	Thorne, Elizabeth, and Thomas Underhill,.	"	xxviii.	146
1769. July 8.	Thorne, Hannah, and Gilbert Field,	"	xiv.	144
1768. Mar. 21.	Thorne, Hannah, and Smith Pine,	"	xiii.	54
1770. Nov. 20.	Thorne, Jacob, and Ida Suydam,	"	xvi.	264
1769. Nov. 3.	Thorne, John, and Mary Allen,	"	xv.	77
1664. Mar. 9.	Thorne, John, and Mary Passill,	G. E.,	i.	98
1780. Jan. 20.	Thorne, John, and Mary Van Wyck,	M. B.,	xxviii.	200
1757. Jan. 25.	Thorne, John, and Susannah Bullock,	"	i.	426
1672. Feb. 1.	Thorne, Joseph, and Anna Lawrenson,	G. E.,	iv.	251
1769. Jan. 9.	Thorne, Joseph, and Phebe Allen,	M. B.,	xiv.	9
1763. Oct. 7.	Thorne, Lanckford, and Mary Roe,	"	vii.	380
1759. Jan. 2.	Thorne, Lydia, and Joseph Thorn,	"	ii.	298
1781. Oct. 18.	Thorne, Mary, and Francis I'Ans,	"	xxxiii.	108
1764. Dec. 3.	Thorne, Mary, and James Sell,	"	viii.	434

DATE.		NAMES.	RECORD.	VOL.	PAGE.
1783.	Jan. 22.	Thorne, Mary, and William Forbes, ...	M. B.,	xxxviii.	24
1737.	Sept. 8.	Thorne, Obediah, and Susannah Thorne, ...	"	i.	7
1762.	Dec. 3.	Thorne, Philip, and Abigal Rowland, ...	"	viii.	433
1779.	Aug. 5.	Thorne, Philip, and Elizabeth Cheeseman,..	"	xxviii.	47
1764.	Dec. 7.	Thorne, Rachel, and George Bloodgood,....	"	viii.	442
1738.	June 8.	Thorne, Richard, and Mary Hyatt,........	"	i.	9
1767.	Dec. 5.	Thorne, Richard, and Sarah Waters,.......	"	xii.	107
1777.	June 25.	Thorne, Sarah, and Phillip Allen, Jr., ...	"	xxiv.	107
1762.	May 4.	Thorne, Stephen, and Elizabeth Hicks,.....	"	vi.	141
1773.	Oct. 14.	Thorne, Stephen, Jr., and Sarah Platt,.....	"	xxi.	141
1667.	July 10.	Thorne, Susannah, and John Ockeson,.....	O. W. L.,	ii.	134
1737.	Sept. 8.	Thorne, Susannah, and Obediah Thorne, ...	M. B.,	i.	7
1763.	Aug. 12.	Thorne, Thomas, and Abigail Caverly,.....	"	vii.	297
1777.	May 1.	Thorne, Thomas, and Abigail Sands,.......	"	xxiv.	80
1738.	Sept. 28.	Thorne, Thomas, and Mary Dodge,........	"	i.	11
1761.	Dec. 23.	Thorne, William, and Elizabeth Gardiner,...	"	v.	297
1779.	Mar. 27.	Thorne, William, and Elizabeth Wood, ...	"	xxvii.	80
1760.	Jan. 25.	Thornhill, Hannah, and James Corrin, ...	"	iii.	7
1765.	July 8.	Thornton, Mary, and Michael Halenbeck, ..	"	ix.	199
1760.	April 16.	Thornton, Rachael, and Jacob Ten Eyck,...	"	iii.	111
1757.	Nov. 17.	Thornycraft, Phebe, and Thomas Frost,....	"	i.	704
1759.	Oct. 6.	Thorp, Daniel, and Prudence Thorp,.......	"	ii.	451
1758.	Mar. 29.	Thorp, Daniel, and Rachel Van Nort,......	"	i.	865
1783.	April 26.	Thorp, Eunice, and James Gray,..........	"	xxxviii.	117
1761.	May 21.	Thorp, John, and Eleanor O'Neil, ...	"	iv.	202
1759.	May 16.	Thorp, John, and Elizabeth Bedford, ...	"	ii.	285
1759.	Oct. 6.	Thorp, Prudence, and Daniel Thorp,.......	"	ii.	451
1761.	Dec. 23.	Thorp, Sarah, and Mathew Paterson,......	"	v.	295
1783.	Nov. 13.	Thuresson, Laurence, and Anne Todd, ...	"	xl.	112
1762.	July 8.	Thurman, Gertry, and Daniel Dunscomb,...	"	vi.	230
1737.	May 20.	Thurman, John, and Nealta Quick,........	"	i.	6
1775.	Sept. 19.	Thurston, Catharine, and James Galloway, .	"	xxiii.	158
1770.	Aug. 6.	Thurston, Elizabeth, and Thomas Cornwell,.	"	xvi.	155
1763.	July 3.	Thurston, Lovit, and Catherine Dobbs,.....	"	vi.	223
1782.	May 8.	Thurston, Lucretia, and Francis De Weder,.	"	xxxv.	153
1764.	Jan. 4.	Thurston, Palatiah, and Tabitha Marston,...	"	viii.	4
1736.	Nov. 30.	Tibout, Marytie, and John Pierce,.........	"	i.	3
1761.	May 2.	Tice, Gilbert, and Christiana Van Sleght,...	"	iv.	175
1761.	Sept. 30.	Tice, John, and Elisabeth Ehl,............	"	v.	107
167⅝.	Mar. 14.	Tiddeman, Anne, and William Peartree, ...	W.·O. P.,	iii.	183
1666.	Sept. 18.	Tiddeman, Thomas, and Hanna Litscho,....	O. W. L.,	ii.	134
1759.	July 6.	Tiebout, Albartus, and Ruth Vanderhoof,...	M. B.,	ii.	350
1766.	June 5.	Tiebout, Cornelius, and Mary Magdalen, ...	"	x.	3
1770.	Dec. 29.	Tiebout, Elizabeth, and Henry Ashworth, ..	"	xvi.	308
1761.	Aug. 25.	Tiebout, Henry, and Margaret Hollock, ...	"	v.	55

DATE.		NAMES.	RECORD.	VOL.	PAGE.
1738. May	16.	Tiebout, Maria, and Benjamin Morgan, ...	M. B.,	I.	9
1771. Oct.	31.	Tiebout, Mary, and John Johnson, ...	"	XVII.	234
1768. June	20.	Tiers, Catherine, and John Harbeck, ...	"	XIII.	135
1764. April	7.	Ties, Margaret, and Robert Bohownen, ...	"	VIII.	140
1781. Nov.	21.	Tiginer, Levina, and Jacob Hewlick, ...	"	XXXIV.	53
1765. Mar.	18.	Tigley, Catharine, and John Hun, ...	"	IX.	70
1779. April	11.	Tillary, James, and Brachey Gleaves, ...	"	XXVII.	105
1764. Oct.	1.	Tillee, Catharine, and Amos Pine, ...	"	VIII.	330
1738. Aug.	16.	Tillee, Elizabeth, and Isaac Bussen, ...	"	I.	10
1765. Mar.	7.	Tillenborough, Catharine, and George Ni- cholls, ...	"	IX.	65
1759. Jan.	27.	Tillet, Joseph, and Elizabeth Pearse, ...	"	II.	167
1773. April	6.	Tillew, Anne, and Edmond Butler, ...	"	XX.	84
1755. Oct.	3.	Tilley, David, and Mary Hopkins, ...	"	I.	187
1763. Oct.	31.	Tilley, Edward, and Margaret Vandewater,.	"	VII.	415
1678. Sept.	26.	Tilley, Samuel, and Mary Limkins, ...	G. E.,	XXXII.	3
1757. Feb.	22.	Tillier, Hanah, and David Mersereau, ...	M. B.,	I.	447
1777. Aug.	11.	Tillman, William, and Charity Hutchins, ...	"	XXIII.	123
1756. Nov.	30.	Tillot, Sarah, and Thomas Place, ...	"	I.	367
1763. Dec.	12.	Tillott, Joseph, and Sarah Dischow, ...	"	VII.	504
1760. April	26.	Tillou, Catharine, and George Richey, ...	"	III.	127
1761. Nov.	14.	Tillou, William, and Mary Childs, ...	"	V.	217
1761. Mar.	13.	Tillow, Anne, and Donald Wilkinson, ...	"	IV.	101
1762. Aug.	13.	Tilly, Elizabeth, and James Neal, ...	"	VI.	273
1679. May	15.	Tilton, Abigail, and Ralph Warner, ...	O. W. L.,	II.	408
1762. July	1.	Tilton, Peter, and Phebe Mills, ...	M. B.,	VI.	220
1665. April	22.	Tilton, Peter, and Rebeccah Brazier, ...	G. E.,	I.	113
1781. June	22.	Tilton, William, and Elizabeth Anderson, ..	M. B.,	XXXII.	96
1778. July	7.	Tilton, William, and Margaret Crannell, ...	"	XXV.	121
1781. Sept.	14.	Timen, Elizabeth, and Jean Cotheret, ...	"	XXXIII.	65
1761. Mar.	9.	Timms, Samuel, and Mary Vider, ...	"	IV.	92
1771. April	13.	Timoson, Peter, and Geertruy Creegier, ...	"	XVII.	56
1781. Nov.	14.	Timothy, Mary, and George Benison, ...	"	XXXIV.	32
1777. Feb.	8.	Timpany, Robert, and Sarah Clark, ...	"	XXIV.	26
1764. Aug.	3.	Timpson, Thomas, and Susannah Jacobs, ...	"	VIII.	274
1738. Oct.	8.	Timson, Thomas, and Hester Rousen, ...	"	I.	2
1738. Oct.	9.	Tines, Samuel, and Mary Brughman, ...	"	I.	11
1779. Dec.	6.	Tingill, Rebecca, and Christian Werner, ...	"	XXVIII.	161
1765. Oct.	5.	Tingley, Abigall, and William Malcolm, ...	"	IX.	291
1761. Feb.	9.	Tingley, Agnes, and Adolph Bras, Jr., ...	"	IV.	59
1764. Aug.	20.	Tingley, Elizabeth, and Samuel Hanshaw, ..	"	VIII.	288
1734. Mar.	4.	Tingley, Samuel, and Agnus Blank, ...	"	I.	5
1767. Nov.	6.	Tingley, Samuel, and Susannah Clem, ...	"	XII.	78
1737. Sept.	7.	Tinover, Sarah, and John Jansey, ...	"	I.	7
1773. July	19.	Tippet, Darkes, and Harman Rutgers, ...	"	XXI.	46

DATE.	NAMES.	RECORD.	VOL.	PAGE.
1770. Mar. 30.	Tippet, Martha, and Anthony Glean,	M. B.,	XXVII.	85
1763. June 9.	Tippet, Philena, and Ezekiel Archer,	"	· VII.	219
1775. April 21.	Tippey, Sarah, and Samuel Zeller,	"	XXIII.	15
1759. Aug. 11.	Tippit, Gilbert, and Susannah Clover,	"	II.	382
1783. Oct. 22.	Tire, Batey, and John Niper,	"	XL.	87
1767. Feb. 18.	Tisen, Mary, and William Lake,	"	XIV.	37
1765. Aug. 2.	Titchbourn, William, and Elizabeth Lawrence,	"	IX.	229
1761. Nov. 20.	Titis, Martha, and Samuel Brush,	"	V.	235
1778. July 11.	Titley, John, and Betty Boss,	"	XXV.	124
1782. Oct. 21.	Tittle, Mary, and John Teare,	"	XXXVII.	57
1766. July 28.	Titts, John, and Elizabeth Northen,	"	X.	64
1776. Mar. 8.	Titus, Abiel, and Ruth Wood,	"	XXIII.	280
1781. Nov. 14.	Titus, Ame, and Richard Leverich,	"	XXXIV.	33
1761. April 14.	Titus, Ann, and John Blank,	"	IV.	149
1757. April 7.	Titus, Anna, and Rem Underdanck,	"	I.	492
1771. Aug. 6.	Titus, Benjamin, and Ruth Bryan,	"	XVII.	154
1766. Oct. 11.	Titus, Catherine, and John Connell,	"	X.	120
1761. Nov. 12.	Titus, Charles, and Margaret Titus,	"	V.	212
1770. July 2.	Titus, Cretia, and Abraham Polhemus,	"	XVI.	132
1760. Dec. 3.	Titus, Elizabeth, and George Polhemus,	"	III.	452
1780. June 28.	Titus, Elizabeth, and John Meserole, Jr.,	"	XXIX.	100
1778. Dec. 14.	Titus, Elizabeth, and Peter Miller,	"	XXVI.	120
1759. Dec. 18.	Titus, Elizabeth, and Richard Hallett,	"	II.	548
1770. June 13.	Titus, Elizabeth, and Samson Crooker,	"	XVI.	109
1781. Nov. 27.	Titus, Frans, and Catharine Voortman,	"	XXXIV.	50
1772. Aug. 20.	Titus, Frans, and Mary Wikhoff,	"	XIX.	27
1783. Nov. 5.	Titus, Hannah, and Gabriel Duryee,	"	XL.	104
1779. Mar. 10.	Titus, Henry, and Jane Robbins,	"	XXVII.	64
1768. Nov. 5.	Titus, Henry, and Martha Simmons,	"	XIII.	226
1769. Mar. 4.	Titus, Jacob, and Martha Keen,	"	XIV.	45
1783. Feb. 28.	Titus, Jacob, and Ruth Rogers,	"	XXXVIII.	58
1758. Sept. 12.	Titus, Jane, and Isaac Conklin,	"	II.	14
1761. April 11.	Titus, Jannetie, and Thomas Skillman,	"	IV.	144
1779. Jan. 26.	Titus, Jemime, and John Boerum,	"	XXVIII.	203
1756. Nov. 30.	Titus, John, and Elizabeth Buerum,	"	I.	366
1780. Jan. 10.	Titus, John, and Mary Hannah Birdsell,	"	XXVIII.	190
1775. Sept. 12.	Titus, John, and Sarah Norton,	"	XXIII.	154
1770. Dec. 10.	Titus, Jonas, and Rhode Sammons,	"	XVI.	286
1761. June 12.	Titus, Jonathan, and Sarah Brash,	"	IV.	236
1775. April 5.	Titus, Joseph, and Martha Moore,	"	XXIII.	2
1772. Oct. 17.	Titus, Judah, and Luke Ramsen,	"	XIX.	74
1761. Nov. 12.	Titus, Margaret, and Charles Titus,	"	V.	212
1770. Mar. 24.	Titus, Margaret, and Isaac Robbins,	"	XVI.	39
1771. Oct. 18.	Titus, Martha, and Samuel Balding,	"	XVII.	213

DATE.	NAMES.	RECORD.	VOL.	PAGE.
1762. Mar. 29.	Titus, Mary, and Ezekiel Conckling,.......	M. B.,	VI.	458
1782. Sept. 17.	Titus, Mary, and Jonathan Williams, ...	"	XXXVII.	4
1761. Dec. 19.	Titus, Mary, and Richard Townsend, ...	"	V.	289
1765. Jan. 3.	Titus, Peter, and Elizabeth Mudge,........	"	IX.	4
1736. April 8.	Titus, Richard, and Mary Peters, ...	"	I.	1
1782. Sept. 10.	Titus, Ruth, and Samuel Titus, ...	"	XXXVI.	142
1773. Nov. 4.	Titus, Samuel, and Abigal Robbins, ...	"	XXII.	13
1782. Sept. 10.	Titus, Samuel, and Ruth Titus, ...	"	XXXVI.	142
1761. Feb. 25.	Titus, Samuel, and Ruth Townsend,.......	"	IV.	81
1767. Aug. 22.	Titus, Sarah, and George Norton, Jr.,......	"	XII.	21
1757. April 18.	Titus, Sarah, and Isaac Rushmore, ...	"	I.	503
1779. Oct. 22.	Titus, Sarah, and Jesse Dickinson, ...	"	XXVIII.	117
1764. Sept. 19.	Titus, Sarah, and Joseph Doty, ...	"	VIII.	317
1738. Mar. 27.	Titus, Susanah, and Nowell Furman, ...	"	I.	9
1760. Jan. 28.	Titus, Susannah, and Ephraim Mors, ...	"	III.	8
1762. Feb. 13.	Titus, Susannah, and Jonathan Furman,....	"	VI.	50
1759. April 14.	Titus, Susannah, and William Mucklevain,..	"	II.	241
1736. Sept. 22.	Titus, Timothy, and Mary Fitch,..........	"	I.	2
1783. June 21.	Titus, William, and Mary Hannah Birdsell, .	"	XXXIX.	65
1760. Feb. 27.	Titus, Zebulon, and Phebe Weekes,.... ...	"	III.	54
1759. Sept. 7.	Tobias, Christian, and Catharine Filkin, ...	"	II.	414
1782. July 16.	Tobias, Joseph, Jr., and Hannah Whippo, ..	"	XXXVI.	85
1781. June 14.	Tobias, Margery, and John Fleet, ...	"	XXXII.	86
1781. April 20.	Tobias, Ruth, and Samuel Walters,........	"	XXXII.	11
1777. Nov. 20.	Tobias, Thomas, and Jenny Van Kleeck, ...	"	XXII.	38
1780. April 25.	Tobin, James, and Catharine Lashore,......	"	XXIX.	35
1760. Feb. 7.	Tobin, Mary, and Samuel Gamble, ...	"	III.	25
1769. April 20.	Tobin, Peter, and Susannah Ackerman, ...	"	XIV.	78
1773. July 30.	Tobin, Set, and Hannah Best, ...	"	XXI.	54
1770. Oct. 15.	Tocloan, Mary, and Hendrick Scankel;.....	"	XVI.	214
1779. Nov. 1.	Tod, James, and Mary Hetly, ...	"	XXVIII.	125
1783. Nov. 13.	Todd, Anne, and Laurence Thuresson,......	"	XL.	112
1781. Oct. 15.	Todd, John, and Elizabeth Foster,.....,....	"	XXXIII.	102
1756. Sept. 6.	Todd, Margaret, and William Whetten,....	"	I.	287
1782. Mar. 4.	Toddy, Susannah, and John Johnson,......	"	XXXV.	73
1770. May 13.	Tody, Mary, and David Henderson, ...	"	XVII.	83
1775. Dec. 12.	Toffey, John, and Abigail Akin, ...	"	XXIII.	228
1780. July 28.	Toffey, Sarah, and Thomas Smith,........ .	"	XXIX.	123
1763. April 28.	Toffy, Mary, and Joseph Woolley, ...	"	VII.	162
1773. Sept. 14.	Tol, Sarah, and Stephanus Vealy,.........	"	XXI.	109
1758. Oct. 11.	Tole, Elizabeth, and Matthew Cowper,.....	"	II.	48
1762. Nov. 12.	Toll, Ann, and William Kittle,............	"	VI.	428
1775. June 16.	Toll, Daniel, and Susannah Switts, ...	"	XXIII.	67
1764. Oct. 5.	Toll, John, and Anna Catrina Vedder, ...	"	VIII.	334
1781. May 4.	Tollckimett, Johan, and Dorothy Morrison, .	"	XXXII.	31

DATE.		NAMES.	RECORD.	VOL.	PAGE.
1761. July	27.	Tolmie, Normand, and Phebe Barnes, ...	M. B.,	v.	10
1759. Mar.	6.	Tom, Christian, and John Driskill, ...	"	II.	210
1779. June	22.	Tom, Mary, and David Haviland, ...	"	XXVIII.	1
1773. Aug.	18.	Tom, Nathaniel, and Elizabeth R. Hicks,...	"	XXI.	71
1768. May	25.	Tom, Sarah, and Pepperell Bloodgood,.....	"	XIII.	113
1780. Dec.	9.	Tom, Thomas, and Catharine Farrington,...	"	XXX.	147
1768. June	24.	Tomkins, John, and Ann Montanye,.......	"	XIII.	137
1758. Oct.	27.	Tomkins, Jonathan Griffin, and Sarah Hyatt,	"	II.	70
1762. July	21.	Tomkins, Susannah, and Clement Place,....	"	VI.	250
1764. Jan.	30.	Tomlingson, James, and Catherene Legget, .	"	VIII.	44
1758. April	24.	Tomlinson, John, and Ann Giraud,........	"	I.	883
1779. April	20.	Tomlinson, Russel, and Agness Cortelyou,..	"	XXVII.	112
1761. Aug.	18.	Tompkins, Elisabeth, and Robert Crosby, ..	"	v.	48
1760. Sept.	4.	Tongue, William, and Dorothy Lyneal, ...	"	III.	283
1761. Jan.	23.	Tonkins, Susannah, and Benjamin Farrington,	"	IV.	27
1771. Nov.	23.	Tonnery, Sarah, and Joseph Haston, ...	"	XVII.	267
1770. April	6.	Tooker, Damarius, and Gerardus Hardenbrook, ...	"	XVI.	50
1670. June	20.	Tooker, Hannah,* and Richard Smith, Jr.,..	C. A.,	II.	550
1761. Sept.	11.	Tooker, William, and Mary Satturly,.....	M. B.,	v.	80
1762. Oct.	2.	Torn, Christopher, and Elizabeth Rynees, ..	"	VI.	343
1759. Dec.	19.	Torrell, Peter, and Jane McDonnick, ...	"	II.	551
1766. June	11.	Torry, James, and Elizabeth Van Embrie,..	"	X.	9
1759. Oct.	17.	Torry, John, and Jennett De Laney,.......	"	II.	462
1760. Nov.	12.	Totten, Anna, and William Place,.........	"	III.	406
1769. Aug.	29.	Totten, Elizabeth, and Gilbert Forbes,.....	"	XV.	92
1736. Mar.	4.	Totten, Hannah, and Richard Smith, ...	"	I.	5
1756. Sept.	3.	Totten, James, and Mariam Bedell,........	"	I.	282
1781. Sept.	15.	Totten, John, and Anne Vandeventer,.....	"	XXXIII.	67
1780. Dec.	20.	Totten, Joseph, and Mary Androvet, ...	"	XXX.	159
1761. June	29.	Totton, Jacob, and Rachel Van Cots, ...	"	IV.	267
1772. Jan.	31.	Totton, Mary, and Jacob Suydam,.........	"	XVIII.	24
1759. Sept.	15.	Totton, Sarah, and Procolus McCown,.....	"	II.	424
1779. April	10.	Totty, Ann, and Francis Wood,..........	"	XXVII.	101
1771. July	26.	Toung, Ann, and James Clark,...........	"	XVII.	145
1758. April	28.	Tourneur, Henry, and Margaret Blawfield,..	"	I.	889
1759. Aug.	3.	Tout, Robert, and Mary Alstyn, ...	"	II.	370
1769. July	17.	Tovow, Lettice, and Bartholemew Coxelter,	"	XIV.	154
1758. Feb.	9.	Tower, Joseph, and Susanah Spranger, ...	"	I.	815
1760. Dec.	5.	Towers, Catherine, and John Van Varck,...	"	III.	458
1761. July	9.	Towers, Jemima, and Daniel Salders, ...	"	IV.	291
1757. Jan.	15.	Towers, Joseph, and Janitje Duyckman,....	"	I.	414
1770. June	7.	Townsend, Ann, and Jeronimus Van Vorheis,	"	XVI.	105

* The name of the woman is not mentioned in the Record. It is taken from Thompson's History of Long Island, vol. ii., p. 452.

DATE.	NAMES.	RECORD.	VOL. . PAGE.
1777. Feb. 18.	Townsend, Ann, and Thomas Hanford, ...	M. B.,	xxv. 24
1781. June 4.	Townsend, Anna, and James Morgan,......	"	xxxii. 71
1758. May 30.	Townsend, Benjamín, and Elizabeth Weyman, ...	"	i. 915
1778. Oct. 23.	Townsend, Daniel, and Rebecca Ward, ...	"	xxvi. 67
1779. July 30.	Townsend, Deborah, and Peter R. Kissan,..	"	xxviii. 37
1782. April 29.	Townsend, Doborah, and Uriah Hoff,......	"	xxxv. 144
1769. Sept. 28.	Townsend, Edward, and Mary Stevens,....	"	xv. 47
1761. June 3.	Townsend, Elisabeth, and John McCoun,...	"	iv. 225
1775. Aug. 26.	Townsend, Elizabeth, and Lewis Carpenter,	"	xxiii. 135
1765. Aug. 1.	Townsend, Elizabeth, and Philip Pinkney,..	"	ix. 225
1771. Sept. 4.	Townsend, Esther, and Samuel Townsend, .	"	xvii. 174
1760. Jan. 31.	Townsend, Ethalinda, and Peter Underell,..	"	iii. 12
1777. Jan. 3.	Townsend, Hanah, and Joseph Green, ...	"	xxiv. 2
1776. Feb. 16.	Townsend, Hester, and William Thorn, ...	"	xxiii. 270
1762. Jan. 22.	Townsend, James, and Freelove Townsend Wilmot,............................	"	vi. 23
1757. Mar. 15.	Townsend, James, and Mary Hicks,.	"	i. 469
1775. June 28.	Townsend, Jane, and George Fowler, ...	"	xxiii. 80
1775. May 12.	Townsend, Jemima, and Tetus Tetus,......	"	xxiii. 34
1769. Oct. 23.	Townsend, John, and Jane Giew,.........	"	xv. 60
1767. July 31.	Townsend, John, and Judith Townsend, ...	"	xii. 4
1779. Oct. 18.	Townsend, John, and Sarah Birdsall, ...	"	xxviii. 115
1738. July 24.	Townsend, John, and Sarah Wright, ...	"	i. 10
1766. Oct. 20.	Townsend, John, and Susannah Morgan,...	"	x. 128
1763. April 8.	Townsend, Joseph, and Margaret Weekes, .	"	vii. 119
1775. Aug. 12.	Townsend, Jotham, and Deborah Kirk, ...	"	xxiii. 125
1767. July 31.	Townsend, Judith, and John Townsend, ...	"	xii. 4
1763. April 28.	Townsend, Latitia, and Benjamin Underhill,	"	vii. 149
1765. Mar. 20.	Townsend, Margaret, and Daniel Thorn,.. .	"	ix. 71
1763. Oct. 31.	Townsend, Margaret, and Stephen Sneden,.	"	vii. 413
1770. Oct. 18.	Townsend, Martha, and John Pasen, ...	"	xvi. 224
1763. Feb. 28.	Townsend, Mary, and James Burk,........	"	vii. 79
1738. June 20.	Townsend, Mary, and John Jackson, ...	"	i. 10
1762. June 11.	Townsend, Mary, and William Jones, Jr., ..	"	vi. 187
1760. Dec. 24.	Townsend, Merrybe, and Micajah Townsend,	"	iii. 491
1763. Dec. 23.	Townsend, Micajah, and Anne Frost,......	"	vii. 519
1760. Dec. 24.	Townsend, Micajah, and Merrybe Townsend,	"	iii. 491
1769. June 28.	Townsend, Nathaniel, and Martha Cornell, .	"	xiv. 134
1780. Aug. 10.	Townsend, Nelley, and Francis Stevenson,..	"	xxix. 138
1761. Feb. 14.	Townsend, Peter, and Hannah Hawkshurst,	"	iv. 64
1762. Jan. 25.	Townsend, Phebe, and Abel Noble, ...	"	vi. 26
1764. Mar. 17.	Townsend, Phebe, and Joseph Lawrence, ..	"	viii. 108
1781. Mar. 15.	Townsend, Phebe, and Samuel Talman, ...	"	xxxi. 71
1775. Nov. 30.	Townsend, Richard, and Abigal Willis, ...	"	xxiii. 224

DATE.		NAMES.	RECORD.	VOL.	PAGE.
1775. Aug.	2.	Townsend, Richard, and Deborah Underhill,	M. B.,	XXIII.	118
1781. April	20.	Townsend, Richard, and Mary Hewlitt, ...	"	.XXXII.	9
1761. Dec.	19.	Townsend, Richard, and Mary Titus, ...	"	V.	289
1770. Oct.	17.	Townsend, Richard, and Rosetta Seaman,..	"	XVI.	218
1765. July	30.	Townsend, Roger, and Keziah Gale,.......	"	IX.	223
1768. Nov.	12.	Townsend, Roseannah, and Daniel Cock,...	"	XIII.	233
1761. Feb.	25.	Townsend, Ruth, and Samuel Titus,.......	"	IV.	81
1770. Jan.	2.	Townsend, Samuel, and Elizabeth Smith, ..	"	XVI.	1
1771. Sept.	4.	Townsend, Samuel, and Esther Townsend,.	"	XVII.	174
1759. Nov.	3.	Townsend, Samuel, and Merriby Allen,....	"	II.	487
1773. Sept.	10.	Townsend, Samuel, and Sarah Horton, ...	"	XXI.	104
1773. July	5.	Townsend, Sarah, and Jaques Cortelyou,...	"	XXI.	29
1778. Feb.	7.	Townsend, Sarah, and William McCowen,..	"	XXV.	18
1764. Dec.	5.	Townsend, Silvanus, and Theodotia Frost,..	"	VIII.	438
173⅞. Feb.	7.	Townsend, Timothy, and Sarah Hulit, ...	"	I.	8
1773. Dec.	31.	Townshend, Elijah, and Mary Treadwell,...	"	XXII.	90
1763. May	2.	Townshend, Elizabeth, and Thomas Brown,	"	VII.	160
1773. Oct.	22.	Townshend, Martha, and Isaac Ward, ...	"	XXI.	146
1759. Feb.	26.	Townshend, Phillip, and Mary Winn,......	"	II.	202
1773. May	29.	Townshend, Temperance, and Elijah Cock, .	"	XX.	131
1763. June	6.	Tows, John, and Anne Van Ondar, ...	"	VII.	213
1778. Nov.	14.	Towse. Francis, and Susanah Frost, ...	"	XXVI.	87
1766. Sept.	15.	Towt, Robert, and Sarah Burdett,.........	"	X.	96
1783. Oct.	2.	Traford, Deborah, and Aaron White, ...	"	XL.	58
1757. July	9.	Trapaulier, Sarah, and Joseph Colly,.......	"	I.	587
1760. Dec.	19.	Traplager, Jane, and James Hendrie,......	"	III.	484
1767. Feb.	13.	Trappagar, Henry, and Jemima Duyckman,.	"	XI.	25
1762. April	19.	Travellier, Peter, and Mary Avery,........	"	VI.	115
1781. Mar.	13.	Travis, Elizabeth, and Robern Cunard,.....	"	XXXI.	70
1756. Dec.	20.	Travis, Hezekias, and Margaret McIntire, ..	"	I.	395
1758. Jan.	17.	Traux, Andries, and Elizabeth Van Vranke,	"	I.	787
1771. Dec.	11.	Treaddle, Phebe, and James Morgan, ...	"	XVII.	290
1773. June	3.	Treadwell, Edward, and Ann Morgan, ...	"	XX.	138
1782. May	22.	Treadwell, James, and Rachel Valentine,...	"	XXXVI.	17
1767. July	27.	Treadwell, Johannah, and Peter Stouten-burgh, ...	"	XII.	2
1666. Mar.	6.	Treadwell, John, and Elizabeth Starre, ...	O. W. L.,	II.	134
1773. Dec.	31.	Treadwell, Mary, and Elijah Townsend,....	M. B.,	XXII.	90
1763. Oct.	14.	Treddell, Mary, and Benjamin Stevens, ...	"	VII.	386
1773. Jan.	30.	Treddle, Phebe, and Thomas Woolley, ...	"	XX.	30
1762. Oct.	8.	Treddle, Samuel, and Dorothy Anderson, ..	"	VI.	354
1762. Nov.	24.	Tredwell, Benjamin, and Elizabeth Seabury,	"	VI.	450
1770. Feb.	8.	Tredwell, Hannah, and Daniel Phœnix, ...	"	XVI.	14
1769. Jan.	5.	Tredwell, John, and Mary Jackson, ...	"	XIV.	4
1755. Nov.	27.	Tredwell, John, and Peggy Cornell, ...	"	I.	217

DATE.	NAMES.	RECORD.	VOL.	PAGE.
1783. Sept. 11.	Tredwell, John, and Pheby Pell, ...	M. B.,	XL.	36
1763. Jan. 21.	Tredwell, Mary, and Ebenezer Haviland,...	"	VII.	27
1762. Mar. 15.	Tredwell, Phebe, and Samuel Searing,.....	"	VI.	68
1759. May 3.	Tredwell, Samuel, and Elizabeth Lispenard,.	"	II.	265
1764. Nov. 21.	Tredwell, Samuel, and Susannah Hewlett,..	"	VIII.	416
1765. Oct. 22.	Tredwell, Sarah, and Benjamin Hulsted,....	"	IX.	311
1761. Jan. 21.	Tredwell, Sarah, and Uriah Platt,.........	"	IV.	24
1783. June 12.	Tredwell, Susannah, and George Tucker,...	"	XXXIX.	53
1765. Oct. 23.	Tredwell, Thomas, and Ann Hazard, ...	"	IX.	314
1738. Dec. 14.	Tredwell, Timothy, and Mary Platt,.......	"	I.	12
1770. Feb. 15.	Tremain, Jonathan, and Abigail Stout,.....	"	XVI.	17
1783. May 30.	Trembles, Moses, and Elizabeth Parker,....	"	XXXIX.	29
1768. July 26.	Trempen, Jacob, and Annatje Trompbour,..	"	XIII.	165
1760. Nov. 3.	Tremper, Helena, and Abram Kip, ...	"	III.	392
1759. Jan. 19.	Tremper, Jacob, and Catherine Deal, ...	"	II.	159
1767. Mar. 2.	Tremper, Michael, and Leah Van Duesen,..	"	XI.	38
1773. Aug. 20.	Trenchard, Elisabeth, and Peter Ganter,....	"	XXI.	78
1762. Nov. 2.	Trepegar, Elizabeth, and William Shortell,..	"	VI.	406
1770. Nov. 13.	Treyner, Catherine, and Thomas Pepson,...	"	XVI.	249
1767. April 6.	Tribe, William, and Elenor Regan, ...	"	XI.	57
1738. July 25.	Triby, John, and Jane Edmondson,........	"	I.	10
1783. April 8.	Trigleth, Edward, and Barsheba Fuller, ...	"	XXXVIII.	87
1779. April 12.	Triglith, Sarah, and William Hargill, ...	"	XXVII.	106
1783. Mar. 21.	Trinder, James, and Elizabeth Withers,....	"	XXXVIII.	72
1768. April 8.	Tripp, John, and Hannah Hopkins,........	"	VI.	97
1768. July 26.	Trompbour, Annatje, and Jacob Trempen,..	"	XIII.	165
1772. July 10.	Trophauga, Catarene, and Peter Ratclift,...	"	XVIII.	164
1668. Aug. 17.	Trott, Susannah, and William Clarke,......	O. W. L.,	II.	223
1760. Sept. 10.	Trotter, Catharine, and Bernard Lintot,....	M. B.,	III.	308
1772. Aug. 31.	Trotter, Catherine, and John Jones, ...	"	XIX.	38
1760. Sept. 15.	Trotter, John, and Rebecca Crispel.........	"	III.	316
1771. Feb. 25.	Trotter, Mary, and John Walter Wendell, ..	"	XVII.	22
1780. Dec. 7.	Trotter, Peter, and Margaret Reid, ...	"	XXX.	142
1780. Sept. 27.	Trotter, Sarah, and William Branthwaite, ..	"	XXX.	44
1667. Sept. 28.	Trotter, William, and Alice Ebell,....	O. W. L.,	II.	185
1737. May 22.	Troup, Robert, and Elinor Bisset,.........	M. B.,	I.	6
1760. April 24.	Trout, Adam, and Ann Hutchens,.........	"	III.	123
1756. July 22.	Troy, Elizabeth, and Peter Martin,........	"	I.	260
1738. Sept. 5.	Truan, Antie, and Rycard Van Wrank, ...	"	I.	11
1771. June 7.	Truax, Abraham, and Elizabeth Van Sice,..	"	XVII.	105
1770. April 10.	Truax, Abraham, and Sarah Vedder, ...	"	XVI.	55
1765. July 17.	Truax, Christiana, and John Collins,.......	"	IX.	207
1761. Oct. 28.	Truax, Isaac, and Elizabeth Van Olinda, ...	"	V.	174
1770. May 26.	Truax, Margaret, and John Van Driesen,...	"	XVI.	96
1782. Sept. 3.	Truesdell, John, and Abigail Ward, ...	"	XXXVI.	136

DATE.	NAMES.	RECORD.	VOL. PAGE.
1760. April 24.	Truman, Catharine, and Thomas Jackson, ..	M. B.	III. 328
1765. Aug. 5.	Truman, Peter, and Elizabeth Harris,......	"	IX. 231
1773. May 24.	Truman, Peter, and Rebekah Montanye,....	"	XX. 122
1765. April 24.	Trumpole, Mary, and Simon Isaac Cole,....	"	IX. 107
1780. Aug. 9.	Trumpour, Paul, and Deborah Emery, ...	"	XXIX. 137
1761. Nov. 25.	Truxtun, Thomas, and Elizabeth Harrison, .	"	V. 248
1759. Sept. 25.	Tubbs, Mary, and Edward Dillen,.........	"	II. 432
1782. June 3.	Tucker, Debby, and Thomas Green, ...	"	XXXVI. 35
1783. July 3.	Tucker, Deborah, and Dennis Van Tuyl,....	"	XXXIX. 80
1772. Aug. 4.	Tucker, Elinor, and Samuel White,........	"	XIX. 11
1779. May 7.	Tucker, Elizabeth, and Robert Galbreath, ..	"	XXVII. 127
1783. Jan. 12.	Tucker, George, and Susannah Tredwell,...	"	XXXIX. 53
1782. Jan. 21.	Tucker, Joseph, and Caturah Davis, ...	"	XXXV. 26
1779. Jan. 23.	Tucker, Sarah, and Michael Hyer,.........	"	XXVIII. 5
1768. Mar. 21.	Tucker, Thomas, and Hannah Bartow,.....	"	XIII. 52
1770. July 14.	Tuckey, Elizabeth, and Jonathan Meredith,...........................	"	XVI. 140
1762. Dec. 18.	Tuckey, William, and Catharine Bussey, ...	"	VI. 487
1778. Aug. 22.	Tuften, Susanah, and Mark Mullen,........	"	XXVI. 10
1780. Sept. 23.	Tull, Joshua, and Mary Tharp,............	"	XXX. 38
1767. Jan. 2.	Tulle, Margaret, and John McClanahan,....	"	XI. 1
1782. Feb. 1.	Tullock, Peter, and Christian Douglass, ...	"	XXXV. 41
1782. June 14.	Tully, John, and Mary Barret,...........	"	XXXVI. 50
1781. July 28.	Tungate, Robert, and Sarah Berrow, ...	"	XXXIII. 13
1759. Nov. 19.	Tur Bose, John, and Jamime Green, ...	"	II. 504
1762. Dec. 16.	Turck, Cornelius, and Agnes Rapalje,......	"	VI. 482
1759. Jan. 13.	Turck, Lettey, and Andrew Elliott,........	"	II. 155
1764. Nov. 12.	Turck, Teuntje, and John Mahany,...	"	VIII. 404
1759. May 9.	Turell, Ebenezer, and Magdelena Bergen, ..	"	II. 273
1783. June 28.	Turett, Mary, and John Lockerman,.......	"	XXXIX. 70
1766. June 9.	Turk, Ahasuerus, and Magdalen Van Sice,..	"	X. 10
1774. Jan. 19.	Turk, Annamarytie, and Nicholas Kiersted,.	"	XXII. 110
1736. Sept. 1.	Turk, Annatie, and Gerrit Van Slyck, ...	"	I. 2
1738. Oct. 18.	Turk, Anne, and Victor Veeker,...	"	I. 11
1770. July 28.	Turk, Cornelius, and Mary Hazard, ...	"	XVI. 148
1773. April 29.	Turk, Cornelius, and Mary Moscholick,....	"	XX. 101
1765. Oct. 31.	Turk, Eleanor, and Samuel Jones,.........	"	IX. 339
1780. Jan. 31.	Turk, Elizabeth, and Benjamin Parker,.....	"	XXVIII. 205
1767. June 13.	Turk, Elizabeth, and Jacob Brouwer, Jr., ..	"	XI. 108
1768. Mar. 15.	Turk, Hannah, and Ichabod Higgins,......	"	XIII. 49
1764. Sept. 14.	Turk, Jacob, and Helena Low, ...	"	VIII. 308
1771. Oct. 25.	Turk, Jannetje, and William Schepmus,....	"	XVII. 224
1778. Jan. 22.	Turnbull, George, and Catherine Clopper, ..	"	XXIV. 18
1780. Mar. 7.	Turnbull, James, and Susannah Perry, ...	"	XXVIII. 218
1682. Feb. 5.	Turnecre, Daniel, and Ann Woodhull, ...	E.,	XXXIII. 36

400 NEW YORK MARRIAGES.

DATE.	NAMES.	RECORD.	VOL.	PAGE.
1772. Dec. 22.	Turner, Ann, and Silas Henrys,	M. B.,	XIX.	161
1738. May 27.	Turner, Anne, and John Peterson,	"	I.	9
1757. Nov. 27.	Turner, Catherine, and Daniel Waldron,	"	II.	518
1759. June 9.	Turner, Cornelius, and Penelope Peneur,	"	II.	317
1760. Feb. 9.	Turner, Francis, and Sarah Gray,	"	III.	27
1760. Feb. 26.	Turner, Jacob, and Agnetie Wagener,	"	III.	52
1780. Feb. 7.	Turner, Jane, and Nathaniel Cooper,	"	XXVIII.	209
1783. Nov. 8.	Turner, Jessee, and Catharine Beck,	"	XL.	109
1779. Feb. 20.	Turner, John, and Christian Moncrieff,	"	XXVII.	45
1782. June 23.	Turner, Levin, and Hannah Brown,	"	XXXVI.	65
1759. Aug. 30.	Turner, Margaret, and Richard Blake,	"	II.	401
1670. Mar. 2.	Turner, Martha, and Edward Hubbard,	C. A.,	II.	655
1782. Aug. 13.	Turner, Mary, and James McAlpine,	M. B.,	XXXVI.	106
1782. July 17.	Turner, Mary, and John Jakways,	"	XXXVI.	86
1762. May 27.	Turner, William, and Sarah Adams,	"	VI.	170
1759. June 21.	Turwilegen, Arantje, and Cornelius Schonmaker,	'	II.	334
1757. June 6.	Tusener, Mary, and Patrick McDonnell,	"	I.	553
1772. Aug. 5.	Tuthill, Hannah, and John Sweet,	"	XIX.	13
1782. Nov. 16.	Tweedle, Mary, and John Brevoort,	"	XXXVII.	82
1772. June 4.	Tweedy, Samuel, and Catherine Vredenburgh,	"	XVIII.	131
1757. Sept. 17.	Tweedy, Sarah, and Philip Cuyler,	"	I.	635
1738. Aug. 28.	Tweck, Neilie, and Lawrence Roome,	"	I.	10
1759. Dec. 31.	Twigg, Mary, and Thomas Clark,	"	II.	563
1777. Aug. 21.	Twine, Ann, and James Wiggan,	"	XXIV.	139
1753. April 16.	Tybout, Tunis, and Elizabeth Lamb,	"	I.	24
1763. Aug. 13.	Tylee, Nathaniel, and Hannah McDowall,	"	VII.	300
1767. Nov. 20.	Tylee, Rebecka, and David Branson,	"	XII.	89
1761. Jan. 6.	Tyler, David, and Sarah Smith,	"	IV.	3
1761. Nov. 12.	Tyler, Jacob, and Elisabeth Johnson,	"	V.	211
1782. Dec. 18.	Tyler, Joannah, and James Cave,	"	XXXVII.	125
1775. June 16.	Tyler, John, and Elizabeth Furman,	"	XXIII.	64
1762. April 30.	Tyms, Samuel, and Jane Van Patten,	"	VI.	138
1761. Feb. 13.	Tyrrel, Jane, and Lewis Pens,	"	IV.	61
1762. July 1.	Tyrrel, Mary, and John Hubbard,	"	VI.	221
1764. Jan. 27.	Tysen, David, and Alice Decker,	"	VIII.	40
1780. Dec. 30.	Tysen, John, and Mary Houseman,	"	XXX.	174
1764. Jan. 27.	Tysen, Martha, and Aron Dupuy,	"	VIII.	41
1783. May 9.	Tysen, Mary, and Hendrick Barger,	"	XXXIX.	6
1757. June 7.	Tytus, Frans, Jr., and Cornelia Duryee,	"	I.	554

U.

DATE.		NAMES.	RECORD.	VOL.	PAGE.
1777. Feb.	24.	Udall, Catherine, and Blackwell Smith, ...	M. B.,	XXIV.	34
1782. Mar.	11.	Udall, Daniel, and Katurah Carl,..........	"	XXXV.	85
1776. Mar.	16.	Udall, Thomas, and Susannah Valentine,...	"	XXIII.	285
1779. Mar.	27.	Ullick, Lanah, and Andrew Rode, ...	"	XXVII.	78
1757. April	7.	Underdanck, Rem, and Anna Titus, ...	"	I.	492
1771. Sept.	18.	Underdunk, Entye, and John Gasnar, ...	"	XVII.	185
1771. Dec.	11.	Underdunk, Mary, and John Riker, ...	"	XVII.	289
1772. Dec.	16.	Underdunk, Sarah, and Phillip Searvent,...	"	XIX.	156
1760. Jan.	31.	Underell, Peter, and Ethalinda Townsend,..	"	III.	12
1774. Feb.	22.	Underhill, Amos, and Mary Woodhull, ...	"	XXII.	133
1783. July	13.	Underhill, Anthony Lispenard, and Clarince Bartow,.............................	"	XXXIX.	90
1782. Jan.	24.	Underhill, Barruck, and Elisabeth Burr,....	"	XXXV.	31
1767. Sept.	2.	Underhill, Benjamin, and Elizabeth Bernet,.	"	XII.	25
1768. Dec.	16.	Underhill, Benjamin, and Elizabeth Bonnet,	"	XIII.	266
1763. April	28.	Underhill, Benjamin, and Latitia Townsend,	"	VII.	149
1756. Jan.	6.	Underhill, Daniel, and Sarah Frost,........	"	I.	407
1775. Aug.	2.	Underhill, Deborah, and Richard Townsend,	"	XXIII.	118
1781. Nov.	23.	Underhill, Edmund, and Frances Carpenter,.	"	XXXIV.	57
1757. Dec.	10.	Underhill, Elizabeth, and Gilbert Drake, ...	"	I.	734
1781. Sept.	21.	Underhill, Elizabeth, and John B. Coles,...	"	XXXIII.	72
1779. July	19.	Underhill, Elizabeth, and Thaddeus Avery,.	"	XXVIII.	25
1759. Mar.	14.	Underhill, Helena, and James Morgan, ...	"	II.	215
1761. Mar.	4.	Underhill, Israel, and Abigail Lispenard, ...	"	IV.	90
1760. April	17.	Underhill, Jacob, and Catharine Willets, ...	"	III.	113
1777. Nov.	24.	Underhill, Jonathan, and Hanah Hyatt,....	"	XXIV.	184
1772. April	16.	Underhill, Lancaster, and Eudocia Hunt,...	"	XVIII.	80
1761. Jan.	9.	Underhill, Margaret, and Robert Angues,...	"	IV.	6
1757. April	7.	Underhill, Martha, and Benjamin Smith, ...	"	I.	490
1778. Jan.	26.	Underhill, Martha, and Stephen Lines,.....	"	XXV.	12
1782. Nov.	18.	Underhill, Mary, and Horatio Wright,.....	"	XXXVII.	86
1782. Nov.	27.	Underhill, Sarah, and Daniel Burr, ...	"	XXXVII.	94
1761. Sept.	30.	Underhill, Sarah, and Noah Bishop,.......	"	V.	110
1761. Oct.	14.	Underhill, Sarah, and Pen Frost,..........	"	V.	135
1779. Nov.	25.	Underhill, Thomas, and Elizabeth Thorne,..	"	XXVIII.	146
1778. June	17.	Ungerer, Nicodemus, and Mary Smelzel, ...	"	XXV.	109
1738. May	11.	Updike, John, and Mary Bregaw,.........	"	I.	9
1760. Dec.	29.	Upham, John, Jr., and Weamthy Estilltine,.	"	III.	495
1764. Aug.	23.	Upham, Mary, and Peter Van Valkenburgh,	"	VIII.	292
1736. May	1.	Upton, Thomas, and Anne Lupton,........	"	I.	1
1779. Nov.	10.	Uragden, Shadrick, and Mary Davis, ...	"	XXVIII.	135

51

DATE.	NAMES.	RECORD.	VOL. PAGE.
1780. Jan. 20.	Ustick, Elizabeth, and Lawrence Hartshorne,	M. B.,	XXVIII. 199
1764. June 9.	Ustick, Henry, and Elizabeth Brower, ...	"	VIII. 222
1772. Dec. 29.	Ustick, Thomas, and Hannah Whitear,.....	"	XIX. 165
1757. June 15.	Ustick, William, and Susannah Pelletreau,..	"	I. 563
1763. Sept. 20.	Utt, Judith, and Barrent Speer, ...	"	VII. 351
1761. May 29.	Utt, Mary, and Thomas Johnston, ...	"	IV. 195
1764. June 2.	Utten, Hannah, and William Stead, ...	"	VIII. 205
1762. July 21.	Uzza, Judith, and Isaac Labagh, ...	"	VI. 248

V.

1758. Sept. 5.	Vail, Daniel, and Else Maddox,...........	"	II. 4
1762. April 22.	Vail, Esther, and Rueben Garman, ...	"	VI. 126
1759. Feb. 26.	Vail, Hannah, and David Pugsly, ...	"	II. 203
1783. April 1.	Vail, Robert, and Mary Cogill,............	"	XXXVIII. 84
1764. Mar. 23.	Valantine, William, and Ruth Smith,......	"	VIII. 116
1783. July 25.	Valentine, Abigail, and Selah Wood, ...	"	XXXIX. 100
1776. Jan. 5.	Valentine, Abigal, and Richard Manee,.....	"	XXIII. 260
1773. Nov. 24.	Valentine, Abraham, and Jenny Oder,.....	"	XXII. 42
1759. Mar. 6.	Valentine, Ann, and Obadiah Vallentine,...	"	II. 211
1778. Feb. 6.	Valentine, Caleb, and Ann North,..... ...	"	XXV. 17
1762. Jan. 22.	Valentine, Charles, and Mary Frost,.......	"	VI. 24
1674. Mar. 10.	Valentine, Deborah, and William Foster,...	W. O. P.,	III. 60
1777. Nov. 15.	Valentine, Elizabeth, and John Freeman,...	M. B.,	XXIV. 182
1763. June 13.	Valentine, Jacob, and Sineche Teller,......	"	VII. 227
1762. Aug. 5.	Valentine, Jane, and Garardus Vermilya,...	"	VI. 265
1753. July 28.	Valentine, Jonathan, and Elizabeth Wright,.	"	I. 80
1767. Sept. 15.	Valentine, Mary, and Eliphilet Stratton, ...	"	XII. 33c
1758. Dec. 2.	Valentine, Mathew, and Applony Willson, .	"	II. 111
1763. Nov. 30.	Valentine, Nathan, and Sarah Carle,.......	"	VII. 483
1759. Mar. 6.	Valentine, Obadiah, and Ann Vallentine,...	"	II. 211
1769. Nov. 23.	Valentine, Phebe, and Thomas Ireland, ...	"	XV. 102
1783. Sept. 7.	Valentine, Philip, and Jane Willis,........	"	XL. 28
1782. May 22.	Valentine, Rachel, and James Treadwell,...	"	XXXVI. 17
1762. April 14.	Valentine, Ruth, and William Crooker, ...	"	VI. 109
1777. June 12.	Valentine, Sarah, and George Chapman, ...	"	XXIV. 102
1761. Feb. 17.	Valentine, Sarah, and Joseph Hicks,.......	"	IV. 67
1763. July 14.	Valentine, Sarah, and Levi Hunt, ...	"	VII. 264
1758. Mar. 10.	Valentine, Sarah, and William Crooker,.. .	"	I. 842
1776. Mar. 16.	Valentine, Susannah, and Thomas Udall,...	"	XXIII. 285
1738. Dec. 14.	Valet, Nicholas, and Judah Prossing, ...	"	I. 12
1762. Aug. 26.	Valing, Catharine, and Aron Smith, ...	"	VI. 292
1763. May 19.	Valintine, Peter, and Mary Willse, ...	"	VII. 192
1757. Feb. 2.	Valk, Christian, and Jane Delanoy,........	"	I. 432

DATE.	NAMES.	RECORD.	VOL.	PAGE.
1768. June 14.	Valk, Christina, and David Van Plank, ...	M. B.,	XIII.	127
1782. Nov. 17.	Vallance, John, and Elisabeth Southard, ...	"	XXXVII.	84
1765. June 13.	Valleau, Catherine, and James Lakerman, ..	"	IX.	167
1761. April 7.	Valleau, Isaiah, and Mary Moore,...... ...	"	IV.	136
1760. Dec. 12.	Valleau, Jane, and James Kip, Jr.,........	"	III.	473
1770. Feb. 23.	Valleau, Magdalen, and William Charda-voyne,...............................	"	XVI.	23
1769. Jan. 31.	Vallentine, Jacob, and Elizabeth Rushmore,.	"	XIV.	24
1779. Jan. 30.	Vallentine, Obadiah, and Rachel Walters,...	"	XXVII.	32
1782. May 2.	Vallentine, Peter, and Ann Stives, ...	"	XXXV.	147
1767. June 5.	Vallentine, Phebe, and Obadiah Seaman,...	"	XI.	105
1762. Dec. 14.	Vallintine, Mary, and William Butler,......	"	VI.	478
1761. Sept. 18.	Van Aelstyn, Abraham, and Maritee Van Alen,..............................	"	V.	87
1760. Sept. 17.	Van Aelstyn, Peter, and Maritie Conyn,...	"	III.	317
1773. Sept. 1.	Van Aernam, Abraham J., and Annete Bo-gert,....................................	"	XXI.	93
1765. June 17.	Van Aernam, Aeltje, and John Groesbeck,..	"	IX.	173
1757. Oct. 27.	Van Aernam, Jacob, and Annatje Van Vran-ken, ...	"	I.	683
1757. Oct. 27.	Van Aernam, Jacob, Jr., and Catrina Banker,	"	I.	684
1766. Sept. 27.	Van Alen, Abraham, and Catherine Van Buren, ...	"	X.	111
1771. Feb. 18.	Van Alen, Abraham E., and Mary Fryen-moet,...............................	"	XVII.	18
1760. June 23.	Van Alen, Alida, and Peter S. Van Alstine,.	"	XIV.	128
1752. Nov. 28.	Van Alen, Annanetje, and Johannis Vos-burgh, ...	"	I.	18
1752. Nov. 28.	Van Alen, Catherine, and Lucas Wingard,..	"	I.	17
1773. Nov. 30.	Van Alen, Elberty, and Jacobus Hogeboom,	"	XXII.	55
1775. May 31.	Van Alen, Elizabeth, and Derick Gardenier,	"	XXIII.	50
1771. July 15.	Van Alen, Garret, and Engeltie Van Al-stine, ...	"	XVII.	132
1761. Feb. 23.	Van Alen, Garret, and Marytie Oosterhout,.	"	IV.	75
1761. April 21.	Van Alen, Hendrick, and Susannah Winne,.	"	IV.	157
1767. Nov. 24.	Van Alen, Johannes I., and Mary Goes,....	"	XII.	97
1758. Mar. 18.	Van Alen, John, and Annatje Herkimer,...	"	I.	856
1767. Nov. 24.	Van Alen, John, and Catherine Clopper, ...	"	XII.	95
1771. April 30.	Van Alen, John E., and Ann Fryenmoet, ..	"	XVII.	72
1772. Oct. 30.	Van Alen, Lucas, and Hillitye Vosburgh, ..	"	XIX.	95
1761. Sept. 18.	Van Alen, Maritie, and Abraham Van Ael-styn,................................	"	V.	87
1766. Sept. 29.	Van Alen, Mary, and Peter Wetbeck, ...	"	X.	110
1775. Sept. 6.	Van Alen, Mary L., and Barent Vosburgh, .	"	XXIII.	148
1769. Oct. 24.	Van Alen, Stephen, and Angeltie Witbeck,.	"	XV.	63

DATE.	NAMES.	RECORD.	VOL. PAGE.
1768. Oct. 4.	Van Allan, Catherine, and Abraham Van Alstile,......	M. B.,	XIII. 203
1776. Jan. 27.	Van Allen, Andrew, and Ann De Bevois,..	"	XXIII. 255
1763. June 30.	Van Allen, Catrina, and Peter Van Ness,...	"	VII. 251
1765. Sept. 10.	Van Allen, Jacobus, Jr., and Christina Van Bueren,............................	"	IX. 259
1761. Jan. 6.	Van Allen, Jane, and Abraham Lyle,......	"	IV. 5
1761. Oct. 15.	Van Allen, John, and Christina Van Dyke,.	"	V. 142
1762. Dec. 29.	Van Allen, John, and Margaret Koolaback,.	"	VI. 501
1764. May 11.	Van Allen, Lena, and Jacobus Vander Pool,	"	VIII. 186
1764. Oct. 23.	Van Allen, Stephen, and Rachael Huyck, ..	"	VIII. 370
1769. Nov. 13.	Van Alnor, Alabart, and Gysbert Sharp,....	::	XV. 91
1757. Dec. 29.	Van Als, Hester, and Allin Elsom, ...	"	I. 758
1762. Dec. 29.	Van Alst, Catharine, and Henry Jacobs, ...	"	VI. 508
1767. Sept. 29.	Van Alst, Catherine, and Abraham Brakaw,	"	XII. 48
1763. Mar. 4.	Van Alst, Hannah, and Samuel Waldron, Jr.,	"	VII. 89
1762. June 8.	Van Alst, Jane, and Charles Hardenberg, ..	"	VI. 183
1759. Oct. 18.	Van Alst, John, and Latie Van Alst, ...	"	II. 463
1759. June 8.	Van Alst, John, and Lettia Van Alst,......	"	II. 312
1759. Oct. 18.	Van Alst, Latie, and John Van Alst, ...	"	II. 463
1763. June 16.	Van Alst, Latitia, and Josiah Ferris,.......	"	VII. 231
1759. June 8.	Van Alst, Lettia, and John Van Alst,......	"	II. 312
1761. Dec. 24.	Van Alst, Margaret, and John Parsall, ...	"	V. 299
1771. May 11.	Van Alstein, Janetie, and William Winne, Jr.,	"	XVII. 82
1768. Oct. 4.	Van Alstile, Abraham, and Catherine Van Allan, ...	"	XIII. 203
1773. Nov. 8.	Van Alstin, Jonas, and Sarah Vander Pool,.	"	XXII. 16
1772. Dec. 1.	Van Alstine, Alexander, and Sarah Widbeek,	"	XIX. 139
1771. July 15.	Van Alstine, Engeltie, and Garret Van Alen, ...	"	XVII. 132
1763. June 23.	Van Alstine, Peter S., and Alida Van Alen,	"	XIV. 128
1763. April 28.	Van Alstyn, Abraham, and Engeltje Slingerland, ...	"	VII. 148
1768. Feb. 15.	Van Alstyn, Cathalina, and Gerret A. Lansing,	"	XIII. 37
1768. Feb. 23.	Van Alstyn, Emmetje, and Samuel Tenbroeck,	"	XIII. 44
1761. June 29.	Van Alstyn, Mary, and Philip Van Alstyn,.	"	IV. 268
1761. June 29.	Van Alstyn, Philip, and Mary Van Alstyn,.	"	IV. 268
1761. April 10.	Van Alstyn, Sarah, and Robert Hoffman, ..	"	IV. 143
1762. Sept. 17.	Van Alstyn, William, and Catharine Kinnickerbacker, ...	"	VI. 320
1767. Sept. 24.	Van Alstyn, Wynant, and Margaret Risedurpe, ...	"	XII. 44
1773. July 16.	Van Alstyne, Abraham A., and Catlyna Van Ness, ...	"	XXI. 40
1775. July 7.	Van Alstyne, Eve, and Leonard Witbeeck,.	"	XXIII. 88

DATE.		NAMES.	RECORD.	VOL. PAGE.
1775. July	28.	Van Alstyne, Heletje, and Abraham Van Hoesen,	M. B.,	XXIII. 110
1775. Sept.	21.	Van Alstyne, Jacob, and Annatie Lansingh,	"	XXIII. 162
1763. Sept.	20.	Van Alstyne, John, and Lena Sharp,	"	VII. 344
1755. Sept.	23.	Van Alstyne, Lambert, and Kalleticot Ousterhout,	"	I. 182
1772. July	15.	Van Alstyne, Leonard, and Elizabeth Gose,.	"	XVIII. 167
1767. Nov.	6.	Van Alstyne, Mary, and Augustinus Scharp,.	"	XII. 77
1772. Oct.	23.	Van Alstyne, Mary, and John Paterson, ...	"	XIX. 90
1775. May	1.	Van Alstyne, Piertje, and Peter Deforeest, .	"	XXIII. 19
1780. Dec.	16.	Van Alts, Carie, and William Parsell.	"	XXX. 154
1737. Dec.	27.	Vaname, Simon, and Elizabeth Garrison,...	"	I. 8
1761. April	11.	Van Anden, Esther, and John Storm,	"	IV. 147
1761. April	18.	Van Anden, Jane, and Jaen Vandervoort,..	"	IV. 154
1769. Mar.	25.	Van Ander, Catherine, and Peter Allburtus,	"	XIV. 60
1769. Nov.	2.	Van Ander, Elsie, and Lambert Vander Voort,	"	XV. 75
1759. Oct.	29.	Van Antwarp, Catharina, and John Rikey, .	"	II. 478
1772. July	8.	Van Antwerp, Anna, and John Arksen, ...	"	XVIII. 158
1764. Oct.	18.	Van Antwerp, Arent, and Hester Cregier,..	"	VIII. 361
1772. Oct.	22.	Van Antwerp, Daniel, and Gerritje Widbeeck,	"	XIX. 86
1759. Sept.	7.	Van Antwerp, Harrejantie, and Lenck Corner,	"	II. 412
1761. Nov.	20.	Van Antwerp, Mary, and Orre Le Grange, .		V. 237
1761. Oct.	21.	Van Antwerp, Simon, and Mariah Denbagh,	"	V. 157
1766. July	14.	Van Antwerpen, Daniel, and Dirckie Winne,	"	X. 49
1761. Nov.	16.	Van Antwerpen, Elisabeth, and John B. Wendell,	"	V. 224
1765. July	8.	Van Antwerpen, Sarah, and John Bradt,...	"	IX. 196
1771. Feb.	23.	Van Antwerpen, Simon Jansen, and Helena Veedder,	"	XVII. 21
1758. Mar.	11.	Van Arder, Hannah, and Peter Moulton, ..	"	I. 843
1761. May	29.	Van Arnem, Anne, and Isaac Lansing,	"	IV. 212
1757. Nov.	9.	Van Arnem, Hannah, and Thomas Isbuster,	"	I. 700
1777. Dec.	22.	Van Assendelff, William, and Mary Perry, .	"	XXIV. 203
1763. June	8.	Van Auke, Peter, and Rachel Sleght,	"	VII. 217
1782. Nov.	29.	Vanauly, Ann, and George De Bevoise,....	"	XXXVII. 97
1776. April	18.	Van Avery, Ryneer, and Rebecca Deforrest,	"	XXIII. 297
1738. Nov.	11.	Van Banthonsen, Garat, and Frances Lewis,	"	I. 11
1772. June	3.	Van Banthousen, Cornelia, and Obadiah Lansingh,	"	XVIII. 130
1762. June	22.	Van Beaven, Annatje, and Volkert Wijetbeck,	"	VI. 202
1639. Sept.	29.	Van Beets, Maritje Frans, and Tomas de Conine,	A. R.,	II. 67

DATE.		NAMES.	RECORD.	VOL. PAGE.
1759. Feb.	19.	Van Bentheuysen, Barent, and Gertruy Halenbeck, ...	M. B.,	II. 197
1759. April	9.	Van Bentheuysen, Jacob, and Rachel Van Vreedenbergh, ...	"	II. 237
1762. Aug.	5.	Van Benthuysen, Baltus, and Sarah Vielen,	"	VI. 266
1756. Oct.	9.	Van Benthuysen, Christiena, and Barent Lewis, ...	"	I. 323
1767. Sept.	21.	Van Benthuysen, Jacob, and Lillis Forryster,	"	XII. 39
1761. Nov.	20.	Van Bergen, Anthony, and Mary Salisbury,	"	V. 236
1766. June	23.	Van Bergen, Elenor, and Martin Van Bergen, Jr., ...	"	X. 25
1771. Nov.	22.	Van Bergen,Elizabeth, and Hermanus Cuyler,	"	XVII. 263
1763. Nov.	11.	Van Bergen, Henry, and Elinor Salsbury,..	"	VII. 444
1766. June	23.	Van Bergen, Martin, Jr., and Elenor Van Bergen, ...	"	X. 25
1765. Aug.	27.	Van Bergen, Nancy, and Isaac Van Volkenbury, ...	"	IX. 249
1760. Nov.	11.	Van Bergen, Neltie, and Henry Outhout, ..	"	III. 401
1768. Dec.	13.	Vanbergen, Peter, and Christina Weaver, ..	"	XIII. 261
1765. Sept.	10.	Van Beuren, Christina, and Jacobus Van Allen, Jr., ...	"	IX. 259
1763. June	10.	Van Beuren, Harman, and Eva Van Slyeck,	"	VII. 221
1779. Jan.	19.	Van Beuren, James, and Else Lott,........	"	XXVII. 18
1782. Aug.	21.	Van Beuren, John, and Sarah Van Duyn,..	"	XXXVI. 116
1760. April	26.	Van Beuren, John M., and Maria Bries,....	"	III. 126
1777. April	27.	Van Beuren, Magdalen, and George Hogg, .	"	XXIV. 75a
1782. Feb.	14.	Vanbeuren, Mary, and Peter Heaton,......	"	XXXV. 55
1773. Sept.	6.	Van Beuren, Philip, and Annatie Hoffman,.	"	XXI. 100
1773. June	8.	Van Beverhoudt, Margaret, and Thomas Duncan,.............................	"	XX. 139
1772. Nov.	21.	Van Beverhoute, Mary, and James Barclay,	"	XIX. 122
1757. Dec.	10.	Van Blaercum, Rebeccah, and Henry Stanton,	"	I. 733
1770. Nov.	7.	Van Blarcum, Marrietje, and Andrew Van Orden, ...	"	XVI. 241
1781. Dec.	28.	Vanblarkam, Sarah, and John Purdy, ...	"	XXXIV. 109
1764. Aug.	6.	Van Bomel, Leonard, and Antje Sprung,...	"	VIII. 275
1783. Oct.	7.	Van Bomlen, Ann, and Mathias Luyster,...	"	XL. 67
1763. May	13.	Van Bommell, Elizabeth, and Henry Ellis, ..	"	VII. 184
1764. April	12.	Van Bommell, Hilah, and James Cooper,...	"	VIII. 152
1782. June	1.	Van Boskerk, Lourens, and Cathaline Bonta,.	"	XXXVI. 33
1738. Aug.	16.	Van Bossom, Catherine, and Robert Benson,	"	I. 10
1763. Nov.	2.	Van Brokle, James, and Agnes Bennet, ...	"	VII. 424
1760. Jan.	3.	Van Brunt, Andrew, and Eanquelty Rapelye,	"	II. 566
1756. June	21.	Van Brunt, Catherine, and Daniel Hendrickson, ...	"	I. 242

DATE.	NAMES.	RECORD.	VOL.	PAGE.
1782. Nov. 23.	Van Brunt, Cornelius, and Jean Adriance,..	M. B.,	xxxvii.	92
1775. Nov. 14.	Van Brunt, Elizabeth, and George Bevois,..	"	xxiii.	208
1759. Dec. 11.	Vanbrunt, Elizabeth, and Hendrick Johnson,	"	ii.	537
1769. July 1.	Van Brunt, Elizabeth, and Nicholas Van Dycke,..............................	"	xiv.	139
1775. June 14.	Van Brunt, Hannah, and John Blake,......	"	xxiii.	60
1775. May 25.	Van Brunt, Jaques, and Maria Johnson,....	"	xxiii.	45
1764. Dec. 19.	Van Brunt, Joost, and Elisabeth Wortman,.	"	viii.	459
1757. June 8.	Van Brunt, Joost, and Lydia Griggs, ...	"	i.	555
1757. June 19.	Van Brunt, Lena, and Richard Prest, ...	"	i.	593
1769. Jan. 20.	Van Brunt, Manica, and George Neefus,....	"	xiv.	16
1737. April 7.	Vanbrunt, Maria, and Joris Lott,..........	"	i.	5
1778. June 13.	Van Brunt, Maria, and Robert Chesley,....	"	xxv.	101
1779. April 6.	Van Brunt, Maritie, and Robert Magaw, ...	"	xxvii.	95
1768. Dec. 19.	Van Brunt, Nicholas, and Catherine Nafius,.	"	xiii.	267
1779. Dec. 20.	Van Brunt, Nicholas, and Magdalen Van Nuys, ...	"	xxviii.	174
1783. Mar. 4.	Van Brunt, Nicholas, and Mary Emmons,..	"	xxxviii.	61
1757. June 8.	Van Brunt, Rutger, and Mary Cortelyou, ..	"	i.	556
1782. May 27.	Van Brunt, Rutgert, and Abigail Vander Bilt,	"	xxxvi.	25
1782. June 10.	Vanbrunt, Rutgert, and Lametje Barraga, ..	"	xxxvi.	47
1760. June 18.	Van Brunt, Sarah, and Court Van Voorhease, ...	"	iii.	190
1766. Sept. 29.	Van Bueren, Ariantie, and Johannes Van Valkenbergh, ...	"	x.	114
1756. Dec. 24.	Van Bueren, Beekman, and Elizabeth Gilbert,	"	i.	398
1773. Aug. 28.	Van Bueren, Catharine, and John Hilton, ..	"	xxi.	89
1761. Sept. 30.	Van Bueren, Frans, and Johanna Van Slieck, ...	"	v.	108
1772. May 19.	Vanbueren, Gose, and Meritie E. Alstyne,..	"	xviii.	112
1738. Aug. 30.	Vanbueren, Hendrick, and Gertruyt Wilbeek,	"	i.	11
1761. Oct. 6.	Van Bueren, Magdelain, and William Schermerhorn, ...	"	v.	127
1764. Jan. 21.	Van Bueren, Mary, and Guilliam Varick,...	"	viii.	28
1768. June 11.	Vanbueren, Mary, and Lucas Salisbury,....	"	xiii.	126
1766. July 13.	Van Bueren, Peter, and Catherine Quackenboss, ...	"	xi.	133
1761. Oct. 3.	Van Bueren, Peter, and Janneka Van Salsberg, ...	"	v.	119
1768. Feb. 1.	Van Bueren, Peter, and Margaret Halenbake, ...	"	xiii.	26
1772. Jan. 13.	Van Bueren, Tobias, and Albertie Hueick,..	"	xx.	8
1783. Jan. 30.	Vanbumlen, Jane, and Benjamin Bennett,..	"	xxxviii.	32
1761. Aug. 25.	Van Bunscoten, Cathalintie, and Isaac Conkling, ...	"	v.	56

DATE.	NAMES.	RECORD.	VOL. PAGE.
1765. Oct. 1.	Van Bunscouten, Sarah, and Abraham Duryea,	M. B.,	IX. 283
1757. Oct. 14.	Van Buren, Abigail, and Jacobus Abeel, ...	"	I. 670
1776. April 17.	Van Buren, Annanitia, and Nanning Vissier,	"	XXIII. 296
1766. Sept. 27.	Van Buren, Catherine, and Abraham Van Alen,	"	X. 111
1758. Nov. 22.	Van Buren, Cornelius, and Majeka Hun, ...	"	II. 102
1757. Dec. 2.	Van Buren, Ephraim, and Catalintje Van Volkenburgh,	"	I. 722
1765. Feb. 4.	Van Buren, Garret, and Mary Woodbeek, ..	"	IX. 43
1773. Dec. 24.	Van Buren, Hendrickje, and Jacob Pruyn, ..	"	XXII. 87
1766. Nov. 15.	Van Buren, Hendrickie, and John H. Beekman,	"	X. 165
1761. Sept. 5.	Van Buren, Hendrickie, and Martin Van Buren,	"	V. 68
1775. Aug. 14.	Van Buren, Johannes, and Catharine Vanderpool,	"	XXIII. 126
1771. Feb. 4.	Van Buren, John, and Littish Smith, ...	"	XVII. 13
1755. Nov. 25.	Van Buren, Judith, and Tobias Ten Eyck, ..	"	I. 216
1761. Sept. 5.	Van Buren, Martin, and Hendrickie Van Buren,	"	V. 68
1765. Feb. 4.	Van Buren, Mary, and Jacob Van Schaick, .	"	IX. 44
1759. April 2.	Van Buren, Mase, and Cathalyna Van Valkenburgh,	"	II. 232
1771. Sept. 12.	Van Buren, Peter, and Dorothy Fryenmoet,	"	XVII. 183
1738. Aug. 10.	Van Buren, Rachel, and Anthon Schuyler, .	"	I. 10
1762. Dec. 22.	Van Bursen, Abigail, and John McCarter, ..	"	VI. 494
1769. Nov. 13.	Vanbury, Elizabeth, and Garret Ryckman, .	"	XV. 89
1770. Aug. 9.	Van Bury, Ephraim, and Margaret Holland,	"	XVI. 156
1770. July 12.	Van Bury, Mary, and Henry Lion, ...	"	XVI. 138
1782. Jan. 14.	Van Buskerk, Abraham, and Hetty Kingsland,	"	XXXV. 17
1738. Oct. 14.	Van Buskerk, Hilie, and John Roll, ...	"	I. 11
1774. Feb. 5.	Van Buskerk, John, Jr., and Jane Van Horne,	"	XXII. 122
1738. Sept. 4.	Van Buskerks, Katherine, and Staats De Groots,	"	I. 11
1782. Mar. 21.	Van Buskirk, Sarah, and Richard Combauld,	"	XXXV. 93
1782. Dec. 21.	Van Buskirk, Silvester, and Mary Lowrear, .	"	XXXVII. 128
1772. Oct. 17.	Van Bussgarrick, Margaret, and John Vandewater,	"	XIX. 75
1761. Aug. 6.	Vance, Elenor, and David Carmick, ...	"	V. 28
1762. Jan. 30.	Vance, James, and Elizabeth Craven, ...	"	VI. 31
1771. Jan. 8.	Vance, John, and Mary Perry, ...	"	XVII. 3
177-. Oct. 7.	Vance, Mary, and John Harris, ...	"	XXVI. 49
1779. Dec. 31.	Van Cleaf, Ann, and Joseph Payne, ...	"	XXVIII. 184
1783. July 4.	Van Cleaf, Cornelius, and Ann Daryea, ...	"	I. 70

DATE.	NAMES.	RECORD.	VOL.	PAGE.
1767. May 12.	Van Cleaf, Elizabeth, and Abraham Egberts,	M. B.,	XI.	83
1775. Sept. 2.	Van Cleeck, Sarah, and Simeon Frear,.....	"	XXIII.	145
1771. Dec. 11.	Van Cleef, Hendrick, and Ide Williamson,..	"	XVII.	287
1768. June 20.	Van Cleef, Phebe, and Jacobus Van Deventer,	"	XIII.	133
1777. Jan. 3.	Van Clef, John, and Mary Van Dyck, ...	"	XXIV.	6
1761. Sept. 8.	Van Clefe, Daniel, and Martha Marshall, ...	"	V.	75
1764. Nov. 8.	Van Cleff, Garrit, and Jamima Cooper,.....	"	VIII.	395
1775. July 24.	Van Cleft, Cornelius, and Elizabeth Garrison, ...	"	XXIII.	104
1775. Sept. 8.	Van Clief, Greetie, and Barrent Johnson, Jr.,	"	XXIII.	152
1755. Nov. 27.	Van Clief, Jannetie, and Rem Adrianse,....	"	I.	218
1762. Oct. 26.	Van Clief, Mary, and William Johnson, ...	"	VI.	385
1760. Oct. 11.	Van Cliegh, Eleanor, and Edmond Welch,..	"	III.	359
1737. Mar. 26.	Van Cortlandt, Anne, and John Chambers,.	"	I.	6
1763. Nov. 8.	Van Cortlandt, Augustus, and Catharine Barclay,..............................	"	VII.	434
1760. April 19.	Van Cortlandt, Augustus, and Elsie Cuyler,.	"	III.	115
1775. Dec. 20.	Van Cortlandt, Catharine, and Abraham Van Wyck,..............................	"	XXIII.	233
1761. May 13.	Van Cortlandt, Eve, and Henry White,....	"	IV.	187
1738. May 6.	Van Cortlandt, Stephen, and Mary Walton Rickels, ...	"	I.	9
1765. Jan. 3.	Van Cortlandt, William Ricketts, and Elizabeth Kortright,......................	"	IX.	3
1761. Oct. 23.	Van Cot, David, and Martha Chichester, ...	"	V.	163
1700. Oct. 4.	Van Cots, Rachael, and Abraham Molaran,.	"	III.	344
1761. June 29.	Van Cots, Rachel, and Jacob Totton,......	"	IV.	267
1783. Nov. 17.	Van Cott, John, and Ann Probasco, ...	"	XL.	120
1782. June 16.	Vancott, Martha, and Samuel Walter, ...	"	XXXVI.	54
1781. Mar. 24.	Van Cotts, David, and Hester Tetis,.......	"	XXXI.	83
1665. Nov. 4.	Van Cowenhoven, Peter, and Alice Sybrants,.............................	O. W. L.,	II.	18
1769. Mar. 25.	Van Dalsam, Ann, and William I. Elsworth,	M. B.,	XIV.	59
1757. Aug. 31.	Van Dam, Cornelia, and John Wallace,....	"	I.	626
1761. Aug. 11.	Van Dam, Nicholas, and Elethe Rhodes, ...	"	V.	40
1753. June 13.	Van Dam, Sarah, and James White,.......	"	I.	60
1782. May 28.	Vandebargh, Hannah, and Thomas Gibson,.	"	XXXVI.	28
1757. Oct. 31.	Van de Belt, Idey, and Rem Hagerman, ...	"	I.	690
1737. Oct. 6.	Vandebelt, Margaret, and Jeremiah Dodge,.	"	I.	7
1770. Nov. 14.	Van de Bogaard, Margrieta, and Philip Vedder, ...	"	XVI.	252
1761. Mar. 25.	Van De Bogart, Catherine, and Martin Randall, ...	"	IV.	119
1753. Sept. 29.	Vandebogert, Catherin, and John Morricen,	"	I.	128
1772. Nov. 30.	Vandeburgh, Elizabeth, and Martin Cornell,	"	XIX.	137

52

DATE.		NAMES.	RECORD.	VOL. PAGE.
1769. Aug.	18.	Van Deboger, Claus, and Elizabeth Merselies,	M. B.,	xv. 26
1761. Nov.	28.	Van Deckar, Annatje, and Johannes Van Hoesen,	"	v. 255
1761. Oct.	21.	Van Denbargh, William, and Ann Van Derwercker,	"	v. 155
1761. Sept.	11.	Vandenberg, Christina, and Garret Oostrander,	"	v. 81
1760. Sept.	19.	Van Denberg, Engeltie, and Isaac Van Valkenburgh,	"	iii. 322
1762. Sept.	11.	Vandenbergh, Alida, and Garret Vandenbergh,	"	vi. 314
1771. Sept.	5.	Van Den Bergh, Altje, and Hendrick Van Schoonhoven,	"	xvii. 176
1773. Mar.	30.	Van Den Bergh, Anna, and Abraham H. Lansingh,	"	xx. 60
1760. April	10.	Van Denbergh, Annatje, and Walter Deridder,	"	iii. 102
1772. July	8.	Van Denbergh, Barran, and Maria Haen,...	"	xviii. 159
1770. Mar.	26.	Van Den Bergh, Castentie, and Harmanus A. Wendell,	"	xvi. 42
1765. Sept.	24.	Vandenbergh, Catharine, and Lewis Van Woirt,	"	ix. 271
1766. Oct.	21.	Van Den Bergh, Catrina, and Garret Waldron,	"	v. 156
1737. May	7.	Vandenbergh, Cornelius, and Anken Vrantur,	"	i. 6
1753. May	30.	Van Den Bergh, Cornelius, and Elizabeth De Hart,	"	i. 43
1766. Oct.	20.	Vandenbergh, Cornelius C., and Catherine Lansingh,	"	x. 129
1764. Dec.	10.	Vandenbergh, Ebetye, and Æneas McIntosh,	"	viii. 446
1775. May	12.	Van Den Bergh, Elizabeth, and Volkert Van Veghten,	"	xxiii. 32
1757. June	1.	Vandenbergh, Folkie, and Adderyaen Kwackenbush,	"	i. 546
1762. Sept.	11.	Vandenbergh, Garret, and Alida Vandenbergh,	"	vi. 314
1756. Oct.	7.	Vandenbergh, Gerret, and Hannah Mandevel,	"	i. 322
1775. May	18.	Van Den Bergh, Gerrit A., and Anna Schams,	"	xxiii. 38
1771. Oct.	31.	Van Den Bergh, Gysbert, and Jannetye Widbeeck,	"	xvii. 236
1765. Oct.	2.	Vandenbergh, Hannah, and Isaac Varian, ..	"	ix. 286
1769. Nov.	24.	Vandenbergh, Johannes I., and Mayekie Onderkerk,	"	xv. 105

DATE.	NAMES.	RECORD.	VOL. PAGE.
1758. Nov. 1.	Vanden Bergh, Lydia, and Peter Ryckman,	M. B.,	II. 76
1769. Nov. 27.	Vandenbergh, Margretje, and John Marcellis,	"	XV. 107
1761. Nov. 21.	Van Den Bergh, Maria, and Nicholas Van Den Bergh,	"	V. 240
1771. Feb. 4.	Van Den Bergh, Mary, and Hendrick Ostrander,	"	XVII. 12
1762. Mar. 1.	Vandenbergh, Mary, and Peter Simon Veeder,	"	VI. 59
1761. Nov. 21.	Van Den Bergh, Nicholas, and Maria Van Den Bergh,	"	V. 240
1771. Jan. 28.	Vanden Bergh, Rachel, and Gerrit I. Visger,	"	XVII. 10
1770. Nov. 17.	Vanden Bergh, Sanakie Clausie, and Isaac Fonda,	"	XVI. 262
1762. April 6.	Vandenbergh, Sarah, and Henry Pels,	"	VI. 90
1760. July 19.	Vandenbergh, Susannah, and Peter Winne,	"	III. 220
1759. Dec. 31.	Vandenbergh, Wynant W., and Maria Ridder,	"	II. 562
1782. May 11.	Vandenburgh, Mary, and John Odell,	"	XXXV. 159
1782. April 22.	Vandenburgh, Richard, and Syntje Rapalje,	"	XXXV. 131
1780. May 30.	Van Denham, Rebecca, and William Geree,	"	XXIX. 72
1760. Nov. 17.	Vandensee, Helligont, and David Hoghtelin,	"	III. 419
1756. Oct. 25.	Van Depoel, Melgert, and Jantie Van Valkenburgh,	"	I. 334
1769. Nov. 9.	Vanderbarrack, Garret, and Rebecca Fonda,	"	XV. 83
1761. Oct. 26.	Vanderbeeck, Ann, and Benjamin Yals,	"	V. 168
1766. Nov. 12.	Vanderbeek, Dorothy, and George Barnes,	"	X. 161
1783. June 24.	Vanderbeek, Peter, and Sarah Dickenson,	"	XXXIX. 67
1771. Nov. 10.	Vanderbeek, Rachel, and Solomon Freley,	"	XVII. 247
1737. April 22.	Vanderbeek, Ram, and Augenistie Bennet,	"	I. 6
1772. Oct. 2.	Vanderbelt, Altje, and John Baptist Dumont,	"	XIX. 65
1779. Nov. 15.	Vanderbelt, Ann, and Abraham Spier,	"	XXVIII.140a
1757. Mar. 4.	Vanderbelt, Cornelia, and Daniel Mersereau,	"	I. 455
1765. Sept. 26.	Vanderbelt, Eleanor, and Nathaniel Johnson,	"	IX. 277
1782. July 30.	Vanderbelt, Elizabeth, and James Carhartt,	"	XXXVI. 95
1759. Nov. 23.	Vander Belt, Elliner, and Marmaduke Foster,	"	II. 513
1769. Jan. 10.	Vanderbelt, Ellinor, and Joseph George,	"	XIV. 10
1783. April 5.	Vander Belt, Gertrude, and John Meserole,	"	XXXVIII. 85
1783. Sept. 17.	Vander Belt, Gertrude, and John Meserole,	"	XL. 43
1778. Dec. 16.	Vanderbelt, Hendrick, and Elizabeth Duryee,	"	XIII. 265
1766. Dec. 20.	Vanderbelt, John, and Belitje Bayte,	"	X. 204
1773. Dec. 31.	Vanderbelt, Phebe, and Abraham Britten,	"	XXII. 91
1766. Sept. 26.	Vanderbelt, Sarah, and George Van Norstrandt,	"	X. 108
1778. Oct. 14.	Vanderbelt, Sitie, and John Hegeman,	"	XXVI. 59
1765. June 5.	Vanderberg, Cornelius, and Mayeke Ouderkerk,	"	IX. 158

DATE.		NAMES.	RECORD.	VOL.	PAGE.
1772. April	6.	Vanderberg, Miritae, and Martin Cornelius Withbeck, ...	M. B.,	XVIII.	69
1758. May	29.	Vanderbergh, Elizabeth, and Hendrick Hagerman, ...	"	I.	913
1764. Nov.	3.	Vanderbergh, Gertruyd, and Philip Bovee, .	"	VIII.	390
1762. June	8.	Vanderbergh, Magdalen, and Thomas Pooley,	"	VI.	184
1782. May	27.	Vander Bilt, Abigail, and Rutgert Van Brunt,	"	XXXVI.	25
1764. Dec.	5.	Vanderbilt, Art, and Annetie Nagle, ...	"	VIII.	439
1757. Mar.	18.	Van Der Bilt, Cornelius, and Elenor Van Tyle,	"	I.	473
1762. Oct.	13.	Vanderbilt, Elizabeth, and Joost Debevoise, .	"	VI.	360
1782. July	3.	Vanderbilt, Jacob, and Rachel Dennis, ...	"	XXXVI.	73
1765. April	17.	Van Der Bilt, Jannitje, and George Martin,	"	IX.	99
1762. Aug.	2.	Van Der Bilt, Jeremiah, Jr., and Antee Ryerson, ...	"	VI.	260
1764. April	4.	Van Derbilt, John, and Elisabeth Abrams, ..	"	VIII.	131
1763. Feb.	1.	Vanderbilt, John, and Elizabeth Broome, ...	"	VII.	43
1777. Dec.	23.	Vanderbilt, John, and Fanny Lawrence, ...	"	XXIV.	205
1778. Mar.	12.	Vanderbilt, John, and Maritie Ditmars, ...	"	XXV.	40
1773. Nov.	15.	Van Der Bilt, Laco, and Peter Stoothoff, ...	"	XXII.	29
1765. April	17.	Van Der Bilt, Lammatje, and John Lefferts, .	"	IX.	98
1778. Oct.	15.	Vanderbilt, Oliver, and Sarah King, ...	"	XXVI.	60
1769. Nov.	2.	Van Der Bilt, Peter, and Annatje Garretson,	"	XV.	74
1772. Mar.	30.	Vanderbilt, Peter, and Helen Hooglandt, ..	"	XVIII.	64
1761. Dec.	10.	Vander Bilt, Pieter, and Jane Van Nuys, ...	"	V.	273
1782. Sept.	27.	Van Der Bilt, Sarah, and Jacobus Hageman,	"	XXXVII.	16
1766. July	8.	Vanderbilt, Sarah, and Matthias Van Dyke, .	"	X.	44
1766. Dec.	31.	Vanderbogart, Arriantie, and Freeman Schermerhorn, ...	"	X.	209
1761. April	13.	Vanderbogert, Rachel, and Cornelius Burheyt,	"	IV.	145
1779. July	15.	Vanderburgh, Hester, and Ephraim Griffin, .	"	XXVIII.	23
1767. Oct.	6.	Vanderburgh, James, and Ellinor Clark, ...	"	XII.	56
1753. Sept.	5.	Vander Burgh, James, and Margaret Noxon,	"	I.	107
1771. April	8.	Van D. Carr, Dirck, and Hillitie Muller, ...	"	XVII.	51
1771. Mar.	11.	Vander Cook, Michel, and Sarah Du Bois, ..	"	XVII.	31
1763. Nov.	23.	Vander Cor, Marytie, and Albert Vander Zee,	"	VII.	466
1736. Mar.	23.	Vanderheule, Henry, and Anne Brested, ...	"	I.	1
1759. Nov.	16.	Van Der Heyden, Alida, and Barent Vrooman, ...	"	II.	501
1760. Sept.	2.	Vanderheyden, Battia, and Matthias Bavee, .	"	III.	277
1770. Mar.	5.	Vanderheyden, Catherine, and Levinus Lansingh, ...	"	XVI.	29
1773. Mar.	13.	Van Der Heyden, Esther, and Cornelius Lansingh, ...	"	XX.	61
1771. Nov.	22.	Vanderheyden, Elisabeth, and John P. Hansen, ...	"	XVII.	264

DATE.		NAMES.	RECORD.	VOL.	PAGE.
1758. Nov.	8.	Vander Heyden, Rachel, and Samuel Stringer,	M. B.,	II.	86
1736. Sept.	8.	Vanderhiden, John, and Catherine Ward, ..	"	I.	2
1777. June	10.	Vanderhoever, Mary, and Thomas Pearsall,.	"	XXIV.	98
1737. Aug.	6.	Vanderhoof, Chatie, and Enock Earle,......	"	I.	7
1759. July	12.	Vanderhoof, Jane, and William Carman,....	"	II.	354
1761. Nov.	19.	Vanderhoof, Mary, and Stephen Allen, ...	"	V.	230
1759. Oct.	3.	Vanderhoof, Mary, and Thomas Dods, ...	"	II.	445
1759. July	6.	Vanderhoof, Ruth, and Albartus Tiebout,...	"	II.	3ь0
1783. June	11.	Vanderhoof, Sarah, and Samuel Thomas,...	"	XXXIX.	50
1782. July	2.	Van Derhooven, Elenor, and John Vendyne,	"	XXXVI.	72
1770. Dec.	7.	Vanderhover, Catherine, and John Polhemus,	"	XVI.	290
1773. May	17.	Vanderhuffen, Zena, and George Losee,....	"	XX.	116
1756. July	12.	Vanderhuyl, Mary, and Jacobus Lefferts, Jr.,	"	I.	254
1762. Aug.	18.	Vanderhyden, Leah, and George Masten,...	"	VI.	278
1762. Sept.	1.	Van Der Kar, Johannes, and Hillitie Van Der Zee, ...	"	VI.	302
1762. Aug.	9.	Vanderkarr, Mary, and Garret Hardick,....	"	VI.	269
1762. Mar.	8.	Vanderkarre, Fitie, and Johannes A. Huycke,	"	VI.	67
1775. July	10.	Vander Ker, Arent, and Rebecca Fonda,...	"	XXIII.	93
1763. Nov.	9.	Vander Lyn, Jacobus, and Esther Hoffman,.	"	VII.	439
1768. Dec.	9.	Vanderlyn, Nicholas, and Saretje Tappen,..	"	XIII.	258
1758. Nov.	18.	Vander Lyn, Niclaas, and Sarah Pick, ...	"	I.	359
1770. Nov.	15.	Vanderpoel, Jacobus, and Lucretia Van Vleck, ...	"	XVI.	255
1761. Jan.	26.	Vander Pole, Catherine, and Jacob Jacob Van Valkenburgh,....................	"	IV.	31
1738. Oct.	26.	Vanderpool, Abraham, and Elizabeth Queman, ...	"	I.	11
1764. Sept.	21.	Van Der Pool, Abraham, and Marija Van Volkenburgh,......................	"	VIII.	320
1759. July	4.	Vanderpool, Anatie, and Henry F. Van Valkenburgh, ...	"	II.	345
1775. July	28.	Vanderpool, Andrew, and Catherine A. Van Valkenburgh, ...	"	XXIII.	109
1775. Aug.	14.	Vanderpool, Catharine, and Johannes Van Buren,..............................	"	XXIII.	126
1767. Oct.	27.	Vanderpool, Catherine, and John Pruyne,..	"	XII.	70
1764. May	11.	Vander Pool, Jacobus, and Lena Van Allen,	"	VIII.	186
1775. May	.8.	Vanderpool, Margaret, and John I. Van Valkenburgh, ...	"	XXIII.	25
1762. Nov.	19.	Vander Pool, Maria, and Lourens Van Dyck,	"	VI.	443
1766. Nov.	4.	Vanderpool, Mary, and Daniel Schermerhorne, ...	"	X.	151
1765. Sept.	30.	Vanderpool, Mary, and John Johannas Huyck, ...	"	IX.	280

Date.	Names.	Record.	Vol.	Page.
1773. Nov. 8.	Vander Pool, Sarah, and Jonas A. Van Alstin,	M. B.,	xxii.	16
1765. June 5.	Vander Poole, Catherine, and James Van Dyck,	"	ix.	154
1736. Nov. 8.	Vanderpoole, Johannes, and Sarah Staats,..	"	i.	3
1760. Nov. 24.	Vanderrife, Letty, and Timothy Shields,....	"	iii.	440
1770. Dec. 19.	Vander Ruff, Catherine, and Thomas Outwater,	"	xvi.	302
1757. Oct. 31.	Van Dersee, Eghtje, and Garret T. Slingerlant,	"	i.	689
1758. Nov. 22.	Vandersee, Eigje, and John Fonda,........	"	ii.	101
1738. Aug. 7.	Vanderspiegel, Sarah, and Joseph Scott,....	"	i.	10
1769. Aug. 29.	Vanderspiegle, Mary Ann, and Jeremiah Platt,	"	xv.	33
1682. May 12.	Vanderveen, Margarett, and Issack Stevenson,	O. W.,	xxxii½.	119
1781. April 4.	Van Der Veer, Abraham, and Charity Bennet,	M. B.,	xxxi.	93
1779. Dec. 15.	Van Der Veer, Ann, and Tarlton Wooden,..	"	xxviii.	172
1764. Nov. 8.	Vander Veer, Catherine, and John Strycker,	"	viii.	396
1761. Nov. 17.	Van Der Veer, Cornelius, Jr., and Leah Van Kirk,	"	v.	225
1768. April 19.	Van Derveer, Hendrick, and Mary Voorhuys,	"	xiii.	82
1777. Jan. 20.	Vanderveer, Ida, and Jacob Lefferts,.......	"	xxiv.	14
1765. May 18.	Vander Veer, Jan, Jr., and Margaret Elder,.	"	ix.	130
1753. Oct. 3.	Vandervolver, Elizabeth, and Johannes Heamstraat, ..	"	i.	130
1768. Dec. 21.	Vandervoort, Abraham, and Elizabeth Gibson,	"	xiii.	270
1762. Sept. 4.	Vander Voort, Angletie, and Leonard Rigler,	"	vi.	308
1781. Jan. 30.	Vandervoort, Catharine, and Peter Storm,..	"	xxxi.	33
1763. June 25.	Vander Voort, Gabriel, and Margaret Coe,..	"	vii.	241
1761. April 18.	Vandervoort, Jaen, and Jane Van Anden, ..	"	iv.	154
1758. Dec. 13.	Vandervoort, Jane, and Simon Duryee, ...	"	ii.	127
1766. Aug. 28.	Vandervoort, John, and Elizabeth Pettit,...	"	x.	85
1780. Dec. 2.	Vandervoort, John, and Jane Latten,......	"	xxx.	135
1766. Nov. 17.	Vandervoort, John, and Rebecka Edwards,.	"	x.	167
1769. Nov. 2.	Vonder Voort, Lam Borth, and Elsie Van Ander,	"	xv.	75
1736. April 13.	Van Der Voort, Madalena, and Benjamin Van De Water,	"	i.	5
1766. Dec. 6.	Vandervoort, Paul, and Gitty Polhemus,...	"	x.	194
1771. Sept. 3.	Van Der Voort, Peter, and Anna Kouwenhoven,	"	xvii.	173
1781. Dec. 6.	Vandervort, John, and Mary Wilsey, ...	"	xxxiv.	74
1760. Oct. 17.	Van Der Vort, Leah, and Teunis Boogaert,.	"	iii.	367
1765. July 29.	Vander Vort, Phebe, and Benjamin Fish,...	"	ix.	220

DATE.	NAMES.	RECORD.	VOL. PAGE.
759. June 8.	Vanderwater, Cornelia, and Henry Ezeler,..	M. B.,	II. 313
778. Dec. 22.	Vanderwater, Elizabeth, and Thomas Fairchild,...............................	"	XXVI. 129
1779. April 9.	Vanderwater, Mary, and James Lewis,.....	"	XXVII. 107
1761. Oct. 21.	Van Derwercker, Ann, and William Van Denbargh,.........................	"	V. 155
1773. May 15.	Vanderwerg, Johannes, and Hannah Bogardus, ...	"	XX. 114
1758. April 26.	Vander Werken, Albert, and Anna Winne,.	"	I. 885
1763. Nov. 23.	Vander Zee, Albert, and Marytie Vander Cor, ...	"	VII. 466
1764. Nov. 12.	Vander Zee, Albert, Jr., and Hester Hooghtelin, ...	"	VIII. 402
1762. Sept. 1.	Van Der Zee, Hillitie, and Johannes Van Der Kar, ...	"	VI. 302
1762. Feb. 18.	Van Deurer, Elizabeth, and Frederick Lans,	"	VI. 54
1765. July 3.	Van Deursen, Ann, and George Dean,.....	"	IX. 192
1778. Dec. 15.	Vandeursen, Ann, and Francis Dominick, ..	"	XXVI. 121
1763. Oct. 27.	Van Deursen, Ann, and Lodwick Inslar, ...	"	VII. 407
1769. Nov. 24.	Van Deursen, Johannes, and Maritie Bronck,	"	XV. 104
1762. Nov. 11.	Van Deursen, Lucas, and Jannetje Van Slyck,	"	VI. 425
1764. Jan. 16.	Van Deursen, Mary, and Anthony E. Bradt,	"	VIII. 18
1765. July 30.	Van Deursen, Mary, and John Van Hoesen,	"	IX. 222
1759. June 9.	Van Deusen, Altje, and Thomas Young,....	"	II. 318
1764. Nov. 29.	Van Deusen, Annatje, and John Van Hoesen,	"	VIII. 432
1761. Oct. 21.	Van Deusen, Baatja, and Thomas Hunn, ...	"	V. 160
1770. May 16.	Van Deusen, Elizabeth, and William Dunbar,	"	XVI. 89
1769. Dec. 4.	Van Deusen, Peter, and Catherine Ways, ..	"	XV. 113
1758. Nov. 20.	Vandevender, Mary, and William Bennet,..	"	II. 97
1763. Jan. 18.	Van Deventer, Abraham, and Mary Simonson, ...	"	VII. 19
1781. Sept. 15.	Vandeventer, Anne, and John Totten,.....	"	XXXIII. 67
1756. June 15.	Vandeventer, Ida, and Garrit Stryker,.....	"	I. 241
1768. June 20.	Van Deventer, Jacobus, and Phebe Van Cleef,	"	XIII. 133
1761. Oct. 10.	Van De Volgen, Petrus, and Gertrude Mynderse,...............................	"	V. 132
1758. Mar. 8.	Vandevoort, Mietje, and Nickklas Blom, ...	"	I. 836
1762. May 28.	Vande Water, Albertus, and Elisabeth Skillman,...............................	"	VI. 171
1763. Mar. 3.	Vandewater, Ann, and John Harper,......	"	VII. 87
1773. April 9.	V d Water, Barnardus, and Phebe Simons, ..	"	XX. 91
1772. Aug. 10.	Vandewater, Bauffe, and Andrew Van Horne,	"	XIX. 17
1737. April 13.	Van De Water, Benjamin, and Madalena Van Der Voort, ...	"	I. 5
1758. Jan. 10.	Vandewater, Benjamin, and Ruth Hopson, .	"	I. 779

DATE.		NAMES.	RECORD.	VOL. PAGE.
1763. Oct.	28.	Van De Water, Catharine, and Lucas Burbanck,	M. B.,	VII. 410
1761. Jan.	9.	Van De Water, Cornelius, and Mary Burtis,	"	IV. 7
1757. Sept.	24.	Vandewater, Elizabeth, and Jeremiah Brewer,	"	I. 644
173⅞. Feb.	9.	Vandewater, Henry, and Catherine Collier,.	"	I. 9
1769. Feb.	1.	Vande Water, Henry, and Margaret Breasted,	"	XIV. 25
1772. Oct.	17.	Vandewater, John, and Margaret Vanbussgarrick,	"	XIX. 75
1759. Jan.	3.	Vandewater, Levinus, and Janetje Losee,...	"	II. 144
1763. Oct.	31.	Vandewater, Margaret, and Edward Tilley,.	"	VII. 415
1737. Oct.	5.	Vandewater, Margaret, and Frederick Hire,	"	I. 7
1770. Dec.	18.	Vandewater, Mary, and William De Lamanter,	"	XVI. 300
1768. Dec.	2.	Vandewater, Peter, and Elizabeth Steed,...	"	XIII. 253
1758. Mar.	13.	Vandewater, Sarah, and Joseph Keys,	"	I. 846
1762. May	17.	Van De Water, Sarah, and Luke C. Quick, .	"	VI. 162
1763. Oct.	13.	Van de Zee, Cornelius, and Anjenetye Wetbeck,	"	VII. 385
173⅚. Feb.	9.	Vandike, Catherine, and Lewis Dubois, ...	"	I. 5
173⅞. Feb.	13.	Vandike, Cornelius, and Margaret Bradt,...	"	I. 9
1757. Jan.	22.	Van Dike, Francis, and Elizabeth Bowns, ..	"	I. 425
1765. Aug.	22.	Van Dike, Jacob, and Mayeka Van Kirk, ..	"	IX. 248
1737. Sept.	22.	Van Dike, Maria, and Johannes Rapellie, ..	"	I. 7
1736. Dec.	20.	Vandike, Peter, and Christina Peterson,....	"	I. 5
1782. Nov.	11.	Vandine, Anne, and Ezekiel Feley,........	"	XXXVII. 78
1756. Sept.	20.	Vandine, Charity, and John Combs,.......	"	I. 298
1781. May	2.	Van Dine, Demenicas, and Hannah Furman,	"	XXXII. 26
1777. Dec.	2.	Van Dine, Douw, and Hannah Springsteen,	"	XXIV. 188
1780. Dec.	16.	Vandine, Jane, and Peter Bogert,.........	"	XXX. 155
1778. Oct.	2.	Van Dine, Sarah, and Bernard Ward,......	"	XXVI. 42
1732. June	8.	Vandine, Syntje, and William Furman, ...	"	XXXVI. 43
1766. Aug.	20.	Vandle, Sarah, and Jacob Rynders,........	"	X. 77
1758. Jan.	6.	Vandolfsen, Theunus, and Elizabeth Holland,	"	I. 773
1771. Sept.	9.	Vandooser, Maria, and Cloudea De La Marter,	"	XVII. 179
1771. Oct.	11.	Van Dresin, Henry, and Hanny Jansen,....	"	XVII. 204
1773. Nov.	27.	Vandrie, William, and Jane Van Law,.....	"	XXII. 52
1770. May	26.	Van Driesen, John, and Margaret Truax,...	"	XVI. 96
1736. Oct.	22.	Van Driesen, John, and Margarita Oethout,.	"	I. 3
1773. Feb.	24.	Van Driesen, Mary, and Henry Grevorate, .	"	XX. 52
1764. Mar.	26.	Van Driesen, Mary, and Thomas Ellis,.....	"	VIII. 119
1738. June	22.	Van Driesen, Peter, and Angeltie Vrooman,	"	I. 10
1770. Dec.	15.	Vandrill, Susanah, and James Armitage, ...	"	XVI. 297
1759. Nov.	9.	Vandue, Leanah, and John Floyd, ...	"	II. 491
1758. June	15.	Van Dueren, Mary, and Johannes Roorback,	"	I. 926

DATE.		NAMES.	RECORD.	VOL.	PAGE.
1771.	Oct. 24.	Vanduersen, Esther, and James Leadbetter,	M. B.,	XVII.	221
1767.	April 24.	Van Duersen, Lucretia, and John Fredherring,	"	XI.	70
1759.	April 24.	Van Duersen, Lucretia, and Robert Watts,..	"	II.	253
1764.	April 17.	Van Duersen, Mary, and Dirck Schuyler, Jr.,.	"	VIII.	160
1755.	Sept. 12.	Vanduersen, Sarah, and Derick Huick,.....	"	I.	174
1771.	Nov. 14.	Van Duesan, Anna, and John Vanhoesan,..	"	XVII.	256
1760.	June 2.	Van Duesen, Helena, and Mathew Goes, ...	"	III.	171
1767.	Mar. 2.	Van Duesen, Leah, and Michael Tremper,..	"	XI.	38
1759.	Nov. 29.	Vanduresen, Susannah, and Shadrach Mur-			
		chant.	"	II.	521
1771.	Mar. 30.	Va: .sen, Jacob, and Else Lansingh,.....	"	XVII.	45
1759.	July 4.	Van Duyn, John, and Magdalene Van Nuys,	"	II.	347
1782.	Aug. 21.	Van Duyn, Sarah, and John Van Beuren, ..	"	XXXVI.	116
1774.	Feb. 15.	Van Duzer, Andrew, and Emilia Early, ...	"	XXII.	128
1761.	Oct. 1.	Van Duzer, Catharine, and John Stagg,....	"	V.	113
1762.	April 10.	Van Duzer, Isaac, and Rachel Begoom, ...	"	VI.	101
1770.	Sept. 21.	Van Dyck, Ann, and James Bennet,.......	"	XVI.	265
1761.	July 2.	Van Dyck, Arent, and Jemmima Hooff,....	"	IV.	273
1782.	Feb. 23.	Vandyck, Catharine, and Joseph Taylor,....	"	XXXV.	61
1775.	July 31.	Van Dyck, Catherine, and James Finglass,..	"	XXIII.	114
1762.	May 21.	Van Dyck, Cornelius, and Tomica Yates,...	"	VI.	165
1762.	April 24.	Van Dyck, Cornelius, and Tomica Yeats,...	"	VI.	130
1760.	July 18.	Van Dyck, Derick, and Elizabeth Strope,...	'	III.	217
1780.	July 18.	Van Dyck, Elizabeth, and Obadiah Bowne,.	"	XXIX.	115
1753.	May 28.	Van Dyck, Hendrick, and Angeltje Maybee,	"	I.	42
1753.	Sept. 27.	Van Dyck, Jacobus, and Elinor Van Hook,	"	I.	127
1765.	June 5.	Van Dyck, James, and Catherine Vander			
		Poole, ...	"	IX.	154
1781.	June 14.	Van Dyck, Jane, and Daniel Jones,..... ...	"	XXXII.	85
1769.	Mar. 29.	Van Dyck, John, and Martha Johnson, ...	"	XIV.	61
1762.	Nov. 19.	Van Dyck, Lourins, and Maria Vander Pool,	"	VI.	443
1768.	Sept. 28.	Van Dyck, Martha, and Adolf Benson, ...	"	XIII.	200
1772.	Mar. 26.	Van Dyck, Mary, and John Moore, ...	"	XVIII.	60
1777.	Jan. 3.	Van Dyck, Mary, and John Van Clef,......	"	XXIV.	6
1756.	July 27.	Van Dyck, Sarah, and Hendrick Oudenaarde,	"	I.	262
1772.	April 21.	Van Dyck, Soncha, and Solomon Saltus, ...	"	XVIII.	88
1759.	Sept. 3.	Van Dyck, Wessell, and Annatje Neuwkerk,	"	II.	406
1777.	Jan. 3.	Van Dyck, William, and Jane Denyse,.....	"	XXIV.	4
1769.	July 1.	Van Dycke, Nicholas, and Elizabeth Van			
		Brunt, ...	"	XIV.	139
1761.	Oct. 15.	Van Dyke, Christina, and John Van Allen,.	"	V.	142
1769.	April 17.	Vandyke, Francis, and Agnes Maurkwat, ..	"	XIV.	76
1738.	April 1.	Vandyke, Mathias, and Orionta Hooffa,....	"	I.	9
1766.	July 8.	Van Dyke, Matthias, and Sarah Vanderbilt,.	"	X.	44
1773.	Aug. 18.	Vandyne, Mintje, and Wyneat Bennet,....	"	XXI.	73

DATE.	NAMES.	RECORD.	VOL. PAGE.
1763. April 11.	Van Elting, Sarah, and Bartholomew Van Volkenburg, ...	M. B.,	VII. 123
1766. July 7.	Van Embrie, Elizabeth, and James Torry,..	"	X. 9
1761. Mar. 17.	Van Emburg, Christeen, and John McChain,	"	IV. 105
1765. Jan. 31.	Van Emburgh, Joseph, and Jemima Lewis,.	"	IX. 40
1737. Aug. 17.	Vanenburgh, Catherine, and Richard Gibb,.	"	I. 7
1736. July 23.	Vanenburgh, Peregrine, and Cornelia Provoost, ...	"	I. 2
1760. Sept. 12.	Van Eppe, Mary, and Andrew Mitchell, ...	"	III. 312
1761. Oct. 27.	Van Eps, Abraham, and Margaret Vêder, ..	"	V. 171
1763. Aug. 17.	Van Eps, Elinor, and Saunders Lansingh, ..	"	VII. 303
1770. Sept. 13.	Van Eps, Geertruy, and William Stevens,..	"	XVI. 186
1766. Nov. 6.	Van Eps, Helena, and William Teller, ...	"	X. 156
1765. July 25.	Van Eps, Helena J., and Arent N. V. Petten,	"	IX. 204
1764. Nov. 27.	Van Eps, Jacob, and Engeltje Wendell,....	"	VIII. 430
1760. Nov. 21.	Van Eps, John Baptist, and Jannetie Lansing, ...	"	III. 430
1773. June 30.	Van Eps, John Jacob, and Margaret Peeck,	"	XXI. 27
1761. Oct. 23.	Van Eps, Nieltje, and Rynier Van Evera,..	"	V. 164
1761. Oct. 29.	Van Etta, Leah, and Barent Lewis,........	"	V. 176
1772. Oct. 2.	Vanetten, Jacobus J., and Rachel Van Wagoner, ...	"	XIX. 66
1783. Mar. 22.	Van Evendor, Mary, and David La Tourrette, ...	"	XXXVIII. 73
1783. July 30.	Van Ever, Eleanora, and Mathew Taylor,..	"	XXXIX. 105
1762. June 5.	Van Evera, Cornelia, and Thomas Roberts,.	"	VI. 182
1780. Dec. 27.	Van Evera, Frances, and John Ross, ...	"	XXX. 170
1770. Nov. 17.	Van Evera, Jacob, and Ratie Marinus,.....	"	XVI. 261
1766. Oct. 24.	Van Evera, Mary, and Archibald Gatfield,..	"	X. 140
1761. Oct. 23.	Van Evera, Rynier, and Nieltje Van Eps, ..	"	V. 164
1782. July 23.	Van Evere, Jane, and John Latham,.......	"	XXXVI. 91
1775. Dec. 22.	Van Every, Andrew, and Hannah Pitt,....	"	XXIII. 235
1770. Dec. 3.	Van Evra, Helena, and Samuel Paddy, ...	"	XVI. 282
1763. Nov. 30.	Van Evra, Mindert, and Rachel Lamb,.....	"	VII. 484
1764. July 7.	Van Evre, Garret, and Catharine Bogard, ..	"	VIII. 249
1764. Dec. 21.	Van Evre, Sarah, and John Van Orden,....	"	VIII. 462
1774. Jan. 12.	Van Fleet, Catherine, and Garrit Harsin,...	"	XXII. 100
1775. June 14.	Van Fleet, Charity, and Abraham Freligh,..	"	XXIII. 61
1765. Jan. 21.	Van Francke, Garrit R., and Alida Ryly,....	"	IX. 26
1767. Nov. 27.	Van Fronker, Maritje, and Michael Bassett,	"	XII. 99
1770. June 6.	Van Gaasbeek, Sarah, and Joseph Oosterhout, ...	"	XVI. 104
1767. Nov. 28.	Van Gaasbeek, Sarah, and Philip Whiteaker,	"	XII. 101
1770. Aug. 17.	Van Gaesbeek, Rachel, and Peter Eltinge,..	"	XVI. 161
1783. Oct. 3.	Van Garden, Jane, and Nicklas Meed,.....	"	XL. 60

DATE.		NAMES.	RECORD.	VOL.	PAGE.
1766. Oct.	16.	Van Gasbeek, Jacobus, and Deborah Kierstada,	M. B.,	x.	125
1758. Sept.	7.	Van Gelder, Abraham, and Ann Fisher,	"	II.	8
1757. July	4.	Van Gelder, Ann, and William Quick,	"	I.	581
1758. Jan.	3.	Van Gelder, Ary, and Jane Gamble,	"	I.	764
1771. Nov.	5.	Van Gelder, Catherine, and William Forbes,	"	XVII.	240
1772. Nov.	16.	Van Gelder, Elizabeth, and George Harsin,	"	XIX.	114
1782. April	27.	Vangelder, Elizabeth, and Thomas Henning,	"	XXXV.	141
1738. Nov.	16.	Van Gelder, Hannah, and William Steddiford,	"	I.	11
1763. April	29.	Van Gelder, Henry, and Mary Carpenter,	"	VII.	319
1765. Feb.	22.	Van Gelder, Isaac, and Ann Hyer,	"	IX.	56
1753. April	16.	Van Gelder, Johannah, and Thomas Collins,	"	I.	23
1763 Dec.	4.	Van Gelder, Martha, and Marmaduke Earle,	"	VII.	489
1757. May	25.	Van Gelder, Peter, and Aeltie Hendrickson,	"	I.	541
1770. Nov.	5.	Van Geyseling, Peter, and Mary Schermerhorne,	"	XVI.	240
1773. May	5.	Van Giesling, Jacobus, and Janety Vealen,	"	XX.	103
1737. Nov.	24.	Van Goosbeck, Catherina, and Anthony Hoffman,	"	I.	8
1766. July	2.	Van Gosbeck, Ann, and Isaac Hasbrook,	"	x.	40
1764. Jan.	30.	Van Groesbeek, Garret, and Maria Groesbeck,	"	VIII.	43
1765. July	17.	Van Guilder, Effe, and Luke Kierstead,	"	IX.	209
1669. Jan.	14.	Van Gunst, Jan Hendrick, and Helena Pieters,	C. A.,	II.	450
1736. May	5.	Van Hall, Dirick, and Cathrina Johana Tenbrook,	M. B.,	I.	1
1775. Sept.	25.	Vanhaugel, Martin, and Judith Carroll,	"	XXIII.	163
1771. Nov.	14.	Vanhoesan, John, and Anne Van Duesan,	"	XVII.	256
1766. Oct.	14.	Van Hoese, Sarah, and John Becker,	"	x.	122
1775. July	28.	Van Hoesen, Abraham, and Helletje Van Alstyne,	"	XXIII.	110
1765. April	18.	Van Hoesen, Catharine, and Lambert Boghart,	"	IX.	102
1771. Jnly	17.	Van Hoesen, Fitie, and Peter J. Vosburgh,	"	XVII.	134
1763. Aug.	25.	Van Hoesen, Harme, and Trintje Witbeek,	"	VII.	310
1764. Nov.	15.	Van Hoesen, Jacob, and Maria Esiel,	"	VIII.	409
1765. July	30.	Van Hoesen, Jan, and Mary Van Deursen,	"	IX.	222
1761. Nov.	28.	Van Hoesen, Johannes, and Annetje Van Deckar,	"	V.	255
1764. Nov.	29.	Van Hoesen, John, and Annatje Van Deusen,	"	VIII.	432
1773. July	23.	Vanhoesen, Maratje, and Martin Vosburgh,	"	XXI.	50
1760. Mar.	15.	Vanholer, Jacob, and Neltje Brinckerhoff,	"	III.	78
1771. Mar.	30.	Van Hook, Arondt, and Abigail Stevens,	"	XVII.	44
1753. Sept.	27	Van Hook, Elinor, and Jacobus Van Dyck,	"	I.	127

DATE.	NAMES.	RECORD.	VOL. PAGE.
1773. Sept. 10.	Van Hook, Mary, and Joel Baldwin, ...	M. B.,	XXI. 105
1765. Oct. 21.	Van Hook, Mary, and Riter Amerman, ...	"	IX. 309
1760. Oct. 28.	Vanhoosen, Anatie, and Jeremiah Hogeboom,	"	III. 384
1764. Feb. 20.	Van Hoosen, Bridget, and Mathias Austin, .	"	VIII. 64
1771. Nov. 28.	Vanhoosen, Conradt, and Elizabeth Van Volkenburgh, ...	"	XVII. 272
1772. Aug. 10.	Van Horn, Andrew, and Bauffe Vandewater, ...	"	XIX. 17
1758. Jan. 11.	Van Horn, Cornelius, and Elizabeth Van Horn, ...	"	I. 781
1758. Jan. 11.	Van Horn, Elizabeth, and Cornelius Van Horn, ...	"	I. 781
1781. July 2.	Vanhorne, Ann, and William Waymnan,...	"	XXXII. 101
1765. Feb. 13.	Van Horne, Augustus, and Anne Marston, .	"	IX. 52
173⅞. Jan. 11.	Van Horne, Catherine, and Peter Rock,....	"	I. 8
1778. April 24.	Van Horne, Catherine, and Samuel Bayard,	"	XXV. 67
1769. Mar. 9.	Vanhorne, Elizabeth, and James Rivington,	"	XIV. 49
1765. Jan. 10.	Van Horne, Eva, and Daniel Lawrence,....	"	IX. 13
1781. May 11.	Van Horne, Gabriel, and Mary Basly, ...	"	XXXII. 44
1779. Feb. 3.	Van Horne, Gitty, and Edward Patten,....	"	XXVII. 35
1783. May 3.	Van Horne, Hannah, and John Deforest,...	"	XXXVIII. 124
1768. Dec. 2.	Van Horne, James, and Mayeke Lott,......	"	XIII. 252
1774. Feb. 5.	Van Horne, Jane, and John Van Buskerk, Jr.,	"	XXII. 122
1757. Aug. 10.	Van Horne, Jannetje, and Cornelius Garbrants, ...	"	I. 610
1756. Aug. 11.	Van Horne, Margaret, and Garrit V. H. De Witt, ...	"	I. 271
1737. Nov. 7.	Vanhorne, Margett, and Simon Johnson,...	"	I. 8
1781. Feb. 3.	Van Horne, Mary, and David M. Clarkson,.	"	XXXI. 35
1782. Jan. 5.	Van Horne, Mary, and James Stringham, ..	"	XXXV. 10
1763. Feb. 19.	Van Horne, Mary, and Levinus Clarkson, ..	"	VII. 69
1782. June 7.	Van Horne, Mary, and Michael Huck, ...	"	XXXVI. 41
1760. May 16.	Vanhorne, Sarah, and John Mason,........	"	III. 157
1738. June 22.	Van Horne, Sarah, and Michael Henderson,	"	I. 10
1684. Dec. 10.	Van Horrow, Helekin, and Oliver Cranesburgh, ...	C. M.,	XXXIII. 70
1782. April 24.	Vanhourn, Jacob, and Catherine Feilding, ..	M. B.,	XXXV. 134
1736. April 13.	Van Housen, Marietia, and Jacobus De Bevois, Jr., ...	"	I. 1
1773. Oct. 2.	Van Houser, Henry, and Elizabeth Everson,	"	XXI. 129
1778. July 11.	Van Houte, John, and Rachel Demare, ...	"	XXV. 127
1764. June 21.	Van Houten, Mary, and Charles De Bevois,	"	VIII. 245
1765. July 26.	Van Houten, Roilf, and Margaret Sharer,...	"	IX. 217
1738. May 5.	Van Hoven, Cornelius, and Mary Boiss,....	"	I. 9
1759. June 27.	Van Husen, Agnes, and Robert Osbourn,...	"	II. 341

DATE.		NAMES.	RECORD.	VOL.	PAGE.
1759. Sept.	15.	Van Ingen, Derick, and Margaret Van Syse,	M. B.,	II.	425
1759. June	2.	Van Kats, Maritje, and Benjamin Nisbit, ...	"	II.	297
1760. Sept.	22.	Vankeuren, Elizabeth, and Benjamin Bevier,	"	III.	334
1761. Nov.	17.	Van Kirk, Leah, and Cornelius Van Der Veer, Jr., ...	"	V.	225
1765. Aug.	27.	Van Kirk, Mayeka, and Jacob Van Dike, ..	"	IX.	248
1768. Dec.	8.	Van Kleack, Cabachay, and Joshua Carman, Jr., ...	"	XIII.	257
1764. Dec.	10.	Van Kleck, Barent, and Helena Palmetier,..	"	VIII.	449
1773. Jan.	6.	Van Kleck, Peter, and Catherine Outen Bogert, ...	"	XX.	3
1764. Dec.	31.	Van Kleeck, Alida, and Lewis Duboys, ...	"	VIII.	470
1770. Nov.	15.	Van Kleeck, Catherine, and Francis Pells,..	"	XVI.	258
1771. Oct.	16.	Van Kleeck, Baltis, and Catherine Jones, ..	"	XVII.	211
1771. July	23.	Van Kleeck, Baltus, and Ann Lawrence,...	"	XVII.	140
1764. May	16.	Van Kleeck, Baltus, and Cornelia Crook,...	"	VIII.	190
1761. Aug.	8.	Van Kleeck, Baltus, and Josyntje Buis, ...	"	V.	35
1771. Mar.	19.	Van Kleeck, Barent B., and Catharine Outwater, ...	"	XVII.	38
1772. Mar.	4.	Van Kleeck, Elizabeth, and Gerret Lefferts,	"	XVIII.	47
1775. Nov.	13.	Van Kleeck, Elizabeth, and Martin Wiltse,.	"	XXIII.	207
1738. Aug.	28.	Van Kleeqk, Elizabeth, and William Low,..	"	I.	10
1763. Oct.	5.	Van Kleeck, Hugh, and Mary Everitt,.....	"	VII.	372
1773. Aug.	10.	Van Kleeck, Jacoba, and Myndert Van Kleeck, ...	"	XXI.	64
1767. Nov.	23.	Van Kleeck, Jane, and Jacobus Low,......	"	XII.	93
1773. Nov.	20.	Van Kleeck, Jenny, and Thomas Tobias,...	"	XXII.	38
1763. Sept.	14.	Van Kleeck, John, and Mary Ellis,........	"	VII.	336
1769. Feb.	15.	Van Kleeck, Lawrence, and Cornelia Livingston, ...	"	XIV.	34
1773. Aug.	10.	Van Kleeck, Leonard, and Jane Crook, ...	"	XXI.	63
1773. Aug.	10.	Van Kleeck, Myndert, and Jacoba Van Kleeck, ...	"	XXI.	64
1767. June	26.	Van Kleeck, Myndert, and Mary De Groff,.	"	XI.	114
1761. April	7.	Van Kleeck, Peter, and Ann Lewis,.......	"	IV.	137
1759. Oct.	15.	Vanklceck, Sarah, and George Stewart, ...	"	II.	461
1762. Nov.	17.	Van Kleef, Baletje, and Peter Van Steenbergh, ...	"	VI.	436
1761. Jan.	30.	Van Kleek, Alitije, and David Ward, ...	"	IV.	41
1755. Oct.	15.	Van Kleek, Catharine, and Peter Palmetier,	"	I.	193
1757. Aug.	24.	Van Kleek, Magdalen, and Francis Cameron,	"	I.	621
1757. Dec.	9.	Van Law, Elizabeth, and Henry Lane,.....	"	I.	731
1773. Nov.	29.	Van Law, Jane, and William Vandrie,.....	"	XXII.	52
1782. April	2.	Van Law, John, and Agness Dodds,.......	"	XXXV.	106
1778. June	17.	Van Lew, Ann, and Edward Willet,.......	"	XXV.	108

422   NEW YORK MARRIAGES.

DATE.	NAMES.	RECORD.	VOL. PAGE.
1763. Sept. 27.	Van Lew, John, and Martha Denton,......	M. B.,	VII. 355
1757. April 9.	Van Lew, Mary, and Barnabe Cade,.......	"	I. 496
1769. Feb. 11.	Vanlew, Mary, and Johannis Polhemus,....	"	XIV. 31
1762. June 28.	Van Liew, Catharine, and John Dorlandt, ..	"	VI. 210
1755. Sept. 30.	Van Loan, Albertus, and Maria Van Loan, .	"	I. 185
1755. Sept. 30.	Van Loan, Maria, and Albertus Van Loan, .	"	I. 185
1769. Oct. 23.	Van Lone, Elizabeth, and Jacob Hallenbeck,	"	XV. 61
1762. Oct. 8.	Van Lone, Trintie, and John Buskerk,.....	"	VI. 353
1764. Nov. 9.	Van Loo, Latitia, and Thomas Smith,......	"	VIII. 397
1763. June 1.	Van Loon, Christina, and Peter A. Fonda,..	"	VII. 209
1763. July 21.	Van Loon, Isaac, and Catharine Halenbeek,	"	VII. 277
1762. Oct. 13.	Van Loon, John, and Mary Van Loon,.....	"	VI. 361
1762. Oct. 13.	Van Loon, Mary, and John Van Loon,.....	"	VI. 361
1759. May 14.	Van Louwe, John, and Dorothy Lott,......	"	II. 283
1766. Sept. 17.	Van Lue, Susannah, and Garrit Dorland,...	"	X. 99
1759. June 6.	Van Maple, Susannah, and William Adams,.	"	II. 304
1738. April 25.	Van Name, Arent, and Mary McClean, ...	"	I. 9
1764. Jan. 7.	Van Name, Mary, and John Dehart,.......	"	VIII. 10
1782. June 27.	Vannamer, Mary, and Peter Post,.........	"	XXXVI. 59
1782. June 8.	Van Namer, Moses, and Mary Legrange,...	"	XXXVI. 42
1782. Nov. 13.	Vannamor, Elizabeth, and Garret Bush,....	"	XXXVII. 80
1763. Jan. 22.	Vannaple, Mary, and Francis Staple, ...	" •	VII. 30
1776. Mar. 9.	Vannass, Isaac, and Catharine Stoutenburgh,	"	XXIII. 282
1773. Nov. 12.	Van Nass, Tark, and Gertruy Knut,.......	"	XXII. 24
1761. Nov. 21.	Van Ness, Annatie, and John Ouderkerk,..	"	V. 239
1773. July 16.	Van Ness, Catlyna, and Abraham A. Van Alstyne, ...	"	XXI. 40
1764. July 13.	Van Ness, Catlyna, and Dirck Van Veghten,	"	VIII. 258
1756. July 12.	Van Ness, Catolintie, and Tunis Bratt,.....	"	I. 251
1770. Aug. 14.	Van Ness, David, and Catherine Heermans,	"	XVI. 160
1765. Aug. 27.	Van Ness, Garret, and Sarah De Garmo,...	"	IX. 246
1759. Aug. 23.	Van Ness, Hendrick, and Magdalena Vrooman, ...	"	II. 388
1759. Feb. 5.	Van Ness, Jane, and John Wharton, ...	"	II. 174
1765. Mar. 5.	Van Ness, Jane, and Robert Yates, ...	"	IX. 62
1762. Nov. 27.	Vanness, John, and Esther Garretse, ...	"	VI. 464
1773. Sept. 30.	Van Ness, John, and Margret Van Voort, ..	"	XXI. 127
1763. May 26.	Van Ness, John, and Rebecca Bogart, ...	"	VII. 203
1763. June 30.	Van Ness, Peter, and Catrina Van Allen, ..	"	VII. 251
1766. Sept. 27.	Van Ness, Peter, and Elbertie Hogeboom,..	"	X. 112
1759. July 17.	Van Ness, Philip, and Lenah Ten Brook,...	"	II. 357
1738. Oct. 28.	Van Nesse, Cornelius, and Susannah Switts,	"	I. 11
1776. Feb. 24.	Van Nest, Rynier, and Catherine Goetschius,	"	XXIII. 273
1765. Oct. 16.	Van Nice, Maria, and John Murphy, ...	"	IX. 301
1761. Dec. 18.	Van Noorstrandt, Altje, and Michael Golder,	"	V. 285

DATE.	NAMES.	RECORD.	VOL.	PAGE.
1762. Jan. 29.	Van Noorstrandt, Ann, and William Watts,	M. B.,	VI.	29
1762. Nov. 1.	Van Noorstrandt, Egbertje, and Adrian Hegeman,	"	VI.	398
1769. July 20.	Van Noorstrandt, George, and Hyletje Durland,	"	XV.	1
1762. Sept. 30.	Van Noorstrandt, Wyntje, and Garret Noorstrandt,	"	VI.	341
1771. Feb. 5.	Vannoorstrant, Anthony, and Marcey Hendrickson,	"	XVII.	14
1780. Mar. 29.	Van Nordan, Gabriel, and Margaret Main, .	"	XXIX.	8
1766. Oct. 14.	Van Norden, Jacobus, and Elizabeth Dawson,	"	X.	123
1760. June 10.	Van Norden, Jaconimtie, and Evert Kipp, .	"	III.	184
1783. Feb. 20.	Van Norden, John, and Magdaleen Maine, .	"	XXXIX.	98
1783. Feb. 28.	Van Norden, Luke, and Sophia Keys, ...	"	XXXVIII.	59
1760. April 3.	Vannorden, Wassal, and Hannah Devou, . . .	"	III.	96
1759. Aug. 8.	Van Norder, Anne, and John Pero, ...	"	II.	380
1758. Sept. 3.	Van Norder, Catherine, and John Bleak, . . .	"	II.	37
1758. Mar. 29.	Van Norder, Elizabeth, and William Marener,	"	I.	866
1760. June 4.	Vannorst, Aaron, and Sarah Poyer, ...	"	III.	176
1764. Mar. 17.	Van Norstrandt, Altje, and Cornelius Smith,	"	VIII.	109
1766. Sept. 26.	Van Norstrandt, George, and Sarah Vanderbelt,	"	X.	108
1763. July 4.	Van Norstrant, Albert, and Eva Longenvyck,	"	VII.	255
1773. June 11.	Van Norstrant, Albert, and Sarah Hagaman,	"	XX.	145
1758. Mar. 29.	Van Nort, Rachel, and Daniel Thorp, ...	"	I.	865
1781. Feb. 19.	Vannorttwick, Sener, and Walker Lyon, . . .	"	XXXI.	50
1773. Oct. 9.	Vannoss, George, and Anne Messerol, ...	"	XXI.	134
1779. April 7.	Vannostran, John, and Sarah Pettit, ...	"	XXVII.	98
1763. Dec. 7.	Vannostrand, Aaron, and Susanna Cornell, . .	"	VII.	496
1778. Oct. 22.	Vannostrand, Albert, and Abigail Searing, . .	"	XXVI.	66
1769. Jan. 31.	Van Nostrand, Cornelius, and Catherine Durlin,	"	XIV.	23
1773. Mar. 29.	Van Nostrand, Cornelius, and Millisent Betts,	"	XX.	75
1780. Mar. 1.	Van Nostrand, Isaac, and Patty Simonson, .	"	XXVIII.	214
1777. Mar. 29.	Van Nostrand, John, and Elenor Lefferts, .	"	XXIV.	54
1767. Nov. 23.	Van Nostrant, Sarah, and David Lamberson,	"	XII.	92
1770. Mar. 28.	Van Nuys, Annetie, and Simon Lott, ...	"	XVI.	43
1761. Dec. 10.	Van Nuys, Jane, and Peter Van Der Bilt, . .	"	V.	273
1779. Dec. 20.	Van Nuys, Magdalen, and Nicholas Van Brunt,	"	XXVIII.	174
1759. July 4.	Van Nuys, Magdalene, and John Van Duyn,	"	II.	347
1781. Jan. 3.	Van Nuys, Sarah, and William Van Nuys, . .	"	XXXI.	7
1777. Dec. 20.	Van Nuys, William, and Elenor Blew, ...	"	XXIV.	201
1781. Jan. 3.	Van Nuys, William, and Sarah Van Nuys, . .	"	XXXI.	7
1764. Oct. 10.	Van Nyss, Magdalen, and Jacob Stellenwerf,	"	VIII.	346

DATE.	NAMES.	RECORD.	VOL. PAGE.
1764. Oct. 10.	Van Nyss, Margaret, and Johannes Lott,...	M. B.,	VIII. 347
1783. Jan. 22.	Vanolaracom, Uriah, and Frances Bradey,..	"	XXXVIII. 27
1761. Oct. 28.	Van Olinda, Elizabeth, and Isaac Truax,....	"	V. 174
1761. Sept. 26.	Van Ordan, Wolvert, and Magdalen De Lanoy,.......................	"	V. 100
1763. Aug. 26.	Van Orde, Lawrence, and Helena Van Sickle,	"	VII. 314
1770. Nov. 7.	Van Orden, Andrew, and Maritje Van Blarcum,...................	"	XVI. 241
1764. Feb. 28.	Van Orden, Elisabeth, and Richard Dauson,.	"	VIII. 85
1764. Dec. 21.	Van Orden, John, and Sarah Van Evre,....	"	VIII. 462
1772. Feb. 7.	Van Orden, Magdalen, and Thomas Tippet Warner, ...	"	XVIII. 30
1783. June 12.	Van Orden, Mary, and Charles McNeal,....	"	XXXIX. 52
1763. Oct. 22.	Van Orden, Synthia, and Abraham Steymets,	"	VII. 400
1763. Sept. 15.	Van Orland, Mary, and Abram Rowan,....	"	VII. 337
1773. Dec. 9.	Vanorse, Hester, and Henry Jacobs,.......	"	XXII. 67
1768. Nov. 22.	Van Orst, John, and Hannah Bennet,......	"	XIII. 241
1760. Sept. 30.	Vanosdall, John, and Catherine Mills,......	"	III. 337
1761. Nov. 26.	Van Osdall, Nicholas, and Jane Brinkerhoff,.	"	V. 249
1781. Sept. 22.	Vanostrandt, Foster, and Charity Ketcham,.	"	XXXIII. 76
1763. June 6.	Van Oudar, Anne, and John Tows,........	"	VII. 213
1770. June 30.	Van Patte, Sophia, and Arent Veader,.....	"	XVI. 127
1758. Mar. 18.	Van Patten, Catharine, and Arent Veder, ..	"	I. 855
1762. Feb. 10.	Van Patten, Engeltje, and John Groot, ...	"	VI. 45
1762. April 13.	Van Patten, Jane, and Samuel Tyms,......	"	VI. 138
1763. June 15.	Van Patten, Susanna, and John Cuyler,....	"	VII. 228
1765. Mar. 29.	Van Patter, Philip, and Deborah Vielee, ...	"	IX. 77
1764. Mar. 1.	Vanpelt, Aaron, and Sarah Van Voorhies,..	"	VIII. 89
1770. Nov. 30.	Van Pelt, Arent, and Phebe Steellinwarf, ..	"	XVI. 278
1757. May 21.	Van Pelt, Ariantje, and Nicholas Barrington,	"	I. 538
1771. Oct. 15.	Van Pelt, Barbara, and John Mercereau,...	"	XVII. 207
1781. July 27.	Van Pelt, Elizabeth, and Johannes Cowenhoven, ...	"	XXXIII. 17
1782. Oct. 7.	Van Pelt, Ellenor, and John McFee, ...	"	XXXVII. 33
1759. Feb. 12.	Van Pelt, Hannah, and George Barnes, ...	"	II. 190
1779. June 10.	Van Pelt, Hannah, and William Bennet, ...	"	XXVII. 163
1762. Sept. 18.	Vanpelt, Jacob, and Elizabeth Meril, ...	"	VI. 322
1778. Mar. 18.	Van Pelt, John, and Famitie Duyree,......	"	XXV. 46
1758. Mar. 7.	Van Pelt, John, and Margaret Lewis,......	"	I. 835
1767. Nov. 17.	Van Pelt, Mary, and Peter Prall,..........	"	XII. 87
1761. Mar. 19.	Van Pelt, Mary, and William Bennet,......	"	IV. 109
1761. April 24.	Van Pelt, Nieltje, and Niccasie Couwenhoven,	"	IV. 166
1771. June 19.	Van Pelt, Peter, and Sarah Lawrence,.....	"	XVII. 116
1783. Feb. 8.	Van Pelt, Rachel, and William Bedell, ...	"	XXXVIII. 37
1767. Nov. 27.	Van Pelt, Ram, and Ida Lefferts, ...	"	XII. 100

DATE.	NAMES.	RECORD.	VOL.	PAGE.
1777. Oct. 15.	Van Pelt, Susanah, and Abraham Stilwill,..	M. B.,	XXIV.	163
1783. Sept. 5.	Van Pelt, Teunis, and Mary Laforge,......	"	XL.	27
1782. Oct. 2.	Van Pelt, William, and Sarah Sanders,.....	"	XXXVII.	24
1763. June 30.	Van Pelt, Winant, and Mary Hyer, ...	"	VII.	247
1763. Feb. 23.	Van Pelts, Joseph, and Elizabeth Egberts,..	"	VII.	76
1765. July 12.	Van Petten, Arent N., and Helena J.Van Eps,	"	IX.	204
1762. June 12.	Van Petten, John, and Eleanor Vedder,....	"	VI.	189
1738. Aug. 19.	Van Petten, Nicholas, and Ariantie Bratt,..	"	I.	10
1761. Jan. 12.	Van Petten, Sarah, and Abraham Bratt,....	"	IV.	11
1768. June 14.	Van Plank, David, and Christina Valk, ...	"	XIII.	127
1765. Sept. 18.	Van Ranselaer, Henry, and Rachel Douw,..	"	IX.	268
1766. Sept. 26.	Van Ranst, Abraham, and Catherine Roose-velt,...............................	"	X.	107
1779. April 2.	Van Ranst, Catherine, and Henry Rogers,..	"	XXVII.	90
1769. April 25.	Van Ranst, Cornelius, and Catherine Duryee,	"	XIV.	85
1762. Oct. 9.	Van Ranst, John, and Mary Willett,.......	"	VI.	356
1770. Feb. 17.	Van Ranst, Mary, and Augustine Graham, .	"	XVI.	18
1772. Sept. 18.	Van Ranst, Mary, and Evert Byvanck, Jr.,.	"	XIX.	52
1761. Dec. 15.	Van Ranst, Sarah, and Nicholas Roosevelt, Jr.,	"	V.	281
1760. July 19.	Van Rants, Mary, and George Codwise,....	"	III.	218
1761. May 19.	Van Rantz, Rachel, and Derick Brincker-hoff, Jr., ...	"	IV.	201
1773. Nov. 25.	Vanrelser, Daniel, and Elizabeth Beedle, ...	"	XXII.	45
1775. July 12.	Van Renselaer, Catharine, and Eilardus Wes-terlo, ...	"	XXIII.	95
1755. Sept. 4.	Van Renselaer, Catherin, and Philip John Schuyler,...........................	"	I.	160
1771. June 19.	Van Renselaer, Catherine, and William Hen-ry Ludlow, ...	"	XVII.	114
1764. Sept. 19.	Van Renselaer, Hendrick K., and Alida Bratt,..............................	"	VIII.	314
1762. Oct. 8.	Van Renselaer, Henry, and Alida Rutsen,..	"	VI.	355
1775. May 13.	Van Renselaer, Killian, Jr., and Mary White,	"	XXIII.	33
1762. Sept. 3.	Van Renselaer, Margaret, and Francis Nicoll,	"	VI.	305
1765. April 23.	Van Renselaer, Robert, and Cornelia Rutser,	"	IX.	104
1764. Jan. 19.	Van Renselaer, Stephen, and Catherine Liv-ingston,............................	"	VIII.	22
1768. Feb. 15.	Van Renselaer, Stephen, and Maria Saun-ders,...............................	"	XIII.	38
1764. Feb. 11.	Van Rensselaer, Jeremiah, Jr., and Helena Lansingh, ...	"	VIII.	57
1760. July 3.	Van Rensselear, Jeremiah, and Judith Ba-yard, ...	"	III.	203
1769. Sept. 18.	Van Rensselaer, Killyaen, and Mary Low,..	"	XV.	40
1780. June 29.	Van Riper, Harman, and Mary Van Riper, .	"	XXIX.	103

54

DATE.	NAMES.	RECORD.	VOL.	PAGE.
1780. June 29.	Van Riper, Mary, and Harman Van Riper, .	M. B.,	XXIX.	103
1783. Aug. 25.	Vanripey, Anne, and Jacob Vanripey, ...	"	XL.	10
1783. Aug. 11.	Vanripey, Jacob, and Anne Vanripey,.....	"	XL.	10
1783. Aug. 11.	Van Rype, Cornelius, and Elizabeth Devenport,...............................	"	XXXIX.	124
1761. July 27.	Van Ryper, Christian, and James Linford,..	"	V.	9
1756. Nov. 5.	Vans, Alexander, and Helena Drinkwater, .	"	I.	346
1761. Oct. 3.	Van Salsberg, Jannika, and Peter Van Bueren, ...	"	V.	119
1758. Dec. 18.	Van Sant, James, and Mary Brooks,.......	"	II.	132
1765. Oct. 26.	Van Sante, Elizabeth, and Thomas Barret,..	"	IX.	323
1759. Oct. 2.	Van Sante, Geysbert, and Rebecca Winne,.	"	II.	440
1763. Oct. 3.	Van Sante, Rachel, and Isaac Hoghkarck,..	"	VII.	369
1770. Feb. 19.	Van Santford, Rebecca, and Cornelius Eckerson,...............................	"	XVI.	21
1770. June 12.	Van Santford, Rebeccah, and Christopher P. Yates, ...	"	XVI.	110
1760. Mar. 17.	Van Schaack, Henry, and Jane Holland,...	"	III.	80
1773. Sept. 8.	Van Schaaick, Anna, and Henry Merselis,..	"	XXI.	103.
1773. Mar. 26.	Van Schaick, Alida, and Anthony Bratt,...	"	XX.	74
1757. June 24.	Van Schaick, Andries, and Alida Hogan,...	"	I.	574
1773. Sept. 30.	Van Schaick, Cathalina, and John Groosbeek,	"	XXI.	128
1773. May 14.	Van Schaick, Catherina, and Cornelius Douw,	"	XX.	111
1772. Dec. 1.	Van Schaick, Cornelius, and Angeltie Yates,	"	XIX.	138
1760. Oct. 7.	Van Schaick, Cornelius, and Judith Wurmer,................................	"	III.	351
1760. Nov. 26.	Van Schaick, David, and Catherine Van Valkenburgh, ...	"	III.	446
1767. July 17.	Van Schaick, Elizabeth, and William Elsworth, ...	"	XI.	135
1760. Nov. 21.	Van Schaick, Garretie, and John I. Bleecker,	"	III.	431
1764. Nov. 27.	Van Schaick, Goose, and Catharine Bleecker,	"	VIII.	426
1770. Nov. 15.	Van Schaick, Goose, and Mary Ten Broeck,	"	XVI.	256
1767. Sept. 9.	Van Schaick, Gosen, and Elcie Roseboom, .	"	XII.	31
1757. June 24.	Van Schaick, Gosen, and Elizabeth Wendel,	"	I.	571
1761. Nov. 9.	Van Schaick, Goshen, and Margaret Schuyler,................................	"	V.	199
1765. Feb. 4.	Van Schaick, Jacob, and Mary Van Buren,.	"	IX.	44
1764. Aug. 16.	Van Schaick, Jane, and Peter Sylvester,....	"	VIII.	284
1768. April 18.	Van Schaick, Lydia, and Isaac Van Vleck,..	"	XIII.	79
1762. July 2.	Van Schaick, Ryeke, and Peter W. Douw, .	"	VI.	222
1772. Nov. 27.	Van Schaick, Sarah, and Peter I. Bogaerdt,.	"	XIX.	131
1772. Jan. 26.	Van Schayck, Cathalyna, and John Stevens,	"	XVIII.	17
1766. Nov. 17.	Van Schayck, Gerret, and Elizabeth Van Slyck, ...	"	X.	170

DATE.		NAMES.	RECORD.	VOL.	PAGE.
1771. Sept.	5.	Van Schoonhoven, Hendrick, and Altie Van Den Bergh,	M. B.,	XVII.	176
1764. Dec.	24.	Van Schoonhoven, Jacobus, and Elisabeth Clout,	"	VIII.	465
1764. Sept.	20.	Van Schoonhoven, Susannah, and Rutger Lansingh,	"	VIII.	318
1767. Oct.	31.	Van Schurliunse, Cornelius, and Elizabeth Roseboom,	"	XII.	73
1765. Oct.	31.	Van Scise, Martha, and Abraham Bockee,..	"	IX.	345
1763. May	2.	Van Sice, Cornelius, and Frances Bloom,...	"	VII.	162
1771. June	7.	Van Sice, Elizabeth, and Abraham Truax,..	"	XVII.	105
1766. July	9.	Van Sice, Jacobus, and Elizabeth Gerbrant,	"	X.	45
1757. July	2.	Van Sice, Hannah, and Patrick Hyne,.....	"	I.	570
1766. June	9.	Van Sice, Magdalene, and Ahasuerus Turk,.	"	X.	10
1759. May	14.	Van Sice, Mary, and George Hopkins,.....	"	II.	282
1763. Dec.	6.	Van Sickelen, Fardeandis, and Cornelia Lagier,	"	XIII.	254
1763. Aug.	26.	Van Sickle, Helena, and Lawrence Van Orde,	"	VII.	314
1782. May	24.	Van Sicklen, Abraham, and Cornelia Cornell,	"	XXXVI.	21
1769. April	10.	Van Sicklen, Arreantje, and Jacobus Suydam,	"	XIV.	70
1772. July	18.	Van Sickler, Jane, and Lewis Guest, ...	"	XIX.	1
1768. Oct.	20.	Van Siclen, John, and Catelinetie Van Wycke,	"	XIII.	214
1769. Aug.	1.	Van Siclen, Mary, and Samuel Lininton,...	"	XV.	13
1771. June	11.	Van Siklen, Cornelius, and Catherine Johnson,	"	XVII.	110
1771. Mar.	12.	Van Sinderen, Ulpianus, and Magdalen Bancker,	"	XVII.	32
1760. July	10.	Van Sise, John, and Elizabeth Clement,....	"	III.	210
1762. Nov.	3.	Van Sise, Judith, and Jacobus Bogert, ...	"	VI.	408
1778. May	21.	Van Size, Margaret, and Garret Willumson,	"	XXV.	89
1765. Sept.	23.	Van Sleek, Jantie, and Garret Groosback,..	"	IX.	270
1761. May	2.	Van Sleght, Christiana, and Gilbert Tice,...	"	IV.	175
1765. Oct.	29.	Van Sleght, Sarah, and Coenradt Hooghtelingh,	"	IX.	333
1761. Sept.	30.	Van Slieck, Johanna, and Frans Van Bueren,	"	V.	108
1763. June	13.	Van Slik, Johannis, and Helena Gardiner,..	"	VII.	252
1761. April	21.	Van Slik, Tobias, and Sentje Wheeler,.....	"	IV.	159
1737. Sept.	3.	Van Slyck, Direck, and Christina Tenbrooke,	"	I.	7
1766. Nov.	17.	Van Slyck, Elizabeth, and Gerret Van Schayck,	"	X.	170
1736. Sept.	1.	Van Slyck, Gerrit, and Annatie Turk, ...	"	I.	2
1765. June	5.	Van Slyck, Harmanus, and Annatje Sanderse Glen,	"	IX.	159

DATE.	NAMES.	RECORD.	VOL. PAGE.
1763. Sept. 8.	Van Slyck, Isaac, and Catharine Huyck,...	M. B.,	VII. 329
1772. Nov. 12.	Van Slyck, Jane, and Garret Hyer, ...	"	XIX. 111
1773. Sept. 1.	Van Slyck, Janetie, and Edward Robinson,.	"	XXI. 96
1755. Sept. 12.	Van Slyck, Jannetie Jacobuse, and Philip Ryley, ...	"	I. 175
1762. Nov. 11.	Van Slyck, Jannetje, and Lucas Van Deursen, ...	"	VI. 425
1762. Oct. 14.	Van Slyck, Jesse, and Jacomyntje Groot,...	"	VI. 365
1753. Oct. 5.	Van Slyck, Jochaim, and Cornelia Van Valkenburgh, ...	"	I. 131
1773. April 5.	Van Slyck, Martin, and Helena Vrooman,..	"	XX. 82
1765. July 30.	Van Slyck, Mary, and Arent Samuel Bratt,.	"	IX. 221
1760. Nov. 25.	Van Slyck, Peter, and Seyentie Gardinier,..	"	III. 443
1776. Feb. 15.	Van Slycke, Cornelius Ad., and Elizabeth Yates, ...	"	XXIII. 268
1772. Nov. 17.	Van Slycke, Harmanus, and Mary Vrooman,	"	XIX. 116
1763. June 10.	Van Slyeck, Eva, and Harman Van Bueren,	"	VII. 221
1759. April 28.	Van Slyk, William, and Dorothy Vasbergh,.	"	II. 260
1767. Mar. 30.	Van Slyke, Anthony; and Claertye Van Slyke, ...	"	XI. 53
1767. Mar. 30.	Van Slyke, Claertye, and Anthony Van Slyke, ...	"	XI. 53
1760. Aug. 14.	Van Solingen, Catharine, and Thomas Livingston, ...	"	III. 253
1767. July 10.	Van Stanvoord, Anna, and James Dole,....	"	XI. 131
1757. Dec. 12.	Van Steenbergh, Benjamin, and Rebeccah Cole, ...	"	I. 737
1765. April 11.	Van Steenbergh, Gertrude, and Evert Roos,	"	IX. 89
1757. June 2.	Van Steenbergh, Johanna, and Simon Westfall, ...	"	I. 547
1773. Sept. 6.	Van Steenbergh, John, and Catherine Masten,	"	XXI. 102
1757. Dec. 12.	Van Steenbergh, Margaret, and John Teller,	"	I. 736
1762. Nov. 19.	Van Steenbergh, Margarit, and Evert Wynkoop Swart, ...	"	VI. 445
1765. May 28.	Van Steenbergh, Mary, and Richard Leaycraft, ...	"	IX. 143
1771. Dec. 3.	Van Steenbergh, Mathew, and Hilake Witeker, ...	"	XVII. 283
1762. Nov. 17.	Van Steenbergh, Peter, and Balitje Van Kleef, ...	"	VI. 436
1773. Feb. 2.	Van Steenbergh, Samuel, and Annatje Swartwout, ...	"	XX. 35
1763. Nov. 9.	Van Steenbergh, Tobias, and Nieltje Crispel,	"	VII. 440
1769. Oct. 19.	Van Steen Bergh, Wilhelmus, and Gerrity Schermerhorne, ...	"	XV. 57

DATE.		NAMES.	RECORD.	VOL.	PAGE.
1737. Sept.	20.	Van Stimberg, Tobias, and Sarah Pierson,..	M. B.,	I.	7
1759. Sept.	15.	Van Syse, Margaret, and Derick Van Ingen,	"	II.	425
1781. July	9.	Vansyth, Frances, and John Ketler, ...	"	XXXIII.	2
1770. Aug.	25.	Vantassel, Susannah, and Rem Monfoort, ..	"	XVI.	170
1760. July	4.	Vantassell, Lena, and William Waldron,....	"	III.	225
1765. April	17.	Vantessell, Peter, and Catharine Acker,....	"	IX.	101
1765. Oct.	28.	Vantine, Rachel, and Cornelius Brett, ...	"	IX.	328
1761. Mar.	13.	Van Toorah, Catharine, and James Allison,.	"	IV.	99
1773. Aug.	7.	Van Tuyl, Andrew, and Mary Bogert,.....	"	XXI.	59
1780. July	3.	Van Tuyl, Dennis, and Deborah Tucker, ...	"	XXXIX.	80
1757. Mar.	18.	Vantuyl, Henry, and Phebe Van Tuyl, ...	"	I.	474
1757. Mar.	18.	Van Tuyl, Phebe, and Henry Vantuyl, ...	"	I.	474
1772. May	9.	Vantuyl, Phebe, and Peter Barberie, ...	"	XVIII.	105
1757. Mar.	18.	Vantuyle, Elenor, and Cornelius Van Der Bilt, ...	"	I.	473
1763. Aug.	13.	Van Tyne, Catharine, and Henry Filkine, ..	"	VII.	301
1737. July	19.	Van Ulitt, Cornelia, and Mathew Edward Thompson, ...	"	I.	6
1757. Nov.	11.	Van Vaghten, Cornelius, and Ann Pensinger,	"	I.	702
1761. Jan.	26.	Van Valkenberg, Jacob Jacob, and Catherine Vander Pole, ...	"	IV.	31
1763. Oct.	31.	Van Valkenbergh, Catlyntie, and Laurence Fonda,.............................	"	VII.	416
1758. Jan.	17.	Van Valkenbergh, Jane, and Joseph Guillot,	"	I.	785
1773. Aug.	20.	Van Valkenbergh, Jane, and Matthew Gose,	"	XXI.	79
1768. May	6.	Van Valkenbergh, Peter, and Angetje Witbeck, ...	"	XIII.	95
1764. Aug.	23.	Van Valkenbergh, Peter, and Mary Upham,	"	VIII.	292
1757. Dec.	2.	Van Valkenburgh, Abraham L., and Eva Van Veghten,.............................	"	I.	721
1775. Aug.	14.	Van Valkenburgh, Ariantje, and Isaac Wessells, ...	"	XXIII.	127
1761. April	13.	Van Valkenburgh, Bartholomew, and Christiana Van Valkenburgh,..............	"	IV.	146
1771. Aug.	8.	Van Valkenburgh, Baushe, and John Davis,	"	XVII.	155
1757. Dec.	2.	Van Valkenburgh, Catalintje, and Ephraim Van Buren,.......................	"	I.	722
1759. April	2.	Van Valkenburgh, Cathalyna, and Mase Van Buren,.............................	"	II.	232
1759. July	4.	Van Valkenburgh, Catharine, and Isaac Van Valkenburgh, ...	"	II.	346
1775. July	28.	Van Valkenburgh, Catharine A., and Andrew Vanderpool, ...	"	XXIII.	109
1769. Oct.	23.	Van Valkenburgh, Catlyne, and Gabriel Esselstyne, ...	"	XV.	62

DATE.	NAMES.	RECORD.	VOL.	PAGE.
1761. April 13.	Van Valkenburgh, Christiana, and Bartholomew Van Valkenburgh, ...	M. B.,	IV.	146
1753. Oct. 5.	Van Valkenburgh, Cornelia, and Jochaim Van Slyck, ...	"	I.	131
1760. Nov. 25.	Van Valkenburgh, Deborah, and Henry H. Clauw, ...	"	III.	442
1759. Nov. 26.	Van Valkenburgh, Dozote, and Hendryck Kettel, ...	"	II.	516
1765. Oct. 31.	Van Valkenburgh, Eve, and John Oosterhout,	"	IX.	346
1768. Feb. 29.	Van Valkenburgh, Eve, and John Vernor, .		XIII.	48
1771. May 27.	Van Valkenburgh, Geretie, and Jacob Schenkall, ...	..	XVII.	94
1759. July 4.	Van Valkenburgh, Henry F., and Annatie Vanderpool, ...	"	II.	345
1768. July 11.	Van Valkenburgh, Isaac, and Annatje Ostrande, ...	"	XIII.	155
1759. July 4.	Van Valkenburgh, Isaac, and Catharine Van Valkenburgh, ...	"	II.	346
1760. Sept. 19.	Van Valkenburgh, Isaac, and Engeltie Van Denbergh, ...	"	III.	322
1776. Feb. 8.	Van Valkenburgh, Jane, and Johannis Schinckel, ...	"	XXIII.	265
1760. Jan. 14.	Van Valkenburgh, Jannetye, and Peter Barheyt, ...	"	II.	580
1756. Oct. 25.	Van Valkenburgh, Jantie, and Melgert Van Depoel, ...	"	I.	334
1738. Aug. 2.	Van Valkenburgh, Jochem, and Maria Hoogeboom, ...	"	I.	2
1775. May 8.	Van Valkenburgh, John I., and Margaret Vanderpool, ...	"	XXIII.	25
1764. Mar. 19.	Van Valkenburgh, Margaret, and John Taylor, ...	"	VIII.	111
1775. May 11.	Van Valkenburgh, Margaret, and Joseph Lawrence, ...	"	XXIII.	30
1769. July 10.	Van Valkenburgh, Mathew, and Hannah Skinkel, ...	"	XIV.	146
1768. Sept. 19.	Vanvalkenburgh, Peter, and Maritje Schermerhorn, ...	"	XIII.	190
1769. Nov. 13.	Van Valkenburgh, Rachel, and Abraham A. Fonda, ...	"	XV.	90
1764. April 10.	Van Valkinburgh, Elizabeth, and Thomas Lynott, ...	"	VIII.	147
1775. April 6.	Van Varck, Ann Mary, and Jonathan Skinner, ...	"	XXIII.	3
1773. Aug. 19.	Van Varck, Dinah, and Thomas P. Periam, .	"	XXI.	76

DATE.	NAMES.	RECORD.	VOL. PAGE.
1772. Jan. 23.	Van Varck, Effee, and John Stout,........	M. B.,	XVIII. 16
1760. Nov. 15.	Van Varck, James, and Elizabeth Bogart,..	"	III. 417
1760. Dec. 5.	Van Varck, John, and Catherine Towers, ..	"	III. 458
1766. Oct. 26.	Van Vecgtan, Anna, and Ignas Kip,.......	"	X. 130
1765. Aug. 22.	Van Vechte, Janetie, and Isaac Whitbeek, .	"	IX. 243
1765. April 25.	Van Veghte, Ann, and Thomas Shipboy,...	"	IX. 108
1757. Nov. 8.	Van Veghte, Cornelius, and Annatje Knickerbacker,............................	"	I. 699
1755. Sept. 8.	Van Veghte, Effie, and John Goar, ...	"	I. 169
1765. May 4.	Van·Veghte, Lydia, and Francis Salisbury, .	"	IX. 120
1757. Mar. 19.	Van Veghten, Angeltie, and Stephen Schuyler, ...	"	I. 475
1770. April 20.	Van Veghten, Anthony, and Mary Fonda,..	"	XVI. 65
1758. Oct. 12.	Van Veghten, Derick, and Aleda Kernickerbacker, ...	"	II. 50
1764. July 13.	Van Veghten, Dirck, and Catlyna Van Ness,	"	VIII. 258
1757. Dec. 2.	Van Veghten, Eva, and Abraham I. Van Valkenburgh,.............	"	I. 721
1761. Nov. 30.	Van Veghten, John, and Ann Williams, ...	"	V. 256
1764. Feb. 27.	Van Veghten, Lydia, and Jacob Cuyler,....	"	VIII. 94
1775. May 12.	Van Veghten, Volckert, and Elizabeth Van Den Bergh,........................	"	XXIII. 32
1762. Nov. 17.	Van Veghten, Volkert, and Jane Hunn, ...	"	VI. 440
1770. June 12.	Van Veighten, Derick T., and Petertie Yates,	"	XVI. 108
1757. Dec. 15.	Van Vicklaer, Garrit, and Maria Duryee,....	"	I. 746
1757. Jan. 21.	Van Vie, Catharine, and Jan Eghbersen,...	"	I. 423
1771. Dec. 14.	Van Vlackreh, Catrina, and Dirck Brinkenhoff, Jr., ...	"	XVII. 294
1772. Nov. 20.	Van Vleck, Abraham H., and Elizabeth Aroe,	"	XIX. 134
1768. April 18.	Van Vleck, Abraham I., and Jane Vosburgh,	"	XIII. 80
1769. Oct. 21.	Van Vleck, Abraham K., and Margaret Cantine,..............................	"	XV. 59
1759. Feb. 7.	Van Vleck, Catharine, and Laurens Eman,..	"	II. 181
1779. Aug. 7.	Van Vleck, Elizabeth, and Cornelius Cook,.	"	XXVIII. 49
1764. Dec. 31.	Van Vleck, Evert, and Catharine Van Volkenburgh, ...	"	VIII. 472
1768. April 18.	Van Vleck, Isaac, and Lydia Van Schaick,.	"	XIII. 79
1772. Nov. 20.	Van Vleck, Isaac, and Margaret Roosevelt,.	"	XIX. 133
1770. Nov. 15.	Van Vleck, Lucretia, and Jacobus Vander Poel, ...	"	XVI. 255
1770. Aug. 30.	Van Vleck, Mary, and Henry Minthorne, ..	"	XVI. 176
1753. July 4.	Van Vleck, Mary, and William Stoutenburgh,	"	I. 71
1769. Oct. 21.	Van Vleck, Samuel, and Catherine Compton,	"	XV. 58
1767. July 4.	Van Vlecker, Deentie, and Daniel Hasbrouck,	"	XI. 124
1762. Nov. 8.	Van Vliet, Teunis, and Lamatje Romine,...	"	VI. 419

DATE.		NAMES.	RECORD.	VOL.	PAGE.
1753. July	12.	Van Volkenbergh, Jannetie, and Barent Hoes,	M. B.,	I.	75
1766. Sept.	29.	Van Volkenbergh, Johannes, and Ariantie Van Bueren,	"	X.	114
1763. April	11.	Van Volkenburgh, Bartholomew, and Sarah Van Elting,	"	VII.	123
1767. Aug.	15.	Van Volkenburgh, Batta, and Johannes Vinhage,	"	XII.	18
1764. Dec.	31.	Van Volkenburgh, Catharine, and Evert Van Vleck,	"	VIII.	472
1765. April	15.	Van Volkenburgh, Catharine, and Frederick Mynderse,	"	IX.	93
1762. Nov.	19.	Van Volkenburgh, Catrina, and Lambert Van Volkenburgh,	"	VI.	444
1771. Nov.	28.	Van Volkenburgh, Elizabeth, and Conradt Vanhoosen,	"	XVII.	272
1758. May	10.	Van Volkenburgh, Eva, and John Schram, .	"	I.	898
1765. Oct.	1.	Van Volkenburgh, Eve, and Cornelius Schermerhorn,	"	IX.	284
1763. May	9.	Van Volkenburgh, Jane, and Charles Charles Cruck,	"	VII.	172
1764. Jan.	23.	Van Volkenburgh, John, and Elisabeth Minderson,	"	VIII.	32
1762. Nov.	19.	Van Volkenburgh, Lambert, and Catrina Van Volkenburgh,	"	VI.	444
1759. Oct.	15.	Van Volkenburgh, Lydia, and James Bloodgood,	"	II.	458
1764. Sept.	21.	Van Volkenburgh, Marija, and Abraham Van Der Pool,	"	VIII.	320
1772. May	25.	Van Volkenburgh, Peter, and Jane Ducolon,	"	XX.	126
1771. Oct.	29.	Van Volkenburgh, Polly, and Bartholomew Hogeboom,	"	XVII.	231
1757. Sept.	1.	Van Volkenburgh, Rachal, and Hugh Deniston,	"	I.	628
1765. Aug.	27.	Van Volkenbury, Isaac, and Nancy Van Bergen,	"	IX.	249
1771. Oct.	29.	Van Volkinburgh, Cloudea, and Christina Smith,	"	XVII.	228
1760. June	18.	Van Voorhease, Court, and Sarah Van Brunt,	"	III.	190
1763. Dec.	19.	Van Voorhees, Jannetje, and Zebulon Southerd,	"	VII.	510
1760. Oct.	10.	Van Voorhees, Mary, and Peter De Bois, ..	"	III.	358
1765. Aug.	7.	Van Voorhees, Phebe, and Johannes Schut,	"	IX.	232
1761. Nov.	13.	Van Voorhees, Sarah, and Daniel Southard, .	"	V.	215
1764. Mar.	1.	Van Voorhies, Sarah, and Aaron Vanpelt, ..	"	VIII.	89

DATE.	NAMES.	RECORD.	VOL.	PAGE.
1764. June 7.	Van Voorhies, Sarah, and Francis Brett, ...	M. B.,	VIII.	215
1769. April 26.	Van Voorhis, Daniel, and Sarah Brett,.....	"	XIV.	90
1768. Oct. 19.	Van Voorhis, Ellinore, and Christopher Dubois, Jr., ...	"	XIII.	212
1762. April 15.	Van Voorhis, John, and Johanna Rowe, ...	"	VI.	110
1773. Aug. 6.	Van Voorhis, Stephen, and Elizabeth Mathewman, ...	"	XXI.	58
1772. Jan. 21.	Van Voorhis, Zachariah, and Anna Lawrence,	"	XVIII.	15
1766. Oct. 24.	Van Voorhuyse, Ann, and Lamber Cuyper,.	"	X.	139
1769. July 28.	Van Voorhys, Jacob, and Sarah White, ...	"	XV.	7
1762. Nov. 1.	Van Voorst, Jacobus, Jr., and Clara Meurenus, ...	"	VI.	402
1759. April 12.	Van Voorst, Sarah, and Samuel Bourdet,...	"	II.	240
1763. May 13.	Van Voort, Annatje, and Arent Becker, ...	"	VII.	187
1773. Sept. 30.	Van Voort, Margrit, and John Van Ness,..	"	XXI.	127
1762. Oct. 5.	Van Voort, Mary, and Benjamin Forsey,...	"	VI.	346
1763. Oct. 31.	Van Voort, Nicholas, and Maria Staats,....	"	VII.	418
1759. Feb. 24.	Van Voorte, Elizabeth, and John Freyer, ..	"	II.	201
1755. Aug. 12.	Van Vorhees, Barnardus, and Ann Griggs,	"	I.	145
1770. June 7.	Van Vorheis, Jeronimus, and Ann Townsend,	"	XVI.	105
1763. April 21.	Van Vorst, Elizabeth, and John Henry,....	"	VII.	135
1772. July 20.	Van Vorst, Hannah, and Jacobus C. Peck, .	"	XIX.	3
1766. Nov. 25.	Van Vorst, John, and Mary Adams,........	"	X.	182
1763. Oct. 26.	Van Vorst, Sarah, and Teunis Swart,......	"	VII.	404
1753. June 29.	Van Vranck, Johannis, and Hannah Fort,..	"	I.	66
1763. Nov. 17.	Van Vranka, Mary, and Isaac Rose,.......	"	VII.	453
1772. Jan. 8.	Van Vrankan, Lawrence, and Angelica Veeder, ...	"	XVIII.	6
1762. Sept. 7.	Van Vranke. Ann, and Simon Fort,.	"	VI.	309
1758. Jan. 16.	Van Vranke, Barberie, and Peter Peterse Bogert, ...	"	I.	784
1758. Jan. 17.	Van Vranke, Elizabeth, and Andries Fraux,	"	I.	787
1763. Jan. 18.	Van Vranke, Gerret, and Breghtie Gislingh,.	"	VII.	21
1763. Oct. 26.	Van Vranke, Rebecca, and John De Graff, .	"	VII.	403
1764. June 8.	Van Vranke. Rykert, and Catharine Dunbar, ...	"	VIII.	217
1757. Oct. 27.	Van Vranken, Annetje, and Jacob Van Aernam, ...	"	I.	683
1770. Nov. 17.	Van Vranken, Gerrit G., and Gartruy Visscher, ...	"	XVI.	260
1762. Nov. 12.	Van Vranken, Jannetje, and William Felench,	"	VI.	429
1762. Nov. 1.	Van Vranken, Hyllegont, and Robert Winne,	"	VI.	401
1760. April 3.	Van Vranken, Ryckart R., and Maria Marselis,.....................	"	III.	95
1770. Nov. 14.	Van Vrankin, Jane, and Barent Mynderse, .	"	XVI.	250

DATE.	NAMES.	RECORD.	VOL. PAGE.
1737. May 7.	Van Vrantur, Anken, and Cornelius Vandenbergh, ...	M. B.,	I. 6
1759. April 9.	Van Vredenburgh, Rachel, and Jacob Van Bentheuysen, ...	"	II. 237
1763. Sept. 27.	Van Vroncka, Christeena, and Albert Slingerland, ...	"	VII. 354
1771. Nov. 12.	Vanvroncka, Margaretta, and Hendrick Waldron, ...	"	XVII. 248
1782. April 4.	Vanvyck, Phebe, and Henry Sheaff, ...	"	XXXV. 115
1738. Aug. 22.	Van Vyve, Madelane, and Burger Mynders,	"	I. 10
1736. May 5.	Van Wagen, Simon, and Neltie Whitaker,.	"	I. 1
1781. April 11.	Van Wagenen, Agness, and Joseph Griffiths,	"	XXXI. 101
1782. Nov. 11.	Van Wagenen, Ann, and Casparus Prior,...	"	XXXVII. 79
1755. Aug. 20.	Van Wagenen, Bailtie, and Johannis Merselis, ...	"	I. 150
1762. May 13.	Van Wagenen, Elizabeth, and Cornelius Decker, ...	"	VI. 160
1762. Jan. 8.	Vanwagenen, Hendrick, and Ann Stillwell,	"	VI. 4
1761. June 25.	Van Wagenen, Henry, and Jane Pintard, ..	"	IV. 263
1773. Oct. 28.	Van Wagenen, Huybert, and Dorothy Lewis, ...	"	XXII. 2
1764. Oct. 29.	Van Wagenen, Jacob, and Mary Ewetse, ..	"	VIII. 381
1770. April 6.	Van Wagenen, Leah, and Abraham Leuwes,	"	XVI. 51
1775. Dec. 14.	Van Wagenen, Mary, and Jacob Kipp, ...	"	XXIII. 230
1768. Oct. 27.	Van Waghanan, Rachel, and Cornelius Hendricks, ...	"	XIII. 217
1780. June 20.	Vanwaglum, Sealeah, and John Johnson,...	"	XXIX. 90
1772. Nov. 26.	Van Wagoner, Maria, and Benjamin Peters,	"	XIX. 130
1772. Oct. 2.	Van Wagoner, Rachel, and Jacobus I. Vanetten, ...	"	XIX. 66
1782. Oct. 7.	Vanwart, Jacob, and Mary Fouler, ...	"	XXXVII. 34
1762. Nov. 1.	Van Wee, Agnes, and Hendrick Bradt, ...	"	VI. 400
1759. Aug. 23.	Van Wee, Johannes, and Magdalena Luke,.	"	II. 389
1764. Oct. 23.	Van Wee, Tryntie, and Casparus Conine,...	"	VIII. 369
1759. May 12.	Van Wenkell, Henry, and Jane Brower, ...	"	II. 281
1780. June 26.	Van Why, Jemime, and Matthew Lownds, .	"	XXIX. 98
1774. Jan. 24.	Vanwi, Peter, and Mary Ellis, ...	"	XXII. 114
1780. Sept. 13.	Van Wick, Sarah, and Nathaniel Foster,...	"	XXX. 26
1762. July 22.	Van Wickel, Garret, and Phebe Coover, ...	"	VI. 252
1776. Jan. 13.	Van Wickeler, Catherine, and Robert Hill, .	"	XXIII. 246
1767. Sept. 28.	Van Wickler, Sarah, and Jan Monfoort, ...	"	XII. 47
1762. Aug. 21.	Van Wie, Gerrit, and Catharine Lansingh,..	"	VI. 282
1772. June 17.	Van Wie, Magdalena, and Phillip Look,....	"	XVIII. 141
1767. May 11.	Van Wie, William, and Jannatie Lansingh,.	"	XI. 80
1772. April 4.	Vanwinckel, John, and Mary Kenedy, ...	"	XVIII. 67

DATE.	NAMES.	RECORD.	VOL.	PAGE.
1783. Oct. 14.	Van Winckle, Sarah, and Jacob Aplee, ...	M. B.,	XL.	79
1780. Sept. 6.	Van Winkel, Abraham, and Ann Clandenny,	"	XXX.	19
1782. Oct. 26.	Van Winkel, Daniel, and Anne Winner, ...	"	XXXVII.	66
1763. June 22.	Van Winkle, Ann, and Cornelius Voorhes, .	"	VII.	240
1779. Sept. 18.	Vanwinkle, Martha, and Josiah Martin, ...	"	XXVIII.	79
1763. Oct. 26.	Van Winkle, Mary, and John Lamb, ...	"	VII.	402
1757. Jan. 26.	Van Winkler, Catharine, and John Williams,	"	I.	427
1773. Aug. 5.	Van Woert, Henry, and Catherine Aights, .	"	XXI.	57
1770. June 8.	Van Woert, John, Jr., and Catharine Lansingh, ...	"	XVI.	106
1763. Sept. 24.	Van Woirt, Lewis, and Catharine Vandenbergh, ...	"	IX.	271
1761. Feb. 28.	Van Woort, Catharine, and Alexander Wilson, ...	"	IV.	85
1760. Nov. 27.	Van Woort, Eva, and Isaac Slingerlandt, . . .	"	III.	449
1760. Oct. 7.	Van Woort, Petrus Jacob, and Rachel Ridder, ...	"	III.	352
1760. Aug. 19.	Van Woort, Rebecca, and Harme Fort, ...	"	III.	260
1738. Sept. 5.	Van Wrank, Rycard, and Antie Truan, ...	"	I.	11
1760. Oct. 7.	Van Wurmer, Judith, and Cornelius Van Schaick, ...	"	III.	351
1775. Dec. 20.	Van Wyck, Abraham, and Catharine Van Cortlandt, ...	"	XXIII.	233
1761. June 23.	Van Wyck, Abraham, and Elisabeth Wright,	"	IV.	256
1772. Mar. 31.	Van Wyck, Abraham, and Sarah Coffin, ...	"	XVIII.	65
1703. Nov. 22.	Van Wyck, Ann, and Isaac Browne, ...	"	VII.	404
1753. June 15.	Van Wyck, Catherine, and Johannis Terbos, Jr., ...	"	I.	62
1764. April 16.	Van Wyck, Christiana, and John Johnson, . .	"	VIII.	157
1764. Oct. 9.	Van Wyck, Cornelius, and Abigail Whitehead, ...	"	VIII.	340
1769. June 3.	Van Wyck, Cornelius, and Sarah Hicks, . . .	"	XIV.	115
1764. May 2.	Van Wyck, Cornelius, Jr., and Sarah Carman, ...	'	VIII.	179
1772. Oct. 20.	Van Wyck, Dinah, and Obadiah Cooper, . . .	"	XIX.	79
1759. May 31.	Van Wyck, Elizabeth, and Benjamin Hogelent, ...	"	II.	296
1758. May 30.	Van Wyck, Elizabeth, and William Provoost,	"	I.	919
1768. Jan. 14.	Van Wyck, Gilbert, and Abigail Seabury, . .	"	XIII.	8
1777. Sept. 30.	Van Wyck, Gilbert, and Sarah Rierson, ...	"	XXIV.	155
1768. July 9.	Vanwyck, Hannah, and Stephen Vanwyck,	"	XIII.	153
1771. Mar. 4.	Van Wyck, Helena, and Henry C. Bogart, .	"	XVII.	23
1759. Sept. 13.	Van Wyck, John, and Anna Vorhiss, ...	"	II.	419
1736. Jan. 24.	Van Wyck, John, and Deborah Laurence, . .	"	I.	5
1763. April 28.	Van Wyck, Mary, and Abraham Lott, ...	"	VII.	151

DATE.	NAMES.	RECORD.	VOL.	PAGE.
1762. April 10.	Van Wyck, Mary, and Barnardus Van Vorhys, ...	M. B.,	VI.	100
1737. Oct. 5.	Vanwyck, Mary, and Francis Brett, ...	"	I.	7
1779. Mar. 29.	Van Wyck, Mary, and Jacob Duryee, ...	"	XXVII.	81
1762. Mar. 22.	Van Wyck, Mary, and John Polhemus, ...	"	VI.	82
1780. Jan. 20.	Van Wyck, Mary, and John Thorne, ...	"	XXVIII.	200
1761. Nov. 23.	Van Wyck, Mary, and Zephaniah Platt, Jr.,	"	V.	243
1775. June 17.	Van Wyck, Neltje, and Zacharias Hoffman,.	"	XXIII.	68
1779. Jan. 11.	Van Wyck, Rhoda, and Isaac Hewlett, ...	"	XXVII.	11
1766. Aug. 30.	Van Wyck, Samuel, and Hannah Hewlet,..	"	X.	86
1762. July 5.	Van Wyck, Sarah, and Abraham Duryee,..	"	VI.	227
1763. Feb. 8.	Van Wyck, Sarah, and John Wright, ...	"	VII.	55
1763. May 10.	Van Wyck, Sarah, and Simon Cortelyou,...	"	VII.	173
1768. July 9.	Vanwyck, Stephen, and Hannah Vanwyck,	"	XIII.	153
1764. Nov. 7.	Van Wyck, Theodorus, and Jane Hasbrouck,	"	VIII.	394
1760. Mar. 10.	Vanwyck, Theodorus, and Martha Robbins,.	"	III.	71
1768. Oct. 20.	Van Wycke, Catelinetie, and John Van Siclen, ...	"	XIII.	214
1772. June 25.	Van Wyk, Hannah, and Petrus Bogardus, Jr.,	"	XVIII.	151
1737. Nov. 16.	Vanwyk, Theodorus, and Mary Ruskey, ...	"	I.	8
1766. June 25.	Van Wyke, Abigail, and Charles Arding,...	"	X.	32
1759. July 26.	Van Yeveren, Rynear, and Deborah Fielding,	"	II.	363
1772. Jan. 29.	Van Yeveron, Rynear, and Hannah Hogan,	"	XVIII.	21
1765. May 30.	Van Zandt, Catherine, and John Crawley,..	"	IX.	146
1771. July 16.	Van Zandt, Catherine, and William A. Forbes,	"	XVII.	133
1763. Jan. 28.	Van Zandt, John, and Mary Hopson, ...	"	VII.	38
1768. April 9.	Van Zandt, Mary, and Barnt Deklyn, ...	"	XIII.	69
1758. Jan. 9.	Van Zandt, Peter, and Sarah Maerschalk, ..	"	I.	776
1766. Aug. 16.	Van Zandt, Peter Praa, and Mary Johnson,.	"	X.	76
1783. Feb. 15.	Van Zant, Jane, and John Cooper, ...	"	XXXVIII.	42
1760. Jan. 24.	Van Zant, Wynant, and Jane Colgan,..:...	"	III.	6
1738. April 21.	Varck, Andrew, and Effia Ten Eyck, ...	"	I.	9
1756. Oct. 6.	Varck, Ann, and William Bishop, ...	"	I.	320
1773. Dec. 14.	Vardill, Mary, and Thomas Bartow, ...	"	XXII.	74
1781. May 9.	Vardill, Thomas, and Susannah Jauncey,...	"	XXXII.	39
1759. Feb. 16.	Varian, James, and Deborah Dibble, ...	"	II.	192
1764. Oct. 31.	Varian, Joseph, and Rachel White, ...	"	VIII.	386
1772. Feb. 25.	Varian, Michael, and Cornelia Horser, ...	"	XVIII.	42
1761. June 27.	Varian, Richard, and Susannah Gardinear,..	"	IV.	265
1764. Jan. 21.	Varick, Guilliam, and Mary Van Beuren,...	"	VIII.	28
1780. Jan. 12.	Varick, John, and Mary Kip, ...	"	XXVIII.	192
1777. April 28.	Varnet, Elenor, and Thomas Cairns, ...	"	XXIV.	76
1781. Dec. 2.	Varnill, Phebey, and Peter Whealey, ...	'	XXXIV.	67
1759. April 28.	Vasbergh, Dorothy, and William Van Slyk,.	"	II.	260
1770. Mar. 29.	Vassall, Richard, and Mary Clarke, ...	"	XVI.	41

NEW YORK MARRIAGES. 437

DATE.	NAMES.	RECORD.	VOL.	PAGE.
1756. Dec. 20.	Vatar, Thomas, and Elizabeth Wilson, ...	M. B.,	I.	394
1772. June 24.	Vaughan, Ann, and Cornelius W. Sullivan, .	"	XVIII.	150
1769. June 21.	Vaughton, Mary, and Peter Wessells, ...	"	XIV.	124
1779. Dec. 1.	Vaullintine, Jacob, and Sarah Schenck, ...	"	XXVIII.	155
1770. June 30.	Veader, Arent, and Sophia Van Patte, ...	"	XVI.	127
1773. May 5.	Vealen, Janety, and Jacobus Van Giesling, .	"	XX.	103
1773. Sept. 14.	Vealy, Stephanus, and Sarah Tol, ...	"	XXI.	109
1778. Nov. 30.	Veasey, Joseph, and Isabella Patterson, ...	"	XXVI.	103
1738. Sept. 11.	Vedder, Albert, and Catrina Vila, ...	"	I.	11
1763. May 13.	Vedder, Albert, and Gertruy Swart, ...	"	VII.	186
1761. Jan. 29.	Vedder, Albert S., and Nieltje Banker, ...	"	IV.	38
1773. Oct. 11.	Vedder, Angenitie, and Nicholas Swart, ...	"	XXI.	135
1765. Feb. 4.	Vedder, Ann, and John Shea, ...	"	IX.	42
1764. Oct. 5.	Vedder, Anna Catrina, and John Toll, ...	"	VIII.	334
1770. Oct. 9.	Vedder, Annatie, and Harmanus Vedder, ..	"	XVI.	206
1765. Oct. 11.	Vedder, Catherine, and Alexander Campbell,	"	IX.	297
1766. Oct. 25.	Vedder, Hannah, and Abraham Delamont, ..	"	X.	142
1770. Oct. 9.	Vedder, Harmanus, and Annatie Vedder, ..	"	XVI.	206
1762. Oct. 13.	Vedder, Mary, and Jacob Schermerhorne, ..	"	VI.	397
1764. Oct. 25.	Vedder, Nicholas, and Eva De La Mont, ...	"	VIII.	376
1770. Nov. 14.	Vedder, Philip, and Margrieta Vande Bo-gaard, ...	"	XVI.	252
1770. April 10.	Vedder, Sarah, and Abraham Truax, ...	"	XVI.	55
1764. Oct. 10.	Vedder, Sarah, and Myndert Wimple, ...	"	VIII.	349
1763. Oct. 26.	Vedder, Volkert, and Rebecca Smith, ...	"	VII.	405
1750. Mar. 10.	Veder, Arent, and Catharine Van Patten, ..	"	I.	855
1761. Oct. 27.	Veder, Margaret, and Abraham Van Eps, ..	"	V.	171
1761. Dec. 2.	Veder, Maritie, and William Hall, ...	"	V.	260
1755. Sept. 10.	Veder, Simon H., and Elizabeth Bancker, ..	"	I.	173
1771. Feb. 23.	Veedder, Helena, and Simon Jansen Van Antwerpen, ...	"	XVII.	21
1773. Nov. 20.	Veeder, Abraham, and Sarah Hansen, ...	"	XXII.	37
1772. Jan. 8.	Veeder, Angelica, and Lawrence Van Vran-kan, ...	"	XVIII.	6
1757. Sept. 2.	Veeder, Barent, and Jannetye Schemerhorne,	"	I.	630
1759. May 4.	Veeder, Catharine, and John Glen, Jr., ...	"	II.	266
1762. June 12.	Veeder, Eleanor, and John Van Petten, ...	"	VI.	189
1772. Oct. 22.	Veeder, Frances, and Mary Bezee, ...	"	XIX.	87
1761. Feb. 24.	Veeder, Geesie, and Jochem Isaac Staats, .	"	IV.	79
1759. June 8.	Veeder, Johannis Myndertse, and Magda-lene P. Vrooman, ...	"	II.	315
1762. Aug. 26.	Veeder, Maria, and Anthony De Bratt, ...	"	VI.	289
1762. Mar. 1.	Veeder, Simon Peter, and Mary Vanden-bergh, ...	"	VI.	59
1763. Jan. 29.	Veeder, Susannah, and John Roseboom, ...	"	VII.	40

DATE.	NAMES.	RECORD.	VOL. PAGE.
1766. Oct. 28.	Veeder, Volkert, and Susannah Minderse, ..	M. B.,	x. 144
1770. July 13.	Veele, Philip, and Rachel Fonda,...	"	xvi. 139
1766. Nov. 17.	Veeler, Lowickes, and Affie Tell, ...	"	x. 169
1767. Aug. 21.	Veghte, Mary, and William Jackson, Jr.,...	"	xii. 19
1782. Oct. 4.	Veil, Susannah, and Jacob Brush,.........	"	xxxvii. 27
1736. Aug. 27.	Veldtman, Gertruya, and John Pinhorne, ..	"	i. 2
1766. July 16.	Veldtman, Machtel, and John Richy, ...	"	x. 54
1773. Sept. 14.	Veley, Hannah, and Garret Winne,........	"	xxi. 108
1781. Jan. 9.	Velsey, Cornelius, and Amy Williams,.....	"	xxxi. 19
1763. April 22.	Velthousen, Christopher, and Ann Dellemont,	"	vii. 136
1771. Nov. 6.	Venderwater, Nelly, and Jonathan Cowdrey,	"	xvii. 242
1766. June 23.	Vendine, Gerret, and Mary Debevois,......	"	x. 24
1771. Oct. 10.	Vendine, John, and Melly Mortisoe,.......	"	xvii. 200
1760. Feb. 23.	Ven Durson, Margaret, and John Bergen,..	"	iii. 43
1782. July 2.	Vendyne, John, and Elenor Van Derhooven,	"	xxxvi. 72
1764. Jan. 20.	Venice, Mary, and Charles Mel,...........	"	viii. 25
1780. Dec. 18.	Vennell, Henry, and Hester Foster,........	"	xxx. 157
1782. April 24.	Venning, William, and Sarah Andrews,....	"	xxxv. 136
1737. Oct. 24.	Vergerean, Peter, and Susannah Bondmot, .	"	i. 7
1782. Feb. 13.	Verity, Hannah, and William Wood, ...	"	xxxv. 52
1763. May 27.	Vermillie, Frederick, and Catharine Nodine,	"	vii. 204
1767. April 13.	Vermillyea, Jane, and Edward Pryor,......	"	xi. 60
1773. June 15.	Vermilya, Jacob, and Mary Dyckman, ...	"	xxi. 10
1762. Aug. 5.	Vermilye, Garrardus, and Jane Valentine,..	"	vi. 265
1765. Oct. 15.	Vermylie, Rebecca, and William Maharry,..	"	ix. 300
1766. June 12.	Vernor, Elizabeth, and Robert Henry, ...	"	x. 15
1762. April 22.	Vernor, Johannes Cornelius, and Mary Bevier,...............................	"	vi. 129
1768. Feb. 29.	Vernor, John, and Eve Van Valkenburgh,..	"	xiii. 48
1766. Sept. 15.	Vernoye, Cornelius C., and Cornelia Dubois,	"	x. 97
1753. Sept. 26.	Ver Planck, Abigail, and Sander J. Lansingh,	"	i. 126
1772. June 20.	Verplanck, Abraham, and Helena Lansingh,	"	xviii. 145
1761. June 8.	Verplanck, Abraham, and Mary Bogart,....	"	iv. 232
1773. Aug. 19.	Verplanck, Anne Mary, and William Bailey,	"	xxi. 75
16⅞₉. Mar. 13.	Verplanck, Helligond, and David Ackerman,	G. E.,	xxxii. 72
1772. Sept. 29.	Ver Planck, John, and Catherine Huck,....	M. B.,	xix. 61
1764. April 6.	Verplanck, Philip, Jr., and Effe Beeckman, .	"	viii. 139
1669. April 20.	Verplanck, Susannah, and John Garland,...	O. W. L.,	ii. 417
1759. June 20.	Verplanck, William, and Lydia Leverson,...	M. B.,	ii. 333
1760. Sept. 3.	Verplank, Anne, and Gabriel G. Ludlow,...	"	iii. 279
1768. June 6.	Verplank, Arriantje, and Abraham Gardinier,	"	xiii. 129
1737. Sept. 6.	Verplank, Guilian, and Mary Cromline, ...	"	i. 7
1760. June 25.	Vertruyck, Jannetie, and Abraham Haring,.	"	iii.195b
1757. Dec. 24.	Vervey, Catharine, and John Brewer, ...	"	i. 753
1758. Nov. 9.	Vesey, William, and Jane Steward, ...	"	ii. 87

DATE.	NAMES.	RECORD.	VOL.	PAGE.
1756. Aug. 26.	Vesterveldt, Osseltie, and Guilliam Bertholf,	M. B.,	I.	277
1770. Nov. 3.	Vianey, Peter, and Mary Fowlkes,	"	XVI.	239
1757. April 21.	Vicary, John, and Jane Lovell,	"	I.	507
1761. Mar. 9.	Vider, Mary, and Samuel Zimms,	"	IV.	92
1760. July 26.	Viel, Nicolas, and Martha Rogers,	"	III.	227
1758. Oct. 31.	Viele, Anneke, and Francis Winne,	"	II.	74
1753. Aug. 1.	Viele, Catherine, and Daniel Higgins,	"	I.	82
1765. May 1.	Vielee, Baltus, and Catharine Losee,	"	IX.	117
1765. Mar. 29.	Vielee, Deborah, and Philip Van Patter, ...	"	IX.	77
1770. Sept. 10.	Vielen, Abraham, and Ann Knickerbacker, .	"	XVI.	184
1775. July 21.	Vielen, Geesje, and Lowrance Schermerhorn, .	"	XXIII.	101
1759. Aug. 30.	Vielen, John, and Geesye Slingerlant,	"	II.	402
1762. Aug. 5.	Vielen, Sarah, and Baltus Van Benthuysen, .	"	VI.	266
1756. Sept. 27.	Vielle, Lawis Hogose, and Maria Vielle, ...	"	I.	307
1756. Sept. 27.	Vielle, Maria, and Lawis Hogose Vielle, ...	"	I.	307
1738. Sept. 11.	Vila, Catrina, and Albert Vedder,	"	I.	11
1772. June 11.	Vilia, Philip G., and Mary Bratt,	"	XVIII.	138
1761. Oct. 6.	Villanaux, Mary, and Francis Peasley,	"	V.	129
1764. Oct. 31.	Villee, Ann, and Joseph Peirson,	"	VIII.	385
1769. July 21.	Villee, Rachel, and Henry Staats,	"	XV.	3
1760. Mar. 22.	Villiock, William, and Elizabeth Frazier, . . .	"	III.	87
1759. Jan. 11.	Vincent, Lewis, and Abigail Fowler,	"	II.	151
1764. May 1.	Vincent, Margaret, and Joseph Beck, ...	"	VIII.	176
1773. Jan. 28.	Vincent, Phebe, and Benjamin Rosekranz, . .	"	XX.	27a
1762. Oct. 19.	Vindlern, Appolonia, and Jacob Ott,	"	VI.	372
1767. Aug. 15.	Vinhage, Johannes, and Batta Van Volkenburgh,	"	XII.	18
1765. April 6.	Vischer, Barent, and Sarah Vischer,	"	IX.	83
1763. April 20.	Vischer, John, and Elisabeth Bratt,	"	VII.	131
1764. May 17.	Vischer. Maritie, and John Wemp,	"	VIII.	191
1765. April 6.	Vischer, Sarah, and Barent Vischer,	"	IX.	83
1753. June 8.	Viscount, Elizabeth, and Benjamin Davies, . .	"	I.	53
1771. Jan. 28.	Visger, Gerrit I., and Rachel Van Den Bergh,	"	XVII.	10
1759. June 8.	Visgher, John, and Susanah Schermerhorn, .	"	II.	314
1762. Nov. 9.	Visher, Elisabeth, and Henry Glen,	"	VI.	422
1762. June 14.	Visher, Jannetie, and Jacob Lansing,	"	VI.	192
1776. April 17.	Vissier, Nanning, and Annanitia Van Buren,	"	XXIII.	296
1758. Dec. 21.	Vogel, George, and Anna Fox,	"	II.	137
1776. Feb. 5.	Volantine, Abigal, and Joshua Willis,	"	XXIII.	259
1772. Nov. 24.	Volentine, Anna, and James Smith,	"	XIX.	124
1768. Jan. 30.	Volentine, Dorothy, and Vincent Fowler, . . .	"	XIII.	20
1772. Dec. 10.	Volentine, Jane, and John Carman,	"	XIX.	152
1773. July 15.	Volentine, Richard, and Mary Oakley,	"	XXI.	38
1781. July 24.	Volintine, Pheby, and John Golden,	"	XXXIII.	14
1737. Mar. 12.	Volkert, Johannes, and Jonale Boshert, ...	"	I.	8

DATE.		NAMES.	RECORD.	VOL.	PAGE.
1772. Jan.	9.	Vollentine, Gilbert, and Mary Morgan, ...	M. B.,	XVIII.	10
1753. May	12.	Vollenwyder, Jacob, and Mary Bratt, ...	"	I.	29
1781. May	2.	Von Altenstein, Joham Carl, and Elizabeth Grim, ...	"	XXXII.	28
1736. Jan.	14.	Vonck, Cornelius, and Elizabeth Provoost, ..	"	I.	5
1761. April	10.	Vonck, Gertrey, and Vincent Montanye, ...	"	IV.	142
1756. Dec.	16.	Von Weissenfels, Fridrig, and Mary Shurmur, ...	"	I.	388
1759. April	23.	Vooght, Michael, and Uliana Claus, ...	"	II.	250
1770. May	24.	Voorhas, Oke, and Mary Carshauw, ...	"	XIII.	112
1780. Oct.	25.	Voorhees, Abigail, and Hugh King, ...	"	XXX.	79
1756. Dec.	16.	Voorhees, Adriaen, and Adriantie Hubbard, .	"	I.	387
1762. June	29.	Voorhees, Barnardus, and Famitie Laten, ..	"	VI.	215
1764. Sept.	8.	Voorhees, Deborah, and William Kowenhoven, ...	"	VIII.	300
1778. Mar.	19.	Voorhees, Ida, and Teunis Suydam, ...	"	XXV.	48
1778. June	29.	Voorhees, John, and Ransie Wyckoff, ...	"	XXV.	117
1762. May	13.	Voorhees, Mary, and Gerret Stoothoff, ...	"	VI.	158
1765. June	17.	Voorhees, Peter, and Mary Sewell, ...	"	IX.	172
1761. Aug.	8.	Voorhees, Sithia, and Isaac Denyse, ...	"	V.	33
1753. Oct.	9.	Voorhees, Stephen, and Mary Lake, ...	"	I.	134
1767. May	19.	Voorhees, Stephen, and Phebe Rider, ...	"	XI.	91
1770. Feb.	17.	Voorheis, John, and Jane Ryder, ...	"	XVI.	20
1762. June	22.	Voorhes, Cornelius, and Ann Van Winkle, ..	"	VII.	240
1780. April	1.	Voorhies, Ann, and William Bernard Gifford,	"	XXIX.	11
1781. July	31.	Voorhies, Catharine, and William Jones, ...	"	XXXIII.	23
1763. Nov.	19.	Voorhies, Cornelius, and Catherin Boerum, .	"	VII.	458
1761. Dec.	12.	Voorhies, Cornelius, and Mary Ditmars, ...	"	V.	276
1762. Nov.	24.	Voorhies, Hellitje, and William Stoothoff, ..	"	VI.	451
1760. Jan.	8.	Voorhies, John, and Anna Schank, ...	"	II.	573
1769. Jan.	26.	Voorhies, Luke, and Mary Voorhies, ...	"	XIV.	20
1769. Jan.	26.	Voorhies, Mary, and Luke Voorhies, ...	"	XIV.	20
1760. June	30.	Voorhis, Cornelia, and Alltie Hoppar, ...	"	III.	201
1773. Jan.	19.	Voorhis, Dorothy, and Cornelius Bennet, ...	"	XX.	14,
1767. June	27.	Voorhis, John, and Phebe Bennet, ...	"	VII.	242
1773. April	7.	Voorhis, Mary, and Powel Amerman, ...	"	XX.	85
1770. April	19.	Voorhuys, Maria, and Hendrick Van Derveer,	"	XIII.	82
1762. April	10.	Voorhys, Bernardus, and Mary Van Wyck,	"	VI.	100
1781. Nov.	27.	Voortman, Catharine, and Frans Titus, ...	"	XXXIV.	59
1771. Dec.	5.	Vorhis, Cornelia, and Cobus Springsteen, ...	"	XVII.	286
1781. June	19.	Vorhis, Sarah, and Isaac Bennet, ...	"	XXXII.	90
1769. Sept.	13.	Vorhiss, Anna, and John Van Wyck, ...	"	II.	419
1779. Jan.	8.	Voris, Simon, and Esther Pettit, ...	"	XXVII.	8
1781. Mar.	21.	Voris, Stephen, and Hannah Roads, ...	"	XXXI.	79
1756. Aug	28.	Vors, Mary, and Samuel Maghee, ...	"	I.	280

DATE.		NAMES.	RECORD.	VOL.	PAGE.
1756. Oct.	22.	Vorse, Hannah, and Joseph Lynsen,.......	M. B.,	I.	331
1760. Sept.	19.	Vosburg, Johannes, and Neiltie Gardinier, .	"	III.	321
1768. Nov.	17.	Vosburgh, Abraham C., and Margrieta Hugeny,.............................	"	XIII.	229
1760. Dec.	6.	Vosburgh, Barent, and Annetje Gerretie,...	"	III.	462
1775. Sept.	16.	Vosburgh, Barent, and Mary L. Van Alen,.	"	XXIII.	148
1768. Oct.	13.	Vosburgh, Bartholomew, and Elliner Ryan,	"	XIII.	209
1765. Sept.	18.	Vosburgh, Cornelia, and Johannis Gardenier,	"	IX.	267
1765. Mar.	11.	Vosburgh, Cornelius, and Annatje Borgart,.	"	IX.	66
1771. Mar.	11.	Vosburgh, Eitie, and Cornelius A. Huyck,..	"	XVII.	30
1766. Nov.	21.	Vosburgh, Elizabeth, and Johannis Goes, Jr.,	"	X.	174
1773. Nov.	30.	Vosburgh, Evert, and Joanna Gardinier, ...	"	XXII.	54
1775. Oct.	14.	Vosburgh, Hartry, and Jacobus De Lamater,.....	"	XXIII.	180
1772. Oct.	30.	Vosburgh, Hillitye, and Lucas Van Alen, ..	"	XIX.	95
1771. Nov.	28.	Vosburgh, Isaac, and Nancy Dickson, ...	"	XVII.	271
1763. June	30.	Vosburgh, Jacob, and Gertrude Legget,....	'	VII.	250
1768. April	18.	Vosburgh, Jane, and Abraham I. Van Vleck,	"	XIII.	80
1767. Sept.	7.	Vosburgh, Jane, and Henry Hous, ...	"	XII.	28
1752. Nov.	28.	Vosburgh, Johannis, and Annanetje Van Alen,............................ . .	"	I.	18
1765. May	15.	Vosburgh, John Abraham, and Sarah Gardiner,.............................	"	IX.	127
1766. Nov.	19.	Vosburgh, Martin, and Cornelia Gilbert, ...	"	X.	171
1760. June	12.	Vosburgh, Martin, and Geertruy Litsjer, ...	'	III.	187
1773. July	23.	Vosburgh, Martin, and Maratje Vanhocsen, ...	"	XXI.	50
1769. Nov.	9.	Vosburgh, Mary, and Abraham Hogeboom,	"	XV.	86
1766. June	24.	Vosburgh, Mathew, and Janetie Gardiner,..	"	X.	28
1767. Dec.	2.	Vosburgh, Myndert, and Syntiche Wheeler,	"	XII.	104
1771. July	17.	Vosburgh, Peter J., and Fitie Van Hoesen,	"	XVII.	134
1761. June	29.	Vosburgh, Sarah, and Cornelius Hogeboom,	"	IV.	269
1759. July	25.	Vralandt, Margaret, and Jacob Brouwer,...	"	II.	362
1736. June	30.	Vredenbergh, Apolonia, and James Byers,..	"	I.	1
1762. Oct.	4.	Vredenbergh, Eleanor, and Peter Bortell, ..	"	VI.	345
1778. Aug.	12.	Vredenbergh, Elizabeth, and Zachariah Busler,..............................	"	XXVI.	3
1777. Dec.	9.	Vredenbergh, John, and Jane Dyckman,...	"	XXIV.	192
1764. Mar.	15.	Vredenburgh, Jannetje, and Frederick Bassett, ...	"	VIII.	105
1772. June	4.	Vredenburgh, Catherine, and Samuel Tweedy,	"	XVIII.	131
1779. April	7.	Vredenburgh, Catherine, and Samuel Wentworth, ...	"	XXVII.	96
1767. Mar.	4.	Vredenburgh, Isaac, and Nelly Montanye,..	"	XI.	39
1765. Oct.	25.	Vredenburgh, John, and Mary Rodbin, ...	"	IX.	320

DATE.		NAMES.	RECORD.	VOL.	PAGE.
1736. May	4.	Vreden Burgh, Mary, and John Asselstyn,..	M. B.,	I.	1
1757. Mar.	3.	Vredenburgh, Mary, and John Outenbogert,	"	I.	454
1765. Oct.	9.	Vredenburgh, Matthias, and Rebecca Benson, ...	"	IX.	293
1775. April	20.	Vredenburgh, William, Jr., and Catharine Myer, ...	"	XXIII.	12
1759. June	27.	Vreedenbergh, Willemeyntje, and Theophilus Anthony, ...	"	II.	342
1781. Aug.	17.	Vreeland, Hannah, and Jasper Zabriske, ...	"	XXXIII.	40
1762. May	11.	Vreelenhuesen, Elisabeth, and Peter Roosevelt, ...	"	VI.	155
1780. Oct.	21.	Vreland, George, and Jane Brinkerhoff,....	"	XXX.	74
1761. April	3.	Vroman, Adam B., and Janetje Zulle,.....	"	IV.	130
1760. Oct.	30.	Vroman, Engettie, and Albert Meebie,.....	"	III.	387
1757. Oct.	26.	Vroman, John Hendrickse, and Jannetje Swits, ...	"	I.	682
1761. April	3.	Vroman, Peter B., and Sartje Swart, ...	"	IV.	129
1771. Oct.	15.	Vroom, Deborah, and Thomas Wood,.....	"	XVII.	210
1771. Sept.	26.	Vroom, Jinnie, and Isaac Ditmars, ...	"	XVII.	193
1781. July	31.	Vroom, John, and Jane Ditmars,.....	"	XXXIII.	24
1761. July	9.	Vroom, Sarah, and Douwe Ditmars,.....	"	IV.	290
1738. June	22.	Vrooman, Angettie, and Peter Van Driesen, ...	"	I.	10
1762. Aug.	21.	Vrooman, Ann P., and Jacobus Schermerhorne, ...	"	VI.	283
1759. Nov.	16.	Vrooman, Barent, and Alida Van Der Heyden, ...	"	II.	501
1762. April	20.	Vrooman, Geesse, and John Clute,.....	"	VI.	118
1764. Oct.	10.	Vrooman, Geetje, and Peter Steers,.....	"	VIII.	348
1773. April	5.	Vrooman, Helena, and Martin Van Slyck,..	"	XX.	82
1758. Oct.	14.	Vrooman, Jacob Simonsen, and Margarita Wemple, ...	"	II.	57
1759. Aug.	23.	Vrooman, Magdalena, and Hendrick Van Ness, ...	"	II.	388
1759. June	18.	Vrooman, Magdalene P., and Johannis Myndertse Veeder,.....	"	II.	315
1772. Nov.	17.	Vrooman, Mary, and Harmanus Van Slycke,	"	XIX.	116
1773. Jan.	27.	Vrooman, Sarah, and Lymon I. Schermerhorn, ...	"	XX.	22
1776. April	22.	Vroome, Cathrina, and Benjamin Schoonmaker,.....	"	XXIII.	299

W.

DATE.	NAMES.	RECORD.	VOL.	PAGE.
1736. April 30.	Waldron, Gerardus, and Elizabeth Rose, ...	M. B.,	I.	1
1773. June 15.	Waldron, Hannah, and George Stevens,....	"	XXI.	7
1771. Nov. 12.	Waldron, Hendrick, and Margareta Van-vroncka, ...	"	XVII.	248
1779. Oct. 9.	Waldron, Hilah, and Abraham Willson,....	"	XXVIII.	109
1762. Mar. 19.	Waldron, James, and Elizabeth Holland,...	"	VI.	79
1753. Sept. 12.	Waldron, Jane, and Richard Ebbets,.......	"	I.	116
1772. Nov. 9.	Waldron, John, and Elizabeth Oakes,......	"	XIX.	103
1761. April 21.	Waldron, Joseph, and May Fashee,........	"	IV.	156
1759. Jan. 31.	Waldron, John, and Rebeccah Bussing, ...	"	II.	170
1775. Oct. 3.	Waldron, Mary, and Elias Nexsen,........	"	XXIII.	171
1760. June 10.	Waldron, Nishie, and Ida Hannigan,.......	"	III.	183
1764. Aug. 14.	Waldron, Peter, and Anne Auterkerck,....	"	VIII.	280
1765. Jan. 21.	Waldron, Peter, Jr., and Angeltje Myer, ...	"	IX.	25
1763. Mar. 4.	Waldron, Samuel, Jr., and Hannah Van Alst,	"	VII.	89
1757. Dec. 22.	Waldron, Susannah, and Cornelius Romme,.	"	I.	750
1760. July 24.	Waldron, William, and Lena Vantassell, ...	"	III.	225
1780. Dec. 6.	Waley, Margaret, and Henry Hurst,.......	"	XXX.	139
1778. May 11.	Walker, Andrew, and Ann Hicks, ...	"	XXV.	79
1769. May 16.	Walker, Ann, and James Flynn, ...	"	XIV.	102
1780. Aug. 24.	Walker, Benjamin, and Hannah Bunts, ...	"	XXIX.	148
1763. Oct. 19.	Walker, Catharine, and Ronil McDannil,....	"	VII.	392
1783. July 28.	Walker, Dorothy, and Samuel Ellis, Jr.,....	"	XXXIX.	103
1763. April 30.	Walker, Elizabeth, and Emmanuel Easton, .	"	VII.	157
1761. Oct. 27.	Walker, Elizabeth, and John Davis, ...	"	V.	172
1762. Feb. 1.	Walker, Elizabeth, and Ralph Hodge,......	"	VI.	32
1763. Aug. 25.	Walker, Elizabeth, and William White, ...	"	VII.	311
1738. Sept. 23.	Walker, Hester, and Thomas Frazier,......	"	I.	11
1758. June 16.	Walker, John, and Catharine Bussey,......	"	I.	927
1760. Aug. 7.	Walker, John, and Mary Brockus, ...	"	III.	241
1779. Dec. 6.	Walker, John, and Rachael Whitney,......	"	XXVIII.	163
1666. Dec. 22.	Walker, Mary, and Robert Seely, ...	O. W. L.,	II.	{105 / 134}
1760. July 23.	Walker, Mary, and Francis Daunt, ...	M. B.,	III.	224
1781. Feb. 14.	Walker, Mary, and John Baldwin, ...	"	XXXV.	56
1765. Feb. 7.	Walker, Mary, and John Webster, ..., ...	"	IX.	48
1757. June 21.	Walker, Mary, and Thomas Kerby, ...	"	I.	569
1760. Nov. 12.	Walker, Mary, and Thomas Patterson,.....	"	III.	404
1770. Nov. 30.	Walker, Peter, and Margaret Waters,......	"	XVI.	277
1760. Oct. 2.	Walker, Samuel, and Elizabeth Callahan,...	"	III.	340
1782. Oct. 21.	Walker, Sarah, and John Brinan, ...	"	XXXVII.	54
1768. Jan. 2.	Walker, Sarah, and Samuel Chambers, ...	"	XIII.	1
1778. Dec. 10.	Walker, Sarah, and Thomas Thompson,....	"	XXVI.	116
1759. April 27.	Walker, Thomas, and Mary Bennit,.......	"	II.	258
1737. May 18.	Walker, William, and Hester Jones,.......	"	I.	6

DATE.	NAMES.	RECORD.	VOL.	PAGE.
1773. Feb. 15.	Wall, Abigail, and Moses Spicer,	M. B.,	xx.	43
1761. Aug. 10.	Wall, Catharine, and Thomas Ffoster,	"	v.	36
1760. Mar. 24.	Wall, Christene, and George Myer,	"	iii.	89
1758. Mar. 31.	Wall, Elizabeth, and William Jones,	"	i.	869
1759. Jan. 11.	Wall, James, and Catherine Kelly,	"	ii.	150
1777. Dec. 4.	Wall, John, and Hanah Winslow,	"	xxiv.	189
1760. May 16.	Wall, John, and Mary Smith,	"	iii.	156
1780. June 1.	Wall, Patrick, and Margaret Brush,	"	xxix.	76
1778. Aug. 31.	Wall, Sally, and Gabriel Furman,	"	xxvi.	17
1769. Sept. 5.	Wallace, Cornelia, and Hugh Gaine,	"	xv.	37
1760. Nov. 20.	Wallace, Dorothy, and John Kirby,	"	iii.	429
1781. Mar. 27.	Wallace, Dorothy, and William Cock,	"	xxxv.	100
1770. June 27.	Wallace, John, and Chloe Dickinson,	"	xvi.	125
1757. Aug. 31.	Wallace, John, and Cornelius Van Dam,	"	i.	626
1761. June 25.	Wallace, John, and Jane Crawford,	"	iv.	262
1783. June 5.	Wallace, Rebecca, and John Allen,	"	xxxix.	40
1779. April 27.	Wallace, Sarah, and Michael Kellie,	"	xxvii.	120
1765. May 20.	Wallace, William, and Agness Hunter,	"	ix.	134
1763. Jan. 3.	Wallagrave, Magdalen, and Samuel Godwin,	"	vii.	4
1764. Mar. 26.	Wallegrave, Susannah, and John Burroughs,	"	viii.	118
1783. Jan. 6.	Wallenburgh, Margaret, and William Maxly,	"	xxxviii.	7
1762. Oct. 6.	Waller, John, and Mary Day,	"	vi.	349
1762. Jan. 20.	Waller, Peter, and Mary McKlen,	"	vi.	18
1775. May 27.	Wallgrove, Elizabeth, and Joseph Jenkins,	"	xxiii.	47
1767. May 6.	Wallis, Thomas, and Jane Edgar,	"	xi.	82
1775. Nov. 22.	Walmsley, John, and Jane Miller,	"	xxiii.	218
1774. Jan. 7.	Walsh, Catherine, and William Geamester,	"	xxii.	96
1737. Dec. 30.	Walsh, Diana, and John Walsh,	"	i.	8
1775. Nov. 16.	Walsh, Hugh, and Catharine Armstrong,	"	xxiii.	216
1737. Dec. 30.	Walsh, John, and Diana Walsh,	"	i.	8
1758. Jan. 20.	Walter, Elizabeth, and Welhelmus Poppels-dorff,	"	i.	793
1763. April 26.	Walter, John, and Mary Ten Eyck,	"	vii.	142
1782. June 16.	Walter, Samuel, and Martha Vancott,	"	xxxvi.	54
1757. May 4.	Walters, John, and Hannah Brush,	"	i.	524
1780. Feb. 3.	Walters, Peter, and Zophia Place,	"	xxviii.	207
1778. Jan. 30.	Walters, Rachel, and Obadiah Vallentine,	"	xxvii.	32
1781. April 20.	Walters, Samuel, and Ruth Tobias,	"	xxxii.	11
1766. Aug. 6.	Walton, Abraham, and Grace Williams,	"	x.	70
1781. Jan. 3.	Walton, Ann, and William Fyers,	"	xxxi.	9
1761. Sept. 19.	Walton, Rebecca, and Cornelius Martineau,	"	v.	90
1671. Dec. 16.	Walton, Thomas, and —— Lawrence,	G. E.,	iv.	73
1769. Dec. 22.	Walton, William, and Anne Egberts,	M. B.,	xv.	130
1757. Oct. 3.	Walton, William, Jr., and Mary De Lancey,	"	i.	655
1770. July 2.	Wamsley, Isaac, and Leah Taylor,	"	xvi.	133

DATE.		NAMES.	RECORD.	VOL.	PAGE.
1763. Dec.	17.	Wamsley, Jane, and Richard Warner,......	M. B.,	VII.	508
1758. Jan.	19.	Wandel, John, and Jane Woodford,.......	"	I.	791
1761. July	4.	Wandel, John, and Letitia Swan,.........	"	IV.	275
1783. Feb.	25.	Wandel, John, and Susannah Latteretee,...	"	XXXVIII.	52
1772. April	4.	Wandel, Mary, and Abraham Warner, ...	"	XVIII.	68
1771. Mar.	26.	Wandell, Catherina, and Arthur Hellme, ...	"	XVII.	41
1768. May	2.	Wandell, Margaret, and Abraham N. Cuyler,	"	XIII.	89
1758. Dec.	6.	Wandewater, Ruth, and James Rigby,.....	"	II.	116
1760. May	9.	Wanshaer, John, Jr., and Helena Schoonma-ker, ...	"	III.	147
1782. Nov.	9.	Wanton, Ruth, and Christopher Darby, ...	"	XXXVII.	76
1782. Sept.	3.	Ward, Abigail, and John Truesdell, ...	"	XXXVI.	136
1778. Oct.	2.	Ward, Bernard, and Sarah Van Dine,......	"	XXVI.	42
1756. July	31.	Ward, Catharine, and Henry Grigg,.......	"	I.	264
1736. Sept.	8.	Ward, Catherine, and John Vanderhiden, ..	"	I.	2
1770. May	9.	Ward, Catherine, and Peter Webbers, ...	"	XVI.	82
1775. May	1.	Ward, Daniel, and Mary Wood, ...	"	XXIII.	18
1761. Jan.	30.	Ward, David, and Alitije Van Kleek, ...	"	IV.	41
1779. May	8.	Ward, Elinor, and James Da Van, ...	"	XXVII.	131
1781. May	9.	Ward, Elizabeth, and John Boerum,.......	"	XXXII.	38
1760. Oct.	17.	Ward, Elizabeth, and John Ford, ...	"	III.	348
1757. July	22.	Ward, Elizabeth, and Samuel Robinson,....	"	I.	598
1782. Jan.	9.	Ward, Gabriel, and Catharine De Vooe,....	"	XXXV.	12
1736. Nov.	8.	Ward, Gartha, and Samuel Craig,.........	"	I.	3
1773. Oct.	22.	Ward, Isaac, and Martha Townshend, ...	"	XXI.	146
1737. June	4.	Ward, John, and Elizabeth Hunter, ...	"	I.	6
1781. Oct.	19.	Ward, John, and Sarah Day,.............	"	XXXIII.	110
1762. May	3.	Ward, Mary, and Joshua Kay, ...	"	VI.	140
1765. Aug.	5.	Ward, Monson, and Catherine Florentine,..	"	IX.	253
1777. May	17.	Ward, Moses, and Abigail Fowler, ...	"	XXIV.	89
1767. Dec.	26.	Ward, Phebe, and Caleb Morgan, ...	"	XII.	123
1778. Oct.	23.	Ward, Rebecca, and Daniel Townsend, ...	"	XXVI.	67
1756. Oct.	2.	Ward, Rebeccah, and John Johns,.........	"	I.	315
1755. Aug.	28.	Ward, Samuel, and Addra Guyon, ...	"	IX.	250
1782. Oct.	16.	Ward, Samuel, and Catharine Barraga, ...	"	XXXVII.	42
1781. May	18.	Ward, Sarah, and John Guyon,...........	"	XXXII.	52
1762. Dec.	23.	Ward, Sarah, and John Needham, ...	"	VI.	495
1753. Sept.	7.	Ward, Stephen, and Ruth Kidney,........	"	I.	109
1783. Sept.	5.	Ward, Uzal, and Rachael Brouwer,........	"	XL.	25
1781. Sept.	1.	Ward, William, and Alise Parker,.........	"	XXXIII.	55
1756. Dec.	31.	Ward, William, and Charity Marteneau,....	"	I.	405
1777. Oct.	21.	Warden, George, and Mary Kippen,.......	"	XXIV.	166
1681. Sept.	3.	Wardrope, Alexander, and Elizabeth Corbett,	O. W.,	XXXII½.	67
1757. Nov.	3.	Ware, Margaret, and Joseph Dunlap, ...	M. B.,	I.	695
1760. Nov.	5.	Waring, Solomon, and Harriantie Snedeker,	"	III.	394

Date.	Names.	Record.	Vol.	Page.
1759. May 31.	Warne, Robert, and Almy Seamon, ...	M. B.,	II.	293
1756. June 26.	Warne, Robert, and Deborah Cole,........	"	I.	243
1759. June 15.	Warne, Sarah, and Peter Tanare, ...	"	II.	325
1678. Feb. 7.	Warner, Abigail, and William Scott,.......	G. E.,	XXXII.	21
1766. June 19.	Warner, Abraham, and Elizabeth Pettit, ...	M. B.,	x?	21
1772. April 10.	Warner, Abraham, and Mary Wandel,.....	"	XVIII.	68
1773. Dec. 9.	Warner, Dorothy, and Peter Post, ...	"	XXII.	69
1760. April 5.	Warner, Elizabeth, and Edward Barden, ...	"	III.	99
1770. Dec. 22.	Warner, Elizabeth, and Peter Galatian, ...	"	XVI.	305
1768. Aug. 10.	Warner, James, and Hannah Hawse,......	"	XIII.	172
1782. Jan. 19.	Warner, Jane, and Lawrence Lacy, ...	"	XXXV.	25
1765. June 28.	Warner, Jesse, and Luke Fish,...........	"	IX.	189
1760. Dec. 29.	Warner, John, and Elizabeth Fowler,.... .	"	III.	494
1767. Feb. 5.	Warner, John, and Jane De Lanoy, ...	"	XI.	20
1778. Dec. 23.	Warner, Mary, and John B. Dash, ...	"	XXVI.	131
1760. Sept. 26.	Warner, Matthias, and Mary Gallasha,.....	"	III.	330
1763. Mar. 26.	Warner, Phebe, and Joseph Jadwin, ...	"	VII.	108
1669. May 15.	Warner, Ralph, and Abigail Tilton,........	O. W. L.,	II.	408
1763. Dec. 17.	Warner, Richard, and Jane Wamsley, ...	M. B.,	VII.	508
1756. Nov. 17.	Warner, Samuel, and Mary Dodge, ...	"	I.	357
1759. Sept. 19.	Warner, Samuel, and Phebe Hunt,........	"	II.	427
1761. July 24.	Warner, Sarah, and Joseph Jadwill, ...	"	V.	7
1767. Feb. 17.	Warner, Thomas, and Elizabeth Brown,....	"	XI.	28
1772. Feb. 7.	Warner, Thomas Tippet, and Magdalen Van Orden,......................	"	XVIII.	30
1765. Jan. 17.	Warner, William, and Jane Chardevoin,....	"	IX.	19
1780. April 18.	Warren, Jane, and Adam Davie,..........	"	XXIX.	27
1783. Oct. 9.	Warrick, Henry, and Ellinor Ellison, ...	"	XL.	75
1737. June 2.	Wartnabey, Altia, and Stunford Cormichael,	"	I.	6
1770. Aug. 23.	Wartt, Hendrick, and Maria Eackker, ...	"	XVI.	168
1767. Dec. 11.	Washbun, Hannah, and Richard Hallett, ...	"	XII.	112
1767. June 3.	Wassbrouck, Helena, and Cornelius Depue,.	"	XI.	104
1777. Feb. 3.	Waters, Angelica, and Isaac Wood, ...	"	XXIV.	25
1760. Feb. 26.	Waters, Ann, and Robert McKay, ...	"	III.	51
1766. June 23.	Waters, Catherine, and Christophel Yates,..	"	X.	26
1781. May 28.	Waters, Elizabeth, and Jacob Moore, ...	"	XXXII.	57
1779. April 11.	Waters, Hanah, and Jacob Moore, ...	"	XXVII.	104
1763. June 23.	Waters, Hannah, and William Carman, ...	"	XI.	113
1779. May 13.	Waters, James, and Elinor Schenck,.	"	XXVII.	134
1768. Aug. 27.	Waters, Joanna, and Jabez Johnson, ...	"	XIII.	179
1776. Dec. 7.	Waters, John, and Jane Morton,....	"	XXIII.	315
1781. Mar. 17.	Waters, John, and Mary Hallett, ...	"	XXXI.	72
1775. June 23.	Waters, John Treadwell, and Ann Betts, ..	"	XXIII.	74
1770. Nov. 11.	Waters, Margaret, and Peter Walker,......	"	XVI.	277
1763. April 18.	Waters, Maritie, and Garrit Welp, ...	"	VII.	118

DATE.	NAMES.	RECORD.	VOL.	PAGE.
1780. Sept. 11.	Waters, Mary, and James Lefford, ...	M. B.,	xxx.	22
1773. Aug. 28.	Waters, Mary, and John Latham, ...	"	xxi.	88
1760. May 7.	Waters, Mary, and Thomas Smith, ...	"	iii.	142
1778. Sept. 17.	Waters, Oliver, and Jane Tallman, ...	"	xxvi.	30
1769. April 5.	Waters, Sarah, and Henry Wisner, ...	"	xiv.	65
1767. Dec. 5.	Waters, Sarah, and Richard Thorne, ...	"	xii.	107
1770. Dec. 15.	Waters, Susannah, and John Watts, ...	"	xvi.	295
1773. June 25.	Waters, Thomas, and Jane Boyle, ...	"	xxi.	22
1778. Mar. 2.	Waters, William, and Hanah Hallet, ...	"	xxvii.	53
1779. Nov. 11.	Watkins, Ann, and William Gowey, ...	"	xxviii.	136
1782. Aug. 31.	Watkins, Thomas, and Elizabeth Webb, ...	"	xxxvi.	131
1783. June 11.	Watson, Adam, and Deborah Hawking, ...	"	xxxix.	49
1768. Nov. 29.	Watson, Alexander, and Abigail Stevenson,	"	xiii.	248
1781. Jan. 3.	Watson, Alexander, and Margaret Fletcher,	"	xxxi.	8
1758. Oct. 1.	Watson, Ann, and Daniel Morson, ...	"	ii.	75
1776. Jan. 31.	Watson, Eleanor, and Alexander McLean, ..	"	xxiii.	257
1770. Nov. 12.	Watson, Henry, and Jane Betty, ...	"	xvii.	249
1781. Aug. 16.	Watson, James, and Elizabeth McCutchen, .	"	xxxiii.	39
1780. Aug. 26.	Watson, James, and Margaret Cumming, ...	"	xxx.	4
1777. Aug. 21.	Watson, Jane, and William Fowler, ...	"	xxiv.	138
1770. Dec. 31.	Watson, John, and Catherine King, ...	"	xvi.	312
1671. Feb. 26.	Watson, John, and Mary Gray Ramsden, ..	G. E.,	iv.	102
1780. Feb. 1.	Watson, John, and Mary Parker, ...	M. B.,	xxviii.	206
1780. Sept. 28.	Watson, Joshua, and Sarah Pell, ...	"	xxx.	46
1777. Sept. 4.	Watson, Margaret, and John Thomas, ...	"	xxiv.	143
1770. Oct. 31.	Watson, Mary, and David Cornwell, ...	"	xvi.	236
1778. July 11.	Watson, Sarah, and John Collins, ...	"	xxv.	125
1783. June 11.	Watt, Ann, and James Holden, ...	"	xxxix.	51
1761. Sept. 12.	Watt, Francis, and Margaret Conckling, ...	"	v.	82
1781. Sept. 1.	Watt, John, and Charity Earl, ...	"	xxxiii.	53
1737. Nov. 1.	Watters, Rachel, and Joseph Bennet, ...	"	i.	7
1765. July 10.	Watters, William, and Mary Bowman, ...	"	ix.	201
1674. Feb. 15.	Watton, Anthony, and Elizabeth Bollin, ...	W. O. P.,	iii.	53
1769. April 26.	Watts, Ann, and Archibald Kennedy, ...	M. B.,	xiv.	89
1761. Oct. 30.	Watts, Catharine, and John Betten, ...	"	v.	179
1770. Jan. 17.	Watts, John, and Ruth Smith, ...	"	xvi.	6
1770. Dec. 15.	Watts, John, and Susannah Waters, ...	"	xvi.	295
1775. Oct. 2.	Watts, John, Jr., and Jane De Lancey, ...	"	xxiii.	170
1777. July 3.	Watts, Margaret, and Micael Demott, ...	"	xxiv.	110
1764. April 25.	Watts, Nicholas, and Phebe Burtis, ...	"	viii.	169
1759. April 24.	Watts, Robert, and Lucretia Van Duersen, .	"	ii.	253
1768. May 2.	Watts, Robert, and Margaret Smith, ...	"	xiii.	91
1765. May 7.	Watts, Robert, and Sarah Smith, ...	"	ix.	121
1770. July 4.	Watts, Susannah, and Philip Kearny, ...	"	xvi.	134
1773. Mar. 23.	Watts, Susannah, and Terence Reilly, ...	"	xx.	69

DATE.	NAMES.	RECORD.	VOL.	PAGE.
1762. Jan. 29.	Watts, William, and Ann Van Noorstrandt,	M. B.,	VI.	29
1778. Nov. 26.	Watts, William A., and Mary Pearson, ...	"	XXVI.	99
1763. May 11.	Waugh, James, and Mary Bell, ...	"	VII.	175
1779. April 24.	Wauters, Garrit, and Garritye Post, ...	"	XXVII.	118
1757. Oct. 13.	Way, Elenor, and Miles Ash, ...	"	I.	668
1769. Nov. 4.	Way, James, and Hester Hillyer, ...	"	XV.	78
1760. Mar. 9.	Way, Jane, and William Lowndes, ...	"	III.	246
1772. Nov. 16.	Way, John, and Mary Betts, ...	"	XIX.	115
1783. Oct. 7.	Way, Mary, and Charles Farrington, ...	"	XL.	69
1757. Mar. 7.	Way, Mary, and James Killmaster, ...	"	I.	459
1783. Sept. 7.	Way, Richard, and Catharine Evans, ...	"	XL.	30
1773. Dec. 13.	Way, Sarah, and Samuel Spragg, ...	"	XXII.	70
1764. Feb. 24.	Waylin, Ann, and Hugh McConnel, ...	"	VIII.	76
1781. July 2.	Waymnan, William, and Ann Vanhorne,...	"	XXXII.	101
1779. Oct. 4.	Wayne, Joseph, and Mary Shelly, ...	"	XXVIII.	101
1769. Dec. 4.	Ways, Catherine, and Peter Van Duesen, ..	"	XV.	113
1782. Mar. 16.	Wealbanch, Margaret, and John Dunn, ...	"	XXXV.	88
1769. Nov. 21.	Weaudell, James, and Rebecca Lefoy, ...	"	XV.	100
1757. Dec. 28.	Wearerlen, Maria, and Peter Klump, ...	"	I.	755
1778. July 1.	Weatherby, Henry, and Phœbe Parks, ...	"	XXV.	118
1771. Nov. 18.	Weaver, Catherine, and John Sax, ...	"	XVII.	258
1768. Dec. 13.	Weaver, Christina, and Peter Vanbergen, ..	"	XIII.	261
1772. Aug. 28.	Weaver, Gedey, and Henry Fach, ...	"	XIX.	31
1769. May 3.	Weaver, John, and Ann Burge, ...	"	XIV.	91
1763. Sept. 27.	Weaver, Michael, and Barbara Kaiser, ...	"	VII.	353
1779. Mar. 20.	Weaver, Michael, and Elizabeth Baar, ...	"	XXVII.	70
1782. Mar. 2.	Weaver, William, and Ann Habberton, ...	"	XXXV.	68
1762. Oct. 29.	Webb, Abigail, and Achilles Preston, ...	"	VI.	395
1765. April 15.	Webb, Alice, and Samuel Roberts, ...	"	IX.	92
1779. July 28.	Webb, Elizabeth, and John Embree, ...	"	XXVIII.	31
1782. Aug. 31.	Webb, Elizabeth, and Thomas Watkins, ...	"	XXXVI.	131
1782. May 22.	Webb, John, and Anne Batten, ...	"	XXXVI.	19
1760. Sept. 29.	Webb, Joseph, and Deborah Shaw, ...	"	III.	336
1780. June 2.	Webb, Joseph, and Sarah Taylor, ...	"	XXIX.	80
1779. Dec. 9.	Webb, Mary, and Richard Nicolson, ...	'	XXVIII.	167
1780. June 16.	Webb, Richard, and Anne Haughwout, ...	"	XXXIX.	60
1781. Mar. 12.	Webb, Richard, and Darcas Bardine, ...	"	XXXI.	69
1761. Mar. 25.	Webb, Richard, and Leah Kemp, ...	"	IV.	117
1761. Oct. 3.	Webb, Samuel, and Elizabeth Ferris, ...	"	V.	120
1764. June 28.	Webb, Sarah, and Nemiah Donaldson, ...	"	VIII.	242
1760. Nov. 7.	Webb, Susannah, and Charles Ellis, ...	"	III.	398
1760. Aug. 29.	Webb, Thomas, and Mary Arding, ...	"	III.	274
1764. Nov. 23.	Webb, William, and Dorothy Tannely, ...	"	VIII.	422
1779. Oct. 6.	Webber, Margaret, and Thomas Knowlin, ..	"	I.	189
1762. Mar. 15.	Webber, Margaret, and William Laffraa, ...	"	VI.	69

57

DATE.	NAMES.	RECORD.	VOL.	PAGE.
1761. April 13.	Webber, Mary, and Luke Shippy,.........	M. B.,	IV.	148
1762. Oct. 29.	Webber, Oliver, and Anne Burns,.........	"	VI.	394
1762. Dec. 10.	Webber, William, and Jane Lackey,.......	"	VI.	473
1760. Nov. 7.	Webbers, Hellegont, and David Banter,....	"	III.	397
1770. May 9.	Webbers, Peter, and Catharine Ward, ...	"	XVI.	82
1759. May 2.	Webern, Catharine, and John Michael Gotz,	"	II.	264
1770. May 1.	Webers, Margaret, and Nicholas Fletcher, ..	"	XVI.	74
1762. Nov. 16.	Webster, Francis, and Martha Mail, ...	"	VI.	435
1781. May 29.	Webster, Hugh, and Sarah Moore, ...	"	XXXII.	61
1782. Oct. 17.	Webster, John, and Elizabeth Bussing, ...	"	XXXVII.	47
1765. Feb. 7.	Webster, John, and Mary Walker, ...	"	IX.	48
1778. Nov. 21.	Webster, Phebe, and Sampson Ridge, ...	"	XXVI.	95
1782. Jan. 31.	Webster, Susannah, and David Lennox,....	"	XXXV.	40
1760. Nov. 21.	Wedder, Courset, and Neltie Bourch,......	"	III.	432
1780. Sept. 26.	Wedders, John, and Susannah Miller,......	"	XXX.	43
1770. Nov. 27.	Wedge, Hannah, and Jacob Davis, ...	"	XVI.	272
1761. Oct. 21.	Weeden, William, and Mary Burwell, ...	"	V.	159
1759. May 12.	Weekes, Ann, and George Baker,.........	"	II.	279
1757. Nov. 12.	Weekes, Augustine, and Elizabeth Lattin,..	"	I.	703
1772. Jan. 8.	Weekes, Elizabeth, and Penn Cock, ...	"	XVIII.	8
1777. Oct. 27.	Weekes, George, and Freelove Weeks, ...	"	XXIV.	171
1761. Feb. 14.	Weekes, George, and Sarah Parsley, ...	"	IV.	62
1762. Nov. 26.	Weekes, James, and Margaret Campbell,...	"	VI.	456
1761. Aug. 4.	Weekes, Jemima, and William Lyset,......	"	V.	24
1761. Nov. 11.	Weekes, Levy, and Mary Burtis,..........	"	V.	207
1763. April 8.	Weekes, Margaret, and Joseph Townsend,..	"	VII.	119
1772. May 3.	Weekes, Margaret, and Phillip Skidmore, ..	"	XVIII.	121
1782. April 18.	Weekes, Martha, and Peter Wheelor,......	"	XXXV.	128
1764. June 8.	Weekes, Mary, and Timothy Cornish, ...	"	VIII.	216
1761. May 4.	Weeks, Anne, and Richard Latin,.........	"	IV.	179
1770. Dec. 5.	Weeks, Bissett, and Catherine Speece,.....	"	XVI.	284
1760. May 16.	Weeks, Catharine, and William Goforth, ...	"	III.	155
1779. Feb. 2.	Weeks, Catherine, and Joshua Willis,......	"	XXVII.	34
1782. Aug. 10.	Weeks, Elizabeth, and Richard Cheesman,..	"	XXXVI.	105
173⅘. Jan. 3.	Weeks, Filina, and Jonathan Smith, ...	"	I.	5
1777. Oct. 27.	Weeks, Freelove, and George Weekes,.....	"	XXIV.	171
1736. July 3.	Weeks, Freelove, and Joseph Cole,....... ..	"	I.	2
1758. Feb. 14.	Weeks, George, and Sarah Hall, ...	"	I.	821
1768. Feb. 11.	Weeks, Hannah, and Abraham Coles, ...	"	XIII.	34
1757. April 4.	Weeks, Isabel, and Robert Reynolds,......	"	I.	485
1783. Dec. 31.	Weeks, Jacob, and Violetta Cocks,........	"	XL.	126
1781. Oct. 3.	Weeks, John, and Jane Simmons,.........	"	XXXIII.	83
1768. June 18.	Weeks, John, and Rebecka Coles,...	"	XIII.	132
1781. May 1.	Weeks, Martha, and Adam Hall,..........	"	XXXII.	25
1761. Sept. 10.	Weeks, Mary, and Cornelius Stratton, ...	"	V.	78

DATE.		NAMES.	RECORD.	VOL.	PAGE.
1782. Jan.	15.	Weeks, Mary, and Jabez Benedict,........	M. B.,	xxxv.	18
1757. Nov.	30.	Weeks, Mary, and Timothy McNamar, ...	"	I.	720
1779. Jan.	18.	Weeks, Nathaniel, and Sarah Place,.......	"	xxvii.	16
1762. July	20.	Weeks, Nicholas, and Rhody Craft, ...	"	vi.	246
1760. Feb.	27.	Weeks, Phebe, and Zebulon Titus, ...	"	iii.	54
1770. April	12.	Weeks, Rhode, and William Bogle, ...	"	xvi.	61
1774. Feb.	3.	Weeks, Rose, and Isaac Kane,...........	"	xxii.	121
1737. June	16.	Weeks, Sarah, and Jacob Bursell, ...	"	I.	6
1756. July	10.	Weeks, Sarah, and James Seamans, ...	"	I.	249
1782. Sept.	6.	Weeks, Simon, and Elizabeth Hare, ...	"	xxxvi.	138
1770. Aug.	6.	Weeks, Stephen, and Sarah McDowell, ...	"	xvi.	154
1779. Jan.	20.	Weeks, Temperance, and Hachaliah Purdy,.	"	xxvii.	20
1779. Nov.	19.	Weeks, Willet, and Dorathy Mudge, ...	"	xxviii.	144
1780. May	19.	Weeks, Ziprey, and Thomas Place,........	"	xxix.	62
1772. June	16.	Weetershang, Daniel, and Christina Wolfe, .	"	xviii.	140
1779. Nov.	25.	Weger, Catherine, and Henry Flack,......	"	xxviii.	147
1764. Aug.	24.	Weigand, John, and Hannah Reyder,......	"	viii.	293
1758. Dec.	2.	Welch, Ann, and Nathaniel Taylor,........	"	ii.	110
1760. Oct.	11.	Welch, Edmond, and Eleanor Van Cliegh,..	"	iii.	359
1757. Jan.	17.	Welch, Edward, and Margaret Manley, ...	"	I.	419
1763. April	26.	Welch, Elizabeth, and John Dent,.........	"	vii.	144
1757. July	5.	Welch, Elizabeth, and Joseph Backer, ...	"	I.	584
1760. April	30.	Welch, James, and Hannah Hapey,........	"	iii.	132
1761. June	29.	Welch, James, and Mary Seperson, ...	"	iv.	270
1757. Nov.	22.	Welch, Philip, and Ann Edwards, ...	"	I.	711
1760. July	3.	Welch, Philip, and Elizabeth Cayton,......	"	iii.	204
1761. Mar.	19.	Welch, Sarah, and John Dimes, ...	"	iv.	108
1761. Jan.	22.	Welch, Thomas, and Anne Buckler, ...	"	iv.	25
1783. June	14.	Welch, Thomas, and Mary Murphy,........	"	xxxix.	58
1780. Aug.	12.	Welch, William, and Hannah Tenbrook, ...	"	xxix.	139
1781. April	12.	Weldrige, Elizabeth, and John Holland,....	"	xxxii.	1
1767. Mar.	9.	Wellean, Ann, and Edmund Sweeny, ...	"	xi.	41
1764. May	4.	Welles, Henry, and Hannah Stout,........	"	viii.	199
1780. July	28.	Wellham, Thomas, and Sarah Richardson, ...	"	xxix.	121
1771. Dec.	18.	Wellin, Elizabeth, and John Hathorn, ...	"	xvii.	300
1760. Nov.	13.	Welling, Elizabeth, and James Hallett,.....	"	iii.	410
1765. April	16.	Welling, Jane, and James Snedicker, ...	"	ix.	97
1778. Feb.	10.	Welling, Samuel, and Elizabeth Tanner,....	"	xxv.	20
1775. Oct.	27.	Welling, Sarah, and John Wheeler, ...	"	xxiii.	188
1777. April	22.	Welling, Sarah, and Peter Rierson,........	"	xxiv.	70
1771. April	24.	Welling, Thomas, and Ann Tanner, ...	"	xvii.	67
1765. April	10.	Wells, Helena, and James Wilson, ...	"	ix.	88
1758. Nov.	29.	Wells, James, and Ann Deforeest,........	"	ii.	108
1780. July	4.	Wells, John, and Jane Evans, ...	"	xxix.	105

DATE.	NAMES.	RECORD.	VOL.	PAGE.
1765. June 21.	Wells, Maritje, and William Ray, ...	M. B.,	IX.	177
1760. Mar. 24.	Wells, Mary, and Reuben Fairchild, ...	"	III.	91
1773. June 15.	Wells, Rebecca, and Samuel Gale, ...	"	XXI.	5
1768. Nov. 4.	Wells, Robert, and Mary Dunlap, ...	"	XIII.	225
1758. Oct. 28.	Wells, Sarah, and Thomas Wright, ...	"	II.	71
1765. Oct. 11.	Wells, William, and Catrina Dumont, ...	"	IX.	298
1768. Nov. 7.	Welor, John, and Mary Cooper, ...	"	XIII.	230
1763. April 8.	Welp, Garrit, and Maritie Waters, ...	"	VII.	118
1764. Dec. 18.	Welp, Jane, and Andrew Ten Eyck, ...	"	VIII.	457
1772. Dec. 2.	Welp, Wilhelmena Mary, and Walter Bicker,	"	XIX.	141
1736. Sept. 2.	Welsh, Elizabeth, and Henry Clarke, ...	"	I.	2
1770. July 30.	Welsh, John, and Jane Allen, ...	"	XXIV.	125
1771. Aug. 1.	Welsh, Ralph, and Jane Beekman, ...	"	XVII.	147
1759. Dec. 20.	Welsh, Robert, and Jane Ross, ...	"	II.	552
1770. July 25.	Welsh, Thomas, and Jane Kane, ...	"	XVI.	146
1761. Jan. 29.	Wemp, Folke, and John Bratt, ...	"	IV.	37
1764. May 17.	Wemp, John, and Maritie Vischer, ...	"	VIII.	191
1771. Feb. 23.	Wemp, John Isaac, and Mary Swits, ...	"	XVII.	20
1756. Nov. 11.	Wempel, Catlyna, and Johannes Emptye, ..	"	I.	351
1757. Oct. 25.	Wempell, John R., and Margaret Mabee,...	"	I.	678
1758. Oct. 14.	Wemple, Margaritia, and Jacob Simonsen Vrooman, ...	"	II.	57
1737. Nov. 1.	Wendal, Ame, and Jacob Denyke, ...	"	I.	8
1736. Oct. 14.	Wendall, Abraham E., and Gertruyd Bleeker,	"	I.	3
1753. Sept. 11.	Wendall, John, and Ann Anderisen, ...	"	I.	112
1761. May 15.	Wendall, John, and Barbery Summer, ...	"	IV.	191
1757. June 24.	Wendel, Elizabeth, and Gosen Van Schaick,	"	I.	571
1772. Oct. 21.	Wendel, Engeltje, and James Howetson,...	"	XIX.	82
1763. Jan. 10.	Wendell, Anna, and Cornelius Cuyler, ...	"	VII.	13
1765. Mar. 26.	Wendell, Annatje, and Philip P. Schuyler,.	"	IX.	74
1757. Oct. 29.	Wendell, Annatje, and Volkert Douw, ...	"	I.	687
1762. Mar. 2.	Wendell, Catharin, and Abraham Cuyler,...	"	VI.	72
1760. July 29.	Wendell, Catherina, and Nanning Fisher,...	"	III.	231
1768. July 13.	Wendell, Cornelius, Jr., and Anna Lansing,.	"	XIII.	157
1761. July 16.	Wendell, Elisabeth I., and Thomas I. Hun,.	"	IV.	299
1759. Dec. 22.	Wendell, Elizabeth, and Barent Staats, ...	"	II.	555
1775. Oct. 4.	Wendell, Elizabeth, and Jacob Bleeker, Jr.,.	"	XXIII.	173
1764. Nov. 27.	Wendell, Engeltje, and Jacob Van Eps,....	"	VIII.	430
1761. July 4.	Wendell, Evert, and Mary Bratt, ...	"	IV.	276
1771. Oct. 10.	Wendell, Fanny, and Peter Brooks, ...	"	XVII.	201
1763. Feb. 28.	Wendell, Hannah, and James Sharpe, ...	"	VII.	83
1762. May 21.	Wendell, Harmanus, and Catharine Glen, ..	"	VI.	163
1770. Mar. 26.	Wendell, Harmanus A., and Castentie Van Den Bergh, ...	"	XVI.	42
1757. April 12.	Wendell, Hendrick, and Maria Lansing,....	"	I.	497

DATE.	NAMES.	RECORD.	VOL.	PAGE.
1759. Mar. 2.	Wendell, James, and Mary Edsall, ...	M. B.,	II.	204
1761. Nov. 16.	Wendell, John Bt., and Elizabeth Van Antwerpen, ...	"	V.	224
1772. Dec. 9.	Wendell, John I., and Alla Hogkirk, ...	"	XIX.	148
1772. Feb. 25.	Wendell, John Walter, and Mary Trotter, ..	"	XVII.	22
1761. Feb. 24.	Wendell, Mary, and Barent Romanse, ...	"	IV.	80
1759. July 10.	Wendell, Mary, and David Scott, ...	"	II.	351
1765. July 17.	Wendell, Philip, and Catalina Groesbeck, ..	"	IX.	208
1765. Feb. 4.	Wendle, Elizabeth, and Jacob Becker, ...	"	IX.	45
1757. Dec. 31.	Wenman, Richard, and Ann Bush, ...	"	I.	763
1736. Nov. 3.	Wenshaer, John, and Christian Egberts,....	"	I.	3
1774. Mar. 2.	Wentworth, Anna, and Peter Kip,........	"	XXII.	137
1779. April 7.	Wentworth, Samuel, and Catherine Vredenburgh, ...	"	XXVII.	96
1774. Oct. 27.	Wentworth, Samuel, and Frances Maney, ..	"	XVI.	232
1779. Dec. 6.	Werner, Christian, and Rebecca Tingill,....	"	XXVIII.	161
1760. Dec. 8.	Wesbrook, Jane, and Peter Schoenmaker,..	"	III.	466
1760. June 6.	Wesner, Elizabeth, and Silvanus Smith,....	"	III.	179
1773. Aug. 16.	Wessel, Henreck, and Anna Savenah Pemper, ...	"	XXI.	68
1769. Jan. 9.	Wessells, Alleta, and Mervin Perry, ...	"	XIV.	8
1778. Nov. 25.	Wessells, Elizabeth, and John B. Moore, ...	"	XXVI.	93
1762. Dec. 7.	Wessells, Francis Van Dyck, and Rachel Ellison, ...	"	VI.	469
1736. Nov. 29.	Wessells, Henry, and Guntye Sleigh,......	"	I.	3
1775. Aug. 14.	Wessells, Isaac, and Ariantje Van Valkenburgh, ...	"	XXIII.	127
1760. Nov. 8.	Wessells, John, and Margare Chadeyn,.....	"	III.	400
1761. April 22.	Wessells, Lawrence, and Ann Chardavoine,.	"	IV.	161
1776. April 3.	Wessells, Margaret, and Benjamin Moore, Jr.,	"	XXIII.	295
1780. Dec. 7.	Wessells, Mary, and John Devine, ...	"	XXX.	145
1769. June 21.	Wessells, Peter, and Mary Vaughton,......	"	XIV.	124
1770. Oct. 25.	Wessells, Rachel, and John Grant, ...	"	XVI.	228
1761. Sept. 7.	Wessells, Sarah, and Daniel Cornu,........	"	V.	69
1756. Dec. 7.	Wessels, Ann, and John Ent, ...	"	I.	376
1775. July 8.	Wessels, Matthias, and Hester Butler, ...	"	XXIII.	90
1755. Sept. 20.	Wessels, Peter, and Elizabeth Hope,.......	"	I.	180
1761. Nov. 26.	West, Deborah, and Samuel Leonard,......	"	V.	250
1684. Oct. 25.	West, John, and Ann Rudgards,.	C. M.,	XXXIII.	54
1757. Dec. 8.	West, Margery, and William Hibben,......	M. B.,	I.	729
1778. July 18.	West, Matthew, and Hanah Johnson,......	"	XXV.	132
1783. April 28.	West, Moses, and Jemime Haws, ...	"	XXXVIII.	119
1715. July 12.	Westerlo, Eilardus, and Catharine Van Renselaer, ...	"	XXIII.	95
1762. June 11.	Westerveldt, John, and Mary Mabey,.....	"	VI.	188

DATE.	NAMES.	RECORD.	VOL.	PAGE
1757. June 2.	Westfall, Simon, and Johanna Van Steenbergh, ...	M. B.,	I.	547
1772. Dec. 19.	Westfalt, Frederick, and Catharina Myer, ..	"	XIX.	158
1779. Jan. 14.	Weston, Thomas, and Elizabeth Myford, ...	"	XXVII.	13
1781. Nov. 5.	Westwick, Robert, and Margaret McGee, ..	"	XXXIV.	18
1763. Oct. 13.	Wetbeck, Angenetye, and Cornelius Vande Zee, ...	"	VII.	385
1767. Jan. 15.	Wetherhead, John, and Rachael Fisher, ...	"	XI.	8
1783. Mar. 17.	Wethershien, Nicholas, and Catharine Moorewise, ...	"	XXXVIII.	67
1762. Sept. 29.	Wetmore, Esther, and David Brown, ...	"	VI.	340
1777. Sept. 11.	Wetmore, George, and Rachell Ogden, ...	"	XXIV.	145
1775. Aug. 30.	Wetmore, Isaiah, and Amy Brush, ...	"	XXIII.	141
1782. Aug. 15.	Wetmore, Jane, and Jesse Lamoreuex, ...	"	XXXVI.	107
1766. Sept. 9.	Wetsell, Anna, and Sebastian Bowman, ...	"	X.	93
1777. Dec. 11.	Wettmore, George, and Rachel Wragge, ...	"	XXIV.	195
1765. May 31.	Wey, Margaret, and James Gardner, ...	"	IX.	149
1768. Dec. 21.	Wey, Sarah, and Thomas Betts, ...	"	XIII.	272
1775. June 20.	Weygand, Hannah, and Richard McDonald,	"	XXIII.	70
1775. June 20.	Weygand, Sarah, and Joseph Hoff, ...	"	XXIII.	69
1762. Aug. 18.	Weyley, Mary, and Daniel Bernard, ...	"	VI.	277
1758. May 30.	Weyman, Elizabeth, and Benjamin Townsend, ...	"	I.	915
1737. July 22.	Weynat, William, and Lia Quackinbush, ...	"	I.	7
1757. Dec. 15.	Weyser, Catharine, and John Butler, ...	"	I.	744
1777. Oct. 23.	Whaler, Mary, and Richard Drowmey, ...	"	XXIV.	170
1782. Aug. 2.	Whaley, Hannah, and Jacob Smith, ...	"	XXXVI.	98
1757. Aug. 23.	Whaley, Sarah, and Stephen Johnson, ...	"	I.	620
1759. Feb. 5.	Wharton, John, and Jane Van Ness, ...	"	II.	174
1781. Dec. 2.	Whealey, Peter, and Phebey Varnill, ...	"	XXXIV.	67
1782. Aug. 20.	Wheat, Sarah, and Samuel Date, ...	"	XXXVI.	115
1782. Dec. 11.	Wheate, Jacob, and Mary Shaw, ...	"	XXXVII.	115
1779. Sept. 4.	Wheaton, Daniel, and Sarah Rankin, ...	"	XXVIII.	67
1780. April 25.	Wheaton, Hester, and Joseph Scars, ...	"	XXIX.	36
1779. May 25.	Wheaton, Sarah, and Henry Brevoort, ...	"	XXVII.	148
1769. Mar. 17.	Wheekes, Freelove, and Townsend Wheekes,	"	XIV.	54
1769. Mar. 17.	Wheekes, Townsend, and Freelove Wheekes,	"	XIV.	54
1757. Dec. 29.	Wheeler, Abigail, and Joseph Kendall, ...	"	I.	759
1764. Aug. 11.	Wheeler, Abraham, and Dorcas Betts, ...	"	VIII.	278
1765. Sept. 8.	Wheeler, Abraham, and Margaret Plumsted,	"	IX.	49
1760. Sept. 25.	Wheeler, Altje, and William Fitch, ...	"	III.	329
1776. Mar. 20.	Wheeler, Amaziah, and Hester Cooper, ...	"	XXIII.	286
1758. Nov. 8.	Wheeler, Anne, and Stephen Le Fever, ...	"	II.	85
1767. Sept. 2.	Wheeler, Catherine, and John Holliday, ...	'	XII.	24
1757. Jan. 6.	Wheeler, Charles, and Dorothy Plumstead, .	"	I.	408

DATE.		NAMES.	RECORD.	VOL.	PAGE.
1781. Feb.	12.	Wheeler, Charles, and Mercey Smith,	M. B.,	XXXI.	21
1757. Oct.	5.	Wheeler, Eliphalet, and Hebseba Smith,	"	I.	654
1759. Oct.	22.	Wheeler, Elizabeth, and Andrew Campbell.	"	II.	467
1775. Oct.	27.	Wheeler, John, and Sarah Welling,	"	XXIII.	188
1736. Aug.	31.	Wheeler, Josiah, and Mary Platt,	"	I.	2
1757. June	16.	Wheeler, Mary, and Isaac Sherwood,	"	I.	565
1760. Sept.	19.	Wheeler, Mary, and William Colegrove,	"	III.	323
1771. Nov.	19.	Wheeler, Nathaniel, and Mary Foresayth,	"	XVII.	259
1761. May	15.	Wheeler, Rachel, and Edward Runshaw,	"	IV.	189
1771. April	25.	Wheeler, Sarah, and John Adams,	"	XVII.	68
1761. April	21.	Wheeler, Sentje, and Tobias Van Slik,	"	IV.	159
1767. Dec.	2.	Wheeler, Syntiche, and Myndert Vosburgh,	"	XII.	104
1782. April	18.	Wheelor, Peter, and Martha Weekes,	"	XXXV.	128
1757. July	20.	Whemp, Deborah, and Dow Funda,	"	I.	595
1738. Aug.	3.	Wherry, Jane, and George Monell,	"	I.	10
1761. Aug.	7.	Whery, Robert, and Elizabeth Blanford,	"	III.	240
1759. May	15.	Whetbeck, Maria, and Jacob Moore,	"	II.	284
1761. July	6.	Wheten, Benjamin, and Phebe Freeman,	"	IV.	280
1765. Feb.	25.	Whethall, Elizabeth, and Jacob I. Schermer- horn,	"	IX.	58
1781. Nov.	7.	Whetstone, Robert, and Mary Neman,	"	XXXIV.	22
1778. Feb.	10.	Whetten, Charity, and Joseph Airs,	"	XXV.	21
1756. Sept.	6.	Whetten, William, and Margaret Todd,	"	I.	287
1738. Oct.	26.	Whibben, John, and Anne Manner,	"	I.	11
1756. July	12.	Whiley, Margery, and Henry Case,	"	I.	252
1763. Feb.	22.	Whitemen, Matthew, and Rhode Forman,	"	VII.	74
1782. Jan.	18.	Whitman, Jarvis, and Deborah Wood,	"	XXXV.	23
1762. April	21.	Whipple, John, and Jane Morrell,	"	VI.	121
1782. July	16.	Whippo, Hannah, and Joseph Tobias, Jr.,	"	XXXVI.	85
1763. Jan.	26.	Whippo, James, and Keziah Mott,	"	VII.	37
1772. Jan.	10.	Whippo, John, and Deborah Elison,	"	XVIII.	11
1781. Nov.	14.	Whiston, Ruth, and Willets Powell,	"	XXXIV.	31
1765. Sept.	16.	Whit, Anne, and William Boyd,	"	IX.	263
1766. Nov.	14.	Whitaker, Catherine, and Abraham Ten Broeck,	"	X.	163
1769. May	4.	Whitaker, Edward, and Elizabeth Dewitt,	"	XIV.	93
1763. April	20.	Whitaker, Elizabeth, and Jacob Burhans,	"	VII.	133
1736. May	5.	Whitaker, Neltie, and Simon Van Wagen,	"	I.	1
1757. June	8.	Whitbeck, Elizabeth, and Thomas Houghte- ling,	"	I.	558
1765. Jan.	7.	Whitbeeck, John, and Cornelia Huck,	"	IX.	11
1765. Aug.	22.	Whitbeek, Isaac, and Janetie Van Vechte,	"	IX.	243
1769. Aug.	1.	Whitbeek, John, and Elizabeth Delamatter,	"	XV.	14
1780. Oct.	2.	White, Aaron, and Deborah Traford,	"	XL.	58
1780. Feb.	4.	White, Ann, and Paul Jappa,	"	XXVIII.	208

DATE.			NAMES.	RECORD.	VOL.	PAGE.
1762.	Jan.	9.	White, Ann, and William Palmer,.........	M. B.,	VI.	6
1768.	Jan.	30.	White, Ann, and William Scobey, ...	"	XIII.	23
1760.	Aug.	18.	White, Catharine, and John Montonje,.....	"	III.	243
1782.	Aug.	24.	White, Charles, and Catharine Belton, ...	"	XXXIII.	45
1763.	Nov.	30.	White, Daniel, and Euphamia Bartow, ...	"	VII.	485
1769.	June	22.	White, Deborah, and Robert Ross, ...	"	XIV.	125
1779.	April	1.	White, Dorcas, and Thomas Laprevick, ...	"	XXVII.	89
1772.	Mar.	19.	White, Ebenezer, and Helena Barto, ...	"	XVIII.	55
1758.	May	1.	White, Elizabeth, and Benjamin Mapes,....	"	I.	890
1769.	Nov.	21.	White, Elizabeth, and John Frederick,.....	"	XV.	101
1768.	May	5.	White, Elizabeth, and Samuel Arthur, ...	"	XIII.	94
1761.	May	13.	White, Henry, and Eve Van Cortlandt, ...	"	IV.	187
1762.	Nov.	13.	White, Henry, and Margaret Saunders, ...	"	VI.	431
1775.	Jan.	7.	White, Ignatius Peter, and Catherine McFarlan,.................................	"	XI.	4
1753.	June	13.	White, James, and Sarah Van Dam,.......	"	I.	60
1779.	June	11.	White, John, and Elizabeth Cornell,.......	"	XXVII.	164
1682.	Aug.	28.	White, John, and Elizabeth Dyer,.........	O. W.,	XXXII½.	159
1778.	Oct.	16.	White, John, and Elizabeth Ferris,........	M. B,	XXVI.	64
1763.	April	30.	White, John, and Hannah Cox,...........	"	VII.	156
1778.	Aug.	8.	White, John, and Juliet Ross, ...	"	XXV.	146
1765.	Jan.	2.	White, John, and Margaret Ogden,........	"	IX.	1
1771.	Dec.	23.	White, Margaret, and Patrick Dennis, ...	"	XVII.	303
1781.	Nov.	18.	White, Martha, and Philip Sammis, ...	"	XXXIV.	47
1763.	Feb.	15.	White, Mary, and Elisha Chase, ...	"	VII.	64
1757.	June	2.	White, Mary, and Hayes Pounell,.........	"	I.	548
1775.	May	13.	White, Mary, and Killiam Van Rensselaer, Jr.,...............................;..........	"	XXIII.	33
1759.	Jan.	6.	White, Nicholas, and Ann Starkes,........	"	II.	146
1761.	Aug.	7.	White, Nicholas, and Catharine Van Slyke,.	"	V.	31
1779.	Nov.	9.	White, Nicholas, and Sarah Forbes, ...	"	XXVIII.	133
1780.	Sept.	1.	White, Peggy, and Peter Noostrant, ...	"	XXX.	14
1760.	Mar.	13.	White, Peter, and Elizabeth Burbank, ...	"	III.	75
1763.	Dec.	5.	White, Peter, and Jane Orchard,..........	"	VII.	492
1771.	April	7.	White, Phebe, and Richard Dutton,........	"	XXVII.	99
1764.	Oct.	31.	White, Rachel, and Joseph Verrien, ...	"	VIII.	386
1772.	Aug.	4.	White, Samuel, and Elinor Tucker,........	"	XIX.	11
1738.	Oct.	27.	White, Sarah, and Anthony Munltsby,.....	"	I.	11
1760.	April	18.	White, Sarah, and Charles Jeffry, ...	"	III.	114
1769.	July	28.	White, Sarah, and Jacob Van Voorhies,....	"	XV.	7
1776.	April	20.	White, Sarah, and Thomas Dickson,.......	"	XXIII.	298
1780.	Nov.	18.	White, Sarah, and Thomas Jennings, ...	"	XXX.	114
1757.	July	21.	White, Simon, and Phaba Wright, ...	"	I.	597
1760.	May	7.	White, Thomas, and Anne Hinson,........	"	I.	822
1760.	Dec.	19.	White, Thomas, and Dinah Lippingcutt, ...	"	III.	486

DATE.	NAMES.	RECORD.	VOL.	PAGE.
1762. July 31.	White, Thomas, and Margaret Hind,.......	M. B.,	VI.	259
1771. June 26.	White, William, and Alice Gordon,........	"	XVII.	122
1763. Aug. 25.	White, William, and Elizabeth Walker, ...	"	VII.	311
1669. Aug. 23.	White, William, and Katherine Dower, ...	O. W. L.,	II.	523
1765. Feb. 2.	White, Wright, and Mary Barker,.........	M. B.,	IX.	60
1767. Nov. 28.	Whiteaker, Philip, and Sarah Van Gaasbeek,	"	XII.	101
1772. Dec. 29.	Whitear, Hannah, and Thomas Ustick, ...	"	XIX.	165
1764. Mar. 29.	Whitefield, Thomas, and Hannah George, ..	"	VIII.	123
1782. Sept. 10.	Whitehand, John, and Elizabeth Mott,.....	"	XXXVI.	143
1780. Dec. 5.	Whitehand, Sarah, and Archibald Gilles, ...	"	XXX.	138
1764. Oct. 9.	Whitehead, Abigail, and Cornelius Van Wyck,	"	VIII.	340
1766. Nov. 20.	Whitehead, Abigail, and Richard Alsop,....	"	X.	172
1764. Dec. 20.	Whitehead, Abigal, and Samuel Skidmore, .	"	VIII.	460
1764. June 23.	Whitehead, Benjamin, Jr., and Ann Carpenter,.................................	"	VIII.	233
1765. June 28.	Whitehead, Charity, and Jacob Field,......	"	IX.	190
1780. Oct. 14.	Whitehead, Charles, and Hanah Platt, ...	"	XXX.	65
1771. Mar. 7.	Whitehead, Daniel, and Catherine Willet, ..	"	XVII.	25
1762. Sept. 4.	Whitehead, Eleanor, and Stephen Field, ...	"	VI.	307
1782. Dec. 14.	Whitehead, Elizabeth, and John Laughton, .	"	XXXVII.	121
1737. Mar. 15.	Whitehead, Sarah, and John Betts,........	"	I.	9
1765. Feb. 22.	Whitehead, Sarah, and Joseph Horsfield,...	"	IX.	57
1738. April 21.	Whitehead, Susannah, and Benjamin Hulet,	"	I.	9
1761. Nov. 14.	Whitehouse, Joseph, and Elizabeth Gray,..	"	V.	219
1766. July 3.	Whitehouse, Solomon, and Sarah Martin,...	"	X.	41
1770. April 11.	Whiteman, Joseph, and Merebe Chichester,.	"	XVI.	60
1771. June 19.	Whiteman, Sophia, and Philip Jacobs, ...	"	XVII.	117
1777. Aug. 20.	Whitewood, Charles, and Elizabeth Curry,..	"	XXIV.	137
1775. Nov. 3.	Whitfield, Catharine, and Thomas Ogilvie,..	"	XXIII.	198
1765. Sept. 12.	Whitfield, Elizabeth, and Giles Cooper, ...	"	IX.	261
1761. Jan. 10.	Whitfield, Elizabeth, and Richard Robinson,	"	IV.	9
1768. May 11.	Whitfield, John, and Catherine Burger, ...	"	XIII.	101
1761. April 26.	Whiting, Elizabeth, and John Cornell, ...	"	IV.	167
1778. July 10.	Whiting, Robert, and Sarah Carr, ...	"	XXV.	123
1767. May 28.	Whitman, Eliphelet, and Martha Smith,....	"	XI.	100
1775. April 12.	Whitman, Jesse, and Hannah Brush, ...	"	XXIII.	8
1758. Jan. 6.	Whitman, Joseph, and Hannah Brush,.....	"	I.	775
1773. Dec. 17.	Whitman, Margaret, and Zopher Brush,....	"	XXII.	78
1764. Jan. 26.	Whitman, Phebe, and James Nostrand,.....	"	VIII.	38
1782. Nov. 29.	Whitman, Phebe, and Isaiah Jarvis,.......	"	XXXVII.	98
1762. July 14.	Whitman, Ruth, and Eliphalet Jarvis,......	"	VI.	237
1763. April 27.	Whitmen, Nathaniel, and Martha Smith,...	"	VII.	146
1764. Oct. 29.	Whitmey, Leonard, and Judith Parent, ...	"	VIII.	378
1736. Dec. 10.	Whitmon, Jerusha, and Joshua Hitcham,...	"	I.	3
1763. June 21.	Whitnell, William, and Elizabeth Euen,....	"	VII.	238

DATE.	NAMES.	RECORD.	VOL. PAGE.
1762. Sept. 26.	Whitney, Isaac, and Catharine Bowman,...	M. B.,	VI. 337
1779. Dec. 6.	Whitney, Rachael, and John Walker,......	"	XXVIII. 163
1770. April 2.	Whitney, Ruth, and John Boom, ...	"	XVI. 46
1782. Dec. 1.	Whitney, Samuel, and Anne Guire, ...	"	XXXVII. 103
1763. Mar. 14.	Whitney, Sarah, and Nathaniel Beek, ...	"	VII. 99
1772. Dec. 29.	Whitney, Sarah, and William Mekeel, ...	"	XIX. 166
1775. Oct. 18.	Whitson, Rachel, and Benjamin Mott, ...	"	XXIII. 184
1781. Mar. 28.	Whitson, Sarah, and Charles Jackson, ...	"	XXXI. 88
1772. Aug. 10.	Whitson, Silas, and Sarah Powell, ...	"	XIX. 18
1783. Aug. 6.	Whooley, Hannah, and Benjamin Platt,....	"	XXXIX. 112
1767. Nov. 3.	Whyley, Jane, and Mathew McDanel, ...	"	XII. 75
1763. Dec. 17.	Whyte, Alexander, and Elizabeth Eagan,...	"	VII. 507
1752. Nov. 27.	Wick, Elizabeth, and Zebulon Cooper,.....	"	I. 13
1769. May 20.	Wickam, Dorothy, and John De Lancey,...	"	XIV. 104
1766. Dec. 12.	Wickes, Elijah, and Kissia Davis, ...	"	X. 202
1781. Nov. 20.	Wickes, Mary, and Moses Bears,..........	"	XXXIV. 52
1771. Oct. 29.	Wickham, Eleanor, and Peter Fountain, ...	"	XVII. 232
1767. Sept. 7.	Wickham, Thomas, and Sarah Denton, ...	"	XII. 26
1768. Feb. 24.	Wickham, William, and Sarah Duncan, ...	"	XIII. 42
1781. April 5.	Wickoff, Sarah, and Hendrick Plas, ...	"	XXXI. 94
1757. Aug. 13.	Wickoff, Willemtie, and Nicholas Schenck, .	"	I. 613
1673. April 25.	Wicks, John, and Hesther Ketcham, ...	G. E.,	IV. 280
1770. Oct. 17.	Wicks, Lemuel, and Ann Carpenter,.......	M. B.,	XVI. 220
1766. July 17.	Wicks, Meriam, and Steven Jagger, ...	"	X. 56
1772. Oct. 22.	Widbeeck, Gerritje, and Daniel Van Antwerp,	"	XIX. 86
1763. Oct. 31.	Widbeeck, Jannetye, and Gysbert Van Den Bergh, ...	"	XVII. 236
1772. Dec. 1.	Widbeek, Sarah, and Alexander Van Alstine,	"	XIX. 139
1779. Aug. 2.	Widner, Mary, and James Hines, ...	"	XXVIII. 43
1781. Jan. 13.	Widowson, Alice, and George Brown,.....	"	XXXI. 22
1778. Aug. 20.	Wiely, Robert, and Catherine Margeson, ,..	"	XXVI. 7
1782. Oct. 23.	Wier, Elizabeth, and Joseph Holdstock,....	"	XXXVII. 63
1764. Feb. 27.	Wiesener, Johann Christian, and Catharine Groesehanck, ...	"	VIII. 82
1775. Nov. 4.	Wiessmer, Peter, and Elizabeth Kortz, ...	"	XXIII. 199
1775. Dec. 16.	Wiessmer, Pieter, and Mary Sharp, ...	"	XXIII. 231
1777. Aug. 21.	Wiggans, James, and Ann Twine, ...	"	XXIV. 139
1761. Nov. 16.	Wiggins, Benajah, and Elisabeth Green, ...	"	V. 221
1765. June 27.	Wiggins, Charles, and Elizabeth Haff,......	"	IX. 191
1766. Nov. 5.	Wiggins, Daniel, and Phebe Platt, ...	"	X. 153
1761. Feb. 2.	Wiggins, Hannah, and Isaac Leggett,......	"	IV. 47
1765. July 9.	Wiggins, Mary, and Gabriel Leggett, ...	"	IX. 200
1764. April 14.	Wiggins, Thomas, and Elizabeth Goodwin, .	"	VIII. 155
1757. Jan. 17.	Wiggins, Thomas, and Sarah Bailey,.......	"	I. 440
1779. May 15.	Wighton, George, and Rachel Emmot,.....	"	XXVII. 137

DATE.		NAMES.	RECORD.	VOL.	PAGE.
1778. Feb.	24.	Wigmore, Catherine, and Thomas Hill, ...	M. B.,	xxv.	32
1759. Dec.	24.	Wigmore, John, and Margaret Lean, ...	"	ii.	558
1773. May	21.	Wigram, John, and Mary Schermerhorn,...	"	xx.	120
1772. Aug.	20.	Wikhoff, Mary, and Frans Titus, ...	"	xix.	27
1738. Aug.	30.	Wilbeek, Gertruyt, and Hendrick Vanbueren, ...	"	i.	11
1783. June	7.	Wilcocks, Catharine, and Tady Cronin, ...	"	xxxix.	46
1769. Dec.	21.	Wilcocks, Elizabeth, and George Brinckerhoff, ...	"	xv.	128
1763. Mar.	26.	Wilcocks, Rossil, and Jemima Halstead, ...	"	vii.	107
1782. May	18.	Wilcocks, Sarah, and William Melvin, ...	"	xxxvi.	11
1763. July	21.	Wilcox, Elisabeth, and Ennis Graham, ...	"	vii.	279
1771. May	27.	Wilcox, Keziah, and James Hall, ...	"	xvii.	93
1763. Dec.	15.	Wilder, Hannah, and John Miller, Jr., ...	"	vii.	505
1759. Sept.	7.	Wildungen, Charles, and Mary Magdalena Daniels, ...	"	ii.	413
1779. Nov.	3.	Wile, John, and Cicile Magee, ...	"	xxviii.	127
1769. Nov.	20.	Wiley, Alexander, and Elizabeth Kerr, ...	"	xv.	99
1773. Dec.	21.	Wiley, Alexander, and Gertruyd Hike, ...	"	xxii.	80
173⅚. Mar.	16.	Wiley, Alexander, and Jane Bell, ...	"	i.	5
1767. Jan.	28.	Wiley, Elizabeth, and John Snell, ...	"	xi.	16
1761. May	29.	Wiley, Esther, and Thomas Hart, ...	"	iv.	213
1738. Sept.	30.	Wiley, James, and Elizabeth Logan, ...	"	i.	11
1763. May	3.	Wiley, Jane, and Joseph Gildersliove, ...	"	vii.	163
1762. July	30.	Wiley, John, and Gertruy Long, ...	"	vi.	256
1737. Aug.	11.	Wiley, John, and Mary Postley, ...	"	i.	7
1760. Oct.	14.	Wiley, Mary, and David Hoome, ...	"	iii.	364
1773. April	8.	Wiley, Mary, and Robert Halsted, ...	"	xx.	89
1763. Feb.	24.	Wiley, Mary, and William Randcl, ...	"	vii.	77
1773. Dec.	28.	Wilie, Cornelius, and Ariantje Palmateer, ..	"	xxii.	88
1781. April	20.	Wilkee, John, and Sarah Roose, ...	"	xxxii.	10
1761. Dec.	17.	Wilkens, Obadiah, and Sarah Lake, ...	"	iii.	481
1780. Oct.	28.	Wilkie, Edward, and Frances Martin, ...	"	xxx.	83
1778. June	17.	Wilkie, Elizabeth, and John Clarke, ...	"	xxv.	107
1759. Aug.	13.	Wilkie, James, and Elizabeth Noble, ...	"	ii.	383
1771. Dec.	2.	Wilkins, Ann, and Robart Grace, ...	"	xvii.	278
1762. Nov.	16.	Wilkins, Isaac, and Isabella Morris, ...	"	vi.	415
1764. Sept.	27.	Wilkins, Isaac, and Mary Burchel, ...	"	viii.	323
1762. May	29.	Wilkins, Jacob, and Hannah Betts, ...	"	vi.	176
1761. Feb.	20.	Wilkins, Jacob, and Keziah Hunt, ...	"	iv.	73
1760. Sept.	8.	Wilkins, James, and Anne Bull, ...	"	iii.	304
1684. Dec.	5.	Wilkins, Matthew, and John Briggs, ...	C. M.,	xxxiii.	56
1669. July	28.	Wilkins, Sarah, and Dennis Holdren, ...	O. W. L.,	ii.	492
1783. Oct.	16.	Wilkinson, Christianna, and John Hanstein, ...	M. B.,	xl.	82

DATE.	NAMES.	RECORD.	VOL.	PAGE.
1763. Jan. 12.	Wilkinson, Edward, and Elizabeth Tanner,.	M. B.,	VII.	14
1759. Dec. 15.	Wilkinson, Elizabeth, and John Radliff,....	"	II.	546
1763. Nov. 22.	Wilkinson, John, and Content Moore,......	"	VII.	462
1775. Aug. 11.	Wilkinson, Martha, and John St. John,....	"	XXIII.	124
1780. Oct. 25.	Wilkinson, Mary, and John Anderson,.....	"	XXX.	80
1773. Dec. 14.	Wilkinson, Richard, and Emelia Everit,....	"	XXII.	75
1763. April 20.	Wilkinson, Stephen, and Christiana Flood,..	"	VII.	134
1781. Feb. 19.	Wilkinson, Susannah, and Dominick Dougherty,...............................	"	XXXI.	51
1761. Mar. 30.	Wilkison, Daniel, and Anne Tillow, ...	"	IV.	101
1759. May 4.	Wilks, Sarah, and William Smith,.........	"	II.	267
1761. Nov. 25.	Will, Henry, and Magdaline Haan,........	"	V.	246
1781. Mar. 23.	Willabe, Joseph, and Sarah Smith,........	"	XXXI.	82
1771. Oct. 5.	Willes, Jane, and Nicholas Halenbeeck, ...	"	XVII.	199
1778. June 12.	Willet, Aletta, and John Dunbar, ...	"	XXV.	99
1760. Oct. 3.	Willet, Anna Statia, and Thomas McIlworth, ...	"	III.	343
1770. Oct. 29.	Willet, Catharine, and John Applegate,....	"	XVI.	233
1771. Mar. 7.	Willet, Catherine, and Daniel Whitehead,..	"	XVII.	25
1772. Nov. 26.	Willet, Charity, and Job Willet, ...	"	XIX.	129
1778. June 17.	Willet, Edward, and Ann Vanlen,........	"	XXV.	108
1774. Jan. 31.	Willet, Edward S., and Sarah Fryer, ...	"	XXII.	119
1761. Dec. 4.	Willet, Gilbert, and Martha Oakley, ...	"	V.	265
1772. Nov. 26.	Willet, Job, and Charity Willet, ...	"	XIX.	129
1756. Oct. 12.	Willet, Martha, and Thomas Miller, ...	"	I.	327
1737. April 7.	Willet, Mary, and David Simmons,........	"	I.	5
1756. Dec. 2.	Willet, Mary, and Elnathan Field,.........	"	I.	370
1762. Oct. 9.	Willet, Mary, and John Van Ranst,........	"	VI.	356
1779. Mar. 20.	Willet, Patience, and Samuel Myres, ...	"	XXVII.	71
1764. July 10.	Willet, Rachel, and Viner Leaycraft, Jr., ...	"	VIII.	253
1782. Mar. 19.	Willet, Rebeckah, and Timothy Scudden, ..	"	XXXV.	91
1768. Aug. 1.	Willet, Susannah, and Samuel Cornwel,....	"	XIII.	167
1737. Oct. 15.	Willet, Thomas, and Elizabeth Lawrence, ..	"	I.	7
1773. Nov. 19.	Willets, Anna, and Zebulon Powell, ...	"	XXII.	34
1760. April 17.	Willets, Catharine, and Jacob Underhill,....	"	III.	113
1782. Oct. 17.	Willets, Daniel, and Martha Doty, ...	"	XXXVII.	45
1738. May 29.	Willets, David, and Deborah Willets, ...	"	I.	9
1738. May 29.	Willets, Deborah, and David Willets, ...	"	I.	9
1773. Nov. 5.	Willets, Jemima, and Amos Powell,.......	"	XXII.	14
1736. Aug. 25.	Willets, Richard, and Hannah Strong, ...	"	I.	2
1779. June 16.	Willett, Alice, and Henry Nicoll,..........	"	XXVII.	166
1777. Aug. 6.	Willett, Amelia, and George Ogilvie, ...	"	XXIV.	128
1767. Feb. 24.	Willett, Ann, and David Colden,..........	"	XI.	35
1767. Oct. 5.	Willett, Charity, and Jesse Smith,.........	"	XII.	55
1762. Aug. 27.	Willett, Edward, Jr., and Mary Gale,......	"	VI.	294

DATE.		NAMES.	RECORD.	VOL.	PAGE.
1763. Nov.	19.	Willett, Elbert, and Cathlina Abeel,.......	M. B.,	VII.	456
1766. July	26.	Willett, Elizabeth, and Benjamin Booth,....	"	X.	62
1753. Oct.	10.	Willett, Elizabeth, and Joseph Field,.......	"	I.	136
1772. May	6.	Willett, Elizabeth, and Thomas Hallett, ...	"	XVIII.	101
1762. Nov.	2.	Willett, Frances, and Christopher Billopp,..	"	VI.	405
1783. April	12.	Willett, James, and Rachael Kenneday,....	"	XXXVIII.	93
1772. Mar.	5.	Willett, Jane, and Robert Alexander,......	"	XVIII.	49
1782. May	8.	Willett, John, and Mary Nostrand, ...	"	XXXV.	155
1766. Sept.	4.	Willett, Margaret, and William Bethell, ...	"	X.	90
1760. April	2.	Willett, Marinus, and Mary Pearsee,.......	"	III.	94
1781. Jan.	23.	Willett, Marquelet, and Letty Brown, ...	"	XXXI.	27
1767. Nov.	12.	Willett, Sarah, and James Morrell, ...	"	XII.	81
1778. Jan.	11.	Willett, Sarah, and William Tallman, ...	"	XXV.	3
173⁶⁄₇. Feb.	17.	Willett, Thomas, and Abigail Stephenson, ..	"	I.	5
1763. Nov.	23.	Williams, Altie, and John Cornell, ...	"	VII.	465
1781. Jan.	9.	Williams, Amy, and Cornelius Velsey, ...	"	XXXI.	19
1771. Mar.	9.	Williams, Ann, and Gabriel H. Ludlow,....	"	XVII.	27
1761. Nov.	30.	Williams, Ann, and John Van Veghten,....	"	V.	256
1779. Dec.	9.	Williams, Ann, and William McKay, ...	"	XXVIII.	168
1769. Sept.	30.	Williams, Anna, and James Betts,.........	"	XV.	48
1736. April	16.	Williams, Annanekie, and Robert Scott,....	"	I.	1
1783. June	26.	Williams, Anne, and James Baxter, ...	"	XXXIX.	69
1757. Feb.	24.	Williams, Anne, and James Stock, ...	"	I.	449
1758. May	15.	Williams, Anne, and John Solis,..........	"	I.	901
1762. Dec.	9.	Williams, Arthur, and Martha Hatfield, ...	"	VI.	472
1760. Aug.	13.	Williams, Bathsheba, and Josiah Briggs,....	"	III.	251
1772. Nov.	5.	Williams, Benjamin, and Mary Payne,.....	"	XIX.	102
1757. June	3.	Williams, Charity, and Peter Buessing, ...	"	I.	550
1759. May	8.	Williams, Charlot, and Charles Conner, ...	"	II.	269
1783. Aug.	28.	Williams, Daniel, and Anna Hatten,.......	"	XL.	12
1762. Dec.	18.	Williams, Edward, and Elisabeth Murray, ..	"	VI.	489
1764. Feb.	22.	Williams, Elizabeth, and David Russell, ...	"	VIII.	71
1782. Oct.	17.	Williams, Elizabeth, and Isaac Doty, ...	"	XXXVII.	46
1777. April	5.	Williams, Elizabeth, and Patrick King, ...	"	XXIV.	58
1737. June	11.	Williams, Elizabeth, and Sampson Benson, .	"	I.	6
1763. Feb.	21.	Williams, Erasmus, and Eyda Beekman, ...	"	VII.	71
1783. July	7.	Williams, George, and Catharine Colroyd, ..	"	XXXIX.	83
1773. Jan.	15.	Williams, Gilbert, and Euphemia Hunt,....	"	XX.	9
1764. Sept.	19.	Williams, Gilbert, and Sarah Williams,.....	"	VIII.	316
1766. Aug.	6.	Williams, Grace, and Abraham Walton,....	"	X.	70
1769. Nov.	27.	Williams, Hannah, and John Ray, ...	"	XV.	108
1753. June	2.	Williams, Hendrick, and Fransyna Cloet,...	"	I.	47
1779. Aug.	25.	Williams, Isabella, and Joseph Galloway,...	"	XXVIII.	58
1778. Dec.	9.	Williams, Jacob, and Deborah Smith,......	"	XXVI.	115
1766. Nov.	24.	Williams, James, and Mary O'Connor,.....	"	X.	180

DATE.	NAMES.	RECORD.	VOL.	PAGE.
173⁷. Mar. 11.	Williams, Jane, and Henry Simmons,	M. B.,	I.	5
1771. April 29.	Williams, Jane, and Robert McClallen,	"	XVII.	70
1760. Feb. 11.	Williams, Jenkins, and Hunty Gautier,	"	III.	31
1759. Sept. 3.	Williams, Jennet, and David High,	"	II.	407
1771. Oct. 23.	Williams, Jenny, and Nicholas Huck,	"	XVII.	219
1775. May 12.	Williams, John, and Agnes Allen,	"	XXIII.	31
1757. Jan. 26.	Williams, John, and Catharine Van Winkler,	"	I.	427
1762. Nov. 24.	Williams, John, and Mary Cornell,	"	VI.	452
1760. Oct. 27.	Williams, John, and Mary Holdridge.	"	III.	382
1779. Mar. 5.	Williams, Jonathan, and Euphemia Palmer,	"	XXVII.	56
1782. Sept. 17.	Williams, Jonathan, and Mary Titus,	"	XXXVII.	4
1762. June 30.	Williams, Margaret, and Thomas Stymest,	"	VI.	216
1760. Mar. 10.	Williams, Margaret, and William Harper,	"	III.	72
1779. May 13.	Williams, Mary, and Abijah Clark,	"	XXVII.	135
1763. Nov. 11.	Williams, Mary, and George Taylor,	"	VII.	445
1779. April 5.	Williams, Mary, and James Cumming,	"	XXVII.	94
1761. April 27.	Williams, Mary, and James Gleen,	"	IV.	168
1759. June 30.	Williams, Mary, and John Davis,	"	II.	343
1783. July 14.	Williams, Mary, and John Gallaudet,	"	XXXIX.	91
1760. Aug. 26.	Williams, Mary, and Uriah Wright,	"	III.	267
1781. July 28.	Williams, Michael, and Sarah Smith,	"	XXXIII.	19
1765. Oct. 24.	Williams, Nicholas, and Sarah Rogers,	"	IX.	317
1755. Aug. 26.	Williams, Peter, and Elizabeth Fonda,	"	I.	155
1737. Oct. 28.	Williams, Phebe, and John Hawkins,	"	I.	7
1753. Sept. 7.	Williams, Phebe, and John Hunt,	"	I.	110
1760. May 31.	Williams, Rachael, and Thomas Clark,	"	III.	169
1759. Oct. 1.	Williams, Ranselaer, and Catharine Cartwright,	"	II.	438
1763. Dec. 23.	Williams, Richard, and Sarah Lake,	"	VII.	521
1758. Dec. 16.	Williams, Robert, and Anne Marea Peffer,	"	II.	130
1764. Sept. 9.	Williams, Sarah, and Gilbert Williams,	"	VIII.	316
1780. May 1.	Williams, Sarah, and Patrick Dillon,	"	XXIX.	38
1771. April 20.	Williams, Sarah, and William Bull,	"	XVII.	63
1783. July 20.	Williams, Searing, and Sarah Rich,	"	XXXIX.	96
1780. April 8.	Williams, Thomas, and Ellen Hornby,	"	XXIX.	15
1760. Jan. 31.	Williams, Thomas, and Hannah Smith,	"	III.	13
1675. June 15.	Williams, Thomas, and Honor Eustace,	W. O. P.,	III.	97
1683. July 24.	Williams, Thomas, and Margaret Richardson,	E.,	XXXIII.	73
1777. Nov. 12.	Williams, Thomas, and Mary Smith,	M. B.,	XXIV.	180
173⁷. Jan. 25.	Williams, Thomas, and Sarah Smith,	"	I.	5
1765. Aug. 2.	Williams, Thomas Pynn, and Catharine Shauknassy,	"	IX.	227
1777. Mar. 28.	Williams, Valentine, and Elizabeth Robins,	"	XXIV.	53
1767. Sept. 11.	Williams, William, and Catherine Cooper,	"	XII.	33b

DATE.	NAMES.	RECORD.	VOL.	PAGE.
1779. Feb. 2.	Willis, Joshua, and Catherine Weeks,......	M. B.,	XXVII.	34
1777. June 20.	Willis, Joshua, and Sarah Cole,..........	"	XXIV.	106
1782. Dec. 17.	Willis, Mary, and Abraham Chapman, ...	"	XXXVII.	122
1765. Aug. 15.	Willis, Mary, and John McGillivray,.......	"	IX.	238
1779. June 17.	Willis, Oliver, and Sarah Marvin, ...	"	XXVII.	167
1775. Nov. 8.	Willis, Ruth, and Samuel Hulett, ...	"	XXIII.	201
1767. Feb. 7.	Willis, Samuel, and Janet Lees,..........	"	XI.	22
1769. April 20.	Willis, Sarah, and John Somarindyck, ...	"	XIV.	79
1762. Aug. 31.	Willis, Stephen, and Sarah Smith,.........	"	VI.	300
1783. Feb. 24.	Willis, Townsend, and Hannah Bowne,....	"	XXXVIII.	51
1757. Oct. 11.	Willit, Thomas, and Mary Embree,........	"	I.	665
1755. Sept. 4.	Willkenson, Ann, and John Healand,......	"	I.	166
1738. June 19.	Willocks, Cornelia, and Charles Smith,.....	"	I.	10
1762. Oct. 28.	Wills, Thomas, and Eleanor James,........	"	VI.	392
1769. May 6.	Willse, Daniel, and Rebecca Brown,.......	"	XIV.	95
1758. May 11.	Willse, Jacob, and Rebeccah Archer, ...	"	I.	900
1763. May 11.	Willse, Mary, and Peter Valintine, ...	"	VII.	192
1763. Nov. 10.	Willse, Susanna, and Daniel Buckbee,......	"	VII.	443
1765. May 20.	Willsey, Tunis, and Christiana Seacord, ...	"	IX.	133
1756. Sept. 27.	Willsher, John, and Elizabeth McLean,....	"	I.	306
1779. Oct. 9.	Willson, Abraham, and Hilah Waldron,....	"	XXVIII.	109
1782. Sept. 21.	Willson, Abraham, Jr., and Elizabeth Duncan, ...,...............	"	XXXVII.	7
1758. Dec. 2.	Willson, Applony, and Matthew Valentine,.	"	II.	111
1738. Sept. 18.	Willson, Catherine, and John Willson,.....	"	I.	11
1778. July 23.	Willson, Dorothy, and John Smith,........	"	XXV.	137
1777. Sept. 20.	Willson, Gilbert, and Jane Pettit,.........	"	XXIV.	148
1757. April 16.	Willson, James, and Lentie Schermerhorne,.	"	I.	499
1772. Jan. 6.	Willson, John, and Ann McClean,.........	"	XVIII.	4
1780. June 16.	Willson, John, and Catharine Dobson, ...	"	XXIX.	88
1738. Sept. 18.	Willson, John, and Catherine Willson, ...	"	I.	11
1760. April 29.	Willson, John, and Martha Audier,........	"	III.	131
1778. Oct. 9.	Willson, John, and Mary Ann Barry,......	"	XXVI.	52
1782. Mar. 9.	Willson, John, and Sarah Lackerman, ...	"	XXXV.	83
1761. June 22.	Willson, John, and Sarah Morris,..........	"	IV.	254
1757. Mar. 21.	Willson, Mary, and Ezekiel Sneed, ...	"	I.	476
1762. June 12.	Willson, Mary, and Peter Collier, ...	"	VI.	190
1737. May 7.	Willson, Mercy, and John Thorn, ...	"	I.	6
1780. Dec. 1.	Willson, Phiby, and John Begg, ...	"	XXX.	132
1779. Jan. 26.	Willson, Sarah, and James Camplin,.......	"	XXVII.	26
1763. May 12.	Willson, William, and Catharine Connor,...	"	VII.	182
1781. May 28.	Willson, William, and Elizabeth Garish,....	"	XXXII.	58
1760. Dec. 4.	Wilmot, Ann, and Alexander McGrah,. ...	'	III.	453
1780. Nov. 6.	Wilmot, Frances, and Peter Alexander Allaire, ...	"	XXX.	92

DATE.	NAMES.	RECORD.	VOL.	PAGE.
1762. Jan. 22.	Wilmot, Freelove Townsend, and James Townsend, ...	M. B.,	VI.	23
1783. Jan. 3.	Wilmott, Jane, and Uzal Johnson, ...	"	XXXVIII.	2
1767. April 1.	Wilsey, Abigail, and John Montanye,......	"	XI.	54
1781. Dec. 6.	Wilsey, Mary, and John Vandervoort,.....	"	XXXIV.	74
1761. Feb. 28.	Wilson, Alexander, and Catherine Van Woort,.............................	"	IV.	85
1760. May 28.	Wilson, Catharine, and Abram Brouwer,...	"	III.	164
1782. Jan. 12.	Wilson, Cornelia, and John Ritchie, ...	"	XXXV.	16
1781. Nov. 17.	Wilson, David, and Elizabeth Kirk,........	"	XXXIV.	43
1780. Nov. 7.	Wilson, David, and Hannah Dol,..........	"	XXX.	97
1761. Dec. 18.	Wilson, Elizabeth, and Samuel Hallett,.....	"	V.	284
1756. Dec. 20.	Wilson, Elizabeth, and Thomas Vatar,.....	"	I.	394
1770. July 18.	Wilson, Elizabeth, and William Bennet, ...	"	XVI.	141
1761. Jan. 10.	Wilson, Gerthry, and William Hodge, ...	"	IV.	8
1764. Dec. 31.	Wilson, James, and Elenor Redgrove, ...	"	VIII.	468
1765. April 10.	Wilson, James, and Helena Wells, ...	"	IX.	88
1760. Jan. 8.	Wilson, Jane, and Samuel Plumbe,........	"	II.	572
1764. June 23.	Wilson, John, and Mary Moran, ...	"	VIII.	234
1769. Oct. 18.	Wilson, John, and Mary Reddens,.........	"	XV.	56
1775. June 22.	Wilson, Joseph, and Sarah Hubbs, ...	"	XXIII.	73
1783. Nov. 15.	Wilson, Lidia, and John Robinson, ...	"	XL.	114
1769. Nov. 18.	Wilson, Martha, and David Seaman,.......	"	XV.	97
1778. May 5.	Wilson, Martha, and John Thomas,........	"	XXV.	71
1772. Sept. 26.	Wilson, Martha, and Samuel Kempton,....	"	XIX.	58
1750. Nov. 19.	Wilson, Mary, and Alexander Stoofs,......	"	II.	506
1778. Oct. 5.	Wilson, Mary, and Bartlet Goodrich, ...	"	XXVI.	110
1758. Nov. 27.	Wilson, Mary, and John Cothong, ...	"	II.	105
1781. Dec. 15.	Wilson, Merriam, and Daniel Berrien, ...	"	XXXIV.	87
1763. Dec. 8.	Wilson, Peter, and Annatje Peterson, ...	"	VII.	498
1763. Nov. 21.	Wilson, Robert, and Elenor Paulding, ...	"	VII.	459
1773. June 17.	Wilson, Samuel, and Ann Yaricks,........	"	XXI.	15
1781. Aug. 15.	Wilson, Sarah, and Joseph Shotwell, ...	"	XXXIII.	37
1773. Dec. 23.	Wilson, Sarah, and Nicholas Carmer,......	"	XXII.	84
1779. Mar. 6.	Wilson, Stephen, and Ann Rainer,........	"	XXVII.	58
1760. Feb. 11.	Wilson, Stewart, and Jane Gregg, ...	"	III.	32
1763. Feb. 22.	Wilt, George, and Abbyjah Arden, ...	"	VII.	75
1753. May 18.	Wilt, John, and Margaret Still, ...	"	I.	34
1776. April 27.	Wiltse, Elenor, and Andrew Bragaw,......	"	XXIII.	304
1773. Mar. 29.	Wiltse, Elizabeth, and John Connor, ...	"	XX.	77
1773. Feb. 22.	Wiltse, Elizabeth, and William McNeil,....	"	XX.	51
1758. Jan. 28.	Wiltse, Jacob, and Amy Snyder,..........	"	I.	803
1757. April 4.	Wiltse, Jacob, and Mary Collier,..........	"	I.	486
1775. Nov. 13.	Wiltse, Martin, and Elizabeth Van Kleeck,.	"	XXIII.	207
1764. April 2.	Wiltsie, Ida, and Patrick Rogers, ...	"	VIII.	178

59

DATE.		NAMES.	RECORD.	VOL.	PAGE.
1773. Nov.	17.	Wimp, Harantic, and Dirick G. Goot, ...	M. B.,	XXII.	33
1765. Oct.	18.	Wimpel, Andrew, and Helena Bratt, ...	"	IX.	308
1760. Dec.	8.	Wimpell, Susannah, and Harmanus Mabee,.	"	III.	464
1738. Oct.	31.	Wimple, Isaac, and Elizabeth Newkirk,....	"	I.	11
1764. Oct.	10.	Wimple, Myndert, and Sarah Vedder, ...	"	VIII.	349
1782. June	14.	Winance, Mary, and Phineas Harned, ...	"	XXXVI.	49
1757. Mar.	21.	Winant, Abraham, and Mary Mersereau,...	"	I.	477
1782. April	1.	Winant, Daniel, and Mathew Dubois,......	"	XXXV.	103
1761. May	30.	Winant, Deborah, and John Morgan,......	"	IV.	218
1777. Dec.	23.	Winants, Ann, and Charles Du Bois, ...	"	XXIV.	204
1779. April	23.	Winants, Catherine, and Abraham Cole,....	"	XXVII.	116
1780. Oct.	6.	Winants, Jacob, and Catharine Lawrence, ..	"	XXX.	58
1779. Jan.	7.	Winants, Peter, and Anne Cole, ...	"	XXVII.	5
1782. Nov.	3.	Winants, Rebecca, and Jacob Mersereau,...	"	XXXIV.	16
1772. Sept.	29.	Winchel, Lemuel, and Susannah Fulver,....	"	XIX.	64
1684. Oct.	25.	Winder, Samuel, and Margerett Rudgars, ..	C. M.,	XXXIII.	54
1677. April	13.	Winder, Sarah, and John Palmer,.........	W. O. P.,	III.	245
1763. Jan.	3.	Windish, Dorothy, and Samuel Randeker,..	M. B.,	VII.	3
1776. April	25.	Winekoop, Dirck D., and Annatje Eltinge, .	"	XXIII.	301
1777. Nov.	5.	Winepress, Thomas, and Thomas Rainsley, .	"	XXIV.	174
1765. Mar.	28.	Winess, James, and Johanna De Graaf, ...	"	IX.	75
1761. April	21.	Winfield, Margaret, and Sciah Robinson,...	"	IV.	165
1765. Oct.	28.	Winfield, Mary, and Thomas Porter,.......	"	IX.	326
1770. July	6.	Wing, Deboragh, and David Jones,........	"	XVI.	137
1752. Nov.	28.	Wingard, Lucas, and Catherine Van Alen,..	"	I.	17
1757. Oct.	14.	Wingend, Mary, and Albert Slingerland,...	"	I.	671
1759. Feb.	26.	Winn, Mary, and Philip Townshend, ...	"	II.	202
1778. Dec.	1.	Winn, Mary, and William Bowman,.......	"	XXVI.	104
1775. Aug.	15.	Winne, Aga, and John Osterhout,.........	"	XXIII.	128
1758. April	26.	Winne, Anna, and Albert Vander Werken,.	"	I.	885
1767. July	31.	Winne, Antie, and Barent Staats,.........	"	XII.	5
1760. Sept.	26.	Winne, Catherine, and Harman Levison,...	"	III.	331
1761. July	22.	Winne, Daniel, and Catharine Hoghteling,..	"	V.	3
1763. April	22.	Winne, Daniel, and Jane Bancker, ...	"	VII.	137
1766. July	14.	Winne, Dirckie, and Daniel Van Antwerpen, ...	"	X.	49
1758. Oct.	31.	Winne, Francis, and Anneke Viele,........	"	II.	74
1757. Aug.	26.	Winne, Frans, and Maritje Lorway, ...	"	I.	623
1773. Sept.	14.	Winne, Garret, and Hannah Veley,........	"	XXI.	108
1769. April	24.	Winne, Helena, and Hendrick James Lansing,....................................	"	XIV.	83
1756. July	12.	Winne, Jannetie, and Adam Short,........	"	I.	255
1756. Oct.	5.	Winne, John, and Mary Burrough, ...	"	I.	319
1761. Feb.	2.	Winne, Mathew, and Mariah Boom,.......	"	IV.	45
1775. Sept.	5.	Winne, Peter, and Helena Bogart,........	"	XXIII.	146

DATE.	NAMES.	RECORD.	VOL.	PAGE.
1775. May 6.	Winne, Peter, and Mary Osterhout,.......	M. B.,	XXXIII.	23
1760. July 19.	Winne, Peter, and Susannah Vandenbergh,.	"	III.	220
1759. Oct. 2.	Winne, Rebecca, and Geysbert Van Sante,.	"	II.	440
1762. Nov. 1.	Winne, Robert, and Hyllegont Van Vranken,	"	VI.	401
1765. April 9.	Winne, Sarah, and David Groesbeek,......:	"	IX.	257
1761. April 21.	Winne, Susannah, and Hendrick Van Alen,	"	IV.	157
1762. Aug. 17.	Winne, William, Jr., and Huybertje Yates,.	"	VI.	275
1771. May 11.	Winne, William, Jr., and Janetie Van Alstein, ...	"	XVII.	82
1764. Oct. 25.	Winne, Williamtie, and Jacob Lansing, ...	"	VIII.	375
1737. July 22.	Winnegand, Abraham, and Lybety Alstine,.	"	I.	6
1782. Oct. 26.	Winner, Anne, and Daniel Van Winkle,....	"	XXXVII.	66
1760. Oct. 10.	Winner, Margaret, and John Childs,.......	"	III.	357
1767. May 14.	Winslow, Catherine, and Bryan Carty,.....	"	XI.	88
1777. Dec. 4.	Winslow, Hanah, and John Wall,.........	"	XXIV.	189
1783. Sept. 10.	Winslow, Isabella Catharine, and Joseph King, ...	"	XL.	33
1783. Nov. 15.	Winslow, Mary, and James Wyatt,........	"	XL.	116
1759. Sept. 1.	Winter, Cornelia, and Richard Dongan,....	"	II.	500
1771. Mar. 15.	Winter, Daniel, and Elizabeth Wootman,...	"	XVII.	33
1758. Sept. 14.	Winter, Hanah, and Stelle Hull, ...	"	II.	21
1773. Jan. 22.	Winter, Mary, and John Graham,........ .	"	XXI.	19
1737. Mar. 25.	Winter, Rebecca, and Charles Knight,.....	"	I.	5
1783. April 16.	Winters, Elizabeth, and Thomas Jackson, ..	"	XXXVIII.	97
1773. June 21.	Winterton, Jane, and John Johnson, ...	"	XXI.	18
1760. Jan. 17.	Winthrop, Elizabeth, and Patrick Hynes,...	"	II.	584
1781. Dec. 8.	Wintworth, Catharine, and Joseph Homes,.	"	XXXIV.	78
1781. Nov. 28.	Wires, Margaret, and Jacob Seguine, ...	"	XXXIV.	62
1780. April 20.	Wirling, Robert, and Yufins Patterson, ...	"	XXIX.	29
1772. May 25.	Wirtz, George, and Esther Hasbrock,......	"	XVIII.	123
1758. Dec. 21.	Wise, Benjamin, and Elizabeth Knap,......	"	II.	136
1781. Nov. 1.	Wiseham, Samuel, and Ann Borrowes, ...	"	XXXIV.	12
1772. July 10.	Wischam, William, and Jane Bras, ...	"	XVIII.	163
1762. Nov. 17.	Wisely, Thomas, and Mary Flood, ...	"	VI.	438
1766. July 17.	Wisener, Anna, and Richard Dowdle, ...	"	X.	55
1763. Jan. 17.	Wishart, Grace, and William Bussman, ...	"	VII.	18
1761. Feb. 25.	Wisner, Elizabeth, and John Denton,......	"	IV.	82
1769. April 5.	Wisner, Henry, and Sarah Waters,........	"	XIV.	65
1762. Nov. 13.	Wisner, Mary, and Phineas, Helmes,......	"	VI.	433
1768. Jan. 22.	Wisner, Sarah, and Moses Phillips,........	"	XIII.	16
1769. Oct. 24.	Witbeck, Angeltie, and Stephen Van Alen,.	"	XV.	63
1768. May 6.	Witbeck, Angetje, and Peter Van Valkenburgh, ...	"	XIII.	95
1770. Dec. 3.	Witbeck, Annatje, and Wessell Salisbury,..	"	XVI.	281
1771. May 6.	Witbeck, Charlotta, and David McCarty,...	"	XVII.	75

DATE.	NAMES.	RECORD.	VOL.	PAGE.
1771. Jan. 28.	Witbeck, Engeltie, and Hendrick Jacob Mesick,	M. B.,	XVII.	9
1775. May 30.	Witbeeck, Andrew, and Catherine Hornbeeck,	"	XXIII.	48
1770. May 3.	Witbeeck, Elizabeth, and David Deforeest,..	"	XVI.	77
1775. July 7.	Witbeeck, Leonard, and Eve Van Alstyne,.	"	XXIII.	88
1773. April 21.	Witbeck, Thomas L., and Stantia Gose, ...	"	XX.	99
1771. Dec. 3.	Witeker, Hilake, and Matthew Van Steenbergh,	"	XVII.	283
1737. July 2.	Witfield, Henry, and Mary Tenet,	"	I.	6
1772. April 6.	Withbeck, Martin Cornelius, and Miritae Vanderberg,	"	XVIII.	69
1783. Mar. 21.	Withers, Elizabeth, and James Trinder, ...	"	XXXVIII.	72
1772. April 14.	Withten, Joseph, and Catherine Miller, ...	"	XVIII.	76
1777. Sept. 29.	Witnell, William, and Elizabeth Hanah,....	"	XXIV.	153
1762. Aug. 31.	Wittbeck, Jane, and Jacobus Cool,	"	VI.	299
1763. Aug. 25.	Wittbeck, Trintje, and Harme Van Hoesen, Jr.,	"	VII.	310
1761. Nov. 21.	Witteker, Margaret, and Cornelius Elmendorph, Jr.,	"	V.	238
1763. April 30.	Witter, Frances, and James Nicholson, ...	"	VII.	158
1736. Nov. 9.	Witts, George, and Elizabeth Robinson,....	"	I.	3
1782. Mar. 7.	Woderef, Mary, and Harre Okye,	"	XXXV.	78
1782. April 20.	Woertendyck, Frederick, and Frowetje Demaresk,	"	XXXV.	130
1764. Sept. 26.	Woertendyck, Jacob, and Mary Blauvelt, ..	"	VIII.	322
1737. April 30.	Woertman, Sarah, and Cornelius Hooglandt,	"	I.	6
1779. Jan. 22.	Woglam, Elizabeth, and Isaac Pray,	"	XXVII.	25
1761. July 4.	Woglom, Mary, and William Blake,	"	IV.	277
1768. Dec. 9.	Woglom, Peter, and Judah Bird,	"	XIII.	259
1772. June 16.	Wolfe, Christina, and Daniel Weetershang,.	"	XVIII.	140
1765. Aug. 14.	Wolff, Coenradt, and Jenny Goff,	"	IX.	236
1772. May 15.	Wolgrove, George, Jr., and Sebina Shepard,	"	XVIII.	118
1757. Sept. 12.	Woll, Latitia, and Thomas McDaniel,	"	I.	634
1782. Aug. 21.	Wolsey, Hester, and Thomas Palmer,	"	XXXVI.	117
1762. April 1.	Wood, Abigael, and Samuel Oakly,	"	VI.	88
1782. Aug. 17.	Wood, Abner, and Mary Cannon,	"	XXXVI.	113
1773. Jan. 22.	Wood, Amy, and Israel Youngs,	"	XX.	25
1765. May 7.	Wood, Anne, and Joseph Dunkly,	"	IX.	122
1770. Feb. 3.	Wood, Catherine, and Walter Skidmore,...	"	XVI.	12
1764. Jan. 30.	Wood, Charles, and Elizabeth Drake,	"	VIII.	42
1760. Nov. 14.	Wood, Charles, and Sarah Charley,	"	III.	411
1760. Jan. 3.	Wood, Deborah, and Anthony Hoanch, ...	"	II.	564
1782. Jan. 18.	Wood, Deborah, and Jarvis Whitman,	"	XXXV.	23

DATE.	NAMES.	RECORD.	VOL.	PAGE.
1764. Nov. 7.	Wood, Deborah, and Miles Okely, ...	M. B.,	VIII.	393
1769. Jan. 19.	Wood, Ebenezer, and Margaret Hoobbard,..	"	XIV.	15
1765. July 15.	Wood, Elisabeth, and Thomas Lowerer, ...	"	IX.	206
1758. Jan. 18.	Wood, Elizabeth, and Jonathan Bloomfield,	"	I.	788
1779. Mar. 27.	Wood, Elizabeth, and William Thorne, ...	"	XXVII.	80
1782. Aug. 15.	Wood, Epenetus, and Mary Loise,........	"	XXXVI.	108
1779. April 10.	Wood, Francis, and Ann Totty, ...	"	XXVII.	101
1768. July 20.	Wood, Freelove, and Samuel Nichols, ...	"	XIII.	166
1763. Feb. 2.	Wood, Hannah, and Benjamin Barker, ...	"	VII.	49
1757. Dec. 15.	Wood, Henry, and Catherine Panter,......	"	I.	745
1777. Feb. 3.	Wood, Isaac, and Angelica Waters, ,......	"	XXIV.	25
1780. Nov. 4.	Wood, Isaac, and Idar Schenk, ...	"	XXX.	90
1753. Aug. 3.	Wood, Israel, and Mary Prime,..........	"	I.	83
1762. April 8.	Wood, Israel, and Vashty Platt, ...	"	VI.	94
1762. Nov. 30.	Wood, Jacob, and Elizabeth Smith, ...	"	VI.	460
1759. April 28.	Wood, Jane, and John Albertus Still,.	"	II.	261
1782. Nov. 4.	Wood, Jeremiah, and Deborah Helmo,.....	"	XXXVII.	71
1736. Nov. 17.	Wood, Jeremiah, and Elizabeth Pearce,....	"	I.	3
1781. April 11.	Wood, John, and Caturey Ridgway,.......	"	XXXI.	102
1759. Jan. 26.	Wood, John, and Elizabeth Lenerton.......	"	II.	165
1765. April 11.	Wood, John, and Margaret Grondine, ...	"	IX.	90
1761. May 19.	Wood, Jonah, and Sarah Bryan,..........	"	IV.	199
1738. Aug. 24.	Wood, Judah, and Matthew Baker, ...	"	I.	10
1738. Oct. 11.	Wood, Judah, and Samuel Gosline,........	"	I.	11
1768. Oct. 12.	Wood, Margaret, and William Hoogland,...	"	XIII.	207
1775. May 1.	Wood, Mary, and Daniel Ward, ...	"	XXIII.	18
1779. May 1.	Wood, Mary, and James Johnson, ...'	"	XXVII.	125
1778. Mar. 9.	Wood, Mary, and John Palmer, ...	"	XXV.	36
1764. May 3.	Wood, Pearce, and Catharine Childs,......	"	VIII.	181
1736. Aug. 30.	Wood, Phebe, and James Matthews, ...	"	I.	2
1772. April 14.	Wood, Phebe, and Michael Rhemp, ...	"	XVIII.	77
1766. June 27.	Wood, Phœbe, and Abraham Becker,......	"	X.	34
1782. Feb. 23.	Wood, Rhodey, and John Hendrickson,....	"	XXXV.	62
1669. Jan. 16.	Wood, Richard, and Dorothy Clay,........	C. A.,	II.	450
1778. June 27.	Wood, Richard, and Katharine Sparracks,..	M. B.,	XXV.	115
1765. April 4.	Wood, Richard, and Mary Du Pue,.......	"	IX.	82
1763. Feb. 28.	Wood, Richard, and Mary Fowler, ...	"	VII.	84
1776. Mar. 8.	Wood, Ruth, and Abiel Titus,............	"	XXIII.	280
1759. Oct. 8.	Wood, Samuel, and Freelove Wright,......	"	II.	453
1767. Dec. 30.	Wood, Samuel, and Mary Brush, ...	"	XII.	125
1762. Oct. 28.	Wood, Sarah, and.Benjamin Larzelere, ...	"	VI.	391
1764. Sept. 28.	Wood, Sarah, and Henry Latourrette,.....	"	VIII.	325
1783. July 25.	Wood, Selah, and Abigail Valentine, ...	"	XXXIX.	100
1760. Feb. 22.	Wood, Stephen, and Elizabeth Rhodes, ...	"	III.	44
1762. Dec. 23.	Wood, Susannah, and Thomas Carman,....	"	VI.	496

DATE.	NAMES.	RECORD.	VOL.	PAGE.
1760. Sept. 22.	Wood, Susannah, and Thomas Metcalf, ...	M. B.,	III.	324
1763. April 15.	Wood, Sybil, and Sylvanus Mead,.........	"	VII.	129
1771. Oct. 15.	Wood, Thomas, and Deborah Vroom, ...	"	XVII.	210
1775. June 1.	Wood, Thomas, and Lucy Green, ...	"	XXIII.	52
1763. Feb. 24.	Wood, Walter, and Hannah De Groot,.....	"	VII.	78
1763. July 22.	Wood, William, and Ann Branson,........	"	VII.	280
1757. Feb. 21.	Wood, William, and Elizabeth Manual, ...	"	I.	445
1782. Feb. 13.	Wood, William, and Hannah Verity, ...	"	XXXV.	52
1756. Dec. 28.	Wood, William, and Rachel Steenbergh, ...	"	I.	400
1768. May 29.	Woodard, Joanna, and John Hallett, ...	"	XIII.	117
1762. July 17.	Woodard, John, and Mary Swansen, ...	"	VI.	244
1769. May 10.	Woodard, Joseph, and Ruth Nichols, ...	"	XIV.	98
1763. Dec. 6.	Woodard, Samuel, and Deborah Thorne, ...	"	VII.	494
1755. Aug. 20.	Woodard, Thomas, and Sarah Burroughs, ..	"	I.	152
1765. Feb. 4.	Woodbeek, Mary, and Garret Van Buren,..	"	IX.	43
1763. May 9.	Wooden, Elizabeth, and William Cropley,..	"	VII.	171
1762. Jan. 14.	Wooden, Phebe, and Daniel Dodge,.......	"	VI.	13
1761. Nov. 17.	Woodford, Fanny, and William Kester,....	"	V.	228
1758. Jan. 19.	Woodford, Jane, and John Wandel, ...	"	I.	791
1736. Aug. 12.	Woodford, Matthew, and Mary Butler, ...	"	I.	2
1781. Nov. 24.	Woodhull, Abraham, and Mary Smith, ...	"	XXXIV.	58
1682. Feb. 5.	Woodhull, Ann, and Daniell Turneere,.....	E.,	XXXIII.	36
1763. May 11.	Woodhull, Deborah, and Isaac Nicoll,......	M. B.,	VII.	177
1780. Nov. 6.	Woodhull, Elisebeth, and Samuel Hopkins,.	"	XXX.	94
1781. Nov. 17.	Woodhull, Elizabeth, and Henry Nicoll,....	"	XXXIV.	45
1781. Dec. 26.	Woodhull, Hannah, and Samuel Satterly, ..	"	XXXIV.	107
1782. Aug. 23.	Woodhull, James, and Keturah Strong, ...	"	XXXVI.	119
1783. Feb. 18.	Woodhull, Josiah, and Elisebeth Brewster, .	"	XXXVIII.	44
1767. Oct. 1.	Woodhull, Julianna, and Hezekiah Howell,.	"	XII.	52
1774. Feb. 22.	Woodhull, Mary, and Amos Underhill,,....	"	XXII.	133
1768. July 6.	Woodhull, Richard, and Sarah Miller,......	"	XIII.	148
1762. Mar. 2.	Woodhull, Ruth, and William Smith,......	"	VI.	61
1758. Jan. 24.	Woodhull, Sarah, and Fletcher Mathews,...	"	I.	800
1763. April 28.	Woodley, Judith, and Morris Humphries, ..	"	VII.	153
1781. June 9.	Woodruff, Eunes, and Peter Fitzsimmons,..	"	XXXII.	80
1761. June 13.	Woodruff, Jabe, and Mary Dunbar,........	"	IV.	239
1759. Aug. 6.	Woodruff, Joseph, and Elizabeth Owen,....	"	II.	375
1782. July 16.	Woodruff, Nathaniel, and Phebe Morrell,...	"	XXXVI.	84
1782. Feb. 26.	Woods, Isabella, and Daniel Laferty, ...	"	XXXV.	66
1761. Mar. 17.	Woods, John, and Levinah Strang,.... ...	"	IV.	104
1775. July 4.	Woods, John, and Martha Brush, ...	"	XXIII.	83
1782. Sept. 11.	Woods, John, and Sarah Sacket, ...	"	XXXVI.	144
1781. Sept. 29.	Woods, Martha, and John Smith,.........	"	XXXIII.	80
1761. Nov. 26.	Woods, Ruth, and John Rogers, ...	"	V.	251
1779. Dec. 15.	Woodson, Tarlton, and Ann Van Der Veer,.	"	XXVIII.	172

DATE.	NAMES.	RECORD.	VOL.	PAGE.
1778. Nov. 23.	Woodward, Elizabeth, and James Peck,....	M. B.,	XXVI.	92
1675. Mar. 1.	Woodward, Ffrances, and Richard Chew, ..	W. O. P.,	III.	183
1757. Jan. 15.	Woodward, Isaac, and Mary Lawrence,....	M. B.,	I.	417
1668. April 3.	Woodward, James, and Jane Crosse, ...	O. W. L.,	II.	223
1770. Nov. 8.	Woodward, John, and Ann Sylvester,.....	M. B.,	XVI.	243
1770. Aug. 20.	Woodward, John, and Elizabeth Burger,...	"	XVI.	164
1736. Oct. 16.	Woodward, Joseph, and Temperance Ffish,.	"	I.	3
1780. Jan. 29.	Woodward, Judith, and Arnold Fleet, ...	"	XXVIII.	204
1737. April 21.	Woodward, Mary, and Isaac Gardiner,.....	"	I.	6
1782. April 3.	Woodward, Mary, and Phenas Stevans,....	"	XXXV.	112
1778. Sept. 10.	Woodward, Patience, and William Betts,...	"	XXVI.	24
1775. June 24.	Woodward, Sarah, and Matthew Farrington,	"	XXIII.	76
1772. Mar. 2.	Woodward, Temperance, and Gabriel Furman,..............................	"	XVIII.	45
1763. Aug. 1.	Woodward, Thomas, and Ann Kelly,......	"	VII.	287
1781. June 25.	Woodword, Henrietta, and Charles Arno, ..	"	XXXII.	97
1767. Sept. 17.	Wooffendale, Robert, and Martha Stevenson, ...	"	XII.	37
1775. July 19.	Wool, Catherine, and Israel Harriot,.......	"	XXIII.	100
1760. July 28.	Wool, Jeremiah, and Deborah Bratt,.......	"	III.	229
1765. Oct. 31.	Wool, Mary, and Richard Harbert,........	"	IX.	338
1763. April 28.	Wooley, Joseph, and Mary Toffy,.........	"	VII.	152
1773. Jan. 30.	Wooley, Thomas, and Phebe Treddle,......	"	XX.	30
1768. Nov. 30.	Woolley, Benjamin, and Susannah Stocker,.	"	XIII.	249
1762. Sept. 20.	Woolley, Henry, and Miriam Cornell, ...	"	VI.	323
1775. Nov. 17.	Woolley, Samuel, and Margaret Morroll, ...	"	XXIII.	213
1770. Nov. 29.	Woortman, Dirck, and Catherine Fisher,...	"	XVI.	274
1756. Aug. 7.	Woortman, Elizabeth, and John Margesom,.	"	I.	270
1771. Mar. 15.	Wootman, Elisabeth, and Daniel Winter,...	"	XVII.	33
1736. April 17.	Worley, Elizabeth, and George Browington,	"	I.	1
1776. Nov. 25.	Wormoot, Elizabeth, and William Graham,.	"	X.	181
1782. July 27.	Wort, Coneraut, and Mary Small,.........	"	XXXVI.	92
1771. Mar. 18.	Worth, Jonathan, and Mary Edwards,.....	"	XVII.	37
1767. April 15.	Wortman, Aletta, and Hendryck Wyckoff,.	"	XI.	62
1763. Dec. 22.	Wortman, Catharine, and Barent Conselye,.	"	VII.	516
1780. Nov. 14.	Wortman, Elizabeth, and Jarvis Dobbs,....	"	XXX.	103
1764. Dec. 19.	Wortman, Elizabeth, and Joost Van Brunt,,.	"	VIII.	459
1780. Dec. 2.	Wortman, Hannah, and Ambrush Fish, ...	"	XXX.	134
1780. Sept. 9.	Wortman, Hannah, and Heman Clark,.....	"	XXX.	21
1778. Dec. 4.	Wortman, Jane, and Isaac Carpenter,......	"	XXVI.	109
1762. Mar. 15.	Wortman, Johanna, and William Bennet,..	"	VI.	71
1762. July 8.	Wortman, Margaret, and Robert Besswick,.	"	VI.	229
1764. Dec. 17.	Wortman, Mary, and William Richardson,..	"	VIII.	456
1761. June 1.	Wortman, Nicolas, and Hannah Smith, ...	"	IV.	222
1781. May 8.	Wortman, Rebecca, and Jacob Ramson,....	"	XXXII.	36

DATE.	NAMES.	RECORD.	VOL. PAGE.
1778. April 28.	Wortman, Susannah, and Abraham Cannon,	M. B.,	XXV. 69
1759. Dec. 6.	Wortman, Tunis, and Elizabeth Duryee,....	"	II. 530
1759. Oct. 31.	Wortman, Tunis, and Rhode Coles,........	"	II. 483
1760. July 23.	Wouters, Elizabeth, and Isaac Lee,........	"	III. 223
1777. Dec. 11.	Wragge, Rachel, and George Wittmer,.....	"	XXIV. 195
1763. June 10.	Wraxall, Elizabeth, and John Maunsell,....	"	VII. 223
1765. June 6.	Wray, George, and Catharine Ten Broeck, .	"	IX. 161
1762. July 16.	Wright, Abigail, and Robert Rosseter,.....	"	VI. 239
1780. July 7.	Wright, Allison, and Melescent Halsey,....	"	XXIX. 107
1760. Oct. 28.	Wright, Amy, and Edward Colwell,.......	"	III. 385
1766. Sept. 24.	Wright, Ann, and John Bennet,..........	"	X. 103
1778. Aug. 27.	Wright, Ann, and Timothy Prout, ...	"	XXVI. 15
1737. June 24.	Wright, Anne, and Alexander Taylor,.....	"	I. 6
1759. Mar. 7.	Wright, Benjamin, and Martha Fordham, ..	"	II. 212
1738. May 1.	Wright, Benjamin, and Mary Smith, ...	"	I. 9
1780. Sept. 25.	Wright, Bridgett, and Joseph Clark,.	"	XXX. 41
1757. Aug. 22.	Wright, Catharine, and John Nutt,........	"	I. 619
1764. Jan. 6.	Wright, Catherine, and Manasseh Salter,...	"	VIII. 9
1780. April 12.	Wright, Charity, and John Hallett,........	"	XXIX. 12
1764. Nov. 6.	Wright, Charles, and Susannah Palmer,....	"	VIII. 391
1737. April 7.	Wright, Deborah, and Benjamin Ferrington,	"	I. 5
1756. July 14.	Wright, Elizabeth, and Abraham Sleeth, ...	"	I. 256
1761. June 23.	Wright, Elizabeth, and Abraham Van Wyck, ...	"	IV. 256
1765. Mar. 25.	Wright, Elizabeth, and Benjamin James,...	"	IX. 72
1738. Nov. 9.	Wright, Elizabeth, and Jacob Rickew, ...	"	I. 11
1757. Nov. 28.	Wright, Elizabeth, and Jeremiah Blanck,...	"	I. 717
1768. Jan. 30.	Wright, Elizabeth, and Joel Smith,........	"	XIII. 22
1753. July 28.	Wright, Elizabeth, and Jonathan Valentine,.	"	I. 80
1760. July 28.	Wright, Elizabeth, and William Scott, ...	"	III. 228
1783. Feb. 6.	Wright, Elizabeth, and William Wright,....	"	XXXVIII. 35
1761. Aug. 4.	Wright, Freelove, and Nathan Horton, ...	"	V. 23
1759. Oct. 8.	Wright, Freelove, and Samuel Wood,......	"	II. 453
1769. Nov. 17.	Wright, Gilbert, and Phebe Jackson,......	"	XV. 82
1758. May 4.	Wright, Hannah, and Daniel Barnes, ...	"	I. 893
1765. Oct. 28.	Wright, Hannah, and Moses Drake, ...	"	IX. 322
1772. April 15.	Wright, Hannah, and Moses Sackrider, ...	"	XVIII. 79
1762. Feb. 8.	Wright, Hila, and Austin Reynolds,.......	"	VI. 231
1782. Nov. 18.	Wright, Horatio, and Mary Underhill, ...	"	XXXVII. 86
1736. June 22.	Wright, Isaac, and Ruth Lee,.............	"	I. 1
1777. Oct. 30.	Wright, Jacob, and Rebecca McDonell, ...	"	XXIV. 172
1765. Mar. 12.	Wright, Jane, and Thomas Skidmore, ...	"	IX. 67
1780. Jan. 12.	Wright, John, and Catharine Somendyck,...	"	XXVIII. 195
1757. May 19.	Wright, John, and Elizabeth Sellars,.......	'	I. 536
1757. Nov. 9.	Wright, John, and Jane Montanye, ...	'	I. 701

DATE.	NAMES.	RECORD.	VOL.	PAGE.
1761. Dec. 22.	Wright, John, and Jane Nixon,...........	M. B.,	v.	291
1783. Jan. 4.	Wright, John, and Margaret Floyd, ...	"	xxxviii.	5
1760. May 16.	Wright, John, and Mary Brady, ...	"	iii.	158
1763. Nov. 14.	Wright, John, and Rachel Lawrence,......	"	vii.	449
1763. Feb. 8.	Wright, John, and Sarah Van Wyck,......	"	vii.	55
1736. April 15.	Wright, John, and Surviah Wright,........	"	i.	1
1737. Oct. 28.	Wright, Jonathan, and Amy Alsop, ...	"	i.	7
1680. Jan. 26.	Wright, Jone, and John Copestaffe,.......	O. W.,	xxxii½.	34
1769. Nov. 10.	Wright, Joseph, and Ann Campbell,.......	M. B.,	xv.	88
1771. Aug. 10.	Wright, Joseph, and Mary Lashly,........	"	xvii.	157
173⅞. Mar. 8.	Wright, Joseph, and Timperance Kirk,.....	"	i.	9
1765. Feb. 15.	Wright, Lettice, and William Leadbetter,...	"	ix.	54
1783. Oct. 7.	Wright, Mark, and Sarah Magra, ...	"	xl.	68
1765. Jan. 4.	Wright, Martha, and Joseph Latting, ...	"	ix.	8
1762. Jan. 28.	Wright, Martha, and Thomas Dickson,.....	"	vi.	28
1759. Dec. 8.	Wright, Mary, and George Harvey,.......	"	ii.	535
1764. Nov. 16.	Wright, Mary, and John Brien, ...	"	xvi.	259
1782. Oct. 11.	Wright, Mary, and Loris Noe, ...	"	xxxvii.	39
1758. Jan. 20.	Wright, Milseson, and Thomas Hunt,......	"	i.	794
1777. May 24.	Wright, Obadiah, and Jane Sayre, ...	"	xxiv.	93
1760. Oct. 18.	Wright, Peter, and Margaret Bloome, ...	"	iii.	370.
1757. July 21.	Wright, Phaba, and Simon White, ...	"	i.	597
173⅘. Jan. 12.	Wright, Rache, and John Frost, ...	"	i.	5
1769. Nov. 3.	Wright, Reuben, and Phebe Quinby, ...	"	xv.	76a
1759. Nov. 21.	Wright, Samuel, and Rebecca Bloom,......	"	ii.	511
1738. July 24.	Wright, Sarah, and John Townsend,.......	"	i.	10
1773. June 26.	Wright, Sarah, and Samuel Carman,.......	"	xxi.	24
1764. Sept. 6.	Wright, Sarah, and Samuel Hallett, ...	"	viii.	298
1782. Dec. 18.	Wright, Sarah, and Terence Reilly,........	"	xxxvii.	124
1768. Aug. 26.	Wright, Solomon, and Mary Hawxhurst,...	"	xiii.	177
1736. April 15.	Wright, Surviah, and John Wright, ...	"	i.	1
1755. Nov. 22.	Wright, Thomas, and Elizabeth Rochell,....	"	i.	214
1761. Nov. 9.	Wright, Thomas, and Mary McQuirrey,....	"	v.	200
1758. Oct. 28.	Wright, Thomas, and Sarah Wells,........	"	ii.	71
1760. Aug. 26.	Wright, Uriah, and Margaret Williams, ...	"	iii.	267
1783. Feb. 6.	Wright, William, and Elizabeth Wright, ...	"	xxxviii.	35
1782. May 25.	Wright, William, and Margret Henry, ...	"	xxxvi.	24
1761. Oct. 27.	Wright, William, and Mary Jones, ...	"	v.	170
1781. Sept. 15.	Wright, William, and Zephery Coals,......	"	xxxiii.	66
1763. April 6.	Wright, Winifred, and Jotham Post,.......	"	vii.	114
1760. Feb. 8.	Wrightman, Susannah, and Gilbert Sherer,.	"	iii.	26
1782. Nov. 28.	Wrightmen, Peter, and Elizabeth Loker-man,..................................	"	xxxvii.	95
1783. July 12.	Wrighton, Mary, and Gardner Baker, ...	"	xxxix.	88
1736. Dec. 10.	Write, Jacob, and Catherine Pell,.........	"	i.	3

60

DATE.	NAMES.	RECORD.	VOL. PAGE.
1783. Nov. 15.	Wyatt, James, and Mary Winslow,........	M. B.,	XL. 116
1761. Jan. 22.	Wyce, Henry, and Rachel Campbell, ...	"	IV. 26
1768. July 13.	Wyckof, Femmetje, and Gilliam Cornell, ...	"	XIII. 158
1753. Oct. 9.	Wyckof, Willemtje, and Gerret Luyter,....	"	I. 135
1776. Jan. 4.	Wyckoff, Catharine, and Richard Covert,...	"	XXIII. 239
1767. April 15.	Wyckoff, Hendrick, and Aletta Wortman,..	"	XI. 62
1764. Oct. 24.	Wyckoff, Hendrick, and Sarah Emans,.....	"	VIII. 373
1778. Dec. 1.	Wyckoff, Johanna, and William Kouvenhoven,........... ....·.......	"	XXVI. 106
1781. Feb. 9.	Wyckoff, John, and Margaret Terhune, ...	"	XXXI. 43
1767. Nov. 10.	Wyckoff, John, and Mary Nostrant,.......	"	XII. 79
1768. Dec. 1.	Wyckoff, Joost, and Sarah Luyster, ...	"	XIII. 250
1778. Oct. 23.	Wyckoff, Margaret, and Amos Ryder, ...	"	XXVI. 68
1768. May 19.	Wyckoff, Maria, and Johannes Emans,.....	"	XIII. 106
1775. April 20.	Wyckoff, Mary, and Isaac Eldert,.........	"	XXIII. 13
1768. Dec. 7.	Wyckoff, Peter, and Hillitje Remsen, ...	"	XIII. 255
1772. Oct. 18.	Wyckoff, Peter, and Lammetie Lott, ...	"	XVII. 214
1775. Aug. 2.	Wyckoff, Peter, and Rymerick Denyse,....	"	XXIII. 117
1778. June 29.	Wyckoff, Ransie, and John Voorhes, ...	"	XXV. 117
1769. Sept. 28.	Wydecker, Rachel, and Tobias Swart,.....	"	XVI. 199
1774. Feb. 2.	Wyer, Abigail, and Lewis Dubois, ...	"	XXII. 120
1762. June 22.	Wyetbeck, Volkert, and Annatje Van Beaven,...............	"	VI. 202
1760. Dec. 16.	Wyley, Isabella, and Abijah Taylor, ...	"	XIII. 263
1764. July 3.	Wylle, George, and Ann McCloud,........	"	VIII. 244
1757. Sept. 28.	Wylley, Alexander, and Elizabeth McKichin,	'	I. 651
1757. Oct. 5.	Wylley, Elizabeth, and Robert Ferguson,...	'	I. 658
1763. Mar. 7.	Wylley, Jane, and John Bole, ...	"	VII. 94
1757. Mar. 5.	Wylley, John, and Catherine Peck, ...	"	I. 457
1761. April 16.	Wynkoop, Annatje, and Christopher Tappen, ...	"	IV. 151
1755. Sept. 24.	Wynkoop, Benjamin, and Catharine Boel,..	"	I. 183
1767. Oct. 14.	Wynkoop, Catherine, and Joseph Gasherie, .	"	XII. 62
1760. April 17.	Wynkoop, Cornelius C., and Maria Catherine Ruehle, ...	"	III. 112
1762. April 10.	Wynkoop, Cornelius D., and Leah Dubois,...	"	VI. 98
1766. Aug. 20.	Wynkoop, Cornelius E., and Cornelia Mancius, ...	"	X. 79
1760. Nov. 17.	Wynkoop, Derick, and Sarah Smedus,.....	"	III. 422
1765. Oct. 29.	Wynkoop, Derick D., and Sarah Eltinge,...	"	IX. 331
1767. Jan. 26.	Wynkoop, Elizabeth, and Benjamin Demire,	"	XI. 14
1765. Oct. 17.	Wynkoop, Evert, and Mary Newkirck, ...	"	IX. 304
1760. Aug. 15.	Wynkoop, Garret, and Phebe Anderson, ...	"	III. 255
1774. Jan. 26.	Wynant, John, and Joannah Fisheron, ...	"	XXII. 115
1762. Nov. 30.	Wynant, Peter, and Susanna Reseau,......	"	VI. 459

DATE.	NAMES.	RECORD.	VOL. PAGE.
1759. June 19.	Wynants, Claetje, and Thomas Harriott, ...	M. B.,	II. 321
1763. Oct. 1.	Wyser, Michael, and Elizabeth Murray,....	"	VII. 365
1761. Oct. 29.	Wyser, Michael, and Rachel Devou, ...	"	V. 177
1779. April 10.	Wytt, Margaret, and William Curtis, ...	"	XXVII. 102
1738. July 13.	Wytt, Mary, and John Corry, ...	"	I. 10
1754. Dec. 21.	Wytt, Sarah, and James Lilley,...........	"	I. 210

Y.

1756. Sept. 10.	Yarden, John, and Rachael Barheit, ...	"	I. 294
1764. Oct. 23.	Yardin, Rachael, and John Bogs, ...	"	VIII. 371
1773. June 17.	Yaricks, Ann, and Samuel Wilson,........	"	XXI. 15
1771. June 27.	Yarrow, Eleanor, and Jonathan Delano, ...	"	XVII. 123
1769. April 10.	Yarrow, Thomas, and Elizabeth Surmon,...	"	XIV. 69
1761. July 22.	Yates, Abraham, and Jannetie Bratt,......	"	V. 4
1771. Aug. 31.	Yates, Abytee, and Christopher Barker,....	"	XVII. 171
1772. Dec. 1.	Yates, Angeltie, and Cornelius Van Schaick, Jr.,................	"	XIX. 138
1761. April 8.	Yates, Catherine, and John Mynderson,....	"	XIII. 66
1766. June 23.	Yates, Christophel, and Catherine Waters,..	"	X. 26
1774. Jan. 31.	Yates, Christopher P., and Maria Fry,.....	"	XXII. 118
1770. June 12.	Yates, Christopher P., and Rebeccah Van Santford, ...	"	XVI. 110
1761. Dec. 2.	Yates, Eva, and Johannes Peek, ...	"	V. 261
1669. July 22.	Yates, Francis, and Dorothy Marsh, ...	O. W. L.,	II. 474
1771. Mar. 28.	Yates, Hannah, and William Staats,.......	M. B.,	XVII. 42
1763. Mar. 4.	Yates, Hester, and Isaac Cole,..........	"	VII. 90
1762. Aug. 17.	Yates, Huybertje, and William Winne, Jr.,.	"	VI. 275
1769. April 11.	Yates, Jellis, and Arreyantie Bratt,........	"	XIII. 73
1760. Jan. 21.	Yates, John Gerse, and Catlyna Goewy,....	"	II. 586
1682. Aug. 7.	Yates, Mary, and John Cornelius,.........	O. W.,	XXXII½. 144
1770. June 12.	Yates, Petertie, and Derick T. Van Veighten,.	M. B.,	XVI. 108
1767. July 10.	Yates, Peter W., and Ann Mary Helmes,...	"	XI. 129
1765. Mar. 5.	Yates, Robert, and Jane Van Ness,........	"	IX. 62
1762. May 21.	Yates, Tomica, and Cornelius Van Dyck,...	"	VI. 165
1760. June 30.	Yates, Tryntie, and Anthony Bryes,.......	"	III. 200
1761. Oct. 26.	Yats, Benjamin, and Ann Vanderbeeck,....	"	V. 168
1782. Jan. 8.	Yeamy, Margaret, and John Sarvant,......	"	XXXV. 11
1761. June 17.	Yeates, Christopher, and Catharine Lansing,	"	IV. 245
1761. Oct. 2.	Yeates, Christopher, and Jannetie Bradt,...	"	V. 114
1776. Feb. 15.	Yeates, Elizabeth, and Cornelius Ad. Van Slycke, ...	"	XXIII. 268
1763. Nov. 3.	Yeates, Highbertie, and Samuel Samuelse Bradt, ...	"	VII. 427

DATE.	NAMES.	RECORD.	VOL.	PAGE.
1762. Oct. 7.	Yeates, Mary, and Jacobus Teller,.........	M. B.,	VI.	350
1762. April 24.	Yeats, Tomica, and Cornelius Van Dyck,...	"	VI.	130
1764. April 9.	Yeamans, George, and Ann Lawrence,.....	"	VIII.	144
1760. Aug. 18.	Yeamons, John, and Lydia Himmons, ...	"	III.	259
1769. Feb. 4.	Yelverton, Abijah, and Margaret Dunning, .	"	XIV.	27
1758. Dec. 23.	Yelverton, Anthony, and Phebe Youngs,...	"	II.	139
1761. May 23.	Yelvington, Elisabeth, and Roeluf Ostrum, .	"	IV.	204
1781. Sept. 17.	Yeomans, Cloe, and John Allen,..........	"	XXXIII.	68
1772. June 5.	Yongs, Benjamin, and Mary Farley,.......	"	XVIII.	134
1760. June 2.	Yoole, Christian, and John Fferguson, ...	"	III.	172
1759. Oct. 22.	York, Edward, and Jane Salisbury, ...	"	II.	469
1779. Nov. 12.	York, Elizabeth, and Richard McKildo, ...	"	XXVIII.	137
1779. Dec. 6.	Yorke, Richard Whiston, and Ellena Reley,	"	XXVIII.	162
1764. Sept. 14.	Yorkse, Helena, and Hendreck Blauvelt,...	"	VIII.	306
1760. Oct. 7.	Youll, Christian, and James Finlay, ...	"	III.	349
1761. Nov. 19.	Young, Abjgail, and William Pierce, ...	"	V.	234
1762. April 21.	Young, Birdseye, and Rachel Strong,......	"	VI.	119
1760. Oct. 24.	Young, Daniel, and Hannah Macoun,......	"	III.	380
1779. April 20.	Young, Elizabeth, and Jacob Moell,.......	"	XXVII.	113
1768. Jan. 30.	Young, Elizabeth, and James McCready,...	"	XIII.	21
1775. July 12.	Young, Elizabeth, and Thomas Sample,....	"	XXIII.	96
1759. Sept. 5.	Young, Esther, and John Grahams, ...	"	II.	430
1756. Sept. 21.	Young, Experience, and Garrat Noel,......	"	I.	299
1780. April 21.	Young, Francis, and Rebecca Paul,........	"	XXIX.	32
1779. Aug. 2.	Young, John, and Elizabeth McBride,......	"	XXVIII.	42
1762. Oct. 1.	Young, John, and Elizabeth Swinney, ...	"	VI.	342
1771. Feb. 7.	Young, John, and Johanna Man,..........	"	XVII.	15
1758. Oct. 11.	Young, John, and Mary Jesson, ...	"	II.	49
1753. May 7.	Young, John, and Mary Offenmout,.......	"	I.	25
1760. Sept. 3.	Young, Margaret, and Richard Anderson,..	"	III.	278
1763. May 25.	Young, Martha, and Joseph Sutton, ...	"	VII.	201
1768. Feb. 10.	Young, Mary, and John Roy, ...	"	XIII.	29
1761. Aug. 20.	Young, Mary, and Patrick Allen, ...	"	V.	49
1770. Sept. 30.	Young, Mary, and Safcreenus Bessinger, ...	"	XXI.	126
1779. Aug. 20.	Young, Matthew, and Catherine Frankfort,.	"	XXVIII.	53
1767. Nov. 21.	Young, Moses, and Barbara Christie, ...	"	XII.	91
1760. Nov. 11.	Young, Philip, and Hannah Sickels,.......	"	III.	402
1772. Dec. 23.	Young, Rachel, and Thomas Rafter,.......	"	XIX.	162
1772. April 15.	Young, Rachel, and Zachariah Backas,....	"	XVIII.	78
1738. Dec. 11.	Young, Robert, and Anne Sherwood,......	"	I.	12
1763. Mar. 5.	Young, Sarah, and James Giles, ...	"	VII.	93
1753. Nov. 12.	Young, Seth, and Martha Fairley,.........	"	XXII.	23
1759. June 9.	Young, Thomas, and Altje Van Deusen,....	"	II.	318
1781. May 30.	Young, Thomas, and Nancy Burger,.......	"	XXXII.	65
1781. Nov. 20.	Young, William, and Catharine Brothers,...	"	XXXIV.	49

DATE.		NAMES.	RECORD.	VOL.	PAGE.
1756. Dec.	4.	Young, William, and Mary Thibou,........	M. B.,	I.	372
1781. Nov.	15.	Younghusband, George, and Mary Harned,.	"	XXXIV.	38
1753. Oct.	1.	Youngs, Elizabeth, and John Lawrence,....	"	I.	129
1773. Jan.	27.	Youngs, Isaac, and Amy Wood,..........	"	XX.	25
1772. June	7.	Youngs, Isaac, and Mary Hewlet,.........	"	XX.	5
1758. Dec.	23.	Youngs, Phebe, and Anthony Yelverton,...	"	II.	139
1771. Oct.	29.	Youngs, Philip, and Abigail Carr,.........	"	XVII.	229
1771. Nov.	20.	Youngs, Samuel, and Rebecca Brush,......	"	XVII.	260
1768. Aug.	10.	Youngs, Sarah, and Frederick Hudson, ...	"	XIII.	173
1761. June	11.	Youry, Lydia, and James Hicks,..........	"	IV.	235

Z.

1764. Nov.	20.	Zabrieske, John,and Jane Goelet, ...	"	VIII.	412
1782. Nov.	30.	Zabriske, Altje, and John Christopher,.....	"	XXXVII.	102
1781. Aug.	17.	Zabriske, Jasper, and Hannah Vreeland,...	"	XXXIII.	40
1773. Nov.	13.	Zabriske, John, and Christina Zabriskie, ...	"	XXII.	27
1773. Nov.	13.	Zabriskie, Christina, and John Zabriske, ...	"	XXII.	27
1775. Dec.	7.	Zabriskie, John J., and Leentje Lansingh, ..	"	XXIII.	225
1781. Nov.	29.	Zanay, Joseph, and Frowy Ridly, ...	"	XXXIV.	63
1769. Dec.	30.	Zeegaart, Catherine, and John Gillelan, ...	"	XV.	135
1761. Nov.	13.	Zeegaerd, Andries, and Sophia Rol, ...	"	V.	214
1777. Sept.	25.	Zegers, Adriana, and John S. Jones,..	"	XXIV.	149
1762. Oct.	21.	Zegren, Christiana, and William Zobre, ...	"	VI.	376
1775. April	21.	Zeller, Samuel, and Sarah Tippey, ...	"	XXIII.	15
1762. Oct.	21.	Zobre, William, and Christiana Zegren, ...	"	VI.	376
1761. April	3.	Zulle, Janetje, and Adam B. Vroman, ...	"	IV.	130
1770. May	1.	Zuricher, Mary, and Frederick Eckert,.....	"	XVI.	75

ADDENDA.

DATE.	NAMES.	RECORD.	VOL.	PAGE.
1759. Nov. 17.	Dacon, James, and Mary Dobbs,..........	M. B.,	II.	503
1756. Dec. 6.	Davenport, William, and Eleanor Kelly,....	"	I.	374
1764. June 4.	De Bevois, Charles, and Mary Van Houten,.	"	VIII.	245
1779. Mar. 10.	Dorland, Garret, and Sarah Smith,........	"	XXVII.	62
1761. June 20.	Dorlin, Elias, and Phelena Rushmore,......	"	IV.	249
1764. Jan. 27.	Dupuy, Aron, and Martha Tysen, ...	"	VIII.	41
1737. May 16.	Fenyck, Richard, and Mary Romer, ...	"	I.	6
1781. Dec. 18.	Furman, Polly, and Robert Parsell,........	"	XXXIV.	93
1773. Aug. 26.	Gant, Peter, and Mary Pantine, ...	"	XXI.	86
1779. Nov. 30.	Giffing, William, and Mary Hutton, ...	"	XXVIII.	153
1764. Nov. 22.	Goes, Louris, and Catharine Hoffman, ...	"	VIII.	418
1759. Sept. 25.	Grehams, John, and Esther Young, ...	"	II.	430
1761. Jan. 24.	Habbot, John, and Mary McDougall, ...	"	IV.	28
1770. Oct. 18.	Hagerman, Thomas, and Massey Homan,...	"	XVI.	221
1765. Oct. 31.	Hages, Mary, and William Costelow,......	"	IX.	343
1760. Oct. 20.	Harbert, Richard, and Cornelia Hart, ...	"	III.	374
1762. June 28.	Harps, Henry, and Hannah Pegrem, ...	"	VI.	211
1775. July 19.	Harriot, Israel, and Catherine Wool, ...	"	XXIII.	100
1757. Nov. 28.	Harsin, Garret, and Sarah Kip, ...	"	I.	715
1761. Nov. 30.	Hayt, Moses, and Charity Soper,..........	"	V.	257
1761. May 26.	Heermans, Henry, and Ann Stoutenbergh,..	"	IV.	207
1782. Feb. 2.	Henly, John, and Elizabeth Allen,.........	"	XXXV.	42
1760. Jan. 22.	Heyer, Mathiac, and Maria Shefer, ...	"	III.	2
1780. Dec. 9.	Hillery, Reginal, and Mary Boice,.........	"	XXX.	146
1761. July 30.	Hinton, Phebe, and Thomas Seaman,......	"	V.	17
1762. June 28.	Huff, Wyntje, and Abraham Cronk,.......	"	VI.	207
1780. Oct. 30.	Janes, Mary, and Henry Hallock, ...	"	XXX.	85
1769. Dec. 13.	Johnsline, John, and Ann Gibson, ...	"	XV.	122
1778. July 20.	Jones, Ann Springall, and Henry Davies,...	"	XXV.	135
1771. Oct. 30.	Keteltas, Garret, and Charity Nicoll,.......	"	XVII.	233
1778. Jan. 28.	Mery, Pierre, and Catherine Ledner,.......	"	XXV.	13
1764. April 17.	Myers, Harmanus, and Rachel Hardenbergh,	"	VIII.	158
1771. Nov. 22.	Onderdonck, Adreyoan, and Nelly Snedeker,	'	XVII.	262
1759. May 10.	Palding, James, and Rachel Bassing, ...	"	II.	277
1778. Mar. 28.	Pane, John, and Wilhelmina Dunkle,.... .	"	XXV.	55
1763. June 7.	Rocess, Charles, and Catherine Merriment, .	"	VII.	215

Date.		Names.	Record.	Vol.	Page.
1760. Feb.	25.	Schmidt, Jacob, and Mary Mitchell, ...	M. B.,	iii.	48
1780. May	13.	Seloover, Getty, and John Colls, ...	"	xxix.	54
1763. Mar.	16.	Seloover, James, and Catherine Alstine, ...	"	vii.	100
1781. Oct.	3.	Simmons, Jane, and John Weeks, ...	"	xxxiii.	83
1769. May	19.	Simonson, Charity, and Abraham Martino, .	"	xiv.	103
1759. April	19.	Simorson, Altje, and Harmanus Garretson, .	"	ii.	247
1676. July	27.	Simpson, Elizabeth Wattells, and Jeremiah Reder, ...	W. O. P.,	iii.	203
1759. Nov.	15.	Smith, Edward, and Mary Honeyman, ...	M. B.,	ii.	495
1759. Nov.	3.	Sneden, Abraham, and Rachael Swartout, ..	"	ii.	488
1770. Dec.	19.	Steymets, Christopher, and Rachel Roome, .	"	xvi.	301
1763. Oct.	22.	Steymetz, Abraham, and Synthia Van Orden,	"	vii.	400
1755. Aug.	26.	Stimes, Jasper, and Susannah Brower, ...	"	i.	156
1761. Nov.	19.	Vanausdalla, Lambertie, and Cornelius Amerman, ...	"	v.	233
1773. June	8.	Van Dar Vort, Jacob, and Margaret Bennet,	"	xx.	141
1772. May	30.	Vangwaggenen, Sarah, and Phillip Harmance, ...	"	xviii.	127
1760. Nov.	26.	Van Valkenburgh, Catherine, and David Van Schaick, ...	"	iii.	446
1782. May	17.	Veaber, William, and Catharine Hieth, ...	"	xxxvi.	5
1757. Dec.	30.	Walsh, Peter, and Mary Bennet, ...	"	i.	761
1764. Feb.	21.	Wells, Jane, and James Richey, ...	"	viii.	67
1766. Sept.	29.	Wetbeck, Peter, and Mary Van Alen, ...	"	x.	110
1762. April	30.	Wickes, Thomas, and Sarah Brush, ...	"	vi.	137
1760. Oct.	22.	Wickoff, Nelly, and Peter Luyster, ...	"	iii.	379
1767. May	14.	Wickoff, Nickles, and Ann Rapelyea, ...	"	xi.	87
1761. Jan.	27.	Will, Elizabeth, and Isaac Stoutenburgh, ...	"	iv.	32
1758. Jan.	3.	Winant, Daniel, and Rachel Andrewuet, ...	"	i.	766
1775. April	10.	Winants, Jacob, and Mary Mersereau, ...	"	xxiii.	5

SUPPLEMENTARY LIST

OF

MARRIAGE LICENSES

Reprinted from

University of the State of New York,
State Library Bulletin
History, No. 1, April, 1898

State Library Bulletin

HISTORY No. 1

April 1898

SUPPLEMENTARY LIST OF MARRIAGE LICENSES

PREFACE

Since the publication of the *Names of persons for whom marriage licenses were issued by the secretary of the province of New York previous to 1784,* Albany 1860, to which this volume is a supplement, there have been found three thin folio volumes of marriage bonds which have been bound as v. 41 of the series of *Marriage bonds.* Of this volume p. 1–66 cover the years 1752–53, p. 67–144 the years 1755–56, and p. 145–240 the year 1758. Some of these names were printed by E. B. O'Callaghan in the *New York genealogical and biographical record,* October 1871, 2: 194–200, but they are all entered in this list as in *Marriage bonds,* v. 41. For an account of marriage licenses and description of the original volumes of *Marriage bonds* see introduction to the *Names of persons for whom marriage licenses were issued previous to 1784.*

The names in the present supplement have been obtained from the following sources :

1 *Marriage bonds,* v. 41, above mentioned.

2 Addenda on p. 478–80 of the volume entitled *Names of persons for whom marriage licenses were issued previous to 1784,* Albany 1860. This list of addenda contains names occurring in the original 40 volumes of *Marriage bonds* and overlooked in the

preparation of the printed volume or there given with a different spelling.

3 List of 29 marriages 1683–1751, from various volumes of New York archives, printed by B. Fernow in New York state library *Report*, 1884, 67:35–36. Part of this list is also printed with some variations in *New York genealogical and biographical record*, 1874, 5:174 in a communication from J. J. Latting.

4 List of Staten Island marriages in *New York colonial manuscripts*, 82:62, where the list is accompanied by the following letter from Gov. Hardy to Rev. Richard Charlton of Staten Island :

New York, 28 Janu^y 1756

Sir

Yesterday Major Taylor of your Island came with a Complaint to me, that you had married John Le Conte Junr Son of Judge Le Conte, without a Lycense, he told me that after it was spoke of there, you sent the 30/ you reced, back to M^r Le Conte, and desired him to go himself to the Office for a Lycense which he did and obtained one two days after he had been married by you. These he said are Facts he can prove, and which he said confirmed their Suspicions that you had marryed many others without any License. For wch he said he was determined to prosecute you. I interposed by telling him I would write to you before he proceeded any further : he answer'd 'twas well, but if you did not produce either a Lycense in the Case of those whom he & others thought you had marryed without any, or return ye 30/ in every Case so circumstanced they wou'd by no means be satisfyed. He gave me a Paper containg ye Names of the Persons they imagine have been marryed without a License, a Copy of wch I enclose you. Justice Rezeau came with Major Taylor, but I did not see him. About an hour or two after this application to me, I reced your Letter from your Son, and had done what I probably shou'd have done, if I had received your Letter before I saw Mr Taylor, whose resentm^t appears to be very strong agst you. You will undoubtedly take the most prudent Measures on this Occasion, as if their Suspicions are true or false, it will apparently be of some consequence to your Charrecter.

I am &c

Mr Charlton

The list referred to was printed in the New York state library *Report*, 1884, 67:35, and also in the *New York genealogical and biographical record*, 1894, 25:95-96, though in the latter case it seems to have been based on another copy.

5 List of marriage licenses, 1691-93 from *Records of wills*, v. 4, in the surrogate's office, New York, communicated by J. J. Latting to *New York genealogical and biographical record*, 1873, 4:31.

6 List of New York marriage licenses granted by Lord Cornbury, 1703-6, which are recorded in an old book of records in New York city and were communicated by John S. Gautier to *New York genealogical and biographical record*, 1870, 1:3,13; 1871, 2:25-28.

7 New York marriage licenses, 1692-1701 in the surrogate's office, New York, communicated by E. B. O'Callaghan to *New York genealogical and biographical record*, 1871, 2:141; 1872, 3:91-93.

Although the present supplementary list is properly limited to the record of marriages in the state archives, we add for the assistance of genealogists and students of early New York history, the following references to other lists of New York marriages recorded in the *New York genealogical and biographical record*. Lists containing only a few names are not included.

East Hampton. Records of marriages recorded by Rev. Nathaniel Huntting, 1700-46, 24:184-94.

Hempstead. St George's church, 1725-86, v. 11-15, 24.

Long Island. Marriages from the *Suffolk gazette*, 1804-9, 24:86-88, 159-61; 25:6-8, 89-90.

New York city. First and Second presbyterian churches, 1756-1812, v. 11-16.

——Reformed Dutch church, New York, 1639-1731, v. 6-8, 10-13, 16. Also published with additions to 1801, in New York genealogical and biographical society, *Collections*, 1890, v. 1.

——Reformed Dutch church at Harlem, 1816-36, 8:41-43.

——Society of friends at New York and vicinity, 1663-1766, 6:97-107, 192-93.

All the records referred to are in the New York state library except the *Deeds* which are in the office of the secretary of state.

GEORGE ROGERS HOWELL

Archivist

ALPHABETIC LIST OF NAMES

1703 June 29	Attkins, Bellekie, and Peter Christiense	G.B.R. 2: 25
1702 Nov. 28	Auboyneau, John, and Frances Shukey	G.B.R. 1: 3
1691 Ap. 9	Aukes, Annetie, and Dirck Janse Woertman	G.B.R. 4: 42
1684 Aug. 2	Avens, Janacay, and William Francis	C.M. 34: 28
1756 Feb. 2	Aymar, Jane, and Dennis Wortman	M.B. 41: 83
1758 June 20	Baceheuse, Margaret, and Andrew Coest	M.B. 41:162
1705 Feb. 19	Baily, Abigail, and Robert Reid	G.B.R. 2: 27
1694 Jan. 11	Baily, Rebecca, and Richard More	G.B.R. 3: 91
1700 Ap. 26	Baird, Alexander, and Magdelena Kipp	G.B.R. 3:194
1758 June 21	Baird, Francis, and Esther Eagles	M.B. 41:165
1693 Ap. 10	Baker, Catharine, and Henry Kemble	G.B.R. 2:142
1702 Dec. 12	Baker, Mary, and Richard Harris	G.B.R. 1: 3
1693 Sep. 4	Baker, Roger, and Mary Walkington	G.B.R. 2:142
1699 Aug. 31	Ball, Adam, and Elizth Collins	G.B.R. 2:142
1758 Aug. 16	Ball, Ann, and Robert Anderson	M.B. 41:215
1758 July 7	Ball, Mary, and John Coffram	M.B. 41:175
1694 Sep. 19	Bancker, Maria, and Cornelis de Peyster	G.B.R. 3: 92
1701 June 26	Bant, Peter, and Mary Vanhoven	G.B.R. 3:194
1756 June 2	Banta, Paulus, and Frances Minthorne	M.B. 41:136
1752-56	Baragor, Jacob, and Mary Martennow	C.M. 82: 62
1696 Aug. 31	Barber, Jane, and Henry Jaman	G.B.R. 3: 93
1706 Mar. 30	Barden, Abiny, and John Brown	G.B.R. 2: 28
1695 July 8	Barents, Margt., and Joseph Smith	G.B.R. 3: 92
1783 May 9	Barger, Hendrick, and Mary Tysen	M.B. 39: 6
1753 Jan. 25	Barker, Benjamin, and Mary Rhodes	M.D. 41: 51
1704 Jan. 6	Barker, Sarah, and Philip Bosen	G.B.R. 2: 26
1690 May 1	Barnes, Lawrence, and Eleanor Lawrence	D. 8:244
1699 Dec. 20	Barre, Mary, and Theunis Titus	G.B.R. 3:193
1759 Jan. 10	Barre, William, and Elizabeth Polhemus	M.B. 2:149
1695 Ap. 8	Barnan, Martha, and Peter Cullom	G.B.R. 3: 92
1696 Aug. 1	Barsley, Ann, and William Fisher	G.B.R. 3: 93
1728 July 19	Barton, and -----	C.M. 68: 86
1696 July	Barton, William, and Hannah Hull	G.B.R. 3: 93
1696 June 16	Basford, John, and Damares Lynns	G.B.R. 3: 93
1752-56	Bate, Need, and Mary Lack	C.M. 82: 62
1703 June 27	Battery, Peter, and Janekie Davis	G.B.R. 2: 25
1781 Ap. 24	Bauer, Barnyby, and Roseny Moore	M.B. 32: 13
1697 Oct. 27	Bayard, Ann Mary, and Augustus Jay	G.B.R. 3:192
1703 Dec. 18	Bayard, Jacobus, and Hillyden Deray	G.B.R. 2: 26
1703 Aug. 12	Bayard, Sarah, and Abraham Goesbeck Chambers	
		G.B.R. 2: 25
1695 Sep. 16	Bayer, Mary, and Moses Leuwis	G.B.R. 3: 92
1703 July 14	Bayeux, Thomas, and Magdleleine Boudinot	G.B.R. 2: 25
1705 Nov. 14	Baylie, Allinar, and James Flimming	G.B.R. 2: 28
1752 Dec. 6	Beadle, Hannah, and Joseph Hall	M.B. 41: 10

1758 Aug. 1	Bears, Elizabeth, and Isaac Wheeler	M.B. 41:197
1763 July 2	Beattie, Robert, and Elisabeth McDonald	M.B. 7:254
1758 Aug. 2	Beatty, Jane, and Thomas Pool	M.B. 41:199
1703 Oct. 30	Beck, Caleb, and Hannah Harley	G.B.R. 2: 25
1705 July 14	Bedlow, Isack, and Susannah Brasier	G.B.R. 2: 27
1703 Jan. 16	Bedwell, Isaac, and Hannah Blank	G.B.R. 1: 3
1703 Aug. 26	Beeck, Deborah, and Coenradt Huyblingh	G.B.R. 2: 25
1702 Jan. 20	Beeke, Aeltie, and Thomas Pell	G.B.R. 3:194
1703 May 26	Beekeman, Janeke, and Isaac Lansing	G.B.R. 1: 13
1705 Feb. 1	Beekman, Adry, and Abigail Lispenar	G.B.R. 2:27
1758 June 12	Beekman, Catharine, and James Cebra	M.B. 41:152
1703 Sep. 6	Beekman, Charles, and Ekay Hansant	G.B.R. 2: 25
1704 Jan. 25	Beekman, Christopher, and Maria De Lanoy	G.B.R. 2: 26
1701 Oct. 2	Belline, Mary, and Ferdinand Ravaud	G.B.R. 3:194
1703 Nov. 18	Bend, Margrett, and Zachariah Goscott	G.B.R. 2: 25
1771 May 18	Beneway, John, and Maria Storn	M.B. 17: 85
1758 June 15	Benneway, Eva, and Abraham Fort	M.B. 41:158
1706 Jan. 9	Bensinck, Matthew, and Katherine Provost	G.B.R. 2: 28
1756 Ap. 30	Benson, Benjamin, and Catharine Deronde	M.B. 41:117
1758 Aug. 5	Benson, Catharine, and Terence Conoway	M.B. 41:204
1704 June 8	Benson, Katherine, and John French	G.B.R. 2: 26
1696 Aug. 1	Bentie, John, and Elizabeth Van Clyff	G.B.R. 3: 93
1756 Mar. 23	Bergen, George, and Magdalin Bratt	M.B. 41: 99
1702 Dec. 16	Berkley, William, and Elizabeth Randall	G.B.R. 1: 3
1753 Mar. 30	Berrien, John, and Altie Braisher	M.B. 41: 18
1705 May 2	Bert, Jonimah, and Robt. Williams	G.B.R. 2: 27
1758 Aug. 5	Berton, Peter, and Anne Duncan	M.B. 41:206
1700 Feb. 14	Berton, Peter, and Elizabeth Archambeau	G.B.R. 2:142
1695 Sep. 12	Betterworth, Patrene, and William Finiconie	G.B.R. 3: 92
1701 Oct. 27	Betts, Joseph, and Grace Mott	G.B.R. 3:194
1691 Nov. 7	Bettyes, John, and Susannah Ashfordby	G.B.R. 4: 31
1701 Sep. 15	Biljan, Peter, and Maria Brean	G.B.R. 2:142
1696 Jan. 19	Billian, Peter, and Perkie Hendricke	G.B.R. 3: 93
1697 Nov. 17	Bingham, Mary, and William West	G.B.R. 3:192
1703 July 12	Bissett, Ellen, and John Lesley	G.B.R. 2: 25
1703 May 12	Blagge, Edward, and Johanna Vrikers	G.B.R. 1: 13
1695 June 28	Blanchard, John, and Joanna Gaultier	G.B.R. 3: 92
1703 Jan. 16	Blank, Hannah, and Isaac Bedwell	G.B.R. 1: 3
1703 Feb. 27	Blerkome, Lubert Jansen, and Angell Hendricks	
		G.B.R. 1: 13
1706 Jan. 15	Bley, Dina, and Stephen Van Brackeling	G.B.R. 2: 28
1756 May 20	Bloom, Mary, and George Rapelye	M.B. 41:131
1699 May 19	Blydenburgh, Joseph, and Cathrine Dehart	G.B.R. 3:193
1692 July 8	Blydenburgh, Joseph, and Mary Smith	G.B.R. 4: 32
1696 Feb. 15	Boedann, Helena, and Daniel Letson	G.B.R. 3: 93
1692 Dec. 16	Boelen, Antie, and Abraham Ketteltas	G.B.R. 2:141

1706 Jan. 10	Boerman, Altie I., Jaques Corteleau	G.B.R.	2: 28
1703 Sep. 15	Bogaert, Hendrick, and Ruttie De la Metze	G.B.R.	2: 25
1693 Ap. 10	Bogardus, Catharine, and Cornelius Vielle	G.B.R.	2:142
1756 May 2	Bogardus, Catharine, and John Willson	M.B.	41:135
1704 May 30	Bogardus, Eporordus, and Hannah Dayly	G.B.R.	2: 26
1756 Jan. 28	Bogardus, John, and Mary Du Bois	M.B.	41: 81
1756 Ap. 23	Bogart, James, and Elizabeth Pocock	M.B.	41:112
1756 Mar. 11	Bogert, Isaac, and Mary Strickland	M.B.	41: 94
1756 Jan. 3	Boghart, Lenah, and Lodowick Inslaer	M.B.	41: 69
1699 Mar. 14	Bolen, James, and Elizabeth Godfrey	G.B.R.	3:193
1756 Aug. 21	Booerum, Charles, and Maria Lott	M.B.	1:275
1704 May 5	Books, Phillip, and Mary Carter	G.B.R.	2: 26
1704 Ap. 21	Booth, George, and Mary Rowly	G.B.R.	2: 26
1703 July 12	Boron, Margaret, ffrench, and John Kelly	G.B.R.	2: 25
1756 Ap. 5	Borright, Catherin, and Thomas Noble	M.B.	41:104
1695 Oct. 16	Bosch, Juriaen, and Geshennamah Bruyor	G.B.R.	3: 92
1704 Jan. 6	Bosen, Philip, and Sarah Barker	G.B.R.	2: 26
1703 July 14	Boudinot, Magdleleine, and Thomas Bayeux	G.B.R.	2: 25
1695 Nov. 8	Bougeaud, Lewis, and Mary Anne van Bursum	G.B.R.	3: 93
1756 May 14	Bound, Hannah, and Joshua Ferris	M.B.	41:126
1753 Jan. 20	Bound, Jacob, and Hannah Lawrence	M. B.	41: 44
1706 Feb. 1	Boundinot, Susanna, and Charles D'Val	G.B.R.	2: 28
1705 Dec. 28	Bounn, Aman, and Mary Prudence	G.B.R.	2: 28
1693 Feb. 20	Bourthier, Michael, and Mary English	G.B.R.	2:142
1758 Aug. 1	Bown, Hannah, and Godfreyd Streit	M.B.	41:198
1738 Dec. 18	Bowyer, Samuel, and Mary Cloudy	M.B.	1: 12
1701 Feb. 24	Boyle, Frances, and Robert Elliott	G.B.R.	3:194
1693 Feb. 8	Boyle, Jane, and Andrew Groves	G.B.R.	2:142
1758 Aug. 21	Bradt, Catherine, and Richard Green	M.B.	41:221
1753 Mar. 30	Braisher, Altie, and John Berriem	M.B.	41: 18
1698 Nov. 26	Branch, Cathrine, and Thomas Petit	G.B.R.	3:193
1761 June 12	Brash, Sarah, and Jonathan Titus	M.B.	4:236
1758 July 13	Brasher, Abraham, and Helena Kortright	M.B.	41:184
1756 May 3	Brasier, Catharine, and Albert Ryckman	M.B.	41:119
1705 July 14	Brasier, Susannah, and Isack Bedlow	G.B.R.	2: 27
1752 Dec. 1	Bratt, Jane, and Stephen Van Shaik	M.B.	41: 5
1756 Mar. 23	Bratt, Magdalin, and George Bergen	M.B.	41: 99
1756 June 9	Bratt, Tryntie, and Jacob De Foreest	M.B.	41:140
1697 Sep. 16	Brazier, Mary, and Philip Wilkinsen	G.B.R.	3:192
1699 May 10	Breadstead, John, and Margaret Peters	G.B.R.	3:193
1701 Sep. 15	Brean, Maria, and Peter Biljan	G.B.R.	2:142
1738 May 11	Bregaw, Mary, and John Updike	M.B.	1: 9
1737 Aug. 23	Brested, Garret, and Catherine Provoost	M.B.	1: 7
1703 Aug. 28	Bresty, Mary, and Alexander Watkay	G.B.R.	2: 25
1697 Sep. 9	Brett, Mary, and Capt. John Tuder	G.B.R.	3:192
1703 Nov. 25	Brett, Roger, and Katharine Rumbout	G.B.R.	2: 25

1756 Mar. 25	Brinckerhoff, Daniel, and Ann Montfort	M.B. 41:100
1758 July 10	Brinckerhoff, Elizabeth, and John A. Brinckerhoff	M.B. 41:178
1756 Ap. 10	Brinckerhoff, John, and Mary Luyster	M.B. 41:107
1758 July 10	Brinckerhoff, John A., and Elizabeth Brinckerhoff	M.B. 41:178
1695 Mar. 9	Britten, Rebecca, and Abram Cole	G.B.R. 3: 92
1704 Ap. 5	Britton, Anne, and Nathan Whitman	G.B.R. 2: 26
1696 Aug. 12	Brookesbanck, ——, and Humphrey Tregenny	G.B.R. 3: 94
1753 Jan. 5	Brookman, Catherine, and Alexander Phoenix	M.B. 41: 40
1706 Jan. 10	Broughton, Andrew, and Mary Mansey	G.B.R. 2: 28
1705 Dec. 24	Broughton, Samson, and Mary Ravaud	G.B.R. 2: 28
1752 Dec. 22	Brower, William, and Mocletia Van Duyn	M.B. 41: 35
1752 Dec. 20	Brown, Abigail, and Joshua Mersereau	M.B. 41: 32
1753 Jan. 24	Brown, Hannah, and Benjamin Quereau	M.B. 41: 50
1706 Mar. 30	Brown, John, and Abiny Barden	G.B.R. 2: 28
1704 July 29	Brown, Mary, and Hendrick Jansen	G.B.R. 2: 26
1705 Dec. 24	Brughman, Harmanus, and Allite Stevense	G.B.R. 2: 28
1695 Oct. 16	Bruyor, Geshennamah, and Juriaen Bosch	G.B.R. 3: 92
1698 Nov. 10	Bryan, Elizabeth, and John Durend	G.B.R. 3:193
1763 Oct. 26	Bryant, Jesse, and Mary Ketcham	M.B. 7:406
1696 May 7	Buckenhoven, Stephen, and Anna van Holst	G.B.R. 3: 94
1703 Dec. 9	Buckley, Elizabeth, and John Huttkins	G.B.R. 2: 26
1695 Oct. 11	Budd, Joseph, and Sarah Underhill	G.B.R. 3: 92
1758 July 22	Bufflere, Jacob, and Margaret Simonsen	M.B. 41:191
1698 Dec.	Bunt, Mary, and Christian Lawrier	G.B.R. 3:193
1705 Nov. 21	Bunting, Benjamin, and Cornelia Carolein	G.B.R. 2: 28
1693 Sep. 4	Burch, William, and Hanna Robinson	G.B.R. 2:142
1758 June 5	Burdett, Susannah, and John Low	M.B. 41:146
1696 June 30	Burger, Eva, and George Hulgrow	G.B.R. 3: 93
1704 Sep. 9	Burger, Myndert, and Sarah Dese	G.B.R. 2: 26
1698 Sep. 5	Burle, Joshua, and Judith Sexton	G.B.R. 3:193
1752 Dec. 13	Burnet, John, and Anne Smith	M.B. 41: 24
1758 July 13	Burney, Edward, and Elizabeth Cramshire	M.B. 41:185
1758 Aug. 4	Burns, Elizabeth, and Charles Merry	M.B. 41:202
1753 Jan. 22	Burns, Margret, and Silas Lawrence	M.B. 41: 46
1705 Sep. 15	Burroughs, Mary, and Thomas Oakley	G.B.R. 2: 28
1703 Dec. 13	Burroughs, Raechall, and William Huggen	G.B.R. 2: 26
1695 Nov. 16	Burroughs, Thomas, and Mary Tayler	G.B.R. 3: 93
1704 Ap. 25	Burroughs, Unis, and Nathaniel Lynes	G.B.R. 2: 26
1753 Jan. 23	Burrows, Jeremiah, and Mary Stringham	M.B. 41: 49
1697 Oct. 18	Burt, Richard, and Margaret Glenn	G.B.R. 3:192
1704 Oct. 4	Burtell, Peter, and Margerett Van Clyff	G.B.R. 2: 27
1694 Oct. 11	Burton, Mary Ann, and Hend'k Jansen Vandenbergh	G.B.R. 3: 92
1697 Mar. 1	Busch, Cornelia, and Peter Cavaleer	G.B.R. 3: 93

1758 Aug. 24	Bush, Anne, and Isaac Somendyck	M.B. 41:229
1753 Feb. 19	Bussing, Peter, and Susannah Myers	M.B. 41: 58
1756 June14	Butler, Hannah, and Nathaniel Coles	M.B. 41:143
1758 Aug. 5	Butler, Mary, and Johannes Vanderheyden	M.B. 41:205
1752-56	Butteler, John, and Rachel Winant	C.M. 82: 62
1701 Sep. 15	Buttler, John, and Hanah Saunders	G.B.R. 3:194
1701 Sep. 15	Buttler, John, and Sarah ——	G.B.R. 2:142
1778 June13	Caen, Daniel, and Wyntie Pettit	M.B. 25:100
1758 Aug. 16	Cagill, James, see Cargill, James.	
1756 Mar. 1	Cain, Catherin, and Jeremiah Pundt	M.B. 41: 91
1761 Dec. 23	Caithness, David, and Mary Patten	M.B. 5:296
1765 May 24	Calhown, George, and Mary Sneeden	M.B. 9:139
1758 Sep. 6	Calyer, Peter, and Margarita De Bevois	M.B. 2: 5
1698 May 4	Campell, Jane, and George Gilbert	G.B.R. 3:193
1759 May 17	Cane, Samuel, and Flora	M.B. 2:288
1728 July 19	Cannon, Ab'm, and ——	C.M. 68: 86
1760 Oct. 18	Cannon, Abraham, and Maria Springsteen	M.B. 3:371
1695 Nov. 18	Cannon, Andrew, and Ann Puppyn	G.B.R. 3: 93
1703 Aug. 18	Cantain, Moses, and Mary DeWitt	G.B.R. 2: 25
1753 Aug. 20	Car, Charles, and Sarah Collins	M.B. 1: 93
1758 Aug. 16	Cargill, James, and Ester Earl	M.B. 41:214
1752 Dec. 15	Cargill, John, and Phebe Striker	M.B. 41: 27
1691 Nov. 22	Carhart, Thomas, and Mary Lord	G.B.R. 4: 31
1700 Ap. 27	Carille (or Laville), Adam, and Elizabeth Gizebert	
		G.B.R. 3:104
1695 May 28	Carly, Mary, and James Spencer	G.B.R. 3: 92
1753 Jan. 11	Carman, Amy, and Joseph Drake	M.B. 41: 42
1683 Jan. 20	Carman, John, and Elizabeth Ludlom	C.M. 31: 7
1761 Aug. 6	Carmick, David, and Elenor Vance	M.B. 5: 28
1694 Dec. 12	Carnaby, Nicholas, and Jane Dawning	G.B.R. 3: 92
1705 Nov. 21	Carolein, Cornelia, and Benjamin Bunting	G.B.R. 2: 28
1701 Aug. 29	Carr, Joanna, and Arthur Willis	G.B.R. 2:142
1704 May 5	Carter, Mary, and Phillip Books	G.B.R. 2: 26
1693 Dec. 19	Carter, Zebulon, and Heiltie Sloot	G.B.R. 3: 91
1701 July 23	Cauley, John, and Agenitie Vande Spegel	G.B.R. 3:194
1701 Dec. 22	Cavaleer, Magdalen, and William Chisnall	G.B.R. 3:194
1697 Mar. 1	Cavaleer, Peter, and Cornelia Busch	G.B.R. 3: 93
1753 Jan. 10	Cavalier, Alida, and John Parsons	M.B. 41: 41
1761 Feb. 10	Cavanaugh, Sylvester, and Lucy Moore	M.B. 4: 56
1703 Dec. 3	Cavelir, Adam, and Mary Dalcale	G.B.R. 2: 26
1760 July 3	Cayton, Elizabeth, and Philip Welch	M.B. 3:204
1702 July 29	Cebra, James, and Ann Meyer	G.B.R. 3:195
1758 June12	Cebra, James, and Catharine Beekman	M.B. 41:152
1692 Ap. 28	Cergoe, Margery, and Edw'd Willake	G.B.R. 4: 32
1696 Mar. 10	Ceysler, Hesther, and Barnet Reyners	G.B.R. 3: 93

1705 Dec. 24	Chamberline, Elizabeth, and John Fleet	G.B.R.	2: 28
1703 Aug. 12	Chambers, Abraham Goesbeck, and Sarah Bayard		
		G.B.R.	2: 25
1693 Aug. 17	Chambers, John, and Mary Drummond	G.B.R.	2:142
1702 Dec. 5	Chambers, Mary, and Richard Robinson	G.B.R.	1: 3
1703 Oct. 10	Champion, ffrancis, and John Jusell	G.B.R.	2: 25
1758 Aug. 24	Chapman, Mary, and William Hawhurst	M.B.	41:228
1695 Nov. 27	Chappell, Francis, and Ann Fromanteel	G.B.R.	3: 93
1705 Jan. 8	Charleton, John, and Hester Gleve	G.B.R.	2: 27
1696 Sep. 8	Cheek, Elizabeth, and John Moore	G.B.R.	3: 93
1758 Aug. 11	Child, Gertruy, and Abraham Leggett	M.B.	41:209
1694 Sep. 18	Childers, Delia, and Johannes Groenendyke	G.B.R.	3: 92
1701 Dec. 22	Chisnall, William, and Magdalen Cavaleer	G.B.R.	3:194
1703 Ap. 8	Chiswell, Jane, and Augustine Graham	G.B.R.	1: 13
1703 June 29	Christiense, Peter, and Bellekie Attkins	G.B.R.	2: 25
1686 Oct. 27	Clare, Katherine, and Jeremy Kittle	L.W.	63
1752 Dec. 16	Clark, Daniel, and Elizabeth McGuire	M.B. 41:	28
1703 June 23	Clarke, Eliza, and William Glenrosse	G.B.R.	2: 25
1694 May 10	Clatworthy, John, and Mary Leeson	G.B.R.	3: 92
1753 Feb. 10	Claus, Leannehand, and William Atkinson	M.B. 41:	57
1761 Feb. 14	Cleghorne, Wilet, and David Ramsey	M.B. 4:	63
1753 Jan. 22	Clement, Elizabeth, and James Farrington	M.B. 41:	45
1696 July 2	Clement, James, and Sarah Hinchman	G.B.R.	3: 93
1699 Sep. 24	Clerke, Charity, and Richard Lawrence	G.B.R.	2:142
1758 Aug. 14	Cline, William, and Joanna Underwood	M.B.	41:213
1704 Jan. 11	Clottworthy, Hanna, and Johannes Johnson	G.B.R.	2: 26
1702 Oct. 26	Clouder, Mary, and Ralph Thurman	G.B.R.	1: 3
1698 July 18	Clowes, Samuel, and Kathrine Douw	G.B.R.	3:193
1694 Jan.	Coats, Edward, and Sarah Thornson	G.B.R.	3: 91
1686-87 Jan.21	Cobbitt, Ann, and Samuell Henry	L.W.	86
1696 Aug. 28	Cobbitt, Lydia, and Thomas Wright	G.B.R.	3: 93
1756 May 6	Cobham, Robert, and Mary Gereau	M.B.	41:122
1756 Jan. 27	Cock, Abraham, and Hilah Minthorne	M.B. 41:	80
1702 Oct. 20	Cock, Catherine, and Conradus Vanderbeeck	G.B.R.	1: 3
1701 Oct. 25	Cockling, Thomas, and Deborah Smith	G.B.R.	2:142
1703 May 12	Coderese, Rachell, and Adolphe De Groosse	G.B.R.	1: 13
1695 Ap. 6	Coel, Lydia, and Peter Masett	G.B.R.	3: 92
1736 June 3	Coen Oven, John, and Jane Briant	M.B. 1:	1
1703 Aug. 9	Coenraats, Octave, and Mary Longfield	G.B.R.	2: 25
1701 May 22	Coerten, Henry, and Elizabeth De Riemer	G.B.R.	3:194
1758 June 20	Coest, Andrew, and Margaret Baceheuse	M.B.	41:162
1758 July 7	Coffram, John, and Mary Ball	M.B.	41:175
1705 May 19	Colburne, Frances, and John Riggs	G.B.R.	2: 27
1695 Mar. 9	Cole, Abram, and Rebecca Britten	G.B.R.	3: 92
1758 June 8	Cole, Catharine, and John Needham	M.B.	41:148
1706 Feb. 1	Cole, Rose, and John Townsend	G.B.R.	2: 28

1752-56	Cole, Susannah, and John Marshal	C.M. 82: 62
1698 July 27	Coleman, Henry, and Eleanor Hunt	G.B.R. 3:193
1691 Dec.	Coleman, Henry, and Mary Meads	G.B.R. 4: 31
1753 Mar. 27	Coleman, Thomas, and Elizabeth Roe	M.B. 41: 15
1756 June 14	Coles, Nathaniel, and Hannah Butler	M.B. 41:143
1757 Ap. 4	Collier, Mary, and Jacob Wiltse	M.B. 1:486
1699 Aug. 31	Collins, Elizth, and Adam Ball	G.B.R. 2:142
1692 Ap. 17	Collins, James, and Elizabeth Kennedy	G.B.R. 4: 32
1701 Oct. 27	Collins, John, and Margaret Verplank	G.B.R. 3:194
1705 Sep. 29	Colsen, Robert, and Elizabeth Jones	G.B.R. 2: 28
1758 Aug. 5	Coroway, Terence, and Catharine Benson	M.B. 41:204
1694 Aug. 9	Cooley, Deborah, and Nicholas Fielding	G.B.R. 3: 92
1694 Ap. 7	Cooper, Benj., and Helena Wilkins	G.B.R. 3: 91
1702 July 29	Cooper, John, and Hannah Frost	G.B.R. 3:195
1752 Dec. 16	Cooper, John, and Ruth Wilse	M.B. 41: 31
1703 Dec. 14	Corbett, John, and Mary Graham	G.B.R. 2: 26
1699 May 6	Corbitt, John, and Christian Milton	G.B.R. 3:193
1698 June 30	Coreman, Daniel Peterse, and Anna Maria Plevier	
		G.B.R. 3:193
1700 Jan. 19	Corlandt, Ann, and Stephen Delancy	G.B.R. 3:193
1756 May 6	Cornel, Gilliam, and Margaret Schanck	M.B. 41:120
1704 July 20	Cornelise, Altie, and John Foster	G.B.R. 2: 26
1705 Dec. 8	Cornelison, John, and Elizabeth Hazareth	G.B.R. 2: 28
1753 Jan. 31	Cornell, Daniel, and Charity Valentine	M.B. 41: 53
1752 Dec. 20	Cornell, Elizabeth, and Anthony Sarly	M.B. 41: 33
1703 Dec. 6	Cornell, Elizabeth, and Nicholas Stillwell	G.B.R. 2: 26
1703 Dec. 6	Cornell, John, and Letitia Printz	G.B.R. 2: 26
1756 May 15	Cornnell, Joseph, and Sarah Heady	M.B. 41:128
1699 Aug. 14	Cornwell, George, and Ann Merchant	G.B.R. 2:142
1756 May 15	Cornwell, Joseph, and Sarah Heady	M.B. 41:128
1756 June 3	Corsen, Ann, and David Kingsland	M.B. 41:137
1706 Jan. 10	Corteleau, Jaques, and Altie I. Boerman	G.B.R. 2: 28
1752-56	Cortelyou, Cornelous, and Sary Spragg	C.M. 82: 62
1700 Jan. 19	Cortlandt, Ann, and Stephen Delancy	G.B.R. 3:193
1695 June 20	Cortlandt, John, and Anna Mary van Schaick	G.B.R. 3: 92
1703 July 6	Corvard, Hugh, and Patience Throgmorton	G.B.R. 2: 25
1753 Feb. 5	Cosby, Arthur, and Mary Hagins	M.B. 41: 56
1697 Ap. 28	Cosins, Barne, and Grace Sanford	G.B.R. 3: 93
1699 Aug. 9	Coulylie, Margt., and Henry Roof	G.B.R. 2:142
1704 Sep. 21	Courtie, Hmtie, and Peter Roose	G.B.R. 2: 27
1705 Sep. 3	Cowne, Debora, and Richd. Stilwell	G.B.R. 2: 28
1758 Sep. 1	Cox, Anne, and Michael Hay	M.B. 41:237
1786 Nov. 17	Cox, Dorothy, and Richard Harford	L.W. 72
1694 Dec. 31	Cox, Jacobus, and Catharina Davids	G.B.R. 3: 92
1687 Mar. 30	Cox, William, and Juda Martins	L.W. 89
1758 July 13	Cramshire, Elizabeth, and Edward Burney	M.B. 41:185

1756 May 14	Cramshire, Jane, and William Finney	M.B. 41:125
1703 May 16	Crawford, Patrick, and Katherin Potter	G.B.R. 1: 13
1760 Dec. 16	Creed, Benjamin, and Jane Hewlet	M.B. 13:478
1703 Dec. 24	Creed, Jane, and Thomas Whitehead	G.B.R. 2: 26
1701 June 6	Cregers, Mareya, and Johanes Vreland	G.B.R. 3:194
1702 Aug. 28	Cregier, Elizabeth, and Nicholas Dally	G.B.R. 3:195
1702 Aug. 27	Cregier, Martinus, and Margarett Van Dalsen	G.B.R. 3:195
1704 Mar. 4	Crego, Josias, and Anne Ellsworth	G.B.R. 2: 26
1696 June 29	Crego, Richard, and Sarah Stilwell	G.B.R. 3: 93
1752-56	Crips, Richer, and Martha Wolcan	C.M. 82: 62
1700 Nov. 25	Croaker, Robert, and Susannah Peterson	G.B.R. 3:194
1756 Jan. 23	Crocheron, Abm. and Eliz. Du Puy	M.B. 41: 77
1758 June 21	Crosfield, Stephen, and Mary C. Kerbyle	M.B. 41:164
1691 Sep. 7	Crundall, Deborah, and Thomas Lyndall	G.B.R. 4: 31
1703 Mar. 2	Cruyger, John, and Mary Cuyler	G.B.R. 1: 13
1695 Ap. 8	Cullom, Peter, and Martha Barriman	G.B.R. 3: 92
1758 June 10	Cussouw, Jacob, and Famytje Van Kleef	M.B. 41:149
1703 Mar. 2	Cuyler, Mary, and John Cruyger	G.B.R. 1: 13
1693 Oct. 23	Cuyler, Rachel, and Meyndert Schuyler	G.B.R. 2:142
1756 Ap. 12	Cuyper, Rachel, and Dennis Van Dorson	M.B. 41:100
1759 Nov. 17	Dacon, James, and Mary Dobbs	M.B. 2:503
1696 Aug. 13	Daillé, Peter, and Seijtie Duyckinck	G.B.R. 3: 94
1703 Dec. 3	Dalcale, Mary, and Adam Cavelir	G.B.R. 2: 26
1701 May 24	Dale, Robert, and Elizabeth Turner	G.B.R. 3:194
1756 Jan. 16	Dally, Elizabeth, and John Anthony	M.B. 41: 75
1702 Aug. 28	Dally, Nicholas, and Elizabeth Cregier	G.B.R. 3:195
1758 July 19	Dalton, Margaret, and Edward Kaho	M.B. 41:189
1704 Feb. 27	Daniel, Thomas, and Sarah Godfrey	G.B.R. 2: 27
1702 Dec. 24	Daniell, Robt., and Susanne Nicholas	G.B.R. 1: 3
1705 May 25	Dant, Pierre, and Elizabeth Holt	G.B.R. 2: 27
1698 May 25	Darkins, Lydia, and Jacobus Rolloquin	G.B.R. 3:193
1692 Dec. 1	Darvall, Katharina, and Frederick Philips	G.B.R. 4: 32
1702 Oct. 27	Davenport, Thomas, and Magarett Lepenar	G.B.R. 1: 3
1756 Dec. 6	Davenport, William, and Eleanor Kelly	M.B. 1:374
1694 Dec. 31	Davids, Catharina, and Jacobus Cox	G.B.R. 3: 92
1696 July 6	Davies, Engeltie, and Thomas Giles	G.B.R. 3: 93
1758 Aug. 14	Davis, George, and Elizabeth Turner	M.B. 41:212
1693 Mar. 25	Davis, Hester, and John Finch	G.B.R. 2:142
1702 Ap. 30	Davis, James, and Elisbeth Santford	G.B.R. 3:195
1703 June 27	Davis, Janekie, and Peter Battery	G.B.R. 2: 25
1693 Ap. 14	Davis, Mary, and Michael Greenham	G.B.R. 2:142
1703 Ap. 10	Davis, Ruth, and John Shepard	G.B.R. 1: 13
1758 July 22	Davis, Sarah, and Jonas Higby	M.B. 41:193
1699 Feb. 25	Davison, William, and Eleanor Goff	G.B.R. 3:193
1694 Nov. 6	Dawning, James, and Sarah Evans	G.B.R. 3: 92

1694 Dec. 12	Dawning, Jane, and Nicholas Carnaby	G.B.R. 3: 92
1756 June 7	Dawson, Mary, and Myndert Van Evera	M.B. 41:139
1756 Ap. 23	Dawson, Susanna, and Elias Anderson	M.B. 41:114
1705 June 9	Dawson, Thomas, and Mary Thoxter	G.B.R. 2: 27
1704 May 30	Dayly, Hannah, and Eporordus Bogardus	G.B.R. 2: 26
1756 Jan. 13	Dean, Alexander, and Elizabeth Lynch	M.B. 41: 74
1758 Mar. 28	Dean, Daniel, and Charity Odell	M.B. 41:145
1758 July 11	Dean, Elizabeth, and John Welch	M.B. 41:181
1693 Oct. 10	Dean, Hannah, and Benj. Phips	G.B.R. 2:142
1700 July 13	Dean, Hannah, and Joseph Aspinwalle	G.B.R. 3:194
1764 June 4	De Bevois, Charles, and Mary Van Houten	M.B. 8:245
1752-56	Decer [Decker], Eve, and Jeams Wood	C.M. 82: 62
1752-56	Decer [Decker], Sarah, and John Merril	C.M. 82: 62
1756 Feb. 3	Decker, Charles, and Marsey Merril	M.B. 41: 85
1704 June 23	Deerby, Meritie, and Albert Van Winkel	G.B.R. 2: 26
1753 Jan. 5	Deforeest, Isaac, and Alida Fonda	M.B. 41: 39
1756 June 9	De Foreest, Jacob, and Tryntie Bratt	M.B. 41:140
1705 June 23	DeForeest, Joannes, and Tryntie Garretse Ravestein	
		G.B.R. 2: 27
1704 Sep. 20	DeForeest, Sarah, and John Meyer	G.B.R. 2: 27
1753 Jan. 5	Deforeest, Susannah, and Isaac Defunda	M.B. 41: 38
1706 Ap. 11	D'Forest, Mary, and Isaac D'Reymer	G.B.R. 2: 28
1702 Jan. 30	Deforest, Sarah, and Johanes Hanse	G.B.R. 3:194
1753 Jan. 5	Defunda, Isaac, and Susannah Deforeest	M.B. 41: 38
1756 Feb. 12	De Graw, James, and Ann Rapelje	M.B. 41: 87
1705 Dec. 19	De Gray, Anne, and William Warner	G.B.R. 2: 28
1703 May 12	De Groosse, Adolphe, and Rachell Coderese	G.B.R. 1: 13
1703 Sep. 14	De Groot, Aegie, and Gerard Schyler	G.B.R. 2: 25
1703 Feb. 3	De Haeese, Susannah, and Robert Hickman	G.B.R. 1: 13
1701 Oct. 27	De Haert, Elizabeth, and William Van Newenhuysen	
		G.B.R. 2:142
1697 Oct. 9	Dehance, Jan, and Margaret Symonse Uthuse	G.B.R. 3:192
1703 Jan. 5	Dehart, Balthazer, and Margritta Mauritz	G.B.R. 1: 3
1704 Dec. 4	D'Hart, Catalina, and Jacobus Kip	G.B.R. 2: 27
1699 May 19	Dehart, Cathrine, and Joseph Blydenburgh	G.B.R. 3:193
1691 Aug. 22	DeHart, Katherine, and James Larkon	G.B.R. 4: 31
1695 June 27	de Hart, Matthew, and Jannetie Mauritz	G.B.R. 3: 92
1694 Ap. 12	d'Honneur, Johannes, and Johanna Maynard	G.B.R. 3: 91
1702 May 14	De Key, Catherine, and Abram Wandall	G.B.R. 3:195
1694 May 9	Dekey, Jacobus, and Sarah Willet	G.B.R. 3: 92
1704 Mar. 7	De Kleyn, Leonard Huygen, and Susannah Vaughton	
		G.B.R. 2: 26
1705 Nov. 2	De Klyen, Elizabeth, and Anthony Lispenard	G.B.R. 2: 28
1703 Sep. 15	De la Metze, Ruttie, and Hendrick Bogaert	G.B.R. 2: 25
1700 Jan. 19	Delancy, Stephen, and Ann Cortlandt	G.B.R. 3:193
1704 Jan. 25	De Lanoy, Maria, and Christopher Beekman	G.B.R. 2: 26

1696 Feb. 21	DeLanoy, Peter, and Mary Edsall	G.B.R. 3: 93
1692 June 27	De La Plaine, Marie, and Jean Le Chavelier	G.B.R. 4: 32
1696 Aug. 11	De Meyer, Mrs Agnetie, and William Jenoway	G.B.R. 3: 93
1686-87 Jan.20	De Morris, Nicolas, and Eleanor Williams	L.W. 86
1699 Aug. 18	Denham, David, and Mary Elsley	G.B.R. 2:142
1704 Jan. 14	Denike, Mary, and John Denmark	G.B.R. 2: 26
1704 Jan. 14	Denmark, John, and Mary Denike	G.B.R. 2: 26
1753 Jan. 18	Denmark, Mary, and Henry Peckwell	M.B. 41: 43
1756 May 1	Denton, Martha, and Stephen Herriman	M.B. 41:118
1699 Aug. 29	Denton, Phebe, and Richard Thorne	G.B.R. 2:142
1694 Sep. 19	de Peyster, Cornelis, and Maria Bancker	G.B.R. 3: 92
1699 Aug. 18	Depheyster, Cornelia, and Alexander Steuard	G.B.R. 2:142
1752-56	Depue, Elizabeth, and Cornelous Simeson	C.M. 82: 62
1704 June 5	DePuy, Andrew, and Jane Archanbaw	G.B.R. 2: 26
1703 Mar. 30	Deraval, Francis, and Richard Willett	G.B.R. 1: 13
1703 Dec. 18	Deray, Hillyden, and Jacobus Bayard	G.B.R. 2: 26
1706 Ap. 11	D'Reymer, Isaac, and Mary D'Forest	G.B.R. 2: 28
1701 May 22	De Riemer, Elizabeth, and Henry Coerten	G.B.R. 3:194
1705 Ap. 27	De Riemer, Isaac, and Anne Woorfman	G.B.R. 2: 27
1756 Ap. 30	Deronde, Catharine, and Benjamin Benson	M.B. 41:117
1703 Oct. 18	Desbrosses, James, and Hellena Gaudineau	G.B.R. 2: 25
1704 Sep. 9	Dese, Sarah, and Myndert Burger	G.B.R. 2: 26
1705 Feb. 1	D'Val, Charles, and Susanna Boundinot	G.B.R. 2: 28
1758 July 29	Devoe, Aron, and Mary Van Vey	M.B. 41:195
1704 Nov. 8	DeVore, Elizabeth, and Andrew Sweroer	G.B.R. 2: 27
1756 Ap. 5	De Vou, Catherine, and Wm. Van Northstrand	M.B. 41:105
1703 Sep. 14	de Vrees, Albert, and Eunnetie Van Dycke	G.B.R. 2: 25
1698 May 26	Dewind, Lewin, and Ariaentie Moll	G.B.R. 3:193
1703 Aug. 18	DeWitt, Mary, and Moses Cantain	G.B.R. 2: 25
1696 Feb. 15	DeWitt, Sarah, and Christopher Hooglandt	G.B.R. 3: 93
1687 May 31	Dewitt, Sophia, and Humphry Seward	L.W. 92
1703 Jan. 8	DeYou, Elizabeth, and John Journey	G.B.R. 1: 3
1752 Dec. 30	Dike, Mary, and Tobyas Van Zandt	M.B. 41: 36
1752 Nov. 30	Dillingham, Silvanus, and Ann Turner	M.B. 41: 2
1701 Aug. 25	Direcks, Fyche, and Francis Van Dyke	G.B.R. 2:142
1695 Ap. 10	Dischington, Cornelia, and Andrew Law	G.B.R. 3: 92
1699 Aug. 18	Dishington, Cornelia, and Alexander Streard	G.B.R. 3:193
1696 Oct. 15	Dodridg, Philip, and Frances Moore	G.B.R. 3: 93
1691-92 Mar.23	Donaldson, John, and Elizabeth Harmon	G.B.R. 4: 31
1753 Jan. 22	Doran, Thomas, and Sarah Van Law	M.B. 41: 47
1779 Mar. 10	Dorland, Garret, and Sarah Smith	M.B. 27: 62
1761 June 20	Dorlin, Elias, and Phelena Rushmore	M.B. 4:249
1701 Oct. 3	Dorton, William, and Prudence Shelston	G.B.R. 2:142
1705 Ap. 11	Doughty, Hannah, and Samuel Thorn, Junr.	G.B.R. 2: 27
1756 May 20	Douglass, Margaret, and Thomas Fullard	M.B. 41:130
1698 July 18	Douw, Kathrine, and Samuel Clowes	G.B.R. 3:193

1697 Sep. 23	Dow, Hendryck, and Neeltie Meynderts	G.B.R.	3:192
1696 Nov. 11	Downing, Jane, and Edward Lambert	G.B.R.	3: 93
1753 Jan. 11	Drake, Joseph, and Amy Carman	M.B.	41: 42
1704 Mar. 29	Drakes, Sarah, and Arthur Willis	G.B.R.	2: 26
1699 Ap. 17	Drincall, Thomas, and Ann Watson	G.B.R.	3:193
1693 Aug. 17	Drummond, Mary, and John Chambers	G.B.R.	2:142
1699 Mar. 14	Duboies, Anne, and Peter Chevalier Dupin	G.B.R.	3:193
1696 Aug. 28	Dubois, Louis, and Hester Grasset	G.B.R.	3: 93
1756 Jan. 28	Du Bois, Mary, and John Bogardus	M.B.	41: 81
1703 July 6	Dubois, Mary, and John Lafon	G.B.R.	2: 25
1699 July	Du Boy, Anna, and Benjn Funeile	G.B.R.	2:142
1687 Sep. 17	Dudly, Marjary, and Ebenezer Willson	L.W.	101
1758 Aug. 5	Duncan, Anne, and Peter Berton	M.B.	41:206
1758 Aug. 22	Duncan, Frances, and George Duncan Ludlow	M.B.	41:226
1756 Mar. 22	Dunkel, Jan Lodewick, and Sarah Van der Voort		
		M.B.	41: 98
1696 July 8	Dunscomb, Daniel, and Helena Swann	G.B.R.	3: 93
1753 Jan. 22	Dunton, Ebenezer, and Dorothy Field	M.B.	41: 48
1699 Mar. 14	Dupin, Peter Chevalier, and Anne Duboies	G.B.R.	3:193
1764 Jan. 27	Dupuy, Aron, and Martha Tysen	M.B.	8: 41
1756 Jan. 23	Du Puy, Elizabeth, and Abraham Crocheron	M.B.	41: 77
1698 Nov. 10	Durend, John, and Elizabeth Bryan	G.B.R.	3:193
1752 Nov. 30	Duryee, Jacob, and Cornelia Schenck	M.B.	41: 3
1704 Feb. 10	Dushen, Valentine, and Mary Stillwell	G.B.R.	2: 26
1703 June 18	Du Tay, Mary, and William Thibowe	G.B.R.	2: 25
1758 Aug. 22	Dutcher, Elizabeth, and John Polhemus	M.B.	41:224
1696 Aug. 13	Duyckinck, Seijtie, and Peter Daille	G.B.R.	3: 94
1704 Jan. 25	Duyckink, Evert, and Elsie Myer	G.B.R.	2: 26
1756 Ap. 20	Duyckman, Rebecca, and Abraham Hooper	M.B.	41:110
1702 Dec. 12	Dyckhuyse, Swantie, and Arent Schuyler	G.B.R.	1: 3
1695 Sep. 16	Dykeman, Mary, and James Hewett	G.B.R.	3: 92
1758 June 21	Eagles, Esther, and Francis Baird	M.B.	41:165
1758 Aug. 16	Earl, Ester, and James Cargill	M.B.	41:214
1702 Ap. 30	Eaton, John, and Elizabeth Michell	G.B.R.	3:195
1696 Feb. 21	Edsall, Mary, and Peter De Lanoy	G.B.R.	3: 93
1758 Aug. 19	Edwards, Frances, and William Fielding	M.B.	41:220
1698 Jan. 13	Edwards, Robert, and Judith Mosston	G.B.R.	3:193
1701 Mar. 26	Ekles, James, and Rebecca Lynus	G.B.R.	3:194
1753 Mar. 12	Eldert, Rachel, and Thomas Van Wyck	M.B.	41: 65
1701 Feb. 24	Elliott, Robert, and Frances Boyle	G.B.R.	3:194
1758 Aug. 21	Ellis, Elizabeth, and Thomas McBride	M.B.	41:222
1704 Oct. 9	Ellson, Hannah, and John Ogleby	G.B.R.	2: 27
1704 Mar. 4	Ellsworth, Anne, and Josias Crego	G.B.R.	2: 26
1696 June 3	Ellsworth, Johannes, and Anna Peters	G.B.R.	3: 93
1699 Aug. 18	Elsley, Mary, and David Denham	G.B.R.	2:142

1704 July 20	Foster, John, and Altic Cornelise	G.B.R. 2: 26
1752-56	Founten, Antiny, and hannah Garrison	C.M. 82: 62
1758 Aug. 18	Founten, Sarah, and Daniel McSwain	M.B. 41:217
1756 Jan. 7	Foy, John, and Mary Van Pelt	M.B. 41: 71
1684 Aug. 2	Francis, William, and Janacay Arens	C.M. 34: 28
1756 May 14	Frederick, Elsie, and Boudawyn Le Conte	M.B. 41:127
1702 Ap. 25	Fredricks, Isaac, and Hester Van Fleckt	G.B.R. 3:195
1693 Ap. 28	Fredricksen, Kathrine, and John Wicken	G.B.R. 2:142
1705 May 23	Freebody, John, and Sarah Fleet	G.B.R. 2: 27
1705 Aug. 20	Freeman, Bernardus, and Margrieta V. Schayck	
		G.B.R. 2: 28
1704 June 8	French, John, and Katherine Benson	G.B.R. 2: 26
1694 Oct. 21	French, John, and Mary White	G.B.R. 3: 92
1695 Nov. 27	Fromanteel, Ann, and Francis Chappell	G.B.R. 3: 93
1702 July 29	Frost, Hannah, and John Cooper	G.B.R. 3:195
1692 Sep. 12	Frost, Mary, and John Hendrickson	G.B.R. 4: 32
1756 May 20	Fullard, Thomas, and Margaret Douglass	M.B. 41:130
1699 July	Funelle, Benjn, and Anna Du Boy	G.B.R. 2:142
1781 Dec. 18	Furman, Polly, and Robert Parsell	M.B. 34: 93
1756 May 10	Gale, John Junr, and Ann Jones	M.B. 41:123
1692 Nov. 19	Gallais, Mary, and Stephen Vallou	G.B.R. 2:141
1703 Ap. 17	Gallutton, Anne, and Thomas Allison	G.B.R. 1: 13
1753 Jan. 2	Gano, John, and Mary McBride	M.B. 41: 37
1773 Aug. 26	Gant, Peter, and Mary Pantine	M.B. 21: 86
1705 Sep. 3	Gardener, John, and Elizabeth (last name illegible)	
		G.B.R. 2: 28
1753 Mar. 26	Gardiner, Rachael, and Jacob Van Woort	M.B. 41: 13
1703 Nov. 6	Garreau, Jean, and Marie Andere	G.B.R. 2: 25
1704 Ap. 10	Garretson, Ryert, and Gerthryt Lemsen	G.B.R. 2: 26
1752-56	Garrison, Cristifer, and Phebe Vanderbilt	C.M. 82: 62
1752-56	Garrison, Hannah, and Antiny Founten	C.M. 82: 62
1703 Oct. 18	Gaudineau, Hellena, and James Desbrosses	G.B.R. 2: 25
1695 June 28	Gaultier, Joanna, and John Blanchard	G.B.R. 3: 92
1758 Aug. 12	Geraud, Mary, and John Martin	M.B. 41:211
1756 May 6	Gereau, Mary, and Robert Cobham	M.B. 41:122
1693 Oct. 18	Geritse, Elizth, and John Anthony	G.B.R. 2:142
1701 Oct. 12	Gerrete, Nieltje, and Barent Staats	G.B.R. 2:142
1693 June 20	Gerritse, Hannah, and John Peterson	G.B.R. 2:142
1705 May 7	Gettes, Paul, and Mercy Flant	G.B.R. 2: 27
1704 Jan. 7	Gettike, Conradus, and Anna Van Aps	G.B.R. 2: 26
1696 Ap. 13	Gibb, Andrew, and Mrs Hannah Smith	G.B.R. 3: 93
1779 Nov. 30	Giffing, William, and Mary Hutton	M.B. 28:153
1698 May 4	Gilbert, George, and Jane Campell	G.B.R. 3:193
1703 Oct. 27	Gilbert, John, and Cornelia Allison	G.B.R. 2: 25
1696 July 6	Giles, Thomas, and Engeltie Davies	G.B.R. 3: 93

1758 July 8	Gillam, Phebe, and William Peek	M.B. 41:176	
1700 Ap. 27	Gindett, John, and Mary Vincent	G.B.R. 3:194	
1700 Ap. 27	Gizebert, Elizabeth, and Adam Carille (or Laville)		
		G.B.R. 3:194	
1699 Aug. 15	Gleave, Richard, and Han Philip	G.B.R. 2:142	
1705 Sep. 1	Glen, Anne, and Richd. Hunt	G.B.R. 2: 28	
1697 Oct. 18	Glenn, Margaret, and Richard Burt	G.B.R. 3:192	
1703 June 23	Glenrosse, William, and Eliza Clarke	G.B.R. 2: 25	
1705 Jan. 8	Gleve, Hester, and John Charleton	G.B.R. 2: 27	
1698 Dec. 12	Glover, Mary, and Jeremiah King	G.B.R. 3:193	
1699 Mar. 14	Godfrey, Elizabeth, and James Bolen	G.B.R. 3:193	
1705 Feb. 27	Godfrey, Sarah, and Thomas Daniel	G.B.R. 2: 27	
1753 Mar. 27	Goes, Isaac, and Catherina Van Duersen	M.B. 41: 14	
1764 Nov. 22	Goes, Louris, and Catharine Hoffman	M.B. 8:418	
1699 Feb. 25	Goff, Eleanor, and William Davison	G.B.R. 3:193	
1694 Oct. 23	Gore, Dorothy, and Richard Yaresly	G.B.R. 3: 92	
1701 Ap. 1	Gorne, John, and Mary Harris	G.B.R. 3:194	
1703 Nov. 18	Goscott, Zachariah, and Margrett Bend	G.B.R. 2: 25	
1704 June 22	Gouverneur, Isaac, and Sarah Staats	G.B.R. 2: 26	
1699 May 16	Governeur, Abraham, and Mary Milborne	G.B.R. 3:193	
1703 Ap. 8	Graham, Augustine, and Jane Chiswell	G.B.R. 1: 13	
1691 Nov. 3	Graham, Isabella, and Lewis Morris	G.B.R. 4: 31	
1684 July 18	Graham, James, and Elizabeth Windebank	C.M. 34: 28	
1703 Dec. 14	Graham, Mary, and John Corbett	G.B.R. 2: 26	
1701 Aug. 16	Graham, Mrs Sarah, and Robert Hooper	G.B.R. 2:142	
1704 Nov. 1	Grant, William, and Rachell Hardenbrook	G.B.R. 2: 27	
1696 Aug. 28	Grasset, Hesther, and Louis Dubois	G.B.R. 3: 93	
1697 Sep. 24	Graves, Deliverance, and Walter Taylor	G.B.R. 3:192	
1697 Oct. 29	Green, Elizabeth, and Peter King	G.B.R. 3:192	
1758 Aug. 21	Green, Richard, and Catherine Bradt	M.B. 41:221	
1704 Nov. 13	Greenfeild, Richard, and Mary Williams	G.B.R. 2: 27	
1693 Ap. 14	Greenham, Michael, and Mary Davis	G.B.R. 2:142	
1694 Dec. 13	Greg, Robert, and Leena Mourits	G.B.R. 3: 92	
1759 Sep. 25	Grehams, John, and Esther Young	M.B. 2:430	
1702 Nov. 20	Grice, John, and Deborah Hadlock	G.B.R. 1: 3	
1756 Ap. 23	Griffin, Rebecca, and Edward Stevenson	M.B. 41:113	
1694 Sep. 18	Groenendyke, Johannes, and Delia Childers	G.B.R. 3: 92	
1752 Dec. 1	Groesbeck, David, Junr., and Catharin Vader	M.B. 41: 6	
1693 Feb. 8	Groves, Andrew, and Jane Boyle	G.B.R. 2:142	
1752-56	Grudine, Peter, and Ebel Smith	C.M. 82: 62	
1703 Oct. 10	Gunter, Mary, and Thomas Ralph	G.B.R. 2: 25	
1704 Jan. 20	Gunthorpe, Jane, and Thomas Hughes	G.B.R. 2: 26	
1761 Jan. 24	Habbot, John, and Mary McDougall	M.B. 4: 28	
1705 June 30	Hading, Johanne, and Bernardus Smith	G.B.R. 2: 27	
1753 Jan. 31	Hadley, Martha, and Samuel Merryman	M.B. 41: 55	

1702 Nov. 20	Hadlock, Deborah, and John Grice	G.B.R. 1: 3
1770 Oct. 18	Hagerman, Thomas, and Massey Homan	M.B. 16:221
1765 Oct. 31	Hages, Mary, and William Costelow	M.B. 9:343
1753 Feb. 5	Hagins, Mary, and Arthur Cosby	M.B. 41: 56
1753 Mar. 20	Haight, Mary, and John Wilson	M.B. 41: 11
1756 Ap. 7	Hait, Benjamin, and Ann Smith	M.B. 41:106
1752 Dec. 6	Hall, Joseph, and Hannah Beadle	M.B. 41: 10
1703 May 4	Hall, Richard, and Anne Evetts	G.B.R. 1: 13
1756 June 4	Hall, Robert, and Catharine Vredenburgh	M.B. 41:138
1758 June 13	Hall, Sarah, and Wm. Wallace	M.B. 41:155
1704 Oct. 14	Hallett, Hannah, and John Washburne	G.B.R. 2: 27
1703 Feb. 24	Hamill, John, and Christine Rosevelt	G.B.R. 1: 13
1758 Aug. 29	Hamilton, Charles, and Catherine Stillwell	M.B. 41:231
1756 Jan. 26	Hamilton, Mary, and James McGrath	M.B. 41: 79
1692 Ap. 20	Hancock, Anna, and Thomas Shaw	G.B.R. 4: 32
1698 Dec. 8	Hancock, John, and Jane Wells	G.B.R. 3:193
1758 Aug. 9	Hancock, William, and Hannah Sise	M.B. 41:208
1697 Ap. 5	Hanmer, Sarah, and Gabriel Ludlow	G.B.R. 3: 93
1703 Sep. 6	Hansant, Ekay, and Charles Beekman	G.B.R. 2: 25
1702 Jan. 30	Hanse, Johanes, and Sarah Deforest	G.B.R. 3:194
1700 Oct. 20	Harbert, Richard, and Cornella Hart	M.B. 3:374
1696 July 10	Hardenbergh, Johannes, and Helenah Meyer	G.B.R. 3: 93
1699 Sep. 12	Hardenbergh, Johannus, and Cathrine Ruthse	G.B.R. 3:193
1694 June 4	Hardenbergh, Mary, and William Pead	G.B.R. 3: 92
1705 Aug. 20	Hardenbroeck, Catherina, and Josiah Ogden	G.B.R. 2: 28
1704 Oct. 27	Hardenbrook, Cornelia, and John Waldron	G.B.R. 2: 27
1692 May 7	Hardenbrook, Mary, and David Jamison	G.B.R. 4: 32
1704 Nov. 1	Hardenbrook, Rachell, and William Grant	G.B.R. 2: 27
1701 Feb. 21	Hardenburgh, Nulie, and Jacob Tenyck	G.B.R. 3:194
1701 June 21	Hardenbrugh, Peter, and Katherine Vanderpolle	
		G.B.R. 3:194
1786 Nov. 17	Harford, Richard, and Dorothy Cox	L.W. 72
1703 Oct. 30	Harley, Hannah, and Caleb Beck	G.B.R. 2: 25
1700 Feb. 14	Harmensen, Hans, and Mary Van Dyke	G.B.R. 3:194
1691 Mar. 23	Harmon, Elizabeth, and John Donaldson	G.B.R. 4: 31
1762 June 28	Harps, Henry, and Hannah Pegrem	M.B. 6:211
1705 Dec. 8	Harrington, Thomas, and Heila Johnson	G.B.R. 2: 28
1775 July 19	Harriot, Israel, and Catherine Wool	M.B. 23:100
1701 Ap. 1	Harris, Mary, and John Gorne	G.B.R. 3:194
1702 Dec. 12	Harris, Richard, and Mary Baker	G.B.R. 1: 3
1698 Oct. 30	Harrod, Richard, and Mary Jones	G.B.R. 3:193
1757 Nov. 28	Harsin, Garret, and Sarah Kip	M.B. 1:715
1758 Sep. 1	Hart, Catharine, and Christopher Johnson	M.B. 41:240
1695 Aug. 19	Harwood, George, and —— Willemke	G.B.R. 3: 92
1758 Aug. 24	Hawhurst, William, and Mary Chapman	M.B. 41:228
1758 Sep. 1	Hay, Michael, and Anne Cox	M.B. 41:237

1705 May 15	Hays, Sarah, and Francis Warne	G.B.R. 2: 27
1761 Nov. 30	Hayt, Moses, and Charity Soper	M.B. 5:257
1705 Dec. 8	Hazareth, Elizabeth, and John Cornelison	G.B.R. 2: 28
1756 May 15	Heady, Sarah, and Joseph Cornwell (or Cornnell)	M.B. 41:128
1753 Mar. 15	Heaviland, Phoebe, and John Williams	M.B. 41: 66
1702 Nov. 27	Heerman, John, and Sarah Shrieve	G.B.R. 1: 3
1761 May 26	Heermans, Henry, and Ann Stoutenbergh	M.B. 4:207
1696 Jan. 19	Hendricke, Perkie, and Peter Billian	G.B.R. 3: 93
1703 Feb. 27	Hendricks, Angell, and Lubert Jansen Blerkome	
		G.B.R. 1: 13
1695 June 4	Hendricksen, Volckert ,and Elizabeth Paulus	G.B.R. 3: 92
1692 Sep. 12	Hendrickson, John, and Mary Frost	G.B.R. 4: 32
1782 Feb. 2	Henly, John, and Elizabeth Allen	M.B. 35: 42
1694 Jan. 1	Henry, Ann, and Joseph Wright	G.B.R. 3: 91
1696 Feb. 17	Henry, Elizth, and David Vyland	G.B.R. 3: 93
1686-87 Jan.21	Henry, Samuell, and Ann Cobbitt	L.W. 86
1756 May 1	Herriman, Stephen, and Martha Denton	M.B. 41:118
1703 July 21	Heus, Thomas, and Sarah Loyd	G.B.R. 2: 25
1695 Sep. 16	Hewett, James, and Mary Dykeman	G.B.R. 3: 92
1760 Jan. 22	Heyer, Mathias, and Maria Shefer	M.B. 3: 2
1704 Ap. 19	Heymer, John, and Dorothy Leigh	G.B.R. 2: 26
1705 Nov. 16	Hiatt, Margaret, and William Ford	G.B.R. 2: 28
1703 Feb. 3	Hickman, Robert, and Susannah De Haeese	G.B.R. 1: 13
1758 Aug. 18	Higbie, Mary, and Michael Murphy	M.B. 41:219
1758 July 22	Higby, Jonas, and Sarah Davis	M.B. 41:193
1780 Dec. 9	Hillery, Regnal, and Mary Boice	M.B. 30:146
1696 July 2	Hinchman, Sarah, and James Clement	G.B.R. 3: 93
1695 Aug. 24	Hinchman, Sarah, and Thomas Willet	G.B.R. 3: 92
1761 July 30	Hinton, Phebe, and Thomas Seaman	M.B. 5: 17
1704 Ap. 26	Hoar, Anthony, and John [Joan] Huyco	G.B.R. 2: 26
1758 July 10	Hoese, Jannetje, and Harman Pruyn	M.B. 41:180
1702 Nov. 17	Holloway, William, and Elizabeth Holyday	G.B.R. 1: 3
1758 June 29	Holmes, Ann, and Edward Prine	M.B. 41:170
1704 Oct. 16	Holmes, Anne, and Peter Peroyne	G.B.R. 2: 27
1696 Aug. 28	Holmes, Katherine, and George Revedly	G.B.R. 3: 93
1694 Ap. 20	Holst, Hannah, and Richard Pateshal	G.B.R. 3: 91
1705 Nov. 5	Holsworth, Mary, and Thomas Huttall	G.B.R. 2: 28
1705 May 25	Holt, Elizabeth, and Pierre Dant	G.B.R. 2: 27
1702 Nov. 17	Holyday, Elizabeth, and William Holloway	G.B.R. 1: 3
1694 Oct. 6	Honan, Daniel, and Sarah Jones	G.B.R. 3: 92
1688 Feb. 7	Honey, Ann, and Samuel Lipis	G.B.R. 3:193
1696 June 2	Hood, Jaspar, and Kathrine Anderson	G.B.R. 3: 93
1706 Jan. 16	Hoogland, Johannes, and Jannitie Tier	G.B.R. 2: 28
1696 Feb. 15	Hooglandt, Christopher, and Sarah DeWitt	G.B.R. 3: 93
1753 Mar. 29	Hooiwey, Peter Junr., and Mary Young	M.B. 41: 16
1756 Ap. 20	Hooper, Abraham, and Rebecca Duyckman	M.B. 41:110

1701 Aug. 16	Hooper, Robert, and Mrs Sarah Graham	G.B.R.	2:142
1696 Nov. 10	Hoorne, Ann, and William Pruden	G.B.R.	3: 93
1693 June 7	Hope, John, and Isabel Allin	G.B.R.	2:142
1698 July 5	Hopper, John, and Margaret Tindell	G.B.R.	3:193
1758 Aug. 4	Hopper, John, and Sophia Read	M.B.	41:201
1758 Aug. 26	Horrenbrook, Mary, and David Morrishor	M.B.	41:230
1758 June 10	Howlen, Oliver, and Elenor Welch	M.B.	41:151
1695 Dec. 24	Huestis, Abigail, and Josiah Hunt, Jr.,	G.B.R.	3: 93
1762 June 28	Huff, Wyntje, and Abraham Cronk	M.B.	6:207
1703 Dec. 13	Huggen, William, and Raechall Burroughs	G.B.R.	2: 26
1704 Jan. 20	Hughes, Thomas, and Jane Gunthorpe	G.B.R.	2: 26
1709 May 2	Hulgrave, Eve, and John Sunsorke	G.B.R.	1: 13
1696 June 30	Hulgrow, George, and Eva Burger	G.B.R.	3: 93
1696 June 12	Hulin, ffrancis, and Susanna Nicholas	G.B.R.	3: 93
1696 July	Hull, Hannah, and William Barton	G.B.R.	3: 93
1703 Oct. 20	Hunderbeek, Abraham, and Martha Woodett	G.B.R.	2: 25
1703 Nov. 22	Hunirk, Aleda, and Charles Smith	G.B.R.	2: 25
1698 July 27	Hunt, Eleanor, and Henry Coleman	G.B.R.	3:193
1695 Dec. 24	Hunt, Josiah, Jr., and Abigail Huestis	G.B.R.	3: 93
1697 Dec. 20	Hunt, Josiah, Jun., and Batthia fferguson	G.B.R.	3:192
1683 Nov. 22	Hunt, Mary, and Matthew Pugsley	G.R.	6: 73
1705 Sep. 1	Hunt, Richd, and Anne Glen	G.B.R.	2: 28
1703 Nov. 3	Huntrick, Matthew Leana, and Abraham Lanseing		
		G.B.R.	2: 25
1758 June 30	Hutchinson, Judah, and James Alexander	M.B.	41:173
1697 Oct. 29	Hutson, Hannah, and Israel Ward	G.B.R.	3:192
1705 Nov. 5	Huttall, Thomas, and Mary Holsworth	G.B.R.	2: 28
1703 Dec. 9	Huttkins, John, and Elizabeth Buckley	G.B.R.	2: 26
1695 Oct. 28	Hutton, John, and Katrine Strangnish	G.B.R.	3: 92
1703 Aug. 26	Huyblingh, Coenradt, and Deborah Beeck	G.B.R.	2: 25
1704 Ap. 26	Huyco, John [Joan], and Anthony Hoar	G.B.R.	2: 26
1758 Aug. 12	Hyatt, Mary, and Joseph Tomkins	M.B.	41:210
1703 Ap. 12	Hyndes, Christine, and John Allison	G.B.R.	1: 13
1758 July 20	Innes, Elizabeth, and John Wingfield	M.B.	41:190
1756 Jan. 3	Inslaer, Lodowick, and Lenah Boghart	M.B.	41: 69
1756 Feb. 2	Jackson, John, and Charity Tredwell	M.B.	41: 84
1695 Nov. 6	Jacobs, Anna, and Thomas Lynch	G.B.R.	3: 92
1695 July 24	Jacobs, Jannetie, and Caspar Springsten	G.B.R.	3: 92
1705 Ap. 10	Jacobs, Neiltie, and Evert Van Hook	G.B.R.	2: 27
1756 Feb. 27	Jacocks, Francis, and Mary Willsey	M.B.	41: 90
1696 Aug. 31	Jaman, Henry, and Jane Barber	G.B.R.	3: 93
1758 June 14	James, Elizabeth, and Charles Moore	M.B.	41:156
1692 May 7	Jamison, David, and Mary Hardenbrook	G.B.R.	4: 32
1705 Mar. 20	Jamison, James, and Beetie Upton	G.B.R.	2: 27
1703 Jan. 16	Jamisson, David, and Johanna Meech	G.B.R.	1: 3

1756 June 3	Kingsland, David, and Ann Corsen	M.B. 41:137
1703 Nov. 8	Kingsland, Edmund, and Mary Pinnhorne	G.B.R. 2: 25
1701 May 9	Kingston, John, and Dorothy Sandige	G.B.R. 3:194
1697 Jan. 26	Kip, Abraham, and Kathalina Van Vlecq	G.B.R. 3: 93
1696 June 8	Kip, Henricus, and Magdalen van Vlecque	G.B.R. 3: 94
1704 Dec. 4	Kip, Jacobus, and Catalina D'Hart	G.B.R. 2: 27
1705 Oct. 3	Kip, Margrieta, and Samuel Kip	G.B.R. 2: 28
1702 Ap. 22	Kip, Petrus, and Emeltie Van Deycke	G.B.R. 3:194
1705 Oct. 3	Kip, Samuel, and Margrieta Kip	G.B.R. 2: 28
1695 Sep. 30	Kipp, Jesse, and Mary Stevens	G.B.R. 3: 92
1700 Ap. 26	Kipp, Magdelena, and Alexander Baird	G.B.R. 3:194
1686 Oct. 27	Kittle, Jeremy, and Katherine Clare, both of Ulster Co.	
		L.W. 63
1691 Aug. 11	Konning, Elizabeth, and Huybert Arentse	G.B.R. 4: 31
1703 Nov. 4	Konsly, Christopher, and Sarah Kidd	G.B.R. 2: 25
1758 July 13	Kortright, Helena, and Abraham Brasher	M.B. 41:184
1703 Sep. 10	Kyarse, Helena, and John Oky	G.B.R. 2: 25
1752-66	**Lack,** Mary, and Need Bate	C.M. 82: 62
1703 Ap. 17	Laconte, William, and Margaret Mahoo	G.B.R. 1: 13
1703 July 6	Lafon, John, and Mary Dubois	G.B.R. 2: 25
1752-56	Laforge, Adrayon, and Elizerbeth Moor	C.M. 82: 62
1693 Jan. 18	Lafort, Marcus, and Hester Richards	G.B.R. 2:141
1753 Ap. 5	Lagrandie, Geesie, and Johannes Luke	M.B. 41: 20
1696 Nov. 11	Lambert, Edward, and Jane Downing	G.B.R. 3: 93
1695 June 19	Lamberts, Martinus, and Catrina van Newenhuysen	
		G.B.R. 3: 92
1756 May 20	Lambertson, Elenor, and Thomas Maddox	M.B. 41:132
1699 Dec. 29	Lance, Eliz., and John Mayson	G.B.R. 3:193
1758 Aug. 31	Land, Anne, and David Aug. Roche	M.B. 41:235
1706 Feb. 27	Lane, Adrien, and Jannitie Van Seckler	G.B.R. 2: 28
1702 Ap. 25	Langstaffe, Moses, and Mary Sidman	G.B.R. 3:195
1703 Nov. 3	Lanseing, Abraham, and Matthew Leana Huntrick	
		G.B.R. 2: 25
1704 Sep. 7	Lansen, John, and Leana Saunders	G.B.R. 2: 26
1703 May 26	Lansing, Isaac, and Janeke Beekeman	G.B.R. 1: 13
1694 Nov. 2	Larkin, Katharine, and Lancaster Simms	G.B.R. 3: 92
1691 Aug. 22	Larkon, James, and Katherine DeHart	G.B.R. 4: 31
1698 Feb. 7	Latham, Joseph, and Jane Singleton	G.B.R. 3:193
1752-56	Latorat, Peter, and ————	C.M. 82: 62
1700 Ap. 27	Laville (or Carille), Adam, and Elizabeth Gizebert	
		G.B.R. 3:194
1695 Ap. 10	Law, Andrew, and Cornelia Dischington	G.B.R. 3: 92
1690 May 1	Lawrence, Eleanor, and Lawrence Barnes	Deeds 8:244
1703 June 11	Lawrence, Eliza, and Jacobus Kiersteade	G.B.R. 2: 25
1753 Jan. 20	Lawrence, Hannah, and Jacob Bound	M.B. 41: 44

1696 Ap. 6	Lawrence, John, and Janetie Stevenson	G.B.R. 3: 93
1753 Jan. 3	Lawrence, Mary, and Talman Waters	M.B. 41: 25
1699 Sep. 24	Lawrence, Richard, and Charity Clerke	G.B.R. 2:142
1705 Jan. 12	Lawrence, Sarah, and James Tillett	G.B.R. 2: 27
1753 Jan. 22	Lawrence, Silas, and Margret Burns	M.B. 41: 46
1692 Nov. 9	Lawrence, Thomas, and Mary Ferguson	G.B.R. 4: 32
166 4-5 Mar.4	Lawrence, William, and Elizabeth Smith	G.E. 1: 98
1699 Dec.	Lawrier, Christian, and Mary Bunt	G.B.R. 3:193
1692 June 27	Le Chavelier, Jean, and Marie De La Plaine	G.B.R. 4: 32
1756 May 14	Le Conte, Bouwdawyn, and Elsie Frederick	M.B. 41:127
1756 Jan. 9	Le Conte, John Junr., and Catharine Van Horne	M.B. 41: 72
1705 Nov. 10	Lee, Mattee, and Thomas Roger	G.B.R. 2: 28
1694 May 10	Leeson, Mary, and John Clatworthy	G.B.R. 3: 92
1702 Jan. 26	Lefeurt, Bartholomew, and Magdalen Peirott	G.B.R. 3: 19
1758 June 19	Lefferts, Cath., and Peter Luister	M.B. 41:159
1753 Mar. 17	Leffertse, Catrintia, and Nicholas Wyckoff	M.B. 41: 21
1758 Aug. 11	Leggett, Abraham, and Gertruy Child	M.B. 41:209
1704 Ap. 19	Leigh, Dorothy, and John Heymer	G.B.R. 2: 26
1687 June 24	Leislaer, Sussannah, and Michaell Vaughton	L.W. 99
1694 Nov. 26	Leisler, Francis, and Thomas Lewis	G.B.R. 3: 92
1699 Dec. 16	Lelonor, Isaah, and Judith Waldron	G.B.R. 3:193
1704 Ap. 10	Lemsen, Gerthryt, and Ryert Garretson	G.B.R. 2: 26
1702 Oct. 27	Lepenar, Magarett, and Thomas Davenport	G.B.R. 1: 3
1703 July 12	Lesley, John, and Ellen Bissett	G.B.R. 2: 25
1704 Nov. 9	Lessitt, Elizabeth, and Samuel Sands	G.B.R. 2: 27
1703 Ap. 12	Lessonby, Alkey, and John Reemer	G.B.R. 1: 13
1696 Feb. 15	Letson, Daniel, and Helena Boedann	G.B.R. 3: 93
1695 Sep. 16	Leuwis, Moses, and Mary Bayer	G.B.R. 3: 92
1758 Aug. 17	Lewis, James, and Hannah Mullenix	M.B. 41:216
1694 June 22	Lewis, Johanna, and John Van Strydt	G.B.R. 3: 92
1758 June 28	Lewis, Joseph, and Phytie Losier	M.B. 41:169
1694 Nov. 26	Lewis, Thomas, and Francis Leisler	G.B.R. 3: 92
1694 Jan. 6	Lightfoott, Mrs Anna, and John Tasher	G.B.R. 4: 31
1697 Dec. 8	Lipet, Moses, and Sarah Throgmartin,	G.B.R. 3:192
1698 Feb. 7	Lipis, Samuel, and Ann Honey	G.B.R. 3:193
1705 Feb. 1	Lispenar, Abigail, and Adry Beekman	G.B.R. 2: 27
1705 Nov. 2	Lispenard, Anthony, and Elizabeth De Klyen	G.B.R. 2: 28
1758 June 6	Livingston, Margaret, and Peter R. Livingston	M.B. 41:147
1758 June 6	Livingston, Peter R., and Margaret Livingston	M.B. 41:147
1696 July 26	Livingstone, Robt. Junr., and Margaret Schuyler	
		G.B.R. 3: 94
1697 Dec. 30	Lloyd, Kathrine, and George Williams	G.B.R. 3:193
1703 Aug. 9	Longfield, Mary, and Octave Coenraats	G.B.R. 2: 25
1692 Ap. 22	Lookingglasse, Mary, and John Finlison	G.B.R. 4: 32
1691 Nov. 22	Lord, Mary, and Thomas Carhart	G.B.R. 4: 31
169 Ap. 16	Loring, John, and Kath'e Van Clyff	G.B.R. 3: 91

1758 June 28	Losier, Phytie, and Joseph Lewis	M.B. 41:169
1695 July 1	Low, Cornelius, and Margt. van Bursum	G.B.R. 3: 92
1758 June 5	Low, John, and Susannah Burdett	M.B. 41:146
1698 Aug. 22	Low, Matthis, and Janitye van Heyninge	G.B.R. 3:193
1756 Jan. 24	Lowdon, Samuel, and Sarah Oakes	M.B. 41: 78
1703 July 21	Loyd, Sarah, and Thomas Heus	G.B.R. 2: 25
1683	Ludlom, Elizabeth, and John Carman, Col.	M.S. 31: 7
1697 Ap. 5	Ludlow, Gabriel, and Sarah Hanmer	G.B.R. 3: 93
1758 Aug. 22	Ludlow, George Duncan, and Frances Duncan	M.B. 41:226
1758 June 19	Luister, Peter, and Catherine Lefferts	M.B. 41:159
1753 Ap. 5	Luke, Johannes, and Geesie Lagrandie	M.B. 41: 20
1696 June 16	Luwersen, Alkie, and Webley Rasby	G.B.R. 3: 93
1703 May 22	Luyckas, Hellegond, and Ogrbert Suert	G.B.R. 1: 13
1756 Ap. 23	Luyster, Anne, and Peter Luyster	M.B. 41:111
1756 Ap. 10	Luyster, Mary, and John Brinckerhoff	M.B. 41:107
1756 Ap. 23	Luyster, Peter, and Anne Luyster	M.B. 41:111
1700 Feb. 14	Lynch, Ann, and Francis Vincent	G.B.R. 3:194
1756 Jan. 13	Lynch, Elizabeth, and Alex. Dean	M.B. 41: 74
1758 July 22	Lynch, Mary, and Caleb White	M.B. 41:192
1695 Nov. 6	Lynch, Thomas, and Anna Jacobs	G.B.R. 3: 92
1697 Oct. 7	Lyndall, Deborah, and William Andersen	G.B.R. 3:192
1691 Sep. 7	Lyndall, Thomas, and Deborah Crundall	G.B.R. 4: 31
1704 Ap. 25	Lynes, Nathaniel, and Unis Burroughs	G.B.R. 2: 26
1696 June 16	Lynus, Damares, and John Basford	G.B.R. 3: 93
1701 Mar. 26	Lynus, Rebecca, and James Ekles	G.B.R. 3:194
1700 Sep. 17	Lyster, Elizabeth, and Thomas Penestone	G.B.R. 3:194
1756 Feb. 23	**Mabbet**, Samuel, and Ruth Yeomans	M.B. 41: 89
1753 Jan. 2	McBride, Mary, and John Gano	M.B. 41: 37
1758 Aug. 21	McBride, Thomas, and Elizabeth Ellis	M.B. 41:222
1758 Aug. 23	McCarter, Catherine, and Dennis Macmar	M.B. 41:227
1758 June 12	McClane, Daniel, and Ann McNeal	M.B. 41:153
1756 Jan. 28	McDowal, Martha, and Lawrence Sweeny	M.B. 41: 82
1758 Aug. 21	McDugal, Elenor, and Joseph Northup	M.B. 41:223
1753 Ap. 5	McFarlin, Daniel, and Catherin Roy	M.B. 41: 19
1756 Jan. 26	McGrath, James, and Mary Hamilton	M.B. 41: 79
1694 Sep. 10	Macgregere, Catherine, and John Evans	G.B.R. 3: 92
1752 Dec. 16	McGuire, Elizabeth, and Daniel Clark	M.B. 41: 28
1705 Jan. 11	Mackelson, Enoch, and Aphia Van Hoorn	G.B.R. 2: 27
1756 Mar. 18	McKim, William, and Mary Watson	M.B. 41: 96
1693 Mar. 22	Macky, John, and Jane Persons	G.B.R. 2:142
1758 Aug. 23	Macmar, Dennis, and Catherine McCarter	M.B. 41:227
1758 June 12	McNeal, Ann, and Daniel McClane	M.B. 41:153
1756 May 6	McNeill, Arthur, and Barbara McNeill	M.B. 41:121
1756 May 6	McNeill, Barbara, and Arthur McNeill	M.B. 41:121
1758 Aug. 18	McSwain, Daniel, and Sarah Founten	M.B. 41:217

508

1756 May 20	Maddox, Thomas, and Elenor Lambertson	M.B. 41:132
1703 Ap. 17	Mahoo, Margaret, and William Laconte	G.B.R. 1: 13
1697 Dec. 9	Mallyear, Sarah, and John Perrey	G.B.R. 3:192
1758 June 22	Maloney, Huner, and Christ. Sennett	M.B. 41:166
1756 Jan. 20	Mann, Ann, and Abraham Willson	M.B. 41: 76
1753 Feb. 24	Mannell, Andrew, and Catharin Sprong	M.B. 41: 61
1758 Sep. 1	Manney, Wines, and Altie Vandenbergh	M.B. 41:238
1701 Aug. 9	Mans, Adriaen, and ————	
1706 Jan. 10	Mansey, Mary, and Andrew Broughton	G.B.R. 2: 28
1752 Dec. 4	Mapack, Wyenefried, and William Taylor	M.B. 41: 8
1704 Mar. 2	Markman, John, and Elizabeth Farmer	G.B.R. 2: 26
1694 Mar. 31	Marriner, Gilbert, and Jannettie ffloyd	G.B.R. 3: 91
1705 May 21	Marrington, Jane, and Peter Murdock	G.B.R. 2: 27
1752-56	Marshal, John, and Susannah Cole	C.M. 82: 62
1756 Mar. 17	Marshall, Frances, and Paul Mersereau	M.B. 41: 95
1692 Sep. 27	Marshall, Garvas, and Elianor Pey	G.B.R. 4: 32
1752 Nov. 30	Marston, Sarah, and Andrew Yelverton	M.B. 41: 4
1752-56	Martennow, Mary, and Jacob Baragor	C.M. 82: 62
1758 Aug. 12	Martin, John, and Mary Geraud	M.B. 41:211
1687 Mar. 30	Martins, Juda, and William Cox	L.W. 89
1695 Ap. 6	Masett, Peter, and Lydia Coel	G.B.R. 3: 92
1752 Dec. 16	Mason, Ann Sarah, and Carden Proctor	M.B. 41: 29
1752 Dec. 22	Mathews, Susannah, and Francis Thurman	M.B. 41: 34
1695 June 27	Mauritz, Jannetie, and Matthew de Hart	G.B.R. 3: 92
1703 Jan. 5	Mauritz, Margritta, and Balthazer Dehart	G.B.R. 1: 3
1701 Oct. 8	Maynard, George, and Isabella Willson	G.B.R. 2:142
1694 Ap. 12	Maynard, Johanna, and Johannes d'Honneur	G.B.R. 3: 91
1699 Dec. 29	Mayson, John, and Eliz. Lance	G.B.R. 3:193
1691 Dec.	Meads, Mary, and Henry Coleman	G.B.R. 4: 31
1684 July 9	Mecarty, John, and Ann Harman	C.M. 34: 28
1703 Jan. 16	Meech, Johanna, and David Jamisson	G.B.R. 1: 3
1696 Jan. 13	Meek, Elizabeth, and James Wheeler	G.B.R. 3: 93
1758 July 31	Melvin, Catharine, and Mathias Rash	M.B. 41:196
1699 Aug. 14	Merchant, Ann, and George Cornwell	G.B.R. 2:142
1752-56	Merril, John, and Sarah Decer [Decker]	M.B. 82: 62
1756 Feb. 3	Merril, Marsey, and Charles Decker	M.B. 41: 85
1752-56	Merril, Thomas, and Eve Jonge	C.M. 82: 62
1758 Aug. 4	Merry, Charles, and Elizabeth Burns	M.B. 41:202
1753 Jan. 31	Merryman, Samuel, and Martha Hadley	M.B. 41: 55
1752 Dec. 20	Mersereau, Joshua, and Abigail Brown	M.B. 41: 32
1756 Mar. 17	Mersereau, Paul, and Frances Marshall	M.B. 41: 95
1758 Aug. 4	Merven, Hannah, and Epenetus Platt	M.B. 41:200
1778 Jan. 28	Mery, Pierre, and Catherine Ledner	M.B. 25: 13
1758 July 15	Mesereau, Mary, and Simon Van Name	M.B. 41:186
1706 Jan. 31	Messelaer, Abraham, and Agenietie Staats	G.B.R. 2: 28
1693 Mar. 20	Meybi, Cathrina, and John Van Hoorn	G.B.R. 2:142

1702 July 29	Meyer, Ann, and James Cebra	G.B.R. 3:195
1696 July 10	Meyer, Helenah, and Johannes Hardenbergh	G.B.R. 3: 93
1704 Dec. 15	Meyer, Ide, and Anna Ravenstein	G.B.R. 2: 27
1701 May 23	Meyer, Jenitie, and Abraham Provoost	G.B.R. 3:194
1704 Sep. 20	Meyer, John, and Darah De Foreest	G.B.R. 2: 27
1696 Aug. 8	Meyer, Katherine, and Zachariah Weeks	G.B.R. 3: 93
1698 Oct. 25	Meyers, Elsey, and Barnardus Smith	G.B.R. 3:193
1700 Ap. 27	Meyers, Katharine, and John Veet	G.B.R. 3:194
1700 Ap. 18	Meyers, Marytie, and Hendrickes Vander Heule	
		G.B.R. 3:194
1697 Sep. 23	Meynderts, Neeltie, and Hendryck Dow	G.B.R. 3:192
1753 Jan. 27	Michaels, Cornelius, and Catharine Robinson	M.B. 41: 52
1702 Ap. 30	Michell, Elizabeth, and John Eaton	G.B.R. 3:195
1758 June15	Michelsen, Hendrick, and Margaret Wilse	M.B. 41:157
1699 May 16	Milborne, Mary, and Abraham Governeur	G.B.R. 3:193
1704 May 4	Milldrum, John, and Femmetie Van Boursen	G.B.R. 2: 26
1756 Jan. 6	Miller, Dorothy, and Jonathan Mills	M.B. 41: 70
1704 Feb. 1	Miller, Jerusia, and John Wickham	G.B.R. 2: 26
1695 Jan. 31	Miller, Paul, and Antie van der Heyden	G.B.R. 3: 92
1704 Oct. 18	Miller, William, and Geertrey Springsteen	G.B.R. 2: 27
1756 Jan. 6	Mills, Jonathan, and Dorothy Miller	M.B. 41: 70
1699 May 6	Milton, Christian, and John Corbitt	G.B.R. 3:193
1705 Oct. 6	Ming, Thomas, and Mary Vorckinson	G.B.R. 2: 28
1756 June 2	Minthorne, Frances, and Paulus Banta	M.B. 41:136
1756 Jan. 27	Minthorne, Hilah, and Abraham Cock	M.B. 41: 80
1702 Dec. 28	Minviel, John James, and Susanne Papin	G.B.R. 1: 3
1703 Nov. 1	Mole, Jacobus, and Lydia Winne	G.B.R. 2: 25
1703 Oct. 19	Mole, Mary, and James Nicholas	G.B.R. 2: 25
1704 Dec. 8	Moll, Angletie, and Mydar Stone	G.B.R. 2: 27
1698 May 26	Moll, Ariaentie, and Lewin Dewind	G.B.R. 3:193
1705 Feb. 28	Mompesson, Roger, and Martha Sinhorn	G.B.R. 2: 28
1752-56	Mongal, Fiankea, and Jacob Mosharow	C.M. 82: 62
1758 June30	Montanie, Sarah, and Robert Finley	M.B. 41:171
1753 Feb. 9	Montanye, Martha, and Abraham Alner	M.B. 41: 64
1756 Mar. 25	Montfort, Ann, and Daniel Brinckerhoff	M.B. 41:100
1702 Dec. 22	Monvielle, Susanna, and William Smith	G.B.R. 1: 3
1699 July 5	Mool, Anne, and John fforlisson	G.B.R. 3:193
1752-56	Moor, Elizerbeth, and Adrayon Laforge	C.M. 82: 62
1758 June14	Moore, Charles, and Elizabeth James	M.B. 41:156
1696 Oct. 15	Moore, Frances, and Philip Dodridg	G.B.R. 3: 93
1705 June20	Moore, Hannah, and Allane Jarrett	G.B.R. 2: 27
1756 Ap. 17	Moore, Henry, and Neeltie Ploughman	M.B. 41:109
1696 Sep. 8	Moore, John, and Elizabeth Cheek	G.B.R. 3: 93
1694 Jan. 11	More, Richard, and Rebecca Baily	G.B.R. 3: 91
1758 June27	Morey, John, and Mary Williams	M.B. 41:168
1752-56	Morgan, John, and Elisebeth Prine	C.M. 82: 62

1686 Oct. 7	Odell, Sarah, and John Archer of Westcher	L.W.		67
1705 Aug. 20	Ogden, Josiah, and Catherina Hardenbroeck	G.B.R.	2:	28
1756 Feb. 21	Ogden, Nathaniel, and Hannah Mott	M.B.	41:	88
1704 Oct. 9	Ogleby, John, and Hannah Ellson	G.B.R.	2:	27
1703 Sep. 10	Oky, John, and Helena Kyarse	G.B.R.	2:	25
1704 Nov. 7	Oliver, Charles, and Margarett Schuyler	G.B.R.	2:	27
1705 Nov. 28	Oliver, John, and Katherine Peterson	G.B.R.	2:	28
1697 Sep. 17	Olpherts, Suert, and Hilleke Pieters	G.B.R.	3:192	
1701 Nov. 10	Olpherts, Suert, and Janeke Snedeker	G.B.R.	3:194	
1771 Nov. 22	Onderdonck, Adreyoan, and Nelly Snedeker	M.B.	17:262	
1756 Mar. 2	O'Neil, Mary, and Thomas Salter	M.B.	41:	92
1691 May 16	Oort, Sarah, and Capt. William Kidd	G.B.R.	4:	31
1702 Dec. 17	Osborn, Samuel, and Katherine Pullion	G.B.R.	1:	3
1698 Dec. 12	Osborn, William, and Elizabeth Way	G.B.R.	3:193	
1692 Oct. 3	Osburne, Elizabeth, and Jacob Ware	G.B.R.	4:	32
1752 Dec. 4	Ostrander, Abraham, and Elizabeth Ostrander	M.B.	41:	9
1752 Dec. 4	Ostrander, Elizabeth, and Abraham Ostrander	M.B.	41:	9
1756 Mar. 29	Outhout, Jonas, and Eliz. Van Haugle	M.B.	41:101	
1705 June 26	Oyan, Margariet, and William Warren	G.B.R.	2:	27
1759 May 10	Palding, James, and Rachel Bassing	M.B.	2:277	
1752 Dec. 11	Palmer, Basheba, and Thomas Pell Junr.	M.B.	41:	23
1753 Mar. 10	Palmer, Bathseba, and John Thomas Junr.	M.B.	41:	22
1778 Mar. 28	Pane, John, and Wilhelmina Dunkle	M.B.	25:	55
1688 Ap. 17	Pangburne, Susanna, and George Jewell of New York			
		L.W.		105
1698 Ap. 16	Pantry, John, and Elizabeth Plinco	G.B.R.	3:193	
1704 Jan. 26	Pape, Thomas, and Mary Pratt	G.B.R.	2:	26
1702 Dec. 28	Papin, Susanne, and John James Minviel	G.B.R.	1:	3
1697 Aug. 14	Parmiter, Thomas, and Margaret Smith	G.B.R.	3:192	
1753 Jan. 10	Parsons, John, and Alida Cavalier	M.B.	41:	41
1694 Ap. 20	Pateshal, Richard, and Hannah Holst	G.B.R.	3:	91
1703 June 18	Patting, Hannah, and Thomas Adams	G.B.R.	2:	25
1695 June 4	Paulus, Elizabeth, and Volckert Hendricksen	G.B.R.	3:	92
1694 June 4	Pead, William, and Mary Hardenbergh	G.B.R.	3:	92
1702 Mar. 23	Pearsall, Catherine, and Thomas Studd	G.B.R.	3:194	
1753 Jan. 18	Peckwell, Henry, and Mary Denmark	M.B.	41:	43
1701 Ap. 7	Pedley, Roger, and Sarah Thorne	G.B.R.	3:194	
1758 July 8	Peck, William, and Phebe Gillam	M.B.	41:176	
1702 Jan. 26	Peirott, Magdalen, and Bartholomew Lefeurt	G.B.R.	3:194	
1753 Feb. 19	Pell, Hannah, and Daniel Stevenson	M.B.	41:	59
1702 Jan. 20	Pell, Thomas, and Aeltie Beeke	G.B.R.	3:194	
1752 Dec. 11	Pell, Thomas Junr. and Basheba Palmer	M.B.	41:	23
1694 Nov. 23	Pell, William, and Eliz'th Van Teuyl	G.B.R.	3:	92
1700 Sep. 17	Penestone, Thomas, and Elizabeth Lyster	G.B.R.	3:194	
1705 Oct. 13	Pennistone, Thomas, and Allice Wooderop	G.B.R.	2:	28

1702 Mar. 23	Prosser, Joseph, and Elizabeth Verwyde	G.B.R.	3:194
1701 May 23	Provoost, Abraham, and Jenitie Meyer	G.B.R.	3:194
1693 June 14	Provoost, Altie, and Gerryt Van Hoorn	G.B.R.	4: 32
1704 Sep. 21	Provoost, Gerrett, and Altie Roose	G.B.R.	2: 27
1696 July 6	Provoost, Margaret, and Johannes van Brugen	G.B.R.	3: 93
1706 Jan. 9	Provost, Katherine, and Matthew Bensinck	G.B.R.	2: 28
1704 Jan. 18	Provoste, Margaret, and John Kerfbyl	G.B.R.	2: 26
1696 Nov. 10	Pruden, William, and Ann Hoorne	G.B.R.	3: 93
1705 Dec. 28	Prudence, Mary, and Aman Bounn	G.B.R.	2: 28
1758 July 10	Pruyn, Harman, and Jannetje Hoese	M.B.	41:180
1705 Sep. 3	Pruyn, Johannes, and Amilia Sanders	G.B.R.	2: 28
1755 Dec. 31	Pudney, James, and Mary Warner	M.B.	41: 67
1698 Ap. 27	Pugsley, Kathrine, and Richard Wilson	G.B.R.	3:193
1683 Nov. 22	Pugsley, Matthew, and Mary Hunt	G.B.R.	6: 73
1702 Dec. 17	Pullion, Katherine, and Samuel Osborn	G.B.R.	1: 3
1756 Mar. 1	Pundt, Jeremiah, and Catherin Cain	M.B.	41: 91
1753 Mar. 23	Puntine, Mary, and Isaac Morris	M.B.	41: 12
1695 Nov. 18	Puppyn, Ann, and Andrew Cannon	G.B.R.	3: 93
1693 June 27	Purrington, Sarah, and Charles Sleigh	G.B.R.	2:142
1753 Jan. 24	Quereau, Benjamin, and Hannah Brown	M.B.	41: 50
1705 Ap. 11	Rainford, Thomas, and Else Vandenbergh	G.B.R.	2: 27
1703 Oct. 10	Ralph, Thomas, and Mary Gunter	G.B.R.	2: 25
1702 Dec. 16	Randall, Elizabeth, and William Berkley	G.B.R.	1: 3
1756 Feb. 12	Rapelje, Ann, and James De Graw	M.B.	41: 87
1756 May 10	Rappalye, Cornelius, and Cornelia Wyckoff	M.B.	41:124
1756 May 20	Rappelye, George, and Mary Bloom	M.B.	41:131
1696 June 16	Rasby, Webley, and Alkie Luwersen	G.B.R.	3: 93
1758 July 31	Rash, Mathias, and Catharine Melvin	M.B.	41:196
1701 Oct. 2	Ravand [Ravaud], Ferdinando, and Mary Belline		
		G.B.R.	3:194
1701 Oct. 2	Ravaud, Ferdinand, and Mary ————	G.B.R.	2:142
1705 Dec. 24	Ravaud, Mary, and Samson Broughton	G.B.R.	2: 28
1704 Dec. 15	Ravenstein, Anna, and Ide Meyer	G.B.R.	2: 27
1705 June 23	Ravestein, Tryntie Garretse, and Joannes DeForeest		
		G.B.R.	2: 27
1705 Mar. 20	Ray, Richard, and Eleanor Saunders	G.B.R.	2: 27
1758 Aug. 4	Read, Sophia, and John Hopper	M.B.	41:201
1698 Mar. 1	Reade, Mary, and William Vesey	G.B.R.	3:193
1693 Sep. 18	Reay, Kathrine, and Richard Potter	G.B.R.	2:142
1706 Ap. 12	Redott, Elizabeth, and Thomas Walker	G.B.R.	2: 28
1703 Ap. 12	Reemer, John, and Alkey Lessonby	G.B.R.	1: 13
1705 Feb. 19	Reid, Robert, and Abigail Baily	G.B.R.	2: 27
1696 Aug. 28	Revedly, George, and Katherine Holmes	G.B.R.	3: 93
1696 Mar. 10	Reyners, Barnet, and Hesther Ceysler	G.B.R.	3: 93

1753 Jan. 25	Rhodes, Mary, and Benjamin Barker	M.B. 41: 51
1752 Nov. 30	Richard, Elizabeth, and Robert Wilson	M.B. 41: 1
1696 July 20	Richard, Stephen, and Mary van Brughen	G.B.R. 3: 93
1693 Jan. 18	Richards, Hester, and Marcus Lafort	G.B.R. 2:141
1705 May 19	Riggs, John, and Frances Colburne	G.B.R. 2: 27
1696 Nov. 27	Righton, John, and Frances Tuder	G.B.R. 3: 93
1703 Mar. 17	Rivilie, Catharine, and Alexander Stuart	G.B.R. 1: 13
1758 July 28	Robinson, Ann, and Daniel Jones	M.B. 41:194
1753 Jan. 27	Robinson, Catharine, and Cornelius Michaels	M.B. 41: 52
1702 Dec. 16	Robinson, Charles, and Elizabeth Roesdale	G.B.R. 1: 3
1693 Sep. 4	Robinson, Hanna, and William Burch	G.B.R. 2:142
1696 Nov. 21	Robinson, Josiah, and Margarett Nicolls	G.B.R. 3: 93
1702 Dec. 5	Robinson, Richard, and Mary Chambers	G.B.R. 1: 3
1697 Dec. 29	Robinson, Thomas, and Rachell Rosell	G.B.R. 3:193
1763 June 7	Rocess, Charles, and Catherine Merriment	M.B. 7:215
1758 Aug. 31	Roche, David Aug. and Anne Land	M.B. 41:235
1758 Aug. 22	Roe, Amey, and John Myer	M.B. 41:225
1753 Mar. 27	Roe, Elizabeth, and Thomas Coleman	M.B. 41: 15
1687 May 16	Roeloffsen, Margarett, and John fflintsburgh	L.W. 92
1702 Dec. 16	Roesdale, Elizabeth, and Charles Robinson	G.B.R. 1: 3
1705 Nov. 10	Roger, Thomas, and Mattee Lee	G.B.R. 2: 28
1702 Ap. 25	Rollitse, Mereyes, and Deyna Teunisse	G.B.R. 3:195
1698 May 25	Rolloquin, Jacobus, and Lydia Darkins	G.B.R. 3:193
1699 Aug. 9	Roof, Henry, and Margt Coulylie	G.B.R. 2:142
1704 Sep. 21	Roose, Altie, and Gerrett Provoost	G.B.R. 2: 27
1704 Sep. 21	Roose, Peter, and Hmtie. Courtie	G.B.R. 2: 27
1697 Dec. 29	Rosell, Rachell, and Thomas Robinson	G.B.R. 3:193
1703 Feb. 24	Rosevelt, Christine, and John Hamill	G.B.R. 1: 13
1699 Nov. 9	Rosevest, Janitje, and Johannus Vanderhuel	G.B.R. 3:193
1756 May 22	Ross, Charles, and Catharine Ryne	M.B. 41:134
1704 Ap. 21	Rowly, Mary, and George Booth	G.B.R. 2: 26
1753 Ap. 5	Roy, Catherin, and Daniel McFarlin	M.B. 41: 19
1756 Mar. 4	Ruffee, Anna, and Hendrick Nagle	M.B. 41: 93
1703 Nov. 25	Rumbout, Katharine, and Roger Brett	G.B.R. 2: 25
1698 Dec. 23	Rutherse, Anthony, and Hendrycke Vandewater	
		G.B.R. 3:193
1699 Sep. 12	Ruthse, Cathrine, and Johannus Hardenbergh	
		G.B.R. 3:193
1702 May 14	Rutsen, Margaret, and Wm. Notingham	G.B.R. 3:195
1756 May 3	Ryckman, Albert, and Catharine Brasier	M.B. 41:119
1756 May 22	Ryne, Catharine, and Charles Ross	M.B. 41:134
1703 July 26	Saatton, Michael, and Elizabeth Van Tright	G.B.R. 2: 25
1699 May 11	Sackett, Richard, and Majory L. Sleade	G.B.R. 3:193
1756 Mar. 2	Salter, Thomas, and Mary O'Neil	M.B. 41: 92
1693 Oct. 25	Samuell, Ariaentie, and Henryck Symonse	G.B.R. 2:142

1705 Sep.	3	Sanders, Amilia, and Johannes Pruyn	G.B.R.	2: 28
1691 Sep.	20	Sanders, Ann, and James Vanderspiegel	G.B.R.	4: 32
1698 Aug.	30	Sandford, Mary, and William Walton	G.B.R.	3:193
1701 May	9	Sandige, Dorothy, and John Kingston	G.B.R.	3:194
1704 Nov.	9	Sands, Samuel, and Elizabeth Lessitt	G.B.R.	2: 27
1697 Ap.	28	Sanford, Grace, and Barne Cosins	G.B.R.	3: 93
1702 Ap.	30	Santford, Elisbeth, and James Davis	G.B.R.	3:195
1700 Feb.	13	Santfordt, ————, and Jane White	G.B.R.	3:194
1752 Dec.	20	Sarly, Anthony, and Elizabeth Cornell	M.B.	41: 33
1753 Mar.	5	Satterly, Rene, and Abial Titus	M.B.	41: 63
1704 Sep.	7	Saunders, Barent, and Mary Wander	G.B.R.	2: 26
1705 Mar.	20	Saunders, Eleanor, and Richard Ray	G.B.R.	2: 27
1701 Sep.	15	Saunders, Hanah, and John Buttler	G.B.R.	3:194
1704 Sep.	7	Saunders, Leana, and John Lansen	G.B.R.	2: 26
1756 May	6	Schanck, Margaret, and Gilliam Cornel	M.B.	41:120
1705 Aug.	20	Schayck, Margrieta V. and Bernardus Freeman		
			G.B.R.	2: 28
1752 Nov.	30	Schenck, Cornelia, and Jacob Duryee	M.B.	41: 3
1703 Nov.	27	Schenck, Martin, and Cornelia Van Weeselew	G.B.R.	2: 25
1705 Ap.	19	Schenk, Margareta, and Peter Strycker	G.B.R.	2: 27
1703 Aug.	31	Schepmodt, Derrick, and Grittie Tappen	G.B.R.	2: 25
1758 June	10	Schermerhoorn, Lucas, and Wyntie Fitzcharles	M.B.	41:150
1760 Feb.	25	Schmidt, Jacob, and Mary Mitchell	M.B.	3: 48
1758 July	10	Schoonmaker, Annake, and Abraham Post	M.B.	41:179
1702 Dec.	12	Schuyler, Arent, and Swantie Dyckhuyse	G.B.R.	1: 3
1700 May		Schuyler, Cathalina, and Jacobus Schuyler	G.B.R.	3:194
1700 May		Schuyler, Jacobus, and Cathalina Schuyler	G.B.R.	3:194
1696 July	26	Schuyler, Margaret, and Robt. Livingston, Junr.		
			G.B.R.	3: 94
1704 Nov.	7	Schuyler, Margerett, and Charles Oliver	G.B.R.	2: 27
1693 Oct.	23	Schuyler, Meyndert, and Rachel Cuyler	G.B.R.	2:142
1691 Oct.	1	Schuyler, Maj. Peter, and Maria Van Ranselaer		
			G.B.R.	4: 31
1703 Sep.	14	Schyler, Gerard, and Aegie De Groot	G.B.R.	2: 25
1780 May	13	Seloover, Getty, and John Colls	M.B.	29: 54
1763 Mar.	16	Seloover, James, and Catherine Alstine	M.B.	7:100
1696 Aug.	1	Selsby, John, and Sarah Thompson	G.B.R.	3: 93
1758 June	22	Sennett, Christopher, and Huner Maloney	M.B.	41:166
1756 Jan.	10	Serle, John, and Martha Smith	M.B.	41: 73
1687 May	31	Seward, Humphry, and Sophia Dewitt	L. W.	92
1698 Sep.	5	Sexton, Judith, and Joshua Burle	G.B.R.	3:193
1758 Aug.	18	Shadwick, Deborah, and Richard Norwood	M.B.	41:218
1705 Nov.	12	Sharroke, Thomas, and Margaret Poste	G.B.R.	2: 28
1701 Ap.	5	Shaw, Priscilla, and John Stevens	G.B.R.	3:194
1692 Ap.	20	Shaw, Thomas, and Anna Hancock	G.B.R.	4: 32
1701 Oct.	3	Shelston, Prudence, and William Dorton	G.B.R.	2:142

1703 Ap. 10	Shepard, John, and Ruth Davis	G.B.R.	1: 13
1702 Nov. 27	Shrieve, Sarah, and John Heerman	G.B.R.	1: 3
1702 Nov. 28	Shukey, Frances, and John Auboyneau	G.B.R.	1: 3
1702 Ap. 25	Sidman, Mary, and Moses Langstaffe	G.B.R.	3:195
1752-56	Simeson, Cornelous, and Elizabeth Depue	C.M.	82: 62
1781 Oct. 3	Simmons, Jane, and John Weeks	M.B.	33: 83
1706 Mar. 5	Simmons, Solomon, and Mary Mott	G.B.R.	2: 28
1694 Nov. 2	Simms, Lancaster, and Katharine Larkin	G.B.R.	3: 92
1758 July 22	Simonsen, Margaret, and Jacob Bufflere	M.B.	41:191
1769 May 19	Simonson, Charity, and Abraham Martino	M.B.	14:103
1759 Ap. 19	Simorson, Altje, and Harmanus Garretson	M.B.	2:247
1676 July 27	Simpson, Elizabeth Wattells, and Jeremiah Reder		
		W.O.P.	3:203
1698 Feb. 7	Singleton, Jane, and Joseph Latham	G.B.R.	3:193
1703 Feb. 28	Sinhorn, Martha, and Roger Mompesson	G.B.R.	2: 28
1758 Aug. 9	Sise, Hannah, and William Hancock	M.B.	41:208
1700 Feb. 14	Skelding, Tho. and Rebecca Astin	G.B.R.	3:194
1691 Oct. 30	Skelton, Robert, and Alse Throgmorton	G.B.R.	4: 31
1756 Ap. 27	Skinner, Isaac, and Hannah Allen	M.B.	41:116
1694 Dec. 26	Slade, Peter, and Margery Wislake	G.B.R.	3: 92
1699 May 11	Sleade, Majory L. and Richard Sackett	G.B.R.	3:193
1687-88 Jan.17	Slegge, Christopher, and Elizabeth Small	L.W.	103
1758 Aug. 30	Sleght, Johannes, and Gerritje Van Bunschooten		
		M.B.	41:233
1693 June27	Sleigh, Charles, and Sarah Purrington	G.B.R.	2:142
1693 Dec. 19	Sloot, Heiltie, and Zebulon Carter	G.B.R.	3: 91
1758 June13	Slover, Isaac, and Maria Johnson	M.B.	41:154
1687-88 Jan.17	Small, Elizabeth, and Christopher Slegge	L.W.	103
1756 Ap. 7	Smith, Ann, and Benjamin Hait	M.B.	41:106
1698 July 11	Smith, Ann, and Robert Everinden	G.B.R.	3:193
1752 Dec. 13	Smith, Anne, and John Burnet	M.B.	41: 24
1698 Oct. 25	Smith, Barnardus, and Elsey Meyers	G.B.R.	3:193
1704 June30	Smith, Bernardus, and Johanne Hading	G.B.R.	2: 27
1703 Nov. 22	Smith, Charles, and Aleda Hunirk	G.B.R.	2: 25
1701 Oct. 25	Smith, Deborah, and Thomas Cockling	G.B.R.	2:142
1752-56	Smith, Ebel, and Peter Grudine	C.M.	82: 62
1759 Nov. 15	Smith, Edward, and Mary Honeyman	M.B.	2:495
1703 May 6	Smith, Elizabeth, and Epenetus Platte	G.B.R.	1: 13
1697 Nov. 15	Smith, Else, and William Willkission	G.B.R.	3:192
1756 Mar. 19	Smith, Gilbert, and Abigail Vandewater	M.B.	41: 97
1701 June24	Smith, Hanah, and John Thompson	G.B.R.	3:194
1696 Ap. 13	Smith, Mrs Hannah, and Andrew Gibb	G.B.R.	3: 93
1756 Ap. 5	Smith, Henry, and Margery Whiley	M.B.	41:103
1758 June24	Smith, Jemima, and Stephen Wood	M.B.	41:167
1697 Sep. 17	Smith, John, and Hannah Phips	G.B.R.	3:192
1704 Mar. 14	Smith, Johnathan, and Elizabeth Platt	G.B.R.	2: 26

1695 July 8	Smith, Joseph, and Margt Barents	G.B.R. 3: 92
1697 Aug. 14	Smith, Margaret, and Thomas Parmiter	G.B.R. 3:192
1756 Jan. 10	Smith, Martha, and John Serle	M.B. 41: 73
1692 July 8	Smith, Mary, and Joseph Blydenburgh	G.B.R. 4: 32
1753 Feb. 20	Smith, Samuel, and Elizabeth Mott	M.B. 41: 62
1702 Dec. 22	Smith, William, and Susanna Monvielle	G.B.R. 1: 3
1701 Nov. 10	Snedeker, Janeke, and Suert Olpherts	G.B.R. 3:194
1758 Sep. 1	Snedeker, Richard, and Elizabeth Van Bummill	M.B. 41:239
1759 Nov. 3	Sneden, Abraham, and Rachael Swartout	M.B. 2:488
1758 Aug. 24	Somendyck, Isaac, and Anne Bush	M.B. 41:229
1758 July 17	Somerindike, Abigail, and Samuel Wall	M.B. 41:188
1694 July 9	Souward, Mary, and Edmond Thomas	G.B.R. 3: 92
1704 Nov. 14	Sparks, Elizabeth, and John Trevitt	G.B.R. 2: 27
1758 June 21	Speir, Gertruyd, and John Poulison	M.B. 41:163
1695 May 28	Spencer, James, and Mary Carly	G.B.R. 3: 92
1701 July 3	Splinter, Lyntie, and Andrew Ten Brooke	G.B.R. 3:194
1752-56	Spragg, Sary, and Cornelous Cortelyou	C.M. 82: 62
1704 Oct. 18	Springsteen, Geertrey, and William Miller	G.B.R. 2: 27
1695 July 24	Springsten, Caspar, and Jannetie Jacobs	G.B.R. 3: 92
1753 Feb. 24	Sprong, Catharin, and Andrew Mannell	M.B. 41: 61
1706 Jan. 31	Staats, Agenietie, and Abraham Messelaer	G.B.R. 2: 28
1701 Oct. 12	Staats, Barent, and Nieltje Gerrets	G.B.R. 2:142
1704 June 22	Staats, Sarah, and Isaac Gouverneur	G.B.R. 2: 26
1692 May 14	Stale, Katharine, and Anthony Pintard	G.B.R. 4: 32
1703 July 19	Stephance, Lucas, and Catherine Van Dyke	G.B.R. 2: 25
1699 Aug. 18	Steuard, Alexander, and Cornelia Depheyster	G.B.R. 2.142
1701 Ap. 7	Stevens, John, and Priscilla Shaw	G.B.R. 3:194
1695 Sep. 30	Stevens, Mary, and Jesse Kipp	G.B.R. 3: 92
1700 Feb. 14	Stevens, Susanna, and Robert Nesbett	G.B.R. 3:194
1705 Dec. 24	Stevense, Allite, and Harmanus Brughman	G.B.R. 2: 28
1705 Jan. 13	Stevenson, Charity, and Tho. Willett	G.B.R. 2: 27
1753 Feb. 19	Stevenson, Daniel, and Hannah Pell	M.B. 41: 59
1756 Ap. 23	Stevenson, Edward, and Rebecca Griffin	M.B. 41:113
1693 June 26	Stevenson, Elizth, and George Anderson	G.B.R. 2:142
1752 Dec. 1	Stevenson, Elizabeth, and James Stewart	M.B. 41: 7
1696 Ap. 6	Stevenson, Janetie, and John Lawrence	G.B.R. 3: 93
1752 Dec. 1	Stewart, James, and Elizabeth Stevenson	M.B. 41: 7
1703 Aug. 7	Stewart, John, and Rebecca Adams	G.B.R. 2: 25
1770 Dec. 19	Steymets, Christopher, and Rachel Roome	M.B. 16:301
1763 Oct. 22	Steymetz, Abraham, and Synthia Van Orden	M.B. 7:400
758 Aug. 29	Stillwell, Cath. and Charles Hamilton	M.B. 41:231
98 Dec. 23	Stillwell, Mary, and Thomas Walton	G.B.R. 3:193
1704 Feb. 10	Stillwell, Mary, and Valentine Dushen	G.B.R. 2: 26
1703 Dec. 6	Stillwell, Nicholas, and Elizabeth Cornell	G.B.R. 2: 26
1703 Ap. 9	Stillwell, Thomas, and Ellis Throgmorton	G.B.R. 1: 13
1705 Sep. 3	Stilwell, Richd. and Debora Cowne	G.B.R. 2: 28

1696	June 29	Stilwell, Sarah, and Richard Crego	G.B.R. 3: 93
1755	Aug. 26	Stimes, Jasper, and Susannah Brower	M.B. 1:156
1695	July 8	Stollard, Giles, and Elizabeth Tuder	G.B.R. 3: 92
1704	Dec. 8	Stone, Mydar, and Angletie Moll	G.B.R. 2: 27
1758	July 11	Storm, Peter, and Catalintie Van Dyke	M.B. 41:182
1758	June 19	Stout, Abigail, and John Agnew	M.B. 41:161
1756	June 11	Stoutenburg, Annatie, and Jacobus Van Vleck	M.B. 41:142
1704	Aug. 7	Stoutenburgh, Catherine, and Nicholas Vanderspeigel	
			G.B.R. 2: 26
1695	Oct. 28	Strangnish, Katrine, and John Hutton	G.B.R. 3: 92
1704	July 20	Strateham, Thomas, and Altie Finn	G.B.R. 2: 26
1705	Nov. 23	Stratton, Martha, and John Adams	G.B.R. 2: 28
1699	Aug. 18	Streard, Alexander, and Cornelia Dishington	G.B.R. 3:193
1758	Aug. 1	Streit, Godfreyd, and Hannah Bown	M.B. 41:198
1756	Mar. 11	Strickland, Mary, and Isaac Bogert	M.B. 41: 94
1752	Dec. 15	Striker, Proebe, and John Cargill	M.B. 41: 27
1753	Jan. 23	Stringham, Mary, and Jeremiah Burrows	M.B. 41: 49
1702	Nov. 19	Struddle, Elizabeth, and Abram Van Laer	G.B.R. 1: 3
1705	Ap. 19	Strycker, Peter, and Margareta Schenk	G.B.R. 2: 27
1703	Mar. 17	Stuart, Alexander, and Catharine Rivilie	G.B.R. 1: 13
1702	Mar. 23	Studd, Thomas, and Catherine Pearsall	G.B.R. 3:194
1705	June 11	Stuyvesant, Anne, and Tho. Pritchard	G.B.R. 2: 27
1698	Nov. 4	Stuyvesant, Elizabeth, and George Sydenham	G.B.R. 3:193
1703	May 22	Suert, Ogrhert, and Hellegond Luyckas	G.B.R. 1: 13
1756	May 22	Sulvane, John, and Mary King	M.B. 41:133
1703	May 2	Sunsorke, John, and Eve Hulgrave	G.B.R. 1: 13
1703	Sep. 3	Swanenburgh, Hannafan, and John Johnson	G.B.R. 2: 2
1696	July 8	Swann, Helena, and Daniel Dunscomb	G.B.R. 3: 93
1758	June 30	Swart, Dirick, and Annatie Vandesee	M.B. 41:172
1756	Jan. 28	Sweeny, Lawrence, and Martha McDowal	M.B. 41: 62
1704	Nov. 8	Sweroer, Andrew, and Elizabeth DeVore	G.B.R. 2: 27
1698	Nov. 4	Sydenham, George, and Elizabeth Stuyvesant	G.B.R. 3:193
1693	Oct. 25	Symonse, Henryck, and Ariaentie Samuell	G.B.R. 2:142
1703	Aug. 31	Tappen, Grittie, and Derrick Schepmodt	G.B.R. 2: 25
1694	Jan. 6	Tasher, John, and Mrs. Anna Lightfoott	G.B.R. 4: 31
1695	Nov. 16	Tayler, Mary, and Thomas Burroughs	G.B.R. 3: 93
1697	Sep. 24	Tayler, Walter, and Deliverance Graves	G.B.R. 3:192
1752	Dec. 4	Taylor, William, and Wyenefried Mapack	M.B. 41: 8
1706	Jan. 19	Teller, William, and Maria Van Pricht	G.B.R. 2: 28
1699	Aug. 4	Ten Broeck, Effey, and Lodwyck Vander Burgh	
			G.B.R. 2:142
1701	Nov. 3	Ten Broek, Christina, and Johanes Van Allen	G.B.R. 3:194
1696	June 9	Ten Broeke, Cornelia, and Johannus Wynkoop	
			G.B.R. 3: 93
1756	June 10	Ten Brook, Jeremiah, and Maritie Van Alen	M.B. 41:141

1701 July 3	Ten Brooke, Andrew, and Lyntie Splinter	G.B.R. 3:194
1704 June 23	Teneve, Stephen, and Neltie Folleman	G.B.R. 2: 26
1704 Mar. 3	Tennike, Hendrika, and Johannes Van Orde	G.B.R. 2: 26
1701 Feb. 21	Tenyck, Jacob, and Nulie Hardenburgh	G.B.R. 3:194
1758 July 6	Terry, Catharine, and Niel Wilkinson	M.B. 41:174
1702 Ap. 25	Teunisse, Deyna, and Mereyes Rollitse	G.B.R. 3:195
1700 May	Thavet, Peter, and Susannah Vergereau	G.B.R. 3:194
1705 July 19	Theobalds, John, and Euson Tuder	G.B.R. 2: 27
1703 June 18	Thibowe, William, and Mary Du Tay	G.B.R. 2: 25
1694 July 9	Thomas, Edmond, and Mary Souward	G.B.R. 3: 92
1753 Mar. 10	Thomas, John Junr. and Bathseba Palmer	M.B. 41: 22
1701 June 24	Thompson, John, and Hanah Smith	G.B.R. 3:194
1696 Aug. 1	Thompson, Sarah, and John Selsby	G.B.R. 3: 93
1704 Oct. 16	Thong, Walter, and Sarah Van Dam	G.B.R. 2: 27
1705 Ap. 11	Thorn, Samuel, Junr. and Hannah Doughty	G.B.R. 2: 27
1696 Oct. 14	Thorne, Elizabeth, and Rigebell Mott	G.B.R. 3: 93
1699 Aug. 29	Thorne, Richard, and Phebe Denton	G.B.R. 2:142
1701 Ap. 7	Thorne, Sarah, and Roger Pedley	G.B.R. 3:194
1694 Jan.	Thornson, Sarah, and Edward Coats	G.B.R. 3: 91
1705 June 9	Thoxter, Mary, and Thomas Dawson	G.B.R. 2: 27
1697 Dec. 8	Throgmartin, Sarah, and Moses Lipet	G.B.R. 3:192
1691 Oct. 30	Throgmorton, Alse, and Robert Skelton	G.B.R. 4: 31
1703 Ap. 9	Throgmorton, Ellis, and Thomas Stillwell	G.B.R. 1: 13
1703 July 6	Throgmorton, Patience, and Hugh Corvard	G.B.R. 2: 25
1752 Dec. 22	Thurman, Francis, and Susannah Mathews	M.B. 41: 34
1702 Oct. 26	Thurman, Ralph, and Mary Clouder	G.B.R. 1: 3
1706 Jan. 16	Tier, Jannitie, and Johannes Hoogland	G.B.R. 2: 28
1700 Feb. 14	Tiller, Andrew, and Ann Verplanck	G.B.R. 3:194
1694 Oct. 11	Tiller, Helena, and Philip Wilkison	G.B.R. 3: 92
1705 Jan. 12	Tillett, James, and Sarah Lawrence	G.B.R. 2: 27
1704 Ap. 20	Timber, Cornelius, and Cornelia Myer	G.B.R. 2: 26
1701 Aug. 7	Timmer, Jane, and Thomas Evans	G.B.R. 3:194
1698 July 5	Tindell, Margaret, and John Hopper	G.B.R. 3:193
1753 Mar. 5	Titus, Abial, and Rene Satterly	M.B. 41: 63
1699 Dec. 20	Titus, Theunis, and Mary Barre	G.B.R. 3:193
1758 Aug. 12	Tomkins, Joseph, and Mary Hyatt	M.B. 41:210
1706 Feb. 1	Townsend, John, and Rose Cole	G.B.R. 2: 28
1705 Mar. 8	Toy, Daniel, and Frances Wessels	G.B.R. 2: 27
1756 Feb. 2	Tredwell, Charity, and John Jackson	M.B. 41: 84
1696 Aug. 12	Tregenny, Humphrey, and ——— Brookesbanck	G.B.R. 3: 94
1704 Nov. 14	Trevitt, John, and Elizabeth Sparks	G.B.R. 2: 27
1704 Nov. 15	Troup, John, and Elizabeth Tunnwell	G.B.R. 2: 27
1758 Aug. 8	Tucker, Daniel, and Elizabeth Platt	M.B. 41:207
1695 July 8	Tuder, Elizabeth, and Giles Stollard	G.B.R. 3: 92
1705 July 19	Tuder, Euson, and John Theobalds	G.B.R. 2: 27
1696 Nov. 27	Tuder, Frances, and John Righton	G.B.R. 3: 93

1695 Ap. 20	Tuder, John, and Affie Van Hoorn	G.B.R.	3: 92
1697 Sep. 9	Tuder, Capt. John, and Mary Brett	G.B.R.	3:192
1704 Nov. 15	Tunnwell, Elizabeth, and John Troup	G.B.R.	2: 27
1752 Nov. 30	Turner, Ann, and Silvanus Dillingham	M.B.	41: 2
1758 Aug. 14	Turner, Elizabeth, and George Davis	M.B.	41:212
1701 May 24	Turner, Elizabeth, and Robert Dale	G.B.R.	3:194
1758 June 19	Turner, William, and Margaret Weeton	M.B.	41:160

1695 Oct. 11	Underhill, Sarah, and Joseph Budd	G.B.R.	3: 92
1758 Aug. 14	Underwood, Joanna, and William Cline	M.B.	41:213
1705 Mar. 20	Upton, Beetie, and James Jamison	G.B.R.	2: 27
1697 Oct. 9	Uthuse, Margaret Symonse, and Jan Dehance	G.B.R.	3:192

1752 Dec. 1	Vader, Catharin, and David Groesbeck, Junr.	M.B.	41: 6
1753 Jan. 31	Valentine, Charity, and Daniel Cornell	M.B.	41: 53
1692 Nov. 19	Vallou, Stephen, and Mary Gallais	G.B.R.	2:141
1756 June 10	Van Alen, Maritie, and Jeremiah Ten Brook	M.B.	41:141
1701 Nov. 3	Van Allen, Johanes, and Christina Ten Broek	G.B.R.	3:194
1704 Jan. 7	Van Aps, Anna, and Conradus Gettike	G.B.R.	2: 26
1756 Feb. 5	Van Arman, Johannes, and Alida Vanderheyden	M.B.	41: 86
1761 Nov. 19	Vanausdalla, Lambertie, and Cornelius Amerman	M.B.	5:233
1697 Dec. 13	Van Baal, Margaret, and Capt. Nicholas Evorste	G.B.R.	3:192
1704 May 4	Van Boursen, Femmetie, and John Milldrum	G.B.R.	2: 26
1706 Jan. 15	Van Brackeling, Stephen, and Dina Bley	G.B.R.	2: 28
1696 July 6	van Brugen, Johannes, and Margaret Provoost	G.B.R.	3: 93
1696 July 20	van Brughen, Mary, and Stephen Richard	G.B.R.	3: 93
1758 Sep. 1	Van Bummill, Elizabeth, and Richard Snedeker	M.B.	41:239
1758 Aug. 30	Van Bunschooten, Gerritje, and Johannes Sleght	M.B.	41:233
1695 July 1	van Bursum, Margt, and Cornelius Low	G.B.R.	3: 92
1695 Nov. 8	van Bursum, Mary Anne, and Lewis Bougeaud	G.B.R.	3: 93
1693 Feb. 20	Van Clyff, Cornelia, and Benjamin Norwood	G.B.R.	2:142
1696 Aug. 1	Van Clyff, Elizabeth, and John Bentie	G.B.R.	3: 93
1694 Ap. 16	Van Clyff, Kath'e, and John Loring	G.B.R.	3: 91
1704 Oct. 4	Van Clyff, Margarett, and Peter Burtell	G.B.R.	2: 27
1701 Oct. 8	Van Cortlandt, Maria, and Kiliaen Van Renselaer	G.B.R.	2:142
1691 May 7	Van Courtland, Jacobus, and Evah Phillips	G.B.R.	4: 31
1702 Aug. 27	Van Dalsen, Margarett, and Martinus Cregier	G.B.R.	3:195
1756 Ap. 12	Van Dalssen, Dennis, and Rachel Cuyper	M.B.	41:108
1704 Oct. 16	Van Dam, Sarah, and Walter Thong	G.B.R.	2: 27
1773 June 8	Van Dar Vort, Jacob, and Margaret Bennet	M.B.	20:141

1758 Sep. 1	Vandenbergh, Altie, and Wines Manney	M.B. 41:238	
1758 July 12	Vandenbergh, Antje, and Abraham Wimple	M.B. 41:183	
1705 Ap. 11	Vandenbergh, Else, and Thomas Rainford	G.B.R. 2: 27	
1694 Oct. 11	Vandenbergh, Hend'k Jansen, and Mary Ann Burton		
		G.B.R. 3: 92	
1758 Aug. 30	Vandenbergh, Maretje, and Wynant V. Vandenbergh		
		M.B. 41:234	
1758 Aug. 30	Vandenbergh, Wynant V. and Maretje Vandenbergh		
		M.B. 41:234	
1756 Feb. 5	Vandenheyden, Alida, and Johannes Van Arman		
		M.B. 41: 86	
1702 Oct. 20	Vanderbeeck, Conradus, and Catherine Cock	G.B.R. 1: 3	
1752-56	Vanderbilt, Phebe, and Cristifer Garrison	C.M. 82: 62	
1699 Sep. 29	Vander Burgh, Cornelia, and John White	G.B.R. 2:142	
1699 Aug. 4	Vander Burgh, Lodwyck, and Effey Ten Broeck		
		G.B.R. 2:142	
1700 Ap. 18	Vander Heule, Hendrickes, and Marytie Meyers		
		G.B.R. 3:194	
1695 Jan. 31	van der Heyden, Antie, and Paul Miller	G.B.R. 3: 92	
1758 Aug. 5	Vanderheyden, Johannes, and Mary Butler	M.B. 41:205	
1697 Jan. 9	Vanderheyden, Johannes, and Mary Wooden	G.B.R. 3:192	
1758 July 10	Vanderheyder, Derick, and Sarah Wendell	M.B. 41:177	
1699 Nov. 9	Vanderhuel, Johannus, and Janitje Rosevest	G.B.R. 3:193	
1697 Oct. 20	Vanderhule, ffemmie, and Benjamin Wyncoop	G.B.R. 3:192	
1701 June 21	Vanderpolle, Katherine, and Peter Hardenbrugh		
		G.B.R. 3:194	
1697 Feb. 11	Vanderpool, Gerrijt, and Deborah Warm	G.B.R. 3: 93	
1703 Jan. 28	Van derrere [Van Dervere], Dominius, and Maria		
	Margaretta Van Orteck	G.B.R. 1: 13	
1704 Aug. 7	Vanderspeigel, Nicholas, and Catherine Stoutenburgh		
		G.B.R. 2: 26	
1691 Sep. 20	Vanderspiegel, James, and Ann Sanders	G.B.R. 4: 32	
1758 June 30	Vandersee, Annatie, and Dirick Swart	M.B. 41:172	
1756 Mar. 22	Van der Voort, Sarah, and Jan Lodewick Dunkel		
		M.B. 41: 98	
1701 July 23	Vande Spegel, Agenitie, and John Cauley	G.B.R. 3:194	
1756 Mar. 19	Vandewater, Abigail, and Gilbert Smith	M.B. 41: 97	
1698 Dec. 23	Vandewater, Hendrycke, and Anthony Rutherse		
		G.B.R. 3:193	
1702 Ap. 22	Van Deycke, Emeltie, and Petrus Kip	G.B.R. 3:194	
1752-56	Vandick, Kias, and Ann Andrewnat	C.M. 82: 62	
1753 Mar. 27	Van Duersen, Catherina, and Isaac Goes	M.B. 41: 14	
1752 Dec. 16	Vanduerson, Heyla, and John Wright	M.B. 41: 30	
1752 Dec. 22	Van Duyn, Mocletia, and William Brower	M.B. 41: 35	
1703 Sep. 14	Van Dycke, Eunnetie, and Albert de Vrees	G.B.R. 2: 25	
1758 July 11	Van Dyke, Catalintje, and Peter Storm	M.B. 41:182	

1694 June 22	Van Strydt, John, and Johanna Lewis	G.B.R.	3: 92
1694 Nov. 23	Van Teuyl, Eliz'th, and William Pell	G.B.R.	3: 92
1703 July 26	Van Tright, Elizabeth, and Michael Saatton	G.B.R.	2: 25
1760 Nov. 26	Van Valkenburgh, Catherine, and David Van Schaick		
		M.B.	3:446
1753 Jan. 31	Van Vecten, Annatye, and Peter de Wandeler		
		M.B. 41:	54
1758 July 29	Van Vey, Mary, and Aron Devoe	M.B. 41:195	
1756 June 11	Van Vleck, Jacobus, and Annatie Stoutenburgh		
		M.B. 41:142	
1697 Jan. 26	Van Vlecq, Kathalina, and Abraham Kip	G.B.R.	3: 93
1696 June 8	van Vlecque, Magdalen, and Henricus Kip	G.B.R.	3: 94
1703 Nov. 27	Van Weeselew, Cornelia, and Martin Schenck	G.B.R.	2: 25
1704 June 23	Van Winkel, Albert, and Meritie Deerby	G.B.R.	2: 26
1753 Mar. 26	Van Woort, Jacob, and Rachael Gardiner	M.B. 41:	13
1753 Mar. 12	Van Wyck, Thomas, and Rachel Eldert	M.B. 41:	65
1752 Dec. 30	Van Zandt, Tobias, and Mary Dike	M.B. 41:	36
1701 May 10	Varick, Johanna, and Albert Willet	G.B.R.	3:194
1687 June 24	Vaughton, Michaell, and Susannah Leislaer	L.W.	99
1704 Mar. 7	Vaughton, Susannah, and Leonard Huygen De Kleyn		
		G.B.R.	2: 26
1782 May 17	Veaber, William, and Catharine Hieth	M.B. 36:	5
1700 Ap. 27	Veet, John, and Katharine Meyers	G.B.R.	3:194
1700 May	Vergereau, Susannah, and Peter Thavet	G.B.R.	3:194
1756 Ap. 2	Vermilya, Isaac, and Susannah Myer	M.B. 41:102	
1700 Feb. 14	Verplanck, Ann, and Andrew Tiller	G.B.R.	3:194
1701 Oct. 27	Verplank, Margaret, and John Collins	G.B.R.	3:194
1702 Mar. 23	Verwyde, Elizabeth, and Joseph Prosser	G.B.R.	3:194
1698 Mar. 1	Vesey, William, and Mary Reade	G.B.R.	3:193
1693 Ap. 10	Vielle, Cornelius, and Catharine Bogardus	G.B.R.	2:142
1700 Feb. 14	Vincent, Francis, and Ann Lynch	G.B.R.	3:194
1704 May 10	Vincent, Joan, and Frederick Fine	G.B.R.	2: 26
1700 Ap. 27	Vincent, Mary, and John Gindett	G.B.R.	3:194
1705 Oct. 6	Vorckinson, Mary, and Thomas Ming	G.B.R.	2: 28
1756 June 4	Vredenburgh, Catharine, and Robert Hall	M.B. 41:138	
1701 June 6	Vreland, Johanes, and Mareya Cregers	G.B.R.	3:194
1703 May 12	Vrikers, Johanna, and Edward Blagge	G.B.R.	1: 13
1704 Mar. 4	Vrille, Arnold, and Elizabeth Vanfford	G.B.R.	2: 26
1696 Feb. 17	Vyland, David, and Elizth Henry	G.B.R.	3: 93
1705 July 19	**Walcraf, David, and Elizabeth Field**	G.B.R.	2: 27
1704 Oct. 27	Waldron, John, and Cornelia Hardenbrook	G.B.R.	2: 27
1699 Dec. 16	Waldron, Judith, and Isaah Lelonor	G.B.R.	3:193
1706 Ap. 12	Walker, Thomas, and Elizabeth Redott	G.B.R.	2: 28
1693 Sep. 4	Walkington, Mary, and Roger Baker	G.B.R.	2:142
1758 July 17	Wall, Samuel, and Abigail Somerindike	M.B. 41:188	

1758 June 13	Wallace, William, and Sarah Hall	M.B. 41:155
1757 Dec. 30	Walsh, Peter, and Mary Bennet	M.B. 1:761
1698 Dec. 23	Walton, Thomas, and Mary Stillwell	G.B.R. 3:193
1698 Aug. 30	Walton, William, and Mary Sandford	G.B.R. 3:193
1702 May 14	Wandall, Abram, and Catherine De Key	G.B.R. 3:195
1704 Sep. 7	Wander, Mary, and Barent Saunders	G.B.R. 2: 26
1753 Jan. 31	Wanderler, Peter de, and Annatje Van Vecten	M.B. 41: 54
1697 Oct. 29	Ward, Israel, and Hannah Hutson	G.B.R. 3:192
1692 Oct. 3	Ware, Jacob, and Elizabeth Osburne	G.B.R. 4: 32
1697 Feb. 11	Warm, Deborah, and Gerrijt Vanderpool	G.B.R. 3: 93
1705 May 15	Warne, Francis, and Sarah Hays	G.B.R. 2: 27
1755 Dec. 31	Warner, Mary, and James Pudney	M.B. 41: 67
1705 Dec. 19	Warner, William, and Anne De Gray	G.B.R. 2: 28
1705 June 26	Warren, William, and Margariet Oyan	G.B.R. 2: 27
1691 Oct. 30	Washbourne, Sarah, and Isaac Arnold	G.B.R. 4: 31
1704 Oct. 14	Washurne, John, and Hannah Hallett	G.B.R. 2: 27
1753 Jan. 3	Waters, Talman, and Mary Lawrence	M.B. 41: 25
1703 Aug. 28	Watkay, Alexander, and Mary Bresty	G.B.R. 2: 25
1699 Ap. 17	Watson, Ann, and Thomas Drincall	G.B.R. 3:193
1756 Mar. 18	Watson, Mary, and William McKim	M.B. 41: 96
1756 May 19	Watson, Samuel, and Christian Pollort	M.B. 41:129
1705 Dec. 28	Watts, Robert, and Mary Nichols	G.B.R. 2: 28
1698 Dec. 12	Way, Elizabeth, and William Osborn	G.B.R. 3:193
1756 Jan. 2	Webber, Cornelius, and Jane Willson	M.B. 41: 68
1696 Aug. 8	Weeks, Zachariah, and Katherine Meyer	G.B.R. 3: 93
1758 June 19	Weeton, Margt. and William Turner	M.B. 41:160
1758 June 10	Welch, Elenor, and Oliver Howlen	M.B. 41:151
1758 July 11	Welch, John, and Elizabeth Dean	M.B. 41:181
1764 Feb. 21	Wells, Jane, and James Richey	M.B. 8: 67
1698 Dec. 8	Wells, Jane, and John Hancock	G.B.R. 3:193
1758 July 10	Wendell, Sarah, and Derick Vanderheyder	M.B. 41:177
1705 Mar. 8	Wessels, Frances, and Daniel Toy	G.B.R. 2: 27
1694 Jan. 25	West, Mrs Ann, and Robert Wharton	G.B.R. 3: 91
1697 Nov. 17	West, William, and Mary Bingham	G.B.R. 3:192
1766 Sep. 29	Wetbeck, Peter, and Mary Van Alen	M.B. 10:110
1694 Jan. 25	Wharton, Robert, and Mrs Ann West	G.B.R. 3: 91
1758 Aug. 1	Wheeler, Isaac, and Eliz. Bears	M.B. 41:197
1696 Jan. 13	Wheeler, James, and Elizabeth Meek	G.B.R. 3: 93
1756 Ap. 5	Whiley, Margery, and Henry Smith	M.B. 41:103
1758 July 22	White, Caleb, and Mary Lynch	M.B. 41:192
1700 Feb. 13	White, Jane, and —— Santfordt	G.B.R. 3:194
1699 Sep. 29	White, John, and Cornelia Vander Burgh	G.B.R. 2:142
1694 Oct. 21	White, Mary, and John French	G.B.R. 3: 92
1696 July 23	Whitehead, Jonathan, and Sarah ffield	G.B.R. 3: 94
1703 Dec. 24	Whitehead, Thomas, and Jane Creed	G.B.R. 2: 26
1704 Ap. 5	Whitman, Nathan, and Anne Britton	G.B.R. 2: 26

1693 Ap. 28	Wicken, John, and Kathrine Fredricksen	G.B.R. 2: 14
1762 Ap. 30	Wickes, Thomas, and Sarah Brush	M.B. 6:137
1704 Feb. 1	Wickham, John, and Jerusia Miller	G.B.R. 2: 26
1760 Oct. 22	Wickoff, Nelly, and Peter Luyster	M.B. 3:379
1767 May 14	Wickoff, Nickles, and Ann Rapelyea	M.B. 11: 87
1753 Mar. 29	Wieks, Jonathan, and Ann Neitherway	M.B. 41: 17
1699 July 5	Wilde, Edey, and John Yeates	G.B.R. 3:193
1694 Ap. 7	Wilkins, Helena, and Benj. Cooper	G.B.R. 3: 91
1697 Sep. 16	Wilkinsen, Philip, and Mary Brazier	G.B.R. 3:192
1758 July 6	Wilkinson, Niel, and Catharine Terry	M.B. 41:174
1694 Oct. 11	Wilkison, Philip, and Helena Tiller	G.B.R. 3: 92
1761 Jan. 27	Will, Elizabeth, and Isaac Stoutenburgh	M.B. 4: 32
1692 Ap. 28	Willake, Edw'd, and Margery Cergoe	G.B.R. 4: 32
1695 Aug. 19	Willemke, ———, and George Harwood	G.B.R. 3: 92
1701 May 10	Willet, Albert, and Johanna Varick	G.B.R. 3:194
1694 May 9	Willet, Sarah, and Jacobus Dekey	G.B.R. 3: 92
1695 Aug. 24	Willet, Thomas, and Sarah Hinchman	G.B.R. 3: 92
1697 Dec. 22	Willett, Mary, and Richard Willett	G.B.R. 3:192
1703 Mar. 30	Willett, Richard, and Francis Deraval	G.B.R. 1: 13
1697 Dec. 22	Willett, Richard, and Mary Willett	G.B.R. 3:192
1705 Jun. 13	Willett, Tho. and Charity Stevenson	G.B.R. 2: 27
1686-87 Jan.20	Williams, Eleanor, and Nicolas de Morris	L.W. 86
1697 Dec. 30	Williams, George, and Kathrine Lloyd	G.B.R. 3:193
1753 Mar. 15	Williams, John, and Phoebe Heaviland	M.B. 41: 00
1758 June 27	Williams, Mary, and John Morey	M.B. 41:168
1704 Nov. 13	Williams, Mary, and Richard Greenfeild	G.B.R. 2: 27
1705 May 2	Williams, Robt. and Jonimah Bert	G.B.R. 2: 27
1701 Feb. 24	Williamson, Charles, and Mary Woolsey	G.B.R. 3:194
1702 Aug. 17	Williamson, Margarett, and Abram Emmons	G.B.R. 3:195
1701 Aug. 29	Willis, Arthur, and Joanna Carr	G.B.R. 2:142
1704 Mar. 29	Willis, Arthur, and Sarah Drakes	G.B.R. 2: 26
1697 Nov. 15	Willkission, William, and Else Smith	G.B.R. 3:192
1756 Feb. 27	Willsey, Mary, and Francis Jacocks	M.B. 41: 90
1756 Jan. 20	Willson, Abraham, and Ann Mann	M.B. 41: 76
1687 Sep. 17	Willson, Ebenezer, and Marjary Dudley	L.W. 101
1701 Oct. 8	Willson, Isabella, and George Maynard	G.B.R. 2:142
1756 Jan. 2	Willson, Jane, and Cornelius Webber	M.B. 41: 68
1756 May 2	Willson, John, and Catharine Bogardus	M.B. 41:135
1753 Mar. 20	Willson, John, and Mary Haight	M.B. 41: 11
1758 June 15	Wilse, Margaret, and Hendrick Michelsen	M.B. 41:157
1752 Dec. 16	Wilse, Ruth, and John Cooper	M.B. 41: 31
1758 Aug. 29	Wilsey, Susannah, and James Nevin	M.B. 41:232
1698 Ap. 27	Wilson, Richard, and Kathrine Pugsley	G.B.R. 3:193
1752 Nov. 30	Wilson, Robert, and Elizabeth Richard	M.B. 41: 1
1758 July 12	Wimple, Abraham, and Antje Vandenbergh	M.B. 41:183
1758 Jan. 3	Winant, Daniel, and Rachel Andrewuet	M.B. 1:766

1752-56	Winant, Rachel, and John Butteler	C.M. 82: 62
1775 Ap. 10	Winants, Jacob, and Mary Mersereau	M.B. 23: 5
1684 July 18	Windebank, Elizabeth, and James Graham	C.M. 34: 28
1758 July 20	Wingfield, John, and Elizabeth Innes	M.B. 41:190
1703 Nov. 1	Winne, Lydia, and Jacobus Mole	G.B.R. 2: 25
1694 Dec. 26	Wislake, Margery, and Peter Slade	G.B.R. 3: 92
1752 Dec. 14	Withers, Jane, and Archibald Johnson	M.B. 41: 26
1691 Ap. 9	Woertman, Dirck Janse, and Annetie Aukes	G.B.R. 4: 42
1752-56	Wolcan, Martha, and Richer Crips	C.M. 82: 62
1752-56	Wood, Jeams, and Eve Decer [Decker]	M.B. 82: 62
1758 June 24	Wood, Stephen, and Jemima Smith	M.B. 41:167
1697 Jan. 9	Wooden, Mary, and Johannes Vanderheyden	G.B.R. 3:192
1705 Oct. 13	Wooderop, Allice, and Thomas Pennistone	G.B.R. 2: 28
1703 Oct. 20	Woodett, Martha, and Abraham Hunderbeek	G.B.R. 2: 25
1691 Oct. 20	Woodrofe, Elizabeth, and Henry Jordanie	G.B.R. 4: 31
1704 Ap. 14	Wooley, Charles, and Hannah Noell	G.B.R. 2: 26
1701 Feb. 24	Woolsey, Mary, and Charles Williamson	G.B.R. 3:194
1705 Ap. 27	Woortman, Anne, and Isaac DeRiemer	G.B.R. 2: 27
1756 Feb. 2	Wortman, Dennis, and Jane Aymar	M.B. 41: 83
1758 Aug. 31	Wright, Elizabeth, and Jasper Allen	M.B. 41:236
1752 Dec. 16	Wright, John, and Heyla Vanduerson	M.B. 41: 30
1694 Jan. 1	Wright, Joseph, and Ann Henry	G.B.R. 3: 91
1696 Aug. 28	Wright, Thomas, and Lydia Cobbitt	G.B.R. 3: 93
1700 July 20	Wychangham, Tho. and Susanna Fine	G.B.R. 3:194
1756 May 10	Wyckoff, Cornelia, and Cornelius Rapalye	M.B. 41:124
1753 Mar. 17	Wyckoff, Nicholas, and Catrintia Leffertse	M.B. 41: 21
1697 Oct. 20	Wyncoop, Benjamin, and ffemmie Vanderhule	G.B.R. 3:192
1696 June 9	Wynkoop, Johannus, and Cornelia Ten Broeke	G.B.R. 3: 93
1694 Oct. 23	Yaresly, Richard, and Dorothy Gore	G.B.R. 3: 92
1699 July 5	Yeates, John, and Edey Wilde	G.B.R. 3:193
1752 Nov. 30	Yelverton, Andrew, and Sarah Marston	M.B. 41: 4
1756 Feb. 22	Yeomans, Ruth, and Samuel Mabbet	M.B. 41: 89
1753 Mar. 29	Young, Mary, and Peter Hoolwey, Junr.	M.B. 41: 16
1695 May 10	Young, Simon, and Ann Elum	G.B.R. 3: 92

NEW YORK
MARRIAGE LICENSES

By

Robert H. Kelby

NEW YORK
MARRIAGE LICENSES

ORIGINALS IN THE ARCHIVES OF THE NEW YORK
HISTORICAL SOCIETY

CONTRIBUTED BY
ROBERT H. KELBY

REPRINTED FROM
THE NEW YORK GENEALOGICAL AND BIOGRAPHICAL RECORD
BEGINNING JULY, 1915

NEW YORK MARRIAGE LICENSES.

CONTRIBUTED BY ROBERT H. KELBY, Librarian New York Historical Society.

In 1860 the State of New York published a volume containing a list of marriage licenses then on record in the office of the Secretary of State, Albany.

The licenses were issued under the seal of the Prerogative Court, and acted as a dispensation from the proclamation of banns, when it was inconvenient or impossible to comply with the general usage. The information given by the license, and unfortunately not printed in the volume published by the State, consisted of the town of residence and occupation of the parties to the marriage, and the prospective bride was designated as Spinster or Widow as the case might be.

In the fire at the Capitol, March 29, 1911, a number of the original manuscript volumes were saved, but all badly burned.

The following additions and corrections are from 432 original licenses, in the Archives of The New York Historical Society.

The pages mentioned in the additions and corrections refer to the volume published by the State.

ROBERT H. KELBY, LIBRARIAN.

PAGE

1   Ablin, John, N. Y., Mariner, and Charlotte Hall, N. Y., spinster, married July 27, 1775, by Rev. Samuel Auchmuty.

1   For Achyndaey, Alex^r., and Jane Flannagen, read Achyndachy, Alexander, carpenter, H. M. S. Loyalist, and Jane Flannegen, N. Y., widow.

2   1783, April 28, read April 21. Adam, William, N. Y., mariner, and Alley Devoor, N. Y., spinster.

2   Adams, Catherine, N. Y., spinster, and John Mitchell, N. Y.

3   Aget, Agnes, N. Y., spinster, and Thomas Smith, N. Y., joyner.

3   Aikens, John, N. Y., yeoman, and Mary Brooks, N. Y., spinster.

3   Airs, Joseph, N. Y., and Charity Whetten, N. Y., spinster.

4   Allen, Jane, N. Y., widow, and John Welsh, N. Y., mariner.

4 (insert)   1775, April 5, Allen, John, Phila., and Mary Johnston, N. Y., spinster, married April 6, 1775, by Rev. Samuel Auchmuty.

5   for Alloway, John, and Jane Ris, read Alloway, John, sergeant 17th regiment of dragoons, and Anne Rix, of the same regiment, spinster.

5 for Almer, Sarah, and Peter Baker, read Alner, Sarah, N.
   Y., spinster, and Peter Baker, Cow Neck, Queens Co.,
   shipwright.

5 Alsop, Elizabeth, late of Nottingham in Great Britain, but
   now of N. Y., spinster, and Richard Hawkins, Ensign
   27th regiment of foot.

6 Amory, John, N. Y., whipmaker, and Mary De Lamon-
   tagnie, N. Y., widow.

7 Anderson, Mary, N. Y., spinster, and John McDonald, (no
   place mentioned).

7 Anderson, William, N. Y., yoeman, and Elizabeth Mc-
   Bride, N. Y., spinster.

9 Applegate, Isabella, N. Y., spinster, and William Evans,
   N. Y., tailor.

9 Appleton, William, and Mary Huggins, spinster, both of
   35th regiment.

10 Armour, William, N. Y., mariner, and Susannah Richard-
   son, N. Y., widow.

10 Arno, Charles, N. Y., mariner, and Henrietta Woodword,
   N. Y., widow.

11 Ash, Sarah, N. Y., widow and Walter Birk, carpenter in
   His Majesty's Engineer Department.

11 for Askins, William and Elizabeth Campbell, read, Askins, William, N. Y., taylor, and Mary Campbell. The
   latter name is repeated in the license as Elizabeth Mary
   Campbell.

11 Atken, Isaac, N. Y., baker, and Effee Curtis of the Manor
   on Staten Island, widow.

11 Atkins, James, N. Y., mariner, and Catherine Kelsey,
   N. Y., spinster.

12 Babcock, David, N. Y., and Barbara Garlick, N. Y., spinster.

12 Baehr, Christian, N. Y., tailor, and Anna Bennet, N. Y.,
   widow.

12 (insert) 1774, Sept. 30, Bailey, William, Westchester Co.,
   N. Y., farmer, and Mary Barret, same place, spinster.

12 Bain, John, N. Y., vintner, and Mary McClean, N. Y.,
   widow.

13 Baker, Gardner, N. Y., cordwainer, and Mary Wrighton,
   N. Y., spinster.

13 Baker, Peter, Cow Neck, Queens Co., shipwright, and
   Sarah Alner, N. Y., spinster.

13 Baker, William, mariner, on board His Majesty's Ship of
   War Le Sybel, and Joanna Keys, N. Y., spinster.

14 Baldwin, John, Queens Co., carpenter, and Elisabeth
   Thompson, N. Y., spinster.

14 Bancker, Abraham, N. Y., cordwainer, and Abigail King,
   N. Y., spinster.

14 Bancker, Evert, Jr., N. Y., merchant, and Anne Taylor, N. Y., spinster.

15 for Barclay, Charlotte A., and Richard Bailey, read Barclay, Charlotte Amelia, N. Y., spinster, and Richard Bayley, N. Y., physician.

15 (insert) 1774, June 15, Barclay, Helena, N. Y., spinster, and Thomas Moncrieffe, Esq., N. Y.

16 Barham, Martha, N. Y., widow, and John Newsted, N. Y., yeoman.

16 Barker, Jane, N. Y., spinster, and John Rote, N. Y.

17 Barnes, Martha, N. Y., widow, and William Brown, N. Y.

17 Barnett, Joseph, clerk in the ordinance office of His Majesty's Navy Department, and Jane Bosworth, N. Y., spinster.

17 for Barnes, Mary, and Archibald Kerby read Barnes, Mary, N. Y., spinster, and Archibald Kerley, N. Y., merchant.

17 Barratt, John, mariner on board His Majesty's Ship the Lyon, and Hannah Collin, N. Y., widow.

18 (insert) 1774, Sept. 14, Barret, Mary, of Westchester County, spinster, and William Bailey, same place, farmer.

18 for Barry, James, and Mary Berry, read Berry, James, N. Y., shopkeeper, and Mary Berry, N. Y., widow.

18 (insert) 1778, Oct. 30. For Barter, Jane, read Barker, Jane, N. Y., spinster, and John Rote, N. Y.

18 for 1779, Jan. 19, read Jan. 13. Barton, John, N. Y., and Abby Smith, N. Y., spinster.

18 Barton, Elizabeth, N. Y., spinster, and Alexander Morrison, N. Y.

18 Barton, Sarah, N. Y., spinster, and John Rundell, carpenter in His Majesty's Navy.

18 for 1782, Feb. 22, read 1782, Feb. 23. Barton, Joseph, N. Y., gentleman, and Elizabeth Sarly, N. Y., widow.

18 (insert) 1783, Aug. 16. Barton, Joseph Hews, N. Y., mariner, and Anne Bingham, N. Y., spinster.

18 for Barton, Robert, and Ann McGrigor, read Barton, Robert, Quartermaster Sergt. of the 52nd Regiment, and Hanna McGrigor, same regiment, widow.

19 (insert) 1778, Oct. 5. Barwick, Sarah (also written Mary), N. Y., spinster, and Peter Lawrence, N. Y.

19 Basden, Robert, N. Y., and Aletta Shearman, N. Y., spinster.

19 (insert) 1774, Dec. 31. Bassett, James, N. Y., mariner, and Sarah Morrell, N. Y., spinster.

19 (insert) 1769, Jan. 21. Baster, John, N. Y., breeches maker, and Elizabeth Russh, N. Y., spinster.

20 Batten, Anne, N. Y., spinster, and John Webb, N. Y., blacksmith.

535

31   for 1778, May 17, read May 19. Blair, John, N. Y., and Mary Plowman, N. Y., spinster.

31   Blair, Samuel, N. Y., and Sarah Ellis, N. Y., spinster.

35   Bogart, Ann, N. Y., widow, and Forbes Newton, N. Y., tinman.

37 (insert) 1781, Mar. 22. Boileau, Lavina, N. Y., spinster, and John Stevens, N. Y., house carpenter.

38   Bosworth, Jane, N. Y., spinster, and Joseph Barnett, clerk in the Ordinance Office of His Majesty's Navy Department.

38   for Boulia, Lavina, and John Stevens, read Boileau, Lavina, N. Y., and John Stevens, N. Y., house carpenter.

39   Bowman, William, N. Y., and Mary Winn, N. Y., spinster.

39   Bowne, Samuel, N. Y., and Mary Stocker, N. Y., spinster.

40   Bradley, James, N. Y., auctioneer, and Catherine Farrell, N. Y., widow.

41   Brannon, Ann, N. Y., spinster, and Charles Dunn, N. Y.

41 (insert) 1782, Oct. 21. Brannon, John, Quartermaster on Board His Majesty's Ship the Lyon, and Sarah Walker N. Y., widow.

41   Branson, Elizabeth, N. Y., spinster, and Daniel Darby, N. Y., mariner.

42   Branson, Mary, N. Y., spinster, and Stephen Sands, N. Y., watchmaker.

42   Branson, Ware, N. Y., cabinetmaker, and Nancy Palmer, Westchester County, spinster.

42   for Brasher, Hannah, and John Dalton, read Brasher, Hannah, N. Y., and John Dalton, N. Y., surgeon.

43   Bratten, Wilson, N. Y., taylor, and Isabella Ewing, N. Y., widow.

43   Bready, Patrick, of the Commissary Generals Department of the City of New York, and Elizabeth Porter, N. Y., spinster.

45   Bride, John Scot, N. Y., currier, and Jane Mathers, N. Y., spinster.

45   for Bridgeford, Robert and Sarah Smith, read Bridgford, Robert, N. Y., mariner, and Sarah Smith, N. Y., spinster.

45   Briggs, Unice, N. Y., spinster, and John Steuart, N. Y., ferryman.

45   Brigs, John, N. Y., and Ruth Duncan, N. Y., spinster.

45   for Brinan, John, and Sarah Walker, read Brannon, John, Quartermaster on Board His Majesty's Ship the Lyon, and Sarah Walker, N. Y., widow.

46   Bringfield, Sarah, N. Y., spinster, and John Mason, N. Y., mariner.

47   Broadhurst, Benjamin, N. Y., mariner, and Fanny Kenedy, N. Y., spinster.

48   for Brooks, Mary, and John Aikens, read Brooks, Mary, N. Y., spinster, and John Aikens, N. Y., yeoman.

536

537

543

544

545

144   for Francois, John, and Mary Kendrick, read Francois, John, and Mary Carderet. MS. license; no place mentioned.

144   for Fraser, William, and Catherine McDonald, read Frazer, William, 42nd Regiment, and Catherine McDonald, same regiment, widow.

145   Freeborn, Sarah Priscilla, N. Y., widow, and Samuel Harrison, N. Y., innkeeper.

145   Freeman, John, N. Y., mariner, and Elizabeth Valentine, N. Y., spinster. (MS. license, "at present there are no Lycenses signed by His Excellency the Governor.")

146   Frost, Susannah, N. Y., widow, and Francis Towse, N. Y.,

147 (insert)   1774, Aug. 24, Funck, Elizabeth, N. Y., spinster, and David Morris, N. Y., mariner.

147   Funck, John, N. Y., and Priscilla Potter (N. Y.) (imperfect).

147   Galatian, Elizabeth, N. Y., widow, and Charles Christian, master in His Majesty's Navy.

147   Galbreath, Sarah, N. Y., widow, and Thomas Ellis, N. Y., shipwright.

148   for Galilee, Roger, and Ann Simons, read Galilee, Roger, N. Y., mariner, and Hannah Simons, N. Y., widow.

149   Gardiner, Magdalean, N. Y., widow, and William Black, N. Y., house carpenter.

149   Gardiner, Jacob, N. Y., and Catherine Garlick, N. Y., spinster.

149   for 1779, Jan. 22, read 1779, Oct. 2. Gardiner, Susannah, N. Y., spinster, and George Smith, N. Y.

149   Gardner, Isabella, Hempstead, Queens County, spinster, and Walter McDonald, Quartermaster 17th Regiment of Dragoons.

149   Gardner, William, carpenter in His Majesty's Engineer Department, and Magdalean McWhirten, N. Y., widow.

149   Garlick, Barbara, N. Y., spinster, and David Babcock, N. Y.

149   Garlick, Catherine, N. Y., spinster, and Jacob Gardinier, N. Y.

150   Garretson, Allathea, N. Y., widow, and William Carty, N. Y., gentleman.

150   Garrison, Lenah, Richmond County, spinster, and Samuel Stilwell, same place.

151   Gay, Charles, N. Y., blacksmith, and Rebecca Smith, N. Y., widow.

151   Geary, Martha, N. Y., widow, and Stephen Shakespeare, N. Y., storekeeper.

151   Geree, William, Surgeon 38th Regiment of Foot, and Rebecca Van Denham, N. Y., spinster.

151   Gerow, Phebe, N. Y., spinster, and Jonathan Sherwood, N. Y., yeoman.

562

564

448 Watson, Adam, N. Y., mariner, and Deborah Hauking, N. Y., spinster.

448 Watson, Margaret, N. Y., widow, and John Thomas, N. Y., mariner.

448 Watson, Sarah, N. Y., spinster, and John Collins, Esq., of His Majesty's Ship Camilla.

448 Watt, Ann, N. Y., spinster, and James Holden, N. Y., cooper.

449 Wayne, Joseph, N. Y., and Mary Shelley, N. Y., widow.

449 Webb, Elizabeth, N. Y., spinster, and John Embree, Westchester.

449 Webb, John, N. Y., blacksmith, and Anne Batten, N. Y., spinster.

449 Webb, Joseph, N. Y., painter and glazier, and Sarah Taylor, N. Y., spinster.

450 Wedders, John, N. Y., mariner, and Susannah Miller, N. Y., spinster.

451 Wells, John, N. Y., sadler, and Jane Evans, N. Y., widow.

452 Welsh, John, N. Y., mariner, and Jane Allen, N. Y., widow.

453 (insert) 1775, Jan. 19, West, Mary, N. Y., spinster, and John Harris, N. Y., mariner.

454 Wettmore, George, N. Y., and Rachel Wragg, N. Y., spinster.

454 Wheate, Sarah, N. Y., spinster, and Samuel Date, N. Y., mariner.

455 Wheeler, Nathaniel, N. Y., blacksmith, and Mary Foresayth, N. Y., widow.

455 Whetten, Charity, N. Y., spinster, and Joseph Airs, N. Y.

456 for White, Charles, and Catherine Belton, read White, Charles, N. Y., coppersmith, and Mary Belton, N. Y., widow.

457 Whitehead, Charles, N. Y., mariner, and Hannah Platt, N. Y., spinster.

458 Widner, Mary, N. Y., widow, and James Hines, N. Y.

458 Wiely, Robert, N. Y., mariner, and Catherine Margeson, N. Y., widow.

458 for Wiggans, James, and Ann Twine, read Wiggins, James, soldier, 45th Regiment, and Ann Twine, 54th Regiment, widow.

459 Wilcocks, Catherine, N. Y., widow, and Tady Cronin, N. Y., baker.

459 Wilcocks, Sarah N. Y., spinster, and William Melvin, N. Y., labourer.

459 for Wile, John, and Cicile Magee, read Wild, John, N. Y., blacksmith, and Cicile Magee, N. Y., widow.

459 Wilkie, Edward, N. Y., Deputy Pilot of the Port, and Frances Martin, N. Y., spinster.

459 Wilkie, Elizabeth, N. Y., widow, and John Clarke, N. Y., mariner.

UNPUBLISHED MARRIAGE CERTIFICATE OF JOHN PALMER AND REBECCA BAXTER OF THE TOWN OF WESTCHESTER, N. Y., 1700.

(From the original in the archieves of The New York Historical Society, contributed by ROBERT H. KELBY, Librarian.)

These may Certifie all Persons whom it may concerne That I James Mott one of his Majesties Justices of the peace for the County of Westchester in the province of New York did joyn in the Bonds of Matrimony the Person of John Palmer of the borrough and Town of Westchester in the province aforesaid and Rebeckah Baxter daughter of Thomas Baxter Senr of the same place the 31st day of October in the twelf year of his Majesties Raigne And in the year of our Lord one thousand Seven hundred. Given under my hand and Seal in Momorinack this 31st Day of October in the Year of our Lord one thousand seven Hundred.

JAMES MOTT

Entred in the Records of the town of Westchester in Lib. No. 6 folio 50 by me

Justis pese

EDWARD COLLIER, Recorder.

NEW YORK MARRIAGE LICENSES, 1639-1706

By Kenneth Scott

Reprinted from

The New York Genealogical and Biographical Record

Volume XCVIII, Numbers 1 and 2

January and April, 1967

NEW YORK
MARRIAGE LICENSES,
1639-1706

By

Kenneth Scott

In the first two volumes of THE RECORD appeared a list of New York marriage licenses granted by Lord Cornbury and taken "from an old book of records in New York City" (1:3,13; 2:25-28). Also in THE RECORD (2:141,142,194-200; 3:91-94,192-95), E. B. O'Callaghan published other early New York marriage licenses, indicating his source as follows: "These licenses are recorded in the old books of record in the Surrogate's office, New York City." J. J. Latting added thirty-one licenses "from Vol. IV of Records of Wills, Surrogate's Office, N.Y." (REC. 4:31, 32). Finally, in April 1898, the *State Library Bulletin. History. No.1* (which is long out of print) appeared with the title "Supplementary List of Marriage Licenses." It was a supplement to *Names of Persons for Whom Marriage Licenses Were Issued by the Secretary of the Province of New York, Previous to 1784,* usually called "New York Marriages" (NYM), which had been published in 1860. The supplement contained, *inter alia,* the marriage licenses which had been printed in THE RECORD as mentioned above.

The original will libers in the Surrogate's Office in New York City were copied in 1892, and from that date until 1966 the original volumes were not available. Recently, however, most of the early original libers (with the exceptions of libers IV, VI, VIII, and XVIII) have been located and microfilmed by the Historical Documents Collection of the Paul Klapper Library, Queens College of The City University of New York, and microfilm copies are in the libraries of Queens College, The New-York Historical Society, and The New York Genealogical and Biographical Society.

Since it is now possible to check already published transcriptions of the marriage licenses against the originals contained in libers II and V, it has seemed valuable to print the early New York marriage licenses taken from the will books for the following reasons: (1) the copies of the will libers made in 1892 contain very many errors; (2) the licenses as printed in the early numbers of THE RECORD are found to contain frequent mistakes, and there are many omissions both of licenses and of details of genealogical importance, such as residence, trade, or previous marital status; (3) lack of exact volume and page references to the original entries is here rectified, so that it will be possible to check the original (or, where that is missing, the 1892 copy) in cases of doubt concerning any transcription. It has been decided to print marriages and marriage licenses mentioned by E. B. O'Callaghan in his *Calendar of Dutch Manuscripts* (CDM) and his *Calendar of English Manuscripts* (CEM), and then the marriage licenses written in the will libers in New York City. Items from original libers II and V will be so designated, followed by page references. Licenses from the 1892 copies are described as from L.1-2, L.3-4, L.5-6, or L.7, followed by page references. The licenses are listed in chronological order up to and including 12 April 1706.

Although many of the marriages authorized by these licenses were performed in the Reformed Dutch Church of New Amsterdam and New York City, reference has been made to the records of that church (*Collections* of the New York Genealogical and Biographical Society, Volume I [1890], Volume IX [1940]) only to supply a missing name or to check the spelling of an unusual name.

As an indication of errors made by the copyists of 1892 a few examples may be cited: the original and correct Nesbett became Nasbell; Stevens, Stivers; Ravaud, Barnard; Belline, Bettine; Turner, Tanner; Studd, Steed; Doston, Dorton. Similarly, in the early numbers of THE RECORD, Rollogum appeared as Rolloquin, Lethem as Letson, Vilard as Vyland, and Ceysler as Leyster, to cite but a few mistakes. In these same early numbers many marriage licenses were omitted; for example, that of Peter White and Kathrine Cavaleere, of Robert Allison and Hannah Bray, of James Mitchell and Gerritie Van Hoek, of Samuel Taylor and Ann Dunlope, and of John Hoghtelingh and Mary Colevelt.

De Conine, Thomas—Marritje Van Beets—22 Sept. 1639 CDM 69
Jurgens, Peter—Cathrina Lysinck, widow of Jan Bartram, lieut.-comm. at
    Curacao—2 July 1642 CDM 19
Peelen, Brant—Maritje Peters, widow of Claes Sybrantsen—3 July 1643
    CDM 23
Linde, Peter, of Belle, Flanders, widower of Elsje Barents—Martha
    Chambaer, of Newkirk, Flanders, widow of Jan Manje—1 July 1644
    CDM 28
La Montagne, Johannes—Angeneta Gillis, widow of Arent Corsen—18
    July 1647 CDM 111
Joosten, Symon—Marritje Symons, widow of Peter Vreucht, surgeon—19
    July 1647 CDM 38
Nuton, Thomas, of Onckeway—Joan Smith—16 April 1648 CDM 116
Van Steenwyck, Gerrit Jansen, widower—Pietertje Heertjes, widow—1
    Sept. 1654 CDM 57
Van Beecq, Johannis—Maria Verleth—c. late Feb. 1654 in Greenwich,
    Conn.—marriage, performed by Goodman Crab, an unauthorized
    farmer, declared unlawful in New Netherland CDM 135-136, 141
Van Brugh, Johannis—Miss Rodenborgh—1658 CDM 331

Laers (Laurentius Carolus), Finnish priest at Altona—c. 1 Feb. 1662;
marriage declared unlawful 14 April 1662 CDM 340
Rombouts, Francis—Anna Elizabeth, widow of Warnar Wessels, of NY—
6 Aug. 1675 CEM 37
Wharton, Walter (of New Castle ?)—c. May 1678; marriage contested in
court 4, 5 June CDM 355
Gilbert, Thomas—Bethia Young, of Southold—n.d. 1683 CEM 152

1684
Dishington, John—Cornelia Johnson—15 April CEM 154
Mecarty, John, of Piscataway—Ann Harman, of Woodbridge—9 July CEM
130
Francis, William, of Piscataway—Janacay Arense, of NYC—2 Aug. CEM
130
Graham, James—Elizabeth Windebank—18 July CEM 131
Seidman, Thomas—Mary Hunt—20 Aug. CEM 131
Jacobs, Hendrick—Antie Symons, both of NYC—9 Oct. CEM 132
Taylor, Edward—Deliverance Hollitt (Hewitt?)—12 Oct. CEM 132
Owing, William—Mary Cinburne, both of Flushing—22 Oct. CEM 132
Wender, Samuel—Margaret Rudyerd (or Rudgars?)—25 Oct. CEM 132
West, John—Ann Rudyard (or Rudgards?)—25 Oct. CEM 132
Brewerton, George—Anite Blanck—24 Nov. CEM 133
Buckmaster, Edward—Margaret Mathews, both of NY—2 Dec. CEM 132
Briggs, John, of Gravesend—Matthew (*sic!*) Wilkins—5 Dec. CEM 132
Cranesburgh, Oliver—Helekin Van Horrow (or Helekie Van Korrow?),
both of NYC—10 Dec. CEM 133
Levy, Asser—Margaret (or Maria?) Levy, both of NYC—23 Dec. CEM 134

1685
Griffin, Saml.—Eliz. Platt, both of Huntington—7 Jan. CEM 134
Wendall, Thomas—Audy Sharpe—23 March CEM 136
Michells, Cornelis—Neltie Elderts—9 April CEM 136
Cox, Wm.—   —17 April CEM 136
Henry, John—Ann Price, both of NYC—25 May CEM 137
Ashton, Thomas—Elizabeth Gibbs, both of NYC—26 May CEM 137
Tankins, Joh. (or Tankirs, John?)—Janitie Haddock, both of NYC—17
Aug. CEM 139
Hopper, Joseph—Janitie Cornelis—17 Aug. CEM 139
Hall (or Hill?), Thomas—Abigail Wakeman—15 Nov. CEM 141
Gore, Christopher—Eliz. Rogers, both of NYC—26 Dec. CEM 143

1686
Antil, Edward—Elizabeth Bowne—10 Sept. CEM 146
Merritt, John—Jane Lockhartt—17 Sept. CEM 146
Lemonter (or Lemouletz?), Jean—Helena Fell—17 Sept. CEM 146

1687

Blair, Rev. James—Sarah Harrison (dau. of Benjamin Harrison)—[probably shortly before 28 April 1687] CEM 342

1691

Van Courtlandt, Jacobus, of NYC, gentl.—Evah Phillips (dau. of Frederick Philips, of NYC, merchant)—7 May L.3-4:193

Kidd, Capt. William, of NYC—Sarah Oort, widow of John Oort, late of NYC, merchant, deceased—16 May L.3-4:195

Arents, Huybert, of NYC, clerke—Elizabeth Konning, widow—11 Aug. L.3-4:250

Larkon, James, of NYC, merchant—Kathrine De Hart—22 Aug. L.3-4:270

Schuyler, Peter, of Albany, gentl.—Maria Van Renselaer, of Albany (dau. of Jeremiah Van Renselaer)—1 Sept. L.3-4:279

Doome, Claes Dietlow—Maria Hendrix Van Hoven, both of NYC—26 Sept. L.3-4:285

Jordaine, Henry, of NYC. mariner—Eliza. Woodrof, widow—20 Oct. L.3-4:289

Lyndall, Thomas—Deborah Crundall—7 Sept. L.3-4:290

Arnold, Isaac—Sarah Washbourne—30 Oct. L.3-4:292

Skelton, Robert—Alice Throgmorton— 30 Oct. L.3-4:292

Morris, Lewis, of NYC, gentl.—Isabella Graham—3 Nov. L.3-4:296

Bettyes, John, of Esopus—Susannah Ashfordby— 7 Nov. L.3-4:296

Carhart, Thomas, of Staten Island, gentl.—Mary Lord—22 Nov. L.3-4:298

Coleman, Henry, of NYC, butcher—Mary Meade, widow—Dec. L.3-4:299

1691/2

Tasker (or Tasher?), John, purser of the *Lyon*—Mrs. Anna Lightfoot, widow—6 Jan. L.3-4:302

Donaldson, John, of New Castle on Delaware River, merchant—Elizabeth Harmen, of NYC, widow—23 March L.3-4:328

1692

Collins, James, of NYC, chirurgeon—Elizabeth Kennedy, single woman— 17 April L.3-4:328

Shaw, Thomas, of NYC. mariner—Anna Hancock, of NYC, widow—20 April L.3-4:331

Finlison, John—Mary Lookingglasse—22 April L.3-4:333

Wislake, Edward—Margery Crege (or Crego?)—28 April L.3-4:333

Jamison, David—Mary Hardenbrok—7 May L.3-4:333

Pintard, Anthony—Katharina Staleboth, of Neversink, East Jersey—14 May L.3-4:333

Le Chavolier, Jean, of NYC, joyner—Marie De La Plaine, of NYC, single woman—27 June L.3-4:344

Blydenburgh, Joseph, of NYC, gentl.—Mary Smith, of Sontalcet (Seatalcot?), Suffolk Co.—8 July L.3-4:347

Moyon, William, of New Castle, merchant—Mary Perdrian (or Pordrian?) —6 Sept. L.3-4:364

Vanderspiegel, James—Ann Sanders (dau. of Robert Sanders, of Albany, gentl.) 20 Sept. L.3-4:364

Hendricksen, John—Marcy Frost, both of Hempstead—12 Sept. L.3-4:364

Marshall, Garvis—Eleanor Pey—27 Sept. L.3-4:365

Ware, Jacob, of Southampton, Suffolk Co.—Elizabeth Osburne—3 Oct. L.3-4:365

Lawrence, Thomas, of Queens Co., L.I.—Mary Ferguson, of the same place—9 Nov. L.3-4:374

Valleau, Stephen, of Kingston, Ulster Co., cooper—Mary Gallaes (or Gallais?) of NYC, widow—19 Nov. L.3-4:375

Phillips, Fred, of NYC, merchant—Katharina Darvell, of NYC, widow— 1 Dec. L.3-4:387

Ketteltas, Abraham, of NYC, smith—Antie Boelen, of NYC, widow—16 Dec. L.3-4:393

1692/3

Lafort, Marcus—Hesther Richards (dau. of Paul Richards, of NYC, merchant)—18 Jan. L.3-4:406

Groves, Andrew, of NYC, vintner—Jane Boyle, of NYC, widow—8 Feb. L.3-4:414

Bourchner (or Bourchuer, or Bourthier?), Michael, of NYC, silversmith —Mary English, single woman—20 Feb. L.3-4:414

Norwood, Benjamin, of NYC, mariner—Cornelia Van Clyff, single woman —20 Feb. L.3-4:414

Van Hoorn, John, of NYC, merchant—Catharina Moyer, of NYC—20 March L.3-4:417

Macky, John, of NYC, mariner—Jane Parsons, of NYC—20 March L.3-4:417

1693

Finch, John, of NYC, mariner—Hesther Davis—25 March L.3-4:418

Kembell, Henry, of NYC, blacksmith—Kathrine Baker—10 April L.3-4:421

Vielle, Cornelius—Kathrine Bogardus—10 April L.3-4:421

Greenham, Michael, of NYC, mariner—Mary Davie—14 April L.3-4:421

Wicken, John—Katherone Fredricksen—28 April L.3-4:430

Hope, John—Isabella Allin—7 June L.3-4:430

Van Hoorn, Gerryt—Altie Provoost—14 June L.3-4:432

Peterson, John, of NYC, mariner—Hannah Gerrytson—20 June L.3-4:434

Anderson, George—Elizabeth Stevenson—26 June L.3-4:445

Sleigh, Charles—Sarah Purrington—27 June L.3-4:445

Chambers, John, of NYC, butcher—Mary Drummond—17 Aug. L.3-4:465

Potter, Richard—Katherine Reay—18 Sept. L.3-4:469

Burch, William—Hannah Robinson—4 Sept. L.3-4:469
Baker, Roger—Mary Walkington—[n.d., probably Sept. 1693] L.3-4:470
Adolph, Dirck, of NY, baker—Ariaentie Kiersteede—27 Sept. L.3-4:470
Phips, Benjamin—Hannah Dean—10 Oct. L.3-4:478
Anthony, John—Elizabeth Gerrytse—18 Oct. L.3-4:478
Schuyler, Myndert—Rachell Cuyler—23 Oct. L.3-4:478
Symonse, Henryck—Ariaentie Samuell—25 Oct. L.3-4:478
Harris, John—Abigail Berriman—21 Nov. V:10
Davis, William— (—) Coleman—23 Nov. V:9
Allison, Robert—Hannah Bray—24 Nov. V:9
Carter, Zebulon—Heiltie Sloot—19 Dec. V:12

1693/4
Wright, Joseph—Ann Henry—1 Jan. V:17
More, Richard—Rebeccah Baily—11 Jan. V:17
Coats, Edward—Sarah Thomson—Jan. V:20
Wharton, Lt. Robert—Mrs. Ann West—25 Jan. V:20

1694
Gilbert, Moses—Jannitie Floyd—31 March V:30
Cooper, Benjamin, of Southampton, carpenter—Helena Wilkens—7 April
    V:39
D'Honuer, Johannes, of NY, glazier—Johanna Maynard—12 April V:39
Loring, John, mariner—Katherine Van Clyff—16 April V:43
Pateshal, Richard—Hannah Holst—20 April V:45
De Key, Jacobus, of NY, merchant—Sarah Willet, of Queens, Nassau
    Island—9 May V:46
Clatworthy, John—Mary Lursen [or Leersen?]—10 May V:46
Pead, William, mariner—Mary Hardenbergh—4 June V:46
Van Strydt, John—Johanna Lewis—24 June V:47
Thomas, Edmond—Mary Souward—9 July V:49
Feilding, Nicholas—Deborah Cooley—9 Aug. V:52
Evans, John—Katharine Macgregore—10 Sept. V:52
Groenendick, Johannes—Delia Childers—18 Sept. V:54
De Peyster, Cornelis—Maria Banckers—19 Sept. V:54
Honan, Daniel—Sarah Jones—6 Oct. V:54
Wilkison, Philip—Helena Teller—11 Oct. V:54
Vandebergh, Hendryck Jamsen—Mary Anny Burtsen (or Burlsen?)—11
    Oct. V:54
French, John—Mary White—21 Oct. V:54
Yaresley, Richard—Dorothy Gore—23 Oct. V:54
Simms, Lancaster, gentl.—Katharine Larkin, widow—2 Nov. V:58
Dawning, James—Sarah Evans—6 Nov. V:62
Pell, William—Elizabeth Van Teuyl—23 Nov. V:62

Lewis, Thomas—Francis Leisler—26 Nov. V:63
Bill, Benjamin—Geesie Van Fort—5 Dec. V:84
Carnaby, Nicholas, mariner—Jane Dawning—12 Dec. V:89
Greg, Robert—Leena Monntes—13 Dec. V:92
Slade, Peter—Margery Wislake—26 Dec. V:92
Cox, Jacobus—Catharina Davids—31 Dec. V:92

1694/5
Miller, Pawl—Antie Vanderheyden—31 Jan. V:97
Cole, Abram—Rabacca Britten—9 March V:101

1695
Masett, Peter—Lejdia Cocks—5 April V:109
Cullom, Peter—Martha Berriman—8 April V:109
Law, Andrew—Cornelia Dishington—18 April V:112
Tuder, John, younger—Affee Van Hoorn—20 April V:113
Young, Symon—Ann Elum—10 May V:120
Spencer, James —Mary Carley—28 May V:122
Fisher, John—Barbary Morton—1 June V:122
Hendricksen, Volkert—Elizabeth Paulus—4 June V:122
Lambrs, Martinus—Catryna Van Newenhuysen—19 June V:123
Blanchard, John, of New Castle, merchant—Joanna Gaultier, of New
    York—28 June V:123
Cortlandt, John—Anna Mary Van Schaick—20 June V:128
De Hart, Matthias—Janetie Mauritz—27 June V:128
Low, Cornelius—Margaret Van Bursum—1 July V:128
Smith, Joseph—Margaret Barents—8 July V:128
Stollard, Giles—Elizabeth Tuder—8 July V:128
Springsteen, Caspar—Janitie Jacobs—24 July V:128
Harwood, George—Willimkie [?] (—), of Flatbush—19 Aug. V:129
Willet, Thomas, of Queens Co.—Sarah Hinchman, of Flushing—24 Aug.
    V:129
Finisonie, William, mariner—Patience Betterworth—12 Sept. V:130
    [cf. MDC, 80: Willjam Finistone, Mariner, en Patientje Belteworth]
Hewett, James—Mary Deyckman—16 Sept. V:130
Leuwis, Moses—Mary Bayer—16 Sept. V:130
Kipp, Jesse—Mary Stevens—30 Sept. V:132
Budd, Joseph—Sarah Underhill—11 Oct. V:132
Bosch, Juriaen—Geshennamah Bruyn—16 Oct. V:132
Hutton, John, mariner—Katrine Strangnish—28 Oct. V:135
Lynch, Thomas—Anna Jacobs—6 Nov. V:135
Bougraud (or Bongrand?)—Mary Van Bursum—8 Nov. V:138
Burroughs, Thomas—Mary Tayler—16 Nov. V:138
Cannon, Andreis—Ann Puppyn—18 Nov. V:138
Chappell, Francis—Ann Fromanteell—27 Nov. V:138

Ewer, John—Albertie Wessels—10 Dec. L.5-6:105
Hunt, John L., Junior—Abigail Huestis—24 Dec.—L.5-6:106

1695/6
Wheeler, James—Elizabeth Meek—13 Jan. V:145
Billiau, Peter—Perkie Hendricks—17 Jan. V:146
Lethem, Daniel—Helena Bordann—15 Feb. L.5-6:112
Hooglandt, Christopher—Sarah Willett—15 Feb. L.5-6:113
Vilard, David—Eliza. Henry—17 Feb. L.5-6:113
De Lanoy, Peter—Mary Edsall—21 Feb. L.5-6:113
Reyners, Barnett—Hesther Leyster—10 March L.5-6:123

1696
Laurence, John—Janetie Stevensen—6 April V:151
Gibb, Andrew, gentl.—Mrs. Hannah Smith—13 April V:151
Hood, Jasper—Katherine Anderson—2 June V:157
Elsworth, Johannes—Anna Peters—3 June V:157
Wyncoop, Johannes—Cornelia Tienbrooke—9 June V:157
Hulin, Francis—Susanna Nicholas—12 June V:157
Basford, John—Damares Lynns—16 June V:158
Rasby, Webley—Alkie Luwersen—16 June V:158
Crego, Richard—Sarah Stillwell—29 June V:158
Hulgrow, George—Evah Burger—30 June V:158
Clement, James—Sarah Hinchman—2 July V:158
Giles, Thomas—Engeltie Davies—6 July V:159
Van Brugen, Johannes—Margarett Provoost—6 July V:159
Dunscomb, Daniel—Helena Swann—8 July V:159
Hardenbergh, Johannes—Helecent Meyer—10 July V:159 [cf. MDC
    Hillegond]
Richard, Stephen—Mary Van Brughen—20 July V:160
Barton, William—Hannah Hull—probably 20 July V:160
Fisher, William—Anna Barcley—1 Aug. V:160
Brine, John—Elizabeth Van Clyff—1 Aug. V:160
Selsby, John—Sarah Thomson—1 Aug. V:161
Weeks, Zachariah—Kathrine Meyer—18 Aug. V:162
Jenoway, William, gentl.—Mrs. Agnitie De Myre—11 Aug. V:162
Reevely, George—Kathrine Holmes—28 Aug. V:162
Wright, Thomas—Lydia Cobbitt—28 Aug. V:162
Dubois, Louis—Hesther Grasset—28 Aug. V:162
Jaman, Henry—Jane Barber—31 Aug. V:162
Moore, John—Elizabeth Cheek—8 Sept. V:164
Mott, Rigebell—Elizabeth Thorne—14 Oct. V:164
Dodrige, Philip—Francis Moore—15 Oct. V:164
Pinder, William—Ann Hoorne—10 Nov. V:164

Lambert, Edward—Jane Downing—11 Nov. V:165
Robieson, Josiah—Margarett Nicolls—21 Nov. V:165
Righton, John—Frances Tuder—27 Nov. V:169

1696/7
Vandenheyden, Johannes—Mary Wooders—9 Jan. V:173
Kip, Abraham—Kathalina Van Vlecqe—26 Jan. V:190
Vanderpool, Gerryt—Deborah Warm—11 Feb. V:193
Cavaleer, Peter—Cornelia Busch—1 March V:200
White, Peter—Kathrine Cavaleere—2 March V:197

1697
Ludlow, Gabriel—Sarah Hanmer—5 April V:200
Olphardt, Shuerdt, of NYC, yeoman—Heilkea Clopper, widow of Cornelius Clopper, of NYC, blacksmith—23 April II:85
Cosins, Barne—Grace Sanford—28 April V:203
Buckenhoven, Stephen—Anna Van Holst—7 May V:203
Kip, Henricus—Magdalen Van Vlecque—8 June V:210
Florentine, Marke—Ann Corlee—23 June V:211
Whitehead, Jonathan—Sarah Feild—23 July V:223
Livingston, Robert, Junr.—Margarett Schuyler—26 July V:223
Tregenny, Humphrey— (—) Brookesbanck—12 Aug. V:224
Daillé, Peter, minister—Seytie Duyckinck—13 Aug. V:224
Parmiter, Thomas—Margarett Smith—14 Aug. V:224
Tuder, Capt. John—Mr[s] Mary Brett—9 Sept. V:248
Wilkenson, Philip—Mary Brazier—16 Sept. V:250
Olpherts, Suert—Hilleke Pieters—17 Sept. V:250
Smith, John—Hannah Phips—17 Sept. V:250
Dow, Hendryck—Neeltie Meynderts—23 Sept. V:250
Tayler, Walter—Deliverance Graves—24 Sept. V:251
Anderson, William—Deborah Lyndall—7 Oct. V:252
Dehance, Jan—Margarett Symonse Uthuse—9 Oct. V:252
Price, Christopher—Susannah Allyn—15 Oct. V:257
Burt, Richard—Margaret Glenn—18 Oct. V:259
Wyncoop, Benjamin—Femmie Vanderhule—20 Oct. V:259
Jay, Augustus—Ann Mary Bayard—27 Oct. V:259
King, Peter—Elizabeth Green—29 Oct. V:259
Ward, Isreal—Hannah Hutson—29 Oct. V:259
Willkission, William—Else Smith—15 Nov. V:259
West, William—Mary Bingham—17 Nov. V:259
Lypet, Moses—Sarah Throgmortin—8 Dec. V:261
Perrey, John—Sarah Mallyear—9 Dec. V:261
Evertse, Capt. Nicholas—Margaret Van Baal—13 Dec. V:261
Hunt, Josiah, Junior—Batthia Ferguson—20 Dec. V:262
Willett, Richard—Mrs. Mary Willett—22 Dec. V:262

Robinson, Thomas—Rachell Rosell—29 Dec. V:263
Williams, George—Kathrine Lloyd—30 Dec. V:263

1697/8
Edwards, Robert—Judith Mosston—13 Jan. V:263
Latham, Joseph—Jane Singleton—7 Feb. V:264
Lipis, Samuell—Ann Honey—n.d., probably Feb. V:274
Vesey, William—Mrs. Mary Reade—1 March V:274

1698
Pantry, John—Elezabeth Plinco—16 April V:283
Wilson, Richard—Kathrine Pugsley—27 April V:288
Gilbert, George—Jane Campbell—4 May V:289
Rollogum, Jacobus—Lydia Darkins—25 May V:292
Dewind, Lewin—Ariaentie Moll—26 May V:292 [cf. MDC 87: Levinus de
    Windt—Ariaentie Moll]
Mitchel, James—Gerritie Van Hoek—9 June V:294
Hoghtelingh, John—Mary Colevelt—15 June V:294 [cf. MDC 88: Jan
    Hoogteling—Mary Colevelt]
Coreman [or Coleman?], Daniel Peterse—Anna Maria Plevier—30 June
    V:298
Allison, Thomas—Cornelia Johnson— 4 July V:299
Hopper, John, of Flushing, L.I.—Margrett Tindell—5 July V:299
Everinden, Robert—Ann Smith—11 July V:299
Clowes, Samuel—Kathrine Douw—18 July V:299
Coleman, Henry—Elenor Hunt—27 July V:299
Low, Matthis—Janitye Van Heyninge—22 Aug. V:300 [cf. MDC 88: Mat-
    thys Louw—Jannetje Heyninge]
Walton, William—Mary Sandford—30 Aug. V:300
Durend, Dr. John—Eliza. Bryan—10 Sept. V:302
Burle, Joshua—Judith Sexton—15 Sept. V:300
Petit, Thomas—Cathrine Branch—26 Sept. V:304
Smith, Barnardus—Elsey Meyers—25 Oct. V:305
Harrod, Richard—Mrs. Mary Jones—30 Oct. V:304
Sydenham, George—Elezabeth Stuyvesant—4 Nov. V:302
Hancock, John—Jane Wells—8 Dec. V:312
King, Jeremiah—Mary Glover—12 Dec. V:326
Osborn, William—Elizabeth Way—12 Dec. V:326
Rutherse, Anthony—Hendrycke Vandewater—23 Dec. V:326

1698/9
Walton, Thomas—Mary Stillwell—[probably Jan. or Feb. 1698/9] V:327
Davison, William—Elenor Goff—25 Feb. V:327
Dupin, Peter Chavalier—Anne Duboies—14 March V:333

1699

Bolen, James—Elezabeth Godfrey—[probably March or April 1699] V:333

Drincall, Thomas—Ann Watson—27 April V:337

Corbitt, John—Christian Milton—6 May V:340

Breadstead, John—Margrett Peters—10 May V:340

Sackett, Richard—Majory L Sleade—11 May V:340

Blydenburgh, Joseph—Cathrine Dehart—19 May V:344

Governeur, Abraham—Mary Milborne—16 May V:344

Williamson, John—Elzeabeth Litts—26 May V:350

Ten Broock, Hendricus—Trienty Janse—26 May V:350 [cf. MDC 90: Tryntie Jans Van Rommen]

Provoost, Jacobus—Mary Vanderpool—31 May V:350

Taylor, Samuell—Ann Dunlope—24 June V:350

Forlisson, John—Ann Mool—4 July V:354

Yeates, John—Edey Wilde—5 July V:354

Funule (?), Benjamine—Anna Du Boy—July V:357

Vande Bergh, Lodwick—Elsey Ten Brock—4 Aug. V:357

Rooff, Henry—Margritt Conlylee—9 Aug. V:357

Cornwell, George—Ann Merchant—14 Aug. V:357

Gleave, Richard—Han (or Har ?) Philip—15 Aug. V:357

Denham (or Donham?), David—Mary Elsley—16 [or 18] Aug. V:357

Streard, Alexander—Cornelia Dishington [n.d., probably Aug. 1699] V:357

Thorne, Richard—Phebe Denton—29 Aug. V:357

Ball, Adam—Elezebeth Collins—31 Aug. V:357

Bald, Adam—Eliza. Collins—[n.d.] II:2

Hardenbergh, Johannis—Cathrine Ruthse—12 Sept. II:1

Lawrence, Richard—Charity Clerke—24 Sept. V:357

White, John—Cornelia Vande Burgh—29 Sept. V:357

Lawrier, Christian—Mary Bant—Dec. II:11

Letour, Isaak—Judith Waldron—16 Dec. II:11

Titus, Theunis—Mary Barre—20 Dec. II:11

Mayson, John—Eliz. Lance—29 Dec. II:11

1699/1700

De Lancy, Stephen—Ann Cortlandt—17 Jan. II:11

Santfordt, (—)—Jane White—13 Feb. II:11

Harmenson, Hans—Mary Van Dyke—14 Feb. II:11

Berton, Peter—Elizabeth Archambeau—17 Feb. II:11

Teller, Andrew—Ann Verplanck—[n.d.] II:11

Vincent, Francis—Ann Lynch—[n.d.] II:11

Nesbett, Robert—Susanna Stevens—[n.d] II:11
Skelding, Tho.—Rebecca Asten—[n.d.] II:11

1700

Vander Heule, Hendrikes—Marytie Meyers—18 April II:21
Baird, Alexander—Magdelena Kipp—26 April II:22
Gindett, John—Mary Vincent—27 April II:22
Vect, John—Katharine Meyers—27 April II:22
Carille, Adam—Elizabeth Geribaut [or Geribat ?]—27 April II:22
Thavet, Peter—Susannah Verrgereau—27 May II:22
Schuyler, Jacobus—Cathalina Schuyler—[n.d.] II:22
Aspinwalle, Joseph—Hannah Dean—13 July II:40
Wychangham, Tho.—Susanna Fine—20 July II:44
Penestone, Tho.—Elizabeth Lyster—17 Sept. II:48
Croaker, Robt.—Susanah Peterson—25 Nov. II:56

1700/1

Tenyck, Jacob—Neelie Hardenburgh—21 Feb. II:94
Elliott, Robert—Frances Boyle [not granted to him]—24 Feb. II:94
Williamson, Charles—Mary Woolsey—24 Feb. II:94

1701

Ekles, James—Rebecca Lynns—26 March II:94
Gorne, John—Mary Harris—1 April II:94
Pedley, Roger—Sarah Thorne—7 April II:95
Stevens, John—Pricilla Shaw—9 April II:97
Lawrence, John—Jane Gregory—24 April II:97
Eldrdge, Wm.—Elisabeth Evans—3 May II:97
Kingston, John—Dorothy Sandige—9 May II:99
Willet, Albert—Johanna Varick—10 May II:107
Coerten, Henry—Elizabeth De Riemer—22 May II:107
Provoost, Abraham—Jenitie Meyer—23 May II:107
Dale, Robt.—Elizabeth Turner—24 May II:107
Vreland, Johanes—Marya Cregers—6 June II:117
Hardenbrugh, Peter—Katherine Vanderpolle—21 June II:122
Thompson, John—Hanah Smith—24 June II:122
Bant, Peter—Mary Van Hoven—26 June II:122
Ten Brooke, Andrew—Syntie Splinter—3 July II:122
Cauley, John—Agenitie Vandespegel—23 July II:122
Evans, Thomas—Jane Timmer—7 Aug. II:122
Mans, Adriaen— (—)—9 Aug. II:131 [*cf.* MDC 96: Adriaan Man met
     Hester Boerden]
Hooper, Robt.—Mrs. Sarah Graham—16 Aug. II:132
Van Dyke, Francis—Fyche Direcks—25 Aug. II:132
Willis, Arthur—Joana Carr—29 Aug. II:132

Biljan, Peter—Maria Breau—15 Sept. II:132
Buttler, John—Hanah Saunders—15 Sept. II:132
Ravaud, Ferdinando—Mary Belline—2 Oct. II:149
Doston, William—Prudence Shelston—3 Oct. II:149
Van Renselaer, Kilian—Maria Van Cortlandt—8 Oct. II:149
Maynard, George—Issabella Willson—8 Oct. II:149
Staats, Barent—Niellye Gerrets—12 Oct. II:149
Cockling, Thomas—Deborah Smith—25 Oct. II:149
Van Newenhuysen, William—Elizabeth De Hart—27 Oct. II:149
Betts, Joseph—Grace Mott—27 Oct. II:162
Van Allen, Johanes—Christina Ten Broek—3 Nov. II:162
Olpherts, Suert—Janeke Snedeker—10 Nov. II:162
Collins, John—Margaret Verplanck—27 Nov. II:162
Chisnall, William—Magdalen Caveleer—22 Dec. II:162

1701/2

Pell, Thomas—Aeltie Beeke—20 Jan. II:163
Lefeurt, Bartholomew—Magdalen Peirott—26 Jan. II:163
Hanse, Johanes—Sarah Deforest—30 Jan. II:163
Arrowsmith, Joseph—Martha Pollom—1 Feb. II:163
Prosser, Joseph—Eliz. Verwyde—20 March II:163
Studd, Tho.—Catherine Pearsall—23 March II:163

1702

Kip, Petrus—Emeltie Van Deycke—22 April II:163
Rollitse, Mereyes—Deylia Teunisse—25 April II:163
Fredricks, Isaac—Hester Van Fleckt—25 April II:163
Langstaffe, Moses—Mary Sidman—25 April II:163
Eaton, John—Elizabeth Michell—30 April II:163
Davis, James—Elisbeth Santford—30 April II:163
Notingham, Wm.—Margaret Rutsen—14 May II:163
Wendall, Abraham—Catharine Dekey—14 May II:163
Cebra, James, mariner—Ann Meyer—29 July II:164
Cooper, John—Hannah Frost—29 July II:164
Emmons, Abraham, of Kings Co., yeoman—Margarett Williamson, widow
    —17 Aug. II:164
Creigier, Martinus, of NY, bolter—Margarett Van Dalsen—27 Aug. II:164
Dally, Nicholas—Elizabeth Cregier—28 Aug. II:164
Vanderbeeck, Conradus, corne measurer, of NYC—Catherine Cock, wid-
    ow—20 Oct. L.7:45
Thurman, Ralph, of NYC, baker—Mary Clouder, widow—26 Oct. L.7:45
Davenport, Thomas, of NYC, merchant—Margarett Lepenar, single wom-
    an—27 Oct.—L.7:45
Holloway, William, mariner—Elizabeth Holyday—17 Nov. L.7:45

Van Laer, Abraham, of NYC, baker—Elizabeth Struddle—17 Nov. L.7:45
Grice, John, of NYC, yeoman—Deborer Hadlock, single woman—20 Nov. L.7:45
Freeman, John, gentleman—Sarah Shrive, single woman—27 Nov. L.7:47
Auboyneau, John—Frances Stuckey—28 Nov. L.7:47
Robinson, Richard—Mary Chambers—5 Dec. L.7:53
Schuyler, Arent—Swantie Dyckhuyse—12 Dec. L.7:59
Harris, Richard—Mary Baker, widow—12 Dec. L.7:59
Robinson, Charles—Elizabeth Roesdall—16 Dec. L.7:64
Berkley, William—Elizabeth Randall—16 Dec. L.7:64
Osborn, Samuell—Katherine Pullion—17 Dec. L.7:65
Smith, William—Susanna Monvielle—22 Dec. L.7:65
Robert, Daniell—Susanne Nicolas—24 Dec. L.7:66
Minviel, John James—Susanne Papin—28 Dec. L.7:66
Nedry, John—Jane Allen—28 Dec. L.7:66

1702/3

Dehart, Balthazar—Margritta Mauritz—5 Jan. L.7:83
Journey, John—Elizabeth De Yan—8 Jan. L7:83
Bedwell, Isaac—Hannah Blank—16 Jan. L.7:83
Jamison, David—Johannah Meech—16 Jan. L.7:83
Vandervere, Dominicus—Maria Margaretta Van Ortcck—28 Jan. L.7:86
Hickman, Robert—Susannah De Freese—3 Feb. L.7:87
Hamill, John—Christine Rosevelt—24 Feb. L.7:89
Blercome, Lubert Jansen—Angell Hendricks—27 Feb. L.7:89
Cruggor, John—Mary Cuyler—2 March L.7:89
Stuart, Alexander—Catharine Rivilie—17 March L.7:91

1703

Willett, Richard—Frances Deravall—30 March L.7:95
Graham, Augustine—Jane Chiswell—8 April L.7:96
Stillwell, Tho.—Ellis Throgmorton—9 April L.7:109
Shepard, John—Ruth Davis—10 April L.7:109
Remer, John—Askey Lessenby—12 April L.7:109
Allison, John—Christian Hyndert—12 April L.7:109
Allison, Tho.—Anne Yallutton—17 April L.7:109
Laconte, Wm.—Margtt. Mahoo—17 April L.7:109
Schut, Johon Michll.—Mary Fromahyden—20 April L.7:117
Scurlocke, John—Eve Hulgrove—2 May L.7:124
Hall, Richard—Anne Evetts—4 May L.7:124
Platte, Epenetus—Elizab. Smith—6 May L.7:124
De Grooffe, Adolph—Rachell Coderse—12 May L.7:124
Blagge, Edward—Johanna Vickers—12 May L.7:124
Crawford, Patrick—Katherin Potter—16 May L.7:124

Suert, Olphert—Hellegond Luyckas—22 May L.7:124
Lansing, Isaac—Janeke Beekeman—26 May L.7:124
Kiersteade, Jacobus—Eliza. Laurence—11 June L.7:125
Battery, Peter—Jenekie Davis—17 June L.7:125
Thiboux, Wm.—Mary Du Tay—18 June L.7:125
Adams, Tho.—Hannah Patting—18 June L.7:125
Glencrosse, Wm.—Eliza. Clarke—23 June L.7:125
Christionse, Peter—Bellekie Attkins—29 June L.7:125
Lafon, John—Mary Dubois—6 July L.7:125
Coward, Hugh—Patience Throgmorton—6 July L.7:125
Lesley, John—Ellen Bissett—12 July L.7:125
Kelly, John—Margarett Flenchborow—12 July L.7:125
Bayeux, Thomas—Magdleleine Boudinot—14 July L.7:125
Stephance, Lucas—Catherin Van Dyke—19 July L.7:125
Hews, Thomas—Sarah Lloyd—21 July L.7:125
Halton, Michael—Elizabeth Van Tright—26 July L.7:125
Stewart, John—Rebecca Adams—17 Aug. L.7:125
Coenraats, Octave—Mary Longfield—9 Aug. L.7:125
Cantain, Moses—Mary De Witt—18 Aug. L.7:125
Huyblingh, Coenraet—Deborah Beeck—26 Aug. L.7:125
Chambers, Abraham Goesbeck—Sarah Bayard—12 Aug. L.7:126
Mackay, Alexander—Mary Bresty—28 Aug. L.7:126
Schepmoes, Derrick—Grittie Tappen—31 Aug. L.7:126
Kiersted, Cornelius—Sarah Elsworth—2 Sept. L.7:126
Johnson, John—Hanna Van Swanenbrugh—3 Sept. L.7:126
Beekman, Charles—Ekay Van Sant—6 Sept. L.7:126
Okey, John—Helena Ryarse—10 Sept. L.7:128
Schyler, Gerard—Aegie D'Groof—14 Sept. L.7:128
De Vrees, Albert—Emmetie Van Dycke—14 Sept. L.7:128
Bogaert, Hendrick—Ruttie De La Metre—15 Sept. L.7:128
Jusell, John—Francis Champion—10 Oct. L.7:128
Ralph, Thomas—Mary Gunter—10 Oct. L.7:128
Desbrosses, James—Hellena Gaudineau—18 Oct. L.7:128
Nicholas, James—Mary Moll—19 Oct. L.7:137
Hunderbeek, Abram—Martha Woodett—20 Oct. L.7:137
Gilbert, John—Cornelia Allison—27 Oct. L.7:137
Beck, Caleb—Hannah Harley—30 Oct. L.7:137
Moll, Jacobus—Lidia Winua—1 Oct. L.7:137 [should it be 1 Nov.?]
Lanseing, Abraham—Matthew Leana Huntrick—3 Nov. L.7:137
Rousby, Christopher—Sarah Kidd—4 Nov. L.7:137
Garreou, Jean—Marie Andere—6 Nov. L.7:137
Kingsland, Edmund—Mary Pinhorne—8 Nov. L.7:137
Goscott, Zachariah—Margett Bond—18 Nov. L.7:137
Smith, Charles—Aleda Hundrick—22 Nov. L.7:138

Brett, Roger—Katharine Rumbout—25 Nov. L.7:138
Schenck, Martin—Cornelia Van Weeselen—27 Nov. L.7:138
Carelir, Adam—Mary Dalcales—3 Dec. L.7:138
Cornell, John—Letitia Smith—6 Dec. L.7:138
Stillwell, Nicholas—Elizabeth Cornell—6 Dec. L.7:138
Huggen, William—Rachaell Burroughs—13 Dec. L.7:138
Hutchins, John—Elizabeth Buckley—9 Dec. L.7:138
Corbett, John—Mary Graham—14 Dec. L.7:138
Bayard, Jacobus—Hillyden Dekay—18 Dec. L.7:138
Whitehead, Thomas—Jane Creed—24 Dec. L.7:138
Bosen, Phillip—Sarah Berser—26 Dec. L.7:138

1703/4

Tenike, Conradus—Anna Van Aps—7 Jan. L.7:138
Johnson, Johannes—Hanna Clotwerthy—11 Jan. L.7:138
Denmarke, John—Mary Denike—14 Jan. L.7:145 & 161
Kerfbyl, John—Margarett Prevost—18 Jan. L.7:145
Hughes, Thomas—Jane Gunthorp—20 Jan. L.7:145 & 161
Beeckman, Christophell—Maria De La Noy—25 Jan. L.7:145
Duyckink, Evert—Elsie Myer—25 Jan. L.7:145 & 161
Pope, Thomas—Mary Pratt—26 Jan. L.7:145 & 161
Wickham, John—Jerusia Miller—1 Feb. L.7:145 & 161
Du Shaw [or Dushen], Valentine—Mary Stillwell—10 Feb. L.7:145 & 161
Macklenan, John—Elizabeth Farmer—2 March L.7:161
Van Orde, Johannes—Hendrika Tennike—3 March L.7:161
Crego, Josias—Anne Ellsworth—4 March L.7:161
Vielle, Arnold—Elizabeth Van Ford—4 March L.7:161
De Kleyn, Leonard Huyggen—Susannah Vaughton—7 March L.7:161
Smith, Jonathan—Elizabeth Platt—14 March L.7:161
Willis, Arthur—Sarah Drakes—29 March L.7:161

1704

Whitman, Nathan—Anne Britton—5 April L.7:161
Gerritson, Ryert—Gerthryt Lansen—10 April L.7:161
Wooley, Charles—Hannah Noel—14 April L.7:175
Heymer, John—Dorothy Leigh—19 April L.7:175
Timber, Cornelius—Cornelia Myer—20 April L.7:196
Booth, George—Mary Rowly—21 April L.7:196
Lynis, Nathaniel—Unis Burroughs—25 April L.7:196
Hoar, Anthony—Jean Huyco—26 April L.7:200
Milldrum, John—Femmetie Van Boursen—4 May L.7:200
Books, Phillip—Mary Carter—5 May L.7:214
Fine, Frederick—John [*sic!*] Vencent—10 May L.7:214

Bogardus, Ephorordus—Hannah Dayly—30 May L.7:214
De Puy, Andrew—Jane Archanbaw—5 June L.7:225
French, John—Katherine Benson—8 June L.7:225
Governeur, Isaac—Sarah Staats—22 June L.7:225
Van Winckel, Albert—Meritie Deerby—23 June L.7:225
Teneve, Stephen—Neltie Folleman—23 June L.7:225
Foster, John—Altie Cornelise—20 July L.7:225
Stateham, Thomas—Altie Finn—20 July L.7:225
Jansen, Hendrick—Mary Brown—29 July L.7:225
Vanderspeigle, Nicholas—Catherine Stoutenburg—7 Aug. L.7:225
Lansen, John—Lena Saunders—7 Sept. L.7:225
Saunders, Barent—Mary Wander—7 Sept. L.7:225
Berger, Myndart—Sarah J. Dese—9 Sept. L.7:225-226
Jansen, Cornelise—Margerett Van Noostrandt—16 Sept. L.7:226
Meyer, John—Sarah D Foreest—20 Sept. L.7:226
Provoost, Gerrett—Altie Roose—21 Sept. L.7:226
Roose, Peter—Mmtie Courtie—21 Sept. L.7:226
Burtell, Peter—Margerett Van Clyft—4 Oct. L.7:226
Ogleby, John—Hannah Ellson—9 Oct. L.7:226
Wasburn, John—Hannah Hallett—14 Oct. L.7:226
Peroyne, Peter—Anne Holmes—16 Oct. L.7:226
Thong, Walter—Sarah Van Dam—16 Oct. L.7:226
Miller, Wm.—Geertroy Springsteen—18 Oct. L.7:226
Waldron, John—Cornelia Hardenbrook—27 Oct. L.7:226
Grant, Wm.—Rachell Hardenbrook—1 Nov. L.7:226
Oliver, Charles—Margerett Schuyler—7 Nov. L.7:226
Swerver, Andrew—Elizabeth De Vore—8 Nov. L.7:226
Sands, Samuell—Elizabeth Lessitt—9 Nov. L.7:226-227
Greenfield, Richard—Mary Williams—13 Nov. L.7:227
Trevitt, John—Elizabeth Sparks—14 Nov. L.7:227
Troup, John—Elizabeth Tunnwell—15 Nov. L.7:227
Kip, Jacobus—Catalina Dhart—4 Dec. L.7:227
Stone, Myndar—Angletie Moll—8 Dec. L.7:227
Meyer, Ide—Anna Raventcin—15 Dec. L.7:227

1704/5

Charleton, John—Hester Gleve—8 Jan. L.7:227
Mackilson, Enoch—Aphia Van Hoorn—11 Jan. L.7:227
Tillet, James—Sarah Lawrence—12 Jan. L.7:267
Willet, Tho.—Charity Stevenson—13 Jan. L.7:267
Beeckman, Adry—Abigail Lispenar—1 Feb. L.7:267
Reid, Robt.—Abigail Baily—19 Feb. L.7:267
Daniel, Thomas—Sarah Godfrey—27 Feb. L.7:267
Toy [Foy?], Daniel—Frances Wessels—8 March L.7:267

Ray, Richard—Eleanor Saunders—20 March L.7:267
Jamison, James—Bettie Upton—20 March L.7:267

1705

Van Hook, Evert—Neiltie Jacobs—10 April L.7:267
Thorn, Samuel, Junr.—Hannah Doughty—11 April L.7:267
Rainsford, Thomas—Elce Vandenbergh—11 April L.7:267
Strycker, Peter—Margareta Schenk—19 April L.7:267
D Riemer, Isaac—Anne Woortman—27 April L.7:267
Williams, Robt.—Jonimah Birt—2 May L.7:267
Gettos, Paul—Mercy Flant—7 May L.7:267
Warne, Francis—Sarah Hays—15 May L.7:267
Riggs, John—Frances Colburne—19 May L.7:267
Mordock, Peter—Jane Marrington—21 May L.7:267
Freebody, John—Sarah Fleet—23 May L.7:267
Dant, Piere—Elizabeth Holt—25 May L.7:267
Dawson, Thomas—Mary Thoxter—9 June L.7:267
Pritchard, Tho.—Anne Stuyvesant—11 June L.7:268
Jarrett, Allane—Hannah Moore—20 June L.7:268
De Foreest, Johannes—Tryntie Garretse Ravestein—23 June L.7:268
Warren, William—Margariet Oyan—26 June L.7:268
Smith, Bernardus—Johanne Hading—30 June L.7:268
Bedlow, Isack—Susannah Brasier—14 July L.7:268
Theobalds, John—Eufen Tuder—19 July L.7:268
Walcraf, David—Elizabeth Field—19 July L.7:268
Ogden, Josiah—Catherine Hardenbrock—20 Aug. L.7:268
Freeman, Bernardus—Margrieta V. Schayck—20 Aug. L.7:268
Hunt, Richd.—Anne Glen—1 Sept. L.7:268
Stilwill, Richd.—Deborah Cowne—3 Sept. L.7:268
Pruyn, Johannes—Amelia Sanders—3 Sept. L.7:268
Gardiner, John— (—) L.7:268 [cf. MDC 104 m. 9 Sept. John Gardenier
    met Elisabeth Witty]
Oakely, Thomas—Mary Burroughs—15 Sept. L.7:309
Colson, Robert—Elizabeth Jones—29 Sept. L.7:310
Kip, Samuel—Margrieta Kip—3 Oct. L.7:310
Ming, Thomas—Mary Vorekinson—6 Oct. L.7:310
Pennistone, Thomas—Allice Wooderop—13 Oct. L.7:310
Lispanier, Anthony—Elizabeth De Kleyn—2 Nov. L.7:310
Nuttall, Thomas—Mary Holsworth—5 Nov. L.7:310
Roger, Thomas—Mathew Lee—10 Nov. L.7:310
Sharroke, Thomas—Margeret Poste—12 Nov. L.7:310
Himming, James—Allinar Baylie—14 Nov. L.7:310
Ford, William—Mary Hiatt—16 Nov. L.7:310
Bunting, Benjamin—Cornelia Cavelier—21 Nov. L.7:310

Oliver, John—Kathrine Peterson—28 Nov. L.7:310
Cornelison, John—Elizabeth Nazareth—8 Dec. L.7:310
Harrington, Thomas—Heila Johnson—8 Dec. L.7:310
Warner, William—Anne D'Gray—19 Dec. L.7:310
Adams, John—Martha Stratton—23 Dec. L.7:310
Broughton, Sampson—Mary Ravaud—24 Dec. L.7:310
Fleet, John—Elizabeth Chamberline—24 Dec. L.7:310
Brughman, Harmanus—Allitie Stevens—24 Dec. L.7:310
Allard, Francis—Mary Ashfield—26 Dec. L.7:310
Watts, Robert—Mary Nicolls—28 Dec. L.7:310
Bounn, Aman—Mary Prudence—28 Dec. L.7:310

1705/6

Bensinck, Mathew—Katherine Provost—9 Jan. L.7:311
Cortleeau, Jaques—Alltie Boeram—10 Jan. L.7:311
Broughton, Andrew—Mary Mansey—10 Jan. L.7:311
Van Brakeling, Stephen—Dina Bleg—15 Jan. L.7:311
Hooghland, Johannes—Jannitie Pies—16 Jan. L.7:310
Teller, William—Maria Van Tricht—19 Jan. L.7:311
Messelaer, Abraham—Agenietie Staats—31 Jan. L.7:311
Townsend, John—Rose Cole—1 Feb. L.7:311
D'Val, Charles—Susanna Boundinot—1 Feb. L.7:311
Lane, Adrian—Jannitie Van Sekler—27 Feb. L.7:311
Mompesson, Roger—Martha Pinhorn—28 Feb. L.7:311
Simmons, Solomon—Mary Mott—5 March L.7:311

1706

Brown, John—Abiny Barden—30 March L.7:311
Mourice, Paul—Margaret Kettletas—8 April L.7:311
D'Reymer, Isaac—Mary D'Forest—11 April L.7:311
Walker, Thomas—Elizabeth Ridot—12 April L.7:311

INDEX TO
NEW YORK MARRIAGE LICENSES,
1639-1706

By

Kenneth Scott

597

Bedwell, Hannah (Blank) 588
Bedwell, Isaac 588
Beeck, Deborah 589
Beeckman, Abigail (Lispenar) 591
Beeckman, Adry 591
Beeckman, Christophell 590
Beeckman, Maria (De La Noy) 590
Beeke, Aeltie 587
Beekeman, Janeke 589
Beekman, Charles 589
Beekman, Ekay (Van Sant) 589
Belline, --- 576
Belline, Mary 587
Bensinck, Katherine (Provost) 593
Bensinck, Mathew 593
Benson, Katherine 591
Berger, Myndart 591
Berger, Sarah J. (Dese) 591
Berkley, Elizabeth (Randall) 588
Berkley, (Wm.) 588
Berriman, Abigail 580
Berriman, Martha 581
Berser, Sarah 590
Berton, Elizabeth (Archambeau) 585
Berton, Peter 585
Betterworth/Belteworth, Patience/
  Patientje 581
Bettine, --- 576
Betts, Grace (Mott) 587
Betts, Joseph 587
Bettyes, John 578
Bettyes, Susannah (Ashfordby) 578
Biljan, Maria (Breau) 587
Biljan, Peter 587
Bill, Benjamin 581
Bill, Geesie (Van Fort) 581
Billiau, Perkie (Hendricks) 582
Billiau, Peter 582
Bingham, Mary 583
Birt, Jonimah 592
Bissett, Ellen 589
Blagge, Edward 588
Blagge, Johanna (Vickers) 588
Blair, James, Rev. 578
Blair, Sarah (Harrison) 578
Blanchard, Joanna (Gaultier) 581

Blanchard, John 581
Blanck, Anite 577
Blank, Hannah 588
Bleg, Dina 593
Blercome, Angell (Hendricks) 588
Blercome, Lubert (Jansen) 588
Blydenburgh, Cathrine (Dehart) 585
Blydenburgh, Joseph 578, 585
Blydenburgh, Mary (Smith) 578
Boelen, Antie (-) 579
Boeram, Alltie 593
Boerden, Hester 586
Bogaert, Hendrick 589
Bogaert, Ruttie (De La Metre) 589
Bogardus, Ephorordus 591
Bogardus, Hannah (Dayly) 591
Bogardus, Kathrine 579
Boelen, Elezabeth (Godfrey) 585
Boelen, James 585
Bond, Margett 589
Books, Mary (Carter) 590
Books, Phillip 590
Booth, George 590
Booth, Mary (Rowly) 590
Bordann, Helena 582
Bosch, Geshennamah (Bruyn) 581
Bosch, Juriaen 581
Bosen, Phillip 590
Bosen, Sarah (Berser) 590
Boudinot, Magdleleine 589
Bougraud (Bongrand), --- 581
Bougraud (Bongrand), Mary (Van Bur-
  sum) 581
Boudinot, Susanna 593
Bounn, Aman 593
Bounn, Mary (Prudence) 593
Bourchner/Bourchuer/Bourthier,
  Mary (English) 579
Bourchner/Bourchuer/Bourthier,
  Michael 579
Bowne, Elizabeth 577
Boyle, Frances 586
Boyle, Jane (-) 579
Branch, Cathrine 584
Brasier, Susannah 592
Bray, Hannah 576, 580

598

Brazier, Mary 583
Breadstead, John 585
Breadstead, Margrett (Peters) 585
Breau, Maria 587
Bresty, Mary 589
Brett, Katharine (Rumbout) 590
Brett, Mary (-) 583
Brett, Roger 590
Brewerton, Anite (Blanck) 577
Brewerton, George 577
Briggs, John 577
Briggs, Matthew (Wilkins) 577
Brine, Elizabeth (Van Clyff) 582
Brine, John 582
Britten, Rabacca 581
Britton, Anne 590
Brookesbank --- (Miss) 583
Broughton, Andrew 593
Broughton, Mary (Mansey) 593
Broughton, Mary (Ravaud) 593
Broughton, Sampson 593
Brown, Abiny (Barden) 593
Brown, John 593
Brown, Mary 591
Brughman, Allitie (Stevens) 593
Brughman, Harmanus 593
Bruyn, Geshennamah 581
Bryan, Eliza. 584
Buckenhoven, Anna (Van Holst) 583
Buckenhoven, Stephen 583
Buckley, Elizabeth 590
Buckmaster, Edward 577
Buckmaster, Margaret
    (Mathews) 577
Budd, Joseph 581
Budd, Sarah (Underhill) 581
Bunting, Benjamin 592
Bunting, Cornelia (Cavelier) 592
Burch, Hannah (Robinson) 580
Burch, (Wm.) 580
Burger, Evah 582
Burle, Joshua 584
Burle, Judith (Sexton) 584
Burroughs, Mary 592
Burroughs, Mary (Tayler) 581
Burroughs, Rachaell 590

Burroughs, Thomas 581
Burroughs, Unis 590
Burt, Margaret (Glenn) 583
Burt, Richard 583
Burtell, Margerett (Van Clyft) 591
Burtell, Peter 591
Burtsen/Burlsen, Mary Anny 580
Busch, Cornelia 583
Buttler, Hanah (Saunders) 587
Buttler, John 587
Campbell, Jane 584
Cannon, Andreis 581
Cannon, Ann (Puppyn) 581
Cantain, Mary (De Witt) 589
Cantain, Moses 589
Carelir, Adam 590
Carelir, Mary (Dalcales) 590
Carhart, Mary (Lord) 578
Carhart, Thomas 578
Carille, Adam 586
Carille, Elizabeth (Geribaut or
    Geribat) 586
Carley, Mary 581
Carnaby, Jane (Dawning) 581
Carnaby, Nicholas 581
Carr, Joana 586
Carter, Heiltie (Sloot) 580
Carter, Mary 590
Carter, Zebulon 580
Cauley, Agenitie (Vandespegel) 586
Cauley, John 586
Cavaleer, Cornelia (Busch) 583
Cavaleer, Peter 583
Cavaleere, Kathrine 576, 583
Caveleer, Magdalen 587
Cavelier, Cornelia 592
Cavelir (See also Carelir)
Cebra, Ann (Meyer) 587
Cebra, James 587
Ceysler, --- 576
Chamberline, Elizabeth 593
Chambers, Abraham Goesbeck 589
Chambers, John 579
Chambers, Mary 588
Chambers, Mary (Drummond) 579
Chambers, Sarah (Bayard) 589

Champion, Francis 589
Chappell, Ann (Fromanteell) 581
Chappell, Francis 581
Charleton, Hester (Gleve) 591
Charleton, John 591
Cheek, Elizabeth 582
Childers, Delia 580
Chisnall, Magdalen (Caveleer) 587
Chisnall, (Wm.) 587
Chiswell, Jane 588
Christionse, Bellekie (Attkins) 589
Christionse, Peter 589
Cinburne, Mary 577
Clarke, Eliza. 589
Clatworthy, John 580
Clatworthy, Mary (Lursen/
  Leersen) 580
Clement, James 582
Clement, Sarah (Hinchman) 582
Clerke, Charity 585
Clopper, Cornelius 583
Clopper, Heilkea (-) 583
Clotwerthy, Hanna 590
Clouder, Mary (-) 587
Clowes, Kathrine (Douw) 584
Clowes, Samuel 584
Coats, Edward 580
Coats, Sarah (Thomson) 580
Cobbitt, Lydia 582
Cock, Catherine (-) 587
Cockling, Deborah (Smith) 587
Cockling, Thomas 587
Cocks, Lejdia 581
Coderse, Rachell 588
Coenraats, Mary (Longfield) 589
Coenraats, Octave 589
Coerten, Elizabeth (De Riemer) 586
Coerten, Henry 586
Colburne, Frances 592
Cole, Abram 581
Cole, Rabacca (Britten) 581
Cole, Rose 593
Coleman, ---(Miss ?) 580
Coleman, Elenor (Hunt) 584
Coleman, Henry 578, 584
Coleman, Mary (-) 578

Colevelt, Mary 576, 584
Collins, Elezebeth 585
Collins, Eliza. 585
Collins, Elizabeth (Kennedy) 578
Collins, James 578
Collins, John 587
Collins, Margaret (Verplanck) 587
Colson, Elizabeth (Jones) 592
Colson, Robert 592
Conlylee, Margritt 585
Cooley, Deborah 580
Cooper, Benjamin 580
Cooper, John 587
Cooper, Hannah (Frost) 587
Cooper, Helena (Wilkens) 580
Corbett, John 590
Corbett, Mary (Graham) 590
Corbit, Christian (Milton) 585
Corbitt, John 585
Coreman (Coleman ?), Anna Maria
  (Plevier) 584
Coreman (Coleman ?), Daniel
  Peterse 584
Corlee, Ann 583
Cornbury, Lord* 575
Cornelis, Janitie 577
Cornelise, Altie 591
Cornelison, Elizabeth (Nazareth) 593
Cornelison, John 593
Cornell, Elizabeth 590
Cornell, John 590
Cornell, Letitia (Smith) 590
Cornwell, Ann (Merchant) 585
Cornwell, George 585
Corsen, Angeneta (Gillis) 576
Corsen, Arent 576
Cortlandt, Ann 585
Cortlandt, Anna Mary (Van Schaick)
  581
Cortlandt, John 581
Cortleeau, Allitie (Boeram) 593
Cortleeau, Jaques 593
Cosins, Barne 583
Cosins, Grace (Sanford) 583
Courtie, Mintie 591
Coward, Hugh 589

600

601

603

Gardenier, Elisabeth (Witty) 592
Gardiner/Gardenier, John 592
Garreou, Jean 589
Garreou, Marie (Andere) 589
Gaudineau, Hellena 589
Gaultier, Joanna 581
Geribaut/Geribat, Elizabeth 586
Gerrets, Niellye 587
Gerritson, Gerthryt (Lansen) 590
Gerritson, Ryert 590
Gerrytse, Elizabeth 580
Gerrytson, Hannah 579
Gettos, Mercy (Flant) 592
Gettos, Paul 592
Gibb, Andrew 582
Gibb, Hannah (-) 582
Gibbs, Elizabeth 577
Gilbert, Bethia (Young) 577
Gilbert, Cornelia (Allison) 589
Gilbert, George 584
Gilbert, Jane (Campbell) 584
Gilbert, Jannitie (Floyd) 580
Gilbert, John 589
Gilbert, Moses 580
Gilbert, Thomas 577
Giles, Engeltie (Davies) 582
Giles, Thomas 582
Gilles, Angeneta 576
Gindett, John 586
Gindett, Mary (Vincent) 586
Gleave, Han or Har (Philip) 585
Gleave, Richard 585
Glen, Anne 592
Glencrosse, Eliza. (Clarke) 589
Glencrosse, Wm. 589
Glenn, Margaret 583
Gleve, Hester 591
Glover, Mary 584
Godfrey, Elezabeth 585
Godfrey, Sarah 591
Goff, Elenor 584
Gore, Christopher 577
Gore, Dorothy 580
Gore, Eliz. (Rogers) 577
Gorne, John 586
Gorne, Mary (Harris) 586

Goscott, Margett (Bond) 589
Goscott, Zachariah 589
Gouverneur, Abraham 585
Governeur, Isaac 591
Governeur, Mary (Milborne) 585
Governeur, Sarah (Staats) 591
Graham, Augustine 588
Graham, Elizabeth (Windebank) 577
Graham, Isabella 578
Graham, James 577
Graham, Jane (Chiswell) 588
Graham, Mary 590
Graham, Sarah (-) 588
Grant, Rachell (Hardenbrook) 591
Grant, Wm. 591
Grasset, Hesther 582
Graves, Deliverance 583
Green, Elizabeth 583
Greenfield, Mary (Williams) 591
Greenfield, Richard 591
Greenham, Mary (Davie) 579
Greenham, Michael 579
Greg, Leena (Monntes) 581
Greg, Robert 581
Gregory, Jane 586
Grice, Deborer (Hadlock) 588
Grice, John 588
Griffin, Eliz. (Platt) 577
Griffin, Saml. 577
Groenendick, Delia (Childers) 580
Groenendick, Johannes 580
Groves, Andrew 579
Groves, Jane (-) 579
Gunter, Mary 589
Gunthorp, Jane 590
Haddock, Janitie 577
Hading, Johanne 592
Hadlock, Deborer 588
Hall, Abigail (Wakeman) 577
Hall, Anne (Evetts) 588
Hall, Richard 588
Hall, Thomas 577
Hallett, Hannah 591
Halton, Elizabeth (Van Tright) 589
Halton, Michael 589
Hamill, Christine (Rosevelt) 588

604

Hope, John 579
Hopper, Janitie (Cornelis) 577
Hopper, John 584
Hopper, Joseph 577
Hopper, Margrett (Tindell) 584
Huestis, Abigail 582
Huggen, Rachaell (Burroughs) 590
Huggen, (Wm.) 590
Hughes, Jane (Gunthorp) 590
Hughes, Thomas 590
Hulgrove, Eve 588
Hulgrow, Evah (Burger) 582
Hulgrow, George 582
Hulin, Francis 582
Hulin, Susanna (Nicholas) 582
Hull, Hannah 582
Hunderbeek, Abram 589
Hunderbeek, Martha (Woodett) 589
Hundrick, Aleda 589
Hunt, Abigail (Huestis) 582
Hunt, Anne (Glen) 592
Hunt, Batthia (Ferguson) 583
Hunt, Elenor 584
Hunt, John L., Jr. 582
Hunt, Josiah, Jr. 583
Hunt, Mary 577
Hunt, Richd. 592
Huntrick, Matthew Leana 589
Hutchins, Elizabeth (Buckley) 590
Hutchins, John 590
Hutson, Hannah 583
Hutton, John 581
Hutton, Katrine (Strangnish) 581
Huyblingh, Coenraet 589
Huyblingh, Deborah (Beeck) 589
Huyco, Jean 590
Hyndert, Christian 588
Jacobs, Anna 581
Jacobs, Antie (Symons) 577
Jacobs, Hendrick 577
Jacobs, Janitie 581
Jacobs, Neiltie 592
Jaman, Henry 582
Jaman, Jane (Barber) 582
Jamison, Bettie (Upton) 592
Jamison, David 578, 588

Jamison, James 592
Jamison, Johannah (Meech) 588
Jamison, Mary (Hardenbrok) 578
Janse, Trienty 585
Jansen, Cornelise 591
Jansen, Hendrick 591
Jansen, Margerett (Van Noostrandt) 591
Jansen, Mary (Brown) 591
Jarrett, Allane 592
Jarrett, Hannah (Moore) 592
Jay, Ann Mary (Bayard) 583
Jay, Augustus 583
Jenoway, Agnitie (-) 582
Jenoway, (Wm.) 582
Johnson, Cornelia 577, 584
Johnson, Hanna (Clotwerthy) 590
Johnson, Hanna (Van Swanenbrugh) 589
Johnson, Heila 593
Johnson, Johannes 590
Johnson, John 589
Jones, Elizabeth 592
Jones, Mary 584
Jones, Sarah 580
Joosten, Marritje (Symons) 576
Joosten, Symon 576
Jordaine, Eliza. (-) 578
Jordaine, Henry 578
Journey, Elizabeth (De Yan) 588
Journey, John 588
Jurgens, Cathrina (Lysinck) 576
Jurgens, Peter 576
Jusell, Francis (Champion) 589
Jusell, John 589
Kelly, John 589
Kelly, Margarett (Flenchborow) 589
Kembell, Henry 579
Kembell, Kathrine (Baker) 579
Kennedy, Elizabeth 578
Kerfbyl, John 590
Kerfbyl, Margarett (Prevost) 590
Ketteltas, Abraham 579
Ketteltas, Antie (-) 579
Kettletas, Margaret 593
Kidd, Sarah 589
Kidd, Sarah (-) 578

606

Kidd, (Wm.) Capt. 578
Kiersteade, Eliza. (Laurence) 589
Kiersteade, Jacobus 589
Kiersted, Cornelius 589
Kiersted, Sarah (Elsworth) 589
Kiersteede, Ariaentie 580
King, Elizabeth (Green) 583
King, Jeremiah 584
King, Mary (Glover) 584
King, Peter 583
Kingsland, Edmund 589
Kingsland, Mary (Pinhorne) 589
Kingston, Dorothy (Sandige) 586
Kingston, John 586
Kip, Abraham 583
Kip, Catalina (Dhart) 591
Kip, Emeltie (Van Deycke) 587
Kip, Henricus 583
Kip, Jacobus 591
Kip, Kathalina (Van Vlecqe) 583
Kip, Magdalen (Van Vlecque) 583
Kip, Margrieta (Kip) 592
Kip, Petrus 587
Kip, Samuel 592
Kipp, Jesse 581
Kipp, Magdelena 586
Kipp, Mary (Stevens) 581
Konning, Elizabeth (-) 578
Laconte, Margtt (Mahoo) 588
Laconte, Wm. 588
Laers (Laurentius Carolus) 576
Lafon, John 589
Lafon, Mary (Dubois) 589
Lafort, Hesther (Richards) 579
Lafort, Marcus 579
Lambert, Edward 583
Lambert, Jane (Downing) 583
Lambrs, Catryna (Van Newen-
    huysen) 581
Lambrs, Martinus 581
La Montagne, Angeneta (Gillis) 576
La Montagne, Johannes 576
Lance, Eliz. 585
Lane, Adrian 593
Lane, Jannitie (Van Sekler) 593
Langstaffe, Mary (Sidman) 587

Langstaffe, Moses 587
Lanseing, Abraham 589
Lanseing, Matthew Leana (Huntrick)
    589
Lansen, Gerthryt 590
Lansen, John 591
Lansen, Lena (Saunders) 591
Lansing, Isaac 589
Lansing, Janeke (Beekeman) 589
Larkin, Katharine (-) 580
Larkon, James 578
Larkon, Kathrine (De Hart) 578
Latham, Jane (Singleton) 584
Latham, Joseph 584
Latting, J. J.* 575
Laurence, Eliza. 589
Laurence, Janetie (Stevensen) 582
Laurence, John 582
Law, Andrew 581
Law, Cornelia (Dishington) 581
Lawrence, Charity (Clerkc) 585
Lawrence, Jane (Gregory) 586
Lawrence, John 586
Lawrence, Mary (Ferguson) 579
Lawrence, Richard 585
Lawrence, Sarah 591
Lawrence, Thomas 579
Lawrier, Christian 585
Lawrier, Mary (Bant) 585
Le Chavolier, Jean 578
Le Chavolier, Marie (De La Plaine) 578
Lee, Mathew 592
Lefeurt, Bartholomew 587
Lefeurt, Magdalen (Peirott) 587
Leigh, Dorothy 590
Leisler, Francis 581
Lemonter/Lemouletz, Helena (Fell) 577
Lemonter/Lemouletz, Jean 577
Lepenar, Margarett 587
Lesley, Ellen (Bissett) 589
Lesley, John 589
Lessenby, Askey 588
Lessitt, Elizabeth 591
Lethem, --- 576
Lethem, Daniel 582
Lethem, Helena (Bordann) 582

607

Merritt, John 577
Messelaer, Abraham 593
Messelaer, Agenietie (Staats) 593
Meyer, Ann 587
Meyer, Anna (Ravenstein) 591
Meyer, Helecent (Hillegond) 582
Meyer, Ide 591
Meyer, Janitie 586
Meyer, John 591
Meyer, Kathrine 582
Meyer, Sarah (D Foreest) 591
Meyers, Elsey 584
Meyers, Katharine 586
Meyers, Marytie 586
Meynderts, Neeltie 583
Michell, Elizabeth 587
Michells, Cornelis 577
Michells, Neltie (Elderts) 577
Milborne, Mary 585
Milldrum, Femmetie (Van Boursen) 590
Milldrum, John 590
Miller, Antie (Vanderheyden) 581
Miller, Geertroy (Springsteen) 591
Miller, Jerusia 590
Miller, Pawl 581
Miller, Wm. 591
Milton, Christian 585
Ming, Mary (Vorekinson) 592
Ming, Thomas 592
Minviel, John James 588
Minviel, Susanne (Papin) 588
Mitchell, Gerritie (Van Hoek) 576, 584
Mitchel (l), James 576, 584
Moll, Angletie 591
Moll, Ariaentie 584
Moll, Jacobus 589
Moll, Lidia (Winua) 589
Moll, Mary 589
Mompesson, Martha (Pinhorn) 593
Mompesson, Roger 593
Monntes, Leena 581
Monvielle, Susanna 588
Mool, Ann 585
Moore, Elizabeth (Cheek) 582

Moore, Francis 582
Moore, Hannah 592
Moore, John 582
Mordock, Jane (Marrington) 592
Mordock, Peter 592
More, Rebeccah (Baily) 580
More, Richard 580
Morris, Isabella (Graham) 578
Morris, Lewis 578
Morton, Barbary 581
Mosston, Judith 584
Mott, Elizabeth (Thorne) 582
Mott, Grace 587
Mott, Mary 593
Mott, Rigebell 582
Mourice, Margaret (Kettletas) 593
Mourice, Paul 593
Moyer, Catharina 579
Moyon, Mary (Perdrian/Pordrian) 579
Moyon, (Wm.) 579
Myer, Cornelia 590
Myer, Elsie 590
Nasbell, --- 576
Nazareth, Elizabeth 593
Nedry, Jane (Allen) 588
Nedry, John 588
Nesbett, --- 576
Nesbett, Robert 586
Nesbett, Susanna (Stevens) 586
Nicholas, James 589
Nicholas, Mary (Moll) 589
Nicholas, Susanna 582
Nicolas, Susanne 588
Nicolls, Margarett 583
Nicolls, Mary 593
Noel, Hannah 590
Norwood, Benjamin 579
Norwood, Cornelia (Van Clyff) 579
Notingham, Margaret (Rutsen) 587
Notingham, Wm. 587
Nuton, Joan (Smith) 576
Nuton, Thomas 576
Nuttall, Mary (Holsworth) 592
Nuttall, Thomas 592
Oakely, Mary (Burroughs) 592
Oakely, Thomas 592

610

Rosell, Rachell 584
Rosevelt, Christine 588
Rousby, Christopher 589
Rousby, Sarah (Kidd) 589
Rowly, Mary 590
Rudgars, Margaret 577
Rudyard/Rudgards, Ann 577
Rudyerd, Margaret 577
Rumbout, Katharine 590
Rutherse, Anthony 584
Rutherse, Hendrycke (Vande-
water) 584
Ruthse, Cathrine 585
Rutsen, Margaret 587
Ryarse, Helena 589
Sackett, Majory L. (Sleade) 585
Sackett, Richard 585
Samuell, Ariaentie 580
Sanders, Amelia 592
Sanders, Ann 579
Sanders, Robert 579
Sandford, Mary 584
Sandige, Dorothy 586
Sands, Elizabeth (Lessitt) 591
Sands, Samuell 591
Sanford, Grace 583
Santford, Elisabeth 587
Santfordt, --- 585
Santfordt, Jane (White) 585
Saunders, Barent 591
Saunders, Eleanor 592
Saunders, Hanah 587
Saunders, Lena 591
Saunders, Mary (Wander) 591
Schenck, Cornelia (Van Wesselen) 590
Schenk, Margareta 592
Schenck, Martin 590
Schepmoes, Derrick 589
Schepmoes, Grittie (Tappen) 589
Schut, Johon Michll 588
Schut, Mary (Fromahyden) 588
Schuyler, Arent 588
Schuyler, Cathalina (Schuyler) 586
Schuyler, Jacobus 586
Schuyler, Margerett 583, 591
Schuyler, Maria (Van Renselaer) 578

Schuyler, Myndert 580
Schuyler, Peter 578
Schuyler, Rachell (Cuyler) 580
Schuyler, Swantie (Dyckhuyse) 588
Schuyler, Aegie (D'Groof) 589
Schuyler, Gerard 589
Scott, Kenneth* 575
Scurlocke, Eve (Hulgrove) 588
Scurlocke, John 588
Seidman, Mary (Hunt) 577
Seidman, Thomas 577
Selsby, John 582
Selsby, Sarah (Thomson) 582
Sexton, Judith 584
Sharpe, Audy 577
Sharroke, Margaret (Poste) 592
Sharroke, Thomas 592
Shaw, Anna (-) 578
Shaw, Pricilla 586
Shaw, Thomas 578
Shelston, Prudence 587
Shepard, John 588
Shepard, Ruth (Davis) 588
Shrive, Sarah 588
Sidman, Mary 587
Simmons, Mary (Mott) 593
Simmons, Solomon 593
Simms, Katharine (-) 580
Simms, Lancaster 580
Singleton, Jane 584
Skelding, Rebecca (Asten) 586
Skelding, Tho. 586
Skelton, Alice (Throgmorton) 578
Skelton, Robert 578
Slade, Margery (Wislake) 581
Slade, Peter 581
Sleade, Majory L. 585
Sleigh, Charles 579
Sleigh, Sarah (Purrington) 579
Sloot, Heiltie 580
Smith, Aleda (Hundrick) 589
Smith, Ann 584
Smith, Barnardus/Bernardus 584, 592
Smith, Charles 589
Smith, Deborah 587
Smith, Elizab. 588

612

Smith, Elizabeth (Platt) 590
Smith, Else 583
Smith, Elsey (Meyers) 584
Smith, Hanah 586
Smith, Hannah (-) 582
Smith, Hannah (Phips) 583
Smith, Joan 576
Smith, Johanne (Hading) 592
Smith, John 583
Smith, Jonathan 590
Smith, Joseph 581
Smith, Letitia 590
Smith, Margaret (Barents) 581
Smith, Margarett 583
Smith, Mary 578
Smith, Susanna (Monvielle) 588
Smith, (Wm.) 588
Snedeker, Janeke 587
Souward, Mary 580
Splinter, Syntie 586
Sparks, Elizabeth 591
Spencer, Janes 581
Spencer, Mary (Carley) 581
Springsteen, Caspar 581
Springsteen, Janitie (Jacobs) 581
Staats, Agenietie 593
Staats, Barent 587
Staats, Niellye (Gerrets) 587
Staats, Sarah 591
Staleboth, Katharina 578
Stateham, Altie (Finn) 591
Stateham, Thomas 591
Steed, --- 576
Stephance, Catherin (Van Dyke) 589
Stephance, Lucas 589
Stevens, --- 576
Stevens, Allitie 593
Stevens, John 586
Stevens, Mary 581
Stevens, Pricilla (Shaw) 586
Stevens, Susanna 586
Stevensen, Janetie 582
Stevenson, Charity 591
Stevenson, Elizabeth 579
Stewart, John 589
Stewart, Rebecca (Adams) 589

Stillwell, Elizabeth (Cornell) 590
Stillwell, Ellis (Throgmorton) 588
Stillwell, Mary 584, 590
Stillwell, Nicholas 590
Stillwell, Sarah 582
Stillwell, Tho. 588
Stilwill, Deborah (Cowne) 592
Stilwill, Richd. 592
Stivers, --- 576
Stollard, Elizabeth (Tuder) 581
Stollard, Giles 581
Stone, Angletie (Moll) 591
Stone, Myndar 591
Stoutenburg, Catherine 591
Strangnish, Katrine 581
Stratton, Martha 593
Streard, Cornelia (Dishington) 585
Streard, Elexander 585
Struddle, Elizabeth 588
Strycker, Margareta (Schenk) 592
Strycker, Peter 592
Stuart, Alexander 588
Stuart, Catharine (Rivilie) 588
Stuckey, Frances 588
Studd, --- 576
Studd, Catherine (Pearsall) 587
Studd, Tho. 587
Stuyvesant, Anne 592
Stuyvesant, Elezabeth 584
Suert, Hellegond (Luyckas) 589
Suert, Olphert 589
Swann, Helena 582
Swerver, Andrew 591
Swerver, Elizabeth (De Vore) 591
Sybrantsen, Claes 576
Sybrantsen, Maritje (Peters) 576
Sydenham, Elezabeth (Stuyvesant) 584
Sydenham, George 584
Symons, Antie 577
Symons, Marritje 576
Symonse, Arientie (Samuell) 580
Symonse, Henryck 580
Tankins/Tankirs, Janitie (Haddock) 577
Tankins/Tankirs, Joh. 577
Tanner, --- 576

614

617